D0151170

BIOGRAPHICAL DICTIONARY OF AFRO-AMERICAN AND AFRICAN MUSICIANS

THE GREENWOOD ENCYCLOPEDIA OF BLACK MUSIC

BIOGRAPHICAL DICTIONARY OF AFRO-AMERICAN AND AFRICAN MUSICIANS

EILEEN SOUTHERN

Greenwood Press
Westport, Connecticut • London, England

Library of Congress Cataloging in Publication Data
Southern, Eileen.
Biographical Dictionary of Afro-American and African musicians.

(Greenwood encyclopedia of Black music ISSN 0272-0264)
Bibliography: p.
Includes index.
1. Afro-American musicians—United States—Bio-bibliography. 2. Musicians—Africa—Bio-bibliography.
I. Title. II. Series.
ML105.S67 780′.92′2 [B] 81-2586
ISBN 0-313-21339-9 (lib. bdg.) AACR2

Library of Congress Catalog Card Number: 81-2586
ISBN: 0-313-21339-9
ISSN: 0272-0264

First published in 1982

Greenwood Press
A division of Congressional Information Service, Inc.
88 Post Road West, Westport, Connecticut 06881

Printed in the United States of America

10 9 8 7 6 5 4 3 2 1

To my husband

CONTENTS

PREFACE

Although there are biographical dictionaries and encyclopedias that include entries on Afro-American and African professional musicians, there is no single comprehensive volume that attempts to correlate materials related to these musical figures from a historical perspective. I have long felt the need for such a reference work and have attempted to attain that objective in the present volume. It brings together representatives of the various and diverse fields of musical activity who have played a significant role in the history of black music, and of Western music in general. Thus, it documents this history and assesses its achievements and its impact upon world music of contemporary times. It is my hope that the present work will throw into focus the "oneness" of black music—the refusal of its practitioners to fit neatly into traditional categories of folk, popular, jazz, religious, or classical music. Conventional music encyclopedias tend to ignore the "crossover," say, the jazzman who moves into the field of classical music or vice versa. And there is general neglect of men and women who, although not necessarily professional musicians, have made important contributions to black music history—the concert promoters, patrons, and critics, to name a few. But perhaps my most compelling reason for writing this dictionary was a concern for bringing back to memory the legendary figures of the past and for calling attention to significant figures of the present who have overcome the almost insurmountable obstacles erected by slavery and race discrimination to lay the foundation for contemporary black musical activities. Young people today—and, as well, the not-so-young—seem not to realize that there had to be a Sam Lucas before there could be a Sammy Davis, Jr.; that there had to be an Elizabeth Taylor Greenfield before a Leontyne Price; a Sallie Martin, before an Aretha Franklin.

This dictionary draws together widely dispersed and, in many instances, heretofore unpublished information on more than 1500 musicians of African descent, including living persons as well as figures of the past. With regard to chronological coverage, the earliest person for whom I could find career data, Sebastian Rodriguez (c1642-c1726), was used as starting point. To establish a measure of historical perspective, I chose the year 1945 as a cut-off for date of birth, although a few exceptional individuals born after 1945 are included. That year marks the end of an era, as well as the end of World War II, and simultaneously the beginning of a new era that brought profound changes into the life-styles and culture of Afro-Americans and Africans. Granted, it may seem risky to attempt to assess the achievement and appraise the contributions of those who are still living, those whom history has not had time to evaluate, but my reservations on that issue were overridden by my desire to make the dictionary as comprehensive and as representative as possible.

With regard to the criteria for coverage, I relied upon several guiding principles: mainly, the individual should be distinguished, having exerted influence upon others and contributed to the culture of his times; the individual should have made significant achievements during his career; and he should have earned recognition beyond the boundaries of his local community. In some cases, I was unable to apply all the criteria. As early black musicians, for example, have been generally neglected or slighted in existing reference sources, all those born before the Emancipation Proclamation of 1863 were included if even a minimal amount of information could be unearthed about their careers. A similar approach was taken towards women of those years and even later; in contemporary times, women have held their own and needed no such allowances to be made. On the other hand, some areas of activity—such as minstrelsy, vaudeville, blues, jazz, and popular music—have been so dominated by black performers that it was necessary to limit the number of biographees in order to maintain the desired comprehensiveness and, consequently, I applied higher standards for their inclusion than for others.

The first task was to compile a list of names. I began by consulting general biographical dictionaries, such as the *Who's Who in Colored America* series, and such reference works as *Men of Mark* or *Historical Negro Biographies* (see Selected Bibliography on p. 447 for publication details). As I searched for entries on musicians, it became obvious that much is owed the early black editors who compiled directories of eminent black Americans during the long years when American reference literature neglected them. I also acknowledge my indebtedness to the publishers and editors of black newspapers and periodicals, who kept open lines of communication among black communities and reported on the achievements of black Americans during the long years when the white press ignored their existence. By reading through full runs of certain newspapers and magazines, I was able to understand the role played by the various figures in the communities as well as identify their accomplishments. Recently, such standard sources as the Marquis *Who's Who* series, the *Dictionary of American Biography*, and *Current Biography* have begun to include more entries on Afro-Americans, and these sources were used with profit, as were also works pertaining to special fields, such as jazz and blues encyclopedias. In the selection of names for inclusion in the dictionary, I was guided by the choices made in all these sources. Also, I solicited names of noteworthy individuals from musicians and critics of my acquaintance. I believe that the final list is highly representative of the many different kinds of individuals who have contributed to the history of black music, although not all who merit attention could be included. Some pioneered in establishing traditions, some concentrated on preserving traditions, and some devoted their energies to passing on knowledge to the young. All affected the course of history in meaningful ways.

Despite the usefulness of these sources, my investigation posed special problems of research. Very little is available in print about individuals who were active before the 1920s except in outstanding cases, and some areas of activity have been almost totally passed over even up to the present, such as gospel music. I made recourse to a wide variety of archival sources, collected concert and funeral programs for the scraps of biographical data they contain, read every conceivable book and pamphlet that was relevant, examined record-liner notes, and interviewed subjects (either in person or by proxy) and friends and relatives of deceased subjects where possible. To stay *au courant* with the activities of contemporary musicians, I subscribed to a black-press clipping service and persuaded friends to clip from the white press for me, in addition to my own clipping.

All this effort notwithstanding, I am aware that inevitably the dictionary will contain inaccuracies. A surprising number will come from the subjects themselves or their relatives and friends who, in their published interviews and autobiographies, tend to forget important career details (such as, for example, date of birth) and to magnify achievements. Other errors undoubtedly have crept in from my being forced to depend upon unreliable secondary sources. Finally, I was able to uncover only skeletal information for many persons despite extended research. But this is a pioneering venture, and I hope the positive results will outweigh the negative aspects. I also hope that those who possess additional information will send it to me so that biographical sketches can be expanded and inaccuracies minimized in the next edition of the dictionary.

During the course of my research and writing, I observed the emergence of themes that are worthy of note when placed in historical context. The role of the black church in the development of religious music, for example, has been discussed in several places, but little attention has been given to the impact of the black church upon the career development of musicians in general, including even entertainers and bluesmen. It is certainly a subject that calls for further investigation. Another is the role of the black professional organizations in contributing to the development of musicians. But perhaps that is part of a larger topic—the special role taken by certain cities through the years in nurturing black musical activities, the cities where the organizations came into being, along with other institutions that aided the development of the musicians and the various genres. Philadelphia would head the list in the early nineteenth century, succeeded by New York, Washington, D.C., New Orleans, and later Chicago. It is of interest that when a city such as Chicago in the early twentieth century became an important center for jazz, blues, and gospel, it also encouraged classical music activities. The "oneness" of black music!

Another phenomenon to be remarked is that of the master teacher who established rigorous standards for excellence at particular high schools and colleges, which then produced the nation's musical leaders for ensuing decades. Surely one of the pioneers among the secondary-school educators was Major N. Clark Smith, who left his stamp upon Lincoln High School in Kansas City, Sumner High School in St. Louis, Wendell Phillips High School in Chicago, and Tuskegee Institute in Alabama. To compile a list of the musicians who came under the influence of Smith, either directly or indirectly, would be to compile a list of "who's who" among black musicians. Later there was Walter Henri

Dyett at Phillips and DuSable High in Chicago, Alonzo Lewis at Lincoln High, Eugene Mikell in the New York area, and John Whatley in Birmingham, Alabama—to name a few—to which list should be added the names of the legendary college music educators.

Then there is the theme of the musical family which turned out professional musicians from one generation to the next and sent them into various areas of musical activity. The Lew family dynasty, for example, was established by Primus Lew, a fifer in the French and Indian Wars of the 1750s; his descendants were still performing professionally in the mid-twentieth century. Or take the case of the Work family, long associated with Fisk University, which began with the patriarch John Wesley Work I (c1830-1923), a choir director and composer, and produced professional musicians for four generations. The son of Edward Boatner, composer of religious music, became a celebrated jazz saxophonist, Edward ("Sonny") Stitt. A nephew of jazz cornetist Joseph ("King") Oliver became the eminent composer Ulysses Kay. Similar examples of musical families occur frequently among the biographees.

A final phenomenon that comes to mind is that of the organization or production or musical group that served as a kind of career-launching finishing school for hundreds of musicians. Consider, for example, contemporary opera singers. The biographies suggest that, with few exceptions, most of those who succeeded in finding positions in the major companies—the Metropolitan Opera, New York City Opera, La Scala, and others —made their operatic debuts in Gershwin's *Porgy and Bess* or in Virgil Thomson's *Four Saints in Three Acts* or in Scott Joplin's *Treemonisha*. These three operas might be regarded, therefore, as having served as finishing schools for contemporary opera singers. The first two productions have been long-lived, returning to the stage in numerous revivals since their premieres in the 1930s, and the relatively new Joplin opera has been revived since its world premiere in 1972. A parallel situation existed in regard to jazz groups. According to the biographies, most jazzmen of the mid-century years had played in the orchestras of Lionel Hampton, Cab Calloway, Earl Hines, Count Basie, or Duke Ellington or in bands whose leaders had played in those bands. In a similar way, most gospel figures trace their musical ancestry back to Thomas A. Dorsey, Sallie Martin, or Roberta Martin or to gospel figures who got their start with one of those three individuals.

These are but a few of the themes indicated by the biographies.I hope that among the students and scholars who come to this volume for specific information, some will be tempted to browse through it and perhaps begin an investigation of a theme particularly attractive to them. Working on this project has brought me both enjoyment and excitement, notwithstanding the thousands of tedious hours spent in basic research. I have come to regard the biographees, living and dead, as my personal friends, despite the many years that separate some of them from me, and I trust that users of this dictionary will find pleasure in getting to know my friends.

The project also brought me an intense awareness of myself as a black musician. I realize how fortunate I was to spend my formative years in Chicago during the 1920s-30s, where gospel and blues were in the air I breathed, where 35th Street had to be "lined with asbestos to keep the bands from scorching passers-by with their red-hot jazz" (as aptly stated in the *Chicago Defender*), and where classical musicians treasured the music of both black and white composers in their unending concerts. I heard the legendary figures perform before they became legendary! If there was anything additional needed to complete my induction into the world of black music, it was to come into closer contact with my roots, which happened when I went south during the 1940s to teach in black colleges, particularly in Louisiana. All these experiences increased my appreciation of the black heritage and gave support to my work on the project, especially during those periods when I realized I had rushed in where angels would have feared to tread.

Many loyal friends and relatives have contributed to this project over the past ten years. Those who were with me from the beginning, who clipped newspapers and magazines, contributed information, interviewed subjects, photocopied library materials, and otherwise helped in numerous ways include my sisters, Stella Hall and Fanya Wiggins, and professional colleagues D. Antoinette Handy and Dominique-René de Lerma. Among other colleagues who contributed information, investigated special topics, and/or solicited information from others were William Duncan Allen, Barbara Baker, Clarence Boyer, Florence Cadrez Brantley, Tilford Brook, James Braithwaite, Reginald Buckner, Marva Griffin Carter, Earl Calloway, Marion Cumbo, Brazeal Dennard, Samuel Floyd, Andrew Frierson, William Garcia, Oland Gaston, Mary Southern Harper, Roy Hill, Pearl Williams Jones, Angela McLinn, Norman Merrifield, Addison Reed, Geneva Southall, Ralph Williams, and Josephine Wright. Dr. Wright also assumed major responsibility for compiling data about Afro-European musicians. My daughter, April

Reilly, offered helpful suggestions, particularly in regard to rhythm 'n' blues, soul, and the like; my husband, Joseph, assisted me with the enormous correspondence involved with the project and took total charge of preparing the computer-assisted appendices and index.

I am indebted to the various librarians who generously responded to my requests for assistance, particularly Jean Currie (E. Azalia Hackley College, Detroit Public Library), Betty Culpepper (Moorland-Spingarn Collection, Howard University), Barbara Dames and Ruth Hoppe (Harvard University Interlibrary Loan), Donald F. Joyce (Vivian Harsh Collection, Chicago Public Library), Ernest Kaiser and staff (Schomburg Collection, New York Public Library), Frederick Kent (Free Library of Philadelphia), John L. Selch (Indiana State Library), Marion Lonsberry (Denver Public Library), Martha Mahard and her staff (Harvard Theatre Collection), and Wayne Shirley (Music Division, Library of Congress). From the beginning I had the warm encouragement and advice of James T. Sabin, Executive Editor at Greenwood Press, who as a jazz enthusiast gave special attention to my jazz biographies and made helpful suggestions. Production editor Lynn Taylor and copy editor Linda Robinson were helpful in numerous ways and kept a sharp eye open to inconsistencies in the work. Harvard University gave me the gift of time, a leave during the Spring Term, 1979, for which I am appreciative.

These acknowledgements would be incomplete without an expression of gratitude to the musicians who filled out forms and patiently responded to additional requests for information. Most of all, I am indebted to my husband for his forbearance, sympathetic understanding, and active support over a long period of time.

GUIDE TO USE OF THE DICTIONARY

My aim in the biographical sketch is to give a concise, objective account of the individual's professional life. Personal details are included only when relevant to the professional career. Each entry gives facts of birth and death, education, details of career arranged generally in chronological order, and representative compositions or performances. In some cases I have added evaluative comments, particularly where the subject was a pioneer in his field of activity. Each entry carries a bibliography and, when possible, a discography.

NAME.

Most individuals are listed under the names by which they are known professionally. Other names by which the subject may be known are entered in parentheses following the professional name, such as nicknames, titles, and given names that differ from professional names, e.g., **GILLESPIE, JOHN BIRKS ("DIZZY")** or **WASHINGTON, DINAH** (née **RUTH JONES**). In cases where an individual used both pseudonym and given name, both are listed, with a cross-reference to the name that heads the biographical sketch, e.g., **PROFESSOR LONGHAIR.** See **BYRD, HENRY** or **SUNNYLAND SLIM.** See **LUANDREW, ALBERT.** Where individuals preferred to use initials for the first name, or for both first and second given names, brackets are used to indicate such usage, e.g., J. Rosamond Johnson is listed as **J[OHN] ROSAMOND JOHNSON**; S. H. Dudley is listed as **S[HERMAN] H[OUSTON] DUDLEY.** Names can be a source of confusion, particularly among bluesmen and jazzmen. I have made a conscientious effort to track down given names as well as professional names and to indicate the form of the name preferred by the individual. In the case of married women, the form of the listing distinguishes between married and maiden name, with the professional name being used to head the biographical sketch, e.g., the listing **GRAHAM DU BOIS, SHIRLEY** indicates that the subject was known as Graham during her musical career and Du Bois was the married name. The listing **HARE, MAUDE CUNEY** indicates that the married name Hare was used professionally, and Cuney was the maiden name. I have made no effort to identify a married name in instances where the subject did not use it professionally. The same procedures used for identifying individual names are used to denote names of groups and professional organizations.

MUSICAL OCCUPATION.

The vocation of the subject is identified according to how he/she was first known or best known professionally. Many of the subjects were active, however, in more than one field, sometimes because of economic necessity as well as personal choice; these concomitant career activities are discussed in the body of the essays. The concert artist may have had to conduct a music studio and serve as a church musician in order to earn a livelihood from music; invariably concert artists taught privately after retiring from the stage. The practicing musicians and composers who entered into university teaching after earlier careers in composing, jazz, or concert work are identified with their first career choices; whereas persons who began their careers as university teachers are so designated even though they may have toured occasionally as concert artists or played with professional groups. In some fields, particularly the blues and jazz in the early years, it was common for the musician to hold a non-music job along with his musical activity.

In cases where individuals won recognition in two fields, both vocations are listed, joined by a slash, e.g., **WASHINGTON, DINAH.** Gospel/Jazz Singer; **HOLLAND, CHARLES.** Jazz/Opera Singer. In selecting terms to represent the various occupations, I have tried to be as precise as possible. The term *composer*, for example, is applied only to one who wrote art music and/or large-form works in the traditional manner, although I am aware that jazzmen are also composers in the sense that they invent tunes or new sounds as an essential part of their performance. The term *songwriter* is used for the person who wrote primarily popular songs. The terms *musicologist* and *ethnomusicologist* are reserved for individuals who earned advanced degrees in those fields and who published articles in professional journals and/or books in the field.

In a few instances, it proved impossible to use pinpoint precision. I found it necessary, for example, to use the term *jazz* to apply to a variety of musics which fit uncomfortably into the categories of folk, popular, religious, or classical; these musics conventionally have been classified as Dixieland, swing, bebop, avant-garde, and contemporary. Modern jazzmen typically play more than one instrument, and although for the sake of simplicity I have associated individuals with their primary instrument, I realize many are actually multi-instrumentalists who play both electric and accoustic instruments. Another example is my use of the term *entertainer* to refer to the performer who not only sang but also danced and/or used comedy routines in his act. Most frequently the entertainer sang popular music but may have sung rhythm 'n' blues, country-western, or any other of the many kinds of light music. Finally, the term *rhythm 'n' blues* is used to refer to singers of popular music in the black tradition, in the same way as "race music" was used to apply to such music during the 1920s-1940s. The term as used in this work encompasses a wide variety of styles, such as "soul," "funk," and "disco."

Appendix 3, Musical Occupations, gives evidence of the wide variety of musical vocations represented among the biographees, many of whom appear on more than one list.

DATES AND PLACES OF BIRTH AND DEATH.

Whenever possible, I obtained facts of vital statistics from such reliable sources as questionnaires filled out by the subjects, oral and published interviews, official records, and dictionaries that draw upon data provided by the subjects (as in the *Who's Who* books). It should be kept in mind, however, that even information coming from the horse's mouth, so to speak, can be suspect. Performers, particularly, are evasive about giving correct dates of birth; they much prefer to be younger than they actually are until they become octogenarians and nonagenarians. Then they brag about their ages. I found newspapers to be generally reliable in regard to death dates but not always for birth dates, especially where "age at death" was given instead of date of birth. In such instances, my calculations may be off by a year, and I have so indicated by using the prefix *circa* (abbreviated *c*) before the year, e.g., c1920. That form is used also for other educated guesses, and the question mark is used where my information was too scanty to allow for educated guesses. I have made every effort to incorporate the results of my primary-sources research and of the latest research of others into my writing, and occasionally this demands revision of previously accepted data. While I do not pinpoint the sources of the misinformation, it should be remembered that one of my objectives is to update and to correct.

Appendices 1 and 2 provide graphic illustration of the chronological span and geographical spread of this dictionary. As might be anticipated, it was not until the 1860s, when more than four million slaves finally obtained their freedom after two hundred years of suffering, that the creative genius of black Americans was allowed to blossom. With the gradual crumbling of the bars of discrimination, beginning in the 1950s, black musicians finally began to develop to their fullest potential. In view of the wretched conditions under which blacks were forced to live before emancipation, it is miraculous that there should have been any musicians at all before 1863.

DETAILS OF CAREERS.

At the beginning of each essay I have indicated the musical influences brought to bear on the subject through his family, environment, and early training, whenever such information was available. Musical training might be obtained formally in schools or informally through apprenticeship, as was common in the case of bluesmen, gospel singers, and some jazzmen. In the case of apprentices, it should be remembered that individuals underwent training also when they performed alongside experienced players and learned from them; consequently, I have listed the most important group affiliations of the subjects. The asterisk symbol is used to indicate that the biography of the individual mentioned appears elsewhere in this dictionary. Awards and honors associated with popular music, jazz, and gospel are listed as awards from the music or recording industries without any attempt to specify the awardees as winners in *Down Beat*, *Ebony*, or *Metronome* polls; Grammy award winners; recipients of platinum or gold records; or receivers of similar awards distributed by the industry.

In the cases of subjects who received their education formally in schools or through private study, it should be remembered that college attendance by black Americans before the 1940s was relatively rare—as it was, indeed, for all Americans—and that most of our biographees were poor. It may be assumed, therefore, that those who attended college before the mid-century years generally not only were very talented but also the recipients of scholarships and other kinds of awards. Typically, the career development of these persons was aided by individual white patrons and/or black churches and fraternal organizations. This kind of information does not appear in the essays, primarily because it represents the norm, but awards and honors received by biographees after the conclusion of basic education are listed.

A brief representative list of the subject's best-known performances or recordings or compositions or publications is offered in the belief that these evidences of creativity help to place the subject in a musical and/or historical context. In many instances, I could not find dates for compositions; many composers did not even publish their music. Generally, the dates given are dates of composition rather than of publication. The evaluative statements that are added in some cases should further help in explaining why the subject was important and what his specific contributions were to the history of black music. The length of an essay somewhat reflects the importance of the subject, but not invariably so. Some individuals had long, full careers, while others, who may have been just as influential upon their times, died at a young age. Then, too, there was the problem of documentation. Some individuals were too important to exclude, even though the available information was too scanty to allow for a full essay.

BIBLIOGRAPHY AND DISCOGRAPHY.

The references listed in this section represent not only sources I used but also sources to which the user may go for further information. Unpublished materials are listed first—the questionnaires filled out by subjects, correspondence, interviews, and archival sources. The published sources are arranged alphabetically, except that black-press items are grouped together in the alphabetical position of *B*. I have included only such references as contain additional information about the subjects and are easily available in published form or in microform editions. Some titles are represented by abbreviations (see Selected Bibliography for list). Page numbers are given only where the publication has no index or contents page. In the case of the black newspapers, the early issues often had no pagination; but as the papers were characteristically small, consisting of ten or twelve pages, the music-and-stage-news pages are easily located. It was impractical to list some of the most important sources of information—the playbills, programs, obsequies notes, and clippings received from the black-press clipping service. Scholars who wish to consult these materials may apply to me for making appropriate arrangements. It should be remembered that, where my data conflict with previously published information, I have made a conscious effort to correct errors and misinterpretations.

I realize that the most important thing about a musician is the sound of his music, and I regret being unable to find discographies for all subjects. As regards jazz, blues, and gospel (to some extent), a number of fine scholars have produced exemplary work in this field, such as Robert Dixon, Jon Goodrich, Cedric Hayes, Grunnet Jepsen, and Brian Rust, among others (see Selected Bibliography for details). Other areas remain totally neglected. Patricia Turner is the only one, to my knowledge, who has published discographies of black concert and opera artists, and her publications presently are confined to singers. To be sure, Dominique-René de Lerma's forthcoming, multi-volume *Bibliography of Black Music* will include a *Discography of Concert Music*. Frequently, biographical publications include lists of works, discographies, and even filmographies. Such books as the Feather and Kinkle encyclopedias give short lists of recordings for individuals. Finally, users of this dictionary will find that Schwann catalogs can be helpful in locating recordings if the artists' names are known.

Eileen Southern
Harvard University

LIST OF ABBREVIATIONS

(See the Selected Bibliography for reference abbreviations)

A	alto
A.A.	Associate in Arts
AAGO	Associate of the American Guild of Organists
ABC	American Broadcasting Company
AFM	American Federation of Musicians
AID	Agency for International Development
AME	African Methodist Episcopal
AMEZ	African Methodist Episcopal Zion
anon	anonymous
ANTA	American National Theatre and Academy
A&M	Agricultural and Mechanical
A&T	Agricultural and Technical
b.	born
B	bass
B.A.	Bachelor of Arts
BBC	British Broadcasting System
B.E.	Bachelor of Education
B.F.A.	Bachelor of Fine Arts
bibl.	bibliography
B.L.S.	Bachelor of Library Science
B. Mus.	Bachelor of Music
B.Mus.Ed.	Bachelor of Music Education
B.S.	Bachelor of Science
B.W.I.	British West Indies
c	circa
CBS	Columbia Broadcasting System
CME	Colored Methodist Episcopal or Christian Methodist Episcopal
Co.	company
C.O.G.I.C.	Church of God in Christ
comp.	compiled
d.	died
D.C.	District of Columbia
disc.	discography
diss.	dissertation
D.M.A.	Doctor of Musical Arts
D. Mus. Ed.	Doctor of Musical Education
ed.	editor, edited by, edition
FAGO	Fellow of the American Guild of Organists
illus.	illustrated
Inc.	incorporated
incl.	including
intro.	introduction
JATP	Jazz at the Philharmonic
M.A.	Master of Arts
MBS	Mutual Broadcasting System
M.F.A.	Master of Fine Arts
M.L.S.	Master of Library Science
M.Mus.	Master of Music
M. Mus. Ed.	Master of Music Education
M.S.	Master of Science
NAACP	National Association for the Advancement of Colored People
NANM	National Association of Negro Musicians
NBC	National Broadcasting Company
no.	number
NYA	National Youth Adminstration
op.	opus
p.	page(s)

Ph.D.	Doctor of philosophy
QRS	Quality Reigns Supreme
RCA	Radio Corporation of America
Rev.	Reverend
rev.	revised
S	soprano
T	tenor
T.O.B.A.	Theatre Owners Booking Association
transl.	translation, translated by
U.N.	United Nations
UNESCO	United Nations Edcational, Scientific and Cultural Organization
U.S.	United States
USIS	United States Information Service
U.S.O.	United Service Organizations
USSR	Union of Soviet Socialist Republics
vol.	volume
WPA	Works Progress Administration
YM and YWCA	Young Men's and Young Women's Christian Association

A

ABDUL-RAHIM, RAOUL. Writer (b. 7 November 1929 in Cleveland, Ohio). He began his career as a concert baritone; he studied privately with Lola Hayes, Alexander Kipnis, Yves Tinarye, and Adolphe Vogel and at the Vienna [Austria] Academy of Music (1962). He made his debut in April 1955 at Karamu Theatre in Cleveland, Ohio; he made his New York debut in December 1967 at the Carnegie Recital Hall. He toured widely in the United States and abroad (1959-67), appearing in concert halls and at festivals, including the Vienna Theater in Zentrum (1962) and the Bartok Festival in Budapest, Hungary (1962). He also toured as a lecturer and served on panels at meetings of professional organizations and educational institutions. He encouraged music performance in the Harlem community of New York; in 1958 he founded the Coffee Concert Series of Harlem and served as its director for several years (1958-63). He also conducted a voice studio and vocal seminars. Beginning in 1970 he gave increasing attention to writing about the arts. In 1975 he became music critic of the *Amsterdam News* and a member of the Music Critics Association. His honors included awards from the Harold Jackman Memorial Committee (1978) and the National Association of Negro Musicians (1978). His principal music publications were *Famous Black Entertainers of Today* (New York, 1974) and *Blacks in Classical Music* (New York, 1977).

BIBL: ContA, 37-40. WWBA. WWE.

ABRAMS, MUHAL RICHARD LOUIS. Jazz pianist (b. 19 September 1930 in Chicago, Illinois). He taught himself to play piano and several wind instruments. He obtained his musical education at Chicago Musical College (attended four years). His early style development was influenced by Walter ("King") Fleming, William E. Jackson, and the recordings of James P. Johnson.* He began his professional career in 1950, writing and arranging music for King Fleming. In 1955 he was co-founder of a group, called the MJT-3, for which he also was chief arranger and writer. In 1961 he formed a big band, The Experimental Band, in Chicago. During these years he also played with various groups in Chicago and in New York. In 1965 he was one of the founders of the Association for the Advancement of Creative Musicians,* from which developed such groups as the Art Ensemble of Chicago,* the Creative Construction Company, and others. He was an early member of the Creative Construction Company, along with Anthony Braxton,* Leroy Jenkins,* and Leo Smith.* During the 1970s he toured and recorded as a piano soloist and also with others, including the Muhal Richard Abrams Sextet. His best known albums included *Levels and Degrees of Light* (1967), *Young at Heart, Wise in Time* (1969), *Things to Come From Those Now Gone*, *Sightsong*, and *Afrisong*.

BIBL: Questionnaire. ContKey (May 1978). *Downbeat* (15 August 1974). FeaGitJS. Dominique-René de Lerma, ed., *Reflections on Afro-American Music* (Kent, Ohio, 1973).

ACCOOE, WILLIS. Composer (Fl. late nineteenth century; d. April 1904 in New York). Little is known of his career except that he was regarded by his contemporaries as a person of much talent. It may be that the tenor soloist William Accooe who appeared on a Grand Concert in Philadelphia in 1873 should be identified as this biographee. Early in his career he was a pianist with Puggsley's Tennessee Warblers. In 1898 he was appointed the first black musical director of John Isham's Octoroons Company, No. 2, and in 1899 he became musical director of the Robert Cole*/Billy Johnson* *A Trip to Coontown* show and wrote music for the show. In 1901 he wrote music for a Broadway musical, *The Casino Girl*, and for an Off-Broadway production, *The Cannibal King*, the latter with Will

Marion Cook.* In 1902 he joined the George Walker*/ Bert Williams* company as musical director. By December 1903 he had completed a comic opera, which apparently was never produced. His best-known songs were "My Samoan Beauty" and "Society." His wife, Alice Mackey Accooe, was a noted contralto of the period.

BIBL: PaHistSoc: 1G. Black press, incl. IndF, 4 March 1899, 20 April 1901, 28 December 1901, 12 April 1902, 23 April 1904, 1 July 1905.

ACQUAYE, SAKA. Artist/Jazz bandleader (b. 1928 in Accra, Ghana). His father, an amateur musician, played the concertina for his family and acquainted them with hymns, traditional Ga songs, and "highlife." Saka played fife in his school band. He obtained his education at Achimota College, where he studied with Ephraim Amu,* and at the Philadelphia [Pennsylvania] Academy of the Arts in the United States (1954). Although best known as an artist, he was also a musician. In 1951-52 he played saxophone with the Accra Orchestra, and later formed his own Black Beats Band. A few years later he formed Saka Acquaye and His African Ensemble, which made recordings of his compositions that drew upon African themes. In the 1960s he called his group The African Tones. His best-known musicals were *Bö Mong* and *Obadzeng*.

BIBL: *Africa Report* 16 (January 1971). *West African Review* 33 (March 1962), p. 19.

ADAMS, ALTON AUGUSTUS. Military bandmaster (b. 4 November 1889 on St. Thomas, Virgin Islands). He began music study at the age of nine and continued to study privately until he was an adult. He also took correspondence courses from Hugh Clark at the University of Pennsylvania in Philadelphia, the School of Musical Theory at Carnegie Hall in New York, the Royal Academy of Music in London, England, and the University Extension Conservatory of Music in Chicago, Illinois (B. Mus.). At an early age he was apprenticed to a shoemaker, Albert Francis, who was also a bandmaster. Adams's style development was influenced by Francis, from whom he learned to play instruments and also how to conduct a band. In 1910 he organized a band, the St. Thomas Juvenile Band, which he developed into a first-class group. The United States purchased the Virgin Islands in 1917, placing the islands under supervision of the U.S. Navy; upon recommendation of Navy personnel, Adams and his band were taken into the Navy as a unit. Adams was appointed Chief Musician (the sea duty requirement being waived) and thereby became the first black bandmaster in Navy history. He served during the years 1917-34 and 1942-47; his band toured in the United States in 1924 and in the West Indies in 1930. Adams composed a number of marches, of which the best known were "Virgin Island March," "Spirit of the U.S. Navy," and "Governor's Own." Adams also contributed articles to newspapers and periodicals and served as a department editor of such journals as *Jacob's Band Monthly* (1913-17), *Metronome*, and *Army and Navy Musician*. In 1918 Adams organized the public-school music program for the Virgin Islands, and he served as supervisor during the years 1918-31.

BIBL: Black press. BPIM 5 (Fall 1977). WWCA, 1950.

ADAMS, ELWYN ALBERT. Concert violinist (b. 4 August 1933 in Cleveland, Ohio). He came from a musical family: his father played violin, his mother was a singer and piano-accompanist, and his sister Armenta* became a concert pianist. He began violin study at the age of eight in the preparatory department of the New England Conservatory of Music at Boston, Massachusetts. He was inspired and encouraged by Louia Vaughn Jones* to become a concert violinist. He obtained his musical education at the New England Conservatory (B. Mus., 1956) and through private study in Boston with Richard Burgin (1952-56) and in Brussels, Belgium, with Arthur Grumiaux (1956-59) and Ricardo Odvoposoff (1958). He toured widely as a concert violinist in Europe and in the United States, giving recitals and appearing with symphony orchestras. He was concertmaster of the Bordeaux [France] Symphony Orchestra (1963-70) before joining the music faculty of the University of Florida at Gainesville in 1970. Thereafter he combined teaching with playing concerts and performing with orchestral and chamber groups. His honors included first prize at the Fourth International Music Competition in Munich, West Germany (1955); first prize in violin and second prize in chamber music at the Brussels Royal Conservatory Competition (1957); an award from the Eugene Ysaye Foundation (1967); and a Berkshire Music Festival fellowship.

BIBL: Questionnaire.

ADAMS, ISHMAEL KWESI-MENSAH. Choral conductor (b. 8 February 1920 in Accra, Ghana). He obtained his education at the Government Senior Boys' School in Accra; at the Curwen College of Music in London, England (diploma, 1952); and at the Royal School of Church Music in Canterbury, England. In 1954 he began his professional music career as a music assistant at the Ghana Broadcasting Corporation. By 1968 he had been promoted to Assistant Controller of

Programmes (Music). He founded and directed the Trinity Singers (1953-) and the Damas Male Voice Choir (1954-). He also served for a period of time as assistant choirmaster at the Holy Trinity Cathedral Church in Accra. He was an associate of the Curwen Tonic Sol-fa College of Music and published the *Tataleo Choral Journal*.

BIBL: GhanaWW. WWAfrica.

ADAMS HUMMINGS, ARMENTA. Concert pianist (b. 27 June 1936 in Cleveland, Ohio). She came from a musical family: her father played violin, her mother was a singer and piano-accompanist, and her brother Elwyn* became a concert violinist. She began piano study at the age of five in the preparatory department of the New England Conservatory of Music at Boston, Massachusetts. She obtained her musical education at the Juilliard School of Music in New York (M.S., 1962), where she studied with Sascha Gorodnitski. She made her debut as a concert pianist in 1961 at Town Hall in New York. Shortly thereafter she was invited to play in Sierra Leone, West Africa, in ceremonies celebrating its independence; after her performance she toured in other West African countries. During the 1960s-70s she toured widely in the United States, Europe, Australia, India, Pakistan, and Africa, giving recitals and appearing with symphony orchestras. In 1966 she was a featured artist at the World Festival of Negro Arts held at Dakar, Senegal. Her honors included fellowships from the John Hay Whitney and Martha Baird Rockefeller Foundations (1958, 1960), awards from professional music organizations, and a citation from the U.S. State Department for her contributions to American foreign relations.

BIBL: Questionnaire. Black press, incl. AmstN, 27 June 1964.

ADDERLEY, JULIAN EDWIN ("CANNONBALL"). Jazz saxophonist (b. 15 September 1928 in Tampa, Florida; d. 8 August 1975 in Gary, Indiana). He came from a musical family: his father played jazz cornet, and his brother Nathaniel (''Nat'')* became a professional jazz musician. He obtained his musical education in public schools of Tampa, Florida, and Tallahasee, Florida, where he came under the tutelage of high-school bandmaster Leander Kirksey; at Florida A & M College in Tallahasee (B.A., 1948); at the U.S. Naval School of Music (1952); and at New York University (M.A.) He was a teacher and band director at Dillard High School in Fort Lauderdale, Florida, before and after his service in the U.S. Armed Forces (1951-53). In the army he directed jazz groups, the 36th Army Dance Band, and the Army Band at Fort Knox, Kentucky. In the summer of 1955 he went to New York on a visit and was drawn into the world of professional jazz when he filled in for a tardy saxophonist in Oscar Pettiford's* band at the Club Bohemia. His impressive performance brought him overnight celebrity. Thereafter he signed a recording contract and the next spring formed a quintet (1956-57), which included his brother Nat, Sam Jones, Jimmy Cobb, and Julian (''Junior'') Mance. After the group was disbanded, he played with the Miles Davis* Sextet (1957-59) and George Shearing (1959), then reorganized his own group (1959-75). He toured widely throughout the world with his Adderley Quintet and recorded extensively; during the 1960s he enlarged the group to a sextet (1961-65). Those who played with him over the years included his brother Nat, Sam Jones, Louis Hayes, Robert (''Bobby'') Timmons, Barry Harris,* Victor Feldman, Joe Zawinul, Yusef Lateef,* Walter Booker, George Duke, and Charles Lloyd, among others. His well-known performances included ''This here,'' ''Work song,'' ''Sermonette,'' ''Mercy, mercy, mercy,'' and ''Jive samba.'' During the 1960s he became deeply involved in peripheral musical activities. He worked closely with Jesse Jackson's Operation Breadbasket program in Chicago, Illinois, and the later PUSH program, directing musical activities and performing with his group, particularly at Black Expo 1972. He adopted the Reverend Jackson as his ''personal pastor'' and produced in his honor the recordings *Walk Tall* and *The Country Preacher*. He began to add lectures and workshops to his concerts on college campuses, emphasizing the history of black music. He served on panels and committees of professional and government organizations, including the National Endowment for the Arts and the John F. Kennedy Center for the Performing Arts. He actively promoted the career advancement of fellow musicians, among them, Nancy Wilson. In 1974 the Florida House of Representatives offered a resolution in honor of the Adderleys for their musical achievement that reflected glory to their home state. Adderley wrote some of the music played by his group, as did also his brother Nat and other members of the group. His major work was a folk musical written in collaboration with Nat, titled *Big Man* (based on the John Henry legend), which he did not live to see performed on the stage. The album *Big Man* was released posthumously, with Joe Williams* in the title role. Adderley appeared in television shows and was host for a series in 1972; he also appeared in films including *Play Misty For Me* (1971) and *Soul to Soul* (1971). Adderley's style reflected the influence of Charlie Parker* and John Coltrane*; he played both soprano and alto saxophones. He was credited with having invented the concept of, if not the terms, ''soul'' and ''funk'' as applied to jazz. In his later career he showed an interest in electronic instruments and elements of rock 'n' roll. He was married to Olga James, a singer and actress.

BIBL: Black press, incl. CDef, 20 September 1975. FeaEJ. FeaJS. FeaGitJS. MeeJMov. WWA, 1976-77. *Encore* (16 August 1975). *Sepia* (July 1965). CurBiog (January 1961). NYT, 9 August 1975.

DISC: Jep. TudJ.

ADDERLEY, NATHANIEL ("NAT"). Jazz cornetist/Trumpeter (b. 25 November 1931 in Tampa, Florida). He came from a musical family: his father played jazz cornet, and his brother Julian (''Cannonball'')* became a professional jazz musician. He obtained his musical education at Florida A & M College in Tallahasee, Florida (B.A., B.S., 1951). In his childhood he was a boy soprano, then later studied trumpet, baritone horn, and cornet. During his service in the U.S. Armed Forces (1951-53), he played in the 36th Army Dance Band. After his discharge from the army he played professionally with various groups, including Lionel Hampton* (1954-55), his brother (1956-57), James Louis (''J. J.'') Johnson* (1957-58), and Woodrow (''Woody'') Herman (1959), then joined Cannonball permanently in 1960. He toured widely with the Adderley Quintet and recorded extensively. After his brother's death in 1975 he served as artist-in-residence in educational institutions for a period, then returned to jazz performance and formed his own group. His son, Nathaniel, Jr., became a professional jazz musician.

BIBL: FeaEJ. FeaJS. FeaGitJS. *Encore* (7 March 1977). MeeJMov. WWA. WWBA.

DISC: Jep. TudJ.

ADDISON, ADELE. Concert singer (b. 24 July 1925 in New York, New York). Her family moved to Springfield, Massachusetts, when she was a child, and she attended the public schools there. She was encouraged by Dorothy Maynor* to attend the Westminister Choir College at Princeton, New Jersey (B. Mus., 1946). She made her debut as a concert soprano in April 1948 at Jordan Hall in Boston, Massachusetts, and her New York debut in January 1952 at Town Hall. Thereafter she toured in the United States and Canada, giving recitals and appearing with symphony orchestras. In 1963 she toured in the Soviet Union under a cultural exchange program. Her best-known performances were in the world premieres of John La Montaine's *Fragments from Song of Songs* with the New Haven Symphony (1959), Poulenc's *Gloria* with the Boston Symphony (1961), and Foss's *Time Cycle* with the New York Philharmonic (1960). She also sang in oratorio and opera, including the role of Mimi in Puccini's *La Boheme* with the New York City Opera (1955) and the title role of Gershwin's *Porgy and Bess*, along with Richard McFerrin,* on the soundtrack of the film version (1958). She was a member of the New England Opera Company, with whom she sang leading roles in Bizet's *Carmen*, Verdi's *Rigoletto*, and Rossini's *Il Turco in Italia*. She received an honorary doctorate from the University of Massachusetts.

BIBL: AbdulBCM. Black press, incl. AmstN, 10 May 1947, 28 October 1950. WWAW. WWBA.

DISC: Turn.

AFRICAN ROSCIUS, THE. See **ALDRIDGE, IRA.**

AFRO-AMERICAN MUSIC OPPORTUNITIES ASSOCIATION, INC., THE. Professional organization (orig. 1969 at Minneapolis, Minnesota). The organization was founded by C. Edward Thomas* with the support of professional musicians, foundations, and the public. Its purpose was to promote ''the involvement of black musicians in the varied fields of classical music, not only to help black musicians, but to contribute to the enrichment of the quality of serious music throughout the United States and to provide information about it, and to serve as a liaison between talent and opportunity'' (quoted from AAMOA publicity literature). The association published a bimonthly newsletter and reference pamphlets, titled *AAMOA Resource Papers*, under the editorial supervision of Dominique-René de Lerma. During the early 1970s AAMOA sponsored Black Composers Symposia in cooperation with local symphony orchestras and colleges in Baltimore, Maryland (1973), Houston, Texas (1974), and Minneapolis, Minnesota (1975). Beginning in 1974 AAMOA collaborated with Columbia Records to produce a Recorded Anthology of Music by Black Symphonic Composers with the support of various foundations; eight volumes were released before the demise of the project in 1976. The executive director was Thomas, the artistic director and conductor was Paul Freeman,* and the chief consultant was De Lerma. The recordings represented the music of black composers over a period of two centuries, beginning with the Chevalier de Saint-Georges*; and the performers included the leading artists of the nation. AAMOA also released recordings under its own record label. The interest engendered by AAMOA activities led to the organization of a special concert series sponsored by the New York Philharmonic Symphony under the leadership of Leon Thompson* and Freeman, titled A Celebration of Black Composers, at the Lincoln Center in New York on 29 August-2 September 1977. AAMOA made an important contribution to the development of Afro-American music for a period of about ten years (1969-78). Its collaboration with Columbia Records made available for the first time in history an organized series of the symphonic and operatic music of black composers, its sponsorship of national symposia brought about public awareness of this music and stimulated the promotion of similar programs by others, and its publications infused new life into black-music research activities.

AKPABOT, SAMUEL. College professor/Composer (b. 3 October 1931 in Uyo, South Eastern State, Nigeria). His schoolteacher mother "sometimes sang." He sang in the Anglican Cathedral choir (as a boy soprano) at Lagos, Nigeria, for seven years and taught himself to play piano as a child. He first studied piano and organ formally in London, England. He obtained his musical education at King's College in Lagos (diploma, 1954); at the Royal College of Music in London (Associate, 1959), where he studied with Osbourne Peasgood, Ernest Hall, and Herbert Howells of London University; at Trinity College of Music in London (Fellow, 1967); at the University of Chicago [Illinois] (M.A., 1967), where he studied with Howard Brown, Grosvenor Cooper, and Easley Blackwood; and at Michigan State University in East Lansing (Ph.D., 1975). During the years 1959-62 he was Senior Music Producer with the Nigerian Broadcasting Corporation in Lagos. His teaching career included tenures at the University of Nigeria in Nsukka (1962-64, 1967-70), at the University of Ife [Nigeria] (1970-73); at Michigan State University (1973-75); and at the University of Calabar [Nigeria] (1975-). He toured widely as a lecturer in the United States during the 1970s, speaking on the subject of African music. He also contributed articles to such scholarly journals as *African Music*, *African Arts*, *Presence Africaine*, and *The Black Perspective in Music*. His book publications included *Ibibio Music in Nigerian Culture* (Michigan State University Press, 1975) and an article in *Reflections on Afro-American Music* (ed. by Dominique-René de Lerma, Kent State University Press, 1973). Throughout his professional career he was active as a composer. He began to write as early as 1959 and to publish his compositions in 1972. He wrote for a variety of media: orchestra, chorus, chamber groups, and film. His best-known works included *Cynthia's Lament* for wind orchestra, soprano, and six African instruments (1972); *Three Nigerian Dances* for string orchestra and percussion (1975); *Verba Christi*, a cantata for soloists, chorus, narrator, and orchestra (1975, texts based on Synoptic Gospels and congregational hymns); *Festival Fanfare* (1975); *Ofala Festival*, tone poem for wind orchestra and five African instruments (1975); *Jaja of Opobo*, operetta with English and Nigerian texts (1972); and *Three Roads to Tomorrow*, soundtrack for film of same title (1959). His honors included commissions from professional organizations and government institutions in the United States and in Nigeria, prizes won in composition competition, and first prize in a Cannes Film Festival (1956) for a commercial jingle for Barclay's Bank of London.

BIBL: Questionnaire. Black press, incl. *The* [Pittsburgh] *New Courier*, 7 July 1973. BiogNig. WWAfrLit.

ALDRIDGE, AMANDA (also known as **MONTAGUE RING**). Composer (b. 10 March 1866 in Upper Norwood, London; d. 9 March 1956 in London). She came from a musical family: her father, Ira Aldridge,* was an actor and singer, and her sister Irene Luranah* became an opera singer. Encouraged by her father, she studied piano as a child. She attended a convent school in Belgium, then the Royal College of Music in London, England. She studied voice with Jenny Lind and George Henschel, elocution with Madge Kendal, harmony and counterpoint with Frederick Bridge and Francis Gladstone. After a successful concert career, she turned to music teaching when an attack of laryngitis permanently injured her voice. She used the name Montague Ring on her compositions to keep separate her dual careers as singing teacher and composer. Among the singers she coached were Marian Anderson,* Roland Hayes,* and Paul Robeson.* Her best-known compositions were *Three African Dances* (1913), *Three Arabian Dances* (1919), and *Carnival Suite of Five Dances* (1924).

BIBL: Hare. Herbert Marshall and Mildred Stock, *Ira Aldridge, the Negro Tragedian* (London, 1958).

ALDRIDGE, IRA FREDERICK (also known as the **AFRICAN ROSCIUS**). Actor/Entertainer (b. 24 July 1807 in New York, New York.; d. 7 August 1867 at Lodz, Poland). He attended the African Free School No. 2 in New York and obtained his early stage experience with the African Grove Theater company in New York during the years 1821-24. In 1824 he went to Great Britain, working his way across the ocean as a ship steward. He attended the University of Glasgow during the years 1824-25. His first professional engagement was in October 1825 at the Coburg Theater in London, England. He won acclaim for his ability to portray tragic, melodramatic, and comic roles with equal skill; he often whitened his skin to play non-black roles. He also was celebrated for his singing roles, which included Mungo in the ballad opera *The Padlock* (by Bickerstaff and Dibdin) and Alambra in the musical drama *Paul and Virginia* (by Cable, Mazzinghi, and Reeve). As an entertainer he accompanied himself on the Spanish guitar; his repertory included ballads, comic songs, and minstrel songs. His best-known performances were of "Opposum up a gum tree," "The Negro's lament," and "Let me, when my heart is sinking." He was the first black actor to attain international renown; his triumphant tours brought him many honors and awards, including decorations from the King of Prussia, the Czar of Russia, and the King of Sweden. Three of his four children became professional musicians—Ira Frederick, Amanda,* and Irene Luranah.*

BIBL: Black press, incl. the *Anglo-African Magazine* (1860); NYAge, 18 January1890. Herbert Marshall and Mildred Stock, *Ira Aldridge, the Negro Tragedian* (London, 1958). Simm.

ALDRIDGE, IRENE LURANAH. Opera singer (b. 29 March 1860 in London, England; d. 20 November 1932 in London). She came from a musical family: her father, Ira Aldridge,* was an actor and singer, and her sister Amanda* became a composer and voice teacher. As a child she sang with her father. She attended a convent school in Belgium and private schools in Paris, France; Berlin, Germany; and London, England. She settled in Paris and entered a professional career as an opera and concert singer, singing contralto roles in the leading opera houses of Europe. She was reputed to have sung in a Wagerian opera in the Bayreuth [Germany] Festivals at the turn of the century. A tragic illness cut off her career, leaving her an invalid for the last twenty years of her life.

BIBL: Hare. Herbert Marshall and Mildred Stock, *Ira Aldridge, the Negro Tragedian* (London, 1958).

ALEXANDER, BROOKS. Studio teacher (b. c1916; d. July 1976 in New York, New York). He obtained his musical education at Knoxville College in Tennessee and at the Juilliard School of Music in New York. During his service in the U. S. Armed Forces (World War II), he directed army bands at Camp Shanks in New York and at Camp Wheeler in Georgia. He toured widely as a soloist with the Fisk Jubilee Singers* and with the [Leonard] DePaur Singers.* He was musical director of Black Musical Theater Voices, Inc., in New York, which won critical acclaim for its production of the Broadway musical *The Believers* (1968). He conducted a vocal studio; those whom he taught and/or coached in voice included Melba Moore,* Hope Clark, Aretha Franklin,* and Judith DePaul.

BIBL: Black press, incl. AmstN, 7 August 1976.

ALLEN, BETTY LOU (née ELIZABETH LOUISE). Concert singer (b. 17 March 1930 in Campbell, Ohio). Her mother sang in a church choir. She began piano study at an early age and sang with a YWCA glee club. She obtained her musical education at Wilberforce College in Ohio (1944-46), where she studied with Theodore Heimann and sang with the Wilberforce Singers, and at the Hartford College of Music in Connecticut (certificate, 1952). Her teachers included Sarah Peck Moore, Paul Ulanowsky, Carolina Segrera, and Zinka Milanov. In 1951 she attracted the attention of Leonard Bernstein during her study at the Berkshire Music Festival in Tanglewood, Massachusetts, and he invited her to sing in the performance of his *Jeremiah* Symphony. In 1952 she sang the role of St. Teresa II in Virgil Thompson's *Four Saints in Three Acts* in the New York production and repeated the role in a Paris, France, production. In 1958 she made her concert debut (mezzo-soprano) at Town Hall in New York. Thereafter she toured widely in the United States and abroad, giving recitals and appearing with symphony orchestras, singing on radio and television programs, singing at music festivals, and recording for both American and European companies. She also sang oratorio and opera. In 1964 she made her formal operatic debut as Jocasta in Stravinsky's *Oedipus Rex* at the Teatro Colón in Buenos Aires, Argentina. Her other well-known performances were as Ericlea in Monteverdi's *Il Ritorno d' Ulisse*, Monisha in Scott Joplin's* *Treemonisha* (1975), and Landgravine Sophie in Liszt's oratorio *Die Legende von der Heiligen Elisabeth*. Her teaching career included tenures as lecturer or artist-in-residence at the Manhattan School of Music in New York, the Philadelphia [Pennsylvania] Music Academy; the Sibelius Akademie at Helsinki, Finland; and the North Carolina School of the Arts in Winston-Salem. In 1980 she succeeded Dorothy Maynor* as director of the Harlem School of the Arts in New York. Her honors included the Marian Anderson* Award (1952); Martha Baird Rockefeller, John Hay Whitney, and Ford Foundation grants and/or fellowships; and an honorary doctorate from Wittenberg University (1971).

BIBL: *Saturday Review Programs; Philharmonic Hall* (December 1972). NYT, 9 March 1980. WWA. WWAW. WWBA. WWE. WWOpera.

DISC: Turn.

ALLEN, CLEVELAND G. Music journalist (b. March 1887 in Greenville, South Carolina: d. October

1953 in New York, New York). He obtained his musical education in the public schools of Greenville, South Carolina, and New York; at New York University (1920-23); and at the Angelus Academy of Music in New York (1921). He also studied voice privately. He wrote columns for the *New York Age* and served as the New York representative for the *Chicago Defender* and *The Freeman* [Indianapolis]. During the 1920s he was a regular contributor to *Musical America*. He lectured on black folk music and contributed articles to various professional journals.

BIBL: Black press, incl. CDef, 7 May 1927, 3 May 1930. WWCA, 1941-44, 1950.

ALLEN, HENRY JAMES, JR., ("RED"). Jazz trumpeter (b. 7 January 1908 in Algiers, Louisiana; d. 17 April 1967 in New York, New York). He came from a musical family: his father, Henry Allen, Sr. (1877-1952) played trumpet and led a brass band in New Orleans for more than forty years, and two uncles were also professional bandsmen. As a child he played in his father's band. He first played drums, then violin and other instruments, then changed to trumpet, which he studied with his father and Manuel Manetta. He began his professional career in the 1920s and thereafter played with various groups, including George Lewis* (1926), Joseph ("King") Oliver* (1927), Sidney Desvigne and Fate Marable* on Streckfus riverboats (1925, 1928-29), Luis Russell* (intermittently during the years 1929-32), Fletcher Henderson* (1932, 1933-34), Lucius ("Lucky") Millinder* and his Blue Rhythm Band (1934-37; Louis Armstrong* began "fronting" the band in October 1935), and Armstrong (1937-40), among many other groups. He made his recording debut in 1929 and thereafter recorded extensively with his own groups and with others. In late 1929 he recorded with blues singer Victoria Spivey;* later he recorded with a Reverend Gates and his congregation, and in 1933 he teamed with Coleman Hawkins.* Among those who performed with him at one time or another were Jack ("J.C.") Higginbotham,* George ("Pops") Foster,* Hilton Jefferson, William ("Buster") Bailey, Joe Garland, William ("Cozy") Cole,* Lillian ("Lil") Armstrong,* Daniel ("Danny") Barker,* Paul Barbarin,* and William ("Dicky") Wells,* among many others. During the 1940s-60s he toured widely with his groups and as a soloist, appearing at festivals and playing long nightclub residencies in New York; Chicago, Illinois; Boston, Massachusetts; and San Francisco, California. He first toured in Europe with Edward ("Kid") Ory* in 1959, then in the 1960s toured regularly in Europe, particularly in England. He also played on television shows and appeared in the film *The Sound of Jazz* (1957) and documentaries. His best-known performances were solos on "Rug cutter's swing," "Frankie and Johnny," "Body and Soul" (1935), and a passage on "Shakin' the African" that was widely imitated. Allen was regarded as the most important trumpeter in the New Orleans tradition to follow Louis Armstrong. His style was distinctive for its searing melodies; his versatility enabled him to move successfully into the bebop era and modern jazz.

BIBL: ASCAP. ChilWW. FeaEJ. FeaJS. FeaGitJS. MeeJMov. Martin Williams, *Jazz Masters of New Orleans* (New York, 1967).

DISC: Jep. Kink. RustJR. TudJ.

ALLEN, PETER. Military fifer (fl. early nineteenth century; b. in Pennsylvania). He was the company musician for Captain Wyatt's Company, stationed at Huntsville, Texas, during the 1830s. He played flute and banjo. He was among the 300 soldiers massacred on Palm Sunday in 1836 with Colonel James Fannin at Goliad, Texas.

BIBL: GreBD.

ALLEN, RICHARD. Minister/Hymnal compiler (b. 14 February 1760 in Philadelphia, Pennsylvania; d. 26 March 1831 in Philadelphia). He was the founding father of the African Methodist Episcopal Church in 1794 at Philadelphia, Pennsylvania, and was elected its first bishop in 1816 when the church became incorporated as an independent denomination. In 1801 he compiled a hymnal for the exclusive use of his congregation of the Bethel AME Church, titled *A Collection of Spiritual Songs and Hymns Selected from Various Authors by Richard Allen, African Minister* (printed by John Ormrod), which contained texts of fifty-four hymns. Later the same year he published an enlarged edition of sixty-four hymns, *A Collection of Hymns and Spiritual Songs from Various Authors, by Richard Allen, Minister of the African Methodist Episcopal Church* (printed by T. L. Plowman). Allen's hymnals were landmarks in the history of black Americans as the first compiled by a black man for use by black congregations. As folk-selected anthologies, the hymnals denoted the favorite hymns of black Methodists at the beginning of the nineteenth century; many of the hymns served as source materials for the folk composers of the Negro spirituals. In 1818 Allen was a member of the committee, along with Daniel Coker and James Champion, that compiled the first official hymnal of the newly incorporated AME Church.

BIBL: Richard Allen, *The Life Experience and Gospel Labours of the Right Reverend Richard Allen* (Philadelphia, 1887; reprint New York, 1960). EAB.

Carol V. R. George, *Segregated Sabbaths* (New York, 1973). SouMBA. SouRBM. Charles Wesley, *Richard Allen, Apostle of Freedom* (Washington, D.C., 1935).

ALLEN, SANFORD. Symphony violinist (b. 26 February 1939 in New York, New York). His mother was a pianist. He began piano study at the age of five and violin study at seven. When he was ten years old he entered the preparatory department of the Juilliard School of Music in New York, where he studied with Vera Fonaroff. He studied further with Fonaroff at the Mannes College of Music in New York. He obtained his musical education at the High School of Music and Art in New York and at the Berkshire Music Festival school in Tanglewood, Massachusetts (1956), and the Marboro Music Festival school in Vermont (1963). His professional career as a violinist included tenures in the Lewissohn Stadium Orchestra (summers 1959, 61) and in the New York Philharmonic (1962-77), where he was the first permanent black member. He toured widely as a concert violinist, giving recitals and appearing with symphony orchestras. He taught for a short period at Livingston College of Rutgers University in New Brunswick, New Jersey. His honors included the Federation of Music Clubs Award (1956) and the Koussevitsky International Recording Award (1974).

BIBL: AbdulBCM. Black press, incl. AmstN, 25 October 1962, 14 April 1962. WWBA.

ALLEN, WILLIAM DUNCAN. Concert pianist/ Accompanist (b. 15 December 1906 in Portland, Oregon). He came from a musical family: his mother was a pianist, his paternal aunt was a music graduate of Fisk University at Nashville, Tennessee, in 1907, and his sister Connie was an organist-pianist. He began piano study at the age of five. He obtained his musical education at the Oberlin Conservatory in Ohio (B. Mus., 1928; M. Mus, 1936), where he studied with Frank Shaw, and at the Juilliard School of Music (certificate, 1930), where he studied with Gordon Stanley and James Friskin. He studied further with Egon Petri (1935 in England, summers of 1937, 1939 in Poland). His teaching career included tenures at Howard University in Washington, D.C. (1929-35), and Fisk University (1936-43). During the years 1943-53 he toured widely throughout the world as pianist and accompanist with Todd Duncan. Thereafter he settled in San Francisco, California, where he conducted a music studio, served as minister of music at the South Berkeley Community Congregational Church (1953-79), and as music director of the Junior Bach Festival Association of Berkeley, California (1956-76). He also continued his activity as pianist-accompanist; those whom he accompanied over the years included Adele Addison,* Betty Allen,* Gary Burgess, Charlotte Holloman, Elwood Peterson,* Catherine Van Buren,* John Miles, John Patton, George Shirley,* Paul Robeson,* and William Warfield,* among many others. For many years he wrote music columns for San Francisco and Berkeley-Oakland newspapers and contributed articles to music journals such as *Music Journal*, *The Piano Quarterly*, and *The Black Perspective in Music*. His honors included civic and community and church organizations and an honorary doctorate from the Graduate Theological Institute in Berkeley.

BIBL: Questionnaire. Black press, incl. *The Chronicle* [Detroit] 11 October 1975; NYAge, 8 April 1937. NYB, 1952.

ALLISON, LUTHER. Bluesman (b. 17 August 1939 in Mayflower, Arkansas). He taught himself to play guitar by listening to the records of such bluesmen as B. B. King* and Otis Rush,* among others. In 1951 his family moved to Chicago, Illinois. During the late 1950s he formed a blues group, The Four Jivers, which played in local clubs for several years. He developed a local reputation, was called upon to play engagements outside the Chicago area, and began appearing at the various blues festivals, beginning with the Ann Arbor [Michigan] Blues Festival in 1970. In 1972 he signed a recording contract with Motown; thereafter he recorded extensively.

BIBL: BWW. LivBl 14 (Autumn 1973); Robert Neff and Anthony Connor, *Blues* (Boston, 1975).

ALSDORF, DUBOIS B. Society dance-orchestra leader (b. 6 May 1827 in Newburg, New York; d. 3 November 1907 in Newburg). He was the founder of a family, society-dance orchestra, which for eighty-five years provided dance music and dancing classes for Newburg and other places in its vicinity. As a youth he studied with local teachers, then was apprenticed to William "Mons" Appo,* leader of the New York branch of Frank Johnson's* Philadelphia band. After Alsdorf returned to Newburg, he began his career by playing for local dance classes. Later he organized his own dance orchestra, which played at Saratoga, West Point, and other resorts in New York. In 1849 he organized a brass band and, the same year, a dancing school. The next year he began holding annual balls, or "soirees," as he called them. His three sons became professional musicians. The oldest, Charles T. (d. 20 September 1926), gave his attention to the dancing school, which was maintained after he died by his wife until 1930. Ulysses J. was the leader of the Alsdorf orchestra for forty-four years. Simon P. played first violin and clarinet in the orchestra. Dubois Alsdorf was one of the earliest black musicians to become a member of the Musicians Protective Association (AFM Local 291).

BIBL: Black press, incl. NYAge, 7 November 1907, 21 September 1935.

AMMONS, ALBERT C. Boogie-woogie pianist (b. 1907 in Chicago, Illinois; d. 2 December 1949 in Chicago). Little is known of his early life. He played piano in Chicago nightclubs and for "house-rent parties" in the 1920s. His associates were Meade Lux Lewis* and Clarence ("Pine Top") Smith,* who lived in the same apartment house as he. He also played with various groups, including François Moseley's Louisiana Stompers, William Barbee (1930-31), Louis Banks's Chesterfield Orchestra (1930-34), and his own group, the Rhythm Kings. In 1938 he settled in New York. He played with Lewis and Pete Johnson* on John Hammond's celebrated "From Spirituals to Swing" concert at Carnegie Hall on 23 December 1938. Thereafter he played in nightclubs, sometimes with Johnson, sometimes in a trio with Johnson and Lewis, and as a soloist. During the last years of his life he was active in Chicago. His best-known recordings were "Boogie-woogie stomp," "Pine top blues," and "Early morning blues." His son, Eugene ("Jug") Ammons,* was a jazz saxophonist.

BIBL: BPIM 2 (1974), p. 196. ChilWW. FeaEJ. OlivSB.

DISC: DiGod. Jep. RustJR. Kink.

AMMONS, EUGENE ("GENE" "JUG"). Jazz saxophonist (b. 14 April 1925 in Chicago, Illinois; d. 6 August 1974 in Chicago). His father was boogie-woogie pianist Albert Ammons.* He received his musical education in the public schools of Chicago, Illinois, where he came under the tutelage of Walter Dyett* at DuSable High School. He began his professional career in 1943, playing with King Kolax. Thereafter he played with various groups, including William ("Billy") Eckstine* (1944-47) and Woodrow ("Woody") Herman (1949), and with Edward ("Sonny") Stitt* as co-leader (1950-52). He and Stitt attracted wide attention with their "two-tenor [saxophones] musical battles." During the years 1964-69, when he was in prison because of a narcotics charge, he led the prison orchestra and conducted a jazz radio program. In 1969 he formed a group, which recorded extensively and toured widely in the United States and abroad, including appearances at the major jazz festivals. During the 1970s he frequently teamed again with Stitt and also formed a team with Dexter Gordon.* His best-known performances included solos on "Canadian sunset," "Jungle strut," "Didn't we" and "Blues up and down" (with Stitt). His early style development was influenced by Lester Young.* He had a warm, full tone, and his music fused rhythm 'n' blues elements with jazz, particularly in his later years.

BIBL: FeaEJ. FeaJS. FeaGitJS.

DISC: Jep. Kink. TudJ.

AMOAKU, WILLIAM KOMLA. College professor/ Ethnomusicologist (b. 26 June 1940 in Ho [Volta Region], Ghana). As a child he played toy drums in his father's brass band and performed in traditional groups. He obtained his musical education in the lower schools of Legon, Ghana; at the Ghana School of Music and Drama of the University of Ghana (Mus. diploma, 1967); at the Akademia Mozarteum in Salzburg, Austria (Mus. Ed. diploma, 1969); at the University of Illinois in Champaign (M. Mus., 1971); and at the University of Pittsburgh [Pennsylvania] (Ph.D., 1975). His early career development was influenced by Ephraim Amu,* A. A. Mensah, J. H. Kwabena Nketia,* and Fela Sowande*; at a later stage in his career Bruno Nettl was influential. He began study of alto saxophone at an early age and led his own dance band when he was eighteen. During the next decade he was also active in radio and television in Legon. He served in the United Nations Peace Force in Zaire as a member of the Ghanian Army during the years 1960-62. In 1966 he led a student group on a tour of West Germany and Austria in performing traditional African music. During his period of study in Salzburg, he performed with jazz ensembles and in Orff Schulwerk films. He taught at the University of Ghana (1971-73), then settled in the United States in 1973. Thereafter his teaching career included tenures at Howard University in Washington, D. C., (1975-78) and Central State University in Wilberforce, Ohio (1978-). He toured widely as a lecturer on the subject of African music and as a workshop organizer, appearing on college campuses, at conferences of professional organizations, and on radio and television. He contributed articles to scholarly journals and to collected editions, and he published books, including *African Songs and Rhythms for Children* (1971) with accompanying recording. He was also active as a jazz performer, playing with such jazzmen as William ("Billy") Taylor,* Grover Washington,* Richard Davis,* and Atila Zola, among others; he performed in jazz-history films.

BIBL:Questionnaire. Nathan Davis, ed., *Writings in Jazz* (Dubuque, Iowa, 1977).

AMPHION GLEE CLUB. Community glee club (fl. early twentieth century in Washington, D.C.). This community glee club was organized in 1891 in Washington, D.C. Henry J. Lewis* was its long-term director, and perhaps the founder. The Amphion toured widely along the East Coast, frequently giving concerts with other groups or with individuals. Anniversary concerts were given as late as the 1930s.

BIBL: Black press, incl. NYAge, 19 March 1908, 19 August 1938.

AMU, EPHRAIM. College professor/Composer (b. 13 September 1899 in Peki-Avetile, Trans-Volta Region, Ghana). His father was a drummer, who ceased playing when he and his wife became Christians. Amu received his education in schools at Peki-Avetile and Blengo; at the Basel Mission Seminary in Abetifi (1916-20); and at the Royal College of Music in London, England (Associate, 1940). His teaching career included tenures at the Bremen Mission in Peki-Blengo; at the Presbyterian Training College in Akropong; at Achimota College (1934-37, 1942-48); and at the Achimota Teacher Training College (1948-6?), which became a part of the College of Art, Science and Technology at Kumasi in 1951. Amu was the Supervisor of Music in the Department of Teacher Training. After retiring from Kumasi, he joined the University of Ghana faculty as a Senior Research Fellow. He exerted great influence upon the development of Ghanian music education; several of his students later became professional musicians, among them, Guy Warren.* Amu first published musical compositions as early as 1926. His first book-length publication was *Twenty-Five African Songs* (1953), which included traditional songs and some he had written. His best-known compositions were *Traditional Atentenbenj Prelude* for two winds, *Wo nsam mewo* for male voices, *Two Pieces for Bamboo Flute and Piano*, *Twenty Piped Pieces*, and *Enne ye anigyeda*. He was called "the Father of Ghanian Musicology." The University of Ghana gave him an honorary doctorate.

BIBL: Interview of J.H. Kwabena Nketia by E. S. *West African Review* 28 (March 1957), p. 259. RoachBAM.

ANDERSON, "CAT." See **ANDERSON, WILLIAM ALONZO.**

ANDERSON, EDWARD GILBERT. Symphony orchestra conductor (b. 20 February 1874 in Still Pond, Kent County, Maryland; d. 2 December 1926 in Chester, Pennsylvania). He studied music as a child. His family moved to Chester, Pennsylvania, and he conducted a music studio there while still a youth. Later he moved to Philadelphia, Pennsylvania, where in 1904 he became conductor of the Philadelphia Concert Orchestra. About 1914 he went to New York. Thereafter he was active as a conductor of groups of the New Amsterdam Musical Association, of the Clef Club Symphony orchestra, of the Harlem Symphony Orchestra (which he organized), and of the Renaissance Theater Orchestra.

BIBL: Black press, incl. NYAge, 28 February 1925, 11 December 1926, 16 November 1929; PhilaT, 16 March 1912, 18 April 1914, 8 March 1919. Hare.

ANDERSON, HALLIE. Society dance-orchestra leader (b. 5 January 1885 in Lynchburg, Virginia; d. 9 November 1927 in New York, New York). Her family moved to New York when she was three years old, and she received her musical education in the New York public schools, through private study, and at the New York German Conservatory of Music. The black press carried news about her dance orchestras at the turn of the century. In 1905 she gave concerts in association with the New Amsterdam Musical Association Band. Beginning in the same year she promoted an Annual Reception and Ball for many years—perhaps in emulation of Walter Craig's* receptions. At one time she directed an orchestra of 100 pieces, which was integrated by both sex and race. By the second decade of the century large orchestras were no longer popular. In 1919 she directed a Lady Band at the Lafayette Theater in the Harlem community of New York; its members were violinist Mildred Franklin (b. at Boston, Massachusetts), string bassist Olivia Porter* (b. at New Orleans, Louisiana), cornetist Leora Meaux (b. at Louisville, Kentucky), trombonist Della Sutton (b. at Marion, Indiana), and drummer Alice Calloway (b. at Chattanooga, Tennessee). Anderson also was active during the 1920s as a director of theater orchestras in Philadelphia, Pennsylvania.

BIBL: Black press, incl. NYAge, 1905-c1914; CDef, 20 December 1919, 19 November 1927.

ANDERSON, JOSEPH G. Brass-band leader (b. c1816 in Philadelphia, Pennsylvania; d. 30 April 1873 in Philadelphia). He was a longtime member of the Frank Johnson* musical groups. When Johnson died in 1844, Anderson took over leadership of the bands and orchestras, retaining the name The Frank Johnson String and Brass Bands. Anderson played flute, violin, and cornet à piston. He toured widely with his bands and also conducted a music studio in Philadelphia. During the Civil War, he was employed by the government to train brass bands for black regiments that were stationed at Camp William Penn. One of his well-known students was Hamilton A. Moore.*

BIBL: PaHistSoc, Boxes 1G, 13G. Black press, incl. *The Colored American*, 23 January 1841; The PhilaT, 7 September 1912. John W. Cromwell, "Frank Johnson's Military Band" in *Southern Workman* 29 (1900): 532-535; reprinted in BPIM 4 (July 1976). Martin Delany, *The Condition, Elevation, Emigration and Destiny of the Colored People of the United States* (Philadelphia, 1852), pp. 123-124. *The Public Ledger* [Philadelphia], 25 December 1843; 9 April 1844. Trot, p. 309.

ANDERSON, MARIAN. Concert singer (b. 17 February 1902 in Philadelphia, Pennsylvania). She came from a family of musical amateurs: her grandmother played house organ, her mother sang in church choirs as a girl, and her aunt sang in senior church choirs. Her nephew, James DePriest,* became a symphony orchestra conductor. She began singing in the junior choir at her church, the Union Baptist, when she was six years old and joined the adult choir when she was thirteen. She first sang on a public recital at the age of ten, being advertised as "the baby contralto." She obtained her musical education in the public schools of Philadelphia, Pennsylvania. She began singing for local events in the community at an early age, accompanying herself at the piano, and traveled as far as New York to represent her choir on musical programs. When she was in her third year of high school a family friend, actor John Thomas Butler, arranged for her to study with Mary Patterson, who taught her free of charge. She later studied with Agnes Reifsynder, Guiseppe Boghetti (for many years), and Frank La Forge, among others; in London, England, she studied briefly with Raimund von Zur Mühlen, and with Mark Raphael and Amanda Ira Aldrich.* She coached with Michael Rauscheisen in Berlin, Germany. The black community aided her career development: churches and other groups raised money for her voice lessons, and the Philadelphia Choral Society (of which she was a member) provided opportunities for her to perform, as did also the [David] Martin*-Smith School of Music in New York and the National Association of Negro Musicians,* who gave her its first scholarship. Individuals also encouraged her and aided her early career, particularly Roland Hayes* and R. Nathaniel Dett.* She began to sing professionally even before graduating from high school. With William ("Billy") King as her accompanist-manager, she toured the black colleges and the black churches, sang in theaters and school auditoriums under sponsorship of black fraternal organizations, local Y.M.C.A. groups, and similar organizations, and appeared at such conventions as those of the National Baptist Convention and the NAACP. In 1922 she made a debut as a concert contralto at Town Hall in New York, but she was underprepared and critical reviews were unenthusiastic. She continued to study and to tour. In 1925 she won first place in a singing competition held by the New York Philharmonic Symphony for its summer concerts at the Lewissohn Stadium. Her impressive performance in the concert in August won critical acclaim this time and led to increased engagements and professional management. During the next decade she went abroad three times to study further and to give concerts. She sang in many places, but toured extensively in Scandinavian countries (1931, 1933-34), where she acquired European management and an accompanist, Kosti Vehanen, who remained with her until the mid-1930s. On her second visit to Finland she sang for Jan Sibelius, who told her, "My roof is too low for you." In 1935 she made her debut in Paris, France, to critical acclaim. Impresario Sol Hurok attended her third Paris concert in June and offered her a management contract. Later that year she sang a concert at Salzburg, Austria, to which Arturo Toscanini came and afterwards said, "Yours is a voice such as one hears once in a hundred years." In December 1935 she returned to the United States for a second concert at New York's Town Hall, this time as a renowned artist. During the next three decades she toured widely throughout the world and broke down many barriers of racial discrimination. Her growing fame during the 1930s did not protect her, however, from all discrimination. In 1939 she was denied permission to give a concert in Constitution Hall by the DAR (Daughters of the American Revolution) because of color. Public protest over the issue became so great that the White House administration arranged for her to sing an open-air concert on the steps of the Lincoln Memorial in Washington, D.C., and on Easter Sunday morning she sang before an audience of 75,000. She made her television debut, singing a program of sacred music, on the "Ed Sullivan Show" in 1952. In 1953 she made her first tour of Japan; on 7 January 1955 she became the first black artist to sing with the Metropolitan Opera Company, in the role of Ulrica in Verdi's *Un Ballo in maschera*; in 1957 she toured in the Far East as a good-will ambassador for the U. S. State Department and ANTA (American National Theater and Academy).

During the concert season 1964-65 she gave fifty-one farewell concerts across the nation, ending a thirty-year career as "the world's greatest living contralto," with the final concert on Easter Sunday, 19 April 1965, at Carnegie Hall in New York. She had sung before royalty and elected rulers and concert audiences in most of the Western countries and in the Far East, she had sung on radio and television in coast-to-coast broadcasts, and she had recorded extensively. In February 1977 the musical world assembled in Carnegie Hall to pay tribute to her on her seventy-fifth birthday. Rosalynn Carter, wife of the President of the United States, presented her with a Congressional Resolution of Praise, and Mayor Abraham Beame of New York awarded her the New York City Handel Medallion. Anderson's honors included decorations and citations by the governments of France, Finland, Japan, Liberia, Haiti, the Philippines, and Sweden; twenty-three honorary doctorates from educational institutions; and achievement awards from many organizations, foundations, and institutions, including NAACP's Spingarn Medal (1939) and the Bok Foundation (1940). With the $10,000 she received from Bok she established the Marian Anderson Fellowships in 1942, replenishing the fund from time to time. Numerous young musicians of all colors received scholarships, including McHenry Boatwright,* Grace Bumbry,* Gloria Davy,* Mattiwilda Dobbs,* Reri Grist,* Louise Parker,* Rawn Spearman,* Camilla Williams,* and many others who later achieved renown.

She also received awards for service to youth and to the community. In 1958 she served as a member of the U.S. Delegation to the General Assembly of the United Nations. Anderson's concerts typically consisted of lieder, French, and Italian art songs. But audiences would not release her until she had sung their favorites—Schubert's "Ave Maria" and Harry T. Burleigh's "Deep River."

BIBL: Marian Anderson, *My Lord, What a Morning* (New York, 1956). Black press, incl. CDef, 9 August 1919; NYAge, 11 July 1925, 3 January 1929; PhilaT, 3 July 1915, 5 January 1918. EAB. Shirlee Newman, *Marian Anderson, The Lady from Philadelphia* (Philadelphia, 1965). Kosti Vehanen, *Marian Anderson: A Portrait* (New York, 1941). WWA. WWAW. WWE. WWBA. WWCA, 1950.

DISC: Turn.

ANDERSON, PINK. Bluesman (b. 12 February 1900 in Laurens, South Carolina; d. 12 October 1974 in Spartanburg, South Carolina). His family moved to Spartanburg, South Carolina, when he was a child. Self-taught, he began playing guitar at the age of fourteen or fifteen. In 1916 he met guitarist Blind Simmie Dooley, who influenced the development of his style and, after World War I, formed a team with him. Anderson began to play professionally in 1918, joining Dr. W. R. Keer's Indian Remedy [medicine] Show and remaining with the show for over twenty years. He also played with other medicine shows. He first recorded in 1928; thereafter he made several albums and toured widely in the United States.

BIBL: BWW. LivBl 20 (March-April 1974); Kip Lornell, "Peg Pete & His Pals" in LivBl 11 (Winter 1972-73); Oliv.

DISC: Jep. LeS1.

ANDERSON, T. C. ("QUEEN CANDICE"). Gospel singer (b. 1913 in Memphis, Tennessee [?]; d. 1959 in Memphis). She first attracted wide attention about 1941 as the soloist at the East Trigg Baptist Church in Memphis, Tennessee, where W. Herbert Brewster was the minister. When she began singing in the church choir during the late 1920s, Reverend Brewster gave her the name "Queen Candice." She made a special feature of introducing to the public songs written by Brewster, of which the best known were "How I got over," "Move on up a little higher," "I'm leaning and depending on the Lord," and "A sweeter tomorrow."

BIBL: Information from Clarence Boyer. Heil. Horace Clarence Boyer, "The Gospel Song: A Historical and Analytical Study" (M.A. thesis, Eastman School of Music, 1964). Jac.

ANDERSON, T[HOMAS] J[EFFERSON]. Composer/College professor (b. 17 August 1928 in Coatesville, Pennsylvania). His family lived in Washington, D.C., during the years 1932-c1943. He began piano study at the age of five with his mother, a professional musician. He obtained his musical education in the public schools of Washington, D.C., Cincinnati, Ohio, and Coatesville, Pennsylvania; at West Virginia State College in Institute (B.Mus., 1950); at Pennsylvania State University in University Park (M. Mus.Ed., 1951), where he studied with George Ceiga; at the Cincinnati [Ohio] Conservatory of Music (summer 1954), where he studied with T. Scott Huston; at the University of Iowa in Iowa City (Ph.D., 1958), where he studied with Philip Bezanson and Richard Hervig; and at the Aspen School of Music in Colorado (summer 1964), where he studied with Darius Milhaud. His teaching career included tenures in the public schools of High Point, North Carolina (1951-54), West Virginia State College (1955-56), Langston University in Oklahoma (1958-63), Tennessee State University in Nashville (1963-69), and Tufts University in Medford, Massachusetts (1972-). During the years 1969-71 he was composer-in-residence with the Atlanta [Georgia] Symphony, at that time directed by Robert Shaw, and from 1971 to 1972 he was Danforth Visiting Professor at Morehouse College in Atlanta. At an early age he determined to become a bandmaster and music teacher. He played violin as a child, then turned to trumpet in junior high school and formed his own jazz group. During his high school years he toured on summer vacations with a professional jazz orchestra, Tate Wilburn's of Cincinnati. During his early teaching years in North Carolina he worked with both school groups and his own trio, composed of John (''Jackie'') McLean,* Daniel (''Danny'') Richmond, and himself. At graduate school in Pennsylvania he became interested in composition, however, and gave up his teaching goals to write music. He published his first music in 1959 and thereafter worked slowly but steadily, producing three or four works each year. He wrote in a wide variety of musical forms: symphonies, chamber music, works for band, choral works, and vocal and instrumental solos. His mature style reflected the influences of Webern, jazz, spirituals, blues, and various avant-garde techniques. He drew upon both tonal and atonal resources, with a preference for the latter, but avoided serialism. His music was distinctive for its emphasis on linear elements, the use of melodic fragments in constantly shifting melodic and rhythmic patterns, and an intense interest in instrumental colors. His best-known works included the orchestral *Classical Symphony* (1961), *Squares* (1965), *Intervals* (1970) and *Messages, A Creole Fantasy* (1979); the band piece *In Memoriam Zach Walker* (1968); the chamber works *Chamber Symphony* (1961), *Fanfare for Solo Trumpet and Four Mini Bands* (1976), *Transitions* (1971), *Swing Set* for clarinet and piano (1972), and *Variations on a Theme by Alban Berg* for viola and piano (1978); the solo pieces ''Watermelon'' for piano (1971, based on street cries the composer heard as a child in Washington, D.C.) and ''Minstrel Man'' for bass trombone; and the vocal works *Variations on a Theme by M.B. Tolson*, cantata for soprano and chamber ensemble with text by Tolson (1969), *In Memoriam Malcolm X* for mezzo-soprano and orchestra (1974), *Block Songs* for solo voice and children's toys (1972, texts by Pearl Lomax), *Horizon '76* for orchestra and soprano (1976, text by Milton Kessler), and *Re-Creation*, a liturgical music-drama (1978). In 1979 he was commissioned to write an opera by Indiana University's School of Music and Office of Afro-American Affairs: *Soldier Boy, Soldier* (libretto by Leon Forrest). His interests in Afro-American music extended to ragtime: in 1972 he orchestrated Scott Joplin's score for the opera *Treemonisha* for the world premiere at Atlanta, Georgia. His honors included fellowships and grants from the Copley Foundation (1964), McDowell Colony (summers 1960-63, 1968), Fromm Foundation (1964), Rockefeller Foundation (1968), Yaddo Foundation (summers 1970-71), and National Endowment for the Arts (1976) and commissions from individuals, musical organizations, foundations, and educational institutions. In 1978, the year of his fiftieth birthday, friends sponsored ''Retrospective Concerts'' of his music in Chicago, Illinois, and in Cambridge, Massachusetts.

BIBL: Baker. BMI (April 1969). BPIM 1 (Fall 1973). Bull. Gro. Bruce A. Thompson, ''Musical Style and Compositional Techniques in Selected Works of T. J. Anderson'' (Ph.D. diss., Indiana University, 1979).

ANDERSON, WALTER FRANKLIN. College professor (b. 12 May 1915 in Zanesville, Ohio). His early music studies in piano and organ were taken with William Bailey at Capital University in Columbus, Ohio. He obtained his musical education at the Oberlin Conservatory of Music (B. Mus., 1937). In 1938 he became an Associate of the American Guild of Organists. During the 1937-38 season he toured with Catherine Van Buren as accompanist. His teaching career included tenures at Kentucky State College in Frankfort (1939-42); at Karamu House in Cleveland, Ohio (1942); and at Antioch College in Yellow Springs, Ohio (1942-68), where he was head of the music department for many years. In 1968 he was appointed Director of the Music Program for the National Endowment for the Arts in Washington, D.C.; in 1978 he became Special Assistant to the Chairman of NEA. His honors included the Bartol Award (1941), a Rosenwald Foundation fellowship (1948), and an honorary doctorate from Berea College (1970).

BIBL: NYB, 1952. Rom.

ANDERSON, WILLIAM ALONZO ("CAT") Jazz trumpeter (b. 12 September 1916 in Greenville, South Carolina; d. 30 April 1981 in Norwalk, California). He was left an orphan at four years of age, and he obtained his musical training in the Jenkins Orphanage in Charleston, South Carolina, which was celebrated for its Jenkins Orphanage Bands.* He began playing in one of the school bands when he was seven years old and finally settled on the trumpet, which he studied with Alonzo Mills. He first toured with a band in 1929. He also joined with other boys to form a dance orchestra, which played for local dances and acquired the name the Carolina Cotton Pickers. Beginning in the early 1930s the group toured in the South (1932-37). After leaving the orphanage, he played with various groups, including Hartley Toots, the Royal Sunset Orchestra (c1938-41 in New York), Claude Hopkins,* Erskine Hawkins* (1942), Lionel Hampton* (1942, 1944), and William (''Sabby'') Lewis (1943, 1949), among others. His longest tenures were with Edward (''Duke'') Ellington* (1944-47, 1950-59, 1961-71). He also toured with his own groups intermittently. In 1971 he settled in the San Fernando Valley in California. During the next decade he was active in films and television and as a free-lance studio musician, although he continued to tour regularly, appearing in concert halls and nightclubs and at the major jazz festivals. In 1974-75 he toured with an *Ice Capades* show as trumpeter and conductor. He recorded for both American and French companies, wrote songs and instrumental pieces, and published a trumpet manual. He was noted for his high trumpet notes. His best-known performances were solos on ''Trumpets no end,'' ''The eighth veil,'' ''A gathering in a clearing,'' and *Sacred Concerto* and his own album *Cat on a Hot Tin Horn*. His best-known original songs were ''Swinging the cat'' (formerly ''How 'bout that mess''), ''El gato,'' and ''Bluejean beguine.''

BIBL: ASCAP. ChilWW. DanceWDE. FeaEJ. FeaJS. FeaGitJS. MeeJMov.

DISC: Kink. RustJR.

ANIKULAPO-KUTI, FELA (née **FELA RANSOME-KUTI**). ''Afro-beat'' [jazz] bandleader (b. c1938 in Abeokuta, Nigeria). He obtained his education in the schools of Abeokuta and at the Trinity College of Music in London, England (1958-63). He began piano study when he was fourteen years old and also studied saxophone. His early style development was influenced by the calypso-inflected ''high life'' he heard played by Nigerian musicians Victor Olaiya and Roy Chicago. In London he studied trumpet, piano, and voice. He also played with jazz groups in London pubs and nightclubs and became a devotee of the music of John Coltrane,* Charlie Parker,* and Miles Davis.* When he returned to Nigeria in 1963 he formed a group, Koola Lobitos, to play the new music he had developed, called ''Afro–beat,'' from fusing African ''high life'' with Afro-American jazz. After several years the public began to appreciate his new music, and he developed a reputation for brilliant stage shows. In 1969 he visited the United States for the first time and was there introduced to black nationalism. After returning to Nigeria, he began to write politically charged songs. He attracted wide attention in Lagos for his home, called the KalaKuti Republic, and his nightclub, The Shrine, building up a large following among the people. He was the leading popular-music figure in West Africa during the mid-1970s; his role in Nigerian society was similar to that of soul musicians among black Americans, such as James Brown* or Stevie Wonder.* His best-known songs were ''Yellow fever,'' ''Upside down,'' ''Jean Koku,'' and ''Zombie''; his best-known album was *Kalakuta Show*. He used pidgin English for his song lyrics, a universal language in Africa.

BIBL: Black press, incl. AmstN, 2 July 1962, 29 April 1978. NYT, 24 July 1977.

ANING, BEN AKOSA. College professor (b. 4 December 1926 in Dampong, near Bompata, Ashanti Region, Ghana). He obtained his musical education at the University of Ghana at Lagos (1962-64), Columbia University in New York (1964-65), and at the University of California at Los Angeles (diploma in African music, 1966). He was appointed Research Fellow in Music at the University of Ghana in 1966. He contributed articles to professional journals such as the *International Folk Music Journal, Institute of African Studies Papers,* and *The Black Perspective in Music*.

BIBL: GhanaWW.

APPO, ANN. Church organist (b. 1809 in Philadelphia, Pennsylvania; d. December 1828 in Philadelphia). She was the first organist for the St. Thomas African Episcopal Church in Philadelphia, Pennsylvania, which purchased its first organ in 1828. She was a sister of the composer William Appo.*

BIBL. Black press, incl. *Freedom's Journal* (New York), 18 April 1828; 26 December 1828. Gerri Major with Doris E. Saunders, *Black Society* (Chicago, 1976), p. 18.

APPO, WILLIAM. Composer (b. c1808 in Philadelphia, Pennsylvania; d. after 1877 in upper New York state). He and his brother, Joseph, played professionally in the Walnut Street Theater orchestra during the 1820s, according to some reports. He joined the Frank Johnson* band during the 1830s and traveled with the group to England in November 1837 to give concerts. He conducted a music studio in New York for several years, beginning in the 1830s. He may have returned to live in Philadelphia during the 1850s. He played French horn and sang professionally. He was in great demand as a conductor and was called upon to conduct concerts in cities outside New York and Philadelphia. Daniel Payne* referred to him as ''the most learned musician of the race,'' and Martin Delany* and James Trotter* were equally enthusiastic about his talent and achievements. His best-known compositions were the anthem ''Sing unto God'' and a men's choral piece, ''John Tyler's Lamentation,'' which was commissioned by the Utica Glee Club of Utica, New York, during the presidential election campaign of 1844.

BIBL: Black press, incl. *The Colored American*, 2 September 1837, 14 September 1839, 6 March 1841. BPIM 4 (July 1976). Martin Delany, *The Condition,*

Elevation, Emigration and Destiny of the Colored People of the United States (Philadelphia, 1852), p. 125-126. *The Liberator* [Boston], 2 April 1833. SouRBM, p. 67. Trot, p. 302. Gerri Major with Doris E. Saunders, *Black Society* (Chicago, 1976), p. 18.

ARLE-TILZ, CORETTI (née **CORETTA ALFRED).** Concert/opera singer (b. c1870s in New York, New York (?); d. after 1943 in Moscow, USSR). She first attracted attention in 1901 when she joined the "Louisiana Amazon Guards," a vaudeville troupe of seven black women organized by German producer Paule Kohn-Wollner, which included Ollie Burgoyne, Emma Harris, Virginia Shepherd, and Fannie Smith, among others. Little is known of the prior musical experience of the women, except that Alfred sang in the choir of the Mount Olivet Baptist Church in the Harlem community of New York, and Harris (b. 1870 in Augusta, Georgia; d. after 1937 in New York) directed a church choir in Brooklyn. The troupe sailed for Europe in 1901, left Wollner because of her mismanagement, and toured for three years under the management of Burgoyne. In 1904 the troupe arrived in Moscow; the women performed at theaters in St. Petersburg and Moscow for a year, then disbanded in 1905 because of revolutionary activities in Russia. Four of the women eventually returned to the United States, but Harris and Alfred remained. Harris toured widely in Russia as a concert singer for more than a decade, marrying her manager, Ivanovitch Mizikin, in 1911. During World War I she became involved with non-music activities and never returned to the field. In 1933 Harris settled in New York. Some time after 1905 Alfred entered the St. Petersburg Conservatory, where she studied with Elizabeth Zwaninger, and later attended the Moscow Conservatory, where she studied with Maria Vladimir. In 1920 she married a Russian theater director, Tilz. Some time thereafter she began singing professionally as Coretti Arle-Tilz. She toured extensively for more than two decades, particularly in Scandinavian countries and in Eastern Europe. She attracted wide attention with her debut in the title role of Verdi's *Aida* at Kharkov, Russia, in the 1920s, and again during World War II when she toured the Russian army camps singing concerts of spirituals for the Russian troops.

BIBL: Schom, Writer's Program project of the WPA (see under Biographical sketches: Emma Harris). Black press, incl. CDef, 23 June 1934; 18 December 1943. Langston Hughes, *I Wonder As I Wander* (New York, 1956), pp. 82-86.

ARMANT, ALEXANDER. Bandmaster. See **DULF, GEORGE.**

ARMSTRONG, DANIEL LOUIS ("SATCHMO" "DIPPERMOUTH"). Jazz trumpeter (b. 4 July 1900 in New Orleans, Louisiana; d. 6 July 1971 in New York, New York). As a child he formed a quartet that sang on street corners and in cafes for pennies. He obtained his musical education in the public schools of New Orleans, Louisiana, and at the Coloured Waif's Home for Boys (1913-14), where he studied with Peter Davis and played in the Home's brass band. He first played alto horn, then changed to cornet; after a short while he was chosen by Davis to be bandleader. His early style development was influenced by men he heard perform in the community, William ("Bunk") Johnson,* Charles ("Buddy") Bolden,* Freddie Keppard,* and Joseph ("King") Oliver.* Oliver took Armstrong over as his protégé, gave the boy an old cornet, gave him informal lessons on the instrument, and found playing opportunities for "Little Louis." Louis called him "Papa Joe." Armstrong played professionally for a short period when he was fifteen in a local saloon-nightclub, but did not perform regularly until he was seventeen. He formed a six-piece band with Joe Lindsey in 1917; after the band was dissolved he played with various small groups until the summer of 1918, when he joined Edward ("Kid") Ory's* band as a replacement for King Oliver, who had gone to Chicago, Illinois. During his tenure in Ory's band he also played engagements with other groups and with the Tuxedo Brass Band under the leadership of Oscar ("Papa") Celestin.* During the years 1919-22 he played primarily with Fate Marable's* bands on Streckfus Steam Boats, then went to Chicago in the summer of 1922 to join King Oliver (1922-24). Thereafter he played with various groups—Ollie Powers (1924), Fletcher Henderson* (1924-25 in New York and on tour), Lillian ("Lil") Hardin Armstrong's* Dreamland Syncopators (1925-26), Erskine Tate* (1926), Carroll Dickerson* (1926-27, 1928), and Clarence Jones* (1927, 1928). During these years he also led his own groups in 1927 and 1929 and made his recording debut with Oliver in 1923. Thereafter he recorded extensively with others and with his own groups, particularly the Hot Five and the Hot Seven, which performed only in the recording studio (1925-28). The members of these groups included Johnny Dodds,* Warren ("Baby") Dodds,* and Johnny St. Cyr* (all three of whom had played beside him in Marable's riverboat bands), his wife Lil Armstrong, his old bandleader Kid Ory, and Earl Hines,* Lonnie Johnson, Fred Robinson, and Arthur ("Zutty") Singleton,* among others. The recordings attracted wide attention and brought him celebrity status. During the 1930s he toured extensively, generally with the support of bands he fronted rather than with his own groups; these included bands of Luis Russell,* Les Hite,* William (''Chick'') Webb,* Zilner Randolph, and the Mills Blue Rhythm Band.* In 1932 he made his first trip to Europe, touring in England, and acquired his nickname, ''Satchmo,'' from an editor of *The Melody Maker*. Thereafter he toured regularly in Europe, generally using European bands for accompaniment. By the 1940s he had become a world-renowned figure. In 1947 he organized the first of his All-Stars groups, composed of Weldon (''Jack'') Teagarden, Richard (''Dick'') Cary, Sidney (''Sid'') Catlett,* Leon (''Barney'') Bigard,* and Arvell Shaw. Others who played in Armstrong's All Stars groups over the years included Earl Hines, William (''Cozy'') Cole,* Joe Bushkin, Edmond Hall, and Milton Hinton,* among others. During the next two decades and more, Armstrong performed all over the world, from Iceland to Australia, from England to Indonesia; he played at the major jazz festivals and recorded extensively. In 1960 he toured in Africa under sponsorship of the U.S.I.S., playing to an audience of 10,000 at Leopoldville, the Congo. He made recordings in collaboration with such figures as Oscar Peterson,* Ella Fitzgerald,* and Edward (''Duke'') Ellington*, among others. He performed on radio (with his own national network show); on television; in Broadway musicals, *Hot Chocolates* (1929) and *Swingin' the Dream* (1939); and in no fewer than sixty films (including documentaries), among them, *Pennies from Heaven* (1936), *Cabin in the Sky* (1943), *New Orleans* (1947), *The Glenn Miller Story* (1953), *High Society* (1956), *Satchmo the Great* (1956), *Jazz, the Intimate Art* (1968), and *Hello, Dolly* (1969). Armstrong was as much entertainer as jazzman; he was a superb showman; and his gravelly, growling vocal style influenced hundreds of popular singers of his time. His best-known performances included ''Ain't misbehaving,'' which he sang as well as played in *Hot Chocolates* (music by Thomas [''Fats''] Waller); ''Hello, Dolly,'' ''When it's sleepy-time down South,'' ''Dipper mouth blues,'' ''West End blues,'' ''On the sunny side of the street,'' and ''When the saints go marching in,'' among many others. He received numerous awards from the music industry. Armstrong was the genius of jazz, the supreme improviser. He defined jazz cornet-trumpet (he changed to trumpet in 1928), and all trumpeters of his time were directly influenced by his style until the emergence of John Birks (''Dizzy'') Gillespie* in the 1940s. Thereafter he exerted indirect influence on the development of jazz trumpet and, as well, on jazz improvisation in total. No other jazzman was so widely imitated in regard to both instrumental style and vocal style.

BIBL: AlHen. Louis Armstrong, *Swing That Music* (New York, 1936); *Satchmo* (New York, 1954). ASCAP. ChilWW. EAB. FeaEJ. FeaJS. FeaGitJS. Robert Goffin, *Horn of Plenty* (New York, 1947). Max Jones and John Chilton, *Louis: The Louis Armstrong Story, 1900-1971* (London, 1971). MeeJMov. WWCA, 1950.

DISC: Kink. RustJR. TudJ.

ARMSTRONG, LILLIAN (''LIL'') HARDIN. Jazz pianist (b. 3 February 1898 in Memphis, Tennessee; d. 27 August 1971 in Chicago, Illinois). She studied piano as a child. She obtained her musical education at Fisk University in Nashville, Tennessee; at the Chicago [Illinois] College of Music (teacher's certificate, 1928), where she studied with Louis Victor Saar; and at the New York College of Music (diploma, 1929), where she studied with August Fraemche. Her family moved to Chicago in 1917, and she did not return to Fisk to complete her studies. She began her professional career as a song demonstrator in a music shop. She then played with various groups, including Curtis Mosby (c1918), Freddie Keppard* (c1919, 1928), Joseph (''King'') Oliver* (intermittently 1921-24), Elliot Washington (1922), Hugh Swift (c1926), and her own groups. She first met Louis Armstrong* in Joe Oliver's band in 1922, and they married two years later (divorced 1938). During the years 1925-26 she led a group, Madame Lil Armstrong's Dreamland Syncopators, which featured Armstrong. During the same period she recorded with his Hot Five and Hot Seven groups. In the 1930s she was active primarily in New York, where she led all-girl groups and an all-male big band, was staff pianist for a recording company (1937-40), appeared in the Broadway musicals *Hot Chocolates* (1929) and *Shuffle Along of 1933*, and played with her groups on radio programs. During the 1940s-60s she toured as a soloist (to Europe in 1952) and played long residencies in Chicago nightclubs. Those who played in her groups over the years included Leon (''Chu'') Berry,* William (''Buster'') Bailey, Wellman Braud,* Manzie Johnson, Jonah (''Jo'') Jones,* George (''Pops'') Foster,* Jack (''J. C.'') Higginbotham,* Midge Williams, and Joe Thomas. Her recordings included the documentary *Satchmo and Me*. Best known of her songs were ''Brown gal,'' ''Perdido Street blues,'' and ''Struttin' with some barbecue.'' She was performing at a Louis Armstrong Memorial concert in Chicago when she died of a heart attack.

BIBL: ASCAP. FeaEJ. FeaJS. FeaGitJS. Handy. MeeJMov. NYT, 28 August 1971. *Sepia* (September 1965). WWAW, 1970-71.

DISC: Kink. RustJR.

ARMSTRONG, LOUIS. See **ARMSTRONG, DANIEL LOUIS.**

ARROYO, MARTINA. Opera singer (b. 2 February 1936 in New York, New York). She obtained her education in the public schools of New York, where she attended Hunter College High School and later Hunter College of the City University of New York (B.A., 1956), where she sang in the Hunter College Opera Workshop and prepared for a career in opera with Josef Turnau. Her other teachers included Marinka Gurevich, Martin Rich, and Rose Landver. After graduating from college she taught in high school for a year, then worked in the New York Welfare Department as a social worker. In 1958 she made her concert debut as a soprano at Carnegie Hall, singing in the American premiere of Pizzetti's opera, *Murder in the Cathedral*. The same year she won first place in the Metropolitan Opera Auditions and, after study in the Kathryn Long School, made her debut with the Metropolitan singing the Celestial Voice in Verdi's *Don Carlo*—off-stage. She sang only minor roles in Metropolitan productions for the next few years, but she toured widely in Europe, singing in oratorio and opera and giving lieder recitals. Her formal debut at the Metropolitan came in 1965 when she substituted for an ailing Birgit Nilsson on short notice in the title role of Verdi's *Aida*. During the 1960s-80s she sang with the world's leading opera companies and appeared with the world's major symphony orchestras. Her best-known performances were associated with Italian operas: the roles of Leonora in Verdi's *Il Trovatore*, Elizabeth in his *Don Carlo*, and Leonora in his *La Forza del destino*; the title roles of Puccini's *Madame Butterfly* and Ponchielli's *La Gioconda*; and the role of Maddalena in Giordano's *Andrea Chenier*, among others. She was also noted for singing Elsa in Wagner's *Lohengrin* and Lady Macbeth in Verdi's *Macbeth*. She performed at the major music festivals in the United States and in Europe, including the Saratoga, Ravinia, Tanglewood, Vienna, Berlin, and Helsinki. She recorded opera and oratorio extensively. In 1974, however, she recorded spirituals with choirs from Dorothy Maynor's* Harlem School of the Arts, and she occasionally performed and recorded such contemporary works as Stockhausen's *Momente* and Samuel Barber's *Andromache's Farewell*.

BIBL: AbdulFBE. Black press, incl. AmstN, 11 July 1964; NYAge, 21 March 1959. CurBiog (February 1971). "L'Italiana di Harlem" in *Time* (28 September 1970). WWA. WWAW. WWBA. WWOpera.

DISC: Turn.

ART ENSEMBLE OF CHICAGO, THE. Jazz group (orig. 1968 in Chicago, Illinois). The instrumental group was formed in 1968 by members of AACM (the Association for the Advancement of Creative Musicians*), including Joseph Jarman,* Roscoe Mitchell,* Malachi Favors,* Lester Bowie, and Steve McCall. Don Moye joined the group in 1969. The Art Ensemble developed from a group formed by Mitchell in 1966. The group was active in France during the years 1969-71, then settled in Chicago, Illinois. The men played at most of the jazz festivals, on radio and television programs, in concert halls, and on college campuses. They also recorded regularly and appeared in films or on film soundtracks, including *Les stances à Sophie* (1971) and *European Music Revolution* (1970). The Art Ensemble was regarded as one of the leading avant-garde groups in the 1970s. From the mid-1970s on they toured widely in the United States, in Europe, and in Japan. Their best-known albums included *The Paris Sessions* and *Live at Mandel Hall*.

BIBL: FeaGitJS. Black press, incl. CDef, 26 April 1975, 6 May 1975. MeeJMov.

DISC: TudJ.

ASHBY, DOROTHY JEANNE THOMPSON. Jazz harpist (b. 6 August 1932 in Detroit, Michigan). Her father, Wiley Thompson, was a jazz guitarist. She obtained her musical education in the public schools of Detroit, Michigan, where she played in musical groups at the Cass Technical High School, and at Wayne State University in Detroit, where she played harp in the University Orchestra and was also accompanist for choral groups. She first studied piano, then changed to harp in 1952. The next year she began her professional career as a harpist, playing in local Detroit nightclubs. She was active in radio music as a staff harpist and show hostess, particularly during the years 1960-68, and in pit orchestras for musicals produced by her husband, John Ashby, and father (1967). She toured regularly with her Dorothy Ashby Trio, appearing in concert halls, nightclubs, and on television shows. Those with whom she performed over the years included Donald Byrd,* Natalie Cole, Louis Armstrong,* Edward ("Duke") Ellington,* Woodrow ("Woody") Herman, Johnny Mathis,* and Ramsey Lewis,* among many others. She was an active participant in the Detroit Public Schools harp program (1969-). She recorded as a soloist and with her group, and made radio and television commercials. She was a leading jazz harpist of her time.

BIBL: FeaEJ. FeaJS. Handy. WWBA.

DISC: Jep.

ASHFORD & SIMPSON. Songwriting team. See **ASHFORD, NICKOLAS.**

ASHFORD, NICKOLAS. Songwriter/Rhythm 'n' blues singer (b. 4 May 1942 in Fairfield, South Carolina). He grew up in Willow Run, Michigan, and there attended public schools. In the early 1960s he went to New York with aspirations of becoming a professional musician. Soon afterwards he met Valerie Simpson, leader of a gospel group in a Baptist church, and began writing songs for her group. Later Ashford and Simpson formed a song-writing team, which eventually began to write love songs. One of their songs, "Let's go get stoned," attracted wide attention when recorded by Ray Charles (1964) and led to a contract in 1966 with Berry Gordy's Motown Records. Over the years Ashford and Simpson produced songs for such performers as the duo of Marvin Gaye* and Tammi Terrell, Quincy Jones,* Chaka Khan, Gladys Knight* and the Pips, and Diana Ross,* among others. In 1971 Simpson began a recording career as a singer; in 1973 she joined with Ashford to form a duo recording team. Their best-known albums were *So, So Satisfied* and *Send It*. They toured widely, appearing in nightclubs, theaters, and concert halls. Best known of the songs they wrote were "Reach out and touch," "Ain't nothing like the real thing," "Your precious love," "It's my house," and " Ain't no mountain high enough." During the mid-1970s they formed their own publishing and management companies, Nick-O-Val and Hopsack and Silk Productions. They received awards from the music industry.

BIBL: *ASCAP in Action* (Spring 1980). *Ebony* (February 1979). *People* (27 February 1978). WWBA.

ASSOCIATION FOR THE ADVANCEMENT OF CREATIVE MUSICIANS, THE. Professional organization (orig. 1965 in Chicago, Illinois). The organization was founded in May 1965 by Muhal Richard Abrams,* along with others, for the purpose of promoting the music of black musicians. Its program included conducting workshops for young musicians, sponsoring concerts and providing other performance opportunities, and offering training in essential aspects of the music business, among other goals. Although the members of the organization were jazz musicians, they totally rejected the label "jazz" as applying to the music they produced, preferring the terms "creative musicians" and "improvisers." AACM served as the source and, later, umbrella for several groups, including the Creative Construction Company,* Air, the Revolutionary Ensemble,* the Art Ensemble of Chicago,* and the Fred Anderson Sextet. The musicians associated with AACM included Anthony Braxton,* Malachi Favors,* Lester Bowie, Maurice McIntyre, Leroy Jenkins,* Leo Smith,* Steve McCall, Joseph Jarman,* and Roscoe Mitchell,* among many others. The group usually maintained a membership of from thirty to forty musicians. Generally the musicians played many instruments; they were interested in "sounds" rather than exploitation of individual instrument timbres.

BIBL: BPIM 7 (Fall 1979), p. 272. ContKey (May 1978). Dominique-René de Lerma, ed., *Reflections on Afro-American Music* (Kent, Ohio, 1973).

ATKINS, CARL. College professor (b. 4 July 1945 in Birmingham, Alabama). He obtained his musical education at Indiana University in Bloomington (B. Mus., 1967) and at the New England Conservatory of Music in Boston, Massachusetts (M. Mus., 1975). His teaching career included tenures at Elma Lewis's National Center of Afro-American Artists in Boston (1969-70); at Northeastern University in Boston (1969-72); at Brown University in Providence, Rhode Island (1973-76); and at the New England Conservatory (1968-). He toured in the United States and in Europe as a guest conductor of symphony orchestras and as a soloist, appearing with leading symphony orchestras. In 1969 he founded the New England Wind Sinfonia and thereafter served as its director. He was also active as a composer and wrote music for the documentary films *We Are Universal* (1972) and *History of Black Martial Music* (1977).

BIBL: WWBA.

ATKINS, MARJORIE ROBINSON. Music librarian (b. 10 July 1918 in Chicago, Illinois). She obtained her education in the public schools of Chicago, Illinois, at Chicago Musical College (1950-57), and at the University of Chicago (1935-37; M.A. in library science, 1979). She studied voice privately with Lillian Price and Thelma Waide Brown.* She sang in a junior church choir during her school years and later sang in senior church choirs and in a women's quartet. In 1940 she completed her library internship in the Chicago Public Library system and began her professional career as a music librarian. Twelve years later she was appointed Chief of the Music Department (1952-74), and in 1975 she became Chief of the Fine Arts Department (Music and Art). Her innovations included initiating programs for the celebration of National Music Week and sponsoring weekly, live-music concerts at the Main Library (1952-69). Her honors included citations from community and civic organizations and appointments to panels and committees of professional organizations. She published articles in professional journals and published her thesis, *Carl Bismarck Roden and the Chicago Public Library* (Chicago, 1979).

BIBL: Interview by Fanya Wiggins. Questionnaire. "Speaking of People" in *Ebony* (March 1963).

ATKINS, RUSSELL. Poet/Writer (b. 25 February 1926 in Cleveland, Ohio). Although best known as a literary figure, he was also a composer. He began piano study at the age of seven with his mother, a pianist. He obtained his musical education at the Cleveland Music School Settlement, at the Cleveland Institute of Music, and through private study. His career development was influenced by his piano teachers—among them, Murray Adams and J. Harold Brown,* Russell and Rowena Jelliffe, and Walter Anderson,* among others. He began writing music during the 1950s. His best-known compositions were four works for which he used the same title—*Object-Forms*: for violin and piano (1953), cello and piano (1958), concerto for piano and orchestra (1977), for piano (1969)—and *Incidental Music for Riders to the Sea* (Synge, 1950) and *Twenty Spirituals for Piano* (1979). His theory of "psychovisualism" exerted wide influnce upon composers of avant-garde music; it was introduced by Stefan Wolpe at the Darmstadt Festival of Avant-Garde Music in Germany (1956). Atkins published articles in periodicals such as *The Music Review* [England] and *The Saturday Review*. He discussed his music theory in two articles titled "A Psychovisual Perspective for 'Musical' Composition" in *Free Lance* (v. 3, no. 2, 1956; v.5, no.1, 1958). His honors included a Creative Artists Fellowship from the Ohio Arts Council (1978), tributes from professional and civic institutions, and an honorary doctorate from Cleveland State University (1976).

BIBL: *Free Lance* 14 (1970): *The Russell Atkins Issue*. H. H. Stuckenschmidt, "Contemporary Techniques in Twentieth-Century Music" in *The Musical Quarterly* 49 (1963). WWBA.

AUGUSTUS, EDWARD. Brass bandsman (fl. mid-nineteenth century in Philadelphia, Pennsylvania; d.4 (?) December 1881 in Philadelphia). See also **JOHNSON, FRANCIS.** He played double-bass in Frank Johnson's* musical groups. In 1837 when Johnson took an ensemble to give concerts in London, England, he left Augustus in charge of his Quadrille Band and Military Band. Augustus performed with the Johnson band until its disbandment during the 1860s and was active in other areas of Philadelphia's musical life.

BIBL: PaHistSoc, Box IG; Lebanon Cemetery Records: Letter Book of J. C. White. *The Public Ledger* [Philadelphia], 30 October 1837; 6 December 1837.

AUSTIN, LOVIE (née **CORA CALHOUN).** Blues pianist (b. 19 September 1887 in Chattanooga, Tennessee; d. 10 July 1972 in Chicago, Illinois). She studied music at Knoxville College (Tennessee) and Roger Williams College (Nashville, Tennessee). During her early career she toured widely on the vaudeville circuit, including the T.O.B.A. (Theatre Owners' Booking Agency) circuit in The Sunflower Girls and her own Blues Serenaders, which included at one time or another Johnny Dodds,* Tommy Ladnier,* and Kid Ory,* among others. She settled in Chicago, where she worked as a pit pianist for over twenty years at the Monogram Theater and later at the Gem and Joyland Theaters. She first recorded in 1924 and made several recordings thereafter, primarily with her Serenaders. In addition she accompanied many singers on records, either as pianist or with her Blues Serenaders; including Ida Cox,* Alberta Hunter,* Hattie McDaniels,* Gertrude ("Ma") Rainey,* and Ethel Waters,* among others. During the late 1940s she worked as a resident pianist in Jimmy Payne's Dancing School in Chicago. Her film appearances included *The Great Blues Singers* (1961).

BIBL: ChilWWJ. FeaEJ. FeaGitJS. Handy. LivBL 9 (Summer 1972). MeeJMov. Oliv.

DISC: Jep. Kink. RustJR.

AXELSEN, DORIS HOLLAND. Music educator (b. 24 March 1926 in Birmingham, Alabama). She obtained her musical education at Catholic University in Washington, D.C. (B. Mus., 1950); the Cleveland Institute of Music in Ohio (1953-54); Indiana University at Bloomington (1954-55); and the Pius XII Institute in Florence, Italy (M. Mus., 1955). She settled in Europe during the early 1950s. She studied there further at the University of Vienna in Austria (1955-57), at the University of Oslo in Norway (1959-61), and in Sweden at Uppsala University (1970-72) and the Royal Institute of Technology (1972-75), earning advanced degrees in educational psychology. Her piano teachers included Tourgee DeBose,* Emerson Myers, and Arthur Loesser in the United States and Reimar Riefling in Oslo, among others. Her teaching career included tenures at Fort Valley State College in Georgia (1952-53); the Oslo Conservatory of Music (1959-61); in secondary schools of Karlstad and Gothenburg, Sweden (1961-66); at Gothenburg Teachers College (1966-72); and at the Gothenburg Gymnasium (1972-). She toured regularly as a concert pianist in the Scandinavian countries and in England, Austria, and Italy. She was also active as a music critic for Oslo newspapers and various American newspapers and contributed articles to professional European journals. Her book publications included *An Acoustical Correlate to Grain: A Study of Tone Quality* (Uppsala, 1979).

BIBL: Questionnaire.

AYERS, ROY E., JR. Jazz vibraphonist (b. 10 September 1940 in Los Angeles, California). His mother was a music teacher, and he began piano study with her when he was five years old. He obtained his musical education in the public schools of Los Angeles and at Los Angeles City College. He sang in church choirs and played steel guitar in jazz groups until he was seventeen, when he acquired his first vibraharp. He was inspired to play vibes by Lionel Hampton,* whom he heard in live performances as a child, and by Milton Jackson.* He began his professional career in 1961, playing with local groups, such as Curtis Amy and Foreststorn (''Chico'') Hamilton,* among others. He also led his own groups during his college years. Thereafter he toured with Herbie Mann (1966-70), then formed his group called Roy Ayers Ubiquity. Over the years his sidemen included Bernard Purdy, Justo Americo, John Mosely, William Allen, Dennis Davis, Clint Houston, and Billy King, among others. He toured widely and recorded extensively. His music fused elements of rock, jazz, and Latin rhythms; he experimented with exotic sound effects on both acoustic and electronic instruments.

BIBL: FeaJS. FeaGitJS.

DISC: Jep.

AYLER, ALBERT. Jazz saxophonist (b. 13 July 1936 in Cleveland, Ohio; d. 25 November 1970 in New York, New York). He came from a musical family: his father played violin and tenor saxophone, and his brother Donald (''Don'') became a professional jazz trumpeter. The two brothers obtained musical education in the public schools of Cleveland, Ohio, and at the Bennie Miller Music School in Cleveland. During his service in the United States Armed Forces, Albert played with army bands; he spent the last two years of his service in France, where he played with jazz groups in Paris during his off-duty hours. He returned to the United States in 1961. Thereafter he played with Cecil Taylor* (1962), among others, and formed his own Albert Ayler Quintet in 1964. He represented the avant-garde of the 1960s, along with Ornette Coleman,* John Coltrane,* and Taylor. His music belonged to the ''free jazz'' tradition and was distinctive for its loud tones, intricate improvisation, atonality, and intense emotionalism. He employed folk-music elements freely and drew upon rhythm 'n' blues elements as well. His best known recordings included ''Ghosts,'' ''Truth is marching'' (written for Coltrane's funeral), and the album *Spiritual Unity*. After his death his brother formed the Don Ayler Quintet.

BIBL: FeaJS. FeaGitJS. MeeJMov. NYT, 4 December 1970. WWA, 1967-68.

DISC: Jep. TudJ.

AYLER, DONALD (''DON''). Jazz trumpeter (B. 5 October 1942 in Cleveland, Ohio). See **AYLER, ALBERT.**

B

BAILEY, EVANGELINE GERALDINE. Military musician (b. 1949 in Portsmouth, Virginia). She began piano study at the age of five and later studied music at Norfolk State College in Virginia, where she majored in voice and sang in the College Opera Workshop. In May 1972 she made naval history when she was selected as the first female musician—Musician Third Class (Petty Officer), assigned to the Bethesda Naval Medical Center. She performed as a vocalist with the rock group, Port Authority, of the United States Navy Band. She toured with the band to military bases in Europe in the 1970s.

BIBL: GreBD.

BAILEY, JOHN. See **FINNEY, THEODORE.**

BAILEY, PEARL. Jazz singer/Actress (b. 29 March 1918 in Newport News, Virginia). She moved to Philadelphia, Pennsylvania, in 1933, and there attended the William Penn High School. She began her professional career at the age of fifteen after winning first prize in an amateur talent show. She toured in Pennsylvania as a dancer-singer, and later sang on the vaudeville circuit. During the 1940s she sang in nightclubs in New York and toured on the U.S.O. circuit and with various groups, among them, Charles (''Cootie'') Williams* (1943-44), and later William (''Count'') Basie* and Noble Sissle.* She made her debut as an actress in the Broadway musical, *St. Louis Woman* (1946). Thereafter she was active primarily in musicals, including *House of Flowers* (1954) and *Hello, Dolly!* (1967), and the film musicals *Carmen Jones* (1954), *St. Louis Blues* (1958), and *Porgy and Bess* (1959), among many others. She was also noted as an entertainer; she toured widely on the nightclub circuit in the United States and abroad, appeared on radio and television programs, and in 1970 had her own television series on ABC-TV. She received awards from the theater industry, the music industry, civic and government organizations, and citations from Mayor John Lindsay of the City of New York and President Sadat of Egypt. She was appointed special representative in the United States delegation to the United Nations (1975). She published two autobiographical books, *The Raw Pearl* (1968) and *Talking to Myself* (1971), and *Pearl's Kitchen* (1973). She recorded regularly; her best known performances were of ''Tired'' and ''Takes two to tango.'' Her brother William (''Bill'') Bailey was also an entertainer, but later became a minister.

BIBL: ASCAP CurBiog (October 1969). FeaEJ. FeaJS. FeaGitJS. MeeJMov. *Sepia* (April 1971). WWA. WWBA.

DISC: Jep. Kink.

BAKER, DAVID. Jazz cellist/Composer (b. 21 December 1931 in Indianapolis, Indiana). He obtained his musical education in the public schools of Indianapolis, Indiana, where he came under the tutelage of LaVerne Newsome, Russell Brown, and Norman Merrifield* at Crispus Attucks High School; at Jordan Conservatory in Indianapolis, where he studied tuba and trombone; at Indiana University in Bloomington (B. Mus. Ed., 1953; M. Mus. Ed., 1954), where he studied with Bernard Heiden, Thomas Beversdorf, and Juan Orrego-Salas; and at the Berklee School of [Jazz] Music in Boston, Massachusetts, and the School of Jazz at Lenox, Massachusetts (summer 1959). He also studied privately with George Russell* and John Lewis,* among others. He began playing jazz professionally as early as 1948 with local groups. Thereafter he played with various groups, including Maynard Ferguson (1957), Quincy Jones* (1961), George Russell (1962), and others, including John (''Wes'') Montgomery* and Lionel Hampton.* Illness of the jaw forced him to give up wind instruments in 1962, and he turned to jazz cello and double bass. Concomitant with his jazz performing he was pursuing a career in teaching, which included tenures at Lincoln University in Jefferson City, Missouri (1956-57); in the public schools of Indianapolis (1958-59); at Indiana Central College in Indianapolis (1963-64); and at Indiana University (1966-). He was also active in the field of classical music; he performed with symphony orchestras and chamber groups and occasionally was soloist with symphony orchestras. He toured widely with his university jazz groups and his sextet in the United States and abroad. He also toured as a lecturer and conducted workshops on college campuses. He contributed numerous articles on jazz subjects and transcriptions of jazz solos to *Down Beat, Orchestra News*, and similar magazines and published several books, including four manuals on *Jazz Improvisation* (1969-76), four volumes on *Techniques of Improvisation* (1971), and *Jazz Styles and Analysis: Trombone* (1973), among others. He began writing music and arranging for jazz ensembles at an early age. His style is distinctive for its blending of Afro-American elements with traditional European techniques and forms; his composition draws upon jazz, serialism, electronic techniques, gospel, and folk materials. He wrote in a wide variety of forms, including symphonies, symphonies with jazz ensemble, concertos, oratorios and cantatas, chamber works, music for concert band, vocal pieces, instrumental solos, and music for television. His best-known works are the cantata *Black America: To the Memory of Martin Luther King* (1968, later revisions); *The Beatitudes*, for chorus, voices, narrator, jazz ensemble, string orchestra, and dancers (1968); *Levels*, for flutes, horns, strings, solo contrabass, and jazz band, (1973, nominated for the Pulitzer Prize); *Le Chat Qui Perche*, for orchestra, soprano, and jazz quartet (1974); *Two Improvisations for Orchestra and Jazz Combo* (1974); *Sonata for Cello and Piano* (1973); *Concerto for Cello and Chamber Orchestra* (1975); *Ethnic Variations on a Theme of Paganini* (1976); and *Contrasts*, for violin, cello, and piano (1976). His honors included awards from the music industry, appointment to panels and committees of professional and government organizations, and an award from the National Association of Negro Musicians* (1976).

BIBL: BakBCS. *Ebony* (May1970). FeaEJ. FeaJS. FeaGitJS. WWA. WWBA.

BAKER, JOSEPHINE. Entertainer (b. 3 June 1906 in St. Louis, Missouri; d. 12 April 1975 in Paris, France). She left home when she was thirteen to join a touring road show (according to some sources, a Bessie Smith* show). Two years later she found employment in the chorus for the Noble Sissle*/Eubie Blake* Broadway musical, *Shuffle Along* (1921), and there first attracted wide attention, although she did not have a leading role. She next appeared in Sissle and Blake's musical *The Chocolate Dandies* (1924), then in a revue at the Plantation Club in New York. In 1925 she left for Europe with the musical *La Revue Negrè* as a chorus girl and landed in Paris as the star of the show. Originally, Ethel Waters* was to have the leading role, but she decided not to accept. According to the sources, musical director Claude Hopkins* yanked Baker out of the chorus, rehearsed her on the ship passage over, and presented her to Paris in an explosive scene in which she was "entirely nude except for a pink flamingo feather between her limbs" (quoted from NYT; see bibliography). Her career as an entertainer was off to a glowing start; over the next three decades she starred in revues at such nightclubs as the Folies Bergere and the Casino de Paris and won international acclaim. She returned to the United States several times to perform (1935-36 in the Ziegfeld Follies, 1951, 1970s). In 1958 she staged her musical biography, *Paris Mes Amours*, in Paris. Just before she died, she had opened in a new revue that celebrated her fiftieth anniversary in show business. Over her long career she appeared in many French films and made recordings. She published two autobiographies, *Les Memoires de Josephine Baker* (1927) and *Voyages et Aventures de Josephine Baker* (1931).

BIBL: Black press, incl. CDef, 30 June 1934 (re: Claude Hopkins). CurBiog (July 1964, June 1975). *Ebony* (December 1973). *Encore* (7 July 1975). NYT, 13 April 1975.

DISC: RustCED.

BAKER, LAVERN. Rhythm 'n' blues singer (b. 11 November 1928 in Chicago, Illinois). She sang in a church choir as a child and began performing professionally as a rhythm 'n' blues singer during her high-school years. Her early professional experience was at the celebrated Club DeLisa on Chicago's South Side. At seventeen she was well established on the nightclub circuit in Chicago and other Midwestern cities, calling herself "Little Miss Sharecropper." She made her recording debut in the late 1940s but failed to win wide recognition until 1955, when she recorded "That's all I need" and "Tweedle-dee." Thereafter she toured widely, performing in theaters, concert halls, nightclubs, and on television shows in the United States and in Europe. She also recorded extensively. In her early career she sang in the traditional shouting blues style of Gertrude ("Ma") Rainey,* but later she employed more sophisticated arrangements, such as a female background chorus and strings. Some critics felt that her later style anticipated the Motown Sound* of the 1960s. Her best-known performances, in addition to those just cited, included "I can't love you enough," "I waited too long," "I cried a tear," "Jim Dandy," and "See see Ryder."

BIBL: FeaEJ. ShawHS. StamPRS.

DISC: TudBM.

BALLANTA-TAYLOR, NICHOLAS GEORGE JULIUS. Ethnomusicologist (b. 14 March 1893 in Kissy (near Freetown), Sierra Leone; d. 19?). He studied organ as a child and sang in a church choir in his village. In 1917 he passed the first examination for the B.A. degree in music at the Fourah Bay College in Freetown, an affiliate of Durham College in London. As he was unable to travel to London, however, to take the final examination, he did not obtain his degree. In 1921 an American patron, Mrs. Caseley-Hayford, arranged for him to come to the United States to study music. He attended the Institute of Musical Art in New York (now the Juilliard School of Music) and received his diploma in 1924. His other patrons were George Foster Peabody, Frank Damrosch, head of the Institute, and Walter Damrosch, conductor of the New York Symphony. For his thesis he wrote a symphonic work based on African themes, titled *The Music of Africa*. After graduation he went south to collect Negro folksongs and published his collection the next year, *Negro Spirituals of St. Helena's Island* (New York, 1925). During the period he was studying, he produced pageants and published articles about African music. He was the first African to stage African pageants in the United States and to explore the relationships between African and Afro-American folksongs. Later he received a Guggenheim fellowship, which enabled him to collect folksongs in Africa. His best-known work was the choral composition "Belshazzar's Feast" (1919).

BIBL: Black press, incl. NY Age, 22 December 1923, 1 September 1924. *Journal of West Africa* (14 July 1930). *Musical Courier* (June 1922).

BALTHROP, CARMEN. Opera singer (b. 14 May 1948 in Washington, D.C.). She obtained her musical education at the University of Maryland in College Park (B. Mus., 1970) and at Catholic University in Washington, D.C. (M. Mus., 1971). She began singing professionally (soprano) in 1972, appearing in concerts, at music festivals, and as soloist with major symphony orchestras. She also sang with opera companies. In 1975 she attracted wide attention for her performance in the title role of Scott Joplin's *Treemonisha* with the Houston [Texas] Opera Company. The same year she was a finalist in the Metropolitan Opera National Auditions, and in 1978 she made her debut with the Metropolitan Opera. Her recordings included *Treemonisha* and the role of Roggiera in Rossini's *Tancredi*.

BIBL: WWA.

DISC: Turn.

BANKOLE, AYO. Composer (b. May 1935 in Lagos, Nigeria; d. November 1976 in Lagos). He came from a musical family: his father was a church organist, and his mother taught music at the Queen's School in Oyo state. As a youth he played organ in churches of Lagos and organized amateur choral groups. He received his musical education at the Guildhall School of Music and Drama in London, England (1957-60); at Clare College of Cambridge University in England (M.A.); and at the University of California at Los Angeles, where he studied for two years. He was the first Nigerian to study music at Cambridge. During his sojourn in London he was organist-choirmaster at the Church of St. James-the-Less in South London, succeeding Akin Euba* in that position. He also passed the examination for obtaining the Fellowship of the Royal College of Organists. After returning to Nigeria in the mid-1960s he joined the staff of the Nigerian Broadcasting Corporation, then was appointed to the music faculty of the University of Nigeria at Lagos. He began composing at an early age. In London he organized a student choir that performed his compositions, some of which used the Yoruba language. He wrote in a variety of forms, and his style was distinctive for his use of group improvisation. He best-known works were the cantata *Jona* for narrator, singers, dancer, and an unorthodox combination of instruments, including the Indian tambura; his piano sonata No.2 in C, *The Passion* (1959); "The Lord is my Shepherd" for female voice and organ; the Toccata and Fugue for organ; the song collections *Three-Part Songs for Female Choir* and *Three Yoruba Songs for Baritone and Piano*; and *Nigerian Suite* for piano (1960).

BIBL: Information from Akin Euba. *Nigerian Music Review* (No. 1, 1977).

BANKS, BILLY. Entertainer (b. c1908 in Alton, Illinois; d. 19 October 1967 in Tokyo, Japan). Apparently he began his professional career in Cleveland, Ohio; it was there that he first attracted the attention of professional management. In 1932 he recorded with his Rhythmakers or Rhythm Kings. About 1934 he joined Noble Sissle* as singer, remaining with Sissle through his residency at Billy Rose's Diamond Horseshoe club in New York (regularly during the years c1933-50).

During the periods when Sissle was not in residence, Banks remained as singer for an unbroken residency (1938-48). In 1952 he left the United States to tour in Europe, Australia, and Asia. He finally settled in Tokyo, where he was a stage and television entertainer.

BIBL: ChilWW. Langston Hughes and Milton Mercer, *Black Magic* (New York, 1967).

DISC: Jep. RustJR.TudJ.

BAQUET, GEORGE F. Jazz clarinetist (b. 1883 in New Orleans, Louisiana; d. 14 January 1949 in Philadelphia, Pennsylvania). He came from a musical family: his father, Theogene (c1858-c1920), played clarinet professionally, taught music, and directed the local Excelsior Band of New Orleans during the years 1882-1904; his brother Achille (1885-1955) played clarinet with the Reliance Brass Band and other bands of New Orleans. George began his career about 1897 in the Lyre Club Symphony Orchestra. Thereafter he toured with P. T. Wright's* Nashville Students (1902) and the Georgia Minstrels.* He returned to New Orleans about 1905 and thereafter played with various groups, including John Robichaux,* Freddie Keppard,* the Onward Brass Band, the Imperial and Magnolia Orchestras, and occasionally Charles ("Buddy") Bolden.* About 1913 he went to Los Angeles, California, along with Keppard, to join William ("Bill") Johnson's* Original Creole Band and remained with the band through its nationwide tours. After leaving the band in the summer of 1916 he played with various groups, then settled in Philadelphia, Pennsylvania, in 1923. There he performed first with Sam Gordon's Lafayette Players, then in the pit orchestra at the Earle Theater. Thereafter he led his own small groups, one of them called the New Orleans Nighthawks. He recorded during the 1920s with such performers as Bessie Smith* and Ferdinand ("Jelly Roll") Morton.*

BIBL: Black press, incl. CDef,15 July 1916; IndF, 13 February 1915. ChilWW. FeaEJ. Souch.

DISC: Jep. RustJR.

BARAKA, IMAMU AMIRI (née **LEROI JONES**). Writer (b. 7 October 1934 in Newark, New Jersey). Best known as a playwright and author, he is included here because of his books, *Blues People* (New York, 1963) and *Black Music* (New York, 1966), which were widely quoted in music literature of the 1960s-70s. He obtained his education at Howard University in Washington, D.C. (B.A., 1954), at Columbia University in New York, and at the New School for Social Research in New York. His teaching career included tenures at the New School, University of Buffalo in New York, and San Francisco State College in California. Among his many honors were John Hay Whitney and Guggenheim Fellowships (1960, 1965) and selection as a Yoruba Academy Fellow (1965).

BIBL: WWA. WWBA.

BARBARIN, PAUL. Jazz drummer (b. 5 May 1901 in New Orleans, Louisiana; d. 10 February 1969 in New Orleans). He came from a musical family: his father, Isadore (1872-1960), played with the Onward Brass Band almost thirty years and with other brass bands of New Orleans; his brother Louis became a professional musician. Paul first played clarinet, then changed to drums when he was fifteen. His early professional experience was with the Silver Leaf Orchestra and the Young Olympia Band. Beginning in 1917 he gravitated between New Orleans and Chicago, Illinois, for a number of years. In Chicago he played with various groups in local cafes and nightclubs, including Eddie Vincent, Freddie Keppard,* Jimmie Noone,* and Joseph ("King") Oliver* (1925-27), among others; in New Orleans he played with Luis Russell,* Walter Pichon, and Armand Piron,* among others. In 1920 he toured with the Tennessee Ten and with his own group. In 1928 he rejoined Luis Russell (1928-32, 1935 in New York) and thereafter played with various groups, including Louis Armstrong* (1935-38, 1941), Henry ("Red") Allen* (1942-43), Sidney Bechet* (1943-44), and Art Hodes (1953), among others. During these years he also led his own groups for long periods in New Orleans; Springfield, Illinois; New York; and Los Angeles, California. His last group was the Onward Brass Band in the 1960s, in which he was playing when he had a fatal heart attack during the course of a Mardi Gras parade. He recorded extensively with many groups and appeared on television programs and in a film, *World by Night, No.2* (1961).

BIBL: ChilWW. FeaEJ. FeaGitJS. MeeJMov. Souch.

DISC: Jep.Kink. RustJR.

BARBOUR, J. BERNI. Vaudeville pianist/Songwriter (b. 22 April 1881 in Danville, Kentucky; d. 19? in New York, New York). He obtained his musical education at Simmons University, where he was graduated from the normal department in 1896, and studied further at the Schmoll School of Music in Chicago, Illinois (1899). He also studied privately with Carl Liebling, Theodore Thomas, Nicholi Sansone, and Lemmons Sidwell. Early in his career he was musical director for the Gowens Original Nashville Students, and later for the Gideons' Georgia Camp Meeting Musical Comedy Company. In 1903 he founded a music publishing house with N. Clark Smith* in Chicago, possibly the first permanent company to be owned solely by blacks. During the first decades of the twentieth century he played piano in various theaters and nightclubs of Chicago; during the years 1913-18 he toured with his Southland Jubilee Quartet. Some time thereafter he settled in New York, using that city as a base from which he toured. In 1919 he was manager for W. C. Handy's* Memphis Blues Orchestra and toured with the group for a year. He then served as a staff writer for the Pace* and Handy Music Company. He produced dramatic works, several of which he composed—*Arrival of the Negro, Negro Progress,* and *Redemption*—and during 1925-26 he toured with a concert company through Texas, Missouri, and Kansas, staging his works. In 1927 he became a staff member of the Edward B. Marks music publishing company. One of his collaborators was Billy King,* with whom he wrote the shows *Over the Top, They Are Off,* and *Exploits of Africa.*

BIBL: Black press, incl. CDef, 6 June 1914, 16 October 1915; IndF, 2 January 1904. *The Music Master* 2 (March 1920). WWCA, 1930-1941.

BARÈS, BASILE. Composer (b. 2 January 1845 in New Orleans, Louisiana; d. 4 September 1902 in New Orleans). He early showed musical promise and was encouraged to develop his talent by J. A. Perrier, piano dealer and music importer. He studied piano with Eugene Provost, director of the Orleans Theater orchestra, and harmony and composition with a Mr. Pedigram. In 1866 he performed at the Louisiana Fair, including one of his own compositions, "La Seduisante." In 1867 he was sent to Paris, France, on business and remained there for several months in the employ of the firm of Pleyel and Company. During this period he studied music at the Paris Conservatory and played in public concerts. After returning to New Orleans, he established himself as a composer, music teacher, piano tuner, and instrument repairman.

BIBL: Des, p. 87. LaBrew, p. 487. Trot, p. 341; pp. 60-68 of the music section.

BARKER, DANIEL ("DANNY"). Jazz guitarist/Banjoist (b. 13 January 1909 in New Orleans, Louisiana). He came from a musical family: his grandfather, Isidore Barbarin, was a long-time leader of the Onward Brass Band in New Orleans, and his uncle, Paul Barbarin,* was a jazz drummer. He began clarinet study at an early age, taking lessons from Albany ("Barney") Bigard;* he then studied drums with his uncle Paul, and finally changed to guitar and banjo, studying with Bernard Addison. He began playing professionally when he was about fourteen, playing with such local groups as Willie Pajeaud and Lee Collins* (with whom he toured). He settled in New York in 1930. Thereafter he played with various groups, including Stanley ("Fess") Williams,* Albert Nicholas* (1930s, 1948-49), James P. Johnson,* Lucius ("Lucky") Millinder* (1937-38, 1947), Bennett ("Benny") Carter* (1938-39), Cabell ("Cab") Calloway* (1939-46), and Paul Barbarin* (1954-55), among many others. During these years he also led his own groups at intervals and toured with his wife, blues singer Louisa ("Blue Lu") Barker (b. 13 November 1913 in New Orleans, Louisiana). He recorded extensively with various groups, his own Fly Cats, and his wife and other blues singers; he played at jazz festivals and at the New York World's Fair in 1964. In 1965 he resettled in New Orleans. He continued musical activity through the 1960s-70s, playing in nightclubs, lecturing occasionally, appearing at jazz festivals, and working with the New Orleans Jazz Museum as assistant to the curator. He was co-author of *Bourbon Street Black, The New Orleans Black Jazzman* with Jack Buerkle (New York, 1973).

BIBL: ChilWW. FeaEJ. FeaJS. FeaGitJS. Souch.

DISC: Jep. RustJR.

BARNETT, ETTA. See **MOTEN, ETTA.**

BARRETT, EMMA ("SWEET EMMA, THE BELL GAL"). Jazz pianist (b. 25 March 1898 in New Orleans, Louisiana). She began playing professionally about 1923 and thereafter played with leading bands of New Orleans, including Oscar ("Papa") Celestin,* William ("Bebé") Ridgley, George McCullum, Sidney Desvigne, and Armand Piron,* among others. With the revival of public interest in traditional jazz during the 1960s, her career blossomed; she began to record extensively, to appear on television programs, and to tour. From 1961 on she was associated with Preservation Hall in New Orleans. She frequently led her own band, which included Percy Humphrey, Willie Humphrey, Jerry Greene, Jim Robinson, Josiah ("Cié") Frazier, and Narvin Kimball at one time or another. She also sang on recordings and at live performances and appeared in the films *The Cincinnati Kid* (1965) and *Un homme qui me plait* (1969).

BIBL: FeaJS. Handy. MeeJMov. Souch.

BARRETT CAMPBELL, DELOIS. Gospel singer (b. 3 December 1926 in Chicago, Illinois). She began her professional career singing with the Roberta Martin* Singers in Chicago, Illinois, and remained as a lead singer (soprano) with Martin for eighteen years. Others in the group during her tenure included Bessie Folk, Robert Anderson, Willie Webb, Eugene Smith, and Norsalus McKissick, among others. After leaving Martin she formed a trio with her sisters, Billie Greenbey and Rhodessa Porter, called the Barrett Sisters. She toured widely throughout the nation with the Martin Singers and with her trio, recorded regularly, and appeared on radio and television programs, particularly ''Jubilee Showcase'' in Chicago. A member of James Cleveland's* National Gospel Workshop, her honors included citations from civic and community groups. Her best-known performances were ''Climb every mountain,'' ''Born free,'' ''I'll fly away,'' and ''God so loved the world.''

BIBL: Interview by Stella Hall. Heil.

BARRON, KENNETH (''KENNY''). Jazz pianist (b. 9 June 1943 in Philadelphia, Pennsylvania). See **BARRON, WILLIAM.**

BARRON, WILLIAM (''BILL''). Jazz saxophonist (b. 27 March 1927 in Philadelphia, Pennsylvania). He began piano study when he was seven years old and studied tenor saxophone at his school when he was thirteen. He obtained his musical education in the public schools of Philadelphia, Pennsylvania; at the Ornstein School of Music and Combs College of Music (B.A.), both in Philadelphia; and at the University of Massachusetts in Amherst (D. Ed.). During his service in the United States Armed Forces he played in an army band (1944?-1946). After his discharge he returned to Philadelphia, where he played with local groups. In 1958 he settled in New York. Thereafter he played with various groups, including Cecil Taylor* (1958-61), Joseph (''Philly Joe'') Jones* (1961) and Theodore (''Ted'') Curson (as co-leader, early 1960s). During the late 1960s-70s he led his own groups, one of which included his brother Kenneth, and entered into a teaching career, which included tenures as director of the jazz workshop at MUSE (1968-74), a community museum operated by the Brooklyn [New York] Children's Museum, and on the faculty of Wesleyan University in Middletown, Connecticut (1975-). In the 1970s he produced a radio series, ''The Anthology of Black Classical Music,'' on station WNYC. He was also active as panelist and workshop participant in various symposia and at jazz festivals. His honors included a grant from the National Endowment for the Arts in composition. His brother Kenneth was a jazz pianist who played with the James Moody Sextet,* Roy Haynes Quartet,* and John (''Dizzy'') Gillespie* Quintet, among others. In 1973 Kenneth joined the music faculty at Livingston College of Rutgers University in New Brunswick, New Jersey.

BIBL: FeaJS. FeaGitJS. WWBA.

DISC: Jep.

BARTHOLOMEW, DAVE. See **DOMINO, ANTOINE (''FATS'').**

BARTZ, GARY LEE. Jazz saxophonist (b. 26 September 1940 in Baltimore, Maryland). He obtained his musical education in the public schools of Baltimore, Maryland; at the Juilliard School of Music in New York (1957-58); and at the Peabody Conservatory of Music in Baltimore. He began playing alto saxophone when he was eleven years old. During his high-school years he played at parties and later in local clubs, including his father's jazz nightclub. His first professional experience was with the Max Roach* and Abbey Lincoln* Group. Thereafter he played with Art Blakey* (1965-66) and, during the years 1968-69, with McCoy Tyner,* Richard (''Blue'') Mitchell, and again with Max Roach. In 1969 he organized his own group, NTU Troop, but joined Miles Davis* during the years 1970-71. He toured with NTU, appearing at festivals, in concert halls, theaters, and nightclubs, and recorded regularly. He also wrote music for the ABC-TV show *About Time* (1972). His best-known albums were *Home, Harlem Bush Music*, and *I've Known Rivers & Other Bodies*. He received awards from the music industry.

BIBL: Black press, incl. *The Afro-American* [Baltimore], 5 May 1974. FeaGitJS.

BASCOMB, PAUL. Jazz saxophonist (B. 12 February 1910 in Birmingham, Alabama). See **BASCOMB, WILBUR.**

BASCOMB, WILBUR ODELL (''DUD''). Jazz trumpeter (b. 16 May 1916 in Birmingham, Alabama; d. 25 December 1972 in New York, New York). He came from a musical family: his father played drums in local groups; his mother played piano; one brother, Arthur, was a blues pianist; and another brother, Paul, was a jazz saxophonist. He obtained his musical education in the public schools of Birmingham, Alabama, and at the Alabama State Teachers College preparatory high school in Montgomery. He began playing trumpet at his elementary school. He joined the 'Bama State Collegians along with his brother Paul and went to New York in 1934 with the band, which later became the Erskine Hawkins* Band. Dud and Paul were featured soloists with the band until 1944. Thereafter they were co-leaders of first a small group, then a big band (1944-47). After the group's disbandment, Dud played with Edward (''Duke'') Ellington,* then led his own quintet in a long residency at Rahway, New Jersey. Paul moved to the Middle West and was active as a group leader in Detroit, Michigan, and Chicago, Illinois. During the 1950s-60s Dud was active as a free-lancer, particularly in studio recording and as musical director for such entertainers as Sam Cooke,* Wynonie Harris,* Arthur Prysock,* Eddie (''Cleanhead'') Vinson,* and Dinah Washington.* Beginning in 1963 he toured extensively in Japan with Sam (''The Man'') Taylor and in Europe with George (''Buddy'') Tate. He continued to lead his own groups, and he played in pit orchestras for musicals, *Cindy* (1966) and *Purlie* (1970). He also played on soundtracks for films, including *It's a Mad, Mad, Mad, Mad World* (1963) and *Midnight Cowboy* (1969). His son, Wilbur, Jr., became a professional jazzman.

BIBL: ChilWW. DanceWS. FeaEJ. FeaJS. FeaGitJS. MeeJMov.

DISC: Jep. RustJR.

BASIE, WILLIAM (''BILL,'' ''COUNT''). Jazz pianist/Bandleader (b. 21 August 1904 in Red Bank, New Jersey). He first studied music with his mother, a pianist, then later with a local teacher. Later he studied organ (1921) with Thomas (''Fats'') Waller* in New York. He began his professional career playing in clubs in Asbury Park, New Jersey, and in New York; he then toured for several years as an accompanist with vaudeville shows, among them Kate Crippen and Her Kids (c1923), the Gonzell White company, and the Whitman Sisters.* He left the vaudeville circuit in 1927 at Kansas City, Missouri, and found employment there in local theatres and with the Whitmans. He then began playing with jazz bands, first Walter Page's* Blue Devils (1928-29), then Bennie Moten* (1929-35). After Moten's death in 1935, Basie remained with the band briefly under Ira (''Buster'') Moten's leadership, then went to the Reno Club in Kansas City, where he formed his own group. Within a few months he was joined by men with whom he had played in the Blue Devils and Moten's band, including Walter Page, Oran (''Hot Lips'') Page,* James (''Jimmy'') Rushing,* Henry (''Buster'') Smith,* and Lester Young.* He and Smith became co-leaders of the Buster Smith and Count Basie Band of Rhythm, which added more men, including Jesse Price,* Herschel Evans, Clifford McIntyre, and others. The band broadcast nightly over an experimental short-wave station, W9XBY; during this period it acquired a theme song, ''One o'clock jump,'' and Basie acquired his nickname, ''Count.'' In 1936 jazz enthusiast John Hammond heard a broadcast, went to Kansas City to hear a live performance, and later arranged for professional management. After short residencies in Chicago, Illinois, and Buffalo, New York, the Basie band settled in New York and made its debut on 24 December 1936 at the Roseland Ballroom. Personnel changes in the move from Kansas City to New York resulted in the loss of Buster Smith, Jesse Price, and Hot Lips Page, among others, and the addition of Wilbur (''Buck'') Clayton,* Jonathan (''Jo'') Jones,* Freddie Green, Harry Edison,* and others. Blues-singer Rushing was joined by Billie Holiday* (1937-38), then Helen Humes* (1938-42). Slowly Basie established his band as one of the leading groups of the time. It attracted wide attention for its performance on Hammond's celebrated ''From Spirituals to Swing'' concert at Carnegie Hall on 23 December 1938. Basie toured widely with his big band through the 1940s, then had to form a small group in 1950 for economic reasons. He reorganized a big band in 1952 and from that time toured regularly with the big band. The Basie band established its distinctive style over the years, characterized by its blues orientation and use of riff formulas (a heritage from the Kansas City tradition), swinging but precise rhythms (its rhythm section was called ''The All-American Rhythm Section''), and brilliant soloists—among them, in addition to those cited above, William (''Dickie'') Wells,* Victor Dickenson,* Thaddeus (''Thad'') Jones,* Frank Foster,* and Joe Williams,* among others. During the 1960s-70s his band personnel changed frequently. He toured widely throughout the world; appeared with such jazzmen as Frank Sinatra, Tony Bennett, Sammy Davis, Jr.,* and Oscar Peterson,* among others; and performed at jazz festivals, particularly the Newport Jazz Festival/New York. In the 1970s he added playing on cruise ships to his itinerary. Basie made his recording debut in 1929 with Moten and through his long career recorded extensively. He also appeared on innumerable radio and television programs, and in large numbers of films, including *Hit Parade of 1943, Top Man* (1948), *Cinderfella* (1960), and *Made in Paris* (1966), among others. Friends of Basie celebrated his seventieth birthday in 1974 with a gala ''Royal Salute'' in New York. It was by no means a retirement party, however; after more than forty years in jazz, Basie left soon after for his twentieth European tour. He was the grand old man of swing, the only big-band leader of the 1930s still touring regularly through the 1970s. The Basie band undoubtedly exerted wider influence upon contemporary bands than any other band in history, and like the Edward (''Duke'') Ellington* band, it became an American institution. Among his best-known performances were ''April in Paris,'' ''Jumping at the woodside,'' and ''Swinging the blues.'' In 1970 his band produced an album, *Afrique*, which incorporated avant-garde elements into the traditional Basie style. Basie also exerted influence as a pianist. His style development was influenced by Fats Waller, and his economical, subtly timed, chordal interjections were widely imitated by pianists after him. He received numerous awards from the music industry, from civic, community and professional organizations, and an honorary doctorate from the University of Missouri at Kansas City (1978).

BIBL: AlHen. ASCAP. BPIM 2 (Fall 1974). ChilWW. DanceWCB. *Ebony* (December 1974). FeaEJ. FeaJS. FeaGitJS. Ramond Horricks, *Count Basie and His Orchestra* (1957; reprint ed., London: Victor Gollancz Ltd., 1971). MeeJMov. NYT, 1 August 1971. Russ. WWA. WWBA.

DISC: Jep. Kink. RustJR. TudJ.

BASSEY, SHIRLEY. Popular-music singer (b. 8 January 1937 in Cardiff, Wales). She began singing professionally when she was sixteen. She was singing in a local workmen's club when a producer heard her and asked her to audition for a show, "Memories of Jolson." Her successful audition led to engagements in London [England] nightclubs. In 1956 she made her formal debut at the Astor Club in London's West End. During the following decades she slowly established her reputation as an entertainer of international stature. Her performance of the theme song for the James Bond film, *Goldfinger* (1964), brought her wide attention. She also sang theme songs for the films *The Liquidators* (1966) and *Diamonds Are Forever* (1971). She toured widely throughout the world, appearing in theaters, concert halls, nightclubs, and on television shows, and she recorded extensively. Her best-known recordings were "Never, never, never," "Something," and the album *Good, Bad, Beautiful*.

BIBL: Black press, incl. CDef, 19 November 1960, 6 December 1975. WWA.

BATES, CLAYTON ("PEG LEG"). Dancer/Entertainer (b. 11 October 1907 in Fountain Inn, South Carolina). As a child he sang and danced on the streets of his home town. When he was twelve years old he had an accident that forced amputation of his left leg. At fourteen he began dancing with a peg-leg, and at sixteen he was performing professionally. His early experiences were in medicine shows, carnivals, and vaudeville shows, including Eddie Lemon's Revue. During the 1920s he settled in New York. Thereafter he appeared in theaters and Broadway musicals, including Lew Leslie's *Blackbirds of 1928* and *Blackbirds of 1933*. William ("Bill," "Bojangles") Robinson* helped him to perfect his act, and Bates eventually became an entertainer of international stature. He toured widely throughout the world as a single performer and also with groups such as the Harlem Globetrotters (as a pre-game and half-time performer) and the Ed Sullivan Theater Revue (national tour). He also appeared on radio and television programs. After a twenty-five-year career he retired from the entertainment world and built a resort in upper New York state, where he produced his own shows and frequently entertained guests.

BIBL: Black press, incl. NYAge, 24 September 1949; *The Voice* (New York), 5 July 1974. *Sepia* (June 1963).

BATSON BERGEN, FLORA. Concert singer (b. 16 April 1864 in Washington, D.C.; d. 1 December 1906 in Philadelphia, Pennsylvania). She was taken to Providence, Rhode Island, at the age of three and began singing in local church choirs as a child. During the early 1880s she began to appear in local concerts in Providence and in Boston, Massachusetts. In 1885 she became a member of the Bergen Star Concert Company, and eventually its "prima dona soprano," quite by accident: When Nellie Brown,* the leading Bergen soprano, was forced to cancel an appearance in Providence because she was touring in the South, Batson was called in as a last-minute replacement. Already a local favorite, she impressed manager James Bergen so much that he took over her management, made her the leading prima donna of his company, and in 1887 married her. Thereafter she toured widely, after successful debut appearances in New York and Philadelphia, Pennsylvania, in 1885. She made three worldwide tours during her career, which included appearances before Queen Victoria of England, Pope Leo XIII, Queen Lil of Hawaii, the royal family of New Zealand, and other crowned heads. In 1896 she severed her relationship with her husband; thereafter she toured with basso Gerard Millar. The duo gave concerts, appeared as featured artists in an "Operatic Specialties" act with the South Before the War Company, and toured with the Orpheus McAdoo* Minstrels and Vaudeville Company in Australia (1899-1900). She was called "The Double-Voiced Queen of Song" because her wide range enabled her to sing in the baritone register as well as high soprano. Some music critics regarded her as the most successful black concert singer of the nineteenth century after Elizabeth Taylor Greenfield.* Certainly she was one of the three leading black singers of the late nineteenth century, along with Marie Selika* and M. Sissieretta Jones.* Her favorite accompanist was Virginia Montgomery of New York.

BIBL: Black press, incl. NYFreeman, 25 April 1885, 24 October 1885; NYAge, 3 December 1887, 6 December 1906; IndF, 26 December 1896, 24 December 1898, 12 May 1900, 15 February 1901. Maj.

BAZADIER, PHILIP. Military trumpeter (b. 1748 in Guadaloupe; d. 10 June 1848 at Wilmington, North

Carolina). He won wide recognition as the bugler-trumpeter of the Clarendon Horse Guards and the Light Horse Company of Wilmington, North Carolina. He was also the town's "chief musician," who played violin at the balls of the aristocracy and on festive civic occasions.

BIBL: BPIM 8 (Fall 1980), pp. 150-152.

BEACON CHORAL UNION. See **DUPREE, WILLIAM H.**

BEBEY, FRANCIS. Writer/Concert guitarist (b. 16 July 1929 in Douala, Cameroun). He obtained his education at the college in Douala (B. S. in mathematics) and at the Sorbonne in Paris, France. He studied broadcasting at the Studio-école de la Radiodiffusion Outre-Mer in Paris and at New York University. Although best known as a writer, he was also a classical guitarist and composer. He toured widely in the United States, Canada, Europe, and Africa giving solo recitals and lecture concerts. His repertory consisted of African folksong and his own compositions, which generally drew upon African traditional elements. His best-known pieces were "The Ashanti doll is sleeping" (1967), "Black tears" (1963, a poem without words dedicated to those who participated in the March on Washington, D.C.), "The poet's virile prayer" (1973, text by Aimé Cesaire), and "Concert for an old mask" (1965). He published several books, including one about music, *Musique de l'Afrique* (Paris, 1969). Beginning in 1972 he was employed by UNESCO in Paris.

BIBL: WWAfrLit.

BECHET, SIDNEY. Jazz saxophonist (b. 14 May 1897 in New Orleans, Louisiana; d. 14 May 1959 in Paris, France). Two of his brothers, Leonard and Joseph, played musical instruments. He began clarinet study at the age of six with George Baquet.* Later he studied with Lorenzo Tio* and briefly with Louis ("Big Eye") Nelson DeLisle.* He began playing with various local orchestras and brass bands when he was about twelve; thereafter he played in his brother Leonard's band, the Silver Bells Band, and the Young Olympia Band (co-leader with Buddy Petit [née Joseph Crawford]). Later he played with John Robichaux,* the Eagle Brass Band under Willie ("Bunk") Johnson's* leadership (c. 1911), and other groups. In 1914 he left New Orleans in a trio with Clarence Williams* and Louis Wade to tour with a travelling show and remained on the road until 1917, although he did return to New Orleans occasionally to play. He settled in Chicago, Illinois, in 1917; thereafter he played with various groups or persons, including Lawrence Duhé (at the DeLuxe Cafe), Freddie Keppard,* Joseph ("King") Oliver,* Anthony ("Tony") Jackson* (at the Pekin Theater), and Will Marion Cook's* Southern Syncopated Orchestra (1918-20), with which he performed in London, England, in 1919. When Cook returned to the United States, Bechet remained in Europe with a splinter group from the orchestra, performing in London, England, and in Paris, France. He returned to the United States in 1921 and thereafter played in New York with Ford Dabney,* Edward ("Duke") Ellington* (1924), and James P. Johnson.* During the early 1920s he also toured with shows, including Donald Heywood's *How Come* (1921-23), *The Black and White Revue* (1923), *Seven Eleven* (1925), and Mamie Smith's* show. He led his own groups, recorded extensively, and operated a nightclub, Club Basha, for a short period. In the fall of 1926 he sailed to Europe with the show *La Revue Negrè*, which included Claude Hopkins* as the musical director and Josephine Baker* in a leading role. The musical opened in Paris, France, at the Théâtre des Champs Elysées, then toured in Europe. When the show closed, Bechet joined an orchestra that toured in Russia. For more than two decades thereafter he played with groups on both sides of the Atlantic, among them, Noble Sissle* (during the years 1928-38), William ("Willie-the-Lion") Smith,* Tommy Ladnier,* and Arthur ("Zutty") Singleton,* and led his own groups in Paris; Berlin, Germany; Amsterdam, The Netherlands; and other European cities. He also led groups in the United States in New York, Chicago, and Boston during the 1940s, playing in ballrooms, including the Savoy in the Harlem community, in nightclubs, and at jazz festivals. In 1951 he settled permanently in Paris. He was musically active until shortly before his death; using Paris as a base, he toured widely and returned to the United States in 1951 and 1953. He also performed on the vaudeville stage in Paris and appeared in films, including *L'Inspecteur connait la musique* (1955) and *Ah! Quelle èquipe* (1956). Bechet was an important clarinetist in the second generation of the New Orleans school, along with Johnny Dodds* and Jimmie Noone.* His style was distinctive for its heavy vibrato and expressiveness, but it was as a soprano saxophonist that he made his largest contribution to jazz history. He was the pioneer who defined the role of that instrument in the jazz ensemble from the time of his permanent conversion to it in 1919.

BIBL: Sidney Bechet, *Treat It Gentle* (London, 1960). Rudi Blesh, *Combo: U.S.A.* (Philadelphia, 1971). ChilWW. EAB. FeaEJ. MeeJMov. Souch.

DISC: Kink. RustJR. TudJ.

BELAFONTE, HAROLD GEORGE ("HARRY"). Folk singer/Actor (b. 1 March 1927 in New York, New York). Although best known as an actor and producer, he was a singer in his early career. He obtained his education in the public schools of Jamaica, West Indies (where he lived during the years 1935-40), and New York, where he attended high school. After serving in the U. S. Navy (1944-47?), he enrolled in Erwin Piscator's Dramatic Workshop at the New School for Social Research in New York. He attracted favorable attention for a singing role, which led to engagements in New York nightclubs. He soon established himself as a top singer of popular songs, touring widely and recording regularly. In 1950 he left the field of popular music abruptly and turned to folk music. He developed a repertory of folk songs, pursuing research in the Library of Congress Archives of American Folk Song and drawing upon his experiences as a child in the West Indies; in 1951 he made his debut as a folksinger at the Village Vanguard club in New York. Within a short time he won wide recognition as a folksinger of great stature. During the 1950s he toured widely on the nightclub circuit, appeared on numerous television shows, and sang in films, including the role of Joe in *Carmen Jones* (1954). He produced recordings in the mid-1950s that initiated the calypso fad in the United States, such as ''Jamaica farewell,'' ''Day-O (Banana boat song),'' ''Matilda,'' and ''Come back, Liza.'' He also sang Negro spirituals and other folksongs on his recordings and on his live concerts. During the 1960s-70s he devoted more time to straight dramatic roles and to producing films and television shows, many of which treated the subject of black music history and black musicians. He established his own production company, Har Bel, as early as 1959. Later he was president of Belafonte Enterprises. He made an important contribution to the history of black music as folk singer and producer; he also aided the career development of young black performers, among them, Miriam Makeba* and Hugh Masekela.* He received awards from the theater industry and honorary doctorates from Park College (1968) and the New School for Social Research.

BIBL: ASCAP. CurBiog (January1956). StamFCW. WWA. WWBA.

DISC: Kink.

BELL, THOM. Songwriter/Record producer (b. 27 January 1943 in Philadelphia, Pennsylvania). See **GAMBLE, KENNETH.**

BENSON, GEORGE. Jazz guitarist (b. 22 March 1943 in Pittsburgh, Pennsylvania). He sang in an amateur talent contest when he was four years old and won first prize. As a child he sang and played ukelele on street corners and entertained in clubs with his stepfather, a guitarist. When he began formal guitar study at the age of eleven he had already won wide recognition as a performer, had appeared on television shows, and had made recordings. His early style development was influenced by his listening to recordings of Charlie Christian.* During his high-school years he played with local rhythm 'n' blues groups and formed his own group when he was seventeen. Two years later he heard recordings of Charlie Parker* and determined to become a jazz musician. His first jazz experience was with the Jack McDuff Quartet (1962-65); thereafter he played primarily with his own groups. Within a few years he established himself as a jazz singer-guitarist of impressive stature. He toured widely, appearing in concert halls and nightclubs, on television shows, and at festivals, and recorded regularly. His best known albums were *Breezin'*, *The Masquerade*, and *In Flight*. He received many awards from the music industry. His style is distinctive for its fusion of rhythm 'n' blues, jazz, popular music, soul, and bossa nova. He was a pioneer ''crossover'' from jazz to other styles in the 1970s and was credited by some as an important force in bringing about the jazz revival of the 1970s.

BIBL: *Dawn Magazine* (August 1978). *Ebony* (November 1977). FeaJS. FeaGitJS. MeeJMov. WWA. WWBA.

BENSON, NERO. Military trumpeter (fl. mid-eighteenth century in Framingham, Massachusetts). He was enslaved of one Reverend Mr. John Swift, minister of the First Church in Framingham, and was a member of ''full communion'' in the church. He entered His Majesty's service on 27 August 1723 and served as a trumpeter in the company of Captain Isaac Clark of Framingham during the French and Indian Wars in the colonies.

BIBL: Josiah H. Temple, *History of Framingham, Massachusetts* (Framingham, 1887), p 236; Wilkes.

BENTON, BROOK. (née **BENJAMIN FRANKLIN PEAY).** Popular-music singer (b. 19 September 1931 in Camden, South Carolina). As a child he sang in a church choir directed by his father and later sang with local gospel groups. When he was seventeen years old he went to New York to further his career in entertainment. He obtained employment singing on demonstration records for songwriters and publishers and was heard by Nat King Cole* (née Nathaniel Coles), who liked a Benton song, ''Looking back,'' and recorded it. The success of Cole's record brought wide attention to songwriter-singer Benton. In 1955 he met Clyde Otis, and the two men formed a songwriting team, producing songs that were sung by Cole, Patti Page, Roy Hamilton, and Clyde McPhatter,* among others. In 1959 Benton himself sang one of the songs co-written by him, Clyde, and B. Hendricks, ''It's just a matter of time,'' and won wide recognition. During the next few years he released a large number of best-selling songs, some in collaboration with Dinah Washington.* He established himself as one of the most popular ballad singers of the early 1960s; he toured widely on the nightclub and theater circuits and recorded extensively. During the mid-1960s, however, his career as an entertainer reached a low point, although he continued to meet with success in his recording and songwriting, and the Benton-Otis team was dissolved in 1963. In the 1970s Benton made a comeback and began producing top-selling recordings again. In 1978 he was reunited with his songwriting partner Otis. His best known songs, in addition to those cited above, included ''A lover's question,'' ''A rainy night in Georgia,'' ''Shoes,'' and ''Making love is good for you.''

BIBL: *Ebony* (May 1978). *Sepia* (March 1961). StamPRS. WWBA.

DISC: Giv.

BERGEN, FLORA BATSON. See **BATSON BERGEN, FLORA.**

BERRY, CHARLES EDWARD ANDERSON (''CHUCK''). Rock singer (b. 15 January 1926 in San Jose, California.) His family moved to Missouri shortly after his birth. He began piano study at the age of seven and later studied saxophone and guitar. He obtained his musical education in the public schools of Wentzville and St. Louis, where his interest in music was encouraged by Julia Davis at Sumner High School. He sang in a church choir and in his high-school glee club. His style development was influenced by his listening to recordings of Nat King Cole (née Nathaniel Coles),* Louis Jordan,* and Frank Sinatra. Despite his musical activities, he did not enter music as a career until about 1950. His early professional experience was with the Ray Banks orchestra in St. Louis. In 1952 he formed a trio with Johnny Johnson (piano) and Ebby Harding (drums), with himself on guitar. Within three years the trio had established itself as a leading group in St. Louis. He had been writing songs for some time, and in 1955 he went to Chicago, Illinois, to further his career development. He attended a production of Muddy Waters (née McKinley Morganfield)* and was given permission by Waters to ''sit in'' with his group. Waters was impressed by Berry's performance and arranged for a record contract. Berry's first song, ''Maybelline,'' attracted wide attention. Thereafter he recorded extensively. He also toured widely in the United States and abroad and appeared on television shows and in films, including *Rock, Rock, Rock* (1956), *Jazz on a Summer's Day* (1960), and *Let the Good Times Roll* (1973). Berry was regarded as the leading originator of rock 'n' roll; unlike his white imitators, he was both performer and songwriter, and he exerted enormous influence upon the development of popular music in the 1960s and 1970s. His style was distinctive for its high-pitched, brilliant guitar with its use of heavy bass riffs and ''floating piano,'' and its employment of the twelve-bar blues form. His best known songs included ''Wee, wee hours,'' ''Roll over, Beethoven,'' ''Too much monkey business,'' and ''Ding a ling.'' He received awards from the music industry. At the end of the 1960s his career went into a small decline but recovered with the rock 'n' roll revival of the mid-1970s, to which Berry made an important contribution. He was called ''folk poet of the fifties.''

BIBL: CurBiog (April 1977). StamPRS. WWA. WWBA.

DISC: TudBM.

BERRY, LEON (''CHU''). Jazz saxophonist (b. 13 September 1910 in Wheeling, West Virginia; d. 30 October 1941 in Conneaut, Ohio). He came from a musical family, and his brother Nelson became a professional jazz musician. He played alto saxophone during his high-school years, and during the three years he attended West Virginia State College at Bluefield, he played alto and tenor with Edwards' Collegians. He also played with other groups in the area. In 1929 he joined Sammy Stewart and was with the band when it played at the Savoy Ballroom in the Harlem community of New York in 1930. Thereafter he played with various groups, including Bennett (''Benny'') Carter (1932, 1933),* Charlie Johnson (1932-33), Theodore (''Teddy'') Hill (1934-35),* Fletcher Henderson (1934, 1935-37),* and Cabell (''Cab'') Calloway (1937-41).* He was an important tenor saxophonist of the swing era, who played in the tradition of Coleman Hawkins.* His best-known performance was the solo on ''A ghost of a chance.''

BIBL: ChilWW. FeaEJ.

DISC: Kink. RustJR.

BETHUNE, THOMAS GREENE WIGGINS (''BLIND TOM''). Concert pianist/Composer (b. 25 May 1849 near Columbus, Georgia; d. 13 June 1908 in Hoboken, New Jersey). Born a slave—and blind—he early revealed an aptitude for music. His owner, Colonel James N. Bethune, purchased a piano for his family when Tom was about four years old. According to legend, Tom stole into the living room one night and played correctly some of the music that he had heard performed during the day. Thereafter he was allowed free access to the piano, and during this period his owner began to exhibit him to the public. Tom was given informal irregular instruction by the Bethune daughters and Mrs. Bethune, a music teacher before her marriage, which consisted primarily of letting him listen to music to serve as a basis for developing a repertory. In 1858 he was hired out for three years to Perry Oliver, a planter of Savannah, Georgia, who exhibited the slave boy as the "musical prodigy of the age: a Plantation Negro Boy." During the Civil War, Tom's tours were curtailed although, ironically, he was forced to give concerts during the summer of 1861 for the benefit of wounded Confederate soldiers—the enemies of those fighting for the freedom of the slaves. After the war, Tom began a long and arduous career that lasted almost thirty years and carried him throughout the United States, Europe, and South America. His first tour abroad was in 1866. He was continuously subjected to rigorous tests of his extraordinary talent and prodigious memory. His management capitalized upon the controversy his playing aroused by collecting testimonial letters from leading musicians of the time—among them, Ignaz Moscheles and Charles Halle—which they published along with a biographical sketch in a pamphlet, *The Marvelous Musical Prodigy Blind Tom* (New York, n.d.). They procured the best music teachers for him, including one W. P. Howard of Atlanta, Georgia, who accompanied Tom on the first European tour in 1866. By the end of the nineteenth century, Blind Tom had become an American institution; few were the towns where he had not performed, and his name was a household word. He continued to tour widely after his prodigy days had passed; during the 1890s he was more and more often billed as a vaudeville attraction. He retired in 1898, having made fortunes for his original owner; the son, James S. Bethune; Perry Oliver; and the son's widow, who married Albert J. Lerché. Thereafter rumors of his death occasionally appeared in the press, only to be later refuted. During the 1904-05 season he made a "come-back" concert tour.

Tom's repertory supposedly included some 7000 pieces, which he could play upon request; and he is credited with having composed more than 100 pieces, most of them fantasias or variations based upon operatic airs and ballad tunes of the period but also including original compositions. He improvised many pieces that were never published. His output included dances, marches, salon pieces, and the "battle pieces" that were popular during his time. On one occasion he performed his "Battle of Manassas" (in reference to a Civil War battle) so realistically that his audience offered protests. His published music used the pseudonyms J. C. Beckel and Francois Sexalise in addition to his own name. Although most of his music was published after 1870, he was well represented in the *Complete Catalogue of Sheet Music and Musical Works* (published by the Board of Music Trade of the United States of America in 1871). His best-known compositions, in addition to the battle piece cited above, were "Water on the Moonlight," "The Rainstorm," "Wellenlänge" or "Voice of the Waves" (Sexalise), "Imitation of the Sewing Machine," "Marche Timpani," and "Reve Charmant."

BIBL: Black press incl. CleveG. 1 August 1885; IndF, 1 June 1889; NYAge, 18 June 1908, 2 July 1908. See Geneva Southall, *Blind Tom* (Minneapolis: Challenge Productions, Inc., 1979) for a bibliography and complete list of works.

BIBB, CHARLES LEON. Folksinger (b. c1924 in Louisville, Kentucky). As a child he sang in a church choir and later sang in his high-school glee club. After service in the U. S. Armed Forces, he settled in New York, where he began singing professionally, at first in small nightclubs, then in Off-Broadway productions of such shows as *Livin' the Life* (1957), *Lost in the Stars* (1958), *Annie, Get Your Gun* (1958), and *Finian's Rainbow* (1960). Beginning in the late 1950s he toured widely as a folksinger in the United States, and later in Europe (beginning in 1964), singing in concert halls, nightclubs, and at jazz and folk festivals. He also recorded extensively from 1959 on and appeared on radio and television programs. He attracted wide attention for his singing in *A Hand Is at the Gate* (1966). Thereafer he devoted more time to acting and appeared in several films. He gave concerts occasionally in the 1970s. His best-known performances included "Mule skinner," "Sinner man," "On my way to Saturday," and "Lost in the stars."

BIBL: StamFCW. *The Washington Post*, 26 October 1969.

BIGARD, LEON ALBANY ("BARNEY"). Jazz clarinetist (b. 3 March 1906 in New Orleans, Louisiana; d. 27 June 1980 in Culver City, California). He came from a musical family; his brother (uncle?) Emile played violin in New Orleans bands, and his brother Alec became a jazz drummer. He began clarinet study at the age of seven with Lorenzo Tio, Jr.*; later he changed to tenor saxophone. In 1922 he began playing professionally; thereafter he played with Albert Nicholas,* Octave Gaspard, and Luis Russell,* among others. In 1924 he joined Joseph ("King") Oliver* as a saxophonist but began playing clarinet about 1925. After leaving Oliver in 1927 he played with various groups, including Charlie Elgar,* Luis Rusell again, and Edward ("Duke") Ellington (1927-42).* In 1942 he settled in California. Over the years he played with many groups, including Freddie Slack, Edward ("Kid") Ory (1946),* Louis Armstrong (1947-52, 1953-55, 1960-61),* and William ("Cozy") Cole,* among others. He also led his own groups frequently in Los Angeles, California. During the 1940s-70s he toured widely with others at home and abroad, appearing in theaters and concert halls, in nightclubs, on college campuses, and at major jazz festivals. The U. S. State Department sent him to Africa in 1960-61. In the 1970s he played with Arthur ("Art") Hodes, Eddie Condon, William ("Wild Bill") Davison, the New Ragtime Jazzband (1975 in Switzerland), and The Pelican Trio (1978 in Europe). He recorded extensively and appeared on radio and television programs and in films, including *Botta e risposta* (1951), *The Strip* (1951), *St. Louis Blues* (1958), and the documentary made for French television, *Musical Biography of Barney Bigard* (1975). He received awards from the music industry in the United States and in France. He was co-composer with Ellington of "Mood indigo" and several other songs. His style was distinctive for its expressiveness and flowing melodies. He was an important swing clarinetist, although he belonged to the New Orleans tradition; he was one of the few sidemen who played with two of the major giants of jazz, both Ellington and Armstrong.

BIBL: ASCAP. ChilWW. FeaJS. FeaGitJs. Pops Foster, *The Autobiography of a New Orleans Jazzman, as Told to Tom Stoppard* (Berkeley, 1971). MeeJMov.

DISC: Jep. Kink. RustJR.

BILLUPS, KENNETH BROWNE. School music educator/Choral conductor (b. 15 April 1918 in St. Louis, Missouri). He obtained his musical education in the public schools of St. Louis, Missouri; at Lincoln University in Jefferson City, Missouri (B.A., 1940); at Northwestern University in Evanston, Illinois (B. Mus., 1945; M. Mus., 1947); Washington University in St. Louis; and Southern Illinois University at Edwardsville. His teaching career included tenures in the public schools of Webster Groves, Missouri (1943-49); the public schools of St. Louis, Missouri (1950-77), where he taught at Sumner High School and became supervisor of vocal music for the city (1975-77); at the University of Missouri in St. Louis (1971-77, evening sessions); and at the Music and Arts University in St. Louis (1952-54). He also served as visiting professor in various institutions during summer schools, including Northwestern University, Lincoln University, and Texas Southern University in Houston. He was active as a choral director throughout his career. He directed groups during his college years; thereafter he directed the Wings Over Jordan Choir* (Unit 2, 1942-46); the CBS radio group, The Legend Singers (1940-77); choral groups for the Municipal Opera of St. Louis (regularly during the years 1944-76); and local community groups. He toured as a guest choral conductor and also conducted the St. Louis Symphony on occasions. He also served as musical director for stage works from time to time, including *The Three-Penny Opera* in 1965 for the American Theater and Joplin's* *Treemonisha* in 1979 for the National Association of Negro Musicians.* During the 1970s he was active with radio and television programs; he was music director for KSD-TV "Protestant Hour" (1972-73), host for radio station KMOX show "Afro-Americans and Their Music" in 1973, and producer of a weekly program on KTVI-2, "God's Musical World" (1972-77). His honors included awards from civic and professional organizations, an award from the Northwestern University Music Alumni Association, and appointment to boards and executive committees of such organizations. He was president of the National Association of Negro Musicians for six years (1963-69). He published numerous compositions and folksong arrangements for chorus and voice.

BIBL: Questionnaire. WWCA, 1950.

BLACK PATTI. See **JONES, M. SISSIERETTA** and **J. MAYO WILLIAMS.**

BLACK MALIBRAN, THE. See **MARTÍNEZ, MARÍA.**

BLACK SWAN, THE. See **GREENFIELD, ELIZABETH TAYLOR** and **PACE, HARRY.**

BLACKWELL, FRANCIS HILLMAN ("SCRAPPER"). Blues guitarist (b. 21 February 1903 in Syracuse, South Carolina(?); d. 7 October 1962 in Indianapolis, Indiana). See **CARR, LEROY.**

BLAKE, ("BLIND") ARTHUR (née **ARTHUR PHELPS).** Bluesman (b. c1890 in Jacksonville or Tampa, Florida; d. c1933 in Jacksonville). Little is known about his early life except that he was active as a guitarist in Atlanta, Georgia. He recorded in Chicago during the years 1926-29, then went on the road with a show, Happy-Go-Lucky, managed by his friend George Williams. Those with whom he played and/or recorded included Gus Cannon,* Johnny Dodds,* ''Ma'' (Gertrude) Rainey,* Elzadie Robinson, and Irene Scruggs, among others.

BIBL: BWW. CharCB. FeaEJ. Oliv.

DISC: RustEJ. TudBM.

BLAKE, JAMES HUBERT ("EUBIE"). Ragtime/ Musical comedy composer (b. 7 February 1883 in Baltimore, Maryland). He first played on a house pump-organ, then began piano study when he was six years old with local teacher Margaret Marshall. Later he studied with Llewellyn Wilson* (1907-14) and at New York University in the Schillinger System of Composition (1949) with Rudolph Schramm. He also studied informally with Will Marion Cook* (1920s). He began his career as a ragtime pianist about 1898, playing in local bars and brothels of Baltimore, Maryland. His early style development was influenced by the pianists he heard playing in Baltimore, among them Jesse Pickett, William Turk, (''Big'') Jimmy Green, (''One-Leg'') Willie Joseph, and others. Beginning in 1901 he toured with shows, including Dr. Frazier's Medicine Show (1901) and In Old Kentucky (1902), then returned to playing in Baltimore cafes and nightclubs. During the years 1907-15 he was pianist in a hotel, the Goldfield, and played during summers in nearby Atlantic City, New Jersey, where he came into contact with such ragtime pianists as James P. Johnson,* William (''Willie-the-Lion'') Smith,* and William (''Willie'') Gant.* In 1915 he came into contact with Noble Sissle,* and the two men formed a vaudeville act, The Dixie Duo; they toured widely (1915-20) and appeared with James Reese Europe's* Society Orchestra during the years 1916-19. Blake and Sissle wrote songs in collaboration from the beginning; their first song, ''It's all your fault,'' was introduced by white singer Sophie Tucker and became a success. In 1920 Blake and Sissle collaborated with the vaudeville team Flournoy Miller* and Aubrey Lyles* to produce the Broadway musical *Shuffle Along*, which opened in May 1921 on Broadway after two-week try-outs at the Howard Theatre in Washington, D.C., and at the Dunbar Theatre in Philadelphia, Pennsylvania. Miller and Lyles provided the book; Sissle, the lyrics; and Blake, the music. The show was so successful that at one time there were three companies on the road simultaneously; some of its songs proved to be longlasting, including ''I'm just wild about Harry,'' ''Love will find a way,'' and ''Bandanna days.'' The cast included several who would later win wide recognition in the world of music or the stage, among them, Josephine Baker,* Caterina Jarboro,* Florence Mills,* Paul Robeson,* and William Grant Still (in orchestra).* With *Shuffle Along*, Blake entered into a new career, that of writing musical comedies; in addition to Sissle he collaborated with Andy Razaf.* He wrote scores for *The Chocolate Dandies* (1924, originally titled *In Bamville*), Will Morrissey's *Folies Bergere* of 1930, *Blackbirds of 1930*, *Shuffle Along of 1933*, *Swing It* (1937), *Shuffle Along of 1952*, and *Bubbling Brown Sugar* (1976). He also contributed songs to such musicals as *Elsie* (1923), *Charlot's Revue of 1924*, *Hot Rhythm* (1930), and *Tan Manhattan* (1941). When *The Chocolate Dandies* closed in 1925, Blake and Sissle went to England, where they performed on the vaudeville stage and wrote songs for Charles B. Cochran's *Revue of 1926* in London. After returning to the United States, Blake was active during the next decade and a half as songwriter, collaborating with Henry Creamer,* among others, and as vaudeville entertainer with Henry (''Broadway'') Jones, in addition to writing musicals. He and Jones produced a vaudeville revue called *Shuffle Along, Jr.* (1928-29). During the years of World War II Blake toured with U.S.O. shows throughout the nation as a musical conductor (1941-46). He then retired, but the revival of interest in ragtime during the 1950s brought him out of retirement to begin a third career as concert rag pianist and lecturer. He toured throughout the world, appearing in concert halls and theaters, on college campuses, at jazz festivals, and on radio and television shows. He recorded regularly. He had made his recording debut in 1917 and over the years recorded with his orchestra (1920s-30s) and made piano rolls. Then in 1969 he recorded the album *The Eighty-Six Years of Eubie Blake*, and in 1972 he established his own record company, Eubie Blake Music, Inc., which issued recordings of him at the piano and also other performers, including Noble Sissle, Ivan Harold Browning,* and Edith Wilson,* among others. In 1973 he made five piano rolls for the QRS (Quality Reigns Supreme, a subsidiary of the Melville Clark Piano Company), thus drawing his total number to thirty-nine recorded rolls. Throughout his career he wrote music continuously; from his first piano rag in 1898, ''Charleston rag'' (originally titled ''Sounds of Africa''), he wrote more than 350 piano pieces and songs, including waltzes and character pieces as well as rags. Best known of the piano pieces were ''Chevy Chase,'' ''Brittwood rag,'' ''Eubie's boogie,'' ''Troublesome ivories,'' and ''Baltimore todolo.'' His best-known songs included (in addition to those cited above) ''Memories of you,'' ''Lovin' you the way I do,'' ''You were meant for me,'' and

"You're lucky to me." His numerous honors included awards from the music and theater industry, from professional organizations and civic groups, citations from cities and other government units, and honorary doctorates from Brooklyn College of the City University of New York (1973), Dartmouth College (1974), Rutgers University (1974), and the New England Conservatory of Music (1974). He was the subject of a French television musical autobiography; in 1974 he made a documentary film with Sissle titled *Reminiscing with Sissle and Blake*; and in 1978 a musical *Eubie*, based on his music, opened on Broadway. Eubie Blake was a seminal figure in the history of American music as a ragtime pianist and composer and as a composer of musical comedies.

BIBL: Interviews with E.S. ASCAP. BleshR. Rudi Blesh, *Combo: USA* (Philadelphia, 1971). BPIM 1 (Spring, Fall 1973). Lawrence Carter, *Eubie Blake: Keys of Memory* (Detroit, 1979). ChilWW. FeaEJ. FeaJS. Robert Kimball and William Bolcom, *Reminiscing with Sissle and Blake* (New York, 1972). *Ebony* (July 1973). *Jazz Magazine* (Summer 1978). MeeJMov. Al Rose, *Eubie Blake* (New York: Macmillan Co., 1979). WWA.WWBA. WWCA, 1950.

DISC: CRE. Kink. *Record Research* 159/160 (December 1978). RustJR. TudJ.

BLAKEY, ARTHUR ("ART") (also known as **ABDULLAH IBN BUHAINA).** Jazz drummer (b. 11 October 1919 in Pittsburgh, Pennsylvania). He began his professional career playing piano with local groups in Pittsburgh, Pennsylvania, then later changed to drums. Thereafter he played with various groups, including James ("Jimmy") Murray (early 1940s in Pittsburgh), Mary Lou Williams* (1942), Fletcher Henderson* (1943-44), William ("Billy") Eckstine* (1944-47), Lucius ("Lucky") Millinder* (1949), and Boniface ("Buddy") DeFranco (quartet, 1951-53). He also led his own groups from time to time, as in 1941 and 1944 in Boston. In 1955 he formed the Jazz Messengers, which included performers with whom he had played in a cooperative group—Kenneth ("Kenny") Dorham,* Henry ("Hank") Mobley, Horace Silver,* and Douglas Watkins. His group toured widely during the next three decades, although with personnel changes. Many of those who performed in his groups over the years later won wide recognition as jazz artists, among them, Freddie Hubbard,* Wayne Shorter,* Lee Morgan, Curtis Fuller, Theodore ("Sonny") Rollins, Cedar Walton, John ("Jackie') McLean,* and Donald Byrd,* among others. In 1971-72 Blakey toured with the Giants of Jazz, which was composed of six bandleaders, John ("Dizzy") Gillespie,* Thelonious Monk,* Alfred McKibbon, Edward ("Sonny") Stitt,* and Kai Winding. During the 1970s the Jazz Messengers continued to tour in the United States, Europe, and Japan, appearing at festivals, in concert halls, and in nightclubs. He won awards from the music industry. Blakey was one of the foremost drummers, along with Maxwell ("Max") Roach,* in the hard-bop tradition and a pioneer in expanding the possibilities of the contemporary jazz drum. His style was distinctive for its explosive vitality and use of Afro-Cuban elements. He frequently formed all-percussive orchestras or chamber groups for performances. His best-known albums included *A Night at Birdland, Buhaina's Delight,* and *Anthenagin*.

BIBL: AlHen. ChilWW. FeaEJ. FeaJS. FeaGitJS. *Jazz Magazine* (Winter 1979). MeeJMov. WWBA.

DISC: Jep. Kink. ModJ. TudJ.

BLAND, JAMES. Minstrel/Songwriter (b. 23 October 1854 in Flushing, New York; d. 5 May 1911 in Philadelphia, Pennsylvania). His family moved to Philadelphia, Pennsylvania, when he was six, and there he first became interested in music. About 1868 his family relocated in Washington, D.C., when his father was appointed to a civil-service position. After graduation from high school, he entered Howard University in Washington with the intent of studying law but soon deserted the classroom to become a minstrel. He taught himself to play the banjo, found employment in local hotels and at private entertainments, and began writing songs for use in his performances. His composition was influenced by the folksongs of the ex-slaves he heard all about him during this post-Civil War period. White minstrel George Primrose heard some of Bland's songs and arranged to use them for his own shows, which gave Bland an auspicious beginning for his career. It appears that Bland's earliest professional experience was in 1875 with the Original Black Diamonds minstrel troupe of Boston, Massachusetts. Thereafter he performed with various groups, including the Bohee Brothers Minstrels in 1876, which included also Billy Kersands* and Sam Lucas*; Sprague's Georgia Minstrels in 1877; and Haverly's Genuine Colored Minstrels beginning about 1880. He went abroad with this troupe in 1881 but did not return to the United States with the minstrels, remaining abroad along with the Bohee brothers, Billy Allen, and one or two others. Bland toured the continent for almost a decade, singing *without* the traditional minstrel blackface in the leading music halls of Europe and earning for himself the sobriquet, "idol of the music halls." He returned home about 1890 and joined W. S. Cleveland's Colored Minstrels but in 1891 left again for Europe. It is not known when he next returned to the United States; as W. C. Handy* met him at Louisville, Kentucky, in 1897, his return obviously predated that year. In 1898 Bland sang with Black Patti's* Troubadours, in apparently his last public performances. Bland was a prolific songwriter, credited with having written more than 600 songs of all kinds—particularly ballads, comic, and religious for solo voice and ensemble. His best known song is ''Carry me back to old Virginny,'' written when he was twenty-four years old and adopted in 1940 by Virginia as its official state song. Other celebrated songs of Bland are ''Oh, dem golden slippers,'' ''In the evening by the moonlight,'' ''Hand me down my walking cane,'' ''De golden wedding,'' and ''Dandy black brigade.''

BIBL: Free Library of Philadelphia [Pennsylvania] Clipping File. Black press, incl. CDef, 1 July 1911; CleveG, 31 January 1891,16 May 1891; IndF 23 August 1890, 3 December 1898. John J. Daly, *A Song in His Heart* (Philadelphia, 1951). *Etude* (October 1946). W.C. Handy, *Father of the Blues* (New York, 1941). Simond.

BLAND, ROBERT CALVIN ("BOBBY BLUE"). Bluesman (b. 27 January 1930 in Rosemark [near Memphis], Tennessee). He moved to Memphis in 1947, where he first sang with the Pilgrim Travelers, a church group, and later with the Beale Streeters, which included at one time or another Johnny Ace (John Marshall Alexander), Roscoe Gordon, Earl Forrest and Riley (''B. B.'') King.* His first recordings in 1950 revealed his inclination to imitate established entertainers, particularly Nat (''King'') Cole (née Nathaniel Coles)* and B. B. King. After service in the armed forces (1952-54), he returned to Memphis and began recording extensively. He also toured with Herman (''Junior'') Parker (1955-61)* and later with his own group (1961-68). During the mid-1950s he began to develop a distinctive style—rooted in gospel, jazz, and popular ballads in addition to blues—and recorded several successful albums. After a three-year absence from music, he returned to touring in 1971 with a new group, later called the Blue Explosions, and occasionally appeared with others, among them, Albert King* and B. B. King. His music during the later 1970s reflected the influence of disco and country music.

BIBL: BWW. LivBl 4 (Winter 1970-71); LivBl 39 (July-August 1978). Oliv. Charles Keil, *Urban Blues* (Chicago, 1966).

DISC: Jep. TudBM.

BLANTON, CAROL. College professor/Concert pianist (b. 10 January 1911 in St. Helena Island, South Carolina; d. 15 February 1974 in Baltimore, Maryland). She came from a musical family. Her father, Joshua Enoch Blanton, long-time president of Vorhees Institute in South Carolina, traveled during World War I with the War Camp Community Service, entertaining the troops, along with pianist Helen Hagan,* and teaching servicemen to sing Negro spirituals and other folksongs. She obtained her musical education at Spelman College in Atlanta, Georgia (B.A., 1933), where she studied with Kemper Harreld;* at Morehouse College in Atlanta; at the Institute of Musical Art in New York (M. Mus., 1938; now the Juilliard School of Music); and at Catholic University of America in Washington, D. C. She also studied privately with Loony Epstein, Sascha Gorodnitzki, Carl Friedberg, and Hazel Harrison.* Her teaching career included tenures at Dillard Univesity in New Orleans, Louisiana (1936-46); at Hampton Institute in Virginia (1946-47); and at Morgan State University in Baltimore, Maryland (1947-74). Concomitantly with her teaching she toured regularly as a concert pianist.

BIBL: Black press, incl. *The Afro-American* [Baltimore], week of 19-23 February 1974; NYAge, 25 January 1919. NYB, 1952, p. 58.

BLANTON, JAMES ("JIMMY"). Jazz bassist (b. October 1918 in Chattanooga, Tennessee; d. 30 July 1942 in Los Angeles, California). He came from a musical family; his mother, a pianist, led her own band. He studied violin as a child, then changed to double bass when he attended Tennessee State College in Nashville, Tennessee (1934-37), where he played with the State Collegians, led by Samuel (''Sammy'') Lowe in 1935. During his college years he also played with local groups and during vacation periods with Fate Marable's* riverboat bands. In 1937 he went to St. Louis, Missouri, where he played with the [James] Jeter/[Hayes] Pillars orchestra. In 1939 he joined Edward (''Duke'') Ellington* (1939-41), with whom he remained until illness forced him to leave music. Ellington recorded several sets of duets with Blanton (piano and string bass, 1939, 1940) and wrote ''Jack the bear'' especially for Blanton. He was a pioneering jazz bassist who transformed his instrument into a melodic instrument comparable to a horn and revolutionized jazz bass performance, as Charles (''Charlie'') Christian* revolutionized jazz guitar performance.

BIBL: ChilWW. FeaEJ.

DISC: Kink. RustJR.

BLANTON, JOSHUA. See **BLANTON, CAROL.**

BLEDSOE, JULIUS (JULES). Concert singer (b. 29 December 1898 in Waco, Texas; d. 14 July 1943 in Hollywood, California). He sang in church concerts as a child and studied piano. He attended Bishop College in Marshall, Texas (A.B., 1918), and studied further at Virginia Union College in Richmond, Virginia (1918-19), and Columbia University in New York (1919-24), where he entered the school of medicine. During this period in New York he studied voice with Claude Warford, and later with Parisolti and Lazar Samoiloff. Successful appearances on local concerts led him to abandon a medical career; in April 1924 he made his concert debut as a baritone in Aeolian Hall. Thereafter he studied voice for two more years, then made his stage debut in 1926, singing the role of Tizah in Frank Harling's opera *Deep River*. The next year he created the role of Joe in Ziegfeld's production of *Show Boat* and later toured with the show in Europe. In 1927 he also was appointed to the music staff of the Roxy Theater on Broadway, which broadcasted regularly as Roxy's Gang; he was the first black artist to be continuously employed by a Broadway theater. In 1934 Bledsoe sang the title role in Gruenberg's European production of his opera *The Emperor Jones* and repeated his performances in New York. He attracted wide attention as an opera singer; for example, as Amonasro in Verdi's *Aida* in Cleveland in 1932 (Lawrence Productions, Summer Opera) and in the title role of Moussorgsky's *Boris Goudonov* at the Italian Opera in Holland in 1933. Thereafter he toured widely as a concert singer at home and abroad, singing in concert halls and on radio. In 1935 he programmed a special series titled "Songs of the Negro" for the British Broadcasting Company. The next year he starred in the London production of Lew Leslie's *Blackbirds of 1936*. At the time of his death he had just completed a tour of army camps, giving concerts to entertain servicemen. He was perhaps best known by the public for his performance of "Old man river," from *Show Boat*. The critics and his musical contemporaries, however, regarded him as second only to Roland Hayes* during his time. He recorded a number of works and was active as a composer. His best known composition was the *African Suite* for violin and orchestra. His awards included an honorary doctorate from Bishop College (1941).

BIBL: Black press, incl. AmstN, 24 July 1943. CBDict. Hare. WWCA, 1927-44.

DISC: Turn.

BO DIDDLEY. See **McDANIEL, ELLAS.**

BOATNER, EDWARD H. Composer (b. 13 November 1898 in New Orleans, Louisiana; d. 16 June 1981 in New York, New York). His father was an itinerant minister, who took his family with him on his travels from church to church. Boatner was impressed by the singing he heard and began to collect spirituals at an early age. He obtained his education in the public schools of St. Louis, Missouri, where his family lived during his childhood; in the public high schools of Kansas City, Kansas, where his family later moved; at Western University in Quindaro, Kansas; at the Boston Conservatory of Music in Massachusetts; and at the Chicago [Illinois] College of Music (B. Mus., 1932). His teachers included Louis Victor Saar, Felix Deyo, and Rudolph Schramm, among others. His career development was aided by Roland Hayes,* who heard him sing in Kansas and encouraged him to study voice, and by R. Nathaniel Dett,* who took Boatner over as his protégé, coached him, and made a joint concert tour with him in the New England states. Boatner lived in Boston during the years 1917-c1925; he then settled in Chicago. There he was active as a concert singer, church organist-choir director, and director of community choral groups. During the years 1925-31 he was director of music for the National Baptist Convention. In 1933 he was appointed director of music at Samuel Huston College in Austin, Texas. Later he taught at Wiley College in Marshall, Texas, then in the late 1930s settled permanently in New York. There he conducted a music studio, served as music director for various churches, and conducted choral groups. Boatner was best known for his spiritual arrangements, which were widely sung, many of them being first introduced by such singers as Harry T. Burleigh, Roland Hayes, and Marian Anderson* in the 1920s. His best known arrangements were "On ma journey," "Oh, what a beautiful city," "Trampin'," "Soon I will be done," "Let us break bread together," and "I want Jesus to walk with me." He published collections of spirituals, *Book of 30 Choral Afro-American Spirituals*, and a piano manual. He also wrote in the larger forms, including a musical comedy, *Julius Sees Her; Freedom Suite*, for orchestra, chorus, and narrator; and *The Man From Nazareth*, an Afro-American "spiritual musical." His honors included an award from the National Association of Negro Musicians* (1964). His daughter Adelaide and son Clifford became concert artists; his son Edward ("Sonny") Stitt* became a professional jazz musician.

BIBL: Questionnaire. ASCAP. Black press, incl. CDef, 16 July 1927, 30 August 1930, 30 December 1933.

BOATWRIGHT, McHENRY. Concert/Opera singer (b. 29 February 1928 in Tennille, Georgia). He came from a musical family: his father played piano and sang, and a sister studied music at the New England Conservatory of Music in Boston, Massachusetts. He taught himself to play piano as a child before he began formal music study. He obtained his musical education at the New England Conservatory (B. Mus. in piano, 1950; B. Mus. in voice, 1954). In February 1956 he made his debut as a concert baritone at Jordan Hall in Boston. Thereafter he toured widely in the United States and abroad, appearing with symphony orchestras, giving solo recitals, and singing in opera and oratorio. He began winning prizes in vocal competitions in the early 1950s. In 1953 he placed first over 2000 contestants in the *Boston Post* Festival, and the same year he won first place in the International Chicago Festival competition, which earned him an appearance on the Ed Sullivan television show. In 1953 and 1954 he won Marian Anderson* awards. In 1957 he won first place in the National Federation of Music Clubs competition, which gave him a debut recital at Town Hall in New York in January 1958. He made his operatic debut in 1958 with the New England Opera Theater, singing the role of Arkel in Debussy's *Pelléas et Mélisande*. Thereafter he toured widely in the United States, Europe, Canada, Japan and other countries in the Far East, appearing with symphony orchestras, giving concerts, and singing with opera companies. He was noted for his performance of the role of Crown in Gershwin's *Porgy and Bess* and the leading role in Gunther Schuller's *The Visitation*.

BIBL: Black press, incl. CDef, 25 January 1958. CBDict. WWBA.

DISC: Turn.

BOHEE, GEORGE. Entertainer/Minstrel (B. 18?? in Chicago, Illinois; d. 19?? in New York, New York). See **BOHEE BROTHERS.**

BOHEE, JAMES DOUGLASS. Entertainer/Minstrel (B. 18?? in Chicago, Illinois; d. 1 December 1897 in London, England). See **BOHEE BROTHERS.**

BOHEE BROTHERS. Minstrel dance team (fl. late nineteenth and early twentieth centuries). James and George Bohee won wide attention for their soft-shoe dances and skills at playing banjos as they danced. About 1876 they organized their own troupe, called the Bohee Brothers Minstrels, which included James Bland* and Bobby Weston.* Later they performed with various groups, including Callender's Georgia Minstrels and Haverly's Genuine Colored Minstrels, sometimes referred to as the "Black Hundred," with whom they toured abroad. When that troupe returned to the United States in 1882, they remained abroad along with James Bland, Billy Allen, and others. They established themselves as vaudeville performers and conducted a banjo studio in London, advertising themselves as the "Famous Royal Bohee Brothers, banjoists and entertainers to their Royal Highnesses, the prince and princess of Wales, the late King Edward VII and Queen Alexandria." James died in 1897. Some time during the 1920s or 1930s George Bohee returned to the United States and settled in New York. A sister, Laura, was also active in vaudeville; Mayme Bohee may have also been a relative.

BIBL: Black press, incl. NYGlobe, 3 March 1883; CleveG, 8 January 1887; IndF, 24 October 1896. Flet, 41. *New York Clipper Annual*, 1897. Simond. SouMOBA, 260.

BOLDEN, CHARLES JOSEPH ("BUDDY"). Prejazz cornetist (b. 6 September 1877 in New Orleans, Louisiana; d. 4 November 1931 in Jackson, Louisiana). Self-taught, it is believed that he studied music basics with Manuel Hall about 1894. He began playing professionally soon afterwards with the local band of Charles Galloway. By 1897 Bolden had formed his own band, which reached its peak level of performance during the years 1900-1905. His bands played for parades and dances. The band's personnel included at one time or another Willie Cornish (trombone), Jefferson ("Brock") Mumford (guitar), James ("Jimmy") Johnson (double bass), Henry Zeno (drums), Cornelius Tillman (drums), Frank Lewis (clarinet), and William ("Willie") Warner (clarinet). Bolden's health began to deteriorate after 1905, and he was committed to a mental hospital in 1907, where he spent the remainder of his life. Bolden was the most important of the prejazz-era cornetists. His style was distinctive for its powerful tone, and he exerted wide influence on cornetist-trumpeters who followed him. His best-known performances were "Make me a pallet on the floor," "Bucket's got a hole in it," and "Buddy Bolden blues."

BIBL: FeaEJ. Donald M. Marquis, *In Search of Buddy Bolden* (Baton Rouge, Louisiana, 1978).

DISC: Kink.

BONDS, MARGARET ALLISON. Composer (b. 3 March 1913 in Chicago, Illinois; d. 26 April 1972 in Los Angeles, California). She came from a musical family: her mother, Estella Bonds, was a church organist and music teacher. She began piano study at the age of five, at first with her mother, then with local teachers Martha Anderson and T. Theodore Taylor.* She obtained her musical education from Northwestern University (B. Mus., M. Mus.), where she studied with Emily Boettcher Bogue, and at the Juilliard School of Music, where she studied with Roy Harris and Robert

Starer. She also studied with Florence Price* and William L. Dawson.* During the 1930s she was active as a concert musician, appearing with symphony orchestras and giving solo recitals, and as occasional accompanist for such singers as Etta Moten.* She founded the Allied Arts Academy in Chicago for talented black children. About 1939 she went to New York, where she served as editor in the music publishing house of Clarence Williams.* Later she formed a two-piano duo with Gerald Cook, which toured and performed on radio. In 1944 the Bonds-Cook duo played a piano recital series on station WNYC. During the 1960s she settled in Los Angeles, California. She served as musical director for the Inner City Repertory Theatre, taught piano at the Inner City Institute, and wrote arrangements for the Los Angeles Jubilee Singers. She was best known as a composer and began writing music at an early age. When she was nineteen she received a Wanamaker award for composition and later received other awards. Her early style development was influenced by Harry T. Burleigh,* whose style she imitated early in her career, and by Will Marion Cook,* as well as her composition teachers. Her mature style reflected these influences but was distinctively her own, with subtle jazz and folk music inflections. She wrote in a variety of forms: symphonies, musicals, ballets, a cantata, piano music, and numerous songs. Her best-known works were the cantata *Ballad of the Brown King* (1961, text by Langston Hughes); the songs "The Negro speaks of rivers" (1946, text by Hughes) and *Three Dream Portraits* (1959, text by Hughes); the arrangements *Five Spirituals; Spiritual Suite for Piano*; the ballet *Migration*; *Mass in D Minor*; and the musicals *Romey and Julie* and *Shakespeare in Harlem: U.S.A.* Her honors included a Rosenwald Fellowship and awards from the National Council of Negro Women (1962), ASCAP, and the Northwestern University Alumni Association (1967).

BIBL: AbdulBCM. ASCAP. Black press, incl. AmstN, 5 August 1944; CDef, 15 October 1932, 10 December 1938, 4 November 1939; NYAge, 6 May 1944. Margaret Bonds, "A Reminiscence" in *The Negro in Music and Art* (Washington, D.C., 1967). Mildred D. Green, "A Study of the Lives and Works of Five Black Women Composers in America" (Ph.D. diss., University of Oklahoma, 1975). NYB, 1952, p. 58. *Variety* (10 May 1972), p. 86. WilABW. WWAW, 1970-71.

BONNEMERE, EDWARD VALENTINE ("EDDIE"). Jazz pianist (b. 15 February 1921 in New York, New York). He obtained his musical education in the public schools of New York, at New York University (B. Mus. Ed., M. Mus. Ed.) at Hunter College of the City University of New York (M.A., 1966), and at Columbia University Teachers College (professional diploma). During his high-school years he was a church pianist. After service in the U.S. Armed Forces (1942-45), he began playing professionally with various groups, including Claude Hopkins* (1946). Thereafter he performed with his own groups in nightclubs, theaters, and dance halls, particularly the Savoy in the Harlem community. His teaching career included service in the New York public schools for many years. During the 1960s he became interested in writing music for the church; in the following years he composed six masses and several settings of the Lutheran Service. His music combines elements of jazz, Latin rhythms, gospel, and Gregorian chant. He also wrote popular music, of which the best known were the songs "Square dance mambo" and "Roostology." His honors included an honorary doctorate from Susquehanna University (1976).

BIBL: Questionnaire. FeaEJ.

DISC: Jep.

BOOKER T & THE MG's. Rock group. See **JONES, BOOKER T.**

BOONE, JOHN WILLIAM ("BLIND BOONE"). Concert pianist (b. 17 May 1864 in Miami, Missouri; d. 4 October 1927 in Warrensburg, Missouri). He contracted brain fever at the age of six months and lost his sight. After the death of his father, his mother moved to Warrensburg, Missouri. As a child he organized his half-brothers and friends into a band that played on street corners and for local entertainments. He attended the St. Louis School for the Blind for three years, where he studied music with Enoch Donley. After running away from school before completing the course of study, he became a street musician, playing the mouth organ and organizing his own company. In 1878 John Lange heard him play at a Christmas festival and took over management of his career. Boone gave his first professional concert in 1879 in Columbus, Missouri. Black manager Lange (d. 22 July 1916) devoted the rest of his life to developing Boone's career. Boone toured widely for forty-eight years in the United States, Canada, and Mexico with his troupe, the Blind Boone Concert Company; twice the company toured in Europe. The company of five or six singers and instrumentalists included over the years Emma Francess Smith, Jessie Brosius, and Stella May Boone. Boone was also active as a composer of light classical and rag piano pieces; in 1912 he made piano-roll recordings for Q.R.S., which included "Woodland Murmurs," "Sparkling Spring,"

"Rag Medley No. 1," and "Blind Boone's Southern Rag Medley No. 2."

BIBL: Black press, incl. IndF (extensive coverage), 5 September 1891, 14 May 1897; BPIM (Fall 1980), p. 171. Melissa Fuell, *Blind Boone, His Early Life and His Achievements* (Kansas City, Mo., 1915). JaTiRagS. *Negro Digest* (November 1949), p. 52.

BOOTH, ALAN. Concert pianist-accompanist (b. 1920 in New York, New York). He obtained his musical education at the Oberlin [Ohio] Conservatory of Music (B. Mus.) and studied further with Isabelle Vengerova. He toured with Paul Robeson* as an associate artist and toured as assistant artist with Harry Belafonte,* Robert McFerrin,* Edward Matthews,* Aubrey Pankey,* and Muriel Rahn,* among others. He also toured as a concert pianist, appearing with symphony orchestras and giving solo recitals. In 1966 he was one of the founders of the Symphony of the New World;* he served as official pianist for the orchestra for many years.

BIBL: Black press.

BOSTIC, EARL O. Jazz saxophonist/Arranger (b. 25 April 1913 in Tulsa, Oklahoma; d. 28 October 1965 in Rochester, New York). He played clarinet and alto saxophone during his high-school years in Tulsa, Oklahoma, and later studied music at Xavier University in New Orleans, Louisiana. His early professional experiences were with Terrence Holder (1931-32) and Bennie Moten* (1933). In New Orleans he worked with various groups, including Joseph Robichaux (1934) and the Charlie Creath*/Fate Marable* band (1935-36). He played with groups in the North, then settled in New York in 1938. During the next three decades he was active primarily as leader of his own groups and as an arranger. He also played, however, with Oran ("Hot Lips") Page* (1931-1941) and Lionel Hampton* (1939, 1943-44), among others. He recorded regularly and wrote numerous songs, including "The major and the minor," "Let me off uptown," and "Brooklyn boogie." His best-known recordings were "Flamingo," "You go to my head," "Temptation," and "Moonglow." His alto saxophone style was powerful; his music of the 1940s-50s was more rhythm 'n' blues than jazz.

BIBL: ChilWW. FeaEJ. ShawHS.

DISC: Kink.

BOSTIC, JOE WILLIAM. Gospel producer (b. 21 March 1909 in Mt. Holly, New Jersey). He obtained his education at Morgan State College in Baltimore, Maryland (B.A., 1929). He conducted radio programs in Baltimore and was a correspondent for the *Afro-American* before he settled in New York about 1937. There he became active both in journalism and in radio, serving as host for such shows as "Tales from Harlem" (station WMCA, 1937-39) and as a disc jockey on stations WCMW (1939-42) and WLIB (1942-195?). He produced weekly talent shows with live performances by black musicians. In 1950 he made music history when he produced the first all-gospel program at Carnegie Hall in New York. Called Negro Gospel and Religious Musical Festival, it featured Mahalia Jackson* as the lead performer. In 1951 he returned with the Second Annual Negro Gospel and Religious Music Festival, again with Jackson and such other gospel figures as James Cleveland,* Norsalus McKissick, and J. Earle Hines. Thereafter there were annual Carnegie Hall concerts for many years. Beginning in the early 1940s Bostic produced a Sunday morning gospel program, "Gospel Train," on radio station WLIB. In May 1959 he began producing larger festivals with his First Annual Gospel, Spiritual and Folk Music Festival, which played at Madison Square Garden before an audience of 11,000. He was called "the Dean of Gospel Disc Jockeys."

BIBL: Black press, incl. NYAge, 2 May 1959. Laurraine Goreau, *Just Mahalia, Baby* (Waco, Texas, 1975). Heil. *Sepia* (March 1963). WWCA, 1950.

BOWERS, SARAH SEDGWICK. Concert soprano. See **BOWERS, THOMAS.**

BOWERS, THOMAS (also known as **THE COLORED MARIO).** Concert singer (b. c1823 in Philadelphia, Pennsylvania; d. 3 October 1885 in Philadelphia). He obtained his early musical training from his brother, John C. Bowers (1811-1873), who was an organist at the St. Thomas African Episcopal Church in Philadelphia, Pennsylvania. He studied piano and organ; at the age of eighteen he succeeded his brother as organist at St. Thomas. Later he studied voice with Elizabeth Taylor Greenfield,* "The Black Swan." By 1841 he was singing solos (tenor) on local concerts. In 1854 he appeared in a recital with Greenfield; later he was taken under management by the impresario Colonel J. H. Wood and toured widely for that time with Greenfield. He conducted a music studio in Philadelphia and sang professionally until his death. In 1964 there was a revival of interest in his career when he was represented in an episode of the television show *Bonanza*.

His sister, Sarah Sedgwick Bowers, was a professional singer. She toured as a concert soprano, beginning in 1856, and was called "The Colored Nightingale." Later she organized a touring concert company.

BIBL: PaHistSoc, Box 13G. Black press, incl. NYFreeman, 10 October 1885. Trot, 131-137, 310.

BOWMAN, ANDERSON. See **McAFEE, CHARLES.**

BOWMAN, ELMER. Vaudeville songwriter (b. 1870s in Charleston, South Carolina (?); d. 22 July 1916 in New York, New York). Little is known of his early life. He left home with Chris Smith* some time during the 1890s to tour with a medicine show, which became stranded. He and Smith then went to New York, where they formed a vaudeville act that eventually became successful and toured widely on the leading vaudeville circuits. One of the songs they wrote, "I ain't poor no more," became a hit song before 1900. Bowman also collaborated with Al Johns, producing with him several very popular songs, including "Go way back and sit down" in 1901. Bowman was a founding member of the Clef Club* in 1910 and directed Clef-Club orchestras during the years 1912-16. In 1911 he became a member of the Billie Burke [dramatic] Company. The same year one of his songs was featured in the Broadway musical *Madame Sherry* by Elizabeth Murray.

BIBL: Black press, incl. IndF, 24 December 1899, 28 December 1901; NYAge, 15 April 1909, 3 August 1916. Flet, 145.

DISC: Kink.

BOWMAN, EUDAY LOUIS. Rag composer/Pianist (b. 9 November 1887 in Fort Worth, Texas; d. 26 May 1949 in New York, New York). Little is known of his career except that he was an itinerant rag pianist and arranger/composer before he settled in New York during the 1940s. His best-known piece, "Twelfth-Street Rag," was recorded by himself and others.

BIBL: ASCAP. JaTiRags.

DISC: RustJR.

BOYD, EDWARD RILEY ("EDDIE"). Blues pianist (b. 25 November 1914 in Stovall, Mississippi), He left home at the age of fourteen to live in Memphis, Tennessee, where he began his professional career. He taught himself to play guitar by listening to "Memphis Minnie" (Minnie Douglass Lawlers)* on the radio; his main instrument was the piano, however, and the chief influences upon his style were Roosevelt Sykes* and Leroy Carr.* In 1941 he went to Chicago, where he first teamed with Johnny Shines* on guitar, then later with "Sonny Boy Williamson, No. 1" (John Lee Williamson)* on harmonica. Thereafter he played with various bluesmen and recorded regularly. In 1965 he went to Europe with the American Folk Blues Festival and remained there, living first in Paris, France, then in other European capitals until in 1971 he settled in Helsinki, Finland. He continued to be active as a soloist and in recording.

BIBL: BWW. CharLB. LivBl 35, 36, 37 (November-December 1977; January-February 1978; March-April 1978). Oliv.

DISC: LeSl.

BOYER, HORACE CLARENCE. College professor (b. 28 July 1935 in Winter Park, Florida). He obtained his musical education at Bethune-Cookman College in Daytona Beach, Florida (B.A., 1957), and at the Eastman School of Music in Rochester, New York (M.A., 1964; Ph.D., 1973). His teaching career included tenures in the public schools and Brevard Community College of Cocoa, Florida (1957-63, 1965-69); at Albany State College in Georgia (1964-65); Florida Technological University in Orlando (1972-73); and at the University of Massachusetts in Amherst (1973-). As a youth he and his brother James toured as a gospel duo with Alex Bradford,* Mahalia Jackson,* and Rosetta Tharpe.* He also toured with his brother independently in the Famous Boyer Brothers duo. His master's thesis was a study of gospel music; and his doctoral dissertation, an investigation of black church music. He toured widely with the gospel choirs he organized at the institutions where he taught. He also toured as a lecturer, giving special emphasis to the subject of gospel music, conducted choral workshops, and published articles in such professional journals as *The Music Journal* and *The Black Perspective in Music* as well as *Black World* and *First World*. He was active as a organist-choirmaster during his service in the U.S. Armed Forces (1958-60) and later in a church at Macedon, New York (1969-72). During the years 1973-77 he was director of the Voices of New Africa House Workshop Choir. He recorded gospel-music albums, including *Mine Eyes Have Seen the Glory* (1973). His honors included Ford Foundation Fellowships (1969-72).

BIBL: Questionnaire. *The American Negro Reference Book*, ed. by John P. Davis (Englewood Cliffs, New Jersey, 1966), p. 743.

BRACKEN, JAMES ("JIM"). Record producer (b. 1909; d. 1972 in Chicago, Illinois). About 1953 he and Vivian Carter, whom he later married, and her brother Calvin Carter founded the Vee Jay Records, which became the largest black-owned record company in the world by the mid-1960s. They were formerly operators of a record shop in Gary, Indiana. Vivian Carter had been a disc jockey on radio station WWCA in Gary since 1948, and she continued to broadcast on one or another station in Chicago into the 1970s, including talk shows as well as blues and gospel programs. Vee Jay Records had an imposing list of performers during its heyday, including the Spaniels, the Impressions,* El Dorados, the Dells,* John Lee Hooker,* Gladys Knight* and the Pips, Jay McShann,* and Jimmy Reed,* among others. The company also had the American distribution for the English singing group, the Beatles. In 1965 Vee Jay declared bankruptcy and sold or leased many of its masters to other producers. One of the executives, Betty Chiapetta, later reestablished the company in Los Angeles, California, as VJ International; general manager Ewart Abner later became president of Motown. The Brackens started over again after a few years with small labels—he had kept some of his masters and his publishing house, Costuma—but he died before the new company was well established.

BIBL: LivBl 8 (Spring 1972). Jimmy Reed Interview in LivBl 21 (May-June 1975). ShawHS. ShawWS.

BRADFORD, ALEX. Gospel singer (b. 1926 in Bessemer, Alabama; d. 15 February 1978 in Newark, New Jersey). From earliest childhood he was active in music: he performed on the vaudeville stage at the age of four, he sang in gospel groups, and he studied music and dance with local teacher Martha Belle Hall. He obtained his musical education in public schools of Bessemer, Alabama, and was later graduated from the Snow Hill Normal and Industrial Institute in Snow Hill, Alabama. His early style development was influenced by the gospel performers he heard in Bessemer, including Prophet Jones, the Blue Jays gospel quartet, and the Swan Silvertones,* among others. He decided to enter a gospel-music career after hearing a concert in Birmingham, Alabama, in which both the Roberta Martin* and the Clara Ward* Singers performed. During the early 1940s he left school to perform professionally with a group, The Protective Harmoneers, which broadcasted on the local radio station under the sponsorship of the Protective Industrial Insurance Company and also toured. Thereafter he sang with various groups—among them, the Birdettes in Detroit, Michigan; the Banks family in Pittsburgh, Pennsylvania; and his own Bronx Gospelaires in New York. He then returned to Alabama to complete his school studies but continued to perform during summer vacations with gospel groups in New York. After graduating from Snow Hill, he taught school and also became an ordained minister; during this period he acquired the nickname "Professor." During his service in the U.S. Armed Forces (1943-45) he performed on campshow programs. After the war he settled in Chicago, Illinois, where he came into contact with such established gospel figures as Thomas A. Dorsey,* Roberta Martin, and Mahalia Jackson,* and became especially close to Sallie Martin.* He sang with various groups in Chicago, then in 1954 organized his own all-male, eight-man Bradford Specials, which is credited with being the first all-male gospel group in history (as distinguished from the male gospel quartet). He published many of his songs through Roberta Martin's publishing firm and also sang irregularly with her groups. During this period he recorded regularly; one of his songs, "Too close to heaven," was an immediate commercial success and established him as the "Singing Rage of the Gospel Age." He toured widely with his groups across the nation and abroad, singing in churches, theaters, concert halls, and at jazz festivals. Beginning in the 1960s he became active in musical theater. In 1961 he sang a leading role in Langston Hughes's* gospel song-play, *Black Nativity*, which was written especially for him, Marion Williams,* and Princess Stewart. After playing on Broadway, the show went to the Festival of Two Worlds at Spoleto, Italy (July 1962), then toured abroad for four years. Other stage works in which he appeared included *But Never Jam Today* (1969), *Bury the Dead* (1971), *Don't Bother Me, I Can't Cope* (1972), and *Your Arm's Too Short to Box With God* (1975). He collaborated with Vinette Carroll in directing some of the musicals in which he sang. His last ministry was the Greater Abyssinian Church in Newark, New Jersey; at one time he was president of the New Jersey chapter of Dorsey's National Convention of Gospel Choirs. In the 1970s he established his own Creative Movement Repertory Company and began producing his own shows, among them, *Black Seeds of Music*. Those who sang with the Bradford Singers over the years included Madeleine Bell, Charles E. Campbell, Thomas J. Fouse, Isaiah Jones (pianist), Robert E. Williams, and his wife, Alberta Carter Bradford, among others. His numerous honors included awards from the music and recording industries. His best-known songs included "He'll wash you whiter than snow," "Let God abide," "Too close to heaven," "Walking with the King," and "I found the answer." Bradford was one of the first gospel figures to introduce gospel into the secular theater.

BIBL: AbdulFBE. Black press, incl. CDef, 8-14 February 1964. Heil. NYT, 16 February 1978.

DISC: TudBM.

BRADFORD, PERRY ("MULE"). Vaudeville entertainer/songwriter (b. 14 February 1893 in Montgomery, Alabama; d. 20 April 1970 in New York, New York (?)). His family moved to Atlanta, Georgia, when he was six years old. He began playing piano professionally when he was about thirteen, touring as a soloist and with such groups as Allen's New Orleans Minstrels (1907). Later he toured on the vaudeville circuit and performed in musical shows, among them, The Smarter Set.* He formed a special act with a mule, called Jeanette; because of that act he acquired his nickname ''Mule.'' Some time before 1920 he settled in New York, where he became involved in music publishing, the recording industry, and stage productions. In 1920 he was musical director for Mamie Smith* and is credited with having arranged for her to make the first recording of blues by a black singer, ''Crazy blues'' (August 1920), which was written by Bradford himself. Originally white singer Sophie Tucker was to have recorded the song. He made numerous recordings with others and with his own groups, one of them called The Jazz Phools, another Perry Bradford's Mean Four. Those who recorded with him (or whom he accompanied) included Louis Armstrong,* Garvin Bushell,* Johnny Dunn,* Alberta Hunter,* James P. Johnson,* and Sippie Wallace,* among others. Throughout his career he wrote songs and musical revues or comedies, among them, *The Prince of Hayti* (1916), *Made in Harlem* revue (1918), *Put and Take* (Broadway production, 1921), and *Messin' Around* (1929, as lyricist). His best-known songs were ''You need some loving,'' ''That thing called love,'' and ''It's right here for you.'' Bradford's ''Crazy blues'' was immensely successful and started the vogue for ''race records,'' that is, music recorded by black performers.

BIBL: ASCAP. Black press, incl. CDef, 25 November 1916; IndF, 30 June 1917. ChilWW. FeaEJ. FeaJS.

DISC: Kink. RustJR.

BRADSHAW, MYRON ("TINY"). Jazz drummer (b. 1905 in Youngstown, Ohio; d. December 1958 in Cincinnati, Ohio). He attended Wilberforce University in Ohio, where he came into contact with Horace Henderson* and joined Henderson's Collegians (as a singer). Later he went to New York, where he sang with various groups, including the Mills Blue Rhythm Band* (1932-33) and Luis Russell* (1933-34). In 1934 he organized his own group. Thereafter he played long residencies in ballrooms and nightclubs in New York; Philadelphia, Pennsylvania; and Chicago, Illinois, among other cities. He also toured in the United States, Europe, and Japan (sponsored by the U.S.O. in 1945). Illness forced his retirement in the 1950s.

BIBL: AlHen.ChilWW.

DISC: Jep. RustJR.

BRADY, WILLIAM. Composer (fl. mid-nineteenth century in New York, New York; d. March 1854 in New York). Little is known of his career except that he was highly regarded as a composer by his contemporaries. He played double bass in groups that performed in local concerts in New York; he may have also conducted a music studio.

BIBL: Black press, incl. *The Colored American*, 14 September 1839. Trot, p. 302; pp. 4-21 of the music section.

BRAITHWAITE, JAMES ROLAND. College professor (b. 28 February 1927 in Boston, Massachusetts). His mother was a professional musician. He studied piano as a child. He obtained his musical education in the public schools of Boston, Massachusetts; at Boston University (B. Mus., 1948; M.A., 1950; Ph.D., 1957); and at the Union Theological Seminary School of Sacred Music in New York (1953). During his undergraduate study he concentrated on organ; in graduate school he majored in sacred music. He was active in Boston as a church organist in Congregational and Lutheran churches (1945-52) and as organist-choir director at the Episcopal Church of Harvard-Radcliffe (1960-61). He contributed music reviews to the *Boston Herald* (1961) and gave organ recitals regularly. After serving in the U.S. Armed Forces (1950-52), he joined the music faculty at Talladega College in Alabama (1952-), where he remained throughout his teaching career. In addition to serving as the college organist and teaching, he also carried administrative responsibilities as department chairman. In 1974 he was appointed Dean of the College. He wrote music for instruments, voice, and chorus, including the *Talladega College Commencement Processional* (1971) and *Music for the Manger Scene* (1959). His honors included appointments to panels and committees of professional organizations.

BIBL: Questionnaire. *Outstanding Educators of America*, 1973. WWBA.

BRAND, ADOLPH JOHANNES ("DOLLAR") (also known as **ABDULLAH IBRAHIM).** Jazz pianist (b. 9 October 1934 in Capetown, South Africa). He began piano study at the age of seven with his mother, a pianist and church-choir director. He learned several other instruments on his own and began playing professionally with local groups before he was fifteen, later including the Willy Max Band and the Tuxedo Slickers. After completing his high-school studies he toured with groups in Africa and in Europe; he was co-leader of a group with Kippy Moeketsie that included Hugh Masekela* (trumpet) and Jonas Gwangwa (trombone). In 1960 he organized his own group, The Jazz Epistles, which featured Masekela, and which became the leading jazz group in South Africa. In 1962 he settled in Europe with a trio. Soon thereafter he came into contact with Edward (''Duke'') Ellington,* who arranged for Brand to make his first European recording, *Duke Ellington Presents the Dollar Brand Trio*. In 1965 he went to the United States and made his debut at the Newport Jazz Festival; he later toured with Elvin Jones* (1966). Through the 1960s-70s he continued to tour throughout the world and recorded regularly. In 1968 he was converted to Islam and adopted a Muslim name, Abdullah Ibrahim. The same year he returned to South Africa, living in various places over the next few years, including Swaziland (1971-73), where he founded the Marimba School of Music, and in Johannesburg (mid-1970s), as well as Capetown. His touring took him to concert halls, nightclubs, and major jazz festivals, primarily as a soloist (or with his trio). In 1979, however, he toured in Europe and Australia with a big band. Over the years those who performed with him, in addition to those cited above, included flutist Talib Quadr, bassist Victor Ntoni, drummers John Betsch and Nelson Magwaza, and his wife Sathima (Bea Benjamin). His music was intensely emotional and deeply rooted in the folk music of his people. His piano style, which reflected the influence of Ellington and Thelonious Monk,* was distinctive for its use of drum-like, repetitive bass patterns in the left hand against elaborate improvisations in the right hand, which produced dense, polyrhythmic textures on fortissimo levels. His best-known albums included *African Sun* (1968), *The Journey* (1978), *Cape Town Fringe* (1978), *African Piano* (1974), *Soweto* (1979), and *Ode to Duke Ellington* (1979). He received awards from the music industry and was the subject of a documentary film, *Portrait of a Bushman* (1968). In 1980 he maintained homes in both the United States and in Europe, from which he continued to make global tours.

BIBL: Black press, incl. AmstN, 4 March 1978. ContK (May 1980). FeaJS. FeaGitJS. MeeJMov.

DISC: TudJ.

BRAUD, WELLMAN. Jazz bassist (b. 25 January 1891 in St. James Parish, Louisiana; d. 29 October 1966 in Los Angeles, California). (according to Souch, Braud died on 6 June 1967). He began playing violin when he was seven years old; later he played violin and double bass in local string trios (1908-13). In 1917 he settled in Chicago, Illinois, where he played with various groups, including Lawrence Duhé, the Original Creole Orchestra, and Charlie Elgar.* In 1922 he went to Europe with James P. Johnson's* revue, *Plantation Days*; after returning to Chicago, he played with Wilbur Sweatman* (1923), among others, then joined Edward (''Duke'') Ellington* (1926-35). After leaving Ellington he played with various groups, including his Spirits of Rhythm and his trio (1937-41), Oran (''Hot Lips'') Page* (1938), Edgar Hayes (1939), Sidney Bechet* (1940-41), Garvin Bushell* (1944), and Edward (''Kid'') Ory,* among others. Those with whom he recorded over the years included Lillian (''Lil'') Armstrong,* Ferdinand (''Jelly Roll'') Morton,* James (''Jimmie'') Noone,* and Clarence Williams.* In the 1960s he settled in Los Angeles, California. Occasionally he played in big bands on special occasions, as with Ellington (1961), and he toured with pianists on the West Coast. He is credited with having made the first recording with amplified bass, ''Hot and bothered,'' with Ellington (1928). He was presented in Ripley's ''Believe It or Not'' as the world's fastest bassist (probably untrue, even in the 1920s-30s).

BIBL: ChilWW. DanceWDE. FeaEJ. FeaJS. FeaGitJS. Pops Foster, *The Autobiography of a New Orleans Jazzman, as Told to Tom Stoddard* (Berkeley, 1971). MeeJMov. Souch.

DISC: RustJR.

BRAXTON, ANTHONY. Jazz multi-instrumentalist/Composer (b. 4 June 1945 in Chicago, Illinois). He began playing alto saxophone when he was about twelve. He obtained his musical education in the public schools of Chicago, Illinois; at the Chicago School of Music (1959-64), where he studied saxophone with Jack Gell; at Wilson Junior College and Roosevelt University in Chicago. His early style development was influenced by John Coltrane,* Paul Desmond, and Eric Dolphy,* among others. During his service in the U. S. Armed Forces (1964-66) he played in army bands and organized his own small groups. After his discharge he returned to Chicago, where he joined the Association for the Advancement of Creative Musicians* under the influence of Roscoe Mitchell.* He played with one of the subgroups of AACM, the Creative Construction Company, which included Muhal Richard Abrams,* Leroy Jenkins,* and Leo Smith,* and toured with the group in Europe (1969). He also played with others, among them Circle (1970-72), which included Armando (''Chick'') Corea, David Holland, and Barry Altschul. In 1972 he made his debut at Town Hall in New York, performing with chamber groups as well as solo. He toured widely in the United States and abroad and received awards from the music industry at home, in France, and in Japan. His best-known albums were *Three Compositions of New Jazz* (1968), *New York, Fall 1974*, and *Duets 1979*. In his early career he used mathematical diagrams and formulas to represent his compositions rather than titles. He composed for a wide variety of media, from multiple orchestras to solo instruments such as the saxophone. His mature style was representative of free jazz, although he played blues and traditional jazz, and was distinctive for his use of silence and frequent dispensing with a rhythm section.

BIBL: FeaGitJS. Michael Ullman, *Jazz Lives* (Washington, D.C., 1980). WWA.

DISC: TudJ.

BREWSTER, W. HERBERT. Gospel songwriter (b. 2 July 1899 in Somerville, Tennessee). He obtained his education at Roger Williams College. He settled in Memphis, Tennessee, in the 1920s, where he became minister of the East Trigg Baptist Church. Later he served as the Corresponding Executive Secretary of the Educational Board of the National Baptist Convention. Although a singer (bass-baritone), he was best known as a gospel songwriter. His songs were first widely performed by "Queen Candace" Anderson,* Mahalia Jackson,* the Clara Ward* Singers, and his own Brewster Ensemble, among others. He also wrote plays and pageants, which were performed annually at his church. His songs are distinctive for their use of Biblical texts and images, tempo changes, and penchant for melismatic cadenzas. He is credited with being the first to introduce triple meters into gospel music. His best-known songs included "I'm leaning and depending on the Lord," "Move on up a little higher," "Just over the hill," "How I got over," "These are they," and "Surely, God is able" (the first gospel song to use triple meters [12/8] and one of the first two gospel songs to sell over a million copies, along with "Move on up.") His son, W. Herbert, Jr., was also a gospel songwriter.

BIBL: Interview with H. Clarence Boyer. Horace Clarence Boyer, "The Gospel Song: A Historical and Analytical Study" (M.A. thesis, Eastman School of Music, 1964). Heil. BPIM 7 (Spring 1979). Jac.

BRICE, CAROL LOVETTE. Concert singer (b. 16 April 1918 in Sedalia, North Carolina). She came from a musical family: both parents were singers, and her brothers Jonathan and Eugene became professional musicians. She received her musical education at Palmer Memorial Institute in Sedalia, North Carolina, and at the age of fourteen toured with the Institute Singers as a soloist; at Talladega College in Alabama (Mus. B., 1939); and at the Julliard School of Music in New York (1939-44, professional diploma in voice), where she studied with Francis Rogers. During the years 1939-43 she was a soloist at St. George's Episcopal Church in New York, where earlier Harry T. Burleigh* had been soloist (1894-1946). In 1943 she was given the Walter Naumberg Award, the first of her race to receive it. In 1944 she made her debut as a contralto at Town Hall in New York. She toured widely in the United States, Europe, and South America, appearing with symphony orchestras and giving solo recitals in concert halls and on CBS television (1945). She was also active in musicals, including *The Hot Mikado* (1939, New York World's Fair), *Finian's Rainbow* (1960), *Show Boat* (1961 production), and *Gentlemen Be Seated* (1963). She sang the role of the Voodoo Princess in Clarence Cameron White's* opera *Ouanga* (1956) and the role of Maria in Gershwin's *Porgy and Bess* (1961, 1977 productions). She made her recording debut in 1946 and thereafter recorded regularly. Her best-known recordings were Falla's *El Amor Brujo*, Mahler's *Songs of A Wayfarer*, Blitzstein's *Regina*, R. Nathaniel Dett's* *The Ordering of Moses*, Richardson's *The Grass Harp*, and *A Carol Brice Recital*. In her early career she frequently toured and recorded with her brother Jonathan as accompanist. Her brother Eugene (1913-1980), a graduate of Juilliard, sang with the Robert Shaw Chorale, the New York City Opera, and in Broadway musicals. In February 1958 brothers and sister gave a Brice Trio Concert at Town Hall in New York. In the 1970s she was appointed to the music faculty of the University of Oklahoma at Norman. She continued to give recitals and to sing in opera and oratorio along with her teaching; frequently she toured with her husband, Thomas Carey.* Her honors included selection as Woman of the Year by the National Council of Negro Women and the Naumberg Award (cited above). In 1977 she and her husband were named Oklahoma Musicians of the Year.

BIBL: Black press, incl. AmstN, 16 December 1944; NYAge, 27 October 1945, 8 February 1958. NYB, 1952, p. 53. WWAW. WWBA. WWCA, 1950.

DISC: Turn.

BRICKTOP. See **SMITH, ADA LOUISE.**

BRIDGETOWER, GEORGE POLGREEN. Concert violinist (b. 29 February 1780 in Baila, Poland; d. 29 February 1860 in London, England). His father was probably a native of the West Indies. His younger brother, Friedrich, became a concert violoncellist. George Polgreen was a child prodigy. He studied with Giovanni Mane Giornovichi and, reputedly, with Franz Joseph Haydn. He made his debut in Paris, France, at a concert of the Concert Spiritual on 11 April 1789. In the fall of that year he went to London, England, where about 1791 he was taken into the retinue of the Prince of

Wales (later King George IV) at Brighton. In London he studied with Thomas Attwood, Jr., and François-Hippolyte Barthélémon, gave recitals, played first violin in the Prince of Wales's private chamber band (1795-1809), and played in other orchestras in the city. During the years 1802-04 he toured on the Continent. In Vienna, Austria, he was befriended by Beethoven, who wrote the Violin Sonata, Op. 47, the *Kreutzer Sonata*, for him. Bridgetower gave the first performance of the sonata at a concert at the Augarten Theatre on 24 May 1803, with Beethoven himself at the piano. After returning to London, Bridgetower was active as a music teacher and in the Philharmonic and the Professional Music Society of London. In 1811 he earned a B. Mus. degree from Cambridge.

BIBL: Betty Matthews, "George Polgreen Bridgetower" in *Music Review* (February 1968). F. G. Edwards, "George P. Bridgetower and the Kreutzer Sonata" in *The Musical Times* (1 May 1908). Scobie. Josephine R. B. Wright, "George Polgreen Bridgetower: An African Prodigy in England" in *The Musical Quarterly* 66 (January 1980).

BRINDIS DE SALAS, CLAUDIO JOSÉ DOMINGO (the father). Symphony orchestra conductor (b. 30 October 1800 in Havana, Cuba; d. 17 December 1872 in Havana). At an early age he came under the protection of Count Don José Maria Chacon in Havana because of his mother's employment with the family. At fourteen he was sent to study music at an academy run by Ignatius Calvo. He later developed a wide reputation as a singer, violinist, and orchestral conductor. He also served as a dancing teacher to the city's elite youth. He first played one of his compositions in public in 1837, when he was chosen to conduct an orchestra for festivities honoring Governor Michael Tacon. After passing a rigorous examination given by the Corporation of Havana, he earned the right to the title "Maestro Composer and Musician." He was the leading musician in Cuba of his time. His son, Claudio José,* was also a professional musician.

BIBL: *Anglo-African Magazine* (New York, 1860). Hare. LaBrew. Nicolás Guillén, "Claudio José Domingo Brindis de Salas: El Rey de las Octavas" in 3 *Cuadernos de Historia Habanera* (Havana, 1935).

BRINDIS DE SALAS, CLAUDIO JOSÉ DOMINGO (the son). Concert violinist (b. 4 August 1852 in Havana, Cuba; d. 2 June 1911 in Buenos Aires, Argentina). As a child he studied music with his father, Claudio José,* and with another musician in Havana, José Redondo. He first performed in a public concert when he was ten years old. In 1869 he matriculated at the Paris [France] Conservatory of Music, where he studied with Charles Danclas, Félicien David, and Camillo Sivori (violin). About 1872 he returned to Havana, upon the death of his father, but had returned to the Conservatory by 1874, and apparently continued his studies there. During his stay in Europe he gave concerts in various places including Italy, Prussia, Russia, Austria, Poland, and France. It was during these years that he was given the soubriquet "King of the Octaves." By 1886 he had returned to Havana, and thereafter he toured extensively in the Caribbean and in South America. It may well be that he spent some time during the last decades of his life again in Europe. During that period, or the period of his earlier sojourn in Europe, he was decorated by the German Emperor and the King of Italy.

The contemporary press refers to another Cuban violinist, Joseph (or José) R. Brindis, who may have been Claudio's brother (see BIBL: Hare). Joseph toured in the late 1870s with Sprague's Georgia Minstrels, which at that time included James Bland* and Sam Lucas,* among others. Later he toured with the Hyers Sisters* company and was a member of the troupe when it produced *The Underground Railroad* in 1878 and when it appeared in Callender's Minstrel Festival at the Grand Opera House in New York in June 1883. In August 1883 Joseph went to France. Nothing more is known of his career except that he was called "The Colored Remeny in the West."

BIBL: Information from Josephine Wright.* Black press, incl. NYGlobe, 26 May 1883. Hare. Nicolás Guillén, "Claudio José Domingo Brindis de Salas: El Rey de la Octavas" in 3 *Cuadernos de Historia Habanera* (Havana, 1935). LaBrew. *Le Menestrel* 40 (1874), pp. 95, 167. *The New York Clipper*, 9 June 1883, 4 August 1883.

BRINDIS, JOSEPH (or **JOSÉ**) **R.** Concert violinist. See **BRINDIS DE SALAS, CLAUDIO.**

BROOKS, SHELTON. Songwriter (b. 4 May 1886 in Amesburg, Ontario, Canada; d. 6 September 1975 in Los Angeles, California). As a child he taught himself to play on the family house organ while an older brother pumped. He began his professional career at the age of sixteen as a cafe and theater pianist in Detroit, Michigan. Later he settled in Chicago, Illinois, where he continued to play piano—at the Monogram, Pekin, and Grand theaters as well as in nightclubs. He began writing songs about 1909, of which the best known were "Honey gal" (1909), "Some of these days" (1910), "There'll come a time" (1911), and "Darktown strutters ball"(1917). He toured widely as a vaudeville entertainer before the early 1920s. He then turned to the Broadway stage, where he played leading roles in *Plantation Revue* (1922) with Florence Mills,* *Dixie to Broadway* (1924) with Mills, and Ken Murray's *Blackouts of 1949*. He toured in Europe with Lew Leslie's *Blackbirds of 1923*. Later he returned to entertaining in nightclubs.

BIBL: ASCAP. Black press, incl. CDef, 19 February 1910; NYAge, 9 July 1938. NYT, 11 September 1975.

DISC: Kink. RustCED.

BROOKS, TILFORD. College professor (b. 13 June 1925 in St. Louis, Missouri). He obtained his musical education at Southern Illinois University in Carbondale (B.A., 1949) and Washington University in St. Louis, Missouri (M.A., 1960; D. Mus.Ed., 1972). His career development was influenced by his teachers Elwood Buchanan, Bernard Schneider, and Lewis B. Hilton. His teaching career included tenures in the public schools of East St. Louis, Illinois (1950-66), and at Washington University (1969-). He also served as an instructional media specialist in East St. Louis (1966-71) and director of music education (1971-73). He toured widely as a lecturer, particularly on the subject of black composers, presenting papers to college audiences and before professional-society meetings and on radio and television programs; he also toured as a consultant and as an adjudicator for band competitions. He also published articles in such professional journals as *The Music Journal* and *Missouri Music Educators Research Journal*; his book publications included his doctoral dissertation, *A Historical Study of Black Music and Selected Twentieth Century Black Composers* (in press, 1980). Brooks was also active as a performing musician: he played trombone in the Gateway Symphony Orchestra in St. Louis (1964-71), the George Hudson jazz orchestra (1952-73), and in orchestras for special events, such as the Eddie Fisher-Buddy Hackett Show (1969), the Ray Charles* Show (1972), and Nancy Wilson* Shows (1974, 1975), among others.

BIBL: Questionnaire.

BROONZY, WILLIAM LEE CONLEY ("BIG BILL"). Bluesman (b. 26 June 1893 in Scott, Mississippi; d. 14 August 1958 in Chicago, Illinois). He played on homemade string instruments when he was a child. His family moved to Arkansas, where he listened to older relatives singing many kinds of folksongs. After service in the armed forces during World War I, he settled in Chicago in 1920, where he played blues guitar professionally for the first time. Reputedly taught by banjoist ("Papa") Charlie Jackson,* Broonzy recorded as early as 1923 but did not begin recording extensively until 1930. He was one of the important Chicago blues figures (although he maintained a residency in Arkansas) and played and/or recorded with many of the Chicago bluesmen, both as singer and accompanist; among them, Frank Brasswell, "Bumble Bee Slim" (née Amos Easton), "Georgia Tom" (née Thomas A. Dorsey*), ("Little") Walter Jacobs,* ("Cripple") Clarence Lofton,* "Tampa Red" (née Hudson Whittaker*), and ("Brother") John Sellers.* In 1938 and 1939 he performed in the From Spirituals to Swing Concerts produced by John Hammond at Carnegie Hall in New York. He gave his first blues concert abroad in 1951 for the London Jazz Club and thereafter toured widely in Europe and in the United States, both as soloist and with others, among them, Mahalia Jackson.* Later his tours included Africa, South America, and the Far East. He was a seminal figure in the development of urban blues, but his music revealed its rural roots; his delivery was hard-driving and earthy in fast blues, and often poignant in slow blues. He is credited with having written more than 300 blues.

BIBL: BWW. BPIM 2 (Fall 1974), pp. 191-208. CharCB. FeaEJ. MeeJMov. Oliv. StamFCW. Autobiography: *Big Bill Blues*, as told to Yannick Bruynoghe (New York, rev. ed., 1964).

DISC: Jep. DiGod. Kink. LeSl. RustJr. TudBM.

BROWN, ANITA PATTI (née **PATSY DEAN**). Concert singer (b. c1870s-80s in Georgia (?); d. 1950s in Chicago, Illinois). Little is known of her early career. According to the press, she was born in Georgia, spent her childhood in Chattanooga, Tennessee, and began her career singing in an AME Church choir in Indianapolis, Indiana. She apparently settled in Chicago, Illinois, during the first years of the twentieth century. Her appearance at the Chicago Opera House in March 1903 was stated by the press to be her debut (as a soprano). She toured widely through the United States, the West Indies, and South America—so much so that she was called "the globe-trotting prima donna" by the black press. In January 1915 she made her New York debut on Walter Craig's* Pre-Lenten Recital, which also featured Roland Hayes* and Helen Elise Smith (Dett). After World War I she toured as the soloist with the 370th Infantry Band, Eighth Illinois Regiment, known as the "Black Devils," under the leadership of George E. Dulf.* She became one of the first black concert artists to make recordings when she made records for the Victor Phonograph Company in 1916 and for Black Swan Records in 1920. During the early 1920s she studied voice in Europe and also gave recitals during her stay there. By the 1930s she was conducting a vocal studio in Chicago. Her husband, Arthur Brown, was one of the founders of the Umbrian Glee Club.*

BIBL: Interview of Earl Calloway* by Fanya Wiggins. Black press, incl. CDef, 28 June 1913, 7 January 1922, 4 May 1946; IndF, 15 June 1903; NYAge, 28 January 1915, 13 July 1916, 15 May 1920, 25 May 1929.

BROWN, ANNE WIGGINS. Concert singer (b. 9 August 1915 in Baltimore, Maryland). She obtained her musical education at the Institute of Musical Art in New York (certificates in voice 1932, 1934; now Juilliard School of Music), where she studied with Licia Dunham; at Morgan College in Baltimore, Maryland; and at Columbia University Teachers College in New York. She first attracted wide attention in 1935 when she created the role of Bess (soprano) in Gershwin's folk opera *Porgy and Bess*. She also sang in Broadway musicals, including *Mamba's Daughters* (1939) and *La Belle Helene* (1939) and later in the 1942 revival of *Porgy and Bess* and in European productions of *Porgy and Bess* (Sweden, 1947, 1948) and Menotti's *The Medium and the Telephone* (Norway, 1950). During the years 1942-48 she toured widely in the United States, Canada, and Europe (beginning in 1946) as a concert singer, appearing with symphony orchestras and giving solo recitals; she also appeared on television programs. In 1948 she settled in Norway, where she continued to be active as a concert and opera singer and conducted a music studio.

BIBL: Communication from Doris Axelsen.* Black press, incl. CDef, 13 July 1935; NYAge, 8 March 1947. NYB, 1952, p. 53. WWCA, 1950.

DISC: Turn.

BROWN, GEORGE. Military bugler (fl. early nineteenth century). He served as a bugler on the ship *Chesapeake* during the War of 1812 in the United States and took part in the Shannon Encounter in June 1813.

BIBL: Wilkes.

BROWN, JAMES. Rhythm 'n' blues singer (b. 17 June 1928 in Pulaski, Tennessee). His father sang blues and played guitar. His family moved to Augusta, Georgia, when he was a child, and there he attended public schools. He sang in church choirs but did not become seriously interested in music as a career until he was in his early twenties. He then joined with other entertainers to perform in local bars and nightclubs. In 1956 he made a recording, "Please, please, please," that proved an immediate success commercially and led to a contract with a record company. Later recordings he made were equally successful, and within a short period he had established himself as the leading rhythm 'n' blues singer of his time. During this period he earned the nicknames "Soul Brother, No. 1" and "Godfather of Soul." He began touring with his own company, James Brown and the Famous Flames Show, traveling throughout the world with appearances in theaters, nightclubs, concert halls, at festivals, and on radio and television programs. Beginning in 1976 he produced his own weekly syndicated television show from Atlanta, Georgia. He also sang on film soundtracks or produced music for films, including *Black Caesar* (1973) and *Slaughter's Big Ripoff* (1977). He established his own music companies, James Brown Productions and James Brown Enterprises. His best-known performances were "Black is beautiful; say it loud: I'm black and I'm proud," "King heroin," "Try me," and "Get on the good foot," among others. Brown's style was distinctive for its intense emotionalism and militant lyrics. More than any other entertainer, he was representative of "soul" music. He received numerous awards from the music and recording industries as well as citations from civic organizations.

BIBL: *Sepia* (September 1972, December 1978). ShawHS. StamPRS. WWA.

DISC: Giv. Jep. TudBM.

BROWN, J[OHN] HAROLD. Composer/College professor (b. 28 September 1902 in Shellman, Georgia). He obtained his musical education at Fisk University (B.A.,1923); the Horner Institute-Kansas City Conservatory in Missouri (B. Mus., 1926); and Indiana University at Bloomington (M.A., 1931), where he studied with Winfred Merrill. He also studied with Virgil Thomson and Arthur Shepard. His teaching career included tenures in the public schools of Kansas City, Kansas (1923-27), Indianapolis, Indiana (1927-34), and Cleveland, Ohio (1946-55); at Hampton Institute in Virginia (summers 1927-34); at Florida A & M College in Tallahasee (1934-40), where he was director of music; and at Southern University in Baton Rouge, Louisiana (1940-46), where he was also department chairman. In 1946 he settled in Cleveland, where he became active as music director at Karamu House and the Huntington Playhouse. He produced musicals and presented his Karamu Quartet on CBS radio (1950-54), and on national concert tours. He also conducted a music studio. He exerted wide influence as a teacher upon the career development of many who later won recognition in the world of music, including Nicholas Gerren* and Russell Atkins.* Brown won wide attention for his compositions, particularly his vocal and choral works, published under the name J. Harl Brown. His best known compositions were the cantata, *The African Chief*, the oratorio *Job*, the choral *The Saga of Rip Van Winkle*, and his many spiritual arrangements. His honors included six Wanamaker Composition Awards (1927-30) and a Harmon Foundation Award (1929).

BIBL: Questionnare. Matt. NYB, 1952, p. 58. Reginald Buckner, ''A History of Music Education in the Black Community of Kansas City, Kansas, 1905-1954'' (Ph.D. diss. University of Minnesota, 1974).

BROWN, LAWRENCE. Concert accompanist (b. 29 August 1893 in Jacksonville, Florida; d. 25 December 1972 in New York, New York). He studied music privately in Boston, Massachusetts, where he moved in 1914, and later studied composition in London at Trinity College (1920) and voice with Amanda Ira Aldridge.* He first met Roland Hayes* in London and first accompanied Hayes in 1921 at a command performance for King George V of England at Buckingham Palace. Thereafter he toured with Hayes for four years as accompanist. In 1925 he accompanied Paul Robeson* in a recital consisting solely of Negro spirituals at the Greenwich Village Theater in New York This was the first time in history that a concert was given over entirely to Negro spirituals. Brown's collaboration with Robeson lasted thirty-eight years, until illness brought an end to Robeson's career. In addition to accompanying, Brown often sang tenor to Robeson's bass-baritone on recitals. Brown made more than 400 arrangements of Negro folksongs.

BIBL: Black press, incl. AmstN, 28 December 1977.

DISC: RustCED (see under Robeson). Turn (see under Robeson).

BROWN, MARION. Jazz saxophonist (b. 8 September 1935 in Atlanta, Georgia). He obtained his musical education at Howard University in Washington, D.C., and at Wesleyan University in Middletown, Connecticut. He played reed instruments in high school, in an army band during his service in the U.S. Armed Forces, and in college groups. His teaching career included tenures in the public schools of New Haven, Connecticut; and at Colby College in Waterville, Maine; at Brandeis University in Waltham, Massachusetts; and at Bowdoin College in Brunswick, Maine. He left college in 1965 to record in New York with Archie Shepp* and John Coltrane,* playing alto saxophone. Beginning about 1967 he led his own groups, which recorded and toured in Europe. He returned to the United States in summer 1969 and thereafter toured in a duo with Leo Smith* at home and abroad. Later he toured with Steve McCall. He was regarded as an important saxist of the free-jazz movement; he also played other instruments, particularly exotic ones, as did his contemporaries. His best-known works included *Afternoon of a Georgia Faun*, *Geechee Recollections*, and *Sweet Earth Flying*. He was the subject of a documentary film, *See the Music* (1970).

BIBL: BPIM 1 (Spring 1973). FeaJS. FeaGitJS. NYT, 11 August 1974.

BROWN, MORRIS, JR. Choral conductor (b. 1812 in Charleston (?), South Carolina; d. 15 October 1890 in Philadelphia, Pennsylvania). He was a son of Morris Brown (1770-1849), who settled in Philadelphia, Pennsylvania in 1823 and succeeded Richard Allen* as Bishop of the African Methodist Episcopal Church. Little is known of his early life except that he may have studied voice with John Cromwell of Philadelphia during the 1820s. By the 1830s Brown had become increasingly active as a choral conductor and soloist, particularly in regard to sacred music concerts sponsored by black churches of Philadelphia and New York. He also conducted a music studio. He attracted much attention in 1839 (?) when he trained a chorus of 150 to sing Handel's oratorio, *The Messiah*, accompanied by a string orchestra under the direction of Edward Roland.* He also produced sacred music concerts with orchestras directed by Francis Johnson,* Isaac Hazzard,* James Hemmenway,* and Francis Seymour.*

BIBL: PaHistSoc, Box 1G. Black press, incl. *The Colored American*, 23 January 1841; NYAge, 1 November 1890. *The Public Ledger* (Philadelphia), 1 May 1837, 26 June 1843.

BROWN, OSCAR, JR. Entertainer/Composer (b. 10 October 1926 in Chicago, Illinois). He began his professional career as a child actor and entered music relatively late, although he wrote songs and poetry from childhood on. In 1952 his song ''Brown baby,'' attracted wide notice when it was sung by Mahalia Jackson.* His performance of the song on the demonstration record called attention to his singing ability and launched him into a career as an entertainer. He toured widely on the nightclub circuit and appeared on television and radio programs. In 1962 he was host for a television series ''Jazz Scene USA'' and in 1980 for the series ''From Jumpstreet: A Story of Black Music.'' He also produced television specials. During the 1960s-70s he gave more attention to writing music, although continuing his activity as an entertainer. The musicals he wrote and produced, some in collaboration with others, included *Kicks and Company* (1961), *Joy* (1970), the opera *Slave Song* (with Alonzo Levister, 1972), and *In Da Beginning* (1977) among other productions. He received awards from the theater industry. In 1972 he was artist-in-residence at Howard University in Washington, D.C.

BIBL: BMI (Issue 5, 1972). *Encore* (8 March 1976). FeaJS. WWBA.

BROWN, SCIPIO. Military drummer (b. c1757 in Rhode Island; d. 16 February 1834 in Rhode Island). He enlisted on 1 May 1778 in Colonel Christopher Greene's and Jeremiah Olney's black Rhode Island Regiment and served as a drummer during the War of the American Revolution.

BIBL: GreBD. MnBAF. Lorenzo Greene, "Some Observations on the Black Regiment of Rhode Island in the American Revolution" in JNH 37 (April 1952).

BROWN, THELMA WAIDE. College professor (b. 1897 in Ashland, Kentucky; d. 25 August 1975 in Chicago, Illinois). She studied piano as a child with her mother, a teacher in the public schools of Ashland, Kentucky. She obtained her musical education at colleges in Kentucky and at the Chicago [Illinois] Musical College. She settled in Chicago during the late 1920s. Thereafter she was active as a soprano soloist in local productions of operas and oratorios, as a church choir director, and as a studio teacher. She also toured as a concert singer in the United States and in Canada. In 1946 she was appointed a voice teacher at Chicago Musical College of Roosevelt University and remained in the position for more than twenty-six years. Her honors included awards from music and civic organizations and from the National Association of Negro Musicians (1969).

BIBL: Black press, incl. CDef, 3 September 1975.

BROWN, TOM. Vaudeville entertainer (b. 14 June 1868 in Indianapolis, Indiana; d. 20 June 1919 in Chicago, Illinois). Little is known of his early career except that he had been in show business for more than thirty years when he died. He was a member of the George Walker*/Bert Williams* Company during the first decade of the twentieth century, and later he performed with the Lafayette Players, the dramatic company based in Harlem in the city of New York. During the years 1910-12 he toured with J. Rosamond Johnson* in a vaudeville act. In 1915 he organized a touring company with Billy Johnson,* which was disbanded after Johnson's death in 1916.

BIBL: Black press, incl. CDef, 24 July 1915, 8 April 1916, 28 June 1919; IndF, 6 August 1914.

BROWN, WILLIAM ALBERT. Concert/opera singer (b. 29 March 1938 in Jackson, Mississippi). He obtained his musical education at Jackson State University in Mississippi (B. Mus. Ed., 1959), where he studied with Robert Henry; at Indiana University in Bloomington (M. Mus., 1962), where he studied with Charles Keillman and Paul Mattheu; at Peabody Conservatory in Baltimore, Maryland (1966-68), where he studied with Carolyn Long. He also studied with Alice Duschak. In 1961 he made his debut as a concert tenor in Handel's *Judas Maccabeus* with the Fort Wayne [Michigan] Symphony Orchestra; in 1967 he made his New York debut with the Little Orchestra Society's concert performance of Busoni's *Turandot*. In 1962 he made his operatic debut with the North Virginia Opera Company, singing the role of Rodolfo in Puccini's *La Bohème*. In 1968 he made his debut with the New York City Opera in Weisgall's *Nine Rivers from Jordan*. During the years 1970-71 he toured with the Goldovsky Grand Opera Theater. He also toured widely as a concert singer, appearing with major symphony orchestras of the United States and abroad, and performed with opera companies and on television programs, including the world premiere of John LaMontaine's opera *Shephardes Playe* performed by the Washington Opera. His best known operatic performances were as Feste in David Amram's *Twelfth Night*, Nero in Monteverdi's *L'Incoronazione di Poppea*, and Nate in William Grant Still's* *Highway 1, U.S.A.*, in addition to those cited above. He made his recording debut in 1973 and thereafter recorded regularly; his best-known recorded performances were of Olly Wilson's* "Sometime" and arias from operas by Still and Samuel Coleridge Taylor.* As a concert artist he attracted wide attention for his "all black-composer programs." His teaching career included tenures as an Affiliate Artist at Augustana College in Rock Island, Illinois; at Eckerd College in St. Petersburg, Florida; and as professor at the University of North Florida in Jacksonville (1972-). He received awards from the recording industry.

BIBL: Questionnaire. *Outstanding Educators of America*, 1973. *Personalities of the South*, 1975-76. WWA, 1980-81. WWOpera.

BROWN, WILLIAM WELLS. Writer (b. 1814 in Lexington, Kentucky; d. 6 November 1884 in Chelsea, Massachusetts). Although not a musician, he is included here because of his song collection, *The Anti-Slavery Harp* (Boston, 1849), and other books that contain valuable information about musical practices of Afro-Americans in the nineteenth century. Only texts are given in the song collection, but titles of appropriate tunes for the texts are listed, thus providing an index to songs that were popular during the times. *My Southern Home* (Boston, 1860) and *The Negro in the American Rebellion* (Boston, 1880) both contain descriptions of musical performance practices and texts of folksongs. Brown, an active antislavery lecturer, often sang during his presentations.

BIBL: William Edward Farrison, *William Wells Brown, Author and Reformer* (Chicago, 1969).

BROWN MITCHELL, NELLIE. Concert singer (b. 1845 in Dover, New Hampshire; d. January 1924 in Boston, Massachusetts). She studied voice with a local teacher, Caroline Bracker, of Dover and began her professional career as a church soloist at a local Baptist Church, serving during the years 1865-72. Thereafter she was a church soloist in Haverhill, Massachusetts (1872-76), again in Dover (1876-c1878), and in Boston, Massachusetts (1879-86?), where she served also as the musical director at the Broomfield Street Church. She studied in Boston at the New England Conservatory and the School of Vocal Arts, receiving a diploma from that institution in 1879. She began singing in local concerts early in her career and began touring during the 1870s. She made her New York debut in 1874 and her Philadelphia [Pennsylvania] debut in 1882. During the 1880s she was featured as the "prima donna soprano" on Bergen Star Concerts, assisted by such artists as baritone William I. Powell of Philadelphia, soprano Adelaide Smith of Boston, and entertainer Sam Lucas.* In 1885 she made an extended concert tour in the South. The next year she resigned her church position to devote her time to concertizing as a soloist and with her Nellie Brown Mitchell Concert Company, which included her sister, soprano Ednah B. Brown. Her career reached its peak during the 1880s and 1890s; in 1886 the *Cleveland Gazette* called her "America's greatest singer of African descent" and in 1888, "Madame Selika's* only rival." In 1888 she was appointed a vocal instructor at the Hedding Chautauqua Summer School in East Epping, New Hampshire, and taught there many summers. She toured widely for her time, appearing in major cities along the East Coast frequently and in the Middle West. During the late 1890s she left the concert stage and concentrated on studio teaching, advertising that she used the "Guilmette Method" of vocal technique.

BIBL: Black press, incl. NYGlobe, NYFreeman, 14 March 1885, 24 October 1885, 20 March 1886; CleveG, 31 October 1886, 14 April 1888; IndF, 23 August 1890. Trot.

BROWNING, IVAN HAROLD. Vaudeville singer (b. 1891 in Brenham, Texas; d. 20 May 1978 in Los Angeles, California). He first attracted attention when he sang at the San Francisco World's Fair in 1915. During his early career he sang tenor in quartets; about 1917 he began a longtime association with the Four Harmony Kings (until 1933), which included also Charles E. Drayton, W. H. Berry, and W. H. Hann. The Kings toured widely; they were on tour with James Reese Europe* in 1919 when Europe met his death in Boston in May of that year. The Kings also sang in Broadway musicals, including the Noble Sissle*/Eubie Blake* *Shuffle Along* (1921) and *The Chocolate Dandies* (1924). Browning also sang leading roles in musicals. In 1924 the Kings settled in Europe. Browning left the quartet in 1933 to team with Henry Starr in a vaudeville act, which toured theaters and nightclubs in Europe until the outbreak of World War II. He and Starr wrote many of the songs they sang. During his years overseas Browning regularly contributed a column to the *Chicago Defender* titled "Across the Pond." After returning to the United States, Browning settled in California, where he became active in films. In 1971-72 he made a series of recordings with Eubie Blake, singing some of the songs that he had made famous over his long career.

BIBL: Black press, incl. ChgDef, 17 November 1917, 17 May 1919; NYAge, 15 October 1921, 31 December 1927. Jacket notes for *Eubie Blake Music*, v. 1. *Los Angeles Times*, 4 June 1978.

BRYAN, FREDERICK. See **HANDY, W[ILLIAM] C.**

BRYANT, JOYCE. Opera/Popular-music singer (b. 1928 in San Francisco, California). She went to Los Angeles when she was fourteen, won first prize in a talent show at a nightclub, and was offered a singing spot by the bandleader. Thereafter she sang professionally. In her early career she sang with the Flennoy Trio (also known as the Sepianaires), then later toured widely as a soloist, singing in the top nightclubs of the nation. By the 1950s she was one of the leading entertainers of the period; her personal appearance was distinctive for her dyed silver hair. Abruptly in 1955 she left the entertainment field to study at Oakwood College, a Seventh Day Adventist School in Huntsville, Alabama, with the goal of becoming a missionary. ("Little") Richard Penniman* enrolled at Oakwood during her third year and earned his ordination as a minister in the Seventh Day Adventist Church in 1961. Bryant settled at Washington, D.C., in 1959, where she studied voice with Frederick Wilkerson. She began performing as a concert soprano in 1960 and thereafter gave solo recitals, appeared with symphony orchestras, and sang opera. For three years she sang with the New York City Opera, including the title role of Gershwin's *Porgy and Bess* (1961). During the years 1967-77 she sang with various opera companies in Europe. After returning to the United States, she toured again on the nightclub circuit.

BIBL: Black press, incl. CDef, 29 January 1955. NYT, 22 July 1977.

BRYANT, WILLIAM STEVEN ("WILLIE"). Entertainer/Jazz bandleader (b. 30 August 1908 in New Orleans, Louisiana; d. 9 February 1964 in Los Angeles, California). His family moved to Chicago, Illinois, when he was four years old. During the years c1926-33 he toured widely on the vaudeville circuit; he played for five years with the Whitman Sisters* company, including an act with Princess Pee Wee, and with such performers as Bessie Smith* and Buck and Bubbles* (née Ford Lee Washington and John William Sublett). In 1934 he organized a big band (1934-38), which played long residencies in New York and included among its personnel Bennett (''Benny'') Carter,* Eddie Durham,* William (''Cozy'') Cole,* Theodore (''Teddy'') Wilson,* and Ben Webster,* among others. He then turned to entertaining in nightclubs and theaters; he attracted wide attention as the master of ceremonies at the Apollo Theater in the Harlem community, particularly for the celebrated weekly Amateur Nights, and was credited with bringing to the public singers who would later become famous, among them Ella Fitzgerald* and Sarah Vaughan.* In 1943 he was one of the first to take a group abroad under the sponsorship of the USO ''all-colored'' Camp Shows to entertain servicemen during World War II. After the war he again organized a jazz band (1946-48). During the 1950s he was a disc jockey in New York, broadcasting with Ray Carroll on radio station WHOM from the windows of a Harlem nightclub, The Baby Grand. In 1954 he was host for a television series, ''Showtime at the Apollo.'' He settled in California in the late 1950s and was active as a disc jockey there.

BIBL: ASCAP, Black press, incl. AmstN, 13 November 1943; CDef, 11 November 1939. ChilWW. FeaEJ. FeaJS.

DISC: Jep. Kink. RustJR.

BRYMN, JAMES TIMOTHY ("TIM"). Society dance-orchestra and military-band leader (b. 5 October 1881 in Kinston, North Carolina; d. 3 October 1946 in New York, New York). He obtained his musical education at Shaw University in North Carolina and studied further at the National Conservatory of Music in New York. Early in the 1900s he formed a partnership with Cecil Mack* (neé Richard McPherson), and the team was engaged to write songs for the Joseph Stern music publishing company. He was musical director for the George Walker*/Bert Williams* company when it produced *In Dahomey* at London, England, in 1904. In 1906 he became musical director for The Smart Set* company and wrote scores for some of its shows, including *The Black Politician* and *His Honor, the Barber*, which featured Sherman H. Dudley.* Beginning about 1914 he was active as a conductor of Clef Club* orchestras; he also led society-dance bands at the New York Roof Garden and in nightclubs and supper clubs. During World War I he led the 350th Field Artillery Regiment Band and was identified by the press as one of the black bandmasters who ''introduced jazz music into France.'' After the war his band, called the Black Devils, toured the United States; the band's sponsor was opera-diva Ernestine Schumann-Heink, who was called ''godmother of the 350th.''

BIBL: Black press, incl. CDef, 10 December 1911, 24 May 1919; NYAge, 7 May 1914. Emmett J. Scott, *The American Negro in the World War* (Washington, D.C., 1919), 300.

BUCK AND BUBBLES. See **SUBLETT, JOHN.**

BUCKNER, MILTON ("MILT"). Jazz organist (b. 10 July 1915 in St. Louis, Missouri; d. 27 July 1977 in Chicago, Illinois). He came from a musical family: two brothers, Theodore (''Ted'') and George, became professional jazzmen. Left an orphan at nine years old, he went to Detroit, Michigan, to live with an uncle, John Tobias, who taught him piano. He obtained his musical education in the public schools of Detroit and at the Detroit Institute of the Arts. He began playing professionally about 1930 with local Detroit groups. He also made arrangements for bands, among them, Earl Walton and McKinney's Cotton Pickers.* Thereafter he played with Lionel Hampton* for several years (1941-48, 1950-52), also making arrangements for Hampton; he led his own groups also (1948-50), at first a sextet, then a big band. Beginning in late 1952 he concentrated his attention more on the Hammond organ and toured widely with a trio in the United States and abroad. During his career he performed and/or recorded with various jazzmen, including Roy Eldridge,* Illinois Jacquet,* Jonathan (''Jo'') Jones,* Louis Jordan,* George (''Buddy'') Tate, and Jimmy Woode. He was one of the pioneers in playing jazz and rhythm 'n' blues on the Hammond organ, and he made significant contributions to jazz-piano technique in his innovative use of interconnected parallel chords to achieve the effect of horns. The piano style was widely imitated and later popularized by George Shearing. Buckner's best-known performances were "Hamp's boogie woogie" and "Mighty low."

BIBL: ChilWW. FeaEJ. FeaGitJS. MeeJMov. NYT, 30 July 1977.

DISC: Jep. Kink.

BUMBRY, GRACE ANN. Opera singer (b. 4 January 1937 in St. Louis, Missouri). She came from a musical family: her father was a church organist, and her mother was a church pianist. As a child she sang in a church choir and began piano study at the age of seven. She received her musical education in the public schools of St. Louis, Missouri, where she came under the tutelage of Kenneth Billups* at Sumner High School and studied voice with him privately; at Boston [Massachusetts] University (1954-55); at Northwestern University in Evanston, Illinois (1955-56), where she studied with Lotte Lehmann; and at the Music Academy of the West in Santa Barbara, California (1956-59). Later she studied further with Lehmann and with Armand Tokatyan and Pierre Bernac. Her early career development was influenced by Billups and by the National Association of Negro Musicians,* which gave her scholarships. When she was seventeen he encouraged her to enter a talent contest sponsored by radio station KMOX in St. Louis; she won first prize and with it an opportunity to sing on Arthur Godfrey's Talent Scouts national television show. Thereafter she devoted full time to preparing for a career in music. She was greatly inspired by Marian Anderson, whom she heard in live concerts and to whose recordings she listened. It was Lehmann who encouraged her to plan for an opera career. She made her professional debut in 1958 as a mezzo-soprano in San Francisco, California. In 1960 she made her operatic debut in the role of Amneris in Verdi's *Aida* with the Paris [France] Opera Company. Thereafter she toured widely in the United States and in Europe, giving solo recitals and singing with leading opera companies. She attracted wide attention in 1961 when she sang the role of Venus in Wagner's *Tannhauser* at the Bayreuth [Germany] Festival. In 1963 she made her American operatic debut as Venus in Wagner's *Tannhauser* with the Chicago Lyric Opera. In 1965 she made her debut with the Metropolitan Opera Company as Princess Eboli in Verdi's *Don Carlo*. During the 1960s she also was active as a concert singer. In November 1962 she made her debut at Carnegie Hall in New York and thereafter won critical acclaim for her lieder and other art-song recitals. During the 1970s she began singing dramatic soprano roles, although she had begun her career as a mezzo-soprano. Her best-known performances included such roles in Verdi's operas as Lady Macbeth in *Macbeth*, Abigaille in *Nabucco*, and Leonora in *Ernani*; the title roles in Strauss's *Salome*, Janácek's *Jenufa*, and Ponchielli's *La Gioconda*; Sarah in Donizetti's *Roberto Devereux*; and Inez in Meyerbeer's *L'Africaine*. Critics acclaimed her voice for its power, richness, and flexibility.

BIBL: CBDict. *The Crisis* 84 (November 1977). NYT, 2 January 1977. WWA. WWBA. WWOpera.

DISC: Turn.

BURGIE, IRVING LOUIS ("LORD BURGESS"). Songwriter (b. 28 July 1924 in New York, New York). He obtained his musical education at the Juilliard School of Music in New York (1946-48), the University of Arkansas at Pine Bluff (1948-49), and the University of Southern California at Los Angeles (1949-50). During his service in the U.S. Armed Forces (1942-45) he was encouraged to develop his musical skills; he sang in a chapel choir and studied musical theory. After his discharge he began serious music study and was active in New York with the Harlem Writers' Guild. He first attracted wide attention for the songs he wrote for Harry Belafonte* during the years 1956-60, which included "Day O," "Jamaica farewell," "I do adore her," "Angelina," "The wanderer," "Come back, Lisa," and many others. He was a large contributor of songs to Belefonte's album, *Calypso*, one of the first American albums to sell a million copies. He also wrote for The Kingston Trio such songs as "The wanderer," "The Seine," and "El matador." He wrote songs for the film *Island in the Sun* (1957). His other works included the Off-Broadway musical *Ballad for Bimshire* (1963), which he revised and produced again in 1978 with the title *Calalou*. His publications included *The West Indian Songbook* (1972).

BIBL: ASCAP. Black press, incl. AmstN, 16 January 1971, 14 October 1978. WWBA.

BURLEIGH, HENRY THACKER ("HARRY"). Composer (b. 2 December 1866 in Erie, Pennsylvania; d. 12 September 1949 in Stamford, Connecticut). He had no formal music study as a child but revealed talent as a singer, and his mother encouraged his interest in music. The odd jobs at which he worked during his youth provided him with opportunities to hear performances of artists who visited Erie—among them, Italo Campanini, Teresa Carreño, and Rafael Joseffy—and inspired him to become a singer. Eventually he found employment singing in local churches and synagogues. When he was twenty-six he decided to go to New York to further his musical education, and he competed for a scholarship at the National Conservatory of Music in that city. His grades on the entrance examination were not high enough to win him a scholarship, but through the intercession of the registrar, Frances Knapp MacDowell (mother of composer Edward MacDowell), he was given a second audition and awarded the scholarship. Mrs. MacDowell remembered him from his Erie days when he had been the doorman at a recital given by Carreño at the home of Elizabeth Russell. At the Conservatory Burleigh studied voice with Christian Fritsch, harmony with Rubin Goldmark, and counterpoint with John White and Max Spicker. He played in the Conservatory orchestra under Franz van der Stucken. Mrs. MacDowell helped him to find employment; and Jeanette Thurber, founder of the Conservatory, also befriended him. In 1892 composer Antonin Dvorak came to New York from Bohemia (now Czechoslovakia) to head the Conservatory, and Burleigh studied with him. Burleigh also spent many hours outside the classroom with Dvorak, singing spirituals for the composer and copying manuscripts for him (for which Burleigh was paid). Burleigh absorbed the composer's theories that America's Negro and Indian folk music could serve as a basis for the development of a nationalistic school of music in the United States. In addition to working at the Conservatory, Burleigh taught music privately and sang with church choirs in the Harlem community of the city.

In 1894 he competed for a church soloist position at the aristocratic St. George's Protestant Episcopal Church and won over forty-nine other applicants. Despite objections of some members of the church to his color, he was appointed to the position, with strong support from the minister, and remained there for fifty-two years. He established two traditions at St. George's: beginning in 1895 he sang Faure's song ''The Palms'' on every Palm Sunday, and beginning in 1923 he gave an annual concert of Negro spirituals. In 1900 he became the first black soloist at wealthy Temple Emanu-El and remained there for twenty-five years.

In addition to his church positions, Burleigh conducted a music studio and gave concerts. During the two decades after his graduation from the Conservatory in 1896, he toured extensively in the United States and in Europe during at least two summers, where he sang before royalty. During the 1890s he had a brief flirtation with vaudeville: he appeared for a month or so with Black Patti's* Troubadours at the beginning of its first season in the fall of 1896 but left before December of that year. He returned to the stage briefly in 1898 to play in (or direct?) an orchestra for the George Walker*/Bert Williams* show *The Senegambian Carnival* but turned down an offer to become the musical director of the show. In 1911 he became an editor for G. Ricordi music publishers.

He began composing about 1898; at first he wrote in the conventional forms of the period, simple songs and sentimental ballads. As he developed his skills, he began to write art songs. He composed more than 300 songs, including arrangements of spirituals, for solo voice and choral ensemble; several works for violin and/or piano, including *Six Plantation Melodies for Violin and Piano* (1901), *From the Southland* for piano (1914), and *Southland Sketches* for violin and piano (1916); and a collection of hymn arrangements, *Old Songs Hymnal* (1929). His art songs were popular during his time and widely sung by such artists as Lucrezia Bori, Ernestine Schumann-Heink, and John McCormack. Best-known of the songs were ''I love my Jean'' (1914, Robert Burns poem), ''Little mother of mine'' (1917), ''Dear old pal of mine'' (1918), ''In the great somewhere'' (1919), and ''Lovely, dark and lonely one'' (1935, a Langston Hughes* poem). His best-known cycles were *Five Songs of Lawrence Hope* (1919) and *Saracen Songs* (1914). His most important contribution to American music was his arranged spiritual set in the style of an art song for solo voice. His ''Deep river'' (1916) was the first to employ the form; the next year he published a revision of ''Deep river'' along with other solo-voice arrangements and continued to publish groups of the spiritual-arrangements periodically for the next twenty years. The arrangements became immensely popular with concert singers; in 1917 they established a tradition for concluding recitals with a group of spirituals, a tradition which continues to the present, particularly among black artists. He wrote in a neoromantic style; the piano accompaniment in his sensitive song settings was used to set and sustain the mood rather than move on an equal plane with the lyrical melodies. He used Negro folk idioms freely and was regarded as one of the early black nationalistic composers.

Burleigh was the first black composer to win critical acclaim for composing art songs. He was a charter member of ASCAP (American Society of Composers, Authors, and Publishers) and was elected to its Board of Directors in 1941. He received numerous honors, including the Spingarn Medal (1917), a Harmon Foundation Award (1929), and honorary degrees from Atlanta University (M.A., 1918) and Howard University (doctorate, 1920).

BIBL: ASCAP. Baker. BPIM 2 (Spring 1974). CurBiog (August 1941). DAB. Gro. Hare. HNB. Ellsworth Janifer, "Harry T. Burleigh, Ten Years Later" in *Phylon* 21 (1960). MOBA. WWCA, 1927-44. WWW, vol. 2.

BURNETT, CHESTER ARTHUR ("HOWLIN' WOLF"). Bluesman (b. 10 June 1910 in Aberdeen (near West Point), Mississippi; d. 10 January 1976 in Hines, Illinois). He played blues at an early age, developing his style in the late 1920s under the tutelage of Charlie Patton* and Sonny Boy Williamson, No. 2 (Willie ("Rice") Miller*). He was an itinerant bluesman in the Delta region through the 1930s and 1940s, served in the armed forces during World War II, then in 1947 settled in West Memphis, Arkansas, where he became a disc jockey on radio station WKEM. He also organized a band, which included at one time or another James Cotton,* Pat Hare, Willie Johnson, ("Little Junior") Herman Parker,* and Ike Turner,* among others. In 1951 he began to record; in 1952 he moved to Chicago, where he became one of the important post-war blues figures, along with Muddy Waters (McKinley Morganfield)* and Jimmy Reed.* Thereafter he toured widely in the United States and abroad and recorded extensively. He exerted enormous influence upon his contemporaries, particularly in England where rock 'n' roll groups took over his song materials and imitated his style. His best-known songs included "Moanin' at midnight," "How many more tears," "Sittin' on top of the world," "Smoke-stack lightning," and "No place to go." Although a seminal figure in the development of urban blues, his style was earthy, aggressive, and intense, reflecting its rural roots.

BIBL: BWW. LivBl 1 (Spring 1970); LivBl 26 (January-February 1976). MeeJMov. NYT, 12 January 1976. Oliv. ShawHS. StamPRS.

DISC: LeSlBR; TudBM.

BURRELL, KENNETH EARL ("KENNY"). Jazz guitarist (b. 31 July 1931 in Detroit, Michigan). He came from a musical family: three brothers became professional musicians. He began playing guitar when he was twelve years old. He obtained his musical education in the public schools of Detroit, Michigan, and at Wayne University in Detroit (B. Mus., 1955). He studied classical guitar a short while (1952-53) and taught himself to play jazz guitar. He first played professionally during the 1940s with local groups. In the mid-1950s he went to New York; thereafter he played with various groups, including the Oscar Peterson* Trio (1955-57), Benny Goodman (1957-59), and the Jimmy Smith* Trio (1959), among others. He organized his own groups in the early 1950s; in 1960 he toured with the Kenny Burrell Trio, and in 1963 with the Kenny Burrell Quartet. During the 1960s-70s he toured widely throughout the world, making his first tour of Europe in 1969 and of Japan in 1970. In addition to performing with his own groups, he also toured with the Newport All Stars. In 1972 he settled in Los Angeles, California. His activity there included studio work along with live performance, and he also lectured on college campuses. His best-known albums were *Guitar Forms, God Bless the Child, Up the Street*, and *Ode to 52nd Street* (his own compositions). He received many awards from the music industry. He was a leading guitarist in the "hard-bop" style.

BIBL: FeaEJ. FeaJS. FeaGitJS. WWBA.

DISC: Jep.

BURRIS, ANDREW. Composer (fl. mid-nineteenth century in Philadelphia, Pennsylvania; d. after 1865 in Philadelphia). Little is known of his career except that he was highly regarded by his contemporaries for his compositions. He conducted a music studio in Philadelphia, Pennsylvania, and occasionally directed choruses and bands. One of his pupils was Samuel Diton, father of Carl Rossini Diton.* His best-known pieces were "You bid me strike my harp" and "Brotherhood grand march."

BIBL: PaHistSoc, Box 1G. John E. Bruce, "A History of Negro Musicians" in *Southern Workman* 45 (1916). LaBrew.

BUSHELL, GARVIN PAYNE. Jazz clarinetist (b. 25 September 1902 in Springfield, Ohio). He came from a musical family: both parents were voice teachers, and an uncle played clarinet. He began piano study at the age of six and clarinet study at thirteen. He attended Wilberforce University in Ohio and toured with traveling tent shows during vacation periods. In 1919 he settled in New York; thereafter he played in nightclubs and with various groups, including Mamie Smith* and Her Jazz Hounds, Ethel Waters* and Her Black Swan Jazz Masters (1921-22), and Sam Wooding* (1925-28), with whom he toured in Europe (1925-27) in The Chocolate Kiddies revue. After returning to the United States, he played with Wooding another year, was involved in free-lance work, and played in the pit orchestra for Thomas ("Fats") Waller's* Broadway musical, *Keep Shufflin'* (1928), and in New York nightclubs. During the next three decades he played with various groups, including Fletcher Henderson* (1935-36, 1958), Cabell ("Cab") Calloway* (1936-37, 1966), William ("Chick") Webb* (1937-39), and Wilbur DeParis* (1959-64). He led his own groups from time to time, played several times in orchestras for Broadway musicals, and in 1950 played bassoon with the Chicago Civic Orchestra. His touring took him to Europe several times and to Africa in 1964 with Paul Taubman. In 1967 he settled in Puerto Rico, where he conducted a music studio.

BIBL: AlHen. ChilWW. FeaEJ. MeeJMov.

DISC: Jep. RustJR.

BUTCHER, VADA EASTER. University professor/ Ethnomusicologist (b. 6 December 1923 in St. Louis, Missouri). She began piano study at the age of six with her mother, Benne Parks Easter, a concert pianist-music teacher. She obtained her musical education at Fisk University (B.A., 1942; M. Mus., 1946) where she studied with John Work III*; at Chicago [Illinois] Musical College (D.F.A., 1950), where she studied with Rudolph Ganz; at Catholic University of America in Washington, D.C.; and at the Conservatoire de musique in Fontainebleau, France (1950-51), where she studied with Nadia Boulanger. She also studied with Robert Hemingway, Robert Casadesus, and Charles Seeger. Her teaching career included tenures at Howard University in Washington, D.C. (1946-76) and at Bowling Green State University in Ohio (1978-79). During the years 1972-76 she was Dean of the College of Fine Arts at Howard. She was also active as a concert pianist. She made her debut in February 1940 at Kiel Auditorium in St. Louis, Missouri. Thereafter she toured regularly as a concert pianist, particularly on the black-college circuit. She contributed articles to such professional journals as *Music Educators Journal, Journal of Research in Music Education*, and *Journal of the Society for Ethnomusicology* and published books, including *Ethnic Music in General Education* (1977) and *Materials for Courses in African and Afro-American Music for the Undergraduate Student* (1970). She toured as a lecturer, giving particular attention to the subject of African and Afro-American music, and as a workshop consultant. She also served as visiting lecturer at several institutions. Her honors included fellowships from the Ford Foundation (1955), Rosenwald Foundation (1948), Oliver Ditson Foundation (1945), Wooley Foundation (French government, 1951); awards from the *Evening Star* newspaper of Washington, D.C. (1971), and Fontainebleau Conservatory (1950); and appointment to panels and committees of government organizations associated with music. In 1976 she established her own consultant firm.

BIBL: Questionnaire. Beverly Blondell, "Drums Talk at Howard" in *Music Educators Journal* (November 1971). *The Washington Star*, 3 October 1973.

BUTLER, JERRY ("THE ICEMAN"). Rhythm 'n' blues singer (b. 8 December 1939 in Sunflower, Mississippi). His family moved to Chicago, Illinois, in 1942. He sang in church choirs as a child, and when he was twelve years old became a member of the choir of the Traveling Souls Spiritual Church, in which Curtis Mayfield* also sang. Later he and Mayfield sang together in a gospel group, The Modern Jubelaires, and in a rhythm 'n' blues group, The Impressions.* He left The Impressions in 1958 to tour as a solo entertainer and within a few years established himself as one of the leading rhythm 'n' blues singers of his time. For several years Mayfield worked with Butler as guitarist and songwriting collaborator. Butler recorded extensively and toured widely, appearing in theaters, nightclubs, and on television programs. In 1966 the company for which he was recording, Vee Jay,* went out of business; he changed to another and began working with the songwriting team of Kenneth ("Kenny") Gamble* and Leon Huff.* Through the 1970s his popularity remained as high as at the beginning of his career. He earned his nickname, "The Iceman," because of his restrained, although tender, performance style and his eschewing of excessive movement as he sang, unlike most rhythm 'n' blues singers. His best-known songs included "For your precious love" (sung with The Impressions), "Only the strong survive," "He will break your heart," and "Western Union man."

BIBL: *Ebony* (December 1969). ShawHS. StamPRS.

BUTLER, JOHN ("PICAYUNE"). Minstrel banjoist (b. early nineteenth century in the West Indies; d. 18 November 1864 in New York, New York). He settled in New Orleans, Louisiana, during the 1820s and there attracted attention when he played a four-stringed banjo on street corners for "picayunes" or tips. He soon became "known from New Orleans to Cincinnati." On 19 October 1857 he made an impressive showing in a banjo competition held in the Chinese Assembly Rooms in the city of New York. His best-known song, "Picayune Butler's come to town," was published in Phil Rice, *Correct Method for the Banjo* (New York, 1858).

BIBL: BPIM 3 (Spring 1975), p. 78. Ann Charters, *The Ragtime Songbook* (New York, 1965). Henry A. Kmen, *Music in New Orleans: The Formative Years, 1791-1841* (Baton Rouge, 1966). Edward LeRoy Rice, *Monarchs of Minstrelsy* (New York, 1911).

BUTTERBEANS AND SUSIE. See **EDWARDS, JODY AND SUSIE.**

BYARD, JOHN ARTHUR, JR. ("JAKI"). Jazz keyboardist (b. 15 June 1922 in Worcester, Massachusetts). He came from a musical family: his grandmother played theater piano for silent movies, his father played baritone horn in a marching band, and his mother played piano. He began piano study when he was seven years old. He obtained his musical education in the public schools of Worcester, Massachusetts, and later studied at the Schillinger School of Music. During his high-school years he played trumpet with local groups. After service in the U.S. Armed Forces (1942-45), where he played trombone in army bands, he went to Boston, Massachusetts. Thereafter he played with various groups, including Earl Bostic* (1949-50), Herbert Pomeroy (tenor saxophone, 1952-55), and Maynard Ferguson (1959-62), among others. In 1962 he went to New York, where he joined Charles Mingus* as pianist and arranger and later played with other groups of jazzmen, among them Eric Dolphy,* Don Ellis, Kenneth McIntyre,* and Sam Rivers.* He toured in Europe with Mingus (1968-70); he also toured widely as a solo pianist in Europe, Australia, China, and Japan. His teaching career included tenures as a lecturer at the New England Conservatory of Music in Boston (1969-77), at Southeastern Massachusetts University in North Dartmouth (1974-76), at the City College of the City University of New York (1974-76), and at the Hartt School of Music in Hartford, Connecticut (1975-77). He also toured as a lecturer, holding seminars on college campuses and giving lecture-recitals. He served as a conductor at the Elma Lewis* School in Boston (1972-76). He recorded regularly; his best-known albums were *Freedom Together* and *Here's Jaki.* He received awards from the music industry. His style was distinctive for his ability to play all kinds of piano music, from ragtime and stride piano to free jazz.

BIBL: ContK (January 1978). FeaEJ. FeaJS. FeaGitJS. WWBA.

BYAS, CARLOS WESLEY ("DON"). Jazz saxophonist (b. 21 October 1912 in Muskogee, Oklahoma; d. 24 August 1972 in Amsterdam, The Netherlands). He first studied violin, then changed to alto saxophone. He attended Langston University in Oklahoma, where he led his own group, Don Carlos and His Collegiate Ramblers. He left college in 1933 to tour with Bert Johnson's Sharps and Flats, playing tenor saxophone; he left the band in Los Angeles, California. Thereafter he played with various groups, including Lionel Hampton* (1935), Edward ("Eddie") Barefield (1936), Eddie Mallory (1937-38, with whom he went to New York in 1937 in Mallory's accompanying band for Ethel Waters*), Andrew ("Andy") Kirk* (1939-40), William ("Count") Basie* (1941-43), and John ("Dizzy") Gillespie's* quintet (1944), among others. He also played free-lance engagements and led his own group in 1945. The next year he went to Europe with Donald ("Don") Redman,* and settled there, living first in France, then in The Netherlands. He toured widely in Europe, appearing at major jazz festivals and in nightclubs and theaters. He performed in Europe with Edward ("Duke") Ellington* (1950) and with Norman Granz's Jazz at the Philharmonic. In 1970 he returned to the United States to tour and in 1971 he toured in Japan with Arthur ("Art") Blakey.* He was an important tenor saxophonist in the Coleman Hawkins* tradition. He was also an architect of the bebop era; during the early 1940s he played at Minton's Playhouse in the Harlem community with jazzmen who were experimenting with new sounds and rhythms, producing a music that later would be called bebop, along with Gillespie, Oscar Pettiford,* Charlie Christian,* Kenneth ("Kenny") Clarke,* Thelonious Monk,* Milt Hinton,* and others. And he was a member of Gillespie's quintet on 52nd Street in New York that "represented the birth of the bebop era" (quoted from Gillespie, p. 202).

BIBL: ChilWW. FeaEJ. FeaJS. FeaGitJS. Dizzy Gillespie, *To Be Or Not to Bop* (New York, 1979). MeeJMov. Russ.

DISC: Jep. Kink. RustJR.

BYRD, DONALD[SON] T. Jazz trumpeter (b. 9 December 1932 in Detroit, Michigan). His father, a minister and pianist, introduced him to music. Two uncles played saxophone and drums, and his sister played piano. He obtained his musical education in the public schools of Detroit, Michigan; at Wayne University in Detroit (B.A.); at the Manhattan School of Music in New York (B. Mus., 1963); and at Columbia University Teachers College (Ph.D. in college teaching and administration, 1971). He also studied with Nadia Boulanger in Fontainbleau, France (1963). He played with local jazz groups of Detroit in his early career. During his service in the U.S. Armed Forces (1951-53), he played in an Air Force band. After his discharge he settled in New York, where he played with various groups, including Arthur ("Art") Blakey* and Maxwell ("Max") Roach.* In the late 1950s he began touring widely with his own groups and with others, appearing in concert halls and at festivals in the United States and abroad. During the years 1965-66 he was an arranger for the Norwegian Radio Orchestra. His teaching career included tenures in the public schools of New

York; at Howard University in Washington, D.C. (1968-73); and at North Carolina Central College in Durham (1975-). He also served as a lecturer or artist-in-residence at various educational institutions and toured as a lecturer, particularly on the subject of black music. At Howard University he organized a student group, the Blackbyrds, that later became professional and had a successful career. Byrd toured widely with his student group and made recordings with it. He received numerous awards from the music industry. His best-known albums were *Street Lady* and *Black Byrd*. He was a leading performer in the ''hard-bop'' tradition.

BIBL: BMI (April 1971). FeaEJ. FeaJS. FeaGitJS. MeeJMov. *Sepia* (August 1969). WWBA.

DISC: Jep. ModJ. TudJ.

BYRD, HENRY ROELAND (''PROFESSOR LONGHAIR''). Blues pianist (b. 19 December 1918 in Bogalusa, Louisiana; d. 29 January 1980 in New Orleans). He was taken to New Orleans at the age of two months; as a child he studied with his mother, learning guitar and other instruments. During his adolescence he danced with other boys on street corners for money and in local clubs and bars. His musical style development was influenced by local pianists Rocky Sullivan, Robert Bertrand, Isidore (''Tuts'') Washington, and others. Although he began playing piano in public as early as 1939, he regarded his professional career as beginning in 1949, the year in which he also made his first recordings. Thereafter he performed extensively, frequently touring with groups under the management of Dave Bartholomew, and continued to record, though not prolifically. He was a seminal figure of the New Orleans blues school, not only as the inventor of the rhumba blues—in which he superimposed fast triplets on a syncopated rhumba beat—but also because he exerted enormous influence upon other blues pianists, among them, Antoine (''Fats'') Domino,* Jesse Hill, and Earl King. His best-known songs included ''Bye, bye, baby,'' ''Bald head,'' ''Walk your blues away,'' ''Tipitina,'' and ''Go to the Mardi Gras.''

BIBL: BWW. LivBl (incl. disc.), 26 (March-April 1976). *Missouri Friends of the Folk Arts* 5, n. 1 (Winter 1978). Press coverage. ShawHS.

DISC: Jep. TudBM; LeSl.

C

CAESAR, SHIRLEY. Gospel singer (b. c1938 in Durham, North Carolina). Her father, "Big Jim" Caesar, was a professional gospel singer, who sang with the Just Come Four gospel quartet. She obtained her musical education in the public schools of Durham, North Carolina, and at North Carolina State College in Durham (1956-58). She sang in church choirs as a child and began singing professionally when she was fourteen, touring on the church circuit on weekends and during school vacations as "Baby Shirley" with gospel groups, among them The Charity Singers. She also had a professional association with gospel preacher Leroy Johnson. In 1958 she became a full-time evangelist and joined the Caravans (1958-66), at that time under the leadership of Albertina Walker, with whom she toured widely and recorded. In 1966 she formed her own group, the Shirley Caesar Singers, and made her recording debut as a leader. During her tenure with the Caravans, she lived in Chicago, Illinois; after leaving the group she returned to Durham. She was the leading female gospel singer of her generation. Her style was described as "rock-gospel," but unlike many of her contemporaries she limited her repertory to sacred music. Her best-known songs included "Let Jesus fix it," "Put your hand in the hand of the Man from Galilee," "Reach out and touch," and "When the Saviour reached down," among many others. Her honors included awards from the music and recording industries and citations from civic and community groups.

BIBL: BMI (Issue 4, 1977). *Dawn Magazine* (April 1979). *Ebony* (September 1977). GMEncy. Heil. Jac. LivBl 6 (Autumn 1971), p. 38.

CALHOUN, CORA. See **AUSTIN, LOVIE.**

CALLOWAY JONES, BLANCHE. Jazz-band leader (b. 2 February 1902 in Baltimore, Maryland; d. 16 December 1978 in Baltimore). She came from a musical family: her mother was a church organist and two brothers, Cabell ("Cab")* and Elmer, became professional musicians. As a child she studied piano and voice with Llewelyn Wilson.* She also sang in a church choir. She obtained her musical education from Morgan State College in Baltimore, Maryland. She began her professional career in the early 1920s, singing with the 1923 touring companies of the Noble Sissle*/Eubie Blake* musical *Shuffle Along* and the James P. Johnson* show *Plantation Days*. When *Plantation Days* was disbanded in Chicago, Illinois, in 1927, she remained in the city and found employment as a nightclub entertainer. During the years 1931-38 she led her own big band, which included at one time or another William ("Cozy") Cole,* Victor ("Vic") Dickenson, Albert ("Andy") Gibson, and Ben Webster,* among others. During the early 1930s she called her band Blanche Calloway and Her Joy Boys; later it was simply Blanche Calloway and her orchestra. During the late 1930s to mid-1940s she toured primarily as a soloist, except in 1940 when she again organized a big band, an all-girls band. She left the field of musical performance in 1944. During the 1950s she was a disc jockey on Miami [Florida] radio station WMBM. Her best-known songs were "I need loving" and "Growlin' Dan," her band's theme song.

BIBL: AlHen. Black press, incl. CDef, 20 July 1940; *The* [Richmond] *Afro-American*, 30 December 1978. ChilWW. Cab Calloway and Bryant Rollins, *Of Minnie the Moocher & Me* (New York, 1976). Handy.

DISC: RustJR.

CALLOWAY, CABELL ("CAB"). Jazz-band leader/Singer (b. 25 December 1907 in Rochester, New York). He came from a musical family: his mother was a church organist and his brother Elmer and sister Blanche* became professional musicians. His family more, where he studied with Llewelyn Wilson* in his musical education in the public schools of Baltimore, where he studied with Llewelyn Wilson* at the high school. He also studied voice privately with Wilson and with Ruth Macabee. He sang in a church choir at an early age. He also began singing in local nightclubs during his high school years and played drums in a local group. His early style development was influenced by William ("Chick") Webb,* who performed in Baltimore during Calloway's formative years. In 1927 he began singing professionally, joining the musical revue *Plantation Days*, in which his sister Blanche was performing. When the show closed in Chicago, Illinois, he remained in the city; he attended Crane College for a short while and began singing in local nightclubs. By 1929 he had formed his own band, the Alabamians, which toured for a period, then went to New York, where it made its debut at the Savoy Ballroom in the Harlem community. The group was disbanded, however, within two weeks after its opening, and Calloway toured with the *Hot Chocolates* musical in a singing role. He was then invited to lead the Missourians, a group originally from Kansas City, Missouri, but then playing in New York. In the spring of 1930 his band went into the celebrated Cotton Club as a replacement for Edward ("Duke") Ellington.* During his two-year association with the club, the band changed personnel, becoming in reality his band; he broadcast every night from the club. In 1931 he made his recording debut and began writing his own songs, including one that became the theme song of his band, "Minnie the moocher." Within a short time he was firmly established as a successful bandleader. He toured widely with his big bands at home and abroad, recorded extensively, and appeared in numerous films, including *Ali Baba Goes to Town* (1937), *Dixie Jamboree* (1944), and *Stormy Weather* (1943), among many others. In 1947 he was forced to disband his big band for economic reasons; thereafter he worked with small groups, although he occasionally led a big band for special engagements, as in 1951. In 1952 he began a new career as a singing actor; he toured with Gershwin's folk opera *Porgy and Bess* (1952-54), the Harlem Globetrotters (1965, as a halftime show), and the Broadway musical *Hello, Dolly!* (1967-71). Between acting engagements he toured widely with a small group in Europe, South America, the Caribbean, and the United States. He continued to be active musically through the 1970s, singing in theaters, nightclubs, and resort areas; in the mid-1970s he toured with a show, *Sounds of the Forties*. Calloway was an important big-band leader of the 1930s-40s; those who played in his groups included many who would later become celebrated, among them, Leon ("Chu") Berry,* John ("Dizzy") Gillespie,* Daniel ("Danny") Barker,* Milton Hinton,* Tyree Glenn,* Robert ("Jonah") Jones,* Benny Payne, Hilton Jefferson, William ("Cozy") Cole,* Ben Webster,* and others. Although not the first to use "scat singing," he helped to popularize it with his "hi-de-ho." In 1976 he published his autobiography with Bryant Rollins, *Of Minnie the Moocher and Me*.

BIBL: ASCAP. ChilWW. FeaEJ. MeeJMov. WWBA.

DISC: Jep. Kink. RustJR.

CALLOWAY, EARL. Music critic (b. 4 October 1926 in Birmingham, Alabama). He obtained his musical education at Oakwood College in Huntsville, Alabama (1946-47), Chicago [Illinois] Musical College (B. Mus.), and Roosevelt University in Chicago. During his years of service in the U. S. Armed Forces (1951-53), he toured as a concert tenor in Japan and Korea. Thereafter he settled in Chicago, Illinois, where he became active in musical circles. He organized and directed community choirs and church choirs, and he taught music in the public schools. In 1960 he became music critic for the *Chicago Courier* and fine arts editor for the Associated Negro Press. In 1964 he was appointed music editor for the *Chicago Defender* and fine arts editor for the Negro Press International. He also toured as a lyric tenor and as a lecturer.

BIBL: Interview by Fanya Wiggins. WWA.

CAMPBELL, AMBROSE (née **AMBROSE OLADIPO ADEKOYA).** Jazz-band leader (b. 1919 in Lagos, Nigeria). He sang in a church choir as a child. During his school years he learned to play guitar and drums. In 1940 he left Lagos to follow the sea. During a lengthy shore leave in London, England, he formed the first Nigerian dance band in London. In 1944 he formed the Original West African Rhythm Brothers, which included West Indians and Europeans as well as Africans. His band toured widely as an entertainment unit and also as an accompanying group with the Ballets Africaines.

BIBL: *West African Review* (28 November 1959).

CAMPBELL, DELOIS BARRETT. Gospel singer. See **BARRETT CAMPBELL, DELOIS.**

CAMPBELL, LUCIE EDDIE. Gospel songwriter/Educator (b. 1885 in Duck Hill, Mississippi; d. January 1963 in Memphis, Tennessee). Her family moved to Memphis, Tennessee, when she was a child. She obtained her education in the public schools of Memphis; at Rust College in Holly Springs, Mississippi (B.A.); at the University of Chicago (Illinois); Columbia University Teachers College in New York; and at Tennessee A & I College in Nashville (M.A.). She became a public school teacher at an early age and spent the last forty years of her career at the Booker T. Washington High School in Memphis. She was active with the National Baptist Convention for many years (1916-47), serving at one time or another as a vice-president of the National Baptist Music Convention, as president of the National Baptist Choral Society, and as music director of the National Baptist Sunday School and Baptist Training Union Congress. She was also active in the community as church choir director and accompanist. She won wide recognition as a gospel song writer, publishing her first song, "Something within," in 1919. Her best-known songs included "The Lord is my Shepherd," "Heavenly sunshine," "I need Thee every hour," and "He understands, He'll say well done."

BIBL: Communication from Samuel Floyd. Heil. Jac. William E. Washington, ed., *Miss Lucy Speaks* (Nashville: The National Baptist Training Union Board, 1971).

CANNON, GUS ("BANJO JOE"). Bluesman (b. 12 September 1883 in Red Banks, Mississippi; d. 15 October 1979 in Memphis, Tennessee). He played on handmade banjos as a child. At the age of fifteen he began to play for local social entertainments after obtaining a real banjo and receiving a little instruction from Bud Jackson. In 1901 he made a cylinder recording at Belzoni, Mississippi, for the Victor Talking Machine Company—thereby becoming the first bluesman to record. He settled in Memphis, Tennessee, early in his career. In 1916 he began to play regularly in a blues band of Ripley, Tennessee, along with Noah Lewis and Ashley Thompson. Beginning in 1918 he toured every season with medicine shows, generally in a team with Hosie Woods. During his travels with Dr. Willie Lewis's medicine show, he played in a jug band with Walter ("Furry") Lewis,* Jim Jackson, and "Son Brimmer" (Will Shade).* He made his first disc recordings in 1927 with ("Blind") Arthur Blake* (Arthur Phelps) in Chicago; thereafter he recorded with his jug band, Cannon's Jug Stompers, which included at one time or another Elijah Avery, Lewis Thompson, and Hosie Woods, among others. He was musically active past his eighty-sixth birthday. His best-known blues was "Walk right in."

BIBL: BWW. CharCB. FeaEJ. Oliv. LivBl 44 (Autumn 1979).

DISC: DiGod. LeSlBr. RustJR. TudBM.

CAPERS, VALERIE. Jazz pianist/College professor (b. 1937 in New York, New York). She came from a musical family: her father, Alvin Capers, was a professional jazz pianist, and her brother Robert ("Bobby") played tenor saxophone and flute in the Ramon ("Mongo") Santamaria* band. She studied piano as a child. She became blind when she was six years old and attended the New York Institute for the Education of the Blind, where she continued to study piano along with her other studies. Later she attended the Juilliard School of Music (B. Mus., 1959; M. Mus., 1960). Her teaching career included tenures at the Manhattan School of Music in New York and at Bronx Community College of the City University of New York (1973-). She became interested in jazz through the influence of her brother and began her jazz career as a pianist in a local nightclub. Later she formed her own trio and made her recording debut in the 1960s. She began composing jazz pieces thereafter, encouraged by her brother, and in 1970 began writing music for chorus and other media. Her honors included a grant from the National Endowment for the Arts (1976). Her best-known works were the jazz-inflected Christmas cantata *Sing About Love* (1974) and the piece "El Toro."

BIBL: Black press, incl. AmstN, 16 June 1962; NYAge, 30 May 1959. NYT, 17 December 1978.

CARAVANS, THE. Gospel group (orig. 1953 in Chicago, Illinois). The all-female group was formed by Albertina ("Tina") Walker, formerly a lead singer with Robert Anderson's group. When she organized her group she drew upon ex-members of Anderson's group, among others. Over the years personnel of The Caravans included Inez Andrews, Shirley Caesar,* Cassietta George, Imogene Greene, Bessie Griffin,* Dorothy Norwood, and Delores Washington. About 1954 James Cleveland* joined the group and was active not only as a singer but also as a songwriter. Later other men sang with The Caravans, including Eddie Williams and James Herndon, who also were accompanists. Aretha Franklin* was among those who shared concerts or recorded with the group. From the mid-1950s to 1966, The Caravans was a leading gospel group. Its best-known performances included "Soldiers in the army," "The Blood will never lose its power," and "The solid Rock."

BIBL: Heil. Barbara Baker, "Black Gospel Music Styles, 1942-1975" (Ph.D. diss., University of Maryland, 1978).

DISC: Hayes.

CAREY, THOMAS DEVORE. Opera singer/College professor (b. 29 December 1931 in Bennettsville, South Carolina). He obtained his musical education at City College of the City University of New York (1954-58), the Stuttgart [Germany] Musikhochschule (1960-62), and the Munich [Germany] Musikhochschule (1962-65). He also studied with Hans Hotter and Rupert

Grundlach. In 1957 he made his debut as a concert baritone at Town Hall in New York. In 1961 he won prizes in the Munich International Competition and in s'Hertogenbosch International Competition; the next year he won a prize in the Brussels International Competition. In 1962 he made his European operatic debut with the Nederlandsche Opera Company of Amsterdam, The Netherlands, singing the role of Giorgio Germont in Verdi's *La Traviata*. His best-known roles were the title role of Verdi's *Rigoletto*, first sung with the Paris Opera; the role of Mel in Tippet's *The Knot Garden*, with the London Royal Opera (1971); Absolom in the German premiere of Kurt Weill's *Lost in the Stars*, with the Stuttgart Opera (1963); and the role of Joe in the London productions of the Hammerstein/Kern *Show Boat* (1971, 1977). He toured also as a concert singer, frequently with his wife, Carol Brice.* In 1969 he was appointed to the music faculty of the University of Oklahoma at Norman. His honors included awards from the Concert Artist Guild (1957), Marian Anderson Foundation (1961), and the Oklahoma Artist Award (1976); fellowships from such foundations as the John Hay Whitney (1960-62), Walter M. Sullivan (1959), and Martha Baird Rockefeller (1962-64). In 1977 he and his wife were named Oklahoma Musicians of the Year.

BIBL: WWA.

DISC: Turn.

CARLISLE, UNA MAE. Jazz singer (b. 26 December 1918 in Xenia, Ohio; d. 7 November 1956 in New York, New York). She sang in public at the age of three and studied piano as a child. She began her professional career when she was thirteen as a radio pianist in Cleveland, Ohio. She was spending her summer vacation in New York in 1932 when Thomas ("Fats") Waller* heard her perform and later invited her to appear on his show on Cincinnati [Ohio] radio station WWL. Thereafter she became a regular performer on the show and also toured with Waller's company. Her style development was deeply influenced by his pianism. After leaving the show she toured as a soloist on the nightclub circuit. In 1936 she went to Europe with the *Blackbirds of 1936* company, which featured Maude Russell, Jules Bledsoe,* the Nicholas Brothers, and J. Rosamond Johnson* in charge of the sixteen-voice choir. After touring with the show, she remained in Europe to tour as a soloist, returning home in 1940. She also appeared in films, recorded, studied music at the Sorbonne in Paris, and operated her own nightclub in the Montmartre area of Paris. Back in the United States she continued to perform as a nightclub entertainer, recorded, and appeared on radio and television shows. During the late 1940s she had her own radio and television shows. Illness forced her to retire in 1954. She was noted for her songs, of which the best known were "Walking by the river" and "I see a million people."

BIBL: Black press, incl. CDef, 2 May 1936. BMI (Issue No. 4, 1977). ChilWW. FeaEJ. MeeJMov. Maurice Waller and Anthony Calabrese, *Fats Waller* (New York, 1977).

DISC: Jep. Kink. RustJR.

CARNEY, HARRY HOWELL. Jazz saxophonist (b. 1 April 1910 in Boston, Massachusetts; d. 8 October 1974 in New York, New York). As a child he played piano, then clarinet, and finally alto saxophone. He began playing with a local band when he was thirteen; thereafter he played with various groups, including Charlie Holmes and Stanley ("Fess") Williams,* then joined Edward ("Duke") Ellington* (1927-74). After Ellington's death he played for a short period in the band under Mercer Ellington's* leadership. Early in his career he began playing baritone saxophone and later doubled on bass clarinet. He played with a powerful, intense tone and was a pioneer in defining the role of the jazz baritone saxophone. He recorded extensively with various groups and individual jazzmen and received many awards from the music industry.

BIBL: ChilWW. FeaEJ. FeaJS. FeaGitJS. MeeJMov.

DISC: Jep. Kink. RustJR.

CARR, LEROY. Blues pianist (b. 27 March 1905 in Nashville, Tennessee; d. 29 April 1935 in Memphis, Tennessee). Carr and Francis ("Scrapper") Blackwell won recognition as a team rather than as individual performers. Carr was taken to Indianapolis, Indiana, in 1912. Self-taught, he played piano as a child, joined a traveling circus while still a boy, and later served in the army. Blackwell came from a musical family and began playing on homemade guitars as a child. He moved to Indianapolis at the age of three. The two bluesmen met during the late 1920s and recorded together from 1928 to 1935, when Carr died. They complemented each other well: Carr's soft piano style and somewhat sharp voice gave contrast to Blackwell's warmer voice and long, single-string runs on the guitar. The team exerted wide influence on contemporary bluesmen, including "Bumble Bee Slim" (Amos Easton),* William ("Count") Basie,* and Jimmy Rushing, among others. They toured widely through the Middle West. Some blues scholars credit Carr and Blackwell with anticipating the Kansas City school of jazz: Carr's song materials were used by Kansas City bands, and Blackwell's guitar style paved the way for Charlie Christian* and Eddie Durham.

BIBL: BWW. CharCB. FeaEJ. Charles Keil, *Urban Blues* (Chicago, 1966). Oliv.
DISC: DiGod. Kink. LeSl. TudBM.

CARROLL, DIAHANN (née **CAROL DIAHANN JOHNSON**). Actress/Popular music singer (b. 17 July 1935 in New York, New York). Although best known as an actress, she was a performing musician in her early career. She sang in a church choir as a child and obtained her musical education at the High School of Music and Art in New York and at New York University. Encouraged by winning a prize on a television talent show, she began singing professionally in nightclubs in New York. As her career developed she sang in Broadway musicals, including *House of Flowers* (1954), and in film musicals, including *Carmen Jones* (1954), *Porgy and Bess* (1959), and *Paris Blues* (1961). She also sang on television programs and made recordings. During the 1960s she moved into the field of acting, taking leading nonsinging roles in both stage plays and films.
BIBL: NegA. WWA. WWBA.

CARTER, BENNETT LESTER ("BENNY"). Jazz saxophonist/Trumpeter (b. 8 August 1907 in New York. New York). He came from a musical family: his father played guitar, his mother played piano, and a cousin, Theodore ("Cuban") Bennett, was a professional jazz trumpeter. He was inspired to learn trumpet by his cousin and James ("Bubber") Miley,* but settled instead on the saxophone, which he studied with Francis Mikell* and Arthur Reeves. Later in his career he returned to the trumpet. He began playing professionally when he was about seventeen, joining a local group as an alto saxophonist. He played with various other groups thereafter, among them, Billy Paige in New York and Louis Deppe* in Pittsburgh. In 1925 he went to Wilberforce College in Ohio to study theology, but instead he joined Horace Henderson's* Wilberforce Collegians (intermittently 1925-28) and left college to travel with the band when it went on its annual summer tour. Thereafter he played with Fletcher Henderson* (1928-29, 1930-31, 1934), William ("Chick") Webb* (1931), Charlie Johnson (1927), William McKinney's* Cotton Pickers (as musical director, 1931-32), William Bryant (1935), and Charlie Barnet (1935), among others. He also led his own groups at intervals. In 1935 he went to Europe, where he played with Willie Lewis in Paris, France, and later with Henry Hall's BBC Orchestra in London, England, and Freddy Johnson in Amsterdam, The Netherlands. During his three-year sojourn in Europe (1935-38), he also toured as a soloist and was active as an arranger. After returning to the United States he formed a big band, which made its debut at the Savoy Ballroom in the Harlem community of New York in 1940. During the next few years he led big bands and small groups in New York and on the West Coast. In 1945 he settled permanently at Los Angeles, California, and continued to lead his own groups through the 1950s-60s. During those years he also toured abroad with Norman Granz's Jazz at the Philharmonic shows and as a soloist (1961, 1968) and played for a short period with Edward ("Duke") Ellington,* among others. Carter had an active career as an arranger, dating back to his tenure with Fletcher Henderson. Those for whom he arranged over the years included Duke Ellington, Charlie Johnson, Theodore ("Teddy") Hill,* and Benny Goodman, among others. His position with Henry Hall in London was that of arranger rather than instrumentalist. Beginning in the 1940s he gave more and more time to writing and arranging music, particularly for films and later for television shows. His film scores included *A Man Called Adam* (1966), *Red Sky at Morning* (1970), and *Buck and the Preacher* (1972), among others; he wrote music for such television shows as "Ironside," "Name of the Game," "Bob Hope Presents," the Alfred Hitchcock shows, the Chrysler Theater series, and many others. He also appeared in numerous films as soloist, with his band, or on film soundtracks. He was active as musical director for various jazz figures, including Pearl Bailey,* Ray Charles,* and Maria Muldaur, among others. During the 1970s he toured regularly in Europe, and performed in Japan and Australia; in 1976 he toured in the Middle East under sponsorship of the U.S. Department of State. He also became involved in college teaching and served as visiting professor or workshop consultant in several institutions, among them Baldwin-Wallace, Eisenhower College, Yale, Cornell, and Duke University. He was a visiting professor at Princeton three times (1973, 1977, 1979). Carter received several awards from the music industry; his other honors included appointment to panels of professional organizations and an honorary doctorate from Princeton University (1974). Carter was regarded as one of the most versatile musicians of his time. He recorded regularly throughout his career with his own groups and with others. As an alto saxophonist he exerted large influence upon the development of that instrument in the jazz ensemble, along with Johnny Hodges;* his style was lyrical and eloquent. As a bandleader he earned the nickname, "The King." He is credited with having recorded the first flute solo with a big band (Wayman Carver on "Devil's holiday," 1933) and the first to augment the saxophone section to five instruments. As an arranger he helped to lay the foundation for the big band swing orchestra, along with Fletcher Henderson and Donald ("Don") Redman.* He was also noted as a composer. His best-known pieces were "Blues in my heart," "When lights are low," "Cow cow boogie," and the orchestral *Kansas City Suite*, written for William ("Count") Basie.*

BIBL: ASCAP. ChilWW. DanceWS. FeaEJ. FeaJS. FeaGitJS. MeeJMov. WWA.

DISC: Jep. Kink. RustJR. TudJ.

CARTER, BETTY (née **LILLIE MAE JONES**). Jazz singer (b. 16 May 1930 in Flint, Michigan). She studied at the Detroit Conservatory of Music. After winning first prize in an amateur show in 1946, she began singing professionally. She toured with various groups, including Lionel Hampton* (1948-51), Miles Davis* (1958-59), and Theodore ("Sonny") Rollins* (1963 in Japan), among others. She also toured widely as a soloist, appearing in nightclubs and theaters. Beginning in the 1970s she toured on the college circuit and lectured; she also recorded regularly and founded her own record company in 1971. She was credited with expanding the language of swing jazz to include bebop elements in the tradition of Billie Holiday and Ella Fitzgerald. Her best-known albums were *Baby, It's Cold Outside* and *The Invisible Betty Carter* (with Ray Charles*). She received her nickname, "Betty Bebop," during her tenure with Hampton.

BIBL: Black press, incl. CDef, 25 March 1976; PhilaT, 1 December 1973. FeaEJ. FeaJS. FeaGitJS. WWA, 1976-77.

DISC: Jep.

CARTER, BO. Bluesman. See **MISSISSIPPI SHEIKS, THE.**

CARTER, DENNIS DRUMMOND. Brass bandsman (b. in Accomac County, Virginia; fl. in mid-nineteenth century in Philadelphia, Pennsylvania). See also **JOHNSON, FRANCIS.** He was a member of Frank Johnson's* band and was elected chairman after Johnson's death in April 1844. Carter remained with the band, which was directed by Joseph Anderson,* until the early 1850s, when he went west, finally settling in San Francisco, California. There he won wide recognition as a music teacher and band leader.

BIBL: *The Public Ledger* [Philadelphia], 13 April 1844; *Pacific Appeal* [San Francisco], 15 August 1862.

CARTER, RONALD LEVIN ("RON"). Jazz bassist (b. 4 May 1937 in Ferndale, Michigan). He came from a musical family in which all the children played instruments. As a child he played with other siblings in chamber groups. He began playing cello at the age of ten, then changed to string bass during his high-school years in Detroit. He obtained his musical education at the Eastman School of Music in Rochester, New York (B. Mus., 1959), where he played in the Rochester Philharmonic (1958-59) and the Eastman Philharmonia (1959), conducted by Howard Hanson; and at the Manhattan School of Music in New York (M. Mus., 1961), where he played in the institution's symphony orchestra (1960-61). His teaching career included tenures at Washington University in St. Louis, Missouri, and at Manhattan School of Music. He first played professionally in Detroit with local groups and led his own groups during his college years in Rochester. In 1959 he settled in New York. Thereafter he played with various groups, including Foreststorn ("Chico") Hamilton,* Randolph ("Randy") Weston,* Thelonious Monk,* and in a trio with Robert ("Bobby") Timmons and Albert Heath.* He began to record extensively in 1962. During the 1960s-70s he also played with such groups as Miles Davis (1963-68),* Michael Legrand, the New York Bass Choir, and the New York Jazz Quartet. He toured widely in the United States, Europe, and Japan with others, with his own quartets, and as a soloist, appearing on television shows, in concert halls and theaters, nightclubs, on college campuses, and at jazz festivals. From 1975 on he performed largely with his own quartet; in his "new" quartet he played a piccolo bass. Those who played in his groups at one time or another included Kenneth ("Kenny") Barron,* Ben Riley, Charles ("Buster") Williams, and Larry Willis. For his solo appearances, Carter commissioned works from such classical composers as Noel DaCosta* and William Fischer* as well as jazz composers. He published technical manuals, *Building a Jazz Bass Line*, in three volumes. He received numerous awards from the music industry. He was one of the leading bassists of his generation, along with Richard Davis*, and exerted enormous influence upon his contemporaries.

BIBL: *Encore* (8 December 1975). FeaEJ. FeaJS. FeaGitJS. Milt Hinton, "New Giant of the Bass" in *Jazz Magazine* 2 (Winter 1978). MeeJMov. WWA.

DISC: Jep. ModJ.

CARTER, VIVIAN. Disc jockey/Record producer. See **BRACKEN, JAMES.**

CATLETT, SIDNEY ("BIG SID"). Jazz drummer (b. 17 January 1910 in Evansville, Indiana; d. 25 March 1951 in Chicago, Illinois). As a child he played piano, but changed to drums, which he played in a school band. He received his education in an elementary school of Evansville, Indiana, and at Tilden High School in Chicago, Illinois, where he studied drums with Joe Russek. He began playing professionally about 1928 with Darnell Howard.* Thereafter he played with various groups, including Sammy Stewart (1929-30), Elmer Snowden* (1931-32), Bennett ("Benny") Carter* (1932-33), Rex Stewart (1933), the [James] Jeter/[Hayes] Pillars band (1935), Fletcher Henderson* (1936), Donald ("Don") Redman* (1936-38), Louis Armstrong* (1938-41, 1941-42), Benny Goodman (1941), and Theodore ("Teddy") Wilson* (1942-44), among others. He also led his own groups during these years and was active as a free-lancer. During the years 1944-47 he led a quartet, and in 1946 he had a big band for a short period. Thereafter he played with the Louis Armstrong All Stars (1947-49), then was active primarily in nightclubs. Catlett was a highly versatile drummer who could play in all the styles, from New Orleans traditional to bebop, but was especially noted as a swing drummer.

BIBL: AlHen. ChilWW. FeaEJ. Whitney Balliett, *Improvising* (New York, 1977).

DISC: Jep. Kink.

CATO, MINTO. Opera singer (b. 4 September 1900 in Little Rock, Arkansas; d. 26 October 1979 in New York, New York). She obtained her musical education at the Washington Conservatory of Music in Washington, D.C., then under the direction of Harriet Gibbs Marshall.* She taught in public schools in Arkansas and Georgia, then went to Detroit, Michigan, where she conducted a music studio. During the 1920s she began singing professionally and toured widely with her husband's show, Joe Sheftal and his Southland Revue, in Europe, Canada, Mexico, Australia, and the South Sea Islands. After returning to the United States she settled in New York. Thereafter she appeared in Broadway musicals and cabaret revues, including *Keep Shufflin'* (1928), the Connie's Inn revue *Hot Chocolates* (1929), and *Blackbirds of 1930*, among others. During the 1930s-40s she sang mezzo-soprano roles with opera companies, among them Salmaggi's production of Verdi's *Aida* at the New York Hippodrome (1937), and productions of Mary Cardwell Dawson's* National Negro Opera Company, including Verdi's *Il Trovatore* (1944) and *La Traviata* (1947).

BIBL: Black press, incl. AmstN, 3 November 1979; CDef, 16 March 1929; 5 December 1931; 3 April 1937; 11 November 1944.

CELESTIN, OSCAR ("SONNY," "PAPA"). Jazz trumpeter (b. 1 January 1884 in Napoleonville, Louisiana; d. 15 December 1954 in New Orleans, Louisiana). He first played guitar and mandolin, then later changed to trombone and trumpet. He began his professional career at St. Charles, Louisiana, where he played in a brass band. About 1906 he settled in New Orleans, Louisiana. Thereafter he played with various brass bands, including the Algiers, Allen's, the Olympia, and Jack Carey, among others. About 1909 or 1910 he joined the Tuxedo Band, which played at the Tuxedo Dance Hall and, according to George ("Pops") Foster* and other jazzmen of New Orleans, was led by William ("Bebé") Ridgley. There is some controversy as to whether Celestin or Ridgley founded the Tuxedo; for many years they were co-leaders. After they separated in 1925 Celestin formed Celestin's Original Tuxedo Jazz Orchestra. He played long residencies in the city, toured in the South, and made several recordings. During the mid-1930s-40s he was forced to work outside music but continued to lead a band. About 1946 he reentered the field, recorded again, appeared on radio and television, and played residencies in nightclubs. In 1955 his band performed in the film *Cinerama Holiday*. Those who performed in his groups at one time or another included Emma Barrett,* Ricard Alexis, Paul Barnes, Jeanette Salvant, and Alphonse Picou,* among others.

BIBL: ChilWW. FeaEJ. MeeJMov. Souch. *Pops Foster, The Autobiography of a New Orleans Jazzman as Told to Tom Stoddard* (Berkeley, 1971).

DISC: RustJR. Jep.

CHAMBERS, JOSEPH ("JOE"). Jazz drummer (B. 25 June 1942 in Stoneacre, Virginia). See **HAKIM, TALIB RASUL.**

CHAMBERS, PAUL LAURENCE DUNBAR, JR. Jazz bassist (B. 22 April 1935 in Pittsburgh, Pennsylvania; d. 4 January 1969 in New York, New York). He began his professional career about 1949 playing tuba and baritone horn in Detroit, Michigan, then later changed to string bass. He played with various groups during the years 1949-54, including Kenneth ("Kenny") Burrell,* Paul Quinchette, and George Wallington, among others, then joined Miles Davis* (1955-61). Thereafter he toured in a trio with James ("Jimmy") Cobb and Wynton Kelly (1961-65), then was active as a free-lancer. He recorded extensively and received many awards from the music industry. Chambers was a leading bassist of his generation and was credited with being the first to combine arco and pizzicato in his solos. His style was expressive and exploited fully the potential of his instrument.

BIBL: FeaEJ. FeaJS. FeaGitJS. Bill Cole, *Miles Davis* (New York, 1974).

DISC: Jep. ModJ.

CHAMBERS, STEPHEN. See **HAKIM, TALIB RASUL.**

CHAPPELLE, PATRICK HENRY ("PAT"). Vaudeville-troupe manager (b. 7 January 1869 in Jacksonville, Florida; d. 21 October 1911 in Tampa, Florida). He began his professional career playing in a string trio with two other boys. In 1899 he organized the Imperial Colored Minstrels, with which he toured widely. He also took over management of theaters in Jacksonville and Tampa, Florida. In April 1900 he organized a touring company to produce musical comedies, the first of which was a two-act musical titled *A Rabbit's Foot*. Within a few years that title was used to apply to the company itself, as Pat Chappelle's Rabbit Foot Company. Chappelle died at an early age, but his company lived for many years. He was called ''the Black Barnum,'' after circus magnate Phineas Taylor Barnum, because of his achievements as a showman. In 1912 Fred S. Walcott took over management (1912-1951) of Chappelle's Rabbit Foot Company, retaining its original name and using Port Gibson, Mississippi, as its home base. When Gertrude (''Ma'') Rainey* and Bessie Smith* toured with the tent show in 1915, it was still called by its original name. Later, the name was changed to F. S. Walcott's Rabbit Foot Minstrels; the company was touring as late as the 1950s. Those who played in the Rabbit Foot Minstrels over the years included Butterbeans and Susie* (Jody and Susie Edwards), (''Sleepy'') John Estes,* Bertha (''Chippie'') Hill,* Walter (''Brownie'') McGhee,* Louis Jordan,* Willie Nix, Hammie Nixon,* and (''Big'') Joe Williams,* among others.

BIBL: BWW. Black press, incl. CDef, 12 June 1943, 23 June 1956; IndF, 22 April 1899, 16 May 1908, 25 November 1911, 16 November 1912. OlivSB.

CHARIOTEERS, THE. Popular music group (org. in Wilberforce, Ohio; fl. 1930s-40s). Originally called The Southern Black Birds, the vocal quartet was organized during the early 1930s at Wilberforce College in Ohio by a faculty member, Howard Daniel. It was composed of William B. Williams (lead), George Lubers (second tenor), John Harewood (baritone), with Daniel as bass. The group began its professional career singing on Cincinnati radio station WLW (c1933-35). About 1935 the quartet went to New York, where it attracted national recognition. Personnel changes included Edward Jackson for Lubers and Ira Williams for Harewood. In 1938 the Charioteers appeared in the Broadway musical *Hellzapoppin*. During the years 1942-47 the group appeared regularly on the Kraft Music Hall television show. The group toured widely and recorded many albums.

BIBL: Black press, incl. CDef, 1 June 1935.

DISC: Kink.

CHARLES, RAY (née **RAY CHARLES ROBINSON).** Rhythm 'n' blues singer (b. 23 September 1930 in Albany, Georgia). His family moved to Greenville, Florida, when he was an infant. When he was three years old he was given access to a piano in the neighborhood cafe, and he taught himself to play, inspired by the proprietor, Wylie Pitman, a boogie-woogie piano player. He began going blind when he was five years old and within two years was totally blind. He obtained his musical education at the State School for the Blind in St. Augustine, Florida. He left school when his mother died, and at fifteen began his professional career. He first played piano in bars and clubs of Jacksonville, Florida, then moved to other cities in the state. When he was eighteen he settled in Seattle, Washington, where he organized his own group, the McSon Trio. His early style development was influenced by Nat King Cole* (née Nathaniel Coles), both as singer and pianist, and his first group imitated the Cole and Charles Brown sound. The trio played regularly in local places and on radio and television programs. He wrote arrangements for his group and for others; in 1948 he made his first recordings, and he dropped the Robinson from his name. In 1950 he settled in Los Angeles, California. His trio had difficulty in finding engagements, and within a short period his management sent him on tour as a single with Lowell Fulson* (1950-52). After leaving Fulson he toured as a soloist, then formed a seven-piece group in 1954, for which he wrote and arranged the music as well as played piano and alto saxophone, and sang. He developed a distinctive style, combining elements of spirituals and blues in the songs he wrote. His group toured widely, particularly in the South, playing on the black theater circuit. He made his recording debut as a band leader in 1954 and occasionally played for such artists as Ruth Brown. Eventually he established himself as the leading entertainer of his time, whose versatile group could perform jazz, blues, rhythm 'n' blues, or gospel with authority. In 1959 he attracted wide attention for his so-called ''secularized gospel''; in 1962 he combined gospel elements with country and western music, as in the albums *Modern Sounds in Country and Western Music*. In 1976 he combined yet two other styles, transforming patriotic songs into gospel. He toured widely throughout the world with his show, which included a female vocal group, The Raeletts, speciality acts, and a big band (sometimes large orchestras with strings, particularly for recordings). He performed on television shows and in films or on film soundtracks, including *Ballad in Blue* (1964) and *The Cincinnati Kid* (1965). Charles exerted enormous influence upon others as a band leader, composer, and performer. He is credited with having developed the concept of soul, the merging of gospel, rhythm 'n' blues, and popular music into a musical entity. He received numerous awards from the music industry. In 1978 he published his autobiography, *Brother Ray*, with David Ritz.

BIBL: ASCAP. CurBiog (April 1965). ContKey (July 1980). EAB. FeaEJ. FeaJS. FeaGitJS. *Ebony* (September 1960, October 1974). Michael Lydon, *Boogie Lightning* (New York, 1974). MeeJMov. WWA. WWBA.

DISC: Jep. TudBM.

CHARLTON, MELVILLE. Church organist (b. 26 August 1880 in New York, New York; d. 13 November 1973 in New York, New York). He studied piano as a child and obtained his musical education in the public schools. He studied further at the City College of New York and the National Conservatory of Music, where he studied organ and composition with Charles Heinroth and music history with Henry Finck. He also studied choral conducting, taking a course with J. M. Heffenstein of Grace Church. His professional career included tenures as organist at the Jewish Temple of Covenant (1914-24) and the Union Theological Seminary (1911-c40). In 1915 he was the first black American to pass the examination of the American Guild of Organists for admission to the rank of an associate. During the early twentieth century he played regularly in concerts, both as piano or organ soloist and as an accompanist; he frequently toured as accompanist with Harry T. Burleigh.* In 1924 he received an honorary doctorate from Howard University. Over the years his piano piece, "Poem Erotique," has remained popular with concert pianists.

BIBL: Black press, incl. CDef, 29 May 1920; IndF, 8 May 1915; NYAge, 19 January 1905, 1 April 1909. WWCA, 1940-1950.

CHATMAN, PETER ("MEMPHIS SLIM"). Bluesman (b. 3 September 1915 in Memphis, Tennessee). His father played piano and guitar; he began playing piano professionally before he was sixteen. The chief influence upon his piano style was Roosevelt Sykes.* In 1937 he went to Chicago; within a short while he had won recognition as a top blues pianist and in 1940 he began to record. The same year he joined "Big Bill" (William Lee Conley) Broonzy,* whose group also included "Sonny Boy Williamson, No. 1" (John Lee Williamson),* among others. Later he formed his own groups, playing music that at times was only blues-tinged. In 1959 he returned to folk blues; the next few years he toured widely, appearing at the major festivals, and recorded extensively. In 1960 he went to Europe to perform and record; eventually he settled in Paris, France. He had a longtime association with Willie Dixon,* with whom he toured and recorded in the United States and abroad. He and Dixon were responsible for the organization of the American Folk Blues Festival, which made its first European tour in 1962. As a songwriter, he was best remembered for "Everyday I have the blues," popularized first by Lowell Fulson* and later by Joe Williams* with the William ("Count") Basie* orchestra.

BIBL: BWW. CharLB. FeaEJ. FeaJS. MeeJMov. Oliv. ShawWS.

DISC: LeSlBR. TudBM.

CHATMON (aka **CHATMAN), ARMENTER ("BO").** Bluesman (b. 21 March 1893 in Bolton, Mississippi; d. 21 September 1964 in Memphis, Tennessee). See **MISSISSIPPI SHEIKS, THE.**

CHATMON (aka **CHATMAN), SAM.** Bluesman (b. 10 January 1897 in Bolton, Mississippi). See **MISSISSIPPI SHEIKS, THE.**

CHATMON FAMILY. Bluesmen. See **MISSISSIPPI SHEIKS, THE.**

CHAUVIN, LOUIS. Ragtime pianist/Composer (b. 13 March 1881 in St. Louis, Missouri; d. 26 March 1908 in Chicago, Illinois). He was regarded as the best rag pianist of his time, which included such top pianists as Joe Jordan,* Sam Patterson,* and Charlie Warfield.* He began his career, along with his friend Patterson, touring with the Alabama Jubilee Singers in the summer of 1894. Later he and Patterson formed a quartet, the Mozart Comedy Four, which performed locally. He also began to play piano in the tenderloin district during this period. In 1903 he and Patterson collaborated in publishing the song "The moon is shining in the skies," and during the same year wrote a musical, *Dandy Coon*, for which Joe Jordan* served as musical and stage director. The show toured briefly before becoming stranded in Des Moines, Iowa. During the St. Louis World's Fair in 1904, Chauvin and Patterson played piano in a beer hall on the fair grounds; afterwards Chauvin returned to the red-light district. In 1907 he went to Chicago; he was playing in a cafe on Chicago's South Side when he was taken fatally ill.

Chauvin's style development was influenced by Tom Turpin,* an important figure in the St. Louis rag school. In turn, Chauvin is credited with having influenced Scott Joplin;* the two collaborated on the rag "Heliotrope Bouquet."

BIBL: Blesh. BPIM 3 (Spring, Fall 1975). JaTi.

CHEATHAM, ADOLPHUS ANTHONY ("DOC"). Jazz trumpeter (b. 13 June 1905 in Nashville, Tennessee). As a child he played cornet and played in a local church boy's band, where he took lessons from the bandleader. At an early age he began playing in the pit orchestra of the local Bijou Theatre, where the visiting shows included such singers as Clara Smith,* Ethel Waters,* Bessie Smith,* and Gertrude (''Ma'') Rainey.* About 1924 he began touring with bands, playing saxophone as well as trumpet, including Marion Hardy's band for the Sunshine Sammy Revue and later Albert (''Al'') Wynn. In 1926 he settled in Chicago, Illinois, and led his own group for a short period. Thereafter he played with various groups, including William (''Chick'') Webb,* Sam Wooding* (1928-30 in Europe), McKinney's Cotton Pickers* (1931-32), Cabell (''Cab'') Calloway* (1932-39), Theodore (''Teddy'') Wilson* (1939), the Eddie Heywood* Sextet (1943-45), among many others. During the 1950s-70s he played regularly with Latin-American bands, led his own groups at intervals (particularly 1960-65), and conducted a music studio. He also played with Benny Goodman, Wilbur DeParis,* Ricardo Rey, Leonard (''Red'') Balaban, and others. His touring took him frequently to Europe, including Russia, and to South America (1968) and Africa (1960). He played at the major jazz festivals with various groups, including the New York Jazz Repertory Company. In 1971 he worked with the Broadway musical *Two Gentlemen of Verona*. He recorded regularly with many jazz groups and published a manual, *Ad Lib Chord Reading*.

BIBL: ChilWW. DanceWS. Cab Calloway, *Of Minnie the Moocher and Me* (New York, 1976). FeaEJ. FeaGitJS. MeeJMov. Michael Ullman, *Jazz Lives* (Washington, D.C., 1980).

DISC: Jep. Kink.

CHECKER, CHUBBY. See **EVANS, ERNEST.**

CHEEKS, JULIUS ("JUNE"). Gospel singer (b. 7 August 1929 in Spartanburg, South Carolina; died 27 January 1981 in Miami, Florida). He was an ordained minister as well as gospel singer. His early style development was influenced by his hearing live performances of blues singer Albert (''Blind Boy'') Fuller* and recordings of the Dixie Hummingbirds,* The Fairfield Four, and the Soul Stirrers.* In the early 1940s he began singing professionally with a local group, The Baronets. Thereafter he sang with various groups, including the Sensational Nightingales (1946, intermittently through the 1950s), the Soul Stirrers (two years during the late 1940s), his own group, the Sensational Knights (after 1960), and the Mighty Clouds of Joy.* When he sang with the Nightingales group, it included Paul Owens, Jo Jo Wallace, Carl Coates (guitarist), and Howard Carroll; during his tenure in the group he developed many hallmarks of his style that would later exert wide influence upon both gospel and rhythm 'n' blues singers. He wrote and arranged songs for the groups with whom he performed and early added piano to the conventional guitar and drum accompaniment for gospel quartet singing. He was regarded as one of the originators, along with Claude Jeter, of rock- or soul-gospel. His style was distinctive for his free use of falsetto and shouting; he was one of the first gospel singers to move into the audience during a performance and shake hands with the spectators. His best-known performances included solos of ''Burying ground,'' ''Standing at the judgement,'' ''The last mile of the way,'' ''To the end,'' and ''Just crying.''

BIBL: Black press, incl. AmstN, 15 February 1981. Heil.

CHERRY, DONALD EUGENE ("DON"). Jazz trumpeter (B. 18 November 1936 in Oklahoma City, Oklahoma). His family moved to Los Angeles, California, when he was four years old. He began playing trumpet as a child and played with a high-school jazz orchestra led by David Brown. He played professionally with local groups at an early age, among them, Dexter Gordon* and Wardell Gray. About 1955 he came into contact with Ornette Coleman* and joined a group of young musicians with whom Coleman worked out musical ideas in George Newman's garage. Before Coleman organized a formal group, Cherry made recordings with him: *Something Else! The Music of Ornette Coleman* (1958) and *Tomorrow Is the Question* (1958). Thereafter he played in Coleman's quintet (1959-62), going to New York in 1959. Both men attended the School of Jazz in Lenox, Massachusetts, in the summer of 1959. After Coleman's group was disbanded, Cherry played with others, including Steven Lacy and Theodore (''Sonny'') Rollins,* and helped to found the New York Contemporary Five with Archie Shepp* and John Tchicai* (1963). He first toured in Europe in 1963 and returned that year to settle in Paris, France, then later in Sweden. He toured widely in Europe with his own Donald Cherry Quintet and with others, including Albert Ayler,* George Russell,* and Ornette Coleman (1969). He returned frequently to the United States to perform and to record, with the Jazz Composers Orchestra (1968) and Charlie Hayden (1969), among others. He also appeared at jazz festivals on both sides of the Atlantic and in films, both as performer and as composer of music for soundtracks, as in *The Holy Mountain* (1973). He was active as a teacher also on both sides of the Atlantic, serving as an artist-in-residence at Dartmouth College and teaching music for the Workers Educational Guild in Sweden. His best-known albums were *Complete Communion, Symphony for Improvisers*, and *Where Is Brooklyn.* Cherry was called the "poet of free jazz." As a partner for Coleman he was the second major architect of the free jazz movement. He played a cornet-like "pocket trumpet" in an intensely lyrical and elegant style. In his later career he introduced Far Eastern elements and instruments, particularly flutes, into his music for both small groups and his European big bands, such as the Eternal Rhythm Orchestras.

BIBL: BMI (November 1971). FeaEJ. FeaJS. FeaGitJS. A. B. Spellman, *Black Music* (1966; reprint, New York, 1970).

DISC: ModJ. TudJ.

CHILDERS, LULU. College professor (b. 28 February 1870 in Dryridge, Kentucky; d. 6 March 1946 in Howell, Michigan). She was graduated from the Oberlin Conservatory of Music (diploma, 1896; B. Mus., 1906) with a major in piano. She served as director of music at Knoxville College in Tennessee for five years (1900-05), then went to Howard University in Washington, D.C., as a music instructor. In 1912 she became a professor of voice and director of the School of Music. Under her leadership the music program at Howard flourished; the university Choral Society under her direction won critical acclaim for its periodic concerts, particularly its presentations of Handel's *Messiah* and Samuel Coleridge-Taylor's* *Hiawatha* trilogy. In 1940 she retired as Dean of the Howard School of Music, and in 1942 was given an honorary degree by Howard.

BIBL: MSCent. Black press, incl. NYAge, 30 November 1905; IndF, 24 October 1908. Rayford Logan, *Howard University: The First Hundred Years* (New York, 1969).

CHORAL STUDY CLUB. Community choral group (org. in 1900 in Chicago, Illinois). This community chorus was organized by Pedro Tinsley* in 1900. After illness forced him to retire in 1917, George Duncan took over leadership of the group. During the early twentieth century Kemper Harreld* was assistant conductor. Others associated with the group over the years included pianist-accompanists Gertrude Smith Jackson* and Pelargie Blair, organist Walter Gossett,* and director Tom Theodore Taylor,* among others. The Choral Study Club gave annual concerts, for which guest artists often were imported from the East.

BIBL: Black press, incl. CDef, 27 January 1917.

CHRISTIAN, CHARLES ("CHARLIE"). Jazz guitarist (b. 29 July 1916 in Bonham, Texas; d. 2 March 1942 in New York, New York). He came from a musical family: his father played blues guitar, his mother played piano, and his four brothers played musical instruments. His family moved to Oklahoma City, Oklahoma, when he was five years old. As a child he played trumpet; when he was twelve he changed to guitar and played in the family string band. He began playing professionally when he was fifteen with local groups. During the 1930s he played with various groups, including his brother's Jolly Jugglers, Alphonso Trent, Mary Mae Winburn, and the [James] Jeter/[Hayes] Pillars Orchestra, among others. He also formed his own group, and when he was eighteen began playing electric guitar. In 1939 he joined the Benny Goodman Sextet (1939-41), which included Theodore ("Teddy") Wilson* and Lionel Hampton*; he made his first recordings the same year with the Sextet. Thereafter he recorded extensively with Goodman and with others until his fatal illness in 1941. He appeared in John Hammond's legendary From Spirituals to Swing concert at Carnegie Hall in New York in December 1939. During his sojourn in New York he played with jazzmen who were experimenting with new sounds and rhythms at Minton's Playhouse in the Harlem community, producing the music that would later be called bebop, along with John ("Dizzy") Gillespie,* Oscar Pettiford,* Don Byas,* Milton Hinton,* Kenneth ("Kenny") Clarke,* and Thelonious Monk,* among many others. Clarke and Monk were in Minton's house band. Christian redefined the role of the jazz guitar, turning it into an instrument that played solos in the same way as saxophones. Although Eddie Durham* is credited with being the first to use amplified guitar in the jazz ensemble, it was Christian who made such a strong impact with his electric guitar that jazzmen after him discarded their acoustic guitars. As a participant in the jam sessions at Minton's, he was an architect of the bebop era.

BIBL: ChilWW. FeaEJ. Rudi Blesh, *Combo: U.S.A.* (Philadelphia, 1971). Dizzy Gillespie with Al Fraser, *To Be Or Not to Bop* (New York, 1979). MeeJMov. Russ.

DISC: Kink. RustJR. TudJ.

CLARK, EDGAR ROGIE. Music educator (b. 4 April 1913 in Atlanta, Georgia; d. 15 February 1978 in Detroit, Michigan). He obtained his musical education at Clark College in Atlanta, Georgia (B.A., 1935); Columbia University Teachers College in New York (M.A.), Chicago [Illinois] Musical College, the Juilliard School of Music in New York, and the Berkshire

Music Festival in Tanglewood, Massachusetts. His early career development was aided by Kemper Harreld* and Roland Hayes.* During his college years he sang in recitals as a tenor; in later years he sang professionally as a baritone. His teaching career included tenures at Fort Valley [Georgia] State College (1936); in the public schools of the city of New York (1944-47); at Jackson [Mississippi] State College (1949-c51); in the public schools of Toledo, Ohio; at Wayne County Community College in Detroit, Michigan; and in the public schools of Warren Woods, Michigan (1966-78). He toured widely as a lecturer, particularly on folklore, and as a choral conductor, workshop consultant, and concert singer. He was active also as a producer of radio and television programs: in New York he produced the series ''Americans All'' for radio station WNYC; in Detroit he produced a weekly television program for WLBT. He published articles on black folksong in such journals as *Journal of American Folklore, Musical America, Music Journal, Journal of Negro Education*, and *Phylon*, among others. His book-length works included a completed manuscript, ''The Black Bard: A Study of Negro Folk Music.'' He was perhaps best known, however, as a composer. He was a pioneer in publishing song collections by black composers, of which the best known were *Negro Art Songs* and *Copper Sun*. Other well-known works of his included the opera *Ti Yette*, *Fete Creole* for orchestra, *John Henry Fantasy* for band, and the collections *Six Afro-American Carols for Christmas* and *Six Afro-American Carols for Easter*. His honors included fellowships from the Ford Foundation, John Hay Whitney Foundation, National Endowment for the Arts, and an award from the National Association of Negro Musicians* (1973).

BIBL: DetAH. Questionnaire. ASCAP. Black press, including AmstN, 29 June 1944. Ray Lawless, *Folksingers and Folksongs in America* (New York, 1960). WWCA, 1950.

CLARK, JAMES. Military fifer. (b. 1804 in Burke County, Georgia; d. after 1904 in Emanuel County, Georgia). He served with Company K, Twenty-Eighth Georgia Regiment, Confederate Army, as a fifer during the Civil War. According to the record, he was not an enlisted man but was paid by the company for his services as a fifer.

BIBL: GreBD.

CLARK, ROGIE. See **CLARK, EDGAR ROGIE.**

CLARKE, KENNETH SPEARMAN ("KENNY" "KLOOK"). Jazz drummer (b. 9 January 1914 in Pittsburgh, Pennsylvania). He came from a musical family: his father played trombone, and his brothers played drums and string bass. He obtained his musical education in the public schools of Pittsburgh, Pennsylvania, where he studied instruments and theory in high school. He began playing professionally about 1930; he toured with various groups, including Leroy Bradley (c1930-33), Roy Eldridge* (1933), the [James] Jeter/[Hayes] Pillars band in St. Louis, Edgar Hayes (1937-38, including tour in Scandinavia), and Theodore (''Teddy'') Hill* (1938-39), among others. After Hill gave up his band, he became manager of Minton's Playhouse in the Harlem community and hired Clarke to lead the house band, which included Thelonious Monk,* among others. Black musicians from all over the city developed the habit of gathering at Minton's and Clark Monroe's Uptown House after working hours for jam sessions where they experimented with new ideas and/or competed with each other in exhibiting their musical and technical skills. Among those who participated, along with Clarke and Monk, in the experimental music, later to be called bebop, were John (''Dizzy'') Gillespie,* Oscar Pettiford,* Charlie Christian,* Milton Hinton,* Illinois Jacquet,* and many others. During the 1940s-50s Clarke was active with various groups, including Bennett (''Benny'') Carter* (1941-42), John (''Dizzy'') Gillespie (1946, 1948), Henry (''Red'') Allen* (1947), Tadd Dameron* (1948), and William (''Billy'') Eckstine* (1951), as well as his own groups occasionally. During his years of service in the U.S. Armed Forces (1943-45), he played in army bands. In 1952 he was a founding member of the Modern Jazz Quartet and remained with the group three years (1952-55). In 1956 he settled in Paris, France. There he played with various groups, taught privately and at the Conservatory de St. Germain en-Laye, recorded, and appeared in films, including *Lift to the Scaffold* (1957) and *Les liaisons dangereuses* (1959). He also wrote music for film scores, such as *On n'enterre pas le dimanche* (1959) and *La rivière du hibou* (1961). In the 1960s he collaborated with Francy Boland of Belgium to co-lead a big band (1960-73). The Clarke-Boland Big Band toured widely and performed at the major jazz festivals. Clarke returned to the United States occasionally: in 1972 for the inauguration of the Duke Ellington* Fellowship program at Yale University; in 1978 to receive a ''Prez Award'' (for Lester ''Prez'' Young*) from the city of New York in recognition of jazzmen who brought fame to 52nd Street. As a participant in the jam sessions at Minton's, Clarke was an architect of the bebop era. His drum style, which reflected the influence of Jonathan (''Jo'') Jones's* even, four-beat legato approach, laid the foundation for modern drumming.

BIBL: ChilWW. FeaEJ. FeaJS. FeaGitJS. Dizzy Gillespie with Al Fraser, *To Be or Not to Bop* (New York, 1979).

DISC: Jep. Kink. RustJR. TudJ.

CLAYTON, WILBUR ("BUCK"). Jazz trumpeter (b. 12 November 1911 in Parsons, Kansas). His father played trumpet and tuba. He began playing piano when he was six years old, then later changed to trumpet, taking lessons from his father. He began playing professionally in the early 1930s on the West Coast. Under the patronage of Teddy Weatherford,* he led bands in Shanghai, China, for two years (1934-36). After returning to the United States, he settled again in Los Angeles, California, where he played with various groups, then joined William ("Count") Basie* (1936-43). During his service in the U. S. Armed Forces (1943-46), he played in army bands. Thereafter he was active as an arranger for such groups as Basie, Benny Goodman, and Harry James, among others, and he toured at home and abroad. He traveled with the first national tour of Norman Granz's Jazz at the Philharmonic in 1946 and played on several later tours of JATP. From 1947 on he led his own groups primarily and toured frequently in Europe after his first tour in 1949. He also played with others, including Joe Bushkin, James ("Jimmy") Rushing,* Sidney Bechet,* and Albert ("Eddie") Condon, among others. His touring took him to Japan and Australia in 1964 and to the Middle East in 1971 under sponsorship of the U. S. State Department. He appeared at the major jazz festivals on both sides of the Atlantic; recorded extensively, particularly during the 1950s; and appeared in films, including *Jazz on a Summer's Day* (1960), *Buck Clayton and His All Stars* (1961), and *Born to Swing* (1973). Clayton was one of the important trumpeters of the swing era; his style was characterized by a highly individual vibrato and tenderness.

BIBL: ASCAP. BPIM 2 (Fall 1974), p. 199. Cadence (November 1977). ChilWW. FeaEJ. FeaJS. FeaGitJS. MeeJMov.

DISC: Jep. Kink. RustJR. TudJ.

CLEF CLUB, THE. Professional organization (fl. early twentieth century; est. in New York, New York). This musical organization was organized in 1909, incorporated on 21 June 1910 in the state of New York, and was in existence through the mid-1920s. Its purpose was to serve as a booking agent for black musicians and musical groups. Organized by James Reese Europe,* it carried a roster of more than two hundred players during its peak years and boasted that upon request it could furnish a dance orchestra of three or thirty men at any time, day or night. Periodically the organization sponsored its own concerts, in which symphonic music was performed in addition to lighter music. The first Clef Club Symphony Orchestra concert was given in May 1910. The most notable achievements of the organization were its annual concerts, given at Carnegie Hall during the years 1912-15. (In 1914 the musicians called their orchestra the Negro Symphony Orchestra, and in 1915 the Music School Settlement for Colored People was the official sponsor.) These concerts introduced to the public the compositions of black composers, performed by such established artists as Harry T. Burleigh,* J. Rosamond Johnson,* Abbie Mitchell,* and Roland Hayes,* among others. The presidents of the Clef Club were, in succession, James Reese Europe, Dan Kildare (musical director of Gorman's Alabama Troubadours), Fred ("Deacon") Johnson,* Alexander Fenner (a cellist), and Irving ("Kid Sneeze") Williams (an entertainer). During its heyday, the Club sent music groups on tour throughout the world, on all five continents.

BIBL: Black press, particularly NYAge. BPIM (Spring 1978), which includes critical notes of the white press. Flet.

CLEVELAND, JAMES. Gospel singer (b. 5 December 1931 in Chicago, Illinois). He was a boy soprano and began singing in church choirs at an early age. When he was eight years old he attracted wide attention when he sang a solo with the choir of Chicago's Pilgrim Baptist Church, directed by Thomas A. Dorsey.* Later he sang in the church's junior choir. He taught himself to play piano, studied gospel piano with ("Little") Lucy Smith (organist for the Roberta Martin* Singers), and began accompanying local groups during his school years. His early singing style development was influenced by Myrtle Scott, Eugene Smith, and Robert Anderson—all members of the Roberta Martin Singers. Martin encouraged his early efforts at writing gospel songs; she sang his "Grace is sufficient" at an annual meeting of the National Baptist Convention in 1955 and published it for him. The song became very popular. During his formative years, he sang with various groups, including the Thorn Gospel Crusaders, The Caravans,* the Gospelaires (a trio composed of Norsalus McKissick, Bessie Folk, and himself), the Roberta Martin Singers, Mahalia Jackson,* and the Meditation Singers of Detroit, Michigan, among others. His early songs were featured by the Caravans, particularly on a tour in 1956, for which he was pianist-arranger. About 1959 he formed the first of his groups that brought him increasing recognition, the Gospel Chimes, composed of Dorothy Norwood, Imogene Greene, Lee Charles Neely, Jessy Dixon,* and Claude Timmons. A later group, the Cleveland Singers, featured William (''Billy'') Preston* as organ accompanist. In 1960 he recorded a song,''The love of God,'' with the Voices of Tabernacle of Detroit, Michigan, that won him wide recognition and helped to establish him as the leading gospel figure of his time. Further recordings with his own James Cleveland Singers and the 300-voice Angelic Choir of Nutley, New Jersey, particularly ''Peace be still''(1962), earned him such titles as ''Crown Prince of Gospel'' and ''King of Gospel.'' He toured widely in the United States and in Europe during the next decades, appearing in theaters and concert halls, at music festivals, on college campuses, and on television programs. During the early 1960s he became a minister and settled in Los Angeles, California, where he served as pastor to the New Greater Harvest Baptist Church and later founded the Cornerstone Institutional Baptist Church and served as its pastor. In 1968 he founded the Gospel Music Workshop of America, which held annual conventions, bringing together thousands of gospel performers and songwriters (from 15,000 to 20,000) for training in the tradition of black gospel music. In 1969 he organized the Southern California Community Choir, with whom he recorded as well as performed, and as well, the Gospel Girls. He continued to tour widely through the 1970s; he also appeared in the film *Save the Children* (1973). His numerous honors included awards from the music industry, the N.A.A.C.P. Image award (1976), the National Association of Negro Musicians* award (1975), and an honorary doctorate from Temple Bible College. Cleveland was the leading representative of the modern gospel sound, beginning in the 1960s, both as pianist and singer. He exerted enormous influence over those who followed him, among them, Aretha Franklin,* Jessy Dixon, and William (''Billy'') Preston, among others. Over the years he wrote more songs and released more recordings than any other gospel figure of his generation; his songs were published by all the houses and his music became standards in the gospel repertory. His best-known compositions included ''Grace is sufficient,'' ''God specializes'' (with Kenneth Morris), ''He's using me,'' and ''The Man, Jesus.''

BIBL: Barbara Baker, ''Black Gospel Music Styles, 1942-1979'' (Ph.D. diss., University of Maryland, 1978). Horace Boyer, ''The Gospel Song: An Historical and Analytical Study'' (M.A. thesis, Eastman School of Music, 1964). *Dawn Magazine* (April 1979). *Ebony* (November 1968, November 1972). Heil. Jac. *Sepia* (May 1965, May 1972). WWBA.

CLIFF, JAMES (''JIMMY'', née **JAMES CHAMBERS).** Reggae singer (b. 1948 in West Kingston, Jamaica). He was in the troupe of Byron Lee and the Dragonaires of Kingston, Jamaica, when that group performed at the New York World's Fair in 1964, featuring Millie Small as the ska singer. Ska later came to be known as reggae. Thereafter Cliff formed his own groups. He first attracted wide attention in 1971 when he was the leading actor in the first all-Jamaican film, *The Harder They Come*, which used also Desmond Dekker and other reggae singers on the soundtrack. Cliff's best-known recordings were ''Many rivers to cross,'' ''Wonderful world, beautiful people,'' and ''You can get it if you really want to''; his best-known albums were *Jimmy Cliff Unlimited, Music Maker*, and *Follow My Mind*. Reggae music exerted wide influence upon British singers and singers of the United States, particularly Johnny Nash* with his recordings of ''Hold me tight'' and ''I can see clearly now.'' Like other reggae groups, Cliff's musicians belonged to the cult of the Rastafarians. Their music blended elements of rock, calypso, soul, jazz, and blues, with traditional African and religious music.

BIBL: Black press, incl. PhilaT, 31 July 1973. *Essence* (September 1973). *Sepia* (March 1974). NYT, 30 November 1975.

DISC: TudBM.

CLOUGH, ESTELLE PINCKNEY. Concert singer (b. c1860s-70s in Worcester, Massachusetts; d.19? in Worcester (?)). She began her career singing in local concerts in Worcester and Boston, Massachusetts, during the 1880s and gradually appeared as an assisting artist (soprano) during the next decade in concerts in New York and other musical centers of the East. She first attracted wide attention in 1903 when she sang the title role of Verdi's *Aida* in the Theodore Drury* production in New York. In 1904 she sang a solo part in the performance of Samuel Coleridge-Taylor's* *The Childhood of Hiawatha* in Washington, D.C., on the occasion when Coleridge-Taylor came to the United States to conduct a concert of his music. The other soloists were J. Arthur Freeman and Harry T. Burleigh.* She was active as a concert singer through the second decade of the century, if not longer. During the 1930s she conducted a music studio in Worcester.

BIBL: Black press, incl. NYGlobe, 6 January 1883; CDef, 10 May 1919. Hare.

CLOUGH, INEZ. Concert singer (b. c1860s-70s in New England; d. December 1933 in Chicago, Illinois). She first attracted attention during the 1880s when she began singing in local concerts in Worcester, Massachusetts. She sang in John Isham's Oriental America Company during the late 1890s, in the program titled ''Forty Minutes of Grand and Comic Opera,'' and toured with the company in Europe. When it returned to the United States, she remained abroad and toured as an entertainer in music halls for five years. After returning to the United States, she joined the George Walker*/Bert Williams* company and remained through its productions of *In Dahomey* (1902-04), *In Abyssinia* (1906-07), and *In Bandanna Land* (1907-09). During this period she also sang with the Bob Cole*/Johnson brothers* *Shoo Fly Regiment* musical (1906) and appeared in concerts as a soloist in New York, Washington, D.C., and other cities in the East. In 1913 she became a charter member of the Original Lafayette Players. During the 1920s she sang in Broadway musicals, including the Noble Sissle*/Eubie Blake* *Shuffle Along* (1921) and *The Chocolate Dandies* (1924).

BIBL: Black press, incl. NYFree, 17 April 1886; CDef, 28 June 1913, 3 April 1920, 16 December 1933; NYAge, 9 December 1933.

COATES, DOROTHY McGRIFF LOVE. Gospel singer (b. 1930s in Birmingham, Alabama). She sang gospel as a child. Her early style development was influenced by the gospel singers she heard in Birmingham, including Queen C. Anderson,* Georgia Lee Stafford, and J. William Blevins, as well as visitors to the city, such as Sallie Martin* and Mahalia Jackson.* Alex Bradford* was a longtime friend dating back to her school days in Birmingham. In the early 1940s she began singing with the local Original Gospel Harmonettes, a female group composed of Odessa Edwards, Mildred Miller Howard, Vera Kolb, Willie Mae Newberry, and accompanist Evelyn Starks. She remained with the group, except for a period in the late 1940s, until it was disbanded in 1958. The group recorded regularly, and in 1951 her solos on "I'm sealed" and "Get away, Jordan" attracted wide attention. In 1961 she reorganized the Harmonettes, employing Howard, Newberry, Cleo Kennedy, and her sister Lillian McGriff. Over the years her accompanists included Herbert Pickard and Joe Washington. She was as celebrated for her songwriting as for her performance. Her best-known songs were "He's right on time," "You must be born again," "Every day will be Sunday," "Hide me, Jesus," and "I'm trying, Lord." She was twice married to gospel figures; her first husband, Willie Love, sang with the Fairfield Four, and Carl Coates sang with the Nightingales.

BIBL: BMI (Issue 4, 1977). Horace Clarence Boyer, "The Gospel Song: An Historical and Analytical Study." (M.A. thesis, Eastman School of Music, 1964). Heil. Jac.

COBHAM, WILLIAM EMANUEL, JR. ("BILLY"). Jazz drummer (b. 15 May 1944 in the Republic of Panama). His father was a professional jazz pianist. His family moved to New York when he was three years old. By the time he was eight he was playing drums in his father's group; later he played in a Boy Scout's drum corps (1956-58). He obtained his musical education at the High School of Music and Art in New York. During his high-school years he began playing with a local group, the Jazz Samaritans. He played in army bands during his service in the U. S. Armed Forces (1965-68), and began playing with William ("Billy") Taylor* (1967) even before his discharge from the army. Thereafter he played with various groups, including the New York Jazz Sextet, Horace Silver,* his own rock-jazz band called Dreams (1969-70), Miles Davis* (1971), and John McLaughlin's Mahavishnu Orchestra (1972-73). During these years he was also a free-lancer, recorded extensively, and appeared in films, among them, *Jack Johnson* (1970) and *Salsa* (1976). He worked with Billy Taylor on Jazzmobile projects and with Christopher ("Chris") White's* Rhythm Associates, teaching and conducting jazz clinics. From 1974 on he toured primarily with his own groups in the United States and abroad, generally performing music of his own composition. His best-known albums were *Spectrum* and *Crosswinds*. He established himself as a seminal figure in the "rock-jazz" or "progressive rock" style, combining in his music the excitement and urgency of rock with Latin rhythms and free-form jazz improvisation. He received awards from the music industry.

BIBL: Lorraine Alterman, "Who's Afraid of Jazz Rock" in NYT, 26 May 1974. Black press, incl. *New Courier* [Pittsburgh], 12 January 1974, 15 June 1974. FeaEJ. WWA.

DISC: TudJ.

COLE, FRANCES ELAINE. Concert harpsichordist (b. 12 July 1937 in Cleveland, Ohio). As a child she studied piano and violin. She obtained her musical education at Miami University in Oxford, Ohio (B. Mus.), where she was concert mistress of the university orchestra, and at Columbia University Teachers College in New York (M. Mus. Ed., D. Mus. Ed., 1966). She studied privately with Irving Freundlick. During her years of study at Columbia, she was active as a pianist and played violin in local groups, including the National Orchestral Association's orchestra. In 1966 she became interested in the harpsichord and began study with Denise Resout. The next year she began performing publicly as a harpsichordist, appearing with the Gallery Players in Provincetown, Massachusetts, and on television programs. In October 1971 she made her debut at Town Hall in New York. Thereafter she toured widely as a concert artist, including a tour of Europe in 1973, and performed on numerous college campuses and at the Bach Festival in Carmel, California, in 1977. She organized several harpsichord festivals herself, some at institutions where she taught and one at the Lincoln Center in New York in 1975. She also performed in New York supper clubs. In 1979 she appeared regularly on the CBS ''Sunday Morning'' program as a music commentator. Her teaching career included tenures in the public schools of New York; at Temple University in Philadelphia, Pennsylvania; at the Westminister Choir College in Princeton, New Jersey; and at Queens College of the City University of New York.

BIBL: Black press, incl. AmstN, 28 August 1976. Handy. NYT, 6 October1971.

COLE, NAT ("KING") (née **NATHANIEL ADAMS COLES).** Jazz pianist/Popular music singer (b. 17 March 1919 in Montgomery, Alabama; d. 15 February 1965 in Santa Monica, California). He came from a musical family: his mother was choir director for his father's Baptist church, and his three brothers, Ike, Eddie, and Freddie, became professional musicians. He began playing piano at an early age and made his first public appearance when he was four years old in a talent show at the Regal Theater in Chicago. His family moved to Chicago, Illinois, when he was a child. He obtained his musical education in the public schools of Chicago, where he came under the influence of Walter Dyett* at Wendell Phillips High School. He played gospel piano in his father's church and organized his first jazz group, The Musical Dukes, during his high-school years. His first professional experience was as arranger-musical director for the *Shuffle Along* road company in 1936. After the show was disbanded in Los Angeles, California, he remained there and played in nightclubs. In 1939 he formed an instrumental trio with Oscar Moore (guitar), Wesley Prince (bass), and Lee Young (drums), called The King Cole Trio. The trio first attracted wide attention in 1943 with its recording of ''Straighten up and fly right.'' Gradually, Cole left the piano to concentrate on singing and began using larger groups for accompaniment. In 1948-49 he had his own radio series. By 1952 he had entered a new career as an entertainer, singing popular music rather than jazz. He toured widely at home and abroad, recorded extensively, and sang on radio and television programs; in 1956-57 he had his own television series. He appeared in numerous film musicals, among them *Breakfast in Hollywood* (1946), *China Gate* (1957), *St. Louis Blues* (1958, with Cole as W. C. Handy), and *Cat Ballou* (1965). Cole's piano style reflected the influence of Earl Hines*; his vocal style was unique. Cole pioneered in several ways: His group was one of the first jazz ''combos,'' along with that of John Kirby,* and thus foreshadowed the trios, quartets, and quintets that were to become the norm in later years. His trio was the first black instrumental group to have a sponsored radio series, although individual black performers and black singers had been sponsored before his time. Finally, he was one of the first black entertainers in modern times, along with William (''Billy'') Eckstine,* to win international recognition as a singer independent of association with an orchestra—in the same way as James Bland,* for example, in the nineteenth century. He received numerous awards from the music industry. Two daughters, Carole and Natalie, became professional musicians.

BIBL: ASCAP. ChilWW. Maria Cole with Louie Robinson, *Nat King Cole: An Intimate Biography* (New York, 1971). FeaEJ. FeaJS. WWCA, 1950.

DISC: Jep. Kink. RustJR. TudJ.

COLE, COZY. See **COLE, WILLIAM R.**

COLE, ROBERT ALLEN ("BOB"). Entertainer/Lyricist (b. 1 July 1868 in Athens, Georgia; d. 2 August 1911 in New York, New York). At the age of fourteen he went to Atlanta, Georgia, where he obtained his musical education at Atlanta University. He began his professional career in Chicago, Illinois, working at first with Lew Henry* in a vaudeville act, then with Stella Wiley in an act before he and Wiley joined Sam T. Jack's Creole Company in 1895. Produced by white management, this was the first Broadway show to have a black cast; members of the company included Irving Jones,* Mr. and Mrs. Sam Lucas,* and Sylvester Russell,* among others. Sometime during the mid-1890s, Cole became associated with the All-Star Stock Company at Worth's Museum in New York, which probably was the first black dramatic company in the nation. There he came in contact with such leading figures as Gussie Davis,* Will Marion Cook,* and Billy Johnson,* among others; he also wrote dramatic sketches for the company. In 1896 he was engaged to produce a show for M. Sissieretta Jones,* to be called Black Patti's Troubadours, but he left during the first season because of a disagreement with her managers. In partnership with Billy Johnson, he organized a company to produce a musical they had written, *A Trip to Coontown*, which toured for four years (1897-1901). This show is credited with being the first, full-length (three acts) show in a non-minstrel format that was written, produced, and staged by blacks. It received critical acclaim on Broadway and on its tours.

About 1901 Cole and Johnson dissolved their partnership, and Cole entered into an association with J.

Rosamond Johnson* and his brother James Weldon Johnson* (not related to Billy Johnson). This trio wrote a large number of popular songs, most of which were published by Joseph Stern and Edward B. Marks, and produced two successful musicals, *The Shoo-Fly Regiment* (1906-08) and *The Red Moon* (1909-10). These shows established new traditions for black musicals, placing more emphasis on plot than had formerly been done and featuring the singing and dancing of pretty girls. The Cole/Johnson brothers trio also contributed music to Broadway shows with white casts, including *The Belle of Bridgeport* (1900), *The Sleeping Beauty and the Beast* (1901), *The Little Duchess* (1901), *Sally in Our Alley* (1902), *Nancy Brown* (1903), and *In Newport* (1904). Some of the songs written during this period became perennial favorites, including "Oh, didn't he ramble" (under the pseudonym Will Handy), "Under the bamboo tree," and "My castle on the Nile." Cole teamed with J. Rosamond Johnson in vaudeville acts, he as singer and Johnson at the piano, which toured throughout the United States and in Europe. Illness forced Cole's retirement from the stage in 1910.

BIBL: Black press, incl. CDef, 12 August 1911; IndF, 7 October 1899, 30 December 1899; NYAge, 14 July 1910, 20 October 1910.

DISC: Kink.

COLE, WILLIAM RANDOLPH ("COZY"). Jazz drummer (b. 17 October 1909 in East Orange, New Jersey; d. 29 January 1981 in New York, New York). He came from a musical family: three brothers, Theodore, Herbert, and Reuben Jay, became professional jazz musicians. His family moved to Atlantic Highlands, New Jersey, when he was a child, after the death of his mother. He was inspired to play drums by William ("Sonny") Greer,* who played in jazz groups in nearby Long Branch. He played drums in high school and after graduation attended Wilberforce College in Ohio for two years; in the 1940s he attended the Juilliard School of Music in New York, where he studied with Saul Goodman. Earlier he studied with Charlie Brooks and Billy Gladstone in New York, among others. He began playing professionally in 1928, first with Wilbur Sweatman* for a brief period of two weeks, then with various groups, including Blanche Calloway* (1931-33), Bennett ("Benny") Carter* (1933-34), Willie Bryant* (1934-36), Hezekiah ("Stuff") Smith* (1936-38), and Cabell ("Cab") Calloway* (1938-42), among others. During the 1940s-50s he was active in radio, playing with the CBS Orchestra (1942-43); he played with Broadway theater orchestras, performing in the pit orchestra and on stage for *Carmen Jones* and *Seven Lively Arts* (1944) and later with Benny Goodman in theater shows; and he recorded extensively. He toured with the Louis Armstrong* All Stars (1949-53), with an All Star band led by Jack Teagarden and Earl Hines* (1957), and with the Robert ("Jonah") Jones* Quintet (1968). During these years he led his own groups frequently, touring widely—in Africa in 1962-63 under sponsorship by the U.S. State Department—and playing long residencies in New York nightclubs. He appeared in many films, including *Make Mine Music* (1945), *Botta e risposta* (1951), *The Strip* (1951), and *The Glenn Miller Story* (1953). For several years he conducted a drum school in partnership with Gene Krupa (1952-60). Cole was a leading drummer of the swing era, but was also one of the most versatile drummers of modern times; he played equally well in New Orleans traditional style and even recorded with bebop groups.

BIBL: ChilWW. DanceWS. FeaEJ. FeaJS. MeeJMov.

DISC: Jep. Kink. RustJR.

COLE TALBERT, FLORENCE. See **TALBERT, FLORENCE COLE.**

COLEMAN, ORNETTE. Jazz saxophonist (b. 29 March 1930 in Fort Worth, Texas). He received his first instrument, an alto saxophone, when he was fourteen years old. He obtained his musical education in the public schools of Fort Worth, Texas, where he studied saxophone and played in the school band—tenor saxophone in his last year. During his high-school years he played with local groups and formed his own group to play rhythm 'n' blues in local clubs. His fellow musicians included King Curtis* (née Curtis Ousley), Charlie Moffett, and Prince Lasha, among others. After graduating from high school he toured with various groups, including ("Red") Connors, the Silas Green from New Orleans* show, Clarence Samuels, and ("Pee Wee") Crayton, among others. He left Crayton's band in Los Angeles, California, in 1950 and lived there nine years, except for a two-year sojourn again in Fort Worth. He played with various groups in Los Angeles, but also spent much time in study of music theory on his own. He gathered together a group of young musicians—including Billy Higgins, Donald Cherry,* and Edward Blackwell, among others—with whom he exchanged musical ideas in meetings in George Newman's garage. Some of the men formed the nucleus for Coleman's first recordings in 1958, *Something Else: The Music of Ornette Coleman* and *Tomorrow Is the Question*. In 1959 Coleman settled in New York, where he formed a group, composed of Cherry, Higgins, Charlie Hayden, and himself on a plastic alto saxophone, that attracted wide attention because of its revolutionary music. He also attended the School of Jazz at Lenox, Massachusetts, in 1959. Through the 1960s-70s he played avant-garde with his groups of varying sizes, ranging from the trio to the double quartet or larger. An album recorded in 1960, *Free Jazz*, provided a name for the new music he was introducing to the jazz world. He played long residencies in New York nightclubs during the early 1960s, then withdrew from musical activity for three years (1962-65), primarily because of unemployment. In 1965 he went to Europe, where he performed in Germany at the Berlin Jazz Days. He toured in the United States, performing in concert halls and nightclubs, on college campuses, and at jazz festivals. In 1972 his quartet performed his orchestral work, *Skies of America*, with a symphony orchestra (later recorded by the London Symphony). Thereafter he performed with larger groups, the Ornette Coleman Septet in the mid-1970s, and by the end of the 1970s an electric band called Prime Time. He developed his technical skills to include performance on violin, trumpet, or alto saxophone, and his later music reflected the influence of rock. Over the years those who played in his groups included, in addition to those cited above, David Izenzon, Charles Moffett, Dewey Redman, James ("Jimmy") Garrison, Charles Ellerbee, Bern Nix, Ron Shannon, Jamaaladeen Tacuma, James ("Blood") Ulmer, Barbara Huey, and his son Denardo. Coleman was regarded as a leading innovator of the avant-garde in jazz, along with John Coltrane.* He received numerous awards from the music industry and two Guggenheim fellowships for composition (1967, 1974). His mature style was distinctive for its free rhythms, avoidance of conventional chord patterns as the basis for improvisation, unorthodox methods of tone production, and emotionalism. Over the years he developed a special approach to theory, which he called "harmolodic theory" and published a book with that title; he explained it as involving modulation "in range without changing keys." He exerted enormous influence upon the develoment of the avant-garde in jazz. Despite the freedom of his music from restrictions of conventional harmonies and rhythms, some critics felt that it reflected the influence of his roots in the blues.

BIBL: Black press, incl. AmstN, "Recording Session With a Jazz Great," 26 May 1979. FeaEJ. FeaJS. FeaGitJs. MeeJMov. NYT, 11 June 1972; 26 June 1978. A. B. Spellman, *Black Music. Four Lives* (1966; reprint, New York, 1970). WWA. WWBA.

DISC: Jep. ModJ. TudJ.

COLERIDGE-TAYLOR, SAMUEL. Composer (b. 15 August 1875 in Holborn (near London), England; d. 1 September 1912 in Croydon, England). He began study of the violin at the age of five and was a boy soprano in church choirs. He received his musical training at the Royal College of Music in London (1890-97), where he studied with Charles Wood and Walter Parratt, among others. Although he concentrated in violin, he revealed special talent in composition, and the director of the institute, George Grove, recommended that Coleridge-Taylor study composition with Charles Villiers Stanford. He began teaching at the Croydon Conservatory during his student days. In 1897 he was appointed a violin teacher at the college, and the next year he took over the directorship of the Conservatory Orchestral Society (1898-1906). From 1903 until his death he was professor of music at Trinity College of Music in London. He also held part-time positions, teaching at the Crystal Palace School of Art and Music in South London, beginning in 1905, and at the Guildhall School (1910-12). In addition to teaching he was active as a conductor. He organized the Coleridge-Taylor Symphony Concerts (1902-05), which gave performances using guest artists along with its string players; in 1906 he founded the Croydon String Players Club, to which were later added woodwinds and brasses. He also conducted the Royal Rochester Choral Society (1902-07) and the Handel Society in West London (1904-12). Occasionally he was called upon to direct at festivals, particularly in the performance of his own music: the Sheffield Music Festival (1902), the Leeds Festival (1901), and the Hereford Festival (1903). He began composing as a child and published his first composition, the anthem "In Thee, O Lord," when he was sixteen. In 1893 he conducted a concert of his music at the Royal College. A commission received in 1898 from the Committee of the Three Choirs Festival at Gloucester led to his composing "Ballade in A minor" for orchestra, and the success of that led to other commissions. In November 1898 his best-known work, the cantata *Hiawatha's Wedding Feast* (text from Longfellow's *The Song of Hiawatha*), was performed at the College under the direction of Stanford. Later he wrote two additional works using the Longfellow text, *The Death of Minnehaha* (1899) and *Hiawatha's Departure* (1900). From this period on, his works were widely performed in England and abroad. He toured in the United States three times (1904, 1906, 1910), conducting concerts of his music. On the first two occasions he was guest of the Coleridge-Taylor Choral Society of Washington, D.C. (John Turner Layton,* director), and in 1910 he was guest of the Litchfield Choral Union Festival at Norfolk, Connecticut. He toured widely in 1906 and included a concert at Robert Motts's* Pekin Theater in Chicago, Illinois. Those who performed with him on the first two tours included Harry T. Burleigh,* Estelle Clough,* Will Marion Cook,* J. Arthur Freeman, Lola Johnson, Joe Jordan,* N. Clark Smith,* Clarence Cameron White,* and Felix Weir,* among others. Coleridge-Taylor wrote in the neoromantic style common to his time and was highly interested in African, Afro-American, and Indian themes. His interest in Negro folk music was stimulated by two contacts he had with black Americans early in his career. In 1897 he met poet Paul Laurence Dunbar,* who had come to England to read his poems, and the two men gave a series of joint recitals, which included seven musical settings of Dunbar poems (later published as *African Romances*, 1897). In 1899 the composer heard Frederick J. Loudin's Fisk Jubilee Singers,* an experience which served as an inspiration for several works, including the well-known *Twenty-Four Negro Melodies, Transcribed for the Piano* (1905) and *Symphonic Variations on an African Air* (1906, based on the spiritual "I'm troubled in mind"). His best-known works in addition to those cited above were *African Suite* (1898, nos. 1-3 originally for piano and no. 4, "Dance Nègre," for piano quintet, but later orchestrated by the composer); the cantata *The Atonement* (1903); *Kubla Khan* (1905), a rhapsody for solo, chorus, and orchestra; *The Bamboula* (1910), for orchestra; and the violin Concerto in G minor (1911, dedicated to and first performed by Maud Powell). He left a large body of music in a variety of forms, particularly for orchestra, chamber groups, violin, violincello, organ, piano, chorus, and voice. He was the most important composer of African descent of his time, and some of his music retained its popularity over the years, especially the Hiawatha music and the piano pieces. His son Hiawatha (b. 13 October 1900) and daughter Avril (née Gwendolyn, b. 8 March 1903) both became professional musicians and were particularly active as conductors. Avril Coleridge-Taylor was also a composer.

BIBL: Baker. Black press. BPIM 2 (Spring 1974), pp. 57-58. Gro. William C. Berwick Sayers, *Samuel Coleridge-Taylor: His Life and Letters* (London, 1915; 2nd ed., 1927, with works list compiled by J. H. Smithers Jackson). William Tortolano, *Samuel Coleridge-Taylor: Anglo-Black Composer*, 1875-1912 (Metuchen, New Jersey, 1977) includes list of works and discography.

COLLINS, CLEOTA JOSEPHINE. Concert singer (b. 24 September 1893 in Cleveland, Ohio; d. 7 July 1976 in Pasadena, California). As a child she sang in her father's church choir. She obtained her musical education at the Cleveland Conservatory of Music and later studied at Western Reserve University in Cleveland, at Ohio State University, Columbia University Teachers' College in New York, and the Juilliard School of Music in New York. Her voice teachers included E. Azalia Hackley,* Lila Robeson of the Metropolitan Opera, Yeatman Griffith, and Harriet Batterson. Mme. Hackley took on Collins as her protégé and helped the young soprano to obtain financial help for study abroad, which Collins pursued in 1927. During the 1920s she conducted a voice studio in Cleveland and used that city as a base from which she toured extensively. She was a soloist in several of Hackley's Folk Song Festivals and was in wide demand for singing solos in cantatas and oratorios. She entered a teaching career in the 1930s, which included tenures at Sam Huston College in Texas, Bluefield State College in West Virginia, Tuskegee Institute in Alabama, and Virginia State College, where she was appointed head of the voice department in 1940. She retired from college teaching when she married William J. Trent, president of Livingston College in North Carolina. Collins was highly regarded by her contemporaries for her talent and musicianship. She was a charter member of the National Association of Negro Musicians* in 1919.

BIBL: Communication from Altona Trent Johns,* stepdaughter of Cleota Collins. Black press, incl. CDef, 12 June 1920, 1 August 1953; NY Age, 13 March 1920, 5 November 1927.

COLLYMORE, WINSTON. Symphony/Theater violinist (b. 9 May 1913 in New York, New York). He obtained his musical education in the public schools of New York, at the [David] Martin*-Smith School of Music in New York, and at the Juilliard School of Music in New York. In 1921 he made his debut as a concert violinist at Aeolian Hall in New York. Throughout his career he combined concert activity with performance in symphony and theater orchestras. He played in the pit orchestras for such Broadway musicals as *Allegro* (1948), *Porgy and Bess* (1952), *Guys and Dolls* (1965) and *Promises, Promises* (1968). His career also included tenures in the CBS Staff Orchestra (1963-65), the Symphony of the New World* (1964-78), and the Radio City Music Hall Symphony Orchestra (1965-78). He was also active as a free-lance musician with musical groups that accompanied leading jazz artists and entertainers in theaters and concert halls, on television shows, and in the recording studio—frequently with his Winston Collymore Strings. He conducted a music studio in New York. His daughter, Valerie Collymore, was a professional violinist.

BIBL: Questionnaire.

COLORED MARIO, THE. See **BOWERS, THOMAS.**

COLTRANE, ALICE McLEOD. Jazz pianist (b. 27 August 1937 in Detroit, Michigan). She came from a musical family: her mother played piano, and her brother, Ernie Farrow, became a professional jazz bassist. She began piano study when she was seven years old and later studied organ and music theory privately. Her early style development was influenced by Earl (''Bud'') Powell.* She began playing professionally in the 1960s with various groups, including Terry Pollard and the Terry Gibbs Quartet (1961-62). In 1966 she joined John Coltrane's* group (they were married in 1963). After his death in 1967 she toured with her own groups. In 1972 she settled on the West Coast.

BIBL: Bill Cole, *John Coltrane* (New York, 1976). FeaJS (see McLeod). FeaGitJS. Handy.

COLTRANE, JOHN WILLIAM. Jazz saxophonist (b. 23 September 1926 in Hamlet, North Carolina; d. 17 July 1967 in New York). He was born into a musical family: his father played violin and sang, and his mother was a church pianist and also sang in a church choir. Both his grandfathers were ministers in the A.M.E. Zion Church; from earliest infancy he was exposed to black religious music in his maternal grandfather's church. His family moved to High Point, North Carolina, when he was a few months old. He obtained his music education in the public schools of High Point, at the Ornstein School of Music and at Granoff Studios, both in Philadelphia, Pennsylvania. He began clarinet study at the age of twelve in school; a year later he began study of the alto saxophone. After his father's death, his mother moved to Philadelphia, where he began his professional career. In 1945 he began playing in local clubs and bars. During his years of service in the U.S. Armed Forces, he played in a Navy band in the Pacific Arena (1945-46). After the war he returned to Philadelphia, where he played with various groups, including the Joe Webb Blues Band (1946), King Kolax (1946), Eddie (''Cleanhead'') Vinson* (1947), and James (''Jimmie'') Heath* (1948). Leaving Philadelphia, he played with John Birks (''Dizzy'') Gillespie* (1949-51, in both the big band and the quintet), Earl Bostic* (1952-53), Johnny Hodges* (1954-55), and Miles Davis* (regularly during the years 1955-56, 1957-60). Except for Heath's group, the Philadelphia bands played rhythm 'n' blues or traditional blues, as did Bostic's group. During his tenure with Vinson, he changed from alto saxophone to tenor, thus entered jazz formally with a command of both instruments. He made his recording debut in 1949 with Gillespie, and in the next decade recorded and appeared in live performance with a number of jazzmen, including Donald Byrd,* Donald (''Don'') Cherry,* Paul Chambers,* Tadley (''Tadd'') Dameron,* William (''Red'') Garland, John Griffin,* and Thelonious Monk,* among others. He made his recording debut as a band leader in 1957, but it was not until 1960 that he formed his own permanent group—a quartet in which he played soprano saxophone on its first concert. In later years he performed with larger groups, even a big band. He recorded extensively with his groups and with others; played in nightclubs, concert halls, and at festivals; and occasionally toured—to Japan in 1966. Those who performed with him at one time or another included Rashied Ali, Arthur (''Art'') Davis,* Steve Davis, Eric Dolphy,* James (''Jimmy'') Garrison, Roy Haynes,* Billy Higgins, Elvin Jones,* McCoy Tyner,* Reginald (''Reggie'') Workman, and his wife Alice McLeod Coltrane,* among others. Coltrane first attracted wide attention as a member of Miles Davis's group, perhaps with his solo on ''Round about midnight.'' During the 1950s he attracted attention for his ''sheets of sound,'' playing sweeping waves of fast notes that ignored traditional metrical patterns; then came his innovative approach to improvisation and handling of rhythms and forms, his use of Indian, Arabian, and African elements, his concern for spirituality in music, and his intense religiosity. His innovations effected an enlargement of jazz resources that in turn changed the basic character of the music. Along with Ornette Coleman,* he was a seminal figure in the avant-garde movement, the ''free jazz'' era. He received many awards from the music industry. His best-known recordings were *My Favorite Things* (1961), *Giant Steps* (1959), *Africa Brass* (1961), *A Love Supreme* (1964), and *Ascension* (1965).

BIBL: Bill Cole, *John Coltrane* (New York, 1976). *Ebony* (November 1967) FeaEJ. FeaJS. FeaGitJS. MeeJMov. NYT, 29 September 1974. Cuthbert O. Simpkins, *Coltrane* (New York, 1975). J. C. Thomas, *Chasin' the Train: The Music and Mystique of John Coltrane* (New York, 1976). WWA, 1966-67.

DISC: Jep. ModJ. TudJ.

CONNOR, AARON J. R. Composer (fl. mid-nineteenth century in Philadelphia, Pennsylvania; d. 1850 in Philadelphia). He was an early member of the Frank Johnson* band and traveled with the group to England in November 1837 to give concerts. He played trombone, flute, and cornet in the band and also sang solos and in vocal ensembles on Johnson's concerts. He was also active as a music teacher, concert manager, and sometime choral conductor. After Johnson's death in 1844 Connor remained with the Frank Johnson String and Brass Bands under the leadership of Joseph Anderson* for two years. In March 1846 he left to organize his own band. Within a short period he had developed an aristocratic clientele, playing for Philadelphia Assemblies and other society balls, for dancing-school classes, and at Saratoga Springs and other resorts during the summers. In 1844 he began to publish songs and pianoforte arrangements of band pieces. His best-known compositions were the songs "My cherished hope, my fondest dreams" and "Chestnut Street promenade quadrilles," "American polka quadrilles," and "The evergreen polka." Several of his pieces were still in circulation twenty years after his death and were listed in the *Complete Catalogue of Sheet Music and Musical Works, 1870* (published by the Board of Music Trade of the United States of America, 1871; reprint with introduction by Dena Epstein [New York, 1973]).

BIBL: BPIM 4 (July 1976). John E. Bruce, "A History of Negro Musicians" in *Southern Workman* 45 (1916). Martin Delany, *The Condition, Elevation, Emigration and Destiny of the Colored People of the United States* (Philadelphia, 1852), p. 142. LaBrew. *The Public Ledger* [Philadelphia], 24 December 1838; 30 March 1844; 28 March 1846. *The Morning Post* [London], 13 December 1837. Trot, p. 305.

CONTER, JOHN. Military fifer (b. DeKalb, Georgia; fl. early nineteenth century). He was enlisted in the army in April 1847 during the Mexican War and assigned to the Thirteenth Infantry, Fourth Regiment.

BIBL: GreBD.

COOK, J[EAN] LAWRENCE. Jazz pianist (b. 14 July 1899 in Athens, Tennessee; d. 2 April 1976 in Mt. Vernon, New York). He obtained his musical training at the Haines Institute in Augusta, Georgia (1914-19) and studied further at Columbia University (1926-28). He settled in New York during the 1920s and because of his skills in making rolls for player pianos picked up the nickname "Piano Roll Cook." He was one of the first black recording artists hired by the QRS Company (Quality Reigns Supreme) beginning in 1922, and he remained with the company for many years. With the decline of interest in piano rolls during the 1930s, he eventually had to leave the music field in order to earn a living, but he continued to make "J. Lawrence Cook Rolls" for collectors. He also continued to work for his old employer, the Imperial Industrial Company, on a part-time basis. About 1963 there was a revival of public interest in piano rolls, and Cook found employment with the Aeolian Roll Company, which brought back player pianos in 1957. A highlight of 1963 for Cook was his performance on a player piano of a Gershwin performance of "That certain feeling" with the New York Philharmonic Society orchestra, Andre Kostelanetz conducting, at a Lewissohn Stadium concert. Cook continued to make piano rolls for Aeolian until his death. Cook published two manuals: *J. Lawrence Cook's Collection of Modernistic Jazz Arrangements for Piano* and *Modern Popular Piano Playing*.

BIBL: Black press, incl. AmstN, 21 August 1965. NYT, 6 April 1976. WWCA, 1938-40.

COOK, WILL MARION. Composer (b. 27 January 1869 in Washington, D.C.; d. 19 July 1944 in New York, New York). He revealed musical talent at an early age and was sent to study music at the Oberlin Conservatory in Ohio when he was fifteen years old. He studied violin further with Josef Joachim in Berlin, Germany (1887-89), and attended the National Conservatory of Music in New York (1894-95), where he studied with Antonin Dvorak (at that time director) and John White, among others. He began playing violin professionally during his student days at Oberlin, giving his first recitals in 1886. After returning to the United States in the fall of 1889, he made his debut as a concert violinist in Washington, D.C., in December of that year. The next year he was appointed director of a new orchestra, organized by C. A. Fleetwood, who became the manager, with Frederick Douglass as president. The Cook orchestra toured, traveling as far north as Boston, Massachusetts, to play a concert in 1891. In 1893 Cook was identified as a "protégé of Fred Douglass" in the black press (IndF, 11 February 1893), when it was announced that he would be in charge of music for Colored American Day (25 August) at the Chicago World's Fair. The original plans for that program did not materialize, although Cook had prepared for performance (orchestral?) one of his own works, "Scenes from the Opera of Uncle Tom's Cabin." He did appear, however, on another concert in Chicago that August, along with Harry T. Burleigh,* Marie Selika,* and Sidney Woodward.* When he went to New York in the mid-1890s, he came into contact with vaudeville, more than likely for the first time, and was soon caught up in its activities. In 1898 he collaborated with Paul Laurence Dunbar* to write and produce a musical-comedy sketch, "Clorindy, or The Origin of the Cakewalk," which was staged with a cast of forty that featured Ernest Hogan,* at Broadway's Casino Roof Garden for E. E. Rice's "Summer Nights." Although this was not the first appearance of a black-produced show on Broadway—the Bob Cole*/Billy Johnson* show, *A Trip to Coontown*, played in April for a short time—it was the first time a black show had played in a major theater and had attracted such wide attention. By 1899 Cook had formed a close association with the George Walker*/Bert Williams* company, and he served as musical director/composer for the next several years, through the productions of *The Sons of Ham* (1900), *In Dahomey* (1902), *In Abyssinia* (1905), and *In Bandanna Land* (1907). He was active also in other ways. His musical, *The Southerners*, was produced on Broadway in 1904 (with a white cast except for the black chorus). In 1905 he became involved with the Memphis Students, a singing-dancing troupe organized by Ernest Hogan, which was making history with its concerts of ''syncopated music'' at Hammerstein's Victoria Theater on Broadway. In October 1905 he took the group abroad to fulfill an engagement. The black press suggested that Cook abducted the students, and Hogan's lawyers tried unsuccessfully to prevent the performers from sailing with Cook. After the demise of the Walker/Williams company in 1908, Cook turned his attention to the rapidly expanding cultural life of the Harlem community and assumed a position of musical leadership that he maintained for the next two or more decades. He organized Negro Choral Societies, lectured on and published articles about Negro music, conducted ''all-colored composer'' concerts, and collaborated with others to write musicals, including *The Traitors* (1912), *In Darkeydom* (1914), and *The Cannibal King* (1914). He was also active in Washington, D.C., where he sponsored ''Home Concerts,'' which featured black artists who had begun their careers in that city but had later moved elsewhere. In 1918 Cook embarked upon his greatest adventure; he organized the New York Syncopated Orchestra (aka The Southern Syncopated Orchestra), which toured widely throughout the nation. The next year the orchestra toured in England, playing a command performance for King George V at Buckingham Palace. Included in the company were Sidney Bechet,* Tom Fletcher,* Abbie Mitchell,* and Will Tyers,* among others. After returning to the United States in 1922, Cook toured with Clef Club orchestras and continued to promote concerts. Those who performed with him included Georgette Harvey,* Fletcher Henderson,* and Paul Robeson,* among others. In 1924 Cook's Negro Folk Music and Drama Society sponsored a concert series titled ''Negro Nuances'' at the Times Square Theater in New York; the next year there were ''Virginia Nights'' devoted to ''all Negro-music'' programs in a Greenwich Village theater. He collaborated with Will Vodery* to write and produce the musical *Swing Along* (1929) at Harlem's Lafayette Theater, and he wrote an opera, *St. Louis 'ooman*, which apparently was never staged. Cook won wide recognition as a composer and conductor. His best-known works, in addition to musicals, were songs for chorus or solo (although he wrote instrumental pieces), including ''Swing along,'' ''Exhortation,'' ''Red, red rose,'' ''Bon bon buddy,'' and ''The rain song.'' For many decades he was chief music adviser, teacher, coach, and patron to black musicians of New York, among them, Eubie Blake,* Charles (''Lucky'') Roberts,* James P. Johnson,* Will Vodery,* and Edward (''Duke'') Ellington*—who said of ''Dad'' Cook, ''he was master of us all.''

BIBL: Communication from Mercer Cook (son). ASCAP. BPIM 6 (Spring 1978), pp. 71-88. Black press, incl. CleveG, 16 October 1886, 12 March 1887, 9 July 1887, 9 November 1889; IndF, 13 September 1890, 4 July 1891, 12 August 1893, 30 December 1899; NYAge, 31 March 1923, 19 January 1924, 30 March 1929, 29 July 1944. DAB. Flet. Hare. JoBM. NHBul. Simond. WWCR.

COOKE, CHARLES L. (''DOC''). Jazz arranger (b. 3 September 1891 in Louisville, Kentucky; d. 25 December 1958 in Wurtsboro, New York). In his early career he was active in Detroit, Michigan. Some time before 1920 he settled in Chicago, Illinois, where he led his own groups in theaters and nightclubs. He obtained his musical education at Chicago Musical College (B.A.), where he studied with Felix Borowski and Victor Saar, and the Chicago College of Music (D. Mus., 1926). In 1930 he settled in New York. Thereafter he was active as a staff-arranger for RKO and Radio City Music Hall. He was also associated with Broadway musicals, as musical director for Joe Jordan's* *Brown Buddies* (1930) and as arranger for such musicals as *The Hot Mikado* (1939), *Sons o' Fun* (1941), *Cabin in the Sky* (1940), and *Follow the Girls* (1944). His best-known songs were ''Blame it on the blues'' and ''Loving you the way I do.'' During the 1920s Cooke's groups in Chicago were regarded by his contemporaries as second only to Joseph (''King'') Oliver's.*

BIBL: ASCAP. Black press, incl. CDef, 19 June 1926; NYAge, 3 January 1959. ChilWW.

COOKE, SAM (née COOK). Gospel/Rhythm 'n' blues singer (b. 22 January 1935 in Chicago, Illinois; d. 11 December 1964 in Los Angeles, California). As a child he sang in his father's Baptist church choir and in a family quartet, the Singing Children, composed of his two sisters and a brother. He obtained his musical education in the public schools of Chicago, Illinois, where he sang in the glee club of Wendell Phillips High School. During his school years he also sang with a neighborhood quartet, the Highway QC's, associated with the Highway Baptist Church. In 1949 he joined The Soul Stirrers,* which included at that time Silas Roy Crain, Paul Foster, Jesse Farley, T. L. Bruster, and R. B. Robinson (who was the manager-trainer of the QC's). Cooke took the place of Rebert Harris and soon established himself as one of the leading young gospel singers of his time. His best-known performances included "Nearer to Thee," "Touch the hem of His garment," "Wonderful, God is so wonderful," "One more river to cross," and "Jesus, wash away my troubles." In 1957 he made some recordings of rhythm 'n' blues songs and, encouraged by his success, left gospel and moved into the world of entertainment. Within a short time he had become as celebrated a rhythm 'n' blues singer as he had been a gospel singer. His first song, "You send me" (written by his brother, L. C. Cooke), was an immediate success; further recordings added to his popularity. He toured widely and recorded extensively. Settling in Los Angeles, California, he formed his own producing, publishing, and talent-management companies. His best-known recordings (many of the songs written by himself) included "Twistin' the night away," "Having a party," "A change is gonna come," "Cupid," and "Bring it on home to me." His style was distinctive for its emotional intensity, sensuousness, and polish, particularly in regard to phrasing and breath control. Although regarded as a rhythm 'n' blues singer by his contemporaries, he belonged in reality to the transitional period that led to the development of "soul" music. He exerted enormous influence upon such entertainers as Marvin Gaye,* Al Green,* Otis Redding,* and Robert ("Bobby") Womack,* among others. His movement from the world of gospel to the secular world inspired many others to make the "crossover" from sacred to secular.

BIBL: BMI (Summer 1969, June 1971). BPIM 7 (Spring 1979). Horace Clarence Boyer, "The Gospel Song: An Historical and Analytical Study" (M.A. thesis, Eastman School of Music, 1964). Heil. ShawHS. ShawR5.

DISC: TudBM.

COOPER, CLARENCE. Symphony French hornist (fl. mid-twentieth century). He obtained his musical education at the New England Conservatory of Music in Boston, Massachusetts. His orchestral performance career included tenures with the Halifax Symphony of Nova Scotia, Canada, where he was principal French hornist; with the Quebec Symphony of Canada; with the Milwaukee (Wisconsin) Symphony; and with the Denver (Colorado) Symphony (1967-72), where he became Associate Principal in 1970. He also toured as a concert artist, making his debut at Carnegie Recital Hall in New York in March 1971. His teaching career included a tenure at the Metropolitan State College in Denver. During the 1970s he settled in New York.

BIBL: Communication from Marion Lonsberry. Black press, including AmstN, 6 March 1971.

COOPER, JEROME. Jazz drummer (b. 14 December 1946 in Chicago, Illinois). He obtained his musical education in the public schools of Chicago, Illinois, where he studied with Oliver Coleman and Walter Dyett* at DuSable High School; and at the Chicago Loop Junior College (1967-68). During his college year he worked with Oscar Brown, Jr.* During the early 1970s he worked primarily in Europe with various groups, including Rahsaan Roland Kirk* (1970-71, with whom he went to Europe on tour), Alphonso ("Dizzy") Reece, Clifford Jordan,* Steven Lacy, Robin Kenyatta,* and the Art Ensemble of Chicago,* among others. In 1971 he became a member of the Revolutionary Ensemble trio, along with Leroy Jenkins* and Sirone.*

BIBL: FeaGitJs. "Revolutionary Ensemble" in NYT, 15 January 1977.

COOPER, MAURICE. Concert singer/Studio teacher (b. 23 February 1909 in Kansas City, Kansas). His family moved several times during his childhood, living for periods of time in Minneapolis, Minnesota, Omaha, Nebraska, and Des Moines, Iowa, and settling in Chicago, Illinois, in 1924. He received his secondary and post-secondary education in Chicago at Wendell Phillips High School, where he studied with Mildred Bryant Jones;* at Crane Junior College; and at Chicago Musical College, where he studied with Charles Keep. He also studied with Florence Price* and T. Theodore Taylor.* He was involved with music from an early age: he was a boy soprano in Episcopalian church choirs, and at thirteen he sang a leading role in Handel's *Messiah* at the George R. Smith College in Sedalia, Missouri. At seventeen he sang the role of Nanki-Pooh in the Verdi Opera company's production of the Gilbert and Sullivan operetta *The Mikado*. The next year he joined the Williams Jubilee Singers,* with whom he toured (1929-32). In 1932 he won first place in a voice competition sponsored by NBC radio, RKO theaters, and the *Chicago Daily News*; he toured thereafter on the theater circuit. During the years 1934-38 he toured widely in Canada, at first with the Carolina Singers, then with his own Florida Sextet. In the late 1930s he sang in the productions of the Negro Unit of the Chicago WPA Theater Project, including *The Mikado, The Swing Mikado,* and *Chimes of Normandy*. In

1939 he went to New York to sing in the Broadway production of *The Hot Mikado*. He was also active as a concert, opera, and church singer. He made his debut as a lyric tenor in 1934 at Orchestra Hall in Chicago and thereafter appeared regularly in solo or joint recitals and as soloist with choral groups, particularly the J. Wesley Jones* Choir in its annual concerts at Orchestra Hall and the James Mundy* Choir. During the 1940s he sang in productions of Mary Cardwell Dawson's* National Negro Opera Company. In 1932 he became cantor of the St. Thomas Episcopal Church in Chicago and remained there almost fifty years. He conducted a voice studio and was the founder-director of a choral group composed solely of blind singers (1957-), which gave annual concerts.

BIBL: Interview by Fanya Wiggins. ChiVH.

COOPER, WILLIAM BENJAMIN. Church organist/ Music educator (b. 14 February 1920 in Philadelphia, Pennsylvania). He obtained his musical education at the Philadelphia Musical Academy (formerly Zeckwerhahn Conservatory, B. Mus., 1951; M. Mus., 1952); at Trinity College of Music in London, England; the School of Sacred Music of the Union Theological Seminary in New York; and at the Manhattan School of Music in New York. He began playing for church choirs when he was twelve years old. During his school years he also played for dancing classes, performed (viola) with the Philadelphia Concert Orchestra,* and directed community choruses and opera workshops. His teaching career included tenures at Lincoln University in Pennsylvania (1940-43), Hampton Institute in Virginia (summers 1940, 1941), Bennett College in Greensboro, North Carolina (1951-53), and in the public schools of New York (1958-). His career as a church organist-choirmaster included tenures at the St. Philip's Episcopal Church (1958-74) and St. Martin's Episcopal Church (1974-), both in New York. He composed in a wide variety of musical forms and genres, but gave primary attention to sacred music, particularly for the church service (Masses, cantatas, motets, oratorios) and organ music. His secular compositions included concertos for organ and string or wind ensembles, ballets, art songs, operettas, two operas, and works for small orchestra. His best-known work was *The Choral Service of the Episcopal Church Set to African-American Chants* (recorded by the choir of St. Stephen's Church at Petersburg, Virginia).

BIBL: Questionnaire.

CORDERO, ROQUE. Composer/University professor (b. 16 August 1917 in Panama City, Panama). He studied clarinet, viola, and violin as a child. He began composing at an early age, writing first popular songs, then turning to classical music when he was seventeen. In Panama he studied with Máximo Boza, Pedro Rebolledo, Herbert de Castro, and Myron Schaeffer. He received his musical education at Hamline University in St. Paul, Minnesota (B.A., 1947), where he studied with Ernst Krenek. He also studied with Dimitri Mitropoulos, Leon Barzin, and Stanley Chapple at the National Orchestral Association in New York (1946-48) and at the Berkshire Music Center in Tanglewood, Massachusetts (summer 1946). His teaching career included tenures in Panama at the Escuela de Artes y Oficios (1941-43) and the Conservatorio Nacional de Musica de Panama (now Instituto Nacional de Musica de Panama, 1950-66) and in the United States at Indiana University in Bloomington (1966-69) and Illinois State University in Normal (1972-). As a performer he played clarinet in the Banda del Cuerpo de Bomberos de Panama (1933-43), viola in the Orquesta Sinfonica de Panama (1941-43), and viola in the Orchestra of the University of Minnesota at Minneapolis (1943-47). He was conductor of the Orquesta Nacional de Panama (1964-66). He toured widely as a lecturer and consultant from 1957 on; he served as a delegate to the International Music Council of UNESCO (1961-66, 1968). He also published numerous articles in professional journals, such as *La Estrella de Panama, Revista Musical Chilena, Journal of Interamerican Studies*, and *Buenos Aires Musical*. His book publications included a manual, *Curso de Solfeo* (Panama, 1956; Buenos Aires, 1963), and contribution of an article, "El Publico y la Musica Viva," to *Music in the Americas*, edited by George List and Juan Orrego-Salas (Bloomington, 1967). He wrote music in a variety of forms but was best known for his orchestral and chamber works, including three symphonies (1945, 1956, 1965), a violin concerto (1962) and *Doble Concierto sin Orquesta* (with violin, 1979); *Mensajes breves* for orchestra (1959); a number of sonatas and sonatinas for violin and piano, cello and piano; three string quartets and a quintet for flute, clarinet, violin, cello, and piano; and other works for chamber orchestras or chamber ensembles. His best-known works, in addition to those cited above, were *Miniatures* (1948, for orchestra), *Duo 1954* for two pianos (1954), *Cinco Mensajes Breves para Orquesta* (1959), *Concertino* for viola and string orchestra (1968), *Dos Pequeñas Piezas Corales* for *a capella* choir (1966), and *Cantata for Peace* (1979). His style was distinctive for his use of twelve-tone technique, but in a very free way or "in a kind of mitigated serialism" (quote from *Notes*; see below). His chromaticism frequently had tonal allegiances, and his melodic lines recalled neoromantic expansiveness at times. He favored classical forms, which were given solid structure with attention to rich detail. He received his first compositional award in 1937, the National Prize of Panama, for his *Reina de amer* (known as "The Spirit of Panama" in the United States). Thereafter his honors and awards were numerous, including fellowships from the Institute of International Education (1943-44), Berkshire Music Center at Tanglewood (1946), Panamanian Government (1946-48), and the Guggenheim Memorial Foundation (1949); the 1974 Koussevitzky International Recording Award (for his Concerto for Violin and Orchestra) and prizes in the Inter-American Music Competitions; and honorary doctorates from Hamline University (1966) and the University of Chile (1963). He toured widely in the Americas and in Europe as a lecturer and as jurist for International Composition Competitions.

BIBL: Questionnaire. Baker. Gerald Behague, *Music in Latin America* (Englewood Cliffs, New Jersey, 1979). BMI (Issue 3, 1974). *Composers of the Americas* (Washington, D.C., 1962). *Notes* (September 1973), p. 155. Pan Pipes 60, 62, 64-66 (1968, 1970, 1972-74).

CORNMEALI, SIGNOR. Entertainer (fl. early nineteenth century in New Orleans, Louisiana; d. 20 May 1842 in New Orleans). He began as a street vendor selling corn meal, for which he composed his own song, and became so popular that he was invited to sing at the St. Charles Theater in May 1837. Although black actors had appeared with white companies during the late eighteenth century, Old Corn Meal (as he was called) may have been the first black singing-entertainer to perform in an integrated setting. His musical activities were widely covered in the New Orleans press, and a picture was published in the *Picayune* in February 1838. In 1840 he gave another stage performance, this time at the Camp Street Theater. His best-known performances were of "Old Rosin the beau," "My long tail blue," and his own song, "Fresh corn meal." His real name was unknown.

BIBL: Henry Kmen, *Music in New Orleans: The Formative Years, 1791-1841* (Baton Rouge, 1966). Charles H. Day, *Fun in Black* (New York, 1874; excerpt about Cornmeali reprinted in BPIM 3, Spring 1976).

CORONETS, THE. Jazz quartet (orig. 1959 at Zola, South Africa). Eugene Madonsela (b. c1944) formed the vocal group, along with Corlette Xoli Qalaba (b. c1944), during their high-school years and brought in two classmates from Qalaba's Orlando High School, Eric Magashule and Jake Leabua. For many years the quartet toured widely in Rhodesia, Botswana, Lesotho, and South Africa, then disbanded in 1966. Each member became active with other musical groups. In 1972 Madonsela reorganized The Coronets in response to public demand, and the next year the quartet won first place at the Pinaculo Festival at Durban, South Africa. In 1974 it was composed of Madonsela, Qalaba, Alfred Lerefolo (b. c1940) and Andrew Chabeli (b. 1943). Others who sang with the Coronets over the years included Kenny Majozi Sikalo, Ndaba ("Qavile") Mhlongo, and Joe Daku. Madonsela wrote and arranged music for the group as well as served as choreographer. Soweto's big band, The Jazz Clan, frequently accompanied the quartet in performances, particularly in revues such as *Groovy Train* (1973).

BIBL: *Drum*, 8 May 1973.

COSTON MALONEY, JEAN ELIZABETH. Concert pianist (b. 10 May 1916 in Indianapolis, Indiana; d. 20 April 1968 in Chicago, Illinois). She began piano study at the age of five with local teachers, a Miss Halpin and later Ellen Thomas. She obtained her musical education in the public schools of Indianapolis, Indiana; at the Arthur Jordan Conservatory of Music in Indianapolis (1926-32), where she studied with Boman Cramer and Willard McGregor; at the Oberlin Conservatory of Music in Ohio (B. Mus., 1936); and at the Juilliard School of Music in New York (1936-37), where she studied with Carl Friedberg. She also studied with Rudolph Ganz (1948-49), president at that time of Chicago Musical College. She began playing piano publicly on recitals at an early age and won first place in piano competitions when she was twelve (1928) and sixteen (1932). She performed a concerto with the Oberlin Symphony Orchestra at graduation because of having earned honors, and later performed with other symphony orchestras, including the New Orleans Symphony (1952). She toured during the 1930s-50s as a solo recitalist and in concert duos or as an accompanist with others, including Rowena Savage, Jeraldine Patterson Morret, Albert Davis, Warren Dent, and Carol Brice,* among others. Her teaching career included tenures at Howard University in Washington, D.C. (1937-38); Spelman College in Atlanta, Georgia (1938-39); Dillard University in New Orleans, Louisiana (1947-48, 1950-52); and Lincoln University in Jefferson City, Missouri (1949-50). In her later career she conducted a music studio.

BIBL: Questionnaire filled out by Frances Jean Maloney (daughter) and Ray Stanley Colston (brother).

COTTEN, ELIZABETH ("LIBBA"). Blueswoman (b. 1893 in Chapel Hill, North Carolina). Self-taught, she learned to play guitar as a girl. Although she was left-handed, she did not reverse the strings but turned the guitar upside down with the bass strings on the bottom. After moving to Washington, D.C., as an adult, she worked for the Charles Seeger family, and through the Seegers she was launched into a professional career. She recorded and toured widely, particularly in her later years. Her best-known song, "Freight train," has sometimes been erroneously attributed to others.

BIBL: BWW. LivBl, 40 (Sept-Oct 1978); Ray M. Lawless, *Folksingers and Folksongs in America* (1960; 2nd ed., New York, 1965).

DISC: TudBM.

COTTON, JAMES. Blues harmonica player (b. 1 July 1935 in Tunica, Mississippi). His father was a minister, and he sang in the church choir as a child. He also listened to broadcasts of "Sonny Boy Williamson, No. 2" (Willie "Rice" Miller)* from radio station KFFA in Helena, Arkansas, and taught himself to play blues by imitating Williamson. At the age of nine, he ran away from home to join Williamson's band and played with the band for six years. During the late 1940s he played with "Howlin' Wolf" (Chester Burnett),* among others. In 1954 he joined "Muddy Waters" (McKinley Morganfield)* in Chicago and remained for twelve years with the band, which recorded extensively and toured widely at home and abroad. Thereafter, he formed his own groups. His musical style reflected his church roots and his long association with the Mississippi Delta/Chicago bluesmen.

BIBL: BWW. Robert Neff and Anthony Connor, *Blues* (Boston, 1975); Oliv.

DISC: LeSl. TudBM.

COWELL, STANLEY. Jazz pianist (b. 5 May 1941 in Toledo, Ohio). He began piano study when he was four years old. He obtained his musical education in the public schools of Toledo, Ohio; at the Oberlin [Ohio] Conservatory of Music (B. Mus., 1962), where he studied with Emil Danenberg and Richard Hoffman; at the Mozarteum Academy in Salzburg, Austria (1960-61); at the University of Witchita in Kansas (1962-63); at the University of Southern California in Los Angeles (1963-64), where he studied with Ingolk Dahl; and at the University of Michigan in Ann Arbor (M. Mus., 1966). From childhood on he played both jazz and classical music. His earliest jazz influence came from Arthur ("Art") Tatum,* who was a long-time friend of his father and who played in his house when he was six years old. During his school years he played with such jazzmen as Yusef Lateef* and Rahsaan Roland Kirk;* he also appeared as a soloist with the Toledo Youth Orchestra (1955) and the American Youth Symphony in Santa Monica, California (1964). In 1966 he began to play with leading jazz groups, including Marion Brown* (1966-67), Max Roach* (1967-70), Robert ("Bobby") Hutcherson*/Harold Land (1968-71), Charles Tolliver* (1969-73), and the Heath Brothers* (1975-c80), among others. In 1970 he was a founding member of Collective Black Artists; in 1971 he founded the Piano Choir, which used in addition to acoustic pianos a Hammond organ, electric pianos, synthesizers, and drums, harpsichord, and African pianos. Members of the Piano Choir included Nat Jones, Hugh Lawson, Webster Lewis, Harold Mabern, Danny Mixon, Sonelius Smith, along with Cowell. He was also a founding member of Strata-East Records, Inc. (1970), a musician-owned recording company and in 1972 became president of the company. He toured widely as soloist and sometime accompanist (with Max Roach* and Abbey Lincoln*) in the United States, Europe, Japan, Africa, and Brazil. He recorded extensively, appeared at jazz festivals, and on television programs. He received awards from the music industry for performance and also won recognition for composition, including a Creative Artists Service Program grant (1970). His best-known albums were *Handscapes*, vols. 1, 2 (performed by the Piano Choir), *Waiting for the Moment, Musa/Ancestral Streams*, and *Talkin' 'Bout Love* (soundtrack for a musical titled *Karma*).

BIBL: ContKey (June 1979). FeaGitJS. WWBA.

COX, IDA (née **IDA PRATHER**). Blues singer (b. 25 February 1896 in Toccoa, Georgia; d. 10 November 1967 in Knoxville, Tennessee). Her family moved to Cedartown, Georgia, when she was an infant. She sang in a church choir as a child; at the age of fourteen she began singing professionally and touring with traveling shows, among them, White and Clark's Minstrels, Silas Green's* show, and F. S.Wolcott's Rabbit Foot Minstrels,* with whom she remained for many years. She recorded extensively during the years 1923-29, most frequently accompanied by Lovie Austin* on the piano or the Austin Blues Serenaders, but also with her husband Jesse Crump, Fletcher Henderson,* ("Papa") Charlie Jackson,* and others. During the 1920s and 1930s she also toured with her own shows, including *Raisin' Cain* (later called *Darktown Scandals*). In 1939 she performed on the "From Spirituals to Swing" Concert staged by John Hammond at Carnegie Hall in New York. Later she recorded with her own All-Star Orchestra, which included at one time or another Charlie Christian,* Lionel Hampton,* Fletcher Henderson,* J. C. Higginbotham,* James P. Johnson,*

(''Hot Lips'') Oran Page,* and Billy Taylor,* among others. Illness forced her into retirement in 1945, but she returned to music briefly in 1961.

BIBL: BWW. Black press, incl. CDef during 1920s and 1930s. ChilWW. Derrick Stewart-Baxter, *Ma Rainey and the Classic Blues Singers* (New York, 1970). FeaEJ. Oliv.

DISC: DiGod. Jep. Kink. RustJR. TudBM.

COZZENS or **COUSINS, RICHARD.** Military fifer (b. in Africa, fl. late eighteenth century; d. 1829 in Providence, Rhode Island). He served as a fifer in the black Rhode Island Regiment commanded by Colonel Christopher Greene and Jeremiah Olney during the War of the American Revolution.

BIBL: GreBD. Nell, p. 128. Wilkes, p. 36.

CRAIG, WALTER F. Concert violinist/Conductor (b. 20 December 1854 in Princeton, New Jersey; d. 1920's [?] in New York, New York [?]). His family moved to New York when he was seven years old, and he obtained his musical education in the public schools. He began violin study at the age of fifteen. He studied violin further with various teachers, including Franz Sinzheimer, and studied harmony and composition with Carl Christian Müller, Max Spicker, and Charles Heinroth, among others. In 1870 he made his debut as a concert violinist at the Cooper Union in New York. In 1872 he organized a society dance-orchestra, which was later known as Craig's Celebrated Orchestra. Over the more than twenty-five years of its existence, the group consisted of from eighteen to thirty or more members and at times was interracial. His orchestra played for black and white society balls up and down the Eastern seaboard and performed in the major concerts given by black musicians, including the celebrated Bergen Star Concerts. One of the important events of his early career was the occasion of the Grand Cake-Walk Concert at Madison Square Garden in February 1892, which featured the rising young soprano, M. Sissieretta Jones* (later called Black Patti) and her orchestra, among others. In 1886 Craig passed the examination for admittance into the Musical Mutual Protective Union, the first of his race to do so. In 1889 he organized the Schumann Quintet, which sponsored series of chamber concerts over the years. He inaugurated two special concert series that became revered traditions for black New Yorkers: in 1882 he began the practice of holding an annual Christmas Reception, which was continued for more than twenty-five years. In 1905 he began the practice of sponsoring an Annual Pre-Lenten Recital and Assembly, which lasted through 1915 and which gave opportunities for performance to both established musicians and some who would later become famous; among them, Harry T. Burleigh,* Anita Patti Brown,* Melville Charlton,* E. Azalia Hackley,* Roland Hayes,* and Francis Hall Johnson.* Craig's orchestra pioneered in performing the music of black composers—for example, Samuel Coleridge-Taylor*—in addition to the traditional European repertory. He won wide recognition and critical acclaim for his violin playing during the late nineteenth century.

BIBL: PaHistSoc: LGColl, 13G. Black press, incl. ClevG, 27 February 1886; NYAge, 16 November 1889, 24 May 1919. Simm. Trot, p. 304; 2 in music section.

CREACH, (''PAPA'') JOHN. Rhythm 'n' blues violinist (b. 28 May 1917 in Beaver Falls, Pennsylvania). When he was about ten years old, an uncle gave him a violin and taught him the basics of violin playing. He continued to practice on his own, with the help of his sister Ruth, who played piano. When he was eighteen his family moved to Chicago, Illinois, where he studied violin and music theory privately. Eventually he began playing professionally, at first in local nightclubs, then with a trio, The Chocolate Music Bars, in hotels. His repertory was primarily rhythm 'n' blues. In 1943 he changed to amplified violin. In 1945 he settled at San Francisco, California, where he soon formed the Johnny Creach Trio, which toured widely. He was also active as a soloist and as free-lance performer with other groups, particularly blues bands. He played in restaurants and nightclubs, with a ship band on the *S.S. Catalina* for four years, and appeared in films, among them *Cruising Down the River* and *Blue Gardenia*. In 1970 he joined Jefferson Airplane (1970-74); the next year he began touring and recording with Hot Tuna. He made his recording debut in 1971 and thereafter recorded extensively with his own groups and with others. His best-known recordings were ''Papa John Creach,'' ''String jet rock,'' ''I'm the fiddle man,'' and the album *Filthy*. One press release referred to Creach as the ''voodoo violinist'' because he could ''raise the dead'' with his violin. He was noted for his recordings of ''down-home, dirty'' blues.

BIBL: StamPRS (see under Hot Tuna).

CREAMER, HENRY. Songwriter (b. 21 June 1879 in Richmond, Virginia; d. 14 October 1930 in New York, New York). He obtained his musical education in the public schools of New York and through private study. He made his vaudeville debut at New York's Crescent Theater in 1911, singing one of his own songs. Later he joined with J.Turner Layton* to form a vaudeville act, which toured widely in the United States and abroad for about six years. He and Layton wrote many songs, of which the best known were ''After you've gone,'' ''Dear old Southland,'' and '' 'Way down yonder in New Orleans.'' They also contributed songs to Broadway musicals, as early as 1911 to the Zeigfeld Follies for Bert Williams,* and wrote the score for the musical *Strut Miss Lizzie* (1922), in which they also played leading roles. Creamer was one of the founders of the Clef Club in 1910 and an associate of the Gotham-Attucks Music Company founded by Cecil Mack* (née Richard McPherson).

BIBL: ASCAP. Black press, incl. CDef, 13 May 1911; NYAge, 25 October 1930.

DISC: Kink.

CREATH, CHARLES CYRIL (''CHARLIE''). Jazz trumpeter (b. 30 December 1890 in Ironton, Missouri; d. 23 October 1951 in Chicago, Illinois). He came from a musical family: two sisters played piano. He began playing alto saxophone, then changed to trumpet during his high-school years. About 1906 he began touring with various groups, including P. G. Lowery's* orchestra, Drake and Walker's show, and the Hagen Beck-Wallace Circus band, among others. He settled in St. Louis, Missouri, about 1918 and thereafter led his own groups in dance halls and nightclubs and recorded with his Jazz O-Maniacs. He was also a co-leader with Fate Marable* on riverboats (1926, 1930s) and played with Harvey Lankford's Synco High-Hatters (1933). He settled in Chicago, Illinois, during the c1940s, but was largely inactive in music.

BIBL: ChilWW. FeaEJ.

DISC: RustJR.

CROSSMAN, SIMEON. Military drummer (fl. late eighteenth century in Taunton, Massachusetts). He was a drummer during the American Revolutionary War.

BIBL: Wilkes, p. 71.

CROUCH, ANDRAE. Gospel singer (b. 1 July 1942 in Los Angeles, California). As a child he sang in the choir of his father's Holiness church and began playing for church services when he was eleven years old. He also played at an early age on his father's Sunday-night radio broadcasts and performed with the Crouch Trio (composed of his brother, sister, and himself) at his father's preaching engagements. He obtained his education in the San Fernando [California] High School, the Valley Junior College in San Fernando, and later at the Life Bible College in Los Angeles, California. During his school years he performed with a group, The Cogics, which also included William (''Billy'') Preston.* In 1968 he organized his own mixed group, The Disciples, with whom he was lead singer and pianist and which included his twin sister Sandra. He recorded extensively, toured widely in the United States and abroad, and became one of the leading gospel singers of the 1960s-70s. He wrote numerous songs, many of which became standard repertory items for other gospel groups. His best-known songs included ''I don't know why Jesus loved me,'' ''Through it all,'' ''The blood will never lose its power,'' and the albums *Live in London* and *Take Me Back*. Among those who recorded his songs were Elvis Presley and Pat Boone. During the 1970s his group featured gospel singer Danniebelle Hall. His style combined ballad, rock, country-music and soul-music elements with traditional gospel. Beginning in the 1970s he used both acoustic and electronic instruments (including synthesizers) in his accompanying bands. He received awards from the music and recording industries.

BIBL: ContKey (August 1979). GMEncy. Heil. *Sepia* (December 1976). WWA. WWBA.

DISC: TudBM.

CROWDERS (or **CROWDUS), REUBEN.** See **HOGAN, ERNEST.**

CRUDUP, ARTHUR (''BIG BOY''). Blues guitarist (b. 24 August 1905 in Forest, Mississippi; d. 28 March 1974 in Nassawadox, Virginia). His father played guitar, and he began playing blues on the guitar as a child. He played professionally in cafes and bars in Mississippi until 1940, when he went to Chicago. He recorded extensively during the years 1941-56; in 1942 he added an amplifier to his guitar. He was called ''the father of rock 'n' roll'' because so many of his songs were used by rock singers such as Elvis Presley, including ''That's all right, mama,'' ''So glad you're mine,'' and ''My baby left me.'' Crudup did not benefit financially from his song successes, and he left music during the mid-1950s, except for a recording session in 1959. When the blues made a resurgence in the 1960s, he began to perform again, touring widely at home and abroad, appearing on college campuses and at the major blues festivals. His style was distinctive for its plaintive, high-pitched voice and an insistent, cutting guitar.

BIBL: BWW. Mike Jahn, ''The Royalty Cheaters'' in *High Fidelity Magazine* (December 1972). Oliv.

DISC: DiGod. Jep. LeSl. TudBM.

CRUSADERS, THE. (formerly **THE JAZZ CRUSADERS).** (org. 1952 at Houston, Texas; fl. 1950s-

80s). The instrumental group was organized in 1952 and originally included Wilton Felder (bass/saxophone; b. 31 August 1940), Nesbert ("Stix") Hooper (percussion; b. 15 August 1938), Wayne Henderson (trombone; b. 24 September 1939), and Joseph ("Joe") Sample (keyboard; b. 1 February 1939), all natives of Houston, Texas. They formed a rhythm 'n' blues group in junior high school, joined by Hubert Laws* and Henry Wilson in 1954, and remained together through years of attendance in high school and at Texas Southern University in Houston. In 1958 they left college before completing the degree program and went to the West Coast to further the career of the group in the field of jazz. Over the years they used various names: The Swingsters, The Nite Hawks, and beginning in 1960, The Jazz Crusaders. The group recorded regularly and toured widely, frequently performing with others, among them, Herbert Hancock,* Mahalia Jackson,* The Rolling Stones, and Arthur Fiedler and the Boston "Pops" Orchestra. During the 1960s the Jazz Crusaders became a quartet; in 1972 the quartet changed its name to The Crusaders and widened its repertory to include rock and rhythm 'n' blues as well as jazz. Over the years personnel changes brought in Robert ("Pop") Popwell and Larry Carlton; by 1980 only Felder, Hooper, and Sample remained of the original members. The Crusaders received numerous awards from the music industry. Their best-known recordings included "Freedom sound," "Southern comfort," and "Then there was the blues."

BIBL: Black press, incl. AmstN, 29 October 1975.

CUMBO, CLARISSA BURTON. Concert manager (b. 15 January 1903 in Roseau, Dominica, West Indies). She came from a musical family: her father was a church organist and choir director. She studied piano as a child with teachers of the local Catholic schools and later studied voice with Otto Bohanon, Marshall Rusk, and Harry Williams.* In 1917 she went to New York, where she became active in musical circles of the Harlem community and sang in local community choirs. She first became involved in promoting concerts in 1946 as a member of the group that organized an interracial symphony orchestra under the direction of David Mendoza. Later she served on the Board of Directors (1947-48) for Everett Lee's* Cosmopolitan Little Symphony. In 1950 she organized the Community Friends of Music, which promoted concerts that featured black concert artists. Thereafter she was highly active with the Symphony of the New World* (1964-78), for which she organized a Friends of the Symphony group and served on the orchestra's Board of Directors. In 1970 she founded Triad Presentations, along with her husband Marion Cumbo,* which dedicated itself to the promotion of black concert artists and the music of black composers. Those presented by Triad over the years included Thomas Carey,* Carol Brice,* Betty Allen,* Raymond Jackson,* Robert Jordan,* Eugene Moye, Carol Joy, and Frances Walker,* among many others. The organization also sponsored a Triad Chorale group under the direction of Noel DaCosta.

BIBL: Black press.

CUMBO, MARION. Symphony/theater cellist (b. 1 March 1899 in New York). He obtained his musical education in the public schools of New York; at the [David] Martin*-Smith School of Music in New York, where he studied cello with Minnie Brown; at the Institute of Musical Art in New York (now Juilliard School of Music), where he studied with Willem Willeke; and through private study with Leonard Jeter and with Bruno Steindl in Chicago, Illinois. His career development was aided by Brown, who adopted him as her protégé. He began playing in public concerts about 1915 at the Martin-Smith music school and attracted wide attention in 1920 when he played at the annual convention of the National Association of Negro Musicians in New York. During his early career he was active as both a concert artist and theater musician. He performed with the Negro String Quartet (1919-26), which included Arthur Boyd, Felix Weir,* and Francis Hall Johnson.* He also performed with Johnson's choral groups and with such community organizations as the New Amsterdam Orchestra and the Harlem Orchestra. As a theater cellist, he played in pit orchestras for the Midnight Frolics revue at the Amsterdam Theatre (1919) and such Broadway musicals as the Noble Sissle*/Eubie Blake* *Shuffle Along* (touring company, 1922-24), Sissle/Blake's *The Chocolate Dandies* (1924), Joe Jordan's* *Brown Buddies* (1930), Lew Leslie's *Blackbirds of 1938*, and *The Hot Mikado* (1939), as well as for various vaudeville shows. During the 1940s-50s he performed with Everett Lee's* Cosmopolitan Little Symphony (1947-48), The Symphony of the New World* (1964-78), and the Senior Musician's Orchestra of AFM Local 802 (1970s). In 1950 he toured with Eva Jessye's* choral groups. His recording activity included performances with Fletcher Henderson's* Black Swan Orchestra and with Clara Smith.* In 1970 he and his wife, Clarissa Cumbo,* founded Triad Presentations, an organization dedicated to the promotion of black concert artists and the music of black composers.

BIBL: Interview by Angela McLinn. AbdulBCM. AlHen. Black press, incl. AmstN, 12 August 1944; CDef, 28 August 1920; NYAge, 16 October 1920.

CUNEY HARE, MAUD. See **HARE, MAUD CUNEY.**

CUNNINGHAM, ARTHUR. Composer (b. 11 November 1928 in Nyack, New York). He began piano study when he was six years old. He obtained his musical education in the public schools of Nyack, New York; at Fisk University in Nashville, Tennessee (B.A., 1951), where he studied with John Work III; at the Metropolitan Music School in New York (1941-45), where he studied with Wallingford Riegger, Johnny Mehegan, and Theodore ("Teddy") Wilson;* at the Juilliard School of Music in New York (1951-52), where he studied with Henry Brant, Norman Lloyd, Peter Mennin, and Margaret Hillis; and at Columbia University Teachers College (M.A., 1957). He began writing music as a child and performed his pieces in public when he was seven. When he was twelve he organized his own jazz group, for whom he wrote and arranged music. Through his high-school and college years he continued to write for jazz groups, and beginning in the late 1940s he wrote concert music. In 1951 a concert of his compositions for baritone, soprano, and piano was sponsored by the National Association of Negro Musicians; this was the first all-Cunningham concert. During his years of service in the U. S. Armed Forces, he wrote for an army band and toured with a trio, playing the double bass. He toured widely as a guest lecturer and served as an artist-in-residence in various institutions, including North Carolina State College in Greensboro (1973). He wrote in a wide variety of musical forms, including three symphonies, a work for concert band, two concertos, a dozen or more chamber works, two ballets, ten works for chorus, five operas or stage works, pieces for solo instruments such as piano and cello, and numerous art songs. His best-known works included *Adagio for String Orchestra and Oboe* (1954), *Perimeters* for flute, clarinet, vibraharp, and double bass (1965), *Dialogue for piano and chamber orchestra* (1967), *Lullabye for a Jazz Baby* for trumpet and orchestra (1970), *The Walton Statement* for double bass and orchestra (1971), *Theater Piece* for orchestra (1966), *Concentrics* for orchestra (1968); the stage works *House By the Sea* (1966), *Shango* (1969), and *Ostrich Feathers* (1964); the solo pieces *Engram* for piano (1969) and *Ecclatette* for solo cello (1971); the songs *The Prince* for bass-baritone and orchestra (1973) and *Prometheus* for bass and piano (1965); the *Harlem Suite Ballet* (1971); and *Jubilee Songs* (1971). His style was eclectic, drawing upon traditional techniques and forms, serialism, jazz, rock, and gospel. His honors included grants from ASCAP for composition and the National Endowment for the Arts (1974); his orchestral *Concentrics* was nominated for the Pulitzer Prize.

BIBL: Questionnaire. Bull. Gro. WWBA.

D

D'ALBERT, MARC (MARCUS). Concert pianist/Studio teacher (b. 1908 in Chicago (?), Illinois; d. 6 October 1975 in New York, New York). He was a child prodigy at the piano. When he was fourteen he toured as accompanist/pianist with the Buckner Jubilee Singers in Canada, Europe, and Australia. He studied piano with Harmon Walt at the Chicago Piano College. He began to tour as a concert pianist during the 1930s; he gave his first New York recital in April 1930. He also toured with singers and groups, among them, George Garner* and Hall Johnson.* He settled in New York during the 1940s and maintained a piano studio in Carnegie Hall until his death.

BIBL: Black press, incl. AmstN, 15 October 1975; CDef, 27 April 1929; 18 January 1930. NYT, 8 October 1975.

DA COSTA, NOEL. Composer (b. 24 December 1929 in Lagos, Nigeria). His parents, originally from Kingston, Jamaica, moved back to the West Indies when he was three years old. When he was eleven his family moved to New York; he began the study of violin with Barnabas Istok. His high-school teacher, poet Countee Cullen, inspired him to become a creative artist. He obtained his musical education at Queens College of the City University of New York (B.A., 1952) and Columbia University (M.A., 1956). His awards during this period included a Seidl Fellowship in composition from Columbia and a Fulbright Fellowship to study composition with Luigi Dallapiccola in Italy (1956-1958). In 1970 he was appointed to the music faculty of Rutgers University; his previous teaching experience included tenures at Hampton Institute in Virginia (1961-63) and at Queens College and Hunter College of the City University of New York (1963-66). He was active as a violinist; he played with the Symphony of the New World* and in orchestras of Broadway musicals, ballet, and opera. He also conducted choral groups, and in 1974 became the musical director of the Triad Chorale. His first published composition was *Tambourines* (1970, a Langston Hughes* poem) for children's chorus, piano, and electric guitar. His best-known works were the song cycle *The Confession Stone* (1969-70, text by Owen Dodson); "Jes Grew" for solo violin (1973); *Spiritual Set* for organ (1974), *Ceremony of Spirituals* for soprano, saxophone, chorus, and orchestra (1976); and *The Singing Tortoise* (1971), a theater piece for children. The vocal pieces "Two songs for Juli-Ju" are included in *Anthology of Art Songs of Black American Composers* (New York, 1977).

BIBL: Questionnaire. Lorna McDaniel, "Out of the Black Church" in *The American Organist* (May 1979).

DABNEY, FORD THOMPSON. Society dance-band leader/Songwriter (B. 15 March 1883 in Washington, D.C.; d. 21 June 1958 in New York, New York). He came from a musical family: his father and uncle, Wendell P. Dabney,* were professional musicians. His earliest musical instruction was obtained from his father; later he studied privately with Charles Donch, William Waldecker, and Samuel Fabian. During the years 1904-07 he was court pianist to President Noro Alexis of Haiti. After returning to the United States, he organized groups, —among them, Ford Dabney's Ginger Girls with Effie King and Lottie Gee—which toured on the vaudeville circuit, and later became manager of a theater. By 1913 he had settled in New York and allied himself with James Reese Europe's* Clef Club. He also directed his own syncopated orchestra, which was the first black orchestra to play regularly in a Broadway theater (1913-21)—Ziegfeld's Midnight Frolic Show at the New Amsterdam Theater. When Jim Europe resigned from the Clef Club in 1914, Dabney left with him, and the two men organized the Tempo Club. It was this organization that furnished an orchestra for the dance team of Irene and Vernon Castle. Beginning in 1914, Dabney and Europe wrote the music for the Castles until the death of Vernon in 1917. They also toured with the dancers and are credited with having invented the "fox trot," which the Castles introduced to the public at a Clef Club concert on 13 October 1914 at the Manhattan Casino. Dabney recorded with his groups as early as 1917, using various names over the years, including Dabney's Novelty Orchestra, Ford Dabney's Syncopated Orchestra, and Ford Dabney's Military Band. His best-known works were the musicals *The King's Quest* (1909) and *Rang Tang* (1927), an instrumental piece called "The Pensacola Mootch" (1910), and the song "That's why they call me shine" (1910, lyrics by Cecil Mack*).

BIBL: ASCAP. Black press. Douglas Gilbert, *Lost Chords* (New York, 1942). NYT, 23 June 1958.

DISC: RustJR.

DABNEY, WENDELL PHILLIPS. Writer/Studio teacher (b. 4 November 1865 in Richmond, Virginia; d. 3 June 1952 in Cincinnati, Ohio). The details of his early life are not known. He taught in the public schools of Richmond, Virginia (1886-92), and conducted a music studio there. Later he studied music at Oberlin Conservatory in Ohio, then settled in Cincinnati, Ohio, in 1894. There he conducted a studio for the teaching of guitar, banjo, mandolin, and other string instruments. He also directed string dance orchestras, which played for the city's major receptions, balls, and other social entertainments during the turn of the century. He published two manuals, *Dabney's Complete Method of Guitar* and *The Dabney and Roach Mandolin and Guitar Method*. The periodical he founded in 1906, *The Union*, and his book, *Cincinnati's Colored Citizens* (1926), contain information about black musicians. Bandleader Ford Dabney* was his nephew.

BIBL: Wendell P. Dabney, *Cincinnati's Colored Citizens* (Cincinnati, 1926), pp. 177, 209, 360. NYT, 5 June 1952. WWCR.

DAFORA HORTON, ASADATA. Composer (b. 1889 in Freetown, Sierra Leone, West Africa; d. 4 March 1965 in New York, New York). He left home at the age of twenty and traveled in Africa studying folklore for six years. He then went to Europe, where he stayed for six years, studying music and touring with a group of African drummers and German female dancers whom he had trained. During this period he also taught dance in Berlin and Dresden, Germany, and sang at La Scala Opera House in Milan, Italy. In 1929 he went to New York, where he organized a troupe of singers, dancers, and drummers, and presented the group in its American debut in the fall of 1933. He was encouraged by Anne Kennedy, at that time business manager of the Unity Theater, to develop his program into a full-length production with a plot. The resulting folk opera, *Kykuntor (The Witch Woman)*, opened in May 1934 with a mixed cast of Africans and black Americans. Black pianist Margaret Kennerly Upshur assisted him in training the performers and arranging the music. During the next three decades Dafora regularly presented African dance festivals and folk operas in New York; beginning in 1943 he produced annual festivals. In 1959 he joined forces with Les Jazz Modes Quintet to produce shows. He returned to Freetown in 1960—leaving his group, Shogola Aloba, in the charge of Esther Rolle—with plans for becoming cultural director in his country after it gained independence in April 1961. Illness forced him to return, however, to the United States. His best-known works, in addition to *Kykuntor*, were the dance opera *Zunguru* (1940) and the tribal opera *Africa* (1944).

BIBL: Schom. Black press, incl. AmstN, 5 March 1960; NYAge, 20 November 1943. [New York] *Herald Tribune*, 14 December 1943. NYT, 13 June 1954, 24 January 1959, 22 May 1960.

DALE, CLAMMA CHURITA. Opera singer (b. 4 July 1948 in Chester, Pennsylvania). Her father, Granville Dale, was a part-time jazz performer. She studied piano as a child, began playing clarinet during her grade-school years, and sang solos with the school chorus from the time she was eight years old. She began voice study when she was fourteen, attending the Settlement Music School in Philadelphia, Pennsylvania. She obtained her musical education in the public schools of Chester (a suburb of Philadelphia) and at the Juilliard School of Music in New York (B. Mus., 1970; M.S., 1975). She studied voice with Hans Heinz, Alice Howland, and Cornelius Reed. She made her operatic debut (soprano) in September 1975 with the New York City Opera, singing the role of Antonia in Offenbach's *The Tales of Hoffman*. Also in 1975 she won first prize in the Walter W. Naumberg voice competition, and the Naumberg Foundation sponsored her debut recital at the Alice Tully Hall in May 1976. Thereafter she toured as a concert singer and appeared with symphony orchestras as well as sang in opera. In December 1977 she was one of the six soloists in the premiere of Leonard Berstein's *Songfest* with the New York Philharmonic. In her early career she taught in elementary school in New York and held music classes for prison inmates on Rikers Island. She was best known for her roles of Giulietta in *The Tales of Hoffman*, Nedda in Leoncavallo's *I Pagliacci*, Musetta in Puccini's *La Bohème*,

Countess Almaviva in Mozart's *The Marriage of Figaro*, Mistress Ford in Verdi's *Falstaff*, Bess in Gershwin's *Porgy and Bess*, Pamina in Mozart's *The Magic Flute*, and Saint Teresa I in Virgil Thomson's *Four Saints in Three Acts*.

BIBL: Schom. AbdulBCM. CurBiog (April 1979). *People* (22 November 1976).

DISC: Turn.

DAMERON, TADLEY EWING ("TADD"). Jazz pianist/Arranger (b. 21 February 1917 in Cleveland, Ohio; d. 8 March 1965 in New York, New York). Mostly self-taught, he learned music fundamentals from his brother Caesar, a saxophonist. He began his professional career with Freddie Webster, then later played with Zack White and Blanche Calloway.* He began arranging for bands early in his career and was one of the first jazzmen to write and arrange for bebop groups, among them, John ("Dizzy") Gillespie,* Harlan Leonard, and his own groups. During his career he also wrote or arranged music for Benny Goodman, Ted Heath, Milt Jackson,* Jimmy Lunceford,* Edward ("Sonny") Stitt,* and Sarah Vaughan,* among others. Periodically, he led his own bands (1948, 1953). He pioneered in using bebop harmonic and rhythmic elements in big-band arrangements.

BIBL: ASCAP. FeaEJ. FeaJS.

DISC: Jep. ModJ. RustJR. TudJ.

DANDRIDGE, DOROTHY. Popular-music singer (b. 9 November c1923 in Cleveland, Ohio; d. 8 September 1965 in Los Angeles, California). She began performing professionally at the age of five in a family act, which included her mother, her aunt Ruby Dandridge, and her sister Vivian. Later she and her sister toured the vaudeville circuit as the Dandridge Sisters and recorded with Jimmy Lunceford* in 1940. By the time she was sixteen she was singing at the Cotton Club in New York. She dropped out of music for a period, then returned during the 1950s to sing in nightclubs and in films. She was acclaimed for her performances as Carmen in the film musical *Carmen Jones* (1954) and as Bess in the film *Porgy and Bess* (1959). Her career went into a decline thereafter, although she continued to sing in clubs.

BIBL: Black press, incl. CDef, 1950s; AmstN, 18 September 1965. *Ebony* (March 1966).

DISC: RustJR.

DANIEL, BILLIE LYNN. See also **FRIERSON, ANDREW.** Concert singer/Studio teacher (b. 21 May 1932 in New York, New York). She came from a musical family: her father taught college-level music in his early career, and her mother sang. She began piano study at the age of five and voice study when she was fourteen. She received her musical education at the Juilliard School of Music in New York (diploma, 1952) and at the Manhattan School of Music in New York (B. Mus., 1967; M. Mus., 1972). Her early career development was influenced by the recordings of Lily Pons and Dorothy Maynor* to which she listened. She was a protégé of Rose Bampton; others who aided in her career included Sergius Kagen, Wilfred Pelletier, and Ignace Strasvogel. She made her debut as a concert soprano in March 1959 at the Carnegie Recital Hall in New York and made her Town Hall debut in February 1962. She toured as a concert singer and as soloist for opera and oratorio; in 1961 she went to Europe with the *Porgy and Bess* company, singing the role of Serena. During the 1960s she sang in the Frierson Ensemble, formed by her husband, Andrew Frierson.* Occasionally she gave duo recitals with her bass-baritone husband. She also conducted a voice studio and taught at the Henry Street Settlement House in New York. Her honors included a Marion Anderson Award (1964), John Hay Whitney Fellowship, Joy-in-Singing Award (1962), and Euclid W. McBride Award.

BIBL: Questionnaire. NYT, 31 March 1975.

DANIELS, BILLY. See **DANIELS, WILLIAM.**

DANIELS, WILLIAM ("BILLY"). Popular music singer (b. c1915 in Jacksonville, Florida). He sang in a church choir as a child. Later he sang on the local radio station, then left home at seventeen to go to New York, where his first employment was as a singing waiter. In 1938 he sang with the Erskin Hawkins* orchestra; later he began performing as a single act in nightclubs. In 1951 he had his own television show; he also appeared in film musicals and in the Broadway musicals *Golden Boy* (1964), *Hello, Dolly!* (1975), and *Bubbling Brown Sugar* (London, 1977). He toured widely in clubs in the United States and abroad, with Benny Payne as accompanist after 1950. He recorded with Hawkins and others. His best-known performance was of "That old black magic."

BIBL: Black press, incl. AmstN, 23 January 1960; PhilaT, 9 November 1974. *Ebony* (September 1950, August 1955).

DISC: Jep. Kink. RustCED. RustJR.

DASH, ST. JULIAN BENNETT. Jazz saxophonist (b. 9 April 1916 in Charleston, South Carolina; d. 24 February 1974 in New York, New York). During his high-school days he played with local bands. After settling in New York during the 1930s he led his own band in Harlem; in 1938 he joined Erskine Hawkins,* whom he had known during his study at Alabama State College. After over twenty years of performing with Hawkins, he left music, then returned to lead his own quintet in 1970-71 and to tour in Europe in 1972. He recorded with Hawkins and with his own groups. His best-known song was ''Tuxedo junction.''

BIBL: ASCAP. Black press, incl. AmstN, 27 February 1974. ChilWW. FeaEJ. FeaGitJS.

DISC: Jep. RustJR. TudJ.

DAVENPORT, CHARLES (''COW COW''). Boogie-woogie pianist (b. 26 April 1895 in Anniston, Alabama; d. 2 December 1955 in Cleveland, Ohio). He studied theology at Selma University in Alabama, then left for a career in music, touring with vaudeville acts and carnivals (1914-1930). During those years he teamed with Dora Carr and Ivy Smith; he also organized his own act, Cow Cow's Chicago Steppers. In 1937 he settled in Cleveland, although he left occasionally to perform for periods of time in other cities. He was one of the pioneer boogie-woogie pianists; he claimed to have introduced the term ''boogie-woogie'' to Clarence (''Pinetop'') Smith.* Certainly his ''Cow cow blues'' (recorded 1927) was influential in the development of boogie-woogie piano style. Among his other well-known songs were ''I'll be glad when you're dead, you rascal you'' and ''Mama don't allow it.''

BIBL: ASCAP. ChilWW. FeaEJ.

DISC: DiGod. Jep. Kink. LeSl. RustJR. TudJ.

DAVIS, ARTHUR D. Symphony/jazz bassist (b. 5 December 1934 in Harrisburg, Pennsylvania). He began playing bass and tuba during his high-school years. He obtained his musical education at Hunter College of the City University of New York (B.A., 1972), City College of CUNY (M.A., 1976), and New York University (M.A., 1976). His early jazz experience was with Max Roach* (1958); later he played with John Coltrane,* John Birks (''Dizzy'') Gillespie,* Gigi Gryce, and Ahmad Jamal,* among others. He was also active with Broadway-musical, media, and symphony orchestras during this period, including the NBC Staff Orchestra (1962-63), Westinghouse TV Staff Orchestra (1964-69), the CBS Staff Orchestra (1969-70), and the Symphony of the New World* (beginning in 1965). He toured widely in the United States and in Europe as a soloist, with others, and as a lecturer. He taught at Manhattan Community College of CUNY (1971-73) and published a manual, *The Arthur Davis Method for Double Bass* (New York, 1976).

BIBL: FeaEJ. FeaJS. WWBA.

DISC: ModJ.

DAVIS, CLIFTON (''PIKE''). Jazz trumpeter (b. c1895 in Baltimore, Maryland; d. 13 September 1976 in Baltimore). He was taught trumpet by a local musician and toured in his youth with the Ringling Brothers Circus. In 1915 he played with Eubie Blake* and later with Joe Rochester; he then went to New York, where he joined LeRoy Smith's band. In 1923 he went to London with the Broadway musical *Plantation Revue* (1922) and again in 1926. From the 1930s on he played with or was musical director for many shows, including *Rhapsody in Black* (1931-34) and Lew Leslie's Blackbirds Revue (1934), and toured abroad with the shows. He also played with bands, among them, Ford Dabney's.* His own group, the Pike Davis Continental Orchestra, played in such revues as the *Ziegfeld Follies* and *Brown Buddies* (1930). He settled permanently in Baltimore in 1935, where he played with the Rivers Chambers Orchestra through 1975 and thereafter with Earl Bean.

BIBL: ChilWW. FeaEJ. *International Musician* (September 1976).

DAVIS, EDDIE (''LOCKJAW''). Jazz saxophonist (b. 2 March 1921 in New York, New York). Self-taught, his first professional experiences were with New York groups, including Charles (''Cootie'') Williams,* Lucius (''Lucky'') Millinder,* Andy Kirk,* and Louis Armstrong,* during the years 1942-45. Thereafter he led his own group for seven years (1945-52), then joined William (''Count'') Basie* (1952-53). He reorganized his own groups, after 1955 leading a trio that often included Shirley Scott* and Johnny Griffin.* He rejoined Basie (1964-73), touring at home and abroad with the orchestra, but also played with other groups. In 1973 he settled in Las Vegas, Nevada.

BIBL: FeaEJ. FeaJS. FeaGitJS. WWBA.

DISC: Kink. ModJ. TudJ.

DAVIS, ELLABELLE. Concert singer (b. 17 March 1907 in New Rochelle, New York; d. 15 November 1960 in New Rochelle). She sang in a church choir as a girl. She studied with Reina LeZar and began giving joint recitals with her sister Marie, a pianist, during the mid-1920s. Later she sang solos with various groups, among them the Utica Jubilee Singers in a local concert, and began to give solo recitals. In 1942 she made her concert debut as a soprano at Town Hall in New York. She made her operatic debut in 1946 in the title role of Verdi's *Aida* at the Opera Nacionale in Mexico City and repeated the role in 1949 at La Scala opera house in Milan to much acclaim. In 1947 the League of Composers singled her out as the outstanding American singer of the year (1946-47 season) and commissioned

Lukas Foss to write a work for her, which was the cantata *The Song of Songs*, performed by the Boston Symphony with Serge Koussevitzky, conductor. From 1946 on she toured extensively at home, in Europe, South and Central America, Mexico, and Israel, appearing in solo concerts, with symphony orchestras and opera companies, and at festivals, among them, the Sibelius Festival in Helsinki, Finland. Her long-time accompanist was Kelley Wyatt.* She recorded operatic arias, lieder, and spirituals.

BIBL: Black press, incl. AmstN, 1920s-50s, 19 November 1960. CBD. NYB, 1952. NYT, 16 November 1960.

DISC: Turn.

DAVIS, ("BLIND") GARY D. Bluesman (b. 30 April 1896 in Laurens, South Carolina; d. 5 May 1972 in Hammonton, New Jersey). He lost his sight at an early age and studied at the South Carolina School for the Blind. He taught himself to play blues instruments as a child; at the age of fourteen he organized his own blues band, which toured in the Piedmont area. His early style development was influenced by Willie Walker of Greenville, South Carolina. Later he settled in Durham, North Carolina, where he performed and/or recorded with other Piedmont bluesmen, including "Blind Boy" Fuller* (Fulton Allen) and "Sonny" Terry* (Saunders Terrell). In 1933 he was ordained as a minister; thereafter his interest centered more on gospel music than blues, but it was a blues-inflected gospel, sometimes called "holy blues." In 1944 he settled in New York. Although he had recorded as early as 1935, it was during the 1950s and 1960s that he won recognition as a blues guitarist. He toured at home and abroad, appeared at blues festivals and in films, and recorded both gospel music and blues. His wife, Annie Bell Wright, was also a blues singer.

BIBL: BWW. LivBl 8 (Spring 1972). Kip Lornell, "Living Blues Interview: J. B. Long" in LivBl 29 (September-October 1976). MeeJMov. Oliv. Bill Phillips, "Piedmont Country Blues" in *Southern Exposure* (July 1975). *Variety* (10 May 1972).

DISC: DiGod. LeSl. TudBM.

DAVIS, GUSSIE LORD. Songwriter (b. 3 December 1863 in Dayton, Ohio; d. 18 October 1899 in Whitestone [near New York], New York). He obtained his musical education at the Nelson Musical College in Cincinnati, Ohio, through private tutoring. His application for admission was rejected because of his color, but he arranged with the administration to give janitorial services at a salary of $15.00 per month and in turn to receive private lessons. He had difficulty in finding a publisher for the first song he felt was publishable, " 'Neath the maple on the hill." Finally he persuaded Helling & Company to publish the song for a fee of twenty dollars; the song was successful beyond his dreams, and thus he made money on his first venture. He was eighteen years old. Some time thereafter he came under the influence of songwriter James E. Stewart, of whom Davis later said, "I owe all my points and knowledge about songwriting [to him]" (interview published in CleveG, 4 February 1888). Davis's next successful song was "The lighthouse by the sea," which brought him the offer of a contract with J.C. Groene & Company in 1885. Later he signed a contract with George Propheter, who took Davis to New York with him. Within a few years Davis's songs were being published by the leading publishers in Tin Pan Alley (New York's commercial music district). In 1895 Davis entered a contest sponsored by the *New York World* to find the ten best songwriters in the United States and came in second with his song "Send back the picture and the ring," which won him $500 in gold. By the end of the nineteenth century Davis was one of the leading two or three songwriters in the nation; his best-known song, "In the baggage coach ahead," sold more than a million copies. He was also a performer. He played piano on Bergen Star Concerts during the 1880s and toured with his own Davis Operatic and Plantation Minstrels during the mid-1890s. In the fall of 1899, his show, *A Hot Old Time in Dixie*, was successfully launched on its road tour. Davis and Tom McIntosh* were to be the featured performers, but Davis's death left McIntosh to carry on alone. Davis was a prolific songwriter; he wrote in a wide variety of forms—sacred, sentimental, descriptive, comic, Negro, and Irish. His stage works included musicals and the opera *King Herod*.

BIBL: Black press, incl. CleveG, 4 February 1888, 28 October 1899; IndF, 25 December 1897, 12 August 1899. BPIM (Fall 1978), includes list of works and selected songs. Douglas Gilbert, *Lost Chords* (New York, 1942).

DAVIS, MILES DEWEY, JR. Jazz trumpeter (b. 25 May 1926 in Alton, Illinois). His family moved to East St. Louis, Illinois, when he was an infant less than a year old. He first studied trumpet in elementary school; when he was thirteen he was given his own trumpet and thereafter he studied with St. Louis musician Elwood Buchanan. He obtained his musical education in the public schools of East St. Louis and at Juilliard School of Music in New York (1945), where he remained one semester. He began playing jazz professionally before he was sixteen with a local group, the Blue Devils; he also played in his high-school band. His early style development was influenced by Clark Terry,* who was well known in the St. Louis area and whom he heard perform. Settling in New York in 1945, he began playing with various groups, particularly those associated with New York's famed 52nd Street, such as Charlie Parker* and Coleman Hawkins,* and later with Bennett ("Benny") Carter* (1946, including trip to Los Angeles, California), William ("Billy") Eckstine,* and Tadd Dameron* (during the years 1948-50). By 1948 Davis was also leading his own groups in New York nightclubs and attracted wide attention with his nine-piece so-called Capitol Band, named after its recordings in 1949-50 for Capitol Records. This band's unusual instrumentation, using French horn and reviving use of the tuba, produced a unique sound that contributed to the development of "cool jazz." Later the recordings were issued as *The Complete Birth of the Cool*, which became important in the development of the "West Coast" bebop style. Those who were associated with the landmark recordings as arrangers or performers included Lee Konitz, John Lewis,* Max Roach,* Kai Winding, Gerry Mulligan, and Gil Evans, among others. During the next three decades Davis led primarily quartets, quintets, or sextets and toured widely. In 1957, however, he recorded with a big band the album *Miles Ahead*, which brought him wide recognition as an important innovator; and his small-group recording the next year of *Kind of Blue* was a milestone in jazz history in its representation of the essence of the avant-garde in jazz. His music of the mid-1960s and later—with its fusion of jazz, rock 'n' roll, and soul elements, its use of modal melodies and harmonies, its penchant for electronic instruments, and other innovations—is best represented by the album *Bitches Brew* (1969). In the 1970s Davis continued to explore new frontiers in jazz. Many of the jazzmen who trained with him established their own groups and became leading figures, including Ron Carter,* Julian ("Cannonball") Adderley,* John Coltrane,* William ("Bill") Evans, James ("Jackie") McLean,* Paul Chambers,* Herbert Hancock,* Wayne Shorter,* Joseph ("Philly Joe") Jones,* Armando ("Chick") Corea, and David Holland, among many others. Davis brought young unknowns into his groups, giving them ample room to develop ideas as had his former sidemen. He developed new instrumental skills (he had begun playing the flugelhorn earlier) and frequently played keyboards, while at the same time maintaining the lyricism associated with his earlier music. Over his long career he recorded extensively and received numerous awards from the music industry. His best-known albums included, in addition to those cited above, *A Tribute to Jack Johnson*, *On the Corner*, *Live at the Fillmore East*, *Live-Evil*, and *Get Up With It*. He also appeared in films and produced film scores, among them, *Lift to the Scaffold* (1957) and *Jack Johnson* (1970). Davis was regarded as one of the most influential figures in jazz for more than a quarter century, from the bebop era through the avant-garde of the 1970s. As innovator and leader he was compared to Louis Armstrong* and Charlie Parker, except that his enormous influence was exerted over a longer period of time than that of either Armstrong or Parker. As a trumpeter his early style development was influenced by John ("Dizzy") Gillespie,* but his mature style was distinctive for its intense lyricism, sophisticated simplicity with minimal vibrato, and heavy melancholy.

BIBL: *Encore American and Worldwide News* (21 July 1975). Bill Cole, *Miles Davis* (New York, 1974). FeaEJ. FeaJS. FeaGitJS. MeeJMov. WWA. WWBA.

DISC: Jep. Kink. ModJ. TudJ.

DAVIS, RICHARD. Jazz bassist (b. 15 April 1930 in Chicago, Illinois). His first bass teacher was Walter Dyett* at DuSable High School in Chicago, Illinois; later he studied with Rudolph Fahsbender and attended Vandercook College (B. Mus. Ed., 1952). During his youth he played with both symphonic and jazz groups, including the Youth Orchestra of Chicago, Chicago Civic Orchestra, and bands of Eddie King and Walter Dyett. Thereafter he played with various groups and/or individuals, among them, Ahmad Jamal* (1953-54), Don Shirley* (1954-55), Kenny Burrell* (1959), and Sarah Vaughan,* with whom he toured in Europe and South America during the late 1950s. The symphony orchestras with whom he performed included Orchestra U.S.A. (1961-64), the Gunther Schuller Orchestra, American Symphony, Orchestra of America, Belgium Radio TV Orchestra, New York Philharmonic, and Igor Stravinsky. He was equally active with jazz groups during the 1960s, among them, the Eric Dolphy*/Booker Little Quintet (1961), Mel Lewis/Thad Jones* (1966-71), and others, including his own. He recorded extensively and appeared in TV specials and on film tracks. From 1969 on he was "the nucleus" of the New York Bass Violin Choir, according to its director, William James ("Bill") Lee.* His teaching career included a tenure at the University of Wisconsin at Madison.

BIBL: FeaEJ. FeaJS. FeaGitJS. WWBA.

DISC: ModJ. TudJ.

DAVIS, SAMMY, JR. Entertainer (b. 8 December 1925 in New York, New York). He came from a show-business family: his father was the lead dancer in Will

Mastin's vaudeville touring show, *Holiday in Dixieland*, and his mother was the lead chorus girl. He began touring with the troupe before he was three years old, at first as a kind of human prop, then as a performer. When the troupe was reduced from twelve performers to three, he toured with the trio (1930-48), featured as "Little Sammy" with Mastin (his adopted uncle) and his father, Sammy, Sr. After the two older men retired, he continued his career as a solo entertainer. Beginning in 1933 he appeared in numerous film musicals, including *Rufus Jones for President* (1933), *Porgy and Bess* (1959), *Golden Boy* (1964), *A Man Called Adam* (1966), *Sweet Charity* (1968), and *One More Time* (1970), among others. He played leading roles in Broadway musicals, among them *Mr. Wonderful* (1956) and *Golden Boy* (1964). He toured widely on the nightclub circuit in the United States and abroad, sang on radio and on numerous television shows and special programs, and recorded extensively. In 1965 he published an autobiography, *Yes, I Can*. Although best known as a singer, he also played instruments, particularly the vibraharp and drums.

BIBL: CurBiog (July 1978). *Ebony* (October 1954, February 1976). FeaEJ. WWA. WWBA. WWTheater.

DISC: Jep.

DAVIS, WILLIAM STRETHEN ("WILD BILL"). Jazz organist (b. 24 November 1918 in Glasgow, Missouri). He played piano and guitar as a child. He obtained his musical education in the public schools of Parsons, Kansas; at Tuskegee Institute in Alabama (1937-39); and at Wiley College in Marshall, Texas (B.A.). His first professional experience was with Milt Larkin in Houston, Texas, as arranger-guitarist (1940). He then moved to Chicago, Illinois, where he played with and arranged for various groups and for revues, including Earl Hines.* He toured with Louis Jordan* (1945-47) as a pianist, then changed to jazz organ in 1948. In 1951 he organized his own trio, consisting of guitar, drums, and himself on jazz organ. He toured widely in the United States and in Europe, appearing at festivals as well as in nightclubs and theaters; he recorded regularly; and played long residencies in major cities of the nation, particularly New York, Atlantic City, New Jersey, and Los Angeles, California. He wrote arrangements for such jazzmen as Lionel Hampton,* William ("Count") Basie,* and Edward ("Duke") Ellington.* He also toured with Ellington in 1969. During the 1970s he played on jazz cruises. He was the pioneer in bringing the electric organ (the Hammond) into the jazz ensemble, along with Milton Buckner* (who adopted the organ in 1952). He played in the rhythm 'n' blues style as well as jazz and exerted enormous influence upon younger jazz organists, such as Jimmy McGriff, Lonn Smith,* and Shirley Scott,* among others. His best-known arrangement was "April in Paris," made for Basie.

BIBL: ChilWW. FeaEJ. FeaJS. FeaGitJS.

DISC: Jep.

DAVISON WATKINS, HARRIET. Concert violinist (b. 11 December 1923 in Newark, New Jersey; d. 16 June 1978 in Newark). She studied violin as a child and played solo recitals before she was twelve years old. She obtained her musical education at the Oberlin [Ohio] Conservatory (B. Mus.), the Cleveland [Ohio] Conservatory, and the Juilliard School of Music in New York. She first attracted wide attention in 1941 when she performed at the annual convention of the National Association of Negro Musicians. She toured as a concert violinist and also performed with groups, including the Symphony of the New World, the Harlem Philharmonic Symphony, directed by Karl Hampton Porter,* and the New York City Housing Authority Symphony. She founded a chamber group, Music Among Friends. She was married to Julius Watkins.*

BIBL: Communication from Marion Cumbo. Black press, incl. AmstN, 27 March 1937.

DAVY, GLORIA. Opera singer (b. 29 March 1931 in New York, New York). She obtained her musical education in New York at the High School of Music and Art and at the Juilliard School of Music (B.S., 1954). In 1952 she sang in a production of Virgil Thomson's *Four Saints in Three Acts* in Paris, France. In 1954 she made her concert debut as a soprano at Town Hall in New York. Thereafter she toured in Europe for fourteen months with the Gershwin *Porgy and Bess* company, replacing Leontyne Price* for the overseas tours. When the company returned to the United States, she settled in Milan, Italy, where she began an association with La Scala Opera Company, and remained for five years. She sang regularly with the major opera companies in Europe: in 1957 she made her European operatic debut in the title role of Verdi's *Aida* at the Teatre de l'opera in Nice, France; in 1959 she sang with the Vienna [Austria] State Opera; and in 1960 she appeared at Covent Garden in London, England. She returned to the United States in 1958 to make her debut as Aida with the Metropolitan Opera Company. Her best-known performances were in the title roles of *Aida* and Puccini's *Madame Butterfly*, as Leonora in Verdi's *Il Trovatore*, Pamina in Mozart's *The Magic Flute*, Nedda in Leoncavallo's *Il Pagliacci*, and Dido in Purcell's *Dido and Aeneas*. She also won wide recognition for her performances in such works as Schoenberg's *Erwartung*, Stockhausen's *Momente*, and Honegger's *Nicholas de Flue*. She settled in Geneva, Switzerland, in the 1970s.

BIBL: Ernest Dunbar, *The Black Expatriates* (New York, 1968). Black press, incl. NYAge, 21 January 1959, 8 June 1974. WWA, 1976-77. WWBA.

DISC: Turn.

DAWKINS, JAMES HENRY ("JIMMY.") Bluesman (b. 24 October 1936 in Tchula, Mississippi). His family moved to Pascagoula, Mississippi, when he was a child. His interest in blues was stimulated by hearing the bands of Antoine (''Fats'') Domino,* Smiley Lewis, and ''Guitar Slim'' (Eddie Jones); he obtained his first guitar at the age of sixteen or seventeen. In 1955 he went to Chicago to become a professional bluesman; two years later he began playing in local clubs with his own blues band. Over the years his sidemen included Jim Conley, Lester Dorsie, Ernest Gatewood, Otis Rush,* and Sonny Thompson. He toured widely in the United States and abroad, appearing in nightclubs, on college campuses, at blues festivals, in films, and on radio and television. He won awards from the music industry at home and in France. His best-known album was *Fast Fingers* (1971).

BIBL: BWW. LivBl 8 (Spring 1972). Robert Neff and Anthony Connor, *Blues* (Boston, 1975).

DAWSON, MARY CARDWELL. Opera director (b. 14 February 1894 in Meridian, North Carolina; d. 19 March 1962 in Washington, D.C.). She obtained her musical education in the public schools of Pittsburgh, Pennsylvania, where her family moved when she was a child. Later she studied at the New England Conservatory in Boston, Massachusetts, and at Chicago Musical College. In 1927 she founded the Cardwell School of Music in Pittsburgh. She toured frequently with her Cardwell-Dawson chorus, which won prizes in choral competitions, including those associated with the Chicago World's Fair in 1933-34 and the New York World's Fair in 1939-40. She had large numbers of voice students and during the late 1930s became increasingly concerned that her students were denied the opportunity to sing in opera because of race discrimination. In 1941 she founded the National Negro Opera Company at Pittsburgh to provide an outlet for aspiring opera singers and to inspire young artists to study opera. She established NNOC guilds in New York, Chicago, and Washington, D.C., to provide managerial services, choruses, and other support services when she produced operas in those cities. The opera company staged its first production, Verdi's *Aida*, in August 1941 at the annual meeting of the National Association of Negro Musicians in Pittsburgh, with La Julia Rhea* as Aida, William Franklin* as Amonasro, and Napoleon Reed as Rhadames. The company made its official debut in October 1941; the leading roles were sung by Rhea, Franklin, Nellie Dobson Plants, and Jackson Smith, with Frederick Vajda of the Metropolitan Opera Company conducting. Over the twenty-one years of its existence, the opera company produced Verdi's *Aida* and *Traviata*, Clarence C. White's* *Ouanga* (1956, in concert version), and R. Nathaniel Dett's* oratorio *The Ordering of Moses* (1951), among other dramatic works. Among the opera singers who performed in these productions were Minto Cato,* Lillian Evanti,* Edward Boatner,* Joseph Lipscomb, Robert McFerrin,* and Napoleon Reed, among others, in addition to those cited above. Dawson also encouraged the musical development of young people not associated with opera or voice, among them, jazzmen Ahmad Jamal* and Errol Garner.* Dawson was president of the National Association of Negro Musicians during the years 1939-41.

BIBL: Schom. Black press, incl. AmstN, 24 March 1962; CDef, 6 September 1941, 25 October 1941, 24 March 1962. Virgil Thomson, *The Musical Scene* (New York, 1945).

DAWSON, WILLIAM LEVI. Composer/College professor (b. 26 September 1899 in Anniston, Alabama). He obtained his musical education at Tuskegee Institute in Alabama (1914-21), which he entered when he was thirteen years old, and where he played in the band and orchestra, was music librarian, and traveled with the Institute Singers for five years; at Washburn College in Topeka, Kansas (1921-22); at the Horner Institute of Fine Arts in Kansas City, Missouri (B. Mus., 1925); at the American Conservatory of Music in Chicago, Illinois (M. Mus., 1927); and at the Eastman School of Music in Rochester, New York. He also studied privately with Carl Busch. In the summer of 1921 he sang tenor and played trombone with the Redpath Chautauqua. During his stay in Chicago he played first trombone with the Chicago Civic Symphony Orchestra. His teaching career included tenures as director of music at Kansas Vocational College in Topeka (1921-22), at Lincoln High School in Kansas City (1922-27), and at Tuskegee Institute (1931-56). Under his leadership the Tuskegee Choir gained international renown. In 1956 he was sent by the United States Department of State to conduct choral groups in Spain; thereafter he toured widely in the United States and abroad as a guest conductor of choruses and orchestras.

He began to compose when he was sixteen years old and thereafter wrote continuously in a variety of forms. His best-known compositions were his numerous spiritual arrangements—such as "King Jesus is a-listening," "Talk about a child," "Jesus walked this lonesome valley"—*Negro Folk Symphony* (1934); *Negro Worksong for Orchestra*; Trio in A for violin, cello, piano; Sonata in A for violin and piano; and a Scherzo for orchestra. His musical style was neoromantic with use of Negro folk elements. After touring in West Africa in 1952, he revised his *Negro Folk Symphony*, infusing it with African rhythms and idioms. His honors included Wanamaker Awards (1930, 1931), an honorary doctorate from Tuskegee (1955), an Alumni Achievement Award from the University of Missouri at Kansas City (1963), election to the Alabama Arts Hall of Fame (1975), and an American Choral Directors Association Award (1975).

BIBL: HNB. Layne. WWA. WWBA. WWCA, 1927-50.

DE BOSE, TOURGEE. College professor/Concert pianist (b. 20 August 1893 in Gainesville, Florida; d. 10 July 1971 in Baton Rouge, Louisiana). He studied piano as a child. He obtained his musical education at Fisk University in Nashville, Tennessee (B.A., 1913), and at the Oberlin School of Music in Ohio (1916). He studied piano privately with Carl Friedberg and later in Paris, France, at Alfred Cortot's Ecole normale de musique. During the 1920s he was active in New York, where he taught at the [David] Martin*-Smith School of Music and played solo recitals. His teaching career also included tenures at Bethune-Cookman College in Daytona Beach, Florida; Talladega College in Alabama (1926-46), where he was head of the department; and Southern University in Baton Rouge, Louisiana (1946-58), where he was director of the music division. Throughout his teaching career he gave concerts and appeared with symphony orchestras. He was best known for his performance of nineteenth-century piano literature, particularly Chopin and Debussy. His honors included a Rosenwald Fellowship (1931).

BIBL: Questionnaire filled out by son. Black press, incl. NYAge, 2 September 1922, 1 March 1924, 21 April 1928, 10 October 1931. NYB, 1915. WWCA, 1927-40.

DE PARIS, SIDNEY. Jazz trumpeter (b. 30 May 1905 in Crawfordsville, Indiana; d. 13 September 1967 in New York, New York). He came from a musical family: his father was a bandleader-music teacher, and his brother Wilbur* became a professional musician. He studied music with his father. He began playing professionally about 1924 in Washington, D.C., with Sam Taylor. During the next two decades he played with various groups, including Charlie Johnson (1926-27, 1928-31), McKinney's* Cotton Pickers (1929), Fletcher Henderson* (1932), Donald ("Don") Redman* (1932-36, 1939), Arthur ("Zutty") Singleton* (1939-40, 1941), Ferdinand ("Jelly Roll") Morton* (1939), Sidney Bechet* (1940), Bennett ("Benny") Carter* (1940-41), and Roy Eldridge* (1944), among others. During these years he also led his own groups occasionally, played in the pit orchestra for *Blackbirds of 1938*, and played with his brother Wilbur's groups; after 1947 he played regularly with his brother. He made many recordings with leading jazzmen of his time (in addition to those cited above). His style reflected the influence of Joseph ("King") Oliver,* and as a member of his brother's *New* New Orleans Band he contributed to the transferrence of the New Orleans tradition to the Northeast into the era of bebop. In later years he doubled on the tuba and flugel horn.

BIBL: AlHen. ChilWW. FeaEJ. FeaJS. FeaGitJS. MeeJMov.

DISC: Jep. Kink. RustJR. TudJ.

DE PARIS, WILBUR. Jazz trombonist (b. 11 January 1900 in Crawfordsville, Indiana; d. 3 January 1973 in New York, New York). He came from a musical family: his father was a bandleader-music teacher and his brother Sidney* became a professional musician. He studied music with his father as a child, played in his father's carnival band, and later toured on the T.O.B.A. circuit (Theatre Owners Booking Association). About 1922 he went to New Orleans, where he played with Louis Armstrong* and Armand Piron,* among others. In 1925 he settled in Philadelphia, Pennsylvania, where he formed his own group (1925, 1927-28). During the next two decades he also played with others, including LeRoy Smith, Noble Sissle* (1931), Theodore ("Teddy") Hill* (1936-37), Louis Armstrong* (1937-40), Roy Eldridge,* and Edward ("Duke") Ellington* (1945-47), among others. Beginning in 1943 he formed another small group of his own, and after 1947 worked primarily with his own groups, which included his brother Sidney. He also appeared in films, including *The Pirate* (1948) and *Windjammer* (1958) and played in the Broadway show *The Pirate* (1942). He toured abroad three times: in Europe with Sissle in 1931 and with Hill in 1937, and in Africa with his own group in 1957 under sponsorship of the United States Department of State. His group played long residencies in New York clubs during the 1960s-early

1970s. He regarded himself as a carrier of the New Orleans tradition to the Northeast and called his band the *New* New Orleans Band.

BIBL: ChilWW. FeaEJ. FeaJS. FeaGitJS. MeeJMov.

DISC: Jep. Kink. RustJR. TudJ.

DE PAUR, LEONARD. Choral conductor (b. 18 November 1914 in Summit, New Jersey). He received his musical education at the Institute of Musical Art (now Juilliard School of Music) and Columbia University Teachers College. His early professional experience was obtained with the Hall Johnson* Choir (1932-36), for which he served as an assistant conductor. Thereafter he was musical director for the Negro Unit of the Federal Theatre Project in New York (1936-39), including the Orson Welles production of *MacBeth*, among other productions. He was later active as musical director-arranger for Broadway shows. During his service in the United States Armed Forces (1943-46), he was choral director for fifteen months with the Air Force show, "Winged Victory"; he then organized an Infantry Glee Club for the 372nd Regiment, which toured installations in the Asiatic-Pacific Area. After returning to civilian life in 1946 he organized the De Paur Infantry Chorus, which toured widely throughout the world until 1957. During these years he was also active as a choral director for Thomson's opera *Four Saints in Three Acts* (1952 revival), the musical *Carmen Jones* (1956 revival), and other shows on and off Broadway. He reorganized his DePaur Chorus in 1963 and again toured widely until 1969; in 1966 the group sang at the First World Festival of Negro Arts in Dakar, Senegal, and afterwards toured throughout sub-Saharan Africa. His group's repertory included the folk music of all nations and gave special attention to contemporary music. In 1971 he was appointed Director of Community Relations for the Lincoln Center for the Performing Arts, Inc., in New York. His honors included the Harold Jackman Award (1964). His group's best-known recordings were *Songs of the New Nations* (1964), *Calypso Christmas* (1956), and *A Bicentennial Celebration* (1976).

BIBL: AbdulBCM. Black press, incl. NYAge, 16 July 1949. *Ebony* (December 1951). NYT, 24 October 1971.

DISC: Turn.

DE PRIEST, JAMES ANDERSON. Symphony orchestra conductor (b. 21 November 1936 in Philadelphia, Pennsylvania). He came from a musical family: his mother sang, and his aunt was world-renowned contralto Marian Anderson.* As a child he studied piano and percussions. He obtained his musical education in the public schools of Philadelphia, where he played percussions in the City-Wide High School Orchestra; at the University of Pennsylvania (B.S., 1958; M.A., 1961), where he did not major in music but took music electives and played in the university marching band and symphony orchestra; and at the Philadelphia Conservatory of Music (1959-61), where he studied composition with Vincent Persichetti. His Jimmy DePriest Quintet, which he formed during his college years, attracted attention in 1956 as one of the best jazz groups in the East and appeared on Steve Allen's television show. During the year 1962-63 he toured in the Far East for the United States Department of State as a specialist in American music and made his professional debut as a conductor with the Bangkok [Thailand] Symphony Orchestra. Thereafter he was a guest conductor in other places on his tour. An attack of polio forced his return to the United States in 1963, but he nevertheless entered the 1963 Mitropoulos International Conductors Competition and reached the semi-finals. The next year he won first prize in the Competition. His conducting career included tenures with the Bangkok Symphony (1963-64), New York Philharmonic (assistant conductor to Leonard Bernstein, 1965-66), Symphony of the New World* in New York (principal guest conductor, 1968-70), National Symphony Orchestra in Washington, D.C. (associate conductor, 1971-75; principal guest conductor, 1975-76), and L'Orchestre Symphonique de Quebec (musical director, 1976-). During the years 1966-70, he lived in Rotterdam, Holland; in 1969 he made his debut with the Rotterdam Symphony when he took over concerts originally scheduled to be conducted by Edo de Waart. Thereafter he toured widely in Europe and the United States as a guest conductor. He also composed a number of works, particularly ballet scores. His honors included, in addition to the Mitropoulos prizes, a Martha Baird Rockefeller Award (1969), Merit Citation from the City of Philadelphia (1969), and an honorary doctorate from the University of Pennsylvania (1976).

BIBL: AbdulFBE. *Ebony* (December 1972). FeaEJ. NYT, 13 January 1975.WWA. WWBA.

DE WOLFE SISTERS, THE. Concert/vaudeville singers (b. 18?? in Charlotte, North Carolina). Soprano Sadie and contralto Rosa (d. 23 May 1917 in Boston, Massachusetts) settled in Boston early in their careers and first attracted attention there as a duo in local concerts and as members of the Boston Quartet. In 1884 they sang with the Sam Lucas* Concert Company, which was based in Boston at that time. In 1885 they began appearing as assisting artists on Bergen Star Concerts, which featured Flora Batson* as the prima donna soprano; they continued this off and on for the next decade. Later they toured on the vaudeville circuit, singing in the operatic scenes or acts of vaudeville shows with such companies as the Stewart Concert Company, the Georgia Minstrels* (in 1889), and Sam T. Jack's Creole Company (in 1890). In 1896 they sang with Black Patti's* Troubadours. They retired from the stage during the early twentieth century.

BIBL: PaHistSoc, 1G. Black press, incl. NYGlobe, 13 October 1883, 21 June 1884; NYAge, 10 March 1888; IndF, 20 April 1889, 26 September 1896. Hare. Simond.

DÉDÉ, EDMOND. Composer (b. 20 November 1827 in New Orleans, Louisiana; d. 1903 in Bordeaux, France). He early showed musical talent and was encouraged by his parents, who were migrants from the French West Indies. He studied with Constantin Deburque, violinist and director of the Philharmonic Society (composed of ''men of color''), and with L. Gabici, director of the St. Charles Theater orchestra. In 1848 he was sent to Mexico to study further; in 1857 he entered the Conservatory in Paris, France. He studied composition with Jacques-François Halévy and violin with Jean-Delphin Alard. According to some reports, he was befriended by Charles Gounod. About 1868 he went to Bordeaux, France, where he became director of the L'Alcazar Theater orchestra and remained in the position for twenty-five years. In 1893 he returned to the United States, spending several months visiting relatives and giving concerts as far north as Chicago, Illinois. He was joined by notable musicians of New Orleans on a farewell benefit concert in January 1894, including Basile Barés* and William J. Nickerson.* His best-known compositions were ''Les faux mandarins,'' ''La sensitive,'' ''Emilie,'' ''Le palmier overture,'' and the opera *Sultan d'Ispahan*. His son, Eugene Arcade, was also a composer.

BIBL: Des. Hare. LaBrew. Trot, pp. 340-341; pp. 53-59 of the music section.

DEEP RIVER BOYS, THE. Concert group (org. in 1934 in Hampton, Virginia). The male quartet was organized by Noah Ryder,* student director of the college male glee club, at Hampton Institute in Virginia in 1934. Originally called the Hampton Institute Quartet, its members were Harry Douglas, James Lundy, Carter Wilson, and Ryder himself. The group began singing professionally in 1936 after winning first prize on a Major Bowes Family Amateur Hour radio show. They adopted the name ''Deep River Boys'' at the suggestion of actor Rex Ingram, who was impressed by their performance of Harry T. Burleigh's* song ''Deep river.'' By 1939 personnel changes had brought in Vernon Gardner (first tenor), George Lawson (second tenor), Edward (''Mumbles'') Ware (bass), and Charles Ford (pianist-arranger) with Douglas (baritone-lead) the only original member still remaining in the quartet. In 1948 Senior Robinson was the pianist-arranger. The quartet toured widely throughout the world during the 1940-60s; during World War II they toured on the USO circuit (United Service Organizations). They sang in nightclubs and theaters; they sang regularly on radio for many years, first on the CBS national network, then on NBC; and they made recordings. In 1939 the Deep River Boys appeared in the Broadway musical *Swingin' the Dream*, which featured Louis Armstrong* and Maxine Sullivan.* The quartet's repertory originally consisted primarily of spiritual arrangements but later was enlarged to include a variety of song types.

BIBL: Black press, incl. AmstN, 11 December 1948; ÇDef, 8 April 1939, 18 December 1943. Marjorie Johnson, ''Noah Francis Ryder'' in BPIM 6 (Spring 1978).

DELANY, MARTIN ROBISON. Writer (b. 6 May 1812 in Charleston, Virginia; d. 24 January 1885 in Xenia, Ohio). He is included here primarily for the information about black musicians contained in his first book, *The Condition, Elevation, Emigration and Destiny of the Colored People in the United States Politically Considered* (Philadelphia, 1852). Delany also offers descriptions of black folk music in his novel, *Blake, or the Huts of America* (published serially in *The Weekly Anglo-African*, 26 November 1861-May 1862; also in *The Anglo-African Magazine*, January-July 1859. Modern publication: New York, 1970).

BIBL: EAB. Dorothy Sterling, *The Making of an Afro-American: Martin Robison Delany* (New York, 1971).

DELISLE, LOUIS NELSON (''BIG EYE LOUIS''). Jazz clarinetist (b. 28 January 1885 in New Orleans, Louisiana; d. 20 August 1949 in New Orleans). His father taught him to play accordion; later he learned other instruments, specializing on the clarinet, which he studied with Lorenzo Tio, Sr.* He began playing professionally with local groups about 1905, among them, the Imperial Orchestra, The Golden Rule Orchestra, the Superior, the Eagle Band, and Oscar (''Papa'') Celestin.* In 1916 he went to Boston, Massachusetts, to join William (''Bill'') Johnson's* touring

Original Creole Orchestra, replacing George Baquet,* but returned the next year when the group disbanded temporarily. Thereafter he played with local groups again, including John Robichaux (intermittently during the years 1918-24), Willie Pajeaud, and Sidney Desvignes. He also played in theaters and in nightclubs with others and with his own group (1938-48). He was regarded by his musician-contemporaries as one of the leading clarinetists in the first generation of the New Orleans jazzmen.

BIBL: Tom Bethell, *George Lewis: A Jazzman from New Orleans* (Berkeley, 1977). ChilWW. FeaEJ. Souch.

DISC: RustJR.

DELLS, THE. Rhythm 'n' blues group (fl. 1950-70s; orig. in Harvey, Illinois). The male singing-and-dancing group originated in Harvey, Illinois, a suburb of Chicago, with boys who sang in church gospel choirs and who formed a singing group during their high-school days. They sang in school programs and on street corners and after graduation began singing professionally, calling themselves El Rays. Their early style development was influenced by Harvey Fuqua and his Moonglows rhythm 'n' blues group. The group originally included six singers but later settled into a quintet: Vern Allison (second tenor), Chuck Barksdale (bass), Johnny Carter (first tenor), Marvin Junior (lead), and Michael McGill (baritone). El Rays sang in local clubs and on radio programs without making much progress until 1955 when they signed with Vee Jay Records, which changed the group's name to The Dells. Within a short time the group established itself as a leading rhythm 'n' blues group; in later years The Dells sang jazz as well as soul music. Those with whom they toured included Dinah Washington* and Ray Charles.* Their best-known recordings included "Oh, what a night," "Stay in my corner," "The love we had,"and "Give your baby a standing ovation," among others.

BIBL: Black press, incl. CDef, 3-9 January 1970. ShawHS. StamPRS.

DELTA RHYTHM BOYS, THE. Popular-music group (org. c1935 in New Orleans, Louisiana; fl. 1930s-70s). In 1935 Frederick Hall,* director of music at Dillard University in New Orleans, Louisiana, organized the Dillard University [male] Quartette. Hall had known two of the college students as high-school students when he taught at Jackson State College in Mississippi; when he went to Dillard, they followed him, enrolling in the University. Also called the Frederick Hall Quartet, the group was composed of Elmaurice Miller (first tenor, b. in Tulsa, Oklahoma), Traverse Crawford (second tenor, b. in Indianola, Mississippi), Harry Lewis (baritone, b. in New Orleans), and Otho Gaines (bass, b. in Tupelo, Mississippi). In 1937 an Argentinian business man, Adolfo Aviles, heard the quartet sing when he visited the campus and arranged a nine-month tour for the group in South America under sponsorship of radio station LR4 of Buenos Aires, Argentina. The quartet's programs consisted primarily of Hall's arrangements of Negro spirituals and other black folksongs; he sent new arrangements frequently by air mail to the group during the course of its tour. After returning to the United States, the quartet continued to sing off the campus, including appearances on the Major Bowes Original Amateur Hour radio program. After the men graduated from college, they became a professional group, using the name Delta Rhythm Boys. Personnel changes brought in new members, among them, Clinton Howard to replace Miller and Rene DeKnight as pianist-arranger; by 1944 the quartet included Carl Jones (first tenor) and Kelsey Pharr (baritone). The Delta Rhythm Boys toured widely in the United States and abroad, performing in nightclubs and theaters; they sang on radio programs regularly, particularly the "Amos and Andy Show"; they made recordings as a quartet and with various singers; and they appeared in films, including *Crazy House* (1934), *So's Your Uncle* (1943), *Hi' Ya Sailor* (1943), *Night Club Girl* (1945), and *Rock 'n' Roll Revue* (1955). They were active into the 1970s.

BIBL: Black press, incl. CDef, 7 August 1943, 1 June 1944. Violet G. Bowers, "Frederick Douglass Hall" in BPIM (Fall 1980).

DISC: Kink. Rust JR.

DENNIS, A. Brass bandsman (fl. mid-nineteenth century in New York, New York). See **PLET, A.**

DENT, JESSIE COVINGTON. Studio teacher/ Concert pianist (b. 19 May 1904 in Houston, Texas). She began piano study at the age of five. She obtained her musical education in the public schools of Houston, Texas; at the Oberlin [Ohio] Conservatory of Music (B. Mus., 1924), where she studied with George Carl Hastings; and at the Institute of Musical Art in New York (now the Juilliard School of Music, 1924-28, where she studied with James Friskin and Olga Samaroff. During her stay in New York she conducted a music studio, gave solo recitals, and performed on radio programs. After leaving New York she toured as a concert pianist and conducted a studio in Houston (1929). She then went to Bishop College in Dallas, Texas, to head the piano department (1929-31), the first of her race to be appointed to that position. After

1931 she lived in New Orleans, Louisiana, where her husband was president of Dillard University. She taught music privately and continued to give recitals occasionally.

BIBL: Black press, incl. CDef, 27 February 1930; NYAge, 17 July 1937. Handy. WWCA, 1927-40.

DEPPE, LOUIS. Jazz singer (b. 12 April 1897 in Horse Cave, Kentucky; d. 26 July 1976 in Chicago). His family moved to Springfield, Ohio, when he was a child; he began singing in local hotels and nightclubs at an early age. When he was sixteen, he was befriended by Madame C. J. Walker, who took him to New York and arranged for him to study voice briefly with Buzzi Pecci, coach of Enrico Caruso. Deppe sang baritone solos on concerts in several places before he entered the United States Armed Forces in 1918. After the war he toured with Anita Patti Brown* in South America and the West Indies. Thereafter he moved primarily in the jazz world, although he continued to give concerts occasionally. He is credited with having discovered Earl Hines.* After he engaged Hines to accompany him for his first important engagement at the Collins Club in Pittsburgh, Pennsylvania, the two formed a long-time association. During the years c1921-25, he directed his own orchestra, Lois B. Deppe and His Plantation Orchestra. Thereafter he sang in nightclubs and with choral groups until 1927, when he began singing in Broadway musicals, including Lew Leslie's *Blackbirds of 1927*, *Great Day* (1929), and *Hello, Paris* (1931). During the mid-1930s he returned to singing in clubs until his retirement about 1950.

BIBL: Black press, incl. CDef, 21 April 1917; IndF, 13 November 1915. DanceWEH.

DESCENDENTS OF MIKE AND PHOEBE. Concert ensemble (fl. 1970s.; org. in Snow Hill, Alabama). This family ensemble was composed of Consuela Lee Moorehead (b. 1 November 1926 in Tallahassee, Florida), William James Edwards ("Bill") Lee* (b. 23 July 1928 in Snow Hill, Alabama), A. Grace Mims (b. 17 July 1930 in Snow Hill), and A. Clifton ("Cliff") Lee (b. 24 April 1936 in Snow Hill). They came from a musical family, which included three other children; the mother, Alberta Edwards Lee, was a pianist, and the father, Arnold W. Lee, was a bandmaster. All the children received their basic education at the Snow Hill Institute, founded by the maternal grandfather, William James Edwards. All played in a family band as children and began music study at an early age. Consuela studied piano, attended Fisk University in Nashville, Tennessee (B.A., 1948), and Northwestern University in Evanston, Illinois (M. Mus., 1959), and studied further at the Eastman School of Music in Rochester, New York, and the Peabody Conservatory in Baltimore, Maryland. Her teaching career included tenures at Hampton Institute in Virginia and at Norfolk State University in Virginia (1974-). In addition to teaching she toured as a jazz pianist and was active as a composer-arranger. Bill obtained his musical education at Morehouse College in Atlanta, Georgia (see infra). Grace attended Hampton Institute (B.S., 1952), where she studied voice as a minor, and Case Western University in Cleveland, Ohio (MS in Lib. Sci., 1953). She was active in Cleveland as a singer, where she sang with the Cleveland Orchestra Chorus, Robert Shaw's Chamber Chorus, and groups at Karamu House, including the Karamu Opera Theater. During the 1970s she was hostess of a weekly radio program, "Black Arts," devoted to classical music. Cliff obtained his musical education at Xavier University in New Orleans, Louisiana (B.S., 1959) and settled in New York, where he was active as a jazz musician and studio teacher. He won recognition for his trumpet and flugel horn playing and was a member of The Brass Company. During the 1960s members of the Lee family performed together at recitals of The New York Bass Violin Choir. In the early 1970s they founded Descendents of Mike and Phoebe, using names of maternal slave ancestors six generations removed. Their concerts consisted of spirituals, gospel, blues and other secular folksongs, songs composed by Consuela and/or Bill, and generally excerpts from one of Bill's folk-jazz operas; they were assisted by performers on percussions, bass, and other instruments. Occasionally an entire evening was given over to an opera, as *The Depot* in May 1973 or *The Quarters* in October 1977. The Descendents toured widely throughout the United States, particularly on the college circuit and in concert halls. Their best-known record albums were *A Spirit Speaks* and *The Descendents*.

BIBL: Black press, incl. AmstN, 21 October 1978. NYT, 5 July 1971.

DESDUNES, DAN. Bandleader (b. c1870s-80s in New Orleans, Louisiana; d. 24 April 1929 in Omaha, Nebraska). He began his career playing alto horn in the band of P.T. Wright's* Nashville Students company. By 1898 he had become leader of the company's orchestra. He toured with "Skinner" Harris in a vaudeville act in 1899. When bandmaster P.G. Lowery* left the Nashville Students in 1899 to organize his own band, Desdunes went with him. About 1911 Desdunes formed his own band, which earned a wide reputation in the West over the next two decades. He also taught music at Boy's Town in Omaha, Nebraska. During his early career Desdunes played with Henderson Smith* and Harry Prampin. His father, Rudolphe Desdunes,* published a cultural history of "men of color" in New Orleans, *Nos Hommes et notre histoire* (Montreal, 1911).

BIBL: Black press, incl. IndF, 8 January 1898, 22 January 1898, 29 December 1900; CDef, 4 May 1929. Des. Hare.

DESDUNES, RUDOLPHE LUCIEN. Writer (b. 15 November 1849 in New Orleans, Louisiana; d. 14 August 1928 in Omaha, Nebraska). He included in his book *Nos Hommes et notre histoire* (Montreal, 1911) a chapter on music, which includes valuable information about musicians of New Orleans. His son, Dan,* was a practising musician.

BIBL: Dorothea Olga McCants, transl, *Our People and Our History*, with introduction and notes (Baton Rouge, 1973).

DETT, R[OBERT] NATHANIEL. Composer/College professor (b. 11 October 1882 in Drummondsville, Ontario, Canada; d. 2 October 1943 in Battle Creek, Michigan). He came from a musical family: his father played piano and guitar and sang in a church choir; his mother played piano and sang soprano. He first played piano by ear, listening to his mother and two older brothers who took piano lessons. When their piano teacher discovered that Robert could play, she began teaching him free of charge. In 1893 the family moved to the United States side of Niagara Falls (in New York) and he began piano study with local teacher John Weiss. Later he studied with Oliver Willis Halsted, founder of a conservatory in Lockport, New York (1901-03), then enrolled at the Oberlin Conservatory in Ohio (B. Mus., 1908). He began to play in public at an early age, exciting interest among his listeners because of his improvising skills. At fourteen he took a part-time job as a bell-hop in the local Cataract Hotel, where his duties included informally entertaining the guests by playing piano, and somehwat later he added to his part-time work the position of house pianist at the Niagara Falls Country Club. He published his first piano piece in 1900, "After the cake-walk," and followed with others in 1902 and 1903. These early compositions predictably were amateurish but suggested future promise. The first summer he returned home, the Cataract allowed him the use of a salon for his first piano recital, which not only brought in a little money but also attracted the attention of a future patron, Frederic H. Goff of Cleveland, Ohio, who gave him financial aid through his Oberlin years. At the Conservatory he studied piano with Howard Handel Carter, theory with Arthur E. Heacox, and composition with George Carl Hastings. When Carter went to Europe in 1907, Dett continued piano study with Hastings. Dett completed the five-year program in music at Oberlin (concentrating in piano and composition), the first of his race to do so. During his college years he was a choir director in a local church.

His teaching career included tenures at Lane College in Jackson, Tennessee (1908-11); Lincoln Institute (now Lincoln University) in Jefferson City, Missouri (1911-1913); Hampton Institute in Virginia (1913-32); Sam Huston College in Austin, Texas (summer, 1937); and Bennett College in Greensboro, North Carolina (1937-42). During his early career he developed choral-conducting skills along with his teaching skills and occasionally gave piano recitals. His appointment as director of music at Hampton (its first black director) came through the influence of E. Azalia Hackley,* who took a warm interest in his career and encouraged his interest in Negro folk music. Before going to Hampton, he spent the summer of 1913 studying with Karl Gehrkens at Oberlin. Throughout his career he generally spent his summers studying—at Columbia University in New York; the American Conservatory of Music in Chicago, Illinois; Northwestern University in Evanston, Illinois; and the University of Pennsylvania. During the academic year 1919-20 he attended Harvard University, where he studied composition with Arthur Foote, won the Francis Boott Prize for his choral composition "Don't be weary, traveler," and won the Bowdoin Prize for his essay, "The Emancipation of Negro Music." In the summer of 1929 he studied with Nadia Boulanger at the American Conservatory in Fontainebleau, France, and during the year 1931-32 he attended the Eastman School of Music in Rochester, New York (M. Mus., 1932).

Under his leadership the Hampton Choir developed an international reputation; it gave periodic concerts in the leading concert halls of the nation, sang at the Library of Congress and at the White House, and toured in Europe in 1930. In 1932 Dett resigned from Hampton and settled in Rochester, New York, where he taught privately, lectured, composed, and conducted a radio choir (beginning in 1933), which gave weekly broadcasts over the NBC network. In 1937 he developed a fine choir at Bennett, which toured periodically and broadcast on CBS radio. After resigning in 1942, he again settled in Rochester. In 1943 he became a musical adviser for the USO (United Service Organizations) and was assigned to duty at Battle Creek, Michigan, where he began working with a WAC (Women's Army Corps) chorus. He was active musically until his death.

Although remembered today as a composer, Dett was perhaps better known during his lifetime as a concert pianist, choral conductor, and teacher. Immediately after his graduation, the press hailed him as ''A Promising Musician'' (NYAge, 30 July 1908). He first attracted wide attention as a pianist-composer when he performed in the All-Colored Composers' Concerts produced by William Hackney* during the years 1914-16 at Orchestra Hall in Chicago. His interest in Negro folk idioms was stimulated by his contacts with Azalia Hackley and his appreciation of her work. He firmly believed that Negro folk music should be preserved, both in its original forms and in art forms, in the same way as European composers treated their folk music. He constantly promoted this theme in his interviews, lectures, and writings; most of his composed music employs folk idioms. Moreover, he published two sets of spiritual arrangements: *Religious Folksongs of the Negro* (1927) and *The Dett Collection of Negro Spirituals* (1936). His influence as a teacher extended over several generations of promising students who later became professional musicians, including Dorothy Maynor,* Noah Ryder,* and Rudolph Von Charlton,* among others.

Dett was one of the most celebrated black composers of his time, along with Harry T. Burleigh,* Clarence Cameron White,* and Will Marion Cook,* and he made a lasting contribution to American music with his spirituals-infused compositions. Best-known are his choral motets and oratorios, particularly ''Listen to the lambs,'' ''I'll never turn back no more,'' and ''Don't be weary, traveler''; and the larger works *Music in the Mine* (1916), *The Chariot Jubilee* (1921), and *The Ordering of Moses* (1937). His early piano suites—*Magnolia* (1912), *In the Bottoms* (1913) and *Enchantment* (1922)—became perennial favorities of concert pianists; Percy Grainger and Fanny Bloomfield-Zeisler, for example, popularized *In the Bottoms*. Dett wrote in the neoromantic style, using traditional harmonies and rhythms; some of his later works, however, reflect the influence of his exposure to contemporary idioms—such as the piano suites *Tropic Winter* (1938) or the *Eight Bible Vignettes* (1941-43). Like most black composers of his time, he composed and performed many compositions that were never published.

Dett's numerous honors included an award from the Harmon Foundation, honorary doctorates from Howard University in Washington, D.C. (1924) and Oberlin (1926), and the Palm and Ribbon Award from the Royal Belgian Band. A commission from CBS (1938) led to his writing *American Sampler*, one of his few compositions that does not employ Negro folk idioms. *The Ordering of Moses* had several important performances, including one at the Cincinnati Music Festival in 1937, another by Mary Cardwell Dawson's* National Negro Opera Company (1951), and at the 1969 Golden Jubilee Convention of the National Association of Negro Musicians in St. Louis, Missouri. Recordings of the work included one made by the Voice of America for overseas distribution. Dett was one of the founders of the National Association for Negro Musicians in 1919, along with Clarence Cameron White, Nora Holt,* and Henry Grant,* and served as president of NANM during the years 1924-26.

BIBL: ASCAP. BPIM1 (Spring 1973). Baker. Black press, incl. AmstN, 9 October 1943. DAB. Dett, R. Nathaniel, *The Collected Piano Works*, with introductions by Dominique-René de Lerma and Vivian McBrier (Evanston, Illinois, 1973). Gro. Hare. HNB. Vivian Flagg McBrier, *R. Nathaniel Dett: His Life and Works* (Washington, D.C., 1977). WWCA, 1927-41. WWW, Vol. 2.

DIBANGO, MANU (''DIBBS''). Jazz saxophonist (b. 1934 in Douala, Cameroun). His parents sang in church choirs, and he sang in a church choir as a child. When he was fifteen his family settled in Paris, France, where he studied music in school. In 1953 he began saxophone study. He played with various jazz groups during his school years in France and in Belgium, of which many included musicians from Zaire. His style development was influenced by the Zaire jazzmen. He lived in Africa during the years 1964-68, then resettled in Paris. He recorded extensively and toured widely in Europe and in the United States. His performing groups typically included two bassists, two guitarists, two drummers, a conga player, and an organist. His music blended elements of jazz, rhythm 'n' blues, African traditional music, and West Indian music. His best-known albums were *Soul Makossa* (1971) and *Makossa Man* (1974).

BIBL: Black press, including the PhilaT, 10 June 1973.

DICKENSON, VICTOR (''VIC''). Jazz trombonist (b. 6 August 1906 in Xenia, Ohio). His brother Carlos became a professional musician. He first played organ, then changed to trombone at an early age and played with local groups during his high-school days. After his family moved about 1922 to Columbus, Ohio, he played with groups there. He began playing professionally about 1925 in Madison, Wisconsin, with Don Phillips. Thereafter he played with various groups, including Lawrence (''Speed'') Webb (1929-30, band included Roy Eldridge* and Theodore (''Teddy'') Wilson* at that time), Zack Whyte (1930-32), Blanche

Calloway* (1933-36), Claude Hopkins* (1936-39), Bennett (''Benny'') Carter* (1939, 1941), William (''Count'') Basie* (1940), Frankie Newton (1941, 1942), and Eddie Heywood* (1943-45, 1946), among others. He also wrote arrangements for various groups. After 1947 he performed as a soloist and with his own groups in addition to playing with others, among them Bobby Hackett (1951, 1956, 1968-70, 1973), William (''Wild Bill'') Davison* (1961-62), the Saints and Sinners Band (intermittently 1963-68), Earl Hines's* European tour Jazz From a Swinging Era (1967), and The World's Greatest Jazz Band (1970-72), among others. During these years he also played long residencies in New York, Boston, Massachusetts, and on the West Coast. He toured widely in Europe, Japan, and Australia as a soloist and with bands, playing at the major jazz festivals as well as in concert halls, theaters, and night clubs; in 1964 he toured in the South Pacific with Eddie Condon. He made his recording debut in 1931 with Whyte and thereafter recorded regularly; he was also active in television music. Although representative of the swing era in jazz, he was versatile and played also with Dixieland groups. His trombone style was distinctive for its warmth and humor.

BIBL: ChilWW. DanceWEH. DanceWS. FeaEJ. FeaJS. FeaGitJS. MeeJMov.

DISC: Kink. ModJ. RustJR. TudJ.

DICKERSON, CARROLL. Jazz bandleader (b. 1895; d. October 1957 in Chicago, Illinois). A violinist, he led bands in nightclubs and ballrooms of Chicago, Illinois, during the 1920s. In 1924 he toured for forty-two weeks on the Pantages circuit, the first Chicago big band to make such an extended tour. Those who played in his groups included Louis Armstrong,* Darnell Howard,* Earl Hines,* Franz Jackson, and Arthur (''Zutty'') Singleton,* among others. He made recordings with his Savoy [Ballroom] Orchestra and as a director with Armstrong and Oliver groups. In 1929 Dickerson's band went to New York, where it first played under Armstrong's name, then later played a long residency in a New York club under Dickerson. After the group was disbanded in 1930, he played with the Mills Blue Rhythm Band, toured with Joseph (''King'') Oliver,* then returned to Chicago during the 1930s and thereafter led his own groups again. He was active through the 1940s.

BIBL: ChilWW. DanceWEH.

DISC: Kink. RustJR.

DICKERSON, ROGER DONALD. Composer (b. 24 August 1934 in New Orleans, Louisiana). He began piano study when he was eight with local teacher Miriam Panelle. He obtained his musical education in the public schools of New Orleans, Louisiana, where he began playing brass instruments in high school; at Dillard University in New Orleans (B.A., 1955); at Indiana University in Bloomington (M. Mus., 1957), where he studied with Bernard Heiden; and at the Akademie für Musik and Darstellende Kunst in Vienna, Austria (1959-62), where he studied with Karl Schiske. He played jazz professionally during his college years and toured during summer vacations with bluesmen Joe Turner* and ''Guitar Slim'' (née Eddie Jones). He played in the Fort Smith Symphony Orchestra during his service in the United States Armed Forces and later in the U.S. Army Headquarters Band at Heidelberg, Germany. After returning to the United States in 1962, he gave full attention to composing. His early works, *Movement for Trumpet and Piano* and *Quintet for Wind Instruments*, had received first performances in Vienna. Best-known of his later works are the *Essay for Band* (1962), *A Musical Service for Louis* (1972, with reference to Louis Armstrong), *Orpheus an' His Slide Trombone* (1975), and *New Orleans Concerto* (1977). Critics found his mature style to be thoroughly contemporary but not radical; he referred to such ethnic elements as blues, jazz, and soul but transformed and abstracted them to fuse with his contemporary aims. In addition to composing he was active musically in other ways: he was co-founder in 1975 of the Creative Artists Alliance; he taught composition privately; he played occasionally with jazz groups in the French Quarter of New Orleans; and he served as program associate-consultant for various institutions. His honors included Fulbright and John Hay Whitney Fellowships (1959-61, 1964) and the Louis Armstrong Memorial Award. In 1978 he was the subject of a documentary film, ''New Orleans Concerto,'' broadcast on public television.

BIBL: Questionnaire. *The* [New Orleans] *Times-Picayune*, 20 March 1975, 20 January 1977.

DIGGS, CAROL BLANTON. See **BLANTON, CAROL.**

DINWIDDIE COLORED QUARTET. See **JUBILEE SINGERS.**

DITON, CARL ROSSINI. Concert pianist/Singer (b. 30 October 1886 in Philadelphia, Pennsylvania; d. 25 January 1962 in Philadelphia). He first studied music with his father, Samuel James Diton, a professional musician. He studied further at the Institute for Colored Youth in Philadelphia, Central [public] High School, and the University of Pennsylvania (B.S., 1909). In

1909-10 he made a transcontinental concert tour of the United States, the first black pianist to do so. He was encouraged in his music study by E. Azalia Hackley,* who raised funds for a scholarship that enabled him to study piano in Munich, Germany, during the years 1910-11. After returning to the United States, he entered a teaching career, while at the same time continuing his concerts; his teaching included tenures at Paine College in Augusta, Georgia (1912-14); Wiley College in Marshall, Texas (1914-15), and Talladega College in Alabama (1915-18). His first concert after his return from Germany was sponsored by the Washington [D.C.] Conservatory of Music, under the direction of Harriet Gibbs;* throughout his years of teaching in the South he regularly played piano recitals, which included compositions of black composers. He also wrote music and in 1914 won first prize in a New York contest for his arrangement of four Negro spirituals. In 1918 he settled in Philadelphia, Pennsylvania, where he conducted a music studio. In 1923 he made his Philadelphia debut at the Musical Fund Hall. During the mid-1920s his interest in piano began to lag, gradually being replaced by more involvement in vocal music. In 1926 he made his debut as a concert baritone in Philadelphia, and in 1929 he went to New York to study further at the Juilliard School of Music (diploma, 1930). He opened a music studio, became organist/choirmaster at St. Martin's Church, and was active as an accompanist with such singers as Marian Anderson,* Jules Bledsoe,* Caterina Jarboro,* and Ezio Pinza. In 1930 he received the Harmon Award for composition. In addition to his activities as a pianist/composer, Diton is remembered for his leadership in the National Association of Negro Musicians, of which he was a charter member in 1919 and later, the national president (1926-28).

BIBL: Black press, incl. IndF, 23 October 1915; NYAge, 9 February 1929; AmstN, 3 February 1962. Hare. Penman Lovinggood, *Famous Modern Negro Musicians* (1921; reprint, New York, 1978). WWCA, 1929.

DIXIE HUMMINGBIRDS, THE. Gospel quartet (orig. 1928 in Greenville, South Carolina; fl. through the 1970s). The male gospel quartet was formed by James Davis, a childhood friend of folksinger Joshua ("Josh") White.* By the early 1940s the group's personnel had stabilized and consisted of Davis (baritone), Ira Tucker (lead singer, joined in 1939), Beachey Thompson (tenor, joined in 1943), and William Bobo (basso, joined in 1939?). Tucker and Bobo were from Spartanburg, South Carolina, and had sung with gospel groups before joining "The Birds"—Tucker, with his own Gospel Carriers and Bobo, with the Heavenly Gospel Singers. Thompson sang as a child in the choir of the Chestnut Grove Methodist Church in his hometown, Lenis, South Carolina. The Hummingbirds made their recording debut in 1939 in New York, through the promotion of Josh White. In 1942 they settled in Philadelphia, Pennsylvania. They toured extensively, recorded regularly, and sang on radio programs, as both the Jericho Boys and the Swanee Quintet. Personnel changes brought in Paul Owens, Thompson, and later Howard Carroll (guitarist, joined in 1952) and James Walker (lead singer, joined in 1954). Bobo died in 1976, and thereafter a fifth microphone was set up in his memory wherever the Hummingbirds performed. Over its long career the group changed styles and repertories: in the early years they sang hymns, spirituals, and jubilees in unaccompanied, close harmonies; as they moved into the 1960s-70s their music reflected the influence of jazz, blues, and rock and their repertory was dominated by gospel songs. In addition, they wrote much of their material, particularly Tucker and Walker. "The Birds" toured widely through the seventies, appearing in churches, theaters, nightclubs, on television programs, and at festivals. In 1978 they celebrated the fiftieth anniversary of their career with a gala series of concerts across the nation. Their best-known songs included "Only Jesus," "You don't have nothing if you don't have Jesus," "Loves me like a rock," and "Somebody is lying." The best-known albums were *Dixie Hummingbirds: Live* and *Golden Flight*. They received awards from the music and recording industries. The group exerted wide influence on all gospel quartets and as well on rhythm 'n' blues singers, particularly Brook Benton,* Bobby ("Blue") Bland,* and Jackie Wilson.*

BIBL: Barbara Baker, "Black Gospel Music Styles, 1942-1975" (Ph.D. diss., University of Maryland, 1978). *Ebony* (October 1978). Heil. *Sepia* (April 1974).

DISC: DiGod. Hayes. TudBM.

DIXON, BILL. See **DIXON, WILLIAM.**

DIXON, DEAN CHARLES. Symphony orchestra conductor (b. 10 January 1915 in New York, New York; d. 4 November 1976 in Zug, Switzerland). He began violin study before he was four years old. He obtained his musical education in the public schools of New York, at the Juilliard School of Music (B.S., 1936), and at Columbia University Teachers College (M.A., 1939). He also studied privately with Albert Stoessel. He organized his first musical groups, the Dean Dixon Symphony Orchestra and Dean Dixon Choral Society in 1932, when he was only seventeen years old. With the support of the Harlem community his interracial organizations remained active for several years and frequently presented renowned guest artists on their concerts. Later he formed the American Youth Orchestra (1944). His first appearance with a major orchestra was in 1941, when he conducted the NBC Summer Symphony. In 1948 he made his formal debut as a conductor with the New York Philharmonic Orchestra. Thereafter he toured as a guest conducter in the United States. In 1949 he was invited to conduct concerts in Paris, France, by the French National Radio Orchestra. Discouraged by his inability to secure a permanent post in the United States, he decided to settle in Europe and remained there twenty-one years before returning to his homeland (1949-70). His career as a musical director included tenures with the Goeteborg Symphony in Sweden (1953-60), the Hesse Radio Symphony Orchestra in Frankfurt, West Germany (1961-74), and the Sydney Symphony Orchestra in Australia (1964). He toured widely as a guest conductor during these years in Europe and the Far East. In 1970 he returned to the United States to conduct the New York Philharmonic in a summer concert series and was brought back the next year for an extended tour. He was active musically until his retirement because of illness in 1974, when he settled in Ober-Aegeri, Switzerland. Dixon was possibly the first black American to achieve recognition as a conductor of international stature. Although other black conductors preceded him in Europe—for example, Samuel Coleridge-Taylor* and Rudolph Dunbar*—he was the first to hold permanent positions of long duration with symphony orchestras and to tour worldwide as a guest conductor. His honors included a Rosenwald Fellowship (1945-47) and the Alice M. Ditson Award for being "the outstanding American conductor of 1947-48."

BIBL: AbdulBCM. Black press, incl. NYAge, 2 December 1944; CDef, 7 June 1975, 8 November 1976. HNB. Layne. NYT, 5 November 1976. "An American Abroad" in *Time* (4 May 1962). *The Washington* [D.C.] *Star*, 5 November 1976. WWBA, 1975-76.

DIXON, JESSY. Gospel singer (b. 12 March 1938 in San Antonio, Texas). He studied piano as a child and obtained his musical education in the public schools of San Antonio, Texas, where he sang in school musicals, and at St. Mary's College in San Antonio. He became interested in gospel music during his high-school years and formed his own group. His early style development was influenced by his listening to recordings of the Roberta Martin* Singers and hearing live concerts of James Cleveland* and The Caravans. About 1959 he left college and went to Chicago, Illinois, to sing with Cleveland's Gospel Chimes, which included also Dorothy Norwood, Imogene Greene, Lee Charles Neely, and Claude Timmons. In Chicago he came under the direct influence of Sallie Martin,* wrote gospel songs, and was active also as a free-lance studio artist. He remained with the Gospel Chimes five years, then in 1964 took over leadership of The Thompson Community Singers (founded by Milton Brunson); about the same time he became minister of music at the Omega Baptist Church and founded the Omega Singers. When he made his television debut on Chicago's "Jubilee Showcase," he directed three groups: The Tommies (i.e., The Thompson Community Singers, also known as The Chicago Community Choir), The Omega Choir, and his own Jessy Dixon Singers. During the 1970s-80s he toured widely with his groups in the United States, Europe, Australia-New Zealand, and Israel, appearing in theaters, concert halls, churches, at jazz festivals, on college campuses, and on television programs. He was chosen to represent contemporary gospel at the Golden Jubilee Year Celebration of Gospel Music held in Chicago, Illinois, in June 1980. The choral sound of his groups was jazz-inflected and distinctive for its exciting rhythms. His vocal style was in the tradition of James Cleveland, allowing full exploitation of his rich baritone and his high falsetto. His best-known recordings included "Sit at His feet and be blessed," "These old heavy burdens," "I cannot fail the Lord," "Open our eyes," "He ain't heavy," and "Jesus is the answer" (recorded with Mahalia Jackson*). In 1980 he made a film in which he was featured along with Paul Simon. He received awards from the music industry.

BIBL: Black press, including CDef, 31 May 1980. GMEncy. Heil.

DISC: TudBM.

DIXON, LUCILLE. Symphony bassist (b. 27 February 1923 in New York, New York). She studied piano as a child with local teacher Carmen Shepperd and played for her father's church services. During her high-school years she began to play the bass viol and performed in her high school orchestra and in the All-City High School Orchestra of New York. She studied bass with Fred Zimmerman of the New York Philharmonic. Beginning in 1941 she played in various symphonic groups, among them, the National Youth Administration Orchestra (1941-42), National Orchestral Association (1960-64), the Boston Women's Symphony (1964-65), the Symphony of the New World* (1965 on), and in later years the Orchestral Society of Westchester and the Bridgeport Symphony Orchestra. She was also active as a jazz musician. Her first professional experience was with Earl Hines* (1943-45); she then led her own band, the Lucille Dixon Orchestra (1946-60), which included at one time or another Tyree Glenn,* James Taft Jordan, Percival ("Sonny") Payne,* George Matthews, Bill Smith, and George ("Buddy") Tate, among others. During her long career she played with many of her contemporaries, including Ella Fitzgerald,* Billy Daniels,* Tony Bennett, Frank Sinatra, Billie Holiday,* Eubie Blake,* Sarah Vaughan,* and Jan Peerce, among others. She was a founding member of the Symphony of the New World in 1965, and in 1972 she became manager of the orchestra.

BIBL: BPIM 3 (Fall 1975). DanceWEH. NYT, 1 August 1971.

DIXON, WILL. Entertainer (b. c1860s-70s in Wheeling, West Virginia; d. 14 May 1917 in Chicago, Illinois). He was active in Chicago, Illinois, during the 1890s and the turn of the century; he sang with the Diamond and Blackstone Quartets. He also performed with Phil Miller's *Hottest Coon in Dixie* show. About 1904 he settled in New York. In 1905 he joined the Memphis Students* and traveled with the group to England. After returning to the United States in 1906, he entered a vaudeville career as an entertainer. In 1909 he wrote a musical, *The Belle of Bedford* (book by Henry Creamer), which was produced on Broadway. About 1910 he joined the Smart Set* company, then under the leadership of Sherman H. Dudley.* His best-known song was "My Brazilian beauty." His daughter, Frankye Dixon, was a professional musician.

BIBL: Black press, incl. NYAge, 27 May 1909, 7 June 1917; CDef, 10 January 1914, 9 February 1918; IndF, 9 October 1897, 26 May 1917.

DIXON, WILLIAM ROBERT ("BILL"). Jazz trumpeter/College professor (b. 5 October 1925 in Nantucket, Massachusetts). He came from a musical family: his mother was a blues singer. His family moved to New York when he was a child. He obtained his musical education in the public schools of New York, at Boston [Massachusetts] University, and at the Hartnett School of Music (1946-51). He began trumpet study when he was eighteen years old. After service in the United States Armed Forces (1944-46), he settled in New York and began playing professionally. For the most part he performed with his own groups and concentrated upon his own music. Those with whom he occasionally collaborated included Cecil Taylor* and Archie Shepp*. He was active in the jazz avant-garde movement; he helped to found contemporary jazz societies and organized the October Revolution concert series in 1964. His teacher career included tenures at Columbia University Teachers College (1957-70) and Bennington [Vermont] College (1972-). He also toured as a lecturer and from time to time served as a visiting professor or artist-in-residence at various institutions, among them, the University of Wisconsin at Madison, Washington University in St. Louis, Missouri, and Ohio State University in Columbus.

BIBL: FeaJS. WWBA.

DISC: Jep. ModJ.

DIXON, WILLIE JAMES. Bluesman (b. 1 July 1915 in Vicksburg, Mississippi). He was attracted to the blues as a child when he heard performances of "Little Brother" Eurreal Montgomery.* In 1935 he settled in Chicago, Illinois, where he entered professional boxing. But he began singing with "Baby Doo" Leonard Caston, and about 1939 he left boxing to sing and play bass fiddle in local clubs, at first in the Big Three Trio with Caston and Ollie Crawford. He first recorded in 1949 with Robert Nighthawk* and "Muddy Waters" (née McKinley Morganfield).* During the 1950s he began a long association with "Memphis Slim" (neé Peter Chatman*); the two bluesmen recorded and toured together in the United States and abroad. During the early 1960s they organized the American Folk Blues Festival, which made its first European tour in 1962. Dixon also performed and/or recorded with Eddie Boyd,* Chuck Berry,* "Bo Diddley" (née Ellas McDaniel),* and "Sonny Boy Williamson No. 2" (née Willie "Rice" Miller),* among others. In addition to performance, his career included many years as an A & R man (Artist and Repertory) for various record companies and as a record producer and blues promoter. Beginning in the 1960s he led his own band, the Chicago Blues All Stars, and during the 1970s-80s he published a column in *Living Blues* magazine. He was perhaps best known as a songwriter who produced blues for Sam Cooke,* ("Little") Walter Jacobs,* and Muddy Waters, among others.

BIBL: BWW. *Cadence* (February 1977). LivBl 25 (January-February 1976). LivBl 29 (September-October 1976). MeeJMov. Robert Neff and Anthony Connor, *Blues* (Boston, 1975). Oliv. *Record Research* 98 (May 1969). ShawWS.

DISC: Jep. LeSl.

DOBBS, MATTIWILDA. Concert/opera singer (b. 11 July 1925 in Atlanta, Georgia). She began studying piano at the age of seven. She obtained her musical education at Spelman College in Atlanta, Georgia (B.A., 1946), where she studied voice with Naomi

Maise and Willis Lawrence James,* and at Columbia University Teachers College in New York (M.A., 1948). She also studied privately with Lotte Leonard (1946-50); at Mannes Music School (1948-49); the Berkshire Music Festival at Tanglewood, Massachusetts (1950); and in Paris, France, with Pierre Bernac (1950-52). Beginning in 1953 she began to sing professionally and thereafter toured widely in the United States and abroad as a coloratura soprano. She made her debut in March 1954 at New York's Town Hall with Thomas Scherman's Little Orchestra in Strauss's *Ariadne auf Naxos*. She made her operatic debut at La Scala in Milan in 1953 and her American operatic debuts with the San Francisco Opera in 1955 and the Metropolitan Opera in 1956, singing Gilda in Verdi's *Rigoletto*. In 1959 she settled in Stockholm, Sweden; she continued to tour widely both as a concert artist and as opera singer. Her honors included a Marian Anderson* award (1947), John Hay Whitney Fellowship (1950-52), and first prize in the 1951 International Competition for Music Performers at Geneva, Switzerland. After 1973 she returned periodically to the United States to serve tenures as artist-professor in various institutions, including the University of Texas at Austin and Spelman College.

BIBL: Black press, incl. CDef, 10 March 1956; PhilaT, 17 November 1973; *New Courier* [Pittsburgh], 25 August 1973. CurBio 1955. CBDict. Cornelius V. Troupe, *Distinguished Negro Georgians* (Dallas, Texas, 1962). WWBA.

DISC: Turn.

DODDS, BABY. See **DODDS, WARREN.**

DODDS, JOHN ("JOHNNY"). Jazz clarinetist (b. 12 April 1892 in New Orleans, Louisiana; d. 8 August 1940 in Chicago, Illinois). He came from a musical family: his father and uncle played violin, other siblings played various instruments, and his brother Warren ("Baby")* became a professional musician. Inspired by Sidney Bechet,* he began clarinet study when he was seventeen, studying with Lorenzo Tio, Jr.,* and Charlie McCurdy. He began his professional career with Edward ("Kid") Ory* (intermittently c1911-17). He also played with other local groups, with Fate Marable's* riverboat band (1917), and toured with a vaudeville show, Mack's Merrymakers (1917-18). In 1920 he went to Chicago, Illinois, to join Joseph ("King") Oliver* (1920-24), touring with Oliver in California in 1921, where his brother Warren joined the group. After leaving Oliver he played a long residency with his own group (1924-30) fronted occasionally by Freddie Keppard,* at the Kelly Stables club, and during the next decade played at other nightclubs in Chicago. In 1938 he went to New York to make recordings, but spent most of his mature career in Chicago. He made his recording debut with Oliver's Creole Jazz Band in 1923; during the years 1927-40 he recorded extensively with his own groups—his Black Bottom Stompers, Johnny Dodds Trio, or Washboard Band—and with others, among them, Lovie Austin,* Louis Armstrong,* Oliver, Ferdinand ("Jelly Roll") Morton,* Ory, and Ida Cox.* He was one of the three greatest clarinetists of the New Orleans school, along with Sidney Bechet and Jimmie Noone.* His style was distinctive for its warmth, expressiveness, and exuberance.

BIBL: ChilWW. FeaEJ. Lambert, G. E., *Johnny Dodds* (New York, 1971). Souch.

DISC: Kink. RustJR. TudJ.

DODDS, WARREN ("BABY"). Jazz drummer (b. 24 December 1898 in New Orleans, Louisiana; d. 14 February 1959 in Chicago, Illinois). He came from a musical family: his father and uncle played violin, other siblings played various instruments, and his brother Johnny* became a professional musician. He began studying drums when he was about fourteen with Dave Perkins, and later studied with Walter Brundy and Louis Cottrell, Sr. Although he played occasionally with local groups, his first professional experience was with Willie Hightower in New Orleans (c1913). Thereafter he played with various groups, including Manuel Manetta, Frankie Dusen, Oscar ("Papa") Celestin,* and Fate Marable's* riverboat band (1918-21). He then toured with Joseph ("King") Oliver* (1921-23), arriving in Chicago, Illinois, in 1922. During the next two decades he played with many of the Chicago groups, among them, Honore Dutrey,* Freddie Keppard,* Louis Armstrong,* Charlie Elgar,* Ferdinand ("Jelly Roll") Morton,* and others. In 1944 he returned to New Orleans to record with William ("Bunk") Johnson* and remained with Johnson through New York engagements in 1945. He played with Art Hodes during the years 1946-48, played at a jazz festival in Nice, France, in 1948, and during the 1950s played with various jazzmen in New York and in Chicago. During the 1930-40s he also played with his brother for long periods and occasionally led his own Baby Dodds Quartet. He made his recording debut in 1923 with Oliver's group and thereafter recorded extensively. Successive strokes forced him to curtail his musical activities in 1949 and eventually to retire in 1957. He was a pioneer in the development of the jazz drum and was credited with having introduced the "drum break" into the jazz performance. His autobiography was published in 1959, *The Baby Dodds Story, as told to Larry Gara.*

BIBL: Tom Bethell, *George Lewis: A Jazzman from New Orleans* (Berkeley, 1977). ChilWW. FeaEJ. Souch.

DISC: Jep. Kink.RustJR. TudJ.

DOLPHY, ERIC ALLAN. Jazz clarinetist (b. 20 June 1928 in Los Angeles, California; d. 29 June 1964 in Berlin, Germany). He studied clarinet as a child and later studied oboe in a public-school music program. He obtained his musical education in the public schools of Los Angeles, California; at Los Angeles City College; and at the United States Naval School of Music in Washington, D.C. (certificate, 1952). During his high-school years he played in the Los Angeles City School Orchestra and also with small jazz groups. During his service in the United States Armed Forces (1950-53) he played in the Tacoma [Washington] Symphony Orchestra and also in navy bands. After his discharge, he returned to Los Angeles and began to play professionally with local groups, among them, Gerald Wilson, George Brown, William (''Buddy'') Collette, and Eddie Beal (1956). He also led his own groups occasionally, one of them called Eric Dolphy and his Men of Modern Jazz. In 1958 he left Los Angeles to play with the Foreststorn (''Chico'') Hamilton* Quintet (1958-59), and in 1960 he settled in New York. Thereafter he played with various groups, including Charles Mingus* (1960, 1963), John Coltrane* (1961), Freddie Hubbard* (1962), Ornette Coleman* (1962), and many others. He recorded extensively with others and also as group leader. He toured in Europe with Mingus, appeared at the Antibes Jazz Festival at Juan-les-Pins, France, as a soloist and with Coltrane in 1961, and again with Mingus in 1964. He was a charter member of Orchestra U.S.A. (1962-63), which was organized by John Lewis* to perform ''third-stream'' music. During the early 1960s he was also active with his own quintets, which included at one time or another Ron Carter,* Roy Haynes,* Richard Davis,* Bobby Hutcherson,* Booker Little (co-leader), and Donald Byrd* (co-leader), among others. In 1964 Dolphy settled in Paris, France, after completing the Mingus tour; thereafter he played with American jazzmen in Paris and with French jazzmen. Despite his short career Dolphy was regarded as a seminal figure of the jazz avant-garde movement, along with Coltrane and Coleman. He was especially noted for his bass clarinet style and exerted wide influence upon his contemporaries.

BIBL: FeaEJ. FeaJS. MeeJMov. Vladimir Simosko and Barry Tepperman, *Eric Dolphy* (Washington, D.C., 1974).

DISC: Jep. ModJ. TudJ.

DOMINO, ANTOINE (''FATS''). Blues/jazz/rock singer (b. 26 February 1928 in New Orleans, Louisiana). As a child he studied piano with his brother-in-law, Harry Verrett, who played with Edward (''Kid'') Ory* and Oscar (''Papa'') Celestin.* He began playing professionally at the age of twenty and made his first recording in 1949. During the 1950s he became one of the established rhythm 'n' blues entertainers; he recorded extensively and toured widely. For his first recording he went into partnership with Dave Bartholomew, and the two musicians worked together off and on for the next three decades—writing and arranging songs and producing records. During the late 1960s Domino stopped recording and gave more time to touring the nightclub circuit the world over as a singer/pianist. He returned to recording in 1977.

BIBL: BWW. *Ebony* (May 1974). FeaEJ. LivBl 35 (November-December 1977). MeeJMov. ShawHS.

DISC: Jep. TudBM.

DONEGAN, DOROTHY. Jazz pianist (b. 6 April 1926 in Chicago, Illinois). She began piano study at the age of five and obtained her musical education in the public schools of Chicago, Illinois, where she came under the tutelage of Walter Henri Dyett* at DuSable High School; at the Chicago Conservatory of Music; at Chicago Musical College (1942-44); and at the University of Southern California in Los Angeles (1953-54). She was a church organist at an early age but also began playing jazz professionally in local nightclubs during her high-school years. In 1942 she made her debut as a concert pianist at Orchestra Hall in Chicago, playing a program that was half-jazz and half-classical, including ''jazzed-up'' classics. She toured widely as a soloist, playing in all styles from boogie-woogie to contemporary jazz to classical. She appeared in the film *Sensations of 1945* and in the Brodway musical *Star Time* (1944). She made a number of recordings. In 1954 she published a collection of her piano pieces, *Dorothy Donegan's Musical Compositions, 1942-54.* She was one of the virtuoso jazz pianists of her time; her style reflected the influence of Art Tatum,* Earl Hines,* and Errol Garner.* During a long career she moved gracefully from one era to the next, never becoming dated and typically livening her performances with considerable showmanship.

BIBL: Black press, incl. CDef, 10 November 1945; *New Courier* [Pittsburgh], 19 January 1974. FeaEJ. MeeJMov. NYT, 17 May 1975. WWAW. WWBA.

DISC: Kink.

DORHAM, MCKINLEY HOWARD (''KENNY''). Jazz trumpeter (b. 30 August 1924 in Fairfield, Texas;

d. 5 December 1972 in New York, New York). He came from a musical family: his father played guitar, and his mother and a sister played piano. He obtained his musical education in the public schools of Austin, Texas, and at Wiley College in Marshall,Texas, where he played in the college band. After service in the United States Armed Forces, he began playing professionally. Those with whom he played during the 1940s-50s included Russell Jacquet (1943), John Birks ("Dizzy") Gillespie* (1945), William ("Billy") Eckstine* (1946), Lionel Hampton* (1947), Mercer Ellington* (1948), Charlie Parker* (1948-50), the Jazz Messengers* (1955), and Max Roach* (1956-58), among others. During these years he also led his own groups at intervals and was active as a free-lance player, particularly during the years 1951-55. He began writing arrangements for various groups early in his career; he also wrote music for films, including *A Song Is Born* (1948) and *Witness in the City* (1959), and recorded extensively with his own groups and with others. Beginning in 1965 he wrote record reviews for *Down Beat* magazine; in 1969 he published "Fragments of an Autobiography" for the magazine's annual issue. Dorham was regarded as one of the important figures of the bebop era, and particularly of "hard bop" style.

BIBL: FeaEJ. FeaJS. FeaGitJS. MeeJMov.

DISC: Jep. Kink. ModJ. TudJ.

DORSEY, THOMAS ANDREW. Gospel songwriter (b. 1 July 1899 in Villa Rica, Georgia). He came from a musical family: his mother played church organ, one uncle was a church choir director, and another was a roving guitarist who played for country dances. As a child he occasionally traveled with his father, an itinerant minister and revivalist. His family moved to Atlanta, Georgia, when he was about eleven years old. He studied piano with pianists in a local theater where he had a part-time job selling soft drinks—among them, Edward ("Eddie") Heywood, Sr.—and with local teacher Mrs. Graves. He began playing for social events in the community at an early age. He obtained his musical education in the public schools of Atlanta, Georgia; at Wendell Phillips High School in Chicago, Illinois; and at Chicago Musical College. In 1916 he settled in Chicago and found employment playing piano in bars, in wine rooms of saloons, and in music stores as a song demonstrator. In 1923 J. Mayo ("Ink") Williams* asked him to form a band to tour with Gertrude ("Ma") Rainey* on the TOBA* circuit (Theater Owners Booking Association). He remained with her for four years during touring seasons, performing and accompanying with his five-piece Wildcats Jazz Band, making arrangements and writing music, particularly blues, for use in her shows. He continued his musical activities in Chicago when he was not on tour. During the years 1923-24 he was co-leader of a big band, the Whispering Syncopators; he later recorded with a small group called the Famous Hokum Boys; and he was an arranger for Ink Williams's Chicago Music Publishing Company. After leaving Rainey about 1927 he toured and/or recorded with various persons, including "Tampa Red" (née Hudson Whittaker),* Charlie Jackson,* Bertha ("Chippie") Hill,* Frankie Jaxon, and William ("Big Bill") Broonzy,* among others. He and Tampa Red formed a team that performed regularly and wrote songs in collaboration, of which the best known was "It's tight like that." During these years he acquired his nickname "Georgia Tom"; his other nickname, "Barrelhouse Tom," dated from his Atlanta years.

The Great Depression of 1929 dealt a severe blow to blues-jazz musical activities, and Dorsey turned to sacred music. In 1932 he was appointed chorus director at the Pilgrim Baptist Church, where he remained into the 1980s. He began writing sacred songs as early as 1921, becoming inspired when he attended the annual meeting of the National Baptist Convention in Chicago and heard a singer perform A. W. Nix's "I do, don't you." He was also influenced by the gospel hymns of Charles A. Tindley* that he knew, but he resolved to carry over into his sacred songs "the feeling and the pathos and the moans of the blues" (quoted from an interview with Dorsey; *see* LivBl below). One of his early songs was published in *Gospel Pearls*, a publication of the Sunday School Publishing Board of the National Baptist Convention (copyright 1921). He continued to write his special kind of sacred songs through the early 1920s and coined the term "gospel song" (as distinguished from gospel hymn) to refer to the songs. In 1925 he attempted to sell a song, "If you see my Savior, tell him that you saw me," through the mail, sending hundreds of copies to churches all over the nation. The response was meager and discouraging, but in 1930 a singer performed the song at the Jubilee Meeting of the National Baptist Convention (established in 1880) and brought him wide recognition. The Convention's music directors, Lucie Campbell* and E.W.D. Isaac, Jr., gave him official permission to sell his songs at the meeting. In 1931 he organized, along with Theodore Frye,* the world's first gospel chorus at the Ebenezer Baptist Church, and the same year was a co-founder with Frye and Magnolia Lewis Butts of the Chicago Gospel Choral Union, Inc. In 1932 he opened the Dorsey House of Music, the first publishing house to sell solely gospel music of black composers. The same year, along with Sallie Martin,* he founded the National Convention of Gospel Choirs and Choruses, which within a few years had an annual attendance of 10,000 to 15,000 delegates. As early as 1927 he began promoting his songs through selling song sheets on street corners and demonstrating the songs in churches (where ministers would allow it), particularly in storefront churches. He and Martin toured widely during the 1930s, traveling in the Midwest and South, as far west as Los Angeles, California, and as far east as Philadelphia, Pennsylvania, where they were sponsored in 1935 by Gertrude Ward (later of The Famous Ward Singers*). Dorsey was also active as a performer; he toured as the official pianist for Mahalia Jackson* during the years c1940-42.

Dorsey was called "the Father of Gospel Music." Over his long career he wrote nearly a thousand songs and published over half of them. Before the term gospel song entered common usage, his songs were called "Dorseys" (in the same way as the hymns of Isaac Watts were called "Watts" in black churches). His best-known song was "Precious Lord, take my hand," which was translated into more than fifty languages and which he conducted throughout the world. Other well-known songs, in addition to those cited above, included "Search me, Lord," "When I've done my best," "Hide me in Thy bosom," and "Peace in the valley" (written especially for Mahalia Jackson). Dorsey was a pioneer in other ways. In addition to inventing a name for the new sacred music of black Americans, organizing its first chorus, its first annual convention, and founding its first publishing house, he is credited with establishing the tradition of the gospel music concert. In 1936 he promoted a concert at the DuSable High School in Chicago that included a "battle of song" between two celebrated gospel figures, Sallie Martin and Roberta Martin* (not related) as well as performances by others, including Frye, and charged a small admission fee. The concert inaugurated a new trend in gospel-music promotion. Previously it was common practice not to charge admission for church-music concerts, although free-will offerings might be accepted. Dorsey's numerous honors included awards from civic, church, and professional organizations and honorary doctorates from educational institutions.

BIBL: Interview by Fanya Wiggins. Black press, incl. CDef, 7 June 1980. BPIM 7 (Spring 1979). *Black World* (November 1973; July 1974 [Special Dorsey Issue]. Heil. Jac. LivBl 20 (March-April 1975).

DISC: DiGod. RustJR. TudBM.

DORSEY, WILLIAM H. ("BILLY"). Vaudeville bandleader (b. c1880 at Louisville, Kentucky; d. 29 February 1920 in Arizona). He received his early musical education in Louisville, then went to Chicago, Illinois, where he won recognition as an arranger and bandleader. For many years he was leader of the orchestra and pianist at the Monogram Theater. In 1913 his group included Erskine Tate,* Harry Johnson, and George Smith, among others. In 1915 he went to London, heading a vaudeville company that included Lizzie Hart Dorsey (his wife), Joe Jordan,* and twenty others. After the company's engagement had ended, he remained in London, opening a music studio and performing in various nightclubs. Late in 1919 he returned to the United States in poor health and settled in Arizona to recover; he died soon thereafter.

BIBL: Black press, incl. CDef, 22 October 1910, 17 April 1915, 19 October 1918, 1 November 1919, 13 March 1920; IndF, 20 March 1920.

DOUGLAS, MINNIE ("MEMPHIS MINNIE"). Blueswoman (b. 3 June 1896 in Algiers, Louisiana; d. 7 August 1973 in Memphis, Tennessee). Her family moved to Walls, Mississippi (near Memphis, Tennessee), when she was a child. Her father bought her a banjo soon thereafter; by the time she was fifteen she had gained local recognition for her blues guitar as "Kid" Douglas. Beginning in 1916 she toured for several years with the Ringling Brothers Circus. She settled in Chicago during the late 1920s and established herself as one of the top country blues singers in the city. She had a strong voice, good guitar technique, and was one of the few women who accompanied themselves. In 1929 she made her first recordings as "Memphis Minnie," and thereafter she recorded extensively until 1954, successively with one of her three bluesmen husbands—Casey Bill Weldon, "Kansas Joe" McCoy, and "Little Son Joe" (Ernest Lawlers). In 1957 she returned to Memphis, where she continued to perform until a stroke in 1960 forced her into retirement.

BIBL: BWW. FeaEJ; Handy. LivBl 14 (Autumn 1973). LivBl 19 (February 1975). Oliv.

DISC: DiGod. Jep. Kink. LeSl. TudBM.

DOUGLASS, FANNIE HOWARD. Public-school music teacher (b. 21 April 1883 in Atlanta, Georgia). See **DOUGLASS, JOSEPH.**

DOUGLASS, JOHN THOMAS. Concert violinst (b. 1847 in New York, New York [?]; d. 12 April 1886 in New York). There is some confusion about his early career. Undoubtedly he is the Douglass referred to by David Mannes in 1912 (see NYT, 20 March 1912), although Mannes uses an incorrect first name, which he may have forgotten over the years. According to Mannes, Douglass was sent abroad to study violin by rich patrons. James Trotter* refers to a violinist who "played in some of the best orchestras in England," who seems to have been our biographee, although Trotter does not give his name. Douglass won critical acclaim for his violin skills during the 1860s and wrote a three-act opera, *Virginia's Ball*, before he was twenty-two. A copyright notice was entered at the Library of Congress for *Virginia's Ball* in 1868, but the music seems not to be extant. According to the black press, the opera was produced in 1868 at the Stuyvesant Institute on Broadway in New York; leading roles were sung by Emma Magnan, Julia Keblar, Alexander Luca,* and John Luca.* In addition to touring with the orchestra of Callender's Georgia Minstrels* in 1877, Douglass toured widely for that period as a concert violinist. His career was short-lived, however; by the 1880s he rarely appeared as a soloist. He conducted a large studio in New York, and his string orchestra played occasionally for local entertainments. His contemporaries regarded him as "one of the greatest musicians of the race" and as "the master violinist."

Indirectly, Douglass was responsible for the establishment in 1912 of the Music School Settlement for Colored by David Mannes, then first violinist in the New York Philharmonic Society and later founder of the Mannes School of Music. The Music School Settlement was directed first by David Martin* and later by J. Rosamond Johnson.* As a child, Mannes tried to teach himself violin, as he was too poor to study formally. One day, Douglass was walking down a street in New York, heard the sounds of a child's violin playing through an open window, and entered the house to discover the source of the music. When Douglass learned the circumstances of the Mannes family, he offered to teach David Mannes violin. Mannes gave credit to Douglass for giving him the secure foundation upon which Mannes later built a solid career and never forgot his indebtedness to his black violin teacher. Later he established the Settlement in Douglass's memory.

BIBL: Black press, incl. NYGlobe, 17 February 1883; NYFreeman, 24 April 1886. NYT, 20 March 1912—reprinted in BPIM (Spring 1978). Trot, 276, 301; p. 30 of the music section.

DOUGLASS, JOSEPH HENRY. Concert violinist (b. 3 July 1871 in Washington, D.C.; d. 16 December 1935 in Washington). His early interest in music was encouraged by his father and grandfather, abolitionist Frederick Douglass, both of whom played violin. After Joseph taught himself to play his father's violin, his grandfather arranged for music lessons and in 1889 sent him to study at the New England Conservatory in Boston, Massachusetts. After he returned to Washington, D.C., about 1891 he played in the American Orchestral Club; in 1892 he became leader of the orchestra. He planned to go abroad to study at the Conservatory in Brussels, Belgium—and he studied with Joseph Hasper in preparation for his travels—but his plans never materialized. He continued to develop his violin skills, however, and became the first black violinist to make transcontinental concert tours. For more than three decades he toured widely throughout the nation and played at every black educational institution in the United States. For many years he was managed by the Dumas Lyceum Bureau, a black company. Often his wife, Fannie Howard Douglass, accompanied him at the piano. She obtained her musical training at Oberlin and later taught for many years in the public schools of Washington.

He was the first head of the violin department in the School of Music at Howard University. In 1907 he went to New York, where he conducted a violin studio and established the Douglass Lyceum Bureau. During the years 1911-14 he headed the violin department at the Music School Settlement for Colored, then under the direction of David Martin.* He then returned to Washington. In 1921 he was director of the orchestra at the New Republic Theater and also active as a violin teacher. He continued to tour as a concert violinist for the remainder of his life. During his mature career he was regarded by his contemporaries as "the most talented violinist of the race."

BIBL: Black press, incl. CDef, 3 February 1912, 25 September 1915, 17 April 1920; CleveG, 29 December 1894; NYAge, 13 February 1892, 17 October 1907. BPIM (Spring 1974). WWCR.

DOWDY, HELEN. Opera/musicals singer (b. in New York; d. February 1971 in New York). She began her career singing in a Baptist church choir and later toured with the Eva Jessye* Choir. She sang in opera, oratorio, and musicals in both leading and supporting roles, including Lew Leslie's *Rhaposdy in Black* (1931), *Cabin in the Sky* (1940), Hall Johnson's* *Run Little Chillun* (1943 production), and Thomson's *Four Saints in Three Acts* (1952 production), among others. She was best known, however, for her roles of the Strawberry Woman in Gershwin's *Porgy and Bess* (1935, 1942, 1953, 1965 productions) and Queenie in the Hammerstein-Kern *Show Boat* (1946, 1948, 1956 productions). She was also active in community affairs and served as a church organist for an AME church during the 1930s-40s. She played dramatic roles in *Mamba's Daughters* and *Mrs. Patterson*.

BIBL: Black press, incl. AmstN, 24 July 1943, 27 February 1971.

DRA MU OPERA COMPANY. See **SMITH, RAYMOND LOWDEN.**

DRANES, ARIZONA. Gospel singer (fl. 1920s-40s). Blind singer-pianist Arizona Dranes began recording in the mid-1920s; she and Sister Sallie Sanders were the first women to enter the field of professional gospel/spiritual/jubilee singing, which was dominated by male quartets. She was one of the relatively few gospel singers who belonged to the Holiness Church and exerted wide influence upon other members who entered into gospel, particularly Ernestine W. Washington and Rosetta Tharpe.* Dranes's style was distinctive for its sharp diction, nasal voice quality, and ragtime piano. Her best-known performances were of ''Thy servant's prayer,'' ''The storm is over,''and ''I'll go.''

BIBL: BPIM 7 (Spring 1979). Heil.

DISC: DiGod. TudBM.

DREW, KENNETH SIDNEY ("KENNY"). Jazz pianist (b. 28 August 1928 in New York, New York). He began piano study when he was five years old and obtained his musical education at the High School of Music and Art in New York. His first professional experience was as accompanist for Pearl Primus's dancing classes. During the 1950s he played with various groups, including Coleman Hawkins,* Lester Young,* Charlie Parker* (1950-51), Boniface (''Buddy'') DeFranco (1952-53), Art Blakey,* John Coltrane,* Donald Bryd,* and Bernard (''Buddy'') Rich (1958-59), among others. During the decade he also led his own groups in California and toured with Dinah Washington*; he recorded regularly and was active in televison music. In 1961 he went to Europe as a member of the cast of *The Connection* and remained there, settling in Paris, France. In 1964 he moved to Copenhagen, Denmark. Through the 1960s-70s he continued to be highly active, both as performer and composer. He played with visiting jazzmen from the United States, including Dexter Gordon,* Yuseef Lateef,* Theodore (''Sonny'') Rollins,* and Ben Webster,* among others; and he formed duos and trios with European jazzmen which toured widely in Europe and performed at jazz festivals. He also performed on film soundtracks. Drew's early style development reflected the influence of Earl (''Bud'') Powell,* but in his later career he had a distinctive personal style along with his impressive technique.

BIBL: FeaEJ. FeaJS. FeaGitJS. MeeJMov.

DISC: Jep. Kink. ModJ. TudJ.

DRURY, THEODORE. Concert singer/Opera producer (b. 1860s [?]; d. 1940s in Philadelphia, Pennsylvania [?]). Nothing is known of his early life. He began his career as a concert baritone, and during the 1880s he toured in the Northeast and was assisting artist on programs of the Grand Star Concerts in New York, New York. In October 1889 his newly organized Theodore Drury Colored Opera Company made its debut at Brooklyn, New York. The company toured briefly but staged most of its productions in New York and surrounding areas. In 1900 Drury began to produce grand opera, continuing the practice for eight years. Over the years his operas, which were staged at the Lexington Opera House in New York, included Bizet's *Carmen*, Gounod's *Faust*, Verdi's *Aida*, Leoncavallo's *I Pagliacci*, Mascagni's *Cavaleria Rusticana*, and Antonio Carlos Gomez's *Il Guarany*. Those who sang regularly in his operas included Estelle Pickney Clough,* Desseria Plato,* and George Ruffin;* Drury himself usually sang as well as directed. He employed white orchestras and occasionally used white singers. Some time during the first decade of the century he settled at Boston, Massachusetts, where he organized the Drury Musical Arts Club. In December 1911 his Club produced Handel's *Messiah*. In May 1912 he made his concert debut as a tenor at the Palm Garden in Boston. Thereafter he went abroad to study voice. After returning to the United States in 1918, he made a transcontinental tour of the nation, singing scenes from the standard operas. He then resettled in Boston, where he conducted a voice studio and coached professional singers. He continued to be active away from home, however; in October 1928 his Opera Company staged *Faust* in Providence, Rhode Island, and in August 1930 he served on the jury that awarded prizes in the first Wannamaker Music Contests. He spent the last years of his career in Philadelphia, Pennsylvania. In May 1938 he presented the opera *Carmen* with his Drury Opera Company and made plans to stage it in New York; it is not known whether he did so. In 1945 music critic Nora Holt* referred to him as the ''late Theodore Drury'' (AmstN, 5 May).

BIBL: Black press, incl. CDef, 30 March 1918, 13 October 1928; IndF, 12 October 1889, 11 January 1890, 13 November 1897, 24 May 1902, 4 June 1904; NYAge, 4 January 1900, 6 April 1905, 21 May 1908, 7 May 1938; PhilaT, 18 May 1912, 8 June 1912. *Colored American Magazine* (June 1900). WWRC.

DU BOIS, SHIRLEY GRAHAM. See **GRAHAM DU BOIS, SHIRLEY.**

DUDLEY, S[HERMAN] H[OUSTON] ("HAPSY"). Vaudeville entertainer/manager (b. 12 May 1872 in Janesville, Louisiana; d. 29 February 1940 in Washington, D.C.). He began his career performing with traveling carnivals. Later he toured with various groups, including McCabe and Young's Minstrels and Richard and Pringle's Georgia Minstrels, among others. In 1904 he was a member of John Isham's *King Rastus* Company, which featured Billy Kersands,* and later in the same year took over the leading role in the Smart Set Company after the death of Tom McIntosh.* His last appearances with the Smart Set were in the musical comedies *His Honor, the Barber,* which also starred Aida Overton Walker,* and *Dr. Beans from Boston* (1913). In 1912 he settled in Washington, D.C., where he began to organize a vaudeville circuit of theaters, using that city as his headquarters. His plan was to provide vaudeville shows and other kinds of public entertainment to theaters owned or leased by black proprietors throughout the nation. By 1914 no fewer than twenty-three theaters subscribed to his service, as far south as Atlanta, Georgia. As the first black entrepreneur to organize a Negro circuit of theaters, he paved the way for the T.O.B.A.* (Theater Owners Booking Association), and indeed was credited by the black press with founding T.O.B.A. He published a column in black newspapers titled "On the Dudley Circuit," which listed the theaters, names of managers, and titles of the shows being offered each week. After the beginning of T.O.B.A., he remained the representative in Washington, D.C.; representatives in other centers included Charles Turpin (brother of Tom Turpin*) in St. Louis, Missouri, and white representatives Sam E. Reevin (Chattanooga, Tennessee) and Martin Klein (Chicago, Illinois), among others. Dudley also had his own vaudeville company, which featured him in an act billed "Dudley and His Mule" (whose name was Patrick). During the 1930s he was stage manager for the Silas Green tent show. In 1938 he and his son, S. H. Dudley, Jr. organized a new tent show titled "The Sherman H. Dudleys' Ebony Follies."

BIBL: Black press, incl. CDef, 7 November 1914, 22 May 1915, 9 April 1938, 16 March 1940; IndF, 25 December 1897, 27 January 1912, 2 February 1924. Flet, p. 98.

DUKE, GEORGE. Jazz pianist (b. 12 January 1946 in San Rafael, California). He studied piano as a child. He obtained his musical education at the San Francisco [California] Conservatory of Music (B.A., 1967) and at the San Francisco State University (M.A., 1969). He taught himself to play jazz by listening to recordings, and began playing in San Francisco nightclubs during his high-school years. He led his own trio during the years 1965-70, which toured with a vocal group called The Third Wave and later played with such jazz figures as John Birks ("Dizzy") Gillespie,* Kenneth ("Kenny") Dorham,* Robert ("Bobby") Hutcherson,* and Jean-Luc Ponty, among others. After his trio was disbanded, he played with various groups, including Frank Zappa's Mothers of Invention (1970, 1973-75), Julian ("Cannonball") Adderley* (1971-72), and William ("Billy") Cobham* (1975-76). Thereafter he led his own groups. He began playing electric keyboards in 1968, and soon expanded his skills to include all the keyboards and synthesizers. He also began singing with his groups and expanded his repertory to included all the styles, from rock and popular music to traditional and avant-garde jazz.

BIBL: ContKey (July 1977). FeaGitJS.

DULF, GEORGE. Military bandmaster (b. 10 April 1872 in Springfield, Illinois; d. 1943 in Chicago, Illinois). He was a leader of a Knight of Pythias band, along with Alexander Armant, in 1898 in Chicago, Illinois. The entire band was inducted into the United States Armed Forces in 1899, becoming the Eighth Illinois Band (later the Illinois National Guard Regiment Band) with Armant as bandmaster and Dulf as principal musician. Although an army band, it continued to play for parades, social entertainments, and concerts as formerly, touring widely in the Middle West. In 1901 a representative of the American Federation of Musicians invited the band to join Chicago's Local 10, but the majority of the union members voted against admission of the black band. The next year Armant and Dulf organized a black unit of the AFM, Local 208 or the Musicians Protective Union, and received their charter in July 1902. Armant was elected president (1902-04), and Dulf became vice-president. This apparently was the first black AFM unit in the nation. During World War I, Dulf was bandmaster of the 370th Infantry, which was called the "Black Devils" during its service overseas. After the war, the thirty-two-piece band toured the nation, featuring Anita Patti Brown* on its concerts. According to some sources, Dulf played with Will Marion Cook's* American Syncopated Orchestra during the years 1919-22 and accompanied the orchestra to England. After returning to Chicago, he served as a bandmaster for the Chicago Knight Templars Band (1923-43) and the Charles I. Hunt Post Band (1938-43). He also led a ladies orchestra during the 1920s-30s.

BIBL: Black press, incl. CDef 12 April 1919. *Music Master:* Journal of Local 208, AFM (July 1942).

DUMERVÉ, CONSTANTIN. Writer (b. 1880s in Môle St. Nicolas, Haiti; d. 19?? in Port-au-Prince, Haiti). Although a lawyer by profession, he was also active as a musician. His brother Joseph Méretin Dumervé, a medical doctor, played piano, organ, and clarinet on a professional level. Constantin obtained his musical education at the Petit Séminaire Collège St. Martial in Port-au-Prince, Haiti. During the course of his studies, he became interested in journalism, and one of his teachers, Henri Chauvet, suggested that he combine his interests in music and journalism, writing about music. It was Chauvet who inspired Dumervé to write a history of Haiti's music, a task which took thirty-seven years because of the immense amount of research involved. His publications about music included the *Histoire de la Musique de Haiti* (1968), a song collection *Recueil de chants patriotiques* (1952), and articles contributed to *Les Griots*. He also composed songs, including "Haiti" (text by Dominique Hyppolite), and piano pieces, "La baie du Môle Saint Nicolas" and "In memoriam" (for his brother). In 1963 he was elected to honorary membership in the Beethoven Society of Bonn, West Germany.

BIBL: Dumervé.

DUNBAR, PAUL LAURENCE. Poet/Lyricist (b. 27 June 1872 in Dayton, Ohio; d. 9 February 1906 in Dayton). He is included here because of his collaboration with composers on several occasions to produce musicals or other stage works. Perhaps the earliest such work was *Dream Lovers* (1898), an operatic romance with music by Samuel Coleridge-Taylor.* Dunbar met the composer in 1897 when he went to England to read his poems, and the two men gave a series of joint recitals. Coleridge-Taylor set to music several of Dunbar's poems (published in 1897 as *African Romances*, Op. 17). Dunbar's poetry was also the inspiration for Taylor's *African Suite*, Op. 35 (1898). Dunbar's longest association was with Will Marion Cook.* Best known of the musicals they worked on together were *Clorindy, or the Origin of the Cakewalk* (1898), *Jes Lak White Folks* (1900), and *In Dahomey* (1902). The latter two involved the contributions of other writers and composers as well. Dunbar also wrote lyrics for popular songs, including "Good evenin' " and "My little gypsy maid." Over the years composers of art songs made settings of many Dunbar poems.

BIBL: Will Marion Cook, "Clorindy, or the Origin of the Cakewalk"in SouRBM. James V. Hatch and Omanni Abdullah, *Black Playwrights, 1823-1977* (New York, 1977). W. C. Berwick Sayers, *Samuel Coleridge-Taylor, Musician* (London, 1915).

DUNBAR, RUDOLPH. Symphony orchestra conductor (b. 5 April 1907 in Nabaclis, British Guiana). He was apprenticed to the British Guiana Militia Band when he was nine years old, and he toured with the band for three years. He first studied music as a member of the band, and studied clarinet with Sergeant-Major E. A. Carter. When he was twelve his father sent him to the United States to study music; he settled in New York and attended the Institute of Musical Art there, studying clarinet, piano, and composition (diploma, 1924). He was active in the black music community during his stay in New York; he played in the Harlem [Symphony] Orchestra, under director E. Gilbert Anderson,* and in Will Vodery's* Plantation Orchestra, which toured with the Broadway musical *Dixie to Broadway* (1925). In 1925 he settled in Europe, where he engaged in further study, at first in Paris, France, then in Leipzig, Germany, and in Vienna, Austria. His teachers included Louis Cahuzac, Philippe Gaubert, Paul Vidal, and Felix Weingartner. During his years in Paris he also studied journalism and later became a foreign correspondent for the Associated Negro Press. About 1931 he settled in London, England, where he worked with jazz as well as classical groups. He recorded with his African Polyphony and led his orchestra in a London stage show, *Black Rhythm* (1934). In April 1942 he made his conducting debut with the London Philharmonic Orchestra, the youngest conductor ever to lead that orchestra and the first black conductor. Thereafter he toured widely as a guest conductor in the British Isles, on the Continent, and as far south as Egypt. In March 1944 he conducted the Liverpool Philharmonic Orchestra in a program consisting solely of American music for the first time in England. In November 1944 he made his French debut at Paris with L'Association des concerts Pasdeloup; in 1945 he made his German debut with the Berlin Philharmonic Orchestra. During World War II, he conducted concerts for British and American troops. In October 1945 he organized and conducted a festival of American music in Paris for the first time in Europe. He returned to the United States in 1948 to conduct the Hollywood [California] Bowl Orchestra, and toured in the West Indies and in British Guiana during the years 1951-52. Dunbar contributed articles to professional journals, including a regular column to the *Melody Maker* as "Technical Expert" about the clarinet during the years 1931-38. His book publications included *Treatise on the Clarinet* (1939). Beginning in the 1940s he conducted The School of Modern Clarinet Playing in London.

BIBL: Questionnaire. Black press, incl. AmstN, 8 September 1945; CDef, 9 January 1943; NYAge, 9 May 1925. BPIM (Fall 1981). CurBiog (October 1946).

DUNCAN, JOHN. Composer/College professor (b. 25 November 1913 in Lee County, Alabama; d. 15 September 1975 in Montgomery, Alabama). He obtained his musical education from Temple University

(B. Mus., M. Mus) and studied further at New York University. During his stay in Philadelphia he was active in jazz circles, particularly as an arranger. He taught at Samuel Huston College in Texas before going to Alabama State College (now University) in 1939, where he remained until his death. In 1974 he was given an honorary degree by the university. He published articles in professional journals and the press, but he was best known as a composer-teacher. Although few of his compositions were published, they were performed throughout the South and in several northern cities. His best-known works were the Concerto for Trombone and Orchestra, *An Easter Canticle*, the opera *Gideon and Eliza*, and *Black Bards* for flute, cello, and piano.

BIBL: Personal communication.

DUNCAN, ROBERT TODD. Concert/opera singer (b. 12 February 1903 in Danville, Kentucky). As a child he studied piano with his mother. He obtained his musical training at Butler University in Indiana (B.A., 1925) and Columbia University Teachers College (M.A., 1930). He studied voice with Sara Lee, Edward Lippe, and Sidney Dietch. In 1935 he created the role of Porgy in Gershwin's *Porgy and Bess*; thereafter he appeared in a number of Broadway musicals and films, including *The Sun Never Sets* (London production, 1938), *Cabin in the Sky* (1940), revival of *Porgy and Bess* (1942-43), *Lost in the Stars* (1949), and the films *Syncopation* (1942) and *Unchained* (1955), among others. His operatic debut (baritone) was in Mascagni's *Cavalleria Rusticana* at New York's Mecca Temple in 1934. In 1945 he became the first male of his race to sing with a major opera company when he sang the role of Tonio in Leoncavallo's *I Pagliacci* at the New York City Opera Company. The same season he sang Escamillo in Bizet's *Carmen*. In 1944 he made his debut at New York's Town Hall as a concert baritone; the following two decades he toured widely in the United States and abroad, giving solo recitals and appearing with symphony orchestras. His longtime accompanist was William Duncan Allen.* His teaching experience included tenures at Louisville Municipal College for Negroes (1925-30) and Howard University (1931-45). In his late career he maintained a voice studio in Washington, D.C., and continued to give concerts periodically. His honors included the Donaldson and the Critics Awards for his performances in musicals (1950), an NAACP award for his contribution to the theater, and the President of Haiti's Medal of Honor and Merit (1945). In 1978 the Washington Performing Arts Society held a gala Salute to Todd Duncan on the occasion of his seventy-fifth birthday.

BIBL: CBD. *Ebony* (December 1975). HNB. WWBA. WWCA.

DISC: RustCED. Turn.

DUNCAN,TODD. See **DUNCAN, ROBERT TODD.**

DUNHAM, KATHERINE. Dancer/Choreographer (b. 22 June 1910 in Glen Ellyn, Illinois). Although best known as a dancer, she was also a songwriter and folksong collector. Her family moved to Joliet, Illinois, when she was five years old. She obtained her education in the public schools and junior college of Joliet and at the University of Chicago (Ph.B., 1936; graduate work). She studied music and began to dance at an early age. In high school she studied dance, and at the age of fifteen she gave a public performance with a group she had organized. After completing her junior college work she moved to Chicago, Illinois, where she became active in her brother's Cube Theater movement, studied ballet with Ludmilla Speranzeva, and conducted a dance studio. She founded a dance company, Ballet Negre, which made its debut in 1931 at the Chicago Beaux Arts Ball but later was disbanded. After founding another company, the Negro Dance Group, she became interested in exploring the origins of black popular dances. Her career development in this area was aided by Robert Redfield at the University of Chicago and Melville Herskovits at Northwestern University in Evanston, Illinois. A fellowship enabled her to pursue research in the West Indies in 1935. After completing her work for a degree in social anthropology, she decided to enter a full-time dance career. Within a short period she established herself as the leading figure in Afro-American dance and other dance traditions of African origin. She toured widely with her troupes throughout the world, appearing in theaters, opera houses, nightclubs, and at festivals; she lived for periods of time in Europe, Japan, Haiti, and West Africa; and she also toured as a lecturer and served as artist-in-residence in universities and other educational institutions. She appeared in numerous films, both as dancer-choreographer and as musican, arranging music and writing songs for films, such as *Mambo* (1954). Her best-known songs were "New love, new wine" and "Coco da mata." She also appeared in many Broadway musicals and on radio and television shows. In 1980 she was the subject of a television documentary in the series "Great Performances," sponsored by the Public Broadcasting System. Her honors included a Rosenwald Fellowship (1935), the award Chevalier of Haiti, Legion of Honor and Merit (1952), University of Chicago Alumni Association Award (1968), numerous awards from the music and dance industries, honorary doctorates from MacMurray College (1972) and Atlanta University (1977), and the Albert Schweitzer Music Award (1979). She exerted great influence upon the development of modern dance; some called her the "mother of Afro-American dance." Her students included Alvin Ailey, Marlon Brando, Jose Ferrer, Eartha Kitt,* and Camille Yarbrough, among others.

BIBL: Interview by E.S. Black press, incl. AmstN, 12 April 1980; CDef, 10 June 1975. WWA. WWBA. *Sepia* (August 1953).

DUNN, JOHN ("JOHNNY"). Jazz cornetist/trumpeter (b. 19 February 1897 in Memphis, Tennessee; d. 20 August 1937 in Paris, France). He obtained his musical education at Fisk University in Nashville, Tennessee. He began his professional career playing in vaudeville shows in a local theater of Memphis, Tennessee. Thereafter he played with various groups, including W. C. Handy* (c1916-c1920), Mamie Smith's* Jazz Hounds (1920-21), and Will Vodery's* Plantation Orchestra (1922-24). During these years he also performed with his own Original Jazz Hounds in the Broadway musical *Put and Take* (1921) and recorded with such singers as Edith Wilson* and Josie Miles. As a featured soloist he appeared in several shows, including *Plantation Revue* (1922), *From Dover to Dixie* (London, 1923), *Dixie to Broadway* (1924), *Chocolate Kiddies* (1925), and several of the Lew Leslie *Blackbirds* shows. During the late 1920s he toured in the United States as a soloist and with his big band, then settled in Europe in 1928. There he played with Noble Sissle* and John Ricks, among others, and as well with his own New Yorkers. For several years he worked in Holland and Denmark, then returned to Paris, France in 1937.

BIBL: AlHen.ChilWW.

DISC: Kink. RustJr.

DUPREE, WILLIAM H. Brass bandsman (b. 18 March 1838 in Petersburg, Virginia; d. 22 June 1934 in Neponset, Massachusetts). His family moved to Chillicothe, Ohio, when he was a few weeks old, then to Michigan, then back to Ohio in 1853. In 1859 he joined the Union Valley Brass Band of Chillicothe, playing the B-flat baritone and later serving as the band's manager. In 1863 he enlisted in the United States Armed Forces and became manager of the Fifty-Fifth Regiment Band. After the war he settled in Boston, Massachusetts. He was active with community choral groups and during the 1890s was president of the Beacon Choral Union, which sponsored regular concerts. He was also active as a concert promoter and impresario; in 1886 he was manager for Marie Selika.*

BIBL: Black press, incl. CleveG, 11 April 1885, 31 October 1886; NYAge, 10 May 1890, 15 November 1890. Hare. LaBrew. Trot, 315.

DURHAM, EDDIE. Jazz guitarist (b. 19 August 1906 in San Marcos, Texas). He came from a musical family: six brothers formed the Durham Brothers Orchestra, for which he was a co-leader, guitarist, and trombonist. During the 1920s-30s he played with and wrote arrangements for various groups, including Walter Page's* Blue Devils (1928-29), Bennie Moten* (1929-33), James ("Jimmie") Lunceford* (1935-37), and William ("Count") Basie* (1937-38), among others. As a member of Basie's band he performed on the celebrated From Spirituals to Swing concert staged at Carnegie Hall in New York on 23 December 1938. During the next four decades he gave more and more time to arranging music, working for Ina Ray Hutton, Glenn Miller, and Artie Shaw, among others. He was musical director of the International Sweethearts of Rhythm* (1941-43) and led his own groups, including an all-girls group. Those he toured with in later years included Wynonie Harris,* George ("Buddy") Tate, and Larry Darnell. He was a prolific songwriter as well as arranger; his best-known songs were "Swinging the blues," "Good morning, blues," "Sent for you yesterday and here you come today," and "I don't want to set the world on fire" (some of these with co-composers). Durham was a pioneer in developing the potential of the amplified jazz guitar as a solo instrument.

BIBL: ASCAP. ChilWW. FeaEJ. FeaGitJS. MeeJMov. Russ.

DISC: Kink. RustJR. TudJ.

DUTREY, HONORE. Jazz trombonist (b. 1894 in New Orleans, Louisiana; d. 21 July 1935 in Chicago, Illinois). He came from a musical family: two brothers, Sam and Pete, became professional musicians. During his early career he played with various local groups, including the Melrose Brass Band, the Buddy Petit-Jimmie Noone* band, John Robichaux, and the Silver Leaf Orchestra. During World War I he served in the United States Navy. Thereafter he settled in Chicago, Illinois, where he played with Joseph ("King") Oliver* (1920-21, 1922-24), Carroll Dickerson,* Johnny Dodds,* and Louis Armstrong,* and led his own group in nightclubs. He left the field of music about 1930. He first attracted wide attention in Oliver's band, with whom he made his recording debut in 1923. He was a pioneering jazz trombonist in the New Orleans tailgate style.

BIBL: ChilWW. FeaEJ. MeeJMov. Souch.

DISC: RustJR.

DYETT, WALTER HENRI. Bandmaster/Music educator (b. 1 January 1901 in St. Joseph, Missouri; d. 17 November 1969 in Chicago, Illinois). He began piano study at the age of five with his mother. When he was eleven, his family moved to Pasadena, California, and he began violin study there with Hubert Parker, bandmaster of the local high school. He attended the University of California at Los Angeles in a pre-medicine program but also studied orchestral and band instruments there with a Professor Steindorff. He obtained further musical education in Chicago, Illinois, at the Vandercook School of [Band] Music (B. Mus., 1938), Chicago Musical College (M. Mus., 1942), the American Conservatory of Music, Petrowitsak Bissing's Master School of Music, and the Columbia School of Music (1925-30).

He began playing professionally in dance orchestras in 1918. In 1921 he settled in Chicago; thereafter he played with various groups, including Charles Elgar, Erskine Tate,* Dave Peyton,* and Charles Cooke.* He also played violin at local concerts and in church recitals. From 1922 on, however, he specialized in conducting musical groups and arranging music for their performances. He organized concert and dance orchestras, including the Pickford Orchestra (organized 1925), and conducted church choirs. His teaching career included tenures at the Coleridge-Taylor School of Music (1927-31), Wendell Phillips High School (1931-35), and DuSable High School (1935-69); in the public schools he was bandmaster as well as teacher. A captain in the National Guard, he also was a bandmaster with the United States Eighth Infantry Band and the 184th Field Artillery Band from 1934 on. As bandmaster in the two high schools attended by most black students in Chicago during the 1930-60s, he exerted enormous influence over the development of black musicians in the fields of jazz, military, and concert music—much as his predecessor at Phillips High School, N. Clark Smith,* had established strong traditions for excellence at Phillips and later at Sumner High School in St. Louis, Missouri. Those who studied with Dyett or otherwise came under his influence included Eugene Ammons,* Nat King Cole (née Nathaniel Coles),* Richard Davis,* Bennie Green, John Arnold Griffin, and Nelmatilda Ritchie Woodward,* among others.

BIBL: Interview of wife by Fanya Wiggins. ChiVH. Layne. WWCA, 1950.

E

EARTH, WIND AND FIRE. Rhythm 'n' blues group (org. in Chicago, Illinois; fl. 1970s). The male vocal group of nine singers was organized by Maurice White (b. 19 December 1946 in Memphis, Tennessee), a jazz percussionist. He obtained his musical education in the public schools of Chicago, Illinois, and toured as a child with such gospel singers and groups as the Pilgrim Travelers,* James Cleveland,* and the Clara Ward* Singers. During his high-school years he performed with blues, rock, and jazz bands. Later he studied at the Chicago Conservatory of Music, and during the same period, was accompanist for Etta James,* Fontella Bass, and Curtis Mayfield,* among others. Thereafter he played with Ramsey Lewis,* then organized his own groups. Late in 1969 he organized Earth, Wind, and Fire—whose purpose was to sing in a variety of styles, jazz, rock, popular, and soul. Those who sang in the group over the years included Philip Bailey, Michael Bill, Jessica Cleaves, Leslie Drayton, Larry Dunn (née Lawrence Dunhill), Wade Flemons, John Graham, Jacob Ben Israel, Ralph Johnson, Alan McKay, Alex Thomas, Clint Washington, Andrew Woolfolk, and his brothers Verdine (b. 25 July 1951) and Fred White (b. 13 January 1955). Members of the group wrote and arranged most of the music they sang, particularly the White brothers. Among the group's best-known album recordings were *Head to the Sky, That's the Way of the World*, and *Last Days and Time*. The group toured frequently with the Ramsey Lewis Quartet.

BIBL: Black press. *Ebony* (February 1975).

DISC: Giv.

EATON, ADAM ROY. Music businessman/Pianist (b. 14 May 1930 in New York, New York). He began piano study at the age of six and played in a public recital when he was seven. He obtained his musical education at the High School of Music and Art in New York; the City College of the City University of New York (B.S., 1950); the Manhattan School of Music in New York (B. Mus., 1950; M. Mus., 1952), Yale University in New Haven, Connecticut (1950-52); the University of Zurich in Switzerland; and the Conservatory of Lucerne in Switzerland. He also studied privately with Harold Bauer. In 1951 he made his debut with the Chicago Symphony Orchestra, and in 1952 he made his debut in New York at Town Hall. He was active as a concert pianist during the years 1950-55, touring Europe, giving solo recitals and appearing with symphony orchestras. His teaching career included tenures as a piano instructor at City College of the City University of New York, at the Manhattan School of Music, and at the U.S. Armed Forces Institute. Thereafter he was active in music business enterprises, including tenures as music director with Young and Rubicam Advertising (1955-59), Music Makers, Inc., and Benton and Bowles, Inc. (1959-), where he also was vice-president. His honors included the Naumberg Award (1949) and the Kosciuszko Foundation Chopin Award (1950).

BIBL: Black press, incl. AmstN, 10 June 1950; NYAge, 7 November 1959. WWBA. WWHarlem.

ECKSTINE, WILLIAM CLARENCE ("BILLY" "MR. B"). Jazz singer (b. 8 July 1914 in Pittsburgh, Pennsylvania). He sang as a child at local social events and in a church choir for a short period. He obtained his musical education in the public schools of Pittsburgh, Pennsylvania, and Washington, D.C.; at Howard University in Washington, where he majored in physical education for a year; at Shaw University in Raleigh, North Carolina (B.A., 1974); and at the University of Southern California in Los Angeles. Encouraged by winning prizes in amateur shows in Washington theaters, he dropped out of college to sing professionally with bands in nightclubs and theaters. During the mid-1930s he sang in various places, including Buffalo, New York, Detroit, Michigan, and Pittsburgh, then went to Chicago, Illinois, to sing in the DeLisa Club (1937-39). Thereafter he sang with Earl Hines* (1939-43), toured as a soloist, then organized his own band (1944-46), which included John Birks ("Dizzy") Gillespie,* Kenneth ("Kenny") Dorham,* Eugene Ammons,* Art Blakey,* Dexter Gordon,* Albert ("Budd") Johnson,* Theodore ("Fats") Navarro,* John Malachi, Charlie Parker,* Tommy Potter, and Sarah Vaughan,* among others, with himself on trumpet. This band was important historically for its nurturing of the new bebop music and its encouragement of bebop innovators during the transitional period from swing to bop. After 1946 Eckstine toured widely as a soloist, appearing in theaters, nightclubs, at festivals, and beginning in the 1970s on cruise ships and in theaters-in-the-round. He made his recording debut in 1939 with Earl Hines and thereafter recorded extensively as a soloist. He also recorded with others, among them, Edward ("Duke") Ellington,* Maynard Ferguson, Quincy Jones,* and the George Shearing Quintet. He was active in radio and television music and appeared in films, including *Let's Do It Again* (1975). His best-known recordings were "Jelly, jelly," "Everything I have is yours," "Skylark," "My foolish heart," and "A prisoner of love." He received numerous awards from the music industry. His longtime accompanist was Robert ("Bobby") Tucker.* Eckstine pioneered in defining the role of the black solo jazz singer (independent of association with an orchestra) and thereby paved the way for such singers as Nat King Cole* (née Nathaniel Coles) and the ubiquitous black soloist of today with his piano or trio accompaniment. He is also a seminal figure for his role in the development of bebop.

BIBL: Interview by E.S. BPIM 7, 8 (Fall 1979, Spring 1980). CurBiog (July 1952). DanceWEH. FeaEJ. FeaJS. FeaGitJS. MeeJMov. WWA. WWBA.

DISC: Jep. RustJR. Kink. TudJ.

EDET, EDNA SMITH. Jazz bassist/College professor (b. 16 January 1924 in Boston, Massachusetts). She received her musical education at the Manhattan School of Music in New York (B. Mus.; M. Mus., 1956) and Columbia University Teachers College in New York (M.A., 1960; D. Mus. Ed., 1961). She began her musical career as a jazz bassist. During the 1940s she played with the International Sweethearts of Rhythm,* then later with Viola ("Vi") Burnside's Band, and finally with her own Edna Smith Trio for four years, which included former Sweethearts Carline Ray* and Pauline Braddy. She also played piano, trombone, and guitar. During the 1950s she moved into the area of teaching. Her career included tenures in the public schools of New York (1956-61); the University of Nigeria in Nsukka (1961-67), where she was head of the music program; and Queens College and Medgar Evers College (1967-) of the City University of New York. She published articles on the subjects of African music and music education in such professional journals as *African Music*, *Music Educators Journal*, and *West African Journal of Education*. Her book publications included *The Griot Speaks* (New York, 1978).

BIBL: Questionnaire. Handy. IntWWM.

EDISON, HARRY ("SWEETS"). Jazz trumpeter (b. 10 October 1915 in Columbus, Ohio). He began playing trumpet when he was twelve years old. His first professional experience was with local groups in Columbus, Ohio. Thereafter he played with various groups, including Alphonso Trent, the (James) Jeter/(Hayes) Pillar Band (1933-37), Lucius ("Lucky") Millinder* (1937-38), and William ("Count") Basie* (1938-50). He was given the nickname "Sweets" by Lester Young* during his tenure in the Basie band. During the 1950s-70s Edison toured with JATP (Norman Granz's Jazz at the Philharmonic); toured with the Josephine Baker* Revue (1953); played with such groups as James ("Jimmy") Rushing,* Bernard ("Buddy") Rich, Bennett ("Benny") Carter,* and Louis Bellson; was active as a studio musician in Hollywood, California; and led his own groups intermittently. He rejoined Basie several times after Basie's large group was disbanded in 1950. During the 1970s he also was active in television music, both as a performer in orchestras and as music director for the Redd Fox Show: he also performed on film soundtracks, including *Where's Poppa* (1970). He first attracted wide attention as a member of Basie's orchestra, particularly for his elegant, tender swing style.

BIBL: ASCAP. ChilWW. FeaEJ. FeaJS. FeaGitJS. MeeJMov.

DISC: Jep. RustJR.

EDMONDS, SHEPHERD. Vaudeville entertainer/Songwriter (b. 25 September 1876 in Memphis, Tennessee; d. 24 November 1957 in Columbus, Ohio). He began his career in 1895 as a trap drummer with the Al G. Field's Negro Minstrels. In 1897 he joined John W. Vogel's Darkest America company as a songwriter and baritone singer. He attended Ohio State University at Columbus, Ohio. In 1904 he was founder/manager of the Attucks Music Publishing Company in New York, one of the pioneer publishing companies owned by blacks. He wrote a large number of songs, of which the best known are "I'm goin' to live anyhow until I die" and "Just what did I do."

BIBL: ASCAP. Black press, incl. IndF, 25 December 1897, 24 September 1904.

EDWARDS, DAVID ("HONEYBOY"). Bluesman (b. 28 June 1915 in Shaw, Mississippi). He taught himself to play guitar as a youth. When he was seventeen he heard ("Big") Joe Williams* play at Greenwood, Mississippi, and left home to study and travel with Williams for a year or so. Thereafter he traveled widely in the Delta region and the Southwest, playing for country dances and in clubs, and playing with other bluesmen, among them, ("Little") Walter Jacobs,* Tommy McClennan, and Robert Petway. When he settled later in Memphis, Tennessee, he played with the Memphis Jug Band. About 1955 he settled in Chicago and soon established himself as one of the leading blues figures in the city. Those he worked with included "Sunnyland Slim" (Andrew Luandrew)* and Junior Wells.* Blues scholars felt that his style captured the essence of the Delta tradition and reflected the influence of Charley Patton* and Robert Johnson,* although Edwards had not worked directly with them.

BIBL: BWW. Cadence 5 (April 1979). LivBl 4 (Winter 1970-71). Robert Neff and Anthony Connor, *Blues* (Boston, 1975). Oliv.

EDWARDS, JODY AND SUSIE ("BUTTERBEANS AND SUSIE"). Vaudeville entertainers (org. 1914 at Macon, Georgia; fl. 1914-1960s). Jody Edwards (b. 19 July 1895 in Georgia; d. 28 October 1967 in Chicago, Illinois) and Susie Hawthorne (b. 1896? in Pensacola, Florida; d. 5 December 1963 in Chicago, Illinois) formed a vaudeville act about 1914 and began their career together at the Douglass Theatre in Macon, Georgia. According to the black press, they were married on 15 May 1917 on the stage of the Standard Theatre in Philadelphia, Pennsylvania, in a publicity stunt. They toured widely for almost fifty years on the vaudeville circuit with various groups, including the Rabbit Foot Minstrels* and Jimmie Cooper's revues in the 1920s, and later became one of the top attractions of T.O.B.A.* (Theater Owners Booking Association). By the late 1920s they had organized their own vaudeville company; the shows they produced included *Laughing Lightning* (1929), *Ease on Down* (1930),and *Harlem Bound* (1932), among others. Butterbeans and Susie made their recording debut in 1924 and thereafter recorded extensively for their time. In the 1920s they were frequently accompanied by Eddie Heywood* and Clarence Williams.* Those with whom they performed over the years included Mae Barnes, the Nicholas Brothers, Avon Long,* Bessie Smith,* and Ethel Waters,* among others. In 1941 they appeared in the Broadway musical *Cabin in the Sky* with Waters. They were planning for a gala public celebration of their fiftieth anniversary in show business at Chicago in February 1964, but Susie's death forced cancellation of the event.

BIBL: BWW. Black press, incl. AmstN, 28 August 1948; CDef, 7 December 1963.

DISC: RustJR.

EKWUEME, LAZARUS EDWARD NNANYELU. University professor (b. 27 January 1936 in Oko, Nigeria). He obtained his musical education at the St. John's Anglican School in Oko, Nigeria; the Church Missionary Society Central School in Ekwulawbia (1943-48) and Government College at Umuahia (1948-54), both places in Nigeria; at the University of Durham in England (B. Mus., 1964); the Royal College of Music in London, England (M. Mus., 1965); and at Yale University in New Haven, Connecticut, U.S.A., (M.A., Ph.D., 1970). He also earned the Licentiate of Music degree from Trinity College in London. His teaching career included tenures at the University of Nigeria at Nsukka (1964-66), the State University of New York at Stony Brook (U.S.A., 1970-73), the State University of New York at Oneonta (1973-74), and the University of Nigeria at Lagos (1974-). He published widely in professional journals, such as *African Music*, *Journal of African Studies*, and *The Black Perspective in Music*; he toured as a lecturer and guest choral conductor in the United States and in Africa; and he was active as a composer. His best-known works were *Nigerian Rhapsody* for strings, *Dance of the Black Witches* for Quintet, and *Two Igbo Introits* for choir. In 1977 he was a member of the music committee for the Second World Festival of Black and African Arts held at Lagos, Nigeria.

BIBL: Questionnaire. *Nigerian Music Review* (No. 1, 1977). WWAfrica.

EL-DABH, HALIM. Composer/University professor (b. 4 March 1921 in Cairo, Egypt). He obtained his basic musical training at Sulcz Conservatory in Cairo (diploma, 1944) and began composing at an early age, but earned his degree at Cairo University in agricultural engineering (1945). The critical acceptance of a performance of his piano piece, "It is dark and damp on the front," on a concert at All Saints Cathedral in 1949 "changed his entire life"(quoted from Questionnaire), and thereafter he moved entirely into the field of music. In 1950 he went to the United States, where he studied at the Berkshire Festival Center in Tanglewood, Massachusetts, with Aaron Copeland and Irving Fine. He obtained further musical education at the New England Conservatory of Music in Boston, Massachusetts (M. Mus., 1953); at Brandeis University in Waltham, Massachusetts (M.F.A., 1954); and at the University of

New Mexico. Other teachers included Francis Judd Cooke. Among those who influenced his early musical development were Allen Barker, Hussein Helmy, Kamal Iskander, Piere Nouri, Henry Shlala, and his two brothers. His teaching career included tenures at Haile Selassie University in Addis Ababa, Ethiopia (1962-64); at Howard University in Washington, D.C. (1966-68); and at Kent State University in Ohio (1969-). His musical style represents a fusion of traditional African elements (particularly Egyptian) and Western elements with special emphasis upon rhythmic complexities and percussions. In 1959 he made his debut as a solo drummer at the premiere of his composition *Tahmeela for Derabucca and Strings* at the New York Metropolitan Museum, Leopold Stokowski as conductor. El-Dabh's favored musical forms are operas and similar dramatic works, of which the best known are *Opera Flies* (1971) and the triology *Ptah-mose and the Magic Spell: The Osiris Ritual* (1972), *Aton and the Word* (1973), and *The Twelve Hours Trip* (1973). Other musical forms are represented in his works for full and chamber orchestra, *Unity at the Cross Road* (1978) and *Tonography* (1980, a series of chamber works), and in his ballets, *Clytemnestra* (1958), *Cleopatra* (1961), *Black Epic* (1968, for voice, dancers, actors, and orchestra), and *Lucifer* (1975). Martha Graham frequently used his music for her dance productions. He also wrote electronic music, such as *Symphonies in Sonic Vibrations* (1955) and *Leiyla and the Poet* (1959). For some of his compositions he invented new notational systems to be used along with standard notation.

BIBL: Questionnaire. Baker. Gro.

ELDRIDGE, DAVID ROY ("LITTLE JAZZ"). Jazz trumpeter (b. 30 January 1911 in Pittsburgh, Pennsylvania). He came from a musical family: his mother played piano and his brother Joseph became a professional musician. He began playing drums when he was six, then later changed to trumpet, which he studied with local teacher P. M. Williams. He began playing professionally at an early age and at fifteen toured with his own group, named by his managers Roy Elliott and His Panama Band from New York City, although none of the players had ever been to New York. During the 1920s-30s he played with various groups, including the Greater Sheesley Shows carnival band and the *Rock Dinah* revue in 1927, Horace Henderson* (1928), Elmer Snowden,* Lawrence ("Speed") Webb (1929-30), Charles Johnson, Theodore ("Teddy") Hill,* the Original Cotton Pickers, and Fletcher Henderson* (1936). In 1933 he went to Pittsburgh to co-lead a band with his brother. Also during the 1930s he toured with the Hot Chocolates Revue and led his own groups intermittently, in 1935 at the Famous Door club in New York, in 1936 at the Three Deuces in Chicago, Illinois, and in 1939 in a New York ballroom. During the next three decades he played with various groups, including Gene Krupa (1941-43), Artie Shaw (1944-45, 1949), Benny Goodman (1950), Coleman Hawkins* (regularly during the years 1952-69), Ella Fitzgerald* (1963-64), and William ("Count") Basie,* among others. He toured widely in the United States and Europe as a soloist, small-group leader, and with others; he played at jazz festivals and toured with such shows as JATP (Norman Granz's Jazz at the Philharmonic, during the years 1945-51) and Jazz from a Swinging Era (1967). He made his recording debut in 1935 with Teddy Hill and thereafter recorded extensively. He also was active in radio and television music and appeared in films and on film soundtracks. During the 1970s he played long residencies in Chicago and New York nightclubs, although he continued to tour occasionally in Europe and to appear at jazz festivals and on special television programs. Eldridge was one of the leading innovators in jazz trumpet and often cited by historians as the link between Louis Armstrong* and John Birks ("Dizzy") Gillespie.* Although inspired by Armstrong, his unique style was influenced by the saxophone style of Coleman Hawkins* and became distinctive because of his powerful virtuosity.

BIBL: ChilWW. DanceWS. FeaEJ. FeaJS. FeaGitJS. *International Musician* (January 1972). MeeJMov. WWA. WWBA.

DISC: Jep. Kink. RustJR. TudJ.

ELIE, JUSTIN. Composer/Concert pianist (b. 1 September 1883 in Cap-Haitien, Haiti; d. 2 December 1931 in New York, New York). He early showed musical aptitude, and his parents sent him to study music in Paris, France. After several years of preparation he matriculated at the Paris Conservatory of Music, where he studied with de Beriot, Marmontel, Vital, and Pessart. He returned to Haiti in 1905 and thereafter toured widely as a concert pianist in the Caribbean, South America, and North America. He also conducted a music studio in Port-au-Prince. In 1922 he went to New York, New York, where he remained until his death. His best-known compositions included the symphonic suite *Quisqueye*, his two piano concertos, *Légende Créole* for piano and violin, *Grande Valse de Concert* for orchestra, and the songs "Chant des Houssis" and "Hymne à Dambala." He engaged in research of Haitian folk music and used Haitian elements in some of his compositions. His daughter, Lily, was also a concert pianist and toured with her father, giving two-piano concerts.

BIBL: ASCAP. Black press, incl. NYAge, 27 November 1920. Dumervé.

ELLINGTON, EDWARD KENNEDY ("DUKE"). Jazz pianist/Composer (b. 29 April 1899 in Washington, D.C.; d. 24 May 1974 in New York, New York). He came from a musical family: his mother played piano ''by note,'' and his father played piano ''by ear.'' He began piano study when he was about six years old with a local teacher, Miss Clinkscales. He obtained his musical education in the public schools of Washington, D.C., where he came under the tutelage of Henry Grant* at Armstrong High School, and later studied harmony privately with Grant. In his later career he studied with Will Marion Cook* and Will Vodery.* He began playing piano for local social entertainments during his high-school days and at that time acquired his nickname, The Duke. His early style development was influenced by Louis Brown, Louis Thomas, and Oliver (''Doc'') Perry, among others; he listened to them perform and received from them informal lessons in piano technique and style, particularly from Doc Perry. In high school he was an artist as well as a musician, but passed up an opportunity to develop his artistic skills in favor of a career in music. He began playing professionally in various groups, often substituting for a band pianist. By 1919 he had formed a small band, of which the regular members were three Miller brothers (''Bill,'' Felix, and ''Brother''), Chauncey Brown, and later Otto (''Toby'') Hardwick,* Elmer Snowden,* and William (''Sonny'') Greer.* In 1923 his Duke's Serenaders went to New York, where they performed for several weeks with Wilbur Sweatman* in a vaudeville show, then returned to Washington.

Later the same year he settled permanently in New York; in the fall of 1923 his group, The Washingtonians (under the leadership of Snowden), began a four-year residency at the Hollywood Club (later called the Kentucky Club). Ellington took charge of the six-piece band in 1924 and enlarged it to eleven pieces when he began a three-year residency at the Cotton Club in December 1927. (The Cotton Club's first choice was Joseph (''King'') Oliver,* but he turned down the offer.) Through these years Ellington also played at other nightclubs, in theaters, and toured extensively—as far west as California in 1930. During the 1920s he gave considerable attention to writing and arranging music. He had written his first song, ''Soda fountain rag,'' when he was fifteen; in 1923 he sold his first songs to music publishers on Broadway, collaborating with lyricist Joseph (''Joe'') Trent. In 1924 he wrote the score for the musical *Chocolate Kiddies* (1925), which played a long engagement in Germany with music provided by Samuel (''Sam'') Wooding* and his Orchestra. Ellington made his recording debut with his band in 1924 and thereafter recorded under a wide variety of names, among them, the Jungle Band, the Washingtonians, the Whoopee Makers, the Harlem Footwarmers, and others, as well as Duke Ellington. In the following years the Ellington band continued its extensive touring, played for its first Broadway musical, *Show Girl* (1929), appeared in the first of many films, *Check and Double Check* (1930), and made its first European tours (1933, 1939). Ellington won increasing recognition as a musician of stature in regard to both his compositions and his orchestra, which he played upon as an instrument in the same way other men played trumpets or saxophones. His group included men who made unique contributions to the distinctive sound of the orchestra, including Leon (''Barney'') Bigard,* Wellman Braud,* Lawrence Brown, Harry Carney,* Fred Guy, Johnny Hodges,* James (''Bubber'') Miley,* Joe Nanton,* Juan Tizol, Arthur Whetsol, and Charles (''Cootie'') Williams,* among others, in addition to members of the original Washingtonians. In 1939 William (''Billy'') Strayhorn* joined the group and during his twenty-eight years' tenure collaborated with Duke to such an extent in the composing and arranging that he became Duke's alter-ego.

Early in his career Duke began to infuse the jazz ensemble with new vitality because of his innovations: c1926, ''jungle'' effects achieved through use of the growl and plunger by Miley and Nanton; 1927, the human voice used as an instrument in Adelaide Hall's* solo on ''Creole love call''; 1928, amplified bass used in bassist Braud's solo on ''Hot and bothered''; 1932, trombone trio added to the orchestra sound and anticipation of the Swing Era in the performance style of such pieces as ''It don't mean a thing, if it ain't got that swing''; 1937, Cuban or Latin elements introduced in ''Caravan''; 1938, echo-chambers used in Hodges's solo on ''Empty ballroom blues''; 1930s, Rex Stewart's trumpet half-valve technique used for special effects. He continued to introduce similarly new ideas into his music throughout his long career. He was the first jazz composer in the conventional sense, the first to write extended, musically abstract compositions, which used chromaticism, irregular phrasing, unresolved modulations, and other techniques not traditionally associated with jazz at that time. His personal approach to jazz piano—influenced by Harlem rag pianists James P. Johnson,* William (''Willie-the-Lion'') Smith,* and Charles (''Lucky'') Roberts*—also contributed to the unique sound of his music. He was also first to use concerto form in his works, as in ''Concerto for Cootie'' (1939). In a career filled to overflowing with high points, Duke, nevertheless, ascended some peaks higher than others.

One such peak was his inauguration of an annual jazz concert series at Carnegie Hall in New York, for which he wrote a new work each year (1943-55), including *Deep South Suite, Liberian Suite, New World A-Comin'*, and *Black, Brown, and Beige*, among others. Another peak was represented by his sacred music concerts, the first of which was presented on 16 September 1965 at the Grace Cathedral Church in San Francisco, California; the second, on 19 January 1968 at the Cathedral of St. John the Divine in New York, the largest cathedral in the world; and the third, on United Nations Day, 24 October 1973, at Westminster Abbey in London, England. The concert in 1965 was an historical first—the first jazz concert performed in a church—and, like Duke's other innovations, established a tradition. He wrote in a variety of forms: revues or musicals, such as *Jump for Joy* and *Beggar's Holiday*; symphonic suites, such as *Shakespearean Suite, The Far East Suite, New Orleans Suite*, and *Afro-Eurasian Eclipse*; ballets, such as *The River*; film scores, such as *Anatomy of a Murder, Paris Blues*, and *Assault on a Queen*; works for his orchestra with symphony orchestra, such as *Night Creature*; the pageant *My People* (1963); television-show productions, such as *A Drum is a Woman* (CBS, 1957) and the series "Asphalt Jungle"; and innumerable songs, many written in collaboration with others, particularly Strayhorn. Best-known of his more than 2000 compositions were "Take the A-train," "Mood indigo," "Sophisticated lady," "Solitude," "In a sentimental mood," and "I got it bad and that ain't good."

The list of honors that came to him is endless: sixteen honorary doctorates from American universities, including Columbia, Howard, Brown, and Yale; medals from cities and professional organizations, the President's Gold Medal (1966, from Lyndon B. Johnson) and the Presidential Medal of Freedom (1969, from Richard M. Nixon), and the Spingarn Medal (1959); keys to cities in the United States and abroad and election to honorary citizenship by various cities; innumerable awards from the music and recording industries; and awards from professional societies, councils, associations, institutes, music festivals, and individuals, including Pope Paul VI. He received the French Legion of Honor; Duke Ellington Jazz Societies were organized; and a Duke Ellington Fellowship Program was established at Yale University in 1972. In many respects the history of the Duke Ellington Orchestra was synonymous with the history of the big band in its formative years. Duke exerted enormous influence upon the development of big-band style even into the 1970s. His music represented the collective achievement of his sidemen, with himself at the forefront rather than the sole originator of the creative impulse. Many of his men remained with him for several decades; those who came in during his mid-career included William ("Cat") Anderson,* Louis Bellson, Paul Gonsalves, Ray Nance,* Russell Procope, and his son Mercer (trumpet-road manager), among others. Duke Ellington was unique! After his death Mercer Ellington* continued to tour with the Duke Ellington Band.

BIBL: ChilWW. EAB. DanceWDE. FeaEJ. FeaJS. FeaGitJS. MeeJMov. Duke Ellington, *Music Is My Mistress* (New York, 1973). WWA, 1974-75.

DISC: Jep. Kink. RustJR. TudJ.

ELLINGTON, MERCER. Jazz trumpeter (b. 11 March 1919 in Washington, D.C.). His father was Edward Kennedy ("Duke") Ellington,* a major contributor to the history of American music. He obtained his musical education at the Juilliard School of Music in New York and at New York University. His informal music study began at an early age, for he learned how to play various instruments from the musicians in his father's orchestra and often accompanied the orchestra on tours. He played alto saxophone during his high-school days, but later changed to trumpet under the influence of Charles ("Cootie") Williams.* From 1939 to 1960 he played with various groups, led his own groups intermittently, was active in music management and business enterprises, and even left music for a period during 1953. His first band (1939) included John Birks ("Dizzy") Gillespie,* Calvin Jackson, and Clark Terry,* among others. After service in the United States Armed Forces (1943-45), where he played with army bands, he played with Melvin ("Sy") Oliver,* his own groups, with Cootie Williams (1954 as trumpeter-road manager), and with his father (1950, 1955-59); he was musical director for Della Reese*; he established Mercer Records; and he was a disc jockey on New York radio station WLIB (1961-64). In 1965 he joined Duke's orchestra permanently as business manager-trumpeter. After Duke's death in 1974 he became leader of the Duke Ellington Orchestra and took steps to preserve his father's heritage—making arrangements to transcribe more than 3000 manuscripts, cataloguing the memorabilia, returning classics to the active repertory of the orchestra, and bringing in young talented musicians to play alongside the veterans. During the late 1970s he gave his full attention to writing and arranging music for the Ellington orchestra and embarked upon an ambitious recording program. His son, Edward Kennedy II, was also a jazz musician; he attended the Berklee School of Jazz in Boston, Massachusetts (1972-74), and joined the Ellington orchestra as a guitarist in 1974.

BIBL: ASCAP. ChilWW. FeaEJ. FeaJS. FeaGitJS. WWA. WWBA.

DISC: Kink.

ELLINGTON, EDWARD KENNEDY II. Jazz guitarist. See **ELLINGTON, MERCER.**

EMANUEL, WILLIAM HARRISON. Concert violinist. See **HACKLEY, AZALIA.**

EMIDEE. Concert violinist (b. 17?? in Guinea, West Africa; d. 18?? in Falmouth, England). He was sold into slavery in Guinea to Portuguese traders, who took him to Brazil. Later his owner took him to Lisbon, Portugal, where he studied violin. He became skilled enough to play in the orchestra of the Lisbon Opera. English seamen "impressed" him to provide music for the entertainment of Edward Pellew and his crew aboard the frigate *Indefatigable*; he was not allowed to go ashore for seven years. When Pellew was finally appointed to another ship command, Emidee was put ashore at Falmouth, England. He was the best violinist in the small town and soon found himself in great demand to play for dances and to teach string instruments and the flute. Eventually he became leader of chamber ensembles and the Falmouth Harmonic Society. He wrote many instrumental compositions for chamber groups and symphony orchestra. In 1807 one of his patrons presented some of his orchestral and chamber music to Johann Peter Salomon (impresario for Haydn's concerts in London, England, during the 1790s) with a view to obtaining for Emidee a public concert in London. The plans failed to materialize, however, because some of the London musicians felt that racism would prevent Emidee from being successful. He spent the remainder of his life in Falmouth.

BIBL: *Autobiography of James Silk Buckingham* (London, 1855), p. 165 ff; reprinted in BPIM 1 (Fall 1973), pp. 175 ff.

ESTES, JOHN ("SLEEPY"). Bluesman (b. 25 January 1899 in Ripley, Tennessee; d. 5 June 1977 in Brownsville, Tennessee). His family moved to Brownsville, Tennessee, when he was a child. As a boy he lost the sight of one eye: his vision deteriorated thereafter, and he became totally blind in 1949. He was taught to play guitar by his father and a local bluesman, "Hambone" Willie Newbern. In 1927 he formed a team with harmonica player Hammie Nixon* that lasted over fifty years. He began to record in 1929, making his first records with James ("Yank") Rachell,* and recorded extensively thereafter. From the 1930s on he toured widely with Nixon; they went abroad with the American Folk Blues Festival in 1964 and afterwards toured in Japan as well as Europe. The bluesmen with whom they worked over the years included Son Bonds, Lee Brown, John Henry Barbee, Noah Lewis, Charlie Pickett, and "Tampa Red" (Hudson Whittaker),* among others. Estes and Nixon toured widely up to the day of Estes's death. A documentary film, *The Legend of Sleepy John Estes* (1963) brought him wide attention.

BIBL: BWW. FeaJS. LivBl 19 (January-February 1975). LivBl 33 (July-August 1977). MeeJMov. Robert Neff and Anthony Connor, *Blues* (Boston, 1975). Oliv.

DISC: DiGod. LeSl. TudBM.

ESTES, SIMON LAMONT. Opera singer (b. 2 February 1938 in Centerville, Iowa). He was a boy soprano in a church choir from the time he was eight years old and later sang tenor during his high-school years. He attended the University of Iowa (degrees in social psychology and theology), where he failed auditions for the university choir but sang (baritone) with a student group, the Old Gold Singers. He attracted the attention of Charles Kellis on the music faculty, who coached him privately and inspired him to study opera. Later he studied at the Juilliard School of Music in New York and privately in Germany. He began his professional career as a bass-baritone singing in German opera companies, Berlin's Deutsche Opera and companies of Lübeck and Hamburg. In 1965 he won third place in the Munich International Vocal Competition; in 1966 he won the Silver Medal in the First International Tschaikovsky Vocal Competition in Moscow, U.S.S.R. Thereafter he toured widely in Europe and the United States, singing in the leading opera houses, giving solo recitals, performing in oratorio, symphonies, and similar large-form works, and appearing at music festivals. He also recorded regularly. He was best known for his roles of Wotan in Wagner's *Das Rheingold*, King Mark in Wagner's *Tristan and Isolde*, Don Pedro in Meyerbeer's *L'Africaine*, the Friar in Verdi's *Don Carlos*, Banquo in Verdi's *Macbeth*, Ned in Scott Joplin's* *Treemonisha*, and the title roles in Moussorgsky's *Boris Godounov* and Wagner's *The Flying Dutchman*. When he sang in *The Flying Dutchman* at Bayreuth, Germany, in 1978 he was the first male of his race to sing a major role at the festival. (Luranah Aldridge* and Grace Bumbry* sang at Bayreuth earlier.) His honors included invitations to sing at such events as the opening of the International Olympics at Munich, Germany (1972); the opening of the new concert hall in the Kennedy Center for the Performing Arts in Washington, D.C., with the National Symphony Orchestra under Dorati; and the American premiere of Shostakovich's Symphony No. 14 in Philadelphia, Pennsylvania.

BIBL: *Ebony* (February 1972). *High Fidelity/Musical America* (October 1972). Black press, incl. AmstN, 9 September 1978; CDef, 23 September 1976.

DISC: Turn.

EUBA, AKIN. Composer/University professor (b. 28 April 1935 in Lagos, Nigeria). He obtained his musical education at Trinity College of Music in London, England (1952-57); at the University of California in Los Angeles (B.A., 1964; M.A., 1966); and the University of Ghana at Legon (Ph.D., 1974). During his stay in London he was organist-choirmaster at the Church of St. James-the-Less, where Ayo Bankole* succeeded him in 1957. His teaching career included tenures as a fellow at Trinity College and as senior lecturer at the University of Nigeria at Ifè. He began composing concert music during the 1950s and completed his first major work, a String Quartet, in 1957. Thereafter he composed regularly, writing in a variety of forms. In 1967 his symphonic study *Olurounbi* was given a premiere performance by the Portland [Maine] Symphony Orchestra, conducted by Arthur Bennett Lipkin; *Dirges*, consisting of settings of poems by Africans for singers, speakers, instrumentalists, and dancers, received a premiere at the Munich [Germany] Olympics in 1972; his *Festac 77 Anthem*, for choir and jazz ensemble with a text by Margaret Walker, was first performed at the Second World Festival of Black and African Arts held at Lagos, Nigeria, in 1977. Other well-known works of his included *Four Pieces for African Orchestra* (1966), *Scenes from Traditional Life* for piano (1970), *Six Yoruba Songs* for voice and piano (1975), *Two Tortoise Folk Tales in Yoruba* (1975), and *Black Bethlehem* (1979), a setting of the Christmas story for soloists, chorus, jazz enemble, and Nigerian drums. His style combined African elements with Western art forms and techniques. He also published widely in professional journals and books, including the *Journal of the International Folk Music Council* and *Essays on Music and History in Africa* (ed. by K. P. Wachsmann, 1971). In 1977 he was chairman of the music committee for the Second World Festival held at Lagos. He was counted among the leading Nigerian composers of his time, along with Fela Sowande* and Ayo Bankole.

BIBL: Questionnaire. *Nigerian Music Review* (No. 1, 1977). Joshua Uzoigwe, "Akin Euba: An Introduction to the Life and Music of a Nigerian Composer" (M.A. thesis, Queen's University at Belfast, Ireland, 1978).

EUROPE, JAMES REESE ("JIM"). Society danceband and military-band leader (b. 22 February 1881 in Mobile, Alabama; d. 9 May 1919 in Boston, Massachusetts). He came from a musical family: his mother played piano, a sister, Mary,* and a brother, John, became professional musicians. The family moved to Washington, D.C., before he was ten years old. There he obtained his musical education in the public schools and also studied violin privately with Enrico Hurlei and, according to some sources, Joseph Douglass.* About 1905 he went to New York, where he studied further with Melville Charlton* and Harry T. Burleigh.* He first found employment playing piano in local nightclubs; later he became musical director of the Jolly John Larkin Company. He may have been a member of the 1905 edition of the Memphis Students, a group organized by Ernest Hogan* that is credited with having staged the first public jazz concert in the United States. In 1906 Europe became musical director of the Bob Cole*/Johnson brothers* show, *The Shoofly Regiment*, and wrote one of the show's songs, "Gay Lunetta." In 1909 he was musical director of the show, *Mr. Lode of Koal*, for its Broadway stand and for its touring.

In 1910 Europe was one of the founders of the Clef Club, an organization that combined the functions of a union and a music contractor. The Clef Club's symphony orchestra staged its first big concert in October 1910 at the Manhattan Casino. In 1912 a Clef Club Symphony Orchestra of 125 pieces, with Europe as conductor and William H. Tyers* as assistant conductor, gave a concert at Carnegie Hall for the benefit of the Music School Settlement for Colored, at that time under the directorship of David Martin.* In February 1913 Europe and Tyers again conducted a Clef Club Symphony Orchestra concert at Carnegie Hall, this time in honor of the fiftieth anniversary of the Emancipation Proclamation as well as for the benefit of the Music School Settlement. Europe resigned from the Clef Club in 1913; for the third Carnegie Hall concert, in 1914, he conducted his Negro Symphony Orchestra. His practice of featuring the compositions of black composers on these concerts inspired emulation in other places—particularly at Chicago, Illinois, where William Hackney* began to promote All-Colored Composers concerts in 1914.

After leaving the Clef Club, Europe organized the Tempo Club; he used members of that organization to play in his various groups—the National Negro Orchestra, Europe's Society Orchestra (also called the New York Society Orchestra), and Europe's Double Quintet. In 1914 he began an association with dancers Irene and Vernon Castle which lasted until Vernon's death in 1917. Europe's Society Orchestra, with Tyers and Ford Dabney* as assistant conductors, toured at home and abroad with the Castles. In New York Europe played at the club Castles-in-the-Air. The Castles appeared periodically in Europe's concerts at the Manhattan Casino in the Harlem community. A concert in April 1915, for example, featured as guest artists the Castles, Abbie Mitchell,* Sherman H. Dudley,* and J. Rosamond Johnson,* among others.

In 1917 Europe was asked to organize a band for the U.S. Fifteenth Infantry by Colonel William Haywood and was given $10,000 to cover recruitment expenses. Europe brought in men from all over the nation and from Puerto Rico in the Caribbean. The band was the most popular of all army bands overseas during World War I; nicknamed "the Hellfighters," it toured extensively, playing for servicemen, the French people and government officials, and the Congress of Women at Paris in 1918. The French called Jim Europe's music "jazz." After the war the Hellfighters left the armed services in a body and began a nationwide tour of the United States, advertising themselves as "65 Musician Veterans of the Champagne and Argonne." During a performance at Mechanic's Hall in Boston, Massachusetts, in May 1919, a crazed band member killed Europe. All over the country there was deep mourning; the city of New York gave him a public funeral, the first time a black man had been so honored.

Over the years many musicians performed with Europe who would later win distinction for themselves, including in addition to Dabney and Tyers, Al Johns, Leonard Jeter, Noble Sissle* (his drum major overseas), Creighton Thompson, Felix Weir,* and the Four Harmony Kings,* among others. Europe was a prolific composer of marches and dances. He also wrote songs in collaboration with others, among them, Charles Luckyeth Roberts*; and he teamed with Will Marion Cook* and William Vodery* to write the musical *Way Down South* (1915). His groups were undoubtedly the first black bands to make recordings; he recorded as early as 1913 for the Victor Talking Machine Company and made a series of recordings in 1919 for the Pathe Talking Machine and Record Company. An advertisement in the Chicago Defender (28 June 1919) listed more than thirty new pieces recorded by Europe's band.

Europe was one of the leading musicians of his time, along with Harry T. Burleigh, Will Marion Cook, and J. Rosamond Johnson. He was a strong advocate of Negro music, both the folk music and the composed music, and he published widely in newspapers and magazines in support of its originality and virtues. His best-known pieces were "Too much mustard," "Castlehouse rag," "Castle walk," and the song "The victor." He and Dabney were credited with having invented the fox-trot, the turkey-trot, the Castle-walk, and other dances exhibited by the Castles. After his death, *The New York Times* stated in an editorial (12 May 1919), "[Europe] produced an organization which all Americans swore, and some Frenchmen admitted, was the best military band in the world."

BIBL: Black press, incl. CDef, 22 February 1919, 1 March 1919; IndF, 15 May 1915; NYAge, 26 July 1906, 19 December 1909, 9 April 1914, 26 November 1915. Samuel Charters and Len Kunstadt, *Jazz: A History of the New York Scene* (New York, 1962). Arthur Little, *From Harlem to the Rhine* (New York, 1936). Emmett Scott, *Official History of the American Negro in the World War* (Washington, D.C., 1919). SouRBM.

EUROPE, MARY LORRAINE. Music educator (b. 13 October 1884 in Mobile, Alabama; d. 13 October 1947 in Washington, D.C.). She came from a musical family; her mother played piano and two brothers, James Reese* and John, became professional musicians. She obtained her musical education in the public schools of Mobile and Washington, D.C., where her family moved when she was young. She also studied piano privately. Later she attended Howard University in Washington (B. A., 1923) and Columbia University Teachers College (summer sessions, 1913-19). She taught music for many years at the Dunbar High School in Washington, D.C., and also won recognition as an accompanist, organist, and choral director. She was accompanist for the Coleridge-Taylor Choral Society when that group presented concerts of the composer's music in 1904 and 1906, which were conducted by Samuel Coleridge-Taylor* himself.

BIBL: Black press. BPIM (Spring 1974). Layne. WWCA 1928-29.

EVANS, ERNEST ("CHUBBY CHECKER"). Rock singer (b. 3 October 1941 in Philadelphia, Pennsylvania). He was active in nightclubs, on television, in theaters, and in films, including *Twist Around the Clock* (1972) and *Let the Good Times Roll* (1973). He invented his stage name in imitation of "Fats" Domino, whose real name was Antoine Domino.* His best-known recordings were of "The twist"(1960), which set off the "twist" dance craze, the biggest since the Charleston craze of the 1920s; "Let's twist again" (1961), and "Limbo rock" (1962).

BIBL: ASCAP. ShawHS. WWA. WWBA.

EVANS, WILLIAM. See **LATEEF, YUSEF.**

EVANTI, LILLIAN (née LILLIAN EVANS). Opera singer (b. 12 August 1890 in Washington, D.C.; d. 7 December 1967 in Washington). She obtained her musical education at the Howard University School of Music in Washington, D.C. (B. Mus., 1917), where she was the protégé of Lulu Vere Childers.* She first attracted public attention in November 1915 when she gave a concert with violinist Felix Weir* and other assisting artists. After graduation from Howard she toured as a concert artist (soprano), then went abroad for further study. During the years 1925-30 she studied with a Madame Ritter-Ciampi in Paris and Rosa Storchio in Italy. She also sang with opera companies, taking the title role in Delibes's *Lakme* at the Casino Theater in Nice, France (1925) and repeating her performance at the Trianon Lyrique in Paris (1927). Throughout her career she toured widely in the United States, Europe, the Caribbean, and South America. In 1943 she attracted wide attention for her performance of Violetta in Verdi's *La Traviata*, in the production staged by Mary Cardwell Dawson's* National Negro Opera Company at Washington, D.C., directed by Frederick Vajda. At one time she was married to Roy Wilford Tibbs,* organist and college music teacher.

BIBL: Black press, incl. CDef, 27 November 1915, 11 September 1943; NYAge, 31 May 1917, 5 March 1927. Hare. WWCA 1950.

F

F. S. WALCOTT'S RABBIT FOOT MINSTRELS. See **CHAPPELLE, PATRICK.**

FARMER, ARTHUR ("ART"). Jazz trumpeter (b. 21 August 1928 in Council Bluffs, Iowa). See **GOLSON, BENNY.**

FAVORS, MALACHI. Jazz bassist (b. 22 August 1937 in Chicago, Illinois). See **AACM** (Association for the Advancement of Creative Musicians); **ABRAMS, MUHAL RICHARD.**

FAX, MARK. College professor/Composer (b. 15 June 1911 in Baltimore, Maryland; d. 2 January 1974 in Washington, D.C.). He studied music as a child and at the age of fourteen was a theater pit organist in Baltimore's Regent Theater. His early career development was influenced by his high-school teacher, W. Llewellyn Wilson.* He obtained his musical education at Syracuse University in New York (B. Mus., 1933), the Eastman School of Music in Rochester, New York (M. Mus., 1945), and New York University. His teachers included Cecile Genhart, Bernard Rogers, Howard Hansen, and Gregory Tucker, among others. His teaching career included tenures at Paine College in Augusta, Georgia (1934-42), where he organized the first curriculum in music, and at Howard University in Washington, D.C. (1947-73). In 1972 he was named director of the School of Music, a position he held at his death. He wrote in a variety of forms: choral works, songs, piano and organ pieces, operas, and symphonic compositions. His best known works were the operas *A Christmas Miracle* (1958) and *Till Victory is Won* (1967) and *Three Piano Pieces and Toccatina*.

BIBL: Communications from William B. Garcia* and Dominique-René de Lerma. Black press, incl. *Afro-American* [Baltimore], 22 July 1978.

FERRELL, HARRISON HERBERT. College professor/Symphony orchestra leader (b. c1901 in Chicago, Illinois; d. 18 November 1976 in Institute, West Virginia). Although best known as a college language teacher, he was a practicing musician in his early career. He obtained his education in the public schools of Chicago, Illinois, and at Northwestern University in Evanston, Illinois (B.A., 1924; M.A., 1925; Ph.D., 1928). He began violin study when he was eight years old and made his debut at the age of fourteen on a concert with Anita Patti Brown* and Roland Hayes* (in 1915). He studied violin with Ludwig Becker. He toured as a concert violinist and played with local community orchestras. In 1923 he founded the Ferrell Symphony Orchestra. When he left Chicago in 1928 to become head of the language program at West Virginia State College in Institute, he left his assistant conductor Owen Lawson in charge of the orchestra. He returned to the city occasionally to conduct rehearsals and staged concerts with the orchestra in the summers.

BIBL: Communication from D. Antoinette Handy.* Black press, incl. CDef,19 June 1926, 13 September 1930. Layne.

FINNEY, THEODORE. Society dance-band leader (b. 1 September 1837 in Columbus, Ohio; d. May 1899 in Detroit, Michigan). He went to Detroit, Michigan, at the age of twenty and in partnership with John Bailey organized the Bailey and Finney orchestras. After Bailey's death in 1870, Finney became the sole bandleader/manager. He also played in the Detroit City Band. Finney's Famous Orchestra toured extensively in the Middle West. When the orchestra went to Cleveland, Ohio, in April 1901 to give its Fourth Annual Concert and Ball, the members included Benjamin Shook,* Fred C. Stone,* John W. Johnson,* John Ward, Frank Smith, John Smallwood, Frank Mosby,

Edward Beeler, and two singers and a whistler. Ben Shook had replaced the deceased Finney in June 1899. Several of these men had been in the orchestra for many years and were reputable musicians in their own rights. Among others associated with the Finney orchestras over the years were Charles Gillam,* Harry P. Guy,* Clyde Hayes, Floyd Hickman, and Earl Walton. Finney's Orchestra and groups derived from it were active into the 1930s. At one time there were two Finney Orchestras, the one led by Ben Shook and the other, by Fred Stone and his brothers.

BIBL: DetAZ, K. Myers interview with Clyde Hayes. Black press, incl. CleveG, 13 May 1899, 6 April 1901. La Brew.

FISCHER, WILLIAM S. Composer (b. 5 March 1935 in Shelby, Mississippi). He came from a musical family: his grandfather played in riverboat bands. He began piano study at the age of seven; six years later he began study of the saxophone. He obtained his musical education at Xavier University in New Orleans, Louisiana (B.S., 1956) and at Colorado College in Colorado Springs (M.A., 1962). His composition teachers included Clifford Richter, Albert Seay, and Gottfried von Einem, with whom he sudied at the Akademie für Musik und Darstellende in Vienna, Austria (1965-66). His teaching career included tenures at Xavier University (1962-66), the public schools of New York (1967-75), Newport and Cardiff Colleges in Wales, England (as artist-in-residence, 1966-67). He also served as a visiting lecturer at other colleges, among them, the University of Michigan at Ann Arbor (1970), and Norfolk State University in Virginia (1971). He began playing professionally in jazz groups during the 1950s; those with whom he played (saxophone) included Muddy Waters (née McKinley Morganfield),* Ray Charles,* Joe Turner,* Guitar Slim (née Eddie Jones), and ("Ivory") Joe Hunter,* among others. During the 1960s-70s he became increasingly active as a composer-arranger, record producer, musical director, and publisher; he wrote and/or arranged music for several record companies for films and stage productions, and for such individuals as Roberta Flack,* Yuseef Lateef,* David Newman, and Joe Zwinul, among others. He recorded his works at home and abroad. His best-known recording was *The Rise and Fall of the Third Stream*; his best-known concert compositions were *Experience in E* for jazz quintet and orchestra, *Quiet Movement for Orchestra*, *Electronic Music*, and the opera *Jesse*. His honors included a Fulbright Fellowship (1965-66), grants from the Austrian government (1965) and West Germany (1964), and grants from the New York State Council on the Arts (1971). He published *Analysis of Arnold Schoenberg's Fourth String Quartet* (Denver, 1962).

BIBL: ASCAP. FeaGitJS. WWBA.

FISK, CATO. Military drummer (Fl. late eighteenth century; d. 24 March 1824 in Epsom, New Hampshire). He enlisted in 1777 in Captain William Powell's Company, Colonel George Reid's New Hampshire Regiment, and served as a drummer during the War of the American Revolution. He was a fiddler in his home town.

BIBL: GreBD. MacBFA.

FISK JUBILEE SINGERS, THE. Concert choral groups (fl. from 1871 to the present; organized at Fisk University, Nashville, Tennessee). Fisk University was one of several colleges established by the American Missionary Association after the Civil War to assist in the education of over four million ex-slaves. When Fisk opened its doors in 1866, its all-white faculty included George L. White, who was asked by the university president, John Ogden, to devote his leisure time to instructing students in music. White trained the students to sing their own folksongs as well as the traditional European repertory, and in 1867 the students began to sing on local concerts. Later the singers toured in nearby towns. Encouraged by their success, White took the Fisk singers on an extensive tour in the fall of 1871, hoping to raise money for the struggling young institution. His company included chaperone Miss Well, business manager G. D. Pike, and eleven students: Georgia Gordon, Isaac P. Dickerson, Benjamin M. Holmes, Jennie Jackson, Julia Jackson, Mabel Lewis,* Maggie Porter, Thomas Rutling, Ella Sheppard (pianist), Minnie Tate, and Edmund Watkins.

The tour was unsuccessful at first; white audiences expected black singers to be Ethiopian minstrels, and the Fisk students did not conform to the stereotypes. In December 1871 at Columbus, Ohio, White decided to call his group the "Jubilee Singers," after a favorite black folk-saying about "the year of the jubilee." The name was catchy, and eventually audiences became enthusiastic about the students. A typical program consisted of an anthem, several spirituals, selections from operas, and current songs, such as "The temperance medley" or "Home, sweet home." There were changes in the membership even during the first tour (October 1871-May 1874), when the group included as many as fourteen singers for some concerts. One of the high points was the appearance of the singers in July 1872 at Patrick Sarsfield Gilmore's World Peace Jubilee at Boston, Massachusetts. In Europe the singers appeared before royalty and ordinary folk and met acclaim from all. Some of the singers remained in Europe when the group returned to the United States, among them Dickerson and Rutling. The second tour of the Fisk Jubilee Singers (1875-78) took them to the British Isles, Holland, Germany, and Switzerland. After seven years of touring the Singers had earned more than $150,000 for their institution, an enormous sum for that time, and had acquainted the world with the folk-songs of the American black people.

After the second tour the University gave up sponsorship of the Jubilee Singers; undoubtedly it was difficult to arrange the touring because so many bogus groups had sprung up in imitation of the student singers. Frederick J. Loudin, who had joined the Fisk Singers in 1875, took over the direction of the now private group, with Henry Cushing as his business manager. He brought in new singers and persuaded some of the charter members to rejoin. In 1884 Loudin's Fisk Singers embarked upon a six-year tour around the world which brought them fame—and also brought recognition to the University, as most audiences were not aware that Fisk no longer sponsored the singers. Another spin-off group from the Fisk Singers was that of Orpheus McAdoo,* who took his Jubilee Singers to Australia and South Africa. Beginning in 1898 a newly appointed black faculty member at Fisk, John Wesley Work II,* began to organize and train Jubilee Singers groups, using both students and professionals. His first professional group (1898-c1903) was composed of former students. In 1909 he toured with a quartet, consisting of Alfred King, Noah Walker Ryder,* James A. Meyers, and himself. During the years 1905-11 Roland Hayes* sang intermittently with Fisk groups and toured with the quartet during the summer of 1911. In addition to singing with the quartet, Work also toured with student groups to raise funds for the University until his tenure as director of the Fisk Jubilee Singers ended in 1916. During the years 1916-47 the Singers ensemble was professional. Meyers directed it until his death in 1928, and then his widow, Henrietta Crawley Meyers, directed it until 1947. In that year John Wesley Work III,* at that time chairman of the music department at Fisk, was appointed director of the Fisk Jubilee Singers. He converted the group back to a student group and toured widely with it in the United States and in Europe in 1956. Beginning in 1971 Matthew Kennedy* directed the Jubilee Singers.

BIBL: PaHistSoc: LGColl, 1G. Black press, incl. CDef, 3 December 1916; CleveG, 23 December 1883, 8 November 1884, 3 May 1890; IndF, 24 May 1890; NYAge, 24 January 1891. William Garcia, "The Life and Choral Music of John Wesley Work" (Ph.D. diss., University of Iowa, 1973). J. B. T. Marsh, *The Story of the Jubilee Singers with Their Songs* (Boston, 1877). Gustavus D. Pike, *Jubilee Singers and Their Campaign for Twenty-Thousand Dollars* (Boston, 1873).

DISC: BPIM 9 (Spring 1981), p. 90. Turn.

FITZGERALD, ELLA. Jazz singer (b. 25 April 1918 in Newport News, Virginia). She spent most of her formative years in Yonkers, New York, and obtained her musical education in public schools there. In 1934 she won an amateur contest at the Apollo Theatre in the Harlem community of New York, for which the prize was a week's engagement at the theater. The house bandleader, William ("Chick") Webb,* was so impressed by her talent that he took her into his group. After Webb's death in 1939, she led the band for a period, then began touring as a nightclub singer. By the mid-1940s she had established herself as one of the leading jazz singers of the century. She first recorded in 1935, but the first song to attract wide attention was "A tisket, a tasket" in 1938, which she herself wrote, as she did other songs in her repertory over the years. She toured widely in the United States, in Europe (frequently during the years 1948-57 with Norman Granz's Jazz at the Philharmonic shows), in South America, Australia, the Near East, and the Orient, singing in concert halls and theaters, at jazz festivals, on radio and television shows, on the college circuit, and in films or on film tracks, including *St. Louis Blues* (1958) and *Let No Man Write My Epitaph* (1960). Beginning in 1972 she appeared as a soloist with leading symphony orchestras of the nation. She teamed with or was accompanied by such jazzmen or groups as Louis Armstrong,* William ("Count") Basie,* Edward ("Duke") Ellington,* Frank Sinatra, and the Oscar Peterson* Trio. From the mid-1960s on she was most frequently accompanied by a trio composed of William ("Keter") Betts, Bobby Durham, and Tommy Flanagan.* She received numerous awards from the music industry. Her other honors included the Golden Needle Award from East Berlin, Germany, and honorary doctorates from such institutions as Boston University and Washington University in St. Louis. In 1974 an Ella Fitzgerald School of Performing Arts was established at the University of Maryland at Princess Anne. In 1979 she was given Kennedy Center Honors by the White House for lifetime achievement in the performing arts. As the "first lady of jazz," she was noted for her consummate jazz musicianship; she was a pioneer in her employment of "scat" singing, which she developed during a tour with John Birks ("Dizzy") Gillespie* in the 1940s. Her best-known songs (for which she was co-composer) were "You showed me the way," "I fell in love with a dream," and "I found my yellow basket."

BIBL: ASCAP. EAB. FeaEJ. FeaJS. FeaGitJS. MeeJMov. NYT, 24 November 1974. WWA. WWCA, 1950. WWBA.

DISC: Jep. Kink.RustJR. TudJ.

FIVE BLIND BOYS, THE. Gospel groups (orig. in 1930s in Alabama and in Mississippi). There were two groups that used this name. The Five Blind Boys of Alabama (also known as The Happyland Jubilee Singers) was formed at the Talladega Institute for the Deaf and Blind in 1939. The members of the group were: Johnny Fields (b. 9 September 1927 at Lowndesboro, Alabama), Clarence Fountain (b. 24 November 1929 at Tyler, Alabama), George Scott (b. 18 March 1929 at Tuskegee, Alabama), Olice Thomas (b. 5 May 1926 at Gainesville, Alabama), and Velma Traylor (b. 1923; d. 1947). The blind boys studied music at the Institute and sang for local entertainments. In 1945 the boys left school and began a professional career, singing their first engagement in November 1945 at Jacksonville, Florida. They made their recording debut in 1948 and thereafter recorded regularly. Their best-known recordings included "When I lost my mother," "Honey and the rock," and "Something got a hold of me." After the death of Traylor, sighted persons sang with the group, among them, Louis Dix. Scott wrote many of the arrangements used by the Five Blind Boys of Alabama.

The Five Blind Boys of Mississippi was formed in 1939 at Piney Woods, Mississippi. Also known as the Jackson Harmoneers, the group began singing professionally in 1944 and settled at Chicago, Illinois. Lead singer Archie Brownlee (d. February 1960) dominated the group with his highly original style; other original members were J. T. Clinkscales, Sam Lewis, Lawrence Abrams, and Lloyd Woodard. When the Five Blind Boys first recorded, their accompaniment group was composed of Ronald Hall (piano), Maceo Woods (organ), Wayne Bennett (guitar), and drummer. Brownlee is credited with being the first to interject falsetto shrieks and screams into gospel-quartet style (as distinguished from gospel chorus style). The best-known recordings of the group included "Lord, I've tried," "One of these days," "Mother, don't worry if your child should go to war," "Keep your lamp trimmed and burning till your child comes home," and "I'm gonna leave you in the hands of the Lord."

BIBL: Black press, incl. CDef, 29 August 1964. Heil. *Sepia* (October 1963).

DISC: Hayes.

FLACK, ROBERTA. Popular music/Jazz singer (b. 10 February 1939 in Black Mountain, North Carolina). She came from a musical family: both parents played piano, and her mother was a church organist. Her family moved to Arlington, Virginia, when she was five years old. She first studied piano with her mother, then began formal lessons with Alma Blackmon of Washington, D.C., when she was nine. She obtained her musical education at Howard University in Washington (B.A., 1958), then pursued graduate study for a period before entering a teaching career in the public schools of Farmville, North Carolina (1959-60) and Washington, D.C. (1960-67). During this period she also was a church organist and choral director, voice coach, accompanist for opera singers in a local supper-club, and occasional pianist in the club. She also studied voice during these years. In 1968 Les McCann* heard her perform and helped her to launch a career in the entertainment world. She soon established herself as one of the leading singers of jazz and popular music; she toured widely, singing in concert halls and theaters as well as nightclubs; and she recorded extensively, beginning in 1969. During the 1970s she frequently collaborated with Donny Hathaway.* She received many awards from the music industry. Her best-known performances were "The first time ever I saw your face" and "Killing me softly with his song."

BIBL: *Ebony* (January 1971). MeeJMov. *Sepia* (August 1973). WWA. WWBA.

DISC: TudBM.

FLANAGAN, TOMMY LEE. Jazz pianist (b. 16 March 1930 in Detroit, Michigan). His family encouraged his musical interests: his older brother and sister played piano and he began piano study with the same teacher when he was ten years old. He obtained his musical education in the public schools of Detroit, Michigan, where he began clarinet study at the age of six. His early style development was influenced by Henry ("Hank") Jones,* Earl ("Bud") Powell,* and Art Tatum,* whom he heard through recordings and in live performance. During his high-school years he began to play professionally with local Detroit groups. After service in the United States Armed Forces (1951-53), he played for a period again with Detroit groups, including Billy Mitchell, then settled in New York in 1956. Thereafter he played with various groups, including Oscar Pettiford,* Miles Davis,* Harry ("Sweets") Edison,* Coleman Hawkins,* and Roy Eldridge,* among others. He also led his own Tommy Flanagan Trio and toured widely in the United States, Europe, and the Orient with James ("J. J.") Johnson* (1956-57, 1958), Tony Bennett (1966), and Ella Fitzgerald* (1963-65, 1968-78). After leaving Fitzgerald he toured as a soloist on the nightclub circuit. He was a leading bop pianist of his time and an important representative of the Detroit school, along with pianists Hank Jones and Barry Harris.*

BIBL: ContKey (December 1979). FeaEJ. FeaJS. FeaGitJS. Michael Ullman, *Jazz Lives* (Washington, D.C., 1980). MeeJMov.

DISC: Kink.

FLEET, JAMES. Composer (Fl. mid-nineteenth century in Washington, D.C.). According to Daniel Payne, Fleet was the "ablest colored musician in Washington, D.C." during the mid-nineteenth century. He played flute, guitar, and piano and was active as a choral conductor. His wife, Hermione, played piano.

BIBL: Black press. Daniel Payne, *History of the African Methodist Episcopal Church* (Nashville, 1891), p. 456. SouRBM, p. 67.

FLETCHER, TOM. Entertainer (b. 16 May 1873 in Portsmouth, Ohio; d. 13 October 1954 in New York, New York). As a child he sang in local talent shows and played in the Portsmouth fife corps. He began his professional career at fifteen and thereafter performed with various groups, including Howard's Novelty Colored Minstrels, the *In Old Kentucky* show, Ed Winn's minstrel company, and Richard and Pringle's Georgia Minstrels, among others. About 1898 he entered a new career in vaudeville and nightclub and private entertainment, often appearing in an act with Al Bailey called "Bailey and Fletcher, the Minstrel Boys." In 1908 Fletcher played a leading role in the 1908 edition of the Memphis Students at Hammerstein's Victoria Theater in New York, along with Abbie Mitchell* and others. Ernest Hogan,* who had organized and starred in the 1905 performances of the Memphis Students, was too ill to perform this time. In 1919 Fletcher joined Will Marion Cook's* New York Syncopated Orchestra in its American tour. Fletcher was a drummer as well as singer/comedian. His big contribution to American music history was his autobiography, which offers rich detail about black minstrelsy and vaudeville.

BIBL: Tom Fletcher, *100 Years of the Negro in Show Business* (New York, 1954).

FLOYD, SAMUEL, JR. College professor (b. 1 February 1937 in Tallahassee, Florida). He came from a musical family: his father sang with the Fisk Jubilee Singers* and toured on the concert circuit with Rawn Spearman.* He began piano study at the age of six. His family moved to Lakeland, Florida, when he was seven. His musical education was obtained in public schools of Lakeland, where he played percussions in the concert and marching bands and piano and percussions in the jazz band; at Florida A & M College in Tallahasee, Florida (B.S., 1957); and at Southern Illinois University at Carbondale (M. Mus. Ed., 1965; Ph.D. Ed., 1969). He studied trumpet and percussions privately at college, where he played in music groups. His career development was influenced by Lawrence Pope, his high-school band teacher, and Johnny V. Lee and William Foster* at Florida A & M. His teaching career included tenures at Smith-Brown High School in Arcadia, Florida (1959-62), where he also was director of bands; Florida A & M (1962-64), where he was also assistant director of bands; at Southern Illinois University (1968-78); and Fisk University in Nashville, Tennessee (1978-) where he was Director of the Institute for Research in Black American Music. He published articles in professional journals, including *The Chronicle of Higher Education, Music Educators Journal, College Music Symposium, Music Journal,* and *The Black Perspective in Music*. His published books included *99 Street Beats, Cadences, and Exercises for Percussions* (1961), other manuals for teaching percussions (1965, 1975, 1980), *The Great Lakes Experience: An Oral History* (1977), and *An Anthology of the Music of Black American Composers* (1981). His honors included a Newberry Grant (1971) and grants from the National Endowment for the Arts (1976) and the National Endowment for the Humanities (1976-79).

BIBL: Questionnaire. IntWWMusic.

FORBES, KATHLEEN HOLLAND. Church organist (b. 31 December 1892 in Hamilton, Ontario, Canada; d. 1 October 1978 in Cleveland, Ohio). She began playing a reed organ at the age of six. She obtained her musical education at the Hamilton [Ontario] Conservatory of Music (AHCM degree). She began playing professionally in 1916 as church organist at the Hamilton A.M.E. Church; she also conducted a music studio in Hamilton. In 1923 she settled at Cleveland, Ohio, where she later studied organ with Edwin Arthur Kraft and earned the Associate degree of the American Guild of Organists. During her early career she toured in the United States, Canada, and the Caribbean as a concert pianist and as accompanist for Roland Hayes,* Louia Vaughn Jones,* and others. She conducted a music studio in Cleveland, played organ for and directed church choirs for forty-two years, and directed community choral groups and music study clubs. She was also active with local and national music associations, particularly the National Association of Negro Musicians. Her honors included the Citizen's Citation of Merit from Wilberforce University (1956).

BIBL: Personal communication from Evelyn P. Starling. Questionnaire.

FOSTER, FRANK B. Jazz saxophonist (b. 23 September 1928 in Cincinnati, Ohio). He obtained his musical education in the public schools of Cincinnati, Ohio, and at Wilberforce College (1946-49, now Central State College). During his high-school years, he led his own band, for which he also wrote and arranged music, and in college he played with and arranged for the Wilberforce Collegians. He began playing professionally (alto saxophone) in 1949 at Detroit, Michigan, where he played with such groups as Eugene ("Snookie") Young, Wardell Gray, Edward ("Sonny") Stitt,* and Milton ("Milt") Jackson,* among others. During his service in the United States Armed Forces (1951-53), he played in the Seventh Infantry Band in Korea and also in an army dance band. After his discharge, he played with various groups, including William ("Count") Basie* (1953-64), Lloyd Price, Woodrow ("Woody") Herman, and Lionel Hampton,* among others. In 1965 he formed a big band and thereafter toured widely in the United States and in Europe with his own groups. He also toured with others, including the Elvin Jones Quintet in 1970 and intermittently again during the next decade. During the 1970s he became increasingly involved with teaching; his teaching career included tenures in the public schools of New York as a music consultant (1971-72), at the State University of New York at Buffalo (1972-73), Queens College of the City University of New York, and Livingston College of Rutgers University at New Brunswick, New Jersey (1974-78). He was active with such community groups as Jazzmobile, Inc., of New York and Rahsaan Roland Kirk's* Vibration School of Music. He was also active as a lecturer, workshop consultant, and artist-in-residence at various institutions. His best-known groups were The Loud Minority and the ensemble Living Color; his best-known compositions were "Manhattan fever," "Cecilia is love," and "For all intents and purposes."

BIBL: Questionnaire. FeaEJ. FeaJS. FeaGitJS. WWBA.

DISC: Jep.

FOSTER, GEORGE MURPHY ("POPS"). Jazz bassist (b. 18 May 1892 in McCall, Louisiana; d. 30 October 1969 in San Francisco, California). He came from a musical family: the three children formed a family trio, called The Fosters, which played for local social events. He first played cello, then changed to string bass. When he was ten years old, his family moved to New Orleans, Louisiana. From 1906 to 1917 he played with various groups, including the Rozelle Band, Magnolia Band, Freddie Keppard's* Olympia Orchestra, Tuxedo Orchestra, Dutrey brothers band, Buddy Petit, and Armand Piron,* among others. Thereafter he worked for a few years in riverboat bands with Fate Marable,* Charlie Creath,* and Eddie Allen. In 1922 he joined Edward ("Kid") Ory* at Los Angeles, California. Thereafter he played with most of the important jazz groups of his time, either as a regular player or on special occasions, including Dewey Jackson (1925, 1928-29), Luis Russell* (1929-35), Louis Armstrong* (1935-40), Sidney Bechet* (1945-46), and Earl Hines* (1955-60), among others. Frequently he led his own groups during those years. He first recorded in 1924 and thereafter recorded extensively until about 1940. He toured widely in the United States and made several tours of Europe (in 1966 with the New Orleans All Stars). In 1955 he settled in San Francisco, California, where he played with traditional jazz groups until his death. He was a pioneer in the New Orleans tradition who helped to define the role of the string bass in the jazz ensemble.

BIBL: ChilWW. DanceWEH. FeaEJ. FeaJS. FeaGitJS. Pops Foster, *The Autobiography of a New Orleans Jazzman, As Told to Tom Stoddard* (Berkeley, California, 1971).

DISC: Kink. RustJR. TudJ.

FOSTER, WILLIAM. College professor (b. 25 August 1919 in Kansas City, Kansas). He began playing saxophone and clarinet at the age of twelve and studied clarinet privately at the Kansas City Conservatory of Music through his high-school years. He obtained his musical education in the public schools of Kansas City, Kansas; at the University of Kansas in Lawrence (B. Mus. Ed., 1941); Wayne State University in Detroit, Michigan (M.A., 1950); and Columbia University Teachers College in New York (D. Mus. Ed., 1955). His teaching career included tenures in the public schools of Kansas City, Kansas (1941-43), where he was band and choir director at Lincoln High School; at Fort Valley State College in Georgia (1943-44); at Tuskegee Institute in Alabama (1944-46); and at Florida A & M College in Tallahassee (1946-). His FAM-C band at Florida A & M developed a national reputation and toured widely. He also toured as a lecturer, band consultant, and workshop clinician. He published articles in professional journals, among them *Instrumentalist Magazine* and *The Music Journal*. His honors included appointment to boards and panels of professional organizations, elections to offices of national organizations, awards from civic and professional organizations and the University of Kansas Alumni Achievement Award (1971).

BIBL: Reginald Buckner, "A History of Music Education in the Black Community of Kansas City, Kansas: 1905-54" (Ph.D. diss., University of Minnesota, 1974). WWBA.

FOUNTAIN, PRIMOUS III. Composer (b. 1 August 1949 in St. Petersburg, Florida). His family moved to Chicago, Illinois, when he was two years old. He obtained his musical education in the public schools of Chicago, the Kennedy-King Junior College (1967-68), and DePaul University in Chicago (1968-69), where he studied music theory and composition formally for the first time. He studied trumpet and string bass in high school and played with a jazz group, for which he wrote and arranged music. In 1968 he won an award for composition from BMI (Broadcast Music, Inc.). Music critic Earl Calloway* became interested in his talent and introduced him to Quincy Jones,* who gave Fountain financial support for two-and-a-half years so that he could devote full time to composition. In 1969 his compositions were performed at a concert by musicians of AACM* (Association for the Advancement of Creative Musicians). The same year he received a Guggenheim fellowship, the youngest person (at the age of nineteen) ever to receive the fellowship. Within a year or two his works were being performed by leading symphony orchestras of the nation. In 1970 he settled at Madison, Wisconsin. His best-known works were *Manifestation* (1969), which was transformed into a ballet for the Arthur Mitchell Dance Theater of Harlem; *Ritual Dance of the Amaks* for symphony orchestra (1973), Duet for Flute and Bassoon (1974), and Concerto for Cello and Orchestra (1976). His honors included, in addition to those cited above, an ASCAP grant, a second Guggenheim fellowship, and commissions from music foundations and organizations. His style was eclectic; the strongest influences upon his early development were Stravinsky, whose music he first heard when he was fifteen, and Miles Davis.*

BIBL: Black press. WWBA.

FOUR HARMONY KINGS, THE. Male quartet (Fl. c1916-c1933). See **BROWNING, IVAN.**

FRANKLIN, ARETHA. Gospel/rhythm 'n' blues singer (b. 25 March 1942 in Memphis, Tennessee). Her family moved to Buffalo, New York, when she was an infant, then settled in Detroit, Michigan, when she was about seven. She came from a musical family: her mother was a gospel singer, and her father, Clarence Franklin, was a noted evangelist-preacher-singer. As a child she came into contact with gospel and jazz figures who visited in her home or performed in her father's church. James Cleveland* lived with the family when she was nine years old and gave her informal lessons in gospel music. Her early career development was deeply influenced by her father, and she was inspired by the singing of Clara Ward.* She began singing in her father's church choir at an early age and toured with his evangelistic troupe during her high-school years. At fourteen she made her gospel recording debut. When she was eighteen she changed to singing secular music and, encouraged by a family friend, bassist Major ("Mule") Holley, went to New York to begin her new career. After obtaining professional management, she took vocal coaching and made a recording in August 1960, "Rock-a-bye, my baby" that attracted wide attention. Her career failed to develop, however, until 1966, when she signed with a different recording company. Thereafter she recorded extensively for the next decade and toured widely in the United States and abroad, including a tour of Australia in 1975. Her repertory consisted of rhythm 'n' blues, soul, and popular music; she appeared on television shows and received numerous awards from the music industry. Among her best-known performances were "Respect," "Chain of fools," "You make me feel like a natural woman," and "See saw." She was called the Queen of Soul. In the late 1970s her career seemed to languish, and she was relatively inactive. Her honors included awards from civic and community organizations and an honorary doctorate from Bethune-Cookman College (1975).

BIBL: AbdulFBE. *Ebony* (September 1967). FeaJS. FeaGitJS. Michael Lydon, *Boogie Lightning* (New York, 1974). WWA. WWBA.

DISC: Giv. Jep. TudBM.

FRANKLIN, WILLIAM. Jazz/operatic singer (b. 1906 in Memphis, Tennessee). His family moved to Chicago, Illinois, when he was a child, and he received his musical training in the public schools there. He played in musical groups at Wendell Phillips High School, where he was coached by Mildred Bryant Jones.* Thereafter he played trombone and/or sang with various jazz groups, including Clarence Jones,* Dave Peyton,* Stanley ("Fess") Williams,* and Earl Hines* (1928-35). In 1935 he was injured in an automobile accident and, unable to play trombone, decided to study voice. He attended the Chicago Conservatory of Music, where he studied with Alexander Corado, among others. In 1937 he made his operatic debut as a baritone, singing Amonasro in Verdi's *Aida* with the Chicago Civic Opera, with La Julia Rhea* in the title role. Thereafter he toured widely as a concert artist and sang in opera and musicals, including productions of Mary Cardwell Dawson's* National Negro Opera

Company. During the late 1940s he sang with the Southernaires* as a replacement after the death of Stone Toney. He was well known for his singing of the title role in Gilbert and Sullivan's *The Mikado*.

BIBL: Black press, incl. AmstN, 3 July 1948; CDef, 30 October 1937, 25 February 1939, 25 October 1941. DanceWEH.

FRAZIER, JAMES. Symphony orchestra conductor (b. 9 May 1940 in Detroit, Michigan). He began piano study at the age of five; when he was eleven he became a church organist; when he was sixteen he conducted Handel's *Messiah*. Although his baccalaureate degree was earned in chemistry at Wayne State University in Detroit, Michigan, he studied piano at the Detroit Conservatory and studied music at the University of Michigan in Ann Arbor (M. Mus.). After leaving Michigan he taught in the public schools of New York. In 1964 his conducting activities attracted the attention of Eugene Ormandy, director of the Philadelphia Symphony, and Ormandy became influential in his career development. He made his conducting debut in 1964 with the Detroit Symphony. In 1969 he won first prize in the Cantelli Competition sponsored by La Scala Opera Company of Milan, Italy, and made his opera-conducting debut at La Scala. Later he was appointed assistant conductor of the Detroit Symphony, and in 1974, assistant conductor of the Robin Hood Dell concerts sponsored by the Philadelphia Orchestra. In 1971 he conducted the Leningrad [Russia] Philharmonic Orchestra and returned to Russia in 1975 to tour. His concerts in Madrid, Spain, in 1973 were equally successful and led to invitations from leading orchestras to serve as guest conductor. In 1978 he organized the National Afro-American Philharmonic Orchestra, which gave its debut concert in May 1978 at the Philadelphia Academy of Music.

BIBL: Black press, incl. PhilaT, 27 April 1974. NYT, 24 May 1978.

FREEMAN, BERGERT C. Society dance-orchestra leader (b. 1830(?) in Auburn, New York; d. 31 March 1887 in Cleveland, Ohio). He was a violinist; he settled in Cleveland and led a dance orchestra that played for the important balls and other events of the period in Cleveland. See also **McAFEE, CHARLES.***

BIBL: Black press, incl. CleveG, 1883-1887; 9 April 1887.

FREEMAN, HARRY LAWRENCE. Composer (b. 9 October 1869 in Cleveland, Ohio; d. 21 March 1954 in New York, New York). As a child he played piano, organized a boys' quartet, and was serving as an assistant church organist by the time he was ten years old. Later he studied piano with Edwin Schonert and theory, composition, and orchestration with Johann Beck, founder and conductor of the Cleveland Symphony Orchestra. He began his professional career as a church organist in Cleveland, then moved to Denver, Colorado, about 1892. There he began composing, at first dances and marches in the style of the period, then gradually larger works. He completed his first opera, *The Martyr*, in 1893; it was produced in September of that year by the Freeman Grand Opera Company at the Deutsches Theater in Denver. Later the company staged the opera in Chicago, Illinois; Cleveland, and Wilberforce, Ohio. During the first decade of the twentieth century, Freeman became involved in various activities, including teaching music at Wilberforce University (1902-04) and serving as musical director for Ernest Hogan's* *Rufus Rastus* company (1905) and for the Pekin Theater Stock Company in Chicago, for which he wrote the musical score *Captain Rufus*, with Joe Jordan* and James ("Tim") Brymn.* He then went to New York, where he worked with the Bob Cole*/Johnson* brothers *The Red Moon* company. After that show closed in 1910 he left the stage and established the Freeman School of Music in New York. He was also active as a choral conductor with the Negro Choral Society, and he organized the Negro Grand Opera Company, which produced two of his operas, *Vendetta* and *Voodoo*, during the 1920s. Encouraged by the public response to his music, he gave much attention to composing, particularly opera. He revised his second opera, *Zuluki* (1898, originally titled *Nada*), from which scenes had been performed by the Cleveland Symphony in March 1900; and he wrote others over the years of his long career, making a total of fourteen operas. He also wrote two ballets, *Slave Ballet from Salome* (1932) and *Zulu King* (1934), a symphonic poem, *The Slave* (1925), two cantatas, and a large number of songs and instrumental pieces. In 1930 he received a first-place award from the Harmon Foundation; the same year excerpts from nine of his operas were presented in a concert at Steinway Hall. In 1947 his first opera, *The Martyr*, was presented in concert version at Carnegie Hall. His works were also performed on radio. His son, Valdo Freeman (1900-72), produced and directed many of his father's stage works and also sang leading roles in the productions.

BIBL: Black press, incl. IndF, 12 October 1907, 15 July 1911, 8 May 1915. Edward Hipster, *American Opera and Its Composers* (Bryn Mawr, Pennsylvania, 1927). *The Southern Workman* 62 (July 1933).

FREEMAN, PAUL DOUGLAS. Orchestral conductor (b. 2 January 1936 in Richmond, Virginia). He began to study piano at the age of five, the clarinet when he was eight, and the cello when he was thirteen. He obtained his musical education at the Eastman School of Music in Rochester, New York (B. Mus., 1956; M. Mus., 1957; Ph. D., 1963) and at the Hochschule für Musik in Berlin, Germany (1957-59). His teachers included Richard Lert, Ewald Lindemann, and Pierre Monteux, among others. He began to conduct during his college days at Eastman. His conducting career included tenures with the Opera Theater of Rochester (1961-66), the San Francisco Conservatory Orchestra (1966-67), the San Francisco Little Symphony (1967-68), the Dallas [Texas] Symphony as associate conductor (1968-70), and the Detroit [Michigan] Symphony as conductor-in-residence (1970-79). He also served as principal guest conductor for the Helsinki [Finland] Philharmonic Orchestra (1974-76). In 1979 he was appointed musical director of the Victoria [British Columbia] Symphony Orchestra; he also was music director of the Saginaw [Michigan] Symphony and of the Delta Summer Festival of Music and Arts. His honors included the Distinguished Alumni Citation from the University of Rochester (1975), awards in the Dimitri Metropulous International Conductors Competition (1967) and the Koussevitsky International Recording Competition (1974), the Spoleto Festival of Two Worlds Award (1968), and a Fulbright fellowship. He won wide recognition as a promoter and conductor of concerts of music by black composers. In association with AAMOA* (the Afro-American Music Opportunities Association, Inc.) and others, he sponsored annual symposia and concert series devoted to the music of black composers in principal cities of the United States and helped to establish the Black Composers Series of Columbia Records, for which he served as musical director. Beginning in 1977 he was also principal director for Opera Ebony.*

BIBL: WWA. WWBA.

FREEMAN, VALDO. Singer/Actor. See **FREEMAN, HARRY.**

FRIERSON, ANDREW. Concert singer/Studio teacher (b. 29 March 1927 in Columbia, Tennessee). His family moved to Louisville, Kentucky, when he was a child. He began piano study at an early age and later studied violin. He obtained his musical education in the public schools of Louisville, at the Juilliard School of Music in New York (B.S., 1950), and at the Manhattan School of Music in New York (M. Mus., 1970). He began singing during his service in the United States Armed Forces and, encouraged by his success, decided to study voice. His professional development was influenced by Sergius Kagen and Francis Hall Johnson.* In 1949 he made his concert debut as a baritone at Carnegie Recital Hall in New York. Thereafter he toured widely as a concert singer and soloist in opera and oratorio, except for three periods when he was active as a teacher: at Southern University in Baton Rouge, Louisiana (1950-51); at the Henry Street Settlement House in New York (as director, (1970-72); and at the Oberlin School of Music in Ohio (1973-75). In April 1958 he made his operatic debut singing the role of Cal in Blitzstein's *Regina* with the New York City Opera. During the years he was a member of that company (1958-64), he also sang the roles of Caronte in Monteverdi's *Orfeo*, Judge Bell in Carlisle Floyd's *The Passion of Jonathan Wade*, the Messenger in Stravinsky's *Oedipus Rex*, and Yamadon in Puccini's *Madame Butterfly*, among other roles. He was also noted for roles he sang with other companies, such as Monterrone in Verdi's *Rigoletto*, Don Alfonso in Mozart's *Cosi Fan Tutti*, Porgy in Gershwin's *Porgy and Bess*, and Joe in Hammerstein and Kern's *Show Boat*. During the 1960s-70s he toured frequently with the Frierson Ensemble, which included his wife, Billie Daniel,* and instrumentalists Leon Atkinson, Joseph Johnson, and Kelley Wyatt.* His honors included a Rockefeller Foundation grant and awards from civic and professional organizations.

BIBL: Questionnaire.

FRYE, THEODORE. Gospel singer (b. 10 September 1899 in Fayette, Mississippi; d. 26 August 1963 in Chicago, Illinois). He settled in Chicago, Illinois, in 1927 and soon thereafter began a professional association with the Ebenezer Baptist Church. In 1931 he organized the Chicago Gospel Choral Union, along with Thomas A. Dorsey* and Magnolia Butts Lewis; and in 1932 he was a co-founder with Dorsey of the National Convention of Gospel Choirs and Choruses. About 1937 he and Roberta Martin* organized a Junior Gospel Chorus for Ebenezer, which later formed the nucleus of the Martin-Frye Singers. He was also active as a musical director for annual meetings of the National Baptist Convention. In 1948 he and Mahalia Jackson* founded the National Baptist Music Convention as an auxiliary to the main Convention to train church musicians in the traditions of Baptist music. He served as president for many years, and Jackson served as treasurer. In his later career Frye was a gospel-chorus director at the Olivet Batist Church. He was a close associate of Jackson's and frequently toured with her. He wrote many gospel songs and maintained his own publishing house.

BIBL: Black press, incl. CDef, 20 March 1937, 11 September 1943, 12 August 1950, 24-30 August 1963, 7 June 1980 (cf. Thomas A. Dorsey). Laurraine Goreau, *Just Mahalia, Baby* (Waco, Texas, 1975).

FULLER ("BLIND BOY") (née **FULTON ALLEN).** Bluesman (b. 1908 in Wadesboro, North Carolina; d. 13 February 1941 in Durham, North Carolina). His family moved to Rockingham, North Carolina, when he was a child; there he first began playing guitar. He was blinded by an accident when he was in his twenties, but he had been playing professionally on street corners and for dances long before that time in the area of Durham, North Carolina (c1929-34). In 1934 he met harmonica player "Sonny Terry" (Saunders Terrell),* who was also blind, and the two bluesmen formed a team that lasted until Fuller's death. For a period during the 1930s Fuller and Terry toured with ("Blind") Gary Davis,* whose music influenced Fuller's style. He first recorded in 1935 and thereafter recorded rather extensively. Those with whom he played and/or recorded included "Bull City Red" George Washington, Walter "Brownie" McGhee,* and Davis, among others. He was one of the best-known Piedmont bluesmen; his style was distinctive for its strong, rhythmic guitar and gravelly voice.

BIBL: BWW. CharCB. FeaEJ. Kip Lornell. "Living Blues Interview: J. B. Long" in LivBl 29 (September-October 1976). Robert Neff and Anthony Connor, *Blues* (New York, 1975), see under Brownie McGhee. Oliv.

DISC: DiGod. Kink. TudBM.

FULLER, JESSE ("THE LONE CAT"). Bluesman (b. 12 March 1896 in Jonesboro, Georgia; d. 29 January 1976 in Oakland, California). He was a street singer and vaudeville entertainer in his early life. After he went to Oakland, California, in 1917 he began playing blues guitar, but it was not until the early 1950s that he became a professional bluesman. He began as a one-man band, playing guitar, a kazoo and harmonica mounted on a harness, and an instrument of his own invention, the fotdella, which combined a bass fiddle and a washboard. He made his first recording in 1955 at the age of fifty-nine and thereafter recorded extensively. He also toured widely, appearing at the major folk and jazz festivals at home and abroad, and performed in films and on film soundtracks, including *The Great White Hope* (1970).

BIBL: BWW. FeaEJ. LivBl 20 (March-April 1975). LivBl 25 (January-February 1976). MeeJMov. NYT, 1 February 1976.

DISC: Jep. LeSl. TudBM.

FULLER, OSCAR ANDERSON. College music professor (b. 20 September 1904 in Marshall, Texas). He came from a musical family: his father was chairman of a college music department, and an older sister played piano. He began piano study at the age of six. He obtained his musical education at Bishop College in Marshall, Texas (B. Mus., 1924); at the New England Conservatory of Music in Boston, Massachusetts; and at the University of Iowa in Iowa City (M.A., 1934; Ph.D., 1942). He was credited with being the first of his race to earn a Ph.D. degree in music at a major university. His teaching career included tenures at North Carolina A & T College in Greensboro (1924-29), Prairie View College in Texas (1929-1942), and Lincoln University in Jefferson City, Missouri (1942-74). During the early years of his teaching career he learned to play most of the musical instruments in the process of developing instrumental groups for the colleges and he also developed choral-conducting skills. He won wide recognition for the excellence of his college choirs, with whom he toured; he also toured as a choral clinician. His students over his long career included many who later became professional musicians, among them, opera singer Felicia Weathers.*

BIBL: NYB, 1952. *The Sunday News and Times* [Jefferson City, Missouri], 4 March 1978.

FULLER, WALTER ("ROSETTA"). Jazz trumpeter (b. 15 February 1910 in Dyersburg, Tennessee). He came from a musical family: his father played mellophone in a brass band, and his brother became a professional trumpeter. He began playing professionally at the age of twelve. He toured with Dr. Stoll's medicine show during summers for three years, then went to Chicago, Illinois, about 1925. During the decades of the 1920s-30s he played with various groups, including Sammy Stewart (1927-30), Irene Eadey and her Vogue Vagabonds (1930-31), Earl Hines* (1931-37, 1938-40), and Horace Henderson* (1937-38), among others. Thereafter he led his own groups in various cities, among them Chicago; New York; Minneapolis, Minnesota; Los Angeles, California; and San Diego, California, where he settled in 1946. During the late 1950s he replaced his big band with the Walter Fuller Trio, including Eugene Watson (piano) and Hollis Hassell (drums). His recording of "Rosetta" with the Hines band in 1934 brought him wide attention and his nickname.

BIBL: ChilWW. DanceWEH. FeaEJ.

DISC: Kink. RustJR.

FULSON, LOWELL. Bluesman (b. March 1921 in Tulsa, Oklahoma). His family moved to Atoka, Oklahoma (near the Texas border), when he was a child, and there he learned to play guitar; his grandfather played the fiddle and three uncles played guitar. He also taught himself by listening to recordings, particularly of

(''Blind'') Lemon Jefferson.* At the age of seventeen he began to play professionally; he joined the Dan Wright's String Band and a year later went on tour with Alger (''Texas'') Alexander. He left music for a period, although he played for a local Holiness church. After service in the armed forces (1943-45) he settled in California and made his first recordings. He soon established himself as one of the leading Oakland blues figures; he took to the West Coast elements of the Texas/Oklahoma blues tradition, which fused with the traditions of bluesmen from Kansas City to produce a sophisticated West Coast blues. He toured widely in the United States and played and/or recorded with his brother, Martin Fulson, Lloyd Glenn, and Jay McShane,* among others. Until 1953 he had his own blues band. He finally settled in Los Angeles, California.

BIBL: BWW. LivBl 5, 6 (Summer 1971, Autumn 1971). MeeJMov. Oliv. ShawHS.

FURMAN, JAMES B. College professor/Composer (b. 23 January 1937 in Louisville, Kentucky). He studied piano as a child. During his high-school years he won first place in the Louisville (Kentucky) Philharmonic Society's Young Artist Contest (1953), which allowed him to appear as a soloist with the Louisville Symphony. He obtained his musical education in the public schools of Louisville, at the University of Louisville (B. Mus. Ed., 1958; M. Mus., 1965), at Brandeis University in Waltham, Massachusetts (1962-64), and Harvard University in Cambridge, Massachusetts (summer 1966). His teachers in composition included George Perle, Claude Almand, Irving Fine, Arthur Berger, and Harold Shapero. His teaching career included tenures in the public schools of Louisville (1958-59) and Mamaroneck, New York (1964-65), and at Western Connecticut State College in Danbury (1965-). His compositions fall primarily into the categories of choral works, songs, and chamber music. Best-known of his works are the symphonic oratorio *I Have a Dream* (1971), the trio *Variants* (1963), the choral suite *Four Little Foxes* (1965), and *Declaration of Independence* for orchestra and narrator (1977). He was also active as a church organist and choral director.

BIBL: Personal communication. WWBA.

G

GAMBLE, KENNETH. Producer/Songwriter. (b. 11 August 1943 in Philadelphia, Pennsylvania). He obtained his musical education in the public schools of Philadelphia, Pennsylvania, and began his professional career singing with a local group, the Romeos. Leon Huff* obtained his musical education in the public schools of Camden, New Jersey, where he played drums in his high-school band. After graduation he went to New York and became active as a studio musician, playing piano for singing groups. In 1963 he went to Philadelphia, where he met Gamble when both were doing studio work with Cameo-Parkway Records. The two men formed a songwriting partnership, Gamble-Huff Productions, which wrote and produced songs for local groups at first, then expanded its activities to write for other groups and individuals in the entertainment world of popular and soul music. In 1966 Gamble and Huff established Excel Records, later Neptune Records, then Gamble Records. They next formed the Mighty Three Music Group, which included Thom Bell,* a former bandleader (1962-65) for Chubby Checker* (née Ernest Evans) before he became an A & R man (artist and repertoire) for Cameo-Parkway Records (1966-68). In 1969 they organized Gamble-Huff International Productions and Philadelphia International Records, Inc. which was credited with creating "the Philadelphia Sound" in the 1970s in the same way as Berry Gordy* and his company had created "the Motown Sound" (i.e., Detroit, Michigan, the "Motor City") in the 1960s. The groups and entertainers for whom they produced songs included Jerry Butler,* Wilson Pickett,* Joe Simon, Billy Paul,* Aretha Franklin,* Diana Ross,* Dionne Warwick,* the Spinners, the Jacksons,* the O'Jays,* the Intruders, Lou Rawls,* and many others. In 1978 Gamble was a co-founder of the Black Music Association in Philadelphia, a professional trade association with the goal of "preserving and perpetuating black music." The Gamble-Huff-Bell team received many awards from the music industry.

BIBL: BMI (Summer 1975; No. 2, 1978). *Black Enterprise* (December 1979). WWBA.

GARCIA, WILLIAM BURRES. College professor (b. 16 July 1940 in Dallas, Texas). He obtained his musical education in the public schools of Dallas, Texas; at Prairie View University in Texas (1958-61), where he studied with H. Edison Anderson and Rudolphe von Charlton;* at North Texas State University at Denton (B. Mus., 1962, M. Mus. Ed., 1965), where he studied with Kathryn Harvey and Daniel Moe; and at the University of Iowa at Iowa City (Ph. D., 1973). His teaching career included tenures at Philander Smith College at Little Rock, Arkansas (1963-64); Langston University in Oklahoma (1966-69); Miles College in Birmingham, Alabama (1974-77); and Talladega College in Alabama (1977-). He was also active as a church organist and choir director, and his college-teaching assignments included choral conducting at Miles and Talladega and, as well, administrative work. He toured as a lecturer, particularly giving attention to the subject of the John Wesley Work* family of musicians, the subject of his doctoral dissertation. He published articles in professional journals and music dictionaries. His honors included fellowships from the Southern Fellowships Fund (1970s), the Ford Foundation (1971), and the National Endowment for the Humanities (1973), as well as citations by professional organizations.

BIBL: Questionnaire. WW in the South and Southwest.

GARDNER, NEWPORT (née **OCCRAMER MARYCOO).** Composer (b. 1746 in Africa; d. August 1826 in Liberia). He was brought to Newport, Rhode Island, in 1760 and early revealed musical talent. His slaveowner's wife, Mrs. Caleb Gardner, arranged for him to study music for a short while with Andrew Law, composer and itinerant singing-master. He developed his talents to such an extent that he became a proficient singer and composer. In 1791 he won money in a lottery drawing that enabled him to purchase his freedom. Thereafter he conducted a singing school, which attracted large numbers of white and black students, including his former mistress. As early as 1764 he wrote a choral work, titled "Promise Anthem," which was based on the scriptural texts Jeremiah 30:1-3, 10 and St. Mark 7:27-28 and which was widely sung, although it circulated in manuscript form until its publication at Boston in 1826. He also wrote a considerable number of other pieces, which were well received by his contemporaries. He served as headmaster of a school for black children established by the African Benevolent Society in 1808 and helped to organize the first black church in Newport, the Colored Union Church (dedicated 23 June 1824). In 1826 he joined a group of missionaries who set sail from Boston, Massachusetts, on 4 January to establish a church in Monrovia, Liberia. Gardner was possibly the first black singing master in the United States to win recognition beyond his local community.

BIBL: Charles Battle, *Negroes on the Island of Rhode Island* (Newport, Rhode Island, 1932). BPIM 4 (July 1976). Howard Brooks, *The Negro in Newport* (Newport, 1946). SouRBM.

GARLAND, PHYLLIS T. ("PHYL"). Music journalist (b. 27 October 1935 in McKeesport, Pennsylvania). She came from a musical family; her father was a professional jazzman in his early career. She studied piano as a child. She obtained her education at Northwestern University in Evanston, Illinois (B.S. in journalism, 1957). Her early writing experience was with the *Pittsburgh Courier* (1958-65); thereafter she was associated with *Ebony* magazine in various editorial positions. In addition to publishing numerous articles about black musicians and their music, she lectured widely on the subject and published *The Sound of Soul* (1969).

BIBL: WWBA.

GARNER, ERROL L. Jazz pianist (b. 15 June 1921 in Pittsburgh, Pennsylvania; d. 2 January 1977 in Los Angeles, California). He came from a musical family: his father, an amateur, played three musical instruments, his mother was a church pianist, and his brother Linton became a professional musician. Self-taught, he began playing piano when he was three years old and played professionally at the age of seven with a group, The Candy Kids, on Pittsburgh [Pennsylvania] radio station KDKA. He obtained his musical education in the public schools of Pittsburgh, where he played tuba in the school marching band. Even before he entered high school he was playing on riverboats that sailed the Allegheny and in local nightclubs. In 1944 he went to New York, where he played with various groups in nightclubs on 52nd Street and later with the Leroy ("Slam") Stewart Trio. Soon thereafter he formed his own trio, and for the remainder of his career toured widely in the United States and in Europe with his group or as a soloist. His European debut was in 1948 at the Paris Jazz Festival. In March 1950 he made his concert debut as a jazz pianist in Music Hall in Cleveland, Ohio. In 1958 he became the first jazz pianist to be given a contract by impresario Sol Hurok, who managed such artists as Marian Anderson.* In 1958 he was the first pianist to give a jazz concert in New York's Carnegie Hall. He toured on the international concert circuit, appearing with leading symphony orchestras as well as giving solo recitals; he recorded extensively, perhaps more than any other jazz pianist of his time; and he appeared regularly on televison shows at home and abroad. He was a prolific composer. His best known songs were "Misty," "Laura," "Dreamy," "Solitaire," and "Something happens"; his best-known albums were *Concert by the Sea* and *Magician*. His honors included the Prix de disque from the French Academy of Arts and numerous awards from the music industry. His distinctive piano style derived partly from his use of full chords in the left hand against improvisatory melodies in the right hand that lagged slightly behind the beat.

BIBL: ASCAP. Black press, incl. AmstN, 6 January 1977.CurBiog (March 1977). MeeJMov. NYT, 3 January 1977. WWBA. WWA.

DISC: Jep. Kink.

GARNER, GEORGE ROBERT. Concert singer (b. 16 April 1890 in Virginia; d. 8 January 1971 in Los Angeles, California).His mother was a church organist in Virginia, and he began singing in a church choir at an early age. His family moved to Chicago, Illinois, when he was a child. He obtained his musical education in the public schools of Chicago, at Chicago Musical College (diploma, 1918), at the American Conservatory of Music in Chicago (B. Mus., 1926), where he studied with Charles La Berge, and at the University of Southern California in Los Angeles. He also studied with Adolph Muhlmann and Herman DeVries. During the years 1926-29 he studied in London, England, with George Henschel and Louis Drysdale (a native of Kingston, Jamaica, who taught many of the black singers who went to London, including Florence Mills*). Garner toured widely as a concert tenor, frequently accompanied by his wife Netta Paulyn Garner, a pianist, and also sang in opera and oratorio in the United States and in England. He lived in Chicago after returning to the United States in 1929, then settled in Pasadena, California, in 1934. In 1942 he left the field of music and became an ordained minister in the Methodist Episcopal Church.

BIBL: ChiVH. Communication from Florence Cadrez Brantley. Black press, incl. CDef, 16 February 1924, 13 November 1926, 19 May 1928, 4 July 1936, 20 November 1943. Hare.

GASTON, OLAND. Organist/Music educator (b. 15 November 1925 in Chicago, Illinois). He began piano study at the age of seven and played his first solo recital when he was eleven. He obtained his musical education in the public schools of Chicago, Illinois; in the preparatory department of Chicago Musical College; at Wilson Junior College in Chicago; the United States Army Music School (bandleader's certificate, 1944); at the American Conservatory of Music (B. Mus., 1947; M. Mus. 1948); at the Juilliard School of Music (1949-50) and Columbia University Teachers College (1949-51) in New York; and at the Guilmant Organ School in New York. His piano teachers included Edward Collins, Rudolph Ganz, Merle West, and Alfred Mirovitch, among others; his organ teachers included Stella Bonds, Lillian Carpenter, Walter Gossette,* and George Markey. His career development was also influenced by Herman Billingsly, William E. Myrick, and Blanche Smith-Walton. His teaching career included tenures at Johnson C. Smith University in Charlotte, North Carolina (1941-42); in the public schools of New York (1953-); and at Brooklyn College of the City University of New York as a lecturer (1967-75). During World War II he was an officer-bandleader with the 353rd AFS Band (1944-45). As a youth he won prizes in music competitions that brought not only awards but also opportunities to play on programs of professional organizations. In 1949 he made his concert debut at Kimball Hall in Chicago. He began serving as a church organist in Chicago churches at an early age and later earned admission to the American Guild of Organists. After he settled in New York in 1949, he continued his activity as a church organist and choirmaster, concomitant with his teaching. In January 1957 he made his choral conducting debut at Town Hall with the premiere of Irving Mopper's *Creation*, for baritone, chorus, and orchestra (text by James Weldon Johnson*). He also toured as a concert pianist and organist.

BIBL: Questionnaire.

GATLIN, F. NATHANIEL. College professor (b. 5 July 1913 in Summit, Mississippi). He obtained his musical education at the Oberlin School of Music in Ohio (B.S., 1938); at Northwestern University in Evanston, Illinois (M. Mus., 1945); and at Columbia University Teachers College (D. Mus. Ed.). His teaching career included tenures at Bennett College in Greensboro, North Carolina (1938-43); Lincoln University in Jefferson City, Missouri (1943-47); and Virginia State College in Petersburg (1947-78). He won wide recognition for his military and symphonic bands; he toured with his bands in the United States, Canada, and in Europe during the academic year 1971-72. His marching bands also appeared on nationally televised shows of football games. He also toured widely as a concert clarinetist and appeared with a number of symphony orchestras playing concertos. He was active as a band clinician, guest conductor, and workshop consultant. His honors included citations from professional organizations, appointment to boards of professional groups, and an honorary doctorate from Iowa Wesleyan College (1954).

BIBL: Questionnaire. *The School Musician* (April 1975). WWCA, 1950.

GAYE, MARVIN PENTZ. (née **GAY**). Rhythm 'n' blues singer (b. 2 April 1939 in Washington, D.C.). As a child, he sang in the choir of his father's pentecostal church and toured with his father, singing solos. He also studied piano and later learned to play drums at school. He obtained his musical education in the public schools of Washington, D.C.; during his high school years he played in school orchestras and sang with local rhythm 'n' blues groups. In 1956 he sang with the Rainbows, three of whose members later joined with him to form the Marquees—James ("Sally") Nolan, Reese Palmer, and Chester Simmons. After high school, Gaye served in the U.S. Air Force for a short period (1957), then joined the Moonglows, led at that time by Harvey Fuqua. His touring took him to Detroit, Michigan, where he came into contact with Berry Gordy's* Motown Corporation and began a recording career (1961). Within a few years, he had become a leading rhythm 'n' blues singer; over the years he frequently recorded with female singers, among them, Diana Ross,* Tammi Terrell (d. 1970), Mary Wells, and Kim Weston. During the years c1969-1974 he was relatively inactive as a performer, but he continued to record regularly. After returning to the entertainment world in 1974, he toured widely thereafter, appearing in nightclubs and theaters, on college campuses, in films, and on television and radio programs. His mature style was a blend of soul, gospel, jazz, and popular music; he wrote and/or arranged much of his material. His best-known albums included *What's Going On, Stubborn Kind of Fellow,* and *Let's Get It On*; his well-known songs included "Stubborn kind of fellow," "Mercy, mercy me," "I heard it through the grapevine," and

"Can I get a witness," as well as duets with Terrell, "I could build my whole world around you" and "Ain't no mountain high enough" or with Ross, "My mistake was to love you." He received awards from the music industry and civic groups. His film appearances included performance of the theme song in *Save the Children* (1973).

BIBL: Black press, incl. AmstN, 4 January 1975. *Ebony* (November 1974). NYT, 25 August 1974. *Sepia* (January 1965). StamPRS.

DISC: Giv. TudBM.

GEFFRARD, ROBERT. Composer (b. 5 April 1860 in Gonaïves, Haiti; d. 16 July 1894 in Paris, France). He came from a musical family: an ancestor, Nicolas Geffrard, in 1904 wrote the music to "La Dessalinienne" (text by Justin Lhérisson), which later became the Haitian National Hymn. Robert received his musical education at the Petit Séminaire Collegè St. Martial in Port-au-Prince. His best-known compositions were for piano: "Poésie," "La Cascade," and the grande valse "L'Heroine."

BIBL: Dumervé.

GEORGE, MAUDE ROBERTS. Music journalist/Studio teacher (fl. early twentieth century; d. 1940s-50s in Chicago, Illinois). She obtained her musical education in the public schools of Chicago, Illinois, and at Walden University in Nashville, Tennessee. Later she studied voice with Herman DeVries in Chicago. Her teaching experience included tenures at Walden (1909-11) and Lane College in Jackson, Tennessee (1911-13), before she conducted a vocal studio in Chicago. She was active as a concert singer on local concerts, as music editor for the *Chicago Defender* during the 1920s, and with the community musical organizations, particularly the Chicago Music Association, for which she served as president for several years. She was president of the National Association of Negro Musicians for one term (1934-35) and also served that organization in many other official positions.

BIBL: Black press. WWCA 1941-44.

GEORGE, ZELMA WATSON. Sociologist/Opera singer (b. 8 December 1903 in Hearne, Texas). Although best known as a sociologist, she was active as a musician in her early career. She obtained her musical education at the American Conservatory of Music in Chicago, Illinois (1925-27), where she studied voice, and at Northwestern University in Evanston, Illinois (1924-26), where she studied organ. In 1949 she sang the title role of Gian Carlo Menotti's opera *The Medium* at Karamu House in Cleveland, Ohio, and repeated her performance in the opera's Broadway revival of 1950 in New York. She later sang in Menotti's opera *The Consul* and Kurt Weill's *The Three Penny Opera*. Her doctoral dissertation, "A Guide to Negro Music: Towards a Sociology of Negro Music" (New York University, Ph. D. in sociology, 1954), included an "Index to Negro Music" that catalogued almost a thousand titles of music by black composers, music by white composers using Negro thematic materials, folk music collections, and publications treating history and criticism of black music. She published articles about music in professional journals and books, including "Negro Music in American Life" in the *American Negro Reference Book*.

BIBL: Personal communication. CurBiog (October 1961). WilABW. WWA. WWBA.

GEORGIA MINSTRELS, THE. Minstrel troupes (org. 1865; fl. through 1930s). The use of the title Georgia Minstrels in association with a black minstrel troupe apparently was first used in 1865. In April of that year W. H. Lee, a white man, organized a troupe of fifteen ex-slaves at Macon, Georgia. Some time during the same year (later?) black entrepreneur Charles ("Barney") Hicks* organized a minstrel troupe of black men at Indianapolis, Indiana. Lee toured with his troupe in the Northeast and Canada, under management of Pike and Hatch, for more than a year; by July 1866 however, the troupe had been taken over by Sam Hague of Utica, New York. Giving it a new name, Sam Hague's Slave Troupe of Georgia Minstrels, Hague added additional men and took the troupe to England in July 1866. According to the press, he became dissatisfied with the nonprofessionalism of the ex-slaves and over a two-year period, gradually replaced most of them with white men in blackface. Hicks called his troupe the Original Georgia Minstrels, and by the end of 1865 was touring widely in the West and Northeast. When the troupe began its "Fourth Annual Tour" in 1868, it was accompanied by a thirteen-piece brass band and included a number of exotic specialty acts. There is evidence that there was a third touring troupe in 1866 called the Georgia Minstrels, which was managed by Brooker and Clayton. In January 1870 Hicks took a small group of his minstrels to tour in Europe, leaving behind the main company to continue touring in the United States. In the summer of 1870 he joined forces with Hague's troupe, now called Sam Hague's Great American Slave Troupe, at Cork, Ireland, and the combined groups toured together in the British Isles for a year. Hicks and Hague had a disagreement, and in July 1871 Hicks returned to the United States, taking with him at least two members of Hague's group—Japanese Tommy (neé Thomas Dilworth) and Aaron Banks. Hicks and Hague presented their arguments to the public through the *New York Clipper*; Hague was incensed over Hick's use of the title Georgia Minstrels and over the competition offered by the black minstrel manager. Hicks continued to tour with his troupe through 1871, but by March 1872 he had sold his rights to Charles Callender, although he remained as business manager. During the summer of 1872 Callender reorganized the troupe, adding new men and replacing Hicks with white manager George W. Siddons. Over the seven-year life of the Georgia Minstrels under Hicks's management, its members included Charles Anderson, Aaron Banks, Abe Cox, George Danforth, Peter (''Pete'') Devenear, T. Drewette (or Drewitte), James (''Jim'') Grace, Bob Height, Henry B. Johnson, Sam Jones, Dick Little, Louis Pierson, Dave Porter, George Skillings (leader of the orchestra), Charles Sticks, the Torres brothers, Dick Weaver, Billy Wilson, John Wilson (bandleader), and Jake Zabriskie. Some of these men remained with the troupe for a decade or more through changes in management, which included J. H. Haverly in the 1870s-80s and Charles and Gustave Frohman in the 1880s. By the end of the century the name Georgia Minstrels was in common use: there were Sprague and Blodgett's Georgia Minstrels, Richards and Pringle's, and Rusco and Holland's (which combined during the 1890s), among others. In the twentieth century there were McCabe's Georgia Minstrels, the Smart Set* Georgia Minstrels, and J. C. O'Brien's Famous Georgia Minstrels. As late as 1935 there was a touring troupe calling itself Richard & Pringle's Georgia Minstrels.

BIBL: Black press, incl. CDef, 23 November 1935; IndF, 24 December 1898, 6 September 1902, 2 February 1924; NYFreeman, 21 May 1887; NYGlobe, 3 February 1883, 16 June 1883. Flet, p. 83. *The New York Clipper*, 14 April 1866-1880s. Simond. Trot.

GERREN, NICHOLAS L'OUVERTURE. University professor (b. 3 October 1912 in Kansas City, Kansas). He came from a musical family: his mother sang and played piano, as did two brothers. He began violin study as a child. He obtained his musical training in the public schools of Kansas City, Kansas; at the University of Kansas in Lawrence (B. Mus., 1934; B. Mus. Ed., 1935; M. Mus. Ed., 1948; Ph. D., 1953), where he studied with Waldemar Geltch and E. Thayer Gaston; and at the Moscow Conservatory of Music in Russia, where he studied with Boris Ossipovich Sibor. His early career development was influenced by J. Harold Brown,* leader of his junior-high-school orchestra, and by his high-school principal, John A. Hodge, who helped to arrange for his study in Russia. He played violin in the university symphony orchestra at Lawrence and in the Moscow Radio Theater Symphony Orchestra (1935-37). In December 1937 he made his concert debut in the Music Hall of the Municipal Auditorium at Kansas City, Missouri. His teaching career included tenures in the public schools of Kansas City, Kansas (1934-35, 1938-39); Prairie View State College in Texas (1939-42); Bennett College in Greensboro, North Carolina (1945-46); Lincoln University in Jefferson City, Missouri (1946-53); Texas Southern University at Houston (1953-66); and Central State University at Wilberforce, Ohio (1966-77). In most of the institutions he was director of string ensembles; at Texas Southern and Central State he also carried administrative responsibilities as chairman of the music department and dean of music and fine arts schools and/or divisions. He toured extensively as a concert violinist, as a guest conductor, and with his college choirs. During the years 1955-64 he was guest conductor for the Annual Summer Concerts of the Houston Summer Symphony Orchestra. His numerous honors included awards from professional and civic organizations and appointment to national committees and boards of directors of professional organizations, to state art councils, and to national music advisory panels. In 1973 he was sent by the United States Department of State to visit conservatories, schools, and museums in the Soviet Union.

BIBL: Questionnaire. Black press, incl. CDef, 20 August 1938; *Kansas City* [Missouri] *Call*, 1935-1938. Reginald Buckner, ''A History of Music Education in the Black Community of Kansas City, Kansas, 1905-1954'' (Ph. D. dissertation, University of Minnesota, 1974). *The Xenia Daily Gazette*, 1974-1977.

GIBBS, HARRIET. See **MARSHALL, HARRIET GIBBS.**

GIBBS, LLOYD. Concert/vaudeville singer (b. c1866 in Baltimore, Maryland; d. 21 October 1951 in New York, New York). He was one of the leading tenors of his time. He made his debut with Black Patti's* Troubadours in 1900. Thereafter he sang with George Walker*/Bert Williams* companies and toured the vaudeville circuit. His last tour before retiring from the stage was with a quartet in the Henry J. Savage productions.

BIBL: Black press, incl. AmstN, 27 October 1951.

GILLAM, HARRY. Minstrel/Bandleader (b. 1872 in Detroit, Michigan; d. 27 August 1929 in Detroit). His father, Joseph Charles Gillam,* was violin soloist in Theodore Finney's* orchestra for many years. Harry's early professional experience was with P. T. Wright's* Nashville Students. Thereafter he toured with the Georgia Minstrels,* Mahara's Minstrels, and Ernest Hogan's* Rufus Rastus company (1905-07), among other minstrel groups. In 1908 he returned to Detroit, where later he became leader of the Wells Maroon Band and also conducted a school of music.

BIBL: Black press, incl. CDef, 7 September 1929; IndF, 15 January 1898.

GILLAM, JOSEPH (or JOHN) CHARLES. Society dance-band leader (b. 1824 in Geneva, New York; d. June 1890 in Detroit, Michigan). He and Obediah Wood,* both violinists, organized the first black dance orchestra in Detroit, Michigan, some time before March 1844, at which time the group gave a public concert. He and Wood also set themselves up as music dealers, selling music and instruments. In 1847 Gillam and Wood opened a dancing school and inaugurated a series of school-sponsored cotillions. They played for the city's important balls and in 1849 toured through the western part of Michigan. Beginning in the 1850s the press omitted Gillam's name in referring to Wood's Cotillion and Serenade Band; it is not known the exact date Gillam and Wood separated. Later Gillam played in Theodore Finney's* dance orchestra.

BIBL: Black press. LaBrew.

GILLESPIE, JOHN BIRKS ("DIZZY"). Jazz trumpeter (b. 21 October 1917 in Cheraw, South Carolina). He came from a musical family: his father was a pianist-bandleader in his leisure time, whose band played for local dances, and all the children studied piano. He was surrounded with instruments from earliest childhood, for his father kept the band's instruments at his house. He began piano study at an early age, learned trombone at school, then changed to trumpet when he was about twelve years old (his father died when he was ten). He obtained his musical education in the public schools of Cheraw, South Carolina, where he played in a school band that also played for local dances, and at the Laurinburg Technical Institute in Laurinburg, North Carolina, where he also played in musical groups. In 1935 he went to Philadelphia, Pennsylvania, where he played with Frank Fairfax, among others, and acquired the nickname "Dizzy"; in 1937 he settled in New York. Thereafter he played with various groups, including Theodore ("Teddy") Hill* (1937-39, including tour in Europe), Cabell ("Cab") Calloway* (1939-41), Ella Fitzgerald* (1941), Benny Carter* (1941-42), Les Hite,* Earl Hines* (1942), and William ("Billy") Eckstine* (1944), among others. During the 1940s Gillespie led his own groups from time to time; he played for short periods with Edward ("Duke") Ellington* and John Kirby's sextet; and in 1944 he became co-leader of a group on 52nd Street with Oscar Pettiford,* which for him "represented the birth of the bebop era" (quoted from his autobiography, p. 202). Long before this time, however, he had become deeply involved with the new music called bebop. Beginning about 1939 black musicians who played in bands all over the city would gather after working hours at Minton's Playhouse or Clark Monroe's Uptown House in the Harlem community for "jam sessions," where they experimented with new ideas and/or competed in exhibiting their musical and technical skills. Thelonious Monk* and Kenneth ("Kenny") Clarke* played in the house band at Minton's; among the others who made important contributions to the development of the new music were Gillespie, Oscar Pettiford, Charlie Christian,* Milton Hinton,* Illinois Jacquet,* and, beginning in 1942, Charlie Parker.* Parker and Gillespie were regarded as the leaders, and when they joined Eckstine's band at the end of the 1943, they carried the new music with them, thereby turning the band into "the incubator" of bebop. Because of the recording ban imposed by the National Federation of Musicians during the period August 1942-November 1944, very little of this music was recorded. Gillespie invented the name for the new music. His group on 52nd Street played many of his original pieces, for which there were no titles; he would start the playing by humming "Dee-da-pa-da-n-de-bop," and patrons developed the habit of asking for bebop pieces. Eventually the press picked up the name, and Gillespie gave the title "Bebop" to one of his pieces written without a name during that period. From the mid-1940s on Gillespie led both big bands and small groups. He toured widely throughout the world; in 1956 he toured as a goodwill ambassador for the United States Department of State in Europe, the Near East, and Latin America, thereby marking the first time in history that the United States had given official recognition to a jazz orchestra. Frequently he toured as a soloist with special shows, such as JATP (Norman Granz's Jazz at the Philharmonic, 1946, 1950s), The Giants of Jazz (1971-72), and The Musical Life of Charlie Parker (1974). His groups appeared at the major jazz festivals at home and abroad, in concert halls and theaters, in nightclubs, and on university campuses. He was also active as a lecturer and workshop consultant on college campuses. From the time of his recording debut in 1937, he recorded prolifically with many groups as well as his own; he appeared on television programs and wrote music for film soundtracks as well as appeared in films, including *Jivin' in Be-bop* (1947), *The Cool World* (1963), and *Jazz, the Intimate Art* (1968). He wrote tunes steadily, not only for his own groups but also for others, of which the best known were "A night in Tunisia," "Bebop," "Salt peanuts," and "Groovin' high" and the collaborations with Parker, "Anthropology" and "Shaw nuff." His first historic quintet in 1944 included Don Byas,* Oscar Pettiford, Max Roach,* and George Wallington; changes in personnel brought in Albert ("Budd") Johnson* (as co-leader), Clyde Hart, Leonard Gaskin, and later Earl ("Bud") Powell,* Charlie Parker, Dillon ("Curley") Russell, and Ray Brown, among others. The roster of Gillespie's first big band of 1945 would appear to be a "who's who" in jazz a decade later. His honors included numerous awards from the music and recording industries, awards from civic, professional, and educational institutions, citations by cities and state legislatures, and honorary doctorates from Rutgers University (1972) and the Chicago Conservatory of Music (1978).

Gillespie was the major architect of bebop music, along with Charlie Parker, and one of the leading innovators in the history of jazz. He was the first to bring Afro-Cuban rhythms into jazz (1947), to introduce the South American samba or bossa nova to the United States (1957) and he was credited with being one of the first to use the electric string bass in the jazz ensemble (mid-1960s). His style development was influenced by Roy Eldridge;* all trumpeters since his time were shaped directly by him. He moved gracefully from his origin in the bop era to contemporary times and retained his preeminence as the jazz trumpeter without peer. In 1979 he published his autobiography, *To Be, or Not to Bop*, with Al Fraser.

BIBL: ASCAP. BPIM (Spring 1976). ChilWW. CurBiog (April 1957). Dance WEH. *Ebony* (June 1964). FeaEJ. FeaJS. FeaGitJS. *Negro Digest* (June 1949). MeeJMov. WWA. WWBA.

DISC: Jep. Kink. ModJ. RustJR. TudJ.

GILLIAT, SIMEON (also known as **SY**). Dance fiddler (fl. early nineteenth century in Richmond, Virginia; d. 15 October 1820 in Richmond). He was in great demand during the turn of the century to play for the balls of the Virginia aristocracy, along with his companion, London Brigs, who played flute and clarinet. He is represented in a painting (artist unknown) dating from c1820.

BIBL: Samuel Mordecai, *Richmond in By-Gone Days* (Richmond, 1856; excerpt reprinted in SouRBM). Reproduction of the picture in Langston Hughes and Milton Meltzer, *Black Magic* (Englewood Cliffs, New Jersey, 1967), p. 14.

GILPIN, CHARLES SIDNEY. Actor/Vaudeville singer (b. 20 November 1878 in Richmond, Virginia; d. 6 May 1930 in New York, New York). Although best known as an actor, he began his career as a singer. As a child he sang in local shows. His first professional experience was with Brown's Big Spectacular Log Cabin Company, which was stranded soon after he joined the company, as was also the next company with which he performed, the Great Southern Minstrels. He then left the music field for a short while, although he occasionally toured with concert companies or carnivals. During the years 1903-05 he toured with the Carey and Carter Canadian Jubilee Singers. He then worked as a baritone soloist in the George Walker*/Bert Williams* show, *In Abyssinia* (1906), and also with The Smart Set* company (1906). In 1907 he went to the Pekin Theater in Chicago, Illinois, where he played in *Mayor of Dixie*, a play written by Flournoy Miller* and Aubrey Lyles,* which was used later as the basis for the Noble Sissle*/Eubie Blake* musical *Shuffle Along* (1921). Thereafter he made a transcontinental tour with the Pan-American Octette (1911-14) and played in the Alex Roger*/Henry Creamer* musical, *Old Man's Boy* (1914). He settled in New York about 1916 and became a member of the Anita Bush Players at the Lincoln Theater in the Harlem community; soon thereafter he was one of the founders of the Lafayette Theater Stock Company. After that company disbanded he toured on the vaudeville circuit again. His musical career came to a permanent close when he was chosen in 1919 for the part of William Custis in John Drinkwater's play, *Abraham Lincoln*, and in 1920 for the title role in Eugene O'Neill's drama, *The Emperor Jones*. Discussion of his career as an actor is beyond the scope of this work, but it should be pointed out that he received the Drama League Award and the Spingarn Medal in 1921.

BIBL: Black press, incl. CDef, 10 May 1930. DAB. Flet, 183.

GLADYS KNIGHT AND THE PIPS. Rhythm 'n' blues group (orig. in Atlanta, Georgia; fl. 1950s-1970s). See also **KNIGHT, GLADYS.** The family group was informally organized in 1952 at a birthday party for Merald ("Bubba") Knight, when several of the children present offered to provide entertainment. One of the older cousins, James ("Pip") Woods, later formed the children into a quintet, coached the group and named it The Pips, and arranged for performances in local nightclubs. The vocal group, all natives of Atlanta, Georgia, was composed of Gladys Knight (b. 1944), her brother Bubba (b. 1943), and cousins Edward Patten (b. 1940) and William (b. 1941). Former members Brenda Knight and Eleanor Guest left the group in the 1960s, and Patten joined at that time. All members of the group had experience in singing gospel. The group's first national tour was with Sam Cooke* and Jackie Wilson.* They returned to Atlanta to finish high school, then in 1961 went to New York as The Pips Quartet, later as Gladys Knight and the Pips. They recorded extensively and toured widely in the United States, Europe, Australia, and the Far East, appearing in nightclubs and theaters, in concert halls, and on television programs. They also sang on film soundtracks, including *Claudine* (1974), for which the music was written by Curtis Mayfield.* The group began as a gospel-oriented quartet, but later moved into the fields of rhythm 'n' blues, soul, and popular music, using polished dance routines in their acts. Among their best-known performances were "Every beat of my heart," "I don't want to do wrong," "Neither one of us," and "I feel a song." They received numerous awards from the music industry.

BIBL: *Ebony* (June 1973, October 1977). StamPRS.

DISC: TudBM.

GLENN, EVANS TYREE. Jazz trombonist (b. 23 November 1912 in Corsicana, Texas; d. 18 May 1974 in Englewood, New Jersey). He began his career playing with local bands in Texas, then played with Tommy Myles in Washington, D.C. (1934-36). Thereafter he played with various groups, including Charlie Echols, Eddie Barefield, Eddie Mallory (1937-39), Benny Carter* (1939), Cabell ("Cab") Calloway* (1939-46), Don Redman* (1946), Edward ("Duke") Ellington* (1947-51), and Louis Armstrong* (1965-68, 1970-71). He also led his own groups at intervals. During the 1950s-70s he was highly active in television, radio, and studio performance along with his nightclub work, playing both trombone and vibraphone. In addition to touring widely in the United States and Europe with various groups, he also toured in Europe as a soloist (1946-47, 1951). Two sons, Tyree, Jr., and Roger, became professional musicians.

BIBL: ASCAP. Black press, incl. AmstN, 25 May 1974. ChilWW. FeaEJ. FeaJS. FeaGitJS.

DISC: Jep. Kink. RustJR.

GOINES, LEONARD. College professor (b. 22 April 1934 in Jacksonville, Florida). He obtained his musical education from the Manhattan School of Music (B. Mus., 1955; M. Mus, 1956) and Columbia University Teachers College (M.A., 1960; professional diploma, 1961; D. Mus. Ed., 1963). He studied also at the Fontainebleau School of Music in France (1959). His teaching career included tenures at Howard University in Washington, D.C.; Morgan State University in Baltimore, Maryland; and Queens College, York College, and Manhattan Community College of the City University of New York. He was also a lecturer at New York University. He began playing jazz trumpet with various groups at an early age. He was active also as a performer in the Symphony of the New World (1965-77), in studio and Broadway theater orchestras, and with his Leonard Goines Quintet. He contributed articles to professional journals and dictionaries; he also was a jazz consultant for various professional organizations and institutions, including the Smithsonian Institution in Washington, D.C.

BIBL: WWBA.

GOLDEN GATE QUARTETS. (Est. 1890s; fl. into 1960s). Over the years several quartets have used this name. Possibly the earliest was the group organized in Baltimore, Maryland, in 1892 by Arthur ("Dovey") Coates, Sherman Coates, Frank Sutton, and Henry Winfred. They obtained their first professional engagement through Billy McClain,* who hired them to sing with Whallen and Martell's South Before the War Company. Thereafter the group sang in the show *Black America*, staged outdoors in 1895 in Brooklyn, New York, and Boston, Massachusetts. In 1896 the quartet appeared in Sam T. Jack's Creole Show company; in 1899 it sang with the Tom McIntosh*/Gussie Davis* touring company, A Hot Old Time in Dixie; and thereafter with George Walker*/Bert Williams* productions during the early twentieth century. Later the quartet toured on the vaudeville circuit. There was a Golden Gate Quartet during the 1930s, and bluesman Huddie ("Leadbelly") Ledbetter recorded with a quartet by that name in the 1940s. In the mid-1940s a Golden Gate Quartet composed of William Langford, Henry Owens, Willie Johnson, and Orlandus Wilson appeared in the films *Hit Parade of 1943* and *Hollywood Canteen* (1944). These men began singing together during their high-school years in Norfolk, Virginia. By the 1950s Wilson was the only original member remaining with the quartet; the others were Caleb Ginyard, Clyde Riddick, and Clyde Wright, with Glen Burgess as accompanist. Beginning in 1953 the quartet made annual worldwide tours; during the years 1957-59 the tours were sponsored by the United States Department of State. By the 1970s the Golden Gate Quartet was touring widely throughout the world and included two members of the 1940s group, Riddick and Wilson. The repertory of the quartet changed with the times. In the 1930s the men sang spirituals and jubilee songs; in the 1970s the group was a gospel quartet but included popular music on its programs. Golden Gate Quartets were counted among the leading groups of the various historical periods, from the 1890s to the present.

BIBL: Black press, incl. *The Afro-American*, 17 July 1965; CDef, 30 January 1943; IndF, 3 October 1896, 11 February 1899; NYAge, 21 March 1959. Flet, 91.

DISC: *Folk Music in America*, v. 15 (Library of Congress Music Division).

GOLSON, BENNY. Jazz composer/Arranger (b. 25 January 1929 in Philadelphia, Pennsylvania). He began piano study when he was nine years old, then changed to saxophone when he was thirteen. He obtained his musical education in the public schools of Philadelphia, Pennsylvania, and at Howard University in Washington, D.C. Later he studied composition with Henry Brant and Earle Hagen. During the 1950s he played saxophone with various groups, including Benjamin ("Bull Moose") Jackson (1951), Tadd Dameron* (1953), Lionel Hampton* (1953), Johnny Hodges* (1954), Earl Bostic* (1954-56), John Birks ("Dizzy") Gillespie* (1956-58), and Art Blakey* (1958-59), among others. He then organized his own group and later was a co-leader with Arthur ("Art") Farmer* of the Jazztet (1959-62). Beginning in 1963 he gave increasing attention to writing and arranging music. In 1967 he moved to Los Angeles, California, where his first experience in writing film music came with *The Devil's Brigade*. Thereafter he wrote steadily for films and television. His full-length film scores included *Where It's At* (1969); his television music, either themes or scores, included "It Takes a Thief," "Run for Your Life," "Mission: Impossible," "Ironside," "Mannix," and "M*A*S*H," among other shows. He continued to write music for entertainers and jazzmen, such as Dizzy Gillespie, Miles Davis,* Ella Fitzgerald,* Sammy Davis, Jr.,* Peggy Lee, Lou Rawls,* and Nancy Wilson,* among others. He also recorded regularly and performed occasionally. His best-known songs included "Whisper not," "I remember Clifford," and "Stablemates."

BIBL: ASCAP. BMI (January 1971). FeaEJ. FeaJS. FeaGitJS. MeeJMov.

DISC: Jep.

GONZALEZ, BABS (née **LEE BROWN**). Jazz singer (b. 27 October 1919 in Newark, New Jersey; d. 23 January 1980 in Newark). He began piano study at the age of seven. He obtained his education in the public schools of Newark, New Jersey. He played with local groups at an early age and began performing professionally with a group led by Pancho Diggs during his high-school years. After graduation, he lived in Los Angeles, California, for a year or more, then settled in New York late in 1944. Thereafter he combined musical activities with other kinds of employment. In 1946 he organized his own group, called Babs's Three Bips and a Bop, with Tadd Dameron.* Later he was associated with James Moody. He was active not only as a group leader but also as a disc jockey, musical director, and soloist. Those who sang with his group included Melba Moorman, who later became celebrated as entertainer Melba Moore.* He toured widely in the United States and in Europe and settled permanently in Sweden during the 1970s, returning home only a few months before his death. He was one of the first bebop singers and is credited with having invented some bebop vocabulary. His special word was "expubidence," which referred to the joy of life. He also wrote songs, of which the best known were "Oo-pa-pa-da" and "Moody's mood for love." He published two books, *I Paid My Dues* and *Movin' on Down de Line*.

BIBL: Black press, incl. AmstN, 7 March 1964. FeaEJ.FeaGitJS. *The News American* [Baltimore], 27 January 1980.

GORDON, DEXTER KEITH. Jazz saxophonist (b. 27 February 1923 in Los Angeles, California). He obtained his musical education in the public schools of Los Angeles, California. He began clarinet study at the age of thirteen, then changed to alto saxophone when he was fifteen. His early style development was influenced by his teachers John Sturdevant and Lloyd Reese, a member of the Les Hite orchestra. He switched to tenor saxophone when he was seventeen, inspired by the playing of Lester Young.* He began his professional career playing with a local group, the Harlem Collegians, then joined Lionel Hampton* (1940-43). Thereafter he played with various groups, including Louis Armstrong* (briefly in 1944), William ("Billy") Eckstine* (1944-45), Charlie Parker,* Tadd Dameron,* and Wardell Gray (1947, 1950), among others. He also led his own groups on 52nd Street in New York and on the West Coast. In 1960 he composed music for Jack Gelber's play, *The Connection*, and also acted in the play. During the years 1960-62 he lived in Los Angeles, then in 1962 settled in Copenhagen, Denmark. Thereafter he toured widely in Europe and in the Orient (1975), was active in radio and television music, and gave time to writing music and teaching. He made his recording debut in 1947 and thereafter recorded extensively in the United States and abroad. Periodically he returned to the United States to give concerts and to perform in nightclubs and at festivals. In 1978 his American quartet included George Cables, Eddie Gladden, and Rufus Reid. Gordon was a pioneer tenor saxophonist of the bop era, the first to define bop style for his instrument and a transition between Lester Young and such saxophonists of the 1950s as Theodore

(''Sonny'') Rollins* and John Coltrane.* He moved into contemporary jazz gracefully and remained an important figure of his time. He won awards from the music industry.

BIBL: Black press, incl. AmstN, 6 November 1976. BMI (March 1971). *Dawn Magazine* (August 1978). FeaEJ. FeaJS. FeaGitJS. WWA.

DISC: Jep. Kink. ModJ. TudJ.

GORDON, JOSEPH. Brass-bandsman (b. c1815 in Philadelphia (?); fl. mid-nineteenth century in Philadelphia, Pennsylvania). See **JOHNSON, FRANK.**

BIBL: PaHistSoc, Box 1G. *The Colored American* [New York], 23 January 1841; *Daily Chronicle* [Philadelphia], 23 March 1841.

GORDON, ODETTA (née **ODETTA HOLMES;** also known as **ODETTA FELIOUS GORDON).** Folksinger (b. 31 December 1930 in Birmingham, Alabama). Her family moved to Los Angeles, California, when she was seven years old. She obtained her musical education in the public schools of Los Angeles, where she sang in glee clubs and first studied voice, and at Los Angeles City College, where she majored in music. Her first professional experience was as a member of the chorus in a local production of *Finian's Rainbow* (1949). Soon thereafter she became interested in folk music, taught herself to play guitar, and began performing in nightclubs in Los Angeles and San Francisco, California. Her career development was encouraged by Harry Belafonte.* She toured widely throughout the world, appearing on five continents in theaters, nightclubs, concert halls, on television and radio programs, at folk festivals, on college campuses, and in films, including *Cinerama Holiday* (1955) and *Sanctuary* (1960), among others. Her historic tour in the Soviet Union and Eastern Europe in 1974 attracted wide attention for the novelty of a woman performing alone, using only a guitar for accompaniment. She made her recording debut in 1956 and thereafter recorded regularly. Her repertory included folksongs of all types, from spirituals and blues to children's play songs. Her honors included awards from the music industry and a Key to the City from Birmingham (1965).

BIBL: BWW. FeaEJ. FeaJS. MeeJMov. StamFCW.

DISC: TudBM.

GORDON, TAYLOR. Concert singer (b. 29 April 1893 in White Sulphur Springs, Montana; d. 5 May 1971 in White Sulphur Springs). See also **JOHNSON, JOHN ROSAMOND.** He began his career as a vaudeville entertainer, touring on the B.F. Keith circuit during the years 1919-22. He had a short career as a concert tenor, beginning in 1922 when he teamed with J. Rosamond Johnson* to sing concerts of spirituals. In addition to his concert work with Johnson, he also sang with Johnson's vaudeville act called ''The Inimitable Five'' (1925-27). Thereafter he was active primarily in private entertainment and in small parts in Broadway musicals until 1947, after which he left the field of music. He is remembered primarily for his autobiography, *Born to Be* (1929; reprint, Seattle, Washington, 1975, with introduction by Robert Hemenway).

BIBL: WWCA 1940.

GORDY, BERRY, JR. Promoter/Record producer (b. 28 November 1929 in Detroit, Michigan). He obtained his musical education in the public schools of Detroit, Michigan, and began songwriting at an early age. During the early 1950s he gave increasing attention to writing songs, went to New York to develop the necessary contacts, and produced a number of successful rhythm 'n' blues songs. His first music-business experience was as the proprietor of a record shop in Detroit (1953-55). He continued to write songs, often in collaboration with his sister Gwendolyn and Tyron Carlo. In 1959 he formed his own record-producing company, calling it Motown Records (after Detroit's nickname, the ''Motor Town'') with the Tamla label (originally Tammy). His first releases of recordings by William (''Smokey'') Robinson and the Miracles* were widely successful. During the next few years Gordy promoted unknowns and won enormous success with his recordings; those whose records he produced included Diana Ross* and The Supremes,* Martha Reeves and the Vandellas, Marvin Gaye,* The Temptations,* The Four Tops,* Gladys Knight and the Pips,* The Jackson Five,* and Stevie Wonder,* among many others. Eventually the Motown entertainment complex comprised a publishing arm (Jabete), a management company, and the recording studios. At first Motown centered on rhythm 'n' blues, then moved into the field of popular music, particularly with The Supremes. Among the songwriters who contributed to ''the Motown Sound'' were a team called H-D-H* (i.e., Brian Holland, Eddie Holland, and Lamont Dozier), Norman Whitfield, and Barrett Strong. Motown artists were coached not only in singing but also in choreography, developing stage presence, attire and the like. In 1970 Gordy moved his company, Motown Industries, to Hollywood, California. Thereafter he added film directing and producing to his activities; the best-known of his films were *Lady Sings the Blues* (1972), *Mahogony* (1975), and *The Bingo Long Traveling All-Stars and Motor Kings* (1976). Gordy is credited with having moved almost single-handedly so-called race music (i.e., rhythm 'n' blues) into the mainstream of American popular music. His development of "the Motown Sound" forced the music industry to abandon its longtime practice of publishing separate charts for rhythm 'n' blues best-selling records (called "race records" in earlier times) and to mesh all best-selling records into one list of the top recordings.

BIBL: BMI (February 1971). CurBiog (July 1975). NYT, 7 July 1974. ShawWS. StamPRS. WWA. WWBA.

GOSPEL CHIMES, THE. See **CLEVELAND, JAMES.**

GOSPEL HARMONETTES, THE. See **COATES, DOROTHY.**

GOSSETTE, WALTER. Church organist (b. 18 September 1879 in Steubenville, Ohio; d. 6 September 1965 in Chicago, Illinois). He received his musical education in the public schools of Steubenville, Ohio, and through private study. Later he studied with Van Cuert in Cincinnati, Ohio, and at the Wisconsin Conservatory of Music in Milwaukee. His first professional experience was as a pianist with the Ormes Orchestra in East Liverpool, Ohio (1899). In 1902 he went to Cincinnati, where he was active as a church organist. During the years 1906-1908 he toured as accompanist with the American Jubilee Singers and later with William H. Hahn's Jubilee Singers (1908-1912), which included Noble Sissle* in 1911. Gossette went to Evanston, Illinois, in 1912, where he was a church organist, then settled in Chicago, Illinois, in 1914. Thereafter he was active as a church organist and choir director, as accompanist for local groups and performers, and he conducted a music studio. He also played for community groups and for the Chicago Sunday Evening Club, which met at Orchestra Hall. He was among the first black organists to pass the examination of the American Guild of Organists for admission to the rank of associate.

BIBL: ChiVH. Information from Oland Gaston.* Black press.

GRAHAM, GLADYS. Music critic (b. c1913; d. 30 July 1976 in New York, New York). She worked for the Negro Associated Press and the African Press for many years; her syndicated column, "Graham Crackers," was published in black newspapers all over the world. At the time of her death she was a member of the Board of the Music Critics Association. Her honors included the Ophelia Devore Award and a decoration from President Tubman of Liberia, Africa.

BIBL: Black press, incl. AmstN, 7 August 1976.

GRAHAM DU BOIS, SHIRLEY. Writer (b. 11 November 1906 in Indianapolis, Indiana; d. 27 March 1977 in Peking, China). Although best known as a writer, she was a musician in her early career. Little is known of her early musical training. When her father went to Liberia in 1929 to head a mission school there, she went to Paris, France, where she studied music at the Sorbonne. Later she attended Oberlin College (B.A., 1934; M.A., 1935). Her teaching career included tenures at Morgan State College in Baltimore, Maryland (1929-31), and Tennessee A & I State College in Nashville (1935-36). During her study at Oberlin she wrote the opera *Tom Tom* (1932), which was produced the next year by the Cleveland [Ohio] Opera Company with Jules Bledsoe* and Charlotte Murray in the leading roles. She became supervisor of the Negro Unit of the Chicago Federal Theater in 1936, and during her two-year tenure she contributed her own works to the program: in 1937 she composed a children's opera, *Little Black Sambo*, using a libretto based on the story by Helen Bannerman; in 1938 she produced *The Swing Mikado*, based on the Gilbert and Sullivan operetta. She received a Julius Rosenwald Fellowship in creative writing for the years 1938-40 and thereafter centered her attention on a career in writing, except that she wrote incidental music for two plays produced at Yale University by Owen Dodson, *Garden of Time* (1939) and *Divine Comedy* (1940). She was the second wife of W. E. B. Du Bois.

BIBL: *The Crisis* (May 1977). CurBiog (October 1946). WilABW. WWA. WWAW. WWCA, 1950.

GRANT, EARL THOMAS. Popular-music organist/Singer (b. 20 January 1931 in Idabelle, Oklahoma; d. 10 June 1970 in Lordsburg, New Mexico). He came from a musical family: both parents sang in church choirs. His family moved to Kansas City, Missouri, when he was a child. He played piano and organ in church at an early age. He received his musical education in the public schools of Kansas City and attended the Kansas City Conservatory of Music and the University of Southern California at Los Angeles. He made his recording debut in 1958 and soon established himself as one of the leading popular-music organists of the 1960s. He toured widely (sometimes as a singer also) in the United States, Europe, Japan, and Australia, appearing in nightclubs, theaters, on television shows, and in films, among them *Tender is the Night, Imitation of Life,* and *Tokyo Night*. His best-known performances were of "The end" and "Ebbtide."

BIBL: Black press, incl. NYAge, 2 January 1960. NYT, 11 June 1970. *Sepia* (December 1963). StamPRS.

GRANT, MICKI (née **MINNIE PERKINS**). Composer of stage music (b. 30 June 1941 in Chicago, Illinois). She was both dramatist and musician; the present entry centers on her musical career. She first studied music in elementary school with a teacher who gave her free lessons on the double bass. She also studied violin and piano as a child. She obtained her education in the public schools of Chicago, Illinois; at the Chicago School of Music; and at the University of Illinois in Urbana. She played in school orchestras through her school and college years. She left college during her senior year to tour (singing soprano) with the show *Fly Blackbird*, which took her to New York in 1962. Thereafter she performed in stage works, including Langston Hughes's gospel-play *Tambourines to Glory* (1963); was active in television, particularly as Peggy Nolan in the NBC soap opera, "Another World"; and in 1970 became an artist-in-residence with the Urban Arts Corps, founded in 1967 by Vinette Carroll. In 1971 Grant and Carroll collaborated in writing *Don't Bother Me, I Can't Cope*, Grant serving as composer-lyricist and also acting in the production. Thereafter Grant gave full time to writing musicals, of which the best known were *The Prodigal Sister* and *Your Arm's Too Short to Box with God*. She also continued to write songs. She received numerous awards from the music and theater industries.

BIBL: AbdulFBE. BMI (November 1971; Issue No. 5, 1972; Issue No. 4, 1977). *Ebony* (February 1973). NYT, 7 May 1972. WilABW. WWBA.

GREEN, AL. Rhythm 'n' blues singer (b. 13 April 1946 in Forrest City, Arkansas). His family moved to Grand Rapids, Michigan, when he was a child. He obtained his musical education in the public schools of that city. When he was nine years old, he and his brothers formed a gospel quartet that sang in local churches. During his high-school years he organized a rhythm 'n' blues group, Al Green and the Creations, which toured in the South and Midwest. He made his recording debut in 1967 but met only moderate success until he teamed with bandleader Willie Mitchell in Memphis, Tennessee, who helped him find his musical identity. Green became one of the most popular entertainers of the 1970s. He toured widely in the United States and Europe, singing in concert halls, nightclubs, theaters, on television programs, and in prisons; he recorded extensively; and he won numerous awards from the music industry. Eventually he organized his own management-distribution company at Memphis, Al Green Enterprises, which also published his songs. His style development was influenced by the singing of James Brown,* Sam Cooke,* and Jackie Wilson.* He was regarded as a highly individual, even eccentric, soul singer with gospel roots. His best-known performances included "Let's stay together," "How do you mend a broken heart," and "Tired of being alone."

BIBL: Black press, incl. AmstN, 27 October 1973. *Ebony* (November 1973, October 1976). *Sepia* (April 1975). NYT, 15 April 1973.

DISC: Giv. TudBM.

GREENE, JOHN. Concert singer (b. 1901 in Columbus, Georgia; d. 1960s in Los Angeles, California). He acquired his musical education in the public schools of Birmingham, Alabama. He settled in Chicago, Illinois, in the 1920s; he studied at the Cosmopolitan School of Music and privately with T. Theodore Taylor* and George Garner.* He first attracted wide attention in 1931 when he placed first in a Kraft Music Hall competition and won the opportunity to sing on Kraft radio programs on station WMAQ. He won Julius Rosenwald fellowships in 1933 and 1934, which permitted him to study voice further. He was active in Chicago's musical circles and toured widely as a bass-baritone for the National Cash Register Company. During the 1950s he settled in Los Angeles, California.

BIBL: ChiVH. Communication from Florence Cadrez Brantley. Black press, incl. CDef, 14 March 1931, 22 August 1931.

GREENFIELD, ELIZABETH TAYLOR (also known as **THE BLACK SWAN**). Concert singer (b. c1824 in Natchez, Mississippi; d. 31 March 1876 in Philadelphia, Pennsylvania). Born a slave in Mississippi, she was taken to Philadelphia, Pennsylvania, as an infant by her mistress, Elizabeth H. Greenfield, who joined the Society of Friends and manumitted the infant and her parents. She early revealed musical talent and taught herself to play guitar. She studied voice briefly with a local amateur, Miss Price. Her efforts to study further in Philadelphia were unsuccessful, but she nevertheless began to sing in local concerts and in nearby cities. In 1851 she settled in Buffalo, New York, where she found encouragement to develop her talent and a sponsor, the Buffalo Musical Association, for her debut concert as a soprano in October 1851. The Buffalo *Commercial Advertiser* gave her the sobriquet "The Black Swan" after the concert. During the next two years she toured extensively under the management of impresario Colonel J. H. Wood. In 1853 she went to London, England, to study further and acquired the patronage of writer Harriet Beecher Stowe and the Duchess of Sutherland. She studied music with George Smart, organist and composer for Queen Victoria's Chapel Royal. During her stay in England she sang on a number of concerts, including a command performance for the Queen. She returned to the United States in the summer of 1854 and entered into a full career of concertizing and teaching that lasted over two decades. During one period in the 1850s she toured with Thomas Bowers.* She contributed much to the musical life of black Philadelphians and at one time directed an Opera Troupe, which staged programs during the 1860s. She was the first Afro-American concert singer to win acclaim on both sides of the Atlantic.

BIBL: PaHistSoc, Boxes IG, 13G. HNB. Arthur LaBrew, *The Black Swan* (Detroit, 1969). Trot.

GREER, WILLIAM ALEXANDER ("SONNY"). Jazz drummer (b. 13 December 1903 in Long Branch, New Jersey). He obtained his musical education in public schools of Long Branch, New Jersey, where he began playing drums during his high-school years. He first played professionally with local groups, including Wilbur Gardner, Mabel Ross, and Harry Yerek. He then played in Washington, D.C., with Marie Lucas* at the Howard Theatre. In 1919 he met Edward (''Duke'') Ellington,* joined Ellington's band in 1920, and remained with him thirty-one years (1920-1951, with some leaves of absence). Thereafter he played with various groups, including Johnny Hodges* (1951), Henry (''Red'') Allen* (1952-53), Tyree Glenn* (1959), J. C. Higginbotham* (1960s), and Brooks Kerr (1974). He also led his own groups from time to time, recorded with others and under his own name, and appeared in films, among them, *Check and Double Check* (1930), *Cabin in the Sky* (1942), and *The Night They Raided Minsky's* (1968). Although he played solos infrequently in the Ellington band, he contributed a great deal to its unique sound; he surrounded himself with an enormous array of percussions, which he used for novel effects.

BIBL: ChilWW. Duke Ellington, *Music Is My Mistress* (New York, 1973). FeaJS. FeaGitJS. FeaEJ. MeeJMov.

DISC: Jep. Kink. RustJR.

GRIFFIN, BESSIE (née **ARLETTE B. BROIL).** Gospel singer (b. 1927 in New Orleans, Louisiana). As a child she sang in church choirs. Her early style development was influenced by Mahalia Jackson,* to whose recordings she listened, and throughout her career her voice was compared to Mahalia's. Her first professional experience was with the Southern Harps Spiritual Singers (c1941-51), a female gospel quartet, which also included Alberta Johnson and (''Baby Helen'') Linda Hopkins.* In 1951 Griffin attracted wide attention when she sang on the occasion of Mahalia's Twenty-Fifth Anniversary celebration of her gospel-career beginning, held at the Coliseum in Chicago, Illinois. In 1953 she joined a Chicago group, The Caravans,* and remained with them about a year. She then toured with W. Herbert Brewster,* Jr. (1955-56), and after leaving Brewster resettled at New Orleans, where she was active as both singer and disc jockey. In 1959 she played the leading role in *Portraits in Bronze*, a show produced by Robert (''Bumps'') Blackwell at the Cabaret Concert Theatre and credited with being the first gospel musical in history. The show also produced another first—the first time gospel was performed in nightclubs and coffee houses, thus taken out of the church into the secular world. Griffin's success led to appearances on television shows and increased concert engagements, including a residency at Disneyland in Annaheim, California. She toured with her Gospel Pearls, a quintet which included Blackwell (drums) and Eddie Lee Kendrix (piano). She was credited with being the first gospel singer to take gospel into nightclubs and theaters. She sang in the pop-gospel tradition. Her best-known performance included ''The day is past and gone,'' ''It's real,'' ''He lives,'' and ''Come ye disconsolate.'' She was called ''Queen of the South'' and ''Thunderbolt of New Orleans.''

BIBL: BPIM 7 (Spring 1979). Heil. *Sepia* (March 1960).

DISC: TudBM.

GRIFFIN, JOHN ARNOLD. Jazz saxophonist (b. 24 April 1928 in Chicago, Illinois). He came from a musical family: his father played cornet, and his mother was a singer. He obtained his musical education in the public schools of Chicago, Illinois, where he came under the tutelage of Walter Dyett* at DuSable High School and studied woodwinds and saxophone. After graduation from high school he joined Lionel Hampton's* band as a tenor saxophonist (1945-47). Thereafter he played with various groups, including Joe Morris as co-leader of a sextet (1947-50) and Arnett Cobb* (1951). He served in the United States Armed Forces for two years, then returned to Chicago. Thereafter he played with Art Blakey's* Jazz Messengers (1957), Thelonious Monk* (1958), and Eddie (''Lockjaw'') Davis* (1960-62), among others. In May 1963 he settled in Paris, France, where he later worked with such jazzmen as Kenneth (''Kenny'') Drew,* Art Taylor, and Earl (''Bud'') Powell.* He toured widely with his own groups, recorded extensively, and appeared at the major festivals and on radio and television programs. Frequently he was a soloist with the Kenneth (''Kenny'') Clarke*/Francy Boland Big Band. In 1978 he returned to the United States after a fifteen-year absence to play a series of concerts, including performance at the Monterey Jazz Festival and a duo-concert with the Dexter Gordon Quintet. Griffin was a leading representative of hard-bop saxophone style.

BIBL: Black press, incl. AmstN, 9 September 1978. FeaEJ. FeaJS. FeaGitJS. MeeJMov.

DISC: Jep. ModJ.

GRIFFIN SISTERS, THE. Vaudeville act (b. in Louisville, Kentucky; fl. early twentieth century). Emma and Mabel entered the professional field during the mid-1890s as members of John Isham's Octoroons Company. Later they toured with the Al Reeves Company. In 1913 they organized their own musical comedy company, then later entered vaudeville careers. The sister act was broken up in 1918 with the death of Emma (b. c1873; d. 28 August 1918).

BIBL: Black press, incl.CDef, 16 August 1913, 7 September 1918.

GRIST, RERI. Opera singer (b. c1932 in New York, New York). She obtained her musical education in the public schools of New York, where she attended the High School of Music and Art, and at Queens College of the City University of New York (B.A.). She studied voice with Claire Gelda. As a child she danced in Broadway musicals, and her early professional experience was acquired in musicals, including *Carmen Jones* (1956), *Shinbone Alley* (1957), and *West Side Story* (1957). In 1959 she made her operatic debut (soprano) as Blondchen in Mozart's *The Abduction of the Seraglio* with the Santa Fe Opera Company in New Mexico and made her debut with the New York City Opera. She toured widely in Europe thereafter, singing with various opera companies; she was a member of the Zurich [Switzerland] Opera for three years. In 1966 she made her Metropolitan Opera debut singing the role of Rosina in Rossini's *The Barber of Seville*. She was best known for her performances of the Queen of the Night in Mozart's *Magic Flute*, Zerbinetta in Strauss's *Ariadne auf Naxos*, Olympia in Offenbach's *The Tales of Hoffman*, and Norma in Donizetti's *Don Pasquale*. Her honors included Blanche Thebom and Marian Anderson* Awards.

BIBL: Black press, incl. NYAge, 24 January 1959. Ewen. WWBA. WWOpera.

DISC: Turn.

GUTIÉRREZ Y ESPINOSA, FELIPE. Choirmaster/Composer (b. 26 May 1825 in San Juan, Puerto Rico; d. 27 November 1899 in San Juan). He first studied music with his father, Julián Gutiérrez, then later with José Alvarez, both of whom were musicians in the Regimiento Granada. He learned to play all the band instruments by the time he was twenty years old and began his professional career as Principal Musician in the Regimiento Iberia. In 1858 he became chapel master of the San Juan Cathedral and remained in the position forty years (1858-98). He was also a music teacher and served as head of the music academy in San Juan during the years 1871-74. In 1876 he was sent by the government to study in Europe. He was the first Puerto Rican composer to write an opera, and he wrote in a variety of other musical forms. His first opera was *La palma del Cacique* (1856); the other four included *El Bearnés* (libretto by D. Antonio Biaggi) and *Guarionex* (libretto by Alejandro Tapia y Rivera). He wrote no fewer than seventeen Masses and a number of Mass sections (for both the Proper and the Ordinary); several dances for orchestra, including *La Manganilla* and *Aire de Fandango*; other works for orchestra, including *El Pasto de los Montes* and *Tonidón*; *Sonadina de violín* (with piano or orchestra); and a half dozen or more compositions for chorus and orchestra, including *Las Siete Palabras*. His *Tota Pulchra* for chorus and orchestra calls for a saxophone, the first use of that instrument in Puerto Rican composition. His opera *Macías* (libretto by Martin Travieso, based on a novel of the same title [1834] by Mariano José de Larra) received its premiere performance on 19 August 1877 in San Juan.

BIBL: Information from Dominique-René de Lerma. Robert Stevenson, ''Music in the San Juan, Puerto Rico, Cathedral to 1900'' in *Revista/Review Interamericana* 8 (Winter 1978-79).

GUY, GEORGE (''BUDDY''). Bluesman (b. 30 July 1936 in Lettsworth, Louisiana). He taught himself to play guitar, but did not play professionally until he settled in Chicago in 1957. There he was influenced by (''B. B.'') Riley King,* Jimmy Reed,* Aaron (''T-Bone'') Walker,* ''Muddy Waters'' (née McKinley Morganfield),* and ''Howlin' Wolf'' (née Chester Burnett),* among others. His performance in a blues contest in 1958 brought him much attention and a recording contract. Thereafter he toured widely in the United States, in Europe, and in Africa, appearing at the major blues festivals as well as on college campuses, in concert halls, and in clubs. He recorded extensively, frequently with Otis Rush* and Junior Wells,* among others. His showmanship, based on guitar tricks he had learned in the South, along with his virtuosity contributed to his popularity. He was representative of the younger generation of Chicago bluesmen who developed a distinctive urban blues style during the 1950s.

BIBL: BWW. LivBl 2 (Summer 1970). MeeJMov. Robert Neff and Anthony Connor, *Blues* (New York, 1975). Oliv.

DISC: LeSlBR. TudBM.

GUY, HARRY P. Dance-orchestra pianist (b. c1873-75 in Zanesville, Ohio; d. 1950 in Detroit, Michigan [?]). He studied piano, violin, and organ in his youth. He moved to Cincinnati, Ohio, at an early age and later studied piano there with George Schneider. He was an accompanist for the Cincinnati Opera Club. In 1890 he went to New York, where he attended the National Conservatory of Music. During his stay in the city he entered into the musical life of the black community; he conducted a piano studio and performed in local concerts, including a Grand Star Concert at Carnegie Hall in 1890. In 1894 he accepted a teaching position at Paul Quinn College in Waco, Texas. About 1895 he returned North and settled permanently in Detroit, Michigan. He joined the [Theodore] Finney* Famous Orchestra and played in the Detroit City Band.

BIBL: Black press, incl. CleveG, 10 October 1894; NYAge, 8 February 1890, 1 March 1890, 18 October 1890. LaBrew.

H

H-D-H (HOLLAND-DOZIER-HOLLAND). Songwriting combine (org. in Detroit, Michigan, in late 1950s). The songwriting trio, Brian Holland, Lamont Dozier, and Edward Holland, all natives of Detroit, Michigan, were early employees of Berry Gordy's* Motown Records. Brian Holland (b. 15 February 1941) and Dozier (b. 16 June 1941) began writing songs for Gordy in 1959; Eddie Holland (b. 30 October 1939) became a collaborator in 1962. Until 1969 the trio were songwriters, arrangers, and producers at Motown; their songs were sung by Marvin Gaye,* the Marvelettes, Martha and the Vandellas, The Four Tops,* The Supremes,* The Temptations,* and The Miracles,* among others. H-D-H was credited with creating the "Detroit Sound" more than any other person or group and with moving Motown from its rhythm 'n' blues moorings into the more lucrative field of popular music. In 1969 H-D-H organized its own entertainment combine, Invictus Records and Gold Forever Music. The trio received numerous awards from the music industry.

BIBL: BMI (Issue No. 1, 1973). StamPRS.

HACKLEY, EMMA AZALIA SMITH. Concert singer (b. 29 June 1867 in Murfreesboro, Tennessee; d. 13 December 1922 in Detroit, Michigan). Her family moved to Detroit, Michigan, when she was three years old. She first studied piano with her mother, a music teacher; she also studied violin and voice as a child. During her high-school years she played piano with local dance orchestras. She became a member of the Detroit Musical Society and began appearing as a soprano soloist on local recitals at an early age. After marriage in 1894 she settled in Denver, Colorado, where she attended the University of Denver (B. Mus., 1900), taught music, and conducted community and church choral groups. She gave her debut recital at Denver in 1901 and thereafter toured in the Middle West giving recitals. In late 1901 she settled in Philadelphia, Pennsylvania, where she was appointed music director at the Episcopal Church of the Crucifixion. In 1904 she organized a People's Chorus of one hundred voices. She gave her Philadelphia debut recital in 1905, assisted by some of her protégés and students. She then went to Paris to study with Jean de Reszke for a year and returned to Philadelphia for a second major recital. Thereafter she began to neglect her own career to devote time to advancement of talented young black artists. In 1908 she established a scholarship fund to allow promising young musicians to study abroad, raising money through giving concerts and solicitation, and she began to sponsor musicians in debut recitals and place them in good college teaching positions. Among those whose careers she advanced were soprano Cleota Collins,* pianists R. Nathaniel Dett* and Carl Diton,* and violinists Harrison Emmanuel, Kemper Harreld,* and Clarence Cameron White.* About 1910 she began to tour the nation as a concert artist/lecturer, frequently talking about black folk music; she also began to publish articles in the black press about vocal techniques—a series in the *New York Age* (1914-15) was titled "Hints to Young Colored Artists." She settled in Chicago about 1910 and in 1911 gave her "retiring" concert at Orchestra Hall to critical acclaim. The next year she founded the Vocal Normal Institute (1912-16), but left the students in charge of other teachers, beginning in 1914, to travel about the country giving recitals to raise money for the Institute. Later she organized community concerts in the large cities of the nation, gathering together hundreds of voices for her community choruses, and aroused so much enthusiasm for singing Negro folksongs and so much respect for the importance of black folk materials that she earned the soubriquet "Our National Vocal Teacher." In 1920 she travelled to Japan to teach Negro folksongs at a Sunday school convention. Her tour of California the next year was interrupted when she had a fatal collapse.

BIBL: Black press, incl. CDef, 21 October 1911, 7 October 1916; IndF, 23 March 1901, 4 June 1914, 8 January 1916; NYAge, 31 December 1914, 23 December 1922. M. Marguerite Davenport, *The Life of Madame E. Azalia Hackley* (Boston, 1947). LaBrew. NAW.

HACKNEY, WILLIAM. Impresario (fl. early twentieth century in Chicago, Illinois). He is included here because of his role as a promoter of mammoth concerts at Orchestra Hall in Chicago, Illinois, which were given over to the music of black composers. He first attracted attention because of his annual recitals, beginning in 1911, at Institutional Church in Chicago. Although he rarely received good reviews, his assisting artists included young musicians who would later win recognition for their talents, among them, Kemper Harreld.* Hackney was also a regular soloist on the annual concerts of the Choral Study Club, directed by Pedro Tinsley,* for many years. Hackney was inspired to stage his Orchestra Hall concerts by the concerts sponsored by the Music School Settlement for Colored at Carnegie Hall in New York during the years 1912-15. In 1914 he produced the first of his All-Colored Composers' Concerts, advertising it as the "first colored composers' concert to be given in the North West." The artists, who performed the music of black composers, included pianist R. Nathaniel Dett,* soprano Anita Patti Brown,* baritone Ernest Amos, and tenor Hackney, himself. For the 1915 concert, Dett was again engaged, Helen Hagan* played her own piano concerto, Maude Roberts (George)* sang, as did Hackney again, and Will Marion Cook* was to have directed the Umbrian Glee Club of Washington, D.C., but failed to appear because of illness. The Third Annual All-Colored Composers' Concert in May 1916 was the final one, undoubtedly because of the nation's involvement with World War I the next year. Hackney settled in Galveston, Texas, during the early 1920s and became a public-school music teacher; by 1924 he had moved to Kansas City, Missouri.

BIBL: Black press, incl. CDef 8 April 1911, 6 June 1914, 17 April 1915, 3 June 1922, 2 February 1924; IndF, 1 May 1915, 3 June 1916.

HAGAN, HELEN EUGENIA. Concert pianist (b. January 1891 in Portsmouth, New Hampshire; d. 6 March 1964 in New York, New York). She came from a musical family; her mother was a pianist and her father sang baritone. She studied piano as a child with her mother. Her family moved to New Haven, Connecticut, in 1895, and there she obtained her musical education in the public schools and at Yale University (B. Mus., 1912), where she studied with Stanley Knight. She was awarded the Samuel Simmons Sanford Fellowship, which enabled her to study abroad for two years. In Paris, France, she studied with Blanche Selva and Vincent D'Indy, earning a diploma from the Schola Cantorum in 1914. Later she earned an M.A. degree from Columbia University Teachers' College in New York. During the years 1914-18 she toured widely in the United States as a concert pianist. In April 1915 she played her own *Piano Concerto in C minor* at the All-Colored Composers' Concert promoted by William Hackney* at Orchestra Hall in Chicago, Illinois. In 1918 she was invited by the YWCA (Young Women's Christian Association) to go to France to entertain black servicemen in a group that included singer Joshua Blanton* and the Rev. Hugh Henry Proctor,* who led folk sings in the camps. After returning to the United States in 1919, she settled at Chicago. She conducted a music studio in the Mendelssohn Conservatory of Music, the first of her race to teach music in Chicago's downtown district. In October 1921 she gave her New York debut at Aeolian Hall, the first black pianist to give a solo recital in a New York concert hall. Her performance brought critical acclaim and encouragement to continue concertizing. During the 1930s she entered college teaching, serving on the music faculties of Tennessee State A & M College (Agricultural & Mechanical) and Bishop College in Marshall, Texas, where she was dean of the school of music. In 1935 she settled at New York and established the Helen Hagan Music Studio. In addition to teaching and coaching professional singers, she was active in church music at the Grace Congregational Church and gave recitals as late as 1937.

BIBL: Black press, incl. CDef, 17 April 1915, 10 April 1920, 16 July 1921; NYAge, 6 March 1937, 17 September 1949, 14 March 1964. Hare. NYB.

HAILSTORK, ADOLPHUS CUNNINGHAM. Composer/College professor (b. 17 April 1941 in Albany, New York). He studied piano as a child. He obtained his musical education at Howard University in Washington, D.C. (B. Mus., 1963), where he studied with Mark Fax*; at the American Institute at Fontainebleau, France (summer 1963), where he studied with Nadia Boulanger; at the Manhattan School of Music in New York (B. Mus. in composition, 1965; M. Mus. in composition, 1966), where he studied with Ludmila Ulehla, Nicholas Flagello, Vittorio Giannini, and David Diamond; and at the Michigan State University in East Lansing (Ph.D., 1971). He also attended the Electronic Music Institution at Dartmouth College in New Hampshire (summer 1972), where he studied with Jon Appleton and H. Howe; and the Seminar on Contemporary Music (summer 1978) at the State University of New York at Buffalo. His career as a teacher included tenures at Michigan State University (1969-71), Youngstown State University in Ohio (1971-76), and Norfolk State University in Virginia (1976-). He began writing music at an early age; his musical, *The Race for Space*, was performed at Howard University during his senior year in college, and his orchestral work, *Statement, Variations and Fugue* (1966), was performed by the Baltimore [Maryland] Symphony three years later. In his teaching appointments he not only taught composition but also composed for student choral groups that he conducted. After service in the U.S. Armed Forces in Germany (1966-68), he returned to the United States. Thereafter he received commissions from various organizations and individuals, and his music was performed in the United States and abroad. He wrote in a variety of forms: symphonic works and tone poems for orchestra; a concerto; numerous chamber works; duos for such combinations as horn and piano, clarinet and piano, tuba and piano, flute and piano, and others; a large number of songs, including songs for soprano, baritone, mezzo-soprano, some with piano and others with orchestra or chamber group; band works and band transcriptions, and many pieces for piano. His best-known works were "Mourn Not the Dead" for mixed chorus (1969), *Bellevue* for orchestra (1974), *Celebration* for orchestra (1975), *Out of the Depths* for band (1974), *Bagatelles for Brass* (1974), "Spiritual" for brass ensemble (1976), *American Landscape No. 1* for band (1976), *Suite for Organ* (1968), *Sonatina for Flute and Piano* (1972), *Epitaph: For a Man Who Dreamed* for orchestra (1979), *The Pied Piper of Harlem* for unaccompanied flute (1980), and the two songs "A charm at parting" and "I loved you" (published in Willis Patterson's *Anthology of Art Songs by Black American Composers*). His honors included the Lucy E. Moten Travel Fellowship (1963), the Ernest Block Award for choral composition (co-winner, 1970-71), and the 1977 Belwin-Mills/Max Winkler Award for a band composition.

BIBL: Questionnaire.

HAIRSTON, JESTER. Choral conductor (b. 9 July 1901 in Homestead, Pennsylvania). Although best known as an actor, he was also a musician and is so discussed here. He obtained his musical education at Tufts University in Medford, Massachusetts (B.A., 1929) and at the Juilliard School of Music in New York. His first professional experience was in 1929 with the Eva Jessye* Choir. Later he became assistant conductor of the Hall Johnson* Choir (1930-36) and went with the choir to California in 1936 to make the film *The Green Pastures*. When the group returned East, he remained in Los Angeles, where he organized his own choir and became involved in musical activities. Soon thereafter he began touring in the United States and abroad as a choral conductor, workshop clinician, and lecturer. In 1930 he performed in the Broadway musical *Hello Paris*. During the years 1935-49 he arranged choral music for film soundtracks in more than forty films, beginning with *Lost Horizons* (1936) and including *Duel in the Sun* (1946); he also conducted his choir in singing background music for films. In 1945 he made his first tour in Europe with Noble Sissle* and a USO show. Thereafter the United States Department of State sent him abroad several times as a goodwill ambassador to conduct choruses and teach others American music—to Europe in 1961, 1963; three times to Africa in the mid-1960s; and to Scandinavia and Mexico in 1971. He wrote music in a variety of forms but was best known for his spiritual arrangements; he also made arrangements of African and Japanese folksongs. His honors included an honorary doctorate from the University of the Pacific (1964) and citations from civic and social organizations.

BIBL: Information from Marva Carter. ASCAP. *Black Stars* (October 1975).

HAKIM, TALIB RASUL (née **STEPHEN ALEXANDER CHAMBERS**). Composer (b. 8 February 1940 in Asheville, North Carolina). He studied clarinet as a child, and his brother Joseph became a professional jazz drummer. The family moved to Chester, Pennsylvania, when he was young. He sang in a church choir and on street corners with rhythm 'n' blues groups. He obtained his musical education in the public schools of Chester, at the Manhattan School of Music in New York (1958-59), the New York College of Music (1959-63), and the New School for Social Research in New York (1963-65), concentrating in composition, clarinet, and piano. Later he studied further at Adelphi University in Garden City, New York, and at the Mannes College of Music in New York. His teachers included Margaret Bonds,* Robert Starer, William Sydeman, Hall Overton, Chou Wen-Chung, and Ornette Coleman,* among others. During his high-school years he played in all the school's instrumental groups, from marching band to symphony orchestra, and performed with the All-State Orchestra of Pennsylvania. Although he was interested in jazz at an early age, he did not perform with local groups, as did his brother, but developed his interest through listening to music and studying scores. He began writing music in 1963, and his compositions were first performed and published in 1964. He attracted considerable attention during the years 1965-69, when his works were performed on the "Music in Our Time" concert series in New York, directed by Max Pollikoff. His early style development was influenced by the music of Miles Davis,* John Coltrane,* Mozart, and Debussy. During the 1970s he composed steadily, and his music was increasingly performed by university groups, chamber music groups, and symphony orchestras. He toured widely as a lecturer, appeared on radio and television programs, and for a period produced his own radio programs. He also began a teaching career, serving tenures at Pace College in New York (1970-72) and Nassau Community College of the State University of New York in Garden City (1972-). He was an adjunct professor at Adelphi College during the 1970s and a visiting professor at Morgan State University in Baltimore, Maryland, during the academic year 1978-79. His honors included fellowships from the Bennington Composers Conference (1964-69), composer awards from ASCAP (American Society of Authors, Composers and Publishers 1967-73), and grants from the National Endowment for the Arts (1973) and the Creative Artist Public Service Program (1972).

His music employed avant-garde techniques and elements, particularly in its use of unorthodox instruments and unorthodox performance on traditional instruments. He avoided electronic music elements and chance music, but employed "controlled improvisation" in some compositions. Critics found his music to be arresting in its variety, sensitive, and warm. His best-known works were "Sound Gone" for piano (1967), *Placements* for five percussions and piano (1970), *Visions of Ishwara* (1970), *Shapes* for chamber orchestra (1965), and *Recurrences* for orchestra (1977).

BIBL: BakBCS. Eileen Southern, "America's Black Composers of Classical Music" in *Music Educators Journal* (November 1975). WWEast.

HALL, ADELAIDE. Jazz singer (b. 20 October 1910 in New York, New York). Her father was a school music teacher. She began her professional career as a singer (soprano) in the Eubie Blake*/Noble Sissle* musical *Shuffle Along* (1921). During the 1920s-30s she performed in several shows, among them, *Runnin' Wild* (1923), *Chocolate Kiddies* (1925, including the tour in Europe), *Desires of 1927, Blackbirds of 1928* (in which she took over the role of the late Florence Mills*), and *Brown Buddies* (1930). She also performed during these years with Edward ("Duke") Ellington* at the Cotton Club in Harlem, the Mills Blue Rhythm Band,* and other orchestras and as a soloist with such accompanists as Arthur ("Art") Tatum* and Joe Turner.* In 1936 she went to Europe, where she lived first in Paris, France, then settled in London, England, in 1938. She and her husband operated nightclubs in both cities. She sang in nightclubs and on radio programs and was active in film and stage shows, including *The Sun Never Sets* (1938) and *Kiss Me Kate* (1951). Among those who performed in her clubs and/or accompanied her were Thomas ("Fats") Waller,* Bennie Payne,* and Fela Sowande,* among others. In 1957 she returned to the United States to perform in the Broadway musical *Jamaica*. She attracted wide attention in the 1920s with her wordless singing with the Ellington orchestra, particularly in the "Creole love call" (1927).

BIBL: ChilWW. FeaEJ. FeaJS. FeaGitJS. MeeJMov.
DISC: Kink. RustCED.

HALL, EDMOND. Jazz clarinetist (b. 15 May 1901 in New Orleans, Louisiana; d. 11 February 1967 in Boston, Massachusetts). He came from a musical family: his father, Edward, played cornet in the Onward Brass Band, and three brothers—Herbert, Robert, and Clarence—became professional musicians. Self-taught, he first played guitar, then changed to clarinet. From the 1920s through the mid-1940s he played with various groups, including Buddie Petit (née Joseph Crawford, 1921-23), Alonzo Ross and his Deluxe Syncopators (1926-28), Claude Hopkins* (1930-35), Lucius ("Lucky") Millinder* (1936, 1937), Henry ("Red") Allen* (1940-41),and Theodore ("Teddy") Wilson,* among others. Thereafter he led his own sextet for long periods, then joined Louis Armstrong's* All Stars (1955-58). In 1959 he went to Ghana with the intent of settling there but returned after a few months to the United States in December 1959. He recorded extensively from the 1930s on with his groups and with other groups. He also appeared in films, including *High Society* (1956) and *Satchmo the Great* (1956). During the 1960s he toured widely in Europe and Japan with groups and as a soloist and appeared at major jazz festivals at home and abroad. He was a pioneer jazz clarinetist of the New Orleans school and highly regarded for his individualistic tone quality.

BIBL: ASCAP. ChilWW. FeaEJ. FeaJS. FeaGit. MeeJMov. Souch.

DISC: Jep. Kink. RustJR. TudJ.

HALL, FREDERICK DOUGLASS. College professor (b. 14 December 1898 in Atlanta, Georgia). He began piano study at the age of five with his mother, a music teacher. He obtained his musical education in the public schools of Atlanta, Georgia; at Morehouse College in Atlanta (B.A., 1921), where he studied with Kemper Harreld*; Chicago [Illinois] Musical College (B. Mus., 1924); and Columbia University Teachers College (M.A.,1929; D. Ed. Mus., 1952). He studied further in London, England (1933-35), at the Royal Academy of Music, where he earned the Licentiate degree, and at London University. His teaching career included tenures at Jackson College in Jackson, Mississippi (1921-27), where he served also as supervisor of music for the public schools; at Dillard University in New Orleans, Louisiana (1936-41, 1960-74); at Alabama State College in Montgomery (1941-55); and at Southern University in Baton Rouge, Louisiana (1955-59). He was a boy soprano as a child and sang in church choirs. During his high-school years he played various instruments with school groups and also professionally with the Atlanta Theatre Orchestra. He began writing music at an early age, and his pieces were performed on public concerts during his school years. He became a prolific composer of choral music, particularly arrangements of spirituals, which were widely sung by university groups especially. He also wrote music for piano, arrangements of African songs, and alma-mater hymns for both Jackson College and Dillard. During his two-year stay in the British Isles (1933-35), he toured in England, Scotland, and Wales, studying the folk music of the countries. Later he spent six months in West Africa studying its folk music. In the United States he toured widely as a lecturer, choral workshop consultant, and guest choral conductor. His honors included a Julius Rosenwald Fellowship, General Education Board Fellowship, Phelps-Stokes Fund Research Grant, and citations from educational, professional, civic, and government organizations and institutions, including a testimonial read into the Congressional Record of the United States by representative Augustus Hawkins on 30 April 1964.

BIBL: BPIM (Fall 1980). NYB, 1952. WWCA, 1950.

HALL, IAN. Conductor/Composer (b. 18 January 1940 in Georgetown, Guyana). He went to London, England, when he was thirteen years old and there completed his high-school studies at the Archbishop Tenison's School in Islington, where he was assistant organist and conductor of the school orchestra. He obtained his musical education at Oxford University (Keble College: B.A., 1962; M.A. 1966), where he directed the Academia Musica Oxoniensis, a choir, a chamber music group, and played in the university jazz band. Later he passed the examination to become an Associate of the Royal College of Organists. When he was twenty-two years old he was appointed assistant organist at St. Martin-in-the-Fields and, at the same time, chorister at Southwark Cathedral. In 1966 he became organist of the University of London Church of Christ-the-King in Bloomsbury and director of music for the University of London Choir (1966-73). In 1974 he was appointed organist at the Belgravia Church of St. Michael, where Arthur Sullivan had served in the nineteenth century. He was active in radio and television; in the summer of 1972 he directed a major series of television programs titled "Songs that Matter," and on other occasions he served as an assistant program director. He organized several groups over the years, including the Ian Hall Singers, The Ashanti Drummers, The Baroque Brass, and The Afro-Caribbean Enterprise. In 1970 he founded the interracial Bloomsbury Society "to establish better understanding and agreement between black and white" and sponsored music programs and concerts to that end. His teaching career included tenures at the Forest Hill School in London (1962-64), Achimota College in Ghana (1964-66), and the Peckham Girls Comprehensive School in London (1966-). He was best known for his liturgical works, particularly the *Bloomsbury Mass* (1971), which typically included Afro-Caribbean elements fused with traditional European elements. He toured widely as a lecturer and conductor of his own music in Europe, West Africa, and the Caribbean. He was also active with UNESCO musical affairs, participating in seminars, and was chairman of the United Kingdom Committee for the Second World Black and African Festival held at Lagos, Nigeria, in 1977.

BIBL: Personal communication. BPIM (Fall 1976).

HALL, JUANITA. Stage entertainer (b. 6 November 1902 in Keyport, New Jersey; d. 28 February 1968 in Bay Shore, New York). She obtained her musical education at the Juilliard School of Music in New York and through private study. During her youth she sang in local church choirs. Her first professional experience was in the chorus of the Zeigfeld production of Kern and Hammerstein's *Show Boat* (1927). Thereafter she sang roles in various Broadway productions, including Marc Connelly's music drama *The Green Pastures* (1930), Kurt Weill's opera *Street Scene* (1947), and the musicals *St. Louis Woman* (1946), *South Pacific* (1949), and *House of Flowers* (1954), *Flower Drum Song* (1958), among other shows. She also performed in dramatic productions. During the years 1931-36 she was a soloist and assistant director with the Hall Johnson* Choir. Later she organized and directed her own choral groups, including a chorus sponsored (1936-41) by the WPA (Works Progress Administration) and a New York World's Fair chorus in 1941. She was active in radio and television music; she also performed in New York nightclubs and made recordings with her Juanita Hall Choir. She sang in the film versions of *South Pacific* (1958) and *Flower Drum Song* (1961). Her best-known stage role was as Bloody Mary in *South Pacific*.

BIBL: WWCA, 1950.

DISC: Jep. Kink.

HALL JOHNSON CHOIR. See **JOHNSON, FRANCIS HALL.**

HAMILTON, FORESTSTORN ("CHICO"). Jazz drummer (b. 21 September 1921 in Los Angeles, California). He began his professional career as a clarinetist, performing in the early 1940s with such groups as Ernie Royale, Charles Mingus,* Illinois Jacquet,* Lionel Hampton,* and Lester Young,* among others. During his years of service in the United States Armed Forces (1942-46), he studied drums with Jonathan ("Jo") Jones.* After his discharge he played with various groups, including James ("Jimmy") Mundy,* William ("Count") Basie,* Lena Horne* (intermittently 1948-55), Charlie Barnet, and Gerry Mulligan (with whom he organized a quartet in 1952), among others. He also led his own groups from time to time; a quintet formed in 1956 featured the unusual combination of cello and flute. He appeared in films or on film soundtracks with his groups and as a soloist, including *Road to Bali* (1952) and *Sweet Smell of Success* (1957). He also wrote scores for such films as *Confessor* (1968), *Coonskin/Bustin' Out* (1975), *Repulsion* (1965), and others. In 1966 he settled in New York, where he organized his own production company and gave much time to writing music for television, radio, and films. During the mid-1970s he began performing regularly again, appearing in nightclubs and at jazz festivals with his new groups, recording steadily, and producing special television programs.

BIBL: ASCAP. FeaEJ. FeaJS. FeaGitJS. MeeJMov. WWA. WWBA.

DISC: Jep. Kink. TudJ.

HAMMOND, WADE. Military bandmaster (b. 1870s in Alabama; d. 1950s (?) in Phoenix, Arizona). He was graduated from Alabama A & M College (Agricultural and Mechanical) in Huntsville, Alabama (B.A., 1895) and was assigned to the Ninth United States Cavalry Regiment a few years later, possibly in 1898. During the years 1907-09 he was bandmaster at Western University in Quindaro, Kansas. In 1909 he was one of four black bandmasters appointed chief musicians in the United States Armed Forces by special order of President Theodore Roosevelt, the first time in history that Negro regiments were given black bandmasters. Emmett Scott, secretary to Booker T. Washington, waged a heavy campaign for several years to have black bandmasters appointed to the four Negro regiments in the United States Army, and finally in November 1908 the President ruled that the black bandmasters should be appointed as soon as the presently serving white bandmasters could be transferred. The other three appointees were James A. Thomas (Tenth Cavalry), Elbert Williams (25th Infantry), and William Polk (24th Infantry). Hammond remained with the Ninth Cavalry, stationed at Fort A. D. Russell, Wyoming, for more than thirty years. He toured widely as a guest bandleader and in 1925 was invited to Tuskegee Institute in Alabama to work with the band there. After retiring from the army he settled in Phoenix, Arizona.

BIBL: Black press, incl. CDef, 27 October 1928, 7 January 1950; IndF, 18 September 1909; NYAge, 14 November 1925. Greene.

HAMPTON, LIONEL. Jazz vibraharpist (b. 12 April 1909 in Louisville, Kentucky). His father was a professional entertainer (died in World War I). His family moved to Chicago, Illinois, when he was about seven years old. He obtained his musical education at the Holy Rosary Academy in Kenosha, Wisconsin, where he first studied music and learned to play drums; in Catholic schools of Chicago, Illinois, where he came under the tutelage of N. Clark Smith* (bandmaster at Wendell Phillips High School) as a member of the *Chicago Defender* Newsboys Band, which Smith directed; and at the University of Southern California in Los Angeles (1934). His teachers included James ("Jimmy") Bertrand (xylophone) and Clifford ("Snags") Jones (drums). After graduating from high school he played with various local groups in Chicago, then moved to Los Angeles in 1927. Thereafter he played with various groups, including the Spikes Brothers, Paul Howard's Quality Serenaders, and Les Hite* (1930-34), among others. In 1929 he made his recording debut as a drummer with Howard, and the next year recorded his first vibraharp solo with Louis Armstrong,* who was fronting the Hite band at that time. It was Armstrong who suggested to Hampton that he play vibraharp and thereby launched Hampton into a new career. In 1934 Hampton formed his own group, which played in nightclubs of Los Angeles and Oakland, California. During the years 1936-40 he played in the Benny Goodman Quartet, along with Theodore ("Teddy") Wilson* and Gene Krupa. In 1940 Hampton formed his first big band and soon established himself as a dominant figure in the world of jazz. He toured widely throughout the world, playing on all the continents, and recorded prolifically. During the mid-1960s he was forced to disband his large group because of economic problems; in 1965 he organized a sextet, with which he toured as widely as he had in the past with the big band. Frequently he joined with others for reunion concerts, such as the Benny Goodman Quartet and leading jazzmen for the Newport Jazz Festivals in New York. During the 1970s he performed with small ensembles and occasionally with big bands, particularly for jazz festivals. In 1978 he celebrated the fiftieth anniversary of his entering a music career with tremendous enthusiasm and energy. Over his long career he was active in radio and television and appeared in numerous films, among them, *A Song is Born* (1948), *The Benny Goodman Story* (1955), and *Rooftops of New York* (1960). Over the years his bands and ensembles served as a school through which passed dozens of jazzmen who later would become celebrities; he also gave debuts to such singers as Betty Carter* and Dinah Washington.* He was credited with important innovations, among them, the first to establish the vibraharp as a standard instrument of the jazz ensemble (and other musical groups as well) rather than a novelty instrument; the first to add the electric organ to the jazz group (with "Doug" Duke); and the first to add the electric bass (with Roy Johnson). His groups played in a variety of styles—jazz, rhythm 'n' blues, bop, soul—and his music remained sophisticated and contemporary through the various periods of jazz up to the present. His best-known pieces were "Flyin' home" and "Vibraphone blues." His honors included numerous awards from the music industry and civic and professional organizations; "keys" to several cities, the George Frederic Handel Medallion from the City of New York (1966) and the New York Governor's Award for Fifty Years of Music (1978); a Papal Medal from Pope Paul VI; and honorary doctorates from Allen University, Pepperdine University (1975), Xavier University (Louisiana), and Daniel Hale University (1976).

BIBL: BMI (Issue No. 3, 1978). ChilWW. DanceWS. FeaEJ. FeaJS. FeaGitJS. MeeJMov. NYT, 1 July 1979.

DISC: Jep. Kink. RustJR. TudJ.

HAMPTON SINGERS, THE. Concert choral group (fl. from 1872 to the present; organized at Hampton Institute, Hampton, Virginia). The Hampton Normal and Agricultural Institute opened its doors in 1870 at Hampton, Virginia. Inspired by the success of Fisk University in sending out its students, the Fisk Jubilee Singers, to raise money for the institution, Hampton decided to send out a group of student singers also. Thomas P. Fenner, formerly a music teacher at the Conservatory in Providence, Rhode Island, organized and trained the singers. In February 1873 a group of seventeen singers set out for the first concert of their tour at Washington, D.C.: James R. Bailey, William G. Catus, Sallie Davis, Alice Ferribee, Rachel Elliot, James C. Dungey, Robert Hamilton, John Holt, Hutchins Inge, Lucy Leary, Maria Mallette, Joseph Mebane, Mary Norwood, Carrie Thomas, J. B. Towe, James M. Waddy, and Whit Williams. The first tour was successful, the group returning to the campus on 25 December 1873. A smaller, reorganized group made a second tour (February-December 1874) through Canada and the Middle West. When the Hampton singers completed their third tour in July 1875, they had covered eighteen states and Canada and had sung over five hundred concerts. The tradition, once started, continued over the years. During the years 1913-31, R. Nathaniel Dett* was director of the Hampton Choir; his group toured in Europe (1930) and won international acclaim. Later directors included Clarence Cameron White* during the years 1931-35, Noah Francis Ryder* (1941-46), and Roland M. Carter (1970s).

BIBL: Black press. Mrs. M. F. Armstrong and Helen W. Ludlow, *Hampton and Its Students by Two of Its Teachers. With Fifty Cabin and Plantation Songs arr. by Thomas P. Fenner* (New York, 1874). Mrs. E. P. Smith, "An Incident of the Beginning" in *Southern Workman* 23 (May 1894), 72-76.

HANCOCK, EUGENE WILSON. Church organist/College professor (b. 17 February 1929 in St. Louis, Missouri). He obtained his musical training at the University of Detroit in Michigan (B. Mus., 1951), the University of Michigan at Ann Arbor (M. Mus., 1956) and the School of Sacred Music of Union Theological Seminary in New York (D. Sac. Mus., 1967). His teachers included Robert Baker and Marcel Dupre, among others. He was inspired to become a church organist by David Holland, the first black organist he heard play, and his career development was influenced by Alec Wyton, organist/choirmaster at the Cathedral of St. John the Divine in New York, and by Fela Sowande.* In 1966 he passed the examination for the AAGO degree (Associate of the American Guild of Organists). His church-music career included tenures as organist and choirmaster at Lutheran churches in Detroit, Michigan (1943-63); as assistant organist at the Cathedral Church of St. John the Divine (1963-66); as organist-choirmaster at the New Calvary Baptist Church in Detroit (1967-70); and at the St. Philip's Episcopal Church in New York (1974-   ). He was also active as a teacher at the Manhattan Community College of the City University of New York (1970-). He toured as a concert organist; his concerts were notable for the inclusion of music by black composers, and occasionally he played concerts given over totally to the music of black composers. He published articles in professional journals, such as the *Journal of Church Music* and *Pipeline*. He also published compositions, of which the best known were *An Organ Book of Spirituals* (1966), *Spirituals for Young Voices* (1972) and the songs ''Absalom'' and ''Song of Simeon'' (published in *Anthology of Art Songs by Black Composers*, compiled by Willis Patterson*).

BIBL: Questionnaire. Corliss Richard Arnold, *Organ Literature: A Comprehensive Survey* (Metuchen, New Jersey, 1973). IntWWM.

HANCOCK, HERBERT JEFFREY ("HERBIE"). Jazz pianist (b. 12 April 1940 in Chicago, Illinois). He began piano study at the age of seven; when he was twelve he played a concerto with the Chicago Symphony Orchestra. He obtained his musical education in the public schools of Chicago, Illinois; at Grinnell College in Grinnell, Iowa (1956-60), where he was musically active although he majored in engineering; at Roosevelt University in Chicago (1960); and at the Manhattan School of Music (1962) and the New School for Social Research (1967) in New York. During his college years he formed a big band, for which he wrote and arranged music. After returning to Chicago in 1960 he played piano with local groups and visiting bands, among them Coleman Hawkins.* Thereafter he played with various groups, including Donald Byrd* (1960-63), Eric Dolphy,* Phil Woods, Oliver Nelson,* and Miles Davis* (1963-68). In 1968 he organized his first permanent group, the Herbie Hancock Sextet; in 1973 he changed his group to a quartet for economic reasons. He made his recording debut in 1962 and thereafter recorded extensively with his groups and with others. He toured widely in the United States, Europe, and Japan, appearing in concert halls, in nightclubs, on college campuses, and at the major jazz festivals. He was active in television and films, writing scores for such films as *Blow-up* (1966), *The Spook Who Sat by the Door* (1973), and *Death Wish* (1974). During his tenure with Davis he participated in innovative procedures and first began playing electric piano. With his own groups he moved more in the direction of electronic music: his albums *Mwandishi* (1971) and *Crossings* (1972) documented his new style. By the mid-1970s his group was noted for its extensive use of electronic instruments and its use of elements of jazz, rhythm 'n' blues, and soul. He credited Davis with being the major influence on his style development. In December 1972 he settled in Los Angeles, California. The next year he was converted to Nichiren Shoshu Buddhism. He received numerous awards from the music industry. His best-remembered pieces include the songs ''Watermelon man'' and ''Chameleon'' and the albums *Headhunters* and *Thrust; Treasure Chest*.

BIBL: Black press, incl. *The New Courier* [Pittsburgh], 4 January 1975; *Afro-American* [Baltimore], 1 March 1975. ContKey (November 1977). FeaJS. FeaGitJS. MeeJMov. WWA. WWBA.

DISC: TudJ.

HANDY, JOHN RICHARD. Jazz saxophonist (b. 3 February 1933 in Dallas, Texas). His family lived in Los Angeles, California, during the years 1943-44, moved back to Dallas, Texas, then settled in Los Angeles in 1949. Self-taught on the clarinet, he began to play the instrument when he was thirteen years old. He obtained his musical education in the public schools of Dallas and Los Angeles; at City College of the City University of New York (1960), and at San Francisco State College in California (B.A., 1963). He began to play alto saxophone after moving to Los Angeles and soon thereafter began playing with local jazz and rhythm 'n' blues groups. He served in the United States Armed Forces during the years 1953-55, then returning to playing in California. In 1959 he went to New York; during the years 1959-62 he played with various groups, including Charles Mingus* (1958-59), Randolph (''Randy'') Weston* (1959), and Kenneth (''Kenny'') Dorham,* among others. He also led his own groups as early as 1959 and toured in Europe in 1961, performing on television and in films as well as in concert halls and nightclubs. Thereafter he toured widely in the United States and abroad, appearing with symphony orchestras both as soloist and with his groups, on college campuses, in concert halls and theaters, and at the major jazz festivals. He was active as a teacher, including a tenure at San Francisco State College (1968-) and lectureships at other colleges, among them, the University of California at Berkeley, Stanford University in California, and the San Francisco Conservatory of Music. He also toured on the college circuit as a lecturer and was active in educational television. He received numerous awards from the music industry; his other honors included appointment to civic advisory councils. He recorded regularly; best-known of his compositions were ''The Spanish lady'' and *Concerto for Jazz Soloist and Orchestra* (1970).

BIBL: FeaEJ. FeaJS. FeaGitJS. MeeJMov. WWA. WWBA.
DISC: Jep.

HANDY, W[ILLIAM] C[HRISTOPHER] (''FATHER OF THE BLUES''). Composer (b. 16 November 1873 in Florence, Alabama; d. 28 March 1958 in New York, New York). He studied organ as a child and obtained musical training at the Florence District School for Negroes. He taught himself to play cornet and eventually joined a local band. When he was fifteen he joined a touring minstrel troupe, which however became stranded after playing a few towns. He returned to school, then after graduation found employment as a teacher, and later in a pipe-works factory. In 1892 he set out again to begin a career in music and traveled to Chicago with the intent that his quartet should sing at the World's Fair. When the group arrived there, they found the Fair had been postponed. Handy did not return home, but worked at odd jobs in various places and finally settled in Henderson, Kentucky. There he attached himself to the director of a local German singing society, from whom he learned a great deal about music, and began playing with local black orchestras. In 1896 he joined W. A. Mahara's Minstrels as a cornetist; the next year he was promoted to bandleader. During the years 1900-02 he was bandmaster at Alabama A & M (Agricultural & Mechanical) College at Montgomery; he then returned to Mahara's Minstrels for the 1902-03 season. The troupe toured widely throughout the nation and into Canada, Mexico, and Cuba, and Handy gained experience in arranging and composing for his groups as well as conducting both vocal and instrumental forces. In 1903 he settled in Clarksdale, Mississippi; for the next few years he organized and led military and dance bands in the Mississippi Delta region. About 1908 he settled in Memphis, Tennessee. Later he and Harry Pace,* a businessman who wrote song lyrics, established the Pace and Handy Music [publishing] Company. During his Memphis years, he toured widely with his groups and also served as a booking agent for other dance bands, thus practically controlling the music entertainment industry in the Memphis area (in regard to black orchestras). In 1918 the Pace-Handy Company moved to New York, where it became the leading publisher of the music of black songwriters. In 1920, however, Pace and Handy dissolved their partnership; Pace founded the Pace Phonograph Company, which produced the Black Swan Records, and Handy continued his work through the Handy Music Company.

Although Handy had been composing music from an early age, it was not until 1912 that he published his first piece, ''Memphis blues'' (composed 1909), which was written originally for use in an election campaign that made Edward H. Crump mayor of Memphis. The popularity of the piece at dances where his band performed it persuaded him to change its title and publish it. His next published blues, ''St. Louis blues'' (published 1914), was even more successful and eventually became, perhaps, the most widely performed American song in history. His publication of ''The Beale Street blues'' (1917) firmly established him as ''Father of the Blues.'' Throughout his years in Memphis and later in New York he toured extensively with his ''blues'' bands. Among those who worked closely with him were William Grant Still* and Frederick Bryan, called ''the jazz Sousa.'' He first recorded in 1897 on a cylinder machine with his minstrel band. In 1917 his band recorded for the Columbia Phonograph Company under the name Handy's Orchestra of Memphis, thus making him one of the black pioneers in recording. He was a pioneer in other ways as well. The songs he published during the 1920s helped to establish black folk-inflected songs in the realm of popular music; for example, ''A good man is hard to find,'' which was first sung by Alberta Hunter* and later by white singer Sophie Tucker. In 1928 he produced a mammoth program at Carnegie Hall in New York that emphasized the wide variety of black music, from plantation songs to orchestral rhapsodies. He served as a consultant for important concerts of his time, including the ASCAP Silver Jubilee Festival (1939) and musical events associated with the World Fairs at Chicago (1933-34), San Francisco, California (1939-40), and New York (1939-40). All over the nation theaters, schools, and streets were named after him; in 1931 Memphis founded a W. C. Handy Park. In June 1940, for the first time in history a program given over entirely to the music of a black composer, an all-Handy program, was broadcast on a national network, NBC. In 1958 he was the subject of the film *St. Louis Blues*, which featured Nat King Cole* (née Nathaniel Coles) and Billy Preston.* In 1969 the United States Postal Service issued a stamp, ''W. C. Handy, Father of the Blues.''

Handy wrote and published more than 150 songs and arrangements of folksongs, primarily spirituals and blues. His collections included *Blues: an Anthology* (1926; reissued in 1949 as *Treasury of the Blues*) and *Book of Negro Spirituals* (1938). He also published pamphlets and books, including his own *Negro Authors and Composers of the United States* (1936), the autobiography *Father of the Blues* (1941), and *Unsung Americans Sung* (1944). His autobiography documents not only his own career but as well the history of black music during the period covered by the book. He was one of the most celebrated musicians of his time, and he made a lasting contribution to the history of American musicians through his popularization of the Negro folk blues.

BIBL: Black press, incl. CDef, 19 April 1919. BPIM 7, 8 (Fall 1979, Spring 1980), reprints of Handy correspondence. CurBiog (March 1941). EAB. W. C. Handy, "The Heart of the Blues" in *Etude* (March 1940; reprint in SouRBM). JNH 43 (1958), p. 167. NYT, 4 March 1966. MeeJMov. WWCA, 1929-1950.

HANDY (MILLER), D[OROTHY] ANTOINETTE. Concert flutist (b. 29 October 1930 in New Orleans, Louisiana). She began piano study at the age of five with her mother, a music teacher, and violin study at six. She obtained her musical education in the public schools of New Orleans, Louisiana; at Spelman College in Atlanta, Georgia; at the New England Conservatory of Music in Boston, Massachusetts (B. Mus., 1952); at Northwestern University in Evanston, Illinois (M. Mus., 1953); and at the Paris National Conservatory in France (diploma, 1955). She studied trumpet in high school and began study of the flute when she was fourteen. Her teachers included Frank Ribitsch of the New Orleans Philharmonic and Lois Schaefer of the Boston Symphony. She began her professional career as a flutist with the Chicago Civic Orchestra (1952-53). Thereafter she played with various organizations, including the International Orchestra of Paris (1954-55); the Musica Viva Orchestra of Geneva, Switzerland (1955); Symphony of the Air under Leonard Bernstein (formerly NBC Symphony, 1956); the Bach Festival Orchestra in Carmel, California (1957); the Orchestra of America in New York (1960-62) under Richard Korn; the Symphony of the New World* (1968-71); and the Richmond [Virginia] Symphony (1966-76). She also played in orchestras on television programs and in films. She toured widely as a concert flutist in the United States and in Europe, giving solo concerts and appearing with symphony orchestras. In 1955 she toured with her own group, Trio Pro Viva, in Germany under the sponsorship of the USIS (United States Information Service). In 1965 she formed a Trio Pro Viva in the United States, which toured regularly and featured the music of black composers on its programs; its personnel included Mary Lou Gutman and William E. Terry, among others. Her teaching career included tenures as either faculty member or special projects director at Florida A & M University in Tallahassee; at Tuskegee Institute in Alabama; at Jackson State College in Mississippi; and at Virginia State College in Petersburg. She was also active as a lecturer, consultant, project director, and radio commentator; in 1979 she conducted a weekly radio program, "Black Virginia," centered on black composers and performers of classical music. She published articles in professional journals; her book publications included *Black Music: Opinions and Reviews* (1974) and *Black Women in American Bands and Orchestras* (1981).

BIBL: Questionnaire. *Personalities of the South* (1974). IntWWM.

HARDIN, LILLIAN. See **ARMSTRONG, LILLIAN.**

HARDWICK, OTTO ("TOBY"). Jazz saxophonist (b. 31 May 1904 in Washington, D.C.; d. 5 August 1970 in Washington, D.C.). He began his professional career playing string bass, then changed to saxophone. He played with various local groups in Washington, D.C., beginning in the 1920s, including Carroll's Columbia Orchestra, Elmer Snowden,* and Edward ("Duke") Ellington* (1923-28), with whom he went to New York in 1923. In 1928 he toured in Europe with John Ricks, Noble Sissle,* Nekka Shaw, and his own groups. After returning to the United States he led his own groups, played with William ("Chick") Webb* (1929), Thomas ("Fats") Waller,* and Elmer Snowden, then rejoined Ellington (1932-46), with whom he remained until he retired. He was noted for his saxophone solos in the early Ellington band, particularly on "Sophisticated lady" (he was co-composer with Ellington), "Black and tan fantasy," and "Birgmingham breakdown."

BIBL: ChilWW. FeaEJ. FeaGitJS. MeeJMov. Maurice Waller and Anthony Callabrese, *Fats Waller* (New York, 1977).

DISC: Jep. Kink.

HARE, MAUD CUNEY. Writer (b. 16 February 1874 in Galveston, Texas; d. 13 February 1936 in Boston, Mass.). She obtained her musical education at the New England Conservatory in Boston, Massachusetts, and through private study with Emil Ludwig and Edwin Klabre. Her teaching career included tenures at the Texas Deaf, Dumb, and Blind Institute for Colored Youths at Austin, Texas (1897-98), in the Settlement program of the Institutional Church of Chicago, Illinois (1900-01), and at the State Normal and Industrial College for Negroes at Prairie View, Texas (1903-04). During the turn of the century she was active in Chicago, Illinois, but settled in Boston, Massachusetts, in 1906. She toured widely as a concert pianist/lecturer, in later years with baritone William Richardson.* She also was a collector of folk materials and black history data. In Boston she established the Musical Arts Studio (also called the Allied Arts Center), which promoted lectures, concerts, and a little theater movement. Her compositions included incidental music for the play *Antar of Araby* (1926). She contributed to professional journals —among them, the *Musical Quarterly, Musical Observer*, and *Musical America*—and for many years, beginning about 1910, served as editor of the music and arts department of *The Crisis*. She is best remembered for her book *Negro Musicians and Their Music* (Washington, D.C., 1936), which was the first comprehensive survey of black music to appear since James Trotter's* *Music and Some Highly Musical People* in 1878. Her other publications included *Six Creole Folk Songs* (New York, 1921).

BIBL: Black press, incl. NYAge, 15 November 1890, 26 March 1927. Introduction by Clarence Cameron White* in Hare.

HARLEM OPERA COMPANY. Community organization (org. 1950s in New York, New York). The opera company was founded in the early 1950s by opera singers Monty Norris, Vincent Shields, and Charles War. In 1959 bass-baritone Emory Taylor became the director. During the 1960s the company changed its name twice in line with its efforts to explore new musical resources based on the black tradition; for a period it was called the Afro-American Singing Theater, then later, the New World Singing Theater. In 1974 the company became again the Harlem Opera Society. It was noted for the avant-garde jazz style of its dramatic improvisations, improvised operas, and full-length operas about the Afro-American experience; the best-known of the latter were *Solomon and Sheba, Brown's Buckeroos*, and *Hodges & Company*. Those who sang with the company over the years included Beverly Alston, François Clemmons, Robert Donalson, Jeanne (also known as Geanie) Faulkner, Brenda Feliciano, Abbe Mason, Edward Pierson,* Gwen Sumter, and Von Ray. Faulkner and Pierson also sang with the New York City Opera, and Clemmons sang with the Metropolitan Opera. Sam Rivers* was composer-in-residence and musical director from 1968; his avant-garde jazz ensembles attracted much attention. The opera company toured widely, appearing on college campuses and in concert halls and theaters.

BIBL: Schom.

HARRELD, JOSEPHINE. See **LOVE, JOSEPHINE.**

HARRELD, KEMPER. College professor (b. 31 January 1885 in Muncie, Indiana; d. February 1971 in Detroit, Michigan). His family moved to Indianapolis, Indiana, when he was a child. He began violin study at an early age and obtained his musical education in the public schools of Muncie and Indianapolis; at Chicago [Illinois] Musical College, where he studied with Felix Borowski, among others; at the Sherwood Music School; and at the Fredericksen Violin School, where he studied with the school's founder for three years. During his years in Chicago he was active in music circles: he played violin solos on local concerts and served as conductor of the orchestra for the Choral Study Club,* under the direction of Pedro Tinsley.* In 1911 he went to Atlanta, Georgia, to take charge of music at the Atlanta Baptist College (later, Morehouse College) and remained there until his retirement. During the summer of 1914 he studied at the Stern Conservatory in Berlin, Germany. In 1923 he recorded violin solos for the Black Swan* Record Label. In 1927 he took over the chairmanship of the music department at Spelman College in Atlanta, while continuing to teach at Morehouse. Later he organized the Atlanta University-Morehouse-Spelman Chorus and Symphony Orchestra. He also organized a city-wide chorus made up of choirs from twenty-eight churches in Atlanta. He was a founder of NANM (National Association of Negro Musicians) in 1919 and later served as a national president (1937-39). He made a significant contribution to the history of black music through the wide influence he exerted upon his students, who included Fletcher Henderson,* Alex Jackson, Willis Laurence James,* and Edmund Jenkins,* among others.

BIBL: AlHen. Black press, incl. CDef, 1 July 1909, 13 June 1910, 8 May 1920; NYAge, 17 September 1914, 9 May 1936. WWCA, 1929-50.

HARRIS, BARRY DOYLE. Jazz pianist (b. 15 December 1929 in Detroit, Michigan). His mother was a church pianist. He first played piano when he was four years old. Later he studied with a local teacher. He obtained his musical education in the public schools of Detroit, Michigan. During his high-school years he formed a group, which played mostly bebop. His early style development was influenced by Tommy Flanagan,* who played in Detroit during Harris's formative years, by Earl ("Bud") Powell,* and Art Tatum*; he regarded Charlie Parker* and Coleman Hawkins* as his greatest sources of inspiration. During the 1950s he was house-pianist in Detroit nightclubs; he played in back-up groups for visiting jazzmen; he toured briefly with various groups, among them Max Roach* and Julian ("Cannonball") Adderley*; and he conducted a music studio, where he taught jazz theory. In 1960 he settled in New York. Thereafter he led his own groups primarily but also played with Yusef Lateef,* Coleman Hawkins (intermittently, 1965-69), and Charles McPherson; he appeared on television programs and played at jazz festivals. In the late 1970s he toured in Europe and Japan for the first time. He composed much of the music he played; among his best-known recordings were the albums *Luminescence* and *Live at Tokyo*. He was one of the great trio of Detroit pianists, along with Henry ("Hank") Jones* and Tommy Flanagan. Although he played in the Bud Powell tradition, his style was distinctively personal.

BIBL: Cadence (December 1977). ContKey (November 1979). FeaEJ. FeaJS. FeaGitJS.

DISC: ModJ.

HARRIS, CARL GORDON, JR. College professor (b. 14 January 1936 in Fayette, Missouri). He obtained his musical education in the public schools of St. Joseph, Missouri; at Philander Smith College in Little Rock, Arkansas (B.A., 1956); at the Conservatory of Music of the University of Missouri in Kansas City (M.A., 1964; D. Mus. A., 1972); and at the Vienna State Academy of Music in Austria (summer 1969), where he studied with Gunther Theuring and Ferdinand Grossman. His other teachers included W. Everett Hendricks, Robert Shelton, and Jay Decker, among others. His teaching career included tenures at Philander Smith College (1959-68), the University of Missouri Conservatory of Music (1968-71), and Virginia State College (1971-). He also taught in public schools of Columbia, Missouri, and the Johnson Community College in Shawnee-Mission, Kansas. He was director of choral groups at these institutions and served as chairman of the music department at Virginia State. He was also active as an organist-choirmaster and earned a Minister of Music certificate from the United Methodist Church. He toured widely as a lecturer, choral clinician, and guest conductor; he also toured widely with his choral groups. In the summer of 1974 he toured in Europe as a member of a group of distinguished American Choral Conductors on a People-to-People Goodwill Mission and later served on the faculty for the Protestant Church Music Institute in Berchtesgaden, Germany (summers of 1976, 1977). He published articles in professional journals, such as the *Choral Journal* of the American Choral Directors Association, the *Missouri Journal of Research in Music Education*, and *Chant Choral*. His honors included a Distinguished Alumnus Achievement Award from Philander Smith.

BIBL: Questionnaire. IntWWM. WWBA.

HARRIS, EMMA. See **ARLE-TILZ, CORETTI.**

HARRIS, ESTELLE. Vaudeville entertainer. See **OVERSTREET, W. BENTON.**

HARRIS, HILDA. Concert/opera singer (b. c1930 in Warrenton, North Carolina). She obtained her musical education at North Carolina State University in Greensboro. In New York she studied privately with Jonathan Brice and Lola Hayes. She began her professional career singing in Broadway musicals, such as Irving Burgie's* *Ballad for Bimshire* (1963), *Jericho-Jim-Crow* (1964), *Golden Boy* (1964), *Ben Franklin in Paris* (1964), *Mame* (1966), and others. In 1967 she made her debut as a mezzo-soprano at the Carnegie Recital Hall in New York. Thereafter she toured in the United States and in Europe, giving solo recitals, performing in oratorios, and appearing with symphony orchestras. In 1971 she made her European operatic debut in the title role of Bizet's *Carmen* at St. Gallen, Switzerland, and thereafter sang with various opera companies at home and abroad. In 1974 she joined the New York City Opera and in 1977 made her debut with the Metropolitan Opera. During the 1970s she sang frequently with Opera Ebony.* She was best known for her performances as Tituba in Ward's *The Crucible*, Siebel in Gounod's *Faust*, and the title roles in Puccini's *Madame Butterfly* and Bizet's *Carmen*. Her honors included awards from the New York Singing Teachers' Association, the Young Artist Award, and the Shull Bequest Award.

BIBL: *Catalyst* (November 1973), p. 13.

DISC: Turn.

HARRIS, MARGARET R. Conductor/Concert pianist (b. 15 September 1943 in Chicago, Illinois). She was a child prodigy: she first played in public when she was three years old and played a Mozart concerto movement with the Chicago Symphony Orchestra when she was ten. She obtained her musical education in the public schools of Chicago, Illinois; at the Curtis Institute of Music in Philadelphia, Pennsylvania; and at the Juilliard School of Music in New York (B.S., 1964; M.S., 1965). During the 1960s she was active in New York as a musical director for the Negro Ensemble Company and the New York Shakespeare Festival Company and as a teacher at the Dorothy Maynor* School of the Performing Arts. She made her concert debut as a pianist in 1970 at Town Hall in New York, including some of her original compositions on her program. The same year she made her debut as a conductor-musical director with the Broadway musical *Hair*. Thereafter she conducted for a number of musicals, including *Two Gentlemen of Verona* (1971) and *Raisin* (1973). In 1971 she made her debut as a symphony-orchestra conductor with the Chicago Symphony Orchestra in its Grant Park Concert Series. She toured widely at home and abroad as a guest conductor, appearing in concert halls, on college campuses, and at festivals. Frequently she performed two roles, conductor and pianist-composer, playing her own piano concertos. She was active also in radio and television music and served as the music director for Opera Ebony.* Her honors included appointments to national advisory panels and an award from the National Association of Negro Musicians* (1972).

BIBL: Black press, incl. CDef, 6 September 1975. Handy. WWBA. WWE.

HARRIS, WYNONIE ("MR. BLUES"). Blues singer (b. 24 August 1915 in Omaha, Nebraska; d. 14 June 1969 in Los Angeles, California). He obtained his musical education in the public schools of Omaha, Nebraska, and at Creighton University in Omaha. He left college in the early 1930s to become a professional entertainer in local nightclubs; later he taught himself to play drums and performed with his own groups. During the 1940s he was active as a singer, dancer, and sometime producer; he toured with various groups, including Lucius ("Lucky") Millinder* (intermittently 1944-50), Illinois Jacquet,* Lionel Hampton,* ("Big") Joe Turner,* and Wilbur ("Dud") Bascomb,* among others. He was also active in radio and television music. He first attracted wide attention as a "blues shouter" in Millinder's orchestra. In 1949 he established himself as a pioneer of rhythm 'n' blues singers. His best-known performances were of "Good rockin' tonight," "Playful baby," "All she wants to do is rock," and "Lovin' machine."

BIBL: Black press, incl. NYAge, 3 September 1949. BWW. LivBl 4 (Winter 1970-71). ShawHS.

DISC: Jep. TudJ.

HARRISON, FRANK GOODALL. College professor (b. 10 October 1899 in Austin, Texas; d. 10 March 1977 in New York, New York). He received his musical training in the public schools of Austin, Texas, where he was encouraged to enter a music career by a Mrs. Smith, daughter of Bishop Smith of the African Methodist Episcopal Church, and a Mrs. Crosby; at Howard University in Washington, D.C. (B. Mus., 1922), where he studied with Lulu Childers,* who encouraged his career development, as did also Harry T. Burleigh,* who gave him a two-year scholarship; at Columbia University Teachers College and the Institute of Musical Art (now the Juilliard School of Music), both in New York. He made his debut as a concert baritone in April 1924 in New York. Thereafter he combined concert work with studio teaching; he toured widely in the South during the next few years and also engaged in theater work. In 1927 he was appointed to the music faculty of Talladega College in Alabama by Tourgee DeBose* and remained there forty-two years (1927-69). During his long tenure he directed choral activities and served as chairman of the music department in addition to teaching. His students included Carol Brice,* Vera Little,* Theodore ("Teddy") Wilson,* and John Wesley Work IV. In 1972 Talladega awarded him an honorary doctorate.

BIBL: Information from Roland Braithwaite.* Black press, incl. NYAge, 12 April 1924, 1 October 1927.

HARRISON, HAZEL. Concert pianist (b. 12 May 1883 in La Porte, Indiana; d. 29 April 1969 in Washington, D.C.). She revealed musical talent at an early age and studied piano with local teachers Victor Heinz and Richard Pellow as a child. Through Heinz's contacts she was invited in 1904 to play at the Royal Theater in Berlin, Germany, where she remained for several years. She studied piano there with Ferrucio Busoni, gave recitals, and appeared with the Berlin Philharmonic, directed by Artur Nikisch. After returning to the United States, she played a recital at Chicago, Illinois, to critical acclaim and was given an award by two Chicago women (who remained anonymous) to study again in Berlin. This time she remained abroad during the years 1910-14, studying with Busoni. After returning home she continued to study with Victor Heinz in Chicago. In November 1919 she made her Chicago debut at Kimball Hall, and in May 1922 she made her New York debut at Aeolian Hall. Throughout these years she appeared regularly on concerts in various cities—among them, at the annual meeting of the National Association of Negro Musicians at New York in July 1920—and conducted a music studio in Chicago. During the 1920s she toured widely; she also returned to Germany in 1926 for more study with Busoni and Egon Petri; after resettling in the United States she studied with Percy Grainger. In 1931 she was appointed head of the piano department at Tuskegee Institute in Alabama (1931-34). Thereafter she combined college teaching with her concert touring, often taking leaves of absence for a year to tour. She also appeared with leading symphony orchestras during her long career and occasionally gave lecture-recitals. Her teaching career included also tenures at Howard University in Washington, D.C. (1934-59), and at Alabama State A & M College at Montgomery (1959-64). She was the leading black pianist of her time. Her style was described as virtuosic, brilliant, and powerful with the depth of a full orchestra, displaying consummate musicianship.

BIBL: Black press, incl. CDef, 29 November 1919, 14 November 1931, 20 February 1932; IndF, 1 October

1904; NYAge 15 February 1910, 4 December 1920, 30 October 1926, 29 October 1944. Hare. *The Washington Post*, 1 May 1969.

HART, HENRY. Society dance-orchestra leader (b. c1840 in Frankfort, Kentucky; d. 7 December 1915 in Indianapolis, Indiana). He left Frankfort, Kentucky, at the age of fourteen to go to Cleveland, Ohio, where he learned to play violin. His early professional experience was in a white band under the leadership of one Stanton. About 1864 he went to New Orleans, Louisiana, where he played violin in various nightclubs and met his future wife, Sara, who was a professional pianist. In 1867 they settled in Evansville, Indiana. In 1872 he organized a minstrel troupe, the Alabama Minstrels, which toured briefly before disbanding. At one time or another his troupe included Tom McIntosh,* Sam Lucas,* and Jake Hamilton, among others. About 1885 the Hart family settled in Indianapolis, Indiana, where they formed a family string orchestra, which soon was in demand to play for the leading society balls and receptions. Four of the five Hart daughters became professional musicians—Myrtle, Hazel, Willie, and Estelle. Myrtle began study of the harp with her father and continued with Edmond Schnecker, at that time harpist with Theodore Thomas's Symphony Orchestra of Chicago, Illinois. She performed at the Chicago World's Fair in 1893. Thereafter she acquired her own fine harp with the help of one of her father's patrons, Colonel Eli Lilly. Myrtle toured widely (for that period) as a concert harpist, playing in Washington, D.C., New York, Chicago, and other places. In 1905, for example, she was a featured soloist on Walter Craig's* Pre-Lenten Recital and Assembly in New York.

BIBL: Communications from John L. Selch. Black press, incl. IndF, 1 July 1893, 21 November 1896; NYAge, 19 January 1905. Handy. *Indianapolis News*, 6 April 1901. Simond.

HART, MYRTLE. Concert harpist. See **HART, HENRY.**

HARVEY, GEORGETTE. Actress/Singer (b. 1883 in St. Louis, Missouri; d. 17 February 1952 in New York, New York). She went to New York when she was eighteen years old. She began her professional career in stage music in 1905 when Ernest Hogan* arranged for her to sing in *Rufus Rastus*, a musical in which he had the leading role. She formed a female quartet with three other women in the company, called Creole Belles, which was possibly the first black female quartet in the United States. An agent arranged for a European tour of six months for the women, but once abroad they stayed several years. After the group disbanded in St. Petersburg, Russia, the last city on their itinerary, Harvey remained there. Later she operated a nightclub until 1917, when the outbreak of the Russian Revolution forced her to flee. She escaped to the Far East and spent a few years teaching English in China and Japan. In 1921 she returned to the United States and settled again in New York. Thereafter she became involved with the stage and appeared both in drama and in musicals, including *Strut Miss Lizzie* (1922, by Henry Creamer* and J. Turner Layton*), *Runnin' Wild* (1923, by James P. Johnson* and Cecil Mack*), *Blackberries of 1932*, Gershwin's opera *Porgy and Bess* (1935, 1942), and Kurt Weill's *Lost in the Stars* (1949). She also sang with community groups, including Will Marion Cook's* Clef Club company in 1923, and in nightclubs and theaters.

BIBL: Schom. AlHen. Black press, incl. CDef, 7 April 1923. NYT, 18 February 1952. New York *World-Telegram*, 18 March 1939.

HATHAWAY, DONNY. Jazz singer/Composer-arranger (b. 1 October 1945 in Chicago, Illinois; d. 13 January 1979 in New York, New York). As a child he lived with his grandmother, Martha Crumwell, a gospel singer, in St. Louis, Missouri. Because of her influence he played piano and sang gospel at an early age. He obtained his musical education at Howard University in Washington, D.C. (1963-67). During his college years he was active first as a church organist, then later as a nightclub entertainer with his own trio. Within a few years he had established himself as a composer-arranger and musical producer for such figures as Jerry Butler,* Aretha Franklin,* Roberta Flack,* Curtis Mayfield,* and the Staple Singers,* among others. During the years 1968-73 he composed prolifically, including the score for the film *Come Back, Charlestown Blue* (1972), for which he also conducted the music, and the theme for the CBS television show "Maude." He made his recording debut in 1971 and thereafter recorded extensively, frequently in duos with Roberta Flack. Beginning in 1973 he was musically inactive for a few years but returned to the music field in 1977. His best-known songs were "The ghetto," "The closer I get to you," and "You've got a friend." He received numerous awards from the music industry.

BIBL: Black press, incl. 14 July 1973. *Ebony* (April 1979). NYT, 18 January 1979.

DISC: TudBM.

HAVENS, RICHARD PIERCE ("RICHIE"). Folk singer (b. 21 January 1941 in New York, New York). His father played piano. As a child he sang in a church choir and on street corners with boys' groups. He obtained his education in the public schools of New York, New York. During his high-school years he formed his own group, the McCrea Gospel Singers, which performed for local events. He began his professional career about 1962 after having taught himself to play guitar, singing in local cafes in the Greenwich Village area of New York. His early style development was influenced by the singing of Len Chandler, Dino Valenti, Paul Stookey, and Ray Charles.* He made his recording debut in 1963 and thereafter recorded regularly as a soloist and with others. He began touring about the same time, at first appearing primarily in coffee houses, then also on college campuses, at folk, rock, and jazz festivals, and on television shows in the United States and abroad. He also sang in musicals, among them, *Peter and the Wolf* (1969) and *Tommy* (1972), and in films including *Monterey Jazz* (1973), *Catch My Soul* (1973), *Ali the Man* (1975), and *Greased Lightning* (1977). His best-known albums were *Mixed Bag, Somethin' Else Again,* and *Richard P. Havens 1983.*

BIBL: BWW. StamPRS. *Ebony* (May 1969).

HAWES, HAMPTON. Jazz pianist (b. 13 November 1928 in Los Angeles, California; d. 22 May 1977 in Los Angeles). Self-taught on the piano, he learned to play well enough to begin his professional career during his high-school years. During the years 1944-52 he performed with various groups, including Cecil (''Big Jay'') McNeely, Dexter Gordon,* Howard McGhee,* Milton (''Shorty'') Rogers, Wardell Gray, Johnny Otis, and Howard Rumsey, among others. His style development was influenced by the music of Charlie Parker,* with whom he played in McGhee's band. After service in the United States Armed Forces (1952-54), he organized his own trio, which included bassist Keith (''Red'') Mitchell and drummer Charles (''Chuck'') Thompson and toured widely, bringing Hawes national recognition. Personal problems made him inactive during the years 1958-63; thereafter he toured widely again at home and abroad, playing at festivals, in nightclubs and concert halls, on college campuses, and recording. In addition to leading his own groups, he also performed with Jimmy Garrison (as co-leader), Leroy Vinnegar, Carol Kaye, and Joan Baez, among others. During the 1970s he increasingly used electric keyboards and moved stylistically in the direction of contemporary music. He was best remembered, however, as the keystone of the West Coast school of jazz in the 1950s. He published an autobiography, *Raise Up Off Me*, with Don Asher (1974).

BIBL: FeaEJ. FeaJS. FeaGitJS.

DISC: Kink. ModJ. TudJ.

HAWKINS, COLEMAN (''BEAN'' or ''HAWK''). Jazz saxophonist (b. 21 November 1904 in St. Joseph, Missouri; d. 19 May 1969 in New York, New York). He studied piano with his mother, an organist, when he was five years old; at seven he studied cello, and at nine he began playing tenor saxophone. He obtained his musical education in the public schools of St. Joseph, Missouri, and Kansas City, Missouri; at Washburn College in Topeka, Kansas; and through private study in Chicago, Illinois. He began playing with neighborhood bands at an early age, and by the time he was sixteen was playing professionally with bands in Kansas City. In 1921 he joined Mamie Smith* and Her Jazz Hounds, with whom he toured (1921-23) and went to New York. There he played with various groups, then joined Fletcher Henderson* as a regular sideman in 1924 and remained until March 1934. He first recorded in 1922 with Smith's Jazz Hounds, and made his recording debut with his own orchestra in September 1933. In 1934 he toured in Europe for the first time, at first under the sponsorship of impresario-bandleader Jack Hylton, then later as a free-lance soloist (1934-39). He toured widely on the Continent, performing with others and as a soloist; he recorded extensively; and he appeared in films or on film soundtracks, including *In Town Tonight* (1935). After returning to the United States he led big bands for two years (1939-41), then performed primarily with his small groups. When the 1940s ushered in the bebop era, he moved gracefully into the new times; in February 1944 he gathered together leading jazzmen to make the first recording of a bop piece, ''Woody 'n' you'' including the composer, John Birks (''Dizzy'') Gillespie,* and Don Byas,* Albert (''Budd'') Johnson,* Leo Parker, Oscar Pettiford,* and Max Roach,* among others. Hawkins was active primarily as a soloist during the last twenty-five years of his career, performing and recording extensively with others. His touring included performances with JATP (Norman Granz's Jazz at the Philharmonic) during the years 1946-67 in the United States and in Europe, with Illinois Jacquet's* band to American Service Bases in Europe in 1954, with Roy Eldridge* as co-leader of a quintet, and with Oscar Peterson* (1968), among others. He played with a powerful but expressive tone and a heavy vibrato; his most celebrated performance was on ''Body and soul'' (1939), and his best-known album, *The Hawk Flies* (1944-57). He made innumerable recordings over his long career and won many awards from the music industry. Hawkins was a pioneer in defining the role of the tenor saxophone in the jazz ensemble and was called ''the father of the tenor saxophone.'' His influence upon saxophonists of his time and those who came after him was enormous; they played either in the tradition of Coleman Hawkins or of Lester Young,* then moved from that point into their own individual styles.

BIBL: AlHen, ChilWW. DanceWS. FeaEJ. FeaJS. FeaGitJS. Dizzy Gillespie with Al Fraser, *To Be or Not to Bop* (New York, 1979). MeeJMov. NYT, 20 May 1969.

DISC: Jep. Kink. ModJ. RustJR. TudJ.

HAWKINS, EDWIN. Gospel singer (b. c1943 in Oakland, California). In 1967 Edwin Hawkins and Betty Watson founded a gospel group composed of members of his father's Holiness church and other nearby churches to perform at the Annual Youth Congress of the Churches of God in Christ in Washington, D.C. The success of the performance persuaded the singers, who called themselves The Northern California State Youth Choir, to become a permanent group; in 1968 they changed their name to The Edwin Hawkins Singers. A recording made in 1969, "Oh, Happy Day," brought wide attention and helped to establish the group among the leading gospel groups of the time. They toured widely in the United States and abroad, appearing in churches, on college campuses, on television shows, and in concert halls. By 1980 the nucleus of the Hawkins Singers consisted of members of the family; brothers Walter, Daniel, and Edwin; sisters Carole, Freddie, and Lynette; cousin Shirley Miller; nephew Joe Smith; and Walter's wife, Tremaine, who was lead singer. Edwin and Walter played piano and organ in addition to singing and writing and arranging song materials; Daniel played bass and organ; and Smith played bass, drums, and organ. The Hawkins Singers received awards from the music and recording industries. Their best-known albums were *Children Get Together* (1971) and *Love Alive II* (1979). Their music belonged to the tradition of contemporary soul-gospel.

BIBL: Barbara Baker, "Black Gospel Music Styles, 1942-1975" (Ph.D. diss., University of Maryland, 1978). GMEncy. *Sepia* (August 1969). StamPRS.

DISC: TudBM.

HAWKINS, ERSKINE RAMSAY. Jazz trumpeter. (b. 26 July 1914 in Birmingham, Alabama). He began playing drums at the age of seven, later changed to trombone, and then to trumpet when he was thirteen. He played in a neighborhood band as a child. He obtained his musical education in the public schools and Tuggle Institute of Birmingham, Alabama, and at Alabama State Teachers College in Montgomery, where he played with the 'Bama State Collegians. In 1936 he went to New York and made his debut at the Harlem Opera House as a bandleader with the Collegians, who had gone to New York in 1934 fronted by J. B. Sims. His band was very popular for the next two or more decades, particularly at the Savoy Ballroom in the Harlem community where it became virtually the house band after William ("Chick") Webb's* death in 1939. Economic problems eventually forced him to disband his large group, and in the early 1950s he formed a smaller group. From the 1960s on he led a quartet, which performed primarily in hotels and nightclubs, but he occasionally gathered together a big band for special occasions and recording, as for the album *Reunion* (1974). His band was one of the best of the swing era; those who performed with him over the years included Paul and Wilbur ("Dud") Bascomb,* Julian Dash,* Samuel ("Sammy") Lowe, Heywood Henry, Avery Parrish,* and Billy Daniels,* among others. The band's best-known performances were "Tuxedo junction," "You can't escape from me," and "After hours." He first recorded in 1936 and thereafter recorded extensively. His honors included an honorary doctorate from Alabama State (1947).

BIBL: ASCAP. ChilWW. DanceWS. FeaEJ. FeaGitJS. MeeJMov.

DISC: Jep. Kink. RustJR. TudJ.

HAYDEN, SCOTT. Rag pianist/Composer (b. 31 March 1882 in Sedalia, Missouri; d. 16 September 1915 in Chicago, Illinois). He was a protégé of Scott Joplin*; he began piano study with Joplin at the age of fifteen. His first professional experience was playing piano in nightclubs of Sedalia, Missouri, and later in St. Louis, Missouri. In 1902 he settled in Chicago, Illinois, although he returned to St. Louis for a short period in 1903 to perform with the Scott Joplin Ragtime Opera Company. Hayden eventually left the music field in Chicago. He is remembered for the piano rags he wrote in collaboration with Joplin, "Felicity rag," "Sunflower slow drag," and "Kismet rag."

BIBL: Blesh. BPIM 3 (Spring, Fall 1975). JaTiRR.

HAYES, ISAAC. Rhythm 'n' blues singer (b. 20 August 1942 in Covington, Tennessee). His grandparents, with whom he lived, moved to Memphis, Tennessee, when he was a child, and it was there that he obtained his musical education in the public schools. He taught himself to play musical instruments well enough to play in his junior-high-school band. Even before he graduated from high school he began singing and playing piano in local nightclubs. Later he played saxophone with local groups, including the Mar-Keys, then began an association with Stax Records as a studio bandsman. In 1962 he met David Porter at Stax, and the two men formed a songwriting team which became enormously successful. Those for whom they arranged and produced songs included Carla Thomas, William ("Billy") Eckstine,* and Booker T. Jones,* among others. In 1969 he began recording as a soloist; his second album, *Hot Buttered Soul*, won wide attention. Thereafter he recorded regularly and toured widely. His best-known works were his score for the film *Shaft*, which earned him an Academy Award (1972), and the pieces "Baby," "Soul man," and "Black Moses." He received numerous awards from the music industry. Hayes was an important contributor to the "Memphis sound."

BIBL: BMI (December 1971; Issue No.1, 1978). *Ebony* (October 1973). FeaGitJS.

DISC: TudBM.

HAYES, ROBERT ("UNCLE BOB"). Music/drama journalist (b. 23 December 1869 in Memphis, Tennessee; d. 27 July 1944 in Chicago, Illinois). He moved to Chicago, Illinois, in the first decade of the twentieth century with a musical comedy company and later was active as an entertainer in nightclubs and on the vaudeville stage. He contributed to the *Chicago Defender* for more than twenty years, beginning under music/drama editor Tony Langston, and earned the soubriquet "Dean of Theatrical News." His regular column was titled "Here and There."

BIBL: Black press, incl. CDef, 5 August 1944.

HAYES, ROLAND. Concert singer (b. 3 June 1887 in Curryville, Georgia; d. 31 December 1976 in Boston, Massachusetts). His family moved to Chattanooga, Tennessee, when he was about thirteen, and there he sang in a church choir and first began music study. His early career development was influenced by Arthur Calhoun, who introduced him to recordings of Caruso and taught him music fundamentals. He obtained his musical education at Fisk University in Nashville, Tennessee (beginning in the pre-college department, 1905-c1910), and later studied voice with Arthur Hubbard in Boston, Massachusetts (1911-1919), and George Henschel (1922-23 and intermittently through 1929) and Amanda Ira Aldridge* in London, England. He began singing in public during his student days in Chattanooga, appearing in local churches and for social entertainments. In Nashville he sang (tenor) with the Fisk Jubilee Singers,* and after leaving there went to Louisville, Kentucky, where he eventually found employment singing backstage in a theater for silent films. In 1911 he toured with the Fisk Singers (at that time a professional quartet). He settled in Boston in 1911 and thereafter toured widely as a concert singer, while maintaining employment in non-musical occupations. During the years 1912-19 he traveled throughout the eastern part of the nation, appearing on Walter Craig's* concerts and Carnegie Hall concerts in New York, on Henry Hugh Proctor's* Colored Musical Festival Concerts in Atlanta, Georgia, and on other concerts sponsored by black organizations in large cities. He toured the circuit of black churches and black colleges and, as well, gave periodic recitals in Boston halls, the Steinart and Symphony Hall. By 1920 he had accumulated enough money to study abroad; there he combined study with concert work. From his first concert in London's Aeolian Hall (1920) he won wide recognition for the beauty of his voice. By the time he returned to the United States in 1923, he had sung in the major capitals of Europe and before crowned heads and was an international celebrity. Thereafter he toured extensively at home and abroad, singing with leading symphony orchestras as well as in concert halls. He was perhaps the first black singer to sing with a major orchestra when he sang with the Boston Symphony in 1923. In 1950 he was appointed to the music faculty of Boston University. He continued his concert activities through the 1950s, and in 1962 gave a benefit seventy-fifth birthday concert for black colleges. He aided young black concert artists throughout his career, singing recitals with Marian Anderson* at the beginning of her career and coaching and giving financial aid to many, including Aubrey Pankey* and Rawn Spearman,* among others. Hayes was the leading black singer of his time and undoubtedly the leading concert tenor in the world during the 1920s-40s. His repertory was large and richly varied, consisting primarily of lieder but also including songs from the Renaissance to contemporary times, particularly Negro spirituals. He published *My Songs; AfroAmerican Religious Folk Songs* (Boston, 1948). His daughter, Afrika, became a professional singer.

BIBL: Black press, incl. AmstN, 6 May 1950; CDef, 16 November 1912; NYAge, 18 December 1920, 14 May 1921, 13 October 1923, 19 January 1924; PhilaT, 22 January 1916. BPIM 2 (Fall 1974), 5 (Fall 1977), 6 (Spring 1978), pp. 71-88. HNB. NYB, 1921. Cornelius V. Troup, *Distinguished Negro Georgians* (Dallas, 1962). WWCA, 1950.

DISC: Turn.

HAYNES, EUGENE, JR. College professor/Concert pianist (b. 10 March 1928 in East St. Louis, Illinois). He was a piano prodigy at the age of four. He studied first with local teachers in East St. Louis, Illinois, then with Stanley Henderson in St. Louis, Missouri. He obtained his musical education at the Juilliard School of Music in New York (artist diploma, 1947; postgraduate artist diploma, 1949), where he studied with Catherine Bacon and Vittorio Gianini. He also studied privately with Nadia Boulanger in Paris, France (composition, 1951-54), Isador Philippe in Paris (1954-55), Isabella Vengerova in New York (1955), and Edith Skjerne in Copenhagen, Denmark (harpsichord, 1956). In 1958 he made his debut as a concert pianist at Carnegie Recital Hall in New York. Thereafter he toured widely in the United States, Europe, Latin America, and South America, appearing in concert halls, with leading symphony orchestras, and on radio and television programs. His teaching career included tenures at Lincoln University in Jefferson City, Missouri (1960-79), and at the Southern Illinois University in East St. Louis (1979-). He also taught master classes during summers in Copenhagen. During the years 1965-73 he was host to a classical music program, "The Wonderful World of Music with Eugene Haynes," on St. Louis radio station KSD. His honors included an award from the National Association of Negro Musicians* (1974).

BIBL: Questionnaire. Parmenia Migel, *Titania. The Biography of Isak Dinesen* (New York, n.d.). IntWWM. WWA. WWBA.

HAYNES, ROY OWENS. Jazz drummer (b. 13 March 1926 in Boston, Massachusetts). He played drums as a child. During his high-school years he played with various groups in Boston, Massachusetts, then went to New York in 1945, where he played with Luis Russell* (1945-47) at the Savoy Ballroom in the Harlem community. Thereafter he played with various groups, including Lester Young* (1947-49), Charlie Parker* (1949-50), Miles Davis,* Stanley ("Stan") Getz (intermittently 1950-65), Sarah Vaughan* (1953-58), Thelonious Monk* (1958), and Phineas Newborn (co-leader of a quartet, 1960s), among others. He also led his own groups from time to time and during the 1970s performed primarily with his Hip Ensemble, whose personnel included over the years Don Pate, Cedric Lawson, John Mosley, Art Matthews, and William Saxton, among others. He toured widely in the United States, Europe, and Japan, appearing in concert halls and nightclubs, on radio and television programs, and at jazz festivals. He won awards from the music industry and was regarded as one of the most versatile of contemporary jazz drummers.

BIBL: Black press, incl. AmstN, 29 March 1975. FeaEJ. FeaJS. FeaGitJS. MeeJMov.

DISC: Kink.

HAZZARD, ISAAC. Society dance-band leader (b. 1804 in Philadelphia, Pennsylvania; d. c1864 in Philadelphia). Nothing is known of his early life. By the 1830s he had developed a dance orchestra of about twenty men, which was in great demand to play for Philadelphia's dancing schools, military parades, and fancy dress balls and assemblies of the elite. Like his contemporary Frank Johnson,* Hazzard imported new music from Europe in order to provide his clientele with the "latest successes," according to the press. Although his orchestra was primarily a dance orchestra, he occasionally gave concerts, participated in sacred-music concerts sponsored by black churches, and played for the after-dances of concerts given by white musicians. His band apparently had a permanent association with dancing-school master D. L. Carpenter. In addition to performing with his groups, he conducted a music studio. He published a considerable quantity of music, consisting primarily of pianoforte arrangements of his band compositions. His best-known compositions were "Miss Lucy Neale Quadrille," "The Miercken Polka Waltz," and "The Alarm Gun Quadrille." The popularity of some of his pieces lasted into the 1870s; they were listed in the *Complete Catalogue of Sheet Music and Musical Works, 1870* (published by the Board of Music Trade of the United States of America, 1871; reprint with introduction by Dena Epstein [New York, 1973]).

BIBL: BPIM 4 (July 1976), p. 250. *The Public Ledger* [Philadelphia], including 28 September 1837; 16 October 1837; 12 April 1838; 15 February 1839; 13 November 1839. Philip English Mackey, ed. *A Gentleman of Much Promise. The Diary of Isaac Mickle, 1837-1845* (Philadelphia, 1977).

HEATH, ALBERT ("TOOTIE"). Jazz percussionist (b. 31 May 1935 in Philadelphia, Pennsylvania). See **HEATH, PERCY.**

HEATH, JAMES EDWARD ("JIMMY"). Jazz saxophonist (b. 25 October 1926 in Philadelphia, Pennsylvania). He came from a musical family: his father played clarinet in a band, and two brothers, Albert ("Tootie") and Percy,* became professional musicians. He obtained his musical education in the public schools of Philadelphia, Pennsylvania, and at the Theodore Presser School of Music in Philadelphia (1944-45). Later he studied orchestration with Rudolph Schramm. From the mid-1940s to the late-1960s he played tenor saxophone with various groups, including Howard McGhee* (1947-48), John Birks ("Dizzy") Gillespie* (1950-51), Donald Byrd* (1964), Miles Davis,* and Arthur ("Art") Farmer* (co-leader of a quintet, 1965-68). During the 1960s he changed to playing flute and became more involved with jazz projects and teaching. He worked with William ("Billy") Taylor* in Jazzmobile, teaching and producing jazz-lecture concerts. His teaching career included tenures at City College of the City University of New York and at Housatonic Community College in Bridgeport, Connecticut. He also performed with his own groups and gave increased attention to writing music and arranging for such jazzmen as Yusef Lateef,* Clark Terry,* and Billy Taylor. From 1974 he was co-leader of a quartet or quintet with his brother Percy; the members included at one time or another Albert Heath, Stanley Cowell,* Keith Copeland, and Tony Purrone. His best-known composition was *Afro-American Suite of Evolution* (1976).

BIBL: Black press, incl. AmstN, 14 April 1979. FeaEJ. FeaJS. FeaGitJS. WWA. WWBA.

HEATH, PERCY. Jazz bassist (b. 30 April 1923 in Wilmington, North Carolina). See also **MODERN JAZZ QUARTET.** He came from a musical family: his father played clarinet in a band, and two brothers, Albert ("Tootie") and James ("Jimmy"),* became professional musicians. He obtained his musical education in the public schools of Phildelphia, Pennsylvania, where he played violin in school orchestras, and at the Granoff School of Music in Philadelphia, where he studied string bass. During the 1940s he played with various groups, including Howard McGhee,* Miles Davis,* James ("J. J.") Johnson,* and Theodore ("Fats") Navarro,* among others. In 1950 he joined John Birks ("Dizzy") Gillespie* (1950-52), then performed with the Modern Jazz Quartet (1952-74), which toured widely throughout the world and was credited with taking jazz out of the nightclub into the concert hall. During his tenure in MJQ he played during vacation periods with his brother Jimmy's group; after leaving MJQ in 1974 he joined Jimmy as co-leader of a group, whose membership included at one time or another Albert Heath, Stanley Cowell,* Keith Copeland, and Tony Purrone. The group toured widely throughout the world. Percy Heath recorded prolifically and was regarded as one of the top bassists of the time, especially because of his tone and technique. He received awards from the music industry.

BIBL: Black press, incl. AmstN, 14 April 1979. FeaEJ. FeaJS. FeaGitJS. MeeJMov. WWA, 1976-77.

DISC: Kink. ModJ.

HEGAMIN, LUCILLE NELSON. Vaudeville/blues singer (b. 29 November 1894 in Macon, Georgia; d. 1 March 1970 in New York, New York). She began her career in a Leonard Harper stock company at the age of fifteen. In 1914 she went to Chicago and established herself as the "Georgia Peach." After spending a year in Los Angeles, California, where she sang with the band of her husband, Bill Hegamin, she settled in New York in 1919. In August 1920 she became the second black singer in history to record blues—the first was Mamie Smith.* Like Smith, Hegamin was more a vaudeville singer than a blues singer, and the songs she recorded were composed blues rather than folk blues. During the next decade she toured widely and recorded extensively, as a soloist and with groups, including her own Blue Flame Syncopators. She also performed in musicals, including the road company of *Shuffle Along* (1921-22) and *Creole Follies* (1923), and at one time had her own vaudeville act. After the 1930s she was inactive except for a short recording period during the 1960s.

BIBL: BWW. ChilWWJ. Derrick Stewart-Baxter, *Ma Rainey and the Classic Blues Singers* (New York, 1970). Oliv. *Record Research* 40 (January 1962). *Record Research* 104 (March 1970).

DISC: Kink. RustJR.

HEMMENWAY, JAMES. Society dance-band leader (b. 1800 in Philadelphia, Pennsylvania; d. 1849 in Philadelphia). He first attracted wide attention in the Philadelphia press during the 1820s. His band played during the festivities in honor of the visit of General Lafayette to Philadelphia in 1824. He had a permanent association with the city's Washington Hall; his "Philadelphia Hop Waltz" was arranged for pianoforte "as performed at Washington Hall," and the title page of his fifth set of quadrilles identifies him as the "leader of the orchestra at Washington Hall." The rising popularity of the bands of Isaac Hazzard* and Frank Johnson* undoubtedly was responsible for declining interest in Hemmenway's band during the 1830s. It is not clear whether he ever played in Johnson's band. In 1837, when Johnson was preparing to take a small group to England, he announced in the press that Edward Augustus and James Hemmenway would be left in charge of the Johnson quadrille and military bands remaining in Philadelphia, but finally, only Augustus was left in charge. During Hemmenway's late career, his band performed frequently on sacred-music concerts of black churches. He began publishing marches, dances, and songs as early as 1821; the popular song "That rest so sweet like bliss above" was published in a literary journal, *Atkinson's Casket* (October 1829). Other well known compositions were "General LaFayette's Trumpet March and Quickstep," "The Washington Grays' Grand March," "Miss Billing's Waltz," and his Five Sets of Quadrilles. At least one of his pieces, "The New Year and Courtesy Cotillion,'' was in print as late as 1870 (see the *Complete Catalogue of Sheet Music and Musical Works*, published by the Board of Music Trade of the United States of America, 1871; reprint with introduction by Dena Epstein [New York, 1973]).

BIBL: Black press, incl. *The Colored American*, 23 January 1841. *Poulson's American Daily Advertiser*, 4 November 1826. *The Public Ledger* [Philadelphia], including 17 December 1840. Richard J. Wolfe, *Secular Music in America, 1801-1825: A Bibliography* (New York, 1964).

HENDERSON, JR., FLETCHER HAMILTON (''SMACK''). Jazz pianist-arranger (b. 18 December 1897 in Cuthbert, Georgia; d. 28 December 1952 in New York, New York). He came from a musical family: both parents played piano and his brother Horace* became a professional musician. He studied piano from the age of six until he was thirteen years old. He obtained his musical education at the local private school, where his father was a teacher; at the preparatory school of Atlanta [Georgia] University; at Atlanta University, where he majored in the sciences (B.S., 1920) but was active in musical affairs. He played for musical productions directed by Kemper Harreld,* and in the summers he earned money by playing piano at a resort, Woods Hole, Massachusetts. In 1920 he went to New York to attend graduate school but became involved with music when he substituted for an ailing pianist on a Hudson River pleasure boat and later became the regular pianist. During the years 1920-24 he was associated first with the [Harry] Pace* & [W. C.] Handy* Music Company as song-demonstrator, then with the Pace Phonograph Corporation as musical director, accompanist, and bandleader for the company's Black Swan Jazz Masters (which accompanied Ethel Waters*). He also played with various other groups or accompanied singers during these years, making his recording debut in 1921. In 1924 he organized a big band, which played at the Club Alabam, then at the Roseland Ballroom (regularly 1924-36). During the 1930s his group played in other ballrooms and theaters, toured widely, and recorded extensively for that time. He also began to give considerable time to arranging music; in 1939 he disbanded his group and joined Benny Goodman as staff arranger and pianist (he gave up the piano, however, in December 1939). During the 1940s he reorganized his big band several times to play residencies—such as at the Roseland Ballroom or the DeLisa Club in Chicago, Illinois, or the Savoy Ballroom in the Harlem community of New York—and to play for special occasions, as for the revue *Jazz Train* (1950), for which he wrote the music. He spent another period as arranger with Goodman in 1947 and the next year toured with Ethel Waters again (1948-49). He was leading a small group, the Jazz Train Sextet, when a stroke in December 1950 forced his retirement from music.

Those who performed with one of his groups over the years included Louis Armstrong,* Henry (''Red'') Allen,* William (''Buster'') Bailey, Leon (''Chu'') Berry,* Art Blakey,* Garvin Bushnell,* Bennett (''Benny'') Carter,* Sid Catlett,* Coleman Hawkins,* Horace Henderson, Hilton Jefferson, Donald Redman,* and Russell Smith, among others. Henderson is credited with being the first jazzman to organize a big band and therefore counts as a major contributor to the history of jazz. His arrangements for black and white orchestras laid the foundation for the swing era; more than any other person he deserved the title ''King of Swing,'' which he failed, however, to receive. He pioneered in other ways: his was the first black orchestra to broadcast regularly over the radio; his recordings were the first to include examples of ''scat singing'' (Don Redman in ''My papa doesn't two-time no time,'' 1924) and boogie-woogie basses (Fletcher in ''China blues,'' 1923). His band style was distinctive for its antiphonal play between reed and brasses and his penchant for using muted block-chord reed accompaniment behind brass solos and vice versa. He exerted enormous influence upon his contemporaries, particularly through his arrangements, and his innovations passed into the mainstream of popular music in later years.

BIBL: AlHen. ASCAP. ChilWW. FeaEJ. MeeJMov.
DISC: Jep. Kink. RustJR. TudJ.

HENDERSON, HORACE. Jazz pianist-arranger (b. 22 November 1904 in Cuthbert, Georgia). He came from a musical family: both parents played piano and his brother Fletcher* became a professional musician. He obtained his musical education at the local private school, where his father was a teacher; at Atlanta [Georgia] University; and at Wilberforce [Ohio] University (B.A.). He studied piano informally with his mother as a child, then began formal lessons when he was fourteen years old. While at Wilberforce he organized a student band, The Collegians, with whom he began touring during summer vacations as early as 1924. Beginning in 1927 he toured regularly with the Collegians (after graduating from college), then changed the name of his group to The Stompers (1928-31). Those who played in his groups over the years included Myron (''Tiny'') Bradshaw,* Bennett (''Benny'') Carter,* Henry (''Red'') Allen,* Russell Smith, and Freddie Jenkins, among others. He also played with other groups during the 1920s-30s, including Sammy Stewart (1928), Donald (''Don'') Redman* (1931-33), his brother Fletcher (1933-34, 1936, 1943-

44), and Vernon Andrade (1935), among others. Thereafter he was active primarily with his own groups, although he toured with Lena Horne* (1944-45) as musical director and accompanist and with the Billy Williams Revue (1960s). He settled in Denver, Colorado, during the late 1960s. He was highly regarded as an arranger-composer; those for whom he arranged music included Thomas Dorsey, Charlie Barnet, Benny Goodman, Coleman Hawkins,* Earl Hines,* Glen Gray, Jimmy Lunceford,* and his brother Fletcher, among many others.

BIBL: AlHen. ChilWW. FeaEJ.

DISC: Jep. Kink. RustJR.

HENDERSON, ROSA DESCHAMPS. Vaudeville/musicals singer (b. 24 November 1896 in Henderson, Kentucky; d. 6 April 1968 in New York, New York). She began performing professionally about 1913 in her uncle's tent show and thereafter toured with various carnivals, tent, and vaudeville shows. She sang in duo acts with her husband Douglas (''Slim'') Henderson (1927-1928) and in trios with Douglas and John Mason. During the 1920s she was active in theatrical productions in New York, particularly in Harlem theaters —the Lincoln, Lafayette, and New Alhambra. She performed in such shows as *The Harlem Rounders* (1927), *The Seventh Avenue Strollers* (1927), *Blackouts of 1929*, and *Blackberries Revue* (1930), among others. In 1928 she sang in the London, England, production of *Show Boat*. She made her recording debut in 1923 and thereafter recorded prolifically, often with the accompaniment of Fletcher Henderson* on piano or with his Jazz Five. Other accompaniment groups or individuals included Coleman Hawkins,* Cliff Jackson, James P. Johnson,* Elmer Snowden,* and James (''Bubber'') Miley,* among others. She was best known for her blues, which she sang with a strong, vibrant tone. She recorded more extensively during the years 1923-31, perhaps, than any other black woman singer of the time.

BIBL: BWW. AlHen. ChilWW. *Record Research* (April 1966).

DISC: Kink. RustJR.

HENDRICKS, FREDERICK WILMOTH (''KING HOUDINI''). Calypso entertainer/songwriter (b. 25 November 1896 in Port of Spain, Trinidad; d. 6 August 1973 in New York, New York). He obtained his musical education at St. Mary's College of the Immaculate Conception in Trinidad, British West Indies. In 1923 he settled in New York, where his career as an entertainer flourished. He made history in 1946 when he produced his Calypso Carnival at Carnegie Hall in New York; he was the first calypsonian to perform there. His best-known songs were ''Johnny take my wife,'' which was chosen to be the official Carnival song in Trinidad for three consecutive seasons; ''Gin and coconut water''; and ''Stone cold dead in the market,'' made famous by Ella Fitzgerald* and Louis Jordan.* Hendricks is credited with having brought calypso to the United States.

BIBL: ASCAP. Black press, incl. AmstN, 9 August 1973.

HENDRICKS, JOHN CARL (''JON''). Jazz singer (b. 16 September 1921 in Newark, Ohio). As a child he sang in church and at social entertainments in the community. In 1932 his family moved to Toledo, Ohio, where he later sang on radio programs. His career development was encouraged by Arthur (''Art'') Tatum,* a family friend. He obtained his musical education in the public schools of Toledo, Ohio, and at the University of Toledo. He began his professional career after completing high school, singing with Jessie Jones in Detroit, Michigan. During his service in the United States Armed Services (1942-46), he was stationed in Europe, and he toured in several countries as a soloist. After his discharge he studied drums and for several years was active as both singer and drummer with his own groups, for two years in Rochester, New York, and then in Toledo. In 1952 he settled in New York, where he wrote songs in addition to performing and recording. In 1958 he joined with Dave Lambert and Annie Ross to form a vocal trio, which attracted wide attention for its popularization of ''jazz vocaleses,'' a novel approach to singing jazz that was invented by Edgar (''Eddie'') Jefferson* in the 1940s and promoted by King Pleasure (née Clarence Beeks) in the 1950s. The procedure involved setting lyrics to jazz melodies and to improvised solos on jazz recordings. For the Lambert-Ross-Hendricks first album, Hendricks wrote lyrics to the ensembles and all notes of improvised solos of some old recordings of William (''Count'') Basie*; the result, titled *Sing a Song of Basie*, was enormously successful. The trio toured widely and recorded extensively for six years, featuring a repertory of jazz vocaleses; in 1962 Yolande Bavan replaced Ross. In 1964 the trio was disbanded, and thereafater Hendricks toured for a short period with a new group, Jon Hendricks & Company, then as a soloist. From February 1968 he lived in London, England, for several years; using that city as a base, he toured in Europe and in Africa, appearing on television programs in England and in films, including *Jazz Is Our Religion* (1972). He returned to the United States in the 1970s and settled in Mill Valley, California. He toured occasionally with a trio, recorded frequently, continued his songwriting, and taught at California State University at Sonoma and at the University of California at Berkeley. His best-known work was the stage work, *Evolution of the Blues* (1960). Hendricks was important for his development of the jazz vocalese, which he applied not only to traditional jazz improvisation but also to bebop.

BIBL: ASCAP. FeaEJ. FeaJS. FeaGitJS. MeeJMov.

DISC: Jep. TudJ.

HENDRIX, JAMES MARSHALL ("JIMI"). Rock singer (b. 27 November 1942 in Seattle, Washington; d. 18 September 1970 in London, England). He was given a guitar when he was thirteen years old, and he taught himself to play by listening to recordings of Aaron (''T-Bone'') Walker,* Muddy Waters* (née McKinley Morganfield), and Riley (''B. B.'') King,* among others. During his high-school years he played with local groups. During his service in the United States Air Force, he developed a highly original performance style. After his discharge he returned for a short period to Seattle, but left in 1961 to tour with (''Little'') Richard Penniman* and arrived in New York after an eight-month tour. Thereafter he toured with various groups, including Ike and Tina Turner,* (''King'') Curtis Ousley,* the Isley Brothers,* and James Brown's* back-up group, the Famous Flames, among others. In 1966 he was performing in New York nightclubs when he attracted the attention of English musician Charles Chandler, who proposed to take Hendrix to England where he would be appreciated. Jimi formed his Jimi Hendrix Experience with Mitch Mitchell and Noel Redding; made his debut in Paris, France, late in 1966; and attracted wide attention for the group's flashy attire, use of electronic gadgetry, ear-shattering loud music, and antics while performing. Thereafter he toured on the nightclub circuit and recorded extensively. He returned to the United States in 1967 and soon developed an immense following, particularly after his performances at the Monterey [California] Pop Music Festival in 1967 and the Woodstock [New York] Festival in 1969. He recorded extensively after his first American releases in 1967, writing most of the music himself. His best-known recordings included the albums *Are You Experienced, Purple Haze,* and *Band of Gypsies.* He received numerous awards from the music industry. He appeared in several films, including the documentary *Jimi Hendrix* (1973). Hendrix was regarded as probably the most gifted rock musician of the 1960s; he exerted enormous influence upon the development of rock and soul music and, as well, electric guitar style.

BIBL: BWW. *Ebony* (May 1968). Curtis Knight, *Jimi* (New York, 1975). ShawWS. StamPRS. Chris Welch, *Hendrix* (New York, 1972).

HENRY, LEW W. Minstrel/Producer (b. 1870 in Leavenworth, Kansas; d. 19 ? in Cincinnati, Ohio [?]). He joined Scott's Minstrels at the age of ten and remained in the theatrical world, off and on, for the remainder of his career. Over the years he performed with Campbell's Minstrels, [Charles] Hicks* and Sawyer's Minstrels, and contemporary vaudeville companies. He also toured with Bob Cole* and Billy Caldwell in two-man vaudeville acts. In 1910 he became the first manager of the Howard Theater in Washington, D.C. In 1915 he began working with the Sherman H. Dudley* enterprises and became the manager and show producer at the Dudley Theater in Washington. In later years he settled in Cincinnati, Ohio, where he took over management of the Lincoln and Roosevelt Theaters about 1921.

BIBL: Black press, incl. CDef, 23 July 1910; IndF, 20 November 1915. Wendell P. Dabney, *Cincinnati's Colored Citizens* (Cincinnati, 1926), p. 341.

HEWLETT, JAMES. Actor/Entertainer (fl. early nineteenth century in New York, New York; d. 1840s in New York). A native of the West Indies, he settled in New York during the second decade of the nineteenth century and first attracted attention as a singer in an ''ice cream garden,'' called the African Grove, which was operated by black entrepreneur Henry Brown. In 1821 Brown organized the African Grove Theater company, and Hewlett became one of his featured actors and ballad singers. After the African Grove closed, Hewlett toured as a single attraction, singing popular ballads of the period and performing imitations of famous actors. Some time between 1823 and 1825 he went to London, England; thereafter he advertised himself as ''The New York and London Coloured Comedian.'' In 1826 he joined forces with Frank Johnson* of Philadelphia to give benefit concerts. After taking a few additional benefits for himself in New York, he left again for London in the spring of 1826. After his return to the United States, he largely disappeared from public view. Martin Delany* referred to a Hewlett performance at the Old Richmond Hill Theater of New York in 1836, and in his book (published 1852) reported that Hewlett ''died in New York a few years ago.''

BIBL: Martin Delany, *The Condition, Elevation, Emigration and Destiny of the Colored People of the United States* (Philadelphia, 1852), p. 143. Herbert Marshall and Mildred Stock, *Ira Aldridge, the Negro Tragedian* (London, 1958). *The National Advocate* [New York], incl. 3 August 1821, 27 October 1821, 21 September 1821, 25 September 1821. George Odell, *Annals of the New York Stage*, v. 3 (New York, 1927). Simon Snipe, pseud., ''An Evening at the African

Theater'' in *Sports of New York* (New York, 1823) and ''Hewlett at Home'' in *Sports of New York* (New York, 1824). SouMBA.

HEYWOOD, EDWARD, JR., (''EDDIE''). Jazz pianist (b. 4 December 1915 in Atlanta, Georgia). He came from a musical family: his father, Eddie, Sr., was a bandleader-pianist and an uncle, LeRoy Smith, was also a bandleader. He studied piano with his father when he was eight. By the time he was fourteen, he was playing professionally in a local theater. He left Atlanta about 1932 to tour with various groups, including Clarence Love (1934-37), with whom he went to New York. Thereafter he played with several groups, among them Bennett (''Benny'') Carter* (1938-40) and Arthur (''Zutty'') Singleton* (1940-41). In 1941 he formed his own group, which played long residencies in New York nightclubs, then moved to California in 1944. There his group also appeared in films, including *Junior Prom* (1946) and *The Dark Corner* (1946). At times during his career he was forced to retire temporarily from music because of partial paralysis, but he remained active through the 1970s, playing in nightclubs and appearing at festivals and on college campuses. His best-known performance was ''Begin the beguine'' in the mid-1940s, and his best-known composition was ''Canadian sunset.'' He received awards from the music industry.

BIBL: ChilWW. FeaEJ. FeaJS. FeaGitJS. MeeJMov.
DISC: Jep. Kink.

HIBBERT, FREDERICK (''FRED'' ''TOOTS''). Reggae singer (b. 1946 in May Pen, Jamaica). In 1963 Hibbert formed a vocal group in Kingston, Jamaica, later called Toots and the Maytals, composed of Henry (''Raleigh'') Gordon, Nathaniel (''Jerry'') Mathias, and himself. When the group began touring widely, an instrumental accompaniment group was added, including Ansel Collins (keyboards), Rad Bryan (rhythm guitar), Freddie (''Hucks'') Brown (lead guitar), Paul Douglass (drums), Jackie Jackson (bass), and Winston Wright (organ). The music they played was called ska at first (''blue beat'' in England), then later reggae. Hibbert was credited with having been the first one to use the term reggae in association with music and dance in his song ''Let's do the reggay'' (1968). Their best-known recordings were ''I got dreams to remember,'' ''Monkey man,'' ''Reggae got soul,'' ''Rasta man,'' and ''Pressure drop''; the best-known album was *Funky Kingston* (1975). Reggae music exerted wide influence upon British singers and singers of the United States, particularly Johnny Nash* with his recordings of ''Hold me tight'' and ''I can see clearly now.'' The Maytals, like other reggae groups, were devout Rastafarians. Their music blended elements of rock, calypso, soul, jazz and blues, with traditional African and religious music.

BIBL: Black press, incl. AmstN, 17 July 1976. NYT, 30 November 1975. *Sepia* (March 1974).
DISC: TudBM.

HIBBLER, ALBERT (''AL''). Jazz singer (b. 16 August 1915 in Little Rock, Arkansas). Blind from birth, he obtained his musical training at the Conservatory for the Blind in Little Rock, Arkansas. He began his career by winning prizes in amateur contests. He sang (baritone) with several groups before joining Edward (''Duke'') Kennedy Ellington* (1943-51), where he first won national recognition. After leaving Ellington, he toured as a soloist. He recorded with Ellington, William (''Count'') Basie,* Johnny Hodges,* and others. During the 1970s he was active in television music and appeared at jazz festivals. His best-remembered performances included ''Unchained melody,'' ''After the lights go down low,''and ''Pennies from heaven.''

BIBL: FeaEJ.
DISC: Jep. Kink. TudBM.

HICKS, CHARLES (''BARNEY''). Minstrels manager (b. c1840s [?] in Baltimore, Maryland; d. 1902 in Suraboya, Java [now Indonesia]). Nothing is known of his early career. He first attracted attention when he organized a black minstrel troupe in 1865 in Indianapolis, Indiana, which he called the Georgia Minstrels.* During the mid-1860s there were also two other touring minstrel troupes using the same or similar names. By the end of 1865 Hicks's company was fairly well established, and it toured widely during the next five years. When Hicks began his Fourth Annual Tour in 1868 he boasted of having a thirteen-piece brass band and new specialty acts for his Famous Original Georgia Minstrels. The musicians included Lou Johnson, George Dantworth, and George A. Skilling (orchestra leader). In January 1870 Hicks took a few of his minstrels to tour in Europe, leaving the majority to continue traveling about the United States. In the summer of 1870 Hicks joined forces with Sam Hague's Great American Slave Troupe, which had been performing in the British Isles since 1866. The combined groups played together in Ireland and in England, including a longtime residence at Liverpool. In July 1871 Hicks left Hague to return to the United States, taking with him at least two members of Hague's company, ''Japanese Tommy'' (i.e., Thomas Dilworth) and Aaron Banks. Hague and Hicks had a violent disagreement and argued back and forth through the *New York Clipper* for several months. Hicks continued to tour with his Georgia Minstrels until 1872, when he sold his rights in the troupe to Charles Callender. Over the seven years of its existence. Hicks's Georgia Minstrels included (in addition to those cited above) Charlie Anderson, Peter Devenear, T. Drewette (or Drewitte), James ("Jim") Grace, Robert ("Bob") Height, Billy Kersands,* Samuel Jones, Louis Pierson, Dick Weaver, John Wilson, and Jake Zabriskie, among others. According to "Ike" Simond, other members of this pioneer black minstrel troupe were Abe Bishop, Abe Cox, Tom Cornise, Jake Hamilton, James ("Jimmie") Jackson, Fred Lyons, Dick Slighter, and Lem Williams. Hicks continued to work with the Georgia Minstrels as a manager for Callender for some time. In 1877 he became manager of another black company, which he called the Georgia Minstrels and took to Australia for three years. After returning to the United States about 1880, he worked again briefly with Callender's Minstrels (owned at this time by J. H. Haverly), then became manager for a black-owned company, [Tom] McIntosh* and A. D. Sawyer's Colored Minstrels. This company was short-lived but made a comeback in a few years. By mid-1883 Hicks was working for the Frohman brothers (Charles and Gustave), who had taken ownership of Callender's Georgia Minstrels. The Frohmans had ambitious plans for their newly acquired black entertainers. In July 1883 they staged a mammoth Callender Consolidated Minstrel Festival at the Grand Opera House in New York, which featured Sam Lucas,* Billy Kersands, Wallace King,* Joseph Brindis da Salas,* and the Hyers Sisters,* among others, and which later toured the nation as far west as San Francisco. The Frohmans also planned to organize a Colored Opera Troupe to begin productions in the fall of 1883. It was planned that Hicks should sail to Paris, France, in July to arrange for engaging Marie Selika* and her husband, Sampson Williams, as the leading members of the projected opera company, but the plans apparently fell through. During the mid-1880s Hicks managed various minstrel groups, including one led by Billy Kersands. In August 1886 he became manager and co-owner of the Hicks and Sawyer Refined Colored Minstrels, which he took on tour to Australia and the Far East. In 1899 he was reported to be manager of Harmstron's Circus in Auckland, New Zealand, his original minstrels having returned to the United States. In 1900 Hicks was active in Java. In September 1902 *The* [Indianapolis] *Freeman* published a letter from Hicks, which gave his account of the origin of the Original Georgia Minstrels in 1865. In December 1902 the newspaper reported his death in Java.

BIBL: Black press, incl. NYFreeman, 21 May 1887; NYGlobe, 3 February 1883, 19 May 1883, 26 May 1883, 16 June 1883; IndF, 6 September 1902, 13 December 1902. Flet, p. 83. Simond. Trot, pp. 270-282. *The New York Clipper*, 1866-83.

HIGGINBOTHAM, IRENE. Songwriter (b. 11 June 1918 in Worcester, Massachusetts). She came from a musical family: her mother (who died when Irene was two years old) was music teacher, and an uncle, J. C. Higginbotham,* was a professional jazz trombonist. She began piano study at the age of four. She obtained her musical training at the Atlanta [Georgia] University Laboratory School, where she studied with Kemper Harreld* and Frederick Hall.* She began writing songs when she was fourteen; at sixteen she played her compositions in an all-Higginbotham recital. In 1935 she went to New York to pursue a career in songwriting. Her best-known songs included "That did it, Marie," "Harlem stomp," "The boogie beat'll getcha if you don't watch out," and "The caboose."

BIBL: ASCAP. Black press, incl. NYAge, 27 December 1941.

HIGGINBOTHAM, JACK ("JAY C"). Jazz trombonist (b. 11 May 1906 in Social Circle, near Atlanta, Georgia; d. 26 May 1973 in New York, New York). He came from a musical family: two brothers played brass instruments, and a niece, Irene Higginbotham,* was a songwriter. He began playing the bugle as a youth, then changed to trombone, which he played in local Atlanta groups. His professional career began in the mid-1920s when he moved to Cincinnati, Ohio. Thereafter he played with various groups, including Wesley Helvey (c1924) in Cincinnati; groups in Buffalo, New York (1926-28); Luis Russell* (1928-31), Fletcher Henderson* (1931-33, December 1936-37), William ("Chick") Webb* (1933), Mills' Blue Rhythm Band* (1934-36), and Louis Armstrong* (1937-40), among others. During the years 1940-47 he was co-leader of a sextet with Henry ("Red") Allen* but also played with other groups. During the 1950s-early 1960s he was active primarily with his own groups; he toured in the United States and abroad, appearing in nightclubs and at festivals. His first European tour was in 1958 with Sammy Price.* He began recording in 1929 with Russell and thereafter recorded extensively with his own groups and with others. Higginbotham was noted for his powerful, gut-bucket trombone style, and he played an important role in defining jazz trombone.

BIBL: AlHen. ChilWW. FeaEJ. FeaJS. FeaGitJS. MeeJMov.

DISC: Jep. Kink. RustJR. TudJ.

HILL (née HILLE), ANDREW. Jazz pianist (b. 30 June 1937 in Port au Prince, Haiti). His family settled in Chicago, Illinois, in 1941. As a child he sang in public (boy soprano), danced, and played accordion. Later he played piano and baritone saxophone. He began playing professionally in 1949, before he entered high school, and during the next few years performed with various groups, including Paul Williams's rhythm 'n' blues group and Dinah Washington* (1954), among others. His early style development was influenced by the music of Thelonious Monk.* In 1961 he settled in New York. Thereafter he performed with Rahsaan Roland Kirk* (1962) and the Lighthouse Group in Los Angeles, California (1962), then returned to New York in 1963, where he played with Eric Dolphy,* John ("Jackie") McLean,* Kenneth ("Kenny") Dorham,* Johnny Hartman, Albert ("Al") Hibbler,* and Robert ("Bobby") Hutcherson,* among others. He made his first records in 1963 and thereafter recorded regularly, primarily his own compositions. He toured widely in the United States, appearing in nightclubs and concert halls, on college campuses, at festivals, and in prisons (for a program of the New York State Council of the Arts in 1972). During the 1970s he became involved in teaching; he worked with New York's University of the Streets and served as composer-in-residence at Colgate University in Hamilton, New York (1970-71). He also continued to write music; in addition to extended compositions for his groups, he wrote many scores for televison shows. Best-known of his works were the opera *Golden Spook* (1970) and the chamber pieces, String Quartet, No. 1 and *Ecstasy* for brass quartet. His wife, organist Laverne Gabille, was co-composer for some of his pieces. His honors included grants from the National Endowment for the Arts (1971), the Smithsonian Institution (1975), and the Creative Arts Project, and an honorary doctorate from Colgate University (1971). He was regarded as one of the leaders of the second wave of avant-garde jazzmen in the 1970s; to some critics his highly original style reflected the influence of African rhythms.

BIBL: BMI (April 1972). FeaJS. FeaGitJS. WWA. WWBA.

DISC: Jep. ModJ. TudJ.

HILL, BERTHA ("CHIPPIE"). Blues singer (b. 15 March 1905 in Charleston, South Carolina; d. 7 May 1950 in New York, New York). Her family moved to New York when she was a child, and she began singing in Harlem cafes and nightclubs at an early age. Later she toured with Ma Rainey* and on the TOBA* (Theater Owners' Booking Association) circuit. She settled in Chicago, Illinois, during the mid-1920s, where she soon established herself as an important blues figure. She first recorded in 1925, and recorded regularly thereafter, frequently accompanied by guitarist Lonnie Johnson,* Louis Armstrong,* and Richard M. Jones.* During the 1930s and early 1940s she was largely inactive; she returned to professional singing in 1946, appearing in the radio show "This Is Jazz," singing in nightclubs, and recording again, often with Lovie Austin's* Blues Serenaders. In 1948 she appeared at the Paris Jazz Festival. Her career was cut off by an automobile accident.

BIBL: BWW. ChilWWJ. FeaEJ. Oliv. Derrick Stewart-Baxter, *Ma Rainey and the Classic Blues Singers* (New York, 1970).

DISC: DiGod. Kink. TudBM.

HILL, J[OHN] LEUBRIE. Songwriter (b. c1869 in New Orleans, Louisiana; d. 30 August 1916 in New York, New York). He obtained his early musical education in the public schools of Memphis, Tennessee. He began his career in Cincinnati, Ohio; about 1900 he moved to New York, where he soon established a reputation for himself as a songwriter, particularly in collaboration with Alex Rogers,* with whom he had been associated since 1896. He wrote songs for and performed with the George Walker*/Bert Williams* show *In Dahomey* (1902-05), Ernest Hogan's* show *Rufus Rastus* (1905-06), and the Walker/Williams *In Bandanna Land* (1907-09). He had a leading role in Williams's production of *Mr. Lode of Koal* (1909), after which he organized a company to produce his own shows, *My Friend from Dixie* (1911), and later *My Friend from Kentucky* (1913). The success of the latter, staged at the Lafayette Theater in the Harlem community, led to a demand by Florenz Zeigfeld for use of some of its songs in the *Follies of 1913*. Hill's best-known pieces were the two-step novelty "Chief Bunga Boo" (1910), the "Ragtime drummer" (1903), and the songs "At the ball," "My Dahomian queen," and "That's how the cakewalk's done" (the first, used in the *Follies*; the others, from *In Dahomey*).

BIBL: Black press, incl. NYAge 26 December 1913, 7 September 1916; IndF, 4 March 1911, 9 October 1916.

HILL, THEODORE ("TEDDY"). Jazz saxophonist (b. 7 December 1909 in Birmingham, Alabama; d. 19 May 1978 in Cleveland, Ohio). He obtained his musical education in the public schools of Birmingham, Alabama, where he played drums first in school bands, then changed to trumpet. In high school he came under the tutelage of John ("Fess") Whatley* and studied clarinet and saxophone. After graduation from high school, he toured with the Whitman Sisters* (1926-27), then settled in New York, where he played with various groups, including Luis Russell* (1928-29) and James P. Johnson* (1932), among others. In 1932 he organized his own big band, which played long residencies in theaters, nightclubs, and ballrooms, particularly the Savoy Ballroom in Harlem. His band also broadcasted regularly over radio station WJZ. In 1937 he toured in Europe. He continued to perform after returning to the United States, including appearances at the New York World's Fair in 1939, then disbanded his group in 1939. He recorded as early as 1927 (with Frank Bunch in Birmingham), and thereafter recorded with Henry ("Red") Allen,* Louis Armstrong,* Luis Russell, and his own group (1935-37). Those who played with him at one time or another included Leon ("Chu") Berry,* William ("Bill") Coleman, Roy Eldridge,* John Birks ("Dizzy") Gillespie,* Frank Newton, Russell Procope, and William ("Dicky") Wells,* among others. In 1939 he became manager of Minton's Playhouse in Harlem and hired Kenneth ("Kenny") Clarke,* Joe Guy, Nick Fenton, Kermit ("Scotty") Scott, and Thelonious Monk* to play in the house band. During the next few years Minton's became a place where jazzmen gathered after their working hours for "jam sessions," where they experimented with new ideas and/or competed in exhibiting their musical and technical skills. Monday nights were especially exciting, since most musicians did not perform on that night. Hill provided food and encouragement, but no money. Eventually a new music evolved, later called bebop, from the interaction of ideas among Clarke and Monk in the house band and Gillespie, Oscar Pettiford,* Charlie Christian,* Milton Hinton,* and many others. In 1942 Charlie Parker* joined the jam sessions at Minton's. This club and Clark Monroe's Uptown House came to be known as the birthplace of bop.

BIBL: Black press, incl. CDef, 13 July 1935. ChilWW. FeaEJ. Dizzy Gillespie, *To Be Or Not to Bop* (New York, 1979).

DISC: Kink. RustJR.

HILLERY, MABLE. Blues singer (b. 22 July 1929 in LaGrange, Georgia; d. 27 April 1976 in New York, New York). She first won recognition as a spirituals and blues singer in the Georgia Sea Islands when folklorist Alan Lomax went to the islands in 1960 to make a documentary film. In 1961 she joined the Georgia Sea Singers; she toured widely with the group and also as a soloist, appearing on concerts and at folk festivals. In the late 1960s she settled in New York, where she was active in developing teaching materials and tapes that preserved traditional black folksongs, working with cultural projects in Harlem, and holding workshops for prospective teachers.

BIBL: LivBl 28 (July-August 1976). NYT, 2 May 1976.

HINDERAS, NATALIE LEOTA (née **NATALIE HENDERSON**). Concert pianist (b. 15 June 1927 in Oberlin, Ohio). She came from a musical family: her grandfather was a bandmaster, her father was a professional jazzman, and her mother was a conservatory music teacher. She began playing piano when she was three years old and began piano study at the age of six. She also studied violin and voice as a child. She was a child piano prodigy; she played a full-length recital in public when she was eight years old and played a concerto with the Cleveland Women's Symphony when she was twelve. She obtained her musical education in the public schools of Oberlin, Ohio; at the Oberlin School of Music (to which she was admitted as a special student when she was eight; B. Mus., 1945); and at the Juilliard School of Music in New York, where she studied with Olga Samaroff. Later teachers included Edward Steuermann and Vincent Persichetti, with whom she studied composition. In 1954 she made her debut at Town Hall in New York. Thereafter she toured widely as a concert pianist in the United States, Europe, and the West Indies. In 1959 and again in 1964 her tours were sponsored by the United States Department of State and included Africa and Asia as well as Europe. She performed concertos with the leading symphony orchestras of the nation, played on radio and television programs, and appeared at festivals. Her best-known performances were of Ginastera's Piano Concerto, Rachmaninoff's Concerto No. 2 in C minor, the Schumann Piano Concerto, Gershwin's *Rhapsody in Blue*, and George Walker's* Piano Concerto No. 1, which she commissioned in 1975. She attracted wide attention for her performance of the music of black composers on her recitals and recordings. She made her recording debut in 1971, *Natalie Hinderas Plays Music by Black Composers*, and thereafter recorded several albums. Her honors included awards and fellowships from the Leventritt, John Hay Whitney, Julius Rosenwald, and Martha Baird Rockefeller Foundations, and the Fulbright funds; a citation from the Governor of Pennsylvania (1971); and an honorary doctorate from Swarthmore College. During the 1960s she was appointed to the music faculty of Temple University in Philadelphia, Pennsylvania.

BIBL: Black press, incl. CDef, 26 June 1937, 26 August 1944; PhilaT, 14 January 1975. WWA. WWBA.

HINES, EARL KENNETH ("FATHA"). Jazz pianist (b. 28 December 1905 in Duquesne, Pennsylvania).

He came from a musical family: his father played cornet and was leader of a brass band; his step-mother played organ (his mother died when he was three); and his sister Nancy became a professional musician. He began piano study when he was nine years old; by the time he was twelve he was a church organist, he played regularly on public recitals, and competed successfully in piano competitions. He obtained his musical education in the public schools of Pittsburgh, Pennsylvania, where he organized a jazz group during his high-school years. His early style development was influenced by the music of Eubie Blake* and Charles (''Lucky'') Roberts,* who were family friends and played in his aunt's home. His first professional experience was with Louis Deppe* in 1921, whom he accompanied in a local nightclub. After one year there he toured with Deppe's big band (1922). During the next two years he played in Pittsburgh in nightclubs and with his own groups, then moved to Chicago, Illinois, in 1924, where he played in the Elite No. 2 nightclub. Thereafter he played with various groups, including Carroll Dickerson,* Louis Armstrong,* and Jimmie Noone.* He then organized his own big band (1928-48), which played at the opening of the new Grand Terrace nightclub and later broadcasted regularly from the club. During this period he received the nickname ''Fatha'' from a radio announcer. He toured widely with his band and during the 1940s played long residencies in various cities; for a period in 1943 he brought in a string section of girls, including Angel Creasy and Lucille Dixon.* His band of 1942-43 later was called ''the incubator of bop'' because of the harmonic and rhythmic innovations introduced by such sidemen as John Birks (''Dizzy'') Gillespie,* William (''Billy'') Eckstine,* Eugene Ammons,* Bennie Green, Charlie Parker,* Albert (''Budd'') Johnson,* and singer Sarah Vaughan,* among others. Because of the recording ban imposed by the American Federation of Musicians during the period August 1942-November 1944, little of the innovative music was recorded. Hines disbanded his large orchestra in 1947; those who performed with him at one time or another included (in addition to those already cited) Hayes Alvis,* Walter Fuller,* Darnell Howard,* Herb Jeffries,* Ida James, James Mundy,* Ray Nance,* and Quinn Wilson, among many others. He toured with the Louis Armstrong All Stars (1948-51), then worked thereafter primarily with small groups, with which he toured widely throughout the world, including Europe, Japan, Australia, and Latin America. In 1966 the United States Department of State sponsored his tour in Russia. In 1960 he settled at Oakland, California. In 1964 he made his debut as a solo recitalist in New York and thereafter was highly active as a concert pianist as well as small-group leader. He played at jazz festivals at home and abroad, appeared on television programs and in films, and beginning in 1975 on cruise ships. He was one of the most prolific recording jazzmen in history; he made his recording debut in 1928 with Armstrong's Hot Five group and thereafter recorded with most of the leading jazzmen of his time. His best-known pieces were ''Rosetta,'' ''Boogie woogie on the St. Louis Blues,'' ''Deep forest'' (with Reginald Foresythe), ''You can depend on me,'' and ''Jelly, jelly'' (co-composer). Hines was a virtuoso pianist and a definitive force in the development of piano jazz. His style was distinctive for its ''trumpet style,'' in which he emulated Armstrong's trumpet phrasing, using powerful octaves and tremolo to give the effect of vibrato. He exerted enormous influence upon pianists of his time and later, virtually establishing a ''school''—as did the Harlem pianists—out of which came such pianists as Mary Lou Williams,* Theodore (''Teddy'') Wilson,* Earl (''Bud'') Powell,* and Nathaniel (''Nat King Cole'') Coles,* among others.

BIBL: ASCAP. ChilWW. DanceWEH. EAB. FeaEJ. FeaJS. FeaGitJS. MeeJMov. WWA. WWBA.

DISC: Jep. Kink. RustJR. TudJ.

HINES, J. EARLE. Gospel singer. See **MARTIN, SALLIE.**

HINES MATTHEWS, ALTONELL. Theater singer (b. 1905 in Norfolk, Virginia; d. 6 August 1977 in New York, New York). She obtained her musical education at Livingston College in Salisbury, North Carolina (B.A.), and at Columbia University Teachers College in New York (M. Ed.). Her teaching career included tenures at Virginia State College in Petersburg and Howard University in Washington, D.C. By the 1930s she had settled in New York and was active in musical theater. She sang the role of Commère (mezzo soprano) in Virgil Thomson's opera *Four Saints in Three Acts* in the original production (1934) and in a later revival (1952). She also sang in Gershwin's opera *Porgy and Bess*. She toured with Eva Jessye's* Radio and Concert Choir. She was married to Edward Matthews.*

BIBL: NYT, 9 August 1977.

DISC: Turn.

HINTON, MILTON J. (''MILT''). Jazz bassist (b. 23 June 1910 in Vicksburg, Mississippi). His mother was a church organist, and he was immersed in church musical activities from earliest childhood. His family moved to Chicago, Illinois, when he was a child. He obtained his musical education in the public schools of Chicago, where he came under the tutelage of N.Clark Smith* at Wendell Phillips High School. He began piano study with his mother. When he was thirteen he began violin study and later was concertmaster of the high school orchestra. He also played tuba and string bass in school and outside school played in the *Chicago Defender* Newsboy's Band, which was directed by Smith. His first professional experience was a summer job with Darnell Howard,* who directed a segment of the Earl Hines* band. Thereafter he played with various groups, including Eddie South* (intermittently 1931-36), Cladys (''Jabbo'') Smith,* Cassino Simpson (1932), Arthur (''Zutty'') Singleton* (1935) and Cabell (''Cab'') Calloway* (1936-51). During his tenure with Calloway he came into close contact with John Birks (''Dizzy'') Gillespie* and the two men exchanged musical ideas; Hinton also participated in the experimentation at Minton's Playhouse in the Harlem community (1938-42) that produced the new music called bebop. After leaving Calloway, he became increasingly involved with recording and studio work, although he toured with others frequently, among them, Louis Armstrong* (1953, 1954) and in the 1970s Pearl Bailey* (Africa, Far East, and Middle East) and Paul Anka (Puerto Rico and Mexico), among others. He played in television orchestras and Broadway musical pit orchestras; he also played in films, including *In Harm's Way* (1965) and *L'Aventure du jazz* (1969). He played at major jazz festivals at home and abroad, lectured and conducted workshops on college campuses, and from 1974 on was house bassist at a New York club. His honors included awards from the music industry and from civic organizations. He was an important bassist of the swing era who made a successful transition into bebop and contemporary periods.

BIBL: *Cadence* (December 1978). ChilWW. DanceWEH. DanceWS. FeaEJ. FeaJS. FeaGitJS. MeeJMov.

DISC: Jep. Kink.

HITE, LES. Jazz saxophonist (b. 13 February 1903 in DuQuoin, Illinois; d. 6 February 1962 in Santa Monica, California). He obtained his education in the public schools of Urbana, Illinois, and attended the University of Illinois at Urbana. His first professional experience was with his family band as a saxophonist. Thereafter he toured with various groups, then settled in Los Angeles, California, in 1925. There he played with such groups as the Spikes Brothers, Thomas (''Mutt'') Carey, Paul Howard, Curtis Mosby, and Vernon Elkins, among others. In 1930 he began a long residency at Sebastian's Cotton Club, where his band was ''fronted'' by Louis Armstrong* frequently during the years 1930-32. His band also played residencies in other cities, recorded, and was active in films and on filmtracks, including *The Music Goes 'Round* (1936) and *Sing Sinner Sing* (1933). Those who performed with Les Hite at one time or another included Lionel Hampton,* Lawrence Brown, John Birks (''Dizzy'') Gillespie,* and Aaron (''T-Bone'') Walker,* among others. Hite also wrote and arranged music for his group and for others; his best-known song was ''T-Bone blues.''

BIBL: ASCAP. ChilWW. FeaEJ. FeaJS. MeeJMov.

DISC: Jep. Kink. RustJR.

HOBSON, ANN. Symphony harpist (b. 6 November 1943 in Philadelphia, Pennsylvania). She began piano study at the age of six with her mother, a music teacher. Her family spent three years in Germany, when her father was on military assignment, and she studied with local teachers there. She obtained her musical education in the public schools of Philadelphia, Pennsylvania; at the Philadelphia Musical Academy; and at the Cleveland Institute of Music in Ohio (B. Mus., 1966). She began study of the harp in the music program of her high school. During her second year at the Academy she attended the Harp Colony at Camden, Maine. She played in Philadelphia's All-City High School Orchestra and in the Philadelphia Concert Orchestra.* Her teachers included Alice Chalifoux of the Cleveland Symphony. She began her professional career as second harpist in the Pittsburgh [Pennsylvania] Symphony Orchestra (1965-66). Thereafter she played with the National Symphony Orchestra in Washington, D.C. (principal harpist, 1966-69) and the Boston [Massachusetts] Symphony (associate-principal harpist, 1969-). Her teaching career included participation in the Marlboro Music Festival and tenures on the faculty of the Temple University Ambler Music Festival (1968-69) and the New England Conservatory of Music in Boston. In 1971 she organized the New England Harp Trio in Boston. She toured as a concert harpist, appearing with symphony orchestras and giving solo recitals. She also toured with the Boston Symphony and was with the orchestra in 1979 when it toured in China.

BIBL: Handy. WWBA.

HODGES, JOHN CORNELIUS (''RABBIT'' or ''JOHNNY''). Jazz saxophonist (b. 25 July 1906 in Cambridge, Massachusetts; d. 11 May 1970 in New York, New York). He played piano and drums as a child; at fourteen he began saxophone study, and later Sidney Bechet* gave him a few lessons. He obtained his musical education in the public schools of Boston, Massachusetts. One of his earliest professional experiences was playing in a band led by William (''Willie-the-Lion'') Smith* at New York's Rhythm Club (1925). Thereafter he played with groups in Boston, then joined William (''Chick'') Webb* in New York (1926-27), played with Charles ("Lucky") Roberts* (1928), and Edward ("Duke") Ellington,* with whom he played almost forty years (1928-51, 1955-70). During his long tenure in Ellington's band he won wide recognition for his passionate melodic lines, particularly in his ballad playing, and his penchant for glissandos. During the years 1951-55 he led his own groups or small contingents from the Ellington band. He made his recording debut in 1937 and thereafter recorded extensively with his own groups and with others, including William ("Wild Bill") Davis,* Earl Hines,* Lionel Hampton,* and Theodore ("Teddy") Wilson,* among others. He was also active as a songwriter and arranger and played in films or on filmtracks in the Ellington orchestra. His best known song was "I'm beginning to see the light." Although Hodges occasionally played soprano saxophone, he was counted among the pioneer alto saxophonists in the history of jazz, along with Bennett ("Benny") Carter,* who defined the role of the instrument in the jazz ensemble.

BIBL: ASCAP. ChilWW. DanceWS. FeaEJ. FeaJS. FeaGitJS. MeeJMov.

DISC: Jep. Kink. RustJR. TudJ.

HODGES, M. HAMILTON. Concert singer (b. c1869 in Boston, Massachusetts; d. August 1928 in Boston). He began his professional career as a baritone in the [William E.] Lew* Male Quintette during the early 1880s. Thereafter he toured with the Stewart Concert Company and Orpheus McAdoo's* Jubilee Singers, with whom he toured in South Africa, New Zealand, and Australia beginning in 1889. In 1896 he settled in Auckland, New Zealand, where he was active as a concert singer and voice teacher. Over the years he also sang in Australia and returned to the United States to give concerts. He was particularly noted as an oratorio soloist. In 1925 he resettled in Boston.

BIBL: Black press, incl. CDef, 25 August 1928. "In Retrospect: Orpheus Myron McAdoo" in BPIM 4 (Fall 1976). Hare.

HOGAN, ERNEST (REUBEN CROWDUS). Minstrel/vaudeville entertainer (b. 1865 in Bowling Green, Kentucky; d. 20 May 1909 in New York, New York). He began his career touring as a "pickaninny" in an Uncle Tom's Cabin company. Thereafter he toured with various minstrel companies throughout the nation and abroad. In 1890 he was a co-owner of [Henry] Eden and Hogan's Minstrels at Chicago, Illinois. In 1897 he joined Black Patti's Troubadours* as the leading comedian, and the next year he was the star of Will Marion Cook's* Broadway sketch, *Clorindy, or the Origin of the Cakewalk*. In 1899 he went to Australia with the M. B. Curtis All-Star Afro-American Minstrels; after the company was stranded he took over leadership and completed the touring in Australia, New Zealand, and Hawaii. Returning to the United States about 1902 he took a leading role in the show *Southern Enchantment*, the first production of the newly organized The Smart Set* company. Other principals of the show were Billy McClain,* Cordelia McClain,* and his wife, Louise Hogan. Hogan is credited with staging the first "syncopated-music" concert in history in 1905. He organized a group of singers, instrumentalists, and dancers into an act which gave predominance to syncopated music and called it The Memphis Students. With Abbie Mitchell,* Ida Forsyne, and himself in the starring roles, the act was booked into Hammerstein's Victoria Theater on Broadway for two weeks in May, but was so popular that it was held over for five months. In the fall of 1905 Will Marion Cook took over the act and carried it to Europe on tour. Hogan produced *Rufus Rastus*, with himself as star, during the 1905-06 season. At the time of his fatal attack of illness, he was starring in *The Oyster Man* (1909). Hogan advertised himself as "The Unbleached American," and was the highest-paid black vaudeville entertainer of his time. He was as celebrated for his songs as for his acting; his "All coons look alike to me" (1896) brought down upon him the wrath of some of his fellow black vaudevillians, but it was immensely popular with the public. In January 1900 the song was used as a contest piece in the Competition for the Ragtime Championship of the World. His best-known performance was "Say, wouldn't that be a dream."

BIBL: Black press, incl. IndF., 3 July 1897, 25 December 1898, 1 November 1902; NYAge, 24 August 1905, 27 May 1909. Flet, 135. Ann Charters, *The Ragtime Songbook* (New York, 1955).

HOLIDAY, BILLIE ("LADY DAY") (née ELEANORA FAGAN). Jazz singer (b. 7 April 1915 in Baltimore, Maryland; d. 17 July 1959 in New York, New York). Her father, Clarence Holiday, was a professional jazzman. She obtained her musical education in the public schools of Baltimore, Maryland, but went to live in New York when she was about twelve. She began singing professionally at the age of fifteen in nightclubs in the Harlem community. In 1933 she made her recording debut with Benny Goodman through arrangements made by John Hammond. Thereafter she recorded extensively, particularly during the years 1936-42, with various groups, individuals, and as well her own group, Billie Holiday and Her Orchestra. Her recordings with Theodore ("Teddy") Wilson* (1935-39) and her collaboration with Lester Young* on recordings (1937) won her international recognition. During the 1930s she also toured with various groups, including William ("Count") Basie* (1937) and Artie Shaw (1938) among others. Beginning in 1938 she performed primarily as a soloist in nightclubs, theaters, and concert halls. She toured in Europe twice, with Jazz Club U.S.A. (1954) and as a soloist (1958). She also sang on film soundtracks and in films, among them, *Symphony in Black* (1935), *New Orleans* (1947), and *The Sound of Jazz* (1957, originally filmed for television). She sang for servicemen on tours sponsored by the USO (United Service Organizations) during the period of World War II, and at the first Newport Jazz Festival in 1954. Holiday was regarded as the finest jazz singer of her time; her voice was small but deeply expressive, whether projecting despair, bitterness, or humor. She consciously used her voice as if it were a horn, phrasing and improvising with delicate nuance. Her best-known performances were of "Strange fruit," "Fine and mellow," and "Lover man." In 1956 she published her autobiography, *Lady Sings the Blues*, with William Duffy. In 1972 an autobiographical film with the same title was released.

BIBL: Rudi Blesh, *Combo. U.S.A.* (Philadelphia, 1961). ChilWW. *Ebony* (January 1973). FeaEJ. FeaJS. MeeJMov.

DISC: Jep. Kink. RustJR. TudJ.

HOLLAND, CHARLES. Jazz/opera singer (b. c1910 in Norfolk, Virginia). He began voice study when he was fourteen. During his early career he was active as a jazz singer; he toured on the nightclub circuit, sang on radio programs, engaged in studio recording, and sang with jazz orchestras, among them, Fletcher Henderson* (1934) and Bennett ("Benny") Carter* (1934). He also sang in films, including *Hullabaloo* (1941). During the 1930s he toured with the Hall Johnson* Choir, then settled in Hollywood, California, where he studied with Georges Le Pyre. In October 1940 he made his concert debut as a tenor at the Town Hall in New York. Thereafter he began to study opera and oratorio. In 1945 he sang a leading role in the premiere of Marc Blitzstein's *Airborne Symphony* in New York. Thereafter he began singing on concerts in New York as a soloist and with opera and oratorio groups. In 1949 he settled in Europe. He made his European operatic debut in January 1955 at the Opera Comique in Paris, thereby becoming the first of his race to sing there. In later years he sang with the Nederlandsche Opera in Amsterdam, The Netherlands, and the Norske Opera in Oslo, Norway. He was especially known for his performance of the roles of Monostatos in Mozart's *The Magic Flute* and of Nadir in Bizet's *Les Pêcheurs de perles*. During the 1970s he returned to the United States. In February 1981 he gave a retrospective concert at the Carnegie Recital Hall in New York.

BIBL: AlHen. Black press, incl. AmstN, 7 February 1948, 7 March 1981; CDef, 19 February 1955.

DISC: Turn.

HOLLAND, JUSTIN MINER. Composer (b. 1819 in Norfolk County, Virginia; d. 24 March 1887 in Cleveland, Ohio). He early showed musical promise but was unable to obtain instruction because of the isolation of his father's farm in Virginia. In 1833 at the age of fourteen, he went to Boston, Massachusetts, then settled in nearby Chelsea. He studied guitar with Mariano Perez and theory with Simon Knaebel and William Schubert, both members of Ned Kendall's Brass Band. Later he studied flute with a Mr. Pollack. He studied music further at the Oberlin [Ohio] Conservatory (1841-43; 1845) and in Mexico (1844). In 1845 he settled permanently in Cleveland, Ohio, where he was active as a composer/arranger and conducted a music studio. He won wide recognition for his compositions, particularly for the guitar, and his manuals, *Holland's Comprehensive Method for the Guitar* (1874) and *Holland's Modern Method for the Guitar* (1874). His best-known pieces were "Winter evenings," "Bouquet of flowers," "Flowers of melody," and *Gems for the Guitar*. A large number of his pieces was listed in the *Complete Catalogue of Sheet Music and Musical Works*, published by the Board of Music Trade of the United States of America, 1871; reprint with introduction by Dena Epstein (New York, 1973). His son, Justin Miner Holland, Jr, was also a guitarist and composer; he published *Method for the Guitar* (1888).

BIBL: Black press, incl. IndF. 18 May 1889. Philip J.Bone, *The Guitar and Mandolin* (London, 1954). Russell H. Davis, *Black Americans in Cleveland* (Washington, D.C.). Trot.

HOLLAND, JUSTIN MINER, JR. See **HOLLAND, JUSTIN.**

HOLMES, ODETTA. See **ODETTA.**

HOLMES, ROBERT. Composer (b. 29 March 1934 in Greenville, Mississippi). He received his musical education in the public schools of Memphis, Tennessee, where he began studying music during his junior-high-school years; at Tennessee State University in Nashville (B.S., 1956; M.S. 1970); at the University of Iowa in Iowa City (1959); and at Brandeis University in Waltham, Massachusetts (1960). His early career development was encouraged by gospel songwriter Lucie

Campbell.* He began his professional career in 1961 as general manager and composer-arranger for a music company in Nashville and thereafter filled similar positions with other companies, enlarging his activities to become also a producer, musical director, and A & R director (artists and repertoire). He also taught in the Nashville public schools (1958-69) and served as artist-in-residence at Fisk University in Nashville. In 1969 he established his own company, Doorway Music, continuing his activity as a producer, musical director, recording studio musician, and conductor. He toured widely as a lecturer and performed with such jazz figures as Edward ("Duke") Ellington,* Milt Jackson,* Quincy Jones,* William ("Billy") Taylor,* and Clark Terry,* among others. He composed for a variety of media, including films, television, and radio commercial music in addition to music in traditional forms for orchestra, band, chorus, voice, chamber ensemble, and instrumental solo. His best-known works were *Perplexions for Orchestra* (1973), *Evolutions I & II* for flute and piano (1969), *Eye of the Storm* for chorus and orchestra (1971), and *Yesterday's Mansions* for piano, flute, and cello (1972). His documentary films included *The Gift of Black Folk, The House on Cedar Hill*, and *Two Centuries of Black American Art*, among others. His honors included awards from civic and professional organizations, from the media industry, and a grant from the National Endowment for the Arts (1972).

BIBL: Questionnaire. WWBA.

HOLT, NORA. Music critic (b. 1885 in Kansas City, Kansas; d. 25 January 1974 in Los Angeles, California). She obtained her musical education from Western University in Quindaro, Kansas (B.A.), and Chicago Musical College (M. Mus., 1918), where she studied with Felix Borowski. She is credited with being the first black musician to earn the M. Mus. degree. She studied further with Nadia Boulanger at the American Conservatory in Fontainebleau, France (1931). Before settling in Chicago, Illinois, about 1916 she was organist for several years at the St. Augustine's Episcopal Church in Kansas City, Missouri. In Chicago she was active as president (and later in other offices) of the Chicago Music Association, she served as music critic for the *Chicago Defender* (1917-21), and she lectured regularly on Negro Music. She was one of the leaders in the movement to organize the National Association of Negro Musicians in 1919 and was elected vice-president the first year; other officers were Henry Grant* of Washington, D.C. (president), Alice Carter Simmons of Tuskegee, Alabama (secretary), and Fred ("Deacon") Johnson* of New York (treasurer). During the years 1919-21 Holt published a magazine, *Music and Poetry*. From 1922 to 1937 she traveled widely in the United States, Europe, and the Far East; for several years she was a nightclub entertainer, particularly in Shanghai, China. After returning to the United States permanently, she first lived in Los Angeles, California (1938-41), where she taught in the public schools. She then settled in New York, becoming music editor of the *Amsterdam News* in 1944. She produced a classical music program on radio, "Nora Holt's Concert Showcase WLIB," from 1953 until her retirement in 1964. She also staged an annual festival, "American Negro Artists," on radio station WNYC beginning in 1945.

BIBL: Black press, incl. CDef, 18 August 1917, 9 August 1919; NYAge, 30 January 1954. BPIM 2 (Fall 1974). HughesBM. NYT, 29 January 1974.

HOOKER, JOHN LEE. Bluesman (b. 22 August 1917 in Clarksdale, Mississippi). He began playing guitar at the age of thirteen, taught by his stepfather, Willie Moore, a professional bluesman. He also learned by listening to ("Blind") Lemon Jefferson,* Charley Patton,* and others who played in his home and in the community. He left home at fourteen to live in Memphis, Tennessee; later he lived in Cincinnati, Ohio, and finally settled in Detroit, Michigan, by the time he was twenty. In 1948 he began recording and thereafter recorded extensively for many labels and often under assumed names. Notable among the record companies for which he recorded was that of Joseph Von Battle, a pioneer black producer, who was the first to record Aretha Franklin* many years later. The public's awakened interest in blues during the 1960s brought him added recognition. He toured widely at home and in Europe, appearing on college campuses, and at folk festivals as well as in concert halls and nightclubs.

BIBL: BWW. FeaEJ. Michael Lydon, *Boogie Lightning* (New York, 1974). MeeJMov. Robert Neff and Anthony Connor, *Blues* (Boston, 1975). Oliv. StamPRS. WWA. WWBA.

DISC: Jep. LeSL. TudBM.

HOPKINS, CLAUDE. Jazz pianist (b. 24 August 1903 in Alexandria, Virginia). He studied piano when he was seven years old. He obtained his musical education in the public schools of Washington, D.C., at Howard University in Washington (B.A., 1923), and at the Washington Conservatory of Music (director, Harriet Gibbs Marshall*). He later studied privately in Paris, France, with the director of the Champs Elysee Symphony. He began his professional career playing jazz in local nightclubs and in the pit orchestra of the Howard Theatre. His early career development was encouraged by Caroline Thornton and Marie Lucas*;

he was also influenced by James P. Johnson* and Thomas ("Fats") Waller,* to whose piano rolls he listened and emulated. In 1924 he went to New York to play with Wilbur Sweatman.* Later he organized his own group. In 1925 he went to Europe with *La Revue Nègre*, which featured Josephine Baker* as the star. After touring with the show, he toured with his band, returning to the United States in 1927. During the next three decades he toured with the musical *Ginger Snaps* (1927), played long residencies in New York ballrooms and nightclubs, recorded extensively, and appeared in films, among them, *Dance Team* (1931) and *Wayward* (1932). He was also active as an arranger, writing and arranging music for his own groups and for others, such as Phil Spitalny. In 1946 he led a big band but thereafter his groups were primarily quintets or sextets. From the mid-1950s on he worked frequently with such jazzmen as Henry ("Red") Allen,* Herman Autrey, William ("Wild Bill") Davis,* and Roy Eldridge,* among others. During the 1960s he was active in radio and television music and performed at jazz festivals. He continued to perform regularly through the 1970s, including tours in Europe.

BIBL: ASCAP. Black press, incl. CDef, 30 June 1934. ChilWW. DanceWS. FeaEJ. FeaGitJS. MeeJMov. WWCA, 1950.

DISC: Jep. Kink. RustJR. TudJ.

HOPKINS, LINDA. Gospel/blues singer (b. 14 December 1925 in New Orleans, Louisiana). At the age of three she began to sing in a church choir. When she was twelve she was discovered by Mahalia Jackson*; for the next eleven years she sang with the Southern Harp Spiritual Singers* as "Baby Helen." Thereafter she settled in Oakland, California, where she sang in churches and on radio and directed a youth choir. Later she began singing in nightclubs of Oakland and San Francisco. During the 1950s she began recording, and she toured throughout the world with her nightclub act. In 1955 she settled in New York. Thereafter she was active in stage shows, beginning with *Jazz Train* (1959), which toured in Europe, and later with the Broadway musicals *Purlie* (1970) and *Inner City* (1971). She became noted for her portrayal of Bessie Smith,* which she began in 1959 and later developed into one-woman nightclub shows in 1974 and eventually into a musical, *Bessie and Me*, in 1976. As a child of eleven she saw a Bessie Smith performance in New Orleans, which made an indelible impression upon her and influenced the development of her style, as did also her gospel roots.

BIBL: *Encore American & Worldwide News* (22 December 1975). FeaGitJS. WWBA.

DISC: Jep.

HOPKINS, SAM ("LIGHTNIN' "). Bluesman (b. 15 March 1912 in Centerville, Texas). He came from a musical family; two brothers played blues guitar professionally, as did several relatives. He played for local social entertainments at an early age and traveled with ("Blind") Lemon Jefferson* when he was about ten. Later he served an apprenticeship with Alger ("Texas") Alexander, a relative. In 1946 he went to Los Angeles, California, where he made recordings with pianist Wilson ("Thunder") Smith that won him wide recognition and, as well, the nickname "Lightnin'." After a year or so, he returned to Houston and settled there permanently. Thereafer he recorded extensively and toured widely, appearing on college campuses as well as in concert halls, nightclubs, and at the major blues festivals. His style reflected the influence of Jefferson and Alexander in the earthy, harsh, Texas blues tradition. He was regarded as one of the last blues singers in the grand tradition; although neither his voice nor guitar playing were unusual, his personality and handling of rhythms and timbre made for unforgettable performances.

BIBL: BWW. CharCB. CharLB. FeaEJ. MeeJMov. Robert Neff and Anthony Connor, *Blues* (Boston, 1975). Oliv. StamPRS.

HORNE, LENA. Popular-music/theater singer (b. 30 June 1917 in New York, New York). As a child she accompanied her mother on a tour of the Lafayette Stock Players and appeared in the production of *Madame X* when she was six years old. She obtained her musical education in the preparatory school of Fort Valley College, Georgia, where her uncle was dean, and in the public schools of Brooklyn, New York. She began her professional career in 1934 as a chorus girl at the Cotton Club in the Harlem community of New York. Thereafter she sang with Noble Sissle* (1935-36) and Charlie Barnet (1940-41), then was active primarily as a nightclub entertainer. She toured widely in the United States and in Europe, and she appeared in numerous films, including *Cabin in the Sky* (1942), *Stormy Weather* (1943), *Broadway Rhythm* (1944), *Ziegfeld Follies* of 1945 and of 1946, the *Duchess of Idaho* (1950), and *The Wiz* (1978), among others. She made her recording debut in 1936 with Sissle and thereafter recorded extensively as a soloist and with others. She also sang on radio and television and appeared in such Broadway musicals as *Blackbirds of 1939* and *Jamaica* (1957). She was musically active into the 1980s. Although best-known as a singer of popular music, she also sang jazz and maintained ties with the world of jazz. She published her autobiography, *Lena* (1965), with Richard Schickel.

BIBL: Black press, incl. CDef, 17 May 1947, 24 May 1947, 31 May 1947. *Encore American and World-*

wide News (15 August 1977). FeaEJ. HNB. WWA. WWBA. WWCA, 1950.
DISC: Jep. Kink. RustCED.

HOUSE, EDDIE (''SON''). Bluesman (b. 21 March 1902 in Lyon [near Clarksdale], Mississippi). He spent the early years of his life in Algiers, Louisiana, across the river from New Orleans. Although his father had a little dance band, he did not begin playing blues guitar until he was in his mid-twenties. He was an active churchman with primary concern for religious music. His interest in blues developed after he had moved back to Mississippi; he heard some blues performances in a town near Clarksdale, and he taught himself to play with help from local amateurs. A few years later he came into contact with Charley Patton* and Willie Brown, and the three bluesmen began to record together in 1930. The same year they formed a blues band, which included other bluesmen over the years. He recorded extensively during the next decades—in 1941, for a field-recording program of the Library of Congress. He also toured widely, traveling with the first American Folk Blues Festival to Europe in 1962 and appearing in other blues festivals as well as in concert halls, nightclubs, and on college campuses. During one period in the 1950s he returned to the church, serving as a pastor to a Baptist church and later to a CME church (Colored Methodist Episcopal). Along with Patton, he was representative of the powerful, intense Delta blues tradition in its original unfolding.
BIBL: BWW. LivBl 31 (March-April 1977). MeeJMov. Oliv. StamPRS.
DISC: DiGod. LeSl. TudBM.

HOWARD, DARNELL. Jazz clarinetist (b. 25 July c1892 in Chicago, Illinois; d. 2 September 1966 in San Francisco, California). He came from a musical family: his father, Sam Howard, played violin, cornet, and piano, and his mother played piano. He began violin study when he was seven years old. He obtained his musical education in the public schools of Chicago, Illinois. He played with Clarence Jones* (1912) during his high-school years, then began playing professionally in 1913 with John Wickcliffe's Ginger Orchestra. Thereafter he played with various groups, including W. C. Handy* (with whom he went to New York in 1917 to make recordings), Charles Elgar (1921), James P. Johnson's* band for the *Plantation Days* revue (including the London, England, production in 1923), Carroll Dickerson,* Joseph (''King'') Oliver,* Erskine Tate,* and Jimmy Wade, among others. Generally he played clarinet, alto saxophone, or violin, but eventually he specialized on clarinet only. During the 1920s he also led his own groups from time to time and toured in Europe with the Singing Syncopators (1924) and in the Far East with the New York Singing Syncopators (1925). His longest musical association was with Earl Hines* (1931-37, 1955-62). During the 1930s-50s he also played with Horace Henderson* (1937), Fletcher Henderson* (1938-39), Coleman Hawkins,* and in California with Edward (''Kid'') Ory* (during 1945) and Francis (''Muggsy'') Spanier (1948-53), among others; he also led his own groups. In 1966 he toured in Europe with the New Orleans All Stars. During his long career he recorded extensively with his own groups and with leading jazz figures of his time.
BIBL: AlHen. ChilWW. DanceWEH. FeaEJ. FeaGitJS.
DISC: Kink. RustJR.

HOWLING WOLF. See **BURNETT, CHESTER ARTHUR.**

HUBBARD, FREDERICK DEWAYNE (''FREDDIE''). Jazz trumpeter (b. 7 April 1938 in Indianapolis, Indiana). He came from a musical family: his mother played piano, his sister Mildred played trumpet, and his two brothers played piano and saxophone. He obtained his musical education in the public schools of Indianapolis, where he played mellophone, tuba, trumpet, and French horn in high school groups; and at the Jordan Conservatory in Indianapolis. His early style development was influenced by Clifford Brown, whom he emulated. His early professional experience was with the local Montgomery Brothers, with whom he made his recording debut in 1956. In 1958 he went to New York, where he played with various groups, including Locksley (''Slide'') Hampton, Joseph (''Philly Joe'') Jones,* Theodore (''Sonny'') Rollins,* Quincy Jones,* Art Blakey* and the Jazz Messengers (1961-63), and Max Roach,* among others. During the 1960s-70s he also toured widely in the United States, Europe, and Japan with his own group and with others, including Nancy Wilson*; in 1965 he played in an international jazz orchestra in Austria; he became increasingly involved in composition; and he recorded extensively with his own groups and with others, performing much of his own work. He also performed on film soundtracks, including *The Pawnbroker* (1964), *Blowup* (1966), *The Bus Is Coming* (1971), and *Shaft's Big Score* (1972). By the mid-1970s his style incorporated elements of rhythm 'n' blues and rock, and he used electronic instruments. He was regarded as one of the leading trumpeters of the 1970s; his best-known albums were *First Light* and *High Energy*. He won awards from the music industry.
BIBL: FeaJS. FeaGitJS. MeeJMov. WWA. WWBA.
DISC: ModJ. TudJ.

HUFF, LEON. Producer/Songwriter (b. c1942 in Camden, New Jersey). See **GAMBLE, KENNETH.**

HUGHES, LANGSTON. Writer (b. 1 February 1902 in Joplin, Missouri; d. 22 May 1967 in New York, New York). Although best-known as a poet-writer, he was also active musically as a writer of lyrics, librettos for operas and musicals, and books and poems about music. He obtained his education at Columbia University in New York (1921-22) and Lincoln University in Pennsylvania (B.A., 1929). The works for which he wrote librettos (or plays later adapted into librettos) included *Troubled Island* (music by William Grant Still,* 1941; premiere 1949), *Esther* (music: Jan Meyerowitz, 1946), *The Barrier* (Meyerowitz, 1950), *De Organizer* (music: James P. Johnson,* 1939-41), *Soul Gone Home* (music: Ulysses Kay,* 1954) and *Street Scene* (adapted from the play by Elmer Rice; music by Kurt Weill, 1947). The musicals to which he contributed included *The Ballad of the Brown King* (Margaret Bonds,* 1961); *Black Nativity*, a gospel play with spirituals and other folksongs, (1961); *Simply Heavenly* (music by David Martin, 1957); and the gospel song-play *Tambourines to Glory* (1963). Hughes's books about music included *Famous Negro Music Makers* (1955), *The First Book of Jazz* (1955), and *Black Magic* (1967).

BIBL: EAB. FeaGitJS. HNB. WWA. WWCA, 1950.

HUMES, HELEN. Jazz singer (b. 23 June 1913 in Louisville, Kentucky). She studied piano as a child and sang in a church choir. She also sang with the local Booker T. Washington Community Centre Band, which included Jonah Jones* and William (''Dicky'') Wells* at the time. About 1927 she began singing professionally in local theaters, nightclubs, and dance halls. She made her recording debut in 1927 and thereafter recorded extensively. In 1936 she went to Buffalo, New York, where she sang in hotels and clubs. She sang in other cities, including Cincinnati, Ohio, before she went to New York in 1937. During the next few decades she sang with various groups, including Harry James (1937-38), William (''Count'') Basie* (intermittently 1937-52), Red Norvo (née Kenneth Norville) (during the 1950s, including touring in Australia in 1956), and JATP (Norman Granz's Jazz at the Philharmonic), among others; she toured widely in the United States, Europe, and Australia, singing in concert halls and nightclubs; she appeared on radio and television programs at home and abroad; and she sang in films or on film soundtracks, including *Jivin' in Bebop* (1947) and *Harlem Jazz Festival* (1955). She also sang at the major jazz and blues festivals and toured with such groups as the Rhythm 'n' Blues USA revue (1962-63). During the years 1967-73 she was relatively inactive in music, then returned to high activity, particularly in New York and in Europe. Her best-known performance was ''Be baba leba.'' In addition to nightclub and concert work, she appeared in Broadway musicals. Her honors included an award from the music industry of France (1973) and a key to the city of Louisville (1975).

BIBL: Schom. BWW. Cadence (January 1978). ChilWW. FeaEJ. FeaJS. FeaGitJS. MeeJMov.

DISC: DiGod. Kink. RustJR. TudJ.

HUMMINGS, ARMENTA ADAMS. See **ADAMS, ARMENTA.**

HUNT, DARROLD VICTOR. Symphony conductor (b. 29 June 1941 in New Bedford, Massachusetts). As a child he sang in a family troupe, The Rays, which toured in New England singing spirituals at churches. In high school he sang with choral groups and first began to conduct. He obtained his musical education at the Juilliard School of Music in New York (B.S., 1970; M.S., 1971); at Tanglewood in Massachusetts; at Columbia University in New York; and privately with Gregg Smith (1964-65). During the years 1971-73 he was a conducting fellow of the National Orchestral Association under Leon Bazin, with whom he studied privately in the summer of 1974. His teaching career included tenures at the State University of New York at Purchase and at Brooklyn College of the City University of New York. He began to conduct symphonic groups during his student years at Juilliard; in 1970 he organized the Urban Philharmonic Society and, later, an ancillary group, the Urban Philharmonic Community Chorale. The interracial orchestra, composed of about sixty professional musicians, received grants from foundations and art councils that permitted it to give concerts from time to time. During the late 1970s Hunt sought to establish its permanent home in Washington, D.C. His career as a conductor included also tenures as the assistant conductor of the Baltimore [Maryland] Symphony (1973-74) and various community orchestras and choral groups. His experience with choral groups included touring with the Norman Luboff Choir.

BIBL: Paul DiPerna, ''Bringing Classical Music to the Community'' *Encore American and Worldwide News* (20 June 1977). WWBA.

HUNTER, ALBERTA. Blues singer (b. 1 April 1895 in Memphis,Tennessee). She went to Chicago at the age of eleven; by the time she was fifteen she was singing professionally in local clubs. She began to attract wide attention when she sang at Chicago's Dreamland Cafe; her song "Down hearted blues" (1923) also brought her recognition. In 1926 she replaced Bessie Smith* in the leading role of the musical, *How Come?*, and shortly thereafter she toured in Europe, including a leading role in the London production of *Showboat* (1927) along with Paul Robeson.* During the 1930s she sang in Broadway musicals. During World War II she worked with USO (United Service Organizations) entertainment units and toured throughout the world. After the war she returned to the stage, to nightclubs, and to recording. In 1954 she retired from music and began a nursing career. She returned to music in 1977, in her eighties, and again recorded extensively, appeared on radio and television programs, sang on film tracts, and filled long engagements in New York nightclubs.

BIBL: ASCAP. BWW. ChilWW. *Dawn Magazine* (October 1978). FeaEJ. Oliv.

DISC: DiGod. Kink. LeSl. RustJR.

HUNTER, ("IVORY") JOE. Bluesman (b. 1911 in Kirbyville, Texas; d. 8 November 1974 in Memphis, Tennessee). Little is known of his early career except that he was an itinerant blues entertainer in Texas. In 1933 he recorded for the Library of Congress folk-music program as "Ivory" Joe White; during the 1930s he went to California and there began recording in 1937 for professional labels. In 1945 he formed his own record company, organizing The Three Blazers to record with him—Charles Brown, Johnny Moore, and Oscar Moore. He also played piano for Lowell Fulson* on recordings. By the 1950s he had attained major stature in the entertainment world, not only as a blues singer but also in the fields of rhythm 'n' blues, popular music, and later in country and western music. He was a prolific songwriter; several of his more than 7000 songs won him wide recognition, including "I almost lost my mind" (1950) and "Since I met you baby" (1956). As pianist and singer he was important in the development of the West Coast blues style, although he continuously returned to his native Texas and spent his last years in Louisiana.

BIBL: FeaGitJS. LivBl 19 (January-February 1975). NYT, 10 November 1974. StamPRS.

DISC: Jep.

HURT, JOHN ("MISSISSIPPI"). Bluesman (b. 3 July 1893 in Teoc, Mississippi; d. 2 November 1966 in Grenada, Mississippi). He taught himself to play guitar when he was nine years old and soon thereafter began playing for local social entertainments. He spent most of his life in Avalon, Mississippi, which was remote, and he had little opportunity to hear live blues performances. He learned the folksongs of his community, listened to records, and wrote his own songs. He made his first recordings in 1938, but did not record again until 1963. He had continued to perform through the years, however, and was well prepared to resume recording when he was rediscovered during the 1960s with the revival of public interest in the blues. Thereafter he toured widely in the United States—playing in clubs, concert halls, and at the major folk festivals—and he recorded several albums. His music was in the powerful, intense Delta blues tradition.

BIBL: BWW. Oliv. StamFCW.

DISC: DiGod. LeSl. TudBM.

HUTCHERSON, ROBERT ("BOBBY"). Jazz vibraharpist (b. 27 January 1941 in Los Angeles, California). He studied briefly when he was nine years old. He obtained his musical education in the public schools of Pasadena, California. He began playing vibraharp when he was fifteen, inspired by hearing a recording of Milton Jackson.* He studied informally with Dave Pike and Terry Trotter. His first professional experiences were with local groups in Los Angeles; he then toured with the Al Grey-Billy Mitchell group (1960-61). In 1961 he settled in New York. Thereafter he played with various groups, including John ("Jackie") McLean,* Archie Shepp,* Henry ("Hank") Mobley, Charles Tolliver,* Grachan Moncur, and Gerald Wilson, among others. In 1965 he began playing marimba in addition to vibraharp. He resettled in California in 1969 and thereafter was active primarily with his own groups and as a soloist, although he occasionally performed with big bands and co-led a group with Harold Land (1969-71). He received many awards from the music industry; his musical skills earned him the nickname "Mr. Good Vibes."

BIBL: FeaJS. FeaGitJS.

DISC: Jep. TudJ.

HYERS, ANNA MADAH. Concert singer (b. c1853 in Sacramento, California; d. 1920s [?] in Sacramento). See **HYERS SISTERS.**

HYERS, EMMA LOUISE. Concert singer (b. c1855 in Sacramento, California; d. 189? in ?). See **HYERS SISTERS.**

HYERS SISTERS, THE. Concert ensemble (fl. late nineteenth century). Anna Madah (b. 1853?) and Emma Louise (b. 1855?) Hyers early revealed musical talent and studied music first with their parents, who were amateur musicians. Later they studied piano and solfege with Hugo Sank and voice with opera singer Josephine D'Ormy. In April 1867 they made their debut at the Metropolitan Theater in Sacramento, Anna as soprano and Emma as contralto. After more years of study, they began touring the nation from West to East in 1871, assisted by baritone Mr. LeCount and their father. Their programs included primarily operatic arias, duos, trios, and quartets. For concerts in New York and New England, the father engaged tenor Wallace King,* baritone John Luca,* and accompanist A. C. Taylor. The group won critical acclaim, and in 1872 the Hyers Sisters were invited to sing at Patrick S. Gilmore's World Peace Jubilee at Boston, Massachusetts. Their success on that occasion added to their growing fame. By 1875 the Hyers had organized a small concert company, which performed primarily in New England; for the concerts in Boston the group often was supported by a little symphony orchestra conducted by Napier Lothian, director of the Boston Theater Orchestra. According to some sources, Mr. Hyers as business manager enlarged the company in order to produce drama as early as 1876. The company's first production was *Out of Bondage*, written especially for the Hyers. By the late 1870s the Hyers had added two more dramas to their repertory, *Urlina, the African Princess* and *The Underground Railroad* (written by black playwright Pauline E. Hopkins), and were touring extensively throughout the nation, primarily under the sponsorship of the Redpath Lyceum Bureau. The critics praised the company as "one of the best opera-bouffe troupes in America." Over the years the company included Celestine O. Browne, Billy Kersands,* Dora S. King, Grace V. Overall, Sam Lucas,* a Mr. Lyle, Mrs. Francis A. Powell, and pianist-composer Jacob Sawyer,* among others. Early in 1883 the Hyers dramatic company disbanded temporarily; in May of that year the Hyers' reorganized concert company, including Henderson Smith* and Joseph R. Brindis de Salas,* contracted to appear in the Callendar Consolidated Spectacular Minstrel Festival in July at the Grand Opera House in New York, which later toured the nation as far west as San Francisco. Charles and Gustave Frohman, the white owners of the show, had ambitious plans for the black musicians in their employ. They planned to form a Colored Opera Troupe, which would open in the fall of 1883 and would feature the Hyers Sisters, Wallace King, Lewis Brown, W. W. Morris, and Thomas Waddy. There was to be a chorus and orchestra of forty persons. In July Charles ("Barney") Hicks* was to sail to Paris to engage Marie Selika* and her huband, Sampson Williams,* for the company. Nothing ever came of the plans, however. By the fall of 1886 the Hyers had reorganized their dramatic company and were touring again with the *Out of Bondage* show, which featured King and Lucas as in the 1870s. During the early 1890s the names of the Hyers Sisters appeared less frequently in the press; in April 1893 a press notice stated that they were leaving the stage and would appear only for special engagements. Thereafter no press notices to the Hyers as a duo appeared. In 1894 Emma performed with an *Uncle Tom's Cabin* company, and in 1894 Anna Madah joined John Isham's *Octoroons* company. The operatic finales in Isham's productions, called "Thirty Minutes Around the Operas," allowed Anna to continue singing her usual repertory. Some time before 1900 Emma died. In 1899 Anna Madah went on tour in Australia with the M. B. Curtis All-Star Afro-American Minstrels, which also included William ("Billy") McClain,* Ernest Hogan,* and N. Clark Smith,* among others. After returning to the United States she performed with various Isham companies until 1902, when she retired from the stage and settled in Sacramento.

BIBL: Black press, incl. CleveG, 15 September 1883, 25 August 1894; IndF, 15 April 1893, 27 December 1902; NYClipper 1860s-80s. NYFreeman, 14 August 1886; NYGlobe, 26 May 1883. Hare. Simond. Trotter.

I

IMPRESSIONS, THE. Rhythm 'n' blues group (fl. 1960s-70s; orig. in Chicago, Illinois). The male quintet was organized in 1957 and composed of Arthur and Richard Brooks, Jerry Butler,* Sam Gooden, and Curtis Mayfield.* The Brooks brothers and Sam Gooden formerly sang with a group, The Roosters, in Chattanooga, Tennessee, which also included Fred Cash and a female singer. Butler and Mayfield had sung together in a gospel group called the Modern Jubilaires. The newly organized group changed its name from The Roosters to The Impressions, signed a recording contract with Vee Jay Records,* and released a ballad written by Butler and the Brooks brothers, "For your precious love," which attracted considerable attention. Within a short period Butler left the group, and in 1961 Fred Cash came in as his replacement. Mayfield wrote songs for the new Impressions, which soon established itself as a leading group of the 1960s. There were personnel changes over the years; in 1973 the group consisted of Cash, Gooden, Reggie Torian, and Ralph Johnson. The best-known performances of The Impressions included "I'm so proud," "People get ready," "Keep on pushing," and "Finally got myself together."

BIBL: Black press, including CDef, 26 August 1979. BMI (Issue 1, 1973). *Ebony* (December 1969). StamPRS.

INK SPOTS. Popular-music quartet (fl. 1930s-70s; orig. 1934 in Indiana). The male vocal quartet was organized in 1934 with Charles Fuqua (baritone and guitarist), Orville ("Hoppy") Jones (bass and cellist), William ("Bill") Kenny (tenor), and Ivory ("Deek") Watson (tenor and songwriter). The group earned wide recognition first in England, where they were promoted by impresario-bandleader Jack Hylton. After returning to the United States in 1939, their performances of "If I didn't care" and "It's funny to everyone but me" brought wide attention and popularity. During the 1940s-50s they recorded extensively and toured widely, appearing in theaters, nightclubs, and on radio. During World War II they entertained servicemen at home and in Europe. They also appeared in films, including *Great American Broadcast* (1941) and *Pardon My Sarong* (1942). The quartet was distinctive for its smooth harmonies, Kenny's soprano-high tenor, and Jones's deep-voice "talking" choruses. The original group was broken with Jones's death (11 October 1944 in New York), and he was replaced by Herb Kenny, Bill's brother. For a period in 1944 there were two quartets calling themselves The Ink Spots, then Deek Watson was forced to change the name of his split-off group to The Brown Dots. The last original member, Bill Kenny, died in 1978 (on 22 March in New Westminster, British Columbia). The Ink Spots were active through the 1970s. Over the years personnel changes brought in Gayle Davenport, Leon Antoine, Harold Jackson, Jimmy Holmes, Richard ("Dick") Porter, Isaac Royal, and Charles Ward. The best-known performances included "My prayer," "Do I worry," "Whispering grass," "I'll never smile again," and "Java jive." Many groups of the 1940s imitated the quartet, particularly The Ravens.

BIBL: Black press, including CDef, 23 February 1935. 10 February 1945. NYT, 24 March 1978.

DISC: Kink. RustCED. TudBM.

INTERNATIONAL SWEETHEARTS OF RHYTHM, THE. Jazz orchestra (org. in Piney Woods, Mississippi; fl. c1937-1955). See also **THE SWINGING RAYS OF RHYTHM.** The orchestra was one of several groups organized at the Piney Woods Country Life School in Mississippi by the school's founder-president Laurence C. Jones. It was during the 1920s that Jones began to send student vocal groups, called The Cotton Blossoms, on concert tours to earn money for the school in emulation of the Fisk Jubilee Singers,* the

Hampton Institute Singers,* and similar black college groups. When he observed the growing popularity during the 1930s of such all-girl orchestras as Phil Spitalny's and Ina Ray Hutton's, he decided to organize a women's orchestra at his institution, called The International Sweethearts of Rhythm, composed of students from the high-school and junior-college divisions of Piney Woods. He employed musical director Edna Williams and chaperone/singing director Rae Lee Jones to travel with the sixteen-piece group. When the group gave concerts, Jones often appeared on the same program to talk about the school. The orchestra toured widely throughout the United States, appearing in theaters, at state fairs, for community and civic organizations, and participating in various band competitions with male groups, including one at the New York World's Fair in 1940. In April 1941 the orchestra left the sponsorship of Piney Woods School, became incorporated, and acquired professional management with Annie Mae Winburn as bandleader. The new members that joined thereafter included white and oriental musicians. The orchestra toured extensively at home, in Europe, Mexico, and Canada until the mid-1950s. Those who played with the orchestra included Viola ("Vi") Burnside, Pauline Braddy, Carline Ray,* Edna Smith Edet,* and Ruby Young, among others.

BIBL: Black press, including CDef, 5 July 1941. Handy.

ISLEY BROTHERS, THE. Rhythm 'n' Blues group (fl. 1950s-70s; orig. in Cincinnati, Ohio). The Isley brothers came from a musical family: the father, O'Kelly, Sr., was a vaudeville entertainer, and the mother was a church organist and choir director. Inspired by the Mills Brothers, Mr. Isley organized his four older sons into a gospel quartet when they were children. The boys sang in churches of Cincinnati, Ohio, their home town and toured in Kentucky and Tennessee, accompanied on the piano by their mother. During their high-school days, the Isleys added popular music to their repertory. In the mid-1950s an Isley trio, composed of O'Kelly, Jr. (b. 25 December 1937), Rudolph (b. 1 April 1939), and Ronald (b. 21 May 1941)—the fourth original member, Vernon, had a fatal accident as a youth—went to New York to explore the possibilities of a career in music and obtained professional management. After hearing a performance by Frankie Lymon* and The Teenagers, they changed from popular music to rhythm 'n' blues. In 1959 they recorded one of their own tunes, "Shout," which attracted wide attention for its gospel-rock style. In 1969 the group was enlarged to include two more brothers, Ernest and Marvin, and brother-in-law Chris Jasper. The Isley Brothers toured widely and recorded extensively, writing themselves much of the material they performed. Eventually they founded their own production company. Their best-known songs were "It's your thing," "That lady," "Twist and shout," and "Twistin' with Linda." They received awards from the music industry.

BIBL: *Dawn Magazine* (August 1978). *Encore* (3 February 1975). StamPRS.

DISC: TudBM.

J

JACKSON, ANTHONY ("TONY"). Ragtime-vaudeville pianist (b. 5 June 1876 in New Orleans, Louisiana; d. 20 April 1921 in Chicago, Illinois). He began his career about 1892 in New Orleans, playing cornet, then piano in Adam Olivier's orchestra. Thereafter, until 1904, he played in various cafes and houses of prostitution in the Storyville area of the city. During this period he earned the title "the World's Greatest Single-Handed Entertainer"; he was as celebrated for his singing and accompaniment skills as for his ragime piano. In the summer of 1904 he began touring with the Whitman Sisters'* New Orleans Troubadours but left the company at Louisville, Kentucky and made his way back to New Orleans in the fall. In Louisville he met rag pianists Glover Compton and "Piano Price" Davis, both of whom influenced his style development. In 1905 he settled in Chicago, Illinois; he returned to New Orleans, however, during the years 1910-12 to play at Frank Early's cafe. He established himself on Chicago's South Side as a master pianist, playing in the important cafes and in such theaters as the Elite, the Monogram, and the Grand. He worked with many entertainers who later would win fame, among them, Alberta Hunter,* the Panama Trio (including Florence Mills* and Ada "Bricktop" Smith*), and George Mitchell. Jackson was a prolific composer but published few of his songs and piano rags. His song "Pretty baby" was an instant success when featured by Fannie Brice in the Broadway musical *The Passing Show of 1916*. Other well-known songs were "Miss Samantha Johnson's wedding day," "Why keep me waiting so long," and "Sympathizing man."

BIBL: Black press, incl. CDef, 3 October 1914, 30 October 1915, 8 April 1916. Blesh. Souch.

JACKSON, BABY LAWRENCE. See **JACKSON, LAWRENCE.**

JACKSON, BILLBOARD. See **JACKSON, JAMES ALBERT.**

JACKSON, CHARLIE ("PAPA"). Bluesman (b. in New Orleans, Louisiana [?]; d. 1938 in Chicago, Illinois). He was the first singer to record rural blues. He began his career as a minstrel entertainer, singing and playing banjo, and continued to tour on the vaudeville circuit after he had begun recording. He recorded during the years 1924-30 with both blues and jazz groups, including Freddie Keppard,* Hartzell ("Tiny") Parham, and Albert Wynn. He also recorded duets with Ida Cox* and Gertrude ("Ma") Rainey.*

BIBL: BWW. CharCB. Oliv.

DISC: DiGod. RustJR. TudBM.

JACKSON, CLIFTON LUTHER ("CLIFF"). Jazz pianist (b. 19 July 1902 in Culpepper, Virginia; d. 24 May 1970 in New York, New York). He began his professional career in Washington, D.C., then settled in New York about 1923. Thereafter he played with various groups, including Lionel Howard's Musical Aces (1926), Elmer Snowden* (1926), Sidney Bechet* (1940), Eddie Condon (1946), the Garvin Bushnell* Trio (1959), and J. C. Higginbotham* (1960), among others. More frequently, he led his own groups—his Krazy Kats organized in 1927, with which he recorded in 1930, and other groups over the years—or performed as a soloist or accompanist. He played long residencies in New York nightclubs. He also appeared in films, including *L'Aventure du jazz* (1969) and *The Night They Raided Minsky's* (1968). Afer illness forced him to leave full-time music activities he gave occasional concerts with his wife Maxine Sullivan.* He was one of the pioneer Harlem stride pianists.

BIBL: ChilWW. FeaEJ. FeaJS. FeaGitJS. MeeJMov.

DISC: Jep. Kink. RustJR.

JACKSON TAYLOR, GERTRUDE SMITH. Choral accompanist-conductor (b. 24 April 1903 in Chicago, Illinois). She obtained her musical education in the public schools of Chicago, Illinois, and at the American Conservatory of Music in Chicago. She also studied privately with Thelma Waide Brown,* James Mundy,* and Antoinette Thompkins. Over her long career she was active as a church musician, both as organist and choir director. In March 1930 she organized the Imperial Opera Company, which staged opera and operettas and concert versions of operas semiannually (1930s-70s). Her teaching career included a tenure at the Southern Christian Institute in Edwards, Mississippi (1940-44). During the 1940s she toured with the Jacksonian Trio, which included her daughters Catherine Adams and Betty King.*

BIBL: Questionnaire.

JACKSON, GRAHAM W. Jazz accordionist (b. 22 February 1903 in Portsmouth, Virginia). His mother was a professional singer. He first played piano in public when he was three years old; at seven he played pit piano for silent films, and at fourteen he gave solo recitals. After graduating from high school he began his professional career. Later he obtained his musical eduction at Morehouse College in Atlanta, Georgia, where he studied with Kemper Harreld*; at Chicago [Illinois] Musical College; at Hampton Institute in Virginia; and at Loyola University in Chicago. He settled in Atlanta in 1925 and soon thereafter became a teacher in the public schools (1928-40). He first attracted national attention during the 1930s when President Franklin D. Roosevelt selected him as the White House's favorite entertainer, particularly at the "little White House" in Warm Springs, Georgia. Jackson toured widely, playing piano, organ, and accordion—sometimes playing two or three of these insruments simultaneously. During the latter part of his career he entertained in supper clubs of Atlanta. He received numerous awards, including a proclamation in 1971 by the governor at that time of Georgia, Jimmy Carter, (later, President Carter, 1976-80) that he was the official Musician of the State of Georgia.

BIBL: Black press, incl. *The* [Atlanta] *Voice*, 27 September 1975. ChilWW.

JACKSON, ISAIAH. Symphony orchestra conductor (b. 22 January 1945 in Richmond, Virginia). He obtained his musical education at Harvard University in Cambridge, Massachusetts (B.A., 1966) where he first studied conducting; at Stanford University in California (M.A., 1967); and at the Juilliard School of Music in New York (M.Mus., 1969; D.M.A., 1973), where he founded and conducted the Juilliard String Ensemble. The seventeen-piece ensemble toured in the state of New York. His conducting experience included tenures with the American Ballet Company as an associate conductor (1970-71), as music director of the Youth Symphony Orchestra of New York (1969-73), and as associate conductor of the Rochester [New York] Philharmonic (1973-). In 1973 he served as artistic director of the Festival of Three Cities at Vienna, Austria, and made his European debut conducting the Vienna Symphony. In December 1978 he made his debut with the New York Philharmonic. He toured widely as a guest conductor, appearing with leading symphony orchestras in major cities and at the leading festivals, including the Spoleto in Italy. His honors included the First Governor's Award of Virginia (1979).

BIBL: Questionnaire. Black press, incl. [Pittsburgh] *New Courier*, 6 July 1974. *Encore* (December 1974).

JACKSON, JAMES ALBERT ("BILLBOARD"). Music journalist (b. 20 June 1878 in Bellefonte, Pennsylvania; d. 19?? in New York, New York [?]). His father, Abe V. Jackson, was an original member of the McMillen and Sourbeck Jubilee Singers* (later, known as Stinson's Jubilee Singers), one of the first professional groups to emulate the Fisk Jubilee Singers* during the 1870s, which included William ("Billy") Mills, grandfather of the Mills Brothers.* His early professional experience was as an advance man for Ed Wynn's Big Novelty Minstrels. Later he played with Richard and Pringle's Georgia Minstrels, which featured Billy Kersands* at the time. In 1919 he was the first black reporter to be hired by a major theatrical magazine, *Billboard Magazine*. After 1925 he moved into advertising and marketing. Although not a professional musician, he held honorary membership in the Clef Club.*

BIBL: Flet, p. 30. WWCA 1950.

JACKSON, LAWRENCE DONALD ("BABY LAWRENCE"). Jazz tap dancer (b. 24 February 1921 in Baltimore, Maryland; d. 2 April 1974 in New York, New York). He began his career as a singer and toured on the vaudeville circuit as a child, befriended by "Pops" Foster. When he was twelve he sang with the Don Redman* orchestra. Later he added dancing to his act and discontinued the singing. During the 1940s-early 1950s he performed in nightclubs and theaters with such jazz groups as Edward ("Duke") Ellington,* Woodrow ("Woody") Herman, William ("Count") Basie,* and Earl Hines*; he also toured with Art Tatum* and Bill ("Bojangles") Robinson. After a period of inactivity he returned to the entertainment world in 1961, appearing in theaters and jazz festivals in the United States and abroad, touring with various orchestras and dancing on television shows.

BIBL: Black press, incl. AmstN, 13 April 1974.

JACKSON, MAHALIA (née MAHALA). Gospel singer (b. 26 October 1912 in New Orleans, Louisiana; d. 27 January 1972 in Evergreen Park, Illinois). She sang in a church choir as a child and absorbed the music all about her in New Orleans, Louisiana, particularly the parades, and hearing the recordings of Bessie Smith* in the air. She went to Chicago, Illinois, in December 1927. Soon thereafter she began singing in the choir of the Greater Salem Baptist Church and touring the city's small churches with the Johnson Singers, composed of three brothers—Robert, Prince, Wilbur—and Louise Lemon. In 1929 she came into contact with Thomas A. Dorsey* at the nearby Pilgrim Baptist Church, and he persuaded her to sing his songs on her programs. Later she became a Dorsey-song demonstrator, singing and selling songs on street corners as well as in storefront churches. During the 1930s the demand for her services as a church singer grew, and in 1937 she was invited to make a recording for Decca Records. It attracted little attention, however, and it was almost ten years before she again recorded (1946). She and Dorsey formed a partnership (c1940-46): he became her official accompanist and she sang his songs. In 1948 she was co-founder with Theodore Frye* of the National Baptist Music Convention, an auxiliary to the National Baptist Convention, and thereafter served as treasurer. Her career slowly developed; by 1950 she was becoming well-known outside the church circuit, and she was well established within gospel circles. Her close associates included John Sellers* (later known as ''Brother John'' Sellers), Theodore Frye, Willie Webb, Robert Anderson, and her accompanists Mildred Falls (piano) and blind Herbert James Francis (organ). In 1950 she began appearing on television shows and gave the first all-gospel concert at Carnegie Hall in New York, under the management of Joe Bostic.* She recorded regularly after 1946, and her recordings attracted wide attention in Europe, leading to her first European tour in 1952. During the last two decades of her career, she was practically a national institution. She sang in concert halls, at jazz festivals, in theaters, at the White House (including a presidential inauguration in 1961), for important gatherings of Martin Luther King's Civil Rights Movement (including the March on Washington in 1963), and before crowned heads in Europe. She refused, however, to sing in nightclubs or to sing blues and popular music. She appeared in several films, including *St. Louis Blues* (1958), *Imitation of Life* (1959), *The Best Man* (1964), and documentaries. Her best-known recordings included ''Move on up a little higher,'' ''Just over the hill,'' ''How I got over,'' ''I can put my trust in Jesus,'' ''He's got the whole world in His hands,'' and ''Precious Lord.'' She received awards from the music and recording industries. Her style was distinctive for its powerful rich contralto range and emotional intensity. She earned the title, ''Queen of Gospel Singers.''

BIBL: Barbara Baker, ''Black Gospel Music Styles, 1942-75'' (Ph.D. diss., University of Maryland, 1978). Horace Clarence Boyer, ''The Gospel Song: An Historical and Analytical Study'' (M.A. thesis, Eastman School of Music, 1964). CurBiog (October 1957). *Ebony* (March 1959, April 1968). Laurraine Goreau, *Just Mahalia, Baby* (Waco, Texas, 1975). Heil. Mahalia Jackson with Evan McLeod Wylie, *Movin' On Up* (New York, 1966). MeeJMov.

DISC: DiGod. Hayes. TudJ.

JACKSON, MELVIN (''LITTLE SON''). Bluesman (b. 16 August 1915 near Tyler, Texas; d. 30 May 1976 in Dallas, Texas). His father played guitar. As a child he studied guitar with his father and sang in a Holiness Church choir in nearby Tyler, Texas. He was over thirty years old before he began his professional career as a blues singer-guitarist. Friends persuaded him to make a demonstration record in an amusement arcade booth, which was sent to an agent and led to a recording contract. He first recorded professionally in 1948; encouraged by his success, he formed a blues band which toured widely in the South during the 1950s. He continued to record through the decade, then retired from music because of an automobile accident. His best-known song was ''Rockin' and rollin','' which was credited with inspiring later bluesmen to write similar songs.

BIBL: BWW. LivBl 28 (July-August 1976). Oliv.

DISC: LeSL.

JACKSON, MILTON (''MILT'' ''BAGS''). Jazz vibraharpist (b. 1 January 1923 in Detroit, Michigan). He came from a musical family; four of his brothers played musical instruments. He began teaching himself to play piano and guitar when he was seven years old. He studied piano formally when he was eleven and thereafter played for a church and with local groups. He obtained his musical education in the public schools of Detroit, Michigan, and Michigan State University at East Lansing. During his high-school years he played in the band and symphony orchestra and sang in the glee club and choir. He first studied the vibraharp in high school and decided to specialize on the instrument after hearing a performance by Lionel Hampton* in 1941. He began playing professionally the same year with Detroit groups, among them, Clarence Ringo and George E. Lee.* After service in the United States Armed Forces (1942-44), he returned to Detroit and organized his own group, The Four Sharps. He then played with John Birk ("Dizzy") Gillespie* (1945-47, 1950-52), going with him to New York in 1945. He was an original member of MJQ (Modern Jazz Quartet*)—along with Kenneth ("Kenny") Clarke,* Ray Brown, and John Lewis*—from 1947, when it began performing informally with Gillespie's band, until 1974 when it disbanded. During MJQ's annual summer leaves, he was sometimes co-leader of a group with Brown. Thereafter he toured widely as a soloist or with his own small groups, appearing in theaters and nightclubs, with symphony orchestras, on television shows, and at jazz festivals. He also played with various groups before MJQ was formally organized in 1952, including Howard McGhee,* Tadd Dameron,* Thelonious Monk,* and Woodrow ("Woody") Herman (1949-50). In the summer of 1957 he taught at the School of Jazz in Lenox, Massachusetts. He was the leading vibraphonist in contemporary jazz, filling the same position as Lionel Hampton in traditional jazz; his style was particularly distinctive for its improvisational inventiveness. He received numerous awards from the music industry.

BIBL: Black press, incl. AmstN, 9 June 1979; PhilaT, 10 August 1974. *Cadence* (May 1977). FeaEJ. FeaJS. FeaGitJS. MeeJMov. WWA. WWBA.

DISC: Jep. Kink. ModJ. TudJ.

JACKSON, RAYMOND T. College educator/Concert pianist (b. 11 December 1933 in Providence, Rhode Island). He obtained his musical education at the New England Conservatory in Boston, Massachusetts (B. Mus., 1955), and at the Juilliard School of Music in New York (B.S., 1957; M.S., 1959; D.M.A., 1973), where he studied with Beveridge Webster and Sascha Gorodnitzki, among others. He studied also at the American Conservatory of Music at Fontainebleau, France (diploma, 1960), with Nadia Boulanger, Clifford Curzon, and Robert Casadesus and privately in Paris, France, with Jeanne-Marie Darré. In 1959 he made his debut at Town Hall in New York. Thereafter he toured widely in the United States, Europe, and South America, giving recitals, playing on radio and television programs, and appearing with symphony orchestras. In 1965 he won prizes in the Marguerite Long International Piano Competition at Paris and in the International Piano Competition at Rio de Janeiro, Brazil. His teaching experience included tenures at Mannes College of Music in New York, Corcordia College in Bronxville, New York (1973-77), and Howard University in Washington, D.C. (1977-). His numerous honors included the JUGG Town Hall Debut Award (1959), fellowships from the Ford Foundation (1971-73), John Hay Whitney Foundation (1965), the Eliza G.-George A. Howard Foundation (1960, 1963), and election to the Rhode Island Heritage Hall of Fame (1966).

BIBL: Black press.

JACKSON, TONY. See **JACKSON, ANTHONY.**

JACKSON, WILLIAM. Society dance bandsman (fl. mid-nineteenth century in New York, New York). See also **PLET, A.** In 1852 Martin Delany reported Jackson to be "among the leading musicians of New York City and rank[ing] among the most skillful violinists of America."

BIBL: Black press, incl. *The Colored American*, 14 September 1839. Martin Delany, *The Condition, Elevation, Emigration and Destiny of the Colored People of the United States* (Philadelphia, 1852), p. 124. LaBrew.

JACKSON FIVE, THE. Rhythm 'n' blues group (fl. 1960s-70s; orig. in Gary, Indiana). The Joseph Jackson family consisted of a father who wrote songs and played guitar with a local group in his leisure time, a mother whose hobby was singing, and nine musical children. Family songfests became such enthusiastic affairs that a family group began singing for local social events and, in 1965, in nightclubs. They attracted the attention of the then mayor of Gary, Richard Hatcher; in 1969 he contacted Diana Ross,* who arranged for a recording contract with Berry Gordy's* Motown Records, Inc., for the five oldest boys: Sigmund Esco ("Jackie", b. 4 May 1951), Toriano Adaryll ("Tito," b. 15 October 1953), Jermaine (b. 11 December 1954), Marlon David (b. 12 March 1957), and Michael Joe (b. 29 August 1958). The singing-dancing-instrumental group—Tito played guitar and Jermaine, bass—soon established itelf as a leading rock 'n' roll group. The Jackson Five recorded extensively and successfully, beginning with their first albums *I Want You Back* and *ABC*, released in 1969 and 1970; they toured widely throughout the United States, appearing in theaters, nightclubs, concert halls, and on television shows. In the 1971-72 season they had their own animated show on ABC-TV. In later years three other members of the family joined the group: Yvonne LaToya (b. 29 May 1956), Steven Randall ("Randy," b. 29 October 1961), and Janet Damita Jo (b. 16 May 1966). During the early 1970s, Michael and Jermaine began to release solo albums. In 1976 the group left Motown, changing its name to The Jacksons, and the father, Joe, became manager; Jermaine remained with Motown as a soloist. Within a short period the group was again releasing best-selling albums, of which the best known was *Destiny*, with its most popular tune "Shake your body," written by Michael and Randy. The Jacksons continued to tour worldwide and to record extensively. Michael continued to record solo albums, such as *Off the Wall*, and he appeared in the role of the scarecrow in the film musical, *The Wiz* (1978).

BIBL: Black press, incl. [Pittsburgh] *New Courier*, 14 July 1973. *Ebony* (December 1974, September 1979). NYT, 9 February 1975. StamPRS.

DISC: TudBM.

JACOBS, MARION ("LITTLE") WALTER. Blues harmonica player. (b. 1 May 1930 in Marksville, Louisiana; d. 15 February 1968 in Chicago, Illinois). He began playing harmonica when he was eight years old, and in 1942 formed his own group, which played on street corners. Thereafter he played at various places in the Midwest, including on the King Biscuit Time show on Helena, Arkansas, radio station KFFA and on Mother's Best Flour Hour on the same station; in clubs with Houston Stackhouse* in Helena; and in nightclubs of East St. Louis, Illinois, and St. Louis, Missouri. In 1947 he went to Chicago, where he came under the influence of ("Big Bill") William Lee Conley Broonzy*; later he played with "Muddy Waters" (née McKinley Morganfield).* His style development was also influenced by "Sonny Boy Williamson, No. 1" (née John Lee Williamson).* After leaving Waters in 1952, he toured and recorded with his own band, The Jukes, which included Fred Below, Dave Meyers, and Louis Meyers. He also recorded with Robert ("Junior") Lockwood,* ("Baby Face") Leroy Foster, Jimmy Rogers, Luther Tucker, and Waters, among others. During the mid-1950s he won wide recognition as a rhythm 'n' blues performer, recording some of the most successful records of the period. He was credited with being the first blues harpist to electrify his instrument, which he did by cupping the microphone in his hand along with his harmonica. His harmonica style exerted enormous influence on contemporary and later bluesmen.

BIBL: BWW. LivBl 7 (Winter 1971-72). Oliv.

DISC: LeSl. TudBM.

JACQUET, JEAN BAPTISTE ILLINOIS. Jazz saxophonist (b. 31 October 1922 in Broussard, Louisiana). He came from a musical family; his father was a bassist with a railroad-company band, and two brothers, Linton and Robert, became professional musicians. His family moved to Houston, Texas, when he was an infant. He began playing professionally with local groups during the 1930s. In 1941 he joined Floyd Ray; thereafter he played with various groups, including Lionel Hampton* (1940-42), Cabell ("Cab") Calloway* (1943), William ("Count") Basie* (1944-45), and others. He also toured widely with his own big band, which he formed in 1947, appearing in theaters, nightclubs, concert halls, and at jazz festivals. He toured with JATP (Norman Granz's Jazz at the Philharmonic) in 1944, 1945. He also appeared on television shows and in films, including *Jammin' the Blues* (1944), *Monterey Jazz* (1968), and *D.O.A.* (1949). During the 1970s his trio included Milton Buckner* and Jonathan ("Jo") Jones.* His best known performance was "Flying home," with Hampton's orchestra; his best-known compositions were "Robbins nest," "Black velvet," and "Illinois Jacquet flies again." His early style was distinctive for its extended, high range with "honking sounds" and other tricky whistle-like sounds, which influenced rhythm 'n' blues tenor saxophonists. Jacquet, however, remained in the field of jazz and was regarded as a leading hot and swinging saxman of his time.

BIBL: DanceWCB. FeaEJ. FeaJS. FeaGitJS. MeeJMov. WWA.

DISC: Jep. Kink. ModJ.

JAMAL, AHMAD (née **FRITZ JONES).** Jazz pianist (b. 2 July 1930 in Pittsburgh, Pennsylvania). He began playing piano when he was three years old and began piano study with Mary Cardwell Dawson* at the age of seven. He competed successfully in piano competitions by the time he was eleven and performed publicly on recitals. During his high-school years he played in jazz groups, joining the George Hudson band (1948-49) as a professional after he left school. Thereafter he played with The Four Strings (1949-50), then organized his own trio, The Three Strings, in Chicago, Illinois, in 1951. During the early 1950s he was converted to the Islam faith, changed his name to Ahmad Jamal, and used that name for his trio. He recorded extensively, toured widely in the United States, Europe, Central and South America, and played long residencies in nightclubs of New York and Chicago, among other cities. He also was active in television and films and played on film soundtracks, such as *M*A*S*H* (1969). Over the years his trios included Ray Crawford, Israel Crosby,

Vernal Fournier, Frank Gant, and Jamil Nasser, among others. He also toured as a soloist. His best-known album was *But Not for Me*. He played in the avant-garde style and exerted wide influence upon trios of the 1960s-70s.

BIBL: Black press, incl. CDef, 10 September 1975. ContKey (June 1977). FeaEJ. FeaJS. FeaGitJS. MeeJMov.

DISC: Jep.

JAMES, ETTA. Rhythm 'n' blues singer (b. 1938 in Los Angeles, California). As a child she sang in a gospel church choir and studied music with James Hines. During her high-school years she sang with a trio, called Etta and the Peaches. In 1955 she made her first recording, "The wallflower" (also known as "Roll with me, Henry" and "Dance with me, Henry"), with the aid of Johnny Otis and attracted wide attention. During the years 1955-64 she recorded extensively and established hereself as one of the leading rhythm 'n' blues singers, along with Ruth Brown* and Dinah Washington.* Then her career faltered, although she continued to produce best-selling records periodically. In 1973 she returned to professional music activities, entertaining in nightclubs and recording extensively. Her best-known performances, in addition to the above, were "Something's got a hold on me," "Tell mama," and "I've found a love."

BIBL: Black press, incl. [Los Angeles] *Soul*, 16 September 1974. ShawHS. StamPRS.

DISC: Jep.

JAMES, NEHEMIAH ("SKIP"). Bluesman (b. 9 June 1902 in Bentonia, Mississippi; d. 3 October 1969 in Philadelphia, Pennsylvania). He taught himself to play guitar as a child, influenced by local guitarists Rich Griffith and Henry Stuckey. His piano style reflected the influence of Will Crabtree's boogie-woogie playing. He began playing for country social events at an early age in the Delta region, particularly in the Yazoo City area, often with Stuckey and Griffith. In 1930 he made a successful audition for an agent in Jackson, Mississippi, which led to a contract and a period of regular recording. In 1932 he gave up the blues, however, and organized a gospel group, the Dallas Texas Jubilee Singers, which toured with his father, an itinerant preacher. In 1942 he became an ordained minister. With the revival of public interest in the blues during the 1960s, he returned to touring and recording; he appeared at major folk festivals as well as in concert halls and clubs and toured in Europe with the American Folk Blues Festival in 1967. His music was representative of a specialized local style, called the Bentonia blues, which was practiced by few other than himself and Jack Owens.

BIBL: BWW. LivBl 5 (Summer 1971). NYT, 4 October 1969. Oliv. StamEncy.

DISC: DiGod. LeSl. TudBM.

JAMES, WILLIS LAURENCE. College educator/ Folklorist (b. 18 September 1900 in Montgomery, Alabama; d. 27 December 1966 in Atlanta, Georgia). When he was two years old, his family moved to Florida, where he lived in Pensacola and later in Jacksonville. He obtained his education at the Florida Baptist Academy in Jacksonville and at Morehouse College in Atlanta, Georgia (B.A., 1923), where he sang in the Morehouse quartet and glee club and played violin in the college orchestra. He studied further at the University Extension Conservatory in Chicago, Illinois, with Oswald Blake and Edwin Gerschefski. His teaching career included tenures at Leland College in Louisiana (1923-29), Alabama State Teachers College at Montgomery (1929-33), and Spelman College in Atlanta (1933-66). In addition to teaching he also served as choral director and department chairman in two of the institutions. He early showed an interest in black folksong and began collecting folklore during his sojourn in Louisiana, which resulted in a record release in 1927 (now lost) by the Paramount Record Company, for which he transcribed music and sang the songs and James Edward Halligan transcribed the texts. Over the years he continued his investigation of folksong and toured widely as a lecturer, appearing on college campuses, before professional societies, and at the Newport Jazz and Folk Festivals and the Tanglewood Music Festivals. During the 1940s he was a Recording Fellow for the Library of Congress and thereby associated with the production of field and studio recordings of black folksong, some in collaboration with John Work III.* He was co-founder of the Fort Valley [Georgia] State College Folk Festivals (1940-55), along with the college president, Horace Mann Bond, and served as a summer faculty member during the years 1941-44. He published articles in professional journals and record-jacket notes for folksong recordings. His theory that "the cry" was the most distinctive feature of black folksong attracted wide attention; it was discussed in "The Romance of the Negro Folk Cry in America" in *Phylon* 16 (1955). At his death he left a completed manuscript, titled "Stars in the Elements," which consisted of a collection of folklore with analysis. He was also noted for his compositions, particularly his folksong arrangements, which were widely performed by college groups. His honors included awards from the General Education Board and the Carnegie Foundation, an honorary doctorate from Wilberforce University (1955), and appointment to professional panels and boards of professional organizations.

BIBL: Black press, incl. CDef, 30 September 1939; AmstN, 18 August 1951. Rebecca T. Cureau, "Black Folklore, Musicology, and Willis Lawrence (*sic*) James" in NHBul, 43 (January-February-March 1980). NYB, 1952.

JAMIESON, SAMUEL W. Concert pianist. (b. 1855 in Washington, D.C.; d. February 1930 in Boston, Massachusetts). He began to study piano with local teachers at the age of eleven. Later he studied in Boston with Hungarian pianist Fred K. Boscovitz, James M. Tracy, and Benjamin J. Lang, organist of the Handel and Haydn Society. In 1876 he was graduated from the Boston Conservatory and soon thereafter he established a music studio. He began to play professionally while still a student at the Conservatory, and he continued to tour periodically as a concert pianist throughout his career. He also performed as an assisting artist on concerts; during the 1880s he gave duo concerts with baritone George L. Ruffin,* the first black member of the Handel and Haydn Society. Jamieson was best known for his performance of the romantic composers Chopin and Liszt.

BIBL: Black press, incl. NYGlobe, 7 July 1883, 12 April 1884; NYAge, 16 August 1890. Hare. Trot.

JARBORO, CATERINA. (née **CATHERINE YARBOROUGH).** Concert singer (b. 24 July 1903 in Wilmington, North Carolina). She received her musical training in Catholic schools of Wilmington, North Carolina, and at the Gregory Normal School. About 1916 she went to New York to further her study of music. She became involved with the theater and began singing professionally in Broadway musicals, including the James ("Eubie") Blake*/Noble Sissle* *Shuffle Along* (1921) and James P. Johnson's* *Running Wild* (1923). About 1926 she went abroad to study and to sing. In May 1930 she made her operatic debut singing the title role of Verdi's *Aida* at the Puccini Theater in Milan, Italy. She also sang with other European opera companies. In 1932 she returned to the United States; the next year she made her American operatic debut with the Chicago Civic Opera, directed by Alfredo Salmaggi, singing the title role of *Aida* in July and in the fall singing the role of Selika in Meyerbeer's *L'Africaine* at the Hippodrome Theater in New York. She toured widely as a concert singer, but her career failed to develop in the United States as she had hoped, and by 1937 she had returned to Europe, settling in Brussels, Belgium. Using that city as a base, she toured in Europe and sang operatic roles in European houses. She finally settled in New York, New York.

BIBL: Black press, incl. CDef, 12 March 1932, 18 July 1936, 17 February 1938; NYAge, 22 July 1933. HNB. NYB, 1941-46.

JARMAN, JOSEPH. Jazz woodwind player (b. 14 September 1937 in Pine Bluff, Arkansas). His family moved to Chicago, Illinois, when he was an infant. He obtained his musical education in the public schools of Chicago, where he came under the tutelage of Walter Dyett* at DuSable High School; at Wilson Junior College, Chicago City College, and the Chicago Conservatory of Music. During the 1950s he began playing professionally and toured with rhythm 'n' blues, blues, and jazz groups. In 1965 he began an association with AACM (Association for the Advancement of Creative Musicians). In 1969 he joined the Roscoe Mitchell* Art Ensemble, later called the Art Ensemble of Chicago, and toured with the group in Europe (1969-71), which also recorded there extensively and appeared at jazz festivals. Jarman continued to play with the Art Ensemble and other AACM groups after his return to the United States. His best-known compositions were "Imperfections in a Given Space," "Tribute to the Hard Core,"and "Song for."

BIBL: FeaGitJS.

DISC: Jep.

JAZZ CRUSADERS, THE. See **CRUSADERS, THE.**

JEANTY, OCCIDE ("FILS"). Military bandmaster (b. 18 March 1860 in Port-au-Prince, Haiti; d. 28 January 1936 in Port-au-Prince). He came from a musical family: his father, Occilius Jeanty ("Pere"),* was a music teacher and a flutist. Occide obtained his musical education at l'Ecole Polymathique de Coupeaud, at the Lycée Pétion in Port-au-Prince, and at l'Ecole Centrale de Musique, of which his father was founder-director. During the years 1881-85 he studied music at the Paris Conservatory in France, with Arban, Marmontel, and Douillon, among others, giving special attention to the cornet à piston and to harmony and composition. In 1885 he was appointed director of music at the National Palace by President Salomen (with responsibilities equal to those of a national director of music). He also conducted community bands and orchestras. He wrote in a variety of small music forms: marches, waltzes, polkas, meringues, songs, and character pieces. Best-known of his pieces were ''1804,'' ''Les vautours du 6 Décembre,'' and ''Les trompette des anges.'' After his death a street was named for him in Port-au-Prince, and on the centennial anniversary of his birth in 1960, a stamp was issued in his honor.

BIBL: Dumervé.

JEANTY, OCCILIUS (''PERE''). Military bandsman/ Music-school founder (b. 1830 in Port-au-Prince; d. 2 November 1882 in Port-au-Prince). He received his musical education at l'Ecole Wesleyenne and at the Lycée Pétion, both in Port-au-Prince. He studied flute with Franklin Carpentier and began his professional career about 1858 as a fifer in the Grenadiers de la Garde of his Imperial Majesty, Faustin I. Later in his career he was ''chef du Corps.'' He was a music teacher at the Lycée Pétion for many years. In 1876 he founded l'Ecole Centrale de Musique, whose faculty included Charles Fontin (organist at the Cathedral of Port-au-Prince), Théremène Mémès, Felix Aimé, the Scott brothers, and Stéphen Benoit, among others. During the 1870s Jeanty led orchestras which played at official ceremonies at the National Palace. His son, Occide Jeanty,* was a professional musician.

BIBL: Dumervé.

JEFFERSON, EDGAR (''EDDIE''). Entertainer/Jazz singer (b. 3 August 1918 in Pittsburgh, Pennsylvania; d. 9 May 1979 in Detroit, Michigan). His father was an entertainer and aided the son's career development. He obtained his musical education in the public schools of Pittsburgh, Pennsylvania, where he studied tuba. He also learned to play guitar and drums. He began his professional career as a dancer-singer; he performed with various groups, including The Zephyrs at the Chicago World's Fair in 1933, Coleman Hawkins* (1939), and a Sarah Vaughan* show (1950), among others. During the years 1953-73 he toured primarily with James Moody (intermittently), occasionally with Billy Mitchell and Roy Brooks, and as a soloist. He began recording in 1952 and thereafter recorded regularly. He was best known as the inventor of jazz vocalese: he wrote lyrics to the melodies of improvised solos of jazz instrumentalists. His first vocalese was set to the melody of Coleman Hawkins's solo on ''Body and Soul''; his most celebrated vocalese was set to James Moody's solo on ''I'm in the mood for love'' (first recorded by ''King Pleasure''). Other well-known vocaleses of his were settings of solos in Miles Davis's* *Bitches Brew* and Eddie Harris's *Freedom Jazz Dance*. His album releases included *The Main Man* and *The Live-Liest*.

BIBL: *Downbeat* (21 June 1979). FeaEJ. FeaGitJS. *Jazz Magazine* (February 1978).

JEFFERSON, LEMON (''BLIND LEMON''). Bluesman (b. July 1897 near Wortham, Texas; d. December [?] 1929 in Chicago, Illinois). Born blind, he taught himself to play guitar as a child and played for local country dances and picnics at an early age. He left home when he was about twenty years old to sing professionally in Dallas, Texas. During his stay there he met Huddie (''Leadbelly'') Ledbetter,* and the two bluesmen formed a team that performed in local cafes and sometimes traveled to nearby towns to entertain. He strongly influenced the development of Leadbelly's style and, as well, that of (''Lightnin' '') Sam Hopkins* and Josh White,* both of whom traveled with the blind singer when they were children. During the 1920s he performed throughout the South and became well known. In 1925 he made his first recordings, which were not released until the next year, and thereafter he recorded regularly until his death in 1929. His performance was distinctive for its employment of special vocal and guitar effects, and his songs were imaginative, among them, ''Hangman's blues'' and ''Black snake moan.'' He represented the essence of the Texas blues style, along with Alger (''Texas'') Alexander,* Lonnie Johnson,* and Leadbelly.

BIBL: CharCB. MeeJMov. Oliv. *Record Research* 76 (May 1966).

DISC: DiGod. TudBM.

JEFFRIES, HERBERT (''HERB''). Jazz singer (b. 24 September 1916 in Detroit, Michigan). He obtained his musical education in the public schools of Detroit, Michigan. He sang with leading jazz bands of his time, including Erskine Tate,* Lionel Hampton,* Earl Hines,* Blanche Calloway,* and Edward (''Duke'') Ellington* (1940-42), among others. He toured widely as a soloist, performing in nightclubs, theaters, on radio and television programs, and in films. He recorded extensively and wrote many of his own songs. Early in his career he made a specialty of singing falsetto, but later changed to singing in a deep-voice style. He was especially noted for singing ballads; his best-known performances were ''Flamingo'' and ''Cocktails for two.''

BIBL: ASCAP. FeaEJ. MeeJMov.

DISC: Jep. Kink. RustJR.

JENKINS, EDMUND THORNTON. Composer (b. 9 April 1894 in Charleston, South Carolina; d. 12 September 1926 in Paris, France). His father, Daniel Joseph Jenkins (d. August 1937) was a minister and founder of the Jenkins' Orphanage in Charleston, South Carolina, which was celebrated for its boys' bands. Edmund studied music with his father as a child and played in the orphanage bands. By the time he was fourteen he could play all the band instruments. He obtained his musical education at Avery Institute in Charleston and at the Atlanta Baptist College (now Morehouse College) in Atlanta, Georgia, where he studied with Kemper Harreld.* In 1914 he went to London, England, with an Orphanage band to play at the Anglo-African Exposition and remained in London to matriculate at the Royal Academy of Music. During the seven years he studied at the Academy he won scholarships and prizes, including the Charles Lucas Battison Haines Prize for composition and the Oliveria Prescott Prize. After completing his studies he remained in Europe and became involved in professional musical activities. He was assistant teacher at the Academy for a period, he was a church organist, and he played clarinet in the Savoy Theatre orchestra. About 1922 he settled in Paris, France, and thereafter used that city as a base from which he toured. In 1925 two of his works, *African War Dance* for full orchestra and Sonata in A minor for violoncello, won Holstein prizes in New York. The same year his composition *Charlestonia*, a rhapsody for orchestra using Negro themes, was performed at the Kursaal d'Ostend in Belgium. In 1926 his *Negro Symphony* was performed in London (from a manuscript copy) and accepted for performance in Paris the next year. His premature death, however, prevented its performance.

BIBL: Black press, incl. NYAge, 19 January 1924, 2 October 1926. John Chilton, *A Jazz Nursery: The Story of the Jenkins' Orphanage Bands* (London, 1980). NegroYB.

JENKINS, LEROY. Jazz violinist (b. 11 March 1932 in Chicago, Illinois). See also **REVOLUTIONARY ENSEMBLE, THE.** He studied violin as a child and played in a church group. He was first inspired to develop violin skills after hearing performances by Edward ("Eddie") South and Hezekiah ("Stuff") Smith when he was ten years old. He obtained his musical education in the public schools of Chicago, Illinois, where he studied with Walter Dyett,* and at Florida A & M College in Tallahassee (B.S., 1961), where he was greatly influenced by violinist Bruce Hayden. Thereafter he taught in the public schools of Mobile, Alabama (1961-65), and Chicago, Illinois (1965-69); he was also a strings instructor for the Chicago Urban Poverty Corps (1969). In 1966 he began an association with AACM (Association for the Advancement of Creative Musicians) and worked closely with the program as teacher and performer, along with Richard Abrams,* Joseph Jarman,* Anthony Braxton,* Leo Smith,* and Steve McCall, among others. He was also active with the Art Ensemble of Chicago, the Jazz Composers Workshop Orchestra, and the Creative Construction Company (which included Braxton, McCall, and Smith). In 1970 he went to New York, where he was co-founder of The Revolutionary Ensemble,* along with Jerome Cooper and Sirone. The trio toured widely, playing in nightclubs, concert halls, on college campuses, and at jazz festivals. He also performed as a soloist with others, among them, Ornette Coleman,* Alice Coltrane,* Mtume, and Cecil Taylor.* His honors included a grant from the National Endowment for the Arts (1972) and awards from the music industry. He won wide recognition as a member of the avant-garde who developed the potential of improvisatory violin and viola to its utmost. His compositions included *Background to Life* (suite for solo violin), *Shapes, Textures, Rhythms, Moods of Sounds* (for violin, flute, clarinet, French horn, bass clarinet) and a manual for violin, *Musical Thoughts to Ponder*. During the 1970s he established his own publishing company, Outward Visions, Inc.

BIBL: Personal communication. *The Boston Phoenix*, 20 March 1973, Section 2, p. 8. FeaGitJS. *Melody Maker* (31 July 1971). NYT, 15 January 1977.

JENKINS ORPHANAGE BAND. See **JENKINS, EDMUND.**

JESSYE, EVA. Choral conductor (b. 20 January 1895 in Coffeyville, Kansas). She sang as a child and organized a girls' singing group when she was twelve years old. She obtained her musical education in the public schools of Coffeyville, Kansas, and St. Louis, Missouri; at Western University in Quindaro, Kansas (graduated 1914); and at Langston University in Oklahoma. Her career development was aided by Will Marion Cook,* whom she first met when he brought a musical production to her home town, and she, at the age of twelve, helped him copy music for his orchestra. She later studied with him when she went to New York and also with Percy Goetschius. Her teaching career included tenures in the public schools of Taft, Haskell, and Muskogee, Oklahoma; at Morgan State College in Baltimore, Maryland (1919-20), and at Claflin College in Orangeburg, South Carolina. About 1922 she went to New York to further her career in music. She soon became active in musical circles and sang with pit orchestras for musical shows. Within a short time she organized her Original Dixie Jubilee Singers and began appearing in 1925 on the Major Bowes Family Radio Hour. By 1926 her Eva Jessye Choir had established itself as a leading choral group and was touring widely in the United States. The same year she was engaged by NBC and CBS to organize and direct choral groups for performance on radio and later was selected to be choral director for the King Vidor film *Hallelujah* (1929). In 1934 she was choral director for Virgil Thomson's opera *Four Saints in Three Acts*, and the next year she served as choral director of Gershwin's *Porgy and Bess* (1935). She directed the chorus in the many revivals of the opera through the 1960s and toured with the company in Europe. She also toured widely as a lecturer and guest choral conductor, sometimes conducting her own works, for she was a composer. In 1931 her folk oratorio *Paradise Lost and Regained* was broadcast on NBC radio, and in 1972 it was given its premiere stage production in Washington, D.C. Her other works in large form included *The Life of Christ in Negro Spirituals* and *The Chronicle of Job*. In 1972 she contributed materials to establish an Eva Jessye Collection of Afro-American Music at the University of Michigan in Ann Arbor, and in 1979 she established in a similar collection in southeast Kansas. She served as an artist-in-residence at Pittsburg State University in Kansas (1978-). Her honors included an honorary master's degree from Wilberforce University in Ohio and an honorary doctorate from Allen University in South Carolina. Jessye was the first black woman to succeed as a professional choral conductor, based on the evidence. Her success paved the way for others, both male and female. She also exerted wide influence as a teacher in the informal sense; her singers who later won recognition as concert artists included Andrew Frierson,* Muriel Rahn,* and Lawrence Winters,* among others.

BIBL: Personal communications. Black press, incl. CDef, 24 December 1932, 7 June 1941; NYAge, 15 January 1936. *Ebony* (May 1974). Layne. NYT, 7 October 1979. *The Washington Star*, 12 July 1972.

JETER, CLAUDE. See **SWAN SILVERTONES.**

JIMÉNEZ-BERRA, JOSÉ JULIAN. Concert violinist (b. 9 January1833 in Trinidad da Cuba; d. 188? in Havana, Cuba). He toured with his two sons in a family trio during the 1870s in Europe, particularly in France and Germany. He studied violin with Ferdinand David at Leipzig, Germany, and later played in the Leipzig Gewandhaus Orchestra (1870-75) under the direction of Carl Reinecke. His eldest son, Nicasio, was a violoncellist who also studied at the Leipzig Conservatory and played in the Gewandhaus Orchestra. The second son, José Manuel, was a pianist who studied with Ignaz Moscheles in Leipzig and with Antoine-François Marmontel and Augustin Savard at Paris, France. In 1876 he won second prize (harmony) in the Prix de Rome competition, and in 1877 he shared first prize (piano) with two other contestants. During the years 1881-91 José Manuel conducted a music studio in Cinefuegos, Cuba. Later he taught at the Hamburg Conservatory of Music in Germany. [by Josephine R. B. Wright].

BIBL: Fétis. The European press, including *Le* [Paris] *Menestrel* and *Der* [Leipzig] *Musikalisch Wochenblatt*, 1870-77.

JIMÉNEZ-BERRA, JOSÉ MANUEL. Concert pianist (b. 7 December 1855 in Trinidad da Cuba; d. 15 January 1917 in Hamburg, Germany). See **JIMÉNEZ-BERRA, JOSÉ JULIAN.**

JOHNS, ALTONA TRENT. College music educator (b. 21 December 1904 in Asheville, North Carolina; d. 10 July 1977 in Baton Rouge, Louisiana). She studied piano as a child. She obtained her musical education at Atlanta University in Georgia (B.A.), Columbia University Teachers College in New York (M.A.), the University of New Mexico at Albuquerque, the University of Arizona at Tucson, and the Juilliard School of Music in New York. She was the first music instructor at Bennett College in Greensboro, North Carolina, after it became an institution for women in 1926. Her teaching career included also tenures at Alabama State College in Montgomery; in the public schools of Prince Edward County in Virginia; at Virginia State College in Petersburg; and at Paine College in Augusta, Georgia, as a visiting professor. She became interested in the subject of black music early in her career and traveled widely in the United States, Europe, and Africa as a researcher and lecturer-pianist. In 1969 she was co-founder, with Undine Smith Moore,* of the Black Music Center at Virginia State College, which brought to the campus during the years 1969-72 the leading black composers, performers, musical groups, artists, poets, writers, and lecturers in the United States. The program of the Center, titled "The Black Man in American Music," also sponsored symposia, workshops, and seminar-institutes. Johns contributed articles to professional journals and published the collection *Playsongs of the Deep South* (1944).

BIBL: Personal communication. Black press, incl. AmstN, 30 July 1977.

JOHNSON, ALBERT ("BUDD"). Jazz saxophonist (b. 14 December 1910 in Dallas, Texas). He came from a musical family: his father was a church organist and choir director and also played trumpet, and his brother Frederick ("Keg") became a professional musician. He began piano study when he was eight years old, but taught himself to play trumpet. He obtained his musical education in the public schools of Dallas, Texas. While he was still in elementary school, he began playing drums in a local boys' band, which played for school events and eventually, as the Moonlight Melody Six, for local social events. His first professional experiences were during the mid-1920s; he and his brother played with William Holloway (whose band later was taken over by Ben Smith), Eugene Coy, Terrence Holder, and Jesse Stone, among others. During the years 1928-35, he played with various groups—in Kansas City, Missouri, with George E. Lee* and in Chicago, Illinois, with Clarence Moore, Eddie Mallory, and Louis Armstrong,* among others. Thereafter he played with Earl Hines* (1935-36, 1937, 1938-42), Gus Arnheim, briefly with Horace* and Fletcher Henderson,* and with Don Redman.* He also wrote arrangements for Hines. From the mid-1940s through the 1970s he toured as a soloist and with his own groups, recorded extensively, was active as a musical director, played with many groups, and maintained his own publishing house for a period. His touring took him to Europe several times, on college campuses, and to the major jazz festivals. He played with William ("Count") Basie,* Quincy Jones,* Hines again, Benny Goodman, Melvin ("Sy") Oliver,* and the New York Jazz Repertory Company, among others. He also lectured at various institutions, including the University of Connecticut at Storrs and Rutgers University in New Brunswick, New Jersey, and was associated with the Smithsonian Institution in Washington, D.C., as a concert artist and as a music transcriber in its "classic jazz" project. He was an important figure of the swing era, particularly as saxophonist-arranger for Earl Hines, and a pioneer in the bop tradition. In 1944 he helped William ("Billy") Eckstine* to organize the band that was called "the cradle of bop" and later was musical director for the band. Finally, he wrote and/or arranged music for all five of the early bop orchestras: Hines, Eckstine, John Birks ("Dizzy") Gillespie,* Woodrow ("Woody") Herman, and Boyd Raeburn.

BIBL: ChilWW. DanceWEH. FeaEJ. FeaJS. FeaGitJS. MeeJMov.

DISC: Jep. Kink.

JOHNSON, ALONZO ("LONNIE"). Bluesman (b. 8 February 1889 in New Orleans, Louisiana; d. 16 June 1970 in Toronto, Canada). He learned guitar, fiddle, and other instruments as a child; later he and his brother James played professionally in local cafes. In 1917 he joined a musical show in London; after returning to the United States about 1921, he traveled in Texas and eventually settled in St. Louis, Missouri, where he played in theater orchestras. Later he played for two or more years with Charlie Creath's* riverboat band and with Fate Marable,* then left music until 1925. In that year he won a blues contest, was heard by a record talent scout, and given a recording contract. He soon established himself as a major blues figure. In 1932 he moved to Cleveland, Ohio; in 1937, to Chicago, Illinois. He recorded extensively with both bluesmen, particularly Alger ("Texas") Alexander, and jazz groups, including Louis Armstrong,* Johnny Dodds,* and Edward ("Duke") Ellington.* About 1945 he began to use the electric guitar. In 1952 he traveled to England for the first time to give concerts; thereafter he toured widely at home and abroad; he was also an active songwriter. In 1965 he settled in Toronto, Canada. He was one of the few male urban blues singers of the 1920s in a field dominated by women, such as Bessie Smith,* Ida Cox,* and Victoria Spivey,* among others. His style was polished and sophisticated, distinctive for its jazz-inflected guitar. His influence was particularly evident in the music of Robert Johnson* and ("B. B.") Riley King.*

BIBL: BWW. CharCB. ChilWW. LivBl 2 (Summer 1970). MeeJMov. Oliv.

DISC: DiGod. Kink. LeSl. RustJR. TudBM.

JOHNSON, BILL. See **JOHNSON, WILLIAM MANUEL.**

JOHNSON, BILLY. See **JOHNSON, WILLIAM FRANCIS.**

JOHNSON, BUDD. See **JOHNSON, ALBERT.**

JOHNSON, BUNK. See **JOHNSON, WILLIAM GEARY.**

JOHNSON, DEACON. See **JOHNSON, FRED.**

JOHNSON, FRANCIS (also known as **FRANK JOHNSON).** Composer (b. 1792 in Martinique, West Indies; d. 6 April 1844 in Philadelphia, Pennsylvania). Little is known of his early career. According to *The Master Musician* (see bibl. below), he went to Philadelphia, Pennsylvania, in 1809. He first attracted wide attention in 1818 when G. Willig published his "Six Setts" of Cotillions and the press reported that he was encouraged by the public's response to his dance orchestra. A book published in 1819 identified him as "leader of the band at all balls, public and private; sole director of all serenades . . . inventor-general of cotillions" (see Waln in bibliography below). During the 1820s his career blossomed: his groups played for the city's leading dancing schools; he played for balls and private parties of the aristocracy; in 1821 his small military band began an association with the prestigious State Fencibles Regiment; and by 1822 he had become established at the Saratoga Springs resort. When General Lafayette visited Philadelphia in 1824 it was Johnson's band that provided the major share of the music for the parades, the assemblies, and the numerous parties given in the General's honor. It is not known how Johnson obtained his musical instruction. According to one source, he played in a band led by a black bandleader named Black and studied trumpet with the man. The evidence suggests that he also studied with Richard Willis, director of the West Point Military Band of the United States Army. A dedicatory notice in Johnson's song, "The death of Willis" (1830), pays "respect to his memory for the unusual and kind attention to him in forwarding him in a knowledge of that fine and martial instrument, the Kent Bugle, when first introduced in this country." Johnson became celebrated as a keyed-bugle performer and also as a violinist. Johnson's bands and orchestras retained their primacy among Philadelphia's musical groups through the 1830s and early 1840s, until his death in 1844, despite severe competition offered by the bands of James Hemmenway* and Isaac Hazzard,* as well as several first-rate white bands. In addition to playing for dances and military parades of the elite, he played for sacred-music concerts of black churches in Philadelphia, New York, and Boston in cooperation with such choral conductors as Jacob A. Stans and Morris Brown, Jr.* His groups performed for social entertainments given in the black community—balls, literary festivals, debating events —and funerals. In March 1841 Johnson and Brown staged Haydn's *Creation* in its entirety at the First African Presbyterian Church and repeated the performance later for a white church.

In November 1837 Johnson took a small group of his bandsmen to London, England, to give concerts—William Appo,* Aaron J. R. Connor,* Edward Roland,* and Francis V. Seymour.* Reputedly his performances there included a command performance for Queen Victoria, who gave him a silver bugle. While abroad Johnson became acquainted with the current music styles and forms, particularly the waltz styles of Johann Strauss, and introduced the new music to Philadelphia after returning home. More important, he introduced Philippe Musard's concept of the "promenade concert" to Philadelphia in a series of concerts during the Christmas season of 1838 and established a tradition in the United States that has lasted to the present. Thereafter Johnson's activities included the presentation of formal concerts in addition to playing for balls and parades. Beginning in 1838 he toured widely, as far north as Toronto, Canada, and as far south as St. Louis, Missouri. The existence of slavery prevented, of course, any excursions into the deep South. In addition to performing, Johnson's musical activities including teaching and composing. He trained a large number of the black bandsmen of his time and had numerous students, white and black. One of his wealthy white students, Isaac Mickle, described Johnson's music room as follows: "The wall was covered with pictures and instruments of all kinds, and one side of the room was fixed with shelves whereon were thousands of musical compositions, constituting a valuable library. Bass drum, bass viols, bugles and trombones lay in admirable confusion on the floor; and in one corner was an armed composing chair, with pen and inkhorn ready, and some gallopades and waltzes half finished."

Johnson was a prolific composer, leaving over 200 published pieces and untold numbers of manuscripts, many of which were lost. His output included cotillions, quadrilles, marches, and other dances, sentimental ballads, patriotic songs, operatic arrangements, and even minstrel songs. Although most of the publications are pianoforte arrangements of pieces performed by his bands, none of his band music is extant. It may be that Johnson's groups used "head arrangements," as jazz groups do today, rather than written arrangements. His musical style is straightforward, with engaging melodies but simple harmonies and rhythms. Obviously its attraction derived from the way Johnson performed it; he was acclaimed for his "remarkable taste in distorting a sentimental, simple and beautiful song into a reel, jig or country-dance" (see Waln, p. 155). His most celebrated compositions were the "Bird Waltz," "Philadelphia Grays' Quickstep," "Star-Spangled Banner Cotillions," and the "Voice Quadrilles." His music remained popular for decades after his death; a number of the pieces appear in the *Complete Catalogue of Sheet Music and Musical Works, 1870*, published by the Board of Music Trade of the United States of America, 1871; reprint with introduction by Dena Epstein (New York, 1973).

The size and composition of his musical groups changed over the years from the four-piece unit (bugle, fife, small and large drum) that played with the State Fencibles in 1821. His early military band consisted primarily of woodwinds, to which were added a French horn or two, a serpent, cymbals, bells, triangles, and drums. To play for dances, his men substituted strings for winds, thereby becoming Johnson's Quadrille Band. As brass instruments were introduced into the United States, Johnson's groups incorporated them, as well as such exotic instruments as the ophicleide, bell harmonicon, and harp for concert playing. Over the years those who played instrumental solos on Johnson's concerts included William Appo,* Dennis Carter,* Aaron Connor,* Edward Augustus, Joseph Gordon*, Edward Johnson, Robert C. Kennedy, William R. Jackson, James J. Richards, Edward Roland, Francis Seymour, and E. Toulou, among others.

Johnson was counted among the leading performers of his time, and his influence upon the development of musical traditions in Philadelphia was long-lasting. His group was the first American band, according to all evidence, to give concerts abroad. That fact, and his gift of the "promenade concert" to the United States, earned him, along with his compositions, a secure place in the history of American music. In February 1980 Johnson was elected posthumously to honorary membership in the Artillery Corps Washington Grays at Philadelphia.

BIBL: PaHistSoc. Black press, incl. *Freedom's Journal*, 6 April 1827, 23 September 1827; *The Colored American*, 17 August 1838. BPIM 5 (Spring 1977). John Cromwell, "Frank Johnson's Military Band" in SW 29 (1900); reprinted in BPIM 4 (July 1976). Robert E. Eliason, *Keyed Bugles in the United States* (Washington, D.C., 1972). Arthur LaBrew, *Selected Works of Francis Johnson* (Detroit, 1976). Thomas Lanard, *One Hundred Years with the State Fencibles* (Philadelphia, 1913). Philip English Mackey, ed., *A Gentleman of Much Promise: The Diary of Isaac Mickle, 1837-1845* (Philadelphia, 1977). *The Master Musician* 1 (February 1920), p. 8. *The* [Philadelphia] *Bulletin*, 1 March 1980. The [Philadelphia] *Public Ledger*, 1836-1844. Robert Waln [pseud. for Peter Atall], *The Hermit in America on a Visit to Philadelphia* (Philadelphia, 1818; passages about Johnson reprinted in SouRBAM). Richard J. Wolfe, *Secular Music in America*, 1801-1925 (New York, 1964).

JOHNSON, FRANCIS HALL. Composer (b. 12 March 1888 in Athens, Georgia; d. 30 April 1970 in New York, New York). He showed musical talent at an early age and studied piano as a child with an older sister. Inspired by hearing a violin recital given by Joseph Douglass,* he became interested in learning violin. Although he was given a violin when he was fourteen, he was unable to study formally until he attended college, for he could find no one to teach him in Athens. He obtained his musical education at Knox Institute in Knoxville, Tennessee (1903); Atlanta University in Georgia (1904); Allen University in Columbia, South Carolina (1905-08), where his father was president; the Hahn School of Music in Philadelphia, Pennsylvania, and the University of Pennsylvania (B.A., 1910), where he studied composition with Hugh A. Clark; and the Institute of Musical Art (later joined with the Juilliard School of Music), where he studied with Percy Goetschius (1923-24).

He began to play violin professionally about 1910, traveling in February of that year to New York to appear on a concert. By 1914 he had settled permanently in New York and had become a member of the black music establishment. He played in James Reese Europe's* groups that toured with Irene and Vernon Castle; in 1918 he played with Will Marion Cook's* New York Syncopated Orchestra (aka Southern Syncopated Orchestra) but did not accompany the orchestra to Europe the next year. Throughout this period he conducted a music studio, played regularly on local concerts, and performed with theater pit orchestras, including that of the Noble Sissle*/Eubie Blake* musical *Shuffle Along* (1921). In 1923 he organized the Negro String Quartet, composed of violinists Arthur Boyd and Felix Weir,* cellist Marion Cumbo,* and himself on viola. Although active as a string player, his great interest was in choral music; in September 1925 he organized his first permanent choral group. The Hall Johnson Choir made its formal debut in February 1928 at the Pythian Temple and sang again at Town Hall in March of that year. During the next decade the Choir built a solid reputation for itself: it appeared on radio and in theaters; sang with major orchestras; performed on Broadway in Marc Connolly's play *Green Pastures* (1930), for which Johnson was musical director; and sang in films, among them, *Lost Horizon* (1937), *Way Down South* (1939), *Cabin in the Sky* (1943), and *Green Pastures* (1935). The Choir also made recordings, beginning in 1930 for Victor RCA. In 1933 Johnson produced his folk opera, *Run Littl' Chillun*, on Broadway; it received critical acclaim for the music but not for the book. The musical was revived for a Federal Theater Project at Los Angeles, California, in 1935-37, with Clarence Muse* as director. During the early 1930s Johnson also had a Male Sextet. He was active in California during the years 1938-46, where he organized the 200-voice Festival Choir of Los Angeles and restaged his folk opera in that city, San Francisco, and later in New York. In 1946 he resettled in New York and organized the Festival Negro Chorus of New York City. The next year he inaugurated his annual concert series, titled "New Artists," on which were featured such young artists as cellist Kermit Moore* and baritone Robert McFerrin.* In 1951 the United States Department of State sent the Hall Johnson Choir of twenty-seven singers to the International Festival of Fine Arts at Berlin, Germany, and the Choir remained to tour in Europe for several months. Johnson was one of the most important choral directors of his period. His honors included the Simon Haessler Prize from the University of Pennsylvania (1910), Holstein Prizes (1925, 1927), a Harmon Award (1930), an honorary doctorate from the Philadelphia Academy of Music (1934), and the City of New York's Handel Award (197?). His compositions were immensely popular with concert artists and groups, particularly his spiritual arrangements, of which the best known are ''Honor, honor,'' ''His name so sweet,'' ''I've been 'buked,'' and ''Scandalize my name.'' In addition to single pieces he published two collections, *The Green Pastures Spirituals* (1930) and *Thirty Negro Spirituals* (1949). His Easter cantata, *Son of Man* (1946), became a perennial favorite in New York; and his songs ''The courtship'' (1956) and ''Fi-yer'' (1959, revised 1970), became permanent items in the repertory of black concert singers. Johnson lectured on the importance of preserving the spirituals and wrote an article, ''Notes on the Negro Spiritual'' (published in Eileen Southern, ed., *Readings in Black American Music* [New York, 1971]).

BIBL: Interview by E. S. Communications from Marva Griffin Carter. ASCAP. Black press, incl. NYAge, 7 February 1910, 17 September 1949. CurBiog, 1945, 1970. HNB. Cornelius V. Troup, *Distinguished Negro Georgians* (Dallas, Texas, 1962). WWCA 1950.

DISC: Turn.

JOHNSON, FRED (''DEACON''). Music contractor/ Entertainer (b. 12 August 1878 in Pine Bluff, Arkansas; d. 29 March 1944 in New York, New York). He obtained his musical education in Pine Bluff and at McGill University in Montreal, Canada. He began his professional career as an entertainer at the Chicago World's Fair in 1893. He was active in Montreal during the years 1893-1900, toured widely for the next three years with minstrel and vaudeville companies, then settled in New York about 1903. There he established the Deacon Johnson Music Exchange, a music contracting company, which lasted into the 1940s. He was active with the Clef Club* from the time of its origin in 1909 and served as president during the years 1915-19. He wrote a theatrical-news column for the *New York Age* during the 1920s. One of his last big projects was contracting entertainers for performance at the Chicago World's Fair in 1933-34.

BIBL: Black press, incl. AmstN, 8 April 1944; CDef 3 December 1932; NYAge 7 June 1917, 21 May 1921. Flet, p. 264. WWCA 1940, 1941-44.

JOHNSON, GEORGE LEON. See **TAYLOR, THOMAS THEODORE.**

JOHNSON, HALL. See **JOHNSON, FRANCIS HALL.**

JOHNSON, J. J. See **JOHNSON, JAMES LOUIS.**

JOHNSON, J. ROSAMOND. See **JOHNSON, JOHN ROSAMOND.**

JOHNSON, J. C. Jazz pianist (b. 14 September 1896 in Chicago, Illinois; d. 27 February 1981 in New York, New York). He obtained his musical education in the public schools of Chicago, Illinois, and studied piano privately. He began playing professionally in local nightclubs at an early age. Later he led his own musical groups. About 1915 he settled in New York, where he soon became active in musical circles. In 1918 he published his first song; in 1923 he began collaborating with Thomas (''Fats'') Waller* in writing songs. He also collaborated with Nat Burton, Fletcher Henderson,* Andy Razaf,* and George Whiting, among others. He was active as an accompanist and made his first records for Harry Pace's* Black Swan Records label in 1923 accompanying Ethel Waters.* Others for whom he served as accompanist or performed with included Clara Smith* and Clarence Williams,* among others. He also recorded with his Five Hot Sparks. In 1940 he founded the Crescendo Club in New York, an organization of black songwriters. His best-known songs were ''I need loving,'' ''Don't let your love go wrong,'' ''You can't be mine and somebody else's too,'' and ''Empty bed blues.''

BIBL: AlHen. ASCAP. Black press, incl. AmstN, 4 April 1981. Maurice Waller and Anthony Calabrese, *Fats Waller* (New York, 1977).

DISC: Kink. RustJR.

JOHNSON, JAMES LOUIS (''J. J.''). Jazz trombonist/Film composer (b. 22 January 1924 in Indianapolis, Indiana). He began piano study at the age of eleven and trombone study at fourteen. He obtained his musical education in the public schools of Indianapolis, Indiana, where he came under the influence of Norman Merrifield* and LaVerne Newsome at Crispus Attucks

High School. Later he studied with Earl Hagen. During the 1940s he played and arranged music with various groups, including Clarence Love (1941-42), Bennett ("Benny") Carter* (1942-44), William ("Count") Basie* (1945-47), and Illinois Jacquet* (1947-48), among others. During the years 1948-56 he toured with various jazzmen and/or groups, then performed with his own J. J. Johnson Quintet and Sextet for the next few years (1957-61). Thereafter he gave increasing attention to arranging and composing, although he toured with Miles Davis* (1961-62) and in a sextet with Clark Terry* and Edward ("Sonny") Stitt* (1964). In 1970 he settled in Los Angeles, California, where he moved totally into the areas of composing, particularly for television and films, and music business activities. He first attracted wide recognition as a composer when his works, *El Camino Real* and *Sketch for Trombone and Orchestra*, were performed at the Monterey Jazz Festival in 1959. Other well-known works of his were *Scenario for Trombone and Orchestra* (1962) and *Diversions for Six Trombones, Celeste, Harp and Percussion* (1968). His scores for television shows included "Barefoot in the Park," "Mod Squad," "The Bold Ones" and "Harry-O," among others; his film scores included *Man and Boy* (1971), *Across 110th Street* (1972), *Cleopatra Jones* (1973), and *Willie Dynamite* (1973), among others. He conducted music for many of the films for which he wrote scores. During the 1970s he occasionally led groups for special occasions, and he recorded occasionally with others, among them, Kai Winding in trombone duos and Count Basie. He received awards from the music industry. He was regarded as a brilliant trombonist of the bop school, who helped to define the role of bop trombone during his tenure with the Benny Carter band.

BIBL: BMI (April 1971). FeaEJ. FeaJS. FeaGitJS. MeeJMov. WWA. WWBA.

DISC: Jep. Kink. ModJ. TudJ.

JOHNSON, JAMES PRICE ("JAMES P."). Jazz pianist (b. 1 February 1894 in New Brunswick, New Jersey; d. 17 November 1955 in New York, New York). He first studied piano with his mother, a pianist, then later with Ernest Green and Bruto Giannini, among others. When he was in his teens, his family moved to New York. He obtained his musical education in the public schools of New Brunswick and New York. In 1912 he began playing professionally at summer resorts; later he played for "house-rent parties" and in nightclubs of New York; Atlantic City, New Jersey; other cities on the East Coast; and in Toledo, Ohio (1919). His early style development was influenced by the pianism of Eubie Blake,* Luckeyeth ("Lucky") Roberts,* and Richard ("Abba Labba") McLean. Before 1920 he toured rather widely on the vaudeville circuit and at one time was a musical director for Sherman H. Dudley's* The Smart Set* company. He began to cut piano rolls as early as 1916; in 1923 he was one of a select group of black pianists to make piano rolls for the QRS Music company (Quality Reigns Supreme, a subsidiary of the Melville Clark Piano Company), along with J. Lawrence Cook,* Lemuel Fowler, Clarence Jones,* Lucky Roberts, Thomas ("Fats") Waller,* and Clarence Williams* But even before that time, he made his recording debut in 1921 with Harry Pace's* Black Swan label playing piano solos. He also accompanied such singers as Bessie Smith,* Ida Cox,* and Ethel Waters,* among others.

In 1923 he toured in Europe with the *Plantation Days* company. During the 1930s-40s he led his own groups occasionally, performed as a soloist in nightclubs and theaters, and played with various groups, including Stanley ("Fess") Williams* (1936-37) and William ("Wild Bill") Davis* (1943), among others. In 1944 he produced an all-Johnson music concert at Carnegie Hall in New York, which consisted of spiritual arrangements, jazz improvisations, and compositions in the larger forms. He began writing songs and piano rags as early as 1914; his first published piece was the "Mama and Papa blues" (1914). During the 1920s he gave much attention to writing scores for musicals, such as *Plantation Days* (1923), *Runnin' Wild* (1923), *Keep Shufflin'* (with Fats Waller, 1928), and later *Sugar Hill* (1949). He also wrote an opera, *The Organizer*, which used a libretto by Langston Hughes,* and several large-form works, including the rhapsody *Yamekraw* (1927), which was orchestrated by William Grant Still* and given a film adaptation (1930) and the orchestral *Symphonic Harlem* (1932). He was also active in radio music and films; he performed in *St. Louis Blues* (1929) and wrote music for *Emperor Jones* (1933). His best-known songs were "If I could be with you" and "Charleston," which was introduced in the musical *Runnin' Wild* along with the dance that became a fad; his best-known piano pieces were "Harlem strut" and "Carolina shout," which was used as a test piece by rag pianists for many years. A stroke in 1951 forced him to retire from music. Johnson was a pioneer of the Harlem "stride-piano" school, along with Lucky Roberts and William ("Willie-the-Lion") Smith.* In 1920 Johnson came into contact with Fats Waller, took over the younger man's musical training, and exerted the major influence upon Waller's style development. He also exerted influence over other pianists of the time, including Edward (''Duke'') Ellington* and Arthur (''Art'') Tatum.*

BIBL: AlHen. ASCAP. ChilWW. Tom Davin, ''Conversations with James P. Johnson'' in *Jazz Review* (July 1959). FeaEJ. MeeJMov. Willie-the-Lion Smith with George Hoefer, *Music on My Mind* (New York, 1964). Maurice Waller and Anthony Calabrese, *Fats Waller* (New York, 1977). WWCA, 1950.

DISC: Jep. Kink. RustJR. TudJ.

JOHNSON, JAMES WELDON. Writer (b. 17 June 1871 in Jacksonville, Florida; d. 26 June 1938 in Wicasset, Maine). Although not a professional musician, he is included here because of his close collaboration with his brother, J. Rosamond Johnson.* A graduate of Atlanta University in Georgia, he toured in 1897 with the University Quartet in New England. In 1901 he and his brother joined with Robert (''Bob'') Cole* to write songs and musical comedies; they produced many successful songs and two shows for all-black casts, *The Shoo-Fly Regiment* (1906) and *The Red Moon* (1908), which were produced on Broadway. They also wrote songs for white musicals, including *In Newport* (1904), *Humpty Dumpty* (1904), and *Sleeping Beauty and the Beast* (1901), among others. In 1915 Johnson made a translation of Granados's *Goyescas* for use by the Metropolitan Opera Company. He collaborated with his brother on *The Book of American Negro Spirituals* (1925) and the *Second Book of Negro Spirituals* (1926). His book *Black Manhattan* (New York, 1940) included insightful discussion of black musicians and musical practices. Best-known of the songs he wrote with his brother are ''Lift every voice and sing'' (1899, the so-called Negro Anthem), ''Since you went away,'' ''The maiden with the dreamy eyes'' (with Cole), and ''The old flag never touched the ground'' (with Cole).

BIBL: Johnson is included in the standard reference books. ASCAP. EAB.

JOHNSON, J[OHN] ROSAMOND. Composer (b. 11 August 1873 in Jacksonville, Florida; d. 11 November 1954 in New York, New York). He began piano study at the age of four with his mother, a piano teacher. His musical education was obtained at the New England Conservatory, where he studied with Charles Dennee, George Whiting, and David Bispham, among others. He also studied privately in London, England. In 1896 he began teaching in the public schools of Jacksonville, Florida, later becoming a music supervisor. During the summer of 1899 he went to New York and entered the world of vaudeville, but did not leave the public schools permanently until 1908. In 1901 he and his brother, James Weldon Johnson,* joined with Robert (''Bob'') Cole* to produce a number of successful songs and several musical comedies. *The Shoo-Fly Regiment* (1906) and *The Red Moon* (1908) were produced on Broadway by all-black casts. The Johnson brothers and Cole also wrote songs for white Broadway musicals, including *Sleeping Beauty and the Beast* (1901), *In Newport* (1904), and *Humpty Dumpty* (1904), among others. J. Rosamond also wrote songs and musicals with Cole alone, including songs for *Big Indian Chief* (1903), *The Belle of Bridgeport* (1900), and the well-known songs ''The maiden with the dreamy eyes,'' ''Didn't he ramble'' (under the pseudonym Will Handy), and ''Under the bamboo tree.'' Johnson collaborated with several other poets or lyricists—among them, Paul Lawrence Dunbar* for the song ''Li'l gal,'' Bert Williams* for the musical *Mr. Load of Koal* (1909), and J. Leubrie Hill* for the musical *Hello, Paris* (1911). These songs and others for which Johnson wrote music were popularized by such entertainers as Marie Cahill, Anna Held, George Primrose, and Lillian Russell. Johnson and Cole formed a vaudeville act that toured in the United States and abroad until Cole's death in 1911. They were also co-stars in musicals written by the Johnson brothers and Cole. In 1912 Johnson formed a vaudeville act with Charles Hart (whose partner, Daniel Avery, died in February 1912) and went to London, England, where they played a long engagement in a revue, *Come Over Here*, for which Johnson also wrote music. By the time he returned home in February 1914, he had formed a vaudeville act with Tom Brown, which toured widely in the United States.

In the fall of 1914 Johnson became director (1914-19) of the Music School Settlement for Colored in New York, formerly directed by David I. Martin.* After service in the U.S. Armed Forces during World War I, Johnson reentered the world of performing arts. During the 1920s he toured intermittently with Taylor Gordon,* giving concerts of spirituals; he also toured on the vaudeville circuit with his groups—Johnson and Company, The Harlem Rounders, and The Inimitable Five. In 1936 he went to London to become musical director of Lew Leslie's *Blackbirds of 1936*, which featured Jules Bledsoe,* Maude Russell, and the Nicholas Brothers. He was also active in the theater, appearing in *Mamba's Daughters* (1939), *Cabin in the Sky* (1940, for which he trained the chorus), and Gershwin's *Porgy and Bess* (1935). During the last decades of his career he was an arranger/music editor for New York publishing houses, and he published his own music and books, including the well-known collections *Shout Songs*

(1936) and *Rolling Along in Song* (1937). Earlier he published with his brother James Weldon *The Book of American Negro Spirituals* (1925) and *The Second Book of Negro Spirituals* (1926). He was one of the leading songwriters of his time. As early as 1905 his songs were published in such magazines as the *Ladies Home Journal* and, later, the *Etude*. His stage songs became classics that reappeared in films over the years, and his art songs became concert classics, of which the best known were "Since you went away," "Li'l gal," and "Lift every voice and sing" (at one time called the Negro National Anthem).

BIBL: ASCAP. Black press, incl. NYAge, 20 November 1954; PhilaT, 20 April 1912, 26 July 1913. NYT, 12 November 1954. NYB, 1921-22. Burt.

DISC: Cre.

JOHNSON, JOHN W. ("JACK"). Bandmaster (b. 15 February 1865 in Chatham, Ontario, Canada; d. 19?? in Detroit, Michigan [?]). He began studying music as a youth in London, Ontario, where his family moved in 1866. About 1883 he went to Detroit, Michigan, where he played cornet in the Seventh Fusileers Band, then joined the Detroit City Band. During the years 1885-1890 he toured with Richard and Pringle's Georgia Minstrels.* He then returned to Detroit and organized the new Detroit City Band, which included over the years Charles Stone, Fred Stone,* Benjamin Shook, and others. He also played in Theodore Finney's* Famous Orchestra for many years.

BIBL: DetAH, K. Meyers interview with Clyde Hayes. Black press. LaBrew.

JOHNSON, LEW. Minstrel troupe manager (fl. late nineteenth and early twentieth centuries; b. in Chicago, Illinois (?); d. 27 February 1910 in Grand Forks, British Columbia, Canada). He organized a minstrel troupe in Chicago, Illinois, about 1866 or 1867, but was unsuccessful. About 1869 he organized a troupe at St. Louis, Missouri, that was successful and toured widely over the nation. From that time on Johnson was an important figure in black minstrelsy. He handled more black minstrels than any other black manager, and his contemporaries regarded him as the most successful manager of the period. Over the years he gave various names to his groups: Plantation Minstrels (early 1870s), Lew Johnson's Tennessee Jubilee Singers (late 1870s), Black Baby Boy Minstrels (1890s), Original Jubilee Singers (mid-1870s). He also toured with his own Uncle Tom's Cabin Company. In 1870 his troupe included musicians Robert ("Bob") Bodie (flute, piccolo), J. S. Broadwell (cornet-a-piston), V. Heywood (clarionette), Ed Rector (singer and guitar), S. Coleman (double bass), Alf White (musical director), J. L. West (orchestra leader); singers Hardy and George Carlin; and players Johnny Morton, Frank Essex, Charley Delancy, and Frank Maynard. According to some reports, Sam Lucas* played with Johnson in 1869, and during the late 1880s George Walker* and Bert Williams* toured with him. About 1898 he settled in Grand Forks, British Columbia, where he continued musical activities and served as manager of the Grand Forks Opera House.

BIBL: Black press, incl. IndF, 22 February 1896, 8 January 1898, 24 December 1898, 29 June 1901, 12 March 1910. *The* New York *Clipper*, 27 July 1870-1880s. Simond.

JOHNSON, LONNIE. See **JOHNSON, ALONZO.**

JOHNSON, PETE. Boogie-woogie pianist (b. 24 March 1904 in Kansas City, Missouri; d. 23 March 1967 in Buffalo, New York). He began his career as a drummer, playing with local groups (1922-26) led by Louis Johnson and Ernest Nichols; then turned to piano after studying with his uncle, Charles ("Smash") Johnson, and others. Thereafter he performed as a soloist in local clubs, in a team with singer Joe Turner,* and with groups of Clarence Love and Herman Walder. In 1938 he went to New York to perform with Benny Goodman and, later, on the From Spirituals to Swing Concert produced by John Hammond at Carnegie Hall on 23 December. In 1939 he settled in New York, where he began a long association with pianists Albert Ammons* and Meade Lux Lewis* in the Boogie Woogie Trio. He also played and/or recorded with Ammons and Lewis in duos. In 1960 he settled in Buffalo, New York. In addition to playing in local clubs, he continued to record and to tour regularly, including tours with the Piano Parade Show (1952) and the European trip of JATP (Jazz at the Philharmonic) in 1958. Illness curtailed his activities after he suffered a heart attack in 1958, but he continued to play periodically. His last appearance was on a Spirituals to Swing Concert at Carnegie Hall in New York (1967).

BIBL: BPIM 2 (Fall 1974), pp. 191-208. ChilWW. FeaEJ. FeaJS. FeaGitJS. MeeJMov. Oliv.

DISC: Jep. Kink. RustJR.

JOHNSON, ROBERT. Bluesman (b. c1912 in Hazelhurst, Mississippi; d. 16 August 1938 in Greenwood, Mississippi). Little is known of his life except that he was an itinerant bluesman. During the years 1933-35 he traveled with Johnny Shines* and Walter Horton. He made some forty-one recordings during the years 1936-37, which established him as one of the seminal blues figures. His style development was influenced by Eddie ("Son") House, and he in turn exerted enormous influence upon his contemporaries, particularly Elmore James and "Muddy Waters" (née McKinley Morganfield),* as well as on later bluesmen and rock 'n' roll entertainers. His best-known recordings, including 'Hellhound on my trail," "Dust my broom," and "Walking blues," represent the Mississippi Delta blues tradition in its most powerful expression.

BIBL: BWW. CharCB. Samuel Charters, *Robert Johnson* (New York, 1973). LivBl 5 (Summer 1971). Oliv. Pete Welding, "Ramblin' Johnny Shines" in LivBl 22 (July-August 1975).

DISC: DiGod. TudBM.

JOHNSON, TOMMY. Bluesman (b. c1896 in Terry, Mississippi; d. 1 November 1956 in Crystal Springs, Mississippi). He began playing guitar when he was about fourteen, studying informally with his brother, LeDell Johnson. Beginning about 1912 he played professionally in various places throughout Mississippi, sometimes with Charlie Patton,* Walter Vinson* (also known as Walter Vincent), Rubin Lacy, and Ishmon Bracey, among others. He made his first recordings in 1928 at Memphis, Tennessee. During the 1930s he continued to play throughout the Mississippi Delta region and toured with various shows, including Dr. Simpson's Medicine show, along with Bracey. Thereafter he and Bracey frequently teamed together. Johnson was an influential figure among Mississippi bluesmen. His best-known recordings were "Cool drink of water blues," "Maggie Campbell," and "Big road blues."

BIBL: BWW. David Evans, *Tommy Johnson* (London, 1971). Oliv.

DISC: TudBM.

JOHNSON, WILLIAM FRANCIS ("BILLY"). See also **COLE, ROBERT.** Vaudeville entertainer (b. c1858 in Charleston, South Carolina; d. 12 September 1916 in Chicago, Illinois). He began his career in 1881 with J. W. Hyatt's Colored Minstrels. He wrote a song, "The trumpet in the cornfield," for this show that attracted much attention. Thereafter he toured with various companies, including Lew Johnson's* Black Baby Boy Minstrels (1884), Hicks-Sawyer* Minstrels (1887), W. S. Cleveland's Minstrels (1890s), Sam T. Jack's Creole Company (1890s), and John Isham's Octoroons Company (mid-1890s). During the 1896-97 season he toured with Black Patti's* Troubadours, where he came into contact with Bob Cole.* By this time he had won recognition as a talented songwriter, particularly with his songs for the Octoroons and Black Patti. Before the season was over, he and Cole left the Troubadours, organized their own company, and wrote *A Trip to Coontown*. This show is credited with being the first full-length (three acts) show with a non-minstrel format that was written, produced, and staged exclusively by blacks. Willis Accooe* wrote some of the music, along with Johnson. The show included an "operatic finale," which allowed for display of the many fine voices in the cast, among them, tenor Lloyd Gibbs* and soprano Edna Alexander. The show received critical acclaim and toured for four years. About 1902 Cole and Johnson disbanded their company. For some years Johnson played on vaudeville circuits as a single; he then settled in Chicago, Illinois, where he wrote songs and staged shows, including *Twenty Miles from Home*. In 1914 he joined with Tom Brown* to organize a company and to write musicals for its productions.

BIBL: Black press, incl. IndF, 30 December 1899, 27 May 1916, 23 September 1916.

JOHNSON, WILLIAM GEARY ("BUNK"). Jazz cornetist (b. 27 December 1879 in New Orleans, Louisiana; d. 7 July 1949 in New Iberia, Louisiana). He began cornet study at the age of eight with Wallace Cutchey, a teacher at New Orleans University. He also obtained his musical education at the University. His first professional experience was with Adam Oliver's orchestra in 1894. For the next two decades or so he played with various orchestras and brass bands, including the Olympia, Superior, and Frankie Dusen's Eagle Band. (There is no documentation for Johnson's claim that he played in Buddy Bolden's* band; see Marquis below.) He also played in nightclubs and brothels and toured with circuses and traveling shows, among them, P. G. Lowery's* circus band (1901), McCabe's* Minstrels (1903), the Smart Set Georgia Minstrels* (1918), and the Vernon Brothers Circus (1919). He left New Orleans in 1914; thereafter he was active musically in several cities in Louisiana, then settled at New Iberia, Louisiana, in 1920. According to his obituary in the black press, Johnson played in army bands during the Spanish-American War (1898) and World War I (1918). During the 1920s-30s he played with society dance orchestras, with theater orchestras, and taught music under a WPA (Works Progress Administration) program in New Iberia (1933-37). From time to time he toured with various groups. He first attracted wide attention when he was discussed in the book *Jazzmen*, published by jazz enthusiasts Frederic Ramsey and Charles Smith (1939). He made his recording debut in 1942 in New Orleans and thereafter recorded prolifically until 1947. During the 1940s he played residencies in New York; Chicago, Illinois; Boston, Massachusetts; and San Francisco, California. Those who played in his groups over the years—Bunk Johnson's Original Superior Band or his Yerba Buena Jazz Band, Street Paraders, New Orleans Band, V-Disc Veterans, etc.—included Wellman Braud,* Garvin Bushell,* Danny Barker,* Warren (''Baby'') Dodds,* George Lewis,* and Lawrence Marrero, among others. In 1945 he joined forces with Sidney Bechet* to make recordings; in 1947 he played with Paul (''Doc'') Evans's group. Johnson was a pioneer of the New Orleans school and belonged to the first generation of jazz cornetists who defined the role of the cornet/trumpet in the jazz ensemble, along with Buddy Bolden, Freddie Keppard,* and Joseph (''King'') Oliver.* He was an important figure in the so-called New Orleans Revival during the 1940s.

BIBL: Black press, incl. NYAge, 6 August 1949. ChilWW. FeaEJ. Donald Marquis, *In Search of Buddy Bolden* (Baton Rouge, 1978). MeeJMov. Austin Sonnier, Jr., *Willie Geary ''Bunk'' Johnson* (New York, 1977).

DISC: Jep. Kink. RustJR. TudJ.

JOHNSON, WILLIAM MANUEL (''BILL''). Jazz bandleader (b. 10 August 1872 in New Orleans, Louisiana; d. 1960s[?] in Mexico). He began playing guitar at fifteen, then changed to string bass when he joined a trio in 1900 that performed at a Basin Street cafe in New Orleans. He remained there until 1909, but also played with brass bands, including Frankie Dusen's Eagle Band, Theogene Baquet's Excelsior, and the Peerless; for parades he doubled on the tuba. He organized the Original Creole Band some time during 1909 or 1910. In 1911 he left to settle in California; two years later or thereabouts he sent for the band to join him. The Original Creole Band was the first black dance band, and the first from New Orleans, to make transcontinental tours. During the years 1913-17 the band toured widely in the United States and in Canada on the vaudeville circuit, including the Western Vaudeville Association, the Orpheum, and the Pantages. When it played the Grand Theater at Chicago, Illinois, in February 1915, its personnel included George Baquet,* Freddie Keppard,* James Palao, Eddie Vinson, Norwood (''Giggy'') Williams, and comedian H. Morgan Prince. A year later, at a performance in Winnipeg, Canada, Louis Nelson (''Big Eye'') Delisle* had replaced Baquet. Other men known to have played with the band during these years were George Filhe and ''Dink'' Johnson. In 1917 the band broke up for a short while but was reorganized under Keppard's leadership. Johnson organized another group, later led the ''Seven Kings of Ragtime,'' then organized a band at the Royal Gardens on Chicago's South Side, which he invited Joseph (''King'') Oliver* to front. Later Oliver took over leadership of the band, and Johnson remained with the group until 1923. Thereafter he led his own groups again and played with various others, including Johnny Dodds,* Freddie Keppard, Jimmy Wade, and the Smizer Trio. He was active in musical circles until the early 1960s, when he moved to Mexico.

BIBL: Black press, incl. CDef, 15 July 1916; IndF, 13 February 1915, 22 May 1915. ChilWW. Donald Marquis, *In Search of Buddy Bolden* (Baton Rouge, 1978). Souch.

DISC: RustJR (see under both Johnson and Creole Jazz Band).

JOHNSTONE, CLARENCE (''TANDY''). Vaudeville entertainer. See **LAYTON, JOHN TURNER.**

JOLLY, JABEZ. Military drummer (fl. late eighteenth century). He enlisted on 15 May 1777 in Captain John Russell's Company, Fourteenth Massachusetts Regiment, and served as a drummer during the War of the American Revolution.

BIBL: GreBD. Benjamin Quarles, *The Negro in the American Revolution* (Chapel Hill, North Carolina, 1961), p. 77.

JONES, BOOKER T. Rhythm 'n' blues (soul) organist/arranger (b. 12 November 1944 in Memphis, Tennessee). He played piano as a child and began clarinet study at the age of ten. A few years later he studied piano and Hammond organ briefly. He obtained his musical education in Memphis's Booker T. Washington High School, where he studied several instruments and played in school groups, and at Indiana University in Bloomington (B.A., 1966), where he played trombone in the university's symphony orchestra and also played with campus jazz groups. He began playing professionally when he was fourteen. His keyboard style was influenced by Ray Charles,* James (''Jimmy'') Smith, and Eugene (''Jack'') McDuff. When he was sixteen, he and three others produced a recording for the Stax Record Company in Memphis, ''Green Onions,'' that attracted wide attention. Thereafter he recorded regularly, continuing to work during his college years with the Memphis Group, whose permanent members included white guitarist Steve Cropper, white bassist Donald ("Duck") Dunn, and drummer Al Jackson. Others who performed with the MG's (for Memphis Group) during the 1960s included Joe Arnold, Eddie Floyd, Isaac Hayes,* Wayne Jackson, Andrew Love, Wilson Pickett,* and Otis Redding.* The MG's, whose music reflected the influence of blues and gospel, became the most important soul group of the decade and the leading exponent of the Memphis Sound. They toured widely and produced many highly successful records, including the albums *Soul Limbo*, *MeLemore Avenue*, and *Melting Pot*. In 1968 Jones began to write for films; the same year he made his debut as a singer on a sound-track for *Uptight*. In 1972 he left the MG's, although he later rejoined them periodically for reunions. Thereafter he moved almost entirely into the fields of composing, arranging, and producing records. His first releases were with his wife Priscilla, the albums *Booker T and Priscilla* and *Home Grown*. Later he was a producer for Rita Coolidge (his wife's sister), Bob Dylan, Kris Kristofferson, and Paul Simon, among others. He won several awards from the music industry.

BIBL: ContKey, January 1980. *Ebony*, April 1969. StamPRS.

JONES, CLARENCE. Songwriter (b. 15 August 1889 in Wilmington, Ohio; d. 1 June 1949 in New York, New York). He first studied piano with his mother, a music teacher, then later at the Conservatory of Music and with Sueger Young in Cincinnati, Ohio. He also studied with Albino Garni, Louis Adler, and Charles Singer, among others. He began his professional career as a nightclub pianist in Cincinnati. During the years 1914-32 he was active as a pianist/arranger and conductor in Chicago, Illinois, at the Monogram and Owl Theaters. In 1915 Wurlitzer Pianola engaged him to make player-piano rolls. He led various groups of his own during this period, among them, Clarence Jones and His Wonder Orchestra and Clarence Jones and His Sock Four. He also taught at Pauline James Lee's* National University of Music. He was one of the small group of pianists hired in 1923 to make piano rolls for the QRS Music Company, along with J. Lawrence Cook,* James P. Johnson,* Luckyeth Roberts,* Lemuel Fowler, Thomas ("Fats") Waller,* and Clarence Williams.* In 1932 he settled in New York; he was pianist/arranger for the Southernaires* (1932-39). Jones was a prolific songwriter and recorded regularly.

BIBL: ASCAP. Black press, incl. CDef, 5 December 1914, 8 May 1915, 22 February 1919, 18 August 1923; IndF, 23 December 1911; NYAge, 18 June 1949. WWCA 1941.

DISC: RustJR.

JONES, ELAYNE. Symphonic timpanist (b. 30 January 1928 in New York, New York). She began piano study at the age of six with her mother. She received her musical education at the High School of Music and Art in New York, where she began study of the tympani; at the Juilliard School of Music in New York; and at the Tanglewood Music Festival in Lenox, Massachusetts (1949). She played professionally at an early age, beginning in 1949 with the orchestras of the New York City Opera (1949-61) and the New York City Ballet (1949-52). She also played with other orchestras, including the Brooklyn [New York] Philharmonic (1969-71) and the Westchester [New York] Philharmonic (1969-72), both under the direction of S. Landau; the American Symphony Orchestra (1962-72), under Leopold Stokowski; the Dimitri Mitropolous Conducting Competition Orchestra (1961-71); and the San Francisco Symphony (1972-74), under Seiji Ozawa. The refusal of the San Francisco orchestra in 1975 to give Jones a tenured chair aroused heated controversy among the principals concerned and in the press. Jones was also active as a free-lance tympanist and played in orchestras of Broadway musicals, including *Carnival* (1961), *On a Clear Day You Can See Forever* (1965), *Purlie* (1970), and *Greenwillow* (1960), among others. She played in orchestras for Gilbert and Sullivan operettas, New York City Light Opera productions, summer festivals, and various other organizations or groups. In 1965 she was a founding member of the Symphony of the New World* and later served as its president. She toured widely as a lecturer/concert percussionist. Her teaching career included tenures as a lecturer at the Metropolitan Music School in New York, the Bronx Community College of the City University of New York, the Westchester Conservatory, and the San Francisco Conservatory. She was one of the leading black percussionist/tympanists of her time and received awards from civic and professional organizations. In 1965 National Educational Television presented a special program about her titled "A Day in the Life of a Musician."

BIBL: Handy. IntWMM. NYT, 7 September 1975.

JONES, ELVIN RAY. Jazz drummer (b. 9 September 1927 in Pontiac, Michigan). He came from a musical family: his father played guitar, his mother played piano, and two brothers, Henry ("Hank")* and Thaddeus ("Thad"),* became professional musicians. He obtained his musical education in the public schools of Pontiac, Michigan, a suburb of Detroit, where he played in his school band. During his years of service in the United States Armed Forces (1946-49), he played in a military band. Thereafter he played with various groups, including one in Detroit composed of his brother Thad, Billy Mitchell, and others (1949-51). In 1956 he settled in New York, where he played with Earl ("Bud") Powell,* Donald Byrd,* Tyree Glen,* and Harry ("Sweets") Edison,* among others. He first attracted wide attention during the years 1960-66 when he played with John Coltrane* and developed a revolutionary approach to jazz drumming. After leaving Coltrane he toured widely with his own trios or quartets in the United States, Europe, the Orient, and South America (under sponsorship of the United States Department of State in 1973, 1975). He appeared in concert halls, theaters, nightclubs, on college campuses, at festivals, in public schools, and in prisons. He was active also in television and in films, including *Zachariah* (1970). Those who played in his groups over the years included Frank Foster,* Joe Farrell, Wilbur Little, Billy Greene, and Jimmy Garrison, among others. Jones was regarded as one of the most brilliant drummers of the 1960s-70s. He changed the role of the jazz drum from that of an accompanying instrument to a solo instrument with infinite potential for rhythmic and melodic complexity.

BIBL: FeaEJ. FeaJS. FeaGitJS. Albert Goldman, "Jones Drums Up a Hurricane" in NYT, 15 February 1970.

DISC: Jep. ModJ. TudJ.

JONES, HANK. See **JONES, HENRY.**

JONES, HAROLD. Symphony flutist (b. 25 March 1934 in Chicago, Illinois). He obtained his musical education in the public schools of Chicago, Illinois, where he studied flute during his high-school years with David Underwood at DuSable High School; at the Sherwood School of Music in Chicago, where he studied with Emil Eck; and at the Juilliard School of Music (diploma, 1959). He also studied privately with Harold Bennett, Marcel Moyse, and in the Chicago Civic Orchestra (a training orchestra sponsored by the Chicago Symphony) with Julius Baker and Lois Schaefer. In 1966 he made his concert debut at Town Hall in New York. His orchestral career included tenures in the Goldman Band; the American Symphony Orchestra under Leopold Stokowski; the National Orchestral Association, directed by Leon Barzin; the New York Sinfonietta, the Brooklyn Philharmonic, under Lukas Foss and David Amram; the Municipal Concerts Orchestra, under Julius Grossman; Symphony of the New World,* directed by Benjamin Steinberg and Everett Lee; and the Bach Aria Orchestra, directed by Frank Brief, where he was first flutist. He also recorded with various groups, appeared as soloist with symphony orchestras, and played in The New World Trio with Alan Booth* and Harry Smyles.* His teaching career included tenures at the Westchester [New York] Conservatory of Music, Manhattanville College in New York, and Brooklyn College of the City University of New York.

BIBL: Black press, incl. NYAge, 27 June 1959. NYT, 23 January 1980. WWBA.

JONES, HENRY ("HANK"). Jazz pianist (b. 31 July 1918 in Vicksburg, Mississippi). He came from a musical family: his father played guitar, his mother played piano, and two brothers, Elvin* and Thaddeus ("Thad"),* became professional musicians. He obtained his musical education in the public schools of Pontiac, Michigan, a suburb of Detroit. He studied piano as a child. He began playing professionally when he was thirteen with local groups, at first in Pontiac, then in other Michigan cities after he had graduated from high school. In 1944 he went to New York, where he played with various groups, including Oran ("Hot Lips") Page,* John Kirby,* Andy Kirk,* William ("Billy") Eckstine,* Coleman Hawkins,* Howard McGhee,* Artie Shaw's Gramercy Five, and Benny Goodman (tour of Russia in 1962), among others. He also toured with Ella Fitzgerald* as accompanist (1948-52), with JATP (Norman Granz's Jazz at the Philharmonic, 1947, 1951), and the Thad Jones/Mel Lewis big band (1966). During the years 1959-74 he was active primarily as a staff musician with CBS television. After the staff was dissolved, he returned to performance in clubs and concert halls. He also recorded extensively, appeared in films, and, beginning in 1978, in the orchestra for the Broadway musical *Ain't Misbehaving*. Composer and conductor as well as performer, he founded his own music company, Thank Music Corporation. Jones was a leading pianist of the 1960s-70s, versatile in his adeptness in playing in all the styles and possessing keyboard brilliance in the tradition of Art Tatum,* although he came under the influence of Earl ("Bud") Powell* and Al Haig in his early career. He was regarded by some as the elder statesman of the Detroit pianists, of the trio including also Tommy Flanagan* and Barry Harris.*

BIBL: ContKey (December 1979). FeaEJ. FeaJS. FeaGitJS. MeeJMov. WWBA.

DISC: Jep. Kink.

JONES, IRVING. Songwriter/Vaudeville entertainer (b. c1874; d. 11 March 1932 in New York, New York). Little is known of his early life. He first attracted attention as a member of Sam T. Jack's Burlesque Company in 1890 and was a member of Jack's Creole

Company (1890), along with Sam* and Carrie Lucas,* Fred Piper, and Billy Jackson, among others. He then played with John Isham's Octoroons (1895-97); Will Marion Cook's* *Jes Lak White Folks* (summer 1899), which starred Abbie Mitchell*; and Black Patti's* Troubadours (1900). Later in his career he toured with an act, "Irving Jones and Charley Johnson, Two Cut-ups," and another, "Jones, Drew, and Jones." During the late 1920s he toured as a single on the Radio Keith-Orpheum theater circuits. He was noted for his songs of the 1890s, of which the best known was "Possumala" (1894).

BIBL: Black press, incl. CDef, 19 March 1932; IndF, 20 September 1890, 28 November 1896. BPIM, 167. Burton. Flet, 112, 275. James Weldon Johnson, *Black Manhattan* (New York, 1940).

JONES, J. WESLEY. Church choir director (b. 8 September 1884 in Nashville, Tennessee; d. 11 February 1961 in Chicago, Illinois). He obtained his musical education at the Tennessee Industrial School and at Walden College (B.A., 1905) in Nashville, Tennessee. Some time before 1917 he settled in Chicago, Illinois, where he became active as a church organist and choir director, first at Scott Chapel, then at Progressive Baptist Church, and beginning in 1920 at the Metropolitan Community Church. He studied further at Chicago Musical College with Eduard Freund and Felix Borowski, among others. In 1919 he was one of the founders of the National Association of Negro Musicians,* and he served as its national president during the years 1928-32. During the 1920s he published a music column in the *Chicago Defender*. He attracted wide attention for his choir "battles" with the choirs of James Mundy* during the 1930s. For thirty years he was director of the chorus at the annual Chicagoland Music Festivals, and over his long career he directed several community choral groups. In 1954 he was named minister emeritus of Metropolitan Community Church.

BIBL: ChiVH. Black press, incl. CDef, 24 November 1917, 9 October 1920, 25 February 1961.

JONES, JAMES HENRY ("JIMMY"). Jazz pianist (b. 30 December 1918 in Memphis, Tennessee). His family moved to Chicago, Illinois, when he was a child. He obtained his musical education in the public schools of Chicago and at Kentucky State College, where he played in the band and arranged music for it. During the 1940s-50s he played with various groups, including Hezekiah ("Stuff") Smith* (1943-44), James ("J. C.") Heard (1946-47), Sarah Vaughan* (as accompanist, 1947-52, 1954-58), Ben Webster,* and Harry ("Sweets") Edison,* among others. From the late 1950s on he was active primarily in arranging and conducting for such singers as Lena Horne,* Nancy Wilson,* and Ella Fitzgerald.* Occasionally he led his own groups or conducted for others, as on Edward ("Duke") Ellington's* show, *My People*, at Chicago in 1963. He alo wrote and/or arranged music for films and television, including the CBS special "The Strolling Twenties" (1968), "Duke Ellington—We Love you Madly" (1973), and "Cotton Club" (1975). In 1969 he settled in Los Angeles, California.

BIBL: ChilWW. FeaEJ. FeaJS. FeaGitJS.

DISC: Jep. Kink.

JONES, JONAH. See **JONES, ROBERT ELLIOTT.**

JONES, JONATHAN ("JO" "PAPA JO"). Jazz drummer (b. 7 October 1911 in Chicago, Illinois). He studied piano, trumpet, and saxophone as a child. His early professional experiences were with touring carnivals and shows on the Chautauqua circuit. During the late 1920s-mid 1930s he played with Ted Adams, then later played with Harold Brown's Brownskin Syncopators, Walter Page,* Bennie Moten,* and Lloyd Hunter's Serenaders, among others. He made his recording debut with Hunter in 1931. Thereafter he was active in Kansas City, Missouri, where he played with Tommy Douglas (on piano and vibraharp), then primarily with William ("Count") Basie* on drums (1934, 1935-48 with a few leaves of absence). During these years he also worked with the [James] Jeter/[Hayes] Pillar Band (1936). Thereafter he played with Illinois Jacquet* (1948-50), Lester Young* (1950), Joe Bushkin (1952-53), and Ella Fitzgerald*/Oscar Peterson* (European tour, 1957); he toured with JATP (Norman Granz's Jazz at the Philharmonic, 1947, 1951) and led his own groups occasionally (New York residency, 1957-60). During the 1960s-70s he performed extensively and toured widely as a free-lancer; he also worked with Theodore ("Teddy") Wilson,* Claude Hopkins,* Milton ("Milt") Buckner,* and Joe Bushkin, among others. He appeared at jazz festivals, on television programs, and in many films, including *The Unsuspected* (1947) and *Born to Swing* (1973). He recorded prolifically with his own groups and with others. He was a leading innovator of the swing era. He defined the role of swing percussions, using a driving but relatively light drum beat that stressed evenly all four beats of the measure and transferring the basic beat from the drum to the high-hat cymbal with use of a shimmering, wire-brush technique.

BIBL: ASCAP. ChilWW. FeaEJ. FeaGitJS. MeeJMov. Russ.

DISC: Jep. Kink. RustJR.

JONES, JOSEPH RUDOLPH ("PHILLY JOE"). Jazz drummer (b. 15 July 1923 in Philadelphia, Pennsylvania). He studied piano as a child with his mother. He obtained his musical education in the public schools of Philadelphia, Pennsylvania. During his high-school years he played with local groups, which occasionally accompanied visiting jazzmen who came to Philadelphia to perform. In 1947 he went to New York. Thereafter he played with various groups, including Tony Scott, Tadd Dameron,* Gil Evans, and others. During the years 1952-58 he played primarily with Miles Davis.* After leaving Davis, he organized his own groups and toured as a free-lancer. During the years 1967-72 he lived in Europe—at first in London, England, then in Paris, France, and other cities on the Continent. In London he conducted a music studio; in France he taught with Kenneth ("Kenny") Clarke.* He was also active in television, radio, and films; he toured widely with his groups and as a soloist, appearing in concert halls, nightclubs, at festivals, and working with jazz clinics and workshops. Those with whom he performed included Locksley ("Slide") Hampton, the Clarke-Boland Orchestra, and the Franz Black Orchestra, among others. In 1972 he settled in Philadelphia, where he formed a quintet. In 1975 he formed a jazz-rock group, Le Gran Prix. He first attracted wide attention as a member of Davis's first quintet; he was regarded as one of the important and original drummers of the 1950s.

BIBL: FeaEJ. FeaJS. FeaGitJS. MeeJMov.

DISC: Jep. Kink. ModJ.

JONES, LEROI. See **BARAKA, IMAMU.**

JONES, LOUIA VAUGHN. Concert violinist (b. 2 March 1895 in Cleveland, Ohio; d. 1 February 1965 in Washington, D.C.). He revealed musical promise at an early age and began violin study at the age of nine. He played violin in music groups at Central High School and in community organizations. He obtained his musical education at the New England Conservatory (B. Mus., 1918), where he studied with Felix Winternitz; and in Paris, France, where he studied with Lucien Capet at L'Ecole normal de musique (1921-22), with Maurice Hayot (1923), and with Marcel Darrieux (1925). In 1924 he studied in Budapest, Hungary, with Sollaway. During World War I he served overseas as an assistant bandleader of the 807th Pioneer Infantry Band. After the war he returned to the New England Conservatory for postgraduate work before returning to Paris in 1921. During that period he toured with Roland Hayes* and William Lawrence.* While in Europe during the 1920s he played saxophone and violin with a jazz group, The International Five. In addition to studying violin, he gave recitals, including a command performance before Spanish royalty. He returned to the United States in 1927 and was appointed head of the strings department at Howard University in Washington, D.C. (1930-60). He continued to give concerts throughout his teaching career. In 1935 he was soloist with the National Symphony Orchestra in Washington; during the 1940s-60s he frequently gave joint concerts with Warner Lawson* or Camille Nickerson.*

BIBL: MSCent. Black press, incl. NYAge, 25 October 1930. Hare. *Record Research* (May 1968), pp. 3-4. WWCA 1938-1950.

JONES, M. SISSIERETTA ("BLACK PATTI") (née MATILDA S. JOYNER). Concert singer (b. 5 January 1869 in Portsmouth, Virginia; d. 24 June 1933 in Providence, Rhode Island). Her family moved to Providence, Rhode Island, about 1876 and there she began formal study of music. Later she attended the Providence Academy of Music, where she studied with Ada Lacombe. Some time during the 1880s she studied voice at the New England Conservatory and privately with Luisa Capianni and a Mme. Scongia of London, England. She first sang publicly at local private entertainments and at the Pond Street Baptist Church in Providence. By the time she made her first New York appearance—in a Bergen Star Concert at Steinway Hall in April 1888, which featured Flora Batson* as the prima-donna soprano—she had developed a considerable following. The press identified her as "Mme. M. S. Jones, New England's Rising Soprano Star." A month later she made her debut at the Academy of Music in Philadelphia, Pennsylvania. During the summer of 1888 she was signed by the Tennessee Concert Company, along with tenor Will A. Pierce and a sizable company, to tour in the West Indies. Members of the press and others attended the final rehearsal, held at Wallack's Theater prior to the company's sailing on 2 August for Jamaica, and added to the acclaim she had received on previous appearances in New York.

Although she had been called "Black Patti" by Abbey, Schoeffel, and Grau (managers of the Metropolitan Opera), it was during the West Indies tour that the public for the first time acclaimed her by the soubriquet that remained with her for the rest of her career. Thereafter she toured widely, singing in concert halls and churches, most frequently in Bergen Star

Concerts; in 1890 she toured again in the West Indies, this time with the Star Tennessee Jubilee Singers under the management of black impresario Florence Williams. There were low points during the formative years of her career, however; in April 1889 she performed with the Georgia Minstrels* at Dockstader's Theater in New York. By 1892, however, she was firmly established as a prima donna, and her management changed her billing from Mrs. Matilda S. Jones to Madame M. Sissieretta Jones. The 1890s were peak years: she sang at the White House in February 1892; she was the featured singer at New York's Madison Square Garden for a "Grand Negro Jubilee" on 26-29 April 1892, which also starred white cornetist Jules Levy and his American Band, which was so successful that it had to be repeated on 30 April at the Academy of Music; and her concerts drew enormous crowds up and down the Eastern Seaboard. In 1893 she sang at the Pittsburgh (Pennsylvania) Exposition and at the Chicago World's Fair. That year she ran into legal difficulties when she attempted to negotiate better contract terms with her white manager, James B. Pond. By 1894, however, she had finally escaped Pond and signed with black impresario Ednorah Nahor, who also managed Joseph Douglass* and Rachel Walker.* In the fall of 1894 she signed with the Damrosch Orchestra Company, according to the press, which sponsored her in extensive touring at home and abroad.

In 1896 she made an abrupt change in her career and accepted the starring role in a newly organized vaudeville company, called Black Patti's Troubadours, under the management of white proprietors Voelckel and Nolan. During its first year the company included such established vaudeville entertainers as Robert "Bob" Cole,* the DeWolfe sisters,* Lloyd Gibbs,* Stella Wiley, and Mr. and Mrs. Tom McIntosh,* among others. For almost a decade the company traveled throughout the world, presenting unique entertainment, for that time, that combined elements of vaudeville, musical comedy, and opera to enthusiastic audiences. Black Patti's special appearance was in the "Operatic Kaleidoscope" of Part II of the show, where she sang arias from grand operas with support from the company chorus and with the assistance of other soloists for ensemble numbers. Changes in public taste forced her company to disband in February 1915, and she announced her retirement from the stage. But during the fall of 1915 she returned again to the stage as a soloist at the Lafayette Theater in the Harlem area of New York and at the Grand Theater in Chicago, Illinois. Thereafter she was largely inactive, although she occasionally sang for church benefits and for the black soldiers during World War I. Jones was one of the most celebrated singers of her time, and the top singer of her race for almost three decades. Her voice was described as having phenomenal range, great power, and rich lyrical quality; she "executed rapid runs and trills with perfection" (see BPIM and *Record Research* for reprints of press notices).

BIBL: Black press, incl. CDef, 1 July 1933; IndF 30 December 1889, 28 July 1894, 27 October 1894, 4 May 1895; NYAge 14 October 1915. BPIM 4 (July 1976), 7 (Spring 1979). *Boston Chronicle*, 2 April 1932, p.2. NAW. *Record Research* 165/166 (August 1979), 167/168 (October 1979). Scruggs. Simonds.

JONES, MILDRED BRYANT. Educator (Fl. early twentieth century in Chicago, Illinois; d. 1950s in Chicago). She obtained her musical education at Fisk University in Nashville, Tennessee; Northwestern University in Evanston, Illinois; the New England Conservatory in Boston, Massachusetts; and the Lyceum Arts Conservatory in Chicago, Illinois (B. Mus., 1921). She was the first black teacher in Chicago to pass the examination to teach music in the city's high schools. In 1920 she became head of the music program at Wendell Phillips High School and thereafter widely influenced the musical development of a host of black students who passed through Phillips, along with N. Clark Smith* and later Walter Henri Dyett.*

BIBL: Back press, incl. CDef, 15 October 1921, 1 September 1928, 30 October 1937.

JONES, PEARL WILLIAMS. College educator/Gospel musician (b. 28 June 1931 in Washington, D.C.). As a child she sang in the choir of her father's Pentecostal church. She received her musical education at Howard University in Washington, D.C. (B. Mus., 1953; M. Mus., 1957) and studied piano with Hazel Harrison* and Natalie Hinderas.* Her teaching experience included tenures at Albany State College in Georgia (1954-55), public high schools of Philadelphia, Pennsylvania (1958-72), and the University of the District of Columbia in Washington (formerly Federal Teachers College, 1973-). In 1966 she made her debut as a singer-pianist in Afro-American religious music at Town Hall in New York. Thereafter she toured widely in the United States and in Europe, generally with her Pearl Williams-Jones Soul Trio, giving concerts, appearing on television shows, and conducting seminars on black music. She was also active as a consultant at home and abroad in Afro-American gospel music and published articles in professional journals. Her honors included awards from the music industry, a grant from the National Endowment for the Arts for research in gospel (1974), and an honorary docorate from Lycoming College (1972).

BIBL: Dominique-René de Lerma, ed., *Reflections on Afro-American Music* (Kent, Ohio, 1973). *Directory of Significant 20th-Century American Minority Women* (Nashville, Tenn., 1977). IntWWM, 1977.

JONES, PHILLY JOE. See **JONES, JOSEPH.**

JONES, QUINCY DELIGHT, JR. Composer (b. 14 March 1933 in Chicago, Illinois). His family moved to Bremerton, Washington, when he was ten years old. He obtained his musical education in the public schools of Chicago, Illinois, and Seattle, Washington, where he began study of the trumpet during his high-school years; at Seattle University; and at the Berklee School of Music in Boston, Massachusetts. Early influences upon his musical development came from Ray Charles,* whom he met in 1948 and with whom he exchanged musical ideas; Joseph Pole, formerly a member of the Wings Over Jordan* Choir; and Clark Terry.* In later years William (''Billy'') Eckstine* exerted great influence. Jones's first professional experience was as a trumpeter-arranger in Lionel Hampton's* band (1950-53), with whom he toured widely in the United States and in Europe. Thereafter he settled in New York, where he played with various groups. In 1956 he joined John Birks (''Dizzy'') Gillespie* on a tour in the Near and Middle East and South America sponsored by the United States Department of State. During the years 1957-61 he lived in Europe. He served two years as a musical director for Barclay Disques in Paris, France; studied with Nadia Boulanger and Olivier Messiaen; and in 1960 toured widely with his big band, playing in concert halls and nightclubs, on radio and television programs. After returning to the United States, he was first music director, then vice-president for Mercury Records (1961-68). During the 1960s he also recorded extensively, composed and arranged music, and occasionally worked as musical director for such singers as Billy Eckstine, Peggy Lee, and Frank Sinatra. He wrote his first film score in 1961 for a Swedish film, *Boy in the Tree*. Later he composed music for and directed *The Pawnbroker* (1965) and *Mirage* (1965). Encouraged by his success, he decided to move wholly into film work and settled in Los Angeles, California, in 1968. Thereafter he wrote prolifically for films, including *In Cold Blood* (1967), *For the Love of Ivy* (1968), *Cactus Flower* (1969), *Come Back, Charleston Blue* (1972), *The Getaway* (1972), and many others. He also composed for television, including such shows as ''Ironside,'' ''Sanford and Son,'' and ''Roots.'' During the 1970s he was occasionally active as a performer, despite his deep involvement in writing music. He toured with Roberta Flack* in a concert series and also with his own group. In 1971 his *Black Requiem* was performed by the Houston Symphony with an eighty-voice choir and his friend Ray Charles as soloist. In 1973 he produced and directed the television show ''Duke Ellington—We Love You Madly''; in 1979 he was co-founder of the Institute for Black American Music. His honors included numerous awards from the music industry in the United States and abroad and an honorary doctorate from the Berklee School of Music.

BIBL: ASCAP. *Ebony* (June 1972). FeaEJ. FeaJS. FeaGitJS. MeeJMov. *Sepia* (October 1973). StamPRS. WWA. WWBA.

DISC: Jep.

JONES, RICHARD MYKNEE. Jazz pianist (b. 13 June 1892 in New Orleans; d. 8 December 1945 in Chicago, Illinois). He played alto horn in a brass band at the age of thirteen. He began playing professionally in 1908 in brothels of the Storyville district of New Orleans, Louisiana. Thereafter he led his own groups in various nightclubs and also played with others, among them, John Robichaux,* Armand Piron,* and Oscar (''Papa'') Celestin.* In 1918 he settled in Chicago, Illinois, where he became active in music publishing and served as manager for the Clarence Williams* publishing company (1919-21). He made his recording debut in 1923 and thereafter recorded regularly with his Jazz Wizards or, later, Chicago Cosmopolitans. He was a recording director of ''race records'' for the Okeh recording company during the 1920s; he held a similar position with Decca Records during the 1930s, and in 1945 was a talent scout for the Mercury Recording Company. Occasionally he toured with his groups. Throughout his career he gave primary attention to songwriting and arranging; his best-known songs were ''Riverside blues'' and ''Jazzin' babies blues.''

BIBL: ASCAP (b. 1892 in New Orleans). ChilWW (b. 1889 in Donaldsville, Louisiana). FeaEJ. Souch.

DISC: Kink. RustJR.

JONES, ROBERT C. Choral conductor (fl. mid-nineteenth century in Philadelphia, Pennsylvania). Little is known of his career except that he was ''leader of the vocal department of the Sacred Music Society'' of the black Second Presbyterian Church in Philadelphia, Pennsylvania. In December 1840 the Society performed an Overture by Jones on its sacred-music concert. The black New York press identified him as a ''distinguished vocalist'' when he lectured on sacred music there at the Presbyterian Church in 1840. Presumably he was a singer and composer as well as choral conductor.

BIBL: Black press, incl. *The Colored American*, 5 December 1840. *The Public Ledger* [Philadelphia], 17 December 1840. *The Pennsylvania Freeman* [Philadelphia], 19 December 1841.

JONES, ROBERT ELLIOTT ("JONAH"). Jazz trumpeter (b. 31 December 1908 in Louisville, Kentucky). He began study of the alto horn when he was eleven and changed to trumpet two years later. As a member of the local Booker T. Washington Community Center Band, he obtained both his lessons and instruments free of charge. He obtained his education in the public schools of Louisville, Kentucky. Later in his career he studied trumpet with William Vacchiano of the New York Philharmonic. His first professional experience was with Wallace Bryant on a riverboat which sailed the Ohio and the Mississippi Rivers. Thereafter he played with various groups, including Horace Henderson* (1928), Wesley Helvey (1930), James (''Jimmie'') Lunceford* (1931), Hezekiah (''Stuff'') Smith* (1932-34, 1936-40), and Lillian (''Lil'') Armstrong* (1935), among others. During the 1940s-mid-1950s he worked primarily with Bennett (''Benny'') Carter* (1940), Fletcher Henderson* (briefly in 1941), Cabell (''Cab'') Calloway* (1941-52), and Earl Hines* (1952-53). During these years he toured widely with groups in the United States and abroad; he also played in the pit orchestra for the 1953 Broadway revival of Gershwin's *Porgy and Bess*. In 1954 he toured in Europe as a soloist, and in 1955 he organized his own group, which was active through the 1970s. He played long residencies in New York nightclubs, toured throughout the world, including Australia and the Far East, recorded extensively, and appeared on television and at the major jazz festivals. He was an important big-band trumpeter of the swing era who successfully made the transition into later styles.

BIBL: ChilWW. DanceWS. FeaEJ. FeaJS. FeaGitJS. MeeJMov.

DISC: Kink.

JONES, RUTH. See **WASHINGTON, DINAH.**

JONES, SISSIERETTA. See **JONES, M. SISSIERETTA.**

JONES, THADDEUS JOSEPH ("THAD"). Jazz trumpeter (b. 28 March 1923 in Pontiac, Michigan). He came from a musical family: his father played guitar, his mother played piano, and two brothers, Elvin* and Henry (''Hank''),* became professional musicians. He obtained his musical education in the public schools of Pontiac, Michigan, a suburb of Detroit. He began playing professionally during the late 1930s in a group with his brothers, then played with Edward (''Sonny'') Stitt* and other local groups. After service in the United States Armed Forces (1943-46), he played with various groups, including Billy Mitchell, William (''Count'') Basie* (1954-63), the Roland Hanna Quartet (1963), Gerald (''Gerry'') Mulligan (1964), George Russell* (1964), among others, and as well, his own groups. In 1965 he joined with Mel Lewis to form an eighteen-piece big band, composed of New York jazzmen who earned their living primarily as studio or commercial musicians. Eventually the band began to perform outside New York and during the 1970s toured widely in the United States, Europe, and the Orient. Jones recorded extensively with the big band and with other groups and was active in television (CBS) as a staff musician and in films. Although he was best known as a bandleader and multi-instrumentalist, particularly on the fluegelhorn, he was extremely active as an arranger-composer. He wrote for Harry James, Basie, and for his big band. He received awards from the music industry for both performance and arranging.

BIBL: FeaEJ. FeaJS. FeaGitJS. MeeJMov. WWA.

DISC: Jep. Kink. TudJ.

JOPLIN, SCOTT. Composer (b. 24 November 1868 in Bowie County (now Texarkana), Texas; d. 1 April 1917 in New York, New York). He came from a musical family; his father played violin for plantation dances during slavery, his mother played banjo and sang, and four of the six children (in addition to Scott) sang or played strings. He early revealed talent, and his family purchased a used piano for him, which he taught himself to play. Even as a child he began playing for church and local social events; while in his teens he became known for his piano skills throughout southwestern Arkansas and northeastern Texas. Eventually he studied formally with local teachers. In addition to playing piano, he organized a vocal group, which toured in the Southwest and included his brothers Willie and Robert along with Tom Clark and Wesley Kirby. About 1884 he left home, traveled for some time as an itinerant pianist, then settled in St. Louis, Missouri, in 1885. He found employment as a cafe pianist in the city's prostitution district, but also traveled constantly to nearby places to play piano and to listen to other pianists. In 1893 he went to the Chicago World's Fair, where he came in contact with many black pianists—particularly ragtime pianists (''Plunk'') Henry Johnson, Henry Seymour, and Otis Saunders. During his stay in the city he organized a brass ensemble. In 1894 he and Saunders left Chicago together, stopped several places, including St. Louis, and settled eventually at Sedalia, Missouri. There he played second cornet in the Queen City Concert Band, studied theory and composition at the George R. Smith College for Negroes, and conducted a music studio. His two most promising students were Scott Hayden* and Arthur Marshall,* who also attended Smith College. During these years he also toured with a vocal group he had organized, the Texas Medley Quartette, which was actually a double quartet including his brothers and himself. He began to compose and to publish his first pieces, which were in conventional forms—two waltz songs, a piano waltz, and two marches. The Medley Quartette toured on a vaudeville circuit; during its stop in Syracuse, New York, Joplin published his songs; he published the piano pieces at Temple, Texas, when the group sang a concert there. There is little doubt that he composed and arranged pieces for his groups to perform. Although the Quartette was disbanded in 1897, he organized another group, the Sedalia Quartet, which performed off and on through 1904. He also led an instrumental ensemble, for which he arranged music.

In 1898 Joplin took some of his rag pieces to Kansas City publisher Carl Hoffman, who passed up a piece titled ''The Maple Leaf rag'' in favor of ''Original rags,'' which he published in March 1899. The former took its name from a black social club-cafe in Sedalia, whose patrons knew the piece long before it was published from having heard Joplin play it so often. In the summer of 1899, white publisher John Stark heard Joplin play the piece and decided to publish it. ''The Maple Leaf rag'' was enormously successful, and Joplin was encouraged to continue his composing. He began experimenting with larger forms using ragtime idioms and in 1899 completed a ballet, *The Ragtime Dance*, which was given a single night's performance in Sedalia and later published by Stark (1902). By 1903 Joplin had completed a ragtime opera, *A Guest of Honor*, and his Scott Joplin Drama Company gave the opera at least one performance, if not more, with a cast that included his brother Will, Scott Hayden, Arthur Marshall, and Latisha Howell, among others. Although the score is no longer extant, the opera attracted considerable attention at the time. It was advertised in September 1903 (see IndF) as ''the most complete and unique collection of words and music produced by any Negro writer.'' Its big numbers were ''The Dude's Parade'' and ''Patriotic Parade.'' The non-success of the opera failed to discourage Joplin; by 1905 he was at work on a second opera, *Treemonisha*, which he completed by 1907. As in the case of the first opera, he wrote both words and music. Throughout these years he turned out piano rags, which were very popular with the public and earned him the title, ''Ragtime King.''

He lived in Chicago, Illinois, during the years 1906-mid-1907, where he tried to rid himself of frustration and to recover from his baby's death and separation from his wife. In 1907 he settled in New York and immediately set about trying to get his opera produced. Advised to make various revisions to make it more acceptable to producers, he made the changes in both book and music but was still unable to find a producer. While never relinquishing his dream, he nevertheless became involved in other musical activities. He toured on the vaudeville circuit, he made piano-roll recordings of his rags, and he published his music, including a manual, *The School of Ragtime—Six Exercises for Piano* (1908). In May 1911 Joplin himself published the 230-page manuscript of *Treemonisha*, which was scored for eleven voices and piano accompaniment. He published a full description of the opera in the newspapers; his friends gave a party in his honor; and in October of that year a press release advised that Thomas Johnson, formerly president of the Crescent Theater Company, would be producing the opera and had already booked the company for an opening in Atlantic City, New Jersey. Nothing came of the plans, however. The opera did not go unnoticed by the music establishment; the *American Musician* gave it an enthusiastic review, observing that Joplin ''had produced a thoroughly American opera'' (14 June 1911). Two years later the press announced that *Treemonisha* would be produced at the Lafayette Theater in the Harlem community of New York with forty singers and an orchestra of twenty-five. These plans, too, failed to materialize. Joplin was determined to produce his opera; in 1915 he staged it himself in a Harlem hall, without scenery or orchestra, hoping to attract a producer. The press was silent about the production; it was his friend, Sam Patterson, who later told ragtime historians about the production. Joplin published some numbers of the opera separately: ''A real slow drag'' and the prelude to the third act in 1913, and the ''Frolic of the bears'' in 1915. The latter was given a first performance at the eighth annual recital of the Martin-Smith School of Music on 5 May.

Most Joplin biographers have concluded that the failure of *Treemonisha* crushed Joplin, but the evidence suggests otherwise. In September 1915 he advertised in the black press that he had completed a vaudeville sketch, "The Syncopated Jamboree," which would be produced by one Bob Slater in New York. The next April, Joplin made piano rolls for the Connorized label. He must have continued to compose through 1915 and part of 1916, for in September 1916, he advertised that he had completed a musical comedy titled *If* and that he was working on a symphony. Joplin was a proud man and would hardly have advertised in such manner if he were not actually composing. And the black press, equally proud and also knowledgeable about the community, would hardly have discussed seriously the music of an insane person. It is probable that Joplin was active through mid-1916, and even after that time was partly in possession of his faculties until he was taken to Bellevue Hospital in the fall of 1916 (later, he was removed to Manhattan Hospital). Predictably, Joplin left unfinished work, for he tried to compose until the end.

Joplin was a seminal figure in the history of American music. He exerted enormous influence upon his contemporaries, not only upon those who studied with him or collaborated in writing pieces—among them, Louis Chauvin, Hayden, and Marshall—but also upon those who studied his music, particularly James Scott* and Joseph Lamb. His contributions were multiple: he was the first American to write genuinely American folk operas and ballets; he established the piano rag tradition; and he was the first to successfully fuse the Afro-American folk tradition with European art-music forms and techniques. Although called the "King of Ragtime" during his lifetime, Joplin became a forgotten figure after his death, if not before that year. But the publication of *They All Played Ragtime* in 1950 by Rudi Blesh and Harriet Janis brought about a revival of interest in ragtime and its composers, and Joplin shared in its new popularity. Beginning about 1971 concert pianists began to include Joplin pieces on their recitals and to make recordings, particularly Joshua Rifkin and William Balcom, among others. The same year Vera Brodsky Lawrence published *The Collected Works of Scott Joplin* (New York), a complete edition of his extant music except for three piano pieces. Then in 1972 his opera *Treemonisha* was given a world premiere at Atlanta, Georgia, and the Joplin renascence became firmly established. The use of Joplin piano rags for the musical score of the film *The Sting* (1973) added luster to an already golden reputation.

BIBL: Theodore Albrecht, "Julius Weiss: Scott Joplin's First Piano Teacher" in *Symposium*, Journal of the College Music Society 19 (Fall 1979). ASCAP. Black press, incl. IndF, 12 September 1903, 16 January 1915, 18 September 1915, 7 September 1916, 14 April 1917; NYAge, 5 March 1908, 25 May 1911, 2 June 1911, 5 October 1911, 3 April 1913, 14 August 1913, 29 April 1915. Blesh. BPIM 3 (Spring, Fall 1975). Peter Gammond, *Scott Joplin and the Ragtime Era* (New York, 1975). James Haskins, *Scott Joplin* (New York, 1978). JaTiRR. Addison Reed, "The Life and Work of Scott Joplin" (Ph.D. diss., University of North Carolina, 1973).

JORDAN, CLIFFORD LACONIA. Jazz saxophonist (b. 2 September 1931 in Chicago, Illinois). He played piano as a child and studied saxophone beginning at the age of thirteen. He obtained his musical education in the public schools of Chicago, Illinois, where he came under the influence of Walter Dyett* at DuSable High School. He began his professional career playing with local jazz and rhythm 'n' blues groups. During the 1950s he played with various groups, including Max Roach,* Edward ("Sonny") Stitt,* Horace Silver,* and James ("J. J.") Johnson,* among others. In 1961 he organized a quintet with Kenneth ("Kenny") Dorham,* then in 1962 formed his own quartet with Andrew Hill,* J. C. Moses, and Edward Kahn. In later years his groups included Stanley Cowell,* Billy Higgins, and William ("Bill") Lee.* During the 1960s he toured widely in the United States, Europe, and Japan with his own groups and with Roach and Charles Mingus.* He was active as a soloist in Europe during the years 1966-69 and toured in West Africa and the Middle East under the sponsorship of the United States Department of State (1967) and again in West Africa independently (1969). Through the 1970s he continued to tour at home and abroad and to record extensively. He was also active as a teacher and lecturer in New York for Jazzmobile School, for the programs of Jazz Interactions in the public schools, and at the Henry Street Settlement House. He wrote music for television shows and appeared on television; in the 1970s he formed his own music company, called Dolphy Productions. His compositions employed African elements, and his performances were distinctive for his use of double ensembles in the way he had observed in African music groups.

BIBL: FeaEJ. FeaJS. FeaGitJS.

DISC: Jep.

JORDAN, JOE. Ragtime pianist/Composer (b. 11 February 1882 in Cincinnati, Ohio; d. 11 September 1971 in Tacoma, Washington). As a child he learned to play mostly by ear, imitating a sister who played piano. He attended Lincoln Institute in Jefferson City, Missouri, but left about 1900 to go to St. Louis, Missouri. There he played ragtime piano in the cafes and brothels of the tenderloin district and also violin and drums in the Taborian Band. In 1903 he was musical and stage director for a vaudeville show, *Dandy Coon*, written by Louis Chauvin* and Sam Patterson*; the show folded almost immediately when it went on tour. Thereafter Jordan settled in Chicago, Illinois, and although he traveled frequently to other places, he used that city as his home base. In 1904 he was appointed musical director of Robert Mott's* newly established Pekin Music Hall (later called Pekin Theater), and he wrote the score for the Pekin Stock Company's first production, *The Man from Bam*, which featured Flournoy Miller* and Aubrey Lyles* in the leading roles. Over the years he wrote other musicals for the Pekin, including *Mayor of Dixie*, and directed the Pekin orchestra. In the spring of 1905 he was in New York, where he helped to organize, along with Ernest Hogan,* and to direct the Memphis Students, a show credited with being the first "syncopated-music" concert in history. Including singers, dancers, and instrumentalists, the show starred Hogan and Abbie Mitchell.* Jordan wrote the music for the show. The next season, 1905-06, he wrote the musical score for *Rufus Rastus*, which starred Hogan. In 1908 he returned to New York to direct the second edition of the Memphis Students, in which Tom Fletcher* replaced the ailing Ernest Hogan. Throughout this period Jordan was active as a musical director—for the Bob Cole*/Johnson brothers'* show, *The Red Moon*—a composer, and an arranger. His song, "Lovey Joe," written for Fanny Brice, lifted her to stardom when she sang it in the Ziegfeld Follies of 1910.

During the second decade of the century he toured widely in Europe on the vaudeville circuit; in 1915 he was musical director for prizefighter Jack Johnson's European tours. He was also active in New York vaudeville shows, but spent most of his time in Chicago when not in Europe. In 1913 he directed an orchestra for the new States Theater in Chicago and found time to organize a YMCA Symphony Orchestra during the summer. By the 1920s he had settled again in the United States; in 1926 he first recorded with his group, Jordan's Ten Sharps and Flats. He wrote scores for Broadway musicals, including *Strut Miss Lizzie* (1922), *Deep Harlem* (1929), and *Brown Buddies* (1930), among others; he arranged for leading entertainers of the time, Ginger Rogers, Ethel Merman, and Blossom Seeley, among others; and was a musical director for the Miller/Lyles show, *Keep Shufflin'* (1928). During the 1930s he conducted the Negro Unit Orchestra of the WPA Federal Theater Project. In 1932 he was elected to the board of directors of AFM Local 208, the first of his race to serve thus. During World War II he conducted musical activities and entertained servicemen with his groups at Fort Huachaca, Arizona—at first as a member (captain?) of the U.S. Army's Special Services Division and later, after his discharge, for the USO. In 1944 he settled in Tacoma, Washington, where he retired from professional music. He continued to write songs and to conduct a music studio for a limited number of students until his death at the age of eighty-nine. In addition to the music cited above, his best-known pieces were the piano rags "Pekin rag," "J. J. J. rag," and "Morocco blues"; and the songs, "Oh, say, wouldn't it be a dream" (featured by Ernest Hogan), "Rise and shine," "Teasin' rag" (introduced by Blossom Seeley), and "These eyes of mine" (written for Anna Held).

BIBL: ASCAP. Black press, incl. CDef, 20 August 1913, 26 October 1915, 24 December 1932, 11 September 1943; IndF, 12 August 1916; NYAge, 25 June 1908. Blesh. Flet, pp. 129-131. JaTrRR.

DISC: Kink. RustJR.

JORDAN, LOUIS. Rhythm 'n' blues singer/Saxophonist (b. 8 July 1908 in Brinkley, Arkansas; d. 4 February 1975 in Los Angeles, California). He began clarinet study at the age of seven with his father, who was a bandleader and music teacher. He obtained his musical education in the public schools of Brinkley, Arkansas, and at Arkansas Baptist College in Little Rock, Arkansas. His early professional experiences were with Rudy ("Tuna Boy") Williams and the Rabbit Foot Minstrels.* About 1932 he moved to Philadelphia, Pennsylvania, and thereafter he played with various groups, including Charlie Gaines (1932-35), Kaiser Marshall, LeRoy Smith, and William ("Chick") Webb* (1936-38), among others. In 1938 he formed his own group, later called The Tymphany Five. He made his first recordings the same year, and thereafter recorded extensively with his own groups and with others, among them, Louis Armstrong,* Bing Crosby, and Ella Fitzgerald.* During the 1950s he led a big band for a short period, then returned to his small group, which toured widely. After living in Phoenix, Arizona, for several years, he settled in Los Angeles, California, about 1963. He was active musically through the early 1970s, touring extensively in the United States, Europe, and Asia (in 1967, 1968). He was active in radio and films, including *Beware* (1946), *Follow the Boys* (1944), and *Swing Parade of 1946*, among others. His best-known performances were "Saturday night fish fry," "Knock me a kiss,"

"Gonna move to the outskirts of town," "Choo choo ch' boogie," and "Caldonia" (which he wrote himself). Jordan played in all styles—jazz, popular, blues—and more than any other person contributed to the development of rhythm 'n' blues, which led to rock and roll.

BIBL: BWW. ChilWW. FeaEJ. FeaJS. FeaGitJS. MeeJMov. ShawHS. WWCA, 1950.

DISC: Jep. Kink. RustJR. TudBM.

JORDAN, ROBERT. Concert pianist (b. 2 May 1940 in Chattanooga, Tennessee). He obtained his musical education at the Eastman School of Music in Rochester, New York (B. Mus., 1962) and the Juilliard School of Music in New York (M.S., 1965). He studied further at the Hochschule für Musik in Berlin, Germany (1967), and at the Sorbonne in Paris, France (1969). His teachers included Cecile Genhart and Rosina Lhevine. He toured widely in Europe as a concert pianist during the years 1966-70. In 1972 he made his American debut at Alice Tully Hall in New York; during the 1970s he appeared with the major symphony orchestras in the United States and abroad and gave solo recitals at home, in Europe, South America, and Africa. In November 1976 he played a recital at the John F. Kennedy Center in Washington, D.C., as one of thirteen American pianists chosen to appear on a Bicentennial Concert Series and to perform works commissioned from American composers. In 1977 he represented American concert music at the Second World Black and African Festival at Lagos, Nigeria. His teaching career included tenures at Morgan State University in Baltimore, Maryland, as an artist-in-residence for three years; at the University of Delaware in Newark as an artist-in-residence (1979); and at Bronx Community College of the City University of New York (1972-).

BIBL: WWA.

JOYNER, MATILDA S. See **JONES, M. SISSIERETTA.**

JUBA, MASTER. See **LANE, WILLIAM HENRY.**

JUBILEE SINGERS. Vocal mixed ensembles (org. in 1871; fl. through twentieth century). The use of the word *jubilee* in association with a singing group apparently originated with the Fisk Jubilee Singers,* who toured the world during the years 1871-78, giving concerts to raise money for their college, Fisk University at Nashville, Tennessee. From that time on, the word was used (often in combination with other words) to denote a touring, vocal, mixed ensemble whose repertory consisted primarily of sacred music, spirituals and hymns, with a sprinkling of secular songs but not minstrel or vaudeville songs. When Fisk University dropped its sponsorship of the Singers in 1878, Frederick Loudin, a member of the original Singers from 1875 to 1878, took over management of the now-private group, retaining its name and persuading some of the original singers to join him. In 1884 he embarked upon a worldwide tour which was very successful; most audiences were not aware that the Fisk Jubilee Singers were no longer officially connected with the University. The same year a group calling itself the Canadian Jubilee Singers set out from Ontario, Canada, to tour in England for the purpose of raising money to build a theological seminary for black men at Chatham, Ontario. The troupe, composed of four men and four women, who were descendents of slaves who had escaped to Canada during the period of slavery, included a soloist who had formerly toured with the Fisk Singers. A spin-off group from Loudin's troupe was organized in 1889 by Orpheus McAdoo,* who was Loudin's leading baritone during the years 1886-89. He called his group the Virginia Jubilee Singers when he toured around the world, but audiences often failed to distinguish between his group and the Fisk Jubilee Singers. The word *jubilee* came into common usage during the last decades of the nineteenth century. There were the Wilmington [North Carolina] Jubilee Singers, Slayton's Jubilee Singers, the Sheppard Jubilee Singers, and the McMillen and Sourbeck Jubilee Singers* (later called Stinson's Jubilee Singers), among others. Well-known groups of the twentieth century were Williams's Jubilee Singers,* organized in 1904 in Chicago, Illinois; Hahn's Jubilee Singers, organized somewhat later, which included Florence Cole Talbert* and Noble Sissle* among its members at one time; and Eva Jessye's* Original Dixie Jubilee Singers, organized in the 1920s. Later in the century, the word became closely associated with gospel groups.

The first group to make a recording of "Genuine Jubilee and Camp-Meeting Shouts" was the Dinwiddie Colored Quartet for the Victor Talking Machine Company in October 1902. It was composed of Harry Cryer, Clarence Meredith, Sterling Rex, and James H. Thomas.

BIBL: Black press, particularly IndF, 1889-1900. *The Musical World*, 24 May 1884. *The Master Musician* 1 (October 1919). Flet, p. 30.

DISC: Folk Music in America Series. Vol. 1, *Religious Music: Congregational and Ceremonial*, Library of Congress recordings (Dinwiddie Quartet).

JULIUS, JOHN. Society-dance violinist (fl. mid-nineteenth century in Pittsburgh, Pennsylvania). He was active as a violinist and dancing-school master in Pittsburgh, Pennsylvania. He and his wife Edna maintained a ballroom, called Concert Hall, where he gave balls and assemblies for the aristocracy. When President-elect William Henry Harrison visited Pittsburgh in 1840, the receptions for him were held at Concert Hall, and Julius supervised the music and dancing.

BIBL: Martin Delany, *The Condition, Elevation, Emigration, and Destiny of the Colored People* (Philadelphia, 1852), p. 107.

K

KAY, ULYSSES SIMPSON. Composer (b. 7 January 1917 in Tucson, Arizona). He came from a musical family: his father sang about the house, his mother played piano and sang in a church choir, and his maternal uncle, Joseph (''King'') Oliver,* was a celebrated jazzman. He began piano study at the age of six, violin study at ten, and saxophone study at twelve. He obtained his musical education in the public schools of Tucson, Arizona, where he sang in school glee clubs and played in the high-school marching band and dance orchestra; at the University of Arizona in Tucson (B.S. in public school music, 1938), where he studied composition with John Lowell and performed in college music groups; and at the Eastman School of Music in Rochester, New York (M. Mus., 1940), where he studied with Bernard Rogers and Howard Hanson. He also studied privately with Paul Hindemith at the Berkshire Festival in Tanglewood, Massachusetts (summer 1941), and at Yale University in New Haven, Connecticut (1941-42), and with Otto Luening at Columbia University in New York (1946-47). During his years of service in the U. S. Armed Forces (1942-45), he played saxophone in a Navy band and a dance orchestra, learned to play flute and piccolo, and wrote and arranged music. He lived abroad during the years 1949-52, having obtained fellowships that enabled him to study music in Rome, Italy, as an associate of the American Academy there. After returning to the United States, he became an editorial adviser for Broadcast Music, Inc. (1953-68) and later served as a music consultant. His teaching career included tenures as a visiting professor at Boston [Massachusetts] University (summer 1965) and at the University of California in Los Angeles (1966-67) and as a distinguished professor at Lehman College of the City University of New York (1968-   ).

He began writing music during his college years. His early style development was influenced not only by his teachers but also by William Grant Still,* with whom he came into contact during the summers of 1936 and 1937. Still both inspired him and encouraged him to become a composer. His early compositions were performed publicly during his student years at Eastman by Howard Hanson and The Rochester Civic Orchestra and by soloists. His first important pieces were *Ten Essays for Piano* (1939), *Sinfonietta for Orchestra* (1939), and *Concerto for Oboe and Orchestra* (1940). During the early 1940s his music increasingly was heard on concerts of chamber groups, soloists, and choral groups. There was even a ballet suite, *Danse Calinda* (1941), based on a story by Ridgeley Torrence. In 1944 the performance of his overture, *Of New Horizons* (1944), by Thor Johnson and the New York Philharmonic at the Lewissohn Stadium attracted wide attention; it later won the American Broadcasting Company prize (1946) and several performances. Critics remarked on the lyricism of his music, its agreeable thematic materials and its modernism, predicting that the young composer's obvious talent would grow over the years. Kay's mature style continued the emphasis on lyricism and was distinctive for its rhythmic vitality, sensitivity for contrasting sonorities, and predilection for crisp, dissonant counterpoint, though not necessarily atonal. Generally he avoided serialism, atonality, and the use of aleatoric devices or electronic techniques. He represented modern traditionalism with its roots in romanticism and expressionism of the early twentieth century.

He wrote in a wide variety of forms: by 1980 he had completed eighteen or twenty works for symphony orchestra; four operas; six or more works for band; about twenty for chamber groups, including chamber orchestra; fifteen vocal works, including cantatas, compositions for voice and orchestra, and for narrator and orchestra; a number of pieces for solo instruments, such as piano, organ, flute, and guitar; and many songs for solo voice and piano or organ and for chorus (SATB, SSA, TTBB, etc.) and keyboard accompaniment. He wrote his first film score, *The Quiet One*, in 1948 and thereafter wrote many scores for films, documentaries, and televison films. His best-known orchestral works included *A Short Overture* (1946), which won the George Gershwin Memorial Award in 1947; *Portrait Suite* (1948), which won an award; *Serenade for Orchestra* (1954); *Fantasy Variations* (1963); *Markings* (1966), in memory of Dag Hammerskjold; *Theater Set* (1968); and *Southern Harmony* (1975), based on themes and motives from William Walker's *The Southern Harmony* of 1835. Of his chamber works, the best known were *Brass Quartet* (1950); *Six Dances for String Orchestra* (1954); *Trigon* (1961) for wind orchestra; *Aulos* (1967) for solo flute, two horns, string orchestra, and percussion; *Scherzi Musicali* (1968) for chamber orchestra; *Facets* (1971) for piano and woodwind quintet; and *Quintet Concerto* (1974) for five brass soli and orchestra. His well-known choral works included *Song of Jeremiah* (1945) for baritone, chorus, and orchestra; *Inscriptions from Whitman* (1963) for SATB chorus and orchestra; *Stephen Crane Set* (1967) for chorus and thirteen instruments; *A Covenant for Our Time* (1969) for chorus and orchestra; and *Parables* (1970) for chorus and chamber orchestra. His best-known works for band were *Forever Free* (1962), *Concert Sketches* (1965), and *Four Silhouettes* (1972). His well-known works for solo voice included *Fugitive Songs* (1950) for medium voice and piano; *Triptych on Texts of Blake* (1962) for high voice, violin, violoncello, and piano; *The Western Paradise* (1976) for narrator and orchestra with text by Donald Door; and *Jersey Hours* (1978) for voice and harps with texts by Door. Three of his operas, *The Boor* (1955, libretto adapted from Chekov), *The Juggler of Our Lady* (1956, libretto by Alexander King), and *The Capitoline Venus* (1970, libretto after Mark Twain) received premieres at American universities; the fourth, *Jubilee* (1976, libretto based on novel by Margaret Walker), was first performed by Opera/South.*

He received many honors and awards, including the Alice M. Ditson Fellowship (1946), Rosenwald Fellowship (1947), Fulbright Fellowship (1950), Guggenheim Fellowship (1964), and National Endowment for the Arts Grant (1978); he won the Prix de Rome (1949, 1951), an award from the American Academy of Arts and Letters (1947), and an Alumni Award from the University of Rochester (1972); and he was given honorary doctorates by Lincoln College (in Illinois, 1963), Bucknell University (1966), the University of Arizona (1969), and Illinois Wesleyan University (1969). In 1958 he was a member of the first group of musicians sent to the Soviet Union by the U. S. State Department in a cultural exchange program, and he later served many times on cultural missions sent abroad. In 1979 he was elected to the American Academy of Arts and Letters. He was regarded as one of the important American composers of his generation and was the leading black composer of his time.

BIBL: BakBCS. Bull. BMI (February 1970). Gro. Richard Thomas Hadley, ''The Published Choral Music of Ulysses Kay, 1943-1968'' (Ph.D. diss., University of Iowa, 1972). Laurence Melton Hayes, ''The Music of Ulysses Kay, 1939-1963'' (Ph.D. diss., University of Wisconsin, 1971). WWA. WWBA. WWCA, 1950. WWE. Lucius Reynolds Wyatt, ''The Mid-Twentieth Century Orchestral Variation, 1953-1963; An Analysis and Comparison of Selected Works by Major Composers'' (Ph.D. diss., Eastman School of Music, University of Rochester, 1974).

KEMP, EMMERLYNE J.(''EMME''). Entertainer (b. 6 May 1935 in Chicago, Illinois). She studied piano at an early age and first played on a public recital at the age of six. She obtained her musical education at Northwestern University in Evanston, Illinois (1952-54), at the Berklee School of Music in Boston, Massachusetts (1965), and at New York University (1972-73). She also studied piano privately. During the 1940s-mid-1950s she toured widely in the United States as a nightclub pianist. She played with military jazz groups during her service in the United States Armed Forces (1956-59). Thereafter she toured both as a soloist and with her own groups on the nightclub circuit, on college campuses, and in concert halls. In 1965 she settled in New York. She was active as a songwriter, and in 1975 founded a publishing company, Emme Kemp Music. She also recorded regularly and appeared in Broadway musicals. A songwriter, she contributed music to the musical *Bubbling Brown Sugar* (1976).

BIBL: Black press, incl. CDef, 7 February 1976, 15 July 1977. WWBA.

KENDRICKS, EDWARD (''EDDIE''). Entertainer (b. 17 December 1939 in Union Springs, Alabama). His family moved to Birmingham, Alabama, when he was an infant. During his high-school years he decided to become a professional singer and went to Detroit about 1958. He formed a vocal group with other singers, which sang in local nightclubs. Called at first The Cavaliers, then The Primes, the group was signed to a recording contract with Berry Gordy's* Motown Records in 1962, and its name was changed to The Temptations.* Kendricks sang lead tenor with the group, which won an international reputation. After eleven years, he left the group in 1971 to begin a career as a soloist. He toured widely in the United States and abroad and recorded regularly. His best-known record albums were *All by Myself* and *People—Hold On*. He received awards from the music industry.

BIBL: Black press, incl. PhilaT, 7 August 1973. *Ebony* (April 1971). StamPRS.

DISC: TudJ.

KENNEDY, ANNE GAMBLE. College professor (b. 25 September 1920 in Charleston, West Virginia). She came from a musical family; her mother sang with the Fisk Jubilee Singers and later became a piano teacher. She obtained her musical education at Fisk University in Nashville, Tennessee (B.A., 1941), where she studied with William Allen* and John Work, III*; at the Oberlin School of Music in Ohio (B. Mus., 1943); the Juilliard School of Music in New York (1951); and George Peabody Teachers College in Nashville, Tennessee (1970). She also studied piano privately with Ray Lev. She was encouraged to develop her talent by Marian Anderson* and G. Wallace Woodworth. She made her debut in 1950 at Charleston, West Virginia; thereafter she toured widely as a concert pianist in the United States and the Caribbean. During the 1950s-70s she also gave duo-piano recitals with her husband, Matthew Kennedy.* She was an accompanist for the Fisk Jubilee Singers* for fifteen years. Her teaching career included tenures at Tuskegee Institute in Alabama (1943-45), Talladega College in Alabama (1945-48), and Fisk University (1950-).

BIBL: Questionnaire. NYB, 1952. WWBA. WWE. WWWorld Musicians.

KENNEDY, JOSEPH J. ("JOE"), JR. Educator/Symphony/jazz violinist (b. 17 November 1923 in Pittsburgh, Pennsylvania). He studied violin as a child with his grandfather, Saunders Bennett, and was encouraged by his family to prepare for a career in music. He obtained his musical education at Virginia State College (B.S., 1953), Duquesne University in Pittsburgh, Pennsylvania (M. Mus., 1960), and Carnegie-Mellon University in Pittsburgh. He was encouraged to become a jazzman by James ("Jimmy") Lunceford.* His first group, The Four Strings (1948-50), included Ray Crawford, Edgar Willis, Samuel Johnson, and himself as leader-violinist-arranger. In 1949 Ahmad Jamal* replaced Johnson as pianist. Thereafter, Kennedy was musical director-arranger for Jamal for many years. In 1952 Kennedy began teaching in the public schools of Richmond, Virginia, and in 1973 he was appointed Supervisor of Music for the public schools. He also lectured at Virginia Commonwealth University in Richmond (1972-). He began playing violin with the Richmond Symphony Orchestra in 1960 and continued through the 1970s. He toured widely as a guest conductor, concert violinist, lecturer, and workshop coordinator; he also served on national boards of professional organizations, including the American Youth Symphony and Chorus. His best-known compositions were *Suite for Trio and Orchestra* (1965), *Fantastic Vehicle* (1966), and *Dialogue for Flute, Cello and Piano* (1972).

BIBL: Questionnaire. FeaJS. FeaGitJS. Roach. WWBA.

DISC: Jep.

KENNEDY, MATTHEW W. College music educator (b. 10 March 1921 in Americus, Georgia). He came from a musical family; both parents sang in church choirs and his mother played piano. He began piano study when he was six years old. He obtained his musical education in the public schools of Americus, Georgia, and New York. He attended Fisk University in Nashville, Tennessee (B.A., 1946), where he studied with John Work, III*; the Juilliard School of Music in New York (diploma, 1940; M.S., 1950), where he studied with Lois Adler; and the George Peabody College for Teachers in Nashville (1969-70). His teaching career included tenures at Fisk University (1947-48, 1954-), where he was director of the Fisk Jubilee Singers (1957-68, 1971-), and at the National Music Camp at Interlochen, Michigan (summer faculty 1973). In 1958 he made his debut as a concert pianist at Carnegie Recital Hall in New York. Thereafter he toured widely in the United States, Canada, and Europe, and in later years gave duo-piano recitals with his wife, Anne Gamble Kennedy.* He was also active as an accompanist, touring with Nathaniel Dickerson, the Fisk Jubilee Singers,* Oscar Henry, Rawn Spearman,* and Lawrence Winters,* among others. His published music included arrangements of spirituals (1974). His honors included awards from civic and professional organizations and appointments to boards of professional organizations.

BIBL: Questionnaire. Cornelius V. Troup, *Distinguished Negro Georgians* (Dallas, 1962). WWA. WWBA. WWWorld Musicians.

KENYATTA, ROBIN. Jazz saxophonist (b. 6 March 1942 in Charleston, South Carolina). His family moved to New York when he was four years old. He became interested in music during his high-school years and studied trombone at school. Later he studied saxophone, particularly the alto. During his service in the United States Armed Forces (1951-53), he played in an army band in Germany and studied composition with Russ Garcia in Munich, Germany. After his discharge, he was active as a jazz musician, playing with Valerie Capers,* Edward (''Sonny'') Stitt,* William (''Bill'') Dixon,* the Isley Brothers,* and Roswell Rudd, among others. During the years 1970-72 he lived again in Europe, where he recorded regularly in addition to touring. He attracted wide attention in the decade of the 1970s for the blending of jazz and reggae elements in his music, much of which he wrote himself. The best-known example of his jazz/reggae crossover was his album *Terra Nova* (1973). Among those who played in his Robin Kenyatta Ensemble over the years were James (''Jimmy'') Brown, Huks Brown, Worthington Brown, Michael (''Mike'') Carrabello, Winston Grennan, and Sonelius Smith, among others.

BIBL: Black press, incl. *The* [Pittsburgh] *New Courier*, 2 March 1974. BMI (January 1972). *Encore* (May 1974).

KEPPARD, FREDDIE. Jazz cornetist (b. 15 February 1889 in New Orleans, Louisiana; d. 15 July 1933 in Chicago, Illinois). He came from a musical family; his brother Louis became a professional musician. He played mandolin, violin, and accordion before he changed to the cornet, which he studied with Adolphe Alexander. His first professional experience was in 1901 with Johnny Brown. In 1906 he formed the Olympia Orchestra, which included among its personnel at one time or another George Baquet,* Joseph (''King'') Oliver,* Alphonse Picou,* and Armand J. Piron,* among others. He also played with the Eagle Brass Band, led by Frankie Dusen, and in local dance halls with various groups. In 1913 he and other musicians went to Los Angeles, California, to join the Original Creole Orchestra, organized by William (''Bill'') Manuel Johnson,* which toured widely in the United States and Canada on the vaudeville circuit (1913-18). The orchestra was disbanded briefly in 1917, but was reorganized with Keppard as leader. According to jazz legend, the Victor Talking Machine Company wanted to record a New Orleans jazz group and offered a contract to Keppard, but he refused for fear that other bands would steal his musical ideas. Consequently, they offered the contract to a white band, Nick LaRocca's Original Dixieland Jazz Band. Victor made a test recording of a Creole Jazz Band in 1918 (Keppard's?), but never released the recording. When the Creole Orchestra was disbanded again in 1918, Keppard settled in Chicago, Illinois, and thereafter played with various groups, including Oliver, James (''Jimmie'') Noone,* Erskine Tate,* Charles (''Doc'') Cooke* (1922-24, 1925-26), and Charlie Elgar. During the 1920s he also played in local nightclubs and occasionally led his own groups. He first recorded with Erskine Tate's Vendome Orchestra, and thereafter with other groups, including his own Jazz Cardinals in 1926. He was largely inactive during the 1930s because of illness. Keppard was a pioneer jazz cornetist, belonging to the first generation of jazzmen along with cornetists Willie (''Bunk'') Johnson* and King Oliver. His contemporaries regarded him as the legitimate successor to the ''king of cornetists,'' Charles (''Buddy'') Bolden.* He was an important member of the first orchestra to export New Orleans jazz to the rest of the nation, the Original Creole Orchestra.

BIBL: Black press, incl. CDef, 15 July 1916; IndF, 13 February 1915. Sidney Bechet, *Treat It Gentle* (London, 1960). ChilWW. FeaEJ. Donald Marquis, *In Search of Buddy Bolden* (Baton Rouge, 1978). Souch.

DISC: Kink. RustJR. TudJ.

KERR, THOMAS. University professor (b. 1915 in Baltimore, Maryland). He obtained his musical education in the public schools of Baltimore, Maryland, where he came under the tutelage of W. Llewellyn Wilson* during his high-school years, and at the Eastman School of Music of the University of Rochester in New York (B. Mus.). In 1943 he was appointed to the music faculty at Howard University in Washington, D.C., and remained there until his retirement. He toured as a concert pianist, giving solo recitals and appearing with symphony orchestras. Although he did not study organ and composition formally, he gained wide recognition as a composer, particularly of organ pieces. His compositions were performed in churches and cathedrals as well as in concert halls. His best-known works were the organ *Anguished American Easter*, 1968 and the piano ''Easter Monday Swagger, Scherzino'' (1970). His honors included a Rosenwald Fellowship in composition (1942) and first prize in a competition sponsored by Composers and Authors of America (1944).

BIBL: Black press.

KERSANDS, WILLIAM (''BILLY''). Minstrel entertainer (b. 1842 in New York, New York; d. 29 June 1915 at Artesia, New Mexico). He joined the Georgia Minstrels* during its early years when it was owned by

Charles (''Barney'') Hicks* and went on to establish an international reputation as a minstrel star. During his long career he was associated with most of the important minstrel companies of his time, including Callender's Original Georgia Minstrels, Harvey's International Minstrel Company, Sprague's Georgia Minstrels, and the Richard and Pringle Georgia Minstrels. He played on every minstrel stage in the United States and made several worldwide tours, appearing before the crowned heads of Europe and in the Orient and Australia. In 1878 he toured with the Hyers Sisters'* company in *Out of Bondage*; in 1883 he starred in the Callender's Consolidated Spectacular Minstrel Festival, along with the Hyers Sisters, Sam Lucas,* Wallace King,* and others. He and Lucas also played together in other shows, particularly during the years 1872-74. Later he toured with his own companies, with the Hicks and Kersands Minstrels for five years, then with the Kersands Minstrels for four years. In 1901 he played a vaudeville show, starring with Sherman H. Dudley* in *King Rastus*; but the show closed after a year, and Kersands returned to minstrelsy. His last tour abroad was with the Hugo Brothers' Minstrels to Australia in 1912. After returning to the United States, he and his wife, Louise, joined the Nigro and Stevenson show, then later organized their own troupe. He was performing with this troupe at the time of his death. As a minstrel Kersands was both singer and comedian, but his specialty was dancing, particularly the ''buck-and-wing'' and a soft-shoe dance he called the ''Virginia essence,'' which generally was danced to the tune of Stephen Foster's ''Swanee River.''

BIBL: Black press, incl. CDef, 4 May 1912; IndF, 24 July 1915; NYAge, 15 July 1915, 5 August 1915. Flet. Simond.

KILLEBREW, GWENDOLYN. Opera singer (b. c1942 in Philadelphia, Pennsylvania). She studied music as a child. During her high-school years she studied piano, voice, violin, and French horn. She obtained her musical education at Temple University in Philadelphia, Pennsylvania (B. Mus. Ed., 1963), where she studied with Else Fink, and at the Juilliard School of Music in New York (1963-66), where she studied with Hans Heinz and Christopher West. She was active as a school music teacher, social worker, and music therapist before she began her career in opera. She made her first professional appearance as a mezzo-soprano with the Philadelphia Orchestra at Robin Hood Dell in Casals's *El Pessebre* (summer 1963). In 1966 she was a finalist in the Metropolitan Opera National Council's Regional Auditions; the next year she made her operatic debut with the Metropolitan Opera as Waltraute in Wagner's *Die Walküre*. Her best-known performances were as Amneris in Verdi's *Aida*, Ulrica in Verdi's *Un Ballo in Maschera*, Azucena in Verdi's *Il Trovatore*, and Frica in Wagner's *Das Rheingold*. She also sang the title roles in Bizet's *Carmen*, Rossini's *L'Italiana in Algeri*, and Dvorak's *Russalka*.

BIBL: Dan Sullivan, ''This is Gwen's Day'' in NYT, 15 May 1966. WWA. WWOpera.

DISC: Turn.

KILLINGSWORTH, JOHN DEKOVEN. College educator (b. 20 January 1898 in Fort Worth, Texas). He obtained his musical education at the American Conservatory of Music in Chicago, Illinois (B. Mus., 1931), and the Chicago Conservatory of Music (M. Mus., 1937). His teaching career included tenures at Samuel Huston College in Austin, Texas (1918-20), Rust College in Holly Springs, Mississippi (1920-24), Clark College in Atlanta, Georgia (1924-29, 1933-1950), and Brick Junior College in North Carolina (1929-33). He was active as a church organist and choral director, serving as musical director of the Philharmonic Society Choir and the Gammon Theological Seminary Choir in Atlanta, among other groups. In 1936 he was director of music for the Board of Education of the Methodist Episcopal General Conference. He exerted wide influence as a teacher; among his students who later became well known were Ruby Elzy and Luther Saxon.

BIBL: Layne. WWCA, 1950.

KING, ALBERT. Bluesman (b. 25 April 1923 in Indianola, Mississippi). He taught himself to play guitar as a youth and played for local social entertainments and in clubs of Osceola, Mississippi, at an early age. He began playing professionally in the late 1930s in Osceola. Thereafter he was active in various places, including South Bend, Indiana, where he also sang with the Harmony Kings Gospel Quartet; St. Louis, Missouri, and nearby areas; and in Osceola with his own group, the In the Groove Band. In 1951 he went to Gary, Indiana, where he came into contact with bluesmen living in nearby Chicago, Illinois—among them, James (''Jimmy'') Reed,* with whom he frequently teamed to play engagements. He recorded with Reed in 1951 and as a soloist in 1952, but did not begin to record regularly until 1953. After returning south, he finally settled in St. Louis during the mid-1950s, where he organized a new group. By the 1960s he had established himself as one of the leading country-blues singers and, as well, as a rhythm 'n' blues singer. He toured widely in the United States and abroad, appearing at rock, blues, and jazz festivals, in concert halls, on television shows, and in nightclubs. In 1969 he performed with the St. Louis Symphony Orchestra. He played in the Mississippi Delta tradition. His best-known recordings included "Blues at sunrise," "Let's have a natural ball," "Travelin' to California," "Laundromat blues," and "You got me walking."

BIBL: BWW. *Cadence* (May 1977). StamPRS.

DISC: TudBM.

KING, B. B. Bluesman. See **KING, RILEY.**

KING, BETTY JACKSON. Music educator (b. 17 February 1928 in Chicago, Illinois). As a child she studied piano with her mother, Gertrude Smith Jackson.* She began singing in a family trio with her mother and sister Catherine at an early age. She received her musical education in the public schools of Chicago, Illinois, at Wilson Junior College in Chicago, and at Roosevelt University in Chicago (B. Mus., 1950; M. Mus., 1952). She studied further at Oakland University in Rochester, Michigan; Glassboro College in New Jersey; the Peabody Conservatory of Music in Baltimore, Maryland; the Westminister Choir College in Princeton, New Jersey; and the Bank Street College in New York. Her teaching career included tenures at the University of Chicago Laboratory School; Dillard University in New Orleans, Louisiana; and the public schools of Wildwood, New Jersey, where she also served as director of the high-school choir. She was active as a church choir director in Chicago and in New York at the Riverside Church and also as an accompanist for professional groups and voice teachers. She toured as a lecturer and choral clinician. She began composing pieces during her childhood and became seriously interested in composition in college. Her oratorio, *Saul of Tarsus*, received several performances after its premiere in 1952 by members of the Chicago Music Association. In addition to *Saul*, her best-known works were the cantata *Simon of Cyrene*, the choral work *God's Trombones*, and her spiritual arrangements. She served as president of the National Association of Negro Musicians* (1979-). Her honors included awards from civic, community, and professional organizations.

BIBL: Questionnaire. *The Crisis* (December 1979). IntWWMusic. WilABW.

KING, CORETTA SCOTT. Social activist/Concert singer (b. 27 April 1927 in Marion, Alabama). Although best known as a social activist, she prepared for a career in music and toured as a concert singer after graduating from college. She obtained her musical education at Antioch College in Yellow Springs, Ohio (B.A., 1951) and the New England Conservatory of Music in Boston, Massachusetts (B. Mus., 1954). She made her debut as a concert soprano at Springfield, Ohio, in 1948. She toured widely as a concert singer, including concerts in India in 1959. In her later career she gave Freedom Concerts. She taught voice at Morris Brown College in Atlanta, Georgia, in 1962. Among her numerous honors was an honorary doctorate from the New England Conservatory (1971). She was married to Martin Luther King.

BIBL: WWA. WWBA. WWAW.

KING, FREDDIE. Bluesman (b. 3 September 1934 in Gilmer, Texas; d. 28 December 1976 in Dallas, Texas). He began playing guitar at the age of six, studying with his mother and an uncle, Leon King. He moved to Chicago when he was sixteen; there he developed his style under the influence of Sam ("Lightnin' ") Hopkins,* Riley ("B. B.") King* (not a relative), Aaron ("T-Bone") Walker,* "Muddy Waters" (née McKinley Morganfield),* and "Howlin' Wolf" (née Chester Burnett).* He credited Eddie Taylor and James ("Jimmy") Rogers* with having taught him how to use guitar picks. He began playing in local clubs and in 1958 made his professional debut. He first recorded in 1957 but did not record extensively until 1960. Those with whom he recorded and/or performed included Albert King, Walter ("Brownie") McGhee,* "Sonny Terry" (née Saunders Terrell),* Howlin' Wolf, and Muddy Waters. He also toured widely, beginning in 1960, in the United States, Europe, and Australia, appearing in concert halls, nightclubs, and at jazz and blues festivals. In 1963 he settled in Dallas, Texas.

BIBL: BWW. LivBl 6 (Autumn 1971), 31 (March-April 1977). Robert Neff and Anthony Connor, *Blues* (Boston, 1975).

DISC: LeSl. TudBM.

KING, HATTIE McINTOSH. See **McINTOSH, HATTIE.**

KING, JUANITA. Opera singer (b. 2 March 1924 in Macon, Georgia; d. 2 April 1974 in New York, New York). She obtained her musical education at Knoxville College in Knoxville, Tennessee; at Fisk University in Nashville,Tennessee; and at the Sutphin School of Music in New York. She sang leading roles with Mary Cardwell Dawson's* National Negro Opera Company; she also sang with other opera companies, including the New York City Opera and the Baltimore Civic Opera. In her later career she conducted a music studio and was a voice coach. Her honors included a John Hay Whitney Fellowship (1963) and a New York City Arts Award (1964).

BIBL: Black press, incl. AmstN, 27 April 1974.

KING, RILEY B. ("B. B."). Bluesman (b. 16 September 1925 near Indianola, Mississippi). He was born on a plantation between Indianola and Itta Bena, Mississippi. He came from a musical family: his grandfather played ''bottleneck guitar,'' and both parents sang. As a child he sang in a spiritual quartet at school and later sang in church choirs. Self-taught on the guitar, he began playing about 1943; he formed a gospel quartet, the Elkhorn Singers, that sang in local churches. After a brief period of service in the United States Armed Forces (1943), where he sang blues for servicemen, he sang with church groups, including the St. John Gospel Singers in Greenville, Mississippi. In 1946 he went to Memphis, Tennessee, and thereafter sang blues primarily. His early style development was influenced by his listening to recordings of (''Blind'') Lemon Jefferson,* Alonzo (''Lonnie'') Johnson,* Charlie Christian,* and Django Reinhardt. In Memphis he performed with a group composed of Robert (''Bobby Blue'') Bland,* Earl Forrest, and Johnny Ace (née John Alexander); he also played with others, including Alex (''Rice'') Miller* (also known as ''Sonny Boy Williamson, No. 2''). After appearing with Miller on the Hadacol Show on radio station KWEM in West Memphis, he had his own show, the Pepticon Boy Show, on Memphis radio station WDIA. During the years 1950-53 he was a disc jockey on radio station WDIA in Memphis. His billing as Riley King, the Blues Boy from Beale Street, was gradually shortened to Blues Boy, and finally to B. B. He made his first recording in 1949 and thereafter recorded regularly.

His career developed slowly. He toured extensively during the 1950s, playing mostly small clubs; after 1953 he toured with his own group. By the mid-1960s he had established himself as one of the nation's leading blues singers. He appeared in theaters, ballrooms, concert halls, and nightclubs; he sang at the major jazz and blues festivals, and appeared on television shows. In 1969 he made his first European tour, which was eventually followed by regular tours worldwide over the next decade. During the 1970s he toured increasingly on college campuses, sometimes combining concert and lecture, along with other appearances; and he appeared in films, including *Black Music in America* (1970), *Medicine Ball Caravan* (1971), *Blues under the Skin* (1972), and *Let the Church Say Amen* (1973), among others. In 1975 he settled in Las Vegas, Nevada. He received numerous awards from the music and recording industries; awards from civic and government associations, including an Humanitarian Award from the Federal Bureau of Prisons (1972); honorary doctorates from Tougaloo College (1973) and Yale University (1977); appointment to boards and national committees of various organizations and institutions, such as the John F. Kennedy Performing Arts Center (1971); and keys to various cities and indentification of ''B. B. King Days.'' He was called ''King of the Blues,'' in acknowledgment of his towering position as a blues guitarist, possibly the best of his time. His well-known recordings were innumerable, including ''The thrill is gone,'' ''Sweet little angel,'' ''Caldonia,'' and ''I like to live the love I sing about,'' among many others. His publications included the *B. B. King Blues Guitar* (1970), the *B. B. King Songbook* (1971), and *Blues Guitar, A Method by B. B. King* (1973). His cousin was bluesman Booker T. (''Bukka'') White.*

BIBL: BWW. *Ebony* (November 1969). MeeJMov. Oliv. ShawHS. StamPRS. WWA. WWBA.

DISC: LeSlBR. TudBM.

KING, WALLACE. Concert singer (b. c1840 in Newark, New Jersey; d. 20 February 1903 in Oakland, California). He early revealed musical talent and was taken over as a protégé by Peter O'Fake* of Newark, who gave him musical training along with Sylvester Russell.* He first attracted attention in 1871 as the ''silver-voiced tenor'' in the Hyers Sisters'* company, which also included baritone John Luca.* When the Hyers expanded their company about 1876 to produce drama, he remained with the company. In 1883 he performed with Callender's Consolidated Spectacular Minstrel Festival, which also featured the Hyer Sisters and Sam Lucas,* among others, and toured as far west as San Francisco, California. Charles and Gustave Frohman, the white owners of the show, had ambitious plans for organizing a Colored Opera Troupe in the fall of 1883, but their plans never reached fruition. Wallace was to have been a member of the troupe, along with the Hyers, Marie Selika,* and others. By 1886 the Hyers had reorganized their dramatic company, and Wallace again toured with it. About 1888 he joined the Hicks-Sawyer* Minstrels and traveled with the troupe to Australia and the Far East.

BIBL: Black press, incl. NYGlobe, 19 May 1883; CleveG, 1 May 1886, 20 November 1886, 1 June 1887; IndF, 14 March 1903. Simond.

KING, WILLIAM ("BILLY"). Minstrel/Vaudeville entertainer (b. c1875 in Whistler, Alabama; d. 19??). He toured during the 1890s with his own company, the King and Bush Wide-Mouth Minstrels. After the company was disbanded, he joined the Richard and Pringle Georgia Minstrels company, which featured thereafter the ''big four comedians'': King, William (''Billy'') Kersands,* Clarence Powell, and James Crosby. When King left the company, he settled in Chicago, Illinois, where he founded an organization to produce shows, vaudeville acts, and revues. Sometime before 1912 he organized the Billy King Stock Company (also known as King and [Marshall] Rogers' All-Star Revue), which toured widely in the South, then made its debut in 1916 at the Grand Theater in Chicago. Included in his company in its early years were Cordelia McClain,* Hattie McIntosh* (whom he married in 1912), Benton Overstreet,* and Estella Harris* and the Jass Singers. The Jass group left King in 1917, but by 1920 he had formed his own Jazz Babies. Little is known of his later career except that he continued to be active professionally. In 1937 he was elected president of the Colored Actors' Protective Association in New York.

BIBL: Black press, incl. CDef, 6 May 1916, 30 December 1916, 27 December 1919, 8 May 1920; NYAge, 12 April 1937. Flet, pp. 196-197.

KING CURTIS. See **OUSLEY, CURTIS.**

KIRBY, JOHN. Jazz bassist (b. 31 December 1908 in Baltimore, Maryland; d. 14 June 1952 in Hollywood, California). He learned to play trombone as a youth. About 1925 he went to New York, where he later bought a tuba and played with Bill Brown and his Brownies (1928-30). Thereafter he began playing string bass, studying with Wellman Braud* and George (''Pops'') Foster.* During the 1930s Kirby played with various groups, including Fletcher Henderson* (1930-34, 1935-36), William (''Chick'') Webb* (1934-35, 1936), and Lucius (''Lucky'') Millinder* (1936). During the years 1937-50 he led his own sextet in New York nightclubs, theaters, and hotels; he also played long residencies in Chicago, Illinois, and cities on the West Coast. In 1940 he had his own radio series, ''Flow Gently, Sweet Rhythm,'' which featured Maxine Sullivan* (his wife at that time). During the years 1941-42 he appeared regularly on Duffy's Tavern radio show. During the years 1939-42 his sextet was very popular and recorded extensively. Over the years its personnel included William (''Buster'') Bailey, Sidney (''Big Sid'') Catlett,* William (''Billy'') Kyle, Russell Procope, Charlie Shavers, and O'Neil Spencer. In 1950 he organized a quartet, then later played with Henry (''Red'') Allen* and Wilbur (''Buck'') Clayton.* In 1951 he settled in Los Angeles, California, where he played occasionally with Bennett (''Benny'') Carter* before illness forced him to retire from music. Kirby was a pioneer of small-group leaders during the swing era. His band, billed as ''The Biggest Little Band in the Land,'' was distinctive for its lightly swinging style and skillful arrangements, particularly of the classics in swing style.

BIBL: AlHen. ChilWW. FeaEJ. MeeJMov.

DISC: Jep. Kink. RustJR. TudJ.

KIRK, ANDREW DEWEY ("ANDY"). Jazz bandleader (b. 28 May 1898 in Newport, Kentucky). His family moved to Denver, Colorado, when he was a child, and he obtained his musical education in the public schools there. He played piano as a child and later studied alto saxophone. His teachers included Franz Rath, Walter Light, and Wilberforce Whiteman (father of Paul Whiteman), among others. In 1924 he began playing professionally with George Morrison's* band on tuba and bass saxophone. He toured and recorded with Morrison. In 1925 he joined Terrence Holder's band, later called the Dark Clouds of Joy, then Clouds of Joy. When Holder left the band in 1929, Kirk was asked to take over its leadership; the band's first engagement was at Kansas City, Missouri. The band made its first recordings under Kirk the same year. Thereafter he toured widely with his Clouds of Joy, at first primarily in the Middle West, then eventually throughout the nation (1930-48). By the mid-1930s the band had earned international recognition, was recording regularly, and was particularly popular on the college circuit. He managed to keep his big band through the Depression and World War II, but finally had to disband in 1948 because of economic pressures. Thereafter he was active as a hotel manager, but continued to organize big bands for special occasions and local dances. Those who played in his groups at one time or another over the years included Harold (''Shorty'') Baker,* Don Byas,* Howard McGhee,* Edward (''Crackshot'') McNeil, Theodore (''Fats'') Navarro,* Charlie Parker,* George (''Buddy'') Tate, John Williams, Mary Lou Williams,* Ben Webster,* and Lester Young,* among others. His best-known performances were ''Until the real thing comes along'' and ''Cloudy.'' Kirk's Clouds of Joy was an important swing band in the Kansas City tradition; its style was distinctive for its blues orientation and use of riff formulas, to which Mary Lou Williams contributed as one of the early arranger-pianists.

BIBL: ASCAP. ChilWW. FeaEJ. MeeJMov. Russ. WWCA, 1950.

DISC: Jep. Kink. RusJR. TudJ.

KIRK, RAHSAAN ROLAND (née **RONALD T. KIRK**). Jazz saxophonist (b. 7 August 1936 in Columbus, Ohio; d. 5 December 1977 in Bloomington, Indiana). As a child he studied trumpet, then changed to saxophone and clarinet. He received his musical education at the Columbus [Ohio] School for the Blind (he was blind from infancy, but could see light). He began to play professionally during his high-school days; by the time he was fifteen he was leading his own jazz groups. When he was sixteen he had a dream in which he played three instruments simultaneously; thereafter he determined to realize his dream and developed skills to that end, choosing the tenor saxophone, the stritch (similar in sound to an alto saxophone), and the manzello (similar to a soprano saxophone). He produced harmonies through the use of trick fingering. Sometimes he added flutes to the ensemble, using the bell of the saxophone as a storage place. During the 1960s he toured widely in the United States, Canada, Europe, Australia, and New Zealand, and won international recognition for his groups. He also played with others, including Charles Mingus* (1961), Dexter Gordon,* and John Griffin* (1963), among others. He first recorded in 1960, with the help of Webster Lewis in obtaining a contract; thereafter he recorded extensively. He was regarded by his contemporaries as a highly original, even unique, musician. Although criticized at first for his gimmickry, he later won respect for his consummate musicianship. His repertory included the traditional and the avant-garde; although he was a prolific composer, he also adapted popular music, and sometimes classical, for his use. He received numerous awards from the music industry.

BIBL: Black press, incl. AmstN, 4 February 1978. BMI (January 1970). FeaEJ. FeaGitJS. MeeJMov. NYT, 6 December 1977. Michael Ullman, *Jazz Lives* (Washington, D.C., 1980). WWA. WWBA.

DISC: Jep. TudJ.

KITT, EARTHA MAE. Actress/Popular-music singer (b. 26 January 1928 in North, South Carolina). Although best known as an actress, she was a singer in her early career. Her first professional experience was as a soloist with the Katherine Dunham* Dance Troupe in 1948, with whom she toured in the United States and abroad. When the troupe returned home, she remained in Paris, France. Thereafter she toured widely as a nightclub singer in Europe, Turkey, Egypt, and the United States. She appeared in numerous stage works, including some musicals, such as *New Faces of 1952* and *Shinbone Alley* (1957). The film musicals in which she appeared included *New Faces of 1953* and *St. Louis Blues* (1958). She recorded regularly and appeared on radio and television programs. In the 1960s she settled in Los Angeles, California; later she taught dancing classes. Her honors included a citation as "Woman of the Year" by the National Association of Negro Musicians* (1968). She published three autobiographical works: *Thursday's Child* (1956), *A Tart is Not a Sweet* (19?), and *Alone With Me* (1976).

BIBL: Black press, incl. AmstN, 7 January 1978. CurBiog 1955. WWA. WWBA.

KNIGHT, GLADYS M. Rhythm 'n' blues singer (b. 28 May 1944 in Atlanta, Georgia). She came from a musical family; both parents sang with Wings Over Jordan.* She made her first public appearance at the age of four as a gospel singer and won first place in a "Ted Mack Amateur Hour" television show when she was eight. During the years 1950-53 she toured with the Morris Brown [University] Choir of Atlanta, Georgia, and sang regularly on local concerts. In 1953 she became one of the original members of The Pips (later called Gladys Knight and the Pips*), a singing-dancing group, and remained with the group through the 1970s. She also toured as a soloist (contralto) with Lloyd Terry Jazz Ltd. (1959-61). She won many awards from the music industry, both as a soloist and as a member of the Pips.

BIBL: *Ebony* (June 1973, March 1975) StamPRS. WWA. WWBA.

DISC: TudBM.

KNIGHT, MARIE. Gospel singer. See **THARPE, ROSETTA.**

L

LaBELLE, PATTI (née **PATRICIA LOUISE HOLTE).** Rhythm 'n' blues singer (b. 24 May 1944 in Philadelphia, Pennsylvania). She began singing in public at an early age and performed with groups during her high-school years. In 1960 she organized a vocal trio called Patti LaBelle and the Bluebells, which included Nona Hendryx (b. 4 October 1944 in Trenton, New Jersey) and Sarah Dash (b. 18 August 1945 in Trenton). The trio began to record in 1963, thereafter toured widely on the nightclub circuit, and soon attracted national attention. During the mid-1960s Cindy Birdsong (b. 15 December 1944 in Camden, New Jersey) sang with Patti, then left in 1967 to join The Supremes.* During the early 1970s the singing act was reorganized with Patti as a soloist accompanied by an instrumental group and girls' trio and called simply LaBelle. The act was distinctive for its space-age costumes and frenetic rhythm 'n' blues style. By 1973 LaBelle was again a trio with Hendryx and Dash; Hendryx wrote many of the trio's songs. In December 1976 the trio disbanded, and Patti continued her career as a soloist.

BIBL: *Ebony* (September 1978). *Dawn Magazine* (August 1978). StamPRS.

DISC: TudBM.

LaBREW, ARTHUR. Musicologist/Educator (b. 18 January 1930 in Detroit, Michigan). He studied piano as a child. He received his musical education in the public schools of Detroit, Michigan; at the Oberlin Conservatory of Music in Ohio (B. Mus., 1952), where he studied with David Moyer; and the Manhattan School of Music in New York (M. Mus., 1955). He studied further with Leo Podolsky, Ernesto Berumen, and Giovanni d'Alessi (in Treviso, Italy), and at the Mozarteum in Salzburg, Austria. His teaching career included tenures at the District of Columbia Teachers College in Washington, D.C. (1970-72), Southern University in Baton Rouge, Louisiana (1973-75), and lectureships at Wayne County Community College and Highland Park Community College (both in Michigan). During the years 1972-73 he was curator of the E. Azalia Hackley* Memorial Collection of the Detroit Public Library. He toured regularly as a lecturer, speaking at meetings of professional organizations, on college campuses, and for historical societies and institutions. He was active in community-music affairs, served as a church minister of music, and conducted a piano studio. He published many books (privately), including *Elizabeth T. Greenfield**: *The Black Swan* (1969), *Francis Johnson** (1974), *Studies in Nineteenth-century Afro-American Music* (1975), and *Black Musicians in the Colonial Period* (1977). His honors included awards from civic and professional organizations, including the National Association of Negro Musicians* and the Tanglewood Music Festivals.

BIBL: Questionnaire. Robert Stevenson, ed., *Inter-American Music Review* (Spring/Summer 1979).

LACY, CLEOTA COLLINS. See **COLLINS, CLEOTA.**

LADIPO, DURO. Writer/Composer (b. 18 December 1931 in Oshogbo, Western State, Nigeria). He came from a musical family; his grandfather was a celebrated drummer. He sang in his school choir as a child. When he was fifteen years old, he wrote his first play. Thereafter he wrote works that were similar in style to American musicals, folk operas, and religious musicodramas. In 1961 his Easter Cantata, produced at All Saints Church in Oshogbo, provoked controversy because of his introduction of drums into the church. After that he began producing his works in schools, theaters, and on television. In 1962 he was one of the founding members of the Mbari Mbayo Club, an actors-playwrights group. In 1963 he founded his own Duro Ladipo Players, which later became the National Theatre of Nigeria. His early style development was influenced by Ulli Beier, who advised him to use historical themes, traditional drumming, and classical Yoruba poetry in his stage works. Ladipo's best-known folk operas included *Oba Kosa*, *Oba Moro*, *Oba Waja*, *Eda*, and *Moremi*. He toured widely with his theater group in Africa, Europe, and the United States. His productions attracted wide attention at the Berlin Theatre Festival (1964) and at the British Commonwealth Festival (1965). Ladipo was a pioneer in creating a new style of Nigerian modern theater; his dramas incorporated all aspects of traditional African theater—dance, music, mime, poetry, and drama—fused into a whole.

BIBL: Black press, incl. CDef, 3 March 1975. WWAfrLit.

LADNIER, THOMAS ("TOMMY"). Jazz trumpeter (b. 28 May 1900 in Mandeville, Louisiana; d. 4 June 1939 in New York, New York). He studied trumpet with Willie (''Bunk'') Johnson* when he was fourteen. About 1917 he went to Chicago, Illinois; thereafter he played with various groups, including John H. Wickcliffe, Charlie Creath,* Ollie Powers, Joseph (''King'') Oliver,* and Sam Wooding,* among others. During the years 1925-26 he toured with Wooding in Europe, then left the band to play with the Louis Douglas Revue. He returned to the United States in 1926 and for the next decade or so worked with groups at home and in Europe, among them, Fletcher Henderson* (1926-27), Wooding again (1928-29, including tour in Europe), Benton Peyton (1929 in Europe), Noble Sissle* (1930-31 in Europe and in New York), Sidney Bechet* (1931-33), and others. He also led his own group at intervals, both in France (1930) and in the United States; worked with the Berry Brothers dance team (1931); and recorded with Lovie Austin,* Ida Cox,* Bechet, Rosetta Crawford, Gertrude (''Ma'') Rainey,* and Bessie Smith,* among others. He performed with Bechet on John Hammond's From Spirituals to Swing concert at Carnegie Hall in New York on 23 December 1938. He was one of the leading jazz trumpeters of the 1920s-30s in the New Orleans/Chicago traditions.

BIBL: AlHen. ChilWW. FeaEJ. Souch.

DISC: Kink. RustJR.

LAINE, CLEO (née **CLEMENTINE DINAH CAMPBELL).** Jazz singer (b. 28 October 1927 in Southall, Middlesex (near London), England). She began her career in 1953 in a nightclub, singing with a band led by John Dankworth, whom she later married. By 1956 her popularity in England was firmly established. She made her American debut in September 1972 at Alice Tully Hall in New York. Thereafter she toured widely, singing in concert halls and clubs, appearing on television shows, and singing at the major jazz festivals. She also sang in musicals, including the London revival of *Show Boat* (1971-73), in which she sang the role of Julie. Her repertory included a variety of styles: jazz, blues, folk, popular, lieder, and other art songs.

BIBL: *Essence* (November 1975). FeaJS. FeaGitJS.

DISC: Jep.

LAKE, OLIVER. Jazz saxophonist (b. 14 September 1942 in Marianna, Arkansas). His family moved to St. Louis, Missouri, when he was an infant. As a child he played in a drum and bugle corps. Later he studied saxophone and flute. He obtained his musical education at Lincoln University in Jefferson City, Missouri B.A., 1968), Washington University in St. Louis (1970), and through private study with Ron Carter* and Oliver Nelson.* His teaching career included tenures in the public schools of St. Louis (1968-71), at Webster College in St. Louis (1969), and at the Creative Music Foundation at Woodstock, New York (summers, 1975-). He began playing professionally at an early age. In 1967 he formed the Oliver Lake Quartet. During the years 1972-74 he toured in Europe as leader of a BAG band (Black Artist Group); served as a musician-in-residence at the American Center for Artists and Students in Paris, France; studied electronic music in Paris; and performed duo-concerts with Anthony Braxton* and others. After returning to the United States he settled in New York. He recorded regularly, performed as a soloist and with others. He belonged to the avant-garde; he was one of the founders of BAG, an organization of St. Louis musicians with goals similar to those of AACM in Chicago, Illinois (Association for the Advancement of Creative Musicians). In December 1976 he was a co-founder of the World Saxophone Quartet, which included Julius Hemphill, Hamiet Bluiett, and David Murray. His best-known compositions were *Violin Trio* (1972), *Heavy Spirits* (1975, and the multi-media theatre piece, *Life Dance of Is* (1979).

BIBL: Questionnaire. FeaGitJS.

LAMBERT FAMILY. (Fl. in nineteenth century in New Orleans, Louisiana). The father, Richard Lambert, began to attract attention in New Orleans about 1840 as a music teacher and father of talented sons and daughters. Lucien Charles (b. c1828) became a pianist, went to Paris for further study, and attracted wide attention when he performed there in 1854. Some time before 1878 he settled in Brazil, where he became involved in the manufacturing of pianos. Sidney (b. c1838) played piano and composed pieces for piano and other instruments and voice. He settled in Paris, where he conducted a music studio. His son, Lucien Leon Guillaume Lambert (1858-1945), was a composer and performer of considerable note. John (b. c1862) was active as a cornetist and played at one time in the St. Bernard Brass Band of New Orleans. There was also a son, E. Lambert, whom James Trotter* identifies as the leader of the St. Bernard Band.

BIBL: Des, pp. 82-83. LaBrew. Trot, pp. 338-340; pp. 69-80, 86-95 of the music section.

LAMOTHE, LUDOVIC. Concert pianist/Composer (b. 22 May 1882 in Port-au-Prince, Haiti; d. 4 April 1954 in Port-au-Prince). He came from a musical family: his grandfather played violin, and his father played piano. He began music study at an early age with Virginie Sampeur. He obtained his musical education at l'Institution St. Louis de Gonzague, where he studied piano and clarinet. In 1910 he went to France for further study at the Paris Conservatory of Music, where his teacher was Louis Diémer. Thereafter he won recognition as a concert pianist, particularly for his interpretation of Chopin, and as a composer. His best-known compositions were the dance collection *Sous la Tonnelle*, "Les Jasmins," "Fantasies," and two Valses de Concert. He used Haitian elements in his music.

BIBL: Dumervé.

LANE, WILLIAM HENRY ("MASTER JUBA"). Minstrel dancer (b. c1825 in New York (?), New York; d. 1852 in London, England). Reputedly, William Lane was taught his craft by one "Uncle Jim Lowe." He first attracted public attention as a dancer in Almack's dance hall, operated by Pete Williams in the Five Points district of the city of New York. English writer Charles Dickens saw him there on a visit to America in 1842 and later discussed the dancer in his book, *American Notes for General Circulation* (London, 1842). Circus-man Phineas T. Barnum is credited with having introduced Master Juba to the minstrel stage. In 1844 a contest at the Bowery Amphitheater in New York "between the two most renowned dancers in the world, the original John Diamond and the colored boy Juba" brought celebrity to Juba as a breakdown dancer. Soon thereafter he became a member of the Ethiopian Serenaders, the first of his race to join a white minstrel troupe. In 1846 he toured with Charley White's Minstrels as a jig dancer and tambourine player, and later with the Georgia Champion Minstrels. In 1848 he went to London, England, joined Pell's Ethiopian Serenaders, and became a public idol, a status he maintained until his death.

BIBL: George G. Foster, "The Dance-House" in *New York by Gas Light* (New York, 1850; reprint in SouRBM). Charles Dickens, *American Notes*; reprint in BPIM 3 (Spring 1975). Thomas L. Nichols, *Forty Years of American Life* (London, 1964; reprint of section on Juba in BPIM 3 [Spring 1975]). Edward LeRoy Rice, *Monarchs of Minstrelsy* (New York, 1911). Marian Hannah Winter, "Juba and American Minstrelsy" in *Chronicles of the American Dance*, ed. by Paul Magriel (New York, 1948).

LATEEF, YUSEF ABDUL (née **WILLIAM EVANS**). Jazz flutist/oboist (b. 9 October 1920 in Chattanooga, Tennessee). His family moved to Detroit, Michigan, when he was five years old. He first studied musical instruments in the public schools of Detroit and played alto and tenor saxophone in high school. His musical education was obtained at Wayne University in Detroit (1950-54?), the Manhattan School of Music in New York (B.A., M.Mus. Ed.), and the University of Massachusetts at Amherst (D. Mus. Ed., 1975). He also studied at the Teal School of Music in Detroit for two years and privately in New York with various teachers, among them, Harold Jones* and John Wummer. His teaching career included tenures in the Stan Kenton Summer Jazz Clinics (1963) and at Manhattan Community College of the City University of New York (1972-). He began playing jazz professionally after graduating from high school. He first toured briefly with the 'Bama State Collegians, then with various groups, including Lucius ("Lucky") Millinder* (1946), Oran ("Hot Lips") Page,* and John Birks ("Dizzy") Gillespie* (1949). In 1949 he embraced the Islam faith, changing his name to Lateef; a year later he enrolled in college. He began playing flute in 1954 and thereafter developed his skills on oboe, bassoon, and such exotic instruments as the rabat, shanai, and argole. In 1955 he formed the Yusef Lateef Quintet, which played a long residency in a Detroit nightclub. In 1960 he settled in New York, and the same year organized a quartet, whose personnel changed over the years. In 1961 its members were Barry Harris,* Ernie Farrow, and Lex Humphries, along with Lateef; in 1973 the quartet was composed of Kenneth ("Kenny") Barron,* Robert ("Bob") Cunningham, Albert ("Tudi") Heath, and Lateef. In addition to performing with his quartet, he toured with various groups, including Charles Mingus* (1960-61), Babatundi Olatunji* (1961-62), and Julian ("Cannonball") Adderley.* His touring took him throughout the world, including performances as far away as the Tokyo Festival in Japan. Lateef was an important innovator of the 1960s; his music reflects the influence of European, Near Eastern, oriental, jazz, and blues elements. He wrote primarily music for chamber groups in addition to jazz compositions and music for film soundtracks. His best-known compositions were *Trio for Piano, Violin, and Flute* (1965), *Flute Book of the Blues* (1964), and *Symphonic Blues Suite* for quartet and orchestra.

BIBL: Black press, incl. [Pittsburgh] *New Courier*, 20 July 1974. BMI (May 1971). FeaEJ. FeaJS. FeaGitJS. MeeJMov. WWA. WWBA.

DISC: Jep. ModJ.

LAWLERS, MINNIE. See **DOUGLAS, MINNIE.**

LAWRENCE, WILLIAM. Concert accompanist/singer (b. 20 September 1895 in Charleston, South Carolina; d. 17 March 1981 in New York, New York). His father was a church organist. As a child he studied piano with an older sister and later with local teachers. He obtained his musical education at Avery Normal Institute in Charleston, South Carolina; at the New England Conservatory in Boston, Massachusetts; at Boston University; privately with Frances Grover; and in Paris (1929-32). In 1916 he became accompanist for Roland Hayes,* and the next year he toured on the Swarthmore Chautauqua Circuit with the Hayes Trio, which included William Richardson* along with himself and Hayes. Thereafter he taught at South Carolina State College in Orangeburg, then returned to Boston for voice study. In 1923 he toured with Hayes in Europe. Later he settled in New York, where he conducted a music studio for many years and was active as an accompanist. During the 1930s he was co-director, with Alfred Ross, of the Symphonette Orchestra. His best-known arrangement of a spiritual was "Let us break bread together," which was widely sung by Marian Anderson.*

BIBL: Hare. NYT, 21 March 1981.

LAWS, HUBERT. Symphonic/jazz flutist (b. 10 November 1939 in Houston, Texas). He came from a musical family: his mother was a church pianist, his father sang, and his sister Eloise and brother Ronald* ("Ronnie") became professional musicians. He first studied flute in public school and played in the school band. He obtained his musical education at Texas Southern University in Houston (1956-58), Los Angeles State College in California (1958-60), and the Juilliard School of Music in New York (B. Mus., 1964), where he studied with Julius Baker. He also studied flute privately with Clement Barone of the Houston Symphony. In 1957 he was a soloist with the Houston Youth Symphony Orchestra. His early jazz experience was playing alto saxophone with a junior-high-school group, which continued its activity over a long period (1954-60) and included Wilton Felder, Wayne Henderson, Nesbert ("Stix") Hooper, Joseph ("Joe") Sample, and Henry Wilson. The group's first name was the Swingsters, then later it was called The Modern Jazz Sextet, then The Nite Hawks, and finally The Jazz Crusaders.* During the 1960s Laws played with various groups, including W. Mongo Santamaria* (1963), John Lewis's* Orchestra U.S.A. (1964), and the Berkshire Festival Orchestra in Massachusetts (1961), among others. He also played and/or recorded with such entertainers, jazzmen and gospel figures as James Cleveland,* Richard Davis,* Lena Horne,* James ("J. J.") Johnson,* and Arthur Prysock,* among others. During the 1970s he received increasing recognition for his own groups; he gave annual concerts at Carnegie Hall in New York during the years 1973-75 and toured widely in the United States, Europe, Africa, Japan, and Canada, appearing in concert halls, nightclubs, and at the major jazz festivals. He recorded both jazz and classical music, including the twentieth-century composers Stravinsky and Satie. He played in the Metropolitan Opera orchestra (1968-72) and served as an alternate in the New York Philharmonic (1971-74). He was also active as a free-lance studio musician, playing on television shows, in Broadway-musical orchestras, and in commercial music. His publications included a manual titled *Flute Improvisation*. He received many awards from the music industry.

BIBL: FeaJS. FeaGitJS. MeeJMov. WWA. WWBA.

DISC: Jep.

LAWS, RONALD ("RONNIE"). Jazz saxophonist (b. 3 October 1950 in Houston, Texas). See **LAWS, HUBERT.**

LAWSON, RAYMOND AUGUSTUS. Concert pianist (b. 23 March 1875 in Shelbyville, Kentucky; d. February 1959 in Hartford, Connecticut). He came from a musical family; his father played several instruments and was a member of the Shelbyville brass band. He began organ study at the age of seven and was a church organist by the time he was ten. He studied piano with a local teacher, W. J. Harvey, then went to Fisk University at Nashville, Tennessee, for preparatory work and college. He was the first black student to complete the degree program in music at Fisk (diploma, 1895; B.A., 1896). Later he matriculated at the Hartford School of Music in Connecticut (B. Mus., 1901), where he studied with Edward Noyes, and studied privately in Europe with Ossip Gabrilowitsch (1911). In 1896 he settled in Hartford, Connecticut, and established a music studio. He had begun to tour as a concert pianist during the summer of 1895 and continued to tour throughout his career, playing in many of the major cities of the nation over the years. He played with the Hartford Symphony in 1911 and again in 1919; thereafter he appeared regularly with the orchestra. His honors included an honorary doctorate from Howard University (1931).

BIBL: Black press. WWCR 1915.

LAWSON, WARNER. Choral conductor/College professor (b. 3 August 1903 in Hartford, Connecticut; d. 3 June 1971 in Washington, D.C.). He came from a family of professional musicians. His paternal grandfather played in a brass band; his father, Raymond Lawson,* was a concert pianist and music teacher; and his mother was a soprano soloist with the Fisk Jubilee Singers.* He began piano study at the age of five with his father. He obtained his musical education at Fisk University in Nashville, Tennessee (B.A., 1926); at the Yale University School of Music in New Haven, Connecticut (B. Mus., 1929); at Harvard University in Cambridge, Massachusetts (M.A., 1936); and privately with pianist Artur Schnabel in Berlin, Germany (1929-30). His teaching career included tenures at Fisk University (1930-34), North Carolina A & T College at Greensboro (1936-42), and Howard University in Washington, D.C. (1942-71), where he was appointed in 1942 Dean of the School of Music and in 1960 Dean of the College of Fine Arts, which he helped to establish. During his early career he toured as a concert pianist. Later he won national recognition as a choral director and educator. During his stay in Boston he conducted a semi-professional chorus sponsored by the WPA, and he had an excellent college choir at North Carolina A & T. His contemporaries felt that he raised the art of choral singing among black colleges to its highest level with his chorus at Howard University. By 1951 the Howard choir had become the unofficial chorus of the National Symphony Orchestra and sang with the orchestra regularly. In 1960 the choir toured in Europe under sponsorship of the United States Department of State. Lawson toured widely as a lecturer, as a guest choral conductor, and as a conductor of choral workshops for high schools and universities at festivals. His honors included appointments to committees of national professional and government organizations and honorary doctorates from the Hartt College of Music (1954) and Temple University (1966).

BIBL: Black press, incl. AmstN, 8 June 1971. Rayford Logan, *Howard University: The First Hundred Years* (New York, 1969). *The Washington Star*, 8 June 1971. WWCA, 1933-44.

LAYNE, MAUDE WANZER. Music educator (b. 22 December 1899 in Charleston, West Virginia; d. 3 February 1951 in Charleston [?]). She studied piano as a child and was an organist for a local Sunday school. She obtained her musical education at the Macalester College Conservatory of Music in St. Paul, Minnesota (where she completed the regular course of study in 1915), at Denver University in Colorado, Columbia Teachers' College in New York, Chicago Musical College in Illinois (B. Mus. 1923, M. Mus. 1924), and the American Conservatory in Fontainebleau, France (1925). In 1921 she was appointed supervisor of music for the Negro public schools in Charleston, and she remained in that position until her death. She toured as a concert singer and accompanist early in her career; later she toured with the Garnet High School band, which she organized and directed. Her honors included appointments to committees and boards of professional organizations, awards from fraternal organizations and the Urban League (1948), and an honorary doctorate from the New York College of Music (1937). She is best remembered for her book *The Negro's Contribution to Music* (Philadelphia, 1942).

BIBL: Black press, incl. IndF, 17 July 1915. Layne. WWCA 1950.

LAYTON, J[OHN] TURNER, JR. Vaudeville entertainer (b. 2 July 1894 in Washington, D.C.; d. 1978 in London, England [?]). He studied music with his father, John Turner Layton,* and attended Howard University Dental School in Washington, D.C. He settled in New York during the early twentieth century and there played in James Reese Europe's* dance orchestra. Later he formed a vaudeville act and songwriting team with Henry Creamer.* Their best-known songs included "After you've gone," "Dear old Southland," "Way down yonder in New Orleans," and "Strut Miss Lizzie." He and Creamer also contributed songs to Broadway musicals, as early as 1911 to the Zeigfeld Follies and to such musicals of the 1920s as *Three Showers*, *Spice of 1922*, and *Strut Miss Lizzie*. In the early 1920s Layton formed a vaudeville partnership with Clarence ("Tandy") Johnstone, and the two men went to London, England, in 1924. They played long residencies in London theaters and nightclubs and occasionally toured on the continent. Layton was also active as a correspondent for the *Chicago Defender*, writing columns about the activities of black musicians abroad. In 1935 the Layton-Johnstone team was dissolved. Layton continued to perform as a soloist. In later years he became one of London's best-known variety artists of the stage and BBC television.

BIBL: MS. Black press, incl. CDef, 27 September 1927, 13 June 1927, 1 June 1935, 26 February 1955; NYAge, 14 July 1933. Hare.

DISC: Kink.

LAYTON, JOHN TURNER, SR. Music educator (b. c1841 in Freeport, New Jersey; d. 14 February 1916 in Washington, D.C.). Little is known of his early life. He obtained his musical training from the Round Lake Conservatory at Martha's Vineyard, Massachusetts; Northwestern University in Evanston, Illinois; and the New England Conservatory in Boston, Massachusetts. He served in the United States Armed Forces during the Civil War, then after the war settled in Washington, D.C. In 1883 he began teaching music in the public schools there; in 1895 he was appointed the first male director of music for the colored schools and retained the position until his death. His successor in the position was Josephine E. Wormley (during the years 1916-25). He was choir director for the Metropolitan AME Church for forty-three years, beginning in 1873. During his tenure the Church sponsored concerts by the leading black performing artists of the nation. In 1902 he helped to organize the Samuel Coleridge-Taylor Choral Society (incorporated in 1903) and served as its musical director. In November 1904 and again in November 1906 the Society brought Coleridge-Taylor* from England to the United States to conduct concerts of his music. In May 1913 the Society staged a Testimonial Concert in honor of Coleridge-Taylor, with Layton conducting selections from works of the composer. In addition to his activities as music educator and choral director, Layton achieved distinction as a hymn writer. He was responsible for the musical aspects in the compiling and editing of the eleventh edition of the AME hymnal (1897), the first hymnal of that denomination to include music. Layton's best-known hymns were "O God, we lift our hearts to Thee," "We'll praise the Lord," "Saviour, hear us through Thy merit," and the anthem "Jesus, lover of my soul." He received an honorary B.A. degree from Wilberforce University (1906).

BIBL: Black press, incl. IndF, 22 February 1916; *Washington [D.C.] Bee*, 19 February 1916. Frank Metcalf, *American Writers and Compilers of Sacred Music* (New York, 1925).

LEDBETTER, HUDDIE WILLIAM ("LEADBELLY") (aka WALTER BOYD). Bluesman (b. 29 January 1889 in Mooringsport, Louisiana; d. 6 December 1949 in New York, New York). As a child he taught himself to play first a concertina and then the guitar. He began playing at an early age for local social entertainments in Leigh, Texas, where he lived and later as a child in nearby towns. At some time during this period he taught himself to play a twelve-string guitar, and earned the title "King of the Twelve-String Guitarists." His musical development was influenced by the folksongs and field hollers he heard in his community as well as the barrel-house piano playing he heard in Shreveport, Louisiana. His wanderings as an itinerant bluesman took him over Louisiana and Texas, where he met ("Blind") Lemon Jefferson* in Dallas in c1912. The two bluesmen formed a team that played for a period on street corners and in local bars and clubs. Leadbelly was imprisoned several times (1918-25; 1930-34; 1939-40), and he developed a huge repertory of prison songs. He won his freedom in 1925 by writing a song for Texas governor Pat Neff, who gave him a pardon. In 1932 he made recordings from a Louisiana prison for the Library of Congress field expedition of folklorist Alan Lomax. This brought wide recognition of his talent and in 1934 a release for good behavior. The same year he went to New York under Lomax's sponsorship and began performing professionally in 1935. Thereafter he toured extensively in the United States and, beginning in 1949, in Europe, appearing in concert halls, nightclubs, on radio programs, and on college campuses. Those with whom he performed included ("Big Bill") William Lee Conley Broonzy,* Woody Guthrie, "Sonny Terry" (née Saunders Terrell),* and Josh White,* among others. His performances were used on many film soundtracks, although not on the biographical film, *Leadbelly*, produced in 1976. Of the more than seventy songs he wrote (or reshaped), the best-known are "Good morning blues," "Goodnight, Irene," "The midnight special," "Rock Island Line," and "Gray goose."

BIBL: BWW. LivBl 19 (January-February 1975). LivBl 30 (November-December 1976). MeeJMov. Oliv. StamFCW.

DISC: DiGod. Kink. Max Jones and Albert McCarthy, eds., *A Tribute to Huddie Ledbetter* (London, 1946). LeSl. TudBM.

LEE, A. CLIFTON. See **DESCENDENTS OF MIKE AND PHOEBE.**

LEE, BILL. See **LEE, WILLIAM.**

LEE, EVERETT. Symphony orchestra conductor (b. c1919 in Wheeling, West Virginia). He began violin study at the age of nine. He obtained his musical education in the public schools of Cleveland, Ohio; at the Cleveland Institute of Music (B. Mus., 1940), where he studied violin with Joseph Fuchs; at the Berkshire Music School in Tanglewood, Massachusetts; and at the Saint Cecilia Academy in Rome, Italy. He also studied conducting with Dimitri Mitropoulos, Max Rudolph, and Bruno Walter, among others. He first attracted attention as a conductor when he became a substitute conductor for the Broadway musical *Carmen Jones* in 1944. His career development was encouraged by Leonard Bernstein and Boris Goldovsky, with whom he studied conducting at Tanglewood in 1946. Later he founded the Cosmopolitan Little Symphony, which made its debut in 1948 at Town Hall in New York. During the next decade he was active as a guest conductor with various orchestras, including the New York City Opera orchestra and the Louisville [Kentucky] Symphony. In 1956 he settled in Europe. His conducting career there included tenures as musical director with the Munich [Germany] Traveling Orchestra (1957-62) and the symphony orchestra of Norrkoping, Sweden (1962-72). He also toured widely as a guest conductor in Europe, South America, and the United States. In 1973 he returned to live in the United States, accepting the position of musical director of the Symphony of the New World,* with which he remained until its demise in 1977. In 1976 he made his conducting debut with the New York Philharmonic, and he continued to serve as guest conductor for leading orchestras of the nation. In 1979 he became musical director of the symphony orchestra of Bogota, Columbia. His wife was Sylvia Olden Lee.*

BIBL: Black press, incl. AmstN, 11 January 1969, 8 October 1977; CDef, 30 April 1955; NYAge, 29 September 1945, 26 October 1946. Russell Davis, *Black Americans in Cleveland* (Washington, D.C., 1972).

LEE, GEORGE EWING. Jazz bandleader (b. 28 April 1896 in Kansas City, Missouri; d. 2 October 1958 in Los Angeles, California). He came from a musical family: his father was violinist-leader of a string trio, and his sister, Julia Lee,* became a professional musician. Before 1916 Lee had a group that played for local social events. In 1917 he played baritone saxophone in an army band of the United States Armed Forces. After World War I, he organized a trio, which included his sister Julia and drummer Bruce Redd, and played in Kansas City nightclubs. Later he formed big bands, one of which was called George E. Lee and His Novelty Singing Orchestra and another, Lee and His Brunswick Recorders. During the 1920s-30s his groups were the leading groups of Kansas City, along with those of Bennie Moten* and Jay McShann.* Over the years his sidemen included Albert ("Budd") Johnson,* Jesse Stone,* and Charlie Parker,* among others. He won wide recognition for his ballads and novelty songs and was sometimes billed as "Cab Calloway* of the Middle West." His best-known performances were of "If I could be with you," "Paseo strut," and "St. James Infirmary." In 1940 he settled in Detroit, Michigan, and in 1945, moved to Los Angeles, California. Lee's band was the first big band in Kansas City, and he was credited with being the first male singer with a band in the area.

BIBL: Black press, incl. *The Kansas City Call*, 7 November 1958. ChilWW. Russ.

DISC: RustJR.

LEE, JULIA. Jazz pianist (b. 31 October 1902 in Boonesville, Missouri; d. 8 December 1958 in Kansas City, Missouri). She came from a musical family: her father was violinist-leader of a string trio, and her brother, George Lee,* became a professional musician. She began piano study at the age of ten. Before she was fourteen, she was playing in her brother's band, which entertained at local social events. By 1916 the Lee band had become professional; later it was called George E. Lee and His Novelty Singing Orchestra. Julia toured with the band as a vocalist-pianist (1916-33). After Lee's group was disbanded, she toured as a free-lance soloist, performing in nightclubs and theaters and playing long residencies in Kansas City, Missouri (1934-48, 1950s); Los Angeles, California (1948-50); and Chicago, Illinois (1923, 1939). She recorded regularly as a soloist, with her brother, and with such jazzmen as Jay McShann* and Tommy Douglas. Her style was distinctive for its blues-inflected singing and boogie-woogie piano.

BIBL: ChilWW. FeaEJ. Russ.

DISC: Jep.

LEE, PAULINE JAMES. Educator (b. 18?? in Louisiana, Missouri; d. 19?? in Chicago, Illinois). Her family moved to Chicago, Illinois, when she was a child. She obtained her musical education in the public schools of Chicago and at Northwestern University in Evanston, Illinois. She also studied privately with N. Clark Smith,* Herman DeVries, and Mable Roane, among others. During the second decade of the twentieth century she toured widely with E. Azalia Hackley* as accompanist and also as assisting artist, singing contralto solos. In 1920 she founded the Chicago University of Music, which received its state charter in

1921. Over the years her faculty included some of the nation's most renowned black musicians, among them, N. Clark Smith,* Florence Cole Talbert,* Goldie Guy Martin, Walter Gossette,* Clarence Cameron White* (in summers), and Hazel Harrison,* among others. About 1925 opera singer Ernestine Schumann-Heink gave Lee a fine building in which to house the music school.

BIBL: ChiHistSoc. Black press, incl. CDef, 12 February 1916, 15 January 1921, 2 February 1923.

LEE, SYLVIA OLDEN. Concert pianist/Accompanist (b. c1919 in Washington, D.C.). Her mother was a singer and pianist. She first studied piano as a child with her mother, then later with Cecil Cohen and William Allen.* She obtained her musical education at the Oberlin Conservatory of Music in Ohio (B. Mus.), where she studied with Frank Shaw. Her teachers also included Victor Wittgenstein. Her teaching career included tenures at Talladega College in Alabama and Dillard University in New Orleans, Louisiana. She toured extensively during the 1940s with singers Carol Brice* and Paul Robeson.* She also toured in a two-piano team with Thomas Kerr.* She was married to Everett Lee.

BIBL: Black press, incl. AmstN, 29 July 1944.

LEE, WILLIAM JAMES ("BILL"). Jazz bassist (b. 23 July 1928 in Snow Hill, Alabama). He came from a musical family: his father played cornet/trumpet, his mother was a concert singer, and his brother Clifton ("Cliff") and sisters Consuela and Grace became professional musicians. When he was eight years old he played drums in a family band; at the age of eleven he studied flute. He obtained his musical education at the local Snow Hill Institute, which was founded by his maternal grandfather, William James Edwards; and at Morehouse College in Atlanta, Georgia (B.A., 1951), where he studied with Willis Lawrence James* and Kemper Harreld.* In 1950 he began playing string bass. He went to Chicago, Illinois, in 1952; thereafter he played with various groups, including George Coleman, Johnny Griffin, Andrew Hill,* and Clifford Jordan,* among others. In 1959 he settled in New York, where he later worked with such groups as Ray Bryant, Joseph ("Philly Joe") Jones,* and Phineas Newborn and with folk musicians Judy Collins, Theodore Bikel, Odetta,* and Josh White,* among others. In 1968 he founded the New York Bass Violin Choir, composed of Ron Carter,* Richard Davis,* Lisle Atkinson, Milton ("Milt") Hinton,* Samuel ("Sam Home") Jones, and Michael Fleming, along with himself. The Choir employed guest drummers for performances. In 1972 he was co-founder/co-leader of The Brass Company, along with Billy Higgins and William ("Bill") Hardman. He toured widely and recorded with a family group called Descendants of Mike and Phoebe,* which included his sisters Consuela Lee Morehead* (piano), A. Grace Lee Mims* (soprano), brother A. Cliff Lee* (trumpet/fluegelhorn), and himself on bass. His primary composing interest was in theater music, although he wrote in a variety of forms. His best-known works were the folk or jazz operas *The Depot*, *One Mile East*, *Baby Sweets*, and *The Quarters*, and his music for the stage play *A Hand Is on the Gate*.

BIBL: Black press, incl. AmstN, 21 October 1978. FeaGitJS.

LeMON, LILLIAN MORRIS. Music teacher (b. 19 January 1894 in Chicago, Illinois; d. 30 December 1962 in Indianapolis, Indiana). She studied piano as a child with her mother, a music teacher. She obtained her musical education in the public schools of Indianapolis, Indiana; at Jordan Conservatory of Music in Indianapolis (B. Mus., 1917); and at Indiana University in Bloomington. She toured as accompanist with Florence Cole Talbert* and Carl Diton,* among others. In 1919 she founded the Cosmopolitan School of Music and Fine Arts in Indianapolis. She also taught in the public schools there for many years and was active as a choir director and church chorister. She was the sixth president of the National Association of Negro Musicians (1932-34).

BIBL: Information from Bertha Howard. Layne. WWCA, 1927-41.

LEMONIER, TOM. Songwriter (b. 29 March 1870 in New York, New York; d. 14 March 1945 in Chicago, Illinois). He was active with vaudeville companies in New York during the first decades of the twentieth century. He wrote the musical score for *Rufus Rastus* (1905), which starred Ernest Hogan. His best-known song was "Just one word of consolation." During the 1920s he settled in Chicago, Illinois, and began writing church music.

BIBL: ASCAP. Black press, incl. CDef, 11 December 1926, 21 February 1942; IndF, 24 July 1915.

LENOIR, LUCIE. See **WALKER, RACHEL.**

LEON, TANIA. Orchestra conductor (b. 14 May 1944 in Havana, Cuba). She began piano study when she was four years old. She obtained her musical education at the Carlos Alfredo Peyrellade Conservatory in Havana,

Cuba (B.A., 1963); at the National Conservatory in Havana (M.A., 1964); and at New York University (B.S., 1971; B.A., 1971; M.S., 1973). After completing her musical studies in Havana she earned a degree in business administration (1965). In 1967 she went to New York to further her career as a musician. In 1968 she came into contact with Arthur Mitchell when she was called to accompany one of his dancing classes, and he invited her to associate with his Dance Theater of Harlem, which he was then in the process of forming. She became music director (1970-78), with responsibility for conducting the orchestra and for writing music for the ballet corps. During the 1970s she also was active as musical director-conductor for such productions as the Broadway musical *The Wiz* (1978) and a public television series, WNET's "Dance in America" (1977, 1978). She toured as a guest conductor, appearing with orchestras in the United States and in Europe, including orchestras at the Festival of Two Worlds at Spoleto, Italy (1971) and at the Nervi Festival in Genoa, Italy (1972). During the early 1970s she established a summer workshop series to provide performance opportunities for black artists and composers. Over the years the project expanded and eventually found support in the Brooklyn Philharmonia Orchestra, which appointed her musical director and conductor for the Brooklyn Philharmonia Community Concerts annual series (1978-). She was active also as pianist for the orchestra and as assistant conductor to the conductor, Lukas Foss. Her best-known compositions were the ballets *Tones* (1970) and *Haiku* (1974); the score for a play by Mario Pena, *La Ramera de la Cueva* (1974); and *Spiritual Suite*.

BIBL: Questionnaire. Handy. NYT, 22 June 1980.

LESTER, JULIUS B. Writer (b. 27 January 1939 in St. Louis, Missouri). Although a writer by profession, he was also active as a musician, particularly in the field of folk music. He obtained his education at Fisk University (B.A., 1960). He directed the Newport Folk Festival (1966-68), served as associate editor of *Sing Out* (1964-), and published *The 12-String Guitar as Played by Leadbelly* with Pete Seeger (1965). He also sang professionally and recorded folk music.

BIBL: WWA. WWBA.

LEW, BARZILLAI ("ZELAH or ZEAL"). Military fifer and drummer (b. 5 November 1743 in Groton, Massachusetts; d. 19 January 1821 in Dracut, Massachusetts). His father, Priamus (or Primus), was a musician in the French and Indian War of 1745. Barzillai was active as a fifer in the French and Indian War of 1761, serving in Thomas Farrington's Company of Groton, Massachusetts. He also was a fifer in 1775 at the Battle of Bunker Hill as a member of Captain John Ford's Company of the Twenty-Seventh Regiment of Massachusetts; later he served in Captain Varnum's Company, Colonel Iona Reed's Regiment. After the war he formed a dance orchestra with his twelve children and his wife, Dinah Bowman. One contemporary historian reports that the Lew family "formed a complete band, and furnished music on all first-class occasions in this vicinity [Middlesex County, Massachusetts] and were called frequently to Boston and even as far away as Portland [Maine]. After they became celebrated their services were required so much at Boston that some of them made it their home during the winter months" (see Hurd, p. 311). Dinah played the pianoforte; it is probable that she was the first black woman in American history to be identified as a pianist. Primus Lew established a dynasty that produced professional musicians through seven generations. Two of the best known were Frederick P. White* and William E. Lew,* both of them active during the late nineteenth and early twentieth centuries.

BIBL: Interview with Mrs. Adelaide Buzzelle Bonitto, a direct descendant of Primus Lew. Caleb Butler, *History of the Town of Groton* (Boston, 1848). GreBD. pp. 278, 417, 452. Hamilton D. Hurd, *History of Middlesex County, Massachusetts* (Philadelphia, 1890), pp. 302, 309-311.

LEW, WILLIAM EDWARD. College professor (b. 1 July 1865 in Dracut, Massachusetts; d. 30 January 1949 in New York, New York). He belonged to the musical dynasty of the Lew family, whose ancestry reached back into the eighteenth century with Primus and Barzillai Lew.* As a child he and his sister Edith played piano duets on local recitals in Boston, Massachusetts. Beginning in the 1880s he was active as choral conductor, serving at the Charles AME Church in Boston and as director of the Columbia Glee Club, among other groups; as church organist for the Union Baptist Church in Cambridge, Massachusetts; and beginning in 1891 as church soloist (tenor) in Methodist and Episcopal churches in Boston suburban areas. About 1884 he joined the Sam Lucas Concert Company with his Lew Male Quartette, which included J. Bunch Stanton, George H. Barnett, and M. Hamilton Hodges,* along with himself, and toured for several seasons. Later he organized a Lew Quintette and led local dance orchestras. His vocal groups also toured independently of the Lucas Company under the management of the Redpath Lyceum Bureau. During the years 1903-06 he toured as chorus conductor with the original Smart Set* Company. Beginning in 1906 he entered a teaching career, which included tenures at Lane College in Jackson, Tennessee (1906-09), where he was head of the department; at Miles Memorial College in Birmingham, Alabama (1909-12); at Samuel Huston College in Austin, Texas (1912-13); at North Carolina A & T College in Greensboro (1916-18); in the public schools of Washington, D.C., and at Harriet Gibbs Marshall's* Washington Conservatory of Music (1913-15, 1919-27); and in the public schools (after-school program) of New York, New York (1930-4?). During the 1920s he published a monthly newsletter, titled *Musical Mention*. Several descendents of Barzillai Lee were active musicians contemporaneous with William Lew, among them, concert violinist Frederick Elliot Lewis (1846-18?), who played in the orchestra for Patrick S. Gilmore's World Peace Jubilee in 1872; pianist-organist Frederick Perry White (1860s-1940), who toured as accompanist with Joseph Douglass,* Marie Selika,* and M. Hamilton Hodges, among others; and jazz guitarist Frederick ("Freddie") P. White, Jr.

BIBL: Interview with Mae Buzzelle Bonitto, direct descendant of Primus Lee through her mother, Adelaide Lew Buzzelle. Trot, p. 180 ff.

LEWIS, ELMA INA. Music promoter (b. 15 September 1921 in Boston, Massachusetts). Although not a professional musician, she was active in the promotion of musical activities and education. She obtained her education at Emerson College in Boston, Massachusetts (B.A., 1943), and Boston University (M. Ed., 1944). Her teaching career included tenures in public schools of Boston and in a settlement house. In 1950 she founded the Elma Lewis School of Fine Arts in the Roxbury community of Boston. In 1968 she procured new buildings, renamed her institution the National Center of Afro-American Artists and the next year opened its doors to 250 students. By the mid-1970s she had made great progress towards realizing her dream of making the Center a "national platform for black artists" as well as a teaching institution (quoted from interview in *Ebony*; see below). Her honors included awards from professional, civic, and community organizations; the Mayor's Citation of the City of Boston (1970); and honorary doctorates from Emerson College (1968), Anna Maria College (1971), Boston College (1971), and Colby College (1972).

BIBL: *Ebony* (June 1970). WWA. WWBA.

LEWIS, FREDERICK ELLIOT. Symphony violinist. See **LEW, WILLIAM.**

LEWIS, FURRY. See **LEWIS, WALTER.**

LEWIS, GEORGE FRANCIS (née **GEORGE ZENON).** Jazz clarinetist (b. 13 July 1900 in New Orleans, Louisiana; d. 31 December 1968 in New Orleans). He played various reed instruments as a child; at sixteen he obtained his own clarinet and began specializing on that instrument. His early professional experience was with the Black Eagles Band in Mandeville, Louisiana. Thereafter he played with various brass bands of New Orleans, including Chris Kelly, the Eureka, Henry ("Kid") Rena (1927-29), the Pacific, and the Olympia (1929-32). He also played with dance orchestras, among them, Buddy Petit (née Joseph Crawford), Edward ("Kid") Ory,* Willie ("Bunk") Johnson* (1942, 1945-46), and many others. Throughout his career he led his own bands, and after 1946 he rarely played with others. He toured widely in the United States, Europe, and Japan. He was musically active until just before his death. During the 1960s he played frequently in Preservation Hall in New Orleans. He was one of the pioneer clarinetists of the New Orleans school; he recorded extensively for his time with others and with his own groups, such as George Lewis and His New Orleans All Stars, George Lewis' Ragtime Band, or the George Lewis Quartet.

BIBL; ChilWW. FeaEJ. Tom Bethell, *George Lewis* (Berkeley, 1977). Fairbarn, Ann (pseud. for Dorothy Tait), *Call Him George*,(New York, 1969). Souch. Jay Allison Stuart (pseud. for Dorothy Tait), *Call Him George* (London, 1961).

DISC: Jep. Kink. RustJR.

LEWIS, HENRY. Symphony orchestra conductor (b. 16 October 1932 in Los Angeles, California). He began piano study at the age of five; by the time he was sixteen he had won a double-bass chair in the Los Angeles Philharmonic Orchestra, Alfred Wallenstein, conductor. He studied music at the University of Southern California in Los Angeles. During his ten-year tenure in the Los Angeles Philharmonic, he devoted his attention to mastering orchestral instruments. He performed with the Seventh Army Symphony during his service in the United States Armed Forces (1955-56), first as a bassist and then as a conductor. He toured in Europe with the army orchestra and came into contact with eminent conductors, who aided his career development. He made his professional debut as a conductor in 1961, when he replaced the ailing Igor Markevitch to conduct the Los Angeles Philharmonic in two concerts. In 1958 he founded the Los Angeles Chamber Players, which toured widely at home and in Europe in 1963. He also was musical director of the Los Angeles Opera Company (1965-68). He made his European debut as a conductor with La Scala Opera at Milan, Italy, in 1965 and his Metropolitan Opera debut in 1972, conducting Puccini's *La Boheme*. In 1968 he was appointed musical director of the New Jersey Symphony (1968-76). He toured widely as a guest conductor, appearing with the leading orchestras of the United States and Europe.

BIBL: *Opera News* (20 January 1973). *Time* (17 February 1961). WWA. WWBA. WWE.

LEWIS, J. HENRY. Choral conductor (b. 13 November 1860 in Washington, D.C.; d. 19? in Washington). He studied with John Esputa, director of the United States Marine Band. In 1891 he organized the Amphion Glee Club in Washington, D.C., which remained active for over forty years. Another of his groups, the Dvorak Musical Association, produced Gilbert and Sullivan's *The Pirates of Penzance* in 1900 at the Academy of Music in Philadelphia, Pennsylvania.

BIBL: Black press, incl. NYAge, 19 March 1908. *The Colored American Magazine* (August 1901), p. 235.

LEWIS, JOHN AARON. Jazz pianist (b. 3 May 1920 in LaGrange, Illinois). His family moved to Albuquerque, New Mexico, when he was a child. He began piano study at the age of seven, encouraged by his mother, who was a professional singer. He obtained his musical education at the University of New Mexico in Albuquerque (B.Mus., 1942) and the Manhattan School of Music in New York (M. Mus., 1953). He began playing for local dances during his high-school years. His interest in jazz was stimulated by the music he heard on radio and recordings and through personal contacts with jazz musicians who performed in Albuquerque, such as Lester Young.* During his service in the United States Armed Forces (1942-45), he met Kenneth ("Kenny") Clarke,* who encouraged him to enter a jazz career. After his discharge from the army he played with various groups, including John Birks ("Dizzy") Gillespie* (1945-48), Illinois Jacquet* 1948-49), Miles Davis* (1949), Lester Young, Charlie Parker,* and Ella Fitzgerald* (1954). Throughout these years he was composing and arranging; his first large-form work was given a premiere by Gillespie in 1947 at Carnegie Hall in New York. In the late 1940s he and three other members of Gillespie's band—Milton Jackson,* Ray Brown,* and Kenny Clarke—formed a quartet to perform on concerts, which later began to perform as an independent unit. At first called The Milt Jackson Quartet, then later The Modern Jazz Quartet,* the group was active for more than two decades (1952-74), with Lewis as musical director. He also was musical director for the annual Monterey [California] Jazz Festivals (1958-). In 1962 he organized Orchestra U.S.A. (1962-65), which had as its aim to "play contemporary music of all kinds, as well as to make new music in non-jazz and jazz idioms and to perform classical music properly" (quoted from article in NYT; see below). The orchestra's personnel included leading jazz and classical musicians and performed works of Lewis, Gunther Schuller, and Gary McFarland, among others. In 1957 Lewis wrote his first film score, *Sait-on jamais* (the English title was *No Sun in Venice*); thereafter he wrote several film scores, including *Odds Against Tomorrow* (1959), *Una storia Milanese* (1962), and *Cities for People* (a television film, 1975). He also wrote music for television shows and for the play *Natural Affection* by William Inge (1963). During the 1970s he toured and recorded as a soloist and occasionally with other jazz pianists, as in 1976 on a tour of Japan with Henry ("Hank") Jones* and Marian McPartland. His teaching career included tenures at the School of Jazz in Lenox, Massachusetts, (beginning in 1957), where he served as head of the faculty; at Harvard University in Cambridge, Massachusetts (summer of 1975); and at the Davis Center for the Performing Arts at City College of the City University of New York (1974-). His best-known large-form works were the ballet *Original Sin* (1961) and the musical *Mahalia* (1978); best known of his smaller compositions were "Three windows" from the film *Sait-on jamais* and the jazz fugues "Concorde" and "Vendome." Lewis was a seminal figure of Third Stream music; his compositions fused jazz elements with European classical forms and procedures.

BIBL: FeaEJ. FeaJS. FeaGitJS. *International Musician* (January 1972, July 1977). MeeJMov. NYT, 6 October 1968. WWA. WWBA.

DISC: Jep. Kink. ModJ. TudJ.

LEWIS, MABEL SANFORD. Concert singer (b. c1902 in Memphis, Tennessee; d. July 1980 in Atlanta, Georgia). Her family moved to Chicago, Illinois, when she was a child. She obtained her musical education in the public schools of Chicago, at the Chicago Musical College (B. Mus., 1924); at the Chicago College of Music, where she studied with Louis Victor Saar; at DePaul University in Chicago (M. Mus.); and in Paris, France, with Isadore Philippe. She also studied voice with Edward Boatner,* Leo Braun, and Abbie Mitchell.* Her teaching career included tenures at the Kansas Vocational School in Topeka, Kansas; at the Chicago Conservatory of Music; and in the public schools of

Chicago. She made her concert debut as a coloratura soprano at Town Hall in New York in August 1941. Thereafter she toured regularly on the concert circuit. She was active as a church organist and also served as a musical producer, staging *The Swing Mikado* in 1939. She was a music editor for *The Chicago Defender* during the 1940s. About 1960 she settled in Atlanta, Georgia.

BIBL: Information from Fanya Wiggins. Black press, incl. CDef, 28 July 1928, 17 September 1938, 18 March 1939.

LEWIS, MEADE ("LUX"). Boogie-woogie pianist (b. 4 September 1905 in Chicago, Illinois; d. 7 June 1964 in Minneapolis, Minnesota). Little is known of his early life except that he lived for a while in Louisville, Kentucky. Beginning in the early 1920s he played first violin, then piano in local nightclubs of Chicago. His style development was influenced by Clarence (''Pine Top'') Smith,* who lived in his apartment building, as did also Albert Ammons.* In 1927 Lewis recorded his ''Honky-tonk train blues,'' which became a classic of the genre (recorded again in 1935). In 1938 he performed on the From Spirituals to Swing Concert produced by John Hammond at Carnegie Hall on 23 December. Thereafter he joined with Ammons and Pete Johnson* to form the Boogie Woogie Trio, which recorded and played in New York nightclubs. He also played and/or recorded as a soloist and in duos with Ammons and Johnson. In 1941 he settled in Los Angeles, California, where he continued to play in clubs, and on radio and television programs.

BIBL: BPIM 2 (Fall 1974), pp. 191-208. ChilWW. FeaEJ. FeaJS. MeeJMov. Oliv.

DISC: Kink. RustJR.

LEWIS, RAMSEY EMANUEL, JR. Jazz pianist (b. 27 May 1935 in Chicago, Illinois). He began piano study at the age of six. He obtained his musical education at Chicago Musical College (1947-54), where he studied with Dorothy Mendelssohn from the time he was twelve; the University of Illinois at Urbana (1953-54), and DePaul University in Chicago (1954-55). During the mid-1950s he played in a group, The Cleffs, which included ''Red'' Holt and Eldee Young. After The Cleffs was disbanded in 1956, he organized the Ramsey Lewis Trio, with Young on bass, Holt on drums, and himself on piano and vocals. His early style development was influenced by the music of Arthur (''Art'') Tatum,* Earl Garner,* and Oscar Peterson.* His trio made its recording debut in 1958; by the mid-1960s it had established an international reputation. In 1966 Holt and Young left, and Cleveland Eaton and Maurice White replaced them. In 1969 White left to join the group Earth, Wind & Fire,* and Morris Jennings took his place. During the 1970s Lewis continued to tour widely and record extensively, writing most of the music played by his group; his trio performed on college campuses, in concert halls and nightclubs, and at the major jazz festivals. He also appeared on televison shows. His best-known performances were ''The in-crowd'' (1965) and ''Upendo ni pamoja'' (''Love is together'') (1972).

BIBL: FeaEJ. FeaJS. FeaGitJS. MeeJMov. StamPRS. WWA. WWBA.

DISC: Jep.

LEWIS, WALTER ("FURRY"). Bluesman (b. 6 March 1893 in Greenwood, Mississippi). His family moved to Memphis, Tennessee, when he was six years old. He began playing guitar as a child but did not play professionally until 1917. For many years he traveled with medicine shows, at first in a jug band that included Gus Cannon,* Will Shade,* and Jim Jackson. In 1927 he made his first recordings and recorded regularly during the next few years. He was overlooked, however, when the revival of public interest in the blues during the 1960s brought other bluesmen of his generation back into professional music. His music was in the traditional Mississippi Delta style with frequent use of bottle-neck guitar technique.

BIBL: BWW. CharCB. Oliv. MeeJMov.

DISC: DiGod. LeSl. TudBM.

LINCOLN, ABBEY (née **ANNA MARIE WOOLRIDGE;** also known as **GABY LEE, AMINATA MOSEKA).** Jazz singer (b. 6 August 1930 in Chicago, Illinois). Although best known as an actress, she began her professional career as an entertainer. She began singing publicly during her high-school days and later toured in Michigan with a dance band. In 1951 she settled in California, where she sang in various nightclubs using the name Gaby Lee. After a club residency in Hawaii (1952-54), she returned to California, singing in nightclubs of Hollywood. In 1956 she changed her name to Abbey Lincoln; the same year she made her recording debut. During the 1950s-60s she sang with a group led by Max Roach* (to whom she was married until 1970). She settled in Los Angeles, California, in 1970, using that city as a base from which she toured widely as a soloist in Europe, Asia, and Africa. She was also active in television, radio, and musicals, including the road company of *Jamaica* (summer, 1959). In 1975 she adopted the name Aminata Moseka.

BIBL: Black press, incl. AmstN, 23 June 1979. FeaEJ. FeaJS. FeaGitJS. WWA, 1970-71.
DISC: Jep.

LIPSCOMB, MANCE. Bluesman (b. 9 April 1895 in Brazos County, Texas; d. 30 January 1976 in Navasota, Texas). Although he played for local entertainments from an early age, he did not become a professional bluesman until he was sixty-five, the time when he made his first recordings. Thereafter he toured widely in the United States, appearing in clubs, concert halls, dance halls, and at the major folk and jazz festivals. He also recorded extensively, not only blues but also reels, ballads, breakdowns, and drags. In addition to appearing in films and on film soundtracks, he was the subject of a documentary, *A Well Spent Life* (1970). His guitar-singing style exerted influence on several of his younger contemporaries, including Bob Dylan, Janis Joplin, and Taj Mahal,* among others.
BIBL: BWW. LivBl 25 (January-February 1976). LivBl 26 (March-April 1976). MeeJMov. Oliv.

LISTON, MELBA DORETTA. Jazz trombonist (b. 13 January 1926 in Kansas City, Missouri). Her family moved to Los Angeles, California, when she was a child. She obtained her musical education in that city's public schools and through private study. She began her professional career at the age of sixteen, playing in the pit orchestra of a local theater (1942-44). During the next decade she played with various groups or individuals, including William (''Count'') Basie,* John Birks (''Dizzy'') Gillespie,* Albert (''Budd'') Johnson,* Clark Terry,* Gerald Wilson, and Billie Holliday* (1949), among others. She was also active as an arranger-composer for Edward (''Duke'') Ellington,* Abbey Lincoln,* Charles Mingus,* Jon Lucien,* Diana Ross,* Randy Weston,* and others. In 1959 she played in the Quincy Jones* orchestra, then played for the Broadway musical *Free and Easy*. During the 1960s she continued to write, including television commercials and music for films, as *The Marijuana Affair*; she taught youth groups in New York, including the Pratt Institute Youth-in-Action Orchestra and the Harlem Back Street Tour Orchestra; and she helped to establish the Pittsburgh [Pennsylvania] Jazz Orchestra (1964). In 1973 she settled in Kingston, Jamaica, where she directed the Department of Afro-American Pop and Jazz at the Jamaica School of Music of the University of the West Indies. She continued to write music, record, and occasionally tour. She was one of the few black female trombonists in the history of American music.

BIBL: *Ebony* (June 1977). FeaEJ. FeaJS. FeaGitJS.
DISC: Jep.

LITTLE, VERA. Opera singer (b. 10 December 1928 in Memphis, Tennessee). She obtained her musical education at Talladega College in Alabama, where she studied with Frank Harrison,* and at the Paris [France] Conservatory, where she studied with M. Jouatte. She also studied with Bärwinkle and Sängerleitner in Berlin, Germany. She made her debut (mezzo-soprano) in the title role of Bizet's *Carmen* with the Berlin Opera in the 1958-59 season.
BIBL: WWOpera.
DISC: Turn.

LITTLE RICHARD. See **PENNIMAN, RICHARD.**

LOCKE, ALAIN LEROY. Writer (b. 13 September 1886 in Philadelphia, Pennsylvania; d. 9 June 1954 in New York, New York). A professor at Howard University in Washington, D.C., he is cited here as the author of books containing information about black musicians: *The New Negro* (1925) and *The Negro and His Music* (1936). He obtained his education at Harvard University in Cambridge, Massachusetts (B.A., 1907; Ph.D, 1918); Oxford University in England (1907-10), where he was a Rhodes Scholar; and the University of Berlin in Germany (1910-11).
BIBL: EAB. WWCA, 1950.

LOCKWOOD, ROBERT (''JUNIOR'') (née **ROBERT LOCKWOOD, JUNIOR**). Bluesman (b. 15 March 1915 in Marvell, Arkansas). He taught himself to play on his grandfather's pump organ as a child when he was living in Helena, Arkansas. About 1928 he came into contact with Robert Johnson,* who taught him to play guitar and was the main influence upon his style development. In 1936 he played for a period with''Sonny Boy Williamson, No. 2'' (Willie ''Rice'' Miller)* on the King Biscuit Time radio show, station KFFA in Helena. He also performed in other southern cities before he went to St. Louis, Missouri, in 1939. There he performed with Peter (''Doctor'') Clayton and Charley Jordan; in 1940 the three bluesmen went to Chicago, where Lockwood remained off and on until 1961, when he settled in Cleveland, Ohio. He first recorded in 1940 and thereafter recorded regularly through the 1970s. Those with whom he performed and/or recorded included Freddie King,* ''Muddy Waters'' (née McKinley Morganfield),* and Williamson, among others.
BIBL: BWW. *Cadence* 4 (April 1978). LivBl, 12

(Spring 1973). MeeJMov. Robert Neff and Anthony Connor, *Blues* (Boston, 1975).

DISC: DiGod. LeSl. TudBM.

LOFTON, CLARENCE ("CRIPPLE"). Boogie-woogie pianist (b. 28 March 1887 in Kingsport, Tennessee; d. 9 January 1957 in Chicago, Illinois). Nothing is known of his early life. He settled in Chicago about 1917 and soon won a wide reputation as a boogie-woogie pianist. During the years 1937-38 he recorded a number of piano solos, of which the best known were "Strut that thing" (later renamed "I don't know") and "Monkey man blues."

BIBL: BWW. ChilWWJ. FeaEJ. LivBl 4 (Winter 1970-71). MeeJMov.

DISC: DiGod. LeSl. TudBM.

LOGAN, WENDELL. College educator/Composer (b. 24 November 1940 in Thomson, Georgia). As a child he studied music with his father, who developed the first instrumental-music program for the Thomson [Georgia] public schools. His early style development was influenced by the music he heard of touring orchestras, entertainers, and musical shows that performed in the community center operated by his father, among them, James Brown,* Antoine ("Fats") Domino,* ("Little") Richard Penniman,* and Silas Green from New Orleans.* He obtained his musical education at Florida A & M University at Tallahassee (B.S., 1962), where he studied with Johnnie V. Lee, William Foster,* and Olly Wilson;* at Southern Illinois University at Carbondale (M. Mus., 1964); and at the University of Iowa in Iowa City (Ph.D., 1968). His teaching career included tenures at Florida A & M. (1962-63, 1969-70); public schools of Rudyard, Michigan (1964-65); Ball State University in Muncie, Indiana (1967-69), Western Illinois University at Macomb (1970-73), and the Oberlin School of Music in Ohio (1973-). He was active with jazz groups and marching/concert bands as a trumpeter and arranger throughout his college years; as a teacher he directed instrumental groups in addition to teaching classes. At Ball State he founded the New Music Ensemble. He composed in a variety of forms, and many of his works used electronic techniques, as *From Hell to Breakfast*, a mixed media collaboration for dancers, speakers, lights, and magnetic tapes, or *In Memoriam: Malcolm X* for choir and magnetic tape. Some of his compositions were written totally within the jazz idiom. His concert music was first recorded in 1969, and thereafter several works were recorded. His best-known compositions were *Proportions for Nine Players* (1969), *Songs for Our Times* (1969), *Music for Brasses* (1973), *Variations on a Motive by John Coltrane* (1975), *Duo Exchanges* (1979), *Five Pieces for Piano* (1978), and *Three Pieces for Violin and Piano* (1979). His honors included grants from the National Endowment for the Arts, the Martha Baird Rockefeller Fund, and the H. H. Powers Fund. He published articles in professional journals and the book *Primer for Keyboard Improvisation in the Jazz/Rock Idiom* (1980).

BIBL: Questionnaire. *Perspectives of New Music* 9 (Fall/Winter 1970).

LONG, AVON. Actor/Entertainer (b. 18 June 1910 in Baltimore, Maryland). Although best known as an actor and dancer, he also sang. He received his musical education in the public schools of Baltimore, Maryland, where he came under the tutelage of W. Llewelyn Wilson* in high school; at the New England Conservatory of Music in Boston, Massachusetts (1929), and at the Allied Art Center in Boston (1929). He began performing professionally during the 1930s, appearing in such places as the Cotton Club and the Lafayette Theatre. Over the years in addtion to appearing in plays he sang in a number of musicals, including *Black Rhythm* (1936), Connie's Inn *Hot Chocolates* revue (1935 revival), *La Belle Helene* (1941), the role of Sportin' Life in Gershwin's opera *Porgy and Bess* (1942, 1965), *Memphis Bound* (1945), *Carib Song* (1945), *Beggar's Holiday* (1946), *Green Pastures* (1951), *Mrs. Patterson* (1954), *The Ballad of Jazz Street* (1959), *Fly Blackbird* (1962), *Don't Play Us Cheap* (1972), Scott Joplin's* opera *Treemonisha* (1974 production), and *Bubbling Brown Sugar* (1975). He also appeared in film musicals and toured as a soloist and with his own groups. He received awards from the theater industry and a citation as Man of the Year in Baltimore in 1976. He composed a musical, *Dear Harriet Tubman*, and wrote a number of songs.

BIBL: Black press, incl. NYAge, 5 September 1942. WWA.

DISC: Turn.

LONGHAIR, PROFESSOR. See **BYRD, HENRY R.**

LOOKS, SAMUEL. Military musician (b. c1794 in Quebec, Canada., fl. early nineteenth century). He was enlisted into the army on 4 July 1814 and assigned to the Company of Captain Harrison and Captain Deshas during the War of 1812 in the United States.

BIBL: GreBD.

LOUDIN, FREDERICK. See **FISK JUBILEE SINGERS.**

LOVE, HERMIONE HORTENSE. Concert singer (b. 21 November 1910 in Muskogee, Oklahoma). She came from a musical family: her grandmother was a singer, and her brother, Everett Robbins, became a professional songwriter. She began piano study at the age of five and first sang on a public concert when she was nine. She obtained her musical education in the public schools of Muskogee, Oklahoma, and of Chicago, Illinois; at Crane Junior College in Chicago; Northwestern University in Evanston, Illinois (B. Mus.Ed., 1931, 1968-76); at the University of Chicago (1934-35); and at DePaul University in Chicago (M.A., 1941). She studied voice further with Nina Bolmar, Frank Laird Waller, Maria Kurenko, Lazar Somoiloff, and in Paris, France, with Godard-Bouderie. Her teaching career included tenures in the public schools of Okmulgee, Oklahoma, and at the Loop College in Chicago (1966-76). She made her concert debut as a soprano in 1941 at Town Hall in New York. Thereafter she toured regularly in the United States, Europe, and the Caribbean. Hall Johnson* included music written expressly for her in his oratorio *The Son of Man* (1946), and Margaret Bonds* made arrangements of spirituals for her in *The Five Spirituals*. She conducted music studios in New York (1946-57) and in Chicago (1931-38, 1957-). She was also active as a church musician, including appointment as minister of music at the Monumental Baptist Church in Chicago (1967-). Her honors included awards from civic and professional organizations and from the Loop College.

BIBL: Interview by Fanya Wiggins. Black press, incl. CDef, 13 December 1979.

LOVE, JAMES L. ("DADDY"). Minstrel manager (b. 7 July 1861 in Jefferson, Texas; d. 7 April 1904 in Chicago, Illinois). He began his career as an entertainer, then became involved in the management of minstrels and, later, of vaudeville entertainers. In 1893 he trained a chorus to sing on concerts in Chicago, Illinois, during the World's Fair (Columbian Exposition). Later he established Daddy Love's Theatrical Exchange in Chicago. He also wrote a column for the Indianapolis, Indiana, newspaper, *The Freeman*, about theatrical events and persons.

BIBL: Black press, incl. IndF, 16 April 1904. Flet, p. 31.

LOVE, JOSEPHINE HARRELD. Concert pianist/ Studio teacher (b. 11 December 1914 in Atlanta, Georgia). She came from a musical family: her father, Kemper Harreld,* was a concert violinist and college music teacher; her uncle, Lucien White, was a music critic. She studied piano as a child and gave her first solo recital when she was twelve. She obtained her musical education at Spelman College in Atlanta, Georgia (B.A., 1933); the Institute of Musical Art in New York (now the Juilliard School of Music, B. Mus., 1934); and Radcliffe College in Cambridge, Massachusetts (M.A., 1936). During the summer of 1935 she studied at the Mozarteum Academy in Salzburg, Austria. In April 1939 she made her concert debut as a pianist at San Diego, California. She had made her college debut on her eighteenth birthday at Spelman College, assisted by violinist Drew Days, and she began touring before her debut in California. She toured widely for several years thereafter, particularly on the college circuit. In 1942 she settled in Detroit, Michigan. In later years she conducted a music studio and established Your Heritage House.

BIBL: Black press, incl. AmstN, 17 December 1932.

LOVELL, JOHN, JR. College professor (b. 25 July 1907 in Asheville, North Carolina; d. 6 June 1974 in Washington, D.C.). A professor of English literature at Howard University in Washington, D.C., he is cited here as the author of a book on the Negro spiritual, *Black Song: The Forge and the Flame* (1972). He obtained his education at Northwestern University in Evanston, Illinois (B.A., 1926; M.A., 1927), and the University of California at Berkeley (Ph.D., 1938).

BIBL: *The Washington Post*, 8 June 1974. WWBA, 1975-76.

LOVING, WALTER. Military bandmaster (b. 17 December 1872 in Lovingston, Virginia; d. February 1945 in Manila, The Philippines). He enlisted as a cornetist with the 24th Regiment United States Infantry in 1893 after graduation from high school in Washington, D.C., and served for five years. In 1898 he attended the New England Conservatory in Boston, Massachusetts, then served in the U.S. Armed Forces at Camp Capron in Fort Thomas, Kentucky, as a chief musician for a year. In September 1899 he was assigned as a chief musician in the 48th Regiment U.S. Volunteer Infantry and served as bandmaster until June 1901, when the regiment was mustered out of service in the Philippine Islands. In September 1901 he was commissioned to organize a band for the government by William Taft, at that time Governor-General of the Philippines. His Constabulary Band toured widely in the United States and won recognition for its superior performances, particularly at the St. Louis World's Fair in 1904, at Atlantic City, New Jersey, in 1909, at the Seattle, Washington, Exposition in 1915, and at the Panama Pacific Exposition in 1915. Loving retired in

1916 but was called back into service as a bandmaster at Manila in the Philippines during the years 1919-23. According to the press, Loving was killed during a Japanese attack on the Philippines during World War II.

BIBL: Black press, incl. CDef, 22 December 1923, 10 March 1945; IndF, 7 October 1899; NYAge 5 April 1906, 12 August 1909, 10 April 1920; Julia Davis, "Walter Howard Loving" in NHBull (May 1970). Hare. JNH 30 (1945), pp. 244-245. NYB, 1921-22, 1925-26.

LOVINGGOOD, PENMAN. Writer/Concert singer (b. 25 December 1895 in Austin, Texas). His father was the founder of Samuel Huston College at Austin, Texas. He began music study at the age of eight with local teachers and obtained his musical training at Samuel Huston. Later he studied privately with William Happich in Philadelphia, Pennsylvania, and with J. Rosamond Johnson* in New York. Sometime before 1920 he settled in New York, where later he was active as a church soloist, concert tenor, music columnist, and music teacher. He made his debut at Town Hall in New York in November 1925. During the early 1930s he sang in J. Rosamond Johnson's quartet and played in W. C. Handy's* orchestra. In 1936 the American Negro Opera Association produced an opera he composed, *Menelek*, with a cast that included Carl Diton* and Eloise Uggams, among others, and with Abbie Mitchell* assisting with the stage direction. He is best remembered for his modest report on black artists of the Harlem Renaissance period, *Famous Modern Negro Musicians* (Brooklyn, 1921). His honors included a Wanamaker Prize for composition and a Griffith Music Foundation Medal. In 1945 he settled in California.

BIBL: ASCAP. Black press, incl. NYAge, 21 November 1925, 14 November 1936.

LOWERY, P[ERRY] G. Bandleader (b. 11 October c1870 in Reece, Kansas; d. 1930s (?) in Cleveland, Ohio). His family moved to Eureka, Kansas, when he was a child and it was there that he first studied music. He played in the family band, beginning on drums but later changing to cornet. He played with minor bands during the first five years of his professional career, then joined the band of *Darkest America* (1895) through the offices of George Bailey, trombonist in the band. Later Lowery played with the Mallory Brothers Minstrels, the band of the Wallace and Hagenbeck Circus, and P.T. Wright's* Nashville Students Concert Company. He first attracted wide attention as the bandmaster for Wright's company during the mid-1890s. In the summer of 1898 he played solo cornet at the Trans-Mississippi Exposition, and the next summer he studied at the Boston Conservatory in Massachusetts. He then served as bandleader for Richard and Pringle's Minstrels. In 1899 he left Wright to organize his own P. G. Lowery's Famous Concert Band and P. G. Lowery's Vaudeville Company. In 1901, he was back with the Nashville Students, now under the direction of I. W. Swain, but left permanently within the year. For the remainder of his career he led bands for circuses during the circus season, including the Sells Brothers and Forepaugh's Circus, Wallace and Hagenbeck, Ringling Brothers, Cole Brothers, and Barnum and Bailey. During the year 1915-16 his band toured with the Richard and Pringle Minstrels, but returned to circus work thereafter. He settled during the 1920s in Cleveland, Ohio, where he conducted a music studio and worked with community groups during the winters. In 1924 he led the Ladies Silver Seal Band. He was regarded by his contemporaries as the best black cornetist of his time. During the early 1900s he published a column, "The Cornet and Cornetists of Today" in *The Freeman* (Indianapolis, Indiana).

BIBL: Black press, incl. CDef, 19 January 1924, 9 May 1942; IndF, 25 December 1897, 17 May 1902, 25 March 1916. Handy. *The Master Musician* v.1, no. 5 (March 1920).

LUANDREW, ALBERT ("SUNNYLAND SLIM"). Bluesman (b. 5 September 1907 in Vance, Mississippi). He taught himself to play first on a house pump-organ, then on piano and guitar. In 1922 he began playing professionally; in 1923 he left home and finally settled in Memphis, Tennessee, where he came into contact with many bluesmen and took his first piano lessons with P. R. ("Piano") Gibson. For the next two decades he was an itinerant pianist, playing alone in clubs and also with other bluesmen and women, including Peter ("Doctor") Clayton, "Memphis Minnie" Douglas,* "Little Buddy" Doyle, ("Blind Boy") Fuller (née Fulton Allen),* Gertrude ("Ma") Rainey,* and "Sonny Boy Williamson, No. 1" (née John Lee Williamson).* His boogie-woogie style was influenced by "Speckled Red" (née Rufus Perryman).* He visited Chicago briefly in 1933 but could not earn a living with his blues, and he returned South. During the early 1940s he settled in Chicago and soon became an important member of the blues establishment, playing with the original "Muddy Waters" (née McKinley Morganfield)* band. In the 1950s he began using electric piano occasionally. He recorded steadily, if not prolifically, and with the renewed public interest in blues during the 1960s his career spurted forward. He toured widely in the United States and abroad, with his own groups and with others, among them, Miles Davis* and Charles ("Chuck") Berry.*

BIBL: BWW. *Cadence* 3 (October 1977). ContKey (March 1978). MeeJMov. Robert Neff and Anthony Connor, *Blues* (Boston, 1975). Oliv.

DISC: Jep. LeSl. TudBM.

LUCA FAMILY SINGERS. Concert ensemble (orig. in New Haven, Connecticut; fl. mid-nineteenth century). The family singing group was organized during the 1840s by the father, John W. Luca (b. 1805 in Milford, Connecticut; d. after 1877 in Zanesville, Ohio), a shoemaker by trade, who taught music and directed a church choir in New Haven, Connecticut. The group included his wife Lisette, her sister Diana Lewis (who lived with the Lucas), and the four boys: John W., Jr. (b. 1820s; d. 1910), Simeon (b. 1830s; d. 1854), Alexander (b. 1830s; d ?), and Cleveland (1838-1872). All the boys sang in their father's church choir, and the mother and aunt had well-trained voices. The children were taught to play musical instruments at an early age. John played cello and double bass, having to stand on a stool to reach the strings. During his high-school years he played in the local dance orchestra led by George Coe. Simeon and Alexander studied violin as children, and Cleveland studied piano. The Lucas sang and played instruments on their concert programs. They first attracted national attention in May 1850 when they sang at an abolition convention at New York. Thereafter they toured widely until 1860, using a wagon to carry their instruments and the piano. After Simeon's death in 1854, contralto Jennie Allen toured with the Luca Singers. In 1859 the three brothers toured through the Middle West with the Hutchinson Family Singers, a white troupe. In 1860 Cleveland accepted an invitation from President Roberts of Liberia, Africa, to teach music in Africa, and his departure broke up the family troupe. Alexander was active thereafter in New York; details of his later career are unknown. John, Jr., was active as a church soloist and concert singer, at first in Washington, D.C., then at Baltimore, Maryland. In 1870 he settled in New York, where Alexander was then living. Later he joined the Hyers Sisters'* company (1871-c1884) as singer, musical director, and stage manager. He spent the last twenty-five years of his life in St. Paul, Minnesota, where he conducted a music studio, directed church choirs, sang on concerts, and produced stage works. In November 1909 *The* [Indianapolis] *Freeman* published a long letter from John Luca, in which he gave an account of the early years of the family troupe.

BIBL: Black press, incl. IndF, 27 November 1909, 3 December 1910. Trot.

LUCAS, CARRIE MELVIN. Concert/vaudeville entertainer (b. 18?? in Newport, Rhode Island; d. July 1908 in Providence, Rhode Island [?]). She began her professional career as assistant artist to Marie Selika* about 1883, playing violin and cornet solos on Selika's concerts. During the 1880s she toured with the Bergen Star Concert Company, which carried on its roster such "prima donnas" as Nellie Brown* and later Flora Batson.* While on tour with Bergen, she met and married Sam Lucas* (she was his second wife). Together they joined Sam T. Jack's Creole Company in 1890, with which they performed a special act titled "Mr. and Mrs. Sam Lucas." In addition to playing violin and cornet, she played banjo, guitar, and mandolin, and sang contralto solos. Jack took his company to Europe, but when he returned to the United States the Lucases remained and toured on the continent. They were divorced before she died. Marie Lucas* was her daughter and Sam's.

BIBL: Black press, incl. IndF, 20 September 1890, 11 July 1908, 9 January 1909; NYGlobe, 28 July 1883. Flet, 71-74.

LUCAS, MARIE. Society dance-orchestra leader (b. c1880s in Denver, Colorado; d. 26 (?) April 1947 in New York, New York). She came from a musical family: her father was the celebrated minstrel Sam Lucas,* and her mother, Carrie Melvin Lucas,* was a violinist and cornetist. Marie received musical training from her parents, at schools in Nottingham, England, and at the Boston [Massachusetts] Conservatory. She began her professional career in the musical show, *The Red Moon* (1909), written and produced by Robert ("Bob") Cole,* J. Rosamond Johnson,* and James Weldon Johnson*; her father played a leading role in the show. She began to attract wide attention in 1915 as the leader of the Ladies Orchestra at the Lafayette Theatre in the Harlem community of New York. She played piano and trombone and was also an arranger. In 1916 she was appointed musical director of the Quality Amusement Corporation, which managed several black theaters along the Eastern Seaboard. Those who played in her all-women's orchestras, either at the Lafayette or at the Colonial Theatre in Baltimore, Maryland, included Alice Calloway (drums), Nettie Garland (trombone), Olivia Porter* (cello), Ruth Reed (cornet), Santos Riviere (bass viol), Nellie Shelton (bass viol), Evangeline Sinto (violin), Florence Sturgess (drums), and Emma Thompson (clarinet). After World War I she led a male dance band and played a long residency at the Howard Theatre in Washington, D.C. During the 1930s Lucas toured widely with her Merry Makers, an all-male group.

BIBL: Black press, incl. CDef, 3 January 1931; CleveG, 25 August 1883; IndF, 19 August 1916, 23 December 1916; NYAge, 13 May 1915; NYGlobe, 11 August 1883. DanceWS. Flet, pp. 74-76. Handy.

LUCAS, SAM (née **SAMUEL MILADY**). Minstrel entertainer (b. 7 August 1840 in Washington, Ohio; d. 9 January 1916 in New York, New York). He went to Cincinnati, Ohio, when he was nineteen; there he became a barber and taught himself to play guitar. After service in the United States Union Army during the Civil War, he entered into show business. He attended Wilberforce University in Ohio (1869) and later taught school for a short period at New Orleans, Louisiana. His first professional experience was as guitarist and caller with Hamilton's Celebrated Colored Quadrille Band; during the years 1871-73 he performed on and off with Lew Johnson's* Plantation Minstrels. In July 1873 he joined Callendar's Georgia Minstrels* as a ballad singer and toured with the group in the United States and abroad. In 1878 he played the title role in an Uncle Tom's Cabin show, thereby becoming the first black actor to play the role (previously played by whites in blackface). The same year he toured with the Hyers Sisters'* company, which produced the shows *Out of Bondage*, *Urlina, the African Princess*, and *The Underground Railroad* during the next few years. Later he toured with Sprague's Georgia Minstrels, which at that time also included James Bland* and José Brindis de Salas,* among others. By 1882 he had settled in Boston, Massachusetts, where he organized his own Hub Concert Company. Members of the company included the male Walker Quintet, Lena Hopkins, and his wife and daughter; he also called upon others, including the DeWolfe Sisters,* to perform on his concerts. In April 1885 the press reported that the Lucas Hub Concert Company was "booked way ahead." Nevertheless, Lucas found time to work with other groups; he sang in the Callender Consolidated Spectacular Minstrel Festival in 1883, he appeared on Bergen Star Concerts from time to time, and he traveled occasionally with concert or minstrel companies.

During the early 1880s he sang with Haverly's Genuine Colored Minstrels but did not travel to Europe with the group. In the fall of 1886 he rejoined the Hyers Sisters to tour with the show *Out of Bondage*. During the 1890s he performed with various shows, among them, Sam T. Jack's *Creole Show* (1890), in which his wife joined him; John W. Vogel's *Darkest America*, John Isham's *Octoroons*, and the Robert "Bob" Cole*/ Billy Johnson* show, *A Trip to Coontown* (1897-1902). During the early 1890s he and his wife toured the nation in a vaudeville act called "Mr. and Mrs. Sam Lucas." The next decade he played leading roles in Ernest Hogan's* show, *Rufus Rastus* (1905-06) and two shows of Bob Cole/Johnson brothers,* *The Shoo Fly Regiment* (1906-08) and *The Red Moon* (1909-1910). He was active as a single on the Loew vaudeville circuit until his retirement from the stage in 1912. He then entered the movies, playing Uncle Tom in a film version of *Uncle Tom's Cabin*. Lucas was regarded by his contemporaries as the "dean of the colored theatrical profession" and was called "Dad." His best-known performances were of "Grandfather's clock," "Carve dat possum," and "Turnip greens"; there is doubt, however, that he actually wrote the songs. He published two song books, *Sam Lucas' Plantation Songster* (Boston, n.d., c 1875) and *Sam Lucas' Careful Man Songster* (Chicago, 1881).

BIBL: Black press, incl. IndF, 20 September 1890, 23 January 1897; NYGlobe, 26 May 1883, 28 July 1883; NYFreeman, 21 June 1884, 2 May 1885, 14 August 1886; NYAge, 13 January 1916. (All obits. give his age at death as seventy-five, thus his birthdate was 1840, not 1848 as given in some sources.) Flet, pp. 67-76. Simond. Trot, p. 312.

LUCIEN, JON (JON LUCIEN HARRIGAN). Jazz singer (b. 8 January 1942 in Tortola, British Virgin Islands). His father was a musician, and his mother belonged to a family with strong singing traditions. His family moved to St. Thomas, Virgin Islands, when he was a child. He learned to play drums, piano, guitar, and string bass before he was twelve years old, helped by his father. Later he studied informally with Marty Clark. He obtained his education in a Catholic boarding school, which he attended until he was seventeen. He began singing with a local group when he was fifteen; his early style development was influenced by the singing of Jesse Belvin and Nathaniel ("Nat King Cole") Coles,* to whose records he listened. After leaving school he sang professionally until 1962, when he went to the United States. Thereafter he played string bass with various groups, but began to record as a singer in 1966. His album *Rashida* (1970), which consisted of music composed by himself, brought him wide recognition. He toured widely on the nightclub circuit and appeared in concert halls and at major jazz festivals. His style was distinctive for its blending of jazz, calypso, and African elements. His use of a patois scat-singing developed from his employment of the voice as an instrument.

BIBL: *Essence* (October 1974). FeaGitJS. NYT, 20 August 1974.

LUNCEFORD, JAMES MELVIN ("JIMMY"). Jazz bandleader (b. 6 June 1902 in Fulton, Missouri; d. 13 July 1947 in Seaside, Oregon). His father was a choir director. The family moved to Denver, Colorado, when he was a child. He obtained his musical education in the public schools of Denver, where he studied with Wilberforce Whiteman (father of Paul Whiteman); at Fisk University (B. Mus., 1926); and at City College in New York (now a unit of City University of New York). During his vacation periods from college he played with various groups in New York, including Wilbur Sweatman,* Elmer Snowden,* and Fred ("Deacon") Johnson.* (There is no documentation for the often-printed allegation that he played with Fletcher Henderson.)* During the years 1926-29 he taught in the public schools of Memphis, Tennessee, and formed a band with his students. In 1929 his group became professional, augmented by former Fisk students, and toured widely, played in local nighclubs, and broadcast over radio station WREC in Memphis. He recorded extensively for his time and appeared in films, including *Blues in the Night* (1941) and *Class of '44* (on the soundtrack, 1973), among others. His orchestra was an important "hot" band of the 1930s-40s, distinctive for its lightly swinging style, to which arranger-trumpeter Melvin ("Sy") Oliver* contributed. His band's best-known performances were "Jazznocracy," "Rhythm is our business," "Organ grinder's swing," "'Tain't what you do," and "Margie."

BIBL: ASCAP. Black press, incl. NYAge, 19 July 1947. ChilWW. FeaEJ. Layne. NHB, 1949.

DISC: Jep. Kink. RustJR. TudJ.

LUTCHER, NELLIE. Jazz pianist/Singer (b. 15 October 1915 in Lake Charles, Louisiana). She studied piano as a child, encouraged by her father, who played string bass with the Clarence Hart band. She joined the band when she was fifteen years old and toured on the nightclub circuit. In 1935 her family moved to Los Angeles, California; thereafter she performed in local clubs as a soloist, playing piano and singing. She first recorded in 1947 and produced a best-selling record, "Hurry on down," which launched her into a successful career as an entertainer. During the 1940s she was active in New York, performing in theaters and nightclubs, as well as on the West Coast. Later she left music as her primary activity, but returned to New York in 1975 to resume her career as an entertainer.

BIBL: Black press, incl. *The* [Pittsburgh] *New Courier*, 30 March 1974. *Ebony* (December 1949). FeaEJ.

DISC: Jep.

LYLES, AUBREY. Vaudeville entertainer (b. c1883 in Jackson, Mississippi; d. 28 July 1932 in New York). His family moved to Indianapolis, Indiana, when he was a child, and later to Chicago, Illinois. He met Flournoy Miller* when both were students at Fisk University in Nashville, Tennessee, and they formed a partnership in 1903 that lasted over twenty-five years. At Fisk Miller and Lyles wrote their first plays together and took part in college theatricals. About 1905 they joined Robert "Bob" Motts's* Pekin Theater Stock Company in Chicago and wrote the book for the company's first production, *The Man from Bam*, with musical score by Joe Jordan.* Other plays they wrote for the Pekin included *The Husband* and *The Mayor of Dixie*. In 1907 they wrote *The Oyster Man* for Ernest Hogan,* who was starring in the play at the time of his death in 1909. By 1910 Miller and Lyles were touring on the B. F. Keith vaudeville circuit. They toured extensively during the next decade in the United States and abroad (1915). In 1920 they wrote the book for the Noble Sissle*/Eubie Blake* musical *Shuffle Along* (1921). Other successful productions of the 1920s, for which they wrote books, included *Keep Shufflin'* (1928), with music by Thomas "Fats" Waller* and James P. Johnson,* and *Running Wild* (1923), with music by Johnson. They starred in all these shows. They also were featured in other musicals, including *Way Down South* (1915), *In Darkeydom* (1914), *Rang Tang* (1927), and *Sugar Hill* (1931). Their Sam Peck and Amos Brown characters in *Sugar Hill* were the direct inspiration for Amos and Andy in the radio/television shows of the same title. Lyles went to Africa during the late 1920s and remained a year, thereby dissolving the partnership, but he returned to perform with Miller for some time before his death.

BIBL: Black press, incl. CDef, 19 February 1910, 3 November 1917, 6 August 1932; NYAge, 21 October 1915, 6 August 1932. Flet, 185, pp. 201-205. Hare.

DISC: RustCED.

LYMON, FRANKIE. Rhythm 'n' blues singer (b. 30 September 1942 in New York, New York; d. 27 February 1968 in New York). He came from a singing family; all the children sang in school groups, on street corners, and for community social events. During his junior-high-school years he sang in a quintet, called The Teenagers, composed of Sherman Garnes (b. 1941), James Merchant (b. c1941), Joseph Negroni (b. c1940), and Herman Santiago (b. c1940)—all pupils at Junior High School 164 (Stitt) in New York and all born in the city. The group sang on school programs and on street corners. Richard Barrett, a singer with The

Valentines, heard them and arranged for a recording session, which led to a recording contract. During 1956 the group, now called Frankie Lymon and The Teenagers, won wide recognition as a leading rock 'n' roll group. They toured widely in the United States and Europe, and appeared on radio and television shows and in the film *Rock, Rock, Rock* (1956). Lymon left the group when he was fifteen years old to begin a career as a soloist but was unsuccessful. His attempt at a comeback in 1967 failed. The best-known performance of The Teenagers was "Why do fools fall in love" (written by Lymon).

BIBL: *Ebony* (January 1967). ShawHS. StamPRS.

M

MABLEY, JACKIE ("MOMS") (née **LORETTA MARY AIKEN).** Entertainer (b. 19 March 1897 in Brevard, North Carolina; d. 23 May 1975 in White Plains, New York). Although best known as a comedienne, she began her professional career as a singer at the age of fourteen. Her talent attracted the attention of the vaudeville team of Butterbeans and Susie (Jody and Susie Edwards),* who aided in her career development and obtained for her employment with T.O.B.A.* (the Theater Owners Booking Association). She toured widely on the vaudeville circuit, appearing in theaters and nightclubs; she also appeared with such jazz groups as William ("Count") Basie* and Louis Armstrong.* Eventually she moved into the field of comedy, changed her name to Jackie Mabley after a friend, and acquired the sobriquet "Moms" because of her unselfishness and sympathy for fellow performers. She made her recording debut in 1960. She also appeared regularly on television shows and in a few films, including *Amazing Grace* (1973).

BIBL: Black press, incl. CDef, 4-11 January 1963. CurBiog (January 1975). *Ebony* (April 1974). NYT, 23 May 1975, 25 May 1975.

McADOO, ORPHEUS MYRON. Vocal ensemble director (b. 1858 in Greensboro, North Carolina; d. summer 1900 in Sydney, Australia). He obtained his musical education at Hampton Institute in Hampton, Virginia (graduated 1876), and thereafter taught for ten years in Virginia schools, including Hampton. In 1886 he joined the Fisk Jubilee Singers* (as baritone), which at that time no longer was sponsored by Fisk University but was directed by Frederic Loudon, although it was composed primarily of original Jubilee Singers. The group toured for three years (1886-89) throughout the world. After returning to the United States, McAdoo organized his own group, calling them the Virginia Jubilee Singers, and set out on a worldwide tour in the summer of 1889. Composed of former Hampton students, the troupe included his brother Eugene and contralto Mattie Allen (b. c1868 in Columbus, Ohio; d. 7 August 1936 in Washington, D.C.), who would later become his wife. His tours during the next decade included South Africa and Australia, among other countries. By 1897 he had two companies, the McAdoo Jubilee Singers and McAdoo's Original Colored American Minstrel and Vaudeville Company. In 1899 he leased the Palace Theater in Sydney, Australia, as a home for his "colored stock company" and invited black artists to join his company, which would tour as well as stage productions in Australia. Among those who joined McAdoo in Australia were Flora Batson,* Gerard Miller, Wallace King,* Billy McClain*, and Henderson Smith.*

BIBL: Black press, incl. IndF, 22 February 1890, 21 August 1897, 1 April 1899, 1 September 1900, 6 January 1901. BPIM 4 (Fall 1976). JNH 22 (January 1937), p. 131.

McAFEE, CHARLES. Bandleader (fl. late nineteenth century in Cleveland, Ohio; d. 28 August or 4 September 1919 in Cleveland). He was active during the late 1880s in Cleveland as the bandleader of the Excelsior Reed Band. It is probable that he received his early musical experience by playing in the dance orchestra of Bergert C. Freeman.* According to the press, he became a member of the Cleveland Philharmonic in 1886. He also performed on concerts as a hart soloist and as a baritone, frequently with tenor Anderson Bowman, who also played in the Excelsior band. He and Bowman were co-leaders of a dance orchestra, which played for social entertainments of both blacks and whites in the city. McAfee was one of the few black harpists of the nineteenth century, along with Myrtle Hart* and Courtney Ewing.

BIBL: Black press, incl. CleveG 21 March 1885, 23 October 1886, 12 March 1887, 6 September 1919. Simond.

McCANN, LESLIE COLEMAN ("LES"). Jazz pianist (b. 23 September 1935 in Lexington, Kentucky). As a child he sang with local groups and was influenced by music he heard in a Baptist church. Through his high-school years he sang with school glee clubs and other groups. During his service in the United States Navy he heard a performance by Erroll Garner* in 1955 and decided to become a jazz pianist. After his discharge from the Navy, he attended the Westlake College of Music in Hollywood, California, and the Los Angeles City College in California. In 1956 he won first prize in an All-Navy Talent Show as a singer, which earned him an appearance on the Ed Sullivan television show. In 1957 he began to play professionally in nightclubs, and the next year he made his recording debut. In 1962 he attracted wide attention for his appearance at the Antibes Jazz Festival. Thereafter he toured extensively in the United States, Europe, Central America, Africa, and Tahiti, appearing in concert halls, on college campuses, in penal institutions, and at the major jazz festivals. Beginning in 1969 he used electronic keyboards in his group, Les McCann, Ltd., which included Harold Davis, Jimmy Rowser, Buck Clarke, and Miroslaw Kudykowski, among others. His style blended elements of jazz, rhythm 'n' blues, popular, rock, and gospel; he composed much of the music he performed, in both traditional and avant-garde styles. He was also active as a volunteer teacher in Schools for Learning in Mezcales, New Mexico, and Los Angeles and as a founder of the Institute of Black American Music that was associated with the Rev. Jesse Jackson's Operation Bread Basket.

BIBL: ASCAP. ContKey (April 1979). FeaJS. FeaGitJS. MeeJMov. WWA. WWBA.

DISC: Jep.

McCARTY, VICTOR EUGENE. Composer (b. 1821 in New Orleans, Louisiana; d. 25 June 1881 in New Orleans) He studied piano with J. Norres in his youth. In 1840 he went to the Paris Conservatory in France, where he studied vocal music, harmony, and counterpoint. It is not known how long he remained abroad. By 1850 he had returned to New Orleans and established himself as a professional musician. He performed on local concerts, primarily as a singer and dramatist, but also occasionally on the piano.

BIBL: Des. LaBrew. Trot, pp. 344-345.

McCLAIN, BILLY. Minstrel/Producer (b. 12 October 1866 in Indianapolis, Indiana; d. 19 January 1950 in Los Angeles, California) He began his professional career in 1883 with Lew Johnson's Minstrels, but had played cornet as early as 1881 in a local band at Crone's (Crown's?) Gardens. In 1886 he toured with the Sells Brothers and Forepaugh's Circus, including a residency in Hawaii. Later during the 1880s-90s he toured with various other groups, including the Hicks* and Sawyer Refined Colored Minstrels, Blythe's Georgia Minstrels, W. S. Cleveland's Colored Minstrels, P. T. Wright's* Nashville Students, and Black Patti's* Troubadours. McClain was credited with having conceived the idea of producing the show *The South Before the War* and persuading Whallen and Martell of Louisville, Kentucky, to finance the show in 1894. During the 1890s he was also stage manager and talent scout for Sam T. Jack's Creole Show, *Suwannee River*, and John T. Vogel's *Darkest America*. In the summer of 1895 he produced *Black America*, which employed a cast of over 365 black entertainers, including singers, dancers, comedians, and male quartets from all over the nation, as well as the band from the United States Ninth Cavalry. In 1899 he left for Australia to tour with the M.B. Curtis All-Star Afro-American Minstrels; after that company was stranded, he joined Orpheus McAdoo's* Jubilee Singers and Concert Company in Sydney, Australia. When he returned to the United States after three years, he wrote a show titled *The Smart Set** and found a backer in Gustavus Hill. The show's first production in 1902 starred Ernest Hogan* and included, among others, Cordelia McClain*, Billy's wife. This show was regarded as the finest produced by blacks since the Bob Cole*/Billy Johnson* show *A Trip to Coontown* (1897-1901). McClain toured on the vaudeville circuit in Europe during the years 1905-c1915. In 1910 he wrote a letter to *The* [Indianapolis] *Freeman* stating that he was the first to introduce the cake walk in a stage production (*South Before the War*) and the first to produce a black vaudeville show in French. After returning to the United States, he settled in Tulsa, Oklahoma, then moved to Washington, D.C., and finally settled in California in 1932. His wife, Cordelia, was also active in vaudeville. In addition to playing with the original Smart Set company, she performed with the Bob Cole/Johnson brothers* company and the George Walker*/Bert Williams* companies.

BIBL: Black press, incl. CDef, 3 November 1917, 23 February 1924; IndF, 25 August 1894, 24 December 1898, 5 August 1899, 23 September 1899, 1 November 1902, 23 April 1910, 8 January 1916. Flet, pp. 99-101.

McCOY (McCULLUM or McCOLLUM), ROBERT LEE ("ROBERT NIGHTHAWK"). Bluesman (b.

30 November 1909 in Helena, Arkansas; d. 5 November 1967 in Helena, Arkansas). He began playing professionally in the 1920s on the harmonica, then later changed to guitar, receiving his first lessons from his cousin, Houston Stackhouse.* About 1932 he went to Chicago, where he soon became a part of the blues establishment. During the 1930s and 1940s he recorded rather extensively and toured widely, particularly in the South and Southwest. He spent some time in Helena, Arkansas, where he played on station KFFA in 1946 and again beginning in 1965; he also broadcast on stations in the Memphis, Tennessee, area. Those with whom he played and/or recorded included his brother Percy McCullum, Stackhouse, Earl Hooker, Jimmy Rogers, Peetie Wheatstraw (née William Bunch), Joe Willie Wilkins,* ("Big Joe") Williams,* and Sonny Boy Williamson, No. 2 (née Willie "Rice" Miller),* among others. He was among the first bluesmen who adopted the elecric guitar. His style was influenced by "Tampa Red" (née Hudson Whittaker)*; he exerted strong influence upon Chicago slide guitarists, particularly "Muddy Waters" (née McKinley Morganfield)* and ("Hound Dog") Theodore Taylor.* A songwriter, his songs were popular among bluesmen; his "Prowling Nighthawk" gave him the nickname Nighthawk. His son, Sam Carr, won recognition as a blues drummer.

BIBL: BWW. LivBl interview of Jimmy Rogers, 14 (Autumn 1973); LivBl interview of Houston Stackhouse, 17 (Summer 1974). Oliv.

DISC: DiGod. LeSlBR.

McCOY, SETH. Concert/opera singer (b. December 1928 in Sanford, North Carolina). He obtained his musical education at North Carolina A & T College in Greensboro (B.A., 1950). After service in the United States Armed Forces, he settled in Cleveland, Ohio, where he studied with Pauline Tesmacher at the Music School Settlement. During the 1950s-early 1960s he sang regularly in church choirs and with other choral groups in Cleveland and toured with a male quintet, the Jubilee Singers, although he earned his living as a postman. In 1963 he went to New York, where he began a full-time career in concert music. He sang tenor with the Robert Shaw Chorale (1963-65) and performed with leading musical organizations in the United States and Canada, particularly in singing solo roles in oratorios and symphonic-choral works. He also gave solo recitals. In 1973 he made his debut with the Bach Aria Group at Tully Hall in New York and remained a permanent member of the group. In February 1979 he made his operatic debut with the Metropolitan Opera, singing the role of Prince Tamino in Mozart's *The Magic Flute*. He was regarded as one of the foremost oratorio tenors in the United States.

BIBL: *Ebony* (May 1979). *Opera News* (10 February 1979). WWA. WWBA.

DISC: Turn.

McDANIEL, ELLAS ("BO DIDDLEY"). Bluesman/Rock 'n' roll entertainer (b. 30 December 1928 near Magnolia, Mississippi). His mother moved to McComb, Mississippi, when he was a baby; he was taken to Chicago as a child. There he began to study violin at the age of seven, and he taught himself to play guitar at thirteen. Soon thereafter he organized a blues trio that played on street corners. He first played professionally about 1947 and made his first recordings in 1955, music that contained elements of the newly emerging rock 'n' roll along with traditional blues elements. During the next decade or so he toured widely and recorded extensively as a rock 'n' roll star, frequently with Charles ("Chuck") Berry.* In the mid-1960s he settled in the San Fernando valley in California and eventually in Los Lunas, New Mexico. He continued to record regularly and to perform a wide variety of blues musics, including rhythm 'n' blues. Along with ("Little") Richard Penniman,* Berry, and Antoine ("Fats") Domino,* he was one of the founders of rock 'n' roll. It was disc-jockey Alan Freed who first called him Mr. Rock 'n' Roll. Ironically, the public became less interested in his recordings than in those of his imitators, particularly the English groups The Beatles and The Rolling Stones.

BIBL: BWW. FeaEJ. Michael Lydon, *Boogie Lightning* (New York, 1974). MeeJMov. Robert Neff and Anthony Connors, *Blues* (Boston, 1975). Oliv.

DISC: LeSl. TudBM.

McDANIEL, HATTIE. Vaudeville entertainer (b. 10 June 1895 in Wichita, Kansas; d. 26 October 1952 in Los Angeles, California). She came from a musical family: her father had his own touring tent show, the McDaniel Company, and her mother was a gospel singer. Her family moved to Denver, Colorado, when she was a child, and she obtained her musical education in the public schools there. At the age of seventeen she attracted attention when she sang with George Morrison's* orchestra on a radio program. During the 1920s-30s she toured widely on the vaudeville circuit with Morrison (1924-25) and others, singing in stage revues, on radio shows, and in films, including *Show Boat* (1936). She was often billed as "The Female Bert Williams"* or "The Colored Sophie Tucker." She recorded with the Lovie Austin* Serenaders and Richard M. Jones's* Jazz Wizards. During the mid-

1930s she turned to acting, and in 1940 she was the first of her race to win an ''Oscar'' from the Academy of Motion Picture Arts and Sciences for her performance in *Gone with the Wind*.

BIBL: BWW. Black press, incl. AmstN, 28 April 1979. NAW. WWCA, 1950.

DISC: DiGod. RustJR.

McDOWELL, FREDERICK (''MISSISSIPPI FRED''). Bluesman (b. 12 January 1904 in Rossville, Tennessee; d. 3 July 1972 in Memphis, Tennessee). Little is known of his early life. He lived for some time in Memphis, Tennessee, but finally settled in Como, Mississippi. He made his first recordings in 1959 for folklorist Alan Lomax and the Library of Congress folk program. Rooted firmly in the Delta blues tradition, he won wide attention for his distinctive bottle-neck slide guitar style. He toured widely in the United States and in Europe, and his influence extended not only to bluesmen but also to rock 'n' roll groups, among them, the Rolling Stones. He was active also in gospel music; his best-known song was ''You got to move.''

BIBL: BWW. LivBL 9 (Summer 1972). Oliv.

DISC: Jep. LeSl. TudBM.

McFERRIN, ROBERT. Concert/opera singer (b. 19 March 1921 in Marianna, Arkansas). His family moved to St. Louis, Missouri, when he was six years old. As a child he sang in the choir of his father's church. He obtained his musical education in the public schools of St. Louis, where he attended Sumner High School; at Fisk University in Nashville, Tennessee (1940-41); at Chicago [Illinois] Musical College (B.Mus., 1948), where he studied with George Graham; and at the Kathryn Turney Long School in New York (1953). He also studied with Catherine Van Buren.* His teaching career included lectureships or artist-in-residence appointments at the Sibelius Academy in Helsinki, Finland; at Sacramento State College in California; the St. Louis Institute of Music Conservatory in St. Louis; and at Roosevelt University in Chicago. He began singing professionally during the 1940s. In 1942 he won first place in the *Chicago Tribune's* national contest, which gave him an appearance at the Chicagoland Music Festival. Thereafter he toured widely singing with opera companies, in Broadway musicals, and with jazz orchestras. He was active with Mary Cardwell Dawson's* National Negro Opera Company and sang the role of Amonasro in Verdi's *Aida* (1949) and Valentine in Gounod's *Faust* (1952). In 1949 he sang in the New York City Opera Company's production of William Grant Still's* opera, *Troubled Island*; in 1950 he sang with the New England Opera Company. On Broadway in New York he sang in *Lost in the Stars* (1949), *The Green Pastures* (1951), and *My Darlin' Aida* (1952). In 1959 he and Adele Addison* sang the title roles on the soundtrack for the film edition of Gershwin's *Porgy and Bess*. In 1953 his agent applied for an audition with the Metropolitan Opera Company. He won first place in the Metropolitan Auditions of the Air, and in January 1955 made his operatic debut with the Metropolitan singing Amonasro in *Aida*. During his tenure with the Metropolitan he also sang the roles of Valentine in *Faust* and the title role of Verdi's *Rigoletto*, among many others. In his operatic appearances in the United States and abroad, he was best known for his roles as Orestes in Gluck's *Iphigenia in Taurus*, the voodoo priest in Still's *Troubled Island*, and Tonio in Leoncavallo's *I Pagliacci*. During the 1960s he settled at St. Louis, where he conducted a voice studio, taught in the local community college, and participated in local musical productions. Throughout the 1970s he continued his musical activity on a national level as a concert artist, appearing with symphony orchestras, singing in oratorio, and giving solo recitals. He also sang occasionally in opera, as in Scott Joplin's* *Treemonisha*, staged by the National Association of Negro Musicians* at St. Louis in 1979. McFerrin established a landmark in the history of black music in that he was the first black singer to have a *permanent* position with the Metropolitan Opera (although Marian Anderson* preceded him, she sang in only one opera).

BIBL: Black press, incl. AmstN, 15 October 1975; CDef, 7 May 1955; NYAge 1 January 1949. *Ebony* (October 1953). *Sepia* (May 1976). WWBA

McGHEE, HOWARD. Jazz trumpeter (b. 6 February 1918 in Tulsa, Oklahoma). He studied music with his half-brother, and received his musical education in the public schools of Detroit, Michigan. He played clarinet in his high-school band, but later changed to trumpet after being inspired by the playing of Louis Armstrong* and Roy Eldridge*. During the 1940s-early 1950s he played with various groups, including Lionel Hampton,* Andrew (''Andy'') Kirk* (1941-42, 1943-44), Charlie Barnet (1942-43), and Coleman Hawkins* (1944-45), among others. During those years he also led his own groups, toured with JATP (Norman Granz's Jazz at the Philharmonic, 1947, 1948), and with Oscar Pettiford* (1951-52) in the Far East. Thereafter he was largely inactive until the 1960s, when he organized a quartet, toured as a soloist, and in 1966 with his big band. Through the 1970s he led both small ensembles and big band, appeared at jazz festivals, recorded regularly, and appeared in films. He was also active as a writer-arranger. His best-known piece was ''McGhee special.''

BIBL: ASCAP. FeaEJ. FeaJS. FeaGitJS. MeeJMov.
DISC: Jep. Kink. TudJ.

McGHEE, WALTER BROWN ("BROWNIE"). Bluesman (b. 30 November 1915 in Knoxville, Tennessee). He began to study piano with his sister when he was eight years old; later he taught himself guitar, influenced by his guitarist father. He began to play professionally in 1933, touring the small towns throughout the area; he organized a blues band in Knoxville, which included washboards along with guitars, harmonica, and bass. He also played with minstrel groups and medicine shows. In 1939 he met "Blind Boy" Fuller* (née Fulton Allen) and "Sonny" Terry* (née Saunders Terrell); when Fuller died in 1940, he wrote and recorded "The death of Blind Boy Fuller" and was promoted for a period as "Blind Boy Fuller, No. 2," not wholly with his approval. That year he entered into a permanent partnership with harmonica-player Terry. In 1939 he made his first recordings in Chicago, Illinois, but settled in New York during the early 1940s. During the years 1942-50 he operated a music school in Harlem, called Home of the Blues, where songwriters could obtain help with securing copyrights and promoting their songs, and students could study musical instruments and stage techniques. One of his teachers was ("Blind") Gary Davis.* During these years he appeared in films and Broadway plays, including Langston Hughes's* *Simply Heavenly* (1957) and Tennessee William's *Cat on a Hot Tin Roof* (1954). Those with whom he recorded and/or performed during his long career included Huddie ("Leadbelly") Ledbetter,* Mabel ("Big Maybelle") Smith,* and Josh White,* among others. But it was with his longtime partner Sonny Terry that he became best known. They recorded extensively and toured widely in the United States and in Europe—appearing in concert halls and clubs, on college campuses, and at the major blues and jazz festivals.

BIBL: BWW. CharCB. FeaEJ. LivBl 13 (Summer 1973). MeeJMov. Robert Neff and Anthony Connor, *Blues* (Boston, 1975). Oliv. StamFCW.
DISC: DiGod. Jep. Kink. LeSl. TudBM.

McGINTY, DORIS EVANS. University professor (b. 8 February 1925 in Washington, D.C.). She began piano study at the age of seven, encouraged by her mother, who played piano. She obtained her musical education in the public schools of Washington, D.C.; in the Junior Preparatory Department of Howard University in Washington, where she studied with Andres Wheatley; at Howard (B. Mus., 1945; B.A., 1946), where she studied with Warner Lawson*; at Radcliffe College in Cambridge, Massachusetts (M.A., 1947); and at Oxford University in England (Ph.D., 1954), where she studied with Egon Wellesz and Jack Westrup. As a child she played for the Sunday school of the Metropolitan AMF Church and played on public recitals from the age of twelve. In 1947 she was appointed to the music faculty at Howard University and remained there until retirement. She published articles in professional journals and was Book Review Editor for *The Black Perspective in Music* (1975-). She also contributed articles to the *Dictionary of American Negro Biography* and to *Schulfunk Westdeutscher Rundfunk*. Her honors and awards included Fulbright fellowships (1950, 1951), a General Education Board grant (1951), appointment to national boards of professional music organizations, selection as a Phelps-Stokes Caribbean Exchange Scholar (1974), and Outstanding Teacher Awards (1973, 1976). She was credited with being the first American woman to receive a doctorate in musicology from Oxford University.

BIBL: Questionnaire. WWAW, 1958.

McINTOSH, HATTIE. Vaudeville entertainer (b. in Detroit, Michigan; d. 17 December 1919 in Chicago, Illinois). She began her career in 1884 in the McIntosh and Sawyer's Colored Callender Minstrels, a company of which her husband, Tom McIntosh,* was part owner. In 1890 she toured with W. S. Cleveland's Colored Minstrels. Thereafter she and her husband formed a vaudeville act, "Mr. and Mrs. McIntosh in the King of Bavaria," which played with Sam T. Jack's Creole Show in the 1894-95 season, joined the first company of Black Patti's* Troubadours in 1896, then toured with John Isham's *Octoroons* company for a season. She then played a leading role in the *King Rastus* company. During the first decade of the twentieth century she was a member of George Williams*/Bert Walker* companies and went with the *In Dahomey* show to England in 1902. In 1905 she was a charter member of Robert ("Bob") Mott's* Pekin Theater Stock Company in Chicago, Illinois. Her last performance with Williams/Walker was in *Mr. Lode of Koal* (1909). About 1911 she formed a vaudeville act with Cordelia McClain, and the two women joined the Billy King* Stock Company in 1912. She married King the same year. The King Company toured extensively in the South, then made its Chicago debut in 1915 at the Grand Theater.

BIBL: Black press, incl. CDef, 27 December 1919; IndF, 3 January 1920. Simond.

McINTOSH, TOM. Minstrel/Vaudeville entertainer (b. c1841 in Lexington, Kentucky; d. 3 March 1904 near St. Paris, Ohio). He began his professional career during the 1870s, touring with Henry Hart's* Alabama Minstrels (1872), Callender's Georgia Minstrels, and Haverly's Genuine Colored International Minstrels. His attempt in 1883 to organize a minstrel troupe under black management, along with Charles Hicks* and A. D. Sawyer, was unsuccessful. A second effort in 1884 resulted in the McIntosh and Sawyer's Colored Callender Minstrels, with Hicks as business manager, James Johnson as interlocutor and stage manager, and Charles Boyer as music director and bandleader. The troupe, however, was short-lived. During the late 1880s he formed an act with his wife Hattie, titled ''Mr. and Mrs. McIntosh in The King of Bavaria,'' which played with Sam T. Jack's *Creole Show* in the 1894-95 season, with Black Patti's* Troubadours in 1896, and with John Isham's *Octoroons* in 1897. During the next few years the McIntoshes apparently performed as singles, and his activities are unknown. About 1903 he joined the original Smart Set company, replacing Ernest Hogan* in the leading role. He died on a train when his company was en route from Indianapolis, Indiana, to Columbus, Ohio.

BIBL: Black press, incl. CleveG, 12 March 1904; IndF, 12 March 1904; NYGlobe, 3 February 1883: NYAge, 26 October 1911. LaBrew. NYClipper. Simond.

McINTYRE, KENNETH ARTHUR (''KEN''). Jazz saxophonist/College professor (b. 7 September 1931 in Boston, Massachusetts). His father played mandolin, and he studied piano as a child. He obtained his musical education at the Boston Conservatory of Music (B. Mus., 1958; M. Mus., 1959), Boston University, and the University of Massachusetts at Amherst (D. Ed., 1975). He began his professional career playing with local groups in Boston, and during his service in the United States Armed Forces (1952-54) he played piano in jazz groups. His teaching career included tenures in the public schools of New York (1961-67), Central State University in Wilberforce, Ohio (1967-69), Wesleyan University in Middletown, Connecticut (1969-71), and the State University of New York at Old Westbury (1971-), where he was director of the African-American music and dance program. During the 1960s he led his own groups in New York nightclubs and appeared at Newport Jazz Festivals. He first recorded in 1960; he also performed with symphony orchestras, including the Harlem Philharmonic and the Bridgeport Symphony. In 1962 he was composer-arranger for two independent films, *How Wide Is Sixth Avenue* and *Miracle on the BMT*. His honors and awards included a grant from the National Endowment for the Humanities, which enabled him to study in Ghana during the summer of 1971. He was regarded as one of the important early avant-garde jazzmen.

BIBL: BMI (November 1971). FeaJS. FeaGitJS. Michael Ullman, *Jazz Lives* (Washington, D.C., 1980). WWBA.

MACK, CECIL (RICHARD McPHERSON). Songwriter (b. 6 November 1883 in Norfolk, Virginia; d. 1 August 1944 in New York, New York). He attended Lincoln University in Pennsylvania and later studied music privately in New York with Melvin Charlton.* During the first decade of the twentieth century he was active as a song-writer with George Walker*/Bert Williams* companies. He also founded the Gotham-Attucks music publishing company, which lasted about ten years and published, among other songs, Bert Williams's ''Nobody,'' as well as ''The right church but the wrong pew,'' and ''That's why they call me shine.'' His earliest collaborator was James Tim Brymn*; later collaborators were Chris Smith* with whom he wrote ''Good morning, Carrie'' (1901), James P. Johnson,* Ford Dabney,* and Eubie Blake.* He also wrote scores for Broadway musicals, including *Running Wild* (1923, with Johnson) from which came the songs ''Charleston'' and ''Old-fashioned love,'' and *Swing It* (1937, with Eubie Blake). His Cecil Mack Choir was active on Broadway during the 1920s-30s, singing in such musicals as Lew Leslie's *Blackbirds of 1928*.

BIBL: ASCAP. Black press, incl. AmstN, 5 August 1944; NYAge, 26 July 1906.

McKINNEY, NINA MAE. Entertainer (b. 1912 in Lancaster, South Carolina; d. May 1967 in New York, New York). Although best known as an actress, she was also an entertainer. She received her education in the public schools of Philadelphia, Pennsylvania. She went to New York during the 1920s, where she was a dancer in *Blackbirds of 1928* and thereafter sang in many films, including King Vidor's *Hallelujah* (1929). She toured extensively on the nightclub circuit during the 1930s, frequently with Garland Wilson as accompanist.

BIBL: Black press, incl. CDef, 19 January 1929. ChilWW. MeeJMov.

McKINNEY, WILLIAM (''BILL''). Jazz bandleader (b. 17 September 1895 in Cynthia, Kentucky; d. 14 October 1969 in Detroit [?], Michigan). He began his professional career about 1920 as leader and drummer of a group called the Synco Septet, then later, the Synco Jazz Band, in Springfield, Ohio. He became business manager of the band, which played residencies in various places in the Midwest; after 1926 it was billed as

McKinney's Cotton Pickers and was based in Detroit, Michigan. Don Redman* served as musical director during the years 1927-31, and after the band split into two groups, Benny Carter* became the director of one (1931-32). In 1934 the group was disbanded. McKinney formed another group at Boston, Massachusetts, in 1935, but left the field of music during the 1940s. Among those who played with the Cotton Pickers over the years were Adolphus ("Doc") Cheatham,* Coleman Hawkins,* James P. Johnson,* Todd Rhodes,* and Joe Smith,* among others. In 1974 some musicians revived McKinney's Cotton Pickers to perform at the Newport Jazz Festival-New York.

BIBL: AlHen. ChilWW. FeaEJ.

DISC: Kink. RustJR.

McKINNEY'S COTTON PICKERS. See **McKINNEY, WILLIAM.**

McLEAN, JOHN LENWOOD ("JACKIE"). Jazz saxophonist (b. 17 May 1931 in New York, New York). His father was a professional jazz guitarist. At fourteen years of age he began formal study of alto saxophone. He obtained his musical education in the public schools of New York and at North Carolina A & T College in Greensboro, which he attended for a year. His early style development was influenced by tenor saxophonists Dexter Gordon,* Lester Young,* and Ben Webster*; he tried to copy their sounds on his instrument. During his high-school years he played in a jazz group that included Kenneth ("Kenny") Drew,* Andy Kirk, Jr., and Theodore ("Sonny") Rollins,* among others. During the 1950s he played with various groups, including Miles Davis* (with whom he first recorded), Art Blakey,* Paul Bley, and Charles Mingus.* He also led his own groups. During the years 1959-61 he performed with an Off-Broadway play, *The Connection*, which was performed in London in 1961. When the cast returned to the United States, he remained in Paris for a period to play in nightclubs. During the early 1960s he toured widely in Europe and in Japan (1964, with a group that included Reggie Workman,* Cedar Walton, Benny Golson,* and Roy Haynes*), performed in clubs, and recorded prolifically. From the mid-1960s on he became increasingly interested in teaching, at first in community groups, then on the college level. His teaching career included tenures as a bandmaster for the New York State Correction Department (1967), at the University of Buffalo in New York, and the Hartt College of Music at Hartford, Connecticut (1968-); he also taught summers at Vallekilde, Denmark, beginning in 1972. He continued to tour regularly with groups in the United States and in Europe through the 1970s, often with his son René on tenor saxophone. He organized a culture program in Hartford called Artists Collective. His honors included awards from the music industry, the NAACP, and fraternal organizations. McLean was a leading figure of the second generation of bebop jazzmen.

BIBL: FeaEJ. FeaJS. FeaGitJS. MeeJMov. Spell. WWBA.

DISC: ModJ. TudJ.

McLEOD, ALICE. See **COLTRANE, ALICE.**

McLIN, LENA JOHNSON. Educator/Choral conductor (b. 5 September 1928 in Atlanta, Georgia) She came from a musical family; her uncle was Thomas A. Dorsey,* "Father of Gospel Music." She obtained her musical education at Spelman College in Atlanta, Georgia (B.A., 1951); Roosevelt University in Chicago, Illinois; and Chicago State College. She taught in the public schools of Chicago and was head of the music department at Kenwood High School for many years. She was active as a choral conductor with school groups, church groups, and community groups; she founded a small opera company, the McLin Ensemble, and worked with educational films. She was a prolific composer of vocal and choral gospel music. Her honors included awards from civic and community groups, from the National Association of Negro Musicians* (1970), the NAACP, and an honorary doctorate from Virginia Union University (1975).

BIBL: Dominique-René de Lerma, ed., *Black Music in Our Culture* (Kent, Ohio, 1970). WWBA.

McMILLEN AND SOURBECK JUBILEE SINGERS. Concert ensemble (Org. in Bellefonte, Pennsylvania., fl. late nineteenth century). This was one of the several professional groups that sprang up in imitation of the Fisk Jubilee Singers* after that student group met with great success in its touring. According to Fletcher, the group (later known as Stimson's Singers) originally included William ("Billy") Mills, grandfather of the Mills Brothers* quartet, and Abe V. Jackson, father of James ("Billboard") Jackson.*

BIBL: Tom Fletcher, *100 Years of the Negro in Show Business* (New York, 1954), p. 30.

McNAIR, BARBARA. Popular-music singer (b. 4 March 1939 in Racine, Wisconsin). She obtained her musical education in the public schools of Racine, Wisconsin, and at the University of Southern California in Los Angeles. She began her professional career as a nightclub singer in New York. She first attracted wide attention as a singer on the Arthur Godfrey television show. She appeared in many Broadway musicals, including *The Body Beautiful* (1958), *The Merry World of Nat King Cole* (1961), and the touring company of *No Strings* (1962), among others. During the 1960s-70s she was active primarily as an actress on the stage, in films, and on television. She had her own weekly television show during the years 1969-70.

BIBL: WWA. WWBA.

McNEIL, CLAUDIA MAE. Actress/Entertainer (b. 13 August 1917 in Baltimore, Maryland). Although best known as an actress, she was an entertainer in her early career. She obtained her education in the public schools of New York. She began her professional career in 1933 as a nightclub singer. Her career development was aided by Eubie Blake,* John Hammond, and William ("Bojangles") Robinson, among others. She sang in Robinson's nightclub in the Harlem community and toured in his revue, *Hot From Harlem*. During the 1930s-40s she sang in New York theaters, nightclubs, and USO shows (United Service Organizations). She then toured with Katherine Dunham's dance troupe as a singer (1946-51), including residencies in Haiti, West Indies. Her career during the 1950s-70s was in the theater, except for a period (1951-52) as an entertainer and program coordinator for the Jamaican Broadcasting Company. She was best known for her performances in *Simply Heavenly* (1957) and *Raisin in the Sun* (1959). During the late 1970s she returned to her early career activity as a nightclub entertainer.

BIBL: Black press, incl. NYAge, 16 May 1959. John S. Wilson, "A Voice from Harlem's Past" in NYT, 12 May 1978. WWA. WWBA.

McPHATTER, CLYDE LENSEY. Rhythm 'n' blues singer (b. 15 November 1933 in Durham, North Carolina; d. 13 June 1972 in New York, New York). His mother was a church organist. He began singing in his father's church choir at the age of five. During his high-school years he formed a gospel group, the Mt. Lebanon Singers; at seventeen he was lead singer of the group called Billy Ward and the Dominoes (1950-53). In 1953 he organized The Drifters—composed of Gerhart Thrasher, Andrew Thrasher, and Willie Ferbee—which soon established itself as a leading rhythm 'n' blues group. Over the years there were many personnel changes in the group. After service in the United States Armed Forces (1954-56), he toured widely as a soloist at home and abroad. He recorded extensively until the mid-1960s, when his career appeared to go into a decline. His best-known performances were "Sixty-minute man" and "Have mercy, baby" with the Dominoes, "Money, honey" with the Drifters, and "Seven days" as a soloist. He exerted wide influence upon the style development of such entertainers as William ("Smokey") Robinson,* Jackie Wilson,* and Donnie Elbert, among others.

BIBL: NHBull (January 1974). ShawHS. StamPRS.

DISC: Giv. TudBM.

McRAE, CARMEN. Jazz singer (b. 8 April 1922 in New York, New York). She studied piano privately but began her professional career as a singer in 1944 with Benny Carter.* Her early style development was influenced by Billie Holiday,* whom she imitated in her early career. As she matured, she developed her own distinctive sound and became one of the top female jazz singers, along with Sarah Vaughan.* She sang with various groups, including William ("Count") Basie,* Mercer Ellington* (1946-47), and Mat Matthews, among others. From 1954 on she was active primarily as a soloist; she toured widely in the United States and in Europe, appearing in concert halls, nightclubs, theaters, and at major festivals. She also toured frequently in Japan. She made her recording debut in 1946 as Carmen Clarke (she was married at that time to Kenneth ("Kenny") Clarke,* and thereafter recorded extensively. She appeared regularly on television shows and in films, including *The Subterraneans* (1960), *Hotel* (1967), and *Monterey Jazz* (1968). She won numerous awards from the music industry.

BIBL: FeaEJ. FeaJS. FeaGitJS. WWA, 1976-77. WWBA.

DISC: Jep.

McSHANN, JAY ("HOOTIE"). Jazz bandleader. (b. 12 January 1909 in Muskogee, Oklahoma). As a child he played piano. He attended Fisk University in Nashville, Tennessee (but stayed only two months), and Winfield College in Kansas. He played with various groups in the Southwest, including Eddie Hill, then settled in Kansas City, Missouri, in 1937. After playing in local nightclubs for a period, he organized his own group, which included Charlie Parker* among others. For the next four decades he led groups, both small and big band, except during his years of service in the United States Armed Forces (1944-46). He used Kansas City as his base, but played long residencies in New York; Chicago, Illinois; Los Angeles, California; and Toronto, Canada. Beginning in 1969 he made annual tours in Europe, which included East European cities in 1974 with the show, *The Musical Life of Charlie Parker*. He appeared at the major jazz festivals through the 1970s, on television shows, and in the film *The Last of the Blue Devils* (1974). His publications included *Boogie Woogie and Blues Piano Solos and Instruc-*

tions; The Book of the Blues. His best-known recordings were "Confessin' the blues" and "Hootie blues." His band was the last of the important Kansas City groups, and he himself was a leading blues pianist.

BIBL: *Cadence* (September, October 1979). ChilWW. FeaEJ. FeaJS. FeaGitJS. Russ.

DISC: Jep. Kink. RustJR. TudJ.

MADISON, EARL. Symphony cellist (b. 23 March 1945 in Chicago, Illinois). He began study of the violoncello as a child with his father, Earl Madison, a professional cellist. He obtained his musical education in the public schools of Chicago, Illinois, and at Chicago Musical College (B. Mus.), where he studied with Karl Frugh. His professional career as a cellist included tenures in the Chicago Civic Orchestra (the training orchestra for the Chicago Symphony); in the Symphony of the New World* in New York; in the Pittsburgh Symphony, under the direction of William Steinberg; and in the Milwaukee Symphony. He also played for short periods with other symphony orchestras, including the Chicago Grant Park Symphony. In 1970 he performed in the Tschikovsky Cello competition at Moscow, USSR, including a piece commissioned from Arthur Cunningham,* "Eclalette" for unaccompanied cello.

BIBL: Communication from Fanya Wiggins. Black press.

MADONSELA, EUGENE. See **CORONETS, THE.**

MAKEBA, MIRIAM ZENZI. Folksinger (b. 4 March 1932 in Johannesburg, South Africa). Her parents belonged to the Xhosa nation (related to the Zulas). She obtained her musical education at the Methodist-sponsored Kilmerton Training School in Pretoria, South Africa, which she attended for eight years. She sang in the school choir and occasionally sang solos with the choir. After graduation, she began singing for local events and began to win recognition as a singer of talent. She toured with the Black Manhattan Brothers (1954-57), then with a musical revue. In the late 1950s she attracted international attention for her performances in the film *Come Back, Africa* (1958) and the jazz opera *King Kong* (1959). She made her television debut in 1959 on BBC (British Broadcasting Company) in London, England, and the same year became a protégée of Harry Belafonte,* who took her to the United States to tour with his company. She made her American television debut in 1959 on the Steve Allen Show. During the 1960s-1970s she established herself as an international entertainer, including traditional Xhosi songs as well as jazz in her repertory. She received awards from the music industry. During the 1960s she was married to Hugh Masekela.*

BIBL: ASCAP. Black press, incl. NYAge, 5 December 1959. CurBiog (June 1965). FeaEJ. FeaJS. StamFCW.

MANDO, ALFRED F. Music teacher (b. 18 June 1846 in Troy, New York; d. 10 October 1912 in New York, New York). As a child he studied piano with his father, a musician, and at the Hudsonville Institute in Troy (?). In 1868 he went to New York, where he took the Freedman's Board examination with plans to teach ex-slaves in the South. But his plans changed and he settled in New York, studying music further with Louise Krause, H. A. Atwood, and John T. Douglass.* He conducted music studios in local black churches and was the choirmaster of the Shiloh Presbyterian Church. In 1880 he established his Mozart Conservatory; in 1896 he organized the Mozart Conservatory Concert Orchestra, which toured widely along the Eastern seaboard. He also led a society dance orchestra, which toured extensively. He played violin in the People's Symphony Society of New York. He was a member of the Music Teacher's National Association and served as a delegate to the national convention held at Columbia University in 1907. His honors included membership in the Society Universelle Lyrique of Paris, France.

BIBL: Black press, incl. CDef, 6 July 1912; IndF, 6 June 1896; NYAge, 30 August 1890, 8 August 1907; NYGlobe, 6 January 1883. NYB 1913, p. 251.

MARABLE, FATE. Jazz bandleader (b. 2 December 1890 in Paducah, Kentucky; d. 16 January 1947 in St. Louis, Missouri). He came from a family that produced several professional musicians. He studied piano as a child with his mother. When he was seventeen he began playing piano on riverboats, working first with violinist Emil Flindt on a ship that sailed from Little Rock, Arkansas. During the 1920s-1930s he led bands on steamers sailing on the Mississippi and Ohio Rivers, primarily for the Streckfus Steamboat Line. In the mid-1930s Charles Creath* was frequently his co-leader. Among those who played in his bands over the years were Louis Armstrong,* Johnny Dodds,* Warren ("Baby") Dodds,* Henry ("Red") Allen,* Jimmy Blanton,* Arthur ("Zutty") Singleton,* George ("Pops") Foster,* and Albert ("Al") Morgan, among others. In the 1940s he was inactive for a period, then he began playing in nightclubs of St. Louis, Missouri.

BIBL: ChilWW. FeaEJ.

DISC: Kink.

MARGETSON, EDWARD H. Composer (b. 31 December 1891 in St. Kitts, British Virgin Islands; d. 22

January 1962 in New York, New York). He came from a musical family: his father was a choirmaster and church organist, and his mother was a pianist. At the age of fifteen he began his professional career as a church organist. In 1919 he settled in New York. He obtained his musical education at Columbia University (1921-23, 1924-26), where he studied with Daniel Gregory Mason and Seth Bingham. His piano teachers included Sam Lamberson. He was active as a studio teacher and church organist; he served at the Episcopal Church of the Crucifixion for thirty-eight years (1916-54). He was an associate of the American Guild of Organists. In 1927 he founded the Schubert Music Society, a choral group, which gave periodic concerts and toured occasionally. He was also director of the group until he retired in 1954. He was perhaps best known as a composer, particularly for his *Rondo Caprice* for orchestra and Ballade-Valse-Serenade for cello and for the song cycle *Echoes from the Caribbean*. His honors included grants from the American Academy of Arts and Sciences, the Victor Baier Foundation (1925), and the Rosenwald Foundation (1942) and awards from the Harmon Foundation (1927) and the National Council of Negro Women (1962).

BIBL: Black press, incl. AmstN, 19 August 1930, 3 February 1962, 28 May 1977. Hare. WWCA, 1950.

MARLEY, ROBERT NESTA (''BOB''). Entertainer, reggae (b. 6 February 1945 in Rhoden Hall, St. Ann Parish, Jamaica; d. 11 May 1981 in Miami, Florida). His family moved to Kingston, Jamaica, when he was nine years old. He obtained his musical education in the city's public schools. In 1963 he and Alvin (''Secco'') Patterson formed a vocal group, later called The Wailers, which eventually included Peter Tosh (singer), Tyrone Downie (keyboards), and ''Bunny'' Livingston, among others. The same year Bob won a prize in a talent contest with a song he had written and began making recordings. He opened a small record shop, called Wailing Soul, to assist in marketing his recordings. In 1965 Marley took his group to England for the first time. Thereafter the Wailers toured widely in Europe, the Caribbean, South America, and the United States. Their best-known recordings were ''Concrete jungle,'' ''Burnin' and lootin',' ''Rebel music,'' ''Them belly full,'' and ''Better must come''; their best-known albums were *Rastaman Vibrations*, *Exodus*, *Natty Dread*, *Burnin'*, *Catch a Fire*, and *Babylon by Bus*. Reggae music (earlier called ska) exerted wide influence upon British singers and singers of the United States, particularly Johnny Nash* with his recordings of ''Hold me tight'' and ''I can see clearly now.'' The Wailers, like other reggae groups, were devout Rastafarians, and to many peoples of the Third World, Marley was ''a figure of almost messianic proportions'' (quoted from NYT, 14 August 1977). Their music blended elements of rock, calypso, soul, jazz, and blues with traditional African and religious music.

BIBL: Black press, incl. CDef, 17 May 1976. NYT, 30 November 1975, 14 August 1977. *Sepia* (March 1974).

DISC: TudBM.

MARSHALL, ARTHUR. Ragtime pianist/Composer (b. 20 November 1881 in Saline County, Missouri; d. 18 August 1968 in Kansas City, Missouri). He studied music as a child in Sedalia, Missouri, where his family moved when he was an infant. When he was about fifteen, he became a protégé of Scott Joplin* and studied music with the composer. He also attended the George R. Smith College in Sedalia and the Teacher's Institute, where he earned a teacher's license in education. He first played professionally in local cafes, including the Maple Leaf Club; he also played for local social entertainments. During the years 1900-02 he performed off and on with McCabe's Minstrels as a member of Bunk Johnson's* band. In 1903 he was active in association with activities of the St. Louis World's Fair and was a member of the Scott Joplin Ragtime Opera company. In 1906 he left St. Louis for Chicago, Illinois, where he played piano in cafes and saloons for three years. He returned to Sedalia in 1909; moved to St. Louis a year later, where he played in Tom Turpin's* Eureka Club; and settled in 1917 in Kansas City, Missouri. His best-known pieces are ''Swipsey cakewalk'' (in collaboration with Joplin) and ''Lily queen.''

BIBL: Blesh. BPIM 3 (Spring, Fall 1975). JaTiRR.

MARSHALL, HARRIET GIBBS. Director of conservatory (b. 18 February 1869 in Vancouver, British Columbia, Canada; d. 25 February 1941 in Washington, D.C.). She attended public schools in Oberlin, Ohio, and was the first black American to complete the piano course at the Oberlin Conservatory (1889). Later she studied in Boston, Chicago, and with Moritz Moszowski in Paris, France. She toured briefly as a concert pianist before beginning a teaching career at the Normal School in Huntsville, Alabama. Thereafter she established a music school in association with the Eckstein Norton School at Cane Springs, Kentucky. About 1900 she went to Washington, D.C., where she became assistant director of music for the colored public schools under the directorship of John Layton Turner.* In the fall of 1903 she established the Washington Conservatory of Music and served as its director until 1923, when she accompanied her husband to Haiti, where he served as the attaché to the Haitian legation. In Haiti she founded an industrial school and collected folk music. After returning to the United States in 1927, she gave lecture-recitals on Haitian music and published a book, *The Story of Haiti* (1930). In 1933 she again assumed the directorship of the Conservatory; in 1936 she established a National Negro Music Center in association with the Conservatory. Her significant contribution to black music history was her work with the Conservatory, which remained in operation until 1960. During its early years it was unique as an institution owned and operated by black musicians, which offered to its students musical studies at the conservatory level. In its early years the faculty included such leading black musicians as Clarence Cameron White,* E. Azalia Hackley,* Harry Williams,* and J. Hiliary Taylor, among others. Gibbs was a pioneer in bringing black concert artists from all over the nation to Washington, D.C., and in sponsoring other notable musical events.

BIBL: Black press, incl. IndF, 8 June 1895; NYAge, 13 September 1906, 5 March 1908, 15 March 1927. JNH 26 (1941), pp. 410-411. Doris E. McGinty in BPIM 7 (Spring 1979). NHB 4 (May 1941), pp. 175-76.

MARTHA & THE VANDELLAS. Rhythm 'n' blues trio (orig. in Detroit, Michigan; fl. 1960s-70s). Organized in 1962, the vocal trio (all natives of Detroit) was composed of Martha Reeves (b. 18 July 1941), Betty Kelly (b. 16 September 1944), and Rosalind Ashford (b. 2 September 1943). Although Reeves and Ashford sang together in high school for social events, after graduation Reeves took a job as a secretary in Berry Gordy's* Motown Recording Company. She was given opportunity to sing background music for recording sessions and so impressed management that she was asked to form a trio for regular performance of background music for Motown artists. The trio's performance on Marvin Gaye's recording of "Stubborn kind of fellow" attracted wide attention, and Motown signed the girls to a recording contract in 1962. During the 1960s-70s Martha & the Vandellas toured widely in the United States and in Europe and recorded prolifically. There was a period of inactivity, but Reeves reorganized the group in 1971 with Lois Reeves and Sandra Tilley.

BIBL: *Ebony* (June 1967). StamPRS.

MARTIN, DAVID IRWIN, JR. Concert cellist (b. 5 October 1907 in New York; d. 5 May 1975 in New York). See **MARTIN, DAVID IRWIN, SR.**

MARTIN, DAVID IRWIN, SR. Music educator (b. c1880 in Asheville, North Carolina; d. 28 August 1923 in New York). A violinist, he established a violin studio about 1907 in New York, and in 1912 he joined forces with pianist Helen Elise Smith (Dett*) to form the Martin-Smith School of Music, which covered all areas of studio teaching. He was chosen as the first director of the Music School Settlement for Colored when that institution was founded in 1911 by white philanthropists under the leadership of David Mannes of the New York Symphony. He remained as director until the fall of 1914, when he was succeeded by J. Rosamond Johnson.* Martin focused attention on black performers who were neither minstrels nor vaudeville entertainers and called attention to the music of black composers in the annual concerts produced by the Music School Settlement at Carnegie Hall during the years 1912-15 (Johnson directed the 1915 concert). His own music-school concerts began in 1908 and continued until his death. Both concert series brought before the public the leading black artists of the time, including Marian Anderson,* Florence Cole Talbert,* Harry T. Burleigh,* Roland Hayes,* Marie Selika (Williams),* and Abbie Mitchell,* among others. In addition, the concerts featured such groups as symphony orchestras, led by James Reese Europe* and Will Tyers*; choral groups, directed by Will Marion Cook*; chamber groups, such as the Negro String Quartet and the Young Women's Orchestra; and children's ensembles. For the first time there was public performance of the works of Burleigh, Cook, R. Nathaniel Dett,* Carl Diton,* Scott Joplin,* and Montague Ring* (née Amanda Ira Aldridge), among others, in addition to works of the established composer Samuel Coleridge-Taylor.* The concerts inspired emulation in other cities, particularly at Chicago, Illinois, where William Hackney* inaugurated an annual "All Colored Composers" series in 1914 at Orchestra Hall and Erskine Tate* organized a symphony orchestra. Martin also occasionally brought eminent European artists to the Harlem community in concerts. After Johnson resigned from the Music School Settlement in 1919, its activities were transferred to the Martin-Smith School.

The Martin-Smith school served as both a training institution for music teachers and a haven for concert artists; over the years its faculty included such retired artists as Marie Selika and Sidney Woodward* and such young talented performers of promise as Tourgee DeBose,* Frank Harrison,* and Andrew Fletcher Rosemond,* among others. The school also sponsored debut recitals for young artists and occasionally brought eminent European performers to the Harlem community in concerts. The primary purpose of the school was, of course, to instruct the young; during the next few decades most of those who enriched the musical life of Harlem and represented Harlem nationally were trained within the walls of the school. The best representatives of the school were the Martin children: violinist Gertrude, violinist Eugene Mars, and cellist David Irwin Martin, Jr. Gertrude began violin study at the age of six and toured as a concert violinist as well as played with groups. Eugene had the most remarkable career of the three: he gave his first recital at the age of thirteen at Aeolian Hall in New York; and in 1923 he became the first black graduate in violin from the Institute of Musical Art. David, Jr., carried on his father's work and conducted a music studio; at one time he also led an orchestra.

BIBL: Black press, incl. CDef, 19 April 1919, 7 May 1932; NYAge, 30 April 1914, 6 December 1919, 8 January 1921, 1 January 1927. BPIM 6 (Spring 1978, includes reprints of press clippings for Carnegie Hall concerts). Handy. WWCA 1941-44.

MARTIN, EUGENE MARS. Concert violinist (b. 29 June 1904 in New York, New York; d. 23 December 1926 in New York). See **MARTIN, DAVID IRWIN, SR.**

MARTIN, GERTRUDE. Concert violinist (b. 20 April 1910 in New York, New York; d. 6 September 1945 in New York). See **MARTIN, DAVID IRWIN, SR.**

MARTIN, ROBERTA. Gospel singer (b. 12 February 1907 in Helena, Arkansas; d. 18 January 1969 in Chicago, Illinois). Her family moved to Chicago, Illinois, when she was ten years old. She obtained her musical education in the public schools of Chicago, where she came under the tutelage of Mildred Byrant Jones* at Wendell Phillips High School. About 1931 she was called to the Ebenezer Baptist Church to accompany the gospel chorus recently organized by Theodore Frye* and Thomas A. Dorsey.* In 1933 she and Frye organized a Junior Gospel Chorus at Ebenezer, which included Robert Anderson, Willie Webb, James Lawrence, Norsalus McKissick, and Eugene Smith. Eventually these singers became the Martin-Frye Singers and, in 1936, the Roberta Martin Singers. Those who performed with her groups over the years included Anderson, Delois Barrett Campbell,* Lucy Smith Collier, Bessie Folk, Gloria Griffin, Harold Johnson, Alex Bradford,* McKissick, Myrtle Scott, Eugene Smith, and Webb. For a short period during the 1940s she teamed with Sally Martin* (not related) to form the Martin and Martin Singers. Roberta toured widely with her singers in the United States and in Europe; in 1964 they performed at the Festival of Two Worlds in Spoleto, Italy. She established her own publishing-distribution company early in her career. In addition to concert work, she participated in church and community activities. For many years she was the organist-pianist at Ebenezer; after leaving that church she served as minister of music at the Mount Pisgah Baptist Church (1956-68). She worked with Dorsey's National Convention of Gospel Choirs and Choruses (established 1932), particularly as accompanist for Willie Ford Smith's* work with the Soloists Bureau of the Convention. She also accompanied such gospel singers as Robert Anderson, Mahalia Jackson,* and the Barrett Sisters. Martin was one of the leading pioneer gospel figures in Chicago, along with Dorsey, Sallie Martin, and Mahalia Jackson. She defined the role of gospel piano and was the idol of pianists who came after her. Those whom she took under her tutelage as "pupils," formally or informally, included Alex Bradford, James Cleveland,* and Joe Washington, among others. She exerted enormous influence upon all gospel pianists after her time.

BIBL: Barbara Baker, "Black Gospel Music Styles, 1942-1975" (Ph.D. diss. University of Maryland, 1978). Black press, incl. AmstN, 1 February 1969; CDef, 4-10 August 1962, 6-12 June 1964. Heil. Jac. Pearl Williams-Jones, "Roberta Martin (1907-1969): Spirit of an Era" in Program publ. by the Smithsonian Institution, 6-8 February 1981, Washington, D.C.

MARTIN, SALLY. Gospel singer (b. 20 November 1896 in Pittfield, Georgia). Her mother was a singer who toured on the small-church circuit in the South. When she was left an orphan at sixteen, she moved to Atlanta, Georgia, and there joined the Fire Baptized Holiness Church. She moved to Cleveland, Ohio, in 1917 and settled in Chicago, Illinois, in 1919. She sang in church choirs in both cities. In February 1932 she auditioned to sing in a chorus led by Thomas A. Dorsey* at the Pilgrim Baptist Church, was accepted, and began a long professional association with Dorsey. In 1932 she helped Dorsey to establish his National Convention of Gospel Choirs and Choruses, Inc. Beginning in 1933 she traveled with him throughout the Middle West and South, singing his newly composed gospel songs in small and large churches and helping to sell the songs. She also traveled by herself to various cities, as far west as Los Angeles, California, to organize choral groups to sing the Dorsey songs. After leaving Dorsey in 1940 she toured as a soloist, using Ruth Jones (later known as Dinah Washington*) as her accompanist. She then formed an alliance with Roberta Martin* (not related), whom she had met through Dorsey when Roberta accompanied his chorus, and the two singers became co-leaders of the Martin and Martin Singers.

The collaboration lasted only a short period; she soon formed her own all-women's group, the Sally Martin Singers, which included Elaine Simmons and Sally's adopted daughter, Cora Martin. In 1940 she also established a gospel-music publishing house in partnership with Kenneth Morris, who had come to Chicago, Illinois, in 1934 to perform at the Chicago World's Fair and remained as a church musician at the First Church of Deliverance. It was Clarence Cobbs, pastor of the church, who encouraged her business efforts and recommended Morris as a partner. The Martin and Morris Publishing Company prospered and released such successful songs during its early years as "Just a closer walk with Thee." She toured widely with her groups, making several trips to Europe and visiting Africa. During the 1940s-50s she was associated with the St. Paul Baptist Church in Los Angeles, where the choir, under the direction of J. Earle Hines, made the first gospel broadcast on television. Martin performed with Hines's choir and also recorded with his group. She retired from music in 1970 but continued to tour on special occasions. In 1979 she was featured performer, along with Marion Williams,* in a show, "Gospel Caravan," that played a long residency in Paris. Martin was one of the pioneers of black gospel music; she exerted enormous influence upon its development through her touring; her songs; and her "students" (i.e., those who toured with her), among them, Jessy Dixon,* Delois Barrett Campbell,* and Alex Bradford.* Her best-known songs were "The sweetest Name I know" and "Just a few days to labor."

BIBL: Interview by Stella Hall. Horace Clarence Boyer, "The Gospel Song: An Historical and Analytical Study" (M.A. thesis, Eastman School of Music, 1964). Heil. *Chicago Tribune*, 29 April 1979.

MARTIN-SMITH MUSIC SCHOOL. See **MARTIN, DAVID IRWIN, SR.**

MARTÍNEZ, MARÍA LORETTO. Concert singer (b. c1830s in Havana, Cuba; d. 18??). As a child she was taken under the protection of a military officer stationed at Havana, Aguilar y Conde. After her parents' death, Mme. Aguilar took the child to Spain, where she received her musical education at Seville. As a young girl she attracted the attention of Queen Isabella II of Spain and was invited to join the Queen's retinue. She toured widely in Europe, including England, during the 1850s; her repertory included Cuban and Spanish folksongs, and she often accompanied herself on the guitar. Critics acclaimed her soprano voice with its wide compass (into the contralto register), and she was given the title "the Black Malibran," after opera singer Maria Malibran.

BIBL: Information from Josephine Wright. LaBrew. Otto Mayer-Serra, *Música y músicos de Latin-américa*, v.2 (Mexico, Editorial Atlante, 1947), p. 598. *The Musical World* 25 (22 June 1850), p. 392f.

MASEKELA, HUGH. Jazz trumpeter (b. 4 April 1939 in Wilbank [near Johannesburg], South Africa). He attended missionary schools from the age of nine and first studied piano at school. When he was fourteen he was inspired to learn trumpet after seeing the film *Young Man with a Horn* (1949). He began playing with South African dance bands during his high-school years and toured to major cities. In 1959 he went to London, England, where he studied at the Guildhall School of Music. In 1960 he received a scholarship from Harry Belafonte* to study at the Manhattan School of Music in New York (1960-64). During the 1960s he was also active as arranger and music director for Miriam Makeba* (his wife at that time), who toured with Belafonte. In 1964 he organized his own group and the next year made his first recordings. Thereafter he established himself as a leading jazz figure and toured throughout the world with his groups. In 1973 he returned to Africa in a "search for his roots" (quoted from black press), touring through several countries and performing with African musicians. In Ghana he came into contact with Nigerian jazzman Fela Anikulapo-Kuti* and a Ghanian group called Hedzoleh Soundz. He assumed leadership of the group, made recordings in Nigeria with the help of Ransome-Kuti, and toured in the United States in 1974. His best-known recordings were "Grazing in the grass," "I am not afraid," and the album *Masekela: Introducing Hedzoleh Soundz* (1973). His music blended jazz, reggae, popular, and traditional African elements.

BIBL: Black press. StamPRS.

MATHIS, JOHNNY. Popular-music singer (b. 30 September 1935 in San Francisco, California). He obtained his musical education at San Francisco State College in California. He established himself as a leading ballad singer early in his career, first winning wide recognition with his recording of "Wonderful, wonderful" (1957). Thereafter he toured widely in the United States and abroad and recorded prolifically.

BIBL: ShawR5. WWA.

DISC: Jep.

MATHIS, JOYCE. Concert singer (b. 1944 in Chattanooga, Tennessee). As a child she sang with a family troupe, the Mathis Family, which was directed by her mother. She studied music as a child with her mother. She obtained further musical education in the public schools of Chattanooga; at Central State College in Wilberforce, Ohio (B.Mus., 1965); and at the Juilliard School of Music in New York, where she studied with Florence Page Kimball. She made her concert debut as a soprano in March 1969 at Town Hall in New York. Her honors included the Marian Anderson* Award (1967), the International Black Festival Award (1968), and an award from the National Association of Negro Musicians (1966).

BIBL: Black press.

MATTHEWS, ARTIE. Ragtime pianist/Composer (b. 15 November 1888 in Minonk, Illinois; d. 25 October 1958 in Cincinnati, Ohio). His family moved to Springfield, Illinois, when he was a child. He studied piano first with his mother, then with local teachers. About 1905 he began playing rag piano, learning it from Banty Morgan and Art Dunningham, who played in local brothels and clubs. He also began to play professionally at this time with his string trio on street corners and in local cafes and saloons. About 1908 he settled in St. Louis, Missouri; there he arranged music for rag-publisher John Stark and for Tom Turpin,* who produced shows in his Booker T. Washington Theater. During this period Matthews began to publish some of his piano rags, including "Pastime rag, no. 1" and "Weary blues." He traveled to Chicago, Illinois, several times, where he came into contact with Tony Jackson* and Ferdinand ("Jelly Roll") Morton.* In 1915 he settled in Chicago and was active as a church organist and studio teacher. In 1918 he settled permanently in Cincinnati, Ohio, where in 1921 he founded the Cosmopolitan School of Music. The teachers he employed included his wife Anna and Noah W. Ryder (father of Noah Francis Ryder*), among others.

BIBL: Blesh. Dabney, p. 212. JaTiRR.

MATTHEWS, EDWARD. Concert singer (b. 3 August 1907 in Ossining, New York; d. 21 February 1954 in New York, New York). He came from a musical family; his mother was a church soloist, and his sister Inez* became a professional musician. He received his musical education in the public schools of Ossining and at Fisk University in Nashville, Tennessee (B.A. 1926), where he sang in the Fisk Quartet and toured with the Fisk Jubilee Singers* for a year in Europe. Later he studied with Arthur Hubbard at Boston, Massachusetts (1928). In February 1930 he made his debut as a baritone at Jordan Hall in Boston, and in January 1931 he made his New York debut at Town Hall under the sponsorship of Roland Hayes.* During the years 1932–33 he toured widely in the United States and appeared on radio programs; he was a regular member of the Major Bowes Capitol Radio Family on CBS (Columbia Broadcasting System) for seven years, beginning in 1932. In 1934 he created the role of St. Ignatius in Virgil Thomson's opera *Four Saints in Three Acts*, and the next year he created the role of Jake in Gershwin's *Porgy and Bess*. He also sang the roles in revivals of *Porgy and Bess* in 1944 and *Four Saints* in 1952. His teaching career included tenures at Fisk University, Howard University in Washington, D.C., and Virginia State College in Petersburg. His wife, Altonell Hines* Matthews, was also a singer.

BIBL: Information from Inez Matthews. Black press, incl. AmstN, 27 February 1954; CDef, 17 January 1931; NYAge, 16 January 1932, 18 December 1937. Hare. NYT, 22 February 1954.

DISC: Turn.

MATTHEWS, INEZ. Concert/theater singer (b. 23 August 1917 in Ossining, New York). She came from a musical family: her mother was a church soloist, and her brother Edward* became an opera singer. As a child she sang in her father's Baptist church choir and also sang solos, accompanied by her sister Helen. She obtained her musical education in the public schools of Ossining, New York, and through private study. Her teachers included Katherine Moran Douglas, Paula Novikova, and Frederick Wilkerson, among others. Her career development was influenced by Leonard DePaur.* In 1947 she made her concert debut as a mezzo-soprano at Town Hall in New York; the same year she made her Boston [Massachusetts] debut at Jordan Hall and her Chicago [Illinois] debut at Kimball Hall. Thereafter she toured widely in the United States and in Europe as a concert singer, giving solo recitals and appearing with symphony orchestras. She was also active in opera and musicals. She sang the title role in the Broadway production of *Carmen Jones* (1944-46, 1948); the role of Irina in Kurt Weill's *Lost in the Stars* (1950); the role of St. Theresa in Thomson's *Four Saints in Three Acts* (1951 revival), in which her brother also sang a leading role; and the role of Serena in the film production of Gershwin's *Porgy and Bess* (1960). She toured extensively with the Leonard DePaur Singers at home and abroad. Her teaching experience included a tenure at Virginia State College in Petersburg (1965-70), and she was an associate teacher in Frederick Wilkerson's music studio for many years.

BIBL: Questionnaire. Black press, incl. CDef, 22 March 1958; AmstN, 15 November 1947.

DISC: Turn.

MAULTSBY, PORTIA. College professor/Ethnomusicologist (b. 11 June 1947 in Orlando, Florida). She began piano study at the age of five. She obtained her musical education from Benedictine College in Atchison, Kansas (B. Mus., 1968), where she studied with Sister Joachim Holthaus and Hal Tamblyn, and the University of Wisconsin at Madison (M. Mus., 1969, Ph.D., 1974), where she studied with Lois Anderson. Her career development was aided by her teachers and faculty member Herman Hudson at Indiana University in Bloomington, where she began teaching in 1975. She was one of the first black Americans to specialize in ethnomusicology. After completing her doctoral dissertation of the Negro spiritual, she published in professional journals and lectured at meetings of professional societies. In September 1975 she was guest editor of the *Journal of the Society for Ethnomusicology*. She was also active as composer-arranger for a choral group she directed, called Soul Revue, at Indiana University.

BIBL: Questionnaire.

MAY, JOE ("BROTHER"). Gospel singer. See **SMITH, WILLIE.**

MAYFIELD, CURTIS. Rhythm 'n' blues singer (b. 3 June 1942 in Chicago, Illinois). He taught himself to play guitar at the age of nine. At a early age he toured with the Northern Jubilee Singers, a gospel group associated with the church where his grandmother was the minister. Later he sang with a rhythm 'n' blues group, The Alphatones, but left the group when he was fourteen to join The Impressions, which made recordings as Jerry Butler & The Impressions. After Butler left the group in 1958, Mayfield became the lead singer and, at the same time, worked with Butler (1958-60) as guitarist and songwriter. He also wrote songs for The Impressions, several of which were commercially successful. In 1967 he founded Curtom Records, which published songs, produced records, and provided management for musical groups. He left The Impressions in 1970 to tour and make records as a soloist. He was also active on radio and in films, not only as a performer but also as a composer. His music was used on the soundtracks for *Superfly* (1972), *Claudine* (1974), and *Let's Do It Again* (1975).

BIBL: Black press, incl. CDef, 4 October 1975. BMI (March 1971). *Ebony* (July 1973). StamPRS. WWA. WWBA.

DISC: TudBM.

MAYNOR, DOROTHY (née **DOROTHY LEIGH MAINOR).** Concert singer (b. 3 September 1910 in Norfolk, Virginia). She sang in her father's church as a child. She began voice study formally at the age of fourteen, attending Hampton Institute in Virginia. She obtained her musical education also at Hampton (B.S., 1933), where she came under the guidance of R. Nathaniel Dett,* and later attended the Westminister Choir School in Princeton, New Jersey. In 1935 she went to New York, where she studied privately with William Klamroth and John Alan Haughton, among others. Her career development was aided by Serge Koussevitsky, for whom she auditioned in August 1939 at the Berkshire Music Festival in Massachusetts. She made her debut as a soprano in November 1939 at Town Hall in New York, and made her recording debut soon thereafter. She established herself as one of the leading singers of the nation and, among black concert artists, as a member of the select circle which included Marian Anderson,* Roland Hayes,* and Paul Robeson.* She toured widely in the United States, Europe, Australia, and Central and South America and appeared as soloist with the principal symphony orchestras of the western world. She recorded extensively and sang on radio and television programs. After she retired from the concert stage, she founded the Harlem School of the Arts and served as its first director (1965-1980). Her successor was Betty Allen.* She sponsored benefit concerts for the school, frequently leading the school chorus herself, and presented such guest artists as McHenry Boatright,* Louise Parker,* and George Shirley.* Her honors included honorary doctorates from Bennett College in North Carolina (1945), Howard University (1960), Duquesne University (1970), Oberlin College (1971), and Carnegie-Mellon University (1972); awards from the Town Hall Endowment Series (1940) for outstanding performance at Town Hall and from the Hampton Alumni Association (1941) for distinguished service; and appointment to the Metropolitan Opera Board of Directors (1975).

BIBL: Black press, incl. CDef, 26 August 1939, 14 October 1939. *Ebony* (May 1966). NYT, 6 March 1975, 17 May 1975, 9 March 1980. NYB. WWA. WWBA. WWCA, 1950.

DISC: Turn.

MEADOWS, EDDIE SPENCER. College professor (b. 24 June 1939 in La Grange, Tennessee). He obtained his musical education in the public schools of Memphis, Tennessee, where he came under the tutelage of bandmaster Richard ("Tuff") Green at Melrose High School; at Tennessee State University in Nashville (B.S., 1962); at the University of Illinois at Champaign-Urbana (M.S., 1963) and at Michigan State University in East Lansing (Ph.D., 1970). His career development was influenced by Green, Frank T. Greer, T. J. Anderson,* and Anceo Melvin. His teaching career included tenures at Kentucky State College in Frankfort (1963-64); Wiley College in Marshall, Texas (1964-66); public schools in Chicago, Illinois (1966-67); Michigan State University (1970-72); and San Diego University in California (1972-). He also served as visiting professor at various institutions, including the University of California at Berkeley (1978), the University of California at Los Angeles (1978), and the University of Ghana at Accra (1980-81). He studied trumpet and other brass instruments in his youth and played in jazz groups and marching bands in high schools. In 1966 he played in the Theodore ("Red") Saunders* big band and in the Regal Theater band, both in Chicago. In his teaching career he was bandmaster as well as classroom teacher, and at San Diego he directed the University Jazz Lab Band. He contributed articles to professional publications and toured as a lecturer, speaking on the subjects of jazz, folk music, and black music history. His book publications included *Theses and Dissertations on Black American Music* (1980) and *Jazz Reference and Research Materials* (1981). He was appointed to panels and executive committees of professional and civic institutions.

BIBL: Questionnaire.

MEMPHIS MINNIE. See **DOUGLAS, MINNIE.**

MEMPHIS SLIM. See **CHATMAN, PETER.**

MEMPHIS STUDENTS, THE. Vaudeville act (fl. 1905-08 in New York, New York). This musical organization, which included about twenty singers, dancers, and instrumentalists, is credited with being the first to stage a public concert of "syncopated music" (also called jazz in sources) in New York. The group was organized in May 1905 by Ernest Hogan* and gave more than 150 performances at Hammerstein's Victoria Theater. In October 1905 Will Marion Cook* took over the group and carried it to London, England, for a three-months engagement. Joe Jordan* revived the Memphis Students in 1908, and it enjoyed another successful run on Broadway. Performers associated with the groups included Abbie Mitchell,* Ernest Hogan, Will Dixon,* and dancer Ida Forcyne. In the second edition of the Memphis Students, Tom Fletcher* replaced the ailing Hogan.

BIBL: Black press, incl. NYAge 24 August 1905, 26 October 1905. Flet, p. 129 (Fletcher errs in calling the group the Nashville Students). JohnBM.

MENSAH, EMMANUEL TETTEH. Jazz ["highlife"] bandleader (b. 31 May 1919 in Accra, Ghana). He obtained his education at the Accra Government School and at the Accra High School (1935-39). He began music study as a child, playing fife in elementary school and studying organ and saxophone in high school. During his school years he played with Accra's Rhythm Orchestra and with the Accra Orchestra. In 1945 he studied trumpet with Joe Kelly and later played in the Kumasi [Ghana] Philharmonic Orchestra. He also played in an army band during the 1940s, Jack Leopard and His Black and White Spots, that entertained servicemen. In 1947 he formed a dance band, The Tempos, which toured widely in West Africa and Europe; later he also led the Ramblers International Band. In 1956 he was elected president of the Ghana Musicians Union. His honors included the Ghana Arts Award (1972). He was called "King of Hi-Life."

BIBL: GhanaWW. *West African Review* 28 (March 1957, 29 (October 1958). WWAfrica.

MERCER, MABEL. Popular music singer (b. 3 February 1900 in Staffordshire, England). Her mother and aunt were vaudeville entertainers. She made her professional debut at the age of fourteen singing with her aunt. During the 1920s-30s she lived in Paris, France, where she established herself as one of the leading nightclub singers of the city. She first won recognition as a singer in a club owned by Ada ("Bricktop") Smith*; later she toured the continent on the nightclub circuit. In 1938 she went to the United States and in 1941 she settled in New York. Her friends held a gala celebration on the occasion of her seventy-fifth birthday. Her honors included an honorary doctorate from the Berklee College of Music (1975). Her contemporaries called her "a storyteller in song."

BIBL: Black press, incl. *Bay State Banner*, 24 October 1974. CurBiog (February 1973). *Encore American & Worldwide News* (23 May 1977). NYT, 4 February 1975, 23 February 1975.

MERRIFIELD, NORMAN L. Music educator (b. 19 August 1906 in Louisville, Kentucky). He obtained his musical education at Northwestern University in Evanston, Illinois (B. Mus.Ed., 1927; M. Mus.Ed., 1932); Jordan University School of Music in Indianapolis, Indiana; Michigan State University at East Lansing, Michigan; and the Trinity College of Music in London, England. During his service in the United States Armed Forces (1943-46) he attended an Army Band School and was a bandmaster. His teaching career included tenures at Fisk University in Nashville, Tennessee

(1927-28); public schools in Knoxville, Tennessee (1928-31); Florida A & M College in Tallahassee, Florida (1932-34); and Crispus Attucks High School in Indianapolis, Indiana (1934-67), where he was bandleader and chairman of the music department. He published a number of spiritual arrangements for mixed voices and men's chorus in addition to cantatas and a symphony. He also contributed articles to professional journals. He exerted wide influence as a teacher; among those who came under his tutelage or that of his colleagues, LaVerne Newsome and Russell Brown, at Attucks High School were James ("J.J.") Johnson,* Paul Overbey, Richard Overbey, David Baker,* and Robert Womack.

BIBL: Questionnaire. ASCAP. WWCA, 1950.

MEUDE-MONPAS, THE CHEVALIER J. J. O. de. Composer (b. 17?? in Paris, France; d. 17?? in Berlin, Germany (?)). Little is known of his musical career. He served as a musketeer in the service of Louis XVI of France and went into exile with the onset of the turmoil of the Revolution. He studied music in Paris with Pierre La Houssaye and François Giroust. He published six concertos for violin and orchestra (1786), a *Dictionnaire de Musique* (1787), and a book titled *De l'influence de l'amour et de la musique sur les moeurs* . . . (Berlin, n.d.).

BIBL: BPIM 2 (Fall 1974), p. 233. Fétis.

MIDDLETON, GEORGE. Military commander (fl. late eighteenth century). He was the only black commander of a Revolutionary War company. Called the Bucks of America, his Massachusetts company was one of the two all-black colonial companies that fought in the war (the other came from Rhode Island). Colonel Middleton played the violin.

BIBL: Nell, p. 25. Wilkes, p. 32.

MIDDLETON, VELMA. Jazz singer (b. 1 September 1917 in St. Louis, Missouri; d. 10 February 1961 in Sierra Leone, Africa). She began her professional career with the Connie McLean orchestra of the Cotton Club Show in New York and later sang in nightclubs. She sang with Louis Armstrong* for many years (1942-61) and was on tour with Armstrong in Africa when she fell fatally ill.

BIBL: ChilWW. FeaEJ. FeaJS.

MIGHTY, MIGHTY CLOUDS OF JOY, THE. Gospel group (orig. c1959 in Los Angeles, California). The all-male group originally included Ermant Franklin, Jr., Elmer Franklin (not related to Ermant), Willie Joe Ligon (lead), Johnny Martin, Leon Polk, and Richard Wallace (guitar). The singers formed the group during their high-school days; only Martin, however was a native Californian. Others who performed with the group over the years included singer Jimmy Jones and instrumentalists Elmore Nixon (piano), Hampton Carlton (organ), and Wittier Booker (drums). In 1980 the group was composed of Lion, Martin, Wallace, Elmer Franklin, and Paul Beasley. The Mighty, Mighty Clouds of Joy used amplified instruments in their accompaniment groups and represented a gospel style that blended elements of popular music and rhythm 'n' blues with traditional gospel elements.

BIBL: GMEncy. Heil.

DISC: Hayes.

MIKELL, FRANCIS EUGENE. Bandmaster (b. 27 March 1885 in Charleston, South Carolina; d. 19 January 1932 in New York). He studied violin and cornet as a child with local teachers. He attended the Avery Normal and Industrial Institute in Charleston, South Carolina, and later, Tuskegee Institute in Alabama, where he studied with Charles Harris. He studied further at the New York School of Music. He was director of the Jenkins Orphanage Band* of Charleston when it performed at the inauguration of President William Taft in 1909. His teaching career included tenures at South Carolina State College in Orangeburg, and at Cookman Institute and Florida Baptist Institute in Jacksonville, Florida, where he was also director of the Globe Theater. According to the press, he was called to New York in 1917 by Colonel William Haywood to serve as bandmaster to the newly organized band of the Old Fifteenth Infantry Regiment (later the 369th), of which James Reese Europe* was musical director. Abroad, the band earned the nickname of "Hell-Fighters." After World War I, he settled in New York and became active as a conductor with Clef Club groups. After the death of Europe in 1919, he organized some of the original members of Europe's band into a "Hell-Fighter's Band," which gave its first public concert in December 1919. In May 1922 he was appointed bandmaster of the 369th Infantry Band. He also organized a 369th Cadet band, which trained many who would later win recognition for their instrumental talents. During the 1920s he taught at the Martin-Smith* Music School and was a music instructor at the Bordentown Industrial Institute in New Jersey. He also conducted a music studio in New York. During the 1930s he directed the New York Times Choral Society, Band, and Orchestra. He attracted wide attention for his arrangements and compositions, which were performed by his students and various groups. His best-known piece was "That plantation rag." His sons, Otto R. and Francis Eugene, Jr., were also professional musicians.

BIBL: Black press, incl. CDef, 20 November 1919, 30 January 1932; IndF, 15 October 1910; NYAge, 21 June 1919, 17 July 1920, 1 January 1921, 10 June 1922. ChilWW. WWCA 1928-29, 1930-33.

MILBURN, RICHARD JAMES. Whistler (b. c1814 in Maryland; d. ?). A barber by trade, he gave whistling and guitar recitals in Philadelphia, Pennsylvania. He is remembered today as the composer of "Listen to the mocking bird." The song was published in 1855 with identification of Milburn as composer and Alice Hawthorne (pseudonym for Septimus Winner) as arranger. In later printings the name of Milburn was omitted from the title page.

BIBL: BPIM 3 (Spring 1975), p. 95. John E. Bruce, "A History of Negro Musicians" in *Southern Workman* 45 (1916). Hare. SouMBA.

MILEY, JAMES WESLEY ("BUBBER"). Jazz trumpeter (b. 19 January 1903 in Aiken, South Carolina; d. 24 May 1932 in New York, New York). His family moved to New York when he was a child. He first played professionally with local groups, then toured in the early 1920s with Mamie Smith* and Her Jazz Hounds and later with a revue. In 1923 he joined the Washingtonians, at that time under the leadership of Elmer Snowden,* and remained with the orchestra after Edward ("Duke") Ellington* became the leader the next year. He played with Ellington for five years (1924-29) and thereafter, with various groups, including Noble Sissle,* Arthur ("Zutty") Singleton,* Joseph ("King") Oliver,* Ferdinand ("Jelly Roll") Morton,* and Leo Reisman, among others. In 1931 he played in the pit orchestra for the Sweet and Low Revue; later he formed a group to play for the touring company of that revue. He was a major contributor, along with Joseph ("Tricky Sam") Nanton,* to the unique sound of Ellington's "jungle band" of the 1920s. He pioneered in the use of the growl, rubber plunger, and wah-wah mute, and passed on the techniques to the band's trombonists. He also wrote much of the material played by Ellington's band during the years 1927-29, some of it in collaboration with Ellington. His best-known compositions (written with Ellington) were "Black and tan fantasy," "East St. Louis toodle-oo," and "Creole love call."

BIBL: ChilWW. DanceWDE. FeaEJ.

DISC: Kink. RustJR.

MILLER, FLOURNOY ("HONEY"). Vaudeville entertainer (b. 14 April 1887 in Nashville, Tennessee; d. 6 June 1971 in Hollywood, California). He met Aubrey Lyles at Fisk University in Nashville, Tennessee, where both were students. They formed a partnership in 1903, performing in college theatricals and writing together their first plays. Occasionally Miller's brother, Irvin, participated in activities with them. About 1905 Miller and Lyles joined Robert ("Bob") Mott's* Pekin Theater Stock Company at Chicago, Illinois, and wrote the book for the first musical produced at the Pekin, *The Man from Bam*, with musical score by Joe Jordan.* Other plays written for the Pekin included *The Husband* and *The Mayor of Dixie*. In 1907 they wrote *The Oyster Man* for Ernest Hogan,* who starred in the musical until his death in 1909. By 1910 Miller and Lyles were touring on the B. F. Keith vaudeville circuit, and they toured extensively during the next decade, including performances in Europe in 1915. In 1920 they wrote the book for the Eubie Blake*/Noble Sissle* musical, *Shuffle Along* (based on *The Mayor of Dixie*), and also performed leading roles. They also wrote books for other musicals, including *Keep Shufflin'* (1928, music by Thomas ("Fats") Waller* and James P. Johnson*) and *Running Wild* (1923, music by Johnson). They were featured in these shows and as well in others, including *In Darkeydom* (1914-15), *Way Down South* (1915), *Rang Tang* (1927-28), and *Sugar Hill* (1931). Their Sam Peck and Amos Brown characters in *Sugar Hill* were the direct inspiration for Amos and Andy in the radio and, later, television show *Amos and Andy*. The Miller-Lyles partnership was dissolved for a period when Lyles went to Africa in the late 1920s but was revived for their performance in *Sugar Hill*. The duo also performed in such white musicals as *The Charity Girl* (1912) and *Great Day* (1929). After Lyles's death Miller toured with various partners, among them Haintree Harrington.

BIBL: ASCAP. Black press, incl. CDef, 19 February 1910, 3 November 1917; NYAge, 21 October 1915. Flet, pp. 201-05. Hare.

DISC: RustCED.

MILLER, WILLIE (née **ALECK FORD**) **("RICE" "WILLIAMSON, SONNY BOY NO. 2").** Bluesman (b. 5 December 1899 in Glendora, Mississippi; d. 25 May 1965 in Helena, Arkansas). He began his radio-broadcasting career in 1941 on Sonny Boy's Corn Meal and King Biscuit Show, station KFFA in Helena, Arkansas, and remained with the show off and on until his death. Over the years his radio blues bands included James Peck Curtis, Robert ("Junior") Lockwood,*

Willie Love, Dudlow Taylor, and Joe Willie Wilkins,* among others. Throughout his career Miller toured widely in the United States, sometimes settling in various cities for short periods—as he did in Detroit in 1954 and later in Chicago. He also toured in Europe during the 1960s.

BIBL: BWW. "King Biscuit Time 1971" in LivBl 5 (Summer 1971). MeeJMov. Oliv.

DISC: LeSl. TudBM.

MILLINDER, LUCIUS ("LUCKY"). Jazz bandleader (b. 8 August 1900 in Anniston, Alabama; d. 28 September 1966 in New York, New York). He was a rarity in that although a bandleader he was neither instrumentalist nor singer. He obtained his education in the public schools of Chicago, Illinois. He began his professional career as a master of ceremonies in Chicago nightclubs and ballrooms. In 1931 he took a band on tour for the first time. Thereafter he was leader of a band in a Harlem nightclub in New York, and in 1933 he toured in Europe with another band. The next year he took over leadership of the Mills Blue Rhythm Band (1934-38), which later performed and recorded under his name. His bands were also active in films, including *Paradise in Harlem* (1938) and *Boarding House Blues* (1948). He led various groups until 1952, when he left music as a full-time activity. Thereafter he led bands occasionally on special occasions. During the 1950s he was a disc jockey on radio station WNEW in New York. Those who performed with him over the years included Henry ("Red") Allen,* Harry ("Sweets") Edison,* Jack ("Jay C") Higginbotham,* John Birks ("Dizzy") Gillespie,* and ("Sister") Rosetta Tharpe,* among others.

BIBL: ChilWW. FeaEJ. MeeJMov.

DISC: Jep. Kink. RustJR.

MILLS, FLORENCE. Entertainer (b. 25 January 1895 in Washington, D.C.; d. 1 November 1927 in New York, New York). She began her professional career at the age of four when she appeared as a special feature in the Bob Cole*/Billy Johnson* show, *A Trip to Coontown*. The next season she appeared in the George Walker*/Bert Williams* show, *Son of Ham*. Her family moved to New York in 1903; a few years later she and her sisters organized a vaudeville act called "The Mills Trio" or "The Three Mills Sisters." About 1914 she began touring with a vaudeville act, which disbanded in Chicago, Illinois. There she became a nightclub entertainer on Chicago's South Side. In 1916 she attracted special attention as a member of "The Panama Trio," which included Cora Green and Ada ("Bricktop") Smith.* She toured with the trio for three years on the Pantages circuit (Caroline Willliams replaced Ada Smith), then joined the vaudeville company, The Tennessee Ten, where she met her future husband, entertainer/dancer Ulysses S. Thompson. In 1921 her appearance in the Eubie Blake*/Noble Sissle* show *Shuffle Along* attracted wide attention and led to contract offers; she accepted that of Lew Leslie, who remained her manager until her death. He opened the Plantation cabaret on Broadway in 1922 with Mills as the featured performer in *Plantation Revue*, which included Shelton Brooks,* Edith Wilson,* and the Will Vodery* Plantation Orchestra, among others. Mills also began touring on the Keith vaudeville circuit and performed as an extra in the Greenwich Village Follies in 1922. The next year she starred in *Dover Street to Dixie* at the Pavilion Theater in London, England, and returned to the United States in 1924 to star in *Dixie to Broadway*. William Grant Still* wrote a work especially for her, *Levee Land*, which received its premiere in January 1926 at an International Composers' Guild Concert at Aeolian Hall in New York with Mills singing the solo part in the three-movement orchestra work. The same year she starred in Lew Leslie's *Blackbirds of 1926*, which opened in a Harlem theater, then toured in London and Paris, France, and other continental cities. During her stay in London, she studied voice with Louis Drysdale, a native of Jamaica, West Indies, who conducted a vocal studio in the city. She died suddenly after returning to the United States in the fall of 1927. Her most celebrated performance was of 'I'm a little blackbird looking for a bluebird" from *Dixie to Broadway*.

BIBL: Black press, incl. CDef, 1 March 1916, 17 May 1919; NYAge, 9 February 1924, 18 December 1925, 5 November 1927. U.S. Thompson, "Florence Mills" in *Negro: An Anthology*, edited by Nancy Cunard (London, 1934; 2nd edition by Hugh Ford, New York, 1970).

DISC: RustCED.

MILLS BLUE RHYTHM BAND. See **MILLINDER, LUCIUS.**

MILLS BROTHERS, THE. Popular-music singers (fl. late 1920s to 1970s; orig. in Piqua, Ohio). They came from a musical family. The grandfather, Billy Mills, sang in the McMillen and Sourbeck Jubilee Singers* (later called Stinson's Jubilee Singers), one of the first of the professional groups that emulated the Fisk Jubilee Singers of the 1870s. Their parents were musical, and the boys received their early musical training from their mother. They began singing professionally in 1922 for local social entertainments: Herbert, first tenor (b. 2 April 1912); Donald, second tenor (b. 29 April 1915); Harry, baritone (b. 19 August 1913); John, bass (b. 19 October 1910; d. 24 January 1936). In 1925 the boys went to Cincinnati, Ohio, to audition for radio station WLW and won a contract to broadcast. During the next few years they had several sponsors, which was reflected in the names under which they sang—for example, The Steamboat Four for Sohio Motor Oil or the Tasty Yeast Jesters for Tasty Yeast. They also sang as Four Boys and a Guitar and on The Mills Brothers Program and toured widely throughout the nation. In 1929 the quartet signed a three-year contract with CBS, the first black group to win commercial sponsorship on a national network. Thereafter the Mills Brothers toured widely at home and abroad, recorded extensively after their recording debut in 1931, and appeared in films, including *The Big Broadcast of 1932*, *Twenty Million Sweethearts* (1934), *Broadway Gondolier* (1935), and *The Big Beat* (1957), among others. When John, Jr., died in 1936, his father (1889-1967) replaced him in the quartet, and a year later Norman Brown (d. August 1969) became the guitarist. When the father retired in 1954, the Mills Brothers became a trio. The group was celebrated for its unique sound, produced by imitating instruments with their voices and cupped hands. Their best-known songs were "Paper doll," "Lazy river," "You always hurt the one you love," "Glow worm," and "Goodbye blues" (theme song).

BIBL: Black press, incl. NYAge, 1 February 1936. FeaEJ. *Ebony* (September 1969). Flet, p. 30. *Sepia* (January 1970).

DISC: Kink. RustCED.

MIMS, A. GRACE LEE. See **DESCENDENTS OF MIKE AND PHOEBE.**

MINGUS, CHARLES. Jazz bassist (b. 22 April 1922 in Nogales, Arizona; d. 5 January 1979 in Cuernavaca, Mexico). He began trombone study at the age of eight but after a few lessons changed to cello. He obtained his musical education in the public schools of Los Angeles, where he played in the Los Angeles Junior Philharmonic Orchestra. At seventeen he exchanged his cello for a double bass and joined a local jazz group led by Buddy Colette, a fellow high-school student. His teachers included George ("Red") Callender and, later, Herman Rheinschagen. During the 1940s-early 1950s he played with various groups, including Lee Young (1940), Louis Armstrong* (1941-43), Edward ("Kid") Ory,* Alvino Rey, Lionel Hampton* (1946-48), Kenneth ("Red") Norvo (1950-51), William ("Billy") Taylor* (1952-53), and Edward ("Duke") Ellington,* among others. In 1947 he made his recording debut with Hampton's band; in 1952 he, Max Roach,* and others organized a recording company, called Debut, which was one of the first musician-owned companies in the nation. From the mid-1950s on he led his own groups and conducted workshops, both of which were characterized by experimentation with new jazz forms and harmonic approaches. After the mid-1960s he was relatively inactive but returned to music full time in the 1970s, marking his return with a concert of his big band at Lincoln Center's Philharmonic Hall (now Avery Fisher) in New York in February 1972. Thereafter he toured widely in the United States, Europe, and Japan and recorded regularly. He also appeared on television shows and in films, among them, *All Night Long* (1961), the documentary *Mingus* (1968), and *Jazz in Piazza* (1974). Among the musicians who were professionally associated with him at one time or another were George Adams, John ("Jaki") Byard,* Hamiet Bluitt, Shafti Hadi, John Handy,* Milton ("Milt") Jackson,* Clifford Jordan,* James ("Jimmy") Knepper, Rahsaan Roland Kirk,* John Birks ("Dizzy") Gillespie,* Eric Dolphy,* and John ("Jackie") McLean.* His honors included appointment to the Slee Chair of Music at the State University of New York at Buffalo (1972), a Guggenheim Foundation grant (1971), and awards from the music industry. His best-known albums were *Pithecanthropus Erectus* (1956), *Black Saint and Sinner Lady* (1963), *Mingus Moves* (1974), and *Me, Myself and Eye* (1978), which included the composition "Three worlds of drums." He was regarded as one of the leading jazz composers of his time. His style was eclectic, particularly in his later career, encompassing blues and gospel along with the avant-garde and even elements of jazz-rock upon occasion. He pioneered in defining the role of the jazz string bass, elevating the instrument to the level of a solo melodic insrument in the jazz ensemble. His experiments in the 1950s paved the way for the free collective jazz of the 1960s. Like Duke Ellington, he was a bandleader with rare skills and the ability to inspire his sidemen to impressive achievement. He published an autobiography, *Beneath the Underdog* (New York, 1971).

BIBL: Black press, incl. AmstN, 13 January 1979. BMI (October 1969). CurBiog (February 1971). FeaEJ. FeaJS. FeaGitJS. *Jazz Magazine* (Spring 1979). NYT, 9 January 1979. WWA. WWBA.

DISC: Jep. ModJ. TudJ.

MIRACLES, THE. Also known as **SMOKEY ROBINSON AND THE MIRACLES.** (Orig. 1950 in Detroit, Michigan; fl. 1950s-70s). The members of this singing-dancing group began singing together during their high-school days in Detroit, Michigan. Lead singer William (''Smokey'') Robinson (b. 19 February 1940) organized the group in 1953, including guitarist Marv Tamplin along with bass Warren (''Pete'') Moore (b. 19 November 1940), tenor Robert (''Bobby'') Rogers (b. 19 February 1939), and baritone Ronald (''Ronnie'') White (b. 5 April 1939). He also wrote most of their songs, some in collaboration with others of the group. The group first sang for school events, then in local nightclubs. Roger's cousin, Claudette (later, Mrs. Robinson), toured with the Miracles until 1964 and thereafter occasionally recorded with them. Berry Gordy,* then a part-time record producer, gave the Miracles an audition in 1958 and recorded their song ''Get a job,'' which won wide recognition. When Gordy established the Tamla label of Motown Records in 1959, Smokey Robinson and the Miracles were his first artists. Within the next few years the group became one of the top popular-music groups; they toured widely, appeared on television shows, and recorded extensively. In 1972 Robinson left the Miracles because of his heavy administrative reponsibilities as executive vice-president of Motown Industries, and the next year his place was taken by William Griffen (b. 1951 in Baltimore, Maryland). Robinson continued to write songs for the Miracles, however, and as well for such entertainers as Diana Ross* and the Supremes, Marvin Gaye,* Mary Wells, and The Temptations,* among others. Beginning in 1975 he occasionally toured as a soloist. Among the best-known songs of the Miracles were ''Tears of a clown,'' ''You've really got a hold on me,'' ''Mickey's monkey,'' and ''Going to a go-go.'' They received numerous awards from the music industry.

BIBL: Black press, incl. AmstN, 1 March 1975. *Ebony* (October 1971). StamPRS.

DISC: Giv. TudBM.

MISSISSIPPI SHEIKS, THE. Blues group (orig. c1917 in Bolton, Mississippi). The Mississippi Sheiks was a popular group which consisted primarily of members of the Chatmon (also known as Chatman) family at Bolton, Mississippi: Armenter (''Bo''), Bert Charlie, Edgar, Harry, Laurie, Lonnie, Sam, and Willie. An adopted brother, Walter Jacobs Vinson, also played with the group. The Chatmons had a long tradition for family string bands; the father, Henderson Chatmon, and his brothers had played in a band with their father. Several of the third-generation brothers recorded and/or played as soloists and with other groups, particularly Bo, Harry, Lonnie, and Sam. Lonnie, bandleader and violinist, formed a partnership with Vinson in 1928 when the family group began to fall apart; during the years 1930-33 the two bluesmen recorded as The Mississippi Sheiks. Thus the name is attached to both the family group recordings and to the duo recordings. Vinson also recorded as Walter Vincent. A son of Sam, Sam Chatmon, Jr., was a bluesman known as ''Singing Sam.''

BIBL: BWW. LivBl 21 (May-June 1975). Oliv.

DISC: LeSlBR. TudBM.

MITCHELL, ABBIE. Concert singer/Actress (b. 25 September 1884 in New York, New York; d. 16 March 1960 in New York, New York). She attended public schools in Baltimore, Maryland and began appearing in local church entertainments as a child. She began her professional career at fourteen, when she joined Will Marion Cook's* show, *Clorindy, or the Origin of the Cakewalk* during its run in 1898 in Chicago, Illinois. In December of that year she joined Black Patti's* Troubadours. For the next few years she took leading roles in the important shows of the period, starring in Cook's *Jes Lak White Folks* (summer of 1899); in the George Walker*/Bert Williams* show, *In Dahomey* (1902), with which she went to London, England; in the Bob Cole*/Johnson brothers* show, *The Red Moon*. In 1905 she was a member of the original Memphis Students,* touring with the group in Europe, and she starred again in the second edition of the Memphis Students in 1908. During her first years in New York, she studied voice with Harry T. Burleigh*; later she studied with Emilia Serrano and in Paris with Jean de Reszke. She coached with Will Marion Cook and Melville Charlton.* Beginning about 1910 she became involved with the theater; she appeared in plays at the Pekin and Monogram Theaters in Chicago, and was a charter member of the Original Lafayette Players of Harlem in New York in 1914. Through the years she continued to sing, however, and appeared frequently on concerts in New York and Washington, D.C., in particular. In 1919 she toured with Cook's Southern Syncopated Orchestra (aka the New York Syncopated Orchestra) in the United States and abroad. When Cook returned home in 1921, she remained abroad, touring for over a year with an act called ''Abbie Mitchell and Her Full Harmonic Quartet.'' During her stay she again studied voice in Paris, and she returned for more study in 1931. During the 1920s-30s she sang regularly in concerts and in opera, except during the years 1932-34 when she was a voice teacher at Tuskegee Institute in Alabama. In 1934 she sang the role of Santuzza in an Aeolian Opera Association production of Mascagni's *Cavalleria Rusticana*, and in 1935 she made her last musical-stage appearance as Clara in Gershwin's *Porgy and Bess*. Thereafter she was active in music as a teacher and vocal coach, but continued to appear in straight dramatic roles on the stage. Her first husband was Will Marion Cook (1899-1906).

BIBL: Black press, incl. CDef, 13 August 1910, 21 February 1914; IndF, 31 December 1898, 16 March 1915; NYAge 23 July 1923, 20 April 1929, 21 July 1934, 24 November 1934, 14 November 1936. Hare. HNB. NAW.

MITCHELL, LEONA. Opera/concert singer (b. 13 October 1949 in Enid, Oklahoma). She received her musical education in the public schools of Enid and at Oklahoma City University (B.A., 1971), where she studied with Inez Silberg and performed soprano roles in operas produced at the university. In 1972 she won the Kurt Herbert Adler Award of the San Francisco Opera and made her operatic debut as Micaela in Bizet's *Carmen* with the San Francisco Opera. Thereafter she sang with various companies, including the Houston Opera and the Washington [D.C.] Opera Society, and appeared with major symphony orchestras. In August 1975 she sang the role of Bess in Gershwin's *Porgy and Bess* at the Cleveland Orchestra Blossom Festival and later sang the role in the recording of the opera. In December 1975 she made her Metropolitan Opera debut, singing Micaela in *Carmen*. She made her European operatic debut in 1976 with the Geneva [Switzerland] Opera, singing the role of Liu in Puccini's *Turandot*. Other roles for which she won recognition included Donna Anna in Mozart's *Don Giovanni*, the title role in Puccini's *Madame Butterfly*, Musetta in Puccini's *La Bohème*, and Mme. Lidoine in Poulenc's *Dialogues of the Carmelites*, among others. Her honors included grants from the Rockefeller Foundation and the National Opera Institute and a citation as an "Outstanding Oklahoman" (1975) because she was the first native of Oklahoma to sing with the Metropolitan Opera.

BIBL: *Opera News* (10 February 1979). WWO.

DISC: Turn.

MITCHELL, NELLIE BROWN. See **BROWN, MITCHELL NELLIE.**

MITCHELL, ROSCOE. Jazz saxophonist (b. 3 August 1940 in Chicago, Illinois). He obtained his musical education in the public schools of Chicago, Illinois. He played clarinet and baritone saxophone in his high-school band, and during his service in the United States Armed Forces (1958-61), he played alto saxophone in an army band. In 1962 he began an association with Muhal Richard Abrams's* Experimental Band, which later developed into the Association for the Advancement of Creative Musicians* (formally organized in 1965). During the mid-1960s Mitchell began to organize his own groups, of which the first was the Roscoe Mitchell Sextet, composed of Lester Bowie, Malachi Favors, Alvin Fielder, Maurice McIntyre, and Lester Lashley along with himself. In 1969 he settled in Paris, France, with his group called the Art Ensemble of Chicago,* which included Bowie, Favors, Joseph Jarman, and Don Moye. This group won wide recognition, toured and recorded extensively, and appeared at the major jazz festivals. The Art Ensemble returned to the United States in 1971 and continued its extensive activity, including tours in Europe and the Far East. Mitchell was also active as a soloist and composer; his scores for films included *Les stances à Sophie* (1971). Some critics regarded him as a leading contributor to the avant-garde of the 1960s, along with his Chicago colleagues; his album *Sound* (1966) was stated to be the "first coherent statement of the new esthetic" (quoted from NYT). His most important innovations were his employment of multithematic structures, controlled "free improvisation," and introduction of new instruments to the jazz ensemble.

BIBL: Communication from Leo Smith. FeaGitJS. Robert Palmer, "The Innovative Jazz Arsenal of Roscoe Mitchell" in NYT, 26 February 1977.

DISC: TudJ.

MITCHELL, WILLIAM ("BILLY"). Jazz saxophonist (b. 3 November 1926 in Kansas City, Missouri). He studied music at Cass Technical High School in Detroit, Michigan, and later performed with local groups in nightclubs. Thereafter he played for short periods with various groups, including Nat Towles, Milton Buckner,* James ("Jimmie") Lunceford,* Lucius ("Lucky") Millinder* (1948), and Woodrow ("Woody") Herman (1949). In 1949 he returned to Detroit and organized his own groups which included at one time Elvin* and Thaddeus ("Thad") Jones.* During the 1950s-60s Mitchell toured with John Birks ("Dizzy") Gillespie* (1956-57). William ("Count") Basie* (1957-61, 1966-67), and the Kenneth ("Kenny") Clarke*/Francois ("Francy") Boland big band (1963); served as a music director for Stevie Wonder* (née Stevland Judkins), Sarah Vaughan,* Della Reese,* and Gillespie, among others; and co-led a group with Albert ("Al") Grey (1962-64). He became active in teaching during the 1970s, working with jazz workshops, public-schools and college seminars, and such institutions as the Henry Street Settlement House in New York. In 1973 he founded Billy Mitchell, Inc., which was a "cultural conservatory for the musical arts" (quoted from WWBA) and a producing company.

BIBL: FeaEJ. FeaJS. FeaGitJS. WWBA.

MITCHELL'S CHRISTIAN SINGERS. Gospel group (orig. in Kinston, North Carolina; fl. 1930s-40s). The quartet attracted wide attention when it appeared on John Hammond's From Spirituals to Swing Concert at Carnegie Hall in New York, 23 December 1938. Members of the group were William Brown (first tenor), Julius Davis (second tenor), Louis David (baritone), and Sam Bryant (bass). Bryant belonged to the Disciples of Christ Church, and the other three men, to the Free Will Baptist Church. Their best-known recordings included "Let the church roll on," "Walking in the line of my Saviour," "My poor mother died shouting," and "You rise up." Mitchell's Christian Singers represented the pioneering tradition in gospel quartet singing, along with the Heavenly Gospel Singers of Spartanburg, South Carolina. The style was distinctive for its tight harmonies, blues notes, and employment of moans and groans.

BIBL: BPIM 2 (Fall 1974). Heil.

DISC: DiGod.

MODERN JAZZ QUARTET. (orig. c1947 in New York; fl. 1952-74). The group, which was organized informally about 1947 by members of John Birks ("Dizzy") Gillespie's* orchestra, included Milton ("Milt") Jackson,* vibraharp; John Lewis,* piano; Ray Brown, bass; and Kenneth ("Kenny" or "Klook") Clarke,* drums. These men occasionally played together during performances to allow the orchestra's brass players opportunity to rest after particularly demanding music. Eventually the quartet began to play independently of orchestra performances as the Milt Jackson Quartet and, later, as the Modern Jazz Quartet (MJQ). In 1952 MJQ made its first recordings, and Percy Heath* replaced Ray Brown; in 1954 Lewis became the official musical director; in 1955 Connie Kay replaced Kenny Clarke. MJQ toured widely throughout the world during the twenty-two years of its existence and pioneered in several respects. It was the first small jazz ensemble to present formal concerts in concert halls in the same way as Edward ("Duke") Ellington* staged formal concerts with his big band. In 1957 MJQ helped to open European concert halls to jazz performances, which formerly had been generally reserved for classical-music concerts. Its repertory, composed primarily by Lewis, fused jazz with European classical forms and pioneered in the performance of Third Stream music. In 1959 MJQ gave a landmark concert of Third Stream music with the Beau Arts String Quartet at Town Hall in New York; each quartet performed separately, then joined forces for the final group of numbers. In 1961 MJQ appeared with the Cincinnati Symphony, under the direction of Max Rudolph, and thereafer appeared with leading symphony orchestras throughout the nation and abroad. In 1970 MJQ was the first jazz ensemble invited to perform at La Fenice Opera House in Venice, Italy. MJQ performed on television shows in Europe and the United States and appeared in films, including *Sait-on jamais* (1971), *Little Murders* (1971), *Monterey Jazz* (1973), and the documentary *The Modern Jazz Quartet* (1964, originally produced for television). After MJQ disbanded in 1974, Lewis turned to teaching and performing as a soloist, Jackson organized his own group, Heath played in his brother's orchestra, and Kay performed with Paul Desmond.

BIBL: *International Musician* (January 1972; July 1977). NYT, 6 October 1968, 24 November 1974.

DISC: Jep. Kink. ModJ. TudJ.

MONK, THELONIOUS SPHERE. Jazz pianist (b. 10 October 1917 in Rocky Mount, North Carolina). His family moved to New York when he was a child. Self-taught, he began playing piano at the age of six; later he studied privately. As a youth he played piano in a sanctified-church band that toured widely. He first attracted wide attention in the early 1940s as a member of an informal group that played after regular working hours in Minton's Playhouse and Monroe's Uptown House in the Harlem community, along with Kenneth ("Kenny") Clarke,* Charlie Christian,* John Birks ("Dizzy") Gillespie,* Charlie Parker,* and Earl ("Bud") Powell,* among others. The experimental music produced at these informal jam sessions came to be known as bebop, later bop. During the 1940s-50s, Monk played with various groups for short periods, including Lucius ("Lucky") Millinder* (1942), Coleman Hawkins* (1944), and Gillespie, but he worked primarily with his own groups. In 1959 he gave his first big-band concert at Town Hall in New York. Those who performed with him at one time or another over the years included Art Blakey,* Ray Copeland, Milton ("Milt") Jackson,* John Coltrane,* Paul Jeffrey, Lonnie Hillyer, Lawrence ("Larry") Ridley,* Charlie

Rouse, and Thelonious Monk, Jr. During the 1970s he toured with the Giants of Jazz (1971-72), but was relatively inactive because of illness except for occasional appearances at jazz festivals and in New York concert halls. Despite his orientation as a bop pianist, Monk's style reflected the influence of Thomas (''Fats'') Waller,* Earl Hines,* and Edward (''Duke'') Ellington,* along with blues and gospel. He was a highly original pianist with his unorthodox harmonies, irregular phrasing, and angular melodies; he was also a leading jazz composer of his generation. His best-known compositions were ''Misterioso,'' ''Criss-cross,'' ''Evidence,'' ''Epistrophy,'' and ''Round about midnight.'' He received awards from the music industry.

BIBL: CurBiog (October 1964). FeaEJ. FeaJS. FeaGitJS. Russ. WWBA. WWA.

Jep. ModJ. TudJ.

MONTGOMERY, CHARLES (''BUDDY''). Jazz pianist (b. 30 January 1930 in Indianapolis, Indiana). See **MONTGOMERY, WILLIAM HOWARD (''MONK'').**

MONTGOMERY, EURREAL (''LITTLE BROTHER''). Bluesman (b. 18 April 1906 in Kentwood, Louisiana). He began playing piano at the age of four; by the time he was eleven he was playing for local social entertainments, in local clubs, and in churches. He heard blues performances in his father's roadhouse and also in the area's sawmill camps. His piano style was influenced by Ferdinand (''Jelly Roll'') Morton,* who gave him piano lessons as a child. After a period of performing in logging camps in Louisiana, he played in New Orleans, Louisiana, and Vicksburg, Mississippi; he settled in Chicago, Illinois, in 1926. He returned often to the South, however, and at one time had a blues band there during the 1930s. He recorded extensively and toured widely in the United States and in Europe, appearing in concert halls, in clubs, and at the major blues and jazz festivals. His recording of ''Vicksburg blues'' (formerly ''44 Blues'') was influential upon later blues pianists, as were also his performances of ''Make me a pallet on the floor'' and ''No special rider.''

BIBL: BWW. *Cadence* 3 (October 1977). FeaEJ. MeeJMov. Robert Neff and Anthony Connor, *Blues* (Boston, 1975). Oliv.

DISC: DiGod. Jep. LeSl. RustJR. TudBM.

MONTGOMERY, JOHN LESLIE (''WES''). Jazz guitarist (b. 6 March 1925 in Indianapolis, Indiana; d. 15 June 1968 in Indianapolis). See **MONTGOMERY, WILLIAM HOWARD (''MONK'').**

MONTGOMERY, WILLIAM HOWARD (''MONK''). Jazz bassist (b. 10 October 1921 in Indianapolis, Indiana). He first attracted wide attention for his pioneering work with the electric string bass in Lionel Hampton's* orchestra (1948-50). In 1957 he joined with Richard Crabtree, Ben Barth, and his brother Charles (''Buddy'') to form the Mastersounds jazz quartet, which toured from a base on the West Coast. In 1958 his brother John (''Wes'') joined the group. The group toured widely, recorded regularly, and appeared at jazz festivals before disbanding in the early 1960s. Thereafter ''Monk'' Montgomery toured in a trio with his brothers and played with various other groups, including his own quartet in 1969 and a big band in 1974. He was one of the founders of the World Jazz Association in 1975. Wes Montgomery led his own trio and toured with Wynton Kelly after leaving the Montgomery Trio in the 1960s. He developed an original guitar style, using parallel octaves, that exerted wide influence upon jazz guitarists of his time. Buddy Montgomery settled in Milwaukee, Wisconsin, after his brother Wes's death in 1969. Buddy led his own groups and also became involved with teaching, working with youth groups and college jazz workshops, particularly at the Wisconsin College Conservatory, and giving lecture-concerts in prisons.

BIBL: FeaEJ. FeaJS. FeaGitJS. MeeJMov.

DISC: Jep. ModJ. TudJ.

MOORE, CARMAN LEROY. Composer/Writer (b. 8 October 1936 in Lorain, Ohio). His mother was a pianist, and he began piano study as a child. He obtained his musical education at Ohio State University in Columbus (B. Mus., 1958), where he played French horn in the marching band and concert band and cello in the university orchestra; and at the Juilliard School of Music (M. Mus., 1966). His teachers included Lucio Berio, Hall Overton, Vincent Persichetti, and Stefan Wolpe, among others. He was active as a music critic and published regularly in the [New York] *Village Voice*, *The New York Times*, *The Saturday Review*, and other newspapers. His book publications included *Somebody's Angel Child: The Story of Bessie Smith* (1970) and *The Growth of Black Sound in America* (1977). His teaching career included tenures at Manhattanville College in Purchase, New York; Yale University in New Haven, Connecticut; and Queens College and Brooklyn College of the City University of New York. He was best known as a composer. His first publication was ''Youth in a Merciful House'' (1965), for piccolo, bassoons, percussions, vibraphone, and viola. Thereafter he composed steadily and produced works in a variety of forms, primarily for chamber groups in the 1960s. In 1975 two of his symphonies (composed upon commission) were given premieres: *Gospel Fuse* for symphony orchestra and gospel quartet by the San Francisco Symphony and *Wild Fires and Field Songs* by the New York Philharmonic. Other well-known works of his included *Solar Music* for Brass, Percussion, and Synthesizer; *Follow Light* for chorus, sopranos, bass viol, and percussion; and Quartet for Saxophones and Echoplex.

BIBL: Personal communication. AbdulFBE. Black press, incl. AmstN, 10 June 1978. *Newsweek* (3 February 1975). SouRBM. WWA. WWBA.

MOORE, DOROTHY RUDD. Composer (b. 4 June 1940 in New Castle, Delaware). She obtained her musical education at Howard University in Washington, D.C. (B.A., 1963), where she studied with Mark Fax.* She studied further with Chou Wen Chung in New York and Nadia Boulanger at the American Conservatory of Music in Fontainebleau, France. Her teaching career included tenures at New York University and Bronx Community College of the City University of New York. She began composing during her college years. In 1968 she was one of the founders of the Society of Black Composers. She wrote in a variety of forms, including symphonies, chamber music, piano and other instrumental pieces, and songs. Her best-known works were *Three Pieces* for violin and piano (1967), *Modes* for string quartet (1968), *Dirge and Deliverance* for cello and piano (1971), *Dream and Variations* for piano (1974), and the song cycles *Twelve Quatrains from the Rubaiyat* (1962) and *Songs from the Dark Tower* (1970). Among those who gave premieres of her works were Zito Carno, John Anthony, Willis Patterson,* and her husband, Kermit Moore.*

BIBL: Program notes.

MOORE, HAMILTON ARCHIBALD. Military trumpeter (b. 20 March 1834 in Philadelphia, Pennsylvania; d. 19? in Philadelphia). As a youth he studied music with Joseph Anderson,* leader of the Frank Johnson* Bands after Johnson's death in 1844. In 1859 Moore went to England, where he attended Queen's College at Liverpool and studied harmony with Mathis Kellar. He studied trumpet with John Thompson Norton, trumpeter to George IV. For seven years he played trumpet in the Royal Lancaster Artillery, which gave a command performance for Queen Victoria at Aldershott military camp. He played for five years in the orchestra at the Theatre Royal in Liverpool and in orchestras at the Royal Adelphi and the Prince of Wales. In 1874 he returned to Philadelphia, where he conducted a music studio and was active as an arranger.

BIBL: Black press, incl. PhilaT, 7 September 1912. Harrison Wayman, "The Quaker City" in *The Colored American* 6 (November 1903).

MOORE, KERMIT. Concert cellist (b. 11 March 1929 in Akron, Ohio). He obtained his musical education at the Cleveland Institute of Music in Ohio (1951), New York University (M.A.), the Paris Conservatory in France (artist diploma, 1956), and the Juilliard School of Music in New York. His teachers included Felix Salmond, Paul Bazelaire, George Enesco, Nadia Boulanger, and Pierre Pasquier, among others. He toured widely throughout the world, giving concerts and appearing with leading symphony orchestras. His teaching career included tenures at the Hartt School of Music in Hartford, Connecticut, where he was also a member of the String Quartet-in-Residence. He was also active as a conductor, and in 1975 founded the Riverside Symphony in New York. His honors included the Lili Boulanger Award (1953), the Edgar Stillman Kelly Award, and a Queen Elizabeth II Medal (1958). Moore was a founding member of the Symphony of the New World* in 1964 and of the Society of Black Composers in 1968. His wife was composer Dorothy Rudd Moore.

BIBL: Questionnaire. WWBA.

MOORE, MELBA (née **MELBA MOORMAN**). Actress/Popular-music singer (b. 29 October 1945 in New York, New York). She came from a musical family: her mother was a singer, her father was a jazz saxophonist, and her brother Dennis became a professional jazz pianist. She obtained her education at the Arts High School in Newark, New Jersey, and at the Montclair [New Jersey] State Teachers College (B.A.). After graduation from college she taught in the local high school for two years, but during the same period sang with a group, Voices, Inc. She then began her professional career singing in nightclubs and in recording studios as a background-music singer. She first attracted wide attention as the featured singer with Babs Gonzalez's* orchestra in 1964 and for her recording of "Here today and gone tomorrow." During the late 1960s-70s she sang in Broadway musicals and films, including the musicals *Hair* (1968-70), *Purlie* (1970), and *Timbuktu* (1978) and the films *Pigeons* (1971), *Lost in the Stars* (1974), and *Cotton Comes to Harlem* (1970, on the soundtrack). She toured widely in the United States and in Europe as an entertainer, appearing in nightclubs, concert halls, and on television shows. She was also active as a dramatic actress, as in her portrayal of Harriet Tubman in the television show "The American Woman: Portraits of Courage." She recorded extensively; her best-known albums were *Peach Melba* and *A Portrait of Melba*. She won numerous awards from the music and theater industries.

BIBL: Black press, incl. AmstN, 7 March 1964, 4 March 1978, 25 November 1978. CurBiog (January 1973). *Ebony* (July 1970). WWA. WWBA.

MOORE, UNDINE SMITH. Composer (b. 5 July 1904 in Jarrat, Virginia). Her family moved to Petersburg, Virginia, when she was a child, and there she began piano study with Lillian Allen Darden (aunt of William Duncan Allen*). When she was eight years old and only a fifth-grader, she was invited to accompany the singing for the high-school commencement exercises. She obtained her musical education at Fisk University in Nashville, Tennessee (B.A., B. Mus.), where she studied piano and organ with Alice M. Grass; at Columbia University Teachers College in New York (M.A., professional diploma), where she studied with Howard Murphy; at the Juilliard School of Music and the Manhattan School of Music in New York; and at the Eastman School of Music in Rochester, New York. Her teaching career included tenures in the public schools of Goldsboro, North Carolina, where she was supervisor of music, and at Virginia State College in Petersburg (1927-72). She also served as a visiting professor at Carleton College in Northfield, Minnesota; St. Benedict College in St. Joseph, Minnesota; St. Johns University in Collegeville, Minnesota; and Virginia Union University in Richmond. She toured widely as a lecturer, including in West Africa, and coordinated college workshops and seminars. She was co-founder and co-director with Altona Trent Johns* of the Black Music Center at Virginia State (1969-72), which brought to the campus the leading black composers, performers, musical groups, dancers, and lecturers. She wrote music in a variety of forms, but was best known for her choral compositions, including "The Lamb," "Lord, we give thanks to Thee," and "Daniel, Daniel, servant of the Lord" in addition to her spiritual arrangements. Her *Afro-American Suite* for flute, cello, and piano was widely performed. Her honors included honorary doctorates from Virginia State University (1972) and Indiana University (1976), a Certificate of Appreciation from John Lindsay, Mayor of New York, the Seventh Annual Humanitarian Award from Fisk University (1973), the National Association of Negro Musicians Award (1975), and appointment to national boards and committees of professional organizations. In 1975 Petersburg [Virginia] Mayor Remmis Arnold proclaimed 13 April as Undine Moore Day. She won wide recognition as an educator for her curricular innovations at Virginia State and exerted wide influence as a teacher of students who later became celebrated, among them, Camilla Williams,* William ("Billy") Taylor,* and Leon Thompson.*

BIBL: Questionnaire. BakBCS. Carl G. Harris, "A Study of Characteristic, Stylistic Trends Found in the Choral Works of a Selected Group of Afro-American Composers and Arrangers" (Ph.D. diss., University of Missouri at Kansas City, 1971). Dominique-René de Lerma, ed., *Reflections on Afro-American Music* (Kent, Ohio, 1973).

MOOREHEAD, CONSUELA LEE. See **DESCENDENTS OF MIKE AND PHOEBE.**

MORGAN, ALBERT ("AL"). Jazz bassist (b. 19 August 1908 in New Orleans, Louisiana; d. 13 April 1974 in Los Angeles, California). He came from a musical family: three brothers became professional musicians—Sam (b. 1895 in Bertrandville, Louisiana; d. 25 February 1936 in New Orleans, Louisiana), Isaiah (b. 7 April 1897 in Bertrandville; d. 16 May 1966 in New Orleans), and Andrew (b. 19 March 1903 in Pensacola, Florida). As a child he played clarinet and drums, then began studying bass when he was about ten with Simon Marrero. His first professional experience was in the band of his brother Isaiah; thereafter he played with various groups, including Lee Collins,* Fate Marable* (1925-29), Cabell ("Cab") Calloway* (1932-36), Les Hite* (1938-41), Arthur ("Zutty") Singleton* (1941), William ("Sabby") Lewis (1942-44, 1945-47), and Louis Jordan* (1944-45), among others. At intervals during these years he also led his own groups. In 1957 he settled in California, where later he played with Joe Darensbourg, Jack McVea, Nellie Lutcher,* and Buddy Banks. He recorded with many groups and played in film orchestras, including *Going Places* (1938) and *Drum Crazy—The Gene Krupa Story* (1959).

BIBL: ChilWW. FeaEJ. MeeJMov.

DISC: Kink. RustJR.

MORGANFIELD, McKINLEY ("MUDDY WATERS"). Bluesman (b. 4 April 1915 in Rolling Fork, Mississippi). His mother died when he was three years old, and he was sent to live in Clarksdale, Mississippi. He taught himself to play harmonica and guitar at an early age; during the 1930s he played with a string band, and in 1942 he toured with the Silas Green* tent show. In 1940 he recorded blues for folklorists Alan Lomax and John Work.* Although he performed widely during this period, he did not begin his professional career until after he settled in Chicago in 1943. His contacts there with established bluesmen, including

(''Big Bill'') William Lee Conley Broonzy,* changed the sound of his Delta-blues style; in 1945 he began playing electric guitar. In 1946 he made his first recordings, some of them with ''Sunnyland Slim''* (née Andrew Luandrew) and Leroy Foster. He soon won recognition as one of the leading blues figures in Chicago; his band, established in 1941, had a permanent home in a Southside club and included at one time or another some of the city's most talented bluesmen; among them, James Cotton,* Willie Dixon,* Pat Hare, (''Little'') Walter Jacobs,* Jimmy Rogers, Otis Spann,* and Amos (''Junior'') Wells.* During the next three decades he recorded extensively and toured widely in the United States and abroad, appearing in concert halls, posh nightclubs, on college campuses, and at the major blues and jazz festivals. In 1973 his band toured in Australia and New Zealand. In later years his groups included Mojo Buford, Calvin Jones, PeeWee Madison, Sammy Lawhorn, Piney Top Perkins, and Willie Smith. A number of his recordings achieved great commercial success, including ''Hoochie coochie man,'' ''Caledonia,'' and ''Rolling stone.'' The last-named inspired Bob Dylan to write a song, ''Like a rollin' stone''; the selection of a name for the English rock group; and the choice of a title for a commercial rock magazine. By the 1970s Muddy Waters was regarded as a seminal figure in the history of blues, worthy of his soubriquet, Godfather of the Blues. His influence upon the development of post-World War II blues undoubtedly was greater than that of any other bluesman.

BIBL: BWW. CharCB. *Ebony* (March 1972). FeaEJ. MeeJMov. Robert Neff and Anthony Connor, *Blues* (Boston, 1975). Oliv. *Record Research* 83 (April 1967). StamFCW.

DISC: DiGod. Jep. LeSl. TudBM.

MORRIS, STEVELAND. See **WONDER, STEVIE.**

MORRISON, GEORGE. Jazz bandleader (b. 9 September 1891 in Fayette, Missouri; d. 5 November 1974 in Denver, Colorado). He came from a musical family. His grandfather and father were dance fiddlers, and his brother played string instruments. The boys had a group, the Morrison Brother String Band, which played for social entertainments in Fayette, Missouri, and surrounding areas. His family moved to Boulder, Colorado, when he was about ten years old, and the String Band was reorganized to play in the new home. In 1911 he settled in Denver, Colorado. He began violin study at the age of twelve with local teachers. He obtained his musical education in the public schools of Boulder and at the Columbia Conservatory of Music in Chicago, Illinois, where he studied with Carl Decker, among others. After settling in Denver, he played piano in clubs and hotels; in 1916 he organized his own trio. During the years he studied in Chicago, he played in a cabaret and in a theater orchestra directed by Dave Peyton.* Returning to Denver, he organized a larger group, later augmenting it to eleven pieces, which became one of the leading dance orchestras in Denver. Those who played with Morrison over the years included Andrew (''Andy'') Kirk,* James (''Jimmie'') Lunceford,* and Mary Lou Williams,* among others. In 1920 Morrison's band played a residency in New York and made its recording debut. Later he toured widely on the Pantages vaudeville circuit (1924-25) with Hattie McDaniels* as the featured singer. In his late career Morrison taught instrumental music in the public schools and conducted a music studio. His daughter, Marian Morrison Robinson, and son, George Morrison, Jr., were both professional musicians.

BIBL: *Denver Post*, 8 November 1974. *International Musician* (December 1974). Layne. Schuller.

MORTON, FERDINAND (''JELLY ROLL'') (née **FERDINAND JOSEPH MORTON** or **LA MENTHE).** Ragtime, blues pianist/Jazz bandleader (b. 20 September 1885 in New Orleans, Louisiana; d. 10 July 1941 in Los Angeles, California). He taught himself to play various instruments as a child, and by the time he was seven or eight he was playing on street corners in a three-piece boys' string band. At the age of ten he began piano study with local teachers, later studying with William Nickerson.* By the time he was fifteen he had won recognition as one of the leading ragtime and blues pianists in the city—rivaled perhaps only by Anthony (''Tony'') Jackson.* During the years c1909-12 he toured with vaudeville shows, at first on the Benbow circuit out of Memphis, Tennessee, then later with McCabe's Georgia Troubadours. Thereafter he played in various places as a soloist and with groups he formed, beginning in St. Louis, Missouri (1912), then in Chicago, Illinois, for a long period, although he left several times to play residencies in other cities. In 1915 he played at the San Francisco Exposition. During the years 1917-23 he was active primarily on the West Coast, particularly in Los Angeles, but he also led groups or played as a soloist in Vancouver, Canada, and San Diego, California, among other places, and played for a short period with George Morrison* in Denver, Colorado. In 1918 he made his first recordings with a group that included Edward (''Kid'') Ory* and (''Mutt'') Carey. He resettled in Chicago (1923-28) and became heavily involved in recording. He also used that city as a base from which he toured. During these years he recorded extensively with his Red Hot

Peppers and the New Orleans Rhythm Kings (a white group) and made piano rolls for the QRS Company (Quality Reigns Supreme, a subsidiary of the Melville Clark Piano Company). He was also active as a staff arranger for the Melrose Brothers Publishing Company. Occasionally he played with other groups during the 1920s, such as Fate Marable* (1924), W. C. Handy,* and Henry Crowder. About 1928 he settled in New York. His sidemen during the most intense periods of recording (1923-30) included Lee Collins,* Johnny Dodds, André Hilaire, John Lindsay, George Mitchell, Edward (''Kid'') Ory, Omer Simeon,* Arthur (''Zutty'') Singleton,* and Johnny St. Cyr,* among others. For the next few years he toured widely with his group, played long residencies in New York nightclubs and ballrooms, recorded, and occasionally worked with revues, including *Speeding Along* and *Heading for Harlem*. In 1936 he went to Washington, D.C., where he played in local nightclubs. In 1938 he made a long series of records under the direction of Alan Lomax for the Archive of American Folksong of the Library of Congress, which was a veritable history of jazz. The next year he returned to New York, where he recorded with a big band, then settled in Los Angeles. Illness forced him to leave music the year before his death.

Morton's music represented the fusion of ragtime, blues, and brass-band music into the new music called jazz. He was regarded as the first jazz composer in history, the first to write down his jazz arrangements in notation, and the first to publish a jazz arrangement, the ''Jelly roll blues'' (1915). A large number of his compositions became staples in the jazz repertory, of which the best known were ''Wolverine blues,'' ''King Porter stomp,'' ''New Orleans' blues,'' ''Buddy Bolden's blues,'' ''The naked dance,'' ''Frog-i-more rag,'' and ''Blackbottom stomp.'' His recordings of classic jazz reveal his importance as a pioneering jazz bandleader, and the twelve-album saga he recorded for the Library of Congress was perhaps the most important oral history of jazz ever issued.

BIBL: ASCAP. ChilWW. FeaEJ. Alan Lomax, *Mister Jelly Roll* (1950; reprint, Berkeley, (1973.) MeeJMov.

DISC: Kink. RustJR. TudJ.

MORTON, HENRY STERLING (''BENNY''). Jazz trombonist (b. 31 January 1907 in New York, New York). He obtained his musical education in the public schools of New York and began playing professionally with local groups during his high-school years. Beginning about 1924 he played with various groups, including Billy Fowler (c1924-26), Fletcher Henderson* (1926-28, 1931), William (''Chick'') Webb* (1928-31), Donald (''Don'') Redman* (1931-36), William (''Count'') Basie* (1937-40), the Theodore (''Teddy'') Wilson Sextet* (1940-43), and Edmond (''Ed'') Hall* (1944), among others. During the remainder of the 1940s and through the 1950s he led his own group for a period (1944-46), was active as a studio musician, and played in Broadway pit orchestras for several years, with such shows as *St. Louis Woman* (1946), *Memphis Bound* (1945), and *Jamaica* (1957), among others. He also performed in nightclubs. In 1967 he toured in Europe with Top Brass and returned to Europe in 1974 with The World's Greatest Jazzband, with which he played off and on during the years 1972-74. He also played with Henry (''Red'') Allen* (1959-60), William (''Wild Bill'') Davison* (1968-69), and Robert (''Bobby') Hackett (1970). In 1964 he toured in Africa with Paul Taubman's concert orchestra. Morton was regarded as a leading jazz trombonist of the 1930s-40s.

BIBL: AlHen. ChilWW. FeaEJ. FeaGitJS. MeeJMov.

DISC: Jep. Kink. RustJR. TudJ.

MOTEN, BENNIE. Jazz bandleader (b. 13 November 1894 in Kansas City, Missouri; d. 2 April 1935 in Kansas City). His mother was a pianist. At the age of twelve he played baritone horn in Blackburn's Juvenile Brass Band; later he studied piano with local teachers, who were former students of Scott Joplin.* Moten began playing professionally at an early age with local groups, then organized his own, which he called BB & D, using the initials of players Bailey Handcock, himself, and Duke Lankford. About 1921 he organized a six-piece band (later augmented to ten pieces), which played in local nightclubs. When the band made its recording debut in September 1923, it was only the third jazz group in history to record. (The first was the white Original Dixieland Jazz Band in 1917; the second was Edward (''Kid'') Ory's* band in 1921. George Morrison's* band recorded in 1920, but his records were never released.) Moten's band established itself as the leading jazz group in Kansas City, with only the George E. Lee* band as a serious competitor. During the 1920s-30s Moten tourned widely, at first in the Middle West, then beginning in 1928 on the East Coast as well. Over the years his band personnel included his brother, Buster Moten, Eddie Durham,* William (''Bill'' or ''Count'') Basie,* Oran (''Hot Lips'') Page,* Walter Page,* James (''Jimmy'') Rushing,* Henry (''Buser'') Smith,* and Ben Webster,* among others. After Moten's sudden death on the operating table in 1935, Basie took over leadership of the band. Moten's repertory was dominated by blues; his orchestral style laid the foundation for the so-called Kansas City style, with its emphasis on riffs and hard swinging rhythms.

BIBL: ChilWW. FeaEJ. Russ.

DISC: Kink. RustJR. TudJ.

MOTEN BARNETT, ETTA. Actress/Concert singer (b. 5 November 1901 in San Antonio, Texas). Her father, a minister, was transferred to Kansas City, Kansas, when she was a child. She began singing in her father's church choir at an early age. She obtained her musical education in the public schools of Kansas City, Western University in Quindaro, and at the University of Kansas in Lawrence (B.A., 1931). After graduation from college she went to New York, intending to stay only through the summer and to return to a teaching position in Jefferson City, Missouri. She was invited to be a soloist with the Eva Jessye* Choir; although a contralto, her wide range enabled her to handle soprano solos as well. She made a successful audition for a Broadway show, *Fast and Furious*, and became involved in show business. During the 1930s she was active primarily in musicals and films, including *Gold Diggers of 1933* and *Flying Down to Rio* (1934). In 1934 she went to California, where she worked as a staff artist with Meredith Wilson for NBC radio. In 1942 she sang the role of Bess in Gershwin's *Porgy and Bess*, then retired from the stage. During the 1940s-70s she toured as a soloist on the college and lecture circuit. In her later career she was active in television and was hostess for the show "Etta Moten—With Music and Conversation" on Chicago NBC. Her honors included an honorary doctorate from Atlanta University (1976), appointments to boards of civic and professional organizations, and appointment as an Ambassador of Good Will by the United States Department of State.

BIBL: Black press, incl. AmstN, 3 August 1942; CDef, 25 November 1944, 19 May 1976. *Encore* (May 1974). WWCA, 1938-40, 1950.

MOTOWN SOUND, THE. See **GORDY, BERRY.**

MOTTS, ROBERT ("BOB"). Music hall proprietor (b. Washington, Iowa; d. 10 July 1911 in Chicago, Illinois). He was credited with being "the promoter of the first colored theater in the United States" (IndF, 15 July 1911). Originally owner of a saloon, he converted it to a beer garden in 1903 and to a music hall in 1904; in 1905, he razed the building to erect a new one, the Pekin Theater. His Pekin Theater Stock Company not only staged productions in the theater but also toured in the Middle West and East. Joe Jordan* was musical director of the new theater, and Flournoy Miller* and Aubrey Lyles* wrote the first musical, *The Man from Bam* (music by Jordan), produced in the theater. Other musicals included *The Husband* and *Captain Rufus*, which also played in New York. In addition to staging musicals and plays, Motts sponsored "Professional Matinees" and Sacred Concerts, which brought to the Chicago public such celebrated performers as Sissieretta Jones* ("Black Patti"), George Walker* and Bert Williams,* and Bob Cole* and J. Rosamond Johnson.* On 4 December 1906 the Pekin sponsored a concert of the music of Samuel Coleridge-Taylor,* performed by Harry T. Burleigh,* William H. Tyler,* Will Marion Cook,* N. Clark Smith,* and Irene Howard,* among others, in addition to the composer himself and Joe Jordan with the Pekin Orchestra. Over the years the leading artists of the period performed at the Pekin and/or were employed there, including in addition to those already cited Joseph Douglass,* Abbie Mitchell,* and Kemper Harreld,* among others. Efforts were made to keep the Pekin open after Mott's death, but it finally was closed permanently in August 1916.

BIBL: Black press, incl. IndF, 15 July 1911, 19 August 1916; NYAge, 13 July 1911. Blesh.

MUDDY WATERS. See **MORGANFIELD, McKINLEY.**

MUNDY, JAMES ("JIMMY"). Jazz saxophonist/Arranger (b. 28 June 1907 in Cincinnati, Ohio). His father played mandolin and bass viol in a trio and sang baritone. He studied violin as a child and later toured with the Gene Wilson Becton evangelical orchestra, playing tenor saxophone or clarinet. He obtained his musical education at Northwestern University in Evanston, Illinois. He began his professional career in the mid-1920s, playing with the White Brothers at Washington, D.C., and Tommy Myles, among others. In 1933 he went to Chicago to join Earl Hines* (1933-36) on tenor saxophone and as an arranger. Although he played thereafter with various groups, he was active primarily as a writer-arranger, working with Benny Goodman (1936-39), Paul Whiteman (1941-43), William ("Count") Basie,* Lucius ("Lucky") Millinder,* and Gene Krupa, among others. In 1939 he led his own group for a period. Except for his service in the United States Armed Forces (1943-45), he lived in California during the years 1941-48; there he studied with Ernest Toch and wrote for radio shows and films. After returning to New York, he was a free-lance arranger and in 1955 wrote music for the Broadway musical, *The Vamp*. During the years 1959-60 he was musical director for Barclay Disques in Paris, France; he also wrote music for the film *The Man on the Eiffel Tower*. He was one of the leading black arrangers of his generation.

BIBL: ASCAP. ChilWW. DanceWEH. FeaEJ.

DISC: Jep. Kink. RustJR.

MUNDY, JAMES AHLYN. Choral director (b. 9 July 1886 in Maysville, Kentucky; d. 25 December 1978 in Chicago, Illinois). He obtained his musical education through private study in Maysville, Kentucky; at the Simmons University, Normal Department, in Louisville, Kentucky; and at the Cosmopolitan School of Music in Chicago, Illinois. He went to Chicago about 1906 and soon established himself as one of the black community's leading choral directors and studio teachers. In addition to his duties as choirmaster at the Bethel AME Church, beginning in 1913, he organized community choral groups and produced mammoth concerts at Orchestra Hall and the Coliseum. In 1910 he organized the city's black postal clerks and mail carriers into a Federal Glee Club; on 12 February 1913 his Mundy Singers made their debut at Orchestra Hall. In 1915 he conducted choral groups, along with E. Azalia Hackley,* at the Lincoln Jubilee and Half-Century Exposition; in 1919 he conducted groups at the Illinois Centennial in Springfield, Illinois. During the 1920s his Chicago South Side Opera Company produced regular concerts, including Flotow's opera *Martha*. During the 1930s he won wide recognition for the"Battles of the Choirs" between his groups and those of J. Wesley Jones.* The Mundy Chorister-Jubilee Singers performed at the Chicago World's Fair (1933-34). Mundy also wrote music for his groups to perform.

BIBL: Interview by Fanya Wiggins. ChiHistSoc. Black press, incl. CDef, 4 May 1912, 28 March 1914, 3 December 1931, 4 April 1930.

MURRAY, ROBERT. Composer (fl. mid-nineteenth century in Baltimore, Maryland). Little is known of his career except that he was highly regarded by his contemporaries as a composer of dance pieces. He was also leader of a society-dance orchestra during the 1820s. His best-known compositions were "Furioso galop," "Baltimore galop," and "Tedesco polka." Some of his pieces were still current in 1870 and were listed in the *Complete Catalogue of Sheet Music and Musical Works, 1870*, published by the Board of Music Trade of the United States of America, 1871; reprint with introduction by Dena Epstein (New York, 1973).

BIBL: John E. Bruce, "A History of Negro Musicians" in *Southern Workman* 45 (1916). "An African Fancy Ball" in *Philadelphia Monthly Magazine* 2 (April 1828).

MUSE, CLARENCE. Actor/Entertainer (b. 7 October 1889 in Baltimore, Maryland; d. 13 October 1979 in Los Angeles [or Perris?], California). Although best known as an actor, he was also a musician. He obtained his education at Dickenson University in Carlisle Pennsylvania (LL.B.). After graduation he entered show business and toured on the vaudeville circuit. He was one of the founders of the Lafayette Theater Stock Company in New York in 1914 and remained with the company for seven years. In 1929 he settled in Hollywood, California; thereafter he appeared in numerous films and, later, television shows. In 1935 he produced and directed the revival of Hall Johnson's* folk opera *Run Little Chillun* (originally staged on Broadway in 1933) for the Federal Theatre Project. He wrote a considerable amount of music: his symphony, *Harlem Heab'n*, was given a premiere in the Hollywood Bowl; his best-known song was "When it's sleepy time down south" (written in collaboration with Otis and Leon René*). His honors included an honorary doctorate from Bishop College.

BIBL: ASCAP. Black press, including NYAge, 1 August 1942. *Ebony* (September 1972). *Opportunity* (1938), pp. 275-76. WWA, 1976-77. WWBA, 1976-77. WWCA, 1950.

N

NAHOR, EDNORAH. See **JONES, MATILDA SISSIERETTA.**

NANCE, WILLIS ("RAY"). Jazz trumpeter (b. 10 December 1913 in Chicago, Illinois; d. 28 January 1976 in New York, New York). He studied piano as a child and began violin study at the age of nine. He obtained his musical education in the public schools of Chicago, including Wendell Phillips High School, where he came under the tutelage of N. Clark Smith*; at Lane College in Jackson, Tennessee; and at Chicago Musical College, where he studied with Max Fishel. In high school he played trumpet and was also a drum major; in college he played in the band. He began playing professionally in Chicago nightclubs during the 1930s and came under the influence of violinists Hezekiah ("Stuff") Smith* and Edward ("Eddie") South.* He then led his own six-piece group (1932-37), in which the men sang in four-part harmonies in addition to playing their instruments. Later he played with various groups, including Earl Hines* (1937-38), Horace Henderson* (1939-40), and Edward ("Duke") Ellington* (1940-44), then led his own group again (1944) and worked as a soloist (1945). In 1945 he rejoined Ellington and remained for almost twenty years (1945-63). In Henderson's band he had doubled on violin and trumpet, but in 1961 he changed over to cornet. Throughout his career, however, his performance included singing and dancing, and Ellington gave him ample opportunity to exhibit his showmanship. In 1963 he settled in New York, where he led his own groups in nightclubs and at the World's Fair (1964, 1965) and toured occasionally as a soloist (Europe in 1966). Nance was one of the star performers of the Ellington band. He entered the band as a replacement for "growl" trumpeter Charles ("Cootie") Williams,* and he was taught by trombonist Joseph ("Tricky Sam") Nanton* how to produce "growls" by using a plunger mute. His best-known performance was his solo on "Take the A train," which was widely imitated. Other well-known performances were "Things ain't what they used to be," "In a sentimental mood," "Come Sunday," and "Lover, come back to me" with John Birks ("Dizzy") Gillespie.*

BIBL: Black press. ChilWW. DanceWEH. FeaEJ. FeaJS. FeaGitJS. MeeJMov.

DISC: Jep. Kink. RustJR.

NANTON, JOSEPH ("TRICKY SAM"). Jazz trombonist (b. 1 February 1904 in New York, New York; d. 20 July 1946 in San Francisco, California). He obtained his musical training in the public schools of New York. During the 1920s he played with various groups, among them, Cliff Jackson (1921-23, 1925), Earl Frazier's Harmony Five (1923-24), and Elmer Snowden* (1925). He then joined Edward ("Duke") Ellington* (1925-46), where he was taught by James ("Bubber") Miley* how to produce "growls" on his trombone by using a plunger mute. His "wa-wa" solos seemed to have the quality of the human voice; his trombone skills earned him the nickname "Tricky Sam." He and Miley were largely responsible for the jungle effects of the Ellington band in the 1920s-30s.

BIBL: ChilWW. FeaEJ. MeeJMov.

DISC: Kink. RustJR.

NASH, JOHN ("JOHNNY"). Popular-music singer (b. 19 August 1940 in Houston, Texas). As a child he sang in a church choir and came into contact with gospel music. He began performing professionally when he was thirteen, singing popular music and rhythm 'n' blues on television. During the 1950s he became a regular member of the Arthur Godfrey Talent Scouts show on radio and television (1956-63). Thereafter he toured extensively on the nightclub circuit in the United States and abroad and recorded regularly, using a five-man accompaniment group called The Sons of the Jungle. He first began to attract wide attention in the late 1960s when he recorded reggae songs, particularly "Hold me tight" in 1968, "I can see clearly now" (1972), and "Stir it up" (written by reggae songwriter Robert ("Bob") Marley* of Jamaica). Nash played an important role in introducing reggae into the United States. During the 1970s his repertory included blues, rhythm 'n' blues, rock, country-western, reggae, and calypso, along with popular music. His best-known album was *My Merry-Go-Round*.

BIBL: StamPRS. WWA.

DISC: TudBM.

NATIONAL ASSOCIATION OF NEGRO MUSICIANS. Professional organization (organized 1919 in Chicago, Illinois). The association was established for the purpose of "race unity and advancement . . . [for] raising the musical standards of the teaching profession of our race through this country . . . [for] better instruction in music and a systematic means of improving the musical taste of the public" (quoted from the invitational letter, dated 3 March 1916, sent to black musicians by Clarence Cameron White* from Boston, Massachusetts). Apparently White was the first to propose organizing a national association of Negro music teachers. The conference was cancelled, however, because of an influenza epidemic. R. Nathaniel Dett* sent out letters, dated 22 October 1918, explaining the cancellation and suggesting another date to set for an organizational meeting to coincide with the annual music festival at Hampton Institute, Virginia, where he was then teaching. In the spring of 1919, music critic Nora Holt* held a meeting in her home in Chicago, Illinois, in honor of Clarence White, who had come to the city to give a recital, at which plans were made to hold the first convention of the proposed organization in July 1919. Henry Grant* of Washington, D.C., proposed that a preliminary conference be held in that city in connection with the Second Annual Music Festival of Dunbar High School. This meeting was called the Initial Conference of Negro Musicians and Artists. On 29-31 July 1919 the first convention of NANM (National Association of Negro Musicians) was held at Chicago; the second convention was held at New York in 1920, and the third convention, at Nashville, Tennessee, in 1921. Included among the charter members (list incomplete) were Cleota Collins,* R. Nathaniel Dett, Carl Diton,* Lorenzo Dyer, Maude Roberts George,* Henry L. Grant, Nora Holt, Clara Hutchinson, Edwin Hill, James A. Mundy,* Lillian LeMon,* J. Wesley Jones,* Florence Cole Talbert,* and T. Theodore Taylor.* Through the years NANM held annual conventions in the month of August, except in 1942 when its musical activities were suspended because of World War II. In addition to promoting black musicians and their music, NANM gave scholarships to talented young musicians; the first award went to Marian Anderson* in 1921. During the 1960s the organization established the tradition of giving Annual Awards to mature artists, composers, teachers, and music historians for outstanding achievement and contribution to black culture. In 1969 NANM celebrated its Golden Jubilee Anniversary at St. Louis, Missouri. The week's festivities included a performance of Dett's oratorio, *The Ordering of Moses*, with William Dawson* as musical director. The organization returned to St. Louis in 1979 for its Sixtieth Anniversary Convention and, in addition to its customary concerts, lectures, and workshops, produced Scott Joplin's* opera, *Treemonisha*, with Kenneth Billups* as musical director and Katherine Dunham* as artistic advisor. The presidents of NANM were (in chronological order from 1919 to 1979): Henry L. Grant, Clarence Cameron White, R. Nathaniel Dett, Carl Rossini Diton, J. Wesley Jones, Lillian LeMon, Maude Roberts George, Camille Nickerson,* Kemper Harreld,* Mary Cardwell Dawson,* Clarence Hayden Wilson* (two nonconsecutive terms), Roscoe R. Polin, Kenneth Billups, Theodore Charles Stone,* Brazeal Wayne Dennard, and Betty Jackson King.*

BIBL: Black press, incl. CDef, 9 August 1919; NYAge, 17 May 1919. Nora Holt, "The Chronological History of the NANM" in *Music and Poetry* (July 1921); reprint in BPIM (Fall 1974). NANM Convention Journals.

NATIONAL NEGRO OPERA COMPANY, THE. See **DAWSON, MARY CARDWELL.**

NAVARRO, THEODORE ("FATS"). Jazz trumpeter (b. 24 September 1923 in Key West, Florida; d. 7 July 1950 in New York, New York). He studied piano as a child and began study of the trumpet when he was thirteen. He obtained his musical education in the public schools of Key West, Florida. During his high-school years he played with local groups; thereafter he left the city to join Isaac ("Snookum") Russell, with whom he toured (1941-42). During the 1940s he played with various groups, including Andrew ("Andy") Kirk* (1943-44), William ("Billy") Eckstine* (1945-46), Illinois Jacquet* (1947-48), Lionel Hampton,* Coleman Hawkins,* and Tadd Dameron,* among others. Despite his short career, he was regarded as an important trumpeter of the bebop school, and he exerted wide influence upon his contemporaries, among them,

Clifford Brown and McKinley (''Kenny'') Dorham.*

BIBL: FeaEJ. FeaGitJS. MeeJMov.

DISC: Jep. Kink. TudJ.

NELSON, LOUIS ("BIG EYE"). See **DELISLE, LOUIS NELSON.**

NELSON, OLIVER EDWARD. Composer (b. 4 June 1932 in St. Louis, Missouri; d. 27 October 1975 in Los Angeles, California). He came from a musical family; a brother and a sister became professional musicians. He began piano study at the age of six and saxophone at eleven. His early professional experiences were in St. Louis with the [James] Jeter/[Hayes] Pillars band, George Hudson, Nat Towles, and Louis Jordan* (1950-51). During his service in the United States Armed Forces (1952-54) he played in a Marine band. Thereafter he returned to St. Louis, where he studied composition and theory at Washington University (1954-57), at Lincoln University in Jefferson City, Missouri (1957-58), and later privately with Elliot Carter. About 1958 he went to New York; there he played with various groups, including Erskine Hawkins,* William (''Wild Bill'') Davis,* and Louis Bellson, among others. During the 1960s-70s he devoted much of his time to composing all kinds of music—commercial, jazz, popular, and classical—in a variety of forms. In 1967 he settled in Los Angeles, California, where he became involved in writing music for films and television. The television shows for which he wrote music included *Six Million Dollar Man*, *Ironsides*, *It Takes a Thief*, *The Name of the Game*, and others. His scores for films included *Death of a Gunfighter* (1969), Skull-*duggery* (1969), *Istanbul Express* (1968), *Zigzag* (1970), *Last Tango in Paris* (1972), and *Inside Job* (1973). He also conducted music for films, occasionally led his own groups for special events, and occasionally toured (in West Africa in 1969 under sponsorship of the United States Department of State). His best-known works in the larger forms were *Soundpiece* for Jazz Orchestra (1964), *Jazzhattan Suite* (1967), *Dialogues* for Orchestra (1970), and Suite for Narrator, String Quartet and Jazz Orchestra (1970).

BIBL: Baker. BMI (January 1969, January 1974). FeaEJ. FeaJS. FeaGitJS. MeeJMov. NYT, 27 October 1975. WWA, 1976-77.

DISC: Jep.

NEWMAN, JOSEPH DWIGHT ("JOE"). Jazz trumpeter (b. 7 September 1922 in New Orleans, Louisiana). His father, Dwight Newman, was a dance-orchestra pianist. He obtained his musical education at Alabama State Teachers College in Montgomery, where he played with the 'Bama State Collegians and came into contact with Lionel Hampton.* He played with Hampton (1941-43), then with William (''Count'') Basie* (intermittently during the years 1943-46), J. C. Heard, and Illinois Jacquet* (1947). When he rejoined Basie in 1952 he remained with the group for almost ten years (1952-61). Thereafter he settled in New York and led his own groups for the next few years. He also played with Benny Goodman (1962), Orchestra USA (1963), Oliver Nelson* (1964), and others. From the mid-1960s on he was active in teaching; he conducted workshops on college campuses and taught instrumental music in the Young Musicians' Clinic of Jazz Interactions, Inc., a non-profit organization founded to promote appreciation of jazz. In 1967 he became president of the organization. He was active in Broadway-musical pit-orchestras, including *Promises, Promises* (1969-72), *Raisin* (1973-75), and *What Makes Sammy Run* (1964-65), and appeared in television-show orchestras. He first won wide recognition in Basie's orchestra during the 1950s; his style reflected a fusion of swing and bebop traditions.

BIBL: FeaEJ. FeaJS. FeaGitJS. MeeJMov.

NEWSON, ROOSEVELT, JR. Concert pianist (b. 30 August 1946 in Rayville, Louisiana). He began piano study at the age of thirteen. He obtained his musical education at Southern University in Baton Rouge, Louisiana (B. Mus., 1968), where he studied with Jasper Patton, and at the Peabody Conservatory of Music in Baltimore, Maryland (M. Mus., 1971; D.M.A., 1977), where he studied with Walter Hautzig and Leon Fleisher, among others. He began performing as a concert pianist during the 1970s and toured widely throughout the United States, giving solo recitals and appearing with symphony orchestras. In 1975 he was an Affiliate Artist at Southern University under the Sears Roebuck Foundation/National Endowment for the Arts Program, and in later years he served as Affiliate Artist in other institutions. He was also a ''Showcase Musician'' for Young Audiences, Inc. His honors included an award from the Young Artist League of Dallas, Texas, and grants from the Ford Foundation (1972-73). His repertory consisted of the standard keyboard literature but with special emphasis upon the music of American composers, particularly Aaron Copeland, Scott Joplin,* Charles Ives, George Walker* (the subject of his doctoral dissertation), and Olly Wilson.*

BIBL: Questionnaire. WWBA.

NICHOLAS, ALBERT ("AL"). Jazz clarinetist (b. 27 May 1900 in New Orleans, Louisiana; d. 3 September 1973 in Basel, Switzerland). His uncle, Joseph ("Wooden Joe") Nicholas (1883-1957), was a clarinetist-cornetist and bandleader. He began playing clarinet when he was ten years old and studied the instrument with Lorenzo Tio, Jr.,* when he was fourteen. About the same time he began playing professionally with local groups, including Buddy Petit, Manuel Perez, and Arnold Depass. During his service in the United States Armed Forces (1916-19), he played in an army band. Thereafter he played with various groups, including Depass again (1921), Perez (1922-23), Joseph ("King") Oliver* (intermittently, 1924-26), Jack Carter in Shanghai, China (1926-27), Luis Russell (1928-33), Louis Armstrong* (1937-39), and Arthur ("Zutty") Singleton,* among others. He also led his own groups from time to time and played short periods with William ("Chick") Webb,* Sam Wooding,* Bernard Addison, and John Kirby.* During the period December 1927-November 1928 he was active in Cairo and Alexandria, Egypt, and in Paris, France. He left the field of music in 1941, but returned in 1945, thereafter working with Art Hodes, Edward ("Kid") Ory* (1946), and Rex Stewart, among others. He also worked as a soloist in nightclubs of New York and led his own groups in Los Angeles, California (1949-53). In 1953 he settled in France, but continued to tour widely in Europe and returned to the United States to perform in 1969-70. In 1970 he settled in Switzerland. Nicholas was one of the pioneer clarinetists in the New Orleans tradition.

BIBL: ChilWW. FeaEJ. FeaGitJS. Souch.

DISC: Jep. Kink.

NICKENS, WILLIAM. Military drummer (fl. late eighteenth century in Lancaster County, Virginia). He served as a drummer during the American Revolutionary War. He enlisted about 1780.

BIBL: Benjamin Quarles, *The Negro in the American Revolution* (Chapel Hill, 1961), p. 77. Luther P. Jackson, "Virginia Negro Soldiers and Seamen in the American Revolution" in JNH 27 (July 1942).

NICKERSON, CAMILLE LUCIE. College professor (b. 30 March 1888 in New Orleans, Louisiana). She came from a family of professional musicians. Her father, William Joseph Nickerson,* was a violinist, conductor, and music teacher; her mother, Julia Ellen, played violin and cello, was a music teacher, and founded and conducted a ladies' orchestra; her brother Henry became a violinist and jazz bandleader; and her brother Philip played in a local dance orchestra. She studied piano as a child with her father, and also learned to play organ and mandolin. She obtained her musical education at the Oberlin Conservatory of Music in Ohio (B.A., 1916; M.A., 1932), at the Juilliard School of Music in New York, and at Columbia University Teachers College in New York. Her teaching career included tenures at the Nickerson School of Music in New Orleans (1916-26) and Howard University in Washington, D.C. (1926-62). At Howard she established and directed the Junior Preparatory Department, which produced students destined for later renown, such as George T. Walker.* In 1931 Nickerson won a grant from the Rosenwald Foundation, which permitted her to attend graduate school and to develop her interest in collecting creole folksongs. Encouraged by public interest in her work, she began performing the songs in recitals during the 1930s, wearing creole costumes and calling herself "The Louisiana Lady." In 1944 she made her debut (mezzo-soprano) at Times Hall in New York. Thereafter she toured regularly, particularly on the college circuit and in concert halls; in 1954 she toured in France under the sponsorship of the United States Information Agency. She took a wide interest in Afro-American music on the national level; during the years 1935-37 she was president of the National Association of Negro Musicians.* Her honors included appointments to boards of professional and civic organizations (she was a founding member of the Advisory Committee for the John F. Kennedy Center for the Performing Arts in Washington, D.C.), and an award from the National Association of Negro Musicians in 1962. She published many of her creole song arrangements, of which the best known were "Chère, mo lemmé toi," "Lizette, to quitté la plaine," "Danse, conni, conné," "Fais do do," and "Michieu banjo."

BIBL: Questionnaire. BPIM 7 (Spring 1979). Layne. Roach. WWBA.

NICKERSON, WILLIAM JOSEPH. Orchestra conductor (b. 10 November 1865 in New Orleans, Louisiana; d. 7 February 1928 in New Orleans). He studied music with a Professor L'Enfant of the French Opera orchestra in New Orleans. He taught at Straight University in the city, he conducted a private studio for voice and instruments, and he directed a community orchestra which gave concerts regularly and performed in other cities. One of the earliest productions of the Nickerson Orchestra and Concert Company was the opera, *The Chimes of Normandy*, in the late 1890s. In 1900 his orchestra performed at a Great Congress in Atlanta, Georgia, and the next year it performed in Chicago, Illinois. He was credited with two musical inventions: a piano-muffler, which softened the sounds when someone was practicing piano, and a mandolin attachment, which caused the piano to sound like a mandolin. He also wrote songs, of which "The colored soldier boys of Uncle Sam" was popular during World War I. His family was also musical. His wife, Julia (1879-1908), received her musical training at the New England Conservatory in Boston, Massachusetts, and taught music in the public schools of New Orleans until she married. Thereafter she worked alongside her husband and organized and conducted a ladies' orchestra. One son, Henry, studied violin with his father and became leader of a jazz orchestra; another son, Philip, played with the Silver Leaf society dance orchestra in New Orleans; and the daughter, Camille,* became a college music teacher.

BIBL: Camille Nickerson, personal communication. Black press, incl. NYAge, 18 February 1928. BPIM 7 (Spring 1979). George Hamilton, *Beacon Lights of the Race* (1911).

NIGHTHAWK, ROBERT. Bluesman. See **McCOY, ROBERT LEE.**

NIGHTINGALES, THE. Gospel group. See **THE SENSATIONAL NIGHTINGALES.**

NIXON (née **DAVIS), HAMMIE.** Bluesman (b. 22 January 1908 in Brownsville, Tennessee). He taught himself to play harmonica as a child, influenced by harmonica player Noah Lewis of Gus Cannon's* Jug Stompers. When he was eleven years old he began playing for ("Sleepy") John Estes,* and the two formed a partnership that lasted over fifty years—until Estes's death in 1977. They first played on street corners and for local entertainments, then later traveled with medicine shows. In 1934 Nixon went to Chicago with Son Bonds of Brownsville to make his first recordings. Estes soon followed Nixon to Chicago; during the 1930s and 1940s the two men had a jug-washboard band, which played on Chicago streets and included at one time or another John Henry Barbee, Lee Brown, Son Bonds, Charlie Pickett, and "Tampa Red" (Hudson Whittaker*). The Nixon-Estes team recorded regularly, and the revival of public interest in the blues during the 1960s brought about a spurt in their career. They went to Europe with the American Folk Blues Festival in 1964 and thereafter toured widely abroad, in Japan as well as Europe.

BIBL: BWW. *Cadence* 4 (May 1978). LivBl 19 (January-February 1975). "A Sermon on Sleepy John Estes" in LivBl 33 (July-August 1977). Robert Neff and Anthony Connor, *Blues* (Boston, 1975). Oliv.

DISC: LeSl. TudBM.

NKETIA, JOSEPH HANSON KWABENA. University professor/Ethnomusicologist (b. 22 June 1921 in Mampong, Ashanti Region, Ghana). He sang in a school choir as a child. He obtained his musical education in the primary and middle schools of Mampong, at the Teacher Training College in Akropong (teacher's certificate, 1940); at the School of Oriental and African Studies of London [England] University (certificate in phonetics, 1946); at Birkbeck College and Trinity College of Music in London (B.A., 1949); at Columbia University and the Juilliard School of Music in New York (1958-59); and at Northwestern University in Evanston, Illinois (1959). His teaching career included tenures at Akropong College (1940-44, 1949-52); at the University of Ghana at Lagos (1952-), where he was appointed Director of the newly established Institute of African Studies in 1965; and at the University of California at Los Angeles (1969-). He served as director of the musical ensemble for the Ghana Dance Troupe. He began writing music during his college years at Akropong. His best-known compositions were *Suite for Flute and Piano*; *Four Akan Songs; Canzona* for flute, oboe, and piano; and *Chamber Music in the African Idiom*. He toured widely as a lecturer and workshop consultant in Africa, Europe, the Caribbean, and the United States and delivered papers at international gatherings of professional societies. He also contributed numerous articles to such scholarly journals as *African Arts, Africa Report, Yearbook of the International Folk Music Council, Ethnomusicology*, and *The Black Perspective in Music*. His book-length publications included *Funeral Dirges of the Akan People* (1955), *Folk Songs of Ghana* (1962), *African Music in Ghana* (1962), *Drumming in Akan Communities* (1963), and *The Music of Africa* (1974). His honors included fellowships from the Ford Foundation (1961) and the Rockefeller Foundation (1958-59), the Cowell Award from the African Music Society (1958), the Grand Medal of Ghana (1968), the Ghana Arts Award (1972), and election to the Ghana Academy of Arts and Sciences and to the Royal Anthropological Institute of Great Britain (honorary fellow). He served as director for the International Society for Music Education (1967-) and was an executive member of the International Music Society (1968-) and a council member of the Society for Ethnomusicology (1968-). He was the most renowned African musicologist of his time.

BIBL: GhanaWW. Roach. WWAfrica. WWAfrLit.

NOBLE, JORDAN. Military drummer (b. c1796 in Georgia; d. 20 June 1890 in New Orleans, Louisiana). He was taken to New Orleans as a child. He served as a drummer boy in the Seventh Regiment of Andrew Jackson's forces in the War of 1812 and was active in the Battle of New Orleans; he ''beat his drum during all and every fight, in the hottest hell of the fire, and was complimented by [General Andrew] Jackson himself after the battle'' (see King. p. 256). Cited in press notices as ''the matchless drummer'' and the ''drummer of Chalmette Plains,'' he was held in high regard by New Orleans and honored on many occasions during his declining years. He was a veteran of four wars, having fought in 1836 in the Seminole War in Florida under General P. F. Smith, in 1848 under Colonel J. B. Walton in the First Regiment of Louisiana Volunteers in Mexico, and under General Butler with the colored Native Guards (which he organized in 1863) in the Civil War. He frequently gave ''field-music concerts,'' using the drums he had used in wars. He was called ''The Matchless Drummer.''

BIBL: GreBD. Grace King, *New Orleans. The Place and the People* (New York, 1895), pp. 229, 256. *The Daily Picayune* [New Orleans], 21 June 1890. Wilkes, pp. 81-83.

NOLAN, ROBERT L. (''DEAN''). Music critic (b. 25 January 1912 in Cleveland, Ohio). He began piano study when he was four years old with his mother, a pianist. By he time he was eleven, he was a church pianist and the official accompanist for his school. He obtained his musical education at Howard University in Washington, D.C. (B. Mus., 1938), and at the Juilliard School of Music in New York (M. Mus., 1940). After finishing his study at Juilliard, he toured with the Eva Jessye* Choir for a year. In 1941 he settled in Detroit, Michigan, and founded the Robert Nolan School of Music. During the years 1942-60 he served as a ''cooperating-faculty'' member of Wayne State University in Detroit in teaching piano to the university students. He was also active as a church minister of music, director of community choirs, and accompanist. In 1948 he became a music critic-journalist for *The Michigan Chronicle*. His honors included numerous awards from civic, community and professional groups and a NANM award (National Association of Negro Musicians*) in 1966.

BIBL: WWBA.

NOONE, JIMMIE. Jazz clarinetist (b. 23 April 1895 near New Orleans, Louisiana; d. 19 April 1944 in Los Angeles, California). He began studying guitar at the age of ten and began clarinet study at fifteen. In 1910 his family moved to New Orleans, where he later studied with Sidney Bechet* and Lorenzo Tio, Jr.* He began playing professionally in 1912 with Freddie Keppard.* After Keppard went to California the same year to play with the Original Creole Band,* Noone formed the Young Olympia Band with Buddie Petit (1912-17). During these years he also led his own trio and played with Edward (''Kid'') Ory* and Oscar (''Papa'') Celestine,* among others. In 1917 he settled in Chicago, Illinois, but made frequent trips back to New Orleans. He played with various groups, including Freddie Keppard (1917-18), William (''Bill'') Johnson* (1918-20), and Charles (''Doc'') Cooke* (1920-26, 1927), as well as led his own groups from time to time in Chicago nightclubs. He made his recording debut in 1923 and recorded regularly throughout his career. Among those who played with him were Johnny Dodds* and Earl Hines.* During the 1930s-40s he played residencies in various cities—Omaha, Nebraska; San Antonio, Texas; New Orleans; and New York (as co-leader of a group with Wellman Braud* in 1935). About 1943 he settled in California, and thereafter he played with Kid Ory and led his own group. He was important as a pioneer jazz clarinetist who made the transition from the New Orleans school to the classic jazz of the Chicago school.

BIBL: ChilWW. FeaEJ. MeeJMov. Souch.

DISC: Kink. RustJR.

NORMAN, FRED. Jazz arranger/Composer (b. 5 October 1910 in Leesburg, Florida). His mother was a church organist. He obtained his musical education at Fessenden Academy in Florida, at Dunbar High School in Washington, D.C., and at Howard University. He first began trombone study in high school and played in school bands both in Florida and Washington, D.C. His first professional experience was in 1927 with (''Bubber'') Applewhite and his Florida Troubadours. Thereafter he played with various groups, including Duke Eglin, Booker Coleman, Elmer Calloway, and Claude Hopkins* (1932-38). He was active as an arranger and section trombonist, but not as soloist. Through the 1920s-30s he wrote arrangements for dance orchestras, encouraged especially by Hopkins and Benny Carter*; he also studied arranging. After leaving the Hopkins band in 1938 he gave full time to arranging and in 1944 opened his own office. Those for whom he made arrangements included Tommy Dorsey, Benny Goodman, Glenn Miller, Artie Shaw, Charlie Spivak, and Raymond Scott, among others. He also wrote and arranged for radio orchestras and served as a staff member at CBS radio. During the late 1940s he began working for record companies and was musical director for such singers as William (''Billy'') Eckstine,* Brook Benton,* Diahann Carroll,* Leslie Uggams,* Sarah Vaughan,* and Dinah Washington,* among others. He also wrote for films and the stage, including music for *Ol' Man Satan* (1959).

BIBL: ASCAP. ChilWW. DanceWS. MeeJMov.

NORMAN, JESSYE. Concert singer (b. 15 September 1945 in Augusta, Georgia). She came from a musical family; her mother played piano and her father sang in a church choir. She began piano study at an early age. The choral director at her high school encouraged her musical development and gave her special instruction in voice. She became interested in opera through listening to the Metropolitan Opera radio broadcasts and learned to sing arias, which she sang for Girl Scout and PTA (Parent-Teacher Association) gatherings in her home state. At the age of sixteen she entered the Marian Anderson* Foundation auditions; although she failed to win, she attracted the attention of Carolyn Grant, a voice teacher at Howard University in Washington, D.C., who arranged for her to study at Howard (B. Mus., 1967). Later she attended the Peabody Conservatory of Music in Baltimore, Maryland (1967), where she studied with Alice Duschak, and the University of Michigan at Ann Arbor (1967-68), where she studied with Pierre Bernac. In 1968 she won first prize in the International Music Competition held at Munich, Germany. The next year she made her operatic debut (dramatic soprano) as Elisabeth in Wagner's *Tannhauser* with the Deutsche Opera of Berlin. She remained with the German opera company for several years, singing in Verdi's *Aida* and *Don Carlo*, Meyerbeer's *L'Africaine*, and Mozart's *The Marriage of Figaro*. In 1972 she made debuts with other opera companies and with symphonies: singing the title role in *Aida* at La Scala in Milan, Italy, and the role of Cassandra in Berlioz's *Les Troyens* at the Royal Opera House of Covent Garden in London, England; singing songs of Mahler at the Edinburgh [Scotland] Festival, with Rudolf Kempe conducting; singing in a concert version of *Aida* in the Hollywood Bowl in California with James Levine, conductor; and singing in an all-Wagner concert at the Tanglewood [Massachusetts] Festival with Colin Davis and the Boston Symphony. She toured widely in the United States and in Europe and sang in opera and oratorios, as well as lieder. During the 1970s she settled in London, England.

BIBL: CurBiog (February 1976). *Opera News* (17 June 1973). WWA. WWBA. WWOpera.

DISC: Turn.

NORTHERN, CHAUNCEY. Impresario (b. 3 December 1906 in Hampton, Virginia). He obtained his musical education at Hampton Institute in Virginia, where he sang in the Hampton Glee Club. He studied further at the Institute of Musical Art in New York (now the Juilliard School of Music) and in Italy (1927). He early conducted a music studio in the Harlem community of New York and was also a voice coach. Beginning in the 1940s he wrote a column for the *New York Age*. He was well known for his promotion of talented young black artists and his sponsorship of concerts, particularly at Carnegie Recital Hall. During his early career he toured regularly as a concert artist (tenor).

BIBL: Black press, incl. NYAge, 13 March 1926, 27 August 1927. AmstN, 23 January 1943. *Who's Who in Harlem*, compiled by Beresford Sylvester and Briggs Trottman (New York, 1950).

NORTHUP, SOLOMON. Writer (b. July 1808 in Minerva, Essex County, New York; d. c1860 in Glens Falls, New York). Little is known of his early life. He apparently taught himself to play violin at an early age, since he refers to his violin in his autobiography as "the ruling passion of my youth." He played the fiddle for dances in and near Saratoga Springs, New York, where he settled after marriage. In 1841 he was kidnapped and sold into slavery, ending up in Louisiana. He was not rescued until 1853, when he was allowed to return to his family in New York. He immortalized himself by writing an account of his experiences in *Twelve Years a Slave. Narrative of Solomon Northup, A Citizen of New York, Kidnapped in Washington City in 1841 and Rescued in 1853 from a Cotton Plantation near the Red River in Louisiana* (Cincinnati, 1853). His book offers an insightful description of the life of a slave musician.

BIBL: Sue Eaking and Joseph Logsdon, eds., *Twelve Years a Slave* (Baton Rouge, 1968).

NUÑES GARCÍA, JOSÉ MAURÍCIO. Composer (b. 22 September 1767 in Rio de Janeiro, Brazil; d. 18 April 1830 in Rio de Janeiro). As a child he studied music with his mother and her sister. Later he attended the Escola de Santa Cruz , a school founded by the Jesuits, which came to be known as the "Conservatory of the Negroes" because it produced so many black musicians. He was ordained a priest in the Roman Catholic Church in May 1792 and in 1798 was appointed chapel master of the cathedral at Rio de Janeiro. After Prince Regent Dom John (later John VI) established his court in Brazil, he appointed Nuñes García musical director of the Royal Chapel (November 1808). The composer also served the next ruler, Pedro I, and gave the monarch music lessons. Nuñes García left more than 400 compositions, of which the majority were liturgical. His musical style was influenced by the music of Mozart and Haydn; he came to know their music well through his personal contacts with Sigismund Neukomm, who had studied with the two classical masters and who visited in Rio de Janeiro in 1816. Nuñes García was called "the Father of Brazilian Music."

BIBL: Luis H. Corrêa de Azevado, *A Brief History of Music in Brazil* (Washington, D.C., 1948). Albert Luper, *The Music of Brazil* (Washington, D.C., 1943). Cloefe Person de Mattos, *Catálogo temático des obras do Padre José Maurício Nuñes García* (Rio de Janeiro, 1970).

NZEWI, EMEKA MEKI. Ethnomusicologist/University professor (b. 21 October 1938 at Nnewi, Nigeria). He obtained his musical education at the University of Nigeria in Nsukka (B.A., 1965), where his career development was influenced by Edna Smith Edet,* at that time head of the music department, and at Queen's University in Belfast, Ireland (Ph. D., 1977), where he studied with John Blacking. He was active in music from early childhood on, learning to play the Ese tuned drum row and the clarinet. He was appointed to the faculty of the University of Nigeria at Nsukka (1970-). In addition to teaching he was active in musical theater; he organized an Institute of Theatre Arts at the university, called Productions 4-D, which regularly staged productions under his directorship and toured widely in Nigeria. His productions drew upon traditional Igbo dramatic forms and techniques; he himself wrote the musical scores. His best-known works were *Ogbunigwe* (opera-drama, 1968), *The Lost Finger* (opera-drama, 1970), *A Drop of Honey* (musical, 1972), *Mystery is Illusion* (operetta, 1974), and *The Ordeal for Regeneration* (opera-drama, 1980). He also wrote music for choirs, solo voice, instruments, as well as a symphonic poem (1966). He contributed articles to such professional journals as *Ibadan, Conch, African Music, African Arts*, and *The Black Perspective in Music*. His book publications included *Two Fists in One Mouth* (1975) and *Drama Scene in Nigeria* (1980). In November 1980 he was one of two Nigerian professors sent to China on a cultural exchange tour.

BIBL: Questionnaire. *African Arts* 5 (Winter 1972), pp. 36, 68; 7 (Summer 1974), p. 5.

O

O'FAKE, PETER. Society dance-band leader (b. 1820 in Newark, New Jersey; d. 23 January 1884 in Newark). Self-taught, he learned to play violin and flute well enough to enter a professional career. He began playing in public during the 1840s and in 1847 performed on a concert of the Jullien Society in the city of New York. His "society orchestra" played for the balls of the aristocracy in Newark and nearby places, and during the summer months he played at such resorts as West Point, Cozzens, and Schooley Mountains. He conducted a music studio and a dancing school. He was associated with St. Philip's Episcopal Church in Newark as both a chorister and choir director (beginning in 1856). Like most orchestra leaders of the period, he composed and/or arranged the music his group performed. His best-known composition was a quadrille, "The Sleigh Ride." His son, John O'Fake, was active as a music teacher and instrumentalist in Newark during the last decades of the nineteenth century.

BIBL: Black press, incl. IndF, 14 March 1903; NYFreeman, 23 May 1885; NYGlobe, 26 January 1884; *Weekly Anglo-African*, 7 July 1860. Trot, pp. 304-306.

O'JAYS, THE. Rhythm 'n' blues group. (fl. 1950s-70s; orig. in Canton, Ohio). This male, singing-dancing group was formed in 1957 by Robert ("Bobby") Massey, Walter ("Walt") Williams (b. 25 August 1942), Eddie Lavert (b. 16 June 1947), William ("Bill") Isles, and William Powell—all of whom were attending McKinley High School in Canton, Ohio, at the time. Until 1961 they called their group The Mascots; then they changed the name to The O'Jays for their disc-jockey manager Eddie O'Jay. The group first attracted wide attention in 1963 with its recording of "Lipstick traces," written by Allen Toussaint. Thereafter the quintet met with moderate success, but in the 1970s its popularity soared after beginning an association with songwriters Kenneth ("Kenny") Gamble* and Leon Huff.* By 1976 the O'Jays had been reduced to a trio; Isles left in 1965, Massey left in 1972, and Powell died in 1976. Cholly Atkins, their choreographer, found a replacement in Samuel ("Sammy") Strain, who previously had sung with Little Anthony and the Imperials. In 1977 Levert, Massey, and Williams formed their own promotion and record-producing company. Their best-known performances included the songs "Back stabbers" and "Lonely drifter" and the albums *Message in the Music*, *Live in London*, and *Survival*.

BIBL: Black press, incl. AmstN, 16 November 1974. *Dawn* (August 1978). *Ebony* (September 1977). StamPRS.

DISC: Giv.

ODETTA. See **GORDON, ODETTA.**

OFORI, AGYTARE T. ("OSCARMORE"). Folksong collector (b. September 1939 in Odumase Manya Krobo, Ghana). He came from a musical family and was immersed in traditional music during his childhood. As a child he sang in a church choir. He studied music, including guitar, with Kewsi Baiden at the Old Juaben Senior School in Accra, Ghana. His early style development was influenced by saxophonist ("Papa") Joe Kelly, who inspired Ofori to write "highlife" songs. He began playing professionally in 1953 with the Koforidua Royal Orchestra and later played with the Ralchers Dance Band, led by ("Satchmo") Korley. In 1960 he went to Europe for the first time; later he settled in London, England. On his first visit he came into contact with Zoltān Kodāly in Hungary, who inspired him to serious study of music, and with Malcolm Sargent, with whom he studied at the Curwen Memorial College of Music in London. During the 1960s-70s he devoted much time to collecting folk songs. His best-known highlife songs were "Sanbra," "Odobra," "Gyaesu," and "Amabonsu." His best-known album was *Afrika!* (1971). His honors included an award for writing a commercial jingle for the Ghana National Airline Inaugural Celebration (which won him a trip to Europe) and appointment to membership on the ethnomusicological panel of the Royal Institute of Anthropology in London.

BIBL: Communications.

OLATUNJI, MICHAEL BABATUNDE. Folk music drummer (b. c1920s in Ajido-Badagry, Nigeria). He obtained his musical education at the Baptist Academy in Lagos, Nigeria, and at Morehouse College in Atlanta, Georgia (B.A., 1954). During his school years he formed a cultural dance group that toured widely in Nigeria. His early career development was influenced by the drummer Oyewe and the singer Denge. He went to the United States in 1950. In 1954 he settled in New York with plans to pursue graduate studies at New York University but became involved in musical activities. He performed in various theaters and concert halls and on television shows. During the 1960s he established a cultural center-performing arts school, called The Olatunji Center for African Culture, in the Harlem community of New York. Those who cooperated with his organization or performed with his groups included John Coltrane,* Yusef Lateef,* Abbey Lincoln,* and Max Roach.* Olatunji also toured with his troupe, which included dancers and drummers. His best-known albums were *Drums of Passion* and *Zingo* In 1981 he gave a series of farewell concerts, beginning at the Avery Fisher Hall in New York, preparatory to returning to Nigeria to settle there permanently.

BIBL: Black press, incl. AmstN, 17 January 1981; CDef, 9-15 March 1963. *Sepia* (February 1962).

OLIVER, JOSEPH ("KING"). Jazz cornetist (b. 11 May 1885 near Abend, Louisiana; d. 8 April 1938 in Savannah, Georgia). His family moved to New Orleans, Louisiana, when he was young. As a child he played in a boys' band and probably studied music with the bandleader Walter Kinchin. He first played trombone, then later changed to cornet. He began playing professionally about 1904 as a substitute in the Onward Brass Band. Thereafter he played in various local groups, including such brass bands as the Allen, Olympia, Melrose, Eagle, and the Original Superior Orchestra, Richard M. Jones's* Four Hot Hounds (regularly c1912-1918), and Edward ("Kid") Ory* (1918). He also led his own band during these years. Ory was the first to bill him as "King Oliver," and the nickname remained with him for the rest of his career. In 1918 William ("Bill") Johnson* sent for Oliver to come to Chicago, Illinois, to "front" the Johnson band at the Royal Gardens Cafe. Thereafter he settled in Chicago and used the city until 1927 as a base from which he toured. He played with Lawrence Duhé, then organized his own groups by 1920, called King Oliver's Creole Jazz Band and later King Oliver and His Dixie Syncopators. In the summer of 1922 he sent to New Orleans for Louis Armstrong,* thus adding a second trumpeter to his band. In 1923 he made his recording debut and thereafter recorded regularly. In 1927 he settled in New York, using that city also as a base from which he toured. During the years 1927-37 he toured and recorded with his own groups, but he often had no permanent group and therefore had to assemble bands to record or play special engagements. About 1930 he settled in Nashville, Tennessee, then later lived in Savannah, Georgia.

Oliver's band was one of the most celebrated of the 1920s; among those who played with him, in addition to Armstrong, were William ("Buster") Bailey, Johnny Dodds,* Warren ("Baby") Dodds,* Honore Dutrey,* Lillian ("Lil") Hardin Armstrong,* William ("Bill") Johnson, and Johnny St. Cyr. He was the important link between the New Orleans tradition and the so-called classic jazz tradition of Chicago. He was also important in jazz history as a leading figure in the first generation of jazz cornetists-trumpeters, along with Freddie Keppard* and Willie ("Bunk") Johnson,* and as the mentor of Louis Armstrong. He composed as well as arranged jazz pieces, of which the best known were "Dippermouth blues" (with Armstrong; also known as "Sugarfoot stomp"), "West End blues," "Doctor Jazz," "Dixieland shuffle," and "Riverside blues" (with Richard M. Jones; also known as "Jazzin' babies blues"). Oliver's nephew, Ulysses Kay,* was a composer.

BIBL: Communication from Ulysses Kay in regard to birthplace. Walter C. Allen and Brian A. Rust, *King Joe Oliver* (London, 1955). Louis Armstrong, *Satchmo* (New York, 1954). ChilWW. DAB. MeeJMov.

DISC: Kink. RustJR. TudJ.

OLIVER, MELVIN JAMES ("SY"). Jazz arranger/Composer (b. 17 December 1910 in Battle Creek, Michigan). He came from a musical family: his father sang professionally, taught musical instruments, and directed church choirs; his mother was a piano teacher and a church organist. His family moved to Zanesville, Ohio, when he was a child. He began piano study at an early age, but his real interest was in trumpet, which he studied with his father. At fourteen he began playing professionally with Cliff Barnett; at seventeen he joined

Zack Whyte, with whom he toured. In 1930 he settled in Columbus, Ohio, where he taught music, led small groups in local nightclubs, and made arrangements for college bands. During the years 1933-1943 he was active as an arranger as well as performer with James (''Jimmie'') Lunceford* (1933-39) and Tommy Dorsey (1939-43). During his service in the United States Armed Forces (1943-45) he was a bandmaster and played trumpet in army bands. In the following decades he led his own big band occasionally, arranged music intermittently for Dorsey, worked as a musical director and record supervisor for various recording companies, and wrote or arranged music for television programs and films, including *Dubarry Was a Lady* (1943), *Girl Crazy* (1943), *Ship Ahoy* (1942), and *Go, Man, Go* (1954). Those for whom he arranged included Chubby Checker* (née Ernest Evans), Johnny Carson's television show, Bing Crosby, Louis Armstrong,* Ella Fitzgerald,* the Mills Brothers,* Della Reese,* Peggy Lee, and Frank Sinatra, among others. He toured widely at home and abroad with groups and also as a musical director; in 1968 he arranged for the Olympia Theater orchestra in Paris, France. During the 1970s he toured in England with a Tommy Dorsey revival band, led his big band on concerts of the New York Jazz Repertory Company, and played a long residency with his small group at Rockefeller Center's Rainbow Room (beginning in 1975).

He was regarded as one of the leading arrangers of his time. He was credited with contributing enormously to ''the Lunceford sound,'' which was distincive for its bouncy rhythms and innovative saxophone treatment and was widely imitated by dance bands of the 1950s. His best-known pieces were ''Losers, weepers,'' '''Tain't what you do,'' ''Yes, indeed,'' ''Because you're you,'' ''Dream of you,'' and ''The melody man.''

BIBL: BMI (April 1972). ChilWW. DanceWS. *Encore* (October 1975). FeaEJ. FeaJS. FeaGitJS. MeeJMov. NYT (21 May 1978).

DISC: Kink.

OPERA EBONY. Opera company (founded 1974 in Philadelphia, Pennsylvania). This regional opera company was founded in November 1974 by Sister Elise of the Sisters of the Blessed Sacrament, a Catholic Order, along with co-founders Margaret Harris,* Benjamin Matthews, and Wayne Sanders. Its purpose was ''to create opportunities in opera for previously unheralded minority talent'' (quoted from publicity releases). The company's debut performance was Verdi's *Aidi* in 1976 in Philadelphia. Support groups, Friends of National Opera Ebony, were organized in various cities in the East. Over the years the leading principals included conductors Everett Lee* and Leonard DePaur,* and singers William Brown,* Alpha Floyd, Eugene Holmes, Hilda Harris,* Benjamin Matthews, Arthur Thompson,* and James Tyeska, among others.

BIBL: Black press. Publicity releases.

OPERA/SOUTH. Opera company (founded 1970 in Jackson, Mississippi). This regional opera company was founded by Sister Elise of the Sisters of the Blessed Sacrament, a Catholic order, under the sponsorship of three black colleges in or near Jackson, Mississippi: Jackson State University, Utica Junior College, and Tougaloo College, all members of the Mississippi Inter-Collegiate Opera Guild. For its debut in May 1971, the company staged Verdi's *Aida*, using professional artists in the leading roles and college students for the choruses and ballets. In later years Opera/South produced operas by black composers in addition to the standard repertory: *Highway 1 USA* (1972) and *A Bayou Legend* (1974) by William Grant Still* and *The Juggler of Our Lady* (1972) and *Jubilee* (1976) by Ulysses Kay.* Over the years the principals included director Walter Herbert and designer Donald Door; conductors Margaret Harris* and Leonard DePaur;* and singers William Brown,* Alpha Floyd, John Miles, Wilma Shakesnider, Benjamin Matthews, Barbara Conrad, Faye Robinson,* Arthur Thompson,* Robert Mosley, and Eugene Holmes, among others. Opera/South sent several of its leading singers to such major opera companies as the Metropolitan Opera, New York City Opera, and European opera companies.

BIBL: *Ebony* (February 1973). *Time* (25 November 1974).

ORIGINAL CREOLE ORCHESTRA, THE. See **JOHNSON, WILLIAM MANUEL** and **KEPPARD, FREDDIE.**

ORY, EDWARD (''KID''). Jazz trombonist (b. 25 December 1886 in La Place, Louisiana; d. 23 January 1973 in Honolulu, Hawaii). As a child he played banjo and led a boys' band. He began playing professionally in New Orleans, Louisiana, about 1908; from 1913 to 1919 he led one of the most popular bands in the city. In 1919 he settled in California, where he continued to lead his own groups. When he made his recording debut in 1922, it was the first time in history that a black *jazz* band had recorded (black dance bands had recorded earlier). His groups were called Spikes's Seven Pods of Pepper Orchestra or Kid Ory's Sunshine Orchestra. During the years 1925-30 he was active in Chicago, Illinois, where he recorded and/or played with Louis

Armstrong,* Joseph ("King") Oliver* (1925-27), Dave Peyton* (1927), Clarence Black (1928), and Boyd Atkins (1929). In 1930 he resettled in Los Angeles, California; thereafter he played for short periods with various groups, including Thomas ("Mutt") Carey, Charlie Echols, Leon René,* and Freddie Washington, among others. He was musically inactive during the years 1933-43; he then joined Barney Bigard* (summer of 1942) and played string bass and alto saxophone with his own groups and with others. During the years c1944-46 he played residencies in various cities, occasionally toured—nationwide in 1948; in Europe in 1956, 1959 (at the Berlin Jazz Festival)—and appeared on television programs; he returned to his trombone during these years. He also appeared in films, including *Crossfire* (1947), *New Orleans* (1947), and *The Benny Goodman Story* (1955). In 1966 he retired to Hawaii because of ill health. Ory was an important representative of the jazz "tailgate" trombone style and is credited with having transported the New Orleans tradition to the West Coast. His best-known pieces were "Muskrat ramble" and "Savoy blues."

BIBL: ASCAP. ChilWW. FeaEJ. FeaJS. FeaGitJS. MeeJMov. Souch.

DISC: Jep. Kink. Rust. TudJ.

OSEI, TEDDY. Jazz bandleader (b. 17 December 1936 in Kumasi, Ashanti Region, Ghana). He obtained his education in Kumasi schools and learned to play flute and saxophone. In 1962 he went to London, England, where he studied music at the School of Music and Drama. During his stay in London he also led dance bands. He toured with a troupe in Switzerland and in Tunisia, then returned to Ghana. In 1969 he took Mac Tontoh (trumpeter) and Sol Amarfio (drummer) to England. Adding another player, Robert Bailey (keyboards) of Trinidad, he formed a group, called Osibisa, which played residencies in London nightclubs, performed on television shows, and made recordings. During the 1970s the group, enlarged to seven men, toured extensively in Europe and the United States. Over the years Osibisa included, in addition to the original members, Gordon Hunte, Wendell Richardson from Antigua, Jean Mendengue from Grenada, Spartacus R., and Loughty Lasisi Amoa, representing Caribbean countries, Ghana, and Cameroun. Osibisa's music was distinctive for its blend of African elements, jazz, and Latin-American rhythms. The best-known albums were *Osibisa*, *The Dawn*, *Music for Gong, Gong* and *Woyaya*.

BIBL: Black press, incl. AmstN, 29 December 1973. WWGhana.

OSIBISA. See **OSEI, TEDDY.**

OUSLEY, CURTIS ("KING CURTIS"). Rhythm 'n' blues winds player (b. 1934 in Fort Worth, Texas; d. 14 August 1971 in New York). He obtained his musical education in the public schools of Fort Worth, Texas. He began playing alto saxophone when he was twelve years old and tenor saxophone a year later. By the time he was fifteen, he was leading his own group. After graduating from high school he played with Lionel Hampton.* In 1952 he went to New York, where he soon established himself as one of the leading rhythm 'n' blues saxophonists in the city. In addition to recording prolifically with various groups, he also performed with such individuals as Brook Benton,* Nat King Cole (née Nathaniel Coles),* Andy Williams, and the McGuire Sisters, among others. In 1958 he formed his own rhythm 'n' blues group. He was best known for his music for the dance craze of the 1960s, the twist—particularly the recordings titled "Soul twist" (1962) and "Memphis soul stew" (1967). He was also musical director of a television show called "Soul" for a period, for which he wrote the theme music.

BIBL: Black press, incl. AmstN, 11 August 1962. FeaGitJS. *Sepia* (March 1963). StamPRS.

OVERSTREET, W. BENTON. Vaudeville pianist/Songwriter (fl. early twentieth century). Little is known of his early career except that he was one of the first persons to write and arrange music for a group called a "Jaz or Jazz" band. He first attracted attention in the press in May 1916 when his vaudeville act featuring contralto Estelle (also called Stella) Harris (d. 1933 in Chicago, Illinois) and a Jaz Band opened at the Grand Theater in Chicago, Illinois, with the Billy King* Company. Later his act was enlarged into a company composed of Harris, himself as pianist, a band, and singers and dancers. Harris toured with the Smart Set* company and with a trio including Chris Jones and Billy B. Johnson on the Keith and Proctor vaudeville circuit before joining Overstreet's show. She was regarded by some as "the greatest natural rag-song shouter on the American stage" (IndF, 7 October 1916). Overstreet wrote special songs for Harris to sing, among them, "The Alabama todelo," "The new dance," "The Alabama jazzbo band," and "Jazz dance." The latter was reputed to have been used by more vaudeville acts than any other song ever published. After an association with the Billy King company as a musical director for seven years, Overstreet left the stage in 1921 to become manager-musical director of the Standard and other theaters in Philadelphia, Pennsylvania. Later he toured as a pianist with the S. H. Gray company. One of his best-known songs was ''There'll be some changes made'' (written with Billy Higgins).

BIBL: AlHen. Black press, incl. CDef, 6 May 1916, 28 July 1917, 24 May 1919, 30 April 1921, 26 December 1925; IndF, 7 October 1916, 10 June 1933.

DISC: RustJR.

OWENS, JAMES ROBERT ("JIMMY"). Jazz trumpeter (b. 9 December 1943 in New York, New York). He obtained his musical education at the University of Massachusetts in Amherst and through private study. He studied and played with Donald Byrd* (1959-60) in the Newport Youth Band. Thereafter he played short periods with various groups, including Locksley (''Slide'') Hampton, Lionel Hampton,* Bennie (''Hank'') Crawford, Charles Mingus,* and Herbie Mann. In 1965 he was an original member of the Thad Jones*/Mel Lewis big band; during the 1960s-70s he also played with the Clark Terry* big band, New York Jazz Sextet, Symphony of the New World,* and William (''Billy'') Taylor,* among others, and toured in Europe many times. He was a co-founder in 1969 of Collective Black Artists, Inc. In the mid-1970s he toured and recorded with his own quartet, the Jimmy Owens Quartet Plus. His honors included awards from the music industry and appointments to boards and panels of professional and government organizations and foundations.

BIBL: FeaJS. FeaGitJS. WWBA.

P

PACE, HARRY. Insurance executive/Music publisher/Record producer (b. 6 January 1884 in Covington, Georgia; d. 26 July 1943 in Chicago, Illinois). Although best known as an insurance executive—he was president of the Supreme Liberty Life Insurance Company in Chicago, Illinois, at the time of his death—he was also active in the field of music. He obtained his education at the Atlanta [Georgia] Baptist College (now Morehouse College, B.A., 1903). After graduating from college he taught at Lincoln Institute in Jefferson City, Missouri (1906-08), then settled in Memphis, Tennessee, where he worked as a bank cashier. He soon became involved in the city's musical activities, singing solos on church and community concerts. In 1908 he met W. C. Handy,* and the two men began to collaborate in writing songs, with Pace providing the lyrics. Later they founded the Pace and Handy Music Company-Publishers. In 1918 the publishing company moved to New York and scored success with its very first publication, "A good man is hard to find." Pace was president, Charles Handy (brother of W. C.) was vice-president, and W. C. Handy was secretary-treasurer. Among those employed by the company were Fletcher Henderson* as song-plugger and pianist, William Grant Still* as chief arranger, and Fred Bryan* and J. Berni Barbour* as copyists.

In January 1921 Pace and Handy dissolved their partnership, and Pace set up the Pace Phonograph Corporation to produce records on the Black Swan label, named in honor of the nineeenth-century Elizabeth Taylor Greenfield,* who was called "The Black Swan." This was the first Negro-owned recording company in history. The first artist to record was baritone C. Carroll Clark, a native of Denver, Colorado, who sang popular ballads of the time. Thereafter, however, the company included blues, jazz, art songs, spirituals, operatic arias, and instrumental pieces in its releases. Over the three years of its existence, those who recorded included Katie Crippen, Henry Creamer* and J. Turner Layton* in duos, Kemper Harreld,* Alberta Hunter,* Georgette Harvey,* Clara Smith,* Trixie Smith, Florence Cole Talbert,* Ethel Waters,* and Essie Whitman,* among many others. In October 1921 Pace organized The Black Swan Troubadours—composed of Ethel Waters and her Black Swan Jazz Masters led by Fletcher Henderson—to tour the nation on the vaudeville circuit and thereby advertise his record releases. Simpson, the first road manager, was later replaced by Lester Walton,* who had been active in New York musical affairs for many years. About that time William Still joined the company as musical director. Pace was encouraged by his initial success and formed a partnership in April 1922 with John Fletcher, a white man, and purchased a better plant in order to improve his pressing facilities. The new company, called the Fletcher Record Company, was solely responsible for the Black Swan label, while Pace maintained the independence of his Phonograph Corporation. In 1923, however, Pace's business began to falter; in December 1923 Fletcher Records declared bankruptcy, and in March 1924 Pace sold the Black Swan label to Paramount Records. Thereafter he left the music field. Pace was a pioneer among black record producers. Except for the short-lived Black Patti label, it was not until the 1930s that a black-owned record company again appeared on the scene—the René brothers Exclusive/Excelsior label in Los Angeles, California. *The Chicago Defender* commented upon Pace's failure, but observed that the accomplishments of the Black Swan label had forced white recording companies to do three things: to recognize the vast Negro market for recordings, to release "race catalogues," and to advertise in black newspapers. The Black Swan was successful after all.

BIBL: AlHen. Black press, incl. CDef, 19 April

1924, 17 May 1924, 31 July 1943; AmstN, 31 July 1943. W. C. Handy, *Father of the Blues* (New York, 1941). WWCA, 1941-44.

PAGE, ORAN THADDEUS ("HOT LIPS"). Jazz trumpeter (b. 27 January 1908 in Dallas, Texas; d. 5 November 1954 in New York, New York). As a child he studied piano with his mother. He played clarinet, saxophone, and by the time he was twelve years old, trumpet. His first professional experience was with a band that accompanied Gertrude (''Ma'') Rainey's* touring show. Thereafter he worked with various groups, including a T.O.B.A.* show (Theater Owners Booking Association), Troy Flody, the Blue Devils (1928-31), and Bennie Moten* (1931-35), among others. During the 1930s-50s he led his own groups, both small groups and big bands, playing residencies at Kansas City, Missouri; Boston, Massachusetts; Chicago, Illinois; Minneapolis, Minnesota; and New York, among other cities. In 1949 he performed at the Paris Jazz Festival. He returned to Europe for longer tours in 1951 and 1952. During these years he also played and recorded with others, including Bud Freeman, Joe Marsala, Don Redman,* Artie Shaw, and Ethel Waters,* among others. He was a trumpeter and blues vocalist in the style of Louis Armstrong.* His best-known performance was ''Blues in the night.''

BIBL: BWW. ChilWW. FeaEJ. Russ.

DISC: Jep. Kink. RustJR. TudJ.

PAGE, WALTER SYLVESTER. Jazz bassist (b. 9 February 1900 in Gallatin, Missouri; d. 20 December 1957 in New York, New York). In his youth he played tuba and drums in local groups. He obtained his musical education at Lincoln High School in Kansas City, Missouri, where he came under the tutelage of N. Clark Smith* and began playing string bass, and at the University of Kansas at Lawrence. He first played professionally with Dave Lewis; thereafter he played with various groups, including Bennie Moten* (1918-23; 1931-34); the band of the Billy King* Show, led by Emir Coleman (1923-25); William (''Count'') Basie* (1934; 1936-42; 1946-49); the [James] Jeter/[Hayes] Pillars band (1934); Nat Towles (1945); Jesse Price* (1945-46); and Oran (''Hot Lips'') Page* (1949), among others. When Coleman's group disbanded in 1926, Page took it over as his Original Blue Devils, settling at Oklahoma City, Oklahoma (1925-31). During the 1950s he played and/or recorded with Ruby Braff, William (''Wild Bill'') Davison,* Roy Eldridge,* Jimmy Rushing,* and others. He won wide recognition for his bass playing, particularly as a member of the Basie orchestra of the 1930s-40s. He was a major contributor, along with Jonathan (''Jo'') Jones* and Freddie Green, to the distinctive style of the rhythm section, which was called the ''All American Rhythm Section.'' His performance style exerted wide influence upon other swing bassists.

BIBL: ChilWW. FeaEJ. Russ.

DISC: Kink. RustJR.

PANKEY, AUBREY. Concert singer (b. 19?? in Pittsburgh, Pennsylvania; d. 19?? in New York, New York). As a child he sang in an Episcopalian church choir (boy soprano). He obtained his musical education at Hampton Institute in Virginia, where he sang with the college glee club and was encouraged by R. Nathaniel Dett* to enter a music career. Later he studied at the Oberlin [Ohio] Conservatory of Music and at Boston [Massachusetts] University. He also studied privately with Arthur Hubbard in Boston, with John Alan Haughton in New York, with Theodore Lierhammer in Vienna, Austria, and with Oscar Daniel and Charles Panzera in Paris, France. During the years 1931-40 he lived in Europe, where he gave recitals in addition to studying. In 1940 he made his concert debut as a baritone at Town Hall in New York. Thereafter he toured widely in the United States, Europe, and South America; his tour in South America was sponsored by the U.S. Office of the Coordinator of Inter-American Affairs. In 1956 he toured in China at the invitation of the Chinese People's Association for Cultural Relations with foreign countries; he was the first American to tour in China after the Republic was established in 1949.

BIBL: Black press, incl. CDef, 2 January 1937, 5 February 1944, 7 January 1956; NYAge, 23 August 1947, 4 July 1942. Hare.

PARKER, CHARLES CHRISTOPHER ("CHARLIE," "BIRD," "YARDBIRD"). (b. 29 August 1920 in Kansas City, Missouri; d. 12 March 1955 in New York, New York). His father was a professional entertainer. He obtained his musical education at Lincoln High School in Kansas City, where he came under the tutelage of Alonzo Lewis, who succeeded N. Clark Smith* as bandmaster at Lincoln. He played baritone horn in the school band and saxophone in a jazz group called the Deans of Swing. Outside of school he listened to some of the nation's leading jazz reedmen, who were playing in local clubs, among them, Herschel Evans, Ben Webster,* and Lester Young.* He began playing professionally at the age of fourteen and played with various groups, including Tommy Douglas (1936-37), George E. Lee* (summer 1937), and the Jesse Price/Henry (''Prof'') Smith band (1937-38), among others. In 1938 he went to Chicago, then to New York in search of work. His first job, washing dishes in a restaurant, brought him into contact with Arthur (''Art'') Tatum,* who was the featured entertainer. His next job, playing in a taxi-dance hall, forced him to develop a repertory of popular music. He played at other places, but managed nevertheless to spend much time at Clark Monroe's Uptown House in the Harlem community ''jamming'' with other jazzmen and playing for only tips. Late in 1938 he had to return to Kansas City for his father's funeral; he remained to play briefly with the Harlan Leonard Rockets, then later joined the newly organized Jay McShann* orchestra (1939-42), with which he toured, then left to settle in New York. He became a member of an informal group that regularly gathered for jam sessions at Minton's Playhouse in Harlem, managed by Theodore (''Teddy'') Hill,* which included Kenneth (''Klook'') Clark* and Thelonious Monk,* the only ones actually employed as the house band, along with John Birks (''Dizzy'') Gillespie,* Charlie Christian,* Oscar Pettiford,* and many others.

In December 1942 Parker joined Earl Hines's* orchestra, which later was recognized as the ''incubator of bop.'' The orchestra had been disbanded by the end of 1943, but in the spring of 1944 many of its members were reunited in a band led by Eckstine, including Parker who had worked with Noble Sissle* in the interim. Eckstine's band was historically important as the first to play the new music called ''bebop'' (later, bop). In August 1944 Parker joined the Dizzy Gillespie Quintet, which played in clubs on 52nd Street in New York, but also toured. In 1946 the Quintet played an engagement in California; when it returned to New York, Parker remained behind. Sixteen months later he went to New York and formed his Charlie Parker Quintet with Miles Davis,* Duke Jordan, Tommy Potter, and Max Roach.* Later members included Kenny Dorham,* Roy Haynes,* Red Rodney (née Robert Chudnick), and Al Haig, among others. During the next decade his career flourished and he became a celebrity. His quintet won wide recognition: beginning in 1948 he toured intermittently with JATP (Jazz at the Philharmonic), produced by Norman Granz, as a soloist or with his quintet; in 1949 he played at the International Paris Jazz Festival; in December 1949 a nightclub was opened in New York in his honor, called Birdland; in 1950 he made jazz history when his group became the first to record with a chamber orchestra, producing *Charlie Parker with Strings*. He toured three times in Europe, with JATP and as a soloist. He first recorded in 1940 with McShann's orchestra, and thereafter recorded extensively. His best-known recordings were ''Billie's bounce,'' ''Koko,'' ''Parker's mood,'' ''Now's the time,'' ''Anthropology'' and ''Confirmation.'' He won innumerable awards from the music industry and adulation from the public. Parker was the top alto saxophonist of his time and was regarded as one of the four or five geniuses in jazz history. His saxophone style directly influenced the musical development of all important alto saxophonists who came after him. His approach to improvisation changed the roles of all instruments in the jazz ensemble. He was one of the largest contributors to the movement that changed jazz from a dance music to a chamber music demanding serious listening.

BIBL: FeaEJ. Dizzy Gillespie with Al Fraser, *To Be or Not to Bop* (New York, 1979). Ross Russell, *Bird Lives* (New York, 1973). MeeJMov.

DISC: Jep. Kink. ModJ.TudJ.

PARKER, HERMAN (''LITTLE JUNIOR''). Bluesman (b. 27 March 1932 in Clarksdale, Mississippi [?]; d. 18 November 1971 in Blue Island, Illinois). His first professional experiences were with ''Sonny Boy Williamson, No. 2'' (Willie ''Rice'' Miller)* and ''Howlin' Wolf'' (Chester Burnett)* during the late 1940s. Later he became a regular performer on radio station WDIA in Memphis, Tennessee, along with Johnny Ace (Johnny Alexander), Bobby Bland,* Roscoe Gordon, and Earl Forrest. He also toured with ''Big Mama'' (Willie Mae) Thornton* during this period. He made his first recordings as a singer in 1952; when he began playing harmonica on his recordings in 1956, his style revealed the influence of Williamson. He settled in Chicago, Illinois, during the late 1950s. He recorded extensively, and although he had few commercially successful recordings, his music was greatly influential upon other bluesmen. Best known were his ''Mystery train'' and ''Driving wheel.''

BIBL: BWW. LivBl 7 (Winter 1971-72).

DISC: Jep. LeSl.TudBM.

PARKER, LOUISE. Concert singer (b. 1925 in Philadelphia, Pennsylvania). She obtained her musical education in the public schools of Philadelphia, Pennsylvania, and at the Curtis Institute of Music in Philadelphia (B. Mus.), where she studied with Marian Szkeley Fresch. Later she studied in Paris, France, with Pierre Bernac. In her early career she sang with the Paul Roberts Singers of Philadelphia and with the Hall Johnson* Singers, including a tour of Europe in 1951. She toured widely as a concert singer in the United States, Europe, South America, Australia, and the Near East, giving solo recitals and appearing with symphony orchestras. She was also active in opera, appearing with the Chicago Lyric Opera in Wagner's *Die Walküre* (1973), in the Houston, Texas, production of Scott Joplin's *Treemonisha* (1975), and with the San

Diego [California] Opera in the American premiere of Henze's *Der Junge Lord* (1964). Her teaching career included a tenure at Temple University in Philadelphia. Her honors included the Marian Anderson* Award (1944).

BIBL: Black press, incl. AmstN, 20 September 1947; PhilaT, 17 November 1973.

DISC: Turn.

PARKS, GORDON A. Film producer/Composer (b. 30 November 1912 in Fort Scott, Kansas). Although best known as a film director and producer, he was also a composer. He wrote songs, piano sonatas, chamber music, and several symphonic works, of which the best known were the Piano Concerto (1935) and *The Learning Tree Symphony* (1967). He also wrote music for the film *The Learning Tree* (1968). He directed the film *Leadbelly* (1976), an autobiography of blues singer Huddie ("Leadbelly") Ledbetter.*

BIBL: WWA. WWBA.

PARRISH, AVERY. Jazz pianist-arranger (b. 26 January 1917 in Birmingham, Alabama; d. 10 December 1959 in New York). His mother played piano and a brother, Curley, became a professional jazzman. He was a member of the original 'Bama State Collegians at Alabama State Teachers College in Montgomery, Alabama, and in 1934 went with the band to New York, where later Erskine Hawkins* took over the band's leadership. Parrish was pianist-arranger for the band, which played at the Harlem Opera House and became one of the house bands at the Savoy Ballroom in the Harlem community of New York (1938-58). Parrish left the group in California in late 1942 or 1943, however, and settling there, performed as a single until a tragic accident forced his retirement from music about a year later. His best-known composition was "After hours."

BIBL: ASCAP. Black press, incl. NYAge, 15 August 1942. ChilWW. DanceWS.

PATTERSON, SAM. Ragtime pianist/Vaudeville entertainer (b. c1881 in St. Louis, Missouri; d. 1955 in New York, New York). He studied music as a child. In the summer of 1894 he joined with Louis Chauvin to produce an act with the Alabama Jubilee Singers. Later, he and Chauvin formed a quartet, the Mozart Comedy Four, which performed locally in St. Louis, Missouri. Like other young pianists of the time, he learned ragtime in the Rosebud Cafe of Tom Turpin and began to play in the cafes and honky-tonks of the tenderloin district at a young age. In 1903 he and Chauvin collaborated in writing a musical, *Dandy Coon*, with Joe Jordan as musical and stage director. The show toured briefly before becoming stranded in Des Moines, Iowa. Patterson and Chauvin were among those active during the St. Louis World's Fair in 1904 as ragtime pianists in a beer hall on the fair grounds. Patterson left St. Louis about 1906, and later joined William N. Spiller's group, the Six Musical Spillers (1906-11). Later he toured with the Watermelon Trust Company, another vaudeville troupe.

BIBL: Black press, incl. CDef, 5 December 1925; IndF, 13 May 1911. Blesh.

PATTERSON, ULYSSES S. GRANT. Minstrel cornetist (b. 1 January 1867 in Franklin County, Virginia; d. 19??). He obtained his musical education at Tuskegee Institute in Alabama (1885-86) and Virginia Normal and Collegiate Institute at Petersburg (graduated 1891). He served as a bandmaster at the Institute in Virginia for five years and also in the normal department of the Virginia Theological Seminary and College (1893-97). During the summer of 1896 he toured with the W. S. Cleveland Minstrels and Haverly's Mastadon Minstrels. Later he played with A. G. Field's *Darkest America* company (1897-98). In 1899 he settled in Lynchburg, Virginia, where he became musical director of a Baptist church and conducted a music studio. His best-known song was "I never loved until I met you."

BIBL: IndF, 25 December 1897. WWCR 1915.

PATTERSON, WILLIS CHARLES. College professor/Concert singer (b. 27 November 1930 in Ann Arbor, Michigan). He obtained his musical education at the University of Michigan at Ann Arbor (B. Mus., 1958; M. Mus., 1959), where he studied with Chase Baromeo; at the Hochschule für Musik in Freiburg, Germany, where he studied with Horst Gunther; and at the Manhattan School of Music in New York, where he studied with John Brownlee. He was encouraged to develop his musical talents by members of his community, including C. W. Carpenter, Douglas Williams, and Robert Williams. His teaching career included tenures at Virginia State College at Petersburg (1962-68) and the University of Michigan (1969-), where he directed a men's glee club and became an associate dean for academic affairs in the late 1970s. During the years 1963-78 he sang the role of King Balthazar in the annual NBC television presentation of Menotti's opera, *Amahl and the Night Visitors*. He toured in the United States and in Europe as a concert bass, appeared with symphony orchestras, and sang in operas and oratorios. His honors included a Marian Anderson* Award (1975) and awards from professional organizations. He published *Anthology of Art Songs by Black American Composers* (New York, 1978).

BIBL: Questionnaire. WWBA.

PATTON, CHARLEY. Bluesman (b. 1887 near Edwards, Mississippi; d. 28 April 1934 in Indianola, Mississippi). He played guitar with the Chatman family string band at the age of fourteen, before he left his birthplace. His singing style reputedly was influenced by folksinger Henry Sloan, who was active in Cleveland, Mississippi. He was well known in the Delta region before he made his first recordings in 1929; thereafter he developed a wide reputation. In 1933 he settled in Holly Ridge, Mississippi, near Greenville. He made his last recordings in 1934, some of them religious songs with Bertha Lee. Other bluesmen with whom he recorded included Willie Brown, Eddie ("Son") House,* and Henry Sims. He was influential upon other bluesmen, either directly or indirectly through his recordings and his students. His style was distinctive for its harsh, fierce vocal style and its strongly rhythmic guitar.

BIBL: BWW. CharCB. LivBl 31 (March-April 1977). Oliv.

DISC: TudBM.

PAUL, BILLY (née **PAUL WILLIAMS).** Rhythm 'n' blues singer (b. 1 December 1934 in Philadelphia, Pennsylvania). As a child he sang in his father's church. He began singing in public at the age of eleven on Philadelphia radio station WPEN. By the time he was fourteen he was singing in local nightclubs, occasionally in association with such established performers as Sarah Vaughan,* Dinah Washington,* and Leslie Uggams* (at that time a child star). He obtained his musical education at the West Philadelphia Music School, Temple University, and the Granoff School of Music, all in Philadelphia. His early style development was influenced by Charlie Parker* and Vaughan, among others. He sang with Harold Melvin and the Blue Notes and with the Flamingos before he organized his Billy Paul Trio during the 1960s. Later he became associated with Philadelphia International Records, produced by the song-writing team Kenneth ("Kenny") Gamble* and Leon Huff,* and moved into the top ranks of popular-music singers. He toured widely in the United States, Europe, and South America, singing in concert halls, in nightclubs, and at jazz festivals. He received awards from the music industry. His best-known performance was "Me and Mrs. Jones" (1973).

BIBL: Black press, incl. *Black American*, 15 July 1973.

PAYNE (or **PAINE), BENNY.** Jazz pianist (b. 18 June 1907 in Philadelphia, Pennsylvania). See **DANIELS, BILLY** and **CALLOWAY, CABELL ("CAB").**

PAYNE, CECIL MCKENZIE ("ZODIAC"). Jazz saxophonist (b. 14 December 1922 in New York, New York). He studied alto saxophone with Pete Brown. In 1946 he made his recording debut with James ("J.J.") Johnson*; the same year he began playing baritone saxophone with Roy Eldridge. Thereafter he played with various groups, including John Birks ("Dizzy") Gillespie* (1947-50), Tadd Dameron,* James Moody, Illinois Jacquet* (1952-54), Randolph ("Randy") Weston* (1958-60), Machito (née Frank Grillo) (1963-66), Woody Herman (1966-67), and William ("Count") Basie* (1969-71), among others. He also led his own groups at intervals, such as the Jazz Zodiac Quartet in 1971, and toured frequently in Europe. In 1974 he played with the New York Jazz Repertory Orchestra. He was one of the leading baritone saxophonists in the bebop tradition.

BIBL: FeaEJ. FeaJS. FeaGitJS.

DISC: Jep. Kink. TudJ.

PAYNE, DANIEL ALEXANDER. Minister/Writer (b. 24 February 1811 in Charleston, South Carolina; d. 20 November 1893 in Wilberforce, Ohio). He is included here because of his insightful discussions of black music practices in the nineteenth century in his two books *Recollections of Seventy Years* (Nashville, 1888) and *History of the African Methodist Episcopal Church* (Nashville, 1891). His long career in the church included service as minister, bishop, church historian, and college president of Wilberforce University. In writing his histories, he examined "every pamphlet, every Conference minute, Quarterly and Annual, with every scrap of paper that threw a light upon the genesis and progress of the Connection" (i.e., the African Methodist Episcopal Church). He also had access to two journals, that of Richard Allen,* founder and first bishop of the AME Church, and of Joseph Cox, an elder in the Bethel AME Church of Philadelphia.

BIBL: Quoted from *History* . . . , p. vi.

PEKIN THEATER. See **MOTTS, ROBERT.**

PENNIMAN, RICHARD ("LITTLE RICHARD"). Rock 'n' roll singer (b. 25 December 1932 in Macon, Georgia). He sang in a gospel church choir as a child. He began performing professionally when he was fifteen. In 1951 he won first prize in a talent show at a theater in Atlanta, Georgia, and the same year recorded his first songs. Thereafter he toured with various groups, appearing mostly in small nightclubs, but including also a medicine show. In 1954 he recorded a song, "Tutti frutti," that brought him wide recognition. During the mid-1950s-1960s he toured widely and recorded extensively, although there were periods when he was inactive. In 1958 he withdrew from music to attend Oakwood College in Huntsville, Alabama (B.A., 1961) and to earn ordination as a minister in the Seventh Day Adventist Church. In 1963 he returned to the field of music and toured widely in Europe with English groups, particularly the Beatles and the Rolling Stones, who were relatively unknown at the time; he also toured as a soloist. With the revival of interest in rock 'n' roll in the late 1960s, his career spurted forward; once again he was "king of rock 'n' roll," giving concerts in major halls, appearing on television programs, and making best-selling records. Little Richard was a seminal figure in the history of rock 'n' roll. He exerted direct influence upon Elvis Presley, the Beatles, Jefferson Airplane, and the Rolling Stones, among others—all of whom copied his style and sang the songs he wrote. He also influenced the style development of such singers as Otis Redding* and, indirectly, James Brown* and Aretha Franklin.*

BIBL: BWW. ShawR5. ShawHS. StamPRS. WWBA.

DISC: Giv. Jep. TudBM.

PERKINS, NIMROD. Military drummer (b. c1760 in Accomac County, Virginia; d. 1833 in Accomac County). He served as a drummer on the *Diligence* and *Accomac* vessels of the Navy during the American Revolutionary War. He enlisted in 1777 and served throughout the war.

BIBL: Luther P. Jackson, "Virginia Negro Soldiers and Seamen in the American Revolution" in JHN 27 (July 1942), pp. 264, 277, 279.

PERKINSON, COLERIDGE TAYLOR. Composer (b. 14 June 1932 in New York, New York). He first developed a special interest in music as a junior-high-school student. His early development was influenced by Hugh Ross, who directed a chorus in which he sang, by Dimitri Mitropoulos, and Clarence Whiteman.* He obtained his musical education at the High School of Music and Art in New York, at the New York University, and at the Manhattan School of Music (B. Mus., 1953; M. Mus., 1954). He studied further at the Berkshire Music Center for choral conducting in Massachusetts; the Mozarteum in Salzburg, Austria; and the Netherlands Radio Union in Hilversum, where he worked with Dean Dixon (1960-63). Earlier he was a conducting assistant to Hugh Ross. His teaching career included tenures at the Professional Children's School in New York, where he was music director (1952-64); at the Manhattan School of Music; and at Brooklyn College of the City University of New York. As a conductor he served tenures with the Dessoff Choir (1956-57) as an assistant, with the Symphony of the New World* as a founding member and associate conductor (1965-75), with the New York Mandolin Orchestra as conductor, and with the Brooklyn Community Orchestra as conductor. He was the first composer-in-residence for the Negro Ensemble Company in New York (founded 1967) and composed music for several of its productions, including *God Is a (Guess What)?* (1968), *Song of the Lusitanian Bogey* (1967), *Ceremonies in Dark Old Men* (1974), and *Man Better Man* (1969). He also worked with the Alvin Ailey Dance Company and with Arthur Mitchell's Harlem Dance Company, for which he composed the ballet *Ode to Otis*. He served as musical director for Lou Rawls,* Barbara McNair,* Donald Byrd,* Max Roach,* and the Martin Luther King Productions, among others, and also wrote music for television, radio, and films, including *A Warm December* (c1962), *Crossroads Africa* (c1962), *Amazing Grace* (1974), and *The Education of Sonny Carson* (1974). His vocal works include *Nine Elizabethan Love Lyrics* (c1952), *Attitudes* (written in 1962-63 for George Shirley* by commission from the Ford Foundation), and *Thirteen Love Songs in Jazz Settings* (late 1960s). Best known of his orchestral works are the Concerto for Viola and Orchestra (1954) and *Sinfonietta for Strings* (1953).

BIBL: BakBC.

PERRY, JULIA AMANDA. Composer (b. 25 March 1924 in Lexington, Kentucky; d. 24 April 1979 in Akron, Ohio). Her family moved to Akron, Ohio, when she was ten years old. Her father was an amateur pianist, two older sisters studied violin, and she studied piano as a child. She obtained her musical education in the public schools of Lexington, Kentucky, and Akron, at Akron University, at the Westminster Choir College in Princeton, New Jersey (B. Mus., 1947 in voice; M. Mus. in composition, 1948), and studied further at the Juilliard School of Music in New York (1950) and at the Berkshire Music Center in Lennox, Massachusetts (summer, 1951). She spent the years 1951-59 abroad, where she studied composition with Nadia Boulanger, Luigi Dallapiccola, and Henry Switten and studied orchestral conducting with Emanuel Balaban and Alceo Galliera. She also studied conducting at the Accademia Chigiana in Siena, Italy, during the summers of 1956 and 1957. During her stay in Europe she toured as a lecturer on American music under the auspices of the USIS (United States Information Service) and in 1957 organized and conducted a concert series. Her teaching experience included tenures at Florida A & M College (Agricultural and Mechanical) in 1967-68 and Atlanta [Georgia] University in 1968-69. She began to win recognition as a serious composer early in her career and wrote a secular cantata for her master's thesis. Her honors included Guggenheim Fellowships (1954, 1956), a Boulanger Grand Prix, and an award from the National Institute of Arts and Letters (1965).

She was regarded as one of the most talented female composers of her generation in the United States. She wrote in a neoclassical style, combining a sensitive use of harmonic dissonance with a preference for contrapuntal textures and an intense lyricism. She wrote in a variety of forms, including ten symphonies, two piano concertos, several large-form works for band and chamber orchestra, three operas, piano and other instrumental pieces, and songs. Her best-known works were *Stabat Mater* (1951) for contralto and string orchestra; *Pastoral* (1959) for flute and strings; *Homunculus C.F.* (1960) for soprano and percussions; *Homage to Vivaldi* for symphony orchestra; *Frammenti dalle lettere de Santa Caterina* for soprano, chorus, and orchestra; and the operas *The Bottle, The Cask of Amontillado*, and *The Selfish Giant*. From 1973 on she was paralyzed on her right side from a series of strokes, but she taught herself to write with her left hand and continued composing.

BIBL: Questionnaire. Personal correspondence. Bakers. Black press, incl. AmstN, 16 May 1964. Bull. Mildred D. Green, "A Study of the Lives and Works of Five Black Women Composers in America" (Ph.D. diss., University of Oklahoma, 1975). Gro. Matt.

PERRYMAN, RUFUS ("SPECKLED RED"). Blues pianist (b. 23 October 1892 in Monroe, Louisiana; d. 2 January 1973 in St. Louis, Missouri). His family moved to Hampton, Georgia, when he was a child, then later to Atlanta, Georgia, and finally to Detroit, Michigan. His piano style was influenced by Paul Seminole, whom he heard playing in local nightclubs of Detroit. Early in his adult career he went South, where he became an itinerant entertainer, playing in lumber camps as well as rural and urban clubs and bars. He became well known especially for his performance of "The dirty dozens." He also worked for many years with a medicine show called the Red Rose Minstrels. His later career did not benefit from the revival of public interest in the blues during the 1960s as did the careers of other bluesmen of his generation. He made one European tour in 1959 but no additional ones; he did not entertain on the college circuit but continued to play in clubs as he had begun his career and to record regularly. He was one of the last of the barrelhouse pianists in the tradition of Albert Ammons,* Pete Johnson,* and Meade Lux Lewis.*

BIBL: BWW. FeaEJ. LivBl 11 (Winter 1972-73). MeeJMov. Oliv.

DISC: Jep. LeSl. RustJR.

PETERS, BROCK (née **BROCK FISHER**). Stage musical singer (b. 2 July 1927 in New York, New York). Although best known as an actor, he was also a singer. He attended the University of Chicago in Illinois (1944-46), City College of the City University of New York (1946-47), and studied the theatrical arts privately. His appearances in operas and musicals included Gershwin's *Porgy and Bess* (1943 production), *South Pacific* (1943), *My Darlin' Aida* (1952), *Kwamina* (1961), and *Lost in the Stars* (1972), among others. He toured as a bass soloist with Leonard DePaur's* Infantry Chorus during the years 1947-50. Thereafter he performed in film musicals—including *Carmen Jones* (1954) and *Porgy and Bess* (1959)—on radio and television shows, and on the nightclub circuit. He received numerous awards from the theater industry.

BIBL: WWA. WWBA.

PETERSON, ELWOOD. Concert singer/College professor (b. 23 January 1928 in New York, New York). He obtained his musical education in the public schools of New York, New York. He began voice study at the relatively late age of twenty-four. He sang professionally, however, before that time. His first public appearance (lyric baritone) was in 1950 on a concert sponsored by Composers' Forum at Columbia University in New York. He sang art songs of Howard Swanson. During the years 1951-66 he lived in Europe, where he studied voice and gave recitals. His teachers included Helmi Altendorf at Aachen, Belgium (1957), and Gabrielle Gills and Pierre Bernac at Paris, France (1951-53, 1958-61). In June 1951 he received a *Licence de Concert* from L'Ecole normale de musique. His career development was greatly influenced by Howard Swanson, whom he met in Europe and with whom he maintained a close association during his fourteen years abroad. In addition to singing recitals he also sang opera, including the role of Zurga in Bizet's *The Pearl Fishers* at the Teatro Principal, Palma de Mallorca, Spain (1952); the role of the Husband in Menotti's *Amelia Goes to the Ball* at the Casino in Cannes, France (1954), the role of the Devil in Gluck's *L'Ivrogne Corrigé* in Paris (1960), and the role of Ulysses in Monteverdi's *Il Ritorno d'Ulisse in Patria* (1971) at Claremont, California. In 1967 he was appointed to the music faculty of Pomona College at Claremont. He made recordings in Europe, including performances in French operettas in which his name was listed as Emil Peters.

BIBL: Questionnaire. *The* [Oakland] *Post*, 9 May 1973.

PETERSON, OSCAR EMMANUEL. Jazz pianist (b. 15 August 1925 in Montreal, Quebec, Canada). He came from a musical family; the five children formed a family orchestra. He began study of the trumpet at the age of five but had to give it up after contracting tuberculosis; thereafter he studied piano. At fourteen he won first prize in a Montreal radio-show competition and began playing professionally on a weekly radio show, station CKAC. He also began study of jazz piano with Paul DeMarky and began playing with Johnny Holmes's orchestra (1944-49). He organized his own trio, which included Clarence Jones and Ozie Roberts, and toured for the first time outside Canada in 1949 with the concert unit of JATP (Jazz at the Philharmonic), making his debut at a Carnegie Hall concert in New York in September 1949. During the 1950s he toured with JATP in the United States and in Europe, performed with Ella Fitzgerald* in Great Britain (1955), and in 1958 settled in Toronto, Canada. In 1959 he was cofounder of the Advanced School of Contemporary Music in Toronto (1959-63), along with Edmund Thigpen, Ray Brown, and Phil Nimmons. Through the 1960s and 1970s he continued to tour widely throughout the world, primarily with his own trios during the 1960s and then, beginning about 1972, also as a concert soloist. He continued to tour annually with Fitzgerald. In 1974 he ran his own television series on CNC-TV, "Oscar Peterson Presents," which brought well known jazz artists to the public. In 1976 he made a special series, "Oscar Peterson's Piano Party," for BBC-TV in England. He wrote his first film score in 1978 for *The Silent Partner*. He recorded prolifically, after making his recording debut in 1949, as a soloist, with his trios, and with such jazz artists as Ella Fitzgerald, John Birks ("Dizzy") Gillespie,* Billie Holiday,* Roy Eldridge,* Edward ("Sonny") Stitt,* and Clark Terry,* among others. His honors included the Toronto Civic Medal (1971), an honorary doctorate from Carleton University (1973), the Medal of Service of the Order of Canada (1974), the Gold Disc from Japan, and numerous awards from the music industry.

His piano style was a blend of swing and bebop that revealed the influence of Arthur ("Art") Tatum* upon his development. He was regarded as one of the leading jazz pianists of his time.

BIBL: FeaEJ. FeaJS. FeaGitJS. IntM (November 1971). MeeJMov. WWA. WWBA.

DISC: Jep. Kink.

PETTIFORD, OSCAR. Jazz bassist (b. 30 September 1922 in Okmulgee, Oklahoma; d. 8 September 1960 in Copenhagen, Denmark). His family moved to Minneapolis, Minnesota, when he was three years old. The father organized a family orchestra, including the mother along with eleven children, which toured widely in the Midwest from the 1920s to 1941. Oscar played several instruments as a child, learning from his sisters and brothers. At fourteen he began playing string bass in the family band. In 1943 he left Minneapolis to work with Charlie Barnet and settled in New York. He then played short periods with various groups, including Roy Eldridge,* Thelonious Monk,* and John Birks ("Dizzy") Gillespie* (as co-leader of a bebop group in 1943-44). Thereafter he led his own groups (1944), played with Boyd Raeburn briefly, then in 1945 went to California, where he joined Coleman Hawkins* and later Edward ("Duke") Ellington* (1945-48) and Woodrow ("Woody") Herman (1949). He made his first recordings in 1943 and thereafter recorded prolifically. During the 1950s he toured with Louis Bellson-Charlie Shavers and with his own groups in a USO-sponsored tour of Korea and Japan. In 1958 he settled in Europe and worked with various groups, primarily in Copenhagen, Denmark. Among the jazzmen who performed with him over the years were Kenneth ("Kenny") Clarke,* Errol Garner,* Gigi Gryce, Arthur ("Art") Farmer, J. J. Johnson,* Howard McGhee,* Eli ("Lucky") Thompson,* and Ernie Wilkins,* among others.

Pettiford was regarded as one of the three leading bassists of his time—along with Ray Brown and Charles Mingus*—and as a direct inheritor of James ("Jimmy") Blanton's laurels. Indeed, he replaced Blanton in Ellington's orchestra after Blanton's death. Pettiford further developed the solo possibilities of the jazz bass after Blanton, giving it a flexibility formerly associated with the horn. Although he was not the first jazz cellist, he helped to establish the role of the cello in the jazz ensemble. As bassist and cellist he exerted wide influence upon his contemporaries in the United States and in Europe. He won numerous awards from the music industry. His best-known performances were of "The man I love," "Suddenly it jumped," "Swamp fire," and pieces he wrote himself, "Tricrotism," "Swingin' till the girls come home," and "Black-eyed peas and collard greens."

BIBL: FeaEJ. FeaJS. Ira Gitler, *Jazz Masters of the Forties* (New York, 1966). MeeJMov.

DISC: Jep. Kink. ModJ. TudJ.

PEYTON, DAVE. Bandleader (b. c1885; d. May 1955 in Chicago, Illinois). He received his musical training in the public schools of Chicago, Illinois, and through private study. Later he studied at the American College of Music in Chicago. His first professional experience was with Poney Moore's Burlesque Show in 1908. In 1912 he became musical director of the Grand Theater on Chicago's South Side. He was also active as an arranger and became associated with Watterson, Berlin, and Synder Music Publishers about 1911 or

1912. In 1914 he was inspired by performances of the symphony orchestra of James Reese Europe* in New York, and he organized a small symphony orchestra in Chicago. During its first years the orchestra included some fifty or more instrumentalists and gave monthly concerts. During the 1920s Peyton led bands at various theaters and nightclubs and was also active as a music contractor. In the 1930s he led an orchestra at the Regal Theater. Thereafter he played in clubs as a solo pianist. Beginning in 1925 he published a column, "The Musical Bunch," for several years in *The Chicago Defender*.

BIBL: Black press, incl. CDef, 7 November 1914, 29 January 1916, 5 January 1918, 13 August 1955. ChilWW.

PHILADELPHIA CONCERT ORCHESTRA. (org. in Philadelphia, Pennsylvania; fl. early twentieth century). This community orchestra was founded in 1904, and Edward Gilbert Anderson* became its first conductor. After Anderson went to New York about 1917, the orchestra continued its activities under various directors. In 1930 it was reorganized by Raymond L. Smith,* who served as director during the years 1930-1939, and its name was changed to the E. Gilbert Anderson Memorial Symphony Orchestra. In 1944 the name was changed back again to the Philadelphia Concert Orchestra, although the support organization retained its name, the Anderson Symphonic Association. The orchestra frequently gave concerts with the People's Choral Society of Philadelphia (founded in 1908). It was credited with being the first incorporated black orchestra (1908) in the United States.

BIBL: Black press, incl. AmstN, 20 January 1945; NYAge, 11 December 1926; PhilaT, 20 December 1913. Hare.

PHILADELPHIA SOUND, THE. See **GAMBLE, KENNETH.**

PHILLIPS, ESTHER (ESTHER MAE JONES). Blues singer (b. 23 December 1935 in Galveston, Texas). Her parents moved to Houston, Texas, when she was three months old. Later she lived in Los Angeles, California, in the Watts area with her mother. She began singing there in a local sanctified church at the age of six, and by the time she was twelve, she was winning prizes in local theater amateur shows. In 1949 she attracted the attention of Johnny Otis when she won a prize in the nightclub where he was performing. Later the same year she made her first recording on an Otis album. Thereafter she toured as "Little Esther" with the Otis revue, which included Willie Mae ("Big Mama") Thornton,* among others. When the band was dissolved in 1954, she traveled briefly with Locksley ("Slide") Hampton, then toured as a soloist. She recorded extensively, including such commercial successes as "Double-crossing blues," "Release me," and "And I love him," and toured widely in the United States and abroad. After living in New York for ten years, in 1966 she settled in California. Although not a professional pianist, she often accompanied herself in performance (although not on recordings) and also occasionally played drums. Although best known as a blues or rhythm 'n' blues singer, she also sang jazz, rock 'n' roll, and popular songs.

BIBL: BWW. *Ebony* (October 1972). FeaEJ. FeaGitJS. LivBl 17 (Summer 1974). Robert Neff and Anthony Connor, *Blues* (Boston, 1975).

DISC: Jep. TudBM.

PHILLIPS, T. K. E. Nigerian organist/Choirmaster. See **SOWANDE, FELA.**

PICKETT, WILSON. Rhythm 'n' blues singer (b. 18 March 1941 in Prattville, Alabama). As a child he sang in a church choir and later he sang with local gospel groups. His family moved to Detroit, Michigan, when he was fifteen and there he began singing with a gospel group, the Violinaires. After some time he was invited to join the Falcons, a rhythm 'n' blues group, with whom he sang for four years (1959-1963). By the time he left the Falcons to begin an independent career in New York he was an established figure in the field of rhythm 'n' blues. During the 1960s he founded his own publishing company, Erva Music. His style reflected his gospel roots. His best-known performances were "I found a love," "Love dagger," "You're so fine," all of which he wrote himself, and "634-5789" and "Land of a thousand dances."

BIBL: NYT (9 October 1977). StamPRS.

DISC: TudBM.

PICOU, ALPHONSE FLORISTON. Jazz clarinetist (b. 19 October 1878 in New Orleans, Louisiana; d. 4 February 1961 in New Orleans). He began playing guitar at the age of fourteen and clarinet at fifteen. His first professional experience was in 1892 with Bouboul Valentin. Thereafter he played with various groups in New Orleans, including the Lyre Club Symphony, Oscar DuConge (1899), Freddie Keppard's* Olympia Orchestra (1906), Charles ("Buddy") Bolden,* and the Excelsior Brass Band, among others. He also led his own groups, the Accordiana (1894) and the Independence (1897). During the years 1916-1932 he played regularly with the Tuxedo Brass Band, also with John Robichaux, the Golden Leaf Orchestra, and the Camelia, except for a short period in 1917 when he played with

Manuel Perez in Chicago. He was inactive for most of the 1930s but returned to music in the 1940s, thereafter working with the Bloom Philharmonic Orchestra, Oscar ("Papa") Celestin,* the Tuxedo Band, and Henry ("Kid") Rena. He also led his own groups. He was a living legend when he died at the end of a seventy-year career. His best-known performance was his solo "High society," which he recorded with both Celestin and Rena.

BIBL: ChilWW. FeaEJ. FeaJS. Souch.

PIERCE, BILLIE. See **PIERCE, WILHELMINA.**

PIERCE, DE DE. See **PIERCE, JOSEPH.**

PIERCE, JOSEPH DE LA CROIX ("DE DE"). Jazz cornetist (b. 18 February 1904 in New Orleans, Louisiana; d. 23 November 1973 in New Orleans). He began playing professionally in the 1920s with Arnold DePass. Thereafter he played with various groups, including Abby Williams and the Young Tuxedo Brass Band. In 1935 he married Wilhelmina ("Billie") Pierce,* and the two formed a duo that played in nightclubs and bars, occasionally performing with others and touring. When he became blind during the 1950s his career languished, but with the revival of interest in Dixieland jazz during the 1960s and the founding of Preservation Hall in 1961 by Sandra and Allen Jaffre, the fortunes of the Pierces improved. He and Billie became leading figures in the Preservation Hall Jazz Band, along with William Humphrey (clarinet), Cie Frazier (drums), Jim Robinson (trombone), and Jaffre (tuba). The band toured widely, appearing in concert halls, nightclubs, on television and radio programs, at jazz festivals, and on college campuses. The band also made a number of recordings.

BIBL: FeaJS. FeaGitJS. MeeJMov. NYT (27 November 1973). Souch.

DISC: Jep.

PIERCE, WILHELMINA GOODSON ("BILLIE"). Jazz pianist (b. 8 June 1907 in Marianna, Florida; d. 29 September 1974 in New Orleans, Louisiana). Her father and mother were musicians and her sister, Sadie Goodson, became a professional musician. She grew up in Pensacola, Florida. At the age of fifteen she began playing professionally and later toured with Gertrude ("Ma") Rainey,* winning recognition as a blues shouter and pianist. In 1930 she went to New Orleans, Louisiana, where she later married Joseph ("DeDe") Pierce* (1935). They formed a duo that played in nightclubs and bars and occasionally worked with other groups, including on tours. When DeDe became blind in the 1950s, their careers languished, but with the revival of interest in Dixieland jazz during the 1960s and the founding of Preservation Hall in 1961 by Sandra and Allen Jaffre, their fortunes improved. They became leading figures in the Preservation Hall Jazz Band, along with William Humphrey (clarinet), Cie Frazier (drums), Jim Robinson (trombone), and Jaffre (tuba). The band toured widely, appearing in concert halls, nightclubs, on television and radio progams, at jazz festivals, and on college campuses. The band also made a large number of recordings.

BIBL: BWW. FeaJS. FeaGitJS. Handy. MeeJMov. Souch.

DISC: Jep.

PIERCE, WILL. Tenor, Jubilee Singers. See **JONES, SISSIERETTA.**

PIERSON, EDWARD. Opera/concert singer (b. 4 January 1931 in Chicago, Illinois). He obtained his education in the public schools of Chicago and at Roosevelt University in Chicago (B.A., 1954). He studied voice privately in Chicago with Blanche Branche (1956-66) and in New York with Felix Popper (1968-70) and Roland Gagnon (1970-71). Beginning in 1966 he toured widely as a concert bass-baritone; in 1978 he made his New York debut in the Carnegie Recital Hall. He also sang in performances of the standard oratorios and large choral works with leading symphony orchestras of the nation. His best-known operatic roles were Escamillo in Bizet's *Carmen*, Scarpia in Puccini's *Tosca*, Creon in Stravinsky's *Oedipus Rex*, Don Basilio in Rossini's *The Barber of Seville*, the title role in Delius's *Koanga*, Bartolo in Mozart's *The Marriage of Figaro*, and Crown in Gershwin's *Porgy and Bess*. In 1973 he sang in the PBS-television world premiere of Henze's opera *Rachel, La Cubana*. During the 1970s he also sang in Joplin's* *Treemonisha* and Kern's *Show Boat*. His career as a music teacher included tenures in the public schools of Chicago (1954-66); local colleges of Portland, Oregon (1971-74); the University of Wisconsin (1979); and Mannes College in the city of New York (1979). He also conducted a studio in New York (1975-). His honors included finalist-winner awards in a Chicagoland Music Festival (1961) and an Illinois opera competition (1963), and Martha Baird Rockefeller grants (1968, 1969).

BIBL: Questionnaire.

PINDELL, ANNIE PAULINE. Concert singer (b. c1834 in Exeter, New Hampshire; d. 1 May 1901 in Los Angeles, California). She began her musical studies with a local pianist, then later studied with the brother of Wyzeman Marshall. In 1860 she settled in California, where she won recognition as a concert soprano and as a songwriter. Her tours included a command performance for Queen Emma of Hawaii. She also conducted a music studio. Her best-known songs were "Seek the lodge where the red men dwell" and "Ah, foolish maiden." She was called "The Black Nightingale" and/or "Nightingale of the Pacific."

BIBL: Pauline E. Hopkins, "Famous Women of the Negro Race" in *The Colored American Magazine* 4 (November 1901). Songs are listed in *Complete Catalogue of Sheet Music and Musical Works, 1870* (published by the Board of Music Trade of the United States of America, 1871; reprint with introduction by Dena Epstein [New York, 1973]).

PINKARD, MACEO. Songwriter (b. 27 June 1897 in Bluefield, West Virginia; d. 21 July 1962 in New York). He obtained his musical education at Bluefield Institute in West Virginia. Little is known of his early career except that he toured with his own group during the early twentieth century. In 1914 he founded a theatrical agency at Omaha, Nebraska, and in 1915 he published his first song, "When he sang that baritone." Some time before 1920 he settled in New York, where later he founded Pinkard Publications, a sheet-music publishing company. He continued to publish songs and began to write scores for Broadway musicals, of which the best known was *Liza* (1923), in which the Charleston dance was introduced on Broadway. His best-known songs were "Sweet Georgia Brown," "Give me a little kiss, will ya, huh?," "Them there eyes," "Don't cry, little girl," and "Mammy o' mine" (1920), which was featured by Al Jolson.

BIBL: ASCAP. Black press, incl. AmstN, 28 July 1962; NYAge, 5 September 1959.

PIRON, ARMAND JOHN. Jazz bandleader (b. 16 August 1888 in New Orleans, Louisiana; d. 17 February 1943 in New Orleans). He began violin study as a child with his father, an orchestra leader, or with his brother Albert (according to his ASCAP biography). Later he studied with Charles Eldger and attended the local St. Agnes school. He began playing professionally about 1904. By 1908 he was leading his own group, and later played wih the Peerless Orchestra about 1912. When Freddie Keppard* left New Orleans in 1912 to join William ("Bill") Johnson* in Los Angeles, Piron took over leadership of Keppard's Olympia Orchestra. During the next few years he also played with Oscar ("Papa") Celestin,* W. C. Handy* (on one occasion), and Clarence Williams.* About 1915 he and Williams founded a short-lived music publishing company (until c1917). In 1918 he formed his own band, which played long residencies in New Orleans, except in 1923 and 1924, when he played in New York. In May 1924 Piron's New Orleans Orchestra became the first Negro group to play the Roseland Ballroom. It made such a good impression that the management sought another black orchestra to follow it and brought in Fletcher Henderson.* During the 1920s-30s Piron's band was one of the top bands in New Orleans. He wrote a number of songs, of which the best known were "I wish I could shimmy like my sister Kate," "Sudbustin' blues," and "Mama's gone goodbye."

BIBL: AlHen. ASCAP. ChilWW. W. C. Handy, *Father of the Blues* (New York, 1941). Souch.

DISC: RustJR.

PITTMAN, EVELYN LA RUE. Music educator/Composer (b. 6 January 1910 in McAlester, Oklahoma). Her family moved to Oklahoma City, Oklahoma, when she was a child, and there she obtained her musical education in the public schools. Just before she entered the tenth grade, she went to Detroit, Michigan, where she completed her high-school studies. She then attended Spelman College in Atlanta, Georgia (B.A., 1933), where she studied with Kemper Harreld*; Langston University in Langston, Oklahoma (teacher's certificate); the University of Oklahoma at Norman (M. Mus. 1954), where she studied composition with Harrison Kerr; the Juilliard School of Music in New York (1948), where she studied composition with Robert Ward; and studied further in Paris, France (1956-57), with Nadia Boulanger. Her teaching career included tenures in the public schools of Oklahoma City (1935-56) and in the Greenburg District of New York (1958-76). During the many years she taught in Oklahoma City, she conducted weekly broadcasts over the city-schools radio station with her seventy-five voice choir; she also directed a 350-voice interdenominational choir, sponsored by the YWCA (Young Women's Christian Association). During the 1960s she settled in White Plains, New York.

She began composing at an early age and wrote original music for a Greek play during her senior year at college, which was produced by the Morehouse-Spelman Players. During her stay in Paris, she completed an opera, *Cousin Esther*, which was performed there in May 1957, and performed on New York radio station WNYC in 1963 on an American Music Festival program. Best known of her other works are the song collection *Rich Heritage* (1944, second edition, 1968) and the opera *Freedom's Child* (1972), about the life of Martin Luther King.

BIBL: Black press, incl. AmstN, 16 June 1962. Mildred D. Green, "A Study of the Lives and Works of Five Black Women Composers in America" (Ph.D. diss., University of Oklahoma, 1975).

PITTMAN, PORTIA WASHINGTON. Music educator (b. 6 June 1883 in Tuskegee, Alabama; d. 26 February 1978 in Washington, D.C.). Her father, Booker Taliaferro Washington, encouraged her early interest in music and she studied piano as a child. She obtained her musical training at Tuskegee Institute in Alabama, where her father was president; at Wellesley College in Massachusetts, and at Bradford Junior College in Massachusetts, from which she was graduated in 1905. She then went to Berlin, Germany, where she studied piano for two years with Martin Krause. In 1907 she married and settled in Dallas, Texas, where she taught music in the public schools and directed community choirs. She continued to work with her piano, however, and in May 1908 she went to Washington, D.C., to make her debut as a concert pianist in a joint recital with Clarence Cameron White.* Thereafter she toured periodically on the concert circuit. In 1928 she went to Tuskegee as music teacher and choral director and remained there until her retirement in 1944. Her son, Booker Taliaferro Pittman (1909-1969) was a professional jazzman, and her daughter Fannie (1912-1973) who earned a music degree from the Detroit Conservatory of Music, was a piano teacher.

BIBL: Black press, incl. CDef, 6 October 1928; NYAge, 7 May 1908. Roy L. Hill, *Booker T's Child* (Newark, New Jersey, 1974). *The Master Musician*, v.1, no. 5 (March 1920). Ruth Ann Stewart, *Portia: The Life of Portia Washington Pittman* (New York, 1977).

PLATO BROADLEY, DESSERIA. Concert singer (fl. late nineteenth century; d. 28 January 1907 in Genesee, Idaho). Little is known of her career except that she was a leading singer during the 1890s. She first attracted attention as a "prima donna mezzo-soprano" in Signor A. Farini's Grand Creole and Colored Opera and Concert Company in 1891, when she sang the role of Azucena in Farini's production of Verdi's *Il Trovatore* at the Union Square Theater in New York. In 1893 she again attracted wide attention when she substituted for Sissieretta Jones* at a concert given at the Chicago World's Fair on Colored American Day (25 August). Thereafter she sang regularly on the concert stage. In 1896 she joined the operatic troupe of John Isham's Oriental America company, along with Sidney Woodward,* Mattie Wilkes (d. July 1927 in New York), and others.

BIBL: Black press, incl. CDef, 16 July 1927; IndF, 19 August 1893, 2 September 1893, 15 August 1896, 16 February 1907; NYAge, 19 December 1891.

PLATTERS, THE. Rhythm 'n' blues group (Fl. mid-1950s-70s; orig. in Los Angeles, California). The male vocal group was organized in 1953 by Herbert Reed (bass, b. Kansas City, Missouri); at that time it included David Lynch (second tenor, b. St. Louis, Missouri), Paul Robi (baritone, b. New Orleans, Louisiana), and Tony Williams (tenor and lead singer, b. Roselle, New Jersey). The group first recorded in 1954; the success of their song, "Only you," launched them on the road to fame. In 1955 Zola Taylor joined the group as the female lead singer. During the next few years the group toured widely in the United States, Europe, North Africa, Central and South America; they recorded extensively; and they appeared on television and in films, including *The Girl Can't Take It* (1956). During the 1960s there were personnel changes; by 1969 Reed, the last original member, had gone. Manager-songwriter Buck Ram held the group together, however, and it continued its activity through the 1970s. In 1978 the Platters included Geri Holiday as female lead, Edwin Cook, Harold Howard, Monroe Powell, and Gene Williams. The Platters was the first rhythm 'n' blues group to win wide recognition and commercial success. Their best-known performances included "It isn't right," "Magic touch," and "My prayer."

BIBL: Lavinia Reese, "The Platters" in *Disc & That* (February 1979). ShawR5. StamPRS.

PLET, ANASTASE. Society dance-band leader (fl. mid-nineteenth century in New York, New York). Little is known of his career except that he was a bandleader and violinist, generally in association with church-sponsored concerts. On one occasion the press gave names of the members of his orchestra—a concert given in September 1839 at the First Colored Presbyterian Church by the Philomathean and Phoenixonian Societies for the benefit of Cinque and other African captives of the slave ship *L'Amistad*. The mutinous slaves became a *cause celébre*; black organizations in Philadelphia and New York gave benefits to raise money so that the slaves could return to Africa. On this occasion the choir was under the direction of George L. Phillips and Isaac Rodgers. Plet's orchestra was composed of Master William Jackson* (violin); Cherry Plet (clarinet), A. Dennis (clarinet), A. LaCost (flute), J. D. Connor (trombone), W. P. Mariner (violoncello), W. Brady* (double bass), W. Noland (trumpet), and W. Appo* (horn). The program consisted of hymns and an anthem, "Sing Unto God," written by Appo. Some of these musicians were named in the press on other occasions; in 1833 the Plet brothers and Appo performed on a sacred-music concert at St. Philip's Church, along with William Poyer (violin), P. Thompson (violin), Francis Johnson* (violin), Isaac Barbadoes (double bass), William Hameton, Jr. (organ), Jane Vogelsang (organ), and J. D. Connor (assistant vocal conductor). The Plets,

Dennis, and Jackson played with instrumental groups in Boston, Massachusetts. Dennis and Jackson were active into the 1860s.

BIBL: Black press, incl. *The Colored American*, 14 September 1839; *The Weekly Anglo-African*, 14 April 1860. *The Liberator* [Boston], 2 April 1833, 30 April 1833.

POINDEXTER, NORWOOD ("PONY"). Jazz saxophonist (b. 8 February 1926 in New Orleans, Louisiana). He studied clarinet as a child. He obtained his musical training at the Candell Conservatory of Music in Oakland, California. In 1940 he began playing professionally with Sidney Desvigne. Thereafter he played with various groups, including William (''Billy'') Eckstine* (1947-48), Vernon Alley (1950), and Lionel Hampton* (1951-52), among others. During the years 1952-61 he led his own groups on the West Coast, primarily in San Francisco and the Bay area. He then joined a group accompanying Lambert, Hendricks* & Ross (1961-63), led his own groups on the East Coast, then in 1964 settled in Europe. He toured on the nightclub circuit and appeared at the major European jazz festivals. His nickname came from an arrangement he made for William (''Count'') Basie* called ''Little pony.'' He was a leading soprano saxophonist of the 1960s.

BIBL: FeaEJ. FeaJS. FeaGitJS.

POLIN, ROSCOE. Studio teacher (b. 17 May 1909 in Bridgeport, Indiana). His early interest in music was encouraged by his parents, who sang in church choirs, and his aunt. He taught himself to play on a reed organ given him by a church which no longer used it. Later he studied piano. He obtained his musical training in the public schools of Indianapolis, Indiana, where he was active as a singer and pianist; at Indiana University in Bloomington (B.A., 1932; B. Mus., 1934; M.S., 1939; D. Ed. 1949); and at the Milhouse School of Music, Sherwood School of Music, Indianapolis Conservatory, and Jordan Conservatory, all in Indianapolis. Although he taught mathematics in the public schools of Indianapolis, he was highly active in music as a studio teacher, minister of church music, musical director at a local YMCA, and choral director of community groups, particularly the Dett Choral Club which he organized in the 1960s. He also was active with professional musical organizations and served as president of the Indiana State Association of Negro Musicians (1959-77) and the National Association of Negro Musicians (1940-42, 1950-59). His was the longest tenure of any president of NANM. He published *A Basis for an Interculture Education Program in Schools* (Bloomington, Indiana, 1950).

BIBL: Questionnaire. Black press.

PORTER, KARL HAMPTON. Orchestra conductor (b. 25 April 1939 in Pittsburgh, Pennsylvania). He studied music as a child. During his high school years he played both saxophone and bassoon, the latter in the Pittsburgh Youth Symphony Orchestra. He obtained his musical education at the Carnegie-Mellon University in Pittsburgh, Pennsylvania (1958-60), the Peabody Conservatory in Baltimore, Maryland (1960-62), the Juilliard School of Music in New York (1962-63), the Domaine School for Conductors in Hancock, Maine (1961-63), the American Symphony Orchestra League's Institute for Conductors at Orkney, Virginia, and the Berkshire Music Center at Tanglewood, Massachusetts. He played bassoon in various organizations, including the Denver Symphony Orchestra (1964-65), American Wind Symphony (1960-61), Metropolitan Opera National Company orchestra (1965-67), and Gil Evans's jazz band (1967-69). During the late 1960s he founded several groups in the Harlem community of New York; among them, the Harlem Youth Symphony (1968-70), Harlem Philharmonic Orchestra (1969), New Breed Brass Ensemble, Harlem String Quartet, and the Harlem Woodwind Quintet (composed of Kenneth Adams, Joseph Gore, Kenneth Harris, David Miller, and Edward Perry). Some of the musicians in these groups were non-professionals. In 1972 he was appointed conductor of the New York City Housing Authority Orchestra. Also during that year he was music director for Josephine Baker. In 1974 he was appointed conductor of the Massapequa [New York] Symphony Society. His teaching experience included tenures at the Newark [New Jersey] Community Arts Center (1969-71) and the New York City Community College of the City University of New York (1972-). From 1967 he also was active as a free-lance bassoonist and guest orchestral conductor. His honors included grants from the Rockefeller Foundation (1969) and the National Endowment for the Arts (1970).

BIBL: Black press. WWA. WWBA.

PORTER SHIPP, OLIVIA SOPHIE L'ANGE. Dance-band bassist (b. 17 May 1880 in New Orleans, Louisiana; d. 18 June 1980 in New York, New York). As a child she taught herself to play on an old pump organ acquired by her family and played for a church choir. At the beginning of the twentieth century she went to New York, where her sister May had settled earlier. There she found employment in vaudeville shows and began to play cello, studying with various teachers, including Leonard Jeter.* She began an association with David I. Martin's* Martin-Smith School of Music as Jeter's teaching assistant and as a member of the school orchestra. She also played in Charles Elgar's chamber ensembles. About 1916 she began to study the string bass with Buldreni of the New York Philharmonic Orchestra, among others. Beginning in 1917 she played bass in Marie Lucas's* Lafayette Theater Ladies Orchestra and, later, in Lucas's orchestra in Baltimore. During the 1920s she organized Olivia Shipp's Jazz-Mines and, later, the Negro Women's Orchestral Civic Association. She was active as a free-lance performer and played with dance orchestras in New York over several decades. She was married to the son of actor Jesse Shipp.*

BIBL: Handy.

POSTLEWAITE, JOSEPH WILLIAM. Composer (b. 1837 in St. Louis, Missouri; d. 1 January 1889 in St. Louis). Little is known of his early life. He first came to public notice during the 1850s as leader of a four-piece band and owner of a coffeehouse, along with a Frank Beler. Later Postlewaite established a music publishing company, although he apparently published few of his own pieces. During the late 1850s he and Beler advertised themselves as band agents. Over the years he led groups called by such names as Postlewaite's Quadrille Band, the National Band, Postlewaite's Orchestra, the St. Louis Great Western Band, and the Great Western Reed and String Band. His compositions were very popular in his time; his ''St. Louis Greys Quick Step,'' for example, went into a fifteenth printing. Other well-known pieces were the quadrilles titled ''Home circle lancers'' and ''Schottische quadrille''; the waltzes titled ''Bessie,'' ''Eugenia,'' and ''Iola''; and the schottisches ''Dew drop'' and ''Pleyade.'' A large number of his pieces were listed in the *Complete Catalogue of Sheet Music and Musical Works, 1870,* published by the Board of Music Trade of the United States of America, 1871; reprint with introduction by Dena Epstein (New York, 1973).

BIBL: John E. Bruce, ''A History of Negro Musicians'' in *Southern Workman* 45 (1916). Samuel A. Floyd, Jr., ''J. W. Postlewaite of St. Louis'' in BPIM 6 (Fall 1978).

POWELL, BUD. See **POWELL, EARL.**

POWELL, EARL (''BUD''). Jazz pianist (b. 27 September 1924 in New York, New York; d. 31 July 1966 in New York). He came from a musical family: his grandfather and father played piano, and two brothers, William and Richard (''Richie'') became professional musicians. He began piano study at the age of six. During his high-school years he became interested in jazz, influenced by William (''Billy'') Kyle, pianist of the John Kirby* Sextet. At fifteen he began playing professionally in local New York nightclubs and in his brother's group. After work he would join others who gathered to listen to the musical experimentation taking place at Minton's Playhouse in the Harlem community, where his contacts with Thelonious Monk* influenced his style development. He made his first records in 1943, when he was playing with Melvin (''Cootie'') Williams* (1943-44). Thereafter he played with various groups on New York's 52nd Street, including Don Byas,* John Birks (''Dizzy'') Gillespie,* Dexter Gordon,* J. J. Johnson,* and John Kirby, among others. From the mid-1940s on he was frequently inactive because of ill health. In the 1950s he generally led his own trio; from 1959 to 1964 he was active in Paris, France.

He was regarded as the first of the important bebop pianists and, after Arthur (''Art'') Tatum,* as the cornerstone of modern jazz piano. His best-known performances included ''Off minor,'' ''Indiana'' ''Bud's bubble,'' and ''All God's chillun got rhythm.'' Many of his own compositions were widely known, including ''Dance of the infidels,'' ''Un poco loco,'' ''Hallucinations,'' and ''Glass enclosure.''

BIBL: FeaEJ. FeaJS. MeeJMov. Spellman.

DISC: Kink. TudJ.

PRATTIS JENNINGS, PATRICIA. Symphony keyboardist (b. 16 July 1941 in Pittsburgh, Pennsylvania). She began piano study at the age of six and violin study two years later. She obtained her musical education in the public schools of Pittsburgh, Pennsylvania, and at Carnegie-Mellon University in Pittsburgh (BFA, 1963; MFA, 1964). Her teachers included Harry Franklin, Sidney Foster, and Natalie Hinderas.* From the age of twelve she was church organist at the Welsey Center AME Church for several years. During her high-school years she played violin in the school orchestra and in the Pittsburgh All-City High School Orchestra. In 1964 she auditioned successfully for the position of orchestra pianist with the Pittsburgh Symphony. As the orchestra pianist she was expected to play also organ, harpsichord, and celeste. From the mid-1960s on she gave solo recitals and appeared with leading symphony orchestras in addition to performing with the Pittsburgh Symphony. In October 1971 she toured with the World Symphony Orchestra under Arthur Fiedler. In February 1977 she made her television debut, along with the Pittsburgh Symphony, playing Mozart's early four-hand sonatas with André Previn, the orchestra's conductor, at the second piano.

BIBL: Handy.

PRESTON, WILLIAM EVERETT (''BILLY''). Gospel/rhythm 'n' blues keyboardist/Singer (b. 9 September 1946 in Houston, Texas.) His mother was a singer and actress. He began piano study at the age of three with his mother, and organ study when he was six. His family moved to Los Angeles, California, when he was a child, and there he obtained his musical education in the public schools. He sang in gospel choirs, and when he was ten or eleven appeared on a concert with Mahalia Jackson.* His performance led to an invitation to appear in the film, *St. Louis Blues* (1958), in the role of W. C. Handy* as a boy. During his high-school years Preston sang and played piano or organ with gospel groups, including Andrae Crouch's* COGICS. He was also active as a rhythm 'n' blues performer and toured in the United States and in Europe during the early 1960s with ("Little") Richard Penniman* and Sam Cooke,* among others. He made his first recordings during those years, including "Sixteen-year-old-soul" and "The most exciting organ yet." During the mid-1960s he returned to gospel, touring with the James Cleveland* Singers and recording with them "How great thou art," among other pieces, which featured his organ playing. After leaving Cleveland he toured with his own group for a period, then played with Ray Charles* (c1966-69), The Beatles (1969-70), and The Rolling Stones (1974). During the 1970s he established himself as a leading rock 'n' roll entertainer; he toured widely with his own show, which included girl back-up singers and a band, and wrote much of his song materials. He appeared on television shows and in films, including *Let It Be* (1970), *Slaughter* (1972), *Concert for Bangladesh* (1972), and *Mother, Jugs and Speed* (1976). His best-known songs included "I wrote a simple song," "Music is my life," and "Will it go round in circles." He generally included gospel songs on his secular albums and recorded the all-gospel album *Behold*.

BIBL: GMEncy. MeeJMov. StamPRS. WWBA.

PRICE, FLORENCE BEATRICE SMITH. Composer (b. 9 April 1888 in Little Rock, Arkansas; d. 3 June 1953 in Chicago, Illinois). Her mother was musical, and she began piano study with her at an early age. Florence first played on a public recital at the age of four. She received further musical training from her public school teacher, Charlotte Andrews Stephens, who also taught William Grant Still.* She attended the New England Conservatory of Music in Boston, Massachusetts (B. Mus., 1906), where she studied with George Chadwick, at that time director of the Conservatory, and H. M. Dunham, among others. Later she studied at the Chicago [Illinois] Musical College, the American Conservatory in Chicago, Chicago Teachers College, and the University of Chicago; her teachers included Carl Busch, Arthur Olaf Anderson, and Wesley LaViolette. After graduation from college she entered a teaching career, with tenures at Shorter College in North Little Rock, Arkansas (1906-1910), and Clark University in Atlanta, Georgia (1910-1912). She returned to Little Rock to get married and thereafter conducted a music studio.

She began composing as a young girl and published her first composition before she completed her high school work in 1903. Through the ensuing years she continued to write; a symphonic work was performed in Boston during her years at the Conservatory. In 1925 she won a prize in *Opportunity Magazine's* Holstein Prize competition for her piece "In the Land O' Cotton." In 1927 she settled in Chicago, Illinois. There she taught privately, studied at the institutions cited above, and gave as much time to composing as possible. She was fortunate in finding publishers, particularly for her "teaching pieces"; she also found performances for her concert music and a way to earn money by writing commercial music for radio. She entered her works in one competition after another. In 1932 she won first prize in the Wanamaker Music Contest for her Symphony in E Minor and attracted wide attention. The next year the Chicago Symphony, under the direction of Frederick Stock, performed her symphony at the Chicago World's Fair, "A Century of Progress Exhibition"—the first time in history that a major orchestra had performed the symphony of a black woman. Later her orchestral works were performed by other leading orchestras, including the American Symphony, Detroit Symphony, Chicago Women's Symphony, Chicago Chamber Orchestra, Brooklyn [New York] Symphony, and Pittsburgh Symphony, among others. Smaller works were performed by the United States Marine Band and the New York City Symphonic Band; organists played her organ pieces, particularly members of the Chicago Club of Women Organists, and pianists performed her concerto, particularly her pupil Margaret Bonds.* Her songs received wide performance by such singers as Marian Anderson,* Roland Hayes,* Leontyne Price,* and Blanche Thebom, among others. Her style was conservative for her time; she wrote in a neoromantic style and occasionally drew upon black folk-music elements. Some of her piano pieces used Negro dance forms, and she used Negro poetry as texts for songs. She wrote in a variety of forms: four symphonies, a symphonic tone poem, two violin concertos, a piano concerto, two concert overtures (based on Negro spirituals), the *Chicago Suite* for orchestra, *Negro Folksongs in Counterpoint* for string quartet, *Moods* for a trio (flute, clarinet, and piano), an organ sonata and *Passacaglia and Fugue* for organ, *Lincoln Walks at Midnight* for chorus and orchestra, *The Wind and the Sea* for chorus and orchestra, the suites *Three Little Negro Dances* and *From the Canebrakes*, and many songs and piano pieces.

BIBL: ASCAP. Shirley Graham, "Spirituals to

Symphonies'' in *Etude* 54 (November 1936). Mildred D. Green, ''A Study of the Lives and Works of Five Black Women Composers in America'' (Ph. D. diss., University of Oklahoma, 1975). Barbara Garvey Jackson, ''Florence Price, Composer'' in BPIM 5 (Spring 1977). Hare. NAW. WilABW. WWCA, 1941-44.

PRICE, JESSE. Jazz drummer (b. 1 May 1909 in Memphis, Tennessee; d. 19 April 1974 in Los Angeles, California). He began playing professionally at an early age and toured with Sidney Desvignes, W. C. Handy,* and Bessie Smith,* among others, before he arrived in Kansas City, Missouri, in the 1930s as a member of the Georgia Minstrels.* There he played with William (''Count'') Basie,* Thamon Hayes, George E. Lee,* William (''Bill'') Martin, and others, as well as led his own groups periodically. In 1938 he toured with Ida Cox.* During the 1940s he played with various groups, including Harlan Leonard and, for shorter periods, Louis Armstrong,* Basie, Bennett (''Benny'') Carter,* Ella Fitzgerald,* Walter Fuller,* Bulee (''Slim'') Gaillard, Jay McShann,* and William (''Chick'') Webb.* He also led his own groups and recorded regularly, frequently singing the blues. During the late 1940s-60s he was active primarily on the West Coast. He was a participant with his band in the ''Kansas City Revisited'' program at the Monterey [California] Jazz Festival in 1971. His style represented the classic, blues-inflected, Kansas City school.

BIBL: ChilWW. Russ.

DISC: Jep. Kink.

PRICE, JOHN E. Composer (b. 21 June 1935 in Tulsa, Oklahoma). He began piano study at the age of five. He obtained his musical education in the public schools of Tulsa; at Lincoln University in Jefferson City, Missouri (B.A., 1957), where he studied with Oscar Anderson Fuller,* Augusta McSwain, and William Penn, among others; at the University of Tulsa in Oklahoma (M. Mus., 1963), where he studied with Bela Rozsa; and at Washington University in St. Louis, Missouri, where he studied with Robert Wykes and Harold Blumenfeld. His teaching career included tenures at Karamu House in Cleveland, Ohio (1957-59), where he was a staff-pianist, composer-arranger, and voice coach; at Florida Memorial College in Miami (1964-74); and at Eastern Illinois University at Charleston (1974-). He began composing as a child and performed his first piece in public at his sixth-grade commencement ceremonies. During his high-school years he learned to play orchestral instruments and wrote music of all kinds. His compositions were performed at the school and on church concerts. His first extended composition—*Greenwood Rhythm*, a revue for chorus, dancers, actors, and band—was performed in April 1952 at a Hi Jinks [talent] Show. Throughout his teaching career he wrote music for his students and groups he directed. His music was performed by college groups and such professional groups as the Oakland [California] Youth Symphony.

BIBL: Questionnaire. Alice Tischler, *Bio-Bibliography of Black American Composers* (Detroit, 1979). WWIntM.

PRICE, LEONTYNE. Opera singer (b. 10 February 1927 in Laurel, Mississippi). She came from a musical family; her father played tuba in a church band, and her mother sang solos with the church choir. She began piano study at the age of four and later sang in the church choir. At nine she heard a concert by Marian Anderson* in Jackson, Mississippi, and it made a lasting impression upon her, inspiring her to plan for a career in music—at first as a teacher. She obtained her musical training at Central State College in Wilberforce, Ohio (B.S., 1949), and the Juilliard School of Music in New York (1949-52), where she studied voice with Florence Kimball. She attracted the attention of Virgil Thomson when he heard her sing the role of Mistress Ford in a student production of Verdi's *Falstaff*, and he invited her to sing Cecilia in a 1952 Broadway revival of his opera *Four Saints in Three Acts*. Thereafter she was invited to sing the role of Bess in a revival of Gershwin's opera *Porgy and Bess*, and she toured with the company in Europe (1952-54). She made her concert debut as a soprano in November 1954 at Town Hall in the city of New York. Thereafter the honors came swiftly. In February 1955 she sang the title role of Puccini's *Tosca* on NBC television, thereby becoming the first black singer to appear in a television opera. Later she sang in other telecast operas, including Mozart's *The Magic Flute* and Poulenc's *Dialogues of the Carmelites*. In 1957 she made her operatic debut as Madame Lidoine in *Dialogues of the Carmelites* with the San Francisco Opera. In 1958 she made her European operatic debut in the title role of Verdi's *Aida* at the Vienna Staatsoper and thereafter sang with the leading opera companies of Europe. In January 1961 she made her debut at the Metropolitan Opera as Leonora in Verdi's *Il Trovatore* and received an ovation of forty-two minutes, the longest ever given in the house. In 1962 she was invited to open the season at the Metropolitan in the title role of Puccini's *The Girl of the Golden West*; the next year she opened the season as the prima donna in Verdi's *Aida*. When the Metropolitan Opera moved to its new home at Lincoln Center in September 1966, she sang the role of Cleopatra in Samuel Barber's *Anthony and Cleopatra*, which was written expressly for her. During the 1960s she sang in no fewer than 118 operas at the Metropolitan; in the 1970s she decreased the number of her performances there and gave more time to recitals and singing with other opera companies. Her change of activity was supported by her personnel manager, Hugh Dilworth, the only black manager of a opera star. She recorded prolifically after her first release in 1958.

Her numerous honors included honorary doctorates from Dartmouth College (1962), Howard University (1962), Central State College (1968), Rust College (1968), and Fordham University (1969); the Presidential Medal of Freedom (1964); the NAACP Springarn Medal (1965); the Order of Merit from Italy (1965); election to the American Academy of Arts and Sciences; appointments to membership on national boards and committees of professional, civic, and government organizations; numerous awards from the music and recording industries; and citations from various groups such as the YWCA and *Musical America* magazine.

She sang a wide variety of roles during her career. In addition to those cited above, her best-known performances were the title roles in Puccini's *Madame Butterfly* and Bizet's *Carmen*, Donna Anna in Mozart's *Don Giovanni*, and Leonora in Verdi's *La Forza del Destino*. During the late 1970s she began to move away from Italian opera toward such roles as Ariadne in Strauss's *Ariadne auf Naxos*. She was acclaimed as one of the greatest sopranos of her time and called ''the girl with the golden voice'' and ''the Stradivarius of singers.'' She was married to William Warfield (later divorced).

BIBL: CBDict. CurBiog (October 1978). *Ebony* (December 1966). Ewen. H. L. Lyon, *Leontyne Price: Highlights of a Prima Donna* (New York, 1975). *Opera News* (20 January 1979). Stephen E. Rubin, ''I'm Not Scared Any More'' in NYT (16 September 1973). WWA. WWAW. WWBA. WWOpera.

DISC: Turn.

PRICE, SAMUEL BLYTHE ("SAMMY"). Jazz pianist (b. 6 October 1908 in Honey Grove, Texas). As a child he played alto horn in a boys' band in Waco, Texas. His family moved to Dallas, Texas, when he was ten, and he began piano study with Portia Pittman.* At the age of fifteen he won a dancing contest and began performing professionally, first touring with Alphonso Trent. Later he became active as an accompanist. He also led his own big band, played with Lee Collins, and toured with the ''Let's Go Show'' (1927-28) on the TOBA* (Theater Owners Booking Association) circuit. In 1929 he made his first recordings in Dallas, then went to Oklahoma City, Oklahoma, where he helped to establish jazz radio, along with Leonard Chadwick and Lemuel Johnson. During the 1930s-50s he played long residencies in various cities—Dallas; Kansas City, Missouri; Detroit, Michigan; and New York, New York—as a soloist, frequently with his own small groups, and with others, including Henry (''Red'') Allen,* Sidney Bechet,* William (''Bill'') Johnson,* Willie (''Bunk'') Johnson,* and James (''Jimmy'') Rushing,* among others. In 1937 he began a longtime association with Decca Records as a staff pianist; he recorded with blues, gospel, rhythm 'n' blues, and jazz singers, among them, Rosetta Tharpe,* Peetie Wheatstraw* (née William Bunch), and Trixie Smith. He toured frequently in Europe; in 1956 his touring with his Bluesicians included North Africa. His style was representative of the early boogie-woogie piano.

BIBL: ChilWW. FeaEJ. MeeJMov.

DISC: Jep. Kink. TudJ.

PRIDE, CHARLEY. Country-music singer (b. 18 March 1939 in Sledge, Mississippi). As a child he listened to Saturday-night radio broadcasts of the ''Grand Ole Opry'' from Nashville, Tennessee, and sang along with the country singers. At the age of fourteen he taught himself to play guitar, but his ambition was to become a professional baseball player. He first sang in public in 1960 between the innings of a baseball game in East Helena, Montana, where he was playing on the company team of his employer, Anaconda Mining. Encouraged by his reception, he began singing in local nightclubs of Helena and later attracted the attention of country-western singers Clyde (''Red'') Foley and Woodrow (''Red'') Sovine when they came to Helena to give a concert. The contact led to a recording contract in 1964; his first release, ''Snakes crawl at night'' (1966), was a success. Thereafter he recorded prolifically and toured widely, appearing at the major state fairs, on radio and television shows, and in concert halls. In 1967 he made his debut with the ''Grand Ole Opry.'' He won numerous awards from the ''country music'' industry. He was the first of his race to have a successful career in country-western music.

BIBL: CurBiog (1975). *Ebony* (March 1967). George Alex Sewell, *Mississippi Black History Makers* (Jackson, Mississippi, 1977). StamFCW. WWA.

PROCTOR, HENRY HUGH. Music patron (b. 8 December 1868 near Clifton, Tennessee; d. 12 May 1933 in New York (Brooklyn), New York). When pastor of the First Congregational Church in Atlanta, Georgia, he organized the Atlanta Colored Music Festival Association in July 1910 in order to bring to Atlanta ''the best musical talent of the race'' (quoted from concert programs). Although not a professional musician, he participated in musical activities during his college years at Fisk University in Nashville, Tennessee (B. A., 1891) and at Yale University in New Haven, Connecticut (B. Div. 1894). At Yale he organized a quartet of black students who sang throughout New England, earning money to cover university expenses, and he wrote his thesis on the theology of the slave songs. In Atlanta he was outraged that black citizens could not attend public concerts because of race discrimination, and the Festival Association was his solution to the problem. Over the six-year life span of the festivals, the leading black artists of the period were invited to perform in Atlanta, including Anita Patti Brown,* Harry T. Burleigh,* Lulu Vere Childers,* Roland Hayes,* Katherine Skeene Mitchell, Roy W. Tibbs,* Rachel Walker,* and Clarence Cameron White,* among others. N. Clark Smith* brought choral and instrumental groups from Tuskegee Institute to perform on the concerts; John W. Work* brought the Fisk Jubilee Singers every year; Kemper Harreld* and Carl Diton* served as guest conductors for community choruses of children and adults. The Festival programs consisted of a varied repertory, but always included the music of black composers. World War I brought an end to the Festivals. In 1919 Proctor went to France "to sustain the morale of the boys left behind to clean up the debris" (quoted from Proctor's autobiography) and took with him songleader J. E. Blanton* and pianist Helen Hagan* to entertain the colored troops. In 1920 he left Atlanta to become pastor of a church in Brooklyn, New York.

BIBL: Altona Trent Johns in BPIM 3 (Spring 1975). Henry Hugh Proctor, *Between Black and White: Autobiographical Sketches* (Boston, 1925). Files of the Armistad Research Center in New Orleans, Louisiana.

PRYSOCK, ARTHUR. Popular-music singer (b. 2 January 1929 in Spartanburg, South Carolina). He first attracted wide attention as a jazz baritone with Woodrow ("Buddy") Wilson's big band in 1944, which played regularly at the Savoy Ballroom in the Harlem community of the city of New York. After leaving the band about 1952, he toured as a soloist in nightclubs and concert halls, generally accompanied by his brother's group, the Red Prysock Trio. During the 1960s he began to appear frequently on television shows, particularly the "Tonight Show." His mature style blended elements of jazz, rhythm 'n' blues, and popular music; his repertory emphasized romantic ballads. His best-known performances were of "They all say I'm the biggest fool," "The very thought of you," "Let's get it on," and "It's too late, baby, too late."

BIBL: Black press. FeaJS.

DISC: Jep. Kink.

R

RABBIT FOOT MINSTRELS. See **CHAPPELLE, PATRICK.**

RACHELL, JAMES ("YANK"). Bluesman (b. 16 March 1910 near Brownsville, Tennessee). Although he taught himself to play guitar as a child, he later changed to the mandolin. During the late 1920s he teamed with ("Sleepy") John Estes,* and in 1929 the two bluesmen made a recording with Jab Jones. During the next decade Rachell recorded with Dan Smith, and after Smith's death in 1934, with "Sonny Boy Williamson, No. 1" (John Lee Williamson).* In 1938 he left music for five or six years, then returned to play in the Brownsville area until 1958, when he settled in Indianapolis, Indiana. In 1962 he began to record again, at first with Estes and Hammie Nixon,* then later with his own groups, including his Naptown Blues Band. He also toured in the United States and in Europe, appearing in concert halls, nightclubs, and at the major blues and jazz festivals.

BIBL: *Cadence* (August 1977). Dave Helland, "A Naptown Blues Party" in LivBl 13 (Summer 1973). Oliv.

DISC: DiGod. LeSl. TudBM.

RAHN, MURIEL. Concert singer (b. 1911 in Boston, Massachusetts; d. 8 August 1961 in New York, New York). Her family moved to New York when she was a child and she attended public schools there. She obtained her musical education at Tuskegee Institute in Alabama, Atlanta University in Georgia, and the Music Conservatory of the University of Nebraska at Lincoln. She began singing professionally in 1929 with Eva Jessye's* Dixie Jubilee Singers. Thereafter she sang in Broadway musicals, including Lew Leslie's *Blackbirds of 1929*, Connie Inn's *Hot Chocolates* (1929), and *Carmen Jones* (1943-44, singing the title role in alternation with Muriel Smith*). During the 1940s she became involved in opera; she became a member of the opera group of the National Orchestral Association in New York and sang in some of its productions, among them, Mozart's *The Abduction from the Seraglio* and Puccini's *Suor Angelica* and *Gianini Schichi*. In 1948 she sang the title role of Verdi's *Aida* with the Salmaggi Opera and later repeated her performance with the San Carlo Opera in 1949 and with Mary Cardwell Dawson's* National Negro Opera Company. She also sang in American operas, such as Harry Freeman's* *The Martyr* in 1947 and the Jan Meyerowitz/Langston Hughes* opera *The Barrier* in 1950. She was active as a concert singer and toured widely in the United States and in Europe. During the year 1959-60 she was musical director for the German State Theatre's production of *Bells are Ringing* at Frankfurt.

BIBL: Black press, incl. AmstN, 12 August 1961; NYAge, 3 August 1935, 19 November 1938, 5 February 1949. NYB. WWCA, 1950.

RAINEY, ("MA") GERTRUDE PRIDGETT. Blues singer (b. 26 April 1886 in Columbus, Georgia; d. 22 December 1939 in Columbus). She first won recognition when she sang in a local talent show at the age of fourteen, and thereafter she sang professionally. Beginning in 1904 she formed a vaudeville act with her husband, William ("Pa") Rainey, and for many years she toured through the South—either with her husband or as a soloist—with various companies, including the Rabbit Foot, Al Gaines, and C. W. Parks minstrel troupes; the Silas Green* tent show; and the Haines and Tolliver circuses. Later in her career she toured with her own show and her Georgia Band. As early as 1902 she featured the blues in her performances; later she sang to the accompaniment of jug bands; guitarists, such as "Tampa Red" (Hudson Whittaker)* or Aaron ("T-Bone") Walker*; pianists, such as ("Blind") Arthur Blake* or "Georgia Tom" (Thomas A. Dorsey*); and groups, such as Louis Armstrong* or Lovie Austin's* Blues Serenaders. During the years 1923-28 she recorded extensively; her live performances and recordings earned her the sobriquet Mother of the

Blues. In 1935 she retired from the stage and spent her remaining years managing two theaters she owned in Columbus and Rome, Georgia.

BIBL: BWW. ChilWW. CharCB. FeaEJ. MeeJMov. NAW. Oliv. Derrick Stewart-Baxter, *Ma Rainey and the Classic Blues Singers* (New York, 1970).

DISC: DiGod. Kink. RustJR. TudBM.

RAWLS, LOUIS ALLEN ("LOU"). Gospel singer/ Entertainer (b. 1 December 1936 in Chicago, Illinois). He sang in a gospel choir from the age of seven. His first professional experience was with the Chosen Gospel Singers. After serving in the United States Armed Forces (1956-58), he sang with the Pilgrim Travelers, whose members included Sam Cooke* at that time. After the group was disbanded in 1959, he began his career as a nightclub entertainer in Los Angeles, California. He made his recording debut in 1962 and thereafter began to win recognition for his blues singing as well as his ballads. During the 1960s-70s he toured widely in the United States, Europe, Japan, and Australia; he recorded extensively and appeared on radio and television shows, including the special show "Soul" in 1967 and his own show in the summer of 1969. In 1975 he became associated with Philadelphia International Records, under the management of Kenneth ("Kenny") Gamble* and Leon Huff.* He received awards from the music industry. His best-known album was *Stormy Monday*, and his best-known performance was of "You'll never find another love like mine."

BIBL: Black press, incl. *Philadelphia Tribune*, 16 February 1974. BWW. *Ebony* (October 1978). FeaJS. StamPRS. WWA. WWBA.

DISC: Jep.

RAY RUSSELL, CARLINE. Jazz bassist (b. 21 April 1925 in New York, New York). She came from a family of professional musicians: her father played brass instruments, and her mother was a pianist. She obtained her musical education at the Juilliard School of Music in New York (B. Mus., 1946) and the Manhattan School of Music in New York (M. Mus., 1956), where she studied voice with John Brownlee. In her professional career she was active as a singer (contralto), bassist, guitarist, and pianist. She sang with such choral groups in New York as the Schola Cantorum, Musica Aeterna, Camerata Singers, and the Bach Aria Group. She toured as vocalist with Erskine Hawkins* (1948) and sang Emme Kemp's* "Tomorrow's woman" at the Women's Jazz Festival in Kansas City, Missouri, in 1979. As string bassist she toured with the International Sweethearts of Rhythm* (1940s), the Duke Ellington* Band (1976, in the United States, Canada, and Japan), and the Alvin Ailey Dance Company (1970s), among other groups. In 1979 at the Women's Jazz Festival she was bassist and leader of a small group and a seventeen-piece big band, called Big Apple Jazz Women. She played piano in the Edna [Edet] Smith* Trio during the 1950s. She played in orchestras for radio and television shows, Broadway musicals, and recordings, such as Scott Joplin's* *Treemonisha* and Earl Robinson's Ballad for Americans and (as chorister) in Bernstein's *Chichester Psalms* and Stravinsky's *Threni*. Her recordings included an album, *Music for Contralto and Piano* with Bruce Eberle, for the series *Music Minus One*. She held a teaching appointment at the Medger Evers College of the City University of New York. She was married to Luis Russell.*

BIBL: Handy.

RAZAF, ANDY (ANDREAMENTANIA PAUL RAZAFINKERIEFO). Jazz lyricist (b. 16 December 1895 in Washington, D.C.; d. 4 February 1973 in Los Angeles, California). Although not a musician, he was important for his collaboration with others in writing songs and Broadway musicals. His first publication was "Baltimo," which was sung in the Broadway musical, *The Passing Show of 1913*. His chief collaborators were James ("Eubie") Blake,* Thomas ("Fats") Waller,* J.C. Johnson,* and James Price Johnson,* among others. With Waller he wrote *Keep Shufflin'* (1928, also with James P. Johnson and Henry Creamer*) and *Hot Chocolates* (1929); with Blake he wrote *Blackbirds of 1930*. His best-known songs written with Waller were "Ain't misbehavin'," "Honeysuckle rose," and "Keeping out of mischief now." With Blake he wrote "Memories of you." He also wrote the lyrics for such popular songs as "Make believe ballroom," "Knock me a kiss," "Concentrating on you," and "Stompin' at the Savoy." He received awards from the music industry, and in 1972 he was inducted into the Songwriters Hall of Fame.

BIBL: ASCAP. *Ebony* (January 1973). FeaEJ. FeaGitJS. WWCR.

REDDING, OTIS. Rhythm 'n' blues singer (b. 9 September 1941 in Dawson, Georgia; d. 10 December 1967 near Madison, Wisconsin). His family moved to Macon, Georgia, when he was a child. He obtained his musical education in the public schools there and sang in a church choir. He began singing professionally in the early 1960s; by 1965 he had established himself as a leading rhythm 'n' blues singer. He toured widely in the United States and in Europe and recorded extensively. He was killed in a plane crash when at the peak of his career. Among his best-known albums was *Live in Europe*; his last recording was "Sitting on the dock of the bay.'' He won many awards from the music industry.

BIBL: Black press, incl. *Soul* [Los Angeles], 29 April 1974. StamPRS.

DISC: Giv. TudB.

REDMAN, DONALD MATTHEW (''DON''). Jazz arranger/Composer (b. 29 July 1900 in Piedmont, West Virginia; d. 30 November 1964 in New York, New York). He came from a musical family: his father was a music teacher and a brother, Lewis, became a professional musician. He learned to play wind instruments as a child. He obtained his musical education at Storer's Teachers College in West Virginia and at the Boston Conservatory of Music in Massachusetts. During the 1920s he played soprano and alto saxophone with various groups, including Billy Paige's Broadway Syncopators (1923), Fletcher Henderson* (1924-27), and McKinney's Cotton Pickers* (1927-31). He arranged for Henderson and Louis Armstrong* and served as musical director for the Cotton Pickers. He made his recording debut with Henderson in 1923 and thereafter recorded extensively. In 1931 he organized his own band (1931-40), using sidemen from the Cotton Pickers and Horace Henderson's* band, and played long residencies in New York nightclubs, appeared on radio shows—in his own series for ''Chipso'' in 1932—and in films. Thereafter he gave full time to arranging, although he occasionally formed a group for special occasions or to tour (1941, 1943, 1946-47 in Europe). Those for whom he arranged included Paul Whiteman (for thirty-five years), William (''Count'') Basie,* Isham Jones, Jimmy Dorsey, Ben Pollack, and Harry James, among others. In the fall of 1949 he had his own series on CBS television; during the early 1950s he was musical director for Pearl Bailey.* Redman was a pioneer jazz arranger-composer and a leading contributor to the development of the big-band sound of the 1920s-30s, along with Fletcher Henderson.

BIBL: ASCAP. AlHen. Black press, incl. NYAge, 13 August 1949. ChilWW. FeaEJ. MeeJMov.

DISC: Kink. RustJR. TudJ.

REDMAN, WALTER DEWEY. Jazz saxophonist (b. 17 May 1931 in Fort Worth, Texas). He began playing clarinet at the age of twelve. He played in a church band and in his high-school marching band. He obtained his musical education at Tuskegee Institute in Alabama, Prairie View A & M College in Texas (B.S., 1953), and North Texas State College at Denton (M. Ed., 1959). Although his degrees were not in music, he participated in musical activities during his college years. He taught in the public schools of Texas (1956-59), then went to California, eventually settling in San Francisco. During the 1960s he played with various groups, including Pharoah Sanders,* Don Garrett, Wes Montgomery, and Monville (''Monty'') Waters (as a co-leader), among others. He also led his own groups. In 1967 he settled in New York. Thereafter he worked primarily with Ornette Coleman* (1967-74), Charlie Hayden, Keith Jarrett, and his own groups. He was a leading figure in the avant-garde movement of the 1970s and won wide attention for his tenor-saxophone role in the Coleman group as a complement to Coleman's alto saxophone.

BIBL: Black press, incl. *Soul* [Los Angeles], 30 September 1974. FeaGitJS.

DISC: TudJ.

REED, ADDISON W. College professor (b. 22 April 1929 in Stuebenville, Ohio). He obtained his musical education at Kent State University in Ohio (B.A., 1951; B.S., 1953; M.A., 1957) and at the University of North Carolina at Chapel Hill (Ph.D., 1973). His teaching career included tenures at Henderson Institute in Henderson, North Carolina (1953-54); Booker High School in Sarasota, Florida (1958-61); and St. Augustine's College in Raleigh, North Carolina (1961-). He lectured widely and published articles in professional journals, including discussions on the topic of his doctoral dissertation, ''The Life and Works of Scott Joplin.''

BIBL: WWBA.

REED, MATHIS JAMES (''JIMMY''). Bluesman (b. 6 September 1925 in Dunleith, Mississippi; d. 29 August 1976 in Oakland, California). He taught himself to play guitar as a child, helped by Eddie Taylor, with whom he teamed to play for local social entertainments. His earliest influence was ''Sonny Boy Williamson, No. 2'' (Alex ''Rice'' Miller),* whose broadcasts he heard for the King Biscuit Flour Company on radio station KFFA in Helena, Arkansas. About 1942 he went to Chicago, where he played harmonica for the first time, and performed in local clubs. After service in the military (1944-45), he returned to Chicago in 1946 and began to establish himself as a professional. In 1953 he began recording for Vee-Jay Records,* a black-owned company. Thereafter he recorded extensively and toured widely in the United States and in Europe, appearing in concert halls, clubs, on college campuses, and at the major blues and jazz festivals. Those with whom he performed and/or recorded included Riley (''B.B.'') King,* ''Sunnyland Slim'' (Albert Luandrew),* ''Muddy Waters'' (McKinley Morganfield),* and Williamson. He was representative of the Chicago blues style with its heavy ensemble of amplified guitar, harmonica, and bass and its aggressive four-beat basses.

BIBL: BWW. LivBl 21 (May-June 1975). Oliv.

DISC: Jep. LeSl. TudBM.

REESE, DELLA (née **DELLOREESE PATRICIA EARLY**). Gospel/Popular-music singer (b. 6 July 1932 in Detroit Michigan). She obtained her musical education at Wayne University in Detroit, Michigan. She began singing in church choirs at the age of six, and organized a gospel group, the Meditations, during her college years. She toured with Mahalia Jackson* in the summers of 1945-49 and sang at various times also with Beatrice Brown, Roberta Martin,* and the Clara Ward* Singers. In 1954 she moved from gospel into the field of secular music; she first sang professionally in a local Detroit nightclub, where she came into contact with leading figures of the entertainment world. The first orchestra she sang with was that of Erskine Hawkins.* She began to record in 1955 and thereafter she recorded extensively. From 1957 on she was active primarily as a soloist; she toured widely and appeared regularly on radio and television shows. In 1969-70 she was hostess for a television show, titled "Della." She also appeared in films, including *Let's Rock* (1958). Her best-known performances were "In the still of the night" and "And that reminds me." Her style development was influenced most by Dinah Washington.*

BIBL: CurBiog (September 1971). ShawR5. WWA. WWBA.

RENÉ, LEON T. Songwriter/Record producer (b. 6 February 1902 in Covington, Kentucky). Otis,* the older of the two René brothers, obtained his musical education at Wilberforce University in Xenia, Ohio (B.A., 1921), and later earned a degree in pharmacology. Leon attended Xavier University in New Orleans, Louisiana; Southern University in Baton Rouge, Louisiana; and Wilberforce University. In 1922 the two brothers settled in Los Angeles, California, and Leon continued to study music privately. Later he organized an orchestra and began writing songs, with the collaboration of his brother Otis. In the 1930s the brothers founded two record companies, Exclusive Records and Excelsior Records, when they met with difficulties in getting established record companies to accept their songs. By the mid-1940s, they were the leading record producers among the independent companies. Those they recorded included Nat King Cole (née Nathaniel Coles),* Joe Liggins and His Honeydrippers, Johnny Moore's Three Blazers, Herb Jeffries,* and Johnny Otis, among others. The brothers also established publishing companies, Leon René Publications and Recordo Music Publishers. They were credited with producing the first rhythm 'n' blues records. The emergence of rock 'n' roll forced them into a relatively quiet period, but they returned full time to recording in 1957 with a new label, Class Records, and such artists as Bobby Day (née Robert Byrd). Their best-known songs were "When the swallows come back to Capistrano," "When it's sleepy time down south" (with Clarence Muse*), "Someone's rocking my dreamboat," and "Rockin' robin." The last named, first released in 1958, is credited with having initiated the rock 'n' roll revival of the 1970s when it was released for the second time in 1972. The René brothers won awards from the music industry.

BIBL: Communication from William ("Bill") René in regard to vital statistics. ASCAP. ShawHS.

RENÉ, JR., OTIS J. Songwriter/Record producer (b. 2 October 1898 in New Orleans, Louisiana; d. 5 April 1970 in Los Angeles, California). See **RENÉ, LEON.**

REVOLUTIONARY ENSEMBLE, THE. Instrumental jazz trio (fl. 1970s; orig. New York, New York). Founded in 1970, the "multidirectional group" played improvised music primarily. There was no leader; each member of the trio was leader, soloist, and composer at the same time. The original members were drummer Jerome Cooper,* violinist Leroy Jenkins,* and bassist Sirone.* The trio toured in the United States and abroad, appearing in nightclubs, on television programs and at festivals. The group also recorded. The trio's style was avant-garde improvisational; numerous instruments were employed, including electric violin, viola, and piano and a variety of percussions.

BIBL: Personal communication from Leroy Jenkins. Black press, incl. *Soul* [Los Angeles], 13 September 1976. FeaGitJS. NYT, 15 January 1977.

RHEA, LA JULIA. Concert/opera singer (b. 16 March c1908 in Louisville, Kentucky). She began piano study at the age of five. As a child she sang in a church choir, of which her aunt was director-organist. She obtained her musical education in the public schools of Louisville; during her high school years she heard Florence Cole Talbert* sing and was inspired to become a concert singer. When she was sixteen her family moved to Chicago, Illinois, where she studied at the National University of Music, directed by Pauline James Lee,* and at Chicago Musical College (certificate, 1927). She studied voice privately with Victor Chesnais, Herman DeVries, and Talbert, among others. She sang regularly at local recitals and for special events, such as the annual meeting of the National Association of Negro Musicians* in St. Louis, Missouri, in 1927. During the 1920s she developed a repertory of operatic arias along with the traditional concert repertory. In 1929 she made her debut as a soprano at Kimball Hall in Chicago. In 1931 she sang a leading role in the Broadway musical, *Rhapsody in Black*, which featured Ethel Waters* and the Cecil Mack* Choir. In March 1934 she was granted an audition with the Metropolitan Opera Company but was unsuccessful in breaking down racial barriers; it was not until 1955 that the Metropolitan engaged its first black singer, Marian Anderson.* In 1935 she won first place in a Major Bowes radio talent show and was given a leading role in his Amateur Ensemble Group, No. 2, which toured widely throughout the United States. In 1937 she made her operatic debut, singing the title role of Verdi's *Aida* with the Chicago Civic Opera Company, with William Franklin* as Amonasro. During the next decade she sang in other operas, in Gilbert and Sullivan operettas, and in *Aida* again in 1941 with the debut in Pittsburgh, Pennsylvania, of Mary Cardwell Dawson's* National Negro Opera Company. La Julia Rhea retired from music in 1949 but sang occasionally at private recitals.

BIBL: Interviewed by Fanya Wiggins. Black press, incl. CDef, 28 December 1935, 30 October 1937, 6 September 1941, 25 October 1941, 17 October 1942; [Chicago] *Freedom Journal* (May 1974); NYAge, 7 April 1934.

RHODES, TODD WASHINGTON. Jazz pianist (b. 31 August 1900 in Hopkinsville, Kentucky; d. 1965 in Flint, Michigan). His family moved to Springfield, Ohio, when he was a child. He obtained his musical education at the Springfield School of Music and the Erie Conservatory in Erie, Pennsylvania. In 1921 he joined the newly organized Synco Septette, which later became McKinney's Cotton Pickers.* After leaving the group in 1934, he was active as a soloist and, after 1946, with his own groups, with whom he toured widely.

BIBL: ChilWW. FeaEJ.

DISC: Jep.

RICHARDSON, WILLIAM HOWARD. Concert singer (b. 23 August 1869 in Liverpool, Nova Scotia, Canada; d. c1930s in Boston, Massachusetts). He came from a musical family; his paternal grandfather was director of a concert company. His family moved to Boston when he was eleven years old, and he began music study at that time. He studied with George H. Woods, Arthur Hubbard, and Theodore Schroeder, among others. His first professional experiences were in church music, at first in a quartet and later as soloist. He sang with the Philharmonic Society, under the direction of Archibald Davison, for many years. He first sang solos on a concert in 1909 at Steinart Hall in Boston. Thereafter he toured extensively, singing in oratorios, giving art-song recitals, and joining with Maude Cuney Hare* in lecture-recitals on Negro folksong. In the summer of 1915 he toured with the Hayes Trio, including Roland Hayes* and William Lawrence,* on the Chatauqua circuit. In January 1919 he made his formal debut as a concert baritone at Jordan Hall in Boston. He expanded his touring thereafter to include the West Indies as well as the United States. Throughout his career he conducted a music studio.

BIBL: Black press. Hare.

RIDLEY, FLORIDA RUFFIN. Folklorist(?) (fl. late nineteenth century in Boston, Massachusetts; d. March 1943 in Toledo, Ohio). Nothing is known of her musical career except that she was one of the founders of the Society for the Collection of Negro Folklore in Boston, Massachusetts, in March 1890. The Society met at the Revere Street Church. This apparently was the earliest group of black folklorists; white groups interested in the study of black folklore had been organized earlier at Hampton Institute and other places. Her brother, George Lewis Ruffin, was a church organist and concert baritone.

BIBL: Black press, incl. NYAge, 8 March 1890, 2 April 1890, 26 April 1890; AmstN, 27 March 1943. Hare.

RIDLEY, LAURENCE HOWARD, JR. ("LARRY"). Jazz bassist (b. 3 September 1937 in Indianapolis, Indiana). He obtained his musical education at Indiana University in Bloomington and at the Lenox School of Jazz in Massachusetts. His first professional experiences were with local groups in Indianapolis, among them, Frederick ("Freddie") Hubbard,* James Spaulding, and the Montgomery brothers. During the 1960s-70s he was active primarily in New York, where he played with various groups, including Edward ("Duke") Ellington,* John Birks ("Dizzy") Gillespie,* Coleman Hawkins,* John ("Jackie") McLean,* Horace Silver,* the Thad Jones*/Mel Lewis Big Band, Randolph ("Randy") Weston,* and others. He also played with such groups as the Newport All Stars (beginning in 1968), JCOA (Jazz Composers Orchestra Association), Young Giants of Jazz (1973, on a European tour), and the New York Bass Violin Choir, of which he was an original member. During the 1970s he became increasingly involved in college teaching, and in 1971 joined the music faculty of Livingston College of Rutgers University in New Brunswick, New Jersey. He also was active as an artist-in-residence at various institutions, among them Grambling College and Southern University in Louisiana, the University of Iowa at Iowa City, and Creighton University in Omaha, Nebraska. In December 1977 he participated in a first-time, historic jazz festival at Lesotho in South Africa, along with other members of the Rutgers-Livingston Jazz Professors, Kenneth ("Kenny") Barron,* Freddie Waits, Ted Dunbar, and Frank Foster.*

BIBL: FeaJS. FeaGitJS.

RING, MONTAGUE. See **ALDRIDGE, AMANDA.**

RITCHIE, NELMATILDA. See **WOODARD, NELMATILDA.**

RIVERS, CLARENCE JOSEPH. Sacred music composer (b. 9 September 1931 in Selma, Alabama). An ordained priest, Father Rivers is also a musician and as such is discussed here. His family moved to Cincinnati, Ohio, when he was a child and he attended parochial school there. He obtained further education at the St. Mary's Seminary in Cincinnati (B.A., 1952; M.A., 1956) and later studied at Xavier University in Cincinnati; Catholic University in Washington, D.C.; Yale University in New Haven, Connecticut; and the Institut Catholique in Paris, France. During the years 1956-66 he taught in public schools of Cincinnati, then left teaching to work with a program focusing on the performing arts in worship. This led to his founding the Department of Culture and Worship in the National Office for Black Catholics. In 1972 he became the first director of the Department. He made his debut as a composer in August 1964 when he introduced his work, *An American Mass Program* (recorded in 1963), at the meeting of the National Liturgical Conference in St. Louis, Missouri. His Mass, *Brotherhood of Man*, was performed at the Newport Jazz Festival in 1967, with the assistance of the Billy Taylor* Trio, and by the Cincinnati Symphony Orchestra in 1969 at its Third Annual Ecumenical Concert. Another of his well-known works is *Resurrection* for gospel/jazz soloist and chorus, piano or chamber orchestra. He lectured widely to various denominational groups, held workshops, produced concerts, and supervised celebrations for interreligious gatherings. He pioneered in introducing Afro-American elements into music for Catholic worship. His music blended Gregorian chant and other religious music in the European tradition with blues, spirituals, jazz, and gospel. Generally it called for the collaboration of soloist, choir, and congregation. His honors included awards from civic and community organizations and the Gold Medal of the Catholic Art Association (1966).

BIBL: William Garcia, "Church Music by Black Composers" in BPIM (Fall 1974). "A Protestant Looks at Liturgical Week" in *Our Sunday Visitor* [Catholic newspaper], 4 October 1964. "The Sound of Rivers" in *Sign Magazine* (February 1967). WWBA.

RIVERS, SAMUEL CARTHORNE ("SAM"). Jazz Saxophonist (b. 25 September 1930 in El Reno, Oklahoma). He came from a musical family: his mother played piano, and his father sang with a gospel group, the Silvertone Quartet. His grandfather, Marshall Taylor,* published a collection of slave songs and hymns in 1883. He obtained his musical education in the public schools of Chicago, Illinois (where his family lived until he was seven), and Little Rock, Arkansas; at Jarvis Christian College in Hawkins, Texas (B.A.); and at Boston University in Massachusetts. He began playing professionally in the 1940s with local Boston groups. During the 1950s-60s he played with various groups, including John ("Jaki") Byard,* Miles Davis,* Joe Gordon, Andrew Hill,* Gigi Gryce, Herbert Pomeroy, Cecil Taylor,* and McCoy Tyner,* among others. In 1967 he settled in New York in the Harlem community, where he opened a music studio; about 1971 he moved his Studio Rivbea to the Soho community of New York. In addition to serving as a concert hall, his studio was an art gallery and workshop site, where musicians gathered to rehearse and to experiment with new ideas. He formed big bands and small ensembles to perform his compositions and featured such guest artists as Dewey Redman, Clifford Jordan, and Sonny Murray, among others. From 1968 on he was composer-in-residence for the Harlem Opera Company. His best-known works were the jazz-improvisational opera *Solomon and Sheba* (1973), the composition "Evocation," and the album *Streams, Crystals, and Involution*. Rivers was important in the avant-garde movement of the 1960s, along with Ornette Coleman,* Archie Shepp,* and Cecil Taylor, and he continued his role as a leader in the experimental music of the 1970s.

BIBL: Black press, incl. AmstN, 5 February 1977. *Down Beat*, 16 November 1978. FeaJS. FeaGitJS. *The* [New York] *Village Voice*, 14 June 1973. Michael Ullman, *Jazz Lives* (New York, 1980).

ROACH, HILDRED. College professor/Pianist (b. 14 March 1937 in Charlotte, North Carolina). She began piano study at the age of eight. She obtained her musical education at Fisk University in Nashville, Tennessee, (B.A. 1957), Yale University in New Haven, Connecticut, (M. Mus., 1962), the Juilliard School of Music in New York (1958-59), and the University of Ghana at Accra (1969). Her teachers included John W. Work,* Alan Forte, William Masselos, Katherine Bacon, Janet Knapp, J. Kwabena Nketia,* and Bernard Wagenaar, among others. She toured widely as a concert pianist-lecturer. Her teaching career included tenures at Tuskegee Institute in Alabama (1957-60), Fayetteville State College in North Carolina

(1962-66), Howard University in Washington, D.C. (1966-67), Virginia State College in Petersburg (1967-68), and the University of the District of Columbia (formerly Federal Teachers College, 1968-). She published articles in professional journals and the book *Black American Music: Past and Present* (Boston, 1973).

BIBL: Questionnaire. Cynthia Fadool, *Outstanding Educators of America* (Washington, D.C., 1975). J. T. Vickers, *Personalities of the South* (Raleigh, 1976). WWAW, 1975.

ROACH, MAXWELL LEMUEL ("MAX"). Jazz drummer (b. 10 January 1924 in Elizabeth City, North Carolina). He obtained his musical education in the public schools of the borough of Brooklyn in New York and at the Manhattan School of Music in New York. During the early 1940s he joined other musicians in after-hours ''jam sessions'' at Clark Monroe's Uptown House and Minton's Playhouse in the Harlem community, where he came into contact with Charlie Parker,* Kenneth (''Kenny'') Clarke,* John Birks (''Dizzy'') Gillespie,* and Thelonious Monk,* among others. His early style development was influenced by these founders of the bebop school of jazz. In 1944 he became a member of Gillespie's first quintet, along with Don Byas,* Oscar Pettiford,* and George Wallington. The same year he made his first recordings with Coleman Hawkins.* Thereafter he played with various groups, including Benny Carter,* Miles Davis,* Parker, Howard Rumsey, and Lester Young,* among others. In 1954 he organized his own group and led small ensembles at intervals through the 1970s. In 1972 he formed M'Boom Re: Percussion, which used various kinds of percussions, particularly of Africa and Asia. He toured widely as a lecturer on black music with his groups in the United States and in Europe, appearing in concert halls, on college campuses, and at the major jazz festivals. His best-known composition was the *Freedom Now Suite*. He received many awards from the music industry, and a film based on his *Freedom Now Suite* won first prize in a film festival. His teaching career included tenures at the Lenox School of Jazz In Massachusetts (summers from 1957 on) and at the University of Massachusetts at Amherst (1972-78). Roach was an important drummer of the bebob era, and he exerted wide influence upon his contemporaries, particularly in his use of the top cymbal as the chief carrier of the beat rather than the drum. He was a pioneer in exploiting the drums as melodic instruments as well as rhythmic instruments.

BIBL. Black press, incl. NYAge, 11 May 1974, 18 May 1974. BMI (Issue 4, 1980). FeaEJ. FeaJS. FeaGitJS. Dizzy Gillespie with Al Fraser, *To Be or Not To Bop* (New York, 1979). WWA.

DISC: Jep. Kink. ModJ. TudJ.

ROBERTS, CHARLES LUCKEYETH ("LUCKEY"). Jazz pianist (b. 7 August 1887 in Philadelphia, Pennsylvania; d. 5 February 1968 in New York, New York). He played piano at the age of five and toured as a child with an Uncle Tom's Cabin company; later he toured with Gus Seekes's Pickaninnies and Mayme Remington's Ethiopian Prodigies. He first played piano professionally in nightclubs of Philadelphia. About 1910 he settled in New York and soon established himself as one of the leading nightclub pianists in the Harlem community. He studied with Eloise Smith and Melville Charlton.* During the second decade of the century he was associated with the Smart Set* as musical director (during the years 1913-1919) and composer; his musical scores included *My People*. He toured in Europe with James Reese Europe* in 1915 and thereafter led his own society dance orchestras. He began to publish his piano rags about 1913, including the well-known ''Junk man rag'' and ''Pork and beans.'' He also began making piano rolls during this period, and in 1923 was one of the first group of black pianists engaged to cut rolls by QRS (Quality Reigns Supreme, a subsidiary of the Melville Clark Piano Company), along with J. Lawrence Cook,* Lemuel Fowler, Clarence Johnson, James P. Johnson,* Thomas (''Fats'') Waller,* and Clarence Williams.* Through the 1920s-60s he was active as a soloist, bandleader, and composer. He staged two large concerts of his music, in 1939 at Carnegie Hall in New York and in 1941 at Town Hall in New York. In the summer of 1944 he played his composition, *Whistlin' Pete—Miniature Syncopated Rhapsody* for piano and orchestra, at Robin Hood Dell outside Philadelphia, Pennsylvania, with the Philadelphia Orchestra. Over his long career he wrote more than a dozen musicals, including *This and That* (1919) and *Happy Days* (both with Alex Rogers). His best-known piano piece, in addition to the rags, was ''Moonlight cocktail'' (originally titled ''Ripple of the Nile''). He was the oldest of the pianists credited with founding the Harlem stride-piano style, along with James P. Johnson and William (''Willie-the-Lion'') Smith,* and represented the transition from ragtime to jazz piano. At the beginning of his career he played only by ear, and although he later learned to read music, his performance emphasized improvisation.

BIBL: ASCAP. Black press, incl. CDef, 18 August 1932, 1 November 1919; NYAge, 17 June 1915, 18 October 1919, 5 August 1944. ChilWW. FeaEJ. JaTiRR. Flet, pp. 159-163. Willie-the-Lion Smith, *Music on My Mind* (New York, 1964).

DISC: TudJ.

ROBERTS, HOWARD. Choral conductor (b. 18 July 1924 in Burlington, New Jersey). His family moved to Cleveland, Ohio, when he was eight years old. He received his musical education in the public schools of Cleveland; at Baldwin-Wallace College in Berea, Ohio; at Western Reserve University in Cleveland; and at the Cleveland Institute of Music (B. Mus., 1950; M. Mus., 1951). His teachers included Mordecai Bauman, Marie Kraft, Markinka Gurewich, and Otto Herz, among others. He began playing trumpet professionally at the age of seventeen with Lionel Hampton* and later played with Lucius ("Lucky") Millinder*; he then was active as a performer, musical director, choral conductor, and composer-arranger. As a tenor soloist he sang in Broadway musicals and toured widely throughout the United States with the Robert Shaw Chorale and the American Concert Choir. His career development was aided by Roland Hayes,* Paul Robeson,* and Robert Shaw. As a director and/or conductor he was associated with such musicals as *Camino Real* (1966), *Trumpets of the Lord* (1969), *The Great White Hope* (1968), *Raisin* (1973), and *Guys and Dolls* (1976 production), among others. He also worked with the Alvin Ailey American Dance Theatre and the Donald McKayle Dance Company. He toured in Europe with James Baldwin's *The Amen Corner* (1965), Gershwin's *Porgy and Bess* (1952-55), *Black New World* (1967), and other productions. His own company, the Howard Roberts Chorale, was formally organized in 1969 but began singing much earlier. He was active in television also as a musical director and/or conductor as well as arranger. His best-known compositions were the ballets *Burst of Fists* (1969, written for McKayle) and *Blood Memories* (1976, written for Ailey), the cantata *Long Remembrance* (1975), and the theater piece *The Sun Do Move* (1977). His teaching career included tenures at North Carolina Central University in Durham (1957-59) and Morgan State University in Baltimore, Maryland (1959-61).

BIBL: Questionnaire. Black press, incl. AmstN, 26 May 1962, 5 January 1974. NYT, 12 May 1974.

ROBESON, PAUL. Concert singer (b. 9 April 1898 in Princeton, New Jersey; d. 23 January 1976 in Philadelphia, Pennsylvania). Although perhaps best known as an actor and civil-rights activist, he was also renowned as a concert singer and is so discussed here. He obtained his musical education in the public schools of Somerville, New Jersey, where he sang in his high-school chorus, and at Rutgers University (B.A., 1919), where he was not admitted to the college glee club because of his race. After graduation he went to New York to study law at Columbia University (L.L.B., 1923) and there first became involved with the theater and musical activities. He began to accept dramatic roles, at first in a Harlem Y.M.C.A. production of *Simon the Cyrenian* and later on Broadway; he sang in Hall Johnson's* choruses; he appeared with Will Marion Cook's* productions in the Harlem community (1923); and he sang in the chorus for the Eubie Blake*/Noble Sissle* musical *Shuffle Along* (1921). In 1925 he made his debut as a bass-baritone in the Greenwich Village Theatre, singing a concert consisting solely of Negro spirituals. It was the first time in history for such a concert, and the beginning of Robeson's long concert career (1925-60). He carried his program of spirituals all over the world, learning to sing the songs in many languages, and he also developed programs featuring the folksongs of other nations. His accompanist for thirty-five years, Lawrence Brown,* frequently sang tenor with Robeson in song duos. Robeson's extensive dramatic activities included appearances in musicals (both stage and film) as well as plays. In 1928 he sang the role of Joe in the London production of the Hammerstein/Kern musical *Show Boat.* He also sang in the Broadway 1932 revival of *Show Boat*, the second filming of *Show Boat* (1936), and the film *Song of Freedom* (1937). He made his recording debut in 1925 and thereafter recorded regularly in the United States and abroad. Beginning in 1948 his political activism began to interfere with concert activities. In a period dominated by the Cold War, his concerts were boycotted or cancelled, and he was denied a passport (1950-58) so that he could not honor his concert engagements abroad. In 1958 he revived his musical activities abroad, but illness forced him into retirement in 1961.

Robeson was one of the most celebrated persons of his time; during the decade of the 1940s he, Roland Hayes,* and Marian Anderson* were counted among the top ten concert artists of the United States. His numerous honors included honorary doctorates from Hamilton College (1940), Morehouse College (1943), and Howard University (1945), an honorary master's degree from Rutgers University (1932), the Spingarn Medal (1945), and innumerable awards from institutions, professional and civic organizations, and governments from all over the world. His best-known recording was the album *Songs of My People*. His best-known performances were associated with his struggle for the human rights and dignity of all peoples —the Negro spirituals, the labor song "Joe Hill," "Old man river" from *Show Boat*, and the cantata *Ballad for Americans* (text by John Latouche: music by Earl Robinson), which was introduced to the public via radio broadcast in 1939.

BIBL: Black press, incl. AmstN, 4 March 1972, 31 December 1976. CBD. CurBiog (March1941; March 1976). Gloster Current, "Paul Robeson" in BPIM

(Fall 1976). *Ebony* (April 1976). *Freedomways* (1971). NYT, 24 January 1976. *Rutgers Targum* [Rutgers University, New Brunswick, New Jersey], 10 April 1973. WWA, 1974-75. WWCA, 1950.

DISC: Kink. RustCED. Turn.

ROBINSON, FAYE. Opera/concert singer (b. 2 November 1943 in Houston, Texas). She obtained her musical education in the public schools of Houston, Texas; at Bennett College in Greensboro, North Carolina (B.S. in education); at Texas Southern University in Houston, where she studied with Ruth Stewart; and at North Texas State University in Denton. She also studied privately with Ellen Faull in New York. After graduating from college she taught in an elementary school in Houston before matriculating at Texas Southern for graduate study, where Ruth Stewart encouraged her to become an opera singer. In 1972 she made her operatic debut in the role of Micaela in Bizet's *Carmen* with the New York City Opera. She sang the roles of Desdemona in Verdi's *Otello* (1974) and Adina in Donizetti's *L'Elisir d'Amore* (1975) in Opera/South* productions of the operas. In 1974 she won first prize at the International Music Competition in Munich, Germany. She was also well known for her performances of the roles of Violetta in Verdi's *La Traviata* and Gilda in his *Rigoletto* and of Constanze in Mozart's *The Abduction from the Seraglio*.

BIBL: WWOpera.

DISC: Turn.

ROBINSON, FLORENCE CRIM. University professor (b. 26 October 1932 in Carbondale, Illinois). She came from a musical family: her father directed church choirs, her mother was a public-school music teacher, and her brother played jazz instruments. She first studied piano with her mother, then began study with a local teacher when she was eight years old; she gave her first full-length recital at the age of fourteen. She obtained her musical education in the public schools of Carbondale and Springfield, Illinois; at Southern Illinois University in Carbondale (B.A., 1950; Ph.D., 1963), where she accompanied musical groups and played percussions in the symphony orchestra; and at the University of Denver in Colorado (M.A., 1956). She also studied at Northwestern University in Evanston, Illinois; the University of Colorado in Boulder; the University of Maryland in College Park; and piano privately with Antonia Brico, among others. Her teaching career included tenures in the public schools of Denver (1953-65); at the University of Colorado (1962-65); at Southern Illinois University (1965-68); at Bishop College in Dallas, Texas (1968-71); and at Clark College in Atlanta, Georgia (1971-), where she became head of the Division of Arts and Humanities in 1976. Beginning in the 1960s she became increasingly involved in writing and producing for the media, particularly radio and television. She was best known for her "Rocky Mountain Television Music Teacher" series in Denver, station KRMA-ETV (1963-65); "Florence Robinson Show" on the PLOUGH radio network in Atlanta, Georgia (1972-74); and her narration in the nationally syndicated radio series "The Many Sides of Black Music" (1974-76), which originated in Chicago, Illinois, and was aired in cities across the nation under sponsorship of the Carnation Company. She also produced an album titled *The Many Sides of Black Music* (1977) and documentary films, including *The Music of Black Composers* for PBS televison (1969) and *In Search of Improvisation* (1980). She toured as a lecturer and workshop consultant and served on panels and committees of professional and civic organizations, including the Denver Symphony Board, Dallas Symphony Board, state Councils for the Humanities, the National Endowment for the Arts, and the National Advisory Committee to the John F. Kennedy Center for the Performing Arts, among others. Her honors included "Woman of the Year" awards from sororities and other groups, an "Outstanding Colorado Citizens" award (1963), an achievement award from the National Association of Negro Musicians* (1973), and the Bronze Jubilee Award (Atlanta, 1980).

BIBL: Questionnaire, WWA. WWAW. *WW in the South and Southwest*.

ROBINSON, RAY CHARLES. See **CHARLES, RAY.**

ROBINSON, "SMOKEY." See **MIRACLES, THE.**

RODRÍGUEZ, SEBASTIAN. Military drummer (b. c1642 in Rio Llanero, Portuguese Guinea, West Africa; d. c1706-26 in El Paso (?), New Mexico). He served as a drummer for Don Pedro Reneros de Posada for five years (1686-1691), at first in Mexico; he went north with Posada in 1686 to settle in the New Mexican colony of Guadalupe del Paso (later El Paso), where Posada became governor. During the years 1691-96, Rodríguez was drummer in the service of Governor Diego de Vargas, and during the years 1696-1703 he was drummer to Vargas's successor, Governor Cubero. During the early 1700s he was also town crier in El Paso. The latest date in which his name is mentioned in the records is 1706. As his name does not appear in the earliest Santa Fe burial book, 1726, presumably he died in the interim or left the area.

BIBL: Angelico Chavez, "DeVargas' Negro Drummer" in *The Black Military Experience in the American West*, edited by John M. Carroll (New York, 1971).

ROGERS, ALEXANDER C. ("ALEX"). Lyricist/Entertainer, theater (b. 1876 in Nashville, Tennessee; d. 14 September 1930 in New York, New York). He began his professional career when he was eighteen, touring with a minstrel troupe. He left the troupe in Philadelphia, Pennsylvania, where he met James Vaughn.* The two men collaborated on writing *The Sultan of Zulu* (c1900), which was bought by George Walker,* partner of Bert Williams.* Later Rogers settled in New York, where he joined the Walker/Williams company. He was a singer-actor in the musicals, including *In Dahomey* (1903), *In Abyssinia* (1906), and *In Bandanna Land* (1908). He was also chief lyricist for these plays, working in collaboration with Jesse Shipp* and others. In 1909 he wrote lyrics for *Mr. Lode of Koal*, with music by J. Rosamond Johnson.* Later he was lyricist for *The Traitor* (1912), music by Will Marion Cook*; *The Old Man's Boy* (1914); and *My Friend from Kentucky* (1913; shortened version known as Darktown Follies), with J. Leubrie Hill.* Thereafter his chief collaborator was Charles ("Luckey") Roberts,* with whom he wrote the Broadway musicals *This and That* (1923), *Go Go* (1923), *Sharlee* (1923), and *My Magnolia* (1926).

BIBL: Black press, incl. CDef, 20 September 1930. Hare.

ROGERS (née **LANE), JAMES ("JIMMY").** Bluesman (b. 3 June 1924 in Ruleville, Mississippi). Self-taught on the guitar, he began playing professionally as a youth. His style development was influenced by his listening to recordings of Roosevelt Sykes,* "Memphis Slim" (Peter Chatman),* Peetie Wheatstraw, and others; by the music he heard on the King Biscuit Time radio shows, KFFA in Helena, Arkansas; and by the bluesmen with whom he played during the 1930s and 1940s, including "Little" Walter Jacobs,* Robert ("Nighthawk") McCoy,* Sonny Boy Williamson, No. 2 (Willie "Rice" Miller),* and Muddy Waters (McKinley Morganfield),* among others. He was active in several places, including St. Louis and Memphis, before settling in Chicago in 1945. He began recording thereafter; he played with the Muddy Waters band for ten or twelve years, then formed his own band during the early 1950s. He left music during the years 1961-69, but returned to an active career which included extensive recording and wide touring. Over the years he played and/or recorded with Jacobs, "Sunnyland Slim" (Andrew Luandrew),* "Howlin' Wolf" (Chester Burnett),* "Tampa Red" (Hudson Whittaker),* "Memphis" Minnie Douglas,* "Sonny Boy Williamson, No. 1" (John Lee Williamson),* and "T-Bone" Theodore Walker.*

BIBL: BWW. *Cadence* (June 1979). LivBl 14 (Autumn 1973).

DISC: Jep. LeSlBR. TudBM.

ROLAND, EDWARD DE. Brass bandsman (b. 1803 in Haiti; d. 1894 in Philadelphia, Pennsylvania). As a child he attended the Quaker School in Philadelphia. He came under the musical influence of Francis Johnson* at an early age, and was a member of the group that accompanied Johnson to England in November 1837 to give concerts. Presumably, Johnson selected his most experienced and talented men to make the landmark tour. Johnson used Roland as the "leader of the String Band," a role Roland continued after Johnson's death in 1844. During the 1860s Roland played violin in the Philadelphia Quartette Club. He also conducted a music studio and published compositions. His first publication was in 1846, "Philadelphia's Assembly's Grand Polka, As Performed by the late Frank Johnson's Band at Marvin's Assembly Rooms." Thereafter he published his own arrangements and compositions.

BIBL: PaHistSoc, Box 1G. Black press, incl. NYAge, 1 November 1890. John W. Cromwell, "Frank Johnson's Military Band" in *Southern Workman* 29 (1900). Gerri Major with Doris Saunders, *Black Society* (Chicago, 1976).

ROLDÁN, AMADEO. Symphony conductor/Concert violinist (b. 12 July 1900 in Paris, France; d. 2 March 1939 in Havana, Cuba). His parents were natives of Cuba. He began violin study when he was five years old at the Conservatory of Music in Madrid, Spain. Later he studied harmony and composition there with Conrado el Campo. He settled in Havana, Cuba, in 1919. There he continued his studies with Pedro Sanjuan, musical director of the Havana Orquesta Filarmónica. He first attracted attention in 1923 for his composition *Fiestas Galantes*, settings of poems by Verlaine. In 1924 he was appointed concertmaster of the Filarmónica, and after Sanjuan's departure, he became conductor of the orchestra (1932-39). Along with Alejandro García Caturla, he was regarded as one of the founders of the modern school of composition in Cuba. His best-known works included *Oberture sobre temas cubanos* (1925); *Tres pequeños poemas* (1926); the ballets *El milagro de Anaquillé* (1929) and *La rebambaramba* (1928); and the chamber works *Rítmicas I-VI*

(1930), *Tres toques* (1931), *Danza negra* for voice and seven instruments (1929), *Motivos de son* for high voice and nine instruments (1930), the string quartet *Poema negro* (1939), and *Curujey* for chorus, two pianos, and two percussions (1931). He used Afro-Cuban elements in his music.

BIBL: Alejo Carpentier, *La Musica en Cuba* (Mexico, D.F., 1972. c1946). Nicholas Slonimsky, *Music of Latin America* (New York, 1972, c1945).

ROLLINS, THEODORE WALTER ("SONNY"). Jazz saxophonist (b. 7 September 1930 in New York, New York). His father played clarinet. He obtained his musical education in the public schools of New York, beginning study of the alto saxophone in high school. In 1947 he began playing professionally (tenor saxophone). During the next decade or so he played and/or recorded with various groups, including Babs Gonzales (née Lee Brown),* Earl ("Bud") Powell,* Theodore ("Fats") Navarro,* James ("J. J.") Johnson,* Art Blakey,* Miles Davis* (intermittently during 1951-54), and the Max Roach*/Clifford Brown* quintet (1956-57), among others. In 1957 he began leading his own groups, which were generally trios without piano in the late 1950s, then later quartets with piano. He was inactive musically during two periods, 1959-61 and 1968-71, during which he studied and rethought his musical ideas and, in the second period, visited India and Japan, studying Eastern philosophies and theories. He recorded extensively and appeared in films, including the documentaries *Sonny Rollins, Musician* (1968) and *Sonny Rollins Live at Laren* (1973). His performances were distinctive for his long, brilliant, unaccompanied solos. His style reflected the influence of Charlie Parker* and Coleman Hawkins*; he exerted wide influence upon his contemporaries in the late 1950s, particularly in regard to improvisation. In the 1970s he was no longer in the forefront of avant-garde musicians; he employed rhythm 'n' blues or jazz/rock elements at will. His best-known compositions were "Alfie's theme" (from the film *Alfie*, 1966, for which he wrote the score) and "The cutting edge." His honors included a Guggenheim fellowship (1972) and many awards from the music industry in the United States and in France.

BIBL: CurBiog (April 1976). FeaEJ. FeaJS. FeaGitJS. MeeJMov. *The Washington Post*, 29 July 1973. WWA. WWBA.

DISC: Jep. ModJ. TudJ.

ROSEMOND, ANDREW FLETCHER. Concert violinist (b. c1897 in New Orleans, Louisiana; d. 17 January 1976 in Gloucester, Virginia). He began violin study as a child. He obtained his musical education at the [William J.] Nickerson* School of Music and in the high-school department of Straight University (diploma, 1915), both in New Orleans, Louisiana. He also studied privately later with Eugene Gruenberg and Timothee Adamowski of the New England Conservatory of Music in Boston, Massachusetts; with Georges Enesco at the Ecole Normale de Musique in Paris, France; with Marcel Darrieux in Paris; and with Wilhelm Mueller in Berlin, Germany. About 1916 or 1917 he went abroad and remained for eight years, studying violin and giving recitals. For a period of three years he toured widely in the Far East, where he conducted dance orchestras for long residencies in hotels of Shanghai, China; Hong Kong; and Manilla, the Philippines. In 1926 he settled in New York, and the next year was appointed head of the strings department at the [David I.] Martin*-Smith School of Music. He returned to Europe in 1928 for further study and to give recitals. His teaching career included tenures at Tuskegee Institute in Alabama (1931-40), where he conducted an orchestra and chamber groups in addition to teaching strings; at Coppin State Teachers College in Baltimore, Maryland (1940-43); and in the public schools of Baltimore (1940-43), where he was an instructor of strings for high schools and organizer-conductor of student orchestras. Beginning in 1941 he also served as conductor of the Baltimore NYA Negro Symphony Orchestra and of the Baltimore City Colored Chorus and Orchestra. In 1943 he went to Washington, D.C., to work with USO groups.

BIBL: Interview with wife, Roberta Carter, by D. Antoinette Handy. Black press, incl. CDef, 4 February 1928, 6 February 1943; NYAge, 20 March 1926, 22 January 1927, 14 June 1941. Layne.

ROSS, DIANA. Rhythm 'n' blues/Popular-music singer (b. 26 March 1944 in Detroit, Michigan). See also **SUPREMES, THE.** She obtained her musical education in the public schools of Detroit, Michigan. During the years 1961-70 she sang in The Supremes, a female vocal trio. Thereafter she performed as a soloist in nightclubs, concert halls, on television programs, and in films, including *Lady Sings the Blues* (1972) and *Mahogany* (1975). She recorded extensively and received many awards from the music industry.

BIBL: CurBiog (March 1973). *Ebony* (February 1970; February 1972). WWA. WWBA.

DISC: TudBM.

RUFFIN, GEORGE LEWIS. Concert singer. See **RIDLEY, FLORIDA RUFFIN.**

RUSH, OTIS. Bluesman (b. 29 April 1934 in Philadelphia, Mississippi). He taught himself to play guitar and harmonica as a child by listening to records, particularly of John Lee Hooker,* Sam "Lightnin'" Hopkins,* and "Muddy Waters" (McKinley Morganfield),* among others. In 1949 he went to Chicago and soon became involved with the blues world. In 1953 he began playing professionally in nightclubs with his own groups. He and Willie Dixon* were among the first of the Chicago bluesmen to play blues in minor tonalities, and during his early career he worked with Dixon in writing songs. By the mid-1950s he had established himself as a major blues figure. He toured widely in the United States, Europe, and Japan, appearing in concert halls, nightclubs, on college campuses, and at the major jazz and blues festivals. He also recorded extensively.

BIBL: BWW. LivBl 28 (July-August 1976). Oliv.
DISC: LeSl. TudBM.

RUSHING, JAMES ANDREW ("JIMMY"). Jazz-blues singer (b. 26 August 1903 in Oklahoma City, Oklahoma; d. 8 June 1972 in New York, New York). He came from a musical family: his father played trumpet, his mother sang, and an uncle, Wesley Manning, played piano. He obtained his musical education in the public schools of Oklahoma City and at Wilberforce University in Xenia, Ohio. In 1924 he went to Los Angeles, California, where he found employment as a singing-pianist in local nightclubs. During the mid-1920s-1950s he sang with various groups, including Walter Page's* Blue Devils (1925, 1928-29), Bennie Moten* (1929-35), and William ("Count") Basie* (1935-48, 1949-50). He made his recording debut in 1929 with Page and thereafter recorded regularly with his own groups and with others, among them, Benny Goodman, Bob Crosby, and Johnny Otis. He toured with his band (1950-52), then as a soloist (1950-70s) in the United States and abroad. He appeared regularly on radio and television shows and in several films, including *Crazy House* (1943), *The Sound of Jazz* (1957), *The Learning Tree* (1969), and *Monterey Jazz* (1973). His best-known performances were "Mister five by five" (also his nickname), "Sent for you yesterday," and "I'm gonna move to the outskirts of town." He won numerous awards from the music industry.

BIBL: BWW. ChilWW. FeaEJ. FeaJS. MeeJMov.
DISC: Jep. Kink. RustJR. TudBM.

RUSSELL, GEORGE ALLAN. Composer/theorist (b. 23 June 1923 in Cincinnati, Ohio). As a child he played drums in a Boy Scout drum and bugle corps. He obtained his musical education at the Wilberforce University High School in Xenia, Ohio (1940-43), and studied privately with Stephan Wolpe (1949). He began to play professionally during his high-school years in local clubs. His teaching career included tenures at the Lenox School of Jazz in Massachusetts (summers of 1959, 1960); Lund University in Oslo, Norway, and Vaskilde Summer School in Denmark (1968, 1971); and the New England Conservatory of Music in Boston, Massachusetts (1969-). During a long illness in the early 1940s he was forced to remain in bed, and he began to give serious attention to arranging. Later his arrangements were used by Benny Carter,* in whose band he played drums, and by Earl Hines.* In 1945 he went to New York, where he developed his Lydian Chromatic concept of tonal organization and published a book on the subject in 1953 (second edition, 1959). Thereafter he taught the concept privately in New York (1953-68) and at the Festival of the Arts in Finland (1966, 1967). In 1960 he formed a sextet, which toured widely in the United States and in Europe, appearing on radio and television programs, at the major jazz festivals, and before "new music" societies. During the years 1964-69 he lived in Scandinavian countries. His honors included Guggenheim fellowships (1969, 1972), grants from the National Endowment for the Arts (1969, 1976), and American Music Conference Award (1976), appointment to national boards and panels of professional and government organizations, and numerous awards from the music industry. His best-known works were the *Othello Ballet Suite* (1967), *Listen to the Silence* (1971), and *Living Time* (1975). His composition "Cubana-Be and Cubana-Bop" (1947 with John Birks ("Dizzy") Gillespie* as co-composer) was the first written for big band that blended jazz and Afro-Cuban elements. His Lydian Chromatic concept was the first theory that attempted to explain Afro-American music, particularly jazz and blues, in terms of its own immanent laws rather than the laws of European music.

BIBL: BPIM (Spring 1974). FeaEJ. FeaJS. FeaGitJS. WWA. WWBA.
DISC: Jep. ModJ. TudJ.

RUSSELL, LUIS. Jazz bandleader (b. 6 August 1902 near Bocas del Toro, Panama; d. 11 December 1963 in New York, New York). His father was a pianist-organist and a music teacher. He studied several instruments as a child, including piano and organ. His first professional experiences were playing for silent movies in local theaters and later in a nightclub. In 1919 he moved to New Orleans, Louisiana. During the 1920s he played with various groups, including Arnold DePass and Albert Nicholas,* and in Chicago with Charles ("Doc") Cooke* (1924) and Joseph ("King") Oliver* (1925-27), and in New York with George Howe (1927). During this period he also was a bandleader—in 1924 when he took over the Nicholas band for a year, and in 1927 when he was appointed leader of the Howe group. This band accompanied Louis Armstrong* in 1929, then became Armstrong's regular accompanying unit and was billed as his orchestra (1935-43). After leaving Armstrong in 1943, with whom he played piano or trombone, Russell organized his own big band. Thereafter he played long residencies in New York and other cities on the East Coast; he also toured. In 1948 he gave up his band, but continued to occasionally lead small groups and to teach music. Over the years his sidemen included Paul Barbarin,* Barney Bigard,* George ("Pops") Foster,* J. C. Higginbotham,* Johnny St. Cyr,* and William ("Dickie") Wells,* among others. His bands were counted among the good, "hot" bands of the period. His wife was bassist Carline Ray.

BIBL: ChilWW. FeaEJ. Pops Foster, *The Autobiography of a New Orleans Jazzman*, as Told to Tom Stoppard (Berkeley, 1971).

DISC: Jep. Kink. RustJR. TudJ.

RUSSELL, SYLVESTER. Music critic (b. 14 March 1860s (?) in Orange, New Jersey; d. 1 October 1930 in Chicago, Illinois). He sang in church choirs as a child. He retained his high voice as an adult and was advertised as a male soprano, but he himself preferred to use the term counter-tenor. He studied with Peter O'Fake* and Harry Brazan of Duff's Opera Company. His first professional experiences were in a minstrel company of Al G. Fields and in the chorus for a concert by Sissieretta Jones* at Madison Square Garden in New York in 1892. During the same year he settled in Providence, Rhode Island, where he sang in a church choir, studied music at Brown University, and used the city as a base for his touring New England as a concert tenor. About 1898 he began to write music articles, sending his material to *The Freeman* of Indianapolis, Indiana, from the East. In 1906 he settled in Chicago, Illinois. Thereafter he contributed to the *Chicago Defender* (c1910-1911) and *The Freeman* (until the 1920s) as a musical/dramatic editor. He was a pioneer among black critics; his columns bristled with genuine critical commentary, which earned him many enemies. More than once he was physically assaulted because of his criticism, but he stoutly defended his position and refused to join the ranks of those who praised black artists no matter how poor their production. In addition to criticism, he kept readers abreast of events and gossip in the theatrical world, wrote an annual review of that world, and wrote obituaries, which were reliable because he knew everyone of importance. It was he who gave the name "the Stroll" to Chicago's State Street between 31st and 35th Streets, when that area was celebrated for its black music-making. In 1907 he published a short-lived theatrical magazine, *Sylvester Russell's Review* (Hazelton, Pennsylvania), which was unsuccessful despite his urgent advertisement in the black press. He was reputed to have a private publication which listed the names of all the colored entertainers who had "passed" for white and had moved into the white world. After *The Freeman* suspended publication, he was active as a free-lance writer. His contemporaries called him "the old master" and "dean of dramatic critics."

BIBL: Black press, incl. CDef, 28 May 1910, 11 October 1930; IndF, 8 June 1907, 25 March 1911, 24 August 1918; NYAge, 27 April 1889, 19 December 1891.

RYDER, GEORGIA ATKINS. College professor (b. 30 January 1924 in Newport News, Virginia). She began piano study at the age of six. She received her musical training in the public schools of Newport News, Virginia, where she played violin in the high-school orchestra and accompanied the choir and concert band; at Hampton Institute in Virginia (B.S., 1944), where she was accompanist, soloist, and student conductor of the college choir; at the University of Michigan at Ann Arbor (M. Mus., 1946), and at New York University (Ph. D. in Mus. Ed., 1970). She began her teaching career in the public schools of Alexandria, Virgina (1945-48); thereafter she taught at Norfolk State University (formerly the Norfolk Division of Virginia State College, then Norfolk State College). In 1969 she became chairman of the music department and in 1979, dean of the School of Arts and Letters. Her career development was influenced by her former teacher and later husband, Noah Ryder,* by Lyman B. Brooks, and Leonard DePaur.* She published articles in professional journals and encyclopedias, including *Notable American Women*. She also was active as a church music director and university choral director.

BIBL: Questionnaire. IntWWM. [Norfolk] *Ledger-Star*, 24 October 1969, p. B-3. *Notable Americans*, 1978-79. WWAW.

RYDER, NOAH FRANCIS. College educator/Composer (b. 10 April 1914 in Nashville, Tennessee; d. 17 April 1964 in Norfolk, Virginia). He came from a musical family: his father, Noah Walker Ryder, sang with the Fisk Jubilee Singers, toured for a period as accompanist with Roland Hayes,* and was a college music teacher. Noah Francis studied piano and violin as a child. He obtained his musical education in the public schools of Cincinnati, Ohio, at the University of Cincinnati (one term), at Hampton Institute in Virginia (B.A., 1935), and at the University of Michigan in Ann Arbor (M. Mus., 1947). He began organizing singing groups among his friends at an early age, with himself as director and accompanist. During his college years he led his own jazz group, sang in the college choir, and organized a male quartet, which later became a professional group, The Deep River Boys.* His teaching career included tenures in the public schools of Goldsboro, North Carolina (1935-37), Palmer Memorial Institute in Sedalia, North Carolina (1937-39), Winston-Salem Teachers College in North Carolina (1939-41), Hampton Institute (1941-44), and Norfolk State College in Virginia (1947-62, formerly the Norfolk Division of Virginia State College). During his service in the United States Armed Forces (1944-47), he directed a Navy band and a choir. At Norfolk College he established a music-degree program in 1960, led the college's various choral groups, and chaired the music department. He also directed a community male chorus, the Norfolk Staters, composed of men who formerly had been members of his college groups. He was important for his contributions to choral literature and his influence upon students, many of whom later became professional singers or teachers. He began to compose and arrange music during his college career, particularly for his groups to perform. In 1946 he won the grand prize in the Navy War Writers' Board Contest for his compositon "Sea Suite for Male Voices." He was best known for his spiritual arrangements and the piano works *Five Sketches for Piano* (1947) and "Nocturne" (1953). His second wife was Georgia Ryder.*

BIBL: ASCAP. Marjorie S. Johnson, "Noah Francis Ryder: Composer and Educator" in BPIM (Spring 1978).

S

SAINT-GEORGES, THE CHEVALIER DE (née **JOSEPH BOULOGNE).** Composer/Concert violinist (b. 25 December 1739 near Basse Terre, Guadeloupe, West Indies; d. 10 June 1799 in Paris, France). His family moved to Santo Domingo (now in the Dominican Republic) when he was an infant. He began music study at the age of five with local teacher Joseph Platon. About 1749 he went to Paris, France, with his natural father, Joseph Jean-Marie Boulogne. As a youth he studied fencing and won wide recognition for his fencing skills. He also received, however, the traditional classical education of the time, which included music. During the 1760s he gave serious attention to his music, studying with Jean-Marie Leclair and François Gossec. In 1769 Gossec became Director of Instrumental Music for a newly established concert series in Paris, the Concert des Amateurs, and he appointed Saint-Georges concertmaster of his ensemble (1769-81). When Gossec left the position in 1773, Saint-Georges became the Director. In 1775 he was invited to become director of the Académie Royal de Musique (later known as the Paris Opéra), but the offer was withdrawn when members of the opera company protested against having a mulatto director. During the 1770s-80s he was active as a concert violinist and composer in addition to performing in orchestral groups. He began appearing as a soloist in performance of his own concertos in 1772 with the Concert des Amateurs ensemble, and he published his first string quartets in 1773. In July 1777 his first opera, *Ernestine*, received a single performance at the Comédie Italienne; his second opera, *La Chasse*, was similarly unsuccessful in October 1778 at the Comédie Italienne, but later operas were better received. In 1777 he was appointed to a position by Mme. Montesson that involved him in theater activities as a production manager (1777-85). He also performed with amateur dramatic groups during these years. Political unrest in France because of the approaching Revolution brought his musical career almost to a standstill until two years prior to his death.

In 1792 he was appointed colonel of an all-black regiment, the Légion Nationale des Américains et du Midi, also known as the Légion des Hommes du Couleur or the Légion Saint-Georges. He was dismissed in 1793 because of personal conflict with his commanding officers, but managed to prove himself innocent of trumped-up charges and resumed command of his troops in 1795. He left the service, however, in late 1795 and went to Santo Domingo, where he fought in the uprisings there against Spain and the slaveholding colonists. He returned to Paris in 1797, where he led the Cercle d'Harmonie until just before his death. He wrote in a variety of musical forms: ten concertos for violin and orchestra; twelve string quartets (1773); two symphonies (1778); six "symphonies concertantes" (1775, 1777, 1782); four sonatas, for flute and harp, keyboard, violin and keyboard, and two violins; twelve arias and duos with orchestra; and more than 115 songs with keyboard accompaniment. His best-known works, in addition to those cited above, were the String Quartet, Op. 1, no. 1 in C; the Symphony, Op. 11, no. 1 in G; and the Symphonie Concertante, Op. 13 in G. He wrote in the French Classical tradition of his time, which included influence from the Mannheim School. His sonata forms were bithematic and generally included full recapitulations. He wrote knowingly for the violin, his own instrument, and expanded the technical demands of that instrument. While his music revealed no indication of his African origin, his career is of historical interest in that he was one of the first black composers to make a notable contribution to music in the European tradition. Moreover, he wrote some excellent music apart from its historical interest.

BIBL: Barry Brook, *La symphonie française dans la second moitié du XVIIIe siècle* (Paris, 1962). Dominique-René de Lerma, "The Chevalier de Saint-

Georges" in BPIM 4 (Spring 1976). De Lerma, "Two Friends Within the Saint-Georges Songs" in BPIM 1 (Fall 1973). Hare.

SAMPSON, EDGAR MELVIN. Jazz arranger/Composer (b. 31 August 1907 in New York, New York; d. 16 January 1973 in Englewood, New Jersey). He studied violin as a child but during his high-school years played alto saxophone; he also led his own group. He began his professional career about 1924, playing violin in a duo in local nightclubs. Thereafter he played with various groups, including Edward ("Duke") Ellington,* Charlie Johnson (1928-30), Fletcher Henderson* (1931-32), and William ("Chick") Webb* (1934-36), among others. He was then active as an arranger until 1949, except for a short period when he was musical director for Ella Fitzgerald* (1939) and Al Sears (1943). He led his own groups during the years 1949-51, played with various groups, then led his own groups again during the 1950s-60s. He first attracted wide attention as a composer-arranger of the swing era, particularly for Chick Webb. He also arranged for Benny Goodman, Theodore ("Teddy") Hill,* Red Norvo (née Kenneth Norville), Artie Shaw, and Theodore ("Teddy") Wilson,* among others. His best-known pieces were "Stompin' at the Savoy," "Don't be that way," "If dreams come true," and "Lullaby in rhythm." His important contribution to the history of black music was as a jazz arranger.

BIBL: ASCAP. ChilWW. FeaEJ. FeaGitJS.

DISC: Kink. RustJR.

SANCHO, IGNATIUS. Composer (b. 1729 near Guinea, West Africa; d. 14 December 1780 in London, England. He was born on a slave ship en route from Guinea to Cartagena, Columbia, South America, where he arrived an orphan, his parents having died on the crossing. The Bishop of Cartagena christened him Ignatius. When he was two years old, his slaveholder took him to England and gave (sold?) him to three maiden sisters who lived in Greenwich. From them he received his last name Sancho. At an early age he came to the attention of John, Second Duke of Montagu and formerly governor of Jamaica. The Duke was interested in the possibilities of developing intellectual skills of blacks and gave Sancho a traditional education in the classics, including music. After the Duke's death, the Duchess of Montagu became his patron. He remained under the protection of the Montagu family until 1773, at which time illness prevented his continuing in his position as a household servant. Thereafter he conducted a grocery shop to earn a living for his large family. During his musical career he published a *Theory of Music* (dedicated to Charlotte Augusta Matilda, later Queen of Württemberg), which no longer is extant. His music publications were: *A Collection of New Songs Composed by an African, Humbly Inscribed to the Honorable Mrs. James Brudenell by Her Most Humble and Obedient Servant* (c1769); *Minuets, Cotillions & Country Dances for the Violin, Mandolin, German-Flute and Harpsichord* (c1767, dedicated to Henry, Duke of Buccleugh); *Twelve Country Dances for the Year 1779. Set for the Harpsichord* (1779, dedicated to the "Right Honourable Miss North"); and *Minuets, &c., &c., for the Violin, Mandolin, German-Flute, and Harpsichord, with obligato French horn parts* (c1770, dedicated to John, Lord Montagu of Boughton). Sancho wrote in the Classical style of his time. His career is of interest primarily for its historical importance, for Sancho was among the first black composers to publish music in the European tradition. His music merits attention, however, on its own: his melodies are tuneful; the texts are chosen from excellent sources, including Shakespeare and David Garrick; and his dances are sprightly.

BIBL: *Letters of the Late Ignatius Sancho, An African* (London, 1782). Hare. Josephine R. B. Wright, "Ignatius Sancho: An African Composer (1729-1780)" in BPIM 7 (Fall 1979). WWAfrLit.

SANDERS, FARRELL ("PHAROAH"). Jazz saxophonist (b. 13 October 1940 in Little Rock, Arkansas). He came from a musical family; his grandfather and mother were music teachers. He obtained his musical education in the public schools of Little Rock, Arkansas, learning to play wind instruments in his high school, and at Oakland Junior College in Oakland, California. He played in his high-school band and with local groups in Oakland. In 1962 he went to New York, where he later played with Rashied Ali,* Don Cherry,* Billy Higgins, and Sun Ra* (Herman ("Sonny") Blount), among others. In 1966 he joined John Coltrane,* and after Coltrane's death in 1967 he played with Alice Coltrane* (1967-69). Thereafter he led his own groups.

BIBL: BMI (June 1971). FeaJS. FeaGitJS.

DISC: Jep. TudJ.

SANTAMARIA, RAMON ("MONGO"). Jazz percussionist (b. 7 April 1922 in Havana, Cuba). He studied violin as a child, then changed over to drums. His early style development was influenced by his grandfather, who was a native of Africa. He began playing professionally at the age of seventeen in local nightclubs of Havana. In 1950 he went to the United States; thereafter he played with various groups, including Perez Prado, Tito Puente, and Cal Tjader. In

1961 he formed his own group. Those who performed with him over the years included Robert (''Bobby'') Capers,* Hubert Laws,* and ''Sonny'' Fortune, among others. He first recorded in 1955 and thereafter recorded extensively. His best-known performances were of ''Watermelon man'' (written by Herbie Hancock*), ''Lady Marmalade,'' and the album *Afro-Indio*. He won recognition as one of the leading congo-drum performers of his time. His style was based on Latin rhythms with roots in the Afro-Cuban tradition.

BIBL: Black Press, incl. PhilaT, 23 July 1974. FeaJS.

DISC: TudJ.

SAUNDERS, THEODORE D. ("RED"). Jazz drummer (b. 2 March 1912 in Memphis, Tennessee; d. 4 March 1981 in Chicago, Illinois). He obtained his musical training in the public schools of Milwaukee, Wisconsin. He settled in Chicago, Illinois, during the early 1930s; thereafter he played with various groups, including Tiny Parham. Beginning in 1937 he led his own groups, including long residencies at the Club DeLisa (1937-58) and the Regal Theatre (1960-67), and occasionally played with others, among them, Louis Armstrong,* Edward (''Duke'') Ellington,* Woodrow (''Woody'') Herman, Arthur (''Art'') Hodes, and Eurreal (''Little Brother'') Montgomery.* He received awards from the music industry and professional and civic organizations.

BIBL: ChiHistSoc. ChilWW. FeaEJ. WWA, 1976-77. WWBA.

DISC: Jep.

SAWYER, JACOB. Composer (b. c1859 in Boston, Massachusetts [?]; fl. late nineteenth century). Little is known of his career except that he was highly regarded as a pianist-composer during his time. He toured with the Hyers Sisters Company as a pianist in 1878 and wrote songs especially for the company. A press notice in January 1884 referred to him as Boston's ''favorite Professor Jacob Sawyer'' when he played on a local concert. Trotter includes one of Sawyer's pieces, ''Welcome to the Era March,'' in the 1878 survey.

BIBL: Black press, incl. NYGlobe, 19 January 1884. Trot, p.2; 22-25 of the music section.

SCHUYLER, PHILIPPA DUKE. Concert pianist (b. 2 August 1932 in New York, New York; d. 9 May 1967 in Danang, South Vietnam). She began piano study at the age of three with local teachers, including Arnetta Jones, and began playing on public concerts when she was four. As a child she also composed piano pieces. She obtained her musical education in Catholic schools of New York and through private study. She began to win prizes for performance at an early age, and for several years in succession won honors in competitions sponsored by the New York Philharmonic Young People's Society. In 1946 she made her debut with the New York Philharmonic and she performed with the Boston Symphony the same year. Thereafter she toured widely throughout the world as a concert pianist, giving solo recitals and appearing with the leading symphony orchestras of the world. Her best-known compositions were *Manhattan Nocturne* (1943) for symphony orchestra, *Rhapsody of Youth* (1948), *Nile Fantasy* for piano and orchestra (1965), and *Fairy Tale Symphony* (1943). She published several books on non-musical subjects and the article ''Music of Modern Africa'' in *Music Journal* (October 1960).

BIBL: ASCAP. Black press, incl. NYAge, 18 July 1936. HNB. NYB, 1941-46. WWCA, 1950.

SCOTT, ARTHUR ("BUD"). Jazz guitarist (b. 11 January 1890 in New Orleans, Louisiana; d. 2 July 1949 in Los Angeles, California). He played guitar and violin as a child. He began playing professionally in the late 1890s with various groups, including John Robichaux,* Freddie Keppard,* and the Billy King* Traveling Show (1913). He was active in New York and other cities on the East Coast, beginning in 1915, in theater orchestras and Clef Club* groups, including that of Will Marion Cook.* During the 1920s he played in Chicago, Illinois, with Jimmie Noone,* Joseph (''King'') Oliver,* Dave Peyton,* Erskine Tate,* and Stanley (''Fess'') Williams,* among others. In 1929 he settled in Los Angeles, California. There he played with Thomas (''Mutt'') Carey and Edward (''Kid'') Ory,* among others. He made his first recordings in 1923 with King Oliver and recorded with most of the pioneer Chicago groups, including Ferdinand (''Jelly Roll'') Morton.* He belonged to the first generation of jazzmen in the New Orleans school, who developed under the influence of Buddy Bolden* and helped to carry the tradition to Chicago and Los Angeles during the 1920s.

BIBL: ChilWW. FeaEJ. Souch. Donald Marquis, *In Search of Buddy Bolden* (Baton Rouge, 1978).

DISC: Kink. RustJR.

SCOTT, CECIL XAVIER. Jazz saxophonist (b. 22 November 1905 in Springfield, Ohio; d. 5 January 1964 in New York). He came from a musical family; his father played violin and his brother Lloyd became a professional jazz drummer. He began playing professionally during his high-school days, at first in a trio that included his brother, and later in Scott's Symphonic Syncopators. From 1924 on his band toured widely from its base in New York, New York, and as well played long residencies in the city's ballrooms and nightclubs. After the band was dissolved in the early 1930s he played with various groups, including Fletcher Henderson,* Theodore ("Teddy") Hill,* Arthur ("Art") Hodes, Earl Howard, Henry ("Chick") Morrison, Oran ("Hot Lips") Page,* and Clarence Williams,* among others. He also led his own groups at intervals, recorded regularly, and was active as a studio musician. He was an important representative of the Harlem jazz-saxophone tradition of the 1920s-30s.

BIBL: ChilWW. FeaEJ. MeeJMov.

DISC: Jep. Kink. RustJR.

SCOTT, HAZEL DOROTHY. Jazz pianist (b. 11 June 1920 in Port of Spain, Trinidad). Her family moved to New York when she was four years old; she began piano study at the age of five. She obtained her musical education in the public schools of New York and at the Juilliard School of Music. Her mother, a pianist-saxophonist, was leader of an orchestra called the American Creolians (also known as Alma Long Scott's All-Girl Band), and Hazel began playing professionally with the band at an early age. She first appeared professionally as a jazz soloist in 1935 with William ("Count") Basie.* In 1936 she conducted her own radio series. Thereafter she established herself as one of the leading pianist-singers in New York nightclubs and attracted national attention, particularly during the 1940s. She toured widely and appeared in musicals and films, including *Tropicana* (1943), *I Dood It* (1943), and *Rhapsody in Blue* (1945), among others. Later she had her own television show. During the 1960s she was musically inactive in the United States; she spent the years 1962-67 in Paris, France, and in Switzerland. After returning to the United States, she reentered the music world as a nightclub entertainer, organizing her Hazel Scott Trio, and recorded regularly. Her repertory included both classical music and jazz.

BIBL: ASCAP. *Encore* (18 August 1975). FeaEJ. Handy. MeeJMov.

DISC: Jep. Kink.

SCOTT, JAMES SYLVESTER. Ragtime pianist-composer (b. 1886 in Neosho, Missouri; d. 30 August 1938 in Kansas City, Kansas). He studied piano as a child. His family moved to Carthage, Missouri, when he was about fifteen, and there he continued his musical training in the public schools and through private study. He began his professional career playing piano and the steam calliope at a local amusement park. Later he worked as a clerk and song-plugger in a music store (1902-1914). During this period he began to publish piano rag pieces. In 1906 he visited Scott Joplin* in St. Louis, Missouri, and it is believed that Joplin may have worked with him. Certainly Joplin helped him to find a publisher—John Stark, the publisher of Joplin's music. In 1914 Scott moved to Kansas City, Kansas, where he conducted a music studio and in 1916 became pit pianist at the Panama Theater. Later he organized a band, which played for local social entertainments as late as the 1930s. During the 1920s he was a pit organist in the Lincoln and Eblon Theaters, but was finally driven from that occupation because of the emergence of the sound film. He was regarded as the leading rag composer of the period after Scott Joplin. His best-known pieces were "Hilarity rag," "The climax rag," "Grace and beauty," and "Ragtime oriole."

BIBL: Blesh. JaTiRR.

SCOTT, ROBERT ("THE ALBEMARLE MINSTREL"). Minstrel entertainer (b. 1803 in Charlottesville, Virginia; d. 26 September 1899 in Charlottesville). He was born into a musical family; his father, Jesse, played violin, his mother played piano, and his brothers James and Thomas played flute and violin. Jesse Scott played for the balls and other social entertainments of the Virginia aristocracy, for political celebrations and public festivals, and at the fashionable resorts. When his sons grew old enough to play instruments, he carried them along with him to help provide music. The Scott family, including the mother, performed when General Lafayette visited Monticello in 1824. After Jesse died, the three sons carried on the musical traditions of the family band. Eventually Thomas settled in France. In later years Robert Scott formed a family ensemble with his three sons.

BIBL: Orra Langhorne, "Robert Scott, the Albemarle Minstrel" in *Southern Workman* 29 (1900).

SCOTT, SHIRLEY. Jazz organist (b. 14 March 1934 in Philadelphia, Pennsylvania). She began piano study at the age of four. In high school she studied trumpet and played in Philadelphia's All-City High School Band. After graduation from high school, she attended the Ornstein School of Music. In 1955 she began to play professionally, beginning in her father's nightclub with her brother's band. The same year she began to play organ and later toured as an organist with the Eddie ("Lockjaw") Davis* Trio (1956-60). She then organized her own group, which toured widely in the United States and in Europe, appeared on television shows, and recorded regularly. Among those who performed with her at one time or another were Joe Chambers,* George Coleman, Roland Alexander, Billy Higgins, Stanley Turrentine,* and Harold Vick. She was notable as one of the few black women jazz-group leaders of her time. She also composed and arranged for her groups. She was married to Turrentine (1960-71).

BIBL: FeaEJ. FeaJS. FeaGitJS. Handy.

DISC: Jep.

SEARS, ALBERT OMEGA ("AL"). Jazz saxophonist (b. 22 February 1910 in Macomb, Illinois). He came from a musical family; his brother Marion also became a professional musician. He began playing professionally with the Tynestra Club Quartet at Buffalo, New York. Thereafter he played with various groups, including Cliff Barnett and Paul Craig in Buffalo, and in New York with Elmer Snowden,* Zack White, and William (''Chick'') Webb,* among others. During the 1920s-30s he also toured with the Eubie Blake*-Noble Sissle* *Shuffle Along* road company and led his own group at intervals. During the 1940s-50s he played with Andy Kirk* (1941-42), Lionel Hampton* (1943), Edward (''Duke'') Ellington* (1944-49), and Johnny Hodges* (1951-52), as well as his own groups (1942-43). After 1952 he was active primarily as a music publisher. His best-known composition was ''Castle Rock.''

BIBL: ChilWW. FeaEJ. MeeJMov.

DISC: Jep. Kink. RustJR.

SEDRIC, EUGENE HALL ("GENE" "HONEY BEAR"). Jazz saxophonist (b. 17 June 1907 in St. Louis, Missouri; d. 3 April 1963 in New York, New York). His father was a ragtime pianist. As a child he played in a band sponsored by the Knights of Pythias. He first played professionally with Charlie Creath* in the early 1920s. Thereafter he played with various groups, including Fate Marable* on riverboats, Dewey Jackson, and Ed Allen, among others. In 1923 he went to New York with a road show, the Black and White Revue. Thereafter he played with Sam Wooding* (1925-31, 1932, including a tour in Europe), Fletcher Henderson* (1934), and Thomas (''Fats'') Waller* (1934-42, as clarinetist-saxophonist). During these years he also played with others when Waller was on tour as a soloist, including Mezz Mezzrow and Don Redman* (1938-39). During the 1940s-50s he led his own groups (1943, 1946-51), toured with Hazel Scott* (1945), and played with Bobby Hackett, Jimmy McPartland, Mezz Mezzrow, and Conrad Janis. He first recorded in 1934 with Waller and thereafter recorded extensively with others and also as Sedric and His Honey Bears.

BIBL: AlHen. ChilWW. FeaEJ. Maurice Waller and Anthony Calabrese, *Fats Waller* (New York, 1977).

DISC: Jep. Kink. RustJR.

SELIKA, MARIE (MRS. SAMPSON WILLIAMS). Concert singer (b. c1849 in Natchez, Mississippi; d. 19 May 1937 in New York, New York). She was taken to Cincinnati, Ohio, as an infant and there she studied music as a child. A wealthy local family became interested in developing her talent and arranged for her to study with professional musicians. About 1873 or 1874 she went to San Francisco, California; there she studied with a Signora G. Bianchi and made her debut as a concert soprano in 1876. She then went to Chicago, where she studied with a Mr. Farini for a year, and in 1878 she began to give recitals in the East. According to the black press, that year she was called upon in Boston, Massachusetts, to fill the place of operatic soprano Etelka Gerster at a concert and made such a favorable impression that later she was engaged to sing the title role in a stage production of Meyerbeer's *L'Africaine* at the Academy of Music in Philadelphia (CleveG, 28 April 1888). In 1882 she went to England to study further and to sing professionally. There her appearances included singing on a command performance for Queen Victoria at St. James Hall in October 1883. This appearance added luster to her growing reputation. Back in the United States minstrel-troupe owners Charles and Gustave Frohman made plans to organize a Colored Opera Troupe for the fall of 1883, with Selika as the leading prima donna. Charles Hicks* was appointed to meet Selika in Paris, France, in the summer of 1883 to discuss the plans. But these ambitious plans failed to materialize. Selika returned to the United States late in 1885 and immediately began to tour extensively with her husband, Sampson Williams, who was advertised as Signor Velosko, the Hawaiian tenor (sometimes, the Hawaiian baritone). She seems to have had difficulty in securing professional management at times during her career. In the mid-1880s she was managed by William Dupree* and James M. Trotter*; in a later decade she managed her own concerts, according to advertisements in the press. She toured again in Europe during the years 1887-92, spending a year of that period in Germany (1891-92), and also toured again in the West Indies.

About 1893 she settled in Cleveland, Ohio, where she conducted a music studio and used the city as a base for her touring. Despite problems of management, she sang all over the nation and was regarded as the leading prima donna of the race during her prime. She acquired the soubriquet ''queen of staccato'' when she sang the ''Staccato Polka'' at her Philadelphia debut in 1878, and it remained with her for the rest of her career. During the late 1890s critics began to compare her unfavorably to younger singers—Flora Batson* and Sissieretta Jones,* for example—and her career began to languish. After the death of her husband about 1911, she retired from the stage. In 1916 she accepted a teaching position at the Martin-Smith* School of Music in New York. In 1919 the black musical establishment in New York gave her a testimonial concert. In later years she taught only privately but was active until the year before her death at the age of eighty-seven.

BIBL: Black press, incl. CleveG, 12 March 1887, 28 April 1888; NYGlobe, 3 March 1883, 26 May 1883; IndF, 10 October 1886, 24 July 1891, 23 December 1916; NYAge, 24 May 1919, 29 May 1937. Hopkins. Scruggs.

SELLERS, JOHN ("BROTHER JOHN"). Bluesman (b. 27 May 1924 in Clarksdale, Mississippi). As a young child he lived in Greenville, Mississippi, where he sang in a local church choir and heard live performances of such blues singers as Gertrude ("Ma") Rainey* and Ida Cox*; at the age of ten he was taken to Chicago. There he became involved in the entertainment world and performed with minstrel shows. Later he entered the field of gospel; he toured with Emma Jackson and Mahalia Jackson.* In 1941 he began singing professionally in nightclubs as a soloist. Thereafter he toured widely in the United States and abroad, beginning in 1957, appearing in concert halls, clubs, and at some of the blues and jazz festivals. In 1962 he toured under the auspices of the United States Government Cultural Exchange Program. Those with whom he recorded included ("Big Bill") William Lee Conley Broonzy.*

BIBL: ASCAP. BWW. FeaEJ. Oliv. Laurraine Goreau, *Just Mahalia, Baby* (Waco, Texas, 1975).

DISC: Jep. Kink.

SENSATIONAL NIGHTINGALES, THE. Gospel group (orig. 1940s in South Carolina [?]). The original group included Julius Cheeks* (lead), Carl Coates (bass), Jo Jo Wallace (tenor, guitarist), Howard Carroll (baritone), and Paul Owens (tenor). During the 1950s-60s "The Gales" were among the leading gospel quartets. They toured widely, appearing generally at churches but also on television programs, in community auditoriums, and in schools. Frequently they joined with other groups, as in 1957 when they toured on the Gospel Train, under management of Gertrude Ward, with seven other groups. During the 1970s they appeared with such gospel figures as Rosetta Tharpe* and the Dixie Hummingbirds.* Their best-known performances included "See how they done my Lord," "Somewhere to lay my head," and "The Bible's right."

BIBL: Heil. LivBl 12 (Spring 1973).

SEYMOUR, FRANCIS V. Brass Bandsman (fl. mid-nineteenth century in Philadelphia, Pennsylvania). He came under the musical influence of Francis Johnson* at an early age and was a member of the group that accompanied Johnson to England in November 1837 to give concerts. Presumably, Johnson selected his most experienced and talented men to make the landmark tour. In addition to playing violin and ophicleide, Seymour occasionally conducted ensembles, both vocal and instrumental. He was among those who remained active with the Johnson String and Brass Bands after Johnson's death in 1844. In 1858 the press noted that Seymour conducted an "excellent" orchestra for a celebration sponsored by Philadelphia's Banneker Institute.

BIBL: PaHistSoc, Boxes IG, 13G. Black press, incl. *The Colored American*, 23 January 1841. *The Public Ledger* [Philadelphia], 25 December 1843. *The Pennsylvania Freeman* [Philadelphia], 19 December 1841.

SHADE, WILL ("SON BRIMMER"). Bluesman (b. 5 February 1898 in Memphis, Tennessee; d. 18 September 1966 in Memphis). He played guitar as a youth, after receiving a little instruction from a local bluesman, "Te-Wee" Blackman, then organized a three-man blues group that played on Beale Street in Memphis. Later he traveled with medicine shows, including that of Dr. Willie Lewis, where he played in a jug band with Gus Cannon,* Jim Jackson, and Walter ("Furry") Lewis.* In 1926 he and his wife, Jennie Clayton Shade, organized a jug band, the Memphis Jug Band; they were inspired by a Louisville (Kentucky) group, the Dixie Jug Blowers, organized by Clifford Haye. The Memphis Jug Band recorded extensively during the years 1927-34 and included Jennie as singer, Charlie Polk, Ben Ramey, and Charlie Williamson, among others. Shade also performed and/or recorded in duos with Charlie Burse and with such groups as the Memphis Sanctified Singers.

BIBL: BWW. CharCB. FeaEJ. Oliv.

DISC: DiGod. LeSl. RustJR.

SHAVERS, CHARLES JAMES ("CHARLIE"). Jazz trumpeter (b. 3 August 1917 in New York, New York; d. 8 July 1971 in New York). His father played trumpet. As a child he played piano and banjo, then later changed to trumpet. His early professional experiences were with local groups in New York. During the 1930s-40s he played with various groups, including Myron ("Tiny") Bradshaw,* Lucius ("Lucky") Millinder,* John Kirby* (1937-44), and Tommy Dorsey (periodically from 1945 on). He first attracted wide attention as an arranger-composer for Kirby. During the 1950s-60s he led his own groups, but also played with such others as Louis Bellson, Terry Gibbs (1950, as co-leader of a sextet), Benny Goodman (1954), Sam Donahue, and JATP (Jazz at the Philharmonic), produced by Norman Granz. His touring took him to Europe several times and worldwide in 1964 and 1965. He recorded regularly. His best-known composition was ''Undecided.'' His style was distinctive for its brilliance.

BIBL: ChilWW. FeaEJ. FeaJS. FeaGitJS. MeeJMov.

DISC: Jep. Kink. RustJR.

SHEPHERD, BERISFORD ("SHEP"). Jazz drummer (b. 19 January 1917 in Spanish Honduras, Central America). His family moved to Philadelphia, Pennsylvania, when he was an infant. He obtained his musical education in the public schools of Philadelphia and at the Mastbaum Conservatory there. His early professional experience was with Jimmy Gorham's local group (1932-41). Thereafter he played with various groups, including Benny Carter* (1941-42), Cabell (''Cab'') Calloway* (1946), Wilbur (''Buck'') Clayton* (1947), and Earl Bostic* (1947-50). During the years 1943-46 he served in the United States Army, where he played trombone and percussions in army bands and gained experience in jazz arranging. During the 1950s-60s he played with William (''Bill'') Doggett (1952-59), Erskine Hawkins,* and Melvin (''Sy'') Oliver,* and in pit orchestras of Off-Broadway musicals, including *Mr. Kicks & Company*, *America Be Seated*, and *Jericho Jim Crow*. He toured with the road company of the Broadway musical *Here's Love* (1963) and in 1964 settled in San Francisco, California. Thereafter he was active as an entertainer in local nightclubs and shows. His best-known composition was ''Honky tonk'' (composed with Doggett).

BIBL: ChilWW. WWBA.

DISC: Jep.

SHEPP, ARCHIE VERNON. Jazz saxophonist (b. 24 May 1934 in Ft. Lauderdale, Florida). His family moved to Philadelphia, Pennsylvania, when he was seven years old, and he obtained his musical education in the public schools of Philadelphia and at Goddard College in Vermont (B.A., 1959), where he majored in dramatic literature. He began playing saxophone when he was about fifteen. An early influence upon his development was a local jazz workshop, where he came into contact with Lee Morgan and Kenny Rogers, and with them began playing jazz. After graduation from college he settled in New York. Thereafter he played with various groups, including Cecil Taylor* (1960, in concerts and in the orchestra for the musical *The Connection*), William (''Bill'') Dixon* (as a co-leader), the New York Contemporary Five with John Tchicai* and Donald (''Don'') Cherry,* John Coltrane,* and Robert (''Bobby'') Hutcherson,* among others. In 1961 he entered into teaching, which included tenures in the public schools of New York (1961-63) and at the University of Massachusetts in Amherst (1972-). During the 1960s he worked primarily with his own groups, touring in Europe several times and in North Africa (1969). He made his recording debut with Cecil Taylor in 1960, but attracted most attention for his recordings made with, or under the influence of, Coltrane during the mid-1960s. For a period he worked with Cal Massey; he toured abroad with him in 1969 and wrote a musical, *Lady Day: A Musical Tragedy*, in 1972. Those who played in Shepp's groups at one time or another included Dave Burrell, Clifford Jarvis, Grachan Moncur, and Herman Wright, among others. He was a leader among the avant-garde jazzmen of the 1960s. During the 1970s, however, he seemed to reach back to the roots of black music, drawing upon gospel, traditional jazz, other black folksong idioms, and African elements.

BIBL: FeaJS. FeaGitJS. WWA. WWBA.

DISC: ModJ. TudJ.

SHEPPARD, ELLA. See **FISK JUBILEE SINGERS, THE.**

SHINES, JOHN NED (JOHNNY). Bluesman (b. 26 April 1915 in Frayser, Tennessee). His parents moved to nearby Memphis, Tennessee, when he was six years old. As a child he picked up basic guitar techniques from his mother and an uncle, both of whom played religious music, but did not seriously study the instrument until he was seventeen. About that time he came into contact with ''Howlin' Wolf'' (Chester Burnett),* who exerted strong influence upon the development of his style. During the early 1930s he went to Memphis, where he became active in music, at first as director of a church choir, then eventually as a blues performer. In 1933 he went to Helena, Arkansas, where he formed a team with Robert Johnson*; the two bluesmen toured widely although they were together less than two years. Shines returned to Memphis in 1937 and worked with local bluesmen, including David (''Honeyboy'') Edwards,* Walter Horton, Roosevelt Sykes,* and ''Howlin' Wolf.'' In 1941 he settled in Chicago; in 1946 he made his first recordings. Over the next few decades he toured widely in the United States, Europe, and Japan, appearing in concert halls, clubs, on college campuses, and at the major jazz and blues festivals. He performed and/or recorded with his own groups, as well as with others. In 1969 he settled in Holt, Alabama.

BIBL: BWW. *Cadence* 3 (February 1978). LivBl 22, 23 (July-August 1975; September-October 1973). Robert Neff and Anthony Connor, *Blues* (Boston, 1975). Oliv.

DISC: LeSl. TudBM.

SHIPP, JESSE A. Librettist/Vaudeville entertainer (b. c1869 in Cincinnati, Ohio; d. 1 May 1934 in New York). In his early career he toured with a singing group, the Beethoven Quartet. Thereafter he was active in show music, touring with Draper's "Uncle Tom's Cabin" company; the Eureka Minstrels; Primrose and West's minstrels, "Forty Whites and Thirty Blacks"; John Isham's "Octoroons" company, which also included at the time the Hyers sisters,* Fred Piper, and Hattie* and Tom McIntosh*; and the Robert Cole*/Billy Johnson* show, "A Trip to Coontown." About 1898 or 1899 he became associated with the George Walker*/Bert Williams* company and remained with it until it disbanded. He wrote books for and contributed lyrics to *The Sons of Ham* (1900), *In Dahomey* (1902), *In Abyssinia* (1905), *In Bandanna Land* (1907), and *Mr. Lode of Koal* (1909); he also toured with these productions. In 1917 he retired from the stage but returned to perform in *The Green Pastures* (1930). His daughter-in-law was Olivia Porter Shipp.*

BIBL: Black press, incl. CDef, 5 May 1934; NYAge, 12 May 1934. Flet, 231-238. Hare.

SHIRLEY, (née WALBRIDGE) DONALD ("DON"). Jazz/concert pianist (b. 29 January 1927 in Kingston, Jamaica, West Indies). He began piano study at the age of three with his mother. He obtained his musical education at the Leningrad Conservatory in the Soviet Union, where he studied with Mittolovski. He also attended Catholic University in Washington, D.C., and Harvard University in Cambridge, Massachusetts, earning doctoral degrees in both psychology and liturgical arts. He studied music further with Conrad Bernier and Thaddeus Jones.* He first attracted wide attention in 1945 when he played with the Boston Pops Orchestra, conducted by Dean Dixon.* He began touring as a concert pianist in the mid-1950s, giving solo recitals and appearing with symphony orchestras in the United States and in Europe. He made his debut at Carnegie Hall in New York in March 1968. Although trained to be a concert pianist, he eventually entered the field of jazz or, rather, he included jazz as an essential part of his repertory. About 1960 he organized the Don Shirley Trio—composed of a cellist, string bassist, and himself at the organ—which recorded a number of albums. He also won recognition as a composer.

BIBL: FeaEJ. ContK (September 1977).

DISC: Jep.

SHIRLEY, GEORGE IRVING. Concert/opera singer (b. 18 April 1934 in Indianapolis, Indiana). His family moved to Detroit, Michigan, when he was six years old, and it was there that he first studied music. In his youth he gave vocal recitals at neighborhood churches and played baritone horn in a community band. About 1950 he decided to enter music as a career and majored in music education at Wayne State University in Detroit (B.S., 1955). He studied further with Amos Ebersole and Edward Boatner,* and later with Themy S. Georgi and Cornelius Reid, and pursued graduate studies at Wayne. During his service in the United States Armed Forces (1956-59) he sang operatic arias for servicemen, and their encouragement caused him to consider a career in opera. He made his operatic debut as a tenor with the Turnau Opera Players in 1959, singing the role of Eisenstein in Strauss's *Die Fledermaus* at Woodstock, New York. In 1960 he made his European debut singing Rodolfo in Puccini's *La Bohème* at the Teatro Nuovo in Milan, Italy, and the Teatro alla Pergola in Florence, Italy. In 1961 he won first place in the Metropolitan Auditions of the Air and made his television debut on "The Telephone Hour." During the 1960s-70s he toured widely, singing with leading opera companies of the United States, Europe, and South America, and giving solo recitals. He made his Metropolitan Opera debut in 1961 and remained with the company many years (1961-73). He sang at the major festivals, including the Festival of Two Worlds at Spoleto, Italy, and the Glyndebourne Festival in Scotland, where he sang the role of Tamino in Mozart's *Magic Flute* (1966). Over the years he sang in a number of premieres, including title roles in Henze's *The Stag King* (1965) and the American premiere of Cavalli's *L'Egisto* (1975), the role of Romilayu in Kirchner's *Lily* (1977), and roles in the stage-concert premieres of Stravinsky's *Daphne* (1965) and Rameau's *Les Indes Galantes* (1961). His best-known performances, in addition to those cited, were Macduff in Verdi's *Macbeth*, Pelleas in Debussy's *Pelleas and Melisande*, Pinkerton in Puccini's *Madame Butterfly*, Alfredo in Verdi's *La Traviata*, Don Ottavio in Mozart's *Don Giovanni*, and Loge in Wagner's *Das Rheingold*, among others. He also won wide recognition for his performances in Stravinsky's *Oedipus Rex and Persephone*, Haydn's *Orlando Paladino*, Mahler's *Das Lied von der Erde*, Beethoven's Mass in C, and the Mozart and

Verdi Requiem Masses. He began recording in 1962 and thereafter regularly recorded operas, oratorios,, masses, and similar works. His honors included awards from professional organizations, appointments as artist-in-residence in American universities, and an honorary doctorate from Wilberforce University (1967).

BIBL: *Ebony* (January 1966). Ewen. *Opera News* (December 1976). WWA. WWBA. WWOpera.

DISC: Turn.

SHOOK, BEN. Dance bandleader (b. c1876 in Nashville, Tennessee; d. 19?? in Detroit, Michigan [?]). His family moved to Cleveland, Ohio, when he was an infant, and it was there that he first studied music. Later he attended Fisk University in Nashville, Tennessee (1894-99), where he concentrated on the violin. He left Fisk before graduating because he was called to Detroit, Michigan, in the summer of 1899 to take over the leadership of Theodore Finney's* dance orchestra. Eventually he left the field of music, but must have returned during the late 1920s, for the black press stated that he was "back in the musical world" (see CDef below).

BIBL: Black press, incl. CDef, 14 May 1927; CleveG, 11 August 1894, 13 May 1899, 3 June 1899, 6 April 1901.

SHORT, ROBERT WALTRIP ("BOBBY"). Entertainer (b. 15 September 1926 in Danville, Illinois). Mostly self-taught, he learned to play piano as a child and began playing professionally for local social entertainments at an early age. After graduation from high school he settled in New York, New York, where he established himself as a sophisticated nightclub pianist-singer, particularly in New York, Los Angeles, California, and Hollywood, California. During the 1950s he played long residencies in Paris, France, and in London, England. Through the 1960s-80s he toured widely at home and abroad, appeared regularly on television, and played in orchestras for Broadway musicals. In 1971 he published his autobiography, *Black & White Baby*.

BIBL: FeaEJ. FeaGitJS. WWA. WWBA.

DISC: Jep.

SHORTER, WAYNE. Jazz saxophonist (b. 25 August 1933 in Newark, New Jersey). He obtained his musical education at New York University (B.A., 1955) and played with groups during his service in the United States Armed Forces (1956-58). His first significant professional experience was with Horace Silver* and later Maynard Ferguson. Thereafter he played with various groups, including Art Blakey* (1959-63), Miles Davis* (1964-70), and Weather Report (1971-present; co-founder with Josef ["Joe"] Zawinul). He attracted wide attention as a tenor saxophonist with Blakey, and even more when he played soprano saxophone with Davis. But it was as a tenor saxman that he exerted wide influence upon jazz in the 1970s; his style incorporated Latin-American idioms and modal elements and reflected the influence of John Coltrane* as well as Davis. He composed a large number of pieces and recorded extensively under his own name, with others, and with Weather Report. His best-known albums were *Super Nova* and *Odyssey of Iska*.

BIBL: FeaEJ. FeaJS. FeaGitJS.

DISC: Jep. ModJ. TudJ.

SILAS GREEN FROM NEW ORLEANS. Tent show (org. c1890s). ("Professor") Eph Williams was the owner of the tent show in the 1890s; at that time he was reputed to be the only Negro owner of a circus in the United States. After his death the show foundered for a while, then became the property of Charles Collier in 1921, who reorganized it. During the 1930s the touring show included sixty-five persons and traveled with its own special train equipped with every modern convenience. Sherman H. Dudley, Jr.,* became stage manager in 1936. In 1940 Tim Ousley was producer; in 1943 W. P. Jones bought out his partners and became sole owner. Like the similar Rabbit Foot Minstrels,* Silas Green toured primarily in the South; those associated with the show over the years included Princess White, Gertrude ("Ma") Rainey,* Ida Cox,* and ("Jazzlips") Richardson. Silas Green was active through the 1950s.

BIBL: BWW. Black press, incl. CDef, 6 April 1932, 22 August 1936, 12 March 1955; IndF, 10 July 1897.

SILVER, HORACE WARD MARTIN TAVARES. Jazz pianist (b. 2 September 1928 in Norwalk, Connecticut). He began piano study at the age of twelve and played saxophone in high school. He began playing professionally with local groups at an early age. About 1949 he moved to Hartford, Connecticut, where he played in nightclubs and later with Stan Getz (1950-51). Thereafter he settled in New York and played with various groups, including Art Blakey,* Miles Davis,* Coleman Hawkins,* Oscar Pettiford,* and Lester Young,* among others. In 1955 he organized the Horace Silver Quintet, and the same year established Ecaroh Music, Inc. He toured widely with his group in the United States and abroad, appearing in nightclubs and concert halls and at major jazz festivals. He also appeared regularly on televison. In 1974 he settled in Los Angeles, California; the next year he organized a big band. He composed prolifically for his groups and recorded extensively, both with others and with his groups. Among his best-known albums were *Finger Poppin'*, *Horace Silver and the Jazz Messengers* (which included "Doodlin' " and "The preacher"), *Silver 'n' Brass*, and *Silver 'n' Voices*. He received many awards from the music industry and civic associations. His early style reflected the influence of Earl ("Bud") Powell*; later his music combined elements of bebop with traditional jazz.

BIBL: ASCAP. ContK (September 1979). FeaEJ. FeaJS. FeaGitJS.

DISC: Jep. ModJ. TudJ.

SIMEON, OMER VICTOR. Jazz clarinetist (b. 21 July 1902 in New Orleans, Louisiana; d. 17 September 1959 in New York, New York). His family moved to Chicago, Illinois, when he was fourteen; there he studied with Lorenzo Tio, Jr.,* who was living there at that time. In 1920 he began playing professionally, at first in his brother's group, Al Simeon's Hot Six. Thereafter he played with various groups, including Charlie Elgar (intermittently during the years 1923-27), Ferdinand ("Jelly Roll") Morton* (1926), Joseph ("King") Oliver* (1927), Erskine Tate* (1928-30), and Earl Hines* (1931-37) among others. During the 1920s-30s he also played for short periods with Horace Henderson,* Coleman Hawkins,* and Luis Russell.* He first recorded in 1926 and thereafter recorded extensively with various groups. During the 1940s-50s he played with Walter ("Rosetta") Fuller* (1940, 1941-42), James ("Jimmie") Lunceford* (1942-50; he remained with the band after Lunceford's death in 1947), and Wilbur de Paris* (1951-58). His touring took him to Europe in various bands and to Africa in 1957 with Wilbur de Paris. He first attracted wide attention as clarinetist in Morton's group; he represents the best jazz-clarinet tradition in the Chicago school of the 1920s-30s.

BIBL: AlHen. ChilWW. DanceWEH. Souch.

DISC: Jep. Kink. RustJR. TudJ.

SIMMONS, CALVIN. Symphony orchestra conductor (b. April 1950 in San Francisco, California). He came from a musical family; his mother was a church choir director. He began piano study at the age of six with his mother. Later he studied piano with Tillie Amner and William Corbett-Jones and conducting with Ernst Bacon. At the age of nine he joined the San Francisco Opera Boys Chorus, which was directed by Bacon's sister, Madi Bacon. Within a few years he had developed sufficient skills to be able to conduct the Opera Boys Chorus, and at seventeen he became a rehearsal pianist. He obtained his musical education at the Cincinnati College Conservatory of Music, where he studied with Max Rudolf (at that time director of the Cincinnati Conservatory), and at the Curtis Institute of Music in Philadelphia, Pennsylvania, where he worked with Rudolf (who transferred there in 1969) and Rudolf Serkin. He made his conducting debut during the 1975-76 season as assistant conductor of the Los Angeles Symphony. In 1975 he made his European debut at the Glyndebourne Festival Opera in London, England, and thereafter he conducted leading symphony orchestras in the United States and abroad. In 1978 he made his operatic debut with the San Francisco Opera, conducting Puccini's *La Bohème*, and with the Metropolitan Opera, conducting Humperdinck's *Hansel and Gretel*. In 1979 he was appointed musical director of the Oakland Symphony Orchestra; he was only twenty-eight years old. He also served as the associate musical director of the Western Opera Company in San Francisco, California.

BIBL: *High Fidelity/Musical America* (March 1979). *Opera News* (December 1978).

SIMOND, IKE ("OLD SLACK"). Minstrel (b. 1847 in Mount Vernon, Indiana; d. c1892-1905). Little is known of his career; he began traveling with professional troupes at fifteen and toured widely throughout the nation with minstrel groups and circuses as a comedian and banjoist. He earned a secure place in the history of black music for his valuable booklet *Old Slack's Reminiscence and Pocket History of the Colored Profession From 1865 to 1891*, which was one of the first primary sources, along with James Monroe Trotter's* book, and which records information found in no other sources about blacks in the theatrical profession during the post-Civil War period. He did not tour with the big, celebrated companies, but he apparently came into contact with most of the thousand or more minstrels active during his time, and he gave their names and their troupe affiliations in his book. Among the troupes with which he toured were White and Mahoney's Minstrels out of Memphis, Billy Anderson's Minstrels, Robinson's Circus, and Gales and Hagger's Minstrels. For a short time in 1882 he organized his own group to play at the Chautauqua Assembly at Lake Wood, New York. The evidence suggests that Simond died between the years 1892 and 1905. In the latter year, *The Freeman* of Indianapolis, Indiana, published his book in installments titled "Reminiscences of the Colored Profession," but without identifying the author. It is unlikely that Simond would have allowed the newspaper to purloin his material without protest had he been alive.

BIBL: *Old Slack's Reminiscence and Pocket History* . . . (Chicago, n.d. [1892]; reprt. Bowling Green, Ohio, 1974, with preface and introduction by Francis Lee Utley and Robert C. Toll). Black press, incl. IndF, February-March 1905.

SIMONE, NINA (née **EUNICE WAYMON**). Jazz singer (b. 21 February 1933 in Tryon, North Carolina). She played piano at the age of four; at seven she began piano study with a local teacher and began playing organ. She obtained her musical education in the public schools of Asheville, North Carolina; at the Curtis Institute of Music in Philadelphia, Pennsylvania (1950-53), where she studied with Vladimir Sokoloff; and at the Juilliard School of Music in New York (1974), where she studied with Carl Friedberg. Her family moved to Philadelphia when she was seventeen, and while attending classes she worked as an accompanist at the Arlene Smith Studio and conducted a music studio. During the summer of 1954 she sang in a nightclub in Atlantic City, New Jersey, and was encouraged by her success. She changed her name to prevent the parents of her music pupils in Philadelphia from learning of her activity and remained at the club for the rest of the season. Later she moved permanently into jazz and established herself as an entertainer within a few years. She attracted wide attention in 1959 with her recording of "I loves you, Porgy" from Gershwin's *Porgy and Bess*. During the 1960s-early 1970s she toured widely in the United States and in Europe, appearing in concert halls, nightclubs, and at major jazz festivals; she recorded extensively and appeared regularly on television programs. She expanded her repertory to include gospel, popular, African songs, and contemporary forms, using songs written by her brother, Sam Waymon, her husband, Andrew Stroud, and herself. In 1974 she withdrew from music for a period of over three years and travelled widely in other parts of the world, using Europe as her base. Beginning in 1977 she returned to singing occasionally and recorded an album, *Baltimore*. In December 1978 she launched the beginning of her resumed career with a concert at Avery Fisher Hall in New York. Her best-known albums included *Silk and Soul*, *Emergency Ward*, and *It Is Finished*. Called the "high priestess of soul," she received numerous awards from the music industry.

BIBL: ASCAP. Black press, incl. AmstN, 23 December 1978. MeeJMov. *Soul* (October 1973). StamPRS. WWA. WWBA.

DISC: Jep. TudBM.

SIMPSON, EUGENE THAMON. College professor (b. 10 April 1932 in North Wilkesboro, North Carolina). He obtained his musical education at Howard University in Washington, D.C. (B. Mus., 1951); Yale University in New Haven, Connecticut (B. Mus., 1953, M. Mus., 1954); and Columbia University Teachers College in New York (D. Ed., 1968). His teaching career included tenures at Fort Valley [Georgia] State College (1955), in the public schools of New York (1955-56, 1959-68), at Virginia State College in Petersburg (1968-70), Bowie [Maryland] State College (1970-74), and Glassboro [New Jersey] State College (1975-). He was also active as a choral conductor in churches of New Haven (1952-54) and New York (1959-68), and in the New York public schools. During his service in the United States Armed Forces (1956-58) he was an assistant choral director with the Second U.S. Army at Fort Meade, and he toured with his quartet, The Melodaires, in the Army World Tour Show (1958-59). He was also active during the years 1960-68 as a voice teacher-coach, radio, television, and commercial singer in New York. His honors included awards from professional and civic organizations, appointments to national boards of professional societies, and fellowships from councils and professional organizations. During the 1970s he toured as a lecturer, choral-clinic conductor, workshop consultant, and with his college choruses. His wife, Ingres Hill Simpson, was a music teacher.

BIBL: Questionnaire. WWBA.

SIMPSON, FREDERICK W. ("FRED"). Military bandmaster (b. December 1872; d. 1940s [?] in New York, New York). He began his professional career as a trombonist with Richards and Pringle's Georgia Minstrels* in the special act "The Four Brass Men." He was also a bandleader during his tenure with the Georgia Minstrels. In 1917 he joined the Fifteenth Regiment of the U.S. Army, then stationed in New York, as bandmaster with the rank of lieutenant. After World War I members of his band formed a community band, which became affiliated with the Monarch Lodge Elks in 1921 and called itself the Monarch Symphonic Band. In 1932 Simpson began the tradition of sponsoring an annual concert series with his band. Concerts were played each month during the season at which leading black and white musicians were the featured artists.

BIBL: Black press, incl. CDef, 20 December 1924; IndF, 23 December 1911; NYAge, 6 February 1937, 28 February 1939, 20 November 1943.

SIMPSON, VALERIE. Songwriter/Rhythm 'n' blues singer (b. 16 August 1946 in New York, New York). See **ASHFORD, NICKOLAS.**

SINGLETON, ARTHUR JAMES ("ZUTTY"). Jazz drummer (b. 14 May 1898 in Bunkie, Louisiana; d. 14

July 1975 in New York, New York). He moved to New Orleans, Louisiana, as a youth and began playing professionally about 1915 with such groups as Steve Lewis and John Robichaux.* He served in the United States Armed Forces during World War I, then returned to New Orleans, where he played with various groups, including Oscar ("Papa") Celestin,* Louis ("Big Eye") Nelson,* Luis Russell,* Fate Marable* (1921-23, on riverboats), Robichaux, and Charlie Creath* (in St. Louis, Missouri), among others. In 1925 he went to Chicago, Illinois; thereafter he played with Charles ("Doc") Cooke,* Dave Peyton,* Clarence Jones,* Jimmie Noone,* Earl Hines,* Louis Armstrong,* and others. He toured with Carroll Dickerson* (1927-29) and left the band in New York, where he settled. During the 1930s-early 40s he played with various groups, including Thomas ("Fats") Waller,* James ("Bubber") Miley,* Otto Hardwicke, and others; he also led his own groups and played with touring show bands. He resettled in Chicago during the years c1933-37, then returned to New York, where he worked with Mezz Mezzrow (née Milton Mesirow) and Sidney Bechet* and led his own groups in nightclubs. During the years 1943-51 he lived in Los Angeles, California, where he led groups and became active in television and films, including *Stormy Weather* (1943), *Love That Brute* (1950), *New Orleans* (1947), and others. In 1951 he went to Paris, France, to play an engagement and remained to tour the continent and North Africa (1951-53). After returning to the United States he settled again in New York. Thereafter he led his own groups in nightclubs and occasionally toured with others. He received several awards from the music industry. In 1975 the ESC Recording Corporation of Richmond, Virginia, produced an album in honor of his seventy-fifth birthday, under the direction of Eill Singleton, Johnson McRhee, and others. Titled *Drumface*, the album represented rare performances (some never before released) and conversations of Singleton with others on various topics. He best represents the Chicago jazz tradition of the 1920s-30s. Unlike some of his contemporaries, however, he moved successfully into the swing and bebop periods, recording with Charlie Parker* and John Birks ("Dizzy") Gillespie.* He was credited with having been one of the first drummers to use wire brushes in addition to drumsticks.

BIBL: ChilWW. FeaEJ. FeaJS. FeaGitJS. MeeJMov. NYT, 15 July 1975. Souc.

DISC: Jep. Kink. RustJR.

SIRONE (NORRIS JONES). Jazz bassist (b. 28 September 1940 in Atlanta, Georgia). As a child he studied trombone, bass, and theory with local teachers. Early in his career he played with various groups, including Sam Cooke,* Jerry Butler,* and The Group. In 1965 he settled in New York and thereafter played with Albert Ayler,* Marion Brown,* Bill Dixon,* Don Cherry,* Archie Shepp,* and Sun Ra* (née Herman Blount), among others. In 1970 he joined The Revolutionary Ensemble, composed of Leroy Jenkins,* Jerome Cooper,* and himself.

BIBL: FeaGitJS.

SISSLE, NOBLE. Bandleader (b. 10 July 1889 in Indianapolis, Indiana; d. 17 December 1975 in Tampa, Florida). He sang in his father's church choir as a child. He obtained his musical education in the public schools of Indianapolis, Indiana, and Cleveland, Ohio, where his family lived during the years 1909-1913. He studied further at DePauw University in Greencastle, Indiana (1913), and Butler University in Indianapolis (1914-15). He began singing professionally in 1908, touring with the Edward Thomas Male Quartet on the Chautauqua circuit in the Midwest for a period. After graduation from high school in 1911, he toured with Hahn's Jubilee Singers, managed by Thomas. During this period he first met James Reese Europe* and later became Europe's protégé. In 1915 he organized his own group in Indianapolis; it was short-lived, however, and during the same year he sang with Joe Porter's Serenaders and Bob Young in Baltimore, Maryland. There he met Eubie Blake*; the two men formed a songwriter team (with Sissle as lyricist) and won success with their first publication, "It's all your fault," which was introduced at a Baltimore theater by torch-singer Sophie Tucker. In 1916 Sissle went to New York to join Europe's society dance orchestra; in 1917 he joined Europe's 369th Infantry Regimental Band as the drum major and went overseas with the band. After the war, Sissle went on tour with the Europe band, but the tour was cut off by Europe's murder in May 1919.

During the years 1919-20 Sissle and Blake toured as an act on the vaudeville circuit. A chance meeting in Philadelphia, Pennsylvania, in the summer of 1920 with the vaudeville comedy team of Flournoy Miller* and Aubrey Lyles* led to a collaboration in the production of *Shuffle Along* on Broadway in 1921. After tryout performances in Trenton and other cities in New Jersey, Pottstown, Pennsylvania, and Washington, D.C., the show opened at Cort's 63rd Street Music Hall on 23 May and ran for eighteen months. Then touring companies took the show on the road for two more years; at one time there were three such companies on tour. The continued Sissle and Blake collaboration produced more musicals—*Elsie* (1923), *Chocolate Dandies* (1924), songs for Charles B. Cochran's *Revue of 1926* (in London), and *Shuffle Along of 1933*. In 1925 Sissle and Blake toured again on the vaudeville circuit; in 1926 they performed in English and French theaters. They then dissolved the partnership, and Sissle performed as a soloist in Europe. The next year he formed an orchestra which toured in Europe (1928-31), then he returned to the United States and settled in New York. During the years 1933-mid-1950s he led his own Noble Sissle Orchestra and played long residencies at the Billy Rose nightclub. During the World War II period, he toured with a USO Camp Show that staged *Shuffle Along* for servicemen in Europe (1945-46). During the 1940s he wrote columns for the *New York Age* and for the *Amsterdam News*. In 1952 he was a disc jockey on radio station WMGM in addition to leading his orchestra. Occasionally he and Blake collaborated to write songs or perform together. He was active with many professional organizations throughout his career; he was a founder of the Negro Actor's Guild in 1937 and its first president. He received many awards from the music and theater industries and from civic and professional organizations. The best-known Sissle/Blake songs were "I'm just wild about Harry," "Love will find a way," and "Boogie-woogie beguine."

BIBL: ASCAP. Rudi Blesh, *Combo: USA* (Philadelphia, 1971). Robert Kimball and William Bolcom, *Reminiscing with Sissle and Blake* (New York, 1973). MeeJMov. NYT, 18 December 1975. WWCA, 1950.

DISC: Kink. RustJR.

SMART SET, THE. Touring vaudeville/musical comedy company. More than one company used this name. The original Smart Set was organized in 1902 by Billy McClain* and Ernest Hogan* with white producer Gus Hill. McClain and Hogan wrote the first show, *Southern Enchantment*, staged by the company, which featured them and their wives, among others. After Hogan left the company, Tom McIntosh* became the leading performer; and after his death in 1904, Sherman H. Dudley* took the leading role. This company apparently lasted about six or eight years. About 1908 Salem Tutt Whitney* and his brother, J. Homer Tutt, organized a company called The Smarter Set, which was one of the longest-lived of the black touring vaudeville/musical show companies (1908-23). After a few years the black press began to refer to this company as The Smart Set. During the 1920s there was a company called Al Well's Smart Set Show, and occasionally the press referred to a Smart Set company in later decades.

BIBL: Black press. BWW.

SMITH, ADA BEATRICE ("BRICKTOP"). Popular-music singer (b. 14 August 1894 in Alderson, West Virginia). She began singing in nightclubs in New York at the age of sixteen. In 1916 she sang in Chicago, Illinois, as a member of The Panama Girls, along with Cora Greene and Florence Mills.* In 1924 she went to Paris, France, to sing in a Montmartre cafe, but soon began operating her own club—called Chez Bricktop and located on the Rue Pigalle (1926-39). Later she owned clubs in Mexico City, Mexico, and in Rome, Italy, on the Via Veneto (1951-64). The outbreak of World War II brought her back to the United States, but she later returned to Europe. Her clubs attracted the international smart set; Cole Porter wrote a song for her, "Miss Otis regrets, she's unable to lunch today." She retired from cafe society in her seventies, but came out again in 1973. She made a film, *Honeybaby, Honeybaby* (1973) and returned to singing in New York nightclubs.

BIBL: Black press, incl. CDef, 1 March 1916; AmstN, 24 July 1976.

SMITH, ALBERT ("AL"). Blues record producer (b. 23 November 1923 in Bolivar County, Mississippi; d. 7 February 1974 in Chicago, Illinois). He was active in Chicago, Illinois, beginning in the 1950s, as a blues bandleader and record producer. He worked with Vee Jay Records,* BluesWay, and Blues on Blues, among other companies. The bluesmen for whom he was producer or manager included John Lee Hooker,* James Mathis ("Jimmy") Reed,* William ("Lefty") Bates, and ("Snooky") Pyror, among others. He was also a prolific writer of blues.

BIBL: "The Jimmy Reed Story" in LivBl 21 (May-June 1975). LivBl 16 (Spring 1974).

SMITH, AMANDA BERRY. Evangelist (b. 23 January 1837 in Long Green, Maryland; d. 1915 in Harvey, Illinois). She was born into slavery, but her father earned enough money in his free time to eventually buy the freedom of his family. Her family moved to a farm near York, Pennsylvania, when she was a child. She began evangelical work in October 1870, and in 1878 went to England to stay three months, but instead remained abroad for twelve years. She spent three years of that period in India and eight years in Africa. In her autobiography she gives vivid descriptions of her exhortations at various kinds of religious meetings, particularly camp meetings. On all such occasions she sang hymns and religious songs of her people, thus earning the title "the Singing Pilgrim." After returning to the United States in 1890 she founded the Amanda Smith Orphan's Home for Children at Harvey, Illinois (near Chicago).

BIBL: *An Autobiography. The Story of the Lord's Dealings with Mrs. Amanda Smith, The Colored Evangelist* (Chicago: Meyer and Brother, 1893). Sylvia

Dannett, *Profiles of Negro Womanhood* (Yonkers, New York, 1964).

SMITH, BESSIE. Blues singer (b. 15 April 1894 in Chattanooga, Tennessee; d. 26 September 1937 near Clarksdale, Mississippi). She made her first stage appearance at the age of nine in a local theater. Soon thereafter she began to tour with professional companies; she was featured as a child singer with the Rabbit Foot Minstrels* for several years. Later she toured on the T.O.B.A.* circuit (Theater Owner's Booking Association) with groups and as a soloist. Some time during the years 1913-16 she came into contact with Gertrude ("Ma") Pridgett Rainey*—possibly when both performed with the Tolliver Circus and Tent Show. While there is no proof that Ma Rainey actually taught Bessie to sing blues, the older woman had an enormous influence upon the development of Bessie's style. Smith recorded extensively during the years 1923-33 and used the leading jazzmen and jazz groups of the time to accompany her, among them, Louis Armstrong,* Fletcher Henderson,* James P. Johnson,* Don Redman,* and Clarence Williams.* She recorded duets with Clara Smith.* She regularly toured the vaudeville circuit with her own Midnight Stoppers and Harlem Frolic Company; she also had her own jazz band for many years. She was featured in a film, *St. Louis Blues* (1929), and her voice was used on several soundtracks. She was touring in the South with the Broadway Rastus Show when she had a fatal car accident. Smith was the foremost blues singer of her time, perhaps of all time. Her voice was powerful, intensely expressive, and tragic; she used it with consummate skill and exerted enormous influence upon the development of black-music styles. She was called "Empress of the Blues."

BIBL: BWW. Chris Albertson, *Bessie* (New York, 1972). Chil. DAB. FeaEJ. MeeJMov. Carman Moore, *Somebody's Angel Child: the Story of Bessie Smith* (New York, 1969). NAW. Paul Oliver, *Bessie Smith* (London, 1959). Oliv. *Record Research*, the Victoria Spivey column, No. 44 (July 1962); Derrick Stewart-Baxter, *Ma Rainey and the Classic Blues Singers* (New York, 1970). Gunther Schuller, *Early Jazz: Its Roots and Musical Development* (New York, 1968).

DISC: DiGod. Kink. RustJR. TudBM.

SMITH, BUSTER. See **SMITH, HENRY.**

SMITH, CHRIS. Songwriter (b. 12 October 1879 in Charleston, South Carolina; d. 4 October 1949 in New York, New York). He was apprenticed to a baker as a boy but took advantage of every opportunity to perform at local social entertainments, including traveling shows that came to his town. Some time during the 1890s he and his long-time friend, Elmer Bowman,* left home to tour with a medicine show. After the show was stranded, Smith and Bowman formed a vaudeville act and went to New York. They traveled the vaudeville circuit for almost twenty years. About 1911 Smith formed a vaudeville act with Billy Johnson.* Smith collaborated with many lyricists to write songs which became very popular, most frequently with Bowman, Cecil Mack,* and James Tim Brymn.* His best-known songs were "I ain't poor no more" (before 1900), "Never let the same bee sting you twice" (1900), "Good morning, Carrie" (1901), "He's a cousin of mine" (1906, sung by Marie Cahill in the musical *Marrying Mary*), "You're in the right church but the wrong pew" (1908, written for Bert Williams*), and "Ballin' the jack" (1913, revived by Judy Garland in the film *For Me and My Gal*, 1942). Smith's best-known instrumental piece was "Junk man rag."

BIBL: ASCAP. Black press. BPIM 2 (Fall 1974), p. 169. Burton. Flet, 145-48. Kink.

SMITH, CLADYS ("JABBO"). Jazz trumpeter (b. 24 December 1908 in Pembroke, Georgia). He grew up in the Jenkins's Orphanage Home* in Charleston, South Carolina, where he studied trumpet and trombone and toured with the orphanage band from the age of ten. At sixteen he began playing professionally with Harry Marsh in Philadelphia, Pennsylvania. Thereafter he played with various groups, including Gus Aiken, Charlie Johnson (1925-28), James P. Johnson* (1928, including tours with the *Keep Shufflin'* show), Earl Hines,* Erskine Tate* (1929), Carroll Dickerson,* Stanley ("Fess") Williams,* and Claude Hopkins* (1936-38, 1944), among others. He also led his own groups at intervals from the late 1920s on. Among others with whom he played and/or recorded were Edward ("Duke") Ellington,* Sidney Bechet,* Sam Price, Jesse Stone, the Louisiana Sugar Babes, and guitarist Ikey Robinson. Beginning in the 1930s he used Milwaukee, Wisconsin, as the base from which he toured, and he settled there permanently in the 1940s, although he played residencies in other cities from time to time. During the 1970s he toured several times in Europe. He made his recording debut in 1929 with his own group, Jabbo Smith's Rhythm Aces. He was a virtuoso trumpeter, regarded by some as a rival to Louis Armstrong* in the late 1920s-30s.

BIBL: ChilWW. FeaEJ. FeaJS. FeaGitJS.

DISC: Jep. Kink. RustJR. TudJ.

SMITH, CLARA. Blues singer (b. 1894 in Spartanburg, South Carolina; d. 2 February 1935 in Detroit, Michigan). Little is known of her early life. She became established as an entertainer at an early age and was featured as a star on the T.O.B.A.* (Theater Owners' Booking Association) circuit as early as 1918. She recorded extensively during the years 1923-32; on two early records she sang duets with Bessie Smith.* Like other women blues singers of the period, she used jazzmen or jazz groups to accompany her, including Fletcher Henderson,* Louis Armstrong,* and Don Redman,* among others. She toured widely in the United States with her own show and was billed ''The Queen of Moaners.''

BIBL: BWW. ChilWW. CDef, 9 February 1935. Oliv. Derrick Stewart-Baxter, *Ma Rainey and the Classic Blues Singers* (New York, 1970).

DISC: DiGod. Kink. RustJR.

SMITH, CLARENCE (''PINE TOP''). Boogie-woogie pianist (b. 11 June 1904 in Troy, Alabama; d. 15 March 1929 in Chicago, Illinois). He moved to Birmingham, Alabama, as a youth and soon established himself in the music world, touring on the vaudeville circuit as an accompanist with Butterbeans and Susie (Jodie and Susie Edwards*) and as a soloist. In 1924 he went to Chicago with Charles (''Cow Cow'') Davenport* and settled there, living in the same apartment building as pianists Albert Ammons* and Meade Lux Lewis.* In 1928 he made his first recordings, ''Pine Top's boogie woogie'' and ''Pine Top's blues.'' Thereafter he recorded seven more pieces, but his career was cut off by an untimely death. He was one of the pioneers of the boogie-woogie (piano blues) tradition.

BIBL: BWW. ChilWWJ. FeaEJ. Oliv.

DISC: DiGod. Kink. RustJR.

SMITH, HALE. Composer (b. 29 June 1925 in Cleveland, Ohio). He began piano study at the age of seven, and although his family was not musical, they encouraged his interest in music. During his high school years he played in both concert and jazz groups, first beginning to play jazz at fourteen. The same year he began to play professionally by accompanying singers in local nightclubs. His early piano jazz style was influenced by Earl Hines,* Arthur (''Art'') Tatum,* and Theodore (''Teddy'') Wilson.* He obtained his musical education at the Cleveland Institute of Music (B. Mus., 1950; M. Mus., 1952), where he studied with Ward Lewis and Marcel Dick. A grant enabled him to study composition two additional years with Dick. He played string bass and, later, French horn in army bands during his years of service in the United States Armed Forces (1943-45). His teaching career included tenures at C. W. Post College on Long Island, New York, and at the University of Connecticut at Storrs (1970-).

He composed his first piece as a child after hearing a performance of Thurlow Lieurance's ''By the Waters of Minnetonka.'' When his teacher refused to even look at it, telling him that he would have to study many years before he could dream of becoming a composer, she served as a kind of negative inspiration for him. He wrote continuously thereafter. During his undergraduate years at college he began to write chamber music and art songs; his first songs earned him a BMI Student Composer's Award in 1952. In 1958 he settled in New York, where he later served as music editor and/or music adviser for various music publishing companies, including E. B. Marks, the Frank Music Corporation, Sam Fox Music Publishers, and C. F. Peters Corporation. During the 1950s he also was active as an arranger and/or musical director for such jazz artists as Foreststorn (''Chico'') Hamilton,* Oliver Nelson,* Quincy Jones,* Eric Dolphy,* Abbey Lincoln,* and Ahmad Jamal,* among others, and he wrote music for films, radio, and television. During the 1950s his music was performed more and more frequently; in 1955 Karamu House in Cleveland, Ohio, presented a full recital of Smith music, his first all-Smith recital.

His mature style was characterized by free use of contemporary compositional techniques except for electronic devices. He wrote in a variety of forms, including a half dozen or more works for symphony orchestra, many chamber works, works for concert band, for chorus, for piano, and a number of songs set to texts by Langston Hughes, John Donne, Elinor Wylie, Shakespeare, and the Chinese poets Tu Fu and Lu Yün. His best-known works were the orchestral *Contours* (1962), *Orchestral Set* (1952), *Ritual and Incantations* (1974), and *Innerflexions* (1977); the Sonata for Piano and Cello (1955); the chamber works *By Yearning and by Beautiful* for string orchestra (1961), *Epicedial Variations* for violin and piano (1956), Music for Harp and Chamber Orchestra (1967), and Introduction, Cadenzas, and Interludes for Eight Players (1974); the jazz cantata *Comes Tomorrow* (1972; revised 1976); *In Memoriam—Beryl Rubinstein* for chorus and chamber orchestra or piano (1953; orchestrated 1958); and the piano pieces ''Evocation'' (1972), *Anticipations, Introspections, and Reflections* (1971), and the collection *Faces of Jazz* (1968). He toured as a lecturer and consultant and occasionally published articles in professional journals and anthologies.

BIBL: BakBCS. BPIM 3 (Spring 1975). Gro.

SMITH, HARRY C. Bandleader (b. 20 January 1863 in Clarksburg, West Virginia; d. 10 December 1941 in Cleveland, Ohio). He is best known as the founder-publisher of the *Cleveland Gazette* (1883-1941), but he was also a musician. His family moved to Cleveland when he was two years old. He studied music privately, learned most of the orchestral instruments, and became the leader/cornetist of the Excelsior Reed Band in Cleveland. He also wrote guitar pieces and songs, of which the best known was ''Be true, bright eyes.''

BIBL: Black press, incl. NYFreeman, 3 September 1887; CleveG, 23 March 1889. Davis.

SMITH, HENDERSON. Minstrel bandleader (b. 19 April 1858 in Frankfort, Kentucky; d. 21 September 1923 in Chicago, Illinois). When he was a child, his family moved to Warren, Ohio, where he first studied music privately and later at the Dana Musical Institute. His early professional experience was with the Original Oaks Show in 1875. Thereafter he performed with various groups, including Sprague's Original Georgia Minstrels (1876-80), Haverly's Genuine Colored Minstrels (1880-81), and Callender's Consolidated Spectacular Minstrel Festival Show (1883), which included the Hyers Sisters* and Brindis de Salas.* In 1884 he directed the French Band of Chippewa Falls, Wisconsin. Thereafter he was active primarily as a bandleader or vaudeville entertainer. Occasionally he passed for white in order to obtain employment, as when he played with Patrick S. Gilmore's Famous Cornet Band. The groups with which he worked included J. H. Halliday's Minstrels; W. S. Cleveland's Big Minstrels of Chicago, Illinois, which also included James Bland,* Hattie and Tom McIntosh,* and Billy McClain*; and John W. Vogel's *Darkest Africa*, whose band toured in Australia under Smith's leadership with the Orpheus McAdoo* company. In 1901 Smith originated a vaudeville act, Fourteen Black Hussars (later called Ten Black Knights), which toured widely in the United States and in Europe. When he retired from the stage after almost fifty years, he settled in Chicago, where he directed the pit orchestra at the Atlas Theater. Smith was called ''America's black Sousa,'' in reference to bandleader John Philip Sousa.

BIBL: Black press, incl. CDef, 29 September 1923; IndF, 20 March 1887, 20 November 1897, 5 July 1902; NYGlobe, 26 May 1883. Simond. NYB, 1924.

SMITH, HENRY (''BUSTER''). Jazz saxophonist (b. 24 August 1904 in Aldorf, Texas). His mother was a church pianist and his father played guitar. He played a house organ as a child, then changed to guitar, and finally to clarinet when he was eighteen. His early professional experiences were in 1922 with a quintet in a local nightclub of Dallas, Texas, and with the Voddie White Trio, in which he doubled on the alto saxophone. Thereafter he played with various groups, including the Blue Devils (1925-33, led successively by Emir (''Bucket'') Coleman, Walter Page,* and Smith himself), Bennie Moten* (1933-35), William (''Count'') Basie* (1935-36 as co-leader), Claude Hopkins* (1936), and Andy Kirk,* among others. During the years 1937-38 he was co-leader of a band with Jesse Price in Kansas City, Missouri, which included Charlie Parker.* He exerted strong influence upon Parker's musical development at that time. Late in 1938 Smith went to New York; there he played with and/or arranged for various groups, including Basie, Benny Carter,* Gene Krupa, Oran (''Hot Lips'') Page,* Don Redman,* Eddie Durham, and Lawrence (''Snub'') Mosely, among others; he also led his own band at intervals and was active as a free-lance player. In 1943 he resettled in Dallas, Texas. He was musically active into the 1970s.

BIBL: Cadence (June 1978). ChilWW. FeaEJ. Russ.

DISC: Jep. Kink. RustJR.

SMITH, HEZEKIAH LEROY GORDON (''STUFF''). Jazz violinist (b. 14 August 1909 in Portsmouth, Ohio; d. 25 September 1967 in Munich, Germany). His father was a professional musician, who played string and reed instruments. He began violin study with his father at the age of seven and joined his father's band when he was twelve. His first professional experience was with the Aunt Jemima touring show (1924-26). Thereafter he played with various groups, including Alphonso Trent (1926-28, 1929), Ferdinand (''Jelly Roll'') Morton* (1928), and Joe Bushkin (1964). From the 1930s on he was active primarily with his own groups, using Buffalo, New York, as his base of operations. Among the musicians who played with him over the years were Jonah Jones,* Clyde Hart, William (''Cozy'') Cole,* Lloyd Trotman, Erroll Garner,* and William (''Billy'') Taylor,* among others. In 1936 he settled in New York; in 1943 he moved to Chicago, Illinois; during the 1950s he settled in California. He first recorded in 1928 with Alphonso Trent. He made his recording debut as a bandleader in 1936 with his Onyx Club Boys and the same year began playing amplified violin. In 1957 he toured in Europe with JATP (Norman Granz's Jazz at the Philharmonic) and again in 1965-67 as a soloist. He was a pioneer in the use of the electrically-amplified jazz violin; his style was described as ''barrelhouse'' and ''demonic.'' His best-known songs were ''I'se a muggin','' ''Time and again,'' and ''You'se a viper.''

BIBL: ASCAP. ChilWW. DanceWS. FeaEJ. FeaGitJS.

DISC: Jep. Kink. RustJR. TudJ.

SMITH, JABBO. See **SMITH, CLADYS.**

SMITH, JAMES OSCAR (''JIMMY''). Jazz organist (b. 8 December 1928 in Norristown, Pennsylvania). He came from a family of musical amateurs; both parents played piano. He began piano study at an early age and won first place on a Major Bowes Amateur Show when he was nine, which allowed him the opportunity to appear on radio programs. He obtained his musical education in the public schools of Philadelphia, Pennsylvania, and at the Ornstein School of Music there (1946-49). He began his professional career at sixteen in a song-and-dance act with his father, which performed in local nightclubs. After service in the United States Navy, he returned to Philadelphia, where he studied music formally for the first time and played piano with Johnny Sparrow, Don Gardner (1952-54), and others. In 1955 he organized his own trio. He was inspired to learn jazz organ after hearing a performance of William (''Wild Bill'') Davis* in 1953. He developed a virtuoso and highly original style. He first attracted wide attention as an organist in 1956 for his improvisations on John Birks (''Dizzy'') Gillespie's* piece, ''The champ,'' in which he produced the effect of a big band on his organ. He recorded extensively, often with big-band accompaniment, and in 1962 established his own recording company. He toured widely in the United States and abroad, appearing on television programs, at the major jazz festivals, and in films, including *The Swinging Set* (1964) and on the soundtrack of *Where the Spies Are* (1965). He was a prolific composer; his film scores included *Le Metamorphose de Clopertes* (1965). His best-known albums were *The Cat*, *Walk on the Wild Side*, and the soundtrack album for *Who's Afraid of Virginia Woolf*. He was billed as ''The World's Greatest Organist''; his technical skills were compared to those of Earl (''Bud'') Powell* on the piano, and his role in defining the jazz organ was compared to that of Charlie Christian* in defining the jazz guitar. He won numerous awards from the music industry.

BIBL: ContK (August 1978). FeaEJ. FeaJS. FeaGitJS. MeeJMov. WWA. WWBA.

DISC: Jep. TudJ.

SMITH, JOE. Jazz trumpeter (b. 28 June 1902 in Ripley, Ohio; d. 2 December 1937 in New York, New York). He came from a musical family: his father, Luke Smith, was leader of a brass band in Cincinnati, Ohio, and six brothers became professional jazzmen, including Luke and Russell. He studied trumpet with his father and began playing professionally with local groups at an early age. He left home with a touring group and eventually arrived in New York about 1920, where he later played with Kaiser Marshall. During the next few years he played nightclub residencies in Pittsburgh, Pennsylvania; toured with the Black Swan* Jazz Masters (1922, led by Fletcher Henderson*); toured with Mamie Smith's* Jazz Hounds (1922-23); played with Billy Paige's Broadway Syncopators; directed a band for the Eubie Blake*/Noble Sissle* musical *The Chocolate Dandies* (1924); and did freelance playing and recording. He made his recording debut in 1922 on Harry Pace's* Black Swan label and thereafter recorded extensively. He attracted wide attention as a soloist with Henderson and in accompanying groups for blues singers Ida Cox,* Alberta Hunter,* Bessie Smith,* Gertrude (''Ma'') Rainey,* and Ethel Waters.* From the mid-1920s on he played with various groups, including Fletcher Henderson (1925-28, 1930), McKinney's Cotton Pickers (1929-30, 1931-32), Marshall (1931), and Clarence Love (1933). His trumpet style was warm, lyrical, and sensitive. He exerted considerable influence upon trumpeters of his time, and his solo on ''The stampede'' with Fletcher Henderson was widely imitated.

BIBL: AlHen. ChilWW. FeaEJ.

DISC: Kink. RustJR.

SMITH, LEO. Jazz trumpeter/Composer (b. 18 December 1941 in Leland, Mississippi). His musical development was influenced by his step-father, Alex (''Little Bill'') Wallace, who played blues guitar, sang, and recorded with rhythm 'n' blues bands. He received his musical education in the public schools of Leland, Mississippi, and at the Army School of Music at Fort Leonard Wood, Missouri (graduated 1967). He studied further at the Sherwood School of Music in Chicago, Illinois (1967-68), Wesleyan University at Middletown, Connecticut (1974-75), and privately with Henderson Howard and William Babbcott. He began playing trumpet at the age of twelve in a school band, and a year later was playing professionally with local groups. After graduation from high school he toured with blues bands for a year. During his service in the United States Armed Forces he played in army bands and dance orchestras. In 1967 he settled in Chicago, Illinois, and soon thereafter became a member of the Association for the Advancement of Creative Musicians, founded by Muhal Richard Abrams* in 1965. He performed with the AACM Experimental Orchestra; with various groups led by Anthony Braxton,* Maurice McIntyre, LeRoy Jenkins* (1967-70, including a European tour), and Marion Brown* (1970-72, including European tours), among others; and led his own groups. He made his recording debut in 1967, playing his composition ''The bells'' on Braxton's album *Three Compositions of New Jazz*; thereafter he recorded regularly on both sides of the Atlantic. In 1971 he organized his Dalta Ahkri to showcase serious improvisational music. The next year he established his own recording and publishing companies and released his first solo album,

Creative Music - 1. He wrote for a wide variety of orchestral and chamber groups, but preferred to call himself a scorer of improvisations rather than a composer. His best-known works, in addition to those mentioned above, were *Reflectativity* (1974) and *Spirit Catcher* (1979), which included "The burning of stones" and "Images." His honors included a grant from the National Endowment for the Arts for composition (1972).

BIBL: Questionnaire. Cadence (February 1978). FeaGitJS.

SMITH, LONNIE LISTON. Jazz keyboardist (b. 28 December 1940 in Richmond, Virginia). He came from a musical family. His father, Lonnie Liston, Sr., sang with the Harmonizing Four, a spiritual-singing quartet; a brother, Ray, sang with The Jarmels; and another brother, Donald, sang with Lonnie's Cosmic Echoes. He obtained his musical education in the public schools of Richmond, Virginia, and at Morgan State University in Baltimore, Maryland (B. Mus., 1963). At college he played tuba in the band, piano in the orchestra, and sang in the choir. He began his professional career playing with local groups in Baltimore. In 1963 he settled in New York and thereafter played with various groups or individuals, among them, Betty Carter* (1963-64), Rahsaan Roland Kirk* (1965), Arthur ("Art") Blakey* (1966-67), Joe Williams* (1967-68), Pharoah Sanders* (1969-72), Gato Barbieri (1972-73), and Miles Davis* (1973-74). In 1974 he organized his own group, The Cosmic Echoes. He toured widely in the United States and in Europe with Sanders, Barbieri, and his own group. He was a prolific composer and recorded extensively. His best-known albums were *Expansions* and *Cosmic Funk*. His honors included a grant from the National Endowment for the Arts (1973).

BIBL: ContK (April 1978). FeaGitJS. WWBA.

SMITH, MABEL LOUISE ("BIG MAYBELLE"). Blues singer (b. 1 May 1924 in Jackson, Tennessee; d. 23 January 1972 in Cleveland, Ohio). She sang in a local sanctified church choir as a child. Her first professional experiences were with Dave Clark, then with Myron ("Tiny") Bradshaw* (1947-50). During the 1950s she won recognition as a top singer of rhythm 'n' blues, and was one of the few blues singers invited to appear at the first Newport Jazz Festival in 1954 along with Charles ("Chuck") Berry* and ("Big") Joe Turner.* A shouting singer in the tradition of Gertrude ("Ma") Rainey,* she was called "America's Queen Mother of Soul."

BIBL: BWW. FeaEJ. FeaGitJS. LivBl 7 (Winter 1971-72).

DISC: Jep. TudBM.

SMITH, MAMIE (née MAMIE ROBINSON). Blues singer (b. 26 May 1883 in Cincinnati, Ohio; d. 16 September 1946 in New York, New York). She began her professional career as a vaudeville singer; she toured with The Four Dancing Mitchells and Salem Tutt Whitney's Smart Set* show. In 1913 she settled in New York and soon established herself as a leading cabaret singer. On 14 February 1920 she made her first recording and thereby established a landmark in the history of American music: she was the first singer to make a solo blues recording. The General Phonograph Corporation (Okeh label) had planned originally to record Sophie Tucker on a session, but the white singer was unavailable. Perry Bradford,* a black talent scout, persuaded recording manager Ralph Peer to substitute Smith for the ailing Tucker; she sang two songs written by Bradford, "That thing called love" and "You can't keep a good man down." A few months later, on 10 August, she recorded two more Bradford songs, "Crazy blues" and "It's right here for you." It was the commercial success of this recording that established a vogue for "race records" (records intended for distribution in black communities) that has persisted to the present, although in later years such labels as "rhythm 'n' blues," and "soul" were applied to such records by the industry. Smith recorded regularly after her debut until 1931, often accompanied by her Jazz Hounds, which included William ("Buster") Bailey, Johnny Dunn,* Coleman Hawkins,* and James ("Bubber") Miley,* among others. She also widely toured in the United States, appearing in cabarets and on the vaudeville stage. The Great Depression of the 1930s forced a slowdown in her musical activities, as with other black entertainers, but she returned to professional life in 1940. Although widely advertised as a blues singer, the songs she sang were composed blues and ballads rather than genuine folk blues.

BIBL: BWW. ChilWWJ. FeaEJ. MeeJMov. Oliv. *Record Research* 65 (October 1964). Derrick Stewart-Baxter, *Ma Rainey and the Classic Blues Singers* (New York, 1970).

DISC: DiGod. Kink. RustJR.

SMITH, MURIEL. Actress/Theater singer (b. 23 February 1923 in New York, New York). She obtained her musical education at the Curtis Institute in Philadelphia, Pennsylvania, and studied privately with Elizabeth Schumann. She left her musical studies in 1943 to audition for the title role of the Broadway musical

Carmen Jones and won the audition. She made her professional debut in the musical, alternating with Muriel Rahn* in the role. Four years later she sang the role of Ella Hammer in Marc Blitzstein's *The Cradle Will Rock* (1947 production of the 1937 musical). In 1949 she went to London, England, where she sang in Drury Lane productions of Rodgers and Hammerstein musicals, the role of Bloody Mary in *South Pacific* (1951), and the role of Lady Thiang in *The King and I* (1953). She returned to the United States to sing in a revival of *Carmen Jones* (1956), then settled permanently in London. In 1956 she sang the title role in Bizet's *Carmen* at Covent Garden.

BIBL: Black press, incl. AmstN, 22 April 1944; CDef, 3 January 1944, 6 August 1955, 2 June 1956.

DISC: Turn.

SMITH, N[ATHANIEL] CLARK. Music educator/Composer (b. 31 July 1877 in Fort Levenworth, Kansas; d. 8 October 1933 in St. Louis, Missouri). He obtained his musical education in the public schools of Leavenworth, Kansas; at Western University in Quindaro, Kansas (now defunct); at Guild Hall in London, England (1899); Chicago [Illinois] Musical College (B. Mus. 1905), where he studied with the president, Ziegfeld, with Felix Borowski, and John Miller, among others; the University of Kansas at Lawrence; the Horner Institute of Fine Arts in Kansas City, Missouri (1915-16); and the Sherwood School of Music in Chicago (1928). During the mid-1890s he lived in Wichita, Kansas, where he conducted a music studio, led a boy's band, and organized a municipal mail-carrier's band. He was bandmaster of the 8th Illinois Regiment Band during the Spanish-American War in 1898. In 1899 he embarked on an eighteen-month, world wide tour with the M. B. Curtis All-Star Afro-American Minstrels which later became the Ernest Hogan* Concert Company, including stops in Australia, New Zealand, and Hawaii.

After returning to the United States in 1901, he settled in Chicago, where he was bandmaster in the 8th Illinois State Militia, attended Chicago Musical College (1901-05), and was highly active in the community. He organized Chicago's first black symphony orchestra (perhaps the first in the nation), which gave its debut concert in March 1903 with Anita Patti Brown* and William N. P. Spiller* as the featured artists. The same year he founded a music publishing house with J. Berni Barbour,* perhaps the first to be owned solely by black proprietors. In 1904 he organized Smith's Mandolin and String Instruments Club and the N. Clark Smith Ladies Orchestra. He left Chicago in 1907, when he was commissioned a captain in the U.S. Army, and joined the military faculty at Tuskegee Institute in Alabama (1907-13), where he organized a band, an orchestra, glee clubs, and chamber ensembles. He toured widely with his college groups in the Midwest and South, including appearances in the annual Atlanta [Georgia] Colored Music Festivals sponsored by Henry Hugh Proctor.* In 1913 he was commissioned an army major and went to Western University as bandmaster (1913-15). Thereafter his teaching career included tenures at Lincoln High School in Kansas City, Missouri (1916-22), Wendell Phillips High School in Chicago (1925-26), and Sumner High School in St. Louis, Missouri (1930-33). In 1922 he was hired by the Pullman [Railroad] Company to organize musical groups among its black employees at various headquarters; he began his work in Chicago, organizing a Pullman Porter Band, Orchestra, and Glee Club, and continued his activity in other large cities (1922-25). During the years 1926-30 he was active with Chicago groups.

Despite his full career, Smith found time to participate in musical affairs—he was a charter member of the National Association of Negro Musicians* in 1919—and to compose and arrange for his groups. He was best known for his band pieces and spiritual arrangements, of which a number were published, and the "Tuskegee Institute March," *Negro Folk Suite*, and *Negro Choral Symphony* (1933, composed for performance at the Chicago World's Fair). But it was as an educator that he made an enormous contribution to the history of American music, for he exerted wide influence upon the development of black music through his students and those whom he coached and/or trained. He established such strong standards for excellence at the institutions where he taught that the traditions still exist today. He drilled his marching bands until they were the best of their class; his glee clubs and orchestras similarly met the highest standards; and most of all, he made music exciting and important to his students. The teachers who succeeded him (either directly or later) carried on his traditions—William Levi Dawson* and Alonzo Lewis at Lincoln in Kansas City, Walter Dyett* at Phillips in Chicago, and Stanley Lee Henderson at Sumner in St. Louis. Those who came under his direct influence included, among others, Jasper Allen, Eddie Coles (brother of Nathaniel Coles*), Lionel Hampton,* Alvis Hayes,* Milton Hinton,* Harlan Leonard, Bennie Moton,* Walter Page,* Ray Nance,* Quinn Wilson, and Nelmatilda Ritchie Woodard.* To further list those who were influenced by Smith's successors would produce a who's who of jazz.

BIBL: Black press, incl. CDef, 16 January 1915, 22 May 1920, 12 October 1933; IndF, 28 March 1903, 2 January 1904; NYAge, 6 May 1922. Reginald Buckner,

"A History of Music Education in the Black Community of Kansas City, Kansas, 1905-54" (Ph.D. diss., University of Minnesota, 1974). Russ. *The Negro in Chicago* (Chicago, 1929). WWCA, 1933-37.

SMITH, PINETOP. See **SMITH, CLARENCE.**

SMITH, RAYMOND LOWDEN. Symphony orchestra promoter (b. 12 July 1896 in Salisbury, North Carolina; d. 19?? in Philadelphia, Pennsylvania). He obtained his musical education in the public schools of Philadelphia, Pennsylvania, and at the Philadelphia Academy of Music (1922-24), where he studied violin with F. E. Hahn. He also studied violin with Edwin Hill, theory and orchestration with Walter Pfeiffer, and composition with William Happich. He played with the Philadelphia Concert Orchestra (1912-16), the Trouveres String Trio (1922-29), and the E. Gilbert Anderson* Memorial Symphony Orchestra (in 1944 renamed the Philadelphia Concert Orchestra),* which he reorganized in 1930. He also organized the Dra Mu Opera Company in 1945. He was active as a concert promoter and presented symphony-orchestra concerts over a long period, beginning in the 1930s.

BIBL: Black press, incl. CDef, 9 September 1950. WWCA 1950.

SMITH, RICHARD DONALD. Music educator (b. 4 December 1941 in Philadelphia, Pennsylvania). He obtained his musical education in the public schools of Philadelphia, Pennsylvania, at Temple University in Philadelphia (B. Mus., 1965), and at the Juilliard School of Music in New York. He also studied at the Settlement Music School (1965). During his high-school years he played in the All-Philadelphia High School Orchestra and Band (1956-59), and later he was solo flutist with the Pennsylvania All-State Intercollegiate Band and Orchestra (1961-64). His teaching career included tenures in the James Weldon Johnson* Theater Arts Center and the United National International School, both in New York. He was also active as a conductor of orchestras and choirs in Philadelphia and of the Yonkers [New York] Youth Orchestra. He played flute with various orchestras, including the Symphony of the New World,* and conducted his own music studio from 1967 on.

BIBL: WWBA.

SMITH, RICHARD JOSEPH ("RICK"). Music educator (b. 11 May 1909 in Kansas City, Missouri; d. 13 November 1974 in Kansas City). He began violin study at the age of six. He obtained his musical education at the University of Iowa in Iowa City (B.S., 1931). In his college years he played with a jazz group and after graduation, with Harold Jones's Brownskin Syncopators. Later he played with Thamon Hayes. In 1937 he entered teaching, continuing his jazz performance on the side, and had tenures in the public schools of Kansas City, Missouri (1937-43), and the R. T. Coles Veterans Training School (1943-58). In 1958 he became president of the Musicians Protective Union/Local 627 and was a driving force in bringing about the merger of the black union with the white Local 34 in 1974. In his later career he organized the Kansas City Historical Jazz Quintet, which performed in public schools under the auspices of Young Audiences, Inc.

BIBL: ChilWW. *The Kansas City Call*, 22 November 1974.

DISC: Jep.

SMITH, STUFF. See **SMITH, HEZEKIAH.**

SMITH, WARREN I., JR. Jazz percussionist/College professor (b. 14 May 1934 in Chicago, Illinois). He came from a musical family. His father, Warren, Sr., toured with such jazz groups as Noble Sissle* and Jimmie Noone,* and his mother played harp and piano. He began music study as a child, studying reed instruments with his father, harp with his mother, and drums with local teachers. He obtained his musical education in the public schools of Chicago, Illinois; at the University of Illinois in Urbana (B.S., 1957), where he studied percussions with Paul Price; and at Manhattan School of Music in New York (M. Mus., 1958). He also studied privately with Oliver Coleman, Harold Faberman, and Coleridge Taylor Perkinson,* among others. His teaching career included tenures in the public schools of New York (1958-68), at the Third Street Settlement House in New York (1960-67), and at the State University of New York in Old Westbury (1972-). He began playing professionally with local groups at the age of fifteen. Later he performed with various individuals or groups, among them, Gil Evans, Johnny Richards, Nina Simone,* Sam Rivers,* and Max Roach's* M'Boom. He also was active as a music director (touring with Janis Joplin in Europe in 1969) and played in theater orchestras of the Negro Ensemble Company and Broadway musicals *West Side Story* (1968), *Lost in the Stars* (1972), *Raisin* (1973), and others. He was a charter member of the Symphony of the New World* in 1964; he also performed with the American Symphony Orchestra under Leopold Stokowski. He toured widely as a performer, appearing at major jazz festivals and on college campuses, and as a lecturer and workshop clinician. He published musical compositions and manuals, including the books *Begin-*

ning Rhythmic Notation, Professional Percussion Workshop, and *Rhythmic Exercises for Lab Band*.

BIBL: FeaGitJS. WWBA.

SMITH, WILLIAM HENRY JOSEPH BERTHOL BONAPARTE BERTHOLOFF ("WILLIE-THE-LION"). Jazz pianist (b. 25 November 1897 in Goshen, New York; d. 18 April 1973 in New York, New York). He came from a musical family. His maternal grandmother, a banjoist, toured with the Primrose and West Minstrels, and his mother played piano and organ in churches. He began to study music at an early age, at first with his mother on a house organ, then later piano. His family moved to Newark, New Jersey, when he was a child. He obtained his musical training in the public schools there. He began playing professionally when he was about fifteen, at first in local saloons and nightclubs and then in clubs of Atlantic City, New Jersey, and New York. During his years of service in the United States Army (1917-1919) he was drum major of the 350th Field Artillery Band, directed by James (''Tim'') Brymn,* which was called ''The Seventy Black Devils.'' In 1920 he settled in New York and thereafter played long residencies in nightclubs in the Harlem community, as a soloist and also with his groups. He made his recording debut in 1920 with Mamie Smith* and Her Jazz Hounds; thereafter he recorded extensively. During the 1930s he began to play in clubs and theaters in downtown New York; he toured briefly on the vaudeville circuit with Nina Mae McKinney* (1931), played on Eva Taylor's* radio show with her husband, Clarence Williams,* and studied music formally with Hans Steinke. In later years he toured as a lecturer-pianist, particularly on the college circuit, played on radio and television programs, performed at jazz festivals, and appeared in films. Although he began his career as a ragtime pianist, it was as one of the leading figures of the ''Harlem stride piano school'' that he made his greatest contribution to music history, along with James P. Johnson,* Luckeyeth ("Luckey") Roberts,* and Thomas ("Fats") Waller.* His style was characterized by lyricism and delicacy, despite his powerful left hand. His best-known compositions were the piano pieces ''Echoes of spring,'' ''Rippling waters,'' ''Fingerbuster,'' and the song ''Sweeter than the sweetest.''

BIBL: ASCAP. ChilWW. FeaEJ. FeaJS. FeaGitJS. MeeJMov. Willie-the-Lion Smith, with George Hoefer, *Music on My Mind* (New York, 1965).

DISC: Jep. Kink. RustJR. TudJ.

SMITH, WILLIAM McLEISH ("WILLIE"). Jazz saxophonist (b. 25 November 1910 in Charleston, South Carolina; d. 7 March 1967 in Los Angeles, California). He began study of the clarinet at the age of twelve. He obtained his musical education at Case Technical College in Memphis, Tennessee, and at Fisk University in Nashville, Tennessee. His early professional experiences were with the Boston Serenaders in Memphis (1926) and the Beaty Conner Quartet (summer, 1927). While at Fisk he met James (''Jimmie'') Lunceford* and later joined his band (1929-42). Thereafter he played with various groups, including Charlie Spivak (1942-43), Harry James (1944-51, 1954-63), Edward (''Duke'') Ellington* (1951-52), William (''Billy'') May (1952, 1953, 1960s), and Charlie Barnet (1966), among others. During his years in the United States Navy (1943-44) he was a music instructor. In 1953 he toured in Europe with JATP (Norman Granz's Jazz at the Philharmonic), and after returning home toured wih the Benny Goodman all-star band. He also led his own groups in Los Angeles, California, and was active as a studio musician and in films, including *Young Man with a Horn* (1949). He was regarded as one of the leading alto saxophonists of the 1930s-40s, along with Johnny Hodges* and Benny Carter.* His style was powerful and expressive; his best-known performance was his solo on ''Blues in the night'' with the Lunceford band.

BIBL: ChilWW. FeaEJ. FeaJS. FeaGitJS. MeeJMov.

DISC: Jep. Kink. RustJR.

SMITH, WILLIE MAE FORD. Gospel singer (b. 1906 in Rolling Fort, Mississippi). Her family moved to Memphis, Tennessee, when she was a child, then settled in St. Louis, Missouri, when she was twelve years old. The father formed a family quartet, which attracted wide attention when the singers performed in 1922 at the National Baptist Convention. After the family group was disbanded, Willie Mae decided to enter a music career and planned to study further. She changed to the field of gospel music after hearing Artelia Hutchins sing gospel songs at the annual meeting of the National Baptist Convention in 1926. She became an ordained minister in the late 1920s. In 1936 she organized the Soloists Bureau of Thomas A. Dorsey's* National Convention of Gospel Choirs and Choruses and served as director for many years, teaching those who attended to sing in her gospel style and using her own arrangements. Roberta Martin* served as her accompanist for the Soloists Bureau for many years. In 1937 Smith won wide attention when she performed a song she had written, ''If you just keep still,'' at the annual National Baptist Convention. In 1939 she left the Baptist Church to become a member of the Church of God Apostolic. She was one of the pioneer female gospel singers, along with Queen C. Anderson* and Sallie Martin.* Her style was distinctive for her powerful, blues-like contralto (which was often compared to that of Bessie Smith*) and her free use of roars and crooning. She is credited with having established the tradition of offering introductory sermonettes for each song on the gospel program and explications of the texts. She exerted enormous influence upon the development of gospel, although she did little touring but performed primarily in churches and at revival meetings and made relatively few recordings. Her best-known song was "Take your burdens to the Lord." Her protégés included Martha Bass, who sang with The Famous Ward Singers*; Myrtle Scott, who sang with The Roberta Martin* Singers; and "Brother" Joe May, who was called "the Thunderbolt of the Middle West."

BIBL: Heil. Jac. *Sepia* (April 1975).

SMYLES, HARRY. Symphony oboist (b. 4 December 1917 in Kansas City, Missouri). He came from a musical family: both parents were professional singers, who gave duo recitals and were soloists for church choirs. He began piano study with his father when he was eight years old. Later he studied oboe with Philip Kirchner, of the Cleveland Orchestra, beginning in his junior-high-school years and continuing through his college career. His family moved to Cleveland, Ohio, when he was a child. He obtained his musical education in the Cleveland public schools, at Western Reserve University in Cleveland (B.S., 1942), and at the Berkshire Music Center in Tanglewood, Massachusetts (1947-48). His other teachers included D. Ernest Manring and F. Karl Grossman. His career development was aided by his teachers, who were associated with orchestras; by Serge Koussevitzky, who directed the Berkshire Orchestra when he attended Tanglewood; and by Max Goberman, founder-director of the New York Sinfonietta. His professional career included tenures as first oboist (and English hornist) in the Cleveland Philharmonic, under Karl Grossman; the National Orchestral Association orchestra, under Leon Barzin (1948-49); the orchestra for the Sadlers Well Ballet Company (1955); the Symphony of the New World,* under Benjamin Steinberg (1964-76); and the National Afro-American Philharmonic Orchestra, under James Frazier, Jr.* (1978-). He also played in theater orchestras, including those for Menotti's *The Saint of Bleecker Street* (1955) and Bernstein's *Candide* (1956). His activity as a soloist included appearances with chamber groups and with the New York Sinfonietta and other orchestras, including Dimitri Mitropolos's at Town Hall in 1957. He also played in, and recorded with, chamber groups and was an original member of the New World Trio in 1967, along with Harold Jones* (flute) and Alan Booth* (piano). He was a founding member of the Symphony of the New World, remaining in the orchestra until its disbandment, and a charter member of the National Afro-American Philharmonic. His honors included a Rosenwald fellowship (1948).

BIBL: Questionnaire. "An Even Break" in NYT, 22 April 1956. "The Negro and the North" in *Life* (11 March 1957). "The Negro in Search of an Orchestra" in NYT, 26 November 1967.

SNAËR, SAMUEL. Composer (b. c1832 in New Orleans, Louisiana; d. after 1880 in New Orleans). Little is known of his early life. He reached the peak of his career during the 1860s-70s and was highly regarded by his contemporaries as a pianist, violinist, and violoncellist. He conducted a music studio and was organist at St. Mary's Catholic Church in New Orleans. For a period during the 1860s he directed the orchestra at the Theater D'Orleans. His output included music for orchestra, chamber groups, and voice. His best-known piece was the "Sous de fenetre."

BIBL: Des. LaBrew. Trot, pp. 341-43; pp. 127-152 of the music section.

SNOW, VALAIDA. Entertainer/Jazz trumpeter (b. 2 June c1900 in Chattanooga, Tennessee; d. 30 May 1956 in New York, New York). She came from a musical family: her mother was a music teacher and her sisters became professional entertainers. She began her professional career in the early 1920s as a singer-dancer. Thereafter she toured periodically—in Europe and the Middle East (1929-33, 1936-41) and in the Far East (1926, to Shanghai with the Jack Carter band). In the United States she sang and played trumpet in nightclubs and in musical revues and shows: she toured with Will Masten's Revue; sang leading roles in the Eubie Blake*/Noble Sissle* show, *The Chocolate Dandies* (1924), in *Rhapsody in Black* (1931) and in *Blackbirds of 1934*, which also played in England. During the 1930s she also toured in a song-and-dance act with her husband, Ananias Berry, and appeared in films, including *Take It from Me* (193?), *Irresistible You* (1944), *L'Alibi* (1936), and *Pièges* (1939). She made her recording debut in the 1930s and thereafter recorded regularly under her own name and with others. She spent almost two years in a Nazi concentration camp (1941-43) in Germany before she was given an exchange-prisoner release and allowed to return to the United States in the spring of 1943. She returned to performing in nightclubs and theaters in New York, then in 1945 settled in California. Thereafter she used that state as a base from which she toured until her death.

BIBL: AlHen. Black press, incl. CDef, 21 May 1932, 24 April 1943. ChilWW. Handy. MeeJMov.

DISC: Jep. RustJR.

SNOWDEN, ELMER CHESTER ("POPS"). Jazz guitarist (b. 9 October 1900 in Baltimore, Maryland; d. 14 May 1973 in Philadelphia, Pennsylvania). He played guitar, banjo, and mandolin as a child. In 1914 he began playing professionally in a local Baltimore theater; in 1915 he joined Eubie Blake's* band and remained with the group through the period of Joe Rochester's leadership (1916-19). He then went to Washington, D.C., where he played with Louis Thomas at the Howard Theater and with Claude Hopkins,* among others, as well as led his own group. In 1923 he took a small group—William (''Sonny'') Greer,* Otto (''Toby'') Hardwicke,* Artie Whetsol—to New York to fulfill an engagement, which failed to materialize because the pianist promised by the promoter did not show up. Within a week he sent for Edward (''Duke'') Ellington* to play piano with his group, and Ada (''Bricktop'') Smith* helped his group, now called the Washingtonians, to find employment in a nightclub in the Harlem community. From there his band moved to the Hollywood Club (later called the Kentucky Club). The next year he left the group to join ''Broadway'' Jones's band and took over when Jones left. Later he returned briefly to the Washingtonians, now led by Ellington, then led his own groups through the 1930s. During one period he also played for Broadway musicals: Ford Dabney's* *Rang Tang* (1927), Thomas (''Fats'') Waller's*/James P. Johnson's* *Keep Shufflin'* (1928), *Blackbirds of 1930*, and with Claude Hopkins for a white musical, *Make Me Know It* (1929). During the next three decades he played with various groups, among them, Charles Luckeyeth ("Lucky") Roberts* (1935-39) and Melvin ("Turk") Murphy (1963). He toured with his own groups, taught in music institutes, and recorded extensively. In 1963 he settled in California, but returned east to live before his death. In 1968 he toured with George Wein's Newport Guitar Workshop. He was a pioneeer in defining the role of the jazz banjo; his unique tone resulted from his use of Gibson heavy-duty guitar strings on his banjo.

BIBL: ChilWW. DanceWS. FeaEJ. FeaJS. FeaGitJS. MeeJMov.

DISC: Jep. Kink. RustJR.

SOGA, JOHN HENDERSON. Minister/Hymn writer (b. 1859 in Emgwali, South Africa; d. March 1941 in Southampton, England). See **SOGA, TIYO.**

SOGA, TIYO. Minister/Hymn writer (b. 1829 in Gwali, Cape Province, South Africa; d. 12 August 1871 in Tutura, near Butterworth, South Africa). Although best known as an author and minister, he also wrote hymns and collected folksongs. He obtained his education in schools of Gwali, Lovedale, the Glasgow [Scotland] Free Church National Seminary, and the University of Glasgow. He received his clerical training at the United Presbyterian Church in Glasgow. In 1856 he became the first African minister to be ordained in Great Britain. In 1857 he returned to Africa and founded a mission station at Emgwali, among the Ngqika Xhosa people. During the 1850s he began writing hymns, many of which were included in the Xhosa hymnals published by the Glasgow Missionary Society. His best-known hymns were ''Fulfill thy promise,'' ''Open your eyes and behold how great the blessings are,'' and ''We have a great gift which was given us.'' He also contributed articles and occasionally collections of praise songs to *Indaba*, a Lovedale monthly, under the pen name ''the dove of the nation'' (Uninjiba Waseluhlangeni). He was credited with having collected a large number of folksongs, but he did not publish them. His son, John Henderson Soga, was also a minister and hymn writer. He was sent to Glasgow at the age of three and received all his education there. After being ordained in 1893 he returned to South Africa and founded the Mbonde Mission in the Mount Frere district, among the Bhaca people. His hymns were included in the Xhosa Presbyterian Hymnbook (Amaculo aseRabe).

BIBL: WWAfrLit.

SON BRIMMER. See **SHADE, WILL.**

SOUBISE, JULIUS. Entertainer (b. 1754 in St. Kitts, West Indies; d. 1798 in Calcutta, India). When he was ten years old, he was taken to London, England, where he became ''the darling black'' of Catherine, Duchess of Queensberry. He studied music and elocution. As an adult he played violin ''with considerable taste,'' composed songs in the Italian style, and sang well. He was a favorite performer at the Vauxhall pleasure gardens in London. In July 1777 he went to India, where he died at the age of forty-four.

BIBL: Henry Angelo, *Reminiscenses . . . With Memoirs of His Father and Friends* (London, 1930), p. 442 ff. [quotations from Angelo]. Edward Scobie, *Black Britannia* (Chicago, 1972).

SOUL STIRRERS, THE. Gospel group (orig. c1935 in Trinity, Texas). The original group included Jesse Farley (bass), Silas Roy Crain (tenor), T. L. Bruster (tenor), Rebert H. Harris (lead), and R. B. Robinson (baritone). The Soul Stirrers were active in Houston, Texas, during the late 1930s, then settled in Chicago, Illinois, in the 1940s. The group toured widely and introduced several innovations into traditional "quartet" singing. They were the first to add a fifth man to the group, thus enabling the lead tenor to sing solos against a four-part harmony. They were the first to sing gospel songs exclusively—other quartets had repertories of spirituals, hymns, jubilees, topical, even popular songs—and one of the first to use accompaniment (quartet singing was traditionally a capella). The group's style was distinctive for its complex rhythms and syncopation and for its penchant for having the group chanting key words of the lyrics as a background for the lead-singers' verses. Over the years those who sang with The Soul Stirrers included Sam Cooke,* Arthur Crume, Rufus Crume, Dillard Crume, Paul Foster, Martin Jacox, James Davis, Sonny Mitchell (guitarist), Jimmy Outlaw (Outler?), Johnny Taylor, and Willie Rogers. In 1980 The Soul Stirrers consisted of James Davis and the three Crumes. The group, particularly Rebert Harris and Sam Cooke, exerted wide influence on both gospel and popular-music groups. Cooke and Johnny Taylor crossed over wholly into secular music. The Soul Stirrers laid the foundation for modern gospel quartet singing. Their best-known albums were *Going Back to the Lord Again, Sam Cooke with the Soul Stirrers, The Best of the Soul Stirrers*, and *Tribute to Sam Cooke*.

BIBL: GMEncy. Heil. Barbara Baker, "Black Gospel Music Styles, 1942-1975" (Ph.D. diss., University of Maryland, 1978).

DISC: Hayes. TudBM.

SOUTH, EDDIE. Jazz violinist (b. 17 [27?] November 1904 in Louisiana, Missouri; d. 25 April 1962 in Chicago, Illinois). His family moved to Chicago, Illinois, when he was an infant. He began violin study at an early age and later attended the Chicago College of Music. His teachers included Charles Elgar and Darnell Howard,* among others, and he began playing professionally with Elgar when he was sixteen. Thereafter he played with various groups, including Mae Brady, Erskine Tate,* Jimmy Wade (c1924-27), and Gilbert McKendrick. In 1928 he organized his own group, The Alabamians, with whom he toured in Europe until 1930. During this period he also studied further with teachers in Paris, France, and Budapest, Hungary. During the years 1931-37 he was active in the United States with his groups and also as accompanist for others. He then returned to Europe to play a long residency in Paris (1937-38) and short engagements in other cities. In 1938 he settled permanently in the United States, continuing to lead his own groups in longtime residencies in nightclubs and hotels of New York, Chicago, Hollywood, and other places on the West Coast. During the 1940s he had his own radio series; during the 1950s he appeared regularly on television. He first recorded in 1923 with Jimmy Wade's Moulin Rouge Orchestra; thereafter he recorded many albums with his groups and with others. Best known of these are *The Distinguished Violin of Eddie South* and *Django and His American Friends* (recorded with Django Reinhardt and Stephane Grappelly). A pioneer jazz violinist, he was acclaimed for his artistry and technical skills; he was called "The Dark Angel of the Violin."

BIBL: Black press, incl. CDef, 1920s, 28 April 1962. ChilWW. FeaEJ. FeaJS.

DISC: Jep. Kink. RustJR. TudJ.

SOUTHALL, GENEVA HANDY. University professor (b. 5 December 1925 in New Orleans, Louisiana). She studied piano as a child with her mother, a piano teacher. She obtained her musical education in the public schools of New Orleans; at Dillard University in New Orleans (B.A., 1945), where she studied piano with Carol Blanton;* the American Conservatory of Music in Chicago, Illinois (M. Mus., 1956), where she studied with Rudolph Reuter; and the University of Iowa at Iowa City (Ph.D., 1966), where she studied with John Simms. She sang in the Dillard Youth Chorus through her high-school years and was a choir accompanist and chapel pianist throughout her college career. Her teaching career included tenures at Paul Quinn College in Waco, Texas (1957-58), Knoxville [Tennessee] College (1959-61), South Carolina State College at Orangeburg (1962-64), Grambling [Louisiana] College (1967-70), and the University of Minnesota at Minneapolis (1970-). Throughout this period she was also active as a concert pianist, an accompanist, and chamber-group pianist, including a tour with the Pro Viva Trio in Germany (1955) sponsored by the United States Information Service. Beginning in 1970 she began to give considerable attention to musicological research and publication; she published articles in professional journals and in music dictionaries, such as *The New Grove Dictionary of Music and Musicians*. Her honors included awards from civic, community, and professional organizations. In 1980 she published a biography of Thomas Greene Bethune,* titled *The Life and Times of Blind Tom, A Black Pianist-Composer, 1849-1908*.

BIBL: Questionnaire. WWA. WWBA.

SOUTHERN, EILEEN JACKSON. Musicologist/University professor (b. 19 February 1920 in Minneapolis, Minnesota). She came from a family of amateur musicians: her father played violin, a paternal uncle played trumpet, and her mother sang in church choirs. Her family settled in Chicago, Illinois, when she was four years old, and she began piano study a year later with local teacher Muriel Rose. She obtained her public-school education in Chicago (1925-28; 1931-36), Minneapolis (1929), and Sioux Falls, South Dakota (1929-31). She attended the University of Chicago (B.A., 1940; M.A. 1941) and New York University (Ph.D., 1961), where she studied with Gustave Reese, Curt Sachs, and Martin Bernstein. She studied piano at Chicago Musical College, the Juilliard School of Music, and Boston University; her teachers included Meda Zarbelle Steele, Mollie Margolies, and Ernest Hutcheson, among others. She played for church choirs from childhood on and toured with a spiritual quartet for a short period in South Dakota. She gave her first full-length piano recital at the age of twelve. In 1938 she made her debut, playing a concerto with the Chicago Musical College symphony orchestra at Orchestra Hall; thereafter she toured regularly as a concert pianist until 1955. Her teaching career included tenures in public schools of Charlotte, North Carolina (1942-43), and the city of New York (1954-60); at Prairie View State College in Texas (1941-42); Southern University in Baton Rouge, Louisiana (1943-45; 1949-51); Alcorn State College in Mississippi (1945-46); Claflin University in Orangeburg, South Carolina (1947-49); Brooklyn College of the City University of New York (1960-68); York College of CUNY (1968-75); and Harvard University in Cambridge, Massachusetts (1976-). She contributed articles to such professional journals as *Acta Musicologica, Musica Disciplina, Journal of the American Musicological Society*, and *The Black Scholar*, among others, and to such reference works as *Grolier's Encyclopedia, Dictionary of American Biography, Encyclopedia of Black America*, and *The New Grove Dictionary of Music and Musicians*. She was co-founder/publisher (with her husband Joseph) and editor of a scholarly journal, *The Black Perspective in Music* (1973-). Her book publications included *The Buxheim Organ Book* (1963), *The Music of Black Americans: A History* (1971), *Readings in Black American Music* (editor, 1971); *Anonymous Chansons in a Manuscript at El Escorial* (1981); and *Biographical Dictionary of Afro-American and African Musicians* (1982). From 1969 on she toured widely as a lecturer, speaking particularly on the subject of black-American music. Her honors included citations from professional, civic, and government organizations; awards from professional sororities and other women's organizations; appointments to panels and committees of professional and government organizations (including the Board of Directors of the American Musicological Society, 1974-76); the ASCAP Deems Taylor Award (1973); University of Chicago Alumni Achievement Award (1971); National Association of Negro Musicians Award (1971); a grant from the National Endowment for the Humanities (1979-82); and an honorary M.A. degree from Harvard University (1976).

BIBL: Baker. ContA. Gro. WWA. WWAW. WWBA. WWCA, 1950. WWEast.

SOUTHERN HARP SPIRITUAL SINGERS, THE. See **GRIFFIN, BESSIE** and **HOPKINS, LINDA.**

SOUTHERNAIRES, THE. Entertainer group (fl. 1930s-50s; orig. in New York). The male quartet was organized in 1929 for the purpose of singing in local churches and practiced during its early period at the Williams Institutional CME Church. The group included lead soloist and second tenor Lowell Peters (b. at Cleveland, Tennessee), first tenor Homer Smith (b. at Florence, Alabama), baritone Jay Stone Toney (b. in Kentucky), and bass William Edmondson (b. at Spokane, Washington). All had considerable stage experience before joining the quartet: Peters toured with the Knoxville College quartet (of Knoxville, Tennessee) in Europe and sang with the Hall Johnson* Choir; Smith studied voice and sang at Wilberforce College in Ohio; Toney, who attended Tennessee State Normal School, sang with a quartet in Europe after his service in World War I abroad; Edmondson, who attended Spokane College, sang in a touring concert company. The Southernaires toured widely and sang on coast-to-coast radio network programs, beginning their broadcasting in 1930. Pianist/arranger Clarence Jones* worked with the quartet during the years 1932-39. Spencer Odom* became pianist/arranger in 1939, and in 1944 Roy Yates replaced Smith as first tenor.

BIBL: Black press, incl. NYAge, 6 May 1933, 25 May 1936, 1 January 1944. Hare.

SOWANDE, FELA. Composer (b. 29 May 1905 in Oyo, Nigeria). His father, an Anglican priest, was also an organist. His family moved to Lagos, Nigeria, when he was about seven years old, and there he first studied music formally. His teacher, T. K. Phillips, organist and choirmaster at the Christ Church, was the first Nigerian to study music in Europe and a graduate of Trinity College in London, England. Sowande obtained his education at the Mission School and King's College in Lagos, and at London University (B. Mus., 1956) and Trinity College, where he studied with George Oldroyd, George Cunningham, and Edmund Rubbra. He sang in a church choir from earliest childhood until he was an adult. After completing his basic education in Lagos, he taught school for three years, then entered government service. When he was twenty-seven years old, he decided to become a civil engineer and went to London about 1935 to study. After six months, he changed to the study of music. To support himself he played jazz in London nightclubs. He also studied jazz with a white jazzman, Jerry Moore, who assigned him to listen to recordings of Arthur ("Art") Tatum,* Earl Hines,* and Theodore ("Teddy") Wilson,* among others, and to learn to play in their styles. He established himself as one of the leading jazzmen in London and introduced jazz organ to the city, using the Hammond organ. He came into contact with black-Americans who visited the city, including Thomas ("Fats") Waller,* Paul Robeson,* J. Rosamond Johnson,* and Adelaide Hall* (with whom he recorded and played in her cabaret from 1938 until the outbreak of World War II). He toured as a soloist on the vaudeville circuit and performed with *The Blackbirds of 1937*. He also conducted a regular radio-broadcast series, made recordings, and organized a jazz group composed of West Indians living in London.

He began composing in various styles during his first years in London, and during the 1940s he began playing his music in public in the West London Mission of the Methodist Church at Kingsway Hall, where he was organist-choirmaster for many years (1941-50). This led to opportunities for publication and won him attention as a composer. In 1940 he began a radio series, "West African Music and the Possibilities of Its Development," for which he used his own music as illustration. In 1944 the BBC (British Broadcasting Company) Symphony Orchestra performed his *Africana*. During World War II he was Musical Advisor to the Colonial Film Unit. In 1953 he returned to Nigeria as musical director of the Nigerian Broadcasting Service in Lagos. In 1962 he established the Sowande School of Music at Nsukka, Nigeria. He first toured in the United States in 1957, giving organ recitals under the auspices of the United States Department of State. He also toured widely as a guest conductor of symphony orchestras and as a lecturer. Later he settled permanently in the United States. His teaching career included tenures at Ibadan University in Nigeria, Howard University in Washington, D.C., and the University of Pittsburgh in Pennsylvania. His honors and awards included the MBE (Member of the British Empire) from Queen Elizabeth II for "distinguished services in the cause of music" (1956); the MFN (Member of the Federation of Nigeria, 1964); the Traditional Chieftaincy Award, the Bagbile of Lagos, in recognition of his research into Yoruban folklore (1968); a Rockefeller Foundation grant; and an honorary doctorate from the University of Nigeria at Ife (1972). His best-known works, in addition to that cited above, were *African Suite* for strings (1952), *A Folk Symphony* (1960), organ settings of African folk songs and Negro spirituals, and art-song settings of poems by Anthony Granville-Gascoigne. He was the first African composer to combine African elements with Western art forms and styles.

BIBL: Schom. BPIM 4 (Spring 1976). Bill Cole, *John Coltrane* (New York, 1976).

DISC: RustCED (See Adelaide Hall).

SPANN, OTIS. Bluesman (b. 21 March 1930 in Jackson, Mississippi; d. 24 April 1970 in Chicago, Illinois). He was taught to play piano blues by Friday Ford, but his style also reflected the influence of Big Maceo, "Sunnyland Slim" (Albert Luandrew),* and "Blind" John Davis,* among others. In 1947 he settled in Chicago, where he began a longtime association with "Muddy Waters" (McKinley Morganfield).* Spann was one of the few Chicago blues pianists whose playing resisted the influence of rock or country music. He recorded extensively and/or toured widely in the United States and in Europe with Buddy Guy, James Cotton,* "Bo Diddley" (Ellas McDaniel),* Willie Mae ("Big Mama") Thornton,* "Howlin' Wolf" (Chester Burnett),* and Muddy Waters.

BIBL: BWW. FeaJS. FeaGitJS. LivBl, 2 (Summer 1970).

DISC: LeSl. TudBM.

SPEARMAN, RAWN. Concert singer (b. 4 February 1924 in Bexar, Alabama). He came from a musical family. His father, a minister, sang tenor in amateur quartets, and he often went with his father on tours as a child. He began piano study at an early age and later played guitar and recorder. Although not a music major, in high school and college he participated widely in musical activities. He obtained his education at Florida A & M College (Agricultural and Mechanical) in Tallahassee, Florida (B.S. 1942), where he studied music with Rudolph Von Charlton* and Johnnie V. Lee; at Columbia University Teachers College in New York (M.A., 1963; D. Mus. Ed., 1973); at the American Theater Wing in New York (1949-52); and at Fountainbleau (Paris), France. His music teachers included Charles Kingsford, Otto Hertz, Charles Winter Wood, and Eva Gautier, among others. His career development was also influenced by Edward Boatner,* Roland Hayes,* and Theodore Margetson.* During his service in the United States Armed Forces (1942-46), he sang in his infantry's chorus and played in the infantry band. After his discharge he toured with the Fisk Jubilee Singers* (1947-48) as a member of the quartet and also as a soloist. In May 1951 he made his concert debut as a baritone at Times Hall in New York; in October of the next year he made his Town Hall debut. He toured widely as a concert singer and sang with leading symphony orchestras; in November 1955 he sang a leading role in the New York premiere of Stravinsky's *In Memoriam: Dylan Thomas*. He was also active in theater music; he sang in Britten's *Let's Make an Opera*, Thomson's *Four Saints in Three Acts* (the 1952 revival), the Broadway musicals *House of Flowers* (1955) and *Kwamina* (1961), and Gershwin's *Porgy and Bess* (the 1961-62 revival). In April 1979 he sang the role of Mr. Five in the world premiere of Vaclav Nelhybel's opera, *The Station*. He also sang on television programs and recorded regularly. His teaching career included tenures at Hunter College of the City University of New York (1969-73), the Borough of Manhattan Community College of CUNY (1973-76), and the University of Lowell in Massachusetts (1976-). He won wide recognition for his concerts featuring musical settings of the poems of Langston Hughes.*

BIBL: Questionnaire. Black press, incl. AmstN, 1 December 1951; NYAge-Defender, 27 February 1954. NYT, 20 October 1952, 26 July 1954.

SPECKLED RED. See **PERRYMAN, RUFUS.**

SPELLMAN, A. B. Writer (b. 7 August 1935 in Elizabeth City, North Carolina). Although he was not a professional musician, he is included here because of his contributions to black-music literature. He obtained his education at Howard University in Washington, D.C. (B.A.). His best-known work was *Black Music* (New York, 1970; originally published as *Four Lives in the Bebop Business*, New York, 1966). He contributed articles about black music to periodicals and was editor of *The Cricket*.

BIBL: Page.

SPENCER, KENNETH. Concert singer (b. 1913 in Los Angeles, California; d. 25 February 1964 near New Orleans, Louisiana). He obtained his musical education at the Eastman School of Music in Rochester, New York. In 1941 he made his debut as a concert baritone at Town Hall in New York. Thereafter he toured widely, giving recitals, singing with leading symphony orchestras and occasionally with opera companies. He was also active in radio music; in 1942 he gave recitals regularly on CBS radio. During the 1940s he toured with USO (United Service Organization) units in the United States and abroad. He appeared in films, including *Cabin in the Sky* (1942), *Bataan* (1943) and *The Joyous Pilgrim* (1951). About 1950 he settled in Europe. He returned to the United States in 1963 and settled in Los Angeles, California. He was en route to sing at a concert in New Jersey when he was killed in an airplane crash near New Orleans, Louisiana.

BIBL: Black press, incl. CDef, 17 January 1942, 5 December 1944; AmstN, 29 February 1964.

DISC: Turn.

SPILLER, ISABELLE TALIAFERRO. Music educator (b. 18 March 1888 in Abingdon, Virginia; d. 14 May 1974 in New York, New York). As a child she played piano in her father's church. She received her musical education in the public schools of Philadelphia, Pennsylvania; the New England Conservatory of Music at Boston, Massachusetts (1909); Columbia University Teachers College in New York; and the New School for Social Research in New York. During the years 1912-26 she was assistant manager of the Six Musical Spillers, a vaudeville act organized by her husband, William Newmeyer Spiller,* which toured widely in the United States and abroad. She was also the director of the Spiller Music School, which was established in 1926. Her teaching career included tenures at the Howard Orphans Asylum in Brooklyn, New York (1910-11); the Columbus Hill Center (1929-54), and the public schools of New York (1929-54). During the years 1942-54 she was an orchestral supervisor at the Wadleigh High School. She also supervised the music education program for the New York World's Fair in 1939 and a musical therapy program at Bellevue Hospital.

BIBL: Black press, incl. AmstN, 25 May 1974; PhilaT, 1912-1917. Handy. Layne. WWCA, 1950.

SPILLER, WILLIAM NEWMEYER. Vaudeville entertainer (b. 1877 in Hampton, Virginia; d. 3 September 1944 in New York, New York). He obtained his musical education at Spiller Academy in Hampton, Virginia, which was founded by his father, and at Hampton Institute. Little is known of his early career. In 1899 he joined Mahara's Minstrels as a singer but later played tenor saxophone and alto horn in the Mahara band, then under the leadership of W. C. Handy.* Early in 1903 he moved to Chicago, Illinois, where he sang in local concerts produced by N. Clark Smith* during the early years of the century. About 1906 he organized The Six Musical Spillers, a vaudeville act that toured widely in Europe, South America, Africa, and Canada, as well as the United States, until it was disbanded in the 1930s. His wife, Isabelle Taliaferro Spiller,* served as assistant manager for the group and also as co-director of the Spiller Music School (established in 1926).

BIBL: Communication from D. Antoinette Handy. Black press, incl. AmstN, 9 September 1944; CDef, 18

July 1931; IndF, 10 June 1899, 28 March 1903, 16 October 1915. Flet, p. 225.

SPINNERS, THE. Entertainment vocal quintet (fl. 1950s-70s; org. 1955 in Detroit, Michigan). The singing-dancing male group originally consisted of Henry Fambrough, Billy Henderson, Pervis Jackson, and Bobbie Smith, all natives of Detroit, Michigan. They sang in their high-school glee club and began singing together in local bars and on talent shows as The Domingos. By 1957 they were calling themselves The Detroit Spinners and singing in theaters and ballrooms. In 1961 they made their debut recording for a label produced by Harvey Fuqua of the Moonglows.* In 1964 Fuqua's label was absorbed by Gordy Berry's* Motown Industries, and the Spinners along with him (1964-72). The group first attracted wide attention with the recording "That's what girls are made for" in 1961 and with "Sweet thing" in 1966. Charlie Atkins coached them in their dancing routines, as he did other Motown groups, such as the Jackson Five,* The Temptations,* and Gladys Knight* and the Pips, among others. Personnel changes during the 1960s-70s brought in George Cameron and Phil Wynn, but by 1976 Cameron had gone. After leaving Motown in 1972 the Spinners turned to songwriters Leon Huff,* Kenneth ("Ken") Gamble,* and Thom Bell* of Philadelphia International. Their best-known performances were "Could it be I'm falling in love," "Ghetto child," "One of a kind," and "Live." They received numerous awards from the music industry.

BIBL: Black press, incl. AmstN, 15 May 1976. *Ebony* (July 1976). StamPRS.

SPIVEY, ("QUEEN") VICTORIA REGINA. (b. 15 October 1906 in Houston, Texas; d. 3 October 1976 in New York, New York). She came from a musical family; her father and brothers played in a local string band. She began playing piano as a child and early performed with local groups, including "Daddy" Filmore's blues-jazz band and L. C. Tolen's band. In the clubs she came into contact with "Blind" Lemon Jefferson.* In 1926 she made her first recording, "Black snake blues," which won her wide attention. She recorded extensively during the years 1926-37, longer than any of the other classic blues singers of her period, and wrote most of her songs. Those with whom she recorded or performed included "Memphis Minnie" (Minnie Douglas Lawless),* Bessie Smith,* and "Tampa Red" (Hudson Whittaker),* among others; she also had her own band, Hunter's Serenaders. In 1934 she began a long association with dancer Billy Adams, which lasted until 1951 and included touring with Louis Armstrong,* the Olsen and Johnson *Hellzapoppin'* show, and on the vaudeville circuit. In 1952 she left the stage and devoted her time to church activities, although occasionally performing in clubs. In 1961 she returned to blues and toured widely at home and abroad—in 1963 she went to Europe with the American Folk Blues Festival; she appeared at the major festivals, on radio and television programs, and on college campuses. In 1962 she established her own record company, Spivey Records, which reissued her records and recorded many of the leading bluesmen of the period. She also wrote many columns for *Record Research* magazine. Her contemporaries called her "The Queen."

BIBL: BWW. ChilWWJ. Len Kunstadt, "The Queen and Her Knights" in *Record Research* (May 1956). LivBl 29 (September-October 1976). Derrick Stewart-Baxter, *Ma Rainey and the Classic Blues Singers* (New York, 1970). MeeJMov.

DISC: DiGod. Kink. RustJR. TudBM.

ST. CYR, JOHN ALEXANDER ("JOHNNY"). Jazz banjoist/Guitarist (b. 17 April 1890 in New Orleans, Louisiana; d. 17 June 1966 in Los Angeles, California). His father played guitar and flute, and he began playing guitar as a child. During the years c1905-23 he played with various groups, including Jules Baptiste, Manuel Gabriele, Freddie Keppard,* Oscar ("Papa") Celestin,* Edward ("Kid") Ory,* Armand Piron,* Fate Marable* (on riverboats), Ed Allen, Charlie Creath,* and Manuel Perez, among others. Early in his career he also led his own group, called Consumer's Trio. In 1923 he settled in Chicago, Illinois; thereafter he played and/or recorded with Louis Armstrong* Joseph ("King") Oliver,* Charles ("Doc") Cooke* (1924-29), Darnell Howard,* and Ferdinand ("Jelly Roll") Morton,* among others. During the years 1929-55 he lived in New Orleans, then settled permanently in Los Angeles, California. Those with whom he played in New Orleans included Paul Barbarin,* Alphonse Picou,* and Paul Barnes, among others. On the West Coast he played with the New Orleans Creole Jazz Band (1959) and his own group, The Young Men of New Orleans, at Disneyland in the 1960s. He was a pioneer jazz banjoist in the New Orleans tradition, but his contribution was as an ensemble player rather than soloist.

BIBL: ChilWW. FeaEJ. MeeJMov. Souc.

DISC: Jep. Kink. RustJR.

STACKHOUSE, HOUSTON. Bluesman (b. 28 September 1910 in Wesson, Mississippi). Although he was influenced by uncles who played blues guitar, he first studied with Tommy Johnson* and his brothers, Mager and Clarence, who lived in Crystal Springs, where he settled as a young man. He taught himself to play harmonica by listening to his cousin, Robert (''Nighthawk'') McCullum* (aka McCoy), and to play string instruments, violin and mandolin, by listening to Lonnie Chatman and Jimmy Smith. When he began to play guitar in 1926, his style development was influenced by Alger (''Texas'') Alexander, ''Blind'' Arthur Blake,* Lonnie Johnson,* and ''Blind'' Lemon Jefferson.* He began to play professionally during the mid-1930s, joining a group called the Mississippi Sheiks, No. 2. During the following years he also performed and/or recorded with James (''Peck'') Curtis, Earl Hooker, Pinetop Perkins, Robert Nighthawk, Tommy Johnson,* Joe Wilkins Willie,* and ''Sonny Boy Williamson, No. 2'' (Willie ''Rice'' Miller).* In 1946 he settled in Helena, Arkansas, where he began a long association with the King Biscuit Show on radio station KFFA, which was originated by Williamson. Although not as well known as many of his contemporaries, he exerted wide influence on the development of the Delta blues through his radio broadcasts. In 1970 he settled in Memphis, Tennessee, after living a while in Mississippi during 1969.

BIBL: BWW. LivBl 17 (Summer 1974). Oliv.

STANDIFER, JAMES. University professor (b. 14 August 1936 in Itasca, Texas). He obtained his musical education at Fisk University in Nashville, Tennessee (B.A., 1957; M.A., 1958), and at Case Western Reserve University in Cleveland, Ohio (Ph.D. in Mus. Ed., 1968). During his college years he sang with the Fisk Jubilee Singers.* His teaching career included tenures at Morristown Junior College in Morristown, Tennessee (1958-60); the Cleveland public schools (1963-66); Temple University School of Music in Philadelphia, Pennsylvania (1968-70); and the University of Michigan at Ann Arbor (1970-), where he was also curator of the Eva Jessye* Collection of Afro-American Materials. He toured widely as a lecturer and workshop consultant and published articles in professional journals, among them, *The School Musician, Music Educators Journal, Korea Journal,* and *Journal of Research in Music Education.* His book publications included *Source Book of African and Afro-American Materials for Music Educators,* with Barbara Reeder (Washington, D.C., 1972); *The World of Popular Music,* with Sidney Fox (Chicago, 1974); *New Dimensions in Music; Sound, Beat and Feeling,* with Robert Choate and Barbara Kaplan (New York, 1976, rev. ed.); *New Dimensions in Music, Sound, Shape and Symbol,* with Robert Choate and Barbara Kaplan (New York, 1976, rev. ed.). His honors included awards from professional organizations, appointments to national boards of professional organizations, and a grant from the National Endowment for the Humanities (1979).

BIBL: Questionnaire.

STANS, JACOB A. Choral conductor. See **JOHNSON, FRANCIS.**

STAPLE SINGERS, THE. Gospel group (fl. 1950s-70s; org. in Chicago, Illinois). The Staple family moved to Chicago, Illinois, in 1935. The father, Roebuck, and his children began singing for church and community events in the 1940s and, encouraged by friends, organized a gospel group in 1948. Roebuck sang lead and played guitar; Mavis (b. 1941) sang contralto; Cleotha, soprano; Pervis (b. 1937), baritone. About 1965 Yvonne joined the group. During the 1950s The Staples toured widely, performing from a repertory of hymns, spirituals, and gospel. In the late 1960s they moved into the field of popular music. Thereafter they toured throughout the world, appearing in nightclubs, theaters, and concert halls. They also performed on television programs and in films, including *Soul to Soul* (1971). They began to record extensively about 1953, particularly for Vee Jay Records.*

BIBL: Black press, incl. AmstN, 11 August 1962. StamPRS.

DISC: Hayes. TudBM.

STATON, DAKOTA. Jazz singer (b. 3 June 1932 in Pittsburgh, Pennsylvania). She began singing and dancing at the age of five but did not perform professionally until after her graduation from high school. She studied music at the Filion School of Music in Pittsburgh. In 1954 she made her recording debut and thereafter recorded regularly. She also toured widely, singing in nightclubs, theaters, and at jazz festivals. During the late 1960s-early 1970s she lived abroad for five years and performed primarily in Europe, India and Pakistan, the Far East, and Australia. She received many awards from the music industry. Her performing style was in the tradition of Dinah Washington* and Sarah Vaughan.*

BIBL: FeaEJ. FeaGitJS.

DISC: Jep.

STEWART, REX WILLIAM. Jazz cornetist (b. 22 February 1907 in Philadelphia, Pennsylvania; d. 7 September 1967 in Los Angeles, California). His father played violin, and his mother played piano. As a child he studied violin and piano, then alto horn, and finally cornet, which he played in Danny Doyle's Boys Band.

His family moved to Georgetown, Virginia (near Washington, D.C.), when he was seven years old. He began playing professionally at fourteen with various groups, including riverboat bands. Later he played with Ollie Blackwell (1921), The Musical Spillers (1921-22), Jimmy Cooper, Billy Paige, and Elmer Snowden* (1925), among others. Thereafter he played with Fletcher Henderson* (intermittently during the late 1920s-early 1930s), Horace Henderson,* McKinney's Cotton Pickers* (1931, 1932), and Stanley ("Fess") Williams* (1933); he also led his own group in 1933-34. He was best known for his work with Edward ("Duke") Ellington* (1934-45, except during mid-1943), where he introduced the half-valve technique in his solo in "Boy meets horn," which he co-wrote with Ellington. He first recorded in 1934 and thereafter recorded regularly. After leaving Ellington in 1945, he played with Benny Carter* and toured widely with his own groups or as a soloist. In 1960 he settled in Los Angeles, California, where he became active as a disc jockey, although he continued to perform occasionally, appearing at jazz festivals and touring in Europe in 1966. He lectured and published articles in jazz journals. He also was active in radio, television, and films, including *Hellzapoppin'* (1941), *Rendezvous de Juillet* (1949), and the *Sound of Jazz* (1957), among others. Stewart made an important contribution to the sound of the Ellington orchestra, and his half-valve technique was widely imitated. A collection of his best-known compositions, *Jazz Master of the 30s*, was produced posthumously in 1972.

BIBL: AlHen. ChilWW. FeaEJ. FeaJS. FeaGitJS. MeeJMov.

DISC: Kink. RustJR. TudJ.

STILL, WILLIAM GRANT. Composer (b. 11 May 1895 in Woodville, Mississippi; d. 3 December 1978 in Los Angeles, California). Both parents were musical: his father was the village brass-band leader, and his mother played piano. After his father's death when he was an infant, his mother moved to Little Rock, Arkansas. He obtained his musical education in the public schools of Little Rock, where he came under the influence of Charlotte Andrews Stephens, who also taught Florence Price*; at Wilberforce College in Ohio (1911-14); and at the Oberlin Conservatory of Music in Ohio (1917, 1919), where he studied with Friedrich Lehmann and George Andrews. Later he studied privately with Edgar Varèse (1923-25) and George Whitefield Chadwick (1922), at that time director of the New England Conservatory of Music in Boston, Massachusetts. He began violin study during his high-school years and at Wilberforce played in the University String Quartet. He entered college with the intention of preparing for a career in medicine, but soon found himself deeply involved in musical activities—conducting the college band, arranging for various groups, and writing music. In 1914 he began performing professionally with a dance orchestra. He was an arranger for W. C. Handy* during the summer of 1916, and during that period made the first band arrangements of "Beale Street blues" and "St. Louis blues." During his year of service in the U. S. Navy (1918), he played violin for the entertainment of servicemen in the Officers Mess. In 1919 he left Oberlin to work again for Handy, who had moved to New York with his music publishing business. In addition to playing in Handy's bands, Still made arrangements for the dance groups and served as a road manager. In 1921 he left Handy to become arranger and recording manager of Harry Pace's* newly established Phonograph Company, which produced records on the Black Swan label with Ethel Waters* and Fletcher Henderson,* among many others. During the 1920s-30s he also played with orchestras, including the pit orchestras for the Noble Sissle*/Eubie Blake* musical *Shuffle Along* (1921-23) and the musical *Dixie to Broadway*, which starred Florence Mills* (1924), and Leroy Smith in Atlantic City, New Jersey (summer 1926). He wrote arrangements and orchestrations for radio shows, such as Paul Whiteman's "Old Gold Show" (1929) and Willard Robison's "Deep River Hour," and for such individuals as Earl Carroll, Artie Shaw, Donald Vorhees, and Sophie Tucker. In 1934 he settled in Los Angeles, California, where he began writing music for films, including *Lost Horizon* (1935), *Pennies From Heaven* (1936), and *Stormy Weather* (1943), and later for television shows, including "Gunsmoke" and the original "Perry Mason Show."

He first composed music during his college years, primarily pieces for performance by the various musical groups with which he was associated. But he was also inspired to write classical music because of the example set by Samuel Coleridge-Taylor,* whose activities were discussed in the press at great length during that period. At Oberlin his teachers encouraged him to become a composer, particularly because of his setting of a poem, "Good night," by Paul Laurence Dunbar.* Through the years with Handy and Pace, he wrote popular music as necessary, sometimes using the pseudonym Willy M. Grant. Concomitantly, he was writing concert music and finding opportunities for its performance. In January 1926 the International Composers Guild sponsored a performance of his *Levee Land*, a three-movement work for orchestra and soloist Florence Mills,* which blended jazz idioms with traditional European elements. Thereafter performances of his music came regularly, particularly at concerts of Georges Barrere's Little Symphony Orchestra and of the International Composers Guild, but also by other symphony orchestras. His first symphony, the *Afro-American*, was performed on 29 October 1931 by the Rochester Philharmonic Orchestra under the direction of Howard Hanson on an American Composers' concert. This was the first time in history that a major orchestra had played the full symphony of a black composer, and it established a brief vogue of sorts. In 1932 the Chicago Symphony played Florence Price's* first symphony, in 1934 the Philadelphia Orchestra played William Dawson's* *Negro Folk Symphony*, and in 1935 the New York Philharmonic gave Still's *Afro-American* a New York premiere. This work brought wide critical acclaim and led to important commissions —including one from the New York World's Fair Committee (1939-40) to write the theme music for "The City of Tomorrow"—increased opportunities for writing film and television music, and most important of all, fellowships that enabled him to write opera.

He wrote in a variety of musical forms: twenty-five major works for symphony orchestra, including five symphonies; six operas; four ballets; eight works for voice and orchestra; twelve compositions for chamber groups; a dozen or more pieces and suites for piano or accordion; and numerous songs. His style was neo-romantic, and he fully utilized the black folk elements of his time—spirituals, blues, worksongs, ragtime, and jazz. He was undoubtedly the first composer to use a blues melody (which he invented in faithful similarity to a genuine folk blues) as the thematic basis for a symphony and the first to employ the banjo as a symphonic instrument (in the *Afro-American*). His music was distinctive for its ingratiating melody and frequently piquant harmonies. He was well acquainted with avant-garde techniques and employed such in his piano suite *Three Visions*, but generally he relied upon traditional procedures. His best-known works, in addition to those cited above, were the orchestral Symphony in G Minor (1937, the second symphony), *A Deserted Plantation* (1933, a suite), *Old California* (1941, a tone poem), *In Memoriam: The Colored Soldiers Who Died for Democracy* (1943), *Festive Overture* (1944), *Danzas de Panama* (1948), and *The Peaceful Land* (1960); the ballets *La Guiablesse* (1927), *Sahdji* (1930), and *Lenox Avenue* (1937); the compositions for voice and orchestra *And They Lynched Him on a Tree* (1940, for black chorus, white chorus, narrator, and contralto with text by Katherine Garrison Chapin), *Plainchant for America* (1941, with text by Chapin), *The Little Song That Wanted to be a Symphony* (1954, for narrator, three female voices, and orchestra; also scored for band); *From a Lost Continent* (1948); the harp concerto *Ennanga* (1956, also scored for piano and orchestra); the band works *From the Delta* (1945) and *Folk Suite for Band* (1963); the chamber compositions Suite for Violin and Piano (1943), *Incantation and Dance* (1945, for oboe and piano), *Pastorela* (1946, for violin and piano), *Miniatures* (1948, for flute, oboe, and piano), and four Folk Suites (1962, for varying combinations of chamber instruments); the piano pieces *Seven Traceries* (1939) and *Bells* (1944); and the song suite *Songs of Separation* (1949, using texts by Langston Hughes,* Arna Bontemps, Philippe-Thoby Marcelin, Paul Laurence Dunbar,* and Countee Cullen), in addition to individual songs and settings of spirituals. In his later career Still drew upon folk idioms of Latin America and Europe, as in his *Christmas in the Western World* (1967) or *Four Indigenous Portraits* (1957), which used North and South American Indian themes and Negro themes. His favored musical form was opera, and he was fortunate to see performances of three of his during his lifetime. The first, *Troubled Island* (1941, libretto by Hughes), caused racial barriers to crumble when it was performed by the New York Opera Company in 1949, the first time in history a major company had performed the opera of a black composer. *Highway 1, U.S.A.* (1962, libretto by Verna Arvey) was first performed at the University of Miami under the direction of Fabien Sevitzky and later by Opera/South* (1972); *A Bayou Legend* (1941, libretto by Arvey) was given its premiere by Opera/South in 1974.

Numerous honors went to Still over his long career: he received fellowships from the Guggenheim Foundation (1934-35) and the Rosenwald Foundation; he received many prizes, including the Jubilee Prize of the Cincinnati Symphony (1944), a Harmon Foundation Award (1928), a Freedoms Foundation Award (1953), and a prize from the U.S. Committee for the United Nations; and he was given honorary doctorates by Howard University (1941), Oberlin (1947), Bates College (1954), University of Arkansas (1971), Pepperdine University (1973), the New England Conservatory of Music (1973), Peabody Conservatory (1974), and the University of Southern California at Los Angeles (1975). His works were performed all over the world. On the occasions of his sixty-fifth, seventieth, seventy-fifth, and eightieth birthdays, musical organizations and educational institutions held special celebrations of all-Still music concerts. In 1974 he was cited as " a distinguished Mississippian" by the governor of Mississippi; the same year he was among the first composers represented on the Columbia Records/AAMOA (Afro-American Music Opportunities Association)*

Black Composers Series releases. He pioneered in making a place for the symphonic and operatic works of black composers at American concerts and truly deserved the title given him, "Dean of Afro-American Composers."

BIBL: Interviews with Still and his wife, Verna Arvey Still, by E. S. AlHen. ASCAP. Bull. BPIM 3 (May 1975: A Birthday Offering to William Grant Still). Gro. Robert Bartlett Haas, ed., *William Grant Still and the Fusion of Cultures in American Music* (Los Angeles, 1972 [includes discography and list of works]). WWA. WWBA. WWCA, 1950.

STITT, EDWARD ("SONNY"). Jazz saxophonist (b. 2 February 1924 in Boston, Massachusetts). He came from a musical family: his father was Edward Boatner,* the composer; his mother was a piano and organ teacher; and his brother Clifford and sister Adelaide both became concert musicians. He grew up in Saginaw, Michigan, and took the surname of his stepfather. He began piano study at the age of seven, then later changed to clarinet and saxophone. His early professional experiences were with groups in Detroit, Michigan. In 1942 he toured with Myron ("Tiny") Bradshaw. Thereafter he played with various groups, including John Birks ("Dizzy") Gillespie* (1945-46, briefly in 1958), Eugene ("Gene") Ammons* (as co-leader, 1951-53), Norman Granz's JATP (Jazz at the Philharmonic, European tours in 1958, 1959), Miles Davis,* Clark Terry,* and J. J. Johnson* (in sextet tour of Japan, 1964), Giants of Jazz (world tours in 1970-72), and in the touring show *The Musical Life of Charlie Parker* (European tour in 1974). He was also active with his own groups and as a soloist, performing in nightclubs, theaters, concert halls, and at jazz festivals, two of which were recorded in films, *Jazz in Piazza* (1974) and *Jazz on a Summer's Day* (1960). He first recorded in 1945 and thereafter recorded prolifically. He attracted wide attention in the 1950s for his musical battles with saxophonist Ammons, particularly on the piece "Blues up and down." He received numerous awards from the music industry and civic organizations and was elected an Ellington* Fellow at Yale University. He was a leading saxophonist (alto and tenor) of the 1940s-50s; his playing was reminiscent of that of Charlie Parker,* although he had developed his style before he first heard Parker recordings in 1943.

BIBL: FeaEJ. FeaJS. FeaGitJS. MeeJMov. WWA. WWBA.

DISC: Jep. Kink. ModJ. TudJ.

STONE, FRED. Songwriter (b. 22 January 1873 in Chatham, Ontario; d. January 1912 in Detroit, Michigan). His family moved to Detroit, Michigan, when he was a child. Little is known of his early career. During the early 1890s he became a member of the Detroit City Band, under the leadership of John ("Jack") W. Johnson,* and he played piano in Theodore Finney's* Famous Dance Orchestra. He began to publish songs during the 1890s, of which the best known were "Bos'n rag" (1899), "Ma rag time baby" (1898), and the waltzes "A lady of quality" and "At twilight." The Stone brothers, including Will and Charles along with Fred, led dance orchestras in Detroit over a period of many years—at one time using the title Finney's Orchestra.

BIBL: DetAH, K. Myers interview with Clyde Hayes. Black press, incl. CleveG, 6 April 1901. Hare. LaBrew.

STONE, JESSE. Jazz bandleader/Arranger (b. 1901 in Atchison, Kansas). He received his musical education in the public schools of Kansas City, Missouri, and through private study. By 1920 he was leading his own groups, at first called The Blues Serenaders and later, The Jesse Stone Orchestra. In 1928 he went to Dallas, Texas, to work with Terrence Holder in organizing a band; later he became the bandleader and toured with the group for a year. Thereafter he returned to Kansas City, where he was musical director-arranger for the George E. Lee* Orchestra (1929-31) and later pianist-arranger for the Thamon Hayes Kansas City Rockets (1932-34). In 1935 he settled in Chicago, Illinois; using the city as a base he toured regularly with his groups, including a tour of the Far East in 1946 for the USO (United Service Organizations). The Jesse Stone orchestras of the 1920s-30s were noted for their excellent arrangements, precision, and fine intonation; he was important in the development of the Kansas City school of jazz.

BIBL: ChilWW. DanceWEH. Russ.

DISC: Jep. RustJR.

STONE, THEODORE. Music critic (b. 18 November 1911 in Gainesville, Texas). As a youth he sang in church choirs and in his high-school glee club. He obtained his musical education at Samuel Huston College in Marshall, Texas, at Chicago Musical College, and through private study. About 1930 he settled in Chicago, Illinois, where he became involved in musical activities, particularly community programs and the Chicago Music Association, of which he served as president. In 1939 he went to Finland, where he studied voice with Soini Kuuler and others at the Sibelius Academy at Helsinki; during his stay abroad he also gave recitals and command performances for crowned heads in Europe. In 1940 he made his concert debut as a baritone at Town Hall in New York. Thereafter he toured regularly throughout the United States and in Canada. He was also active as a music critic and became a member of the Music Critics Association. During the years 1968-74 he was president of the National Association of Negro Musicians.*

BIBL: Black press, incl. AmstN, 23 September 1944; CDef, 13 January 1940; NYAge, 20 April 1940.

STRAYHORN, WILLIAM ("BILLY" "SWEETPEA"). Jazz arranger (b. 29 November 1915 in Dayton, Ohio; d. 31 May 1967 in New York, New York). He obtained his musical education in the public schools of Hillsboro, North Carolina, and of Pittsburgh, Pennsylvania. In 1938 he met Edward (''Duke'') Ellington* and played one of his compositions for Ellington. In 1939 he played for a short period with Mercer Ellington,* then joined Duke's band as arranger and occasional pianist (1939-67). He wrote many of the pieces for which Duke's band became celebrated, including ''Take the A train,'' ''After all,'' ''Johnny come lately,'' ''Passion flower,'' and ''Midriff.'' He also collaborated with Duke in writing music as, for example, ''Satin doll'' (also with Johnny Mercer), *A Drum Is a Woman* (1956) and *Shakespearean Suite* (1957). He and Duke were so similar in temperament that it was often difficult to distinguish between their styles. A collection of his pieces was recorded in *And His Mother Called Him Bill* (released posthumously). Strayhorn was also active as a bandleader and he recorded under his own name. His greatest contribution was as arranger for the Ellington band and co-developer of the Ellington sound.

BIBL: ASCAP. ChilWW. FeaEJ. FeaJS. FeaGitJS. MeeJMov.

DISC: Jep. Kink. RustJR. TudJ.

SUBLETT, JOHN WILLIAM (known as **BUBBLES).** Vaudeville/Stage-musical singer (b. 19 February 1902 in Louisville, Kentucky). When he was nine years old he formed a song-and-dance team with a friend, Ford Lee (''Buck'') Washington (1903-1955), that as Buck and Bubbles became one of the leading vaudeville acts of its time (1919-53). The team toured widely in the United States on the theater circuit and played in London (1931). Buck and Bubbles appeared in Broadway musicals, including *Ziegfeld Follies of 1921*, Lew Leslie's *Blackbirds of 1930*, *Frolics of 1938*, *Laugh Time* (1943), and *Carmen Jones* (1944), among others. They also appeared in such films as *Cabin in the Sky* (1943) and *A Song Is Born* (1948). John (''Bubbles'') created the role of Sportin' Life in Gershwin's folk opera, *Porgy and Bess*, in 1935. After Washington's death, he was musically inactive, then returned to the entertainment world during the 1960s. He toured in Vietnam with Bob Hope, appeared on television shows, such as Johnny Carson's, and performed in a nightclub act with Anna Maria Alberghetti. He also made recordings.

BIBL: NegA.

DISC: Turn.

SULLIVAN, MAXINE (née **MARIETTA WILLIAMS)** Jazz singer (b. 13 May 1911 in Homestead, Pennsylvania). She began her professional career singing with a group called The Red Hot Peppers in Pittsburgh, Pennsylvania, and on radio shows. In 1937 she made her recording debut with Claude Thornhill. Thereafter she performed with John Kirby* (to whom she was married during the years 1938-41) and recorded with him the song that brought her wide attention, a swing version of ''Loch Lomond''(1937). She was active in television and in films, including *Going Places* (1938) and *St. Louis Blues* (1939). During the 1940s-50s she toured briefly with Benny Carter* and also as a soloist, and played long residencies at nightclubs in New York and in Europe. She was inactive musically for long periods during the 1940s-50s. She returned to music in the late 1950s, playing trombone as well as singing, and toured widely on the nightclub circuit. During the years 1969-75 she toured intermittently in Europe with The World's Greatest Jazz Band.

BIBL: ChilWW. *Ebony* (July 1974). FeaEJ. FeaJS. FeaGitJS. MeeJMov.

DISC: Jep. Kink. RustJR.

SUMMER, DONNA (née **LaDONNA ANDREA GAINES).** Rock-disco singer (b. 31 December 1948 in Boston, Massachusetts). As a child she sang in church choirs. Later she moved into the field of popular music and, by the time she was sixteen, was singing with a rock 'n' roll group called Crow. In 1967 she went to Europe with a touring company of the musical *Hair*, singing the role of Sheila, which had been created by Melba Moore.* During the next eight years she sang in productions of the Vienna [Austria] Volksoper, including Kern's *Showboat* and Gershwin's *Porgy and Bess*, and in productions of the Broadway musicals *Godspell* and *The Me Noboby Knows* in Munich, Germany. There she also became associated with the developers of the new Eurodisc sound, including arrangers Giorgio Moroder and Pete Bellotte, at the Musicland Recording Studios—at first as a backup singer, then as a soloist. Her first recordings were ''Hostage'' and ''Lady of the night.'' In 1975 her album *Love to Love You* attracted wide attention on both sides of the Atlantic and won her the title ''Disco Sex Goddess.'' Thereafter she toured widely, appearing in nightclubs and concert halls, frequently accompanied by a group called Brooklyn Dreams. She also sang in films, including *The Deep* (1977), for which she wrote and sang the theme song, and *Thank God It's Friday* (1978), which also featured The Commodores. Her best-known albums were *A Trilogy of Love, I Remember Yesterday, Once Upon a Time, Wanderer,* and *Bad Girl*; the later ones included popular songs and gospel as well as disco and rock. She was married at one time to Austrian actor Helmut Sommers. She was credited with launching the disco fad of the 1970s.

BIBL: Black press, incl. CDef, 15 November 1980. CurBiog (July 1979). *Dawn Magazine* (August 1978). *Ebony* (October 1977). WWA.

SUN RA (HERMAN "SONNY" BLOUNT, LE SONY' RA). Jazz keyboardist (b. May c1915 in Birmingham, Alabama). He began playing piano when he was about eleven years old. He attended Alabama A & M College in Huntsville and during that time studied music privately with Willa Randolph. His early professional experiences were with the local group Society Troubadours and with Paul Bascomb,* both in Birmingham. About 1934 he settled in Chicago, Illinois, and organized his own group, which performed primarily in Chicago nightclubs. Thereafter he played with Fletcher Henderson* (1946-47), Hezekiah ("Stuff") Smith,* Coleman Hawkins,* and Wynonie Harris,* among others. During the 1950s he changed his name and organized his Solar Arkestra (also called Space Arkestra or Intergalactic Myth-Science Arkestra). In the 1970s the group typically consisted of thirty or more persons, including dancers and singers, and used costumes, films, light shows, and other theatrics in its productions. Among his sidemen who were members of the original Arkestra in 1956 and remained with him for more than twenty years were Marshall Allen, John Gilmore, and Pat Patrick. He toured widely with his show, recorded, and wrote music for films, including *Cry of Jazz* (1959) and *Space is the Place* (1971). He received many awards from the music industry. He was a pioneer in the use of electronic instruments in the jazz ensemble. His music was free-form and experimental; despite its dissonance and free improvisation, however, it included reference to black-music elements.

BIBL: AlHen. *Cadence* (June 1978). ContKey (January 1979). FeaEJ. FeaJS. FeaGitJS. MeeJMov.

DISC: TudJ.

SUNNYLAND SLIM. See **LUANDREW, ANDREW.**

SUPREMES, THE. Rhythm 'n' blues group (fl. 1960s-70s; org. in Detroit, Michigan). The vocal trio, organized during the late 1950s, was composed of Florence Ballard (b. 30 June 1943), Diana Ross* (b. 26 March 1944), and Mary Wilson (b. 6 March 1943). The girls sang rhythm 'n' blues for local social events during their high-school days. After graduating from high school, they signed a recording contract with Berry Gordy* of Motown Record Corporation. Beginning in 1964 their recordings attracted national attention and they began to win awards from the music industry. In 1967 Cindy Birdsong replaced Florence Ballard, and in the same year the group was renamed Diana Ross and the Supremes. The group toured widely, singing in concert halls, nighclubs, theaters, and on television programs. Their style was a blend of rhythm 'n' blues elements with popular music; many of their songs were written by H-D-H* (Holland-Dozier-Holland) during the 1960s. In January 1970 Jean Terrell replaced Diana Ross.

BIBL: *Ebony* (February 1970). ShawWS. StamPRS.

DISC: TudBM.

SUTHERN, ORRIN CLAYTON. College professor/ Organist (b. 11 October 1912 in Renovo, Pennsylvania). He came from a musical family; his father, an Episcopalian priest, sang and his mother played piano. He began piano study as a child, at first with his mother, then with the organist at his father's church. In 1916 his family moved to Cleveland, Ohio; there he attended the public schools, singing in the boys glee club and the high-school chorus. He began organ study when he was ten years old with Edwin Arthur Kraft, remaining with him for about a dozen years. He obtained his musical education at Western Reserve University in Cleveland (B.A., 1933); Columbia University Teachers College in New York (M.A.), where he studied with Carl Weinrich and Seth Bingham; and the Juilliard School of Music in New York, where he studied organ with Lillian Carpenter and conducting with William Strickland. His teaching career included tenures at Tuskegee Institute in Alabama (1934-39), Florida A & M College in Tallahassee (1940-42), Bennett College at Greensboro, North Carolina (1942-45), Dillard University at New Orleans, Louisiana (1945-50), and Lincoln University in Pennsylvania (1950-). In these institutions he was college organist and choir director as well as teacher.

He gave his first organ recital in August 1928 at the Trinity Cathedral in Cleveland. In 1931 he won a contest sponsored by the American Guild of Organists, which won him sponsorship of a recital at Youngstown, Ohio, in October 1931. He began playing organ professionally in 1933, when his family moved to Chicago, Illinois. He made his concert debut in August 1934 at Orchestra Hall in Chicago. Over the years he combined concert touring with his teaching, playing in concert halls, churches, and on college campuses. His honors included awards from the Lindbach Foundation, the Esso Foundation, and New Directions. He was a pioneer in breaking down racial barriers for black organists; he performed with the New Orleans Symphony Orchestra in 1945 and on CBS radio at Tuskegee, Alabama, in 1946.

BIBL: Questionnaire. IntWWM, 1977. NYB. WWCA, 1950.

SWAN SILVERTONE SINGERS, THE. Gospel group (orig. 1938 in West Virginia). The male quartet was organized by Claude Jeter (b. c1914 in Montgomery, Alabama), who later became an ordained minister. His family moved to Kentucky when he was a child, after his father's death, and he completed his high-school studies there. He then went to West Virginia, where he worked in the coal mines. In 1938 he organized a group, which included his brother and two other miners, called The Four Harmony Kings. Later John Myles came into the quartet to replace his brother. The group toured widely on weekends, and in the early 1940s was offered a radio show in Knoxville, Tennessee. Now composed of Jeter, Myles, John Manson, and Henry Bossard, they changed their name, first to The Silvertone Singers, then to The Swan Silvertones after Swan Bakery took over sponsorship of the radio program. Solomon Womack was added to the quartet for the radio broadcasts. In the late 1940s the quartet left Knoxville and began touring more extensively and recording regularly. Over the years those who sang with the Silvertones included Robert Crenshaw, Carl Davis, Bobby Crutcher, William Connor, Louis Johnson, Dewey Young and Paul Owens (formerly of the Dixie Hummingbirds* and The Sensational Nightingales*). The instrumentalists included guitarist Linwood Hargrove, Kirk Davis, and Jerry Weaver; bassist Robert Crenshaw; and drummers Walter Perkins and Al Duncan, among others. Their best-known performances included "An old lady called mother," "I bowed on my knees and cried holy," "Mary, don't you weep," "Saviour, pass me not," and "My rock." Like the Sensational Nightingales, the Silvertones represented modern gospel-quartet tradition. Their early sound was distinctive for smooth, sweet harmonies and Jeter's falsetto; in later years there were growls, shouts, wails, even crooning accompanying the falsetto, and the harmonies were close and contemporary.

BIBL: Heil.

DISC: Hayes.

SWANSON, HOWARD. Composer (b. 18 August 1907 in Atlanta, Georgia; d. 12 November 1978 in New York, New York). His mother played piano and in her early life sang solos on local concerts. He was a boy soprano and won prizes in talent shows when he was six and seven years old. In 1916 his family moved to Cleveland, Ohio, and there he began piano study formally at the age of nine. He obtained his musical education in the public schools of Atlanta, Georgia, and of Cleveland, Ohio; at the Cleveland Institute of Music (B. Mus., 1937), where he studied with Ward Lewis and Herbert Elwell; and at the American Academy in Fontainebleau, France, where he studied with Nadia Boulanger (1938). He remained in Europe until the onset of World War II forced him to return to the United States, living first in Paris (1938-40), then in Spain and Portugal (1940-41). In 1941 he settled in New York, but he studied and traveled again in Europe during the years 1952-66. He decided upon a career in music early in life but planned to become a concert pianist rather than a composer. He had to work full-time, however, as he pursued his college music studies, and he found himself too exhausted to practice the necessary hours to succeed in his ambition. Gradually he became involved with music theory and eventually composition. The Institute symphony orchestra played one of his orchestral works before he was graduated and encouraged him to continue. The first of his compositions to receive public performance were his songs, beginning about 1946. When Marian Anderson* sang his song, "The Negro speaks of rivers" (Langston Hughes* text), in 1949 on a Carnegie Hall concert, he attracted wide attention and critical acclaim. Three years later his *Short Symphony* won the New York Critic's Circle Award as the best work performed during the 1950-51 concert season. The symphony's premiere at Carnegie Hall was conducted by Dimitri Mitropoulos with the New York Philharmonic, as was also a later performance in the summer of 1951 at the Edinburgh Festival in Scotland. Within the next few years the work was performed by leading orchestras in the United States and in Europe, was broadcast on NBC and CBS national networks, and was recorded for two companies, with Dean Dixon* and the Vienna Staatsoper Orchestra and Franz Litchauer and the Vienna Orchestra. Other compositions of his were also being performed and recorded during the early 1950s—notably *Night Music*, *Sound Piece for Brass Quintet* (1952), *Concerto for Orchestra* (1954) and *Concerto for Piano and Orchestra* (1956) and various songs—by such performers as Carl Stern, Eugene Haynes,* Elwood Peterson,* and the Louisville [Kentucky] Symphony. In 1955 Swanson served as a consultant for a concert series of Negro spirituals given at Sainte Chapelle in Paris. In 1966 he settled permanently in New York.

He wrote in a variety of musical forms: three symphonies, a piano concerto, a concerto "for orchestra," eight chamber works, two piano sonatas, three character piano pieces, and thirty or more songs. Some of this music was unpublished at the time of his death. He wrote in a basically neoclassical style, and his music was distinctive for its lyricism, transparent contrapuntal textures, and dissonant (although not atonal) harmonies. Critics remarked upon its elegance, intensity of feeling, and fusions of sophistication and tenderness, of power and delicacy. Nearly always there was a subtle influence of Negro folksong. Although he neither sang in a church choir nor played in a jazz group, as did many black composers, he felt an involvement with spirituals from the time of his early childhood, when he was fascinated by the congregational singing he heard in rural churches outside Atlanta. His best-known works, in addition to those cited, were the Piano Sonata, No. 2 (1972), "The Cuckoo," for piano (1948), *Fantasy Piece* for saxophone and string orchestra (1969), Sonata for violoncello and piano (1973), Symphony No. 3 (1970), the song cycle *Songs for Patricia* (1951, texts by Norman Rosten), *Trio for Flute, Oboe, and Piano* (1976), the anthem *We Delighted, My Friend* (1977, text by Léopold Senghor), and the songs "Montage" (text by Hughes), "Cahoots" (text by Carl Sandburg), "Death song" (text by Paul Laurence Dunbar*), "The junk man" (text by Sandburg), "In time of silver rain" (text by Hughes), "Joy" (text by Hughes), and "Ghosts in love" (text by Vachel Lindsay). Swanson was regarded as the leading black composer of his generation; he represented the transition period from William Grant Still* to such composers as Ulysses Kay* and George Walker.* Although he did not receive the publicity given to others, professional musicians deeply appreciated his exquisite talent. Twice there were "Music of Howard Swanson" concerts given in New York, on 29 October 1971 and on 12 June 1977, the latter in honor of his approaching seventieth birthday. His other honors included a Rosenwald Fellowship (1938), Guggenheim Fellowship (1952), National Academy of Arts and Letters Award (1952), William and Nona Copley Award (1958), and commissions from symphony orchestras, institutions, and individuals in the United States and in Europe.

BIBL: Interviews by E. S. Black press, incl. AmstN. 2 July 1977. Bull. Dorothy Maxine Ennett, "An Analysis and Comparison of Selected Piano Sonatas by Three Contemporary Black Composers: George Walker, Howard Swanson, and Roque Cordero" (Ph.D. diss., New York University, 1973). Raymond Jackson, "The Piano Music of Twentieth-Century Black Americans as Illustrated Mainly in the Works of Three Composers" (D.M.A. diss., Juilliard School of Music, 1973). NYT, 13 November 1978.

SWEATMAN, WILBUR C. Vaudeville entertainer/Bandleader (b. 7 February 1882 in Brunswick, Missouri; d. 9 March 1961 in New York, New York). He began his career in Kansas City, Missouri, playing clarinet in circus bands, including that of P. G. Lowery's* with the Forepaugh and Sells Brothers' Circus. In 1902 he played in W. C. Handy's* band, associated at that time with Mahara's Minstrels. Thereafter he was active in Minneapolis, Minnesota (1902-08), where he directed his own groups. Some time during this period he developed his skills at playing three clarinets at the same time, producing three-tone harmonies. After leaving Minneapolis, he toured with various groups, then settled in Chicago, Illinois, before 1910. There he directed theater orchestras, at first at the Grand Theater and, in 1911, at the Monogram. He moved to New York in 1913 and became active in vaudeville. His specialty of playing three clarinets simultaneously secured engagements for him in leading vaudeville theaters. He was a pioneer black recording artist, beginning as early as 1903 when he made a cylinder recording of Scott Joplin's* "Maple leaf rag" for the Metropolitan Music Store in Minneapolis. In 1916 he recorded clarinet solos for Emerson Records, accompanied by Emerson symphony orchestras. Thereafter he recorded regularly with his various groups, among them, Wilbur Sweatman's Jazz Band or Original Jazz Band, Wilbur Sweatman and his Acme Syncopators, or Wilbur Sweatman's Brownies. During the 1930s he moved into non-music areas but was active in music publishing; during the 1940s he led a trio in New York nightclubs. His best-known songs were "Down home rag" and "Boogie rag."

BIBL: ASCAP. Black press. ChilWW. FeaEJ. Flet, 149-153.

DISC: Kink. RustJR.

SWEETHEARTS OF RHYTHM, THE. See **THE INTERNATIONAL SWEETHEARTS OF RHYTHM.**

SWINGING RAYS OF RHYTHM, THE. Jazz orchestra (org. in Piney Woods, Mississippi; fl. 1940s). Lawrence C. Jones, founder-president of the Piney Woods Country Life School, began to send out student groups, called The Cotton Blossoms, during the 1920s on concert tours to earn money for the school, in emulation of the Fisk Jubilee Singers,* the Hampton Institute Singers,* and other black college groups. During the 1930s he observed the growing popularity of such all-girl groups as Phil Spitalny's and Ina Ray Hutton's orchestras, and in 1937 he organized a girl's orchestra composed of students from the high-school and junior-college divisions of Piney Woods. This group, called the Sweethearts of Rhythm,* toured widely on the concert and theater circuit until 1941, when it became an independent organization. All along Jones had maintained a training group for the Sweethearts, called the Swinging Rays of Rhythm, and after the Sweethearts left Piney Woods, he sent the Swinging Rays out on tour. Among those who worked with the girl orchestras as teachers and/or arrangers were Laurence C. Jones, Jr., James Polite, and Leon Span, all students at Piney Woods. The Swinging Rays won wide recognition during the years 1941-42 and toured extensively throughout the nation.

BIBL: Black press, incl. CDef, 5 July 1941. Handy.

SYKES, ROOSEVELT. Bluesman (b. 31 January 1906 in Elmar, Arkansas). His family moved to St. Louis, Missouri, when he was a child, but after being left an orphan at the age of seven, he returned to Arkansas. He taught himself to play his grandfather's church organ and later the piano. When he left home at fifteen, he played well enough to perform in local clubs and had been influenced by Jesse Bell and Lee Green, among others. For several years he and Green traveled as itinerant bluesmen in the South. In 1929 he recorded his first blues, among them, "Forty-four blues," and thereafter he recorded extensively with his Honeydrippers. He migrated to Chicago sometime during the early 1930s and established himself as one of the leading blues pianists in the city. During the following decades he toured widely in the United States and in Europe, appearing at the major blues and jazz festivals as well as in concert halls, clubs, and on college campuses. He settled in New Orleans, Louisiana, during the 1970s.

BIBL: BWW. LivBl interview, 9 (Summer 1972). MeeJMov. Robert Neff and Anthony Connor, *Blues* (Boston, 1975). Oliv.

DISC: DiGod. Jep. LeSl. RustJR. TudBM.

SYMPHONY OF THE NEW WORLD. (fl. 1965-76; est. in New York, New York). The racially integrated symphony orchestra was founded in 1964 and gave its first concert in May 1965 at Carnegie Hall in New York. The fourteen founding members included two whites (conductor Benjamin Steinberg and violinist Ross Shub) along with violists Alfred Brown and Selwart Clarke; bassists Arthur Davis,* Richard Davis,* and Lucille Dixon*; flutist Harold Jones*; cellist Kermit Moore*; tympanists Elayne Jones* and Frederick King; oboist Harry Smyles*; trumpeter Joseph Wilder*; and Coleridge Taylor Perkinson,* associate conductor. In addition to performing the traditional orchestral repertory, the Symphony gave premiere performances to works of black composers, including Ulysses Kay,* Perkinson, Hale Smith,* Howard Swanson,* and William Grant Still,* among others. Over the decade of its existence, the leading black artists of the nation appeared with the Symphony, some of them in debut concert performances. Steinberg was musical director from 1965 to 1973, and Everett Lee* was musical director during the years 1973-76. Guest conductors included James DePriest,* Paul Freeman,* Denis DeCoteau, Kermit Moore, and Leon Thompson,* among others.

BIBL: BPIM 3 (Fall 1975).

T

T.O.B.A. (THEATER OWNERS' BOOKING ASSOCIATION). See **DUDLEY, S[HERMAN] H[OUSTON].**

TABU, PASCAL ("ROCHEREAU LE SEIGNEUR"). Jazz singer (b. 13 November 1940 in Bandundu, near Kinshasa, Zaire). As a child he accompanied his father on boat voyages on the Congo River and heard traditional singing among the people. He sang in school choirs and won prizes in singing competitions. He also wrote songs, and by the time he was fourteen years old he was known as the youngest griot in his area. He obtained musical training in his secondary school, but majored in secretarial studies and accounting. He first attracted attention as a songwriter in 1956 when the popular singer Kabasele sang his song "Besame muchacha." In 1959 he himself won recognition as a singer with his recording of "Kelia." He performed with The American Jazz Group, under the leadership of Kabasele and Docteur Nico. Later he organized the African Fiesta National Band and served as its director.

BIBL: *Africa Report* 16 (April 1971).

TAJ MAHAL (née **HENRY SAINTE CLAIRE FREDRICKS-WILLIAMS).** Blues singer. (b. 17 May 1940 in New York, New York). He came from a musical family; his father played jazz piano and his mother was a gospel singer. He obtained his education in the public schools of Springfield, Massachusetts, and the University of Massachusetts at Amherst (B.S. in veterinary science). He taught himself to play several instruments, and after graduation from college began to sing blues in clubs and coffeehouses of Boston, Massachusetts. In 1965 he settled in California, where he formed a blues-rock group, the Rising Sons, with Ry Cooder and Jesse Ed Davis, among others. Later the group was disbanded, but Taj continued to perform as a soloist, touring in the United States and in Europe; he appeared at the major folk and jazz festivals, in nightclubs, theaters, concert halls, on college campuses, and in penitentiaries. He also recorded regularly, performed on television shows, and appeared in films or on film soundtracks, including *Clay Pigeon* (1971), *Sounder* (1972), *Fighting for Our Lives* (1974), and *Sounder II* (1976). His best-known recordings were the albums *Happy to Be Like I Am, Recycling the Blues,* and *Other Related Stuff.*

BIBL: BWW. David Jackson, "A Man with Definite Roots" in *Encore American and Worldwide News*, 17 February 1975. MeeJMov. StamPRS. WWBA.

DISC: TudBM.

TALBERT, FLORENCE COLE. Concert singer (b. c1890 in Detroit, Michigan; d. 22 April 1961 in Memphis, Tennessee). Her mother sang with the Fisk Jubilee Singers,* and she studied piano as a child. When she was ten her family moved to Los Angeles, California. There she first studied voice, encouraged by E. Azalia Hackley,* who heard her sing on a local concert. She obtained her musical training at the University of Southern California in Los Angeles and at Chicago Musical College (B. Mus., 1918), where she studied with John B. Miller and Oscar Saenger. She also studied privately with Herman DeVries. She left college during her senior year to tour with Hahn's Jubilee Singers, then under the management of the Midland Lyceum Bureau of Des Moines, Iowa; then later returned to finish her work at Chicago. She made her debut as a concert soprano in 1918 at Aeolian Hall in New York. Thereafter she toured widely for that time. During the years 1925-27 she studied voice in Europe, with Delia Valeri and Vito Carnevale in Rome, Italy, and with Julian Quezada at Milan, Italy. In 1927 she sang the title role in Verdi's *Aida* at the Comunale Theater in Cozenza, Italy, and thereafter toured in southern Italy. After returning to the United States, she entered into teaching with tenures at Bishop College in Marshall, Texas (1930), where she was the first black director of music, and at Tuskegee Institute in Alabama, where she was head of the voice department (1934-1940s). After marriage she settled in Memphis, Tennessee, where she conducted a studio. She was highly active with the National Association of Negro Musicians* and with Mary Cardwell Dawson's* National Negro Opera Company. She wrote the national hymn of the Delta Sigma Theta sorority.

BIBL: Black press, incl. AmstN, 2 November 1927; NYAge, 24 July 1920, 29 October 1927, 8 March 1930, 24 November 1934, 15 January 1936.

TAMPA RED. See **WHITTAKER, HUDSON.**

TAPLEY, DAISY. Studio teacher (b. 1870s [?] in Big Rapids, Michigan; d. 5 February 1925 in New York, New York). Her family moved to Chicago, Illinois, when she was eight years old. She began piano study as a child; later she studied organ with Emil Liebling and Clarence Eddy. She was a church organist at Quinn Chapel Church by the time she was twelve. In the first decade of the twentieth century she sang with The Colored Nightingales, which included the Winslow sisters, Edna, Valetta, and Hattie. About 1910 or 1911 she went to New York, where she soon established herself as an active member of the black musical establishment. She sang mezzo-soprano and contralto solos on local concerts, she performed with local theater companies, and she conducted a music studio. She was well known for her educational music concert series, which she organized with Minnie Brown in the Harlem community about 1918 and continued for several years.

BIBL: Black press, incl. CDef, 14 February 1925, 11 February 1933 (p. 10, "Early Chicagoans").

TAPSCOTT, HORACE. Jazz pianist (b. 6 April 1934 in Houston, Texas). He began piano study at the age of six with his mother, a professional pianist. His family moved to Los Angeles, California, in 1945 and there he obtained his musical education in the public schools. At Jefferson High School, where he came under the tutelage of Samuel R. Browne, he played in a jazz group with Donald ("Don") Cherry,* Dexter Gordon,* William ("Sonny") Criss, and others. He began playing professionally at an early age with local groups. During his service in the United States Armed Forces (1953-57), he played in an Army Air Force Band. Thereafter he organized his own groups, except for a period when he played with Lionel Hampton* (1959-61). In 1961 he was a co-founder of U.G.M.A.A. (Union of God's Musicians and Artists Ascension), which was dedicated to the preservation of black music, black culture, and community education. His Pan African Peoples Arkestra, the musical mouthpiece of U.G.M.A.A., sponsored free concerts for the community in addition to touring. He recorded as a soloist and with others, including the album *The Giant is Awakened* and the piano work *Songs of the Unsung*. He also wrote music in various forms and genres.

BIBL: FeaGitJS.

TATE, ERSKINE. Jazz bandleader (b. 19 December 1895 in Memphis, Tennessee; d. 17 December 1978 in Chicago, Illinois). He came from a musical family; his father was a music teacher, and his brother James became a professional musician. He obtained his musical education in the public schools of Memphis, Tennessee, and at the Mendelssohn Conservatory of Music and the Columbia School of Music, both in Chicago, Illinois. He settled in Chicago about 1913. Soon thereafter he began playing violin in local theater orchestras. Later he organized his own group, which began a long residence at the Vendome Theatre (1917-26), then played at the Metropolitan Theatre (1926-29), and later at the Michigan Theatre (1929-31). During 1931-32 he toured with his Tate's Radio and Recording Orchestra. He continued to play in clubs during the next decade, then conducted a music studio, beginning in 1945, until illness forced his retirement in the 1970s. Those who played in his groups at one time or another included Louis Armstrong,* Darnell Howard,* Earl Hines,* Milt Hinton,* Freddie Keppard,* Omer Simeon,* Eddie South,* Thomas ("Fats") Waller,* and Theodore ("Teddy") Weatherford,* among others. Tate's orchestra was highly regarded by his contemporaries; its status in Chicago was generally equal to that of Fletcher Henderson's* group in New York. His orchestra was highly versatile, playing both light classical music and jazz.

BIBL: Black press, incl. CDef, 18 August 1917. ChiIWW. DanceWEH. FeaEJ. Maurice Waller and Anthony Calabrese, *Fats Waller* (New York, 1977). WWCA, 1930-40.

DISC: Kink. RustJR.

TATUM, ARTHUR ("ART"). Jazz pianist (b. 13 October 1910 in Toledo, Ohio; d. 5 November 1956 in Los Angeles, California). He came from a musical family; his father played guitar and his mother played piano. He studied piano as a child. He obtained his musical education at the Cousino School for the Blind in Columbus, Ohio (he was blind in one eye and had only partial vision in the other), and at the Toledo

School of Music. His style development was influenced by his listening to piano rolls of James P. Johnson* and Thomas ("Fats") Waller.* He began playing professionally in Toledo nightclubs about 1926 and later played in Cleveland, Ohio. In 1932 he went to New York, where he became accompanist to Adelaide Hall* (1932-33). During the 1930s-early 1940s he played club residencies in various cities, as soloist or with his own groups, including Cleveland again, Chicago, Illinois; Hollywood, California; London, England (in 1938); and New York. In 1943 he organized a trio, including Lloyd ("Tiny") Grimes and Leroy ("Slam") Stewart, with which he toured widely on the concert circuit and played in clubs. He recorded extensively, particularly during the 1950s. He received many awards from the music industry. Tatum was regarded as the "grand old man" of jazz pianists. His style, based on the Harlem stride-piano school, represented at once a summation of jazz piano up to his time and a bold new approach. He was noted for his virtuosity —his use of arpeggios and elaborate embellishment reflected the influence of nineteenth-century romanticism —and his daring (for that time) harmonic progressions.

BIBL: ChilWW. FeaEJ. Maurice Waller and Anthony Calabrese, *Fats Waller* (New York, 1977)

DISC: Jep. Kink. RustJR.

TAYLOR, CECIL PERCIVAL. Jazz pianist (b. 15 March 1933 in New York, New York). He came from a musical family; his mother played piano, and an uncle played violin, percussions, and piano. He began piano study at the age of five with local teachers. When Taylor was a child, his uncle took him to hear the leading jazz bands of the time, among others, Cabell ("Cab") Calloway,* Bennie Goodman, James ("Jimmie") Lunceford,* and William ("Chick") Webb.* He obtained his musical education in the public schools of New York and at the New England Conservatory in Boston, Massachusetts (1952-55). He began organizing his own groups as early as 1953 but it was not until 1957 that he had a regular group, which included Steven ("Steve") Lacy, Buell Neidlinger, and Dennis Charles. He also played with various other groups or individuals, among them, Albert Ayler,* Andrew Cyrille,* Earl Griffith, James ("Jimmy") Lyons, James ("Sunny") Murray, Sam Rivers,* Sirone,* and others. In 1964 he was one of the founders of the Jazz Composers Guild, along with William ("Bill") Dixon,* Archie Shepp,* Sun Ra, (née Herman Blount)* and others; in 1968 he recorded with the Jazz Composers Orchestra. He also recorded extensively with his own groups and as a soloist. His teaching career included tenures at the University of Wisconsin at Madison (1970-72), Antioch College at Yellow Springs, Ohio (1972-74), and Glassboro State College in New Jersey. His honors included awards from the music industry and a Guggenheim Fellowship (1973). One of the leading avant-garde jazzmen of the 1950s, his mature style was characterized by atonality, free improvisation, and rhythmic intensity.

BIBL: Cadence (April 1978). ContKey (January 1979). FeaEJ. FeaJS. FeaGitJS. Spell.

DISC: Jep. ModJ. TudJ.

TAYLOR, CORA ("KOKO"). Blues singer (b. 28 September 1938 in Memphis, Tennessee). She sang in church choirs as a child. Her style development was influenced by "Muddy Waters" (McKinley Morganfield),* Elmore James, "Howlin' Wolf" (Chester Burnett),* "Sonny Boy Williamson, No. 2" (Willie "Rice" Miller),* and "Memphis Minnie" (Minnie Douglas Lawlers),* all of whom she heard perform in Memphis. In 1953 she settled in Chicago and began singing professionally in local clubs, frequently with George ("Buddy") Guy* and Amos ("Junior") Wells.* She first recorded in 1963 through a contact made by ("Big") Bill Hill with Willie Dixon.* Thereafter she recorded extensively and toured widely in the United States and in Europe, writing herself many of the songs she sang.

BIBL: BWW. FeaGitJS. Robert Neff and Anthony Connor, *Blues* (Boston, 1975). LivBl interview, 7 (Winter 1971-72).

DISC: Jep. LeSlBR. TudBM.

TAYLOR, MARSHALL W. Minister/Hymnal compiler (b. 1 July 1846 in Lexington, Kentucky; d. 19??). He was an ordained minister in the Methodist Episcopal Church. In addition to preaching, he held a variety of positions and offices in the church, including that of missionary teacher; presiding elder; delegate to the Ecumenical Conference in London, England, in 1881; and editor of a church magazine, *The Southwestern Christian Advocate*. In 1883 he published a hymnal titled *A Collecion of Revival Hymns and Plantation Melodies*. The hymns were those popular among black churches of the time, and the plantation melodies, which he obtained from his mother and contemporaries, were the so-called Negro spirituals. The hymnal is important as one of only three published by black Christians during the nineteenth century for specific use by black congregations. The first was Richard Allen's* *A Collection of Spiritual Songs and Hymns* . . . (Philadelphia, 1801), for use in the African Methodist Episcopal Church; and the second was Peter Spencer's *African Union Hymn Book* (Wilmington,

Delaware, 1822), for use by the Ezion African Union Church. His grandson, Samuel (''Sam'') Rivers,* was a jazz musician.

BIBL: BPIM 4 (Spring 1976). William J. Simmons, *Men of Mark* (1887).

TAYLOR, THEODORE ROOSEVELT (''HOUND DOG''). Bluesman (b. 12 April 1915 in Natchez, Mississippi; d. 17 December 1975 in Chicago, Illinois). He taught himself to play guitar and in 1935 began playing professionally in Tchula, Mississippi. His style development was influenced by Elmore James, ''Lightnin' '' Sam Hopkins,* and ''Sonny Boy Williamson, No. 2'' (Willie ''Rice'' Miller).* For a short period he played in a band with Robert (''Junior'') Lockwood* and Williamson for the King Biscuit Flour Company. In 1940 he went to Chicago and soon became a part of the blues establishment, although he did not record until 1957. His first tour of Europe was with the American Folk Blues Festival in 1967; thereafter he toured widely and recorded extensively. He was one of the first bluesmen to use traditional Delta bottleneck guitar technique on the electric guitar. Although not as celebrated as several of his contemporaries, his music exerted considerable influence on rhythm 'n' blues and rock 'n' roll.

BIBL: BWW. LivBl 4 (Winter 1970-71). LivBl 25 (January-February 1926). Robert Neff and Anthony Connor, *Blues* (Boston, 1975). Oliv.

DISC: LeSlBR.

TAYLOR, TOM THEODORE. Accompanist/Studio teacher (b. c1885 in Cairo, Illinois; d. c1965 in Cairo). He settled in Chicago, Illinois, in 1908. He received his musical training at Chicago Musical College, where he studied with Emil Leibling, and at the American Conservatory of Music in Chicago, where he studied with Silvio Scionti. He had a long association with the Grace Presbyterian Church, first as a choir singer and, after the death of Pedro Tinsley* in 1921, as the choir director. Beginning about 1914 he entered into the field of piano accompanying and thereafter served as accompanist at most of the important recitals given by black artists in Chicago. He also toured as an accompanist with various artists, including Anita Patti Brown,* Joseph Douglass,* Lillian Evanti,* Abbie Mitchell,* Florence Cole Talbert,* and Clarence Cameron White,* among others. He was also active as a baritone soloist; he began singing solos on local concerts within a few years after he went to Chicago, particularly on concerts of the Choral Study Club.* During the 1920s he toured widely with George Leon Johnson throughout the nation, giving joint recitals; the two men made their New York debut in April 1920. He taught music at the Coleridge-Taylor School of Music, at the Abraham Lincoln Center (both in Chicago), and conducted his own studio. In January 1959 he was given a testimonial concert by Chicago musicians in appreciation of his long years of service.

BIBL: Information furnished by Fanya Wiggins. ChiVH. Black press, incl. CDef, 1 June 1910, 30 May 1914; NYAge, 3 April 1920.

TAYLOR, WILLIAM (''BILLY''). Jazz pianist (b. 24 July 1921 in Greenville, North Carolina). He came from a musical family; his father played keyboard and brass instruments and conducted church choirs. His family moved to Washington, D.C., when he was a child; he began piano study at the age of seven with a local teacher and later studied with Henry Grant,* who also was a high-school bandmaster. His early style development was influenced by recordings of Thomas (''Fats'') Waller* and Arthur (''Art'') Tatum* and live concerts of leading jazzmen at the Howard Theatre. He obtained his musical education in the public schools of Washington, D.C., at Virginia State College in Petersburg (B. Mus., 1942), where he studied with Undine Smith Moore,* and at the University of Massachusetts at Amherst (D. Ed., 1975). He settled in New York about 1954 and soon thereafter began playing with various groups, including John Birks (''Dizzy'') Gillespie* and Ben Webster* and later (in Chicago) Eddie South* and Hezekiah (''Stuff'') Smith.* During the mid-1940s he worked in small ensembles with Leroy (''Slam'') Stewart, William (''Cozy'') Cole,* Machito (née Frank Grillo), and Bob Wyatt, among others. Later in 1946 he toured in Europe with Don Redman* and remained in Paris for a period to make recordings and perform as a soloist. In 1951 he organized the Billy Taylor Trio, which performed regularly on the nightclub circuit. He was also active as a radio disc jockey (1952-66) and program director (1966-69). During the 1960s-early 1970s he was active in television, hosting his own show in 1966 and serving as a musical director for the David Frost Show (1969-72). In the 1970s he founded his own company, Billy Taylor Productions. His teaching career included tenures as a lecturer in public schools, at the C. W. Post College in Greenvale, New York; Manhattan School of Music in New York; the Berkelee College of Music in Boston, Massachusetts; Howard University in Washington, D.C., and other institutions. In 1965 he was a co-founder of Jazzmobile in New York's Harlem community; the organization sponsored free outdoor jazz concerts and presented jazz-lecture concerts for communities and public schools. He contributed articles about jazz to periodicals and wrote a regular column for *Contempo-*

rary Keyboard in the 1970s-80s. He published more than twelve jazz manuals. His honors included numerous awards from the music industry; honorary doctorates from Virginia State University, Fairfield University and Clark College; and appointments to music commissions and national boards of professional, civic, and government councils. A prolific composer and arranger, he was called "Mr. Jazz."

BIBL: Black press, incl. CDef, 22-28 September 1962. ContKey (December 1976). FeaEJ. FeaJS. FeaGitJS. WWA. WWBA.

DISC: Jep. TudJ.

TAYLOR WILLIAMS, EVA. Vaudeville/Popular-music singer (b. 22 January 1896 in St. Louis, Missouri; d. 31 October 1977 in Mineola, New York). She began her career at the age of three touring with the vaudeville act Josephine Gassman and her Pickaninnies. She toured widely with the Gassman troupe in the United States and throughout the world during the years 1898-c1919. She also worked occasionally as a chorus girl, as in the musical *Vera Violetta* (1911), which featured Al Jolson. In 1921 she settled in New York. Thereafter she sang in her husband's groups—the Clarence Williams* Trio, Quartet, Blue Five, and others. She also performed in musicals, including the Noble Sissle*/Eubie Blake* *Shuffle Along* (1921), *Queen O' Hearts* (1928), *Bottomland* (1927), and the Thomas ("Fats") Waller*/James P. Johnson* *Keep Shufflin'* (1928), among others. She made her recording debut on Harry Pace's* Black Swan label in 1921 and thereafter recorded extensively as a soloist, with her husband's groups, and with others. She recorded under various names, among them, Irene Gibbons, Irene Williams, and Catherine Henderson. She began her long radio broadcasting career in 1922 and attracted wide attention as one of the first black women to have her own radio series (NBC network, 1930s). She also sang on television shows at home and in Europe.

BIBL: BWW. ChilWW. Flet, p. 157. WWBA (listed under Williams). WWCA, 1950.

DISC: DiGod. Kink. RustJR.

TCHICAI, JOHN MARTIN. Jazz saxophonist (b. 28 April 1936 in Copenhagen, Denmark). He obtained his musical education in the public schools of Aarhus, Denmark, and at the Aarhus Conservatory and the Copenhagen [Denmark] Conservatory. He began violin study at the age of ten, later studying alto saxophone and clarinet. His style development was influenced by the black American jazzmen who gave concerts in Copenhagen. In 1963 he came to the United States. Along with Archie Shepp* he was a co-founder of the New York Contemporary Five, which included at one time or another Donald ("Don") Cherry,* Ronnie Boykins, Don Moore, James ("Sunny") Murray, and J. C. Moses. When that group was disbanded, he organized the New York Quartet with Milford Graves,* Roswell, and Lewis Worrell. He was also active with the Jazz Composers Guild. After returning to Denmark he organized a group, called Cadentia Nova Danica, which performed until 1971. During the 1970s he entered into a teaching career and thereafter rarely led his own groups, although he continued to play with others.

BIBL: FeaJS. Mike Hames, *John Tshicai in Disc and Tape*. With an introductory conversation by Anthony Barrett (London, 1975).

DISC: ModJ.

TEMPTATIONS, THE. Rhythm 'n' blues group (org. in Detroit, Michigan; fl. 1960s-70s). Organized in 1960, the singing-dancing male quintet was a rhythm 'n' blues group, although most of its members had sung earlier in gospel groups. By the time The Temptations was attracting wide attention in 1965 its members were Melvin Franklin (née David English, b. 12 October 1942 in Mobile, Alabama), Eddie Kendricks (b. 17 December 1939 in Union Springs, Alabama), David Ruffin (b. 18 January 1941 in Meridian, Mississippi), Otis Williams (née Miles, b. 30 October 1941 in Texarkana, Texas), and Paul Williams (b. 2 July 1939 in Birmingham, Alabama; d. 1971). Before joining with Paul Williams to form a rock group, Franklin, Elbridge Bryant (who dropped out in 1963), and Otis Williams had sung with The Distants; Kendricks had sung with the Cavaliers, later called The Primes. After signing a recording contract with Berry Gordy* of Motown Industries, the group was named The Temptations. Its first commercially successful song was "My girl" (1965), written by William ("Smokey") Robinson* and Ronnie White of The Miracles. The quintet toured widely in the United States and in Europe, appearing in nightclubs, ballrooms, theaters, and concert halls. They sang on radio and television shows—including two special television shows in 1969 with The Supremes.* Over the years there were several personnel changes; in 1977 the group included only Franklin and Otis Williams of the original quintet with new members Glen Carl Leonard, Louis Price, and Richard Street. Dennis Edwards and Damon Harris dropped out in the 1970s.

BIBL: Black press, incl. AmstN, 11 June 1977. *Ebony* (April 1971). *Ebony* (July 1975). StamPRS.

DISC: TudBM.

TENNESSEE JUBILEE SINGERS. See **JONES, MATILDA SISSIERETTA.**

TERRELL, SAUNDERS ("SONNY TERRY"). Bluesman (b. 24 October 1911 in Greensboro, Georgia). He lost the sight of one eye at the age of five; an accident when he was eighteen left him almost totally blind. He taught himself to play harmonica as a child, influenced by his father, who also played blues harmonica. At an early age he began to earn money by playing on street corners and for local social entertainments. When he was about fifteen he moved to North Carolina. In 1934 he met "Blind Boy" Fuller (Fulton Allen),* and the two bluesmen later formed a team. He made his first recordings in 1936; from 1938 to 1940 he recorded primarily with Fuller. In 1938 he went to New York to appear in the From Spirituals to Swing concert produced by John Hammond at Carnegie Hall. He met Walter ("Brownie") McGhee* in 1939, and after Fuller's death in 1940, he and McGhee entered into a permanent partnership. During his long career he also performed and/or recorded with "Blind" Gary Davis,* "Big Bill" (William Lee Conley) Broonzy,* "Mississippi John" Hurt,* Eddie ("Son") House,* Nehemiah ("Skip") James,* and Huddie ("Leadbelly") Ledbetter,* among others. In 1942 he settled in New York. He performed in the Broadway musical, *Finian's Rainbow*, and both he and McGhee were in Tennessee Williams's play, *Cat on a Hot Tin Roof* (1955); he also performed on film soundtracks, including *Cisco Pike* (1971) and *Buck and the Preacher* (1972). He and McGhee toured widely in the United States and in Europe, appearing in concert halls, clubs, on college campuses, and at the major blues and jazz festivals. His "crossed" harmonica style was distinctive for its special effects; he imitated train whistles, the cries of hounds and the fox in the blues "Fox chase," and the whine and moans of humans. He developed a particular skill in producing special effects by using his voice at the same time as he played harmonica.

BIBL: BWW. CharCB. FeaEJ. LivBl 13 (Summer 1973). MeeJMov. Robert Neff and Anthony Connor, *Blues* (Boston, 1975). StamFCW.

DISC: DiGod. Jep. Kink. LeSlBR. TudBM.

TERRY, CLARK. Jazz trumpeter (b. 14 December 1920 in St. Louis, Missouri). He began playing trumpet as a child. He obtained his musical education in the public schools of St. Louis, Missouri, where he studied trombone with his high-school bandmaster. At fifteen he played in a local drum and bugle corps. During his service in the United States Armed Forces (1942-45), he played in the Ship's Company Band A at Camp Robert Smalls at Great Lakes, Chicago, Illinois. Among other servicemen in the band who would later become celebrated were Donald White,* Len Bowden (bandmaster), Luther Henderson, Ernie Wilkins,* and Gerald Wilson. During the mid-1940s-50s he played with various groups, including Lionel Hampton,* George Hudson (1945-46), Charlie Barnet, William ("Count") Basie* (1948-51), Fate Marable* (on riverboats), Eddie ("Cleanhead") Vinson,* and Edward ("Duke") Ellington* (1951-59). For many years he was a featured soloist with the NBC-TV Orchestra for the *Tonight Show* (1960-72), but remained in New York when that show moved to California. During the 1960s he also performed and/or toured with various groups, including Quincy Jones* (1960), the J. J. Johnson Sextet* (1964, in Japan), and Ella Fitzgerald* and Oscar Peterson* (1965 in Europe). In 1966 he organized his Big Bad Band, which performed regularly if not extensively through the 1970s. In 1972 he became vice-president of Creative Jazz Composers, Inc., an organization whose purpose was to carry jazz into public schools. He toured as a jazz clinician, and for many years his jazz clinics were sponsored by the Selmer instrument company. His publications included *Let's Talk Trumpet* (1973), *Interpretation of the Jazz Language* (1976), and *Circular Breathing* (1977). He formed his own music publishing and distributing companies as early as 1955. He received numerous awards from the music industry. Terry first attracted wide attention as an Ellington trumpeter; he developed a highly individual swing style, which he carried over into contemporary jazz with some influence of bebop. He was also noted for his wordless vocalizing, called "mumbles."

BIBL: *Cadence* (November 1977). FeaEJ. FeaJS. FeaGitJS. WWA. WWBA.

DISC: Jep.

TERRY, SONNY. See **TERRELL, SAUNDERS.**

THARPE, ("SISTER") ROSETTA (née **ROSETTA NUBIN).** Gospel singer (b. 20 March 1921 in Cotton Plant, Arkansas; d. 9 October 1973 in Philadelphia, Pennsylvania). Her mother, Katie Bell Nubin, was an evangelist of the Holiness church, and Rosetta began traveling with her at an early age. Rosetta began touring as a professional when she was six with evangelist P. W. McGhee on the tent-meeting circuit. She toured widely thereafter, sometimes singing to her mother's accompaniment on a mandolin but generally to her own guitar accompaniment. In 1938 she attracted wide attention when she appeared at the Cotton Club in New York with a show of Cabell ("Cab") Calloway's.* The same year she secured a recording contract with Decca

Records, becoming the first gospel singer to record for a major company. During the 1940s-60s she performed in chuches, concert halls, at folk-jazz festivals, and on radio and television programs, but also in theaters and nightclubs, unlike many of her gospel contemporaries. When she made her debut at the Apollo Theatre in the Harlem community of New York in 1943, she was the first gospel singer to perform in a theater. She toured and/or recorded with jazz groups, particularly Lucius ("Lucky") Millinder,* boogie-woogie pianist Samuel Blythe ("Sammy") Price,* blues-singer Muddy Waters (McKinley Morganfield),* and such gospel groups as The Caravans,* James Cleveland* Singers, and the Dixie Hummingbirds.* In 1946 she formed a partnership with contralto Marie Knight (b. c1924 in Sanford, Florida), who was also a member of the Holiness church; their recording, "Up above my head," was an immediate success. During the two or more years they were together, Knight played piano as well as sang duos with Tharpe. Tharpe was one of the most celebrated of the gospel singers, particularly because of her movement back and forth from gospel to popular music and because she was the first soloist to tour widely in the United States and in Europe. Her best-known performances included "This train," "I looked down the line," "Hide me in Thy bosom," "Didn't it rain," and "End of my journey." She appeared in the film *L'Aventure du jazz* (1969) and in documentaries.

BIBL: Barbara Baker, "Black Gospel Music Styles, 1942-1975" (Ph.D. diss., University of Maryland, 1978). Black press, incl. NYAge, 15 September 1945. *Black World* (November 1973). Heil. FeaEJ. FeaGitJS. MeeJMov.

DISC: DiGod. Hayes. TudJ.

THOMAS, A[LFRED] JACK. Military bandmaster (b. 14 April 1884 in Pittsburgh, Pennsylvania; d. 19 April 1962 in Baltimore, Maryland). He studied music as a child, learning to play mandolin, trumpet, and violin. He obtained his musical education in the public schools of Pittsburgh, Pennsylvania; at Washington and Jefferson College in Pennsylvania; the National Conservatory of Music in Manilla, the Philippines (1906-09); the Institute of Musical Art in New York (diploma, 1914; now the Juilliard School of Music); and the School for Bandmasters at Chaumont, France (1919). He joined the United States Army in 1903, serving in the Tenth Cavalry at Fort McKenzie, Wyoming. After completing his work at the Conservatory in Manilla, he was appointed bandmaster of the Tenth Cavalry. In 1917 he became bandmaster of the 368th Infantry, called The Buffaloes, which was sent in June 1918 to the European theater of World War I. After completing his bandmaster's course in 1919, he was commissioned bandmaster in the Allied Expeditionary Forces. He settled in Baltimore, Maryland, after his discharge from the armed services; soon thereafter he established the Aeolian Conservatory of Music and organized community bands, including Baltimore's first black municipal band in 1921. During the years 1924-27 he was director of music at Morgan College in Baltimore. Beginning in 1936 he was active in New York (although maintaining residence in Baltimore), where he conducted a music studio and in 1939 was associate conductor of the newly organized Negro Symphony Orchestra, directed by Ignatz Waghalter. He returned to Baltimore in 1946 and established the Baltimore Institute of Musical Arts. In 1955 he retired from music.

BIBL: Black press, incl. NYAge, 23 July 1938. James Nathan Jones, "Alfred Jack Thomas, 1884-1962: Musician, Composer, Educator" (M.A. thesis, Morgan State University, 1978). WWCA, 1941-44.

THOMAS, C. EDWARD. See **AFRO-AMERICAN MUSIC OPPORTUNITIES ASSOCIATION, INC.**

THOMPSON, ARTHUR. Opera/concert singer (b. 27 December 1942 in New York, New York). He obtained his musical education in the public schools of New York, the Hartt College of Music in Hartford, Connecticut (B. Mus., 1965), and the Juilliard School of Music (1965-68). He also studied with Adele Addison* and Hans Heinz and was a member of the Metropolitan Opera Studio. During his early career he toured widely as a concert/opera baritone, singing with the smaller companies, as the Juilliard Opera Theater, Chautauqua Opera, Aspen Summer Opera, and the Yale Summer Opera Theater. In 1973 he sang the role of St. Ignatius in Thomson's *Four Saints in Three Acts*, produced by the Mini-Met. In 1974 he attracted wide attention for his performance as Iago in Verdi's *Otello*, produced by Opera/South,* and in the fall of 1974 he made his Metropolitan Opera debut. His honors included the Ezio Pinza Award (1969) and the Marian Anderson* Award (1970).

BIBL: Metropolitan Opera Stagebill (September 1974).

DISC: Turn.

THOMPSON, CHARLES HUBBARD. Ragtime pianist/Composer (b. 19 June 1891 in St. Louis, Missouri; d. 13 June 1964 in St. Louis). Self-taught, he belonged to the group of ragtime pianists active in St. Louis beginning about 1913. Along with Robert Hampton* and Artie Matthews,* he found employment in the cafes of the tenderloin district and a place to exchange ideas with other pianists in Tom Turpin's* Rosebud

Cafe. He attracted special attention as a winner of ragtime competitions. In addition to playing solo piano, he played with such groups as Charlie Creath* and Dewey Jackson. In 1919 he met James P. Johnson* in Toledo, Ohio; thereafter his performance reflected the influence of Johnson. Although he was a prolific composer, only one rag was published, "The lily rag" (1914).

BIBL: Blesh. JaTiRRT

THOMPSON, DEKOVEN. Songwriter (b. 1879 in St. Louis, Missouri; d. 26 May 1934 in New York, New York). His family moved to Chicago, Illinois, when he was an infant. There his father founded the St. Thomas Episcopal Church, and Dekoven and his brother Creighton sang in the church choir as young boys. Little is known of his musical training except that he studied harp. During the early years of the twentieth century he toured in a trio with his brother and Opal Cooper. He began to win attention for his songs before World War I. He was a railroad porter when he came into contact with opera-singer Ernestine Schumann-Heink and showed her some of his songs. She became a kind of patron to him and featured his songs in her recitals, particularly "If I forget thee" (1911), "Love comes but once," and "A heart disclosed." Other well-known songs of his were "Dear Lord, remember me" and "June will come again," the latter featured by Tito Schipa on his recitals. Thompson settled in New York about 1930 and became active in music circles there.

BIBL: Black press, incl. CDef, 5 January 1929, 2 June 1934, 11 November 1939. Hare.

THOMPSON, EGBERT. Bandmaster (b. in Sierra Leone, West Africa; d. 22 August 1927 in Paris, France). He was one of the few black men who won a commission in the United States Army as a bandmaster during the early twentieth century. He was active with Clef Club and Tempo Club groups in New York during the pre-World War I years. He studied at the Institute of Musical Art in New York. During the war he was a bandmaster with the Old Fifteenth Infantry (later renamed 369th). A second lieutenant, he received advanced musical training at the British Band School, Kneller Hall, in Hounslow, England. After the war he settled in Paris, France, where he played in and conducted dance orchestras. Another commissioned bandmaster of the army was First Lieutenant Alfred J. Thompson of the 368th Infantry, who also studied at the Institute of Musical Art.

BIBL: Black press, incl. CDef, 1 March 1919, 17 September 1927; NYAge, 10 September 1927. One source gives his birthplace as Jamaica, West Indies.

THOMPSON, ELI ("LUCKY"). Jazz saxophonist (b. 16 June 1924 in Detroit, Michigan). In his early career he toured as a tenor saxophonist with the 'Bama State Collegians of Alabama State Teachers College in Montgomery, Alabama. He settled in New York during the early 1940s; thereafter he played with various groups, including Lionel Hampton,* Don Redman,* William ("Billy") Eckstine,* Lucius ("Lucky") Millinder,* and William ("Count") Basie,* among others. During the mid-1940s he lived in Los Angeles, California, where he played with John Birks ("Dizzy") Gillespie,* among many others, but he returned to New York by 1948. Beginning in 1951 he led his own groups. Over the years he recorded extensively with his own groups and with others, including Charlie Parker,* Oran ("Hot Lips") Page,* Dinah Washington,* Oscar Pettiford,* and Jack Teagarden. During the 1950s-60s he lived and performed in Europe, primarily in France, for long periods of time. He won wide recognition as a bebop saxophonist; his style was highly individual with a full-bodied tone.

BIBL: FeaEJ. FeaJS. FeaGitJS.

DISC: Kink.

THOMPSON, LEON EVANETTE. Symphony orchestra conductor (b. 1 August 1928 in Richmond, Virginia). He obtained his musical training at Virginia State College in Petersburg, Virginia (B.S. 1948), where he studied with Undine Smith Moore*; at the Eastman School of Music in Rochester, New York (M.Mus., 1952); and at the University of Southern California in Los Angeles (D.M.A., 1966). A Fulbright Fellowship (1955-57) made it possible for him to study in France, where he worked with Nadia Boulanger, among others. His teachers also included Pierre Monteux, Howard Hanson, Jack Westrup, George Szell, and Jean Fournier. His teaching career included a tenure at West Virginia State College in Institute; his conducting career included a tenure as conductor with the Southeast Los Angeles Symphony for three seasons before he joined the staff of the New York Philharmonic in 1970 as Director of Educational Activities and an assistant conductor. During the years 1973-76 he also was principal guest conductor of the Symphony of the New World.* He also toured widely as guest conductor with other orchestras.

BIBL: WWBA.

THORNTON, WILLIE MAE ("BIG MAMA"). Blues singer (b. 11 December 1926 in Montgomery, Alabama.) She won first prize on an amateur show at the age of fourteen, attracted the attention of Sammy Green of Atlanta, Georgia, and was engaged to tour with his show, The Hot Harlem Review. In 1948 she left the show and settled in Houston, where she sang in clubs and worked with local bands. During the early 1950s she joined the Johnny Otis show. She first recorded in 1951, but it was her recording of "Hound dog" in 1953 that brought her wide attention. The song became a rock 'n' roll classic. Thereafter she made numerous recordings and toured extensively in the United States and in Europe. During the late 1950s she settled in Los Angeles, California.

BIBL: BWW. Craig McGregor, "Racism: The Acid That Disfigures Black Artists" in NYT, 10 January 1971. Robert Neff and Anthony Connor, *Blues* (Boston, 1975). Oliv. ShawR5. ShawWS.

DISC: Jep. LeSIBR. TudBM.

TIBBS, ROY WILFORD. College professor (b. 20 August 1888 in Hamilton, Ohio; d. 1 April 1944 in Washington, D.C.). He obtained his musical education at Fisk University (B. Mus. 1912) and the Oberlin Conservatory (M. Mus., 1919). He studied organ further in Paris, France, with Isadore Philippi in 1914. In 1912 he was appointed to the piano faculty of Howard University in Washington, D.C., and remained there until his retirement. For a long period he directed the university choir. Over the years he combined college teaching with occasional concert tours as a pianist. At one time he was married to Lillian Evanti.*

BIBL: Black press, incl. CDef, 20 June 1914; NYAge, 13 March 1920. Rayford Logan, *Howard University: The First Hundred Years, 1867-1967* (New York, 1969).

TIFFANY, CYRUS. Military fifer (b. 1735 in Taunton, Massachusetts; d. 1815 at sea). He served in the American Revolutionary War as a fifer. He remained in the service after the war; in 1797 he was serving on the ship *Alliance*. During the War of 1812 he was active in the Battle of Lake Erie. After the war he lived in Newport, Rhode Island, but later went back to sea and died aboard the ship *Java*. Some reports indicate that his commander was Oliver Perry.

BIBL: Wilkes.

TILGHMAN, AMELIA L. Studio teacher/Concert singer (b. Washington, D.C. [?]; d. Washington, D.C. [?] fl. late 19th century). She was a graduate of the Normal Department of Howard University in Washington, D.C. After graduation she taught in the public schools of Washington and also began to sing professionally in the choir of the Fifteenth Street Presbyterian Church and at local concerts, along with such celebrated singers as Marie Selika,* Anita Patti Brown,* and Adelaide Smith. In December 1880 she made her debut in New York; in June 1881 she was the prima donna soprano of the Sangerfest held at the Grand Opera House in Louisville, Kentucky. The next year she produced the cantata *Queen Esther* at Lincoln Hall in Washington, training the one-hundred-voice choir herself and singing the leading role. In 1883 she had an accident while on a concert tour that temporarily curtailed her activity as a performer. She attended the Boston [Massachusetts] Conservatory in 1885 to study methods for teaching piano, and it is possible that she studied piano with Samuel Jamieson* during that time. In 1885 she settled in Montgomery, Alabama, where she conducted a music studio and began singing on local concerts. Beginning in 1886 she published a music magazine, *The Musical Messenger*, the first such publication by a Negro. Some time before 1891 she resettled in Washington, D.C., and continued to publish her magazine with the help of Lucinda Bragg Adams.

BIBL: Black press, incl. CleveG, 9 April 1887; NYFreeman, 14 March 1886, 21 August 1886; NY Globe, 1 September 1883. Lawson Scruggs, *Women of Distinction* (Raleigh, North Carolina, 1893).

TILLIS, FREDERICK C. Composer/College professor (b. 5 January 1930 in Galveston, Texas). His mother played piano and sang in a church choir. He began trumpet study at the age of seven. Through his high-school years he played trumpet and saxophone in school bands and local jazz groups. He obtained his musical education at Wiley College in Marshall, Texas (B.A., 1949); North Texas State University at Denton (summers, 1969, 1970); and at the University of Iowa in Iowa City (M.A., 1952; Ph.D., 1963). During his years of service in the United States Armed Forces, he was director of the 356th Air Force Band, for which he wrote and arranged music. His teaching career included tenures at Wiley College (1949-51; 1956-61; 1963-64), Grambling College in Louisiana (1964-67), Kentucky State College in Frankfort (1967-69), and the University of Massachusetts in Amherst (1970-). He first became interested in composing as a college junior and in graduate school concentrated his attention on composition. During the 1950s he wrote primarily twelve-tone compositions. Thereafter he developed an eclectic style, drawing upon black music elements, African and Eastern idioms, serialism, and other European styles. He wrote in a variety of forms—for symphony orchestra, chamber music, band, chorus, voice, solo instruments, and jazz ensemble. His best-known works were *Ring Shout Concerto* for percussion and brass (1973), *Spiritual Cycle* for soprano and orchestra (1978, text by Robert Hayden), *Freedom* for mixed chorus (1968), and *Metamorphosis on a Scheme by J.S. Bach* for jazz orchestra (1972).

BIBL: Questionnaire. WWBA.

TINDLEY, CHARLES ALBERT. Gospel songwriter/ Minister (b. 7 July 1859 in Berlin, Maryland; d. 26 July 1933 in Philadelphia, Pennsylvania). He began his career as an itinerant preacher and camp-meeting singer in Maryland. He studied for the ministry at a divinity school in Philadelphia, Pennsylvania, and through a correspondence course from the Boston [Massachusetts] Theological Seminary. Sometime during the late 1870s he settled in Philadelphia and there in 1902 founded the East Calvary Methodist Episcopal Church (now called Tindley Temple). He wrote gospel songs for a number of years before he began to apply for copyrights about 1901. His best-known songs were "I am a poor pilgrim of sorrow," "What are they doing in heaven?" "I have started out to find a better home," "Stand by me" (1905), "We'll understand it better by and by" (1905), and "Take your burden to the Lord and leave it there" (1916). It was the singing of a Tindley song, "I do, don't you?" by A. W. Nix at a Baptist convention in 1921 that directly inspired the writing of gospel songs by Thomas A. Dorsey,* "the father of gospel music."

BIBL: Black press, incl. CDef, 12 August 1933; NYAge, 5 August 1933; PhilaT, 31 March 1917; *The Pittsburgh Courier*, 18 August 1961. Tindley songs appear in the AME Hymnal (Nashville, 1954) and in *Gospel Pearls* (Nashville, 1921).

DISC: DiGod.

TINSLEY, PEDRO T. Choral conductor (b. 1856 in Boston, Massachusetts [?]; d. 23 November 1921 in Chicago, Illinois). He began his career in Boston, Massachusetts, as a cornetist. During the early 1880s he played in the Morris Orchestra and in the Albion Instrumental Quartet, which included also Davis, Feather, and Morris (first names unknown), with Frederick P. White* as accompanist. In 1883 he organized his own band, called Tinsley's Colored Cornet Band or Tinsley's Cornet Band. In December of that year, however, he left Boston to "accept a lucrative position out west," according to the press (NYGlobe, 1 December 1883). "Out west" proved to be Chicago, Illinois, where he immediately became involved in the musical life of the black community, singing baritone solos and playing cornet solos on local concerts. He was also director of choirs at the Institutional Church and the Grace Presbyterian Church and wrote music reviews in the *Chicago Defender*. In 1900 he organized the Choral Study Club,* which became an important institution in the community and inspired the development of other black choral groups. The annual concerts of his group featured well-known soloists of the time, frequently imported from Boston, New York, or Washington, D.C. His long-time associates with the group were accompanists Pelargie Blair and Gertrude Smith Jackson. About 1914 or 1915 he was forced to give up his work because of illness, and George Duncan took over directorship of the Choral Study Club.

BIBL: Black press, incl. CDef, 12 February 1910, 17 November 1917, 3 December 1921; NYAge, 10 December 1921; NYGlobe, 7 April 1883, 18 August 1883; IndF, 5 July 1893.

TIO, LORENZO, JR. Jazz clarinetist (b. 1884 in New Orleans, Louisiana; d. 1 December 1933 in New York, New York). He came from a musical family: his father, Lorenzo, Sr., played clarinet in brass bands of New Orleans from the 1880s on, including the Excelsior, John Robichaux, and a dance band led by Lorenzo and Anthony Doublet. His uncle, Luis ("Papa"), played clarinet with Armand Piron* and the Bloom Philharmonic Orchestra. Lorenzo, Jr., was active early in his career with his father's group and with Theogene Baquet; he also played with the Lyre Club Symphony Orchestra beginning in 1897. Later he played with various groups, including the Onward Brass Band (1910), Oscar ("Papa") Celestin's* Original Tuxedo Orchestra (1913, 1917-18), Manuel Perez (1915-16), Armand Piron* (regularly 1918-28; again in the early 1930s), Gaspard's Maple Leaf Orchestra (1918), and the Tuxedo Brass Band (late 1920s). He was also active as an arranger. He recorded with Ferdinand ("Jelly Roll") Morton,* Piron, and possibly Clarence William's* Harmonizers. Like his father and uncle, however, he was perhaps best known as a teacher; his students included Johnny Dodds,* Leon ("Barney") Bigard,* Albert Nicholas,* Jimmie Noone,* and Omer Simeon,* among others. He settled in New York during the early 1930s and played in nightclubs there.

BIBL: ChilWW. Souc.

DISC: RustJR.

TIO, LORENZO, SR. Brass bandsman (b. c1865 in Mexico; d. 1927 in New Orleans, Louisiana). See **TIO, LORENZO, JR.**

TIO, LUIS ("PAPA"). Brass bandsman (clarinet) (b. c1863 in Mexico; d. c1920 in Jackson, Mississippi). See **TIO, LORENZO, JR.**

TIZOL, JUAN. Jazz trombonist (b. 22 January 1900 in San Juan, Puerto Rico). During his youth he studied music with his uncle, Manuel Tizol, and played in San

Juan's Municipal Band. In 1920 he went to the United States, where he played with various groups in Washington, D.C., including Marie Lucas,* Bobby Lee's Cottonpickers, The White Brothers' Band, and the pit orchestra of the Howard Theatre. In 1929 he joined Edward ("Duke") Ellington,* remaining with him for many years (1929-44, 1951-53, 1960). He also had long tenures with Harry James (1944-51, 1953-59). He was a prolific songwriter/composer. It was his composition *Caravan*, recorded by Ellington in 1937, that began the vogue for so-called Cuban or Latin jazz. Other well-known pieces of his, some written in collaboration with Ellington, were "Moonlight fiesta," "Congo brava," and "Perdido." He retired from music in the 1960s and settled first in Los Angeles, California, and then in Las Vegas, Nevada.

BIBL: ASCAP. ChilWW. FeaEJ. FeaGitJS.

DISC: RustJR.

TROTTER, JAMES MONROE. Writer (b. 8 November 1842 in Grand Gulf, Mississippi; d. 26 February 1892 in (Hyde Park) Boston, Massachusetts). Although not a professional musician, he is included here because of his book, *Music and Some Highly Musical People* (Boston, 1878), which was the first survey of American music published by anyone, black or white, in the United States. He studied music as a child and participated in musical activities through the years. He served in the 55th Regiment, Massachusetts Volunteer Infantry, during the Civil War; after the war he settled in Boston, Massachusetts. He was active in Boston's musical circles. Beginning about 1883 he cooperated with his friend, William Dupree,* in managing dramatic recitals for Henrietta Vinson Davis, which included musicians as assisting artists. On 3 March 1883 he published an insightful article on the career of Marie Selika* in the *New York Globe*.

BIBL: Black press, incl. NYGlobe, 7 July 1884; CleveG, 12 March 1887. Robert Stevenson, "America's First Black Music Historian" in *Journal of the American Musicological Society* 22 (Fall 1973).

TUCKER, IRA. See **DIXIE HUMMINGBIRDS, THE.**

TUCKER, ROBERT NATHANIEL ("BOBBY"). Jazz pianist/Accompanist (b. 8 January 1923 in Morristown, New Jersey). He began piano study at the age of four with local teacher Isabel Pope and sang in a chuch choir from an early age until he was eighteen. After a few years of neglecting the piano, he became seriously interested when he was thirteen and studied with Cecily Knechtel. Later he studied conducting and arranging privately. During his service in the U.S. Armed Forces (1943-46), he was an army bandmaster and he played two-piano recitals with Oland Gaston* on camp shows. His career development was influenced by Theodore ("Teddy") Wilson,* to whose recordings he listened, and by Arthur ("Art") Tatum.* He first came into contact with Tatum about 1945; he would sit beside Tatum in nightclubs on 52nd Street in New York, watching him play and learning from him. Tucker began his professional career in 1946 as an accompanist for Mildred Bailey. Thereafter he served as accompanist-musical director of Billie Holiday* (1946-49) and William ("Billy") Eckstine* (1949-). In addition to playing for Eckstine and conducting accompanying bands, he also wrote arrangements. He toured widely throughout the world with Eckstine, appearing in concert halls, theaters, nightclubs, on radio and television programs, and at jazz festivals. During the 1970s he and Eckstine began performing in theaters-in-the-round and on cruise ships.

BIBL: Interview by E.S. FeaEJ. FeaJS.

TURNER, IKE AND TINA (née **ANNIE MAE BULLOCK).** Rhythm 'n' blues act (organized 1956 in St. Louis, Missouri; fl. 1970s). Ike Turner (b. 5 November 1931 in Clarksdale, Mississippi) taught himself to play piano when he was a child. After graduating from high school in Clarksdale, he organized a group, called Kings of Rhythm, which toured in the area and recorded. During the late 1940s-early 1950s he was active as a blues pianist in West Memphis, Arkansas, where he recorded with "Howlin' Wolf" (née Chester Burnett),* Riley ("B. B.") King,* and Herman ("Little Junior") Parker,* among others. He was also a talent scout for blues recording companies. In 1956 he met Annie Bullock (b. 25 November 1939 in Brownsville, Tennessee). Her family moved to Knoxville, Tennessee, when she was three years old. As a child she sang in church choirs and community talent shows. She moved to St. Louis, Missouri, during the mid-1950s. She began singing with Ike Turner's band in 1956, when his group was performing in a St. Louis nightclub. In 1959 the Turners won wide recognition for their rhythm 'n' blues recording, "Fool in love." Thereafter Ike reorganized his show around Tina, adding a girls' group, the Ikettes, to back her in the singing and dancing. The Turners attracted international attention during the 1960s when they toured in Europe with The Rolling Stones (1966) and later accompanied The Rolling Stones on their American tour. Ike and Tina toured widely with their entertainment act, performing in concert halls, in nightclubs, on television shows, and in films, including *Soul to Soul* (1971). They also recorded extensively.

BIBL: *Ebony* (May 1971). StamPRS. ShawWS.

DISC: Jep. TudBM.

TURNER, JOE. Jazz pianist (b. 3 November 1907 in Baltimore, Maryland). He studied piano when he was five years old with his mother; his early style development was influenced by his listening to piano rolls. About 1923 he settled in New York; thereafter he played piano in nightclubs in the Harlem community and with various groups, including Hilton Jefferson, June Clark, Benny Carter* (1929), and Louis Armstrong* (1930), among others. During the 1930s he toured widely with Adelaide Hall* as accompanist in the United States and abroad. In 1936 he settled in Europe; in 1939 he returned to the United States because of the outbreak of World War II, then in 1949 he resettled in Europe. During his service in the United States Armed Forces (1944-45), he played in an army band led by Melvin ("Sy") Oliver.* He returned to the United States in 1973 to play at a Newport Jazz Festival, and again in 1976 to play a long residency in a New York nightclub. He was one of the original Harlem stride pianists, along with James P. Johnson,* Charles Luckeyeth ("Luckey") Roberts,* William ("Willie-the-Lion") Smith,* and Thomas ("Fats") Waller.* His mature style, however, reflected the influence of later jazz pianists, such as Earl Hines,* Erroll Garner,* and Arthur ("Art") Tatum.*

BIBL: Black press, incl. AmstN, 17 January 1976. ChilWW. FeaEJ. FeaGitJS. NYT, 10 January 1976.

DISC: Jep.

TURNER, JOSEPH VERNON ("BIG JOE"). Bluesman (b. 18 May 1911 in Kansas City, Missouri). He became involved with blues as a child when he led a blind guitarist through the streets of Kansas City. About the age of thirteen he began singing in local clubs, where he came into contact with major blues and jazzmen of the period, including William ("Count") Basie,* Oran ("Hot Lips") Page,* Ben Webster,* and Mary Lou Williams,* among others. Eventually he formed a team with Pete Johnson*; they toured widely and played with a band that gave nightly broadcasts on a local radio station. In 1938 they performed on the From Spirituals to Swing concert produced by John Hammond at Carnegie Hall in New York. The same year they recorded "Roll em, Pete" and "Going away blues," which brought them much attention and influenced the development of rhythm 'n' blues. Thereafter Turner sang with a variety of groups—blues, rhythm 'n' blues, jazz—among them, Edward ("Duke") Ellington* and William ("Count") Basie. He toured widely in the United States and in Europe and recorded extensively. During the early 1940s he settled in Los Angeles, California. In 1947 he and Johnson again performed together, establishing on the West Coast the shouting Kansas City blues. He was active through the 1970s, writing his songs, performing in clubs, and appearing at the major blues and jazz festivals.

BIBL: BWW. ChilWWJ. FeaEJ. FeaGitJS. LivBl 10 (Autumn 1972). MeeJMov. Oliv. ShawR5.

DISC: DiGod. Kink. LeSlBR. TudBM.

TURNER, RACHEL WALKER. See **WALKER, RACHEL.**

TURPIN, THOMAS MILLION ("TOM"). Ragtime pianist/Composer (b. 1873 in Savannah, Georgia; d. 13 August 1922 in St. Louis, Missouri). His family moved to St. Louis, Missouri, during the 1880s. A self-taught pianist, he began his professional career as a pianist in a St. Louis brothel, Babe Connor's Castle Club, where such songs as "Ta-ra-ra-boom-de-ra" and "A hot time in the old town tonight" originated. In 1900 he opened his own saloon, the Rosebud Cafe, which became a gathering place for rag pianists from all over the Midwest. He taught many younger pianists basic rag-playing skills and encouraged the development of others. He and his brother Charles sponsored rag competitions that drew contestants from all over the nation. In later years the Turpin brothers operated the Booker T. Washington Theater, which occasionally produced vaudeville shows as well as staged them. Turpin was the first black man to publish a rag, "Harlem rag" (1897). Best known of his other rags was "St. Louis rag" (1903), written in honor of the St. Louis World's Fair. Turpin also wrote scores for some of the musicals produced at his theater. His brother, Charles, was a manager of T.O.B.A.* (Theaters Owners Booking Association) for many years.

BIBL: Black press. Blesh. JaTiRR.

TURRENTINE, STANLEY. Jazz saxophonist (b. 5 April 1934 in Pittsburgh, Pennsylvania). He came from a musical family: his father, Thomas, Sr., played saxophone with the Savoy Sultans in the 1930s. As a child he studied violoncello but changed to tenor saxophone, taking his first lessons from his father. He began playing professionally when he was seventeen with Lowell Fulson (1951) and thereafter played with various groups, including Ray Charles* (1952), Tadley ("Tadd") Dameron* (1953), Earl Bostic* (1953-56), and Maxwell ("Max") Roach* (1959-60), among others. In 1960 he organized his own group, which featured organist Shirley Scott* for eleven years (1960-71). He was married to her during that period. During the 1970s he toured widely with his Stanley Turrentine Quartet and gradually "crossed over" into the field of popular music, particularly "soul." He recorded regularly, appeared on television shows as well as in nightclubs and theaters, and at the major jazz festivals. Best known of his albums were *Pieces of Dreams*, *In the Pocket*, and *Yester You, Yester Me*.

BIBL: FeaEJ. FeaJS. FeaGitJS.

DISC: Jep.

TUTT, J. HOMER. See **WHITNEY, SALEM TUTT.**

TYERS, WILLIAM H. ("BILL"). Songwriter (b. 27 March 1876 in Richmond, Virginia; d. 18 April 1924 in New York, New York). His family moved to New York when he was twelve years old, and there he first studied music privately. At the age of twenty he toured with a concert company in Europe as a librarian. While there he studied instrumentation at Hamburg, Germany. His first professional experience was in a dancing school, the Metropolitan, where he led his own three-piece group. During the 1890s he also was a staff arranger for music publishers in New York, among them, Joseph Stern & Company, and began to publish his own pieces. He was among the first black musicians who joined the Musicians Protective Union. He became very active with the Clef Club after its organization in 1910 and was an assistant conductor under James Reese Europe* for both Clef Club and Tempo Club groups. He was musical director for Vernon and Irene Castle. In addition, he led an orchestra at Broadway's Strand Roof Garden for many years. In 1919 he was an assistant conductor under Will Marion Cook* with the New York Syncopated Orchestra. His best-known pieces were the instrumental "Panama," "Trocha," "Maori," "A Samoan dance," "Call of the woods," and "Dance of the Philippines." His penchant for Caribbean and South American rhythms perhaps reflected the influence of his father, who was a native of South America.

BIBL: ASCAP. Black press, incl. NYAge, 26 April 1924. Blesh. *The Crisis* 4 (June 1912), p. 68. Flet, pp.278-80. JaTiRRT.

TYLER, JESSE GERALD. Choral conductor/Concert pianist (b. c1879 in Oberlin, Ohio (?); d. 17 May 1938 in Oberlin). He obtained his musical training at the Oberlin Conservatory in Ohio (B. Mus., 1904) and studied further with Oscar Garrison of Washington, D.C., Herbert Witherspoon of New York, and Ernest Kroeger of St. Louis, Missouri. His teaching career included tenures in the public schools of Washington (1904-07) and, during the same period, in Harriet Marshall Gibb's* Washington Conservatory of Music as head of the vocal department; at Lincoln High School in Kansas City, Misouri (1907-11); and at Sumner High School of St. Louis, Missouri (1911-22). In Kansas City he was music supervisor of colored schools, and in St. Louis, he was head of the music department at Sumner as well as music supervisor for colored elementary schools. During his early career he gave piano recitals and later he toured widely as a concert baritone, giving recitals and singing solo parts in oratorios. When Samuel Coleridge-Taylor* conducted a festival of his music in Washington in 1906, Tyler was one of the soloists. He was also active as a church organist/director in St. Louis at the Union Memorial AME Church. Throughout his career he encouraged the development of black concert artists and the performance of the music of black composers. When his Gerald Tyler Choral Society produced the oratorio *Mary Magdalene* in Kansas City in 1909, he imported Harry T. Burleigh,* Carl Diton,* and Inez Clough* from the East to sing the solos. On other occasions he imported such artists as R. Nathaniel Dett* and Anita Patti Brown* to perform on his concerts. Tyler wrote a number of compositions—for piano, chorus, violin, and voice—and also wrote scores for stage works. His best-known compositions were the songs "Ships that pass in the night" (sung by Roland Hayes*), "Syrian lullaby," and "Good-night" and the anthem "Magnificat" for mixed voices. During the early 1920s he gave frequent recitals of his compositions. In 1922 he suffered a stroke which forced his retirement from music, and he resettled in Oberlin, Ohio. During the 1930s, however, he was encouraged to develop piano skills with his left hand, particularly by Clarence Cameron White,* and he became successful enough to be able to give several recitals playing with only his left hand. Tyler made a large contribution to the development of black music in the United States, and particularly in Kansas City and St. Louis, through the high standards that he set for his students, both youths and adults, and the strong traditions of excellence he established in the two cities. Like his successor N. Clark Smith,* Walter Henri Dyett* in Chicago, Illinois, and Eugene Mikell* in New York, his influence as a teacher lasted through several generations and produced some of the most renowned black musical figures of the twentieth century in opera, jazz, composition, and the concert world.

BIBL: Black press, incl. NYAge, 29 April 1909, 13 March 1920; CDef, 20 March 1920. John Cotter, "The

Negro in Music in St. Louis" (M.A. thesis, Washington University [in St. Louis], 1959).

TYLER, VERONICA. Opera/concert singer (b. c1937 in Baltimore, Maryland). She obtained her musical education at the Peabody Conservatory of Music in Baltimore, Maryland (B. Mus., 1960), where she studied with Alice Duschak, and at the Juilliard School of Music in New York, where she studied with Florence Page Kimball. In 1963 she won first place in the International Music (voice) Competitions held at Munich, Germany. In 1964 she made her operatic debut as a soprano in the role of Susanna in Mozart's *The Marriage of Figaro* with the New York City Opera. During the same year she sang in Gershwin's *Porgy and Bess*. In 1966 she won a silver medal in the Tchaikovsky Competitions in Moscow, USSR. Her teaching career included tenures as artist-in-residence at various universities, including the University of Florida at Gainesville (1975-77); the University of Missouri at Columbia (1977-78); the University of Michigan at Ann Arbor (1978-79); and Morgan State University in Baltimore, Maryland (1979-80).

BIBL: Black press, incl. AmstN, 3 October 1964; [Baltimore] *Afro-American*, 16 September 1978.

DISC: Turn.

TYNER, ALFRED MCCOY (aka **SULAIMON SAUD).** Jazz pianist (b. 11 December 1938 in Philadelphia, Pennsylvania). His mother played piano, and he began piano study as a child. By the time he was fifteen he had organized his own group. He began playing professionally with local groups in Philadelphia at an early age, among them, Calvin Massey. Later he played with Benny Golson,* the Golson/Art Farmer* Jazztet, and John Coltrane* (1959-65). Thereafter he performed with his own groups. During the 1970s he toured widely in the United States, Europe, and Japan, and recorded extensively. He first attracted wide attention during the 1960s for his improvisational piano in the Coltrane group, and developed into one of the leading avant-garde pianists of his time. His style development was influenced by Thelonious Monk* and Coltrane, with whom he studied informally. His mature style reflected his use of contemporary elements and his employment of non-Western instruments. He received numerous awards from the music industry. His best-known compositions were *Sahara*, *Enlightenment Suite*, and *Trident*.

BIBL: Bill Cole, *John Coltrane* (New York, 1976). ContKey (October 1976). *Down Beat*, 24 October 1963, p. 18. FeaJS. FeaGitJS.

DISC: ModJ. TudJ.

TYNES, MARGARET. Concert/opera singer (b. 11 September 1929 in Saluda, Virginia). She came from a musical family; her brothers Victor and Morris and her sister Angela [Roberts] became professional musicians. She began singing as a child and won a talent contest at the age of five. She obtained her musical education in the public schools of Greensboro, North Carolina; at North Carolina A & T College (Agricultural and Technical) in Greensboro (B.A.); Columbia University Teachers College in New York (M.A.), and the Juilliard School of Music in New York. Her teachers included Emil Cooper, Lola Hayes, Tullio Serafin, and Guiseppe Pais. She sang in the Broadway revival of Gershwin's *Porgy and Bess* (1952-54), which featured Leontyne Price* and William Warfield,* and toured with the company in Europe. In 1958 she appeared on Ed Sullivan's television show and was invited to go with his company to Russia in 1959 to perform for the Moscow Trade Fair. The same year she made her operatic debut as a spinto soprano in Verdi's *MacBeth* in Montreal, Canada. Thereafter she toured widely as a concert and opera singer in the United States and abroad. In December 1974 she made her Metropolitan Opera debut in the title role of Janacek's *Jenufa*.

BIBL:Black press, incl. NYAge, 13 June 1959, 1 August 1959. WWOpera.

DISC: Turn.

U

UGGAMS, LESLIE. Popular-music singer (b. 25 May 1943 in New York, New York). She obtained her musical training at the Professional Children's School and the Juilliard School of Music (1961-63), both in the city of New York. She began performing professionally at an early age; she began appearing on the "Beulah" television show when she was two years old (1945-50) and sang at the Apollo Theater in the Harlem community when she was nine. As a young adult she first attracted wide attention when she sang on the television show "Sing Along with Mitch" (1961-64). Through the 1960s-70s she was active in radio, television, films, and musical comedies. She also toured widely, singing in concert halls, theaters, nightclubs, and on college campuses. She received awards from the theater and music industries.

BIBL: Black press, incl. AmstN, 21 July 1962. CurBiog (October 1967). WWA. WWBA.

UMBRIAN GLEE CLUB, THE. Community choral organization (fl. twentieth century in Chicago, Illinois). The glee club was founded in 1909 by Edward Morris and Arthur Brown, husband of Anita Patti Brown,* in Chicago. During its early years, there were white directors, among them, E. T. Clissold. The organization gave annual concerts, importing well-known black artists from the East to sing solos or the solo parts in oratorios. Later the group had black directors; one of the most influential was Walter E. Gossette.* The group began to make annual nationwide tours in 1924 under the directorship of R. C. Kelly with T. Tom Taylor* as pianist/accompanist. In May 1964 the glee club staged its fifty-ninth annual concert, with Sidney F. Johnson as director. The singing group was still active in 1980.

BIBL: Black press, incl. CDef, 29 October 1910, 21 March 1925; IndF, 2 May 1914.

UTTERBACH, CLINTON. Gospel singer (b. 1931 in New York, New York). He came from a musical family: both parents were professional gospel singers and his father played in a dance band. He sang in church choirs as a child; at the age of fifteen he was paid soloist for a large church. His style development was influenced by Thomas ("Fats") Waller,* Reginald ("Sonny") Beane, and "Sister" Rosetta Tharpe,* among others—all of whom performed at his church, the Refuge Church in the Harlem community of New York. He obtained his musical education at the City College of the City University of New York and at the Juilliard School of Music in New York. After service in the U.S. Armed Forces (1951-53), he toured with an all-male gospel group. In 1961 he organized the Utterbach Concert Ensemble, which developed a repertory of gospel, spirituals and other folksongs, and popular music. In 1963 his forty-voice choir won the Mahalia Jackson* Award. His choral style was distinctive for its avant-garde arrangements and his vigorous conducting. He wrote and arranged most of the materials performed by his groups, which were pace-setters and widely emulated by contemporary gospel choirs.

BIBL: Pearl Williams Jones, "Afro-American Gospel Music" in Vada Butcher, ed., *Development of Materials for a One-Year Course in African Music* (Washington, D.C., 1970). *Sepia* (October 1965).

V

VAN BUREN, CATHERINE. (b. 10 December 1907 in Morristown, New Jersey). Her family moved to Pittsfield, Massachusetts, when she was a child. She obtained her musical education in the public schools of Pittsfield; at Fisk University in Nashville, Tennessee (B.A., 1931), where she was a soloist with the university choir; and at the Oberlin Conservatory of Music (B. Mus., 1935), where she sang in the a-capella choir. She studied voice with Edgar Schofield, among others. Her early career development was encouraged by Ruth L. Phillips and, later, by Roland Hayes.* After graduating from Fisk, she returned to sing with the Fisk Jubilee Singers* as a soloist. She toured in the United States and in the Caribbean as a concert soprano. She was also active as a church soloist in New York, New York, and sang in the choruses of the Metropolitan Opera and the New York City Opera (1959-63). During World War II she toured with the USO Camp Show Unit, Gershwin's opera *Porgy and Bess*, singing the role of the Strawberry Woman (1944). During the 1950s she toured for almost four years with *Porgy and Bess* in the United States and abroad, including a tour in the USSR. Her teaching career included tenures at Shaw University in Raleigh, North Carolina (1935-36), Talladega College in Alabama (1936-37), Fisk University (1939-41), and Wilberforce University in Ohio (1943).

BIBL: Questionnaire.

VAN PEEBLES, MELVIN. Playwright/Producer/Composer (b. 21 August 1932 in South Chicago, Illinois). Although best known as an actor and producer, he is included here as a singer and composer. He obtained his education in the public schools of Phoenix, Illinois (a suburb of Chicago), and at West Virginia State College in Institute (1949-50) and Ohio Wesleyan in Delaware, Ohio (B.A., 1953). After college he served in the United States Air Force for three-and-a-half years. During the late 1950s he began making films and composing his own film music, although he had no formal training in music. In 1959 he settled in Europe, living first in the Netherlands, then in Paris, France, where he wrote articles for periodicals, wrote novels for himself, and acted, sang, and danced to earn a living. He first attracted wide attention for his film *The Story of a Three-Day Pass* (1967), for which he wrote half of the music. He returned to the United States in the late 1960s. He began to write songs (both music and lyrics) and recorded some albums, including *Brer Soul*, which later were used for his Broadway productions. His first major job in the United States was as director of the film *Watermelon Man* (1970), which starred Godfrey Cambridge. Thereafter he produced films and musicals, including the film *Sweet Sweetback Baadassss Song* (1971), in which he took the leading role, and the Broadway musicals *Ain't Supposed to Die* (1971) and *Don't Play Us Cheap* (1972). He also wrote musicals for television. He received awards from the theater industry.

BIBL: Mel Gussow, "The Baadassss Success of Melvin Van Peebles" in NYT, 20 August 1972. WWBA.

VAUGHAN, SARAH LOU ("SISSY"). Jazz singer (b. 27 March 1924 in Newark, New Jersey). She was born into a family of musical amateurs; her father played guitar and her mother sang in a church choir. She began piano study at the age of seven and later studied organ. She sang in a church choir as a child. When she was sixteen she entered a talent contest at the Apollo Theater in the Harlem community of New York and won first place, which gave her a week's engagement at the theater. Her singing attracted the attention of William ("Billy") Eckstine,* who recommended her to Earl Hines* for membership in his band. She performed with Hines first as a pianist, then as vocalist (1943). Thereafter she sang with Eckstine (1944-45) and John Kirby* (1945), then began performing as a soloist. She toured widely over the next decades throughout the world, giving recitals, singing with symphony orchestras, and appearing in nightclubs. She first recorded in 1944 and thereafter recorded regularly. She was also active in television and in films, including *Jazz Festival* (1956), *Disc Jockey* (1951), *Basin Street Revue* (1956), and the soundtrack of *Cactus Flower* (1962). During the 1970s she frequently sang on college campuses and at the major jazz festivals. She was noted for her improvisatory skills, which reflected the influence of her association with bebop musicians. Her best-known performances were of "Misty," "A foggy day in London," "Poor butterfly," and "Tenderly." She received numerous awards from the music industry. Her contemporaries called her "the divine one" and "Sassy."

BIBL: CurBiog (April 1980). *Ebony* (April 1975). *Essence* (October 1974). FeaEJ. FeaJS. FeaGitJS. MeeJMov. WWA. WWBA.

DISC: Jep. Kink.

VAUGHN, JAMES. Songwriter (b. 1870s [?] in Boston, Massachusetts; d. after 1935 in Boston). He attended the Rindge Technical School in Cambridge, Massachusetts. His first professional experience was with Goodman's Alabama Troubadours. Later he became musical director for the George Walker*/Bert Williams* shows (1902-09) and also wrote songs for the musicals. He went with the show *In Dahomey* to London, England (1902-04), as a member of the cast. After the demise of the Walker/Williams company, he joined J. Leubrie Hill's* company, which produced *My Friend from Dixie* (1911) and *My Friend from Kentucky* (1913) during the three years that Vaughn was with the company. Thereafter he toured with Black Patti's* Troubadours, then in 1915 became musical director of Tutt Whitney's* The Smart Set* company. He wrote scores for the musicals *George Washington Bullion Abroad*, produced by the Smart Set in 1915-16, and *Bamboula* (1920). In 1916 he was active in Chicago as a musical director in nightclubs and theaters. During his tenure at the Club DeLuxe, a trio composed of Cora Green, Ada "Bricktop" Smith,* and Florence Mills* attracted wide attention.

BIBL: Black press, incl. CDef, 1 March 1916, 27 November 1920; IndF, 5 June 1915, 2 October 1915. Hare.

VEE-JAY RECORDS. See **BRACKEN, JAMES.**

VEREEN, BENJAMIN AUGUSTUS ("BEN"). Entertainer (b. 10 October 1946 in Miami, Florida). He early revealed talent and won prizes in talent shows as a child. He obtained his education at the High School of Performing Arts in New York and later studied at the Dance Theater of Harlem school and at the Pentacostal Theological Seminary. Early in his career he sang with the Sensational Twilights, a group active in Brooklyn, New York. His career development was influenced by Vinette Carroll, who taught in the drama department at his high school. His first professional experience was in Langston Hughes's* gospel song-play, *The Prodigal Son* (1965), directed by Carroll. Thereafter he appeared in various musicals, including the production of *Sweet Charity* (1967) at Las Vegas, Nevada; the production of *Hair* (1969) in Los Angeles, California; Charles Gordone's *No Place to Be Somebody* (1970); and the Broadway production of *Pippin* (1972). He was active in television and films and toured widely as a nightclub entertainer. He won awards from the theater industry.

BIBL: CurBiog (April 1978). *Ebony* (May 1973).

VERRETT, SHIRLEY. Opera singer (b. 31 May 1931 in New Orleans, Louisiana). Her family moved to Los Angeles, California, when she was a child. She began singing at the age of six in the Seventh-Day Adventist Church that her family attended. She obtained her musical education in the public schools of Los Angeles, Venture College (A.A., 1951) and the Juilliard School of Music in New York (1956-61, diploma in voice). She studied voice with Anna Fitziu in Los Angeles and with Marian Székély-Fresche at Juilliard. During the years she attended Juilliard, she entered competitions, came to the attention of composers and conductors, and as a result began singing with symphony orchestras, at music festivals, and for special performances before she had made her debut. She attracted wide attention in 1967 when she sang the role of Queen Elizabeth in Donizetti's *Maria Stuarda* at Covent Garden in London, England. In 1968 she made her debut with the Metropolitan Opera in the title role of Bizet's *Carmen*. She was noted for her singing of both soprano and mezzo-soprano roles: as soprano, Princess Selika in Meyerbeer's *L'Africaine*, Lady Macbeth in Verdi's *Macbeth*, the title role in Bellini's *Norma*, Neocle in Rossini's *The Siege of Corinth*, and both Dido and Cassandra in Bizet's *Les Troyens*; as mezzo-soprano, Azucena in Verdi's *Il Trovatore*, Adalgisa in *Norma*, and, of course, Carmen. She also toured as a concert singer; her long-time accompanist was Warren Wilson, who also played for Leontyne

Price* and William Warfield.* Her honors included the Marian Anderson* Award (1955) and Blanche Thebom Award (1960); fellowships from such foundations as the John Hay Whitney (1959), Martha Baird Rockefeller (1959-61), and Ford (1962-63); an Alumni Achievement Award from Venture College (1963); and citations from civic and community organizations.

BIBL: CurBiog (April 1967). *Ebony* (December 1968). NYT Magazine, 30 January 1977. WWA. WWBA.

DISC: Turn.

VINSON, EDDIE (''CLEANHEAD''). Bluesman (b. 18 December 1917 in Houston, Texas). He came from a musical family: his grandfather played violin, and both parents played piano. As a child he sang in church quartets. His early professional experience was obtained with Milton Larkins Band (1936-41). Thereafter he played with various groups, including William (''Big Bill'') Broonzy (1941),* Charles (''Cootie'') Williams* (1942-45, 1954), his own group (1945-49), Jay McShann* (1968-70), Johnny Otis (1970-71), and William (''Count'') Basie* (1972), among others. He recorded with various groups and toured in the United States and in Europe, making his first trip abroad in 1967 with the American Folk Blues Festival. During the late 1960s he settled in Los Angeles, California. He was regarded as a mainstream bluesman, in regard to both his singing and his alto saxophone. His best-known recordings included ''Cherry red,'' ''Kidney stew blues,'' ''Old maid boogie,'' and ''Tune up.''

BIBL: BWW. FeaEJ. FeaGitJS. MeeJMov. Robert Neff and Anthony Connor, *Blues* (Boston, 1975). Oliv.

DISC: Kink.

VINSON (or **VINCENT**), **WALTER JACOB.** Bluesman (b. 2 February 1901 in Bolton, Mississippi; d. 22 April 1975 in Chicago, Illinois). See **MISSISSIPPI SHEIKS.**

VODERY, WILL HENRY BENNETT. Arranger-composer (b. 8 October 1885 in Philadelphia, Pennsylvania; d. 18 November 1951 in New York, New York). His family ran a theatrical boardinghouse in Philadelphia, where he came into contact with leading black entertainers of the period. He studied piano as a child and began playing in local concerts during the 1890s. Later he attended the University of Pennsylvania in Philadelphia, where he studied with Hugh Clark. His early professional experiences were with the George Walker*/Bert Williams* companies. During the first decade of the twentieth century he went to St. Louis, Missouri, as musical director for a Jolly John Larkin show. Thereafter he was active in Chicago, Illinois, as a librarian for the Chicago Symphony Orchestra (1905); during this period he studied harmony and orchestration with Frederick Stock, director of the orchestra. Some time before 1907 he seems to have settled in New York, where he became active as an arranger and songwriter. During the next few years he arranged and/or composed scores for Broadway musicals, including *The Time, the Place and the Girl* (1907); *The Oyster Man* (1909), which starred Ernest Hogan*; and beginning in 1913, for Florenz Ziegfeld's *Follies*. He remained with Ziegfeld productions for twenty years. He was musical director for Hurtig and Seamon's enterprises and arranged music for the company's Dandy Dixie Minstrels. He was also musical director for the George Walker*/Bert Williams* *In Bandanna Land* (1907) and for J. Leubrie Hill's* productions (1911-14), writing the score for Hill's comedy *The Blackville Corporation* (1911) and arranging music for *My Friend from Dixie* (1911). In addition to these activities, he conducted a dance orchestra during these years on the Century Roof Garden in New York, and for a short period led the orchestra at the Howard Theater in Washington, D.C.

During World War I, Vodery attended the Bandmaster's School at Chaumont, France. Thereafter he directed the 807th Pioneer Infantry Band, which performed widely in Europe, appearing before crowned heads of Belgium, and Monaco, and the president of France. After the war, Vodery settled again in New York. In addition to his involvement with Zeigfeld, he led Will Vodery's Plantation Orchestra in various shows featuring Florence Mills,* including *Plantation Revue* (1922), *Dover Street to Dixie* (1923), and *Dixie to Broadway* (1924). In 1929 he collaborated with Will Marion Cook* in writing the musical score for *Swing Along*. In the fall of 1929 he went to Hollywood, California, as an arranger and musical director for Fox Films, the first black musician to fill such a position. After completing musical arrangements for *Virginia City* in 1933, he resettled in New York. During the 1930s he was again active as an arranger, writing orchestrations for *Blackbirds of 1933*, *Shuffle Along of 1933*, and *Virginia* (1937), in addition to Ziegfeld productions. His Will Vodery Singers appeared in the musical *Strike Me Pink* (1933) and his Jubilee Singers in *Show Girl* (1929). One of his last big assignments was as arranger and musical director for *The Cotton Club Parade* revue in 1940, which featured dancer Bill Robinson and Cabell (''Cab'') Calloway's* band. Vodery was highly regarded by his contemporaries for his arranging/orchestration skills; he gave many of the younger musicians informal lessons in orchestration, including Edward ("Duke") Ellington.* He also helped many a black musician to gain a foothold in the musical world, including William Grant Still* and Jules Bledsoe,* among others.

BIBL: ASCAP. Black press, incl. CDef, 6 August 1910, 2 February 1911, 27 March 1915; AmstN, 24 November 1951; NYAge, 28 September 1929, 11 December 1948. Flet, pp. 154-56. Hare. WWCA 1941-44.

VON CHARLTON, RUDOLPH EVERETT. College professor (b. 1912 in Norfolk, Virginia). He obtained his musical education at Hampton Institute in Virginia (B.S., 1931), the University of Michigan at Ann Arbor (M. Mus., 1939), and Columbia University Teachers College in New York (Ph.D., 1948). He also studied at the Juilliard School of Music in New York and the New England Conservatory of Music in Boston, Massachusetts. His piano teachers included R. Nathaniel Dett,* Percy Grainger, and Tobias Matthay. During his college years he toured with the Hampton Choir, then under the leadership of Dett. His teaching career included tenures at Florida A & M (Agricultural and Mechanical) College at Tallahassee (1931-42) and Prairie View State College at Hempstead, Texas (1942-1977), where he was chairman of the department for many years.

BIBL: Black press, incl. NYAge, 27 September 1947. WWCA 1950.

W

WALCOTT'S RABBIT FOOT MINSTRELS, F. S. See **CHAPPELLE, PATRICK.**

WALKER, AARON THIBEAUX ("T-BONE"). Bluesman (b. 28 May 1910 in Linden, Texas; d. 16 March 1975 in Los Angeles, California). Members of his family played guitar or banjo; he began playing guitar when he was thirteen. His style development was influenced by Francis "Scrapper" Blackwell,* Leroy Carr,* and Lonnie Johnson,* to whose records he listened. His family moved to Dallas, Texas, when he was a child, and there he heard live performances of "Blind" Lemon Jefferson,* who was a family friend, and Lonnie Johnson. At sixteen he began playing professionally, at first with Dr. Breeding's Big B Tonic medicine show and Ida Cox's* show. He also played in a high-school band, which continued to perform under the leadership of Lawson Brooks after its members had left school. He first recorded in 1929 but did not record again for several years. He toured widely in the Southwest with Brooks; in 1933 he formed a team with Charlie Christian.* In 1934 he settled in Los Angeles, California. Thereafter he performed in local clubs and also toured widely in the United States and abroad, playing with Les Hite,* among others, and his own groups. In 1935 he became the first blues guitarist to use the electric guitar. His blues written in 1945, "Call it stormy Monday" (later called "Stormy Monday") brought him wide attention, as did later blues, such as "T-Bone blues" and "T-Bone shuffle." He was the pioneer virtuoso on the blues electric guitar, and he exerted enormous influence upon the development of contemporary blues, which is best represented in the music of Riley ("B. B.") King.*

BIBL: BWW. ChilWWJ. FeaEJ. FeaGitJS. LivBl 11, 12 (Winter 1972-73; Spring 1973). LivBl 21 (May-June 1975). MeeJMov. NYT, 17 March 1975.

DISC: Jep. Kink. LeSlBR. RustJR. TudBM.

WALKER, AIDA OVERTON. Entertainer (b. 14 February 1880 in Richmond, Virginia; d. 11 October 1914 in New York, New York). Her family moved to New York when she was a child, and there she received her early musical training. She began her professional career in 1895 as an entertainer in John Isham's *Octoroons* company. In 1896 she went to Black Patti's* Troubadours, and in 1898 she joined the George Walker*/ Bert Williams* company. She and Walker were married in 1899. She appeared in all the Walker/Williams shows, beginning with *The Policy Players* (1899) and continuing through the final one, *In Bandanna Land* (1907-09). After George Walker's death and the disbanding of the company, she joined the Bob Cole*/ Johnson brothers* company, singing a leading role in *The Red Moon* (1908-09). During the 1909-10 season she worked with the Smart Set* company. Thereafter she toured widely as a soloist on the vaudeville circuit. She was regarded by her contemporaries as one of the most talented singer/dancers of the time.

BIBL: Black press, incl. CDef, 17 October 1914, 24 October 1914; IndF, 16 September 1916; NYAge, 14 July 1910, 15 October 1915. Flet, pp. 181-182.

WALKER, GEORGE. Vaudeville entertainer (b. 1873 in Lawrence, Kansas; d. 6 January 1911 in Islip, New York). See also **WILLIAMS, EGBERT "BERT."** He began his career touring with a medicine show. He left the show in San Francisco, California, where he met Egbert ("Bert") Williams.* In 1892 the two men formed a vaudeville act. They worked at Halahan and Homan's Midway in the city, then toured with a minstrel troupe, a medicine show, and finally on the Orpheum vaudeville circuit. During the mid-1890s they went east to advance their careers. In 1896 they appeared in the Broadway musical, *The Gold Bug*; although the musical was unsuccessful, their act won critical acclaim. Thereafter they played a long run at New York's Koster and Bial's Theater, interrupted for a short period for an engagement in London, England. About 1897 they formed an all-black company to produce the show *Senegambian Carnival*, but this proved to be unsuccessful. In 1898 they secured the management of professionals, Hurtig and Seamon, and thereafter produced a series of successful shows: *The Policy Players* (1899), *Sons of Ham* (1900), *Williams and Walker in Dahomey* (1902-05), *Williams and Walker in Abyssinia* (1905-06), and *Williams and Walker in Bandanna Land* (1907-09). *In Dahomey* ran two seasons in England and included a command performance at Buckingham Palace. All these shows provided employment for large numbers of black entertainers, musicians, composers, lyricists, musical directors, stage managers, and others associated with the stage over the years. Those associated with Walker/Williams shows at one time or another included Will Marion Cook,* Paul Lawrence Dunbar,* Lloyd Gibbs,* J. Leubrie Hill,* Jesse Shipp,* Alex Rogers,* Abbie Mitchell,* James Vaughn,* Aida Overton Walker,* Inez Clough,* the Golden Gate Quartet*—to cite but a few names among the many. Walker was married to Aida Overton Walker.

BIBL: Black press, incl. CDef, 14 January 1911; NYAge, 12 January 1911. Flet, pp. 227-38.

WALKER, GEORGE THEOPHILUS. Composer/ College professor (b. 27 June 1922 in Washington, D.C.). He came from a musical family; his father was an amateur pianist, and his sister, Frances Walker Slocum,* became a concert pianist. He began piano study at the age of five. He obtained his musical education in the public schools of Washington, D.C.; in the junior division of the Howard University School of Music in Washington; at the Oberlin [Ohio] Conservatory (B. Mus., 1941); at the Curtis Institute in Philadelphia, Pennsylvania (artist diploma), where he studied with Rudolf Serkin and Rosario Scalero; the American Academy at Fontainebleau, France (artist diploma, 1947), where he studied with Clifford Curzon, Robert Casadesus and Nadia Boulanger; and the Eastman School of Music in Rochester, New York (D. Mus., 1957). He also studied with William Primrose, Gregor Piatigorsky, and Gian-Carlo Menotti. He first attracted wide attention as a pianist when he won the Philadelphia Youth Auditions in 1941 and performed the Rachmaninoff Piano Concerto, No. 3, with the Philadelphia Orchestra under the direction of Eugene Ormandy. In 1945 he made his debut as a concert pianist at Town Hall in New York. During the 1950s he toured extensively in the United States and in Europe under management of National Concert Artists and Columbia Artists, giving recitals and performing with leading symphony orchestras. During the same decade he entered a teaching career, which included tenures at Dillard University in New Orleans, Louisiana (1953-54), the Dalcroze School of Music and the New School for Social Research, both in the city of New York (1960-61); Smith College at Northampton, Massachusetts (1961-68); University of Colorado at Denver (1968-69), and Rutgers University at Newark, New Jersey (1969-). He also served tenures as a guest professor at various institutions, including the Peabody Conservatory in Baltimore, Maryland, and the University of Delaware at Newark, Delaware.

He began composing at an early age and published his first major composition, *Lament for Strings*, in 1946 (later titled *Lyric for Strings*). His mature style was characterized by a fusion of contemporary idioms, including serial techniques, which gave emphasis to engaging melodies, instrumental color, and complex rhythms. He leaned toward the use of such conservative forms as sonatas, concertos, and variations during a period when his contemporaries were employing free forms. His music was infused with a sometimes subtle and other times obvious use of black folk and jazz idioms; for example, his Sonata for Cello and Piano (1957) used a boogie-woogie bass, his song "My luv is a red, red rose" (1971, poem by Burns) was a blues, his *Spirituals for Orchestra* (1974) used Negro spirituals, and his Piano Concerto (1976) "evoked the spirit of Edward ("Duke") Ellington." His best-known works, in addition to those cited, were *Address for Orchestra* (1959), Trombone Concerto (1957), *Variations for Orchestra* (1971), and *Music for Brass—Sacred and Profane* (1976). Of the black composers of his generation, his music was most widely performed, along with that of Ulysses Kay.*

His honors included fellowships and awards—Fulbright (1957), John Hay Whitney (1958), Bok Foundation (1963, grant for concerts in Europe), MacDowell Colony (summers, 1966-69), Guggenheim (1969), Rockefeller (1971, 1974), the National Endowment for the Arts (1972, 1974), and the Hans Kindler Foundation (1975). He also received grants from the American Music League and the Bennington Composers Conference, the Rhea A. Soslund Chamber Music Award (1967), and an Eastman School of Music Alumnus Citation (1961).

BIBL: Questionnaire. BakBC. Bull. Gro. WWBA. WWCA 1950.

WALKER, RACHEL. Concert singer (b. c1873 in Cleveland, Ohio [?]; d. after 1940 in Cleveland). She obtained her musical training in Cleveland, Ohio, where she studied privately with John Underner. As early as 1886 she began to appear on local concerts as a pianist and soprano. During the early 1890s she taught in the public schools of Cleveland, then began to tour as a professional concert singer. In 1893 she joined a black company, the Midnight Star Concert Company (later called the Ednorah Nahar Concert Company). Later she toured in California as the prima-donna soprano with a concert company sponsored by the Henry Wolfson Musical Bureau. In 1895 she left Cleveland for New York in order to study further and to advance her career. The next year she sang at Hammerstein's Olympic Roof Garden, where she was given the sobriquet, "the Creole Nightingale." Thereafter she secured top professional management. In August 1897 she went to London, England, for a long engagement at the Pavillion Theater. She remained abroad for eighteen years, touring with various English concert companies and also as a soloist, using the stage name Lucie Lenoir. The outbreak of World War I brought her back to the United States in 1915. She continued to give recitals for some time after she settled again in Cleveland.

BIBL: Black press, incl. CleveG, 23 October 1886, 8 December 1894; IndF, 15 February 1896, 17 April 1897, 21 May 1898, 7 March 1915, 22 July 1916. Davis.

WALKER SLOCUM, FRANCES. Concert pianist/College professor (b. 6 March 1924 in Washington, D.C.). She came from a musical family: her father was an amateur pianist, and her brother, George Walker,* became a concert pianist and composer. She began piano study at the age of four; she first played in public at the age of five on her teacher's annual student recital. She obtained her musical training in the junior division of the Howard University School of Music in Washington, D.C.; in the public schools of Washington, D.C.; at the Oberlin [Ohio] Conservatory (B. Mus., 1945); the Curtis Institute of Music in Philadelphia, Pennsylvania, where she studied with Rudolph Serkin and Miecyslaw Horszowski; Columbia University Teachers College (M.A., 1952; professional diploma, 1971). She also studied privately with Coeuraad V. Bos and Robert Goldsand. Her teaching career included tenures at Barber-Scotia Junior College at Concord, North Carolina; the Third Street Settlement House in the city of New York; Tougaloo [Mississippi] College; Lincoln University in Pennsylvania (1968-71); Rutgers University in Newark, New Jersey (1971-76); and Oberlin Conservatory (1976-). At the age of seventeen she gave her first full-length recital at Howard University. During her high-school years she played for church choirs; she was also an accompanist for Mary Cardwell Dawson's* National Negro Opera Company. In 1959 she made her debut as a concert pianist at Carnegie Recital Hall in New York. Throughout her career she combined teaching with giving piano concerts, including a tour in Europe in 1971. She also toured with the Symphony of the New World* Ensemble during the 1970s, performing the Schumann Piano Quintet. Her honors included a citation by the National Association of Negro Musicians* (1979) and the Adelaide M. Ayer Fellowship. She was best known for her performances of Brahms, Samuel Coleridge Taylor,* Prokofiev, Rachmaninoff, William Grant Still,* and George Walker.

BIBL: Questionnaire.

WALL, JESSIE or **JESSE.** Military fifer (fl. early nineteenth century. b. c1786; d. after 1863, possibly in Erie, Pennsylvania). He served as a fifer on the ship *Niagara* during the War of 1812; he was active in the Battle of Lake Erie.

BIBL: Wilkes, p. 73.

WALLACE, SIPPIE (née **BEULAH THOMAS**). Blueswoman (b. 11 November 1898 in Houston, Texas). She came from a musical family; a brother, Hersal, and a niece, Hociel Thomas, played blues professionally, and another brother, George, was a songwriter and music publisher. She began performing professionally at an early age and traveled with a tent show during the World War I years. In 1923 she went to Chicago, where she recorded blues until the early 1930s. In 1933 she settled in Detroit, Michigan. Thereafter she was active in church music until the mid-1960s, when she began touring again. In 1966 she toured with the Amercan Folk Blues Festival in Europe and also recorded an album. Those with whom she played and/or recorded during her career included Louis Armstrong,* Buddy Christian, Eurreal ("Little Brother") Montgomery,* Roosevelt Sykes,* and her brother Hersal.

BIBL: BWW. *Cadence* 4 (October 1978). Oliv. *Record Research* 88 (January 1968).

DISC: DiGod. Kink. LeSlBR. RustJR. TudBM.

WALLER, THOMAS WRIGHT ("FATS"). Jazz organist/Composer (b. 21 May 1904 in New York, New York; d. 15 December 1943 near Kansas City, Missouri). He came from a musical family; his paternal grandfather played violin, and his family sang hymns on street corners in the Harlem community of New York. As a child he sang and played harmonium with the family group, taught himself to play piano at the age of six, and later studied piano briefly with a local teacher. He obtained his musical training in the public schools of New York, where he studied string instruments and played piano in the school orchestra and for school assemblies. At an early age he began haunting the local cafés to hear the piano playing of his idols, Russell Brooks, James J. Johnson,* and William Henry ("Willie-the-Lion") Smith.* At fifteen he began playing piano and organ professionally in the local Lincoln Theater. Thereafter he played in local nightclubs, theaters, and at Harlem "rent parties"; he was the protégé of Johnson and Smith, who helped him to master the style that later would be called "Harlem stride piano." Clarence Williams* became his unofficial manager and started him on a recording career in 1922. In 1923 Waller was one of a select group of black pianists hired to make piano rolls by QRS (Quality Reigns Supreme, a subsidiary of the Melville Clark Piano Company), along with J. Lawrence Cook,* Clarence Johnson, James P. Johnson, Lemuel Fowler, Smith, and Williams. In 1926 Waller made his first solo recording; thereafter he recorded extensively as a soloist and with groups. During the 1920s-30s he performed with various groups or individuals, including Erskine Tate* (1927), Fletcher Henderson,* Ted Lewis, Otto Hardwicke,* and Elmer Snowden* (1931-32), as well as played residencies at theaters and nightclubs in Chicago, Illinois, New York, and on the West Coast. He also performed with his own groups, sometimes called Fats Waller and His Buddies or Fats Waller and His Rhythm. In 1932 he played abroad for the first time, in Paris, France, and returned to tour there in 1938 and 1939. He began his long radio broadcasting career in 1930 on station WLW in Cincinnati, Ohio; in 1934 he had his own radio series on CBS.

He began writing songs and piano music at an early age. During the 1920s he began a lifetime collaboration with lyricists and songwriters Clarence Williams, Spencer Williams,* Andy Razaf,* and Johnson, among others. His first musical-comedy score was *Keep Shufflin'* (1927), written with Johnson. Later came *Hot Chocolates* (1929), which included the songs "Ain't misbehaving" and "Honeysuckle rose," and *Early to Bed* (1943). His music was used on film-tracks, and he himself appeared in films, including *Hooray for Love* (1935), *King of Burlesque* (1935) and *Stormy Weather* (1943). Fats Waller became a legend in his own lifetime. He was the first to define the jazz pipe organ and jazz Hammond organ; he established a piano style that influenced countless of those who came after him; and he was a peerless songwriter. His best-known songs, in addition to those cited above, were "Squeeze me," "Keeping out of mischief now," "Blue turning grey over you," and "Stealing apples." Among his celebrated performances were "I'm gonna sit right down and write myself a letter." His instrumental extended compositions included *Boogie-woogie Suite*, *Piano Antics*, *London Suite*, and *Swincopations*. His two sons, Thomas, Jr., and Maurice, became professional musicians. His music enjoyed a revival of public interest with the Broadway production *Ain't Misbehavin'* in 1978.

BIBL: AlHen. ASCAP. ChilWW. FeaEJ. Charles Fox, *Fats Waller* (London, 1960). W. T. Kirkeby, *Ain't Misbehavin': The Story of Fats Waller* (London, 1967). MeeJMov. Maurice Waller and Anthony Calabrese, *Fats Waller* (New York, 1977).

DISC: Jep. Kink. RustJR. TudJ.

WALTON, LESTER AGLAR. Diplomat/Music journalist/director (b. 20 April 1882 in St. Louis, Missouri; d. 23 [?] October 1965 in New York, New York). Although best known as a diplomat and newspaper executive, he was active in musical affairs in the early twentieth century and therefore is included here. He received his education in the public schools and a business college of St. Louis, Missouri. About the turn of the century he began a long association with Ernest Hogan,* taking minor roles in Hogan's productions in order to become knowledgeable about the theater. In 1906 he went to New York, where he later became manager and dramatic editor of the *New York Age* (1908-14, 1917-19). Twice during these years he took over management of the Lafayette Theater in the Harlem community (1914-16, 1919-21). He wrote insightful reviews of concerts and searching editorials on black music and its importance to the community and to the race. He was musically active in other ways as well: he wrote lyrics for and/or helped to direct such musicals as Joe Jordan's* *Rufus Rastus* (1905-06), which starred Ernest Hogan; *The Oyster Man* (1909), also a Hogan musical; Alex Rogers* and Will Marion Cook's* *Black Bohemia* (1911); and Cook's *Darkeydom* (1914-15). In 1922 Walton was touring manager for Harry Pace's* Black Swan Troubadours, which featured Ethel Waters* and Fletcher Henderson* as leader of the Black Swan Jazz Masters. Thereafter Walton was musically inactive.

BIBL: AlHen. Black press, incl. *The Afro-American* [Baltimore], 30 October 1965; CDef, 28 November 1914; NYAge, 5 September 1936. WWWA 4.

WALTON, ORTIZ. Jazz-symphonic bassist (b. 13 December 1933 in Chicago, Illinois). Although a sociologist, he was a professional musician in his early career. He obtained his education at Roosevelt University in Chicago, Illinois (B.S., 1965) and the University of California at Berkeley (M.A., 1970; Ph.D., 1973). He played double bass in the Boston Symphony Orchestra (1957-63) and was the principal double bassist in the Cairo [Egypt] Symphony in 1963. During the 1970s he led a bass trio at Berkeley, called The Hoodoo Jazz Band. His publications included the books *Coronation of the King: Contributions by Duke Ellington to Black Culture* (Berkeley, 1969) and *Music: Black, White and Blue* (New York, 1972) and articles on black music; his compositions included "Night Letter to Duke" and a double-bass sonata.

BIBL: Page. *The Post* [Oakland], 16 December 1971, p. 23. WWBA.

WAR. Rhythm 'n' blues group (fl. 1960s-70s; org. in Long Beach, California). The vocal and instrumental group was organized during the 1960s and first called itself The Creators. The four original members, who sang together for local community social entertainments during their school years, were percussionist Harold Ray Brown (b. 17 March 1946 in Long Beach), guitarist Morris DeWayne ("B.B.") Dickerson (b. 3 August 1949 in Torrance, California), pianist Leroy ("Lonnie") Jordan (b. 21 November 1948 in San Diego, California), and guitarist Howard Scott (b. 15 March 1946 in San Pedro, California). During the mid-1960s Charles Miller (b. 2 June 1939 in Olathe, Kansas) joined the group, which now called itself The Night Shift. Later Thomas Sylvester Allen (also known as "Papa Dee"; b. c1933 in Wilmington, Delaware) and white harmonica player Oskar Lee (b. 24 March 1946 in Copenhagen, Denmark) joined the group, which made its debut in 1969 as a back-up group for white singer Eric Burdon in an act called Eric Burdon and War. The group attracted wide attention in its appearance at the Devonshire Downs rock festival near Newport, California, in 1969. Thereafter it toured widely in the United States and recorded regularly. In 1971 War began touring as an independent act. Its best-known performances were the albums *War*, *The World Is a Ghetto*, *Deliver the Word*, and *War Live*. The performers called their music "street music," a fusion of blues, calypso, Latin rhythms, and free jazz.

BIBL: Black press, incl. AmstN, 28 August 1976. *Ebony* (March 1975). StamPRS.

WARD, CLARA. Gospel singer (b. 21 April 1924 in Philadelphia, Pennsylvania; d. 16 January 1973 in Los Angeles, California). She came from a musical family: her mother, Gertrude Mae Murphy Ward, and her sister, Willa Ward Moultrie, were professional gospel musicians. Her family moved to Philadelphia, Pennsylvania, from South Carolina in the early 1920s. In 1931 Mother Ward began singing professionally, and within a short time she formed a family trio with her two daughters. Clara began piano study when she was eight years old and sang in a church choir from early childhood. She made her first notable professional appearance at the Ebenezer Baptist Church in Philadelphia with The Ward Trio, singing the solo on "When the saints go marching in." The Ward Trio toured widely on the church and revival-meeting circuit; in 1943 they attracted wide attention with their singing at the annual National Baptist Convention. In 1947 new members were added to the group, Marion Williams* and Henrietta Waddy, and the name was changed to The Famous Ward Singers. The Singers began to record and to tour more extensively; during the early 1950s they toured with Cecil Franklin, pastor of the New Bethel Baptist Church in Detroit, Michigan, and father of Aretha Franklin.* Their performance in 1957 at the Newport Jazz Festival won wide attention and led to more concert engagements, as did also their tour the same year with The Gospel Train, which included seven other celebrated gospel groups. In 1958, however, some members left the group, including the brightest star, Marion Williams, who later formed her own group, The Stars of Faith. New members came into the group over the years, including Martha Bass, Frances Steadman, Kitty Parham, Ethel Gilbert, Thelma Bumpess, and Vermettya Royster, among others.

In 1961 Clara made the decisive step of taking her gospel music into nightclubs and theaters, thus following in the lead of Bessie Griffin,* the first gospel singer to do so in 1959. The increased exposure brought more national attention; the Ward Singers performed in such places as Las Vegas and Disneyland in Anaheim, California. Mother Ward retired from singing in 1961, but in 1963 she returned to the field with a new group called The New Ward Singers. Willa formed her own Willa Ward Singers in 1962. In 1963 Clara Ward and her singers became the first gospel group to perform at Radio City Music Hall in New York; the same year she played a leading role in Langston Hughes's* gospel-song play, *Tambourines to Glory*. The singers also appeared in the film *It's Your Thing*. During the 1960s Gertrude and Clara settled in Los Angeles, California; using that city as a base, she continued to tour widely in Europe and in Japan with her Singers and to record regularly. A stroke in 1967 forced her into temporary retirement, but she returned to the nightclub circuit after a short period.

The Ward Singers were the most successful of the pop-gospel groups. The best-known performances of the early group was "Packin' up" and "Surely God is able'' (composed by W. Herbert Brewster* and the first gospel song to use triple rhythms [12/8 meter]). The group that included Marion Williams was well known for her solos on ''Take your burdens to the Lord'' and ''I know it was the Lord.'' Clara's best-known solo was ''How I got over.'' Among their other innovations, the Ward Singers emphasized showmanship and personal attire, discarding the traditional choir robes for elaborate dress and hairstyles. They were highly emulated by both gospel groups and individuals and as well by secular singers; Clara, in particular, exerted strong influence upon Aretha Franklin. The Wards laid the foundation for the development of gospel in the East. They were the first to introduce Thomas Dorsey* and Sallie Martin* to the East when they sponsored a Dorsey-Martin program in 1935 in Philadelphia; and they early established a publishing-distribution company, Ward's House of Music.

BIBL: Barbara Baker, ''Black Gospel Music Styles, 1942-1975'' (Ph.D. diss., University of Maryland, 1978). Boyer in BPIM 7 (Spring 1979). Clarence Boyer, ''The Gospel Song: An Historical and Analytical Study'' (M.A. thesis, Eastman School of Music, 1964). FeaEJ. FeaJS. FeaGitJS. GMEncy. Heil. *Sepia* (January 1960, October 1966, March 1968).

DISC: Hayes. TudBM.

WARFIELD, CHARLES (''CHARLIE''). Ragtime pianist/Composer (b. 1883 in Guthrie, Tennessee; d. 19??). His family moved to Nashville, Tennessee, when he was a child. He went to St. Louis at the age of fourteen. There he found employment as a pianist in the cafes and saloons of the tenderloin district and a place to exchange musical ideas with other rag pianists at Tom Turpin's* Rosebud Cafe. In 1900 he went to Chicago, Illinois, but returned to St. Louis during the World's Fair in 1904 to compete in ragtime competitions. He settled in Chicago thereafter, where he continued his activity as a cafe pianist. He wrote many songs, but in order to find publishers for his pieces he had to allow other names to appear as co-writers of his songs. His best-known song was ''Baby, won't you please come home?'' (1919).

BIBL: Black press, incl. CDef, 11 November 1939. Blesh.

WARFIELD, WILLIAM CAESAR. Concert singer (b. 22 January 1920 in West Helena, Arkansas). His family moved to Rochester, New York, when he was a child. He sang in his father's church choir and studied piano from an early age. After his voice changed to baritone during his high-school years, he began voice study. When a high-school senior he won first place in regional and national auditions of the National Music Educators League competition, which brought him a scholarship to an institution of his choice. He obtained his musical education at the Eastman School of Music in Rochester (B. Mus., 1942), and after service in the United States Armed Forces (1942-45), he returned to Eastman for a year of graduate study (1946). He began singing professionally in 1939; thereafter he gave concerts, sang with various groups, and appeared in musical shows, including the touring company of *Call Me Mister* (1947) and the Broadway productions of Heywood's *Set My People Free* (1948) and Blitzstein's *Regina* (1950). He studied privately with Otto Herz and Yves Tinayre; he made his debut as a concert baritone in March 1950 at the Town Hall in New York. Thereafter he toured widely in the United States and throughout the world—under the sponsorship of the U.S. Department of State more than a half-dozen times, in 1955 as soloist with the Philadelphia Orchestra under the direction of Eugene Ormandy. He also continued to sing in musicals, including the role of Joe in the film production of Kern's *Showboat* (1951) and in the title role of Gershwin's *Porgy and Bess* (1952). He repeated his roles in the opera's revivals in 1961 and 1964 and in the production at Vienna, Austria (1965-72). He also sang in stage productions of *Show Boat* in 1966 and 1971-72 for the Vienna Volksoper. He made numerous appearances on radio and television and recorded prolifically. He appeared with leading symphony orchestras and at the major music festivals, including the Athens [Greece] Festival (1966), the Pacem in Terris II Convocation (1967), and Pablo Casals Festivals (1962, 1963). His honors included an alumnus citation from Eastman (1954), an honorary doctorate from the University of Arkansas (1972), and New York City's George Frederic Handel Medallion. In 1974 he was appointed to the music faculty at the University of Illinois in Champaign; thereafter he combined teaching with concert touring. He was married to Leontyne Price* (divorced 1972).

BIBL: Black press, incl. CDef, 13 March 1976. CBDict. WWA. WWBA. WWCA 1950.

DISC: Turn.

WARREN, GUY. Jazz drummer (b. c1919 in Lagos [?], Ghana). He obtained his musical training at Achimota College in Ghana, where he came under the tutelage of Ephraim Amu.* He was the first African to host a disc-jockey program. He introduced the concept to the Liberian Broadcasting Service and to the Ghana Broadcasting Service. In 1947 he was an original member of The Tempos, directed by Emmanuel Tetteh Mensah.* This was the first band in Africa to use

Afro-Cuban drums. During the 1950s he toured in the United States and introduced the "bintin drum" into jazz ensembles. His best-known album was *Africa Speaks, America Answers*.

BIBL: *West African Review* 28 (June 1957).

WARWICK, DIONNE. Popular-music singer (b. 12 December 1940 in East Orange, New Jersey). She came from a musical family; her mother and maternal relatives were members of a gospel group, The Drinkards. She began piano study at the age of six and as a child sang in church choirs and with family gospel groups. She obtained her musical education in the public schools of East Orange and at the Hartt College of Music in Hartford, Connecticut. During her high school years she was a lead singer with the Gospelaires, which included her sister Dee Dee. After graduation from high school she and her sister went to New York, where they found employment singing background music in recording studios. This led to an audition for her with the songwriting team of Burt Bacharach/Hal David, whose song she recorded at the beginning of her career, "Don't make me over" (1962), and attracted wide attention. She recorded extensively and toured widely in the United States, in Europe, and the Orient, appearing in concert halls, theaters, nightclubs, on college campuses, and at the major jazz festivals. She also appeared on television and in films, including *Slaves* (1969). In 1969 she established the Dionne Warwick Scholarship Fund, which was administered through the National Scholarship and Service Fund for Negro Students. She received numerous awards from the music industry. Her best-known performances were "Move me no mountain," "Take it from me," and "Getting in my way."

BIBL: *Soul Sounds* (5 March 1972). StamPRS. WWA. WWBA.

DISC: Jep.

WASHINGTON, DINAH (née **RUTH JONES**). Gospel/Jazz singer (b. 29 August 1924 in Tuscaloosa, Alabama; d. 14 December 1963 in Detroit, Michigan). Her family moved to Chicago, Illinois, when she was a child. She sang in church choirs and became a choir director at an early age. She began singing popular music during her high-school years; at the age of fifteen she won a talent-show contest at the local Regal Theater and thereafter sang professionally in local nightclubs. The next year, however, she entered the field of gospel music to become an accompanist for Sallie Martin* and later to tour with Martin's gospel group. In 1943 she returned to popular music and had a successful audition with Lionel Hampton,* who changed her name to Dinah Washington. She toured with Hampton (1943-46), then began touring as a soloist on the theater and nightclub circuits. She soon established herself as the leading rhythm 'n' blues singer of her time. She first recorded in 1943 and thereafter recorded extensively. She was active in television and in films, including *Rock and Roll Revue* (1955) and *Jazz on a Summer's Day* (1960). Her singing style, which was characterized as "gutty," reflected the influence of gospel and blues and earned her the soubriquet "Queen of the Blues." Among her best-known performances were "I wanna be loved," "Time out for tears," "What a difference a day makes," and the duos with Brook Benton,* "Baby, you've got what it takes" and the album *The Two of Us*.

BIBL: FeaEJ. FeaJS. MeeJMov. ShawHS. StamPRS.

DISC: Jep. Kink.

WASHINGTON, GROVER. Jazz saxophonist (b. 12 December 1943 in Buffalo, New York). He came from a musical family: his father played tenor saxophone, his mother sang in church choirs, one brother became a church organist, and another played jazz drums professionally. He obtained his first saxophone at the age of ten and began study with Elvin Sheppard, then at the Wurlitzer School of Music in Buffalo. He played in his high-school band and in the Buffalo All-City High School Band. His style development was influenced by his listening to recordings and live performances of John Coltrane,* Benny Golson,* and Stanley Turrentine,* among others. At sixteen he began playing professionally with a group called The Four Clefs (1959-63). He next played with organist Keith McAllister (1963-65), then served in the United States Armed Forces (1965-67), where he played in a marching band at Fort Dix. Thereafter he played with Don Gardner's Sonotones (1967-68), Charles Earland (1971), Joe Jones, Leon Spencer, and Johnny ("Hammond") Smith, among others. He made his recording debut quite by accident: he was a last-minute substitute for Bennie Ross ("Hank") Crawford, and the recording, "Inner city blues," was so successful that it helped to establish him in the music world. He toured widely in the United States with his own groups and abroad, including in Japan.

BIBL: Black press, incl. *Black American*, 2 November 1973; *Eagle*, 14 February 1974. FeaGitJS.

WASHINGTON, RACHEL. Studio teacher (fl. late nineteenth century in Boston, Massachusetts). She is credited with being the first black graduate of the Boston Conservatory. She conducted a music studio in Boston, where she taught several students who later became professional musicians. She also served as organist at the Twelfth Baptist Church. In 1884 she published a manual titled *Musical Truth: The Rudiments of Music*.

BIBL: Black press, incl. NYGlobe, 8 March 1884. Trot, pp. 288-90.

WATERS (née **HOWARD**), **ETHEL.** Blues singer/ Actress (b. 31 October 1896 [1900?] in Chester, Pennsylvania; d. 1 September 1977 in Chats-worth, California). She came from a musical family; her father played piano and her mother and maternal relatives sang. She first sang publicly at the age of five, billed as Baby Star, in a local church program. At the age of seventeen she began singing professionally with a small vaudeville company (although her mother had to sign a paper stating her age as twenty-one). She wanted to sing a new song for her debut and wrote to W. C. Handy* for permission to sing his "St. Louis blues"; consequently she was the first woman (and only the second person) to sing the song professionally, billed as Sweet Mama Stringbean. About 1919 she settled in New York and soon established herself as one of the leading entertainers in the Harlem community. She first recorded in 1921 for Harry Pace's* Black Swan label and attracted wide attention for her "Down home blues" and "Oh, Daddy." Thereafter she recorded prolifically and toured with her Black Swan Jazz Masters, led by Fletcher Henderson.* Later she recorded with Edward ("Duke") Ellington,* Benny Goodman, Russell Wooding, and Eddie Mallory, among others. Beginning in 1927 she appeared in Broadway musicals, including *Africana* (1927), Lew Leslie's *Blackbirds of 1930, Rhapsody in Black* (1931), *As Thousands Cheer* (1933), and *Cabin in the Sky* (1940). She also continued to tour on the vaudeville circuit and to sing in nightclubs. During the years 1935-39 she had her own show. In 1939 she attracted wide attention for her dramatic role in *Mamba's Daughters* and thereafter was active primarily as an actress until the late 1950s. She appeared in nine films during the years 1929-59, beginning with *On With the Show*. During the years 1957-76 she toured with evangelist Billy Graham's various Crusades in the United States and abroad and became celebrated for her singing of "His eye is on the sparrow." She was best remembered, however, for her performance of popular songs and blues, particularly "Stormy weather," "Dinah," "Am I blue," and "Heat wave."

BIBL: AlHen. BWW. ChilWW. FeaEJ. FeaJS. FeaGitJS. MeeJMov. NYT, 2 September 1977. WWA. WWBA, 1975-76. WWCA 1950. Ethel Waters, *His Eye Is On the Sparrow* (New York, 1951), and *To Me It's Wonderful* (New York, 1972).

DISC: DiGod. Kink. RustJR. TudBM.

WATERS, MUDDY. See **MORGANFIELD, McKINLEY.**

WATKINS, JULIUS BURTON. Jazz French hornist (b. 10 October 1921 in Detroit, Michigan; d. 4 April 1977 in Montclair, New Jersey). He began study of the French horn at the age of nine. He attended the Manhattan School of Music in New York and studied privately with Francis Hellstein of the Detroit Symphony Orchestra and Robert Schulze of the New York Philharmonic. He began playing professionally in the early 1940s and worked with various groups, including Ernie Fields (1943-46), Milton ("Milt") Buckner* (1949), Oscar Pettiford,* Les Modes (as co-leader with Charlie Rouse, 1956-59), Johnny Richards, George Shearing (1959), and Quincy Jones* (1960, including European tour). He recorded with several of these groups and also with Kenny Clarke* and "Babs" Gonzalez.* During the 1960s-70s he was active with symphony orchestras in New York, among them, the New York Municipal Orchestra summer concerts, the Harlem Philharmonic under the direction of Karl Hampton Porter,* and the Symphony of the New World.* He also played in Broadway theater orchestras, including those for *Raisin* (1973) and the all-black, 1976 production of *Guys and Dolls*. He won awards from the music industry for his jazz French horn. He was married to Harriette Davison.*

BIBL: Communication from Marion Cumbo. FeaEJ.

DISC: Jep. Kink.

WATTS, ANDRE. Concert pianist (b. 20 June 1946 in Nuremburg, Germany). He began violin study at the age of four on a miniature violin and studied piano at six with his mother, a pianist. When he was eight his family moved to Philadelphia, Pennsylvania. He obtained his education in private schools and at the Philadelphia Academy of Music; later he studied at the Peabody Institute in Baltimore, Maryland. When he was nine years old he won first prize in a competition and appeared with the Philadelphia Symphony on a Children's Concert playing a Haydn concerto. The next year he performed a Mendelssohn concerto with the Orchestra at a summer concert in the Robin Hood Dell, and when he was fourteen he played Franck's *Symphonic Variations* with the Orchestra. At sixteen he played the Liszt E-flat Concerto with the New York Philharmonic Orchestra on a Young People's Concert that was nationally televised by CBS. A few weeks later the Philharmonic's director, Leonard Bernstein, called upon him to perform the concerto at a regular concert (31 January 1963) when the scheduled performer, Glenn Gould, became ill. From that time on, his career spurted forward. In 1966 he made his European debut with the London [England] Symphony Orchestra. In 1967 he made a world tour with the Los Angeles Philharmonic under sponsorship of the U. S. Department of State, and later toured again for the State Department in the Soviet Union (1973). Within a period of ten years he became one of the world's leading pianists. He toured widely throughout the world and recorded extensively. His awards included honorary doctorates from Yale University (1973) and Albright College (1975), an award from the recording industry, the Order of the Zaire from the Congo, Africa, and awards from various professional organizations.

BIBL: Abdul. CurBiog (May 1968). *Encore American & Worldwide News* (9 May 1977). *High Fidelity/Musical America* (February 1973). NYT, 23 October 1977. WWA. WWBA.

WATTS, NELLIE. Impresario/Public school teacher (b. 1889 in Atlanta, Georgia; d. 25 December 1969 in Detroit, Michigan). She obtained her musical education in the public schools of Atlanta, Georgia; Atlanta University, from which she was graduated; and Columbia University Teachers College in New York. She sang in the Azalia Hackley* Chorus during her college years in Atlanta. During the 1920s she settled in Detroit, Michigan, and taught in the public schools there for thirty-nine years. During the 1930s she conceived of a way to contribute to the musical culture of her people and "almost singlehandedly started a new era in the cultural life of her community" (quoted from press clippings). In 1937 she promoted her first concert for a young singer, Marian Anderson,* and thereafter established her Nellie Watts Concert Series, which over the next three decades brought to Detroit more than forty artists as well as dance companies, choirs, and instrumental groups. Those who appeared on her series included Carol Brice,* Todd Duncan,* the DePaur Infantry Chorus,* the Leon Destine Dance Company, Hazel Harrison,* Natalie Hinderas,* Paul Robeson,* and Margaret Tynes,* among others. After the 1943 "race riots" in Detroit, she organized a community-based Patron of the Arts to support her concerts. On 18 March 1967 Detroit honored her with a Nellie Watts Day.

BIBL: Communication and press clippings from Jean Currie, curator, DetAH.

WEATHERFORD, TEDDY. Jazz pianist (b. 11 October 1903 in Bluefield, West Virginia; d. 25 April 1945 in Calcutta, India). He began his professional career in Chicago, Illinois, where he played with Jimmie Wade and Erskine Tate,* among others. He established a reputation as one of the leading pianists on Chicago's South Side. In 1926 he went to the Far East on tour with Jack Carter and remained there for the remainder of his career, except for a short tour in Europe in 1937. His recordings date from 1937 (made in Paris, France) and 1942 (made in Calcutta, India). He led his own groups in such places as Shangai, China; Singapore; Manilla, The Philippines; Celon, Bombay, and Calcutta, India.

BIBL: ChilWW. DanceWEH.

DISC: Jep. RustJR.

WEATHERS, FELICIA (neé **FRANCESS THERESA).** Opera singer (b. 13 August 1937 in St. Louis, Missouri). She first revealed musical talent at the age of four, but when she matriculated at St. Louis University (1953-54), she took courses in preparation for a career in medicine. Later she transferred to Lincoln University in Jefferson City, Missouri (1954-57), where she studied music and developed her vocal skills, encouraged by Oscar Anderson Fuller,* then chairman of the music department. She became seriously interested in opera after winning second place in a Metropolitan Opera audition (1957); thereafter she attended Indiana University at Bloomington (B. Mus., 1961), where she studied with Dorothee Manski and Charles Kullman. In 1961 she went to Europe, where she won first prize in a singing contest in Sophia, Bulgaria. The same year she made her European operatic debut as a dramatic soprano at the Zurich Municipal Opera in Switzerland. Thereafter she sang in the leading opera houses of Europe, including the state operas at Vienna, Austria, and Hamburg and Munich, Germany; Covent Garden in London, England; the Grand Opera in Paris, France; and Teatro Colon in Buenos Aires, Brazil, among others. She also toured widely as a concert singer. In 1965 she made her debut at the Metropolitan Opera singing the role of Lisa in Tchaikovsky's *Pique Dame*. Her best-known performances were the title roles in Verdi's *Aida*, Puccini's *Madame Butterfly*, Strauss's *Salome*, and Janáček's *Jenufa*. She settled in Germany at the beginning of her operatic career. Her awards included honorary doctorates from St. Louis University (1971) and Indiana University (1972) and awards from civic and professional organizations.

BIBL: *Ebony* (May 1970). Ewen. WWA. WWAW. WWOpera

DISC: Turn.

WEBB, CHICK. See **WEBB, WILLIAM.**

WEBB, WILLIAM ("CHICK"). Jazz drummer (b. 10 February 1909 in Baltimore, Maryland; d. 16 June 1939 in Baltimore). He played drums as a child and joined a local boys' band when he was eleven years old. Later he played with riverboat bands. In 1925 he settled in New York, New York, where he played with Edgar Dowell. The next year he organized his own group, which over the years included Benny Carter,* Garvin Bushell, Johnny Hodges,* John Kirby,* Hilton Jefferson, Edgar Sampson,* and John Trueheart, among others. During the 1920s-30s he played in nightclubs, theaters, and ballrooms, winning recognition as one of the leading bands of New York; he also toured regularly and broadcast on a national radio network. In 1930 he toured with the *Hot Chocolates Revue*. From 1931 on, his closest association was with the Savoy Ballroom in the Harlem community, where in 1935 he introduced his protégée, Ella Fitzgerald,* to the public. After his death in 1939, Fitzgerald led and recorded with his orchestra until 1942. According to the *Chicago Defender*, Webb was the first jazz musician to receive an honorary doctorate—from Yale University in New Haven, Connecticut, in 1937. His best-known recordings were "Stompin' at the Savoy," "Don't be that way," "A-tisket, a-tasket" (which featured Fitzgerald), "Holiday in Harlem," and "I found my yellow basket"; he was co-composer of these songs and others.

BIBL: AlHen. Black press, incl. CDef, 26 March 1938. ChilWW. FeaEJ. MeeJMov.

DISC: Kink. RustJR. TudJ.

WEBSTER, BENJAMIN FRANCIS ("BEN"). Jazz saxophonist (b. 27 March 1909 in Kansas City, Missouri; d. 20 September 1973 in Amsterdam, the Netherlands). He studied violin and piano as a child and attended Wilberforce [Ohio] College. Early in his professional career he led a band in Kansas City, Missouri, called Rooster Ben and His Little Red Hens and later played piano for silent movies at Amarillo, Texas (1928). Thereafter he performed with various groups, including Clarence Love, Billie Young, and Dutch Campbell, before he changed to saxophone, inspired and helped by Budd Johnson.* He then played alto or tenor saxophone with such groups as Jasper ("Jap") Allen (1930), Blanche Calloway* (1931), Bennie Moten* (1931-33), Andy Kirk* (1933), Fletcher Henderson* (1934, 1937), Benny Carter* (1934), Willie Bryant (1934), Cabell ("Cab") Calloway* (1936-37), and Theodore ("Teddy") Wilson* (1939-40), among others. During the next ten years he played primarily with Edward ("Duke") Ellington* (1939-43, 1948-49) and others for short periods. He organized his own group late in 1944 and thereafter played in nightclubs in New York, Chicago, and Kansas City. During this period he also worked with Jay McShann,* Bob Wilson, and toured with JATP (Jazz at the Philharmonic). During the 1950s-early 1960s he was active in New York and in Los Angeles, California. In 1965 he settled in Europe, living in Amsterdam, The Netherlands, and later in Copenhagen, Denmark; he played residencies in other European cities, however, during these years. He recorded extensively with others and with his own groups. He also appeared in films, including *The Sound of Jazz* (1957), *Quiet Days in Clichy* (1969), and *Big Ben* (1967, a documentary about him made in Europe). As Ellington's first tenor specialist he established himself as one of the master tenor saxophonists of his time, along with Leon ("Chu") Berry.* Both of them were influenced by Coleman Hawkins.* Webster was celebrated for his warm, emotional performance of ballads, such as "Cottontail," "What am I here for," "All too soon," and "Just a sittin' and rockin'." He exerted wide influence upon his contemporaries.

BIBL: AlHen. ASCAP. ChilWW. DanceWEH. FeaEJ. FeaJS. FeaGitJS. MeeJMov. Russ. WWA. WWBA 1975-76.

DISC: Jep. Kink. RustJR. TudJ.

WEIR, FELIX FOWLER. Concert violinist (b. 8 October 1884 in Chicago, Illinois; d. 9 May 1978 in Fairlawn, New Jersey). He studied violin as a child, encouraged by an uncle who was an amateur musician. He first played on a public concert at the age of eleven. He obtained his musical education at Chicago Musical College; after graduation he went abroad to study at the Conservatory in Leipzig, Germany, but had to return because of death in the family. He was an assisting artist on the concerts of Samuel Coleridge-Taylor's music when that composer visited the United States in 1906. In 1907 he became a teacher in the public schools of Washington, D.C., where his brothers had settled earlier. About 1914 he moved to New York in order to advance his career; there he joined the New Amsterdam Musical Association and performed with Clef-Club groups. He was active also as a concert violinist, playing on concerts in New York, Boston, Massachusetts, Washington, D.C., and other cities on the Eastern Seaboard. About 1915 he formed a duo with cellist Leonard Jeter,which later was expanded to a trio with the addition of pianist Olyve Jeter. He then formed the American String Quartet—composed of Joseph Lymos, Hall Johnson,* Jeter, and himself—which performed regularly on concerts in the East. By the early 1920s his group, renamed the Negro String Quartet, consisted of Arthur Boyd, Marion Cumbo,* Johnson, and himself. These ensembles may have been the first black quartets to tour on the concert circuit. During these years Weir also conducted a music studio. The Weir-Jeter Duo was touring with James Reese Europe* in the spring of 1919 when Europe was murdered by a crazed bandmember on 9 May at Mechanic's Hall in Boston. It was Weir who took over the baton after the fourteenth number and conducted Europe's band through the remainder of the program. Weir was active in theatrical work during the 1920s, playing in and conducting pit orchestras for such Broadway musicals as the Noble Sissle*/Eubie Blake* *Shuffle Along* (1921), James P. Johnson's *Running Wild* (1923), Nicols and Holiner's *Rhapsody in Black* (1931), and Lew Leslie's *Blackbirds of 1928*, for which he conducted the Paris [France] production. During the 1930s he returned to teaching in the public schools of Washington, D.C., and remained there until his retirement.

BIBL: Communication from grandaughter Carolyn Weir. Black press, incl. CDef, 17 May 1919; IndF, 28 November 1896; 28 October 1916; NYAge, 13 September 1906, 4 March 1915.

WELLS, AMOS ("JUNIOR"). Bluesman (b. 9 December 1934 in Memphis, Tennessee). His family moved to Chicago when he was a child. He obtained his first harmonica at the age of twelve; by the time he was fourteen he was playing with ''Tampa Red'' (Hudson Whittaker)* and other established bluesmen. His style development was influenced by (''Little'') Walter Jacobs,* but he later developed his own distinctive amplified-harmonica style, which reflected the carry-over of guitar stylistic elements to his instrument. He first recorded in 1953; by the 1960s he had became one of the major Chicago blues figures. He recorded extensively, most frequently with George (''Buddy'') Guy,* and toured widely.

BIBL: BWW. MeeJMov. Robert Neff and Anthony Connor, *Blues* (Boston, 1975). Oliv. ShawWS.

DISC: Jep. LeSlBM. TudBM.

WELLS, DICKIE. See **WELLS, WILLIAM.**

WELLS, WILLIAM ("DICKIE"). Jazz trombonist (b. 10 June 1909 in Centerville, Tennessee). His family moved to Nashville, Tennessee, when he was a child and settled in Louisville, Kentucky, when he was ten years old. There he first became involved with music, playing baritone, then trombone with the Sunday School band of the Booker T. Washington Community Center and in a small jazz group. Among other performers with the Sunday School band were Jonah Jones,* Buddy Lee, Helen Humes,* and his brother Charlie. His first professional experience was with Lucius Brown, a local group; thereafter he played with various groups, including Ferman Tapp, Lloyd and Cecil Scott, Billy Fowler, Benny Carter* (1932, 1934), Charlie Johnson (1932-33), Fletcher Henderson* (1933), and Theodore (''Teddy'') Hill* (1935-37), among others. During the next decade and more, he played primarily with William (''Count'') Basie* (1938-46, 1947-50), but also for short periods with Lucius (''Lucky'') Millinder* (1946), Melvin (''Sy'') Oliver* (1946-47), Jimmy Rushing* (1952), Earl Hines* (1954), and Ray Charles* (1961-62), among others. Thereafter he was a free-lancer and played with various groups. He toured in Europe several times—with Teddy Hill (1937), Bill Coleman (1953), Wilbur (''Buck'') Clayton* (1959, 1961), George (''Buddy'') Tate (1968), Claude Hopkins* (1978), and as a soloist (1965). He left professional music during the 1970s but returned by the end of the decade. He recorded extensively and appeared in films. He also wrote a number of songs and jazz instrumental pieces. He was one of the leading trombonists of the 1930s-40s and was noted for his romantic style with its distinctive vibrato. He received many awards from the music industry at home and in France.

BIBL: ASCAP. ChilWW. FeaEJ. FeaJS. FeaGitJS. MeeJMov. *The Night People* (Boston, 1971) is Well's autobiography ''As Told to Stanley Dance.''

DISC: Jep. Kink. RustJR. TudJ.

WESTON, BOBBY. See **WESTON, HORACE.**

WESTON, HORACE. Minstrel banjoist (b. c1825 in Derby, Connecticut; d. 23 May 1890 in New York, New York). He came from a musical family; his father, Jube, was a music and dancing-school master, and his brother Bobby became a professional minstrel. He began performing professionally at an early age and had won wide recognition for his banjo skills by the time he was twenty-five years old. In 1863 he joined Buckley's Serenaders minstrel troupe of Boston, Massachusetts. After serving with the Union Army during the Civil War, he joined Charles Hicks's* Georgia Minstrels* in 1867. In 1873 he toured with an Uncle Tom's Cabin Troupe in the United States and abroad. By 1879 he was again a member of the Georgia Minstrels (now managed by Callender), and he remained with the troupe intermittently through the 1880s—when it became Haverly's Genuine Colored Minstrels—including a tour in Europe in 1881-82. During his career, Weston also toured with Barnum and Bailey's Greatest Show on Earth. He was highly regarded by his contemporaries for his banjo skills and banjo pieces; as late as 1969 one of his pieces, ''Minor jig,'' was performed at a concert at New York.

His brother Bobby (d. 19 January 1884) won recognition as a skilled tambourine player; he and Horace toured together extensively. Bobby also toured with the

Bohee* Minstrels and with Jarret and Palmer's U. T. Concert Company.

BIBL: Black press, incl. IndF, 20 April 1889; NYAge, 21 May 1890; NYGlobe, 26 January 1884. Edward Rice, *Monarchs of Minstrelsy* (New York, 1911). Simond. Hannah Winter, "Juba and American Minstrelsy" in *Chronicles of the American Dance*, ed. by Paul Magriel (New York, 1948).

WESTON, RANDOLPH ("RANDY"). Jazz pianist (b. 6 April 1926 in New York, New York). He studied piano as a child. He began to play jazz and rhythm 'n' blues when he was about fourteen; his style development was influenced by recordings or live music of Edward ("Duke") Ellington,* Thelonious Monk,* and Thomas ("Fats") Waller.* He began playing professionally during the late 1940s and played with various groups, including Arthur ("Art") Blakey,* Kenneth ("Kenny") Dorham,* George Hall, "Bull-Moose" Jackson, Cecil Payne,* and Eddie ("Clean-head") Vinson,* among others. From 1955 on he led his own groups, and about 1957 he began touring the college campus circuit with his group and a jazz-dance troupe, working in conjunction with jazz historian Marshall Stearns, who lectured for Weston's demonstrations on the history of jazz. In 1966 he toured Africa with his lecture-concerts under the auspices of the U. S. Department of State. In 1967 he moved to Africa, living in Morocco and Tunisia and finally settling in Tangier, Morocco. In 1969 he opened an African Rhythms Club in Tangier and, using that city as a base, toured extensively in Europe and Africa. He returned to the United States several times to give concerts and play at jazz festivals. He planned to develop a cultural center that would set up an exchange between African countries and Western countries with large Afro-American populations. He first recorded in 1955; the same year his compositions began to reflect the influence of African idioms. His best-known albums were *Tanjah*, *Blues Moses*, *Blues to Africa*, and *African Cookbook*.

BIBL: ASCAP. *Essence* (November 1973). FeaEJ. FeaJS. FeaGitJS. NYT, 7 January 1973.

DISC: Jep. Kink. TudJ.

WHALUM, WENDELL P. College music educator (b. 4 September 1931 in Memphis, Tennessee). He obtained his musical education at Morehouse College in Atlanta, Georgia (B.A., 1952), Columbia University Teachers College (1953, M.A.), and the University of Iowa (Ph.D., 1965). His teaching career included tenures at Morehouse College (1953-) and Atlanta University (summers 1967-77). He was also active as a minister of music in Atlanta churches and as a lecturer and guest choral conductor. He published arrangements of spirituals for mixed voices, men's choir, and solo voice; he also published articles in professional journals and anthologies. His honors included an honorary doctorate from the University of Haiti (1968), awards from civic and professional organizations, and appointment to committees and boards of national music organizations. He played an important role in promoting the premiere of Scott Joplin's* opera, *Treemonisha*, in January 1962 in Atlanta.

BIBL: Questionnaire. WWBA.

WHATLEY, JOHN T. ("FESS"). Music educator (b. c1896 in Tuscaloosa, Alabama; d. 1971 in Birmingham, Alabama). As a child he was inspired to learn cornet when he heard the band of the Ringling Brothers Circus when it came to his town. He obtained his education at the Tuggle Institute in Birmingham, Alabama, where he played in the school band. In 1917 he began to teach at the Industrial High School in Birmingham, serving also as the bandmaster, and remained there until his retirement (the school's name was later changed to Parker High School). He organized the first brass band for black students in the city; over the years his band won wide recognition for its excellence. During the 1920s the band played for President Warren G. Harding. He also led a group called Fess Whatley's Saxo-Society Orchestra. He exerted wide influence as a teacher; many of his students later became celebrated, among them, Erskine Hawkins,* Theodore ("Teddy") Hill,* Wilbur ("Dud") Bascomb,* and Samuel ("Sammy") Lowe, among many others.

BIBL: *The Birmingham Post-Herald Kudzu*, 17 August 1979.

WHISONANT, LAWRENCE. See **WINTERS, LAWRENCE.**

WHITE, ANDREW NATHANIEL. Jazz saxophonist (b. 6 September 1942 in Washington, D.C.). He began study of the saxophone at the age of twelve with John C. Reed in Nashville, Tennessee. He obtained his musical training at Tennessee A & I (Agricultural and Industrial) University in Nashville (1958-60), where he studied with Brenton Banks and played in the symphonic band, and at Howard University in Washington, D.C. (B. Mus., 1964), where he played in the university band and in Symphonetta. In 1960 he began playing professionally and thereafter worked with various groups, including Kenneth ("Kenny") Clarke* (1964-65 in Paris, France), Stanley Turrentine,* and Stevie Wonder* (1968-70), among others. Also during the

1960s he directed the John F. Kennedy Quintet (1961-64) and played in the Howard Theater house orchestra (1966-67), both in Washington, D.C. During the years 1968-70 he played oboe and French horn with the American Ballet Theater orchestra in New York. In 1970 he became bassist for Fifth Dimension. His honors included John Hay Whitney, Rockefeller, and Tanglewood fellowships.

BIBL: FeaGitJS. WWBA. WWE.

WHITE, BARRY. Entertainer/Songwriter (b. 12 September 1944 in Galveston, Texas). His family moved to Los Angeles, California, when he was a child. Although his mother was a music teacher, he taught himself to play piano, beginning at the age of six. He sang in church choirs when he was eight and was playing for community social entertainments by the time he was ten. During his high-school years he sang with a local "soul" quintet. His first professional experience came when he was seventeen; he was paid to perform background music for a Class Records recording by Leon René* (which was never released). His career developed slowly; he sang in small clubs (writing his own songs), was a road manager for singer Jackie Lee for two years, and then was a producer/writer-arranger for Bronco Records. During the late 1960s he moved wholly into the field of entertainment. His first recorded album, *I've Got So Much to Give*, included the highly successful song, "I'm gonna love you." In 1969 he added to his performances a gospel trio, Love Unlimited, composed of Diane Taylor, Glodean James, and Linda James. Their first recording, "Walkin' in the rain with the one I love," established White as a leading entertainer/songwriter in his field. Other well-known albums were *Rhapsody in White*, *Under the Influence of Love*, and *Can't Get Enough of Your Love, Babe*. He received many awards from the music industry.

BIBL: BMI (Summer 1975). *Black Stars* (February 1974).

WHITE, BOOKER WASHINGTON ("BUKKA"). Bluesman (b. 12 November 1909 in Houston, Mississippi; d. 26 February 1977 in Memphis, Tennessee). Self-taught, he received his first guitar at the age of nine from his father. His style development was influencd by Charley Patton,* to whose recordings he listened. He first recorded in 1930 with Napoleon Hairston; during the years 1934-37 he teamed with George ("Bullet") Williams to perform in Mississippi clubs and roadhouses. A murder conviction (self-defense) sent him to the penitentiary (1937-39), where in 1939 he made recordings of prison blues for the Library of Congress field expedition of folklorists John Work and Alan Lomax. After being freed from prison, he returned to blues and continued to record. The revival of public interest in the blues during the 1960s gave his career a spurt forward. Some of his old records were reissued and he made new ones. He toured widely in the United States and in Europe, appearing at the major blues and jazz festivals as well as in concert halls and clubs. His music was representative of the intense, earthy Delta blues tradition and distinctive for its cutting percussive steel guitar.

BIBL: BWW. LivBl 32 (May-June 1977), MeeJMov. NYT, 27 February 1977. Oliv.

DISC: DiGod. Jep. LeSlBR, TudBM.

WHITE, BUKKA. See **WHITE, BOOKER.**

WHITE, CHRISTOPHER ("CHRIS"). Jazz bassist (b. 6 July 1936 in New York, New York). He obtained his musical training in the public schools of the city of New York and through private study with local teachers in the Borough of Brooklyn, New York. His early professional experience was with Cecil Taylor* intermittently through the years 1955-59. Thereafter he played with various groups, including Bernard Peiffer, Nina Simone,* John Birks ("Dizzy") Gillespie* (1962-66), and William ("Billy") Taylor,* among others. Beginning in the late 1960s he was increasingly active with community groups, such as Jazzmobile of the Harlem community, MUSE Jazz Workshop of Brooklyn, and his own music school, Rhythm Associates (founded 1966). His teaching career included lectureships and guest lecturer appointments at Rutgers University in Newark, New Jersey; Wagner College in New York; the University of the West Indies in Kingston, Jamaica; and Antioch College in Yellow Springs, Ohio. During the 1970s he served as the Director of Jazz Studies at Rutgers. He recorded regularly and composed instrumental works and a film score, *Aggro Siezeman* (1975), in addition to songs.

BIBL: FeaJS. FeaGitJS.

WHITE, CLARENCE CAMERON. Composer (b. 10 August 1880 in Clarksville, Tennessee; d. 30 June 1960 in New York, New York). He studied music as a child in Oberlin, Ohio, where he lived with his grandparents. Later he lived with his family in Chattanooga, Tennessee, and in Washington, D.C., where he studied violin with Joseph Douglas* and Will Marion Cook.* He attended Howard University in Washington (1894-95), where he played in the university's Mandolin and Guitar Club and, during the same period, played in Douglas's community symphony orchestra. He studied further at the Oberlin Conservatory of Music in Ohio (1896-1901) and in London, England (summers of 1906, 1908-10), studying composition with Samuel Coleridge-Taylor* and violin with M. Zacharewitsch. His study abroad was made possible by his receiving an E. Azalia Hackley* scholarship. In later years he studied in Paris, France, with Raoul Laparra (1930-32) and at the Juilliard School of Music (summer 1940).

At the age of fifteen he performed one of his own compositions on a local recital in Washington, D.C.; two years later he performed his music at a concert in Chicago, Illinois. He toured widely during the first two decades of the twentieth century, often accompanied at the piano by his wife, Beatrice Warrick White; he was regarded as one of the leading black violinists of the time, along with Joseph Douglas. About 1901 he settled in Washington, where he taught in the public schools (1902-05) and helped his friend, Harriet Gibbs Marshall,* to develop the program of her Washington Conservatory of Music, which opened in 1903. For four years (1903-07) he headed the strings department at the Conservatory. After returning from Europe in 1910 he settled in Boston, Massachusetts, where he conducted a music studio and used the city as a base for periodic concert tours during the years 1912-23. Thereafter he entered a college-teaching career, serving tenures as director of music at West Virginia State College at Institute (1924-30) and at Hampton Institute in Virginia (1932-35). During the 1920s he taught for several summers at Pauline James Lee's* Chicago University of Music. When Hampton discontinued its music school in 1935, he resigned and settled again in Boston, where he conducted a studio, and resumed again his concert touring on a more regular basis than was possible during the years he taught in colleges. During the years 1937-42 he organized community music programs for the National Recreational Association. He settled in New York during the 1950s. Throughout his career he contributed articles to professional journals, including J. Hillary Taylor's *The Negro Music Journal* (1902-03), Nora Holt's* *Music and Poetry* (1919-21), *The Musical Observer*, and *The Etude*, among others.

Samuel Coleridge-Taylor seems to have been the first person to inspire White to become a composer. White corresponded with the Afro-English composer while at Oberlin and played some of Taylor's music on concerts. When Taylor visited the United States in 1904, White performed the composer's *African Dances* on concerts with the composer himself at the piano. Then when White went to London, he not only studied with Taylor but also played in Taylor's String Player's Club. White began to publish little pieces as early as 1912, at first conventional pieces in the salon style of the period, then later compositions that employed Negro folk idioms. During the summer of 1928 he visited Haiti, along with John Matheus, a professor of romance languages at West Virginia State, to study the folklore of the black republic. Later Matheus wrote the play *Tambour*, for which White wrote incidental music, and in 1931 White completed an opera, *Ouanga*, using Matheus's libretto. The opera, depicting the life of Haiti's liberator and first emperor Dessalines, received several performances, including the premiere at South Bend, Indiana, in 1949 by the Burleigh Musical Association and one in Philadelphia, Pennsylvania, in 1950 by the Dra-Mu Negro Opera* Company. In addition, the opera was presented in concert versions, including two performances in 1956 at Carnegie Hall and the Metropolitan Opera House in New York by the National Negro Opera.*

White composed in a variety of forms for violin, piano, solo voice, chorus, orchestra, band, symphony orchestra, organ, and chamber ensemble. In addition to his opera, his best-known works were the violin compositions *Bandanna Sketches* (1919), *Cabin Memories* (1921), and *From the Cotton Fields* (1921); the ballet *A Night in Sans Souci*; the spiritual arrangements *Forty Negro Spirituals* (1927) and *Traditional Negro Spirituals* (1940); the chamber music *Prelude, Dawn, Jubilee, Hallelujah* (1931, string quartet), *Quatuor en do mineur* (1931), *Spiritual Suite* (1956, for four clarinets), *Fantasie* (1954, violoncello), and *Legende d'Afrique* (1955, commissioned and premiered by cellist Kermit Moore*); and the orchestral works *Piece for Strings and Timpani*, *Kutamba Rhapsody* (1942), Symphony in D minor, Violin Concerto in G minor (1945), Concertino in D minor (1952), *Dance Rhapsody* (1955), and *Poem* (1955). White's honors included Rosenwald fellowships (1930-32), a Harmon Foundation Award (1927), the David Bispham Medal for his opera (1932), the Benjamin Award for his orchestral *Elegy* (1954), and honorary degrees from Atlanta University (M.A., 1928) and Wilberforce University in Ohio (D. Mus., 1933). He was a prime mover in the founding of the National Association of Negro Musicians; as early as 1916 he sent out letters suggesting the founding of such an organization and, along with R. Nathaniel Dett* and Nora Holt, laid the foundations for the organizational meeting and first national convention in Chicago in 1919. Later he served as president of NANM (1922-24) and as a member of the board of directors. White was regarded as one of the leading black composers of his time, along with Harry T. Burleigh* and R. Nathaniel Dett.

BIBL: Correspondence from John Matheus. ASCAP. Black press, incl. CDef, 24 April 1920; IndF, 15 May 1897, 16 October 1915; NYAge, 26 September 1926,

15 January 1936. BPIM 9 (Spring 1981). Hare. HNB. NHBul (October-December 1980). WWCA 1927-50. WWWA, v.4.

DISC: Cre.

WHITE, DONALD EDWARD. Symphony cellist (b. 9 July 1925 in Richmond, Indiana). He began study of the cello at the age of sixteen. He obtained his musical education at Roosevelt University in Chicago, Illinois (B.A., 1953), where he studied with Dudley Powers, and at the Hartt School of Music in Hartford, Connecticut (M.A., 1957). His first professional experience was as assistant principal cellist with the Hartford Symphony Orchestra. In 1957 he became a cellist with the Cleveland Symphony, at that time under the direction of George Szell. His teaching career included a tenure at the Cleveland Music School Settlement and private teaching.

BIBL: Black press, incl. NYAge, 21 March 1959. WWBA.

WHITE, FREDERICK PERRY. Concert pianist/Accompanist. See **LEW, WILLIAM.**

WHITE, JOSÉ SILVESTRE DE LOS DOLORES. Concert violinist/Composer (b. 17 January 1836 in Matanzas, Cuba; d. 15 March 1918 in Paris, France). He began music study at the age of ten with his father, Carlos White. Later he studied with José María Roman and Pedro Lecerf. He made his debut in Matanzas in March 1852 as an assisting artist on a program featuring American pianist Louis Gottschalk, who encouraged the young violinist to study further at the Conservatory of Music in Paris, France. White matriculated at the Conservatory in 1855, studying there with Joseph Alard, Henri Reber, and Ferdinand Taite, among others. In 1856 he won the Prix de Rome in Violin. Beginning about 1858 he toured widely in Europe, the Caribbean, South America, and Mexico, giving solo recitals and appearing with musical organizations. He settled in Paris in 1861, where he conducted a music studio in addition to performing. He taught at the Conservatory during the year 1864-65 when his teacher Alard had to take a leave. He made his first tour of the United States during the period 1875-76, and included an appearance with the New York Philharmonic in a performance of Mendelssohn's Violin Concerto. During the years c1881-1891 he was attached to the Imperial Court in Rio de Janeiro, Brazil, as a music teacher. He resettled in Paris in 1891, where he spent the remainder of his life. He was one of the important American violinists of his time and the leading concert artist of Cuban extraction. He left compositions for violin.

BIBL: European press, including *Le Ménestrel*, 1861-1876. Hare. LaBrew. Trot.

WHITE, JOSHUA DANIEL ("JOSH"). Bluesman (b. 11 February 1908 in Greenville, South Carolina; d. 5 September 1969 in Manhasset, Long Island, New York). As a child he sang in the choir of his father's church. He began traveling with blind blues singers when he was seven, leading them along the streets and touring with them from town to town. Over a period of about ten years he led several bluesmen, including "Blind Blake" (Arthur Phelps), "Blind" Lemon Jefferson,* and Joel Taggart, among others, and from them learned to play the guitar. Thereafter he began a professional career, making his first recordings in 1932 in New York. Later he sang with the Southernaires and as a soloist, calling himself "The Singing Christian" when singing gospel and "Pinewood Tom" when singing the blues. He became widely known, recorded extensively, and appeared in Broadway plays, among them *John Henry* (1939), which also featured Paul Robeson.* In 1943 he opened at New York's prestigious nightclub, Cafe Society Downtown, and thereafter popularized the singing of blues and spirituals in clubs. In 1944 he ran his own radio and TV programs. From the 1950s on he toured widely throughout the world, appearing in concert halls and clubs and at folk festivals. His style reflected the influence of Taggart and Jefferson; he favored plaintive songs but had a large repertory, which he delivered with a sophistication not characteristic of the other Piedmont singers. His best-known recordings were "One meatball" and "John Henry."

BIBL: ASCAP. BWW. CurBiog 1944. FeaEJ. FeaGitJS. MeeJMov. NYT, 6 September 1969. Oliv. StamFCW.

DISC: Jep. RustCED. TudBM.

WHITE, PORTIA. Concert singer (b. 24 June 1917 in Truro, Nova Scotia, Canada; d. 1968 in Truro [?]). She began piano study with her mother when she was five years old and sang in her father's church choir from the time she was six. She obtained her musical education at the Halifax Conservatory of Music and studied privately with Ernesto Vinci. In 1941 she made her concert debut as a contralto in Toronto, Canada; in October 1944 she made her New York debut at Town Hall. The next year she appeared in the documentary film *This Is Canada*. She toured widely as a concert singer.

BIBL: Black press, incl. AmstN, 18 March 1944, 28 March 1944. NYB, 1947. CurBiog (March 1945).

WHITE, WILLARD WENTWORTH. Opera singer (b. 10 October 1946 in Jamaica, West Indies). He obtained his musical education at the Juilliard School of Music in New York, where he studied with Beverley Johnson and Giorgio Tozzi. He made his operatic debut (baritone) as Colline in Puccini's *La Boheme* with the New York City Opera Company. In 1975 he attracted wide attention for his role of Ned in Scott Joplin's* *Treemonisha* with the Houston [Texas] Opera Company.

BIBL: WWOpera.

DISC: Turn.

WHITMAN, ALBERTA ("BERT"). Vaudeville entertainer (b. c1888 in Pratt, Kansas; d. June 1964 in Chicago, Illinois). See **WHITMAN SISTERS.**

WHITMAN, ALICE. Vaudeville entertainer (b. c1900; d. 1970s in Chicago, Illinois). See **WHITMAN SISTERS.**

WHITMAN, ESSIE BARBARA. Vaudeville entertainer (b. 4 July 1882 in Osceola, Arkansas; d. 7 May 1963 in Chicago, Illinois). See **WHITMAN SISTERS.**

WHITMAN, MABLE. Vaudeville entertainer (b. c1880 in Lawrence, Kansas; d. 7 May 1942 in Chicago, Illinois). See **WHITMAN SISTERS.**

WHITMAN SISTERS, THE. Vaudeville troupe/company (org. in Kansas City, Missouri; fl. early twentieth century). The Whitman sisters were Mable, Essie Barbara, Alberta or "Bert," and Alice. The father, Albert A. Whitman, was a minister; the three older girls traveled with him at an early age, singing in churches where he preached. They obtained their musical education through private study and at Morris Brown College in Atlanta, Georgia, and the New England Conservatory in Boston, Massachusetts. Mable and Essie began performing professionally during the 1890s, billed as the Daznette Sisters. Will Accooe* wrote a skit for one of their engagements at the Orpheum Theater in Kansas City, Missouri. During the first decades of the twentieth century the Whitmans toured widely on the vaudeville circuit as a family group (including the mother and aunt, according to some sources) in the United States and in Europe. About 1900 the sisters organized their own group, now including Bert and later Baby Alice, and eventually signed with the Independent Family United Circuit. Over the years the sisters used various names for their company, among them, Whitman Sisters Company and Whitman Sisters New Orleans Troubadours. After T.O.B.A.* (Theater Owners Booking Association) was organized during the 1920s, the Whitman sisters company became one of its leading attractions. Mable was the songwriter, and Bert, the male impersonator. The company disbanded in the early 1930s. Essie left the stage in 1933 and became an evangelist. Alice was active at least through the 1930s, appearing in Connies's [Inn] *Hot Chocolates of 1935* and other New York revues and later as a soloist in nightclubs and theaters. Mable toured with the vaudeville act "Pops and Louie" (Pops was her nephew, son of Alice). Over the years those who toured with the Whitman Sisters included Tony Jackson,* William ("Bill") Basie* (later, "Count" Basie), Willie Bryant, and Ferman Tapp, among others. In its heyday the Whitman Sisters company comprised forty-two persons; it played every major vaudeville house in the nation and leading houses in Europe.

BIBL: Black press, incl. CDef, 26 January 1918, 5 March 1927, 4 April 1936, 3 October 1936, 16 May 1942, 27 June 1964; IndF, 25 December 1915; NYAge, 27 April 1935. Blesh. BWW.

WHITNEY, SALEM TUTT. Vaudeville entertainer (b. c1869 in Logansport, Indiana; d. 12 February 1934 in Chicago, Illinois). He began his career in 1894 as a bass singer with the Puggsley Brothers Tennessee Warblers. Thereafter he toured with various groups, including Black Patti's Troubadours,* Eph Williams's "Silas Green from New Orleans,"* and Sherman H. Dudley's* Smart Set company. About 1908 he and his brother, J. Homer Tutt, organized The Smarter Set company, which was one of the most successful and longest-lived (1908-23) of the black touring companies. Over the years the two brothers produced fifteen musicals, including *The Mayor of Newtown, George Washington Bullion Abroad, Darkest Americans, Bamboula,* and *Oh, Joy*. They wrote the books for the shows and frequently contributed song lyrics and music. The musical directors of their shows included James Vaughn,* Charles Luckeyeth ("Luckey") Roberts,* and Clarence Williams,* among others. Perhaps the most successful show was *Bamboula* (1919-20), a two-act "jazzonian operetta" with music written by Vaughn and Edgar Powell. Whitney published a column, "Seen and Heard While Passing," in the Indianapolis *Freeman* for several years and a column in *The Chicago Defender*, "Timely Topics," for sixteen years. In these columns he not only passed on musical gossip and discussed musical events but also gave detailed information about The Smarter Set productions, including names of cast members, titles of songs, and even financial reports occasionally. After the demise of the company he toured on the T.O.B.A.* (Theater Owners Booking Association) circuit until 1928. In 1930 he joined the *Green Pastures* company, with which he played the part of Noah for the three years before his death.

BIBL: Black press, incl. CDef, 17 July 1920, 17 February 1934, 24 December 1934; IndF, 3 January 1914, 5 February 1916, 30 June 1917; NYAge, 17 February 1934.

WHITTAKER (née **WOODBRIDGE), HUDSON ("TAMPA RED").** Bluesman (b. 25 December 1900 in Smithville, Georgia; d. 19 March 1981 in Chicago, Illinois). He spent his childhood in Tampa, Florida. During the mid-1920s he went to Chicago, where he recorded with Gertrude ("Ma") Rainey* and teamed with ("Georgia Tom") Thomas A. Dorsey* to write songs and perform with their groups, variously called The Hokum Boys, The Hokum Trio, and the Hokum Jug Band. They received wide recognition in 1928 for their song "It's tight like that." When Dorsey left the blues world in 1932 to write gospel music, Whittaker organized his Chicago Five group, which included Willie B. James, Arnett Nelson, and "Black Bob" (?), among others. His guitar style was influential with many of his contemporary bluesmen.

BIBL: BWW. FeaEJ. LivBl interview of "Georgia Tom Dorsey," 20 (March-April 1975). Oliv.

DISC: Jep. Kink. LeSlBR. RustJR. TudBM.

WILDER, JOSEPH BENJAMIN ("JOE"). Symphony-jazz trumpeter (b. 22 February 1922 in Colwyn, Pennsylvania). He came from a musical family; his father was a jazz bandleader. He obtained his musical education in the public schools of Philadelphia, Pennsylvania, and attended the Mastbaum School of Music there. He began performing professionally during the 1940s and thereafter played with various groups, including Les Hite* (1941-42), Lionel Hampton* (1942-43, 1945-46), and James ("Jimmy") Lunceford* (1946-47), among others. During the 1950s he played with various groups, played in pit orchestras for Broadway musicals, including *Guys and Dolls* (opened 1950), then joined ABC-television in New York as a staff musician (1957-73). During the 1960s-70s he also played first trumpet in the Symphony of the New World* (1965-71) and toured with Benny Goodman in the Soviet Union (1962). After leaving ABC he became a free-lance studio musician; he worked with various entertainers, appeared on television special programs, and recorded regularly.

BIBL: FeaEJ. FeaJS. FeaGitJS.

DISC: Jep. Kink.

WILKINS, ERNEST BROOKS ("ERNIE"). Jazz saxophonist (b. 20 July 1922 in St. Louis, Missouri). He studied piano as a child but changed to tenor saxophone during his high-school years and began playing with local groups. He obtained his musical training in the public schools of St. Louis, at Wilberforce [Ohio] College, and at the United States Navy School of Music. He played with Clark Terry* and George Hudson in St. Louis before he left to serve in the U. S. Armed Forces at the Great Lakes Naval Training Center (1942-45), where he played with resident bands. In 1944 he was appointed leader of a select group of twenty-five black musicians who were to make history: in January 1945 they became the first black musicians to attend the U.S. Navy Music School. After his discharge from the service, Wilkins played with various groups, including Hudson again, Earl Hines,* and William ("Count") Basie* (1951-55). He then settled in New York, where he established himself as a writer-arranger, working for Basie (for whom he made his first arrangement), Tommy Dorsey, John Birks ("Dizzy") Gillespie,* and Harry James, among others. He also recorded extensively and toured with Gillespie in the Middle East (1956). During the 1960s he became increasingly involved with community programs. He worked with the Phoenix House drug-addict rehabilitation program (1966-69), with Jazzmobile in the Harlem community, and beginning in 1974 with Jazz Interactions. He also was active as a studio musician, as an A & R (artists and repertory) man for a recording company, he led his own groups occasionally, and he played with Clark Terry groups, both big band and the quintet. Wilkins was regarded as one of the leading arrangers of contemporary jazz; his work was in high demand at home and abroad. His original composition included the film score *Stand Up and Be Counted* (1972) and the orchestral work *Four Black Immortals* (1977, a tribute to Paul Robeson,* Jackie Robinson, Malcolm X, and Martin Luther King).

BIBL: FeaEJ. FeaJS. FeaGitJS. Samuel Floyd, "The Great Lakes Experience: 1942-45" in BPIM 3 (Spring 1975). MeeJMov.

DISC: Jep.

WILKINS, JOE WILLIE. Bluesman (b. 7 January 1923 in Davenport, Mississippi; d. 28 March 1979 in Memphis, Tennessee). He began playing harmonica at the age of ten and guitar at twelve, influenced by his father, who played guitar. He also sang in a local church choir as a child. His musical development was influenced by some of the most celebrated bluesmen of the period, including ("Blind") Lemon Jefferson,* Charley Patton,* "Muddy Waters" (McKinley Morganfield),* and Aaron "T-Bone" Walker,* among others—some of whom he heard through live performances and others through recordings. In 1933 he began playing professionally with a blues band; in 1942 he began playing regularly on Willie ("Rice") Miller's* radio show, Sonny Boy's Corn Meal and King Biscuit Show, on station KFFA in Helena, Arkansas. In later years he performed and/or recorded with Riley ("B. B.") King,* Robert ("Junior") Lockwood,* Robert ("Nighthawk") McCoy,* Willie Nix, Roosevelt Sykes,* and Waters, among others. In 1959 he settled in Memphis, Tennessee. His career languished during the 1960s, but he continued to play locally and occasionally appear at blues festivals. During the 1970s he toured with the Memphis Blues Caravan and also with his group, the King Biscuit Boys (later called the Catahula Scound Hounds).

BIBL: BWW. LivBl 42 (January-February 1979). LivBl 11 (Winter 1972-73). Oliv.

WILLIAMS, BERT. See **WILLIAMS, EGBERT.**

WILLIAMS, CAMILLA. Opera singer (b. 1922 in Danville, Virginia). She obtained her musical education at Virginia State College (B.S., 1941) and later studied in Philadelphia, Pennsylvania, with Marian Szekely-Freschl and in New York with Rose Dirman, Sergius Kagen, and Cesare Sodero, among others. She taught in an elementary school in Danville, Virginia, before beginning her career in concert/opera music. In 1943 she won a Marian Anderson* Award. The next year she won first place in a competition that brought her a performance with the Philadelphia Orchestra. In August 1944 she made her radio debut as a soprano on a RCA coast-to-coast network program titled "The Music America Loves Best." In 1946 she made her operatic debut with the New York City Opera, singing the title role of Puccini's *Madame Butterfly*. Thereafter she toured widely at home and abroad, making guest appearances with leading symphony orchestras, giving solo recitals, and singing in the major opera houses. She became best known for her roles of Nedda in Leoncavallo's *I Pagliacci*, Mimi in Puccini's *La Boheme*, Marguerite in Gounod's *Faust*, Princess Ilia in Mozart's *Idomeneo*, and the title role in Verdi's *Aida*, as well as Madame Butterfly. Her African tour in 1958 was sponsored by the U.S. Department of State. During the 1970s she joined the music faculty of Indiana University.

BIBL: Black press, incl. CDef, 19 August 1944; AmstN, 20 January 1962. CBDict. CurBiog (June 1952). WWBA. WWCA 1950.

WILLIAMS, CHARLES MELVIN ("COOTIE"). Jazz trumpeter (b. 24 July 1910 in Mobile, Alabama). He played trombone, tuba, and drums in his school band. Later he taught himself to play trumpet. In his early career he played with various groups, including the Young Family Band (family of Lester Young*), the Eagle Eye Shields, and the Alonzo Ross DeLuxe Syncopators. In 1928 he went to New York with Ross and thereafter played for short periods with William ("Chick") Webb* and Fletcher Henderson,* among others, before joining Edward ("Duke") Ellington* (1929-40). During the next two decades he played with Benny Goodman (1940-41), then toured with his own groups, which were successively a big band, small ensemble, and quartet. He also toured as a soloist during these years. In the 1950s his groups played rhythm 'n' blues as well as jazz. He rejoined Ellington (1962-75), remaining with the orchestra when Mercer Ellington* took it over after Duke's death in 1974. Ill health forced Cootie's retirement in 1975. During his long career he recorded prolifically with Ellington, Theodore ("Teddy") Wilson,* the Goodman Sextet, Lionel Hampton,* and others. Those who performed in his groups over the years, included Pearl Bailey,* Charlie Parker,* Earl ("Bud") Powell,* and Eddie ("Cleanhead") Vinson,* among others. He first attracted wide attention during his tenure in Ellington's orchestra for his distinctive "growl" solos and use of the plunger mute. His best-known performances were on "Saratoga swing," "Ring dem bells," "Echoes of the jungle," and "Concerto for Cootie" (later given lyrics and titled "Do nothing till you hear from me"). He wrote a number of songs, some in collaboration with others, as "Round about midnight" with Thelonious Monk.*

BIBL: ASCAP. ChilWW. FeaEJ. FeaJS. FeaGitJS. MeeJMov.

DISC: Jep. Kink. RustJR. TudJ.

WILLIAMS, CLARENCE. Music publisher (b. 8 October 1893 in Plaquemine Delta, Louisiana; d. 6 November 1965 in New York, New York). His family moved to New Orleans, Louisiana, when he was a child. He began performing professionally at the age of twelve, first touring with a minstrel troupe, then playing piano in the Storyville district of New Orleans. About 1915 he joined with Armand Piron* to form a music publishing business, and the men frequently performed together, particularly in plugging their songs. Later Williams toured on the vaudeville circuit; in 1917 he was musical director of Salem Tutt Whitney's* The Smart Set. Thereafter he moved to Chicago, Illinois, where he operated a music store and sang in local clubs. He also led his own groups, including his Blue Five, Blue Seven, Washboard Five, Jazz Kings, Novelty Four, among others. In 1921 he made his recording debut and thereafter recorded extensively with his groups, his wife Eva Taylor,* and with others. In 1923 he was one of a select group of black pianists invited to make piano rolls for QRS (Quality Reigns Supreme, a subsidiary of the Melville Clark Piano Company), along with J. Lawrence Cook,* Lemuel Fowler, Clarence Johnson, James P. Johnson,* William ("Willie-the-Lion") Smith,* and Thomas ("Fats") Waller.* During the 1920s-40s he produced radio and theater shows, in addition to performing in musicals. He often served as an agent for black talent in the Harlem community, helping to arrange recording sessions for black artists with the major companies. He began publishing his songs early in his career. His best-known songs were "Baby, won't you please come home," "West end blues," "Sugar blues," "Tain't nobody's business if I do," and "Gulf Coast blues."

BIBL: ASCAP. Black press, incl. CDef, 17 May 1919; IndF, 30 June 1917. W. C. Handy, *Father of the Blues* (New York, 1941). Souch. Maurice Waller and Anthony Calabrese, *Fats Waller* (New York, 1977).

DISC: Kink. RustJR.

WILLIAMS, COOTIE. See **WILLIAMS, CHARLES.**

WILLIAMS, EGBERT AUSTIN ("BERT"). Entertainer (b. 12 November 1874 in Antigua, West Indies; d. 5 March 1922 in New York, New York). His family moved to New York when he was a child; later they settled in Riverside, California, where he attended high school. He began his professional career in San Francisco, singing to his own banjo accompaniment. He met George Walker,* and in 1892 the two men formed a vaudeville act. They worked at Halahan and Homan's Midway in the city, then toured with Martin and Sellig's Mastadon Minstrels (1893), with a medicine show, and finally on the vaudeville circuit. During the mid-1890s they went east to further their careers. In 1896 they performed a vaudeville act in the Broadway musical *The Gold Bug*, which attracted wide attention. Thereafter they played a long residency at New York's Koster and Bial's Theater, interrupted for a short period by an engagement in London, England. It was during this period that they introduced the old slave dance, the cakewalk, to the public at home and abroad. About 1897 they formed an all-black company to produce *Senegambian Carnival*, which failed. In 1898 they secured top professional management and thereafter produced a series of successful shows, including *The Policy Players* (1899), *Sons of Ham* (1900), *Williams and Walker in Dahomey* (1902-09), *Williams and Walker in Abyssinia* (1905-06), and *Williams and Walker in Bandanna Land* (1907-08). *In Dahomey* ran two seasons in England and included a command performance for King Edward VII. Illness forced Walker to retire in 1908; thereafter Williams starred in *Mr. Lode of Koal* (1909-10). Over the years the Walker/Williams shows provided employment for large numbers of black entertainers, musicians, composers, lyricists, musical directors, stage managers, and others associated with the stage. Those associated with these shows at one time or another included Will Marion Cook,* Paul Lawrence Dunbar,* Lloyd Gibbs,* J. Leubrie Hill,* Jesse Shipp,* Alex Rogers,* Abbie Mitchell,* James Vaughn,* Aida Overton Walker,* Inez Clough,* and the Golden Gate Quartet*—to cite but a few names. During the years 1910-19 Williams performed as a "single" in the Ziegfeld Follies and thereafter, independently on the vaudeville circuit. He was appearing in Detroit, Michigan, in the musical *Under the Bamboo Tree* when he had a fatal collapse. He was the leading black comedian/entertainer of his time. He recorded extensively for his time and made films. He also wrote songs, of which the best known was "Nobody."

BIBL: Black press, incl. CDef, 18 March 1922; NYAge, 11 March 1922. Douglas Gilbert, *American Vaudeville. Its Life and Times* (New York, 1940). Hare. Mable Rowland, *Bert Williams* (New York, 1923).

DISC: RustCED.

WILLIAMS, FESS. See **WILLIAMS, STANLEY.**

WILLIAMS, FLORENCE. Jubilee Singers manager. See **JONES, SISSIERETTA.**

WILLIAMS, HENRY ("HARRY"). Concert singer (b. 1850s in Cleveland, Ohio [?]; d. 1930s-40s in New York, New York). He received his early musical training through private study with local teachers in Cleveland, Ohio, including John Underner. In 1886 he went to Paris, France, where he studied with Delle Sede and gave concerts. Later he went to London, England, where he studied with Francesco Tosti and came under the patronage of Luigi Denza. He returned to Cleveland in 1888 for a short period, gave some recitals, then returned to London. In 1890 he toured with a British concert company, the Frazier Quintet. He also was given a temporary appointment to the voice faculty of the London Academy of Music. After he returned to Cleveland about 1903 or 1904, he conducted a voice studio. In 1912 he went to Washington, D.C., where he became head of the voice department of Harriet Gibbs Marshall's* Washington Conservatory of Music. During his years in Washington, he conducted a choral society and a symphony orchestra for the Conservatory. During the 1920s he was director of music at the Florida Normal School in St. Augustine. In 1927 he settled in New York, where he conducted a voice studio and occasionally sang at local concerts. In June 1938 the Harlem community honored the octogenarian as the ''Dean of Afro-American voice teachers'' with a testimonial concert.

BIBL: Black press, incl. CDef, 22 February 1913, 22 December 1917, 17 September 1927; CleveG, 29 January 1887, 1 September 1888, 22 March 1890, 9 April 1904; NYAge, 18 June 1938.

WILLIAMS, HENRY F. Composer (b. 13 August 1813 in Boston, Massachusetts; d. July 1903 in Boston). He studied music as a child and was bound out to a music teacher until he was twenty-one, according to some reports. He developed skills in playing violin, cornet, and several other instruments. He also conducted a music studio, but was best known for his arrangements and compositions. He was frequently employed by Patrick Sarsfield Gilmore to arrange music for the Irish bandleader's group. When Frank Johnson's* band lost its leader by death in 1844, the new leader, Joseph Anderson,* invited Williams to arrange music for the band. Williams also toured with the band for a period, then returned to Boston permanently. In 1872 he played doublebass in the mammoth orchestra of one thousand players that assembled to perform for Gilmore's World Peace Jubilee in Boston. Williams was a prolific composer; his output included overtures, dances, marches, songs, and sacred music. His best-known compositions were the ballads ''Lauriette'' and ''Come love and list awhile,'' the ''Parisien Waltzes'' for piano, and the anthems ''O, Give Thanks'' and ''Sing unto God.'' Many of his pieces were listed in the *Complete Catalogue of Sheet Music and Musical Works, 1870*, published by the Board of Music Trade of the United States of America, 1871; reprint with introduction by Dena Epstein (New York, 1973).

BIBL: BPIM 4 (July 1976). Black press, incl. IndF, 18 May 1889. Trot, pp. 106-113; pp. 44-52 of the music section.

WILLIAMS, J. MAYO (''INK''). Record producer (b. 1894 at Monmouth, Illinois; d. 2 January 1980 in Chicago, Illinois). During the 1920s-30s he was the most important black record executive of the period. He was recording director for the so-called race series of three companies: Paramount, Vocalion, and Decca. Paramount issued its series 12000/13000 during the years 1922-30, having taken over Harry Pace's* Black Swan label in April 1924; undoubtedly Williams was responsible for most of the releases and probably all of the field recordings. He also directed recordings for the Vocalion series 1000 (1925-31), and Decca series 7000 (1934-40?). In 1927 Williams produced recordings on his own short-lived label, *Black Patti*—named in honor of M. Sissieretta Jones,* who was called ''the Black Patti.'' Those for whom he directed recordings over the years included William (''Count'') Basie,* Nat (''King'') Cole,* (''Blind'') Arthur Blake,* Ida Cox,* Alberta Hunter,* Mahalia Jackson,* Gertrude (''Ma'') Rainey,* and Muddy Waters (née McKinley Morganfield),* among many, many others. Williams also worked with small independent labels, particularly during the 1940s.

BIBL: LivBl 45/46 (Spring 1980).

WILLIAMS, JOE (née JOSEPH GOREED). Jazz singer (b. 12 December 1918 in Cordele, Georgia). His mother moved to Chicago, Illinois, when he was three years old. There he was widely exposed to church music; his mother and aunt sang in church choirs. He obtained his musical training in Chicago's public schools. At seventeen he began singing professionally with a local group, Johnny Long's orchestra. Thereafter he sang with various groups, including Lionel Hampton* (1943), William (''Count'') Basie* (1950), and Theodore (''Red'') Saunders* (1950s). Later he had a long association with Basie (1954-60), during which period he became well known for his performances of ''Every day I have the blues,'' ''A man ain't supposed to cry,'' and ''All right, okay, you win.'' After leaving Basie he toured widely as a soloist, although he continued to perform with Basie intermittently. He sang at home and abroad, in theaters and concert halls, in nightclubs, and at major jazz festivals. He was also active in television and films, including *The Moonshine War* (1970). His repertory included popular songs and blues, but he was best known for his blues-inflected jazz.

BIBL: FeaEJ. FeaJS. FeaGitJS. MeeJMov.

DISC: Jep. Kink. TudBM.

WILLIAMS, JOE LEE (''BIG JOE'' or ''PO' JOE''). Bluesman (b. 16 October 1903 in Crawford, Mississippi). He played homemade flutes and guitars as a child and grew up in a blues environment. He began singing and playing blues guitar professionally at an early age, wandering from place to place and settling for short periods in Tuscaloosa, Alabama, and West Helena, Arkansas. He toured with the Birmingham Jug Band in F. S. Wolcott's Rabbit Foot Minstrels,* which at that time featured Ethel Waters.* Although he recorded as early as 1928, his recording career began seriously in 1935. Those with whom he performed and/or recorded included Walter Davis, Charlie Jordan, Robert (''Nighthawk'') McCoy,* Charley McFadden,

Roosevelt Sykes,* "Peetie Wheatstraw" (William Bunch), and "Sonny Boy Williamson, No. 1" (John Lee Williamson).* Although he toured widely, he made St. Louis, Missouri, his home base and was an important blues figure in that city.

BIBL: BWW. CharLB. FeaEJ. Oliv.

DISC: Jep. LeSIBr. TudBM.

WILLIAMS, MARION. Gospel singer (b. 29 August 1927 in Miami, Florida). As a child she sang in church choirs and at tent revival meetings. In 1947 she joined The Famous Ward Singers* (1947-58) and became their lead singer. She attracted wide attention for one of the earliest solos she sang, W. Herbert Brewster's* "Surely God is able," the first gospel song to employ triple rhythms (12/8 meter). After leaving the Wards, she and other ex-members of the group formed the Stars of Faith (1959-65), which included Esther Ford, Kitty Parham, Frances Steadman, Henrietta Waddy, Rita Palmer, and Mattie Williams, among others. In 1961 she and her singers played important roles in the gospel musical, *Black Nativity* (text by Langston Hughes),* which was especially written for her, Alex Bradford,* and Princess Stewart. After its Broadway run, the musical toured in Europe and Australia. At Christmastime 1963 *Black Nativity* was produced on national television. In 1965 Williams left the Stars of Faith and began performing as a soloist. She toured widely during the 1960s-70s, including a visit to Africa in 1966, singing in concert halls, on television programs, in theaters and nightclubs, at the World Festival of Negro Arts in Dakar, Senegal (1966), and at the Newport Jazz Festival (1975), and increasingly on college campuses. She was noted for her singing of hymns; she also wrote and arranged gospel songs. Her best-known performances included solos sung with the Ward Singers, such as "Packin' up," "Weeping may endure for a night," and "Take your burdens to the Lord"; her best-known albums were *Prayer Changes Things*, *Gospel Now*, and *The New Message*. Her style was distinctive for the wide range of her voice, from contralto to coloratura soprano, and her improvisatory skills.

BIBL: FeaJS. FeaGitJS. Heil.

DISC: Hayes.

WILLIAMS, MARY LOU (née **MARY ELFREIDA SCRUGGS**). Jazz pianist (b. 8 May 1910 in Atlanta, Georgia; d. 28 May 1981 in Durham, N.C.). Her family moved to Pittsburgh, Pennsylvania, when she was four years old. Her mother was a pianist and she played piano as a child. By the time she was twelve, she was playing for local social entertainments. She obtained her musical education in the public schools of Pittsburgh and through private study. Her early professional experiences were with bands that toured on the vaudeville circuit with shows, including that of Seymour and Jeanette. She then played with John Williams (1926-27), whom she married, and with Andy Kirk* (1931-42). She was Kirk's chief arranger-pianist as early as 1929, however, and occasionally played with his group before becoming a full-time member. During the 1930s she also arranged for other jazz bandleaders, including Louis Armstrong,* Tommy Dorsey, Earl Hines,* Benny Goodman, and Glen Gray, among others. In 1942 she was co-leader of a group with Harold ("Shorty") Baker, her second husband, for a short period. Thereafter she lead her own group, toured six months (1943) with Edward ("Duke") Ellington* as a staff arranger, then began performing as a soloist or with a trio in nightclubs, primarily in New York and in California. She spent the years 1952-53 in Europe, where she played long residencies in London, England, and in Paris, France. After returning to the United States she resumed her nightclub playing; she also appeared at major jazz festivals and toured college campuses. Her teaching career included tenures in the public schools of Pittsburgh, at the University of Massachusetts in Amherst (1975-77), and at Duke University in Durham, North Carolina (1977-81).

She began composing early in her career; her *Zodiac Suite* was played by the New York Philharmonic in 1946. After she embraced Catholicism in 1957, she began writing jazz Masses and other jazz liturgical music, including the well-known "Hymn in honor of St. Martin Porres" (1962), a black saint. One of her three Masses, called "Mary Lou's Mass," was adapted for ballet and given a premiere performance by the Alvin Ailey American Dance Theater in 1971. Williams remained one of the leading jazz pianists of her time through many decades. Her style development was influenced by Earl Hines and Arthur ("Art") Tatum.* She exerted influence upon the development of the so-called Kansas City jazz school through her arrangements for Kirk and other big bands of the 1930s. She moved easily through the transition from swing to bebop, and through her direct contacts with such performers as Thelonious Monk,* Tadd Dameron,* John Birks ("Dizzy") Gillespie,* Miles Davis,* and others, she exerted influence upon the style development of a younger generation. Her honors included a Guggenheim Fellowship (1972) and honorary doctorates from Fordham University, Manhattan College, and Loyola University (New Orleans, Louisiana).

BIBL: Whitney Balliett, *Improvising* (New York, 1977). BPIM 8 (Fall 1980). ChilWW. FeaEJ. FeaJS. FeaGitJS. Handy. MeeJMov. NYT, 30 May 1981. WWA. WWBA. WWCA, 1950.

DISC: Jep. TudJ.

WILLIAMS, ROBERT PETE. Bluesman (b. 14 March 1914 in Zachary, Louisiana; d. 31 December 1980 in Rosedale, Louisiana). He moved to Scotlandville, Louisiana (near Baton Rouge), in 1928. He developed a distinctive country-blues style, which used modal melodies, sparse chords, and flowing rhythms, and frequently avoided the twelve-bar form. In 1956 a murder conviction (in self-defense) sent him to Angola Prison. There he was heard by folklorists Richard Allen and Harry Oster, for whom he made his first recordings in 1958 for the Louisiana Folklore Society. In 1959 he was given a parole and in 1964, full pardon—mainly because of outside interest in his talent. He performed at the Newport Folk Festival in 1964 and thereafter toured widely, playing on college campuses and at the major blues and jazz festivals. During the 1970s he toured with the American Blues Festival in Europe, recorded regularly, and appeared in films, including *Roots of American Music* (1971), *Out of the Blacks Into the Blues* (1972), and *Blues Under the Skin* (1972), among others. His later slide-guitar style was influenced by "Mississippi" Fred McDowell,* whom he met during the 1960s.

BIBL: BWW. CharLB. Terry Pattison, "Louisiana Country Blues" in LivBl 8 (Spring 1972). LivBl 2 (Summer 1970). MeeJMov. NYT, 15 March 1981. Oliv.

DISC: LeSlBR. TudBM.

WILLIAMS, SAMPSON. See **SELIKA, MARIE.**

WILLIAMS, SPENCER. Songwriter (b. 14 October 1889 in New Orleans, Louisiana; d. 14 July 1965 in New York, New York). He obtained his musical education in the public schools of Birmingham, Alabama, where he lived as a child. He began his professional career playing piano in the Storyville district of New Orleans, Louisiana. In 1907 he went to Chicago, Illinois, where he first played piano in the Sans Souci Amusement Park. About 1915 he settled in New York and gave his attention more and more to writing music. One of his first successful songs was "I ain't got nobody" (1916). He also wrote musicals in collaboration with others, including *Put and Take* (1921) and *Tan Topics* (1924). He wrote the musical score of *La Revue Nègre* in 1925 and went with the company, which starred Josephine Baker,* to produce the show in Paris, France. He remained there writing music for Baker's acts at the Folies Bergere until 1931, returned to the United States in that year, then went back to Paris the next year, taking Thomas ("Fats") Waller* with him. Later he settled in London, England. He resettled in the United States during the 1950s. His best-known songs were "Basin Street blues," "Everybody loves my baby," and "I've found a new baby."

BIBL: ASCAP. Black press, incl. AmstN, 24 July 1965. ChilWW. Maurice Waller and Anthony Calabrese, *Fats Waller* (New York, 1977).

DISC: Kink.

WILLIAMS, STANLEY ("FESS"). Jazz clarinetist (b. 10 April 1894 in Danville, Kentucky; d. 17 December 1975 in New York, New York). He studied violin at an early age. He obtained his musical education at Tuskegee [Alabama] Institute (graduated 1914), where he studied with N. Clark Smith* and specialized in clarinet. He taught several years in the public schools of Winchester, Kentucky, where he picked up the nickname "Fess," an abbreviation of the word "professor." He was active with various dance bands on weekends, including Frank Port in Cincinnati, Ohio. During the years 1919-23 he led his own groups. Thereafter he played in Chicago, Illinois, with Ollie Powers and others, then went to New York in 1924. His band played at the opening of the Savoy Ballroom in the Harlem community of New York in 1926. His Royal Flush Orchestra played long residencies at the Savoy and other local dance halls during the mid-1920s-30s. He also toured, recorded regularly during the period 1925-30, performed on NBC radio, and played a long engagement at the Regal Theater in Chicago (1929). He retired from music during the 1940s but continued to lead groups occasionally.

BIBL: Black press, incl. AmstN, 27 December 1975. ChilWW. NYT, 20 December 1975.

DISC: RustJR.

WILLIAMS COLORED SINGERS. Vocal mixed ensemble (org. in Chicago, Illinois [?]; fl. early twentieth century). Also known as the Williams Jubilee Singers, this ensemble was organized in 1904 by Charles Williams (b. in Holly Springs, Mississippi). He obtained his musical education at Rust College in Holly Springs. At the age of eighteen he moved to Chicago, Illinois, where later he joined a touring male quartet. He then organized a group called the Dixie Singers, and soon thereafter, his Jubilee Singers. Originally composed of eight men and eight women, the group toured largely on the circuits of white lyceum bureaus and Chautauqua organizations during the first five years of its existence. In April 1915 the Singers gave their first concert for a black audience at the Manhattan Casino in New York. Thereafter the tours included performances for both black and white audiences. The repertory of the ensemble consisted of ballads, operatic pieces, and "plantation and jubilee songs." The press reported that when the Singers appeared at the Academy of Music in Philadelphia, Pennsylvania, in April 1916, the hall was sold out for the first time in its history. The Singers took their first worldwide tour in 1910-11 and thereafter circled the globe several times during the next decade. While in London, England, where they gave 130 performances, the singers as a group studied voice with Amanda Ira Aldridge.* Those associated with the Singers included Virginia Green, Annis Hackley, Hattie Hobbs, Marie Peek, George Leon Johnson, Fannie Williams (wife of the director), and pianist Ethel Minor, among others.

BIBL: Black press, incl. CDef, 23 April 1910, 23 January 1915; IndF, 8 April 1916; NYAge, 1 April 1915, 13 April 1916, 18 January 1917. *The Chicago Negro Almanac and Reference Book.*

WILLIAMSON, JOHN LEE ("SONNY BOY WILLIAMSON NO. 1.") Bluesman (b. 30 March 1914 in Jackson, Tennessee; d. 1 June 1948 in Chicago, Illinois). He taught himself blues harmonica as a child and played for local social entertainments in the Memphis, Tennessee, area at an early age. During the 1930s he moved to Chicago, Illinois, where despite his youth he soon established himself as one of the leading Chicago bluesmen, along with William Lee Conley ("Big Bill") Broonzy.* He first recorded in 1937; thereafter he recorded regularly, often with James ("Yank") Rachell.* He was noted for his "crossed-harmonica" style, which enabled him to achieve on his instrument the special effects characteristic of vocal blues. His music greatly influenced his contemporaries in both Memphis and Chicago.

BIBL: BWW. FeaEJ. Oliv.

DISC: Jep. LeSlBR. TudBM.

WILLIAMSON, SONNY BOY, NO. 1. See **WILLIAMSON, JOHN LEE.**

WILLIAMSON, SONNY BOY, NO. 2. See **MILLER, WILLIE ("RICE").**

WILSON, EDITH (née **EDITH GOODALL).** Vaudeville/musical singer (b. 2 September 1896 in Louisville, Kentucky; d. 31 March 1981 in Chicago, Illinois). She began singing for local events at thirteen and at sixteen toured in a trio composed of Dan Wilson, his sister Lena, and herself. In New York she met Perry Bradford,* who put her in the musical *Put and Take* (1921) and arranged for a recording contract for her. She made her first recordings in September 1921. Thereafter she toured widely in the United States and in Europe on the nightclub circuit; she also appeared in musicals and revues, including *From Dover Street to Dixie* (1923 in London), *Chocolate Kiddies* (1925 in Europe), Connie's *Hot Chocolates Revue* (1929-30), *Blackbirds of 1926*, *Jazzamania* (1927), *Blackbirds of 1933-34* (New York and London), and *Memphis Bound* (1945), among other shows. During the 1940s-60s she toured extensively as a soloist on the vaudeville circuit, then entered an acting career, primarily on radio and later on television. Her commercial-music activity included advertising Aunt Jemima pancakes for the Quaker Oats Company (1947-65) on television and at festivals. During the 1970s she returned to music, appearing at festivals and on college campuses as well as in nightclubs. She also recorded with Eubie Blake* and Eurreal ("Brother") Montgomery.*

BIBL: BWW. *Cadence* (August 1979). NYT, 1 April 1981. WWBA.

WILSON, GERALD STANLEY. Jazz trumpeter (b. 4 September 1918 in Shelby, Mississippi). His family moved to Detroit, Michigan, when he was about fourteen. He studied piano as a child with his mother, a pianist, and later studied music at the Cass Technical High School in Detroit. His early professional experience was with the Plantation Club Orchestra (1936-37). Thereafter he played with various groups, including Jimmie Lunceford* (1939-42), a United States Navy band at the Great Lakes Naval Training Station during World War II (1943-44), William ("Count") Basie* (1947-49), John Birks ("Dizzy") Gillespie* (1949), and Edward ("Duke") Ellington* (intermittently, 1947-66). He was also an arranger-composer for several bands during these years. He led his own groups during the mid-1940s in Los Angeles, California, and again in the 1950s in San Francisco, California. In the 1960s he toured with a big band, performing in leading concert halls of the nation. His teaching career included tenures as a lecturer at San Fernando Valley State College in California and at California State University at Northridge (1969-). He composed regularly throughout his career. In the 1970s he began to write symphonic works, some of which were performed by the Los Angeles Symphony. He received numerous awards from the music industry.

BIBL: FeaEJ. FeaJS. FeaGitJS. MeeJMov. WWBA.

DISC: Jep.

WILSON, NANCY. Jazz singer (b. 20 February 1937 in Chillicothe, Ohio). She sang in a church choir as a child and through her high-school years. At the age of sixteen she began singing professionally in local nightclubs and later with the Rusty Bryant Band (1956-58).

She went to New York in 1958, where she first sang in small nightclubs. In 1959 she met Julian ("Cannonball") Adderley,* who helped to advance her career. She made her recording debut in the fall of 1959 and thereafter recorded prolifically. She toured widely in the United States and abroad, singing in theaters, concert halls, and on television. For a year she had her own television show on Los Angeles, California, station KNBC (1974-75). She received awards from the music and recording industries, from civic and professional organizations, and an honorary doctorate from Central State University in Ohio.

BIBL: Black press, incl. AmstN, 8 March 1975. FeaEJ. FeaJS. FeaGitJS. WWA. WWBA.

DISC: Jep.

WILSON, OLLY. Composer/College professor (b. 7 September 1937 in St. Louis, Missouri). He came from a musical family; his father sang in the local Harry T. Burleigh* Choral Society, and the family sang spirituals in quartet style around the house. He began piano study at the age of eight; within a few years he was playing for church and accompanying his father's solos at local concerts. When he was ten he began clarinet study at school. He received his musical education in the public schools of St. Louis, where he played in the Sumner High School band and came under the influence of bandmaster Clarence Hayden Wilson; at Washington University in St. Louis (B. Mus., 1959), where he studied with Earl Bates, Henry Lowe, and Robert Wykes; at the University of Illinois in Urbana (M. Mus., 1960), and at the University of Iowa in Iowa City (Ph.D., 1964), where he studied with Robert Kelley and Phillip Bezanson. He studied further at the Studio for Experimental Music at the University of Illinois (1967). His teaching career included tenures at Florida A & M (Agricultural and Mechanical) University in Tallahassee (1960-62), the Oberlin [Ohio] Conservatory of Music (1965-70), and the University of California at Berkeley (1970-).

His early style development was influenced by the spirituals and gospel music he heard at church, the blues he heard on the radio and the streets, and the recordings he listened to of music by Bartok, Schoenberg, Stravinsky, and Varèse as well as Miles Davis* and Charlie Parker,* among others. During his high-school years he led a jazz group, for which he made arrangements and wrote pieces. Also during this period he wrote music for school revues. During his college years he played clarinet in the band; then, changing over to string bass, he played in the college chamber orchestra, the St. Louis Philharmonic, the St. Louis Summer Players, and other semi-professional city groups. In later years he played with the University of Illinois symphony orchestra and with the Cedar Rapids [Iowa] Symphony Orchestra. At Washington University he came into contact with Oliver Nelson,* played in Nelson's jazz group, and developed his jazz-arranging skills with Nelson's help. He first began writing music in the classical tradition at college; in 1958 one of his early compositions, a trio for flute, cello, and piano, was performed at a Midwestern Composer's Symposium in Iowa. Encouraged by its success, he composed regularly thereafter, and gradually his music received more and more public exposure. In 1964 his Three Movements for Orchestra was performed at a Composer's Symposium in Dallas, Texas; in 1967 his Sextet for Winds (1963) was played in a Black Composer's Concert Series in Atlanta, Georgia; in 1968 his *Cetus* for electronic tape won first prize in an international competition for electronic compositions sponsored by Dartmouth College. In 1971-72 and again in 1978 he went to Ghana to study African music.

His mature style reflected the various influences of gospel and spirituals, jazz (particularly bebop) and blues, African music, and music in the European tradition. His early works employed serialism, but later he preferred electronic music and the combining of electronic sounds with acoustical instruments and voice. His music revealed his intense interest in rhythms and instrumental color and his predilection for unorthodox combinations, as *Wry Fragments* (1961) for tenor and percussions, "Chanson innocente" (1965) for contralto and two bassoons, or "Soliloquy" for solo contrabass. His use of black-music idioms was evident in such compositions as *Piece for Four* (1966), which employs a Miles Davis approach to instrumentation; *SpiritSong* (1973), for mezzo-soprano, women's chorus, orchestra (including amplified instruments), and gospel chorus, which employs spirituals in a contemporary context; *Sometimes* (1976), for tenor and electronic tape, which is based on the spiritual "Sometimes I feel like a motherless child." His best-known works, in addition to those cited above, were *Black Martyrs* (1972) for chorus and tape, written in memory of Martin Luther King, Jr., Malcolm X, and Medgar Evers; *Akwan* (1972) for piano, electronic piano, and orchestra; *The Eighteen Hands of Jerome Harris* (1971), an electronic ballet work; *Voices* (1970) for symphony orchestra; "Piano Piece" (1969); *Reflections* (1978) for symphony orchestra; and *Expansions* (1979) for organ. His honors included Guggenheim fellowships (1971-72, 1977-78), awards from the National Academy of Arts and Letters (1974) and civic and professional organizations, and commissions from leading symphonies and concert artists. In addition to teaching and composing he was also active as a conductor of chamber ensembles.

BIBL: BakBC. BPIM 5, 6 (Spring 1977, Spring 1978). Bull. Gro.

WILSON, THEODORE (''TEDDY''). Jazz pianist (b. 24 November 1912 in Austin, Texas). When he was six years old, his family moved to Tuskegee, Alabama, where his parents were appointed to the faculty of Tuskegee Institute. He studied piano as a child, then changed to violin, and in high school learned to play clarinet and oboe. He played piano, however, in the high school band. He obtained his musical education at Tuskegee and Talladega College in Alabama (which he attended for a year). In 1929 he went to Detroit, Michigan, where he played with Lawrence (''Speed'') Webb, and then to Toledo, Ohio, where he played with Milton Senior. At Toledo he met Arthur (''Art'') Tatum*; they became fast friends and exchanged musical ideas. His style development was also influenced by the pianism of Earl Hines* and Thomas (''Fats'') Waller.* In 1931 Wilson moved to Chicago, where he played with various groups, including Erskine Tate,* Clarence Moore, Eddie Mallory, Louis Armstrong,* and Jimmie Noone.* In 1933 he went to New York to play with Benny Carter.* Later he joined Willie Bryant* (1934-35), then played for the Charioteers,* directed small-group recordings for Billie Holiday* (1935), and played solo piano in nightclubs. During the years 1936-39 he played with Benny Goodman, at first as a guest performer with the band, then as a member of the Goodman Trio along with Gene Krupa. Thereafter he led his own big band (1939-40) and later a sextet (1940-44). He played again with Goodman in the Broadway musical *The Seven Lively Arts* (1945) and many times during the next decades for reunions, film appearances, special concerts, and recording. Beginning in 1945 he gave his attention primarily to teaching, studio work, recording, and broadcasting on CBS radio and New York radio station WNEW (1949-52). He taught at the Manhattan School of Music and summer classes at the Juilliard School of Music. Through the 1960s-70s he toured widely throughout the world with his trio, which frequently included bassist Milton (''Milt'') Hinton* and his son Teddy Wilson, Jr., on drums. He appeared regularly on television and played on college campuses as well as in concert halls and nightclubs. His film performances included *Something to Shout About* (1943) *Hollywood Hotel* (1937), *Make Mine Music* (1945), and *The Benny Goodman Story* (1955), among others.

He was a seminal figure in jazz piano over a period of four decades. His sophisticated, elegant, ''swing''-piano style influenced most pianists of his time. His crisp, delicate playing was timeless, and he maintained his popularity over the years, although his style was only minimally affected by bebop and the avant garde. He was also a talented songwriter and arranger, and gave much attention to this aspect of his career from time to time. His numerous honors included awards from the music industry and citations from civic and educational institutions.

BIBL: ASCAP. ChilWW. DanceWEH. FeaEJ. FeaJS. FeaGitJS. Nat Hentoff, ''Dr. Jazz and His Son, the Professor'' in NYT, 14 April 1974. MeeJMov. WWA. WWBA.

DISC: Jep. Kink. RustJR. TudJ.

WILSON, W. LLEWELLYN. School music teacher (b. 9 March 1887 in Baltimore, Maryland; d. September 1950 in Baltimore). When he was four years old he was taken to Boston, Massachusetts, where he lived for three years. After returning to Baltimore, he began working at the age of eight in a church, where he pumped for the organ. Two years later he began playing organ. He studied music with W. G. Oust, at that time music critic for the Baltimore *Sun*. He obtained his musical training in the public schools of Baltimore and at the Colored Normal School (teacher's diploma, 1910). He later studied organ, cello, theory and composition; his teachers included Harold Randolph, John Stainer, Gustav Strube, and Bart Wirtz, among others. He began teaching at the Douglass High School in Baltimore immediately after graduation and remained there forty years. He also conducted a private studio. During the 1930s-40s he wrote a weekly column for *The* [Baltimore] *Afro-American*, titled ''Concords and Discords.'' He was conductor of the city-sponsored Baltimore City Orchestra and Chorus, which gave frequent concerts. He made a significant contribution to the history of black music and exerted wide influence upon the development of black music through his students and those whom he coached or directed in music groups; his students included Eubie Blake,* Cabell (''Cab'') Calloway,* Anne Brown,* Mark Fax,* Ellis Larkins, Avon Long,* and Thomas Kerr,* among others. At one time during the late 1920s all the black music teachers in the Baltimore public schools were his former students.

BIBL: Black press, incl. *The* [Richmond] *Afro-American*, 12 February 1980.

WINGS OVER JORDAN. Church choral group (org. 1937 in Cleveland, Ohio). When Glenn T. Settle (b. 1895 near Reidsville, North Carolina) became pastor of the Gethsemane Church in Cleveland, Ohio, he found there an excellent choir. He studied music in order to take over its direction and then arranged for an audition of the group with the local radio station WGAR. The choir sang its first broadcast in July 1937. By January 1939 the choir's popularity had increased to such an extent that it was broadcasting every Sunday morning on the CBS radio network a program titled "Wings Over Jordan," which was "dedicated to the heart of the Americas" (1937-47). Beginning in 1938 the choir toured widely and recruited new members from all over the nation. The choir's national program ended in 1944, after which it toured for a year to American army camps in the European Theater of World War II. After returning to the United States, Settle remained active with his choir until his death, touring in the South and the far West.

BIBL: Black press, incl. CDef, 6 January 1940. Davis. Layne.

DISC: Turn in BPIM 9 (Spring 1981).

WINTERS, LAWRENCE (née **LAWRENCE WHISONANT**). Concert/opera singer (b. 12 November 1915 in Kings Creek, South Carolina; d. 24 September 1965 in Hamburg [?], Germany). He obtained his musical education in the public schools of Washington, D.C., where he was encouraged to study voice by Mary Europe*; and at Howard University in Washington, D.C. (B. Mus., 1941), where he studied with Todd Duncan,* sang in the college glee club, and was a soloist with the university choir. After leaving Howard he toured with the Eva Jessye* Choir. He first attracted wide attention in 1941 when he sang the role of Dessalines in a concert production of Clarence Cameron White's* opera, *Ouanga*, at the New School for Social Research in New York. During his years of service in the U.S. Armed Forces, he was director of music in the Special Services Division at Fort Huachuca, Arizona, and also an entertainer. In 1947 he made his debut as a concert baritone at Town Hall in New York; in 1948 he made his operatic debut as Amonasro in Verdi's *Aida* with the New York City Opera. Thereafter he toured widely in the Americas (including the Caribbean) and in Europe. In 1951 he sang the Messenger in the world premiere of David Tamkin's *Dybbuk* by the New York City Opera. In 1952 he made his European operatic debut as Amonasro at the Hamburg [Germany] State Opera. In addition to giving concerts and singing in operas, he also appeared in musicals, including the Broadway musical *Call Me Mister* (1946). During the years 1961-65 he was principal baritone at the Hamburg Opera. His best-known performances were as Dr. Miracle in Offenbach's *Tales of Hoffman*, Tschello in Prokofiev's *The Love of Three Oranges*, Marcello in Puccini's *La Boheme*, Canio in Leoncavallo's *I Pagliacci*, and in the title role of Verdi's *Rigoletto*.

BIBL: ChiHistSoc. Black press, incl. NYAge, 22 January 1944, 26 July 1941, 14 November 1959. CBDict.

DISC: Turn.

WITHERS, MAZIE MULLEN. Vaudeville trombonist (b. in Denver, Colorado; d. 14 October 1921 in New York, New York). Little is known of her career except that she was a band trombonist in the late nineteenth century, a period when few women, if any, played the trombone in public. She was active in Chicago, Illinois, early in her career, then moved to New York, where she played in the Lafayette Theater's Ladies Orchestra in the Harlem community. She toured with Will Marion Cook* and his New York Syncopated Orchestra in 1919.

BIBL: Black press, incl. NYAge, 5 November 1921.

WITHERSPOON, JAMES ("JIMMY"). Bluesman (b. 8 August 1923 in Gurdon, Arkansas). He sang in a local church choir as a child. Although he did not sing professionally, his first performances with a band came during the years of his service in the Merchant Marines (1941-43), when he sang with Teddy Weatherford* at Calcutta, India, and later on a Red Cross show. After returning to the United States, he sang with Jay McShann* (1944-48), then recorded and toured with various groups as a soloist. His recording of "Tain't nobody's business" in 1952 won him wide attention; thereafter he recorded extensively and toured at home and abroad, appearing in clubs, concert halls, and at the major blues and jazz festivals. Beginning in the 1970s his touring took him to Japan and other countries in the Far East. He settled in Los Angeles, California, during the same decade. There he organized his own production company. He also was active in films (title role in *The Black Godfather*, 1975), on television, and on radio programs with his own blues disc jockey show. He was a prolific songwriter.

BIBL: BWW. *Cadence* 3 (January 1978). FeaEJ. FeaJS. FeaGitJS. LivBl 33 (July-August 1977). MeeJMov.

DISC: Jep. TudBM.

WOMACK, ROBERT DWAYNE ("BOBBY"). Rhythm 'n' blues singer (b. 4 March 1944 in Cleveland, Ohio). He came from a musical family: his father played guitar and his mother sang. He and three brothers formed a gospel quartet, called The Womack Brothers, which toured on the gospel circuit for ten years. He played guitar and sang the lead. Later the group changed its name to The Valentines and began singing popular music. Their first recordings, "Looking for love" and "It's all over now," attracted wide attention. Womack left the family group to play guitar with Sam Cooke* (c1956-64). After Cooke's death he toured with various entertainers and also with his own groups. He gave primary attention, however, to writing songs, of which some of the best known were "That's the way I feel about cha," "Woman's gotta have it," and "It's all over now." He contributed music to the score for the film *Across 110th Street* (1972), along with J. J. Johnson.* During the 1970s he established his own music publishing company in Hollywood Hills, California. He received awards from the music industry.

BIBL: Black press, incl. AmstN, 7 July 1973. WWBA.

WONDER, STEVIE (née **STEVLAND JUDKINS;** aka **STEVELAND MORRIS, STEVELAND HARDAWAY).** Rhythm 'n' blues singer (b. 13 May 1950 in Saginaw, Michigan). His family moved to Detroit, Michigan, when he was an infant. Blind from birth, he won recognition as a child prodigy at an early age; he played several instruments, sang rhythm 'n' blues, and wrote his own songs. His style development was influenced by the blues he listened to on a local radio-network program titled "Sundown," particularly the singing of Riley ("B.B.") King.* He first played a harmonica, then later piano, organ, and drums. In 1961 Ronnie White of the Miracles* brought Stevie to the attention of Berry Gordy,* who added him to the Motown company (then called "Hitsville"). "Little Stevie Wonder" first attracted national attention in 1963 with his appearance in the Motown Revue at the Apollo Theater in the Harlem community of New York and with the release of his first records. Thereafter he toured widely throughout the world and recorded extensively. He obtained his musical training in the public schools of Detroit and at the Michigan School for the Blind in Lansing, Michigan (graduated 1968); when he was on tour a special tutor accompanied him. During the 1970s he studied further at the University of Southern California in Los Angeles.

He began writing most of the music he performed while still in his teens. Beginning in 1970, with "Signed, sealed, and delivered," he produced his own records. His growing musical maturity was made evident in that he turned away from the romantic ballads he sang in the 1960s towards music of serious content. During the 1970s his popularity increased, despite his temporary retirement from performance because of a near-fatal auto accident. He became one of the leading entertainer-songwriters of his time. He appeared on television and in films; his worldwide touring took him to the Far East and to Africa, where in 1977 he performed at FESTAC, the Second World African and Black Cultural Festival, held in Lagos, Nigeria. He began to use synthesizers during the 1970s and typically combined his own voice in "over-dubbing" style with the music-making of other musicians as background for his performance. After the mid-1970s he took longer and longer periods to prepare his productions. *Songs in the Key of Life* (1976) took more than two years, and *Journey Through the Secret Life of Plants* (1979) took three years. His best known compositions include the songs "Fingertips" (recorded when he was twelve years old), "You are the sunshine of my life," "My cherie amour," and "Uptight," and the albums *Music of My Mind*, *Talking Book*, *Innervisions*, and *Fulfillingness' First Finale*. He received numerous awards from the music industry and from civic and professional organizations. He was regarded by some as the "godfather of disco-soul."

BIBL: Black press, incl. AmstN, 10 November 1979. CurBiog (March 1975). *Ebony* (January 1977). StamPRS. WWA. WWBA.

DISC: TudBM.

WOOD, OBEDIAH. Society dance-band leader (b. c1815 in New York, New York; d. after 1865 in Detroit, Michigan). He went to Detroit, Michigan, some time in or before 1843. He and Joseph Charles Gillam* organized a dance orchestra, which gave a concert in March 1844. He and Gillam also set themselves up as music dealers, selling music and instruments. In 1847 they opened a dancing school and inaugurated a series of school-sponsored cotillions. They played for the city's important balls and in 1849 toured through the western part of Michigan. It is not known when Gillam dissolved his partnership with Wood; beginning in 1852 the press no longer included Gillam's name in referring to the band, O. C. Wood's Cotillion and Serenade Band. Wood continued his activity through the 1850s, then apparently was forced to retire because of the strong competition offered by new black bands in Detroit, especially that of Theodore Finney.*

BIBL: Black press. LaBrewS.

WOODARD, NELMATILDA RITCHIE. Music educator (b. 3 November 1913 in Alton, Illinois). Her family moved to Chicago, Illinois, when she was an infant. She began violin study at the age of six and gave her first solo recital when she was twelve. She obtained her musical education in the Chicago public schools, at the Ziegfeld Conservatory of Music in Chicago, at Northwestern University School of Music in Evanston,

Illinois (B. Mus., 1936; M. Mus. 1937), and at Loyola University, Chicago Musical College, and Chicago Teachers College. Her teaching career included tenures in the Chicago public schools as classroom teacher, music supervisor, and, beginning in the 1960s, director of music for the school system. She also toured as a lecturer and workshop consultant. She received numerous honors and awards from civic, community, and professional organizations as well as appointment to national boards of professional groups.

BIBL: ChiVH. Black press, incl. CDef, 19 June 1926. WWBA.

WOODING, SAMUEL DAVID ("SAM"). Jazz pianist (b. 17 June 1895 in Philadelphia, Pennsylvania). He began his professional career about 1912 in Atlantic City, New Jersey. In 1914 he went to New York, where he played piano for Madison Reid. After service in the United States Armed Forces during World War I, where he played in an army band, he organized his Society Syncopators. He played residencies with his group in Atlantic City, Detroit, Michigan, and New York during the years 1919-25. During this period he also played for a short time in the orchestra of the *Plantation Days* revue (1922), which starred Florence Mills* and Shelton Brooks.* In May 1925 he sailed to Europe with the *Chocolate Kiddies* revue as leader of the orchestra. After playing with the company a year, he toured with his group in Europe and South America. He returned to the United States in 1927, played in some vaudeville theaters but turned down an offer to play in a new nightclub, The Cotton Club, in the Harlem community of New York. The job went to the then-unknown Edward ("Duke") Ellington* and started him on the road to fame. During the years 1928-31 Wooding toured extensively in Europe, then played long residencies in the United States (1932-35), toured with his Southland Spiritual Choir (1937-41), and toured with other vocal groups (c1945-49). During the mid-1930s he attended the University of Pennsylvania in Philadelphia full-time and earned two degrees (B.S., M.Ed.). He taught in the early 1950s, then in 1953 became accompanist-manager for singer Rae Harrison, and thereafter the duo toured extensively throughout the world. In June 1975 he organized a big band, his first in forty years, which made its debut in New York with Harrison as the featured soloist. Wooding is credited with many "firsts" in jazz history: his was the first American band to make recordings in Europe in June 1925 (Paul Whiteman was second, in April 1926); the first black band to play a musical abroad—in the *Chocolate Kiddies* in Berlin, Germany; and the first black band to tour in the Soviet Union (1926) and in Scandinavia (1931). His contemporaries called him the "black dean of jazz."

BIBL: Black press. ChilWW. John S. Wilson, "Jazz Notes" in NYT, 8 June 1975.

DISC: RustJR. TudJ.

WOODWARD, SIDNEY. Concert singer (b. 16 October 1860 in Stockbridge, Georgia; d. 13 February 1924 in New York, New York). He received his musical training at the New England Conservatory in Boston, Massachusetts, where he studied with Edna Hall, among others. He began singing professionally in 1890 and toured extensively that year in the South as a concert tenor. About two years later he attracted the attention of Lillian Nordica, a soprano with the Metropolitan Opera, who was helpful in advancing his career. In 1893 he made his debut at Chickering Hall in Boston; later the same year he sang at the Chicago World's Fair on Colored American Day in August. In 1896 he joined John Isham's Oriental America company as the principal singer in that part of the program titled "Forty Minutes of Grand and Comic Opera"; assisting him were Inez Clough,* Belle Davis, J. Rosamond Johnson,* and Desseria Plato,* among others. During the years c1897-1900 he studied in Germany and received a certificate from the Royal Conservatory in Dresden. He also gave concerts while abroad. After returning to the United States he entered a teaching career, with tenures at the Florida Baptist Academy in Jacksonville, Clark College in Atlanta, Georgia, and the Music Settlement School for Colored in New York (1916-21). He also directed local church choirs. On 19 December 1921 the leading black musicians of the city joined him in a farewell concert at Carnegie Hall to celebrate the thirty-first anniversary of his musical career.

BIBL: Black press, incl. CleveG, 21 October 1893; NYAge, 28 September 1916, 10 December 1921, 23 February 1924.

WORK, FREDERICK JEROME. Folklorist/Music educator (b. 1879 in Nashville, Tennessee; d. 24 January 1942 in Bordentown, New Jersey). He came from a musical family: his father, John Wesley Work I (c1830-1923), was a church choir director in Nashville, Tennessee, who wrote and arranged music for his choirs, of whom some members had sung with the original Fisk Jubilee Singers.* One brother, John Wesley II,* became a composer and college music educator; other siblings followed musical careers; and two nephews, John Wesley III* and Julian,* became professional musicians. He obtained his musical education at Fisk University in Nashville, where he sang with the Fisk Jubilee Singers; at Columbia University Teachers College in New York; and at Temple University in Philadelphia, Pennsylvania. His teaching career included tenures at Prairie View State College in Texas; in the public schools of Kansas City, Missouri; and at the New Jersey Manual Training School in Bordentown, where he was music director for many years (1922-42). He wrote music and arranged spirituals for his school choir, which toured widely on the East Coast and sang regularly on radio programs. Although he composed instrumental works—of which the best known was *Negro Suite* (1936)—he was most noted for his spiritual arrangements and folksong collecting. Beginning in 1901 he and his brother, John Wesley II, published several collections of folksong arrangements, of which the first was titled *New Jubilee Songs as Sung by the Fisk Jubilee Singers*.

BIBL: Black press, incl. NYAge, 24 January 1942. William B. Garcia, "The Life and Choral Music of John Wesley Work III (1901-1967)" (Ph.D. diss., University of Iowa, 1973).

WORK, JOHN WESLEY I. See **WORK, FREDERICK JEROME** and **WORK, JOHN WESLEY II.**

WORK, JOHN WESLEY II. Composer/College professor (b. 6 August 1872 in Nashville, Tennessee; d. 7 September 1925 in Nashville). He came from a musical family: his father, John Wesley Work I (c1830-1923) was a church choir director in Nashville, Tennessee, who wrote and arranged music for his choirs, of whom some members sang with the original Fisk Jubilee Singers.* He attended Fisk University (B.A., 1895, M.A. 1898) in Nashville, Tennessee, where he was active in musical organizations, and Harvard University. In 1898 he was appointed to the Fisk faculty, and in 1906 he became chairman of the history and Latin department. As early as 1898 he began to reorganize Fisk singing groups to tour on the concert circuit and earn money as did the original Fisk Jubilee Singers* in the 1870s. Beginning in 1909 he toured with a Fisk Jubilee Quartet, composed of Alfred G. King, Noah W. Ryder, James A. Meyers, and himself. This group toured extensively and recorded for the Victor Talking Machine Company. Beginning in 1913 he established the tradition of presenting annual Fisk Jubilee Concerts. He also directed the University's Mozart Society (organized 1880), for which leading black artists of the nation were imported to sing solos at concerts. Occasionally he sang tenor solo parts in oratorios and cantatas, particularly at Henry Hugh Proctor's* Atlanta [Georgia] Colored Music Festivals (1910-1916). One of Work's major contributions was his effort to preserve the Negro spiritual. He collected black folksongs at an early age. In 1901 he and his brother, Frederick Jerome,* published the first of several collections of folksong arrangements, *New Jubilee Songs as Sung by the Fisk Jubilee Singers*, and in 1915 he published a treatise, *Folk Songs of the American Negro* (both published in Nashville). He resigned from Fisk in 1923 to accept the presidency of Roger Williams University in Nashville. His son, John Wesley Work, III* became a professional musician.

BIBL: Black press, incl. NYAge, 12 September 1925. William B. Garcia, "The Life and Choral Music of John Wesley Work" (Ph.D. diss., University of Iowa, 1973). HNB.

WORK, JOHN WESLEY III. Composer/College professor (b. 15 June 1901 in Tullahoma, Tennessee; d. 17 May 1967 in Nashville, Tennessee). He came from a family of professional musicians. His grandfather, John Wesley Work I,* was a church choir director in Nashville, Tennessee; he wrote and arranged music for his choirs, of whom some members sang with the original Fisk Jubilee Singers.* His father, John Wesley Work, II,* was a singer, folksong collector-arranger, and college music professor. An uncle, Frederick Jerome,* also collected and arranged folksongs. His mother, Agnes Hayes Work, was a singer, who also helped to train Fisk singing groups, and his brother Julian* became a professional musician. John Wesley participated in musical activities from earliest childhood and began piano study at the age of twelve. He obtained his musical training at the Fisk University laboratory school, the Fisk High School, and the University (B.A., 1923); the Institute of Musical Art (now the Juilliard School of Music) in New York (1923-24), where he studied with Gardner Lamson; Columbia University Teachers College in New York (M.A., 1930), where he studied with Howard Talley and Samuel Gardner; and Yale University in New Haven, Connecticut (B. Mus., 1933), where he studied with David Stanley Smith. He also studied voice privately with Lamson (1924-27). His entire teaching career was spent at Fisk University (1927-66); over the years he served in a variety of positions, as director of choral groups (with which he toured), teacher, lecturer in University-sponsored lecture series, and department chairman. He toured as a lecturer on the subject of black folksong and published articles in professional journals and music dictionaries over a period of more than thirty years; his best-known articles were "Plantation Meistersingers" in *The Musical Quarterly* (January 1940) and "Changing Patterns in Negro Folksongs" in *Journal of American Folklore* (October 1940). His other publications included the book *American Negro Songs and Spirituals* (1940), which contained folksong arrangements in addition to text.

He began composing during his high-school years and continued throughout his career. He wrote in a variety of musical forms—for full orchestra, piano, chamber ensemble, violin, and organ—but his largest output was in choral and solo-voice music. Best known of his instrumental works were *Yenvalou* for orchestra (1946), which used Haitian themes; the piano works *Sassafras* (1946), *Scuppernong* (1951) and *Appalachia* (1954); and the organ suite *From the Deep South* (1936). His best-known choral works were the cantata *The Singers* (1941) and the cycle *Isaac Watts Contemplates the Cross* (1962). His honors included Julius Rosenwald fellowships (1931, 1932), first prize in the 1946 competition of the Federation of American Composers for his cantata, an award from the National Association of Negro Musicians (1947), and an honorary doctorate from Fisk University (1963). His son, John Wesley Work IV, had a brief career as a professional singer.

BIBL: ASCAP. William Burres Garcia, "The Life and Choral Music of John Wesley Work" (Ph.D. diss., University of Iowa, 1973). WWCA 1950.

WORK, JULIAN C. Composer (b. 25 September 1910 in Nashville, Tennessee). See also **WORK, JOHN WESLEY III.** He came from a family of professional musicians. His father, John Wesley Work II,* was a folksong collector, singer, and college music teacher at Fisk University in Nashville, Tennessee. His mother, a singer, helped to train singing groups at Fisk, and his brother, John Wesley III,* was a composer and college music teacher. He studied music as a child with local teacher Mary E. Chamberlain and was involved in musical activities from early childhood along with other members of his family. He obtained his musical education at Fisk University. He began composing as early as 1948, with "Myriorama at Midnight" (performed by the Los Angeles Philharmonic), but did not publish his music until the 1950s. He wrote in many forms but gave primary attention to band and symphonic music. He was also an arranger. His best-known works were *Portraits from the Bible* (1956), "Processional Hymn" (1957), "Autumn Walk" (1957), "Driftwood Patterns" (1961), and "Stand the Storm" (1963).

BIBL: Questionnaire. William Burres Garcia, "The Life and Choral Music of John Wesley Work" (Ph.D. diss., University of Iowa, 1973).

WRIGHT, ANNIE BELL. Blues singer. See **DAVIS, GARY D.**

WRIGHT, JOSEPHINE R. B. College professor/ Musicologist (b. 5 September 1942 in Detroit, Michigan). She came from a musical family: her father, an Episcopalian priest, studied music with R. Nathaniel Dett* at Hampton Institute in Virginia. She began piano study at the age of three with her father. Later she studied piano and organ with Thomasina Talley Greene. She obtained her musical education in the preparatory schools of Lincoln University in Jefferson City, Missouri; in the college department of Lincoln (1959-61); at the University of Missouri (B. Mus., 1963; M.A., 1967), where she studied with Andrew Minor, who encouraged her to become a musicologist; at Pius XII Academy in Florence, Italy (M. Mus., 1964); and at New York University (Ph.D., 1975), where she studied with David Burrows and Jan LaRue. She made her concert debut as a soprano with the Jefferson City Philharmonic in 1967, Carl Burkle, conductor. Her career development as a musicologist was influenced and encouraged by Eileen Southern.* Her teaching career included tenures at York College of the City University of New York (1972-76) and at Harvard University in Cambridge, Massachusetts (1976-). She contributed articles to *The New Grove Dictionary of Music and Musicians* (sixth edition) and to such professional journals as *The Black Perspective in Music* (for which she also served as New Music editor), *The Musical Quarterly*, and *Notes* of the Music Library Association. Her book publications included *The Collected Works of Ignatius Sancho* (New York, 1981). She received fellowships and grants from the Cardinal Spellman Fund (1963), the American Association of University Women (1971), the Clark Fund at Harvard University (1978-80), and the National Endowment for the Humanities (1979-82).

BIBL: Questionnaire. IntWWM, 1975. WWAW.

WRIGHT, P[RESTON] T. Ministrel-troupe manager (b. 1857 in Mexico, Missouri; d. 15 March 1898 in Cincinnati, Ohio). His family moved to McComb, Illinois, when he was a child. A barber by trade, he became involved with show business at an early age and in 1874 joined T. H. Bland's Carolinians, a minstrel troupe, as a basso profundo. About 1884 he organized Wright's Nashville Students and Colored Comedy Company—also called the Nashville University Students and/or P. T. Wright's Colored Concert Company—which developed into one of the leading black touring groups of the late nineteenth century. His wife, Ida Lee Wright, contralto and dancer, assisted him and managed the company for a short period after his death. The Nashville Students served as a training ground for several who would later win recognition for their talents, including Sherman H. Dudley,* Dan Desdunes,* P. G. Lowery,* Harry Prampin, and James White, among others. About 1899 or 1900 the name of the group was changed to W. I. Swain's Nashville Students, after the name of the new manager, and P. G. Lowery served for a short time as the assistant manager.

BIBL: Black press, incl. IndF, 10 June 1893, 25 December 1897, 2 April 1898, 28 December 1901.

WYATT, KELLEY, E. Concert accompanist (b. 9 April 1923 in Fort Smith, Arkansas). He began piano study at the age of seven. He obtained his musical education at Xavier University in New Orleans, Louisiana (B.A., 1947) and Columbia University Teachers College in New York (M.A., 1949; doctoral studies, 1971-75). He studied piano and accompanying further with Maxim Schur, Franz Mittler, Frederick Kurzweil, Otto Herz, and Leo Taubman. He was encouraged to enter a career in accompanying by Sister M. Elise, founder of Opera/South* and Opera Ebony,* concert singers Hortense Love* and Ellabelle Davis,* and voice coach Carolinn S. Holden, among others. In 1954 he made his debut as an accompanist with soprano Helen Phillips at Town Hall in New York. Thereafter he toured widely as an accompanist in the Americas, Europe, and the Middle East. He was musical director for Kurt Weill's *Three-Penny Opera* in its first New York production (1955-57). He was also active as a voice coach and piano teacher; he conducted a private studio and taught at Hunter College of the City University of New York.

BIBL: Questionnaire. Edward J. Dwyer, *Singers in New York* (New York, 1972).

DISC: Turn (cf. Ellabelle Davis).

WYATT, LUCIUS REYNOLDS. University professor (b. 18 August 1938 in Waycross, Georgia). He studied piano as a child with his mother, a pianist, and began trumpet study at the age of twelve. He obtained his musical education in the public schools of Waycross, where he came under the tutelage of E. C. Christian, bandleader at the Central High School; at Florida A & M University in Tallahassee (B.S., 1959), where he studied with William P. Foster,* Johnnie V. Lee, Phillip Cooper, and Lenard C. Bowie, among others; and at the Eastman School of Music in Rochester, New York (M. Mus., 1960; Ph.D., 1974), where he studied with Robert V. Sutton (theory), Frederick Fennell, Sidney Mear, and Donald Hunsberger. He also studied trumpet privately in Philadelphia, Pennsylvania, with Sigmund Hering (1956). He made his first public appearance as a trumpet soloist in 1953 on a television talent show in Detroit, Michigan, station WXYZ-TV. At Florida A & M he played in the FAMU symphonic and marching bands and with the FAMU jazz orchestra. At Eastman he played in the symphony orchestra and in the Eastman Wind Ensemble (first trumpet). During his years of service in the U.S. Armed Forces (1963-65), he toured with the U.S. Army Headquarters Band in Europe. His teaching career included tenures at Tuskegee Institute in Alabama (1960-63; 1965-74) and at Prairie View State University (1974-), where he served as chairman of instrumental music and director of the symphonic band. He toured regularly as a concert trumpeter and as a member of the Prairie View Faculty Brass Quintet, particularly in the Southwest. He contributed articles to professional journals and was active as a composer and arranger. His best-known compositions were *Rondo for Brass Quartet* (1969), *Diversions for Solo Percussionist and Wind Ensemble* (1974), and *Centennial Salute for Symphonic Band* (1978).

BIBL: Questionnaire. *Outstanding Educators of America*, 1974. *WW in the South and Southwest*, 1980.

Y

YANCEY, ESTELLE ("MAMA"). Blues singer (b. 1 January 1896 in Cairo, Illinois. See **YANCEY, JAMES.**

YANCEY, JAMES EDWARD ("JIMMY"). Boogie-woogie pianist (b. 20 February 1898 in Chicago, Illinois; d. 17 September 1951 in Chicago). His father was a guitarist/singer, and a brother, Alonzo, became a pianist. He began performing professionally as a child as a singer and dancer and toured with vaudeville troupes at an early age. He toured in England before World War I. About 1915 he settled in Chicago, where he was active as a club pianist and "house-rent party" pianist; at the same time he worked full-time as a groundskeeper at the Comiskey White Sox (baseball) Park. He first recorded in 1939; his best-known records were "Yancey stomp" and the album *Yancey's Getaway*. His wife, "Mama" Estelle, was a blues singer, but did not sing professionally until the 1940s. In 1943 she made her first recording and thereafter recorded with various others in addition to her husband, among them, Richard M. Jones,* Eurreal ("Little Brother") Montgomery,* and Arthur ("Art") Hodes.

BIBL: BWW. *Cadence* interview of Mama Yancey, 4 (November 1978), ChilWW. FeaEJ. Oliv,

DISC: Kink, LeSIBR. RustJR.

YOUNG, LESTER ("PREZ"). Jazz saxophonist (b. 27 August 1909 in Woodville, Mississippi; d. 15 March 1959 in New York, New York). He came from a family of professional musicians. His father was a bandleader, his mother played piano, and his brother Leonidas ("Lee") became a professional jazz musician. His family moved to New Orleans, Louisiana, when he was an infant. The children studied instruments with their father and played in the Young family band, which toured on the vaudeville circuit and with carnivals and circuses in the Middle West and Southwest. In 1920 the Youngs moved to Minneapolis, Minnesota, which served thereafter as a base for their touring. Lester played drums in the family band, then changed to alto saxophone when he was thirteen. Three years later he left the family band to join Art Bronson's Bostonians (1928-29, 1930), based in Salina, Kansas. Thereafter he played with various groups, including the family band again in 1929, local groups in Minneapolis, the Original Blue Devils (1932-33), and bands in Kansas City, Missouri. During the early 1930s he also played for short periods with Fletcher Henderson* (1934), Andy Kirk,* William ("Count") Basie,* Clarence Love, Bennie Moten,* and Joseph ("King") Oliver.* In 1936 he rejoined Basie (1936-40), accompanying the band to New York, and made his recording debut the same year. Thereafter he recorded extensively, particularly with Billie Holiday*; during this period he acquired his nickname "Prez" (abbreviation for president) from Holiday, whom he called "Lady Day." During the early 1940s he led his own group (1941), co-led a group with his brother Lee (1941-43), which played residencies in Los Angeles, California, and in New York; worked with Al Sears, including a USO (United Service Organizations) tour; played briefly with John Birks ("Dizzy") Gillespie*; then rejoined Basie (1943-44). After serving in the United States Armed Forces (1944-45), he settled in Los Angeles. In 1946 he began a long association with the JATP (Jazz at the Philharmonic) shows, produced by Norman Grantz, and toured intermittently with the shows in the United States and in Europe (1946-59). He performed primarily as a soloist during his late career, although he occasionally led his own groups and played with big bands. His best-known performances were "Taxi war dance," "Jive at five," and "Lester leaps in." He was a seminal figure in the history of the jazz tenor saxophone, along with Coleman Hawkins.* His style was lyrical and tender, though reserved, with smoothly ''swinging'' lines, and he exerted wide influence on tenor players of his time.

BIBL: ASCAP. ChilWW. FeaEJ. MeeJMov. Lewis Porter in BPIM 9 (Spring 1981). Russ.

DISC: Kink. RustJR. TudJ.

Appendix 1

PERIOD OF BIRTH

THE COLONIAL ERA: 1640-1775

Allen, Richard
Bazadier, Philip
Benson, Nero
Brown, George
Brown, Scipio
Cozzens, Richard
Crossman, Simeon
Emidee
Fisk, Cato
Gardner, Newport
Gilliat, Simeon
Jolly, Jabez
Lew, Barzillai
Meude-Monpas, The Chevalier J.J.O de
Middleton, George
Nickens, William
Nunes Garcia, Jose
Perkins, Nimrod
Rodriguez, Sebastian
Saint-Georges, The Chevalier de
Sancho, Ignatius
Soubise, Julius
Tiffany, Cyrus

THE NEW NATION: 1776-1839

Aldridge, Ira
Allen, Peter
Alsdorf, Dubois
Anderson, Joseph
Appo, Ann
Appo, William
Augustus, Edward
Bowers, Thomas
Brady, William
Bridgetower, George Polgreen
Brindis de Salas, Claudio
Brown, George
Brown, Morris, Jr.
Brown, William Wells
Burris, Andrew
Butler, John
Carter, Dennis
Clark, James
Connor, Aaron J. R.
Conter, John
Cornmeali, Signor
Dede, Edmond
Delany, Martin
Dupree, William
Finney, Theodore
Fleet, James
Freeman, Bergert
Gillam, Joseph Charles
Gordon, Joseph
Greenfield, Elizabeth Taylor
Gutierrez y Espinosa, Felipe
Hazzard, Isaac
Hemmenway, James
Hewlett, James
Holland, Justin Miner
Jackson, William
Jeanty, Occilius
Jimenez-Berra, José Julio
Johnson, Francis
Jones, Robert C.
Julius, John
Lambert Family, The
Lane, William
Looks, Samuel
Luca Family, The
McCarty, Victor
Milburn, Richard
Moore, Hamilton A.
Murray, Robert
Noble, Jordan
Northup, Solomon
O'Fake, Peter
Payne, Daniel
Pindell, Annie
Plet, Anastase
Postlewaite, Joseph
Roland, Edward de
Scott, Robert
Seymour, Francis
Smith, Amanda
Snaër, Samuel
Soga, Tiyo
Washington, Rachel
Wall, Jesse
Weston, Bobby
Weston, Horace
White, José Silvestre
Wood, Obediah
Work, John Wesley I

THE ANTEBELLUM PERIOD: 1840-1862

Aldridge, Irene Luranah
Bares, Basile
Bethune, Thomas Green W.
Bland, James
Bohee, George
Bohee, James Douglass
Brindis de Salas, Claudio J. D.
Brindis de Salas, José R.
Brown Mitchell, Nellie
Craig, Walter F.
Desdunes, Rudolphe Lucien
Douglass, John Thomas
Geffrard, Robert
Hart, Henry
Hicks, Charles
Hyers, Anna Madah
Hyers, Emma Louise
Jamieson, Samuel
Jeanty, Occide
Jimenez-Berra, Jose Manuel
Johnson, Lew

1840-1862, continued

Johnson, William Francis
Kersands, William
King, Wallace
Layton, Sr., John Turner
Lewis, Frederick Elliot
Lewis, J. Henry
Loudin, Frederick
Love, James L.
Lucas, Sam
McAdoo, Orpheus Myron
McIntosh, Tom
Mando, Alfred F.
Martinez, Maria Loretto
Russell, Sylvester
Sawyer, Jacob
Selika, Marie
Simond, Ike
Smith, Henderson
Soga, John Henderson
Taylor, Marshall W.
Tilghman, Amelia L.
Tindley, Charles Albert
Tinsley, Pedro T.
Trotter, James Monroe
Washington, Rachel
Williams, Henry
Woodward, Sidney
Wright, Preston T.

POST-EMANCIPATION: 1863-1899

Accooe, Willis
Adams, Alton
Aldridge, Amanda
Allen, Cleveland G.
Amu, Ephraim
Anderson, Edward Gilbert
Anderson, Hallie
Arle-Tilz, Coretti
Armstrong, Lillian Hardin
Austin, Lovie
Ballanta-Taylor, Nicholas
Baquet, George
Barbour, J. Berni
Barrett, Emma
Batson, Flora
Bechet, Sidney
Blake, "Blind Arthur"
Blake, James Hubert
Bledsoe, Julius
Boatner, Edward H.
Bolden, Charles
Boone, John William
Bowman, Elmer
Bowman, Euday Louis
Bradford, Perry
Braud, Wellman
Brooks, Shelton
Broonzy, William Lee
Brown, Anita Patti
Brown, Lawrence
Brown, Thelma Wade
Brown, Tom
Browning, Ivan Harold
Brymn, James Timothy
Burleigh, Henry Thacker
Campbell, Lucie E.
Cannon, Gus
Celestin, Oscar
Chappelle, Patrick
Charlton, Melville
Chatmon, Armenter
Chatmon, Sam
Chauvin, Louis
Childers, Lulu
Clough, Estelle Pickney
Clough, Inez
Cole, Robert Allen
Coleridge-Taylor, Samuel
Collins, Cleota
Cook, Jean Lawrence
Cook, Will Marion
Cooke, Charles L.
Cotten, Elizabeth
Cox, Ida
Creamer, Henry
Creath, Charles
Cumbo, Marion
Dabney, Ford
Dabney, Wendell Phillips
Dafora, Asadata
Davenport, Charles
Davis, Clifton
Davis, Gary D.
Davis, Gussie Lord
Dawson, Mary Cardwell
Dawson, William Levi
De Bose, Tourgee
De Wolfe Sisters, The
Delisle, Louis Nelson
Deppe, Lois
Desdunes, Dan
Dett, Robert Nathaniel
Dickerson, Carroll
Diton, Carl Rossini
Dixon, Will
Dodds, Johnny
Dodds, Warren
Dorsey, Thomas Andrew
Dorsey, William H.
Douglas, Minnie
Douglass, Fannie Howard
Douglass, Joseph Henry
Dranes, Arizona
Drury, Theodore
Dudley, Sherman H.
Dulf, George
Dumervé, Constantin
Dunbar, Paul Laurence
Dunn, John
Dutrey, Honore
Edmonds, Shepherd
Edwards, Jody
Edwards, Susie
Elie, Justin
Ellington, Edward Kennedy
Estes, John
Europe, James Reese
Europe, Mary
Evanti, Lillian
Ferrell, Harrison Hubert
Fletcher, Tom
Forbes, Kathleen Holland
Foster, George Murphy
Freeman, Harry Lawrence
Frye, Theodore
Fuller, Jesse
Garner, George Robert
George, Maude Roberts
Gibbs, Lloyd
Gillam, Harry
Gilpin, Charles Sidney
Gordon, Taylor
Gossette, Walter
Griffin Sisters, The
Guy, Harry
Hackley, Emma Azalia
Hackney, William
Hagan, Helen Eugenia
Hall, Frederick D.
Hammond, Wade
Handy, William C.
Hare, Maud Cuney
Harreld, Kemper
Harrison, Frank
Harrison, Hazel
Hart, Myrtle
Harvey, Georgette
Hayden, Scott
Hayes, Robert
Hayes, Roland
Hegamin, Lucille Nelson
Henderson, Fletcher H.
Henderson, Rosa Deschamps
Hendricks, Frederick W.
Henry, Lew W.
Hill, John Leubrie
Hodges, M. Hamilton
Hogan, Ernest
Holt, Nora

Howard, Darnell
Hunter, Alberta
Hurt, John
Jackson, Anthony
Jackson, Charlie
Jackson, James Albert
Jefferson, Lemon
Jenkins, Edmund Thornton
Jessye, Eva
Johnson, Alonzo
Johnson, Francis Hall
Johnson, Fred
Johnson, J. C.
Johnson, James Price
Johnson, James Weldon
Johnson, John Rosamond
Johnson, John W.
Johnson, Tommy
Johnson, William Geary
Johnson, William Manuel
Jones, Clarence
Jones, Irving
Jones, J. Wesley
Jones, Louia Vaughn
Jones, M. Sissieretta
Jones, Mildred Bryant
Jones, Richard Myknee
Joplin, Scott
Jordan, Joe
Keppard, Freddie
Killingsworth, John Dekoven
Kirk, Andrew Dewey
Lamothe, Ludovic
Lawrence, William
Lawson, Raymond Augustus
Layne, Maude Wanzer
Layton, Jr., John Turner
Ledbetter, Huddie
Lee, George Ewing
Lee, Pauline James
LeMon, Lillian Morris
Lemonier, Tom
Lew, William Edward
Lewis, Walter
Lipscomb, Mance
Locke, Alain Leroy
Lofton, Clarence
Loving, Walter
Lovinggood, Penman
Lowery, Perry G.
Lucas, Carrie Melvin
Lucas, Marie
Lyles, Aubrey
Mabley, Jackie
McAfee, Charles
McClain, Billy
McDaniel, Hattie
McIntosh, Hattie
Mack, Cecil
McKinney, William
Marable, Fate
Margetson, Edward H.
Marshall, Arthur
Marshall, Harriet Gibbs
Martin, David I.
Martin, Sallie
Matthews, Artie
Mikell, Francis Eugene
Miller, Flournoy
Miller, Willie "Rice"
Mills, Florence
Mitchell, Abbie
Morrison, George
Morton, Ferdinand
Moten, Bennie
Motts, Robert
Mundy, James Ahlyn
Muse, Clarence
Nickerson, Camille Lucie
Nickerson, William Joseph
Noone, Jimmie
Oliver, Joseph
Ory, Edward
Overstreet, W. Benton
Pace, Harry
Patterson, Sam
Patterson, Ulysses S. Grant
Patton, Charley
Perryman, Rufus
Peyton, Dave
Phillips, T. K. E.
Picou, Alphonse F.
Pinkard, Maceo
Piron, Armand J.
Pittman, Portia Washington
Plato Broadley, Desseria
Porter, Oliva Shipp
Price, Florence B. Smith
Proctor, Henry Hugh
Rainey, Gertrude P.
Razaf, Andy
Rene, Otis J.
Richardson, William Howard
Ridley, Florida Ruffin
Roberts, Charles L.
Robeson, Paul
Rogers, Alexander C.
Rosemond, Andrew Fletcher
Ruffin, George L.
Scott, Arthur
Scott, James Sylvester
Shade, Will
Shipp, Jesse A.
Shook, Ben
Simpson, Frederick W.
Singleton, Arthur James
Sissle, Noble
Smith, Ada Beatrice
Smith, Bessie
Smith, Chris
Smith, Clara
Smith, Harry C.
Smith, Mamie
Smith, Nathaniel Clark
Smith, Raymond Lowden
Smith, William Henry J.
Spiller, Isabelle T.
Spiller, William Newmeyer
St. Cyr, John Alexander
Still, William Grant
Stone, Fred
Sweatman, Wilbur C.
Talbert, Florence Cole
Tapley, Daisy
Tate, Erskine
Taylor, Eva
Taylor, Tom Theodore
Thomas, Alfred Jack
Thompson, Charles Hubbard
Thompson, Dekoven
Thompson, Egbert
Tibbs, Roy Wilford
Tio, Lorenzo, Jr.
Tio, Lorenzo, Sr.
Tio, Luis
Turpin, Thomas Million
Tyers, William H.
Tyler, Jesse Gerald
Vaughn, James A.
Vodery, Will Henry B.
Walker, Aida Overton
Walker, George
Walker Turner, Rachel
Wallace, Beulah Thomas
Walton, Lester Aglar
Warfield, Charles
Watts, Nellie
Weir, Felix Fowler
Whatley, John T.
White, Clarence Cameron
White, Frederick Perry
Whitman, Alberta
Whitman, Essie Barbara
Whitman, Mable
Whitney, Salem Tutt
Williams, Clarence
Williams, Egbert Austin
Williams, J. Mayo
Williams, Sampson
Williams, Spencer
Williams, Stanley
Wilson, Edith
Wilson, W. Llewellyn
Withers, Mazie Muller

1863-1899, continued
Wooding, Samuel David
Work, Frederick Jerome
Work, John Wesley II
Yancey, Estelle
Yancey, James Edward

EARLY TWENTIETH CENTURY: 1900-1919

Alexander, Brooks
Allen, Henry James
Allen, William Duncan
Ammons, Albert
Anderson, Marian
Anderson, Pink
Anderson, T. C.
Anderson, Walter Franklin
Anderson, William Alonzo
Armstrong, Daniel Louis
Atkins, Marjorie R.
Bailey, Pearl
Baker, Josephine
Banks, Billy
Barbarin, Paul
Barker, Daniel
Bascomb, Paul
Bascomb, Wilbur Odell
Basie, William
Bates, Clayton
Berry, Leon
Bigard, Leon A.
Billups, Kenneth B.
Blackwell, Francis Hillman
Blakey, Art
Blanton, Carol
Blanton, James
Bonds, Margaret
Bostic, Earl
Bostic, Joe William
Boyd, Edward Riley
Bracken, James
Bradshaw, Myron
Brewster, W. Herbert
Brice, Carol
Brown, Anne Wiggins
Brown, John Harold
Bryant, William Steven
Buckner, Milton
Burnett, Chester Arthur
Bushell, Garvin Payne
Byas, Carlos Wesley
Byrd, Henry Roeland
Calloway, Blanche
Calloway, Cabell
Campbell, Ambrose
Carlisle, Una Mae
Carney, Harry Howell
Carr, Leroy
Carter, Bennett Lester
Catlett, Sidney
Cato, Minto
Chatman, Peter
Cheatham, Adolphus Anthony
Christian, Charles
Clark, Edgar Rogie
Clarke, Kenneth Spearman
Clayton, Wilbur
Cole, Nat "King"
Cole, William Randolph
Collymore, Winston
Cooper, Maurice
Cordero, Roque
Coston Maloney, Jean
Creach, John
Crudup, Arthur
Cumbo, Clarissa Burton
D'Albert, Marcus
Dameron, Tadley Ewing
Daniels, William
Dash, St. Julian B.
Davis, Ellabelle
Davis, William Strethen
De Paris, Sidney
De Paris, Wilbur
De Paur, Leonard
Dent, Jessie Covington
Dickenson, Victor
Dixon, Dean
Dixon, Willie James
Dowdy, Helen
Dunbar, Rudolph
Duncan, John
Duncan, Robert Todd
Dunham, Katherine
Durham, Eddie
Dyett, Walter Henri
Eckstine, William Clarence
Edison, Harry
Edwards, David
Eldridge, David Roy
Ellington, Mercer
Fax, Mark
Fitzgerald, Ella
Foster, William
Franklin, William
Fuller, "Blind Boy"
Fuller, Oscar Anderson
Fuller, Walter
Gatlin, F. Nathaniel
George, Zelma Watson
Gerren, Nicholas
Gillespie, John Birks
Glenn, Evans Tyree
Gonzales, Babs
Graham, Gladys
Graham Dubois, Shirley
Greene, John
Greer, William A.
Hairston, Jester
Hall, Adelaide
Hall, Edmond
Hall, Juanita
Hampton, Lionel
Hardwick, Otto
Harris, Wynonie
Hawkins, Coleman
Hawkins, Erskine Ramsay
Henderson, Horace
Heywood, Edward
Hibbler, Albert
Higginbotham, Irene
Higginbotham, Jack
Hill, Bertha
Hill, Theodore
Hines, Earl Kenneth
Hines Matthews, Altonell B.
Hinton, Milton J.
Hite, Les
Hodges, John Cornelius
Holiday, Billie
Holland, Charles
Hooker, John Lee
Hopkins, Claude
Hopkins, Sam
Horne, Lena
House, Eddie James
Hughes, Langston
Humes, Helen
Hunter, Ivory Joe
Jackson, Clifton Luther
Jackson, Gertrude Smith
Jackson, Graham W.
Jackson, Mahalia
Jackson, Melvin
James, Nehemiah
James, Willis Laurence
Jarboro, Caterina
Jefferson, Edgar
Jeffries, Herb
Johns, Altona Trent
Johnson, Albert
Johnson, Pete
Johnson, Robert
Jones, Henry
Jones, James Henry
Jones, Jonathan
Jones, Robert Elliott
Jordan, Louis
Kay, Ulysses
Kerr, Thomas
Kirby, John
Ladnier, Thomas
Lawson, Warner

Lee, Everett
Lee, Julia
Lee, Sylvia Olden
Lewis, George Francis
Lewis, Mabel Sanford
Lewis, Meade
Lockwood, Robert
Long, Avon
Love, Hortense
Love, Josephine Harreld
Lovell, John
Luandrew, Albert
Lunceford, James Melvin
Lutcher, Nellie
McCoy, Robert Lee
McDowell, Frederick
McGhee, Howard
McGhee, Walter
McKinney, Nina Mae
McNeil, Claudia Mae
McShann, Jay
Martin, David Irwin, Jr.
Martin, Eugene Mars
Martin, Gertrude
Martin, Roberta
Matthews, Edward
Matthews, Inez
Maynor, Dorothy
Mensah, Emmanuel Tetteh
Mercer, Mabel
Merrifield, Norman L.
Middleton, Velma
Miley, James Wesley
Millinder, Lucius
Mills Brothers, The
Monk, Thelonious S.
Montgomery, Eurreal
Moore, Undine Smith
Morgan, Albert
Morganfield, McKinley
Morton, Henry Sterling
Moten Barnett, Etta
Mundy, James
Nance, Willis
Nanton, Joseph
Nicholas, Albert
Nixon, Hammie
Nolan, Robert L.
Norman, Fred
Northern, Chauncey
Oliver, Melvin James
Page, Oran Thaddeus
Page, Walter Sylvester
Pankey, Aubrey
Parks, Gordon A.
Parrish, Avery
Payne (or Paine), Benny
Pierce, Joseph D. L.Croix
Pierce, Wilhelmina G.
Pittman, Evelyn La Rue
Polin, Roscoe
Price, Jesse
Price, Samuel Blythe
Rachell, James
Rahn, Muriel
Redman, Donald Matthew
René, Leon T.
Rhea, La Julia
Rhodes, Todd Washington
Roldan, Amadeo
Rushing, James Andrew
Russell, Luis
Ryder, Noah
Sampson, Edgar Melvin
Saunders, Theodore D.
Scott, Cecil Xavier
Sears, Albert Omega
Sedric, Eugene Hall
Shavers, Charles James
Shepherd, Berisford
Shines, John Ned
Simeon, Omer Victor
Smith, Cladys
Smith, Clarence
Smith, Henry
Smith, Hezekiah Leroy G.
Smith, Joe
Smith, Richard Joseph
Smith, William McLeish
Smith, Willie Mae Ford
Smyles, Harry
Snow, Valaida
Snowden, Elmer Chester
South, Eddie
Sowande, Fela
Spencer, Kenneth
Spivey, Victoria Regina
Stackhouse, Houston
Stewart, Rex William
Stone, Jesse
Stone, Theodore
Strayhorn, William
Sublett, John William
Sullivan, Maxine
Sun Ra
Suthern, Orrin Clayton
Swanson, Howard
Sykes,Roosevelt
Tatum, Arthur
Taylor, Theodore R.
Terrell, Saunders
Tizol, Juan
Turner, Joe
Turner, Joseph Vernon
Van Buren, Catherine
Vinson, Eddie
Vinson (or Vincent), Walter Jacob
Von Charlton, Rudolph Everett
Walker, Aaron Thibeaux
Waller, Thomas Wright
Warren, Guy
Waters, Ethel
Weatherford, Teddy
Webb, William
Webster, Benjamin Francis
Wells, William
White, Booker T. Washington
White, Joshua Daniel
White, Portia
Whitman, Alice
Whittaker, Hudson
Williams, Charles Melvin
Williams, Joe
Williams, Joe
Williams, Mary Lou
Williams, Robert Pete
Williamson, John Lee
Wilson, Gerald Stanley
Wilson, Theodore
Winters, Lawrence
Woodard, Nelmatilda R.
Work, John Wesley III
Work, Julian C.
Young, Lester

POST-WORLD WAR I: 1920-

Abdul-Rahim, Raoul
Abrams, Richard Louis
Acquaye, Saka
Adams, Armenta
Adams, Elwyn Albert
Adams, Ishmael Kwesi
Adderley, Julian Edwin
Adderley, Nathaniel
Addison, Adele
Akpabot, Samuel
Allen, Betty Lou
Allen, Sanford
Allison, Luther
Ammons, Eugene
Amoaku, William
Anderson, Joseph G.
Anderson, Thomas Jefferson
Anikulapo-Kuti, Fela
Aning, Ben Akosa
Arroyo, Martina
Ashby, Dorothy Jeanne
Ashford, Nickolas
Atkins, Carl
Atkins, Russell
Axelsen, Doris Holland
Ayers, Roy
Ayler, Albert

1920-, continued

Ayler, Donald
Bailey, Evangeline G.
Baker, David N.
Baker, La Vern
Balthrop, Carmen Arlene
Bankole, Ayo
Baraka, Imamu Amiri
Barrett Campbell, Delois
Barron, Kenneth
Barron, William
Bartz, Gary Lee
Bassey, Shirley
Bebey, Francis
Belafonte, Harold George
Bell, Thom R.
Benson, George
Benton, Brook
Berry, Charles Edward
Bibb, Leon
Bland, Robert Calvin
Boatwright, McHenry
Bonnemere, Edward
Booth, Alan
Boyer, Horace C.
Bradford, Alex
Braithwaite, James Roland
Brand, Adolph J.
Braxton, Anthony
Brewster, W. Herbert
Brooks, Tilford
Brown, James
Brown, Marion
Brown, Oscar, Jr.
Brown, William Albert
Bryant, Joyce
Bumbry, Grace Ann
Burgie, Irving Louis
Burrell, Kenneth Earl
Butcher, Vada Easter
Butler, Jerry
Byard, John A.
Byrd, Donaldson T.
Caesar, Shirley
Calloway, Earl
Capers, Valerie
Carey, Thomas Devore
Carroll, Diahann
Carter, Betty
Carter, Ronald Levin
Chambers, Joseph
Chambers, Paul Laurence, Jr.
Charles, Ray
Cheeks, Julius
Cherry, Donald E.
Cleveland, James
Cliff, James
Coates, Dorothy Love
Cobham, William Emanuel
Cole, Frances Elaine
Coleman, Ornette
Coltrane, Alice McLeod
Coltrane, John William
Cooke, Sam
Cooper, Clarence
Cooper, Jerome
Cooper, William Benjamin
Cotton, James
Cowell, Stanley
Crouch, Andrae
Cunningham, Arthur
Da Costa, Noel
Dandridge, Dorothy
Daniel, Billie Lynn
Davis, Arthur D.
Davis, Eddie
Davis, Miles Dewey, Jr.
Davis, Richard
Davis, Sammy, Jr.
Davison Watkins, Harriette
Davy, Gloria
Dawkins, James
De Priest, James Anderson
Dibango, Manu
Dickerson, Roger
Dixon, Jessy
Dixon, Lucille
Dixon, William Robert
Dobbs, Mattiwilda
Dolphy, Eric Allan
Domino, Antoine
Donegan, Dorothy
Dorham, McKinley Howard
Drew, Kenneth Sidney
Duke, George
Eaton, Roy
Edet, Edna Smith
Ekwueme, Lazarus Edward
El-Dabh, Halim
Estes, Simon Lamont
Euba, Akin
Evans, Ernest
Farmer, Arthur
Favors, Malachi
Fischer, William S.
Flack, Roberta
Flanagan, Tommy Lee
Floyd, Samuel
Foster, Frank B.
Fountain, III, Primous
Franklin, Aretha
Frazier, James
Freeman, Paul D.
Frierson, Andrew
Fulson, Lowell
Furman, James B.
Gamble, Kenneth
Garcia, William
Garland, Phyllis T.
Garner, Errol L.
Gaston, Oland
Gaye, Marvin
Goines, Leonard
Golson, Benny
Gordon, Dexter Keith
Gordon, Odetta
Gordy, Berry, Jr.
Grant, Micki
Grant, Earl
Green, Al
Griffin, Bessie
Griffin, John Arnold
Grist, Reri
Guy, George
Hailstork, Adolphus
Hakim, Talib Rasul
Hall, Ian
Hamilton, Foreststorn
Hancock, Eugene Wilson
Hancock, Herbert Jeffrey
Handy, John
Handy Miller, D. Antoinette
Harris, Carl Gordon
Harris, Hilda
Harris, Margaret R.
Hathaway, Donny
Havens, Richard Pierce
Hawes, Hampton
Hawkins, Edwin
Hayes, Isaac
Haynes, Eugene
Haynes, Roy Owens
Heath, Albert
Heath, James Edward
Heath, Percy
Hendricks, John Carl
Hendrix, James Marshall
Hibbert, Frederick
Hill, Andrew
Hillery, Mable
Hinderas, Natalie
Hobson, Ann
Holmes, Robert
Hopkins, Linda
Hubbard, Frederick D.
Huff, Leon
Hunt, Darrold Victor
Hutcherson, Robert
Isley Brothers, The
Jackson, Isaiah
Jackson, Lawrence
Jackson, Milton
Jackson, Raymond T.
Jackson Five, The

Jacobs, Marion Walter
Jacquet, Jean Baptiste
Jamal, Ahmad
James, Etta
Jarman, Joseph
Jenkins, Leroy
Johnson, Folorunso
Johnson, James Louis
Jones, Elayne
Jones, Elvin Ray
Jones, Harold
Jones, Joseph Rudolph
Jones, Pearl Williams
Jones, Quincy Delight
Jones, Thaddeus Joseph
Jordan, Clifford Laconia
Jordan, Robert
Kemp, Emmerlyne J.
Kendricks, Edward
Kennedy, Anne Gamble
Kennedy, Joseph J.
Kennedy, Matthew W.
Kenyatta, Robin
Killebrew, Gwendolyn
King, Albert
King, Betty
King, Coretta Scott
King, Freddie
King, Frederick
King, Juanita
King, Riley B.
Kirk, Rahsaan Roland
Kitt, Eartha Mae
Knight, Gladys M.
Knight, Marie
Labelle, Patti
Labrew, Arthur Randolph
Ladipo, Duro
Laine, Cleo
Lake, Oliver
Lateef, Yusef
Laws, Hubert
Laws, Ronald
Lee, A. Clifton
Lee, William James
Leon, Tania
Lester, Julius B.
Lewis, Elma Ina
Lewis, Henry Jay
Lewis, John Aaron
Lewis, Ramsey Emanuel
Lincoln, Abbey
Liston, Melba Doretta
Little, Vera
Logan, Wendell
Lucien, Jon
Lymon, Frankie
McCann, Leslie Coleman
McCoy, Seth
McDaniel, Ellas
McFerrin, Robert
McGinty, Doris Evans
McIntyre, Kenneth Arthur
McLean, John Lenwood
McLin, Lena Johnson
McNair, Barbara
McPhatter, Clyde Lensey
McRae, Carmen
Madison, Earl
Madonsela, Eugene
Makeba, Miriam Zenzi
Marley, Robert Nesta
Masekela, Hugh
Mathis, Johnny
Mathis, Joyce
Maultsby, Portia Katrenia
Mayfield, Curtis
Meadows, Eddie Spencer
Mims, Grace Lee
Mingus, Charles
Mitchell, Leona
Mitchell, Roscoe
Mitchell, William
Montgomery, Charles
Montgomery, John Leslie
Montgomery, William Howard
Moore, Carman Leroy
Moore, Dorothy Rudd
Moore, Kermit
Moore, Melba
Moorehead, Consuela Lee
Nash, John
Navarro, Theodore
Nelson, Oliver Edward
Newman, Joseph Dwight
Newson, Roosevelt
Nketia, Joseph H. Kwabena
Nzewi, Emeka Meki
Norman, Jessye
Ofori, Agyare T.
Olatunji, Michael B.
Osei, Teddy
Ousley, Curtis
Owens, James Robert
Parker, Charles C.
Parker, Herman
Parker, Louise
Patterson, Willis Charles
Paul, Billy
Payne, Cecil McKenzie
Penniman, Richard
Perkinson, Coleridge Taylor
Perry, Julia
Peters, Brock
Peterson, Elwood
Peterson, Oscar Emmanuel
Pettiford, Oscar
Phillips, Esther
Pickett, Wilson
Pierson, Edward
Poindexter, Norwood
Porter, Karl Hampton
Powell, Earl
Prattis Jennings, Patricia
Preston, William
Price, John E.
Price, Leontyne
Pride, Charley
Prysock, Arthur
Rawls, Louis Allen
Ray Russell, Carline
Redding, Otis
Redman, Walter Dewey
Reed, Addison W.
Reed, Mathis James
Reese, Della
Reeves, Martha
Ridley, Laurence Howard
Rivers, Clarence Joseph
Rivers, Samuel Carthorne
Roach, Hildred
Roach, Maxwell
Roberts, Howard
Robinson, Faye
Rogers, James
Rollins, Theodore Walter
Ross, Diana
Rush, Otis
Russell, George Allan
Ryder, Georgia Atkins
Sanders, Farrell
Santamaria, Ramon
Schuyler, Philippa Duke
Scott, Hazel Dorothy
Scott, Shirley
Sellers, John B.
Shepp, Archie Vernon
Shirley, Donald
Shirley, George Irving
Short, Robert Waltrip
Shorter, Wayne
Silver, Horace Ward M. T.
Simmons, Calvin
Simone, Nina
Simpson, Eugene Thamon
Simpson, Valerie
Sirone
Smith, Albert
Smith, Hale
Smith, James Oscar
Smith, Leo
Smith, Lonnie Liston
Smith, Mabel Louise
Smith, Muriel

1920-, continued
Smith, Richard Donald
Smith, Warren I.
Southall, Geneva Handy
Southern, Eileen Jackson
Spann, Otis
Spearman, Rawn
Spellman, A. B.
Standifer, James
Staton, Dakota
Stitt, Edward
Summer, Donna
Tabu, Pascal
Taj Mahal
Tapscott, Horace
Taylor, Cecil Percival
Taylor, Cora Walton
Taylor, William
Tchicai, John Martin
Terry, Clark
Tharpe, Rosetta Nubin
Thomas, C. Edward
Thompson, Arthur
Thompson, Eli
Thompson, Leon Evanette
Thornton, Willie Mae
Tillis, Frederick C.
Tucker, Robert Nathaniel
Turner, Ike and Tina
Turrentine, Stanley
Tyler, Veronica
Tyner, Alfred McCoy
Tynes, Margaret
Uggams, Leslie
Utterback, Clinton
Van Peebles, Melvin
Vaughan, Sarah Lou
Vereen, Benjamin A.
Verrett, Shirley
Walker, Frances
Walker, George T.
Walton, Ortiz
Ward, Clara
Warfield, William Caesar
Warwick, Dionne
Washington, Dinah
Washington, Grover
Watkins, Julius Burton
Watts, Andre
Weathers, Felicia
Wells, Amos
Weston, Randolph
Whalum, Wendell P.
White, Andrew Nathaniel
White, Barry
White, Christopher
White, Donald Edward
White, Maurice
White, Willard Wentworth
Wilder, Joseph Benjamin
Wilkins, Ernest Brooks
Wilkins, Joe Willie
Williams, Camilla
Williams, Marion
Wilson, Nancy
Wilson, Olly Woodrow
Witherspoon, James
Womack, Robert Dwayne
Wonder, Stevie
Wright, Josephine
Wyatt, Kelley E.
Wyatt, Lucius

Appendix 2

PLACE OF BIRTH

AFRICA

CAMEROON
Bebey, Francis (Doula)
Dibango, Manu (Doula)

EGYPT
El-Dabh, Halim (Cairo)

GHANA
Acquaye, Saka (Accra)
Adams, Ishmael Kwesi (Accra)
Amoaku, William (Ho)
Amu, Ephraim (Peki-Avetile)
Aning, Ben Akosa (Dampong)
Mensah, Emmanuel Tetteh (Accra)
Nketia, Joseph H. Kwabena (Mampong)
Ofori, Agyare T. (Odumase Manya Krobo)
Osei, Teddy (Kumasi)

NIGERIA
Akpabot, Samuel (Uyo)
Anikulapo-Kuti, Fela (Abeokuta)
Bankole, Ayo (Lagos)
Campbell, Ambrose (Lagos)
DaCosta, Noel (Lagos)
Ekwueme, Lazarus Edward (Oko)
Euba, Akin (Lagos)
Johnson, Folorunso (Lagos)
Ladipo, Duro (Oshogbo)
Nzewi, Emeka Meki (Nnewi)
Olatunji, Michael B. (Ajido-Badagry)
Phillips, T. K. E.
Sowande, Fela (Oyo)
Warren, Guy (Lagos)

SOUTH AFRICA
Brand, Adolph J. (Capetown)
Makeba, Miriam Zenat (Johannesburg)
Masekela, Hugh (Wilbank)
Soga, John Henderson (Emgwali)
Soga, Tiyo (Gwali)

WEST AFRICA
Cozzens, Richard
Emidee (Guinea)
Gardner, Newport
Rodriguez, Sebastian (Rio Llanero, Guinea)
Sancho, Ignatius (Guinea)
Ballanta-Taylor, Nicholas G. J. (Kissy, Sierra Leone)
Dafora, Asadata (Freetown, Sierra Leone)
Thompson, Egbert (Sierra Leone)

ZAIRE
Tabu, Pascal (Bandundu, Kinshasa)

CANADA

Brooks, Shelton (Amesburg, Ontario)
Dett, Robert Nathaniel (Drummondsville, Ontario)
Forbes, Kathleen Holland (Hamilton, Ontario)
Johnson, John W. (Chatham, Ontario)
Looks, Samuel (Quebec)
Marshall, Harriet Gibbs (Vancouver)
Peterson, Oscar Emmanuel (Montreal, Quebec)
Richardson, William (Liverpool, Nova Scotia)
Stone, Fred (Chatham, Ontario)
White, Portia (Truro, Nova Scotia)

CARIBBEAN

ANTIGUA
Williams, Egbert

CUBA
Brindis de Salas, Claudio (Havana)
Brindis de Salas, Claudio J. D. (Havana)
Brindis de Salas, José R. (Havana)
Jimenez-Berra, Jose Julio (Trinidad da Cuba)
Jimenez-Berra, Jose Manuel (Trinidad da Cuba)
Leon, Tania (Havana)
Martinez, Maria Loretto (Havana)
Roldan, Amadeo (Havana)
Santamaria, Ramon (Havana)
White, Jose Silvestre (Matanzas)

DOMINICA
Cumbo, Clarissa (Roseau)

GUADELOUPE
Bazadier, Philip
Saint-Georges, The Chevalier de (Basse Terre)

HAITI
Dumervé, Constantin (Môle St. Nicolas)
Elie, Justin (Cap-Haitien)
Geffrard, Robert (Gonaives)
Hill, Andrew (Port-au-Prince)
Jeanty, Occide (Port-au-Prince)
Jeanty, Occilius (Port-au-Prince)
Lamothe, Ludovic (Port-au-Prince)
Roland, Edward de. (?)

JAMAICA
Cliff, James (West Kingston)
Hibbert, Frederick (May Pen)
Marley, Robert (Rhoden Hall)
Shirley, Donald (Kingston)
White, Willard Wentworth

MARTINIQUE
Johnson, Francis

TRINIDAD
Hendricks, Frederick W. (Port of Spain)
Scott, Hazel Dorothy (Port of Spain)

VIRGIN ISLANDS
Adams, Alton Augustus (St. Thomas)
Lucien, Jon (Tortola)
Margetson, Edward H. (St. Kitts)
Soubise, Julius (St. Kitts)

WEST INDIES: COUNTRY UNKNOWN
Butler, John
Hewlett, James

CENTRAL AMERICA

HONDURAS
Shepherd, Berisford (Spanish Honduras)

PANAMA
Cobham, William Emanuel
Cordero, Roque (Panama City)
Russell, Luis (Bocas del Toro)

EUROPE

BRITISH ISLES
Aldridge, Amanda (Upper Norwood, London)
Aldridge, Irene Luranah (London)
Bassey, Shirley (Cardiff, Wales)
Coleridge-Taylor, Samuel (Holborn)
Laine, Cleo (Southall)
Mercer, Mabel (Staffordshire)

DENMARK
Tchicai, John Martin (Copenhagen)

FRANCE
Meude-Monpas, The Chevalier, J. J. O. (Paris)

GERMANY
Watts, Andre (Nuremburg)

POLAND
Bridgetower, George Polgreen (Baila)

MEXICO

Tio, Lorenzo, Sr.
Tio, Luis

SOUTH AMERICA

BRAZIL
Nunez Garcia, Jose Mauricio N. (Rio de Janeiro)

GUYANA
Dunbar, Rudolph (Nabaclis)
Hall, Ian (Georgetown)

UNITED STATES

ALABAMA
Atkins, Carl (Birmingham)
Axelsen, Doris Holland (Birmingham)
Bascomb, Paul (Birmingham)
Bascomb, Wilbur Odell (Birmingham)
Bradford, Alex (Bessemer)
Bradford, Perry (Montgomery)
Calloway, Earl (Birmingham)
Coates, Dorothy Love (Birmingham)
Cole, Nat "King" (Montgomery)
Davenport, Charles (Anniston)
Dawson, William Levi (Anniston)
Duncan, John (Lee County)
Europe, James Reese (Mobile)
Europe, Mary (Mobile)
Gordon, Odetta (Birmingham)
Hammond, Wade
Handy, William C. (Florence)
Hawkins, Erskine Ramsay (Birmingham)
Hill, Theodore (Birmingham)
James, Willis Laurence (Montgomery)
Kendricks, Edward (Union Springs)
King, Coretta Scott (Marion)
Lee, A. Clifton (Snow Hill)
Lee, William James (Snow Hill)
Millinder, Lucius (Anniston)
Mims, Grace Lee (Snow Hill)
Parrish, Avery (Birmingham)
Pickett, Wilson (Prattville)
Pittman, Portia Washington (Tuskegee)
Rivers, Clarence Joseph (Selma)
Smith, Clarence (Troy)
Spearman, Rawn (Bexar)
Sun Ra (Birmingham)
Thornton, Willie Mae (Montgomery)
Washington, Dinah (Tuscaloosa)
Whatley, John T. (Tuscaloosa)
Williams, Charles Melvin (Mobile)

ARIZONA
Kay, Ulysses (Tucson)
Mingus, Charles (Nogales)

ARKANSAS
Allison, Luther (Mayflower)
Cato, Minto (Little Rock)
Green, Al (Forrest City)
Hibbler, Albert (Little Rock)
Jarman, Joseph (Pine Bluff)
Johnson, Fred (Pine Bluff)
Jordan, Louis (Brinkley)
Lake, Oliver (Marianna)
Lockwood, Robert (Marvell)
McCoy, Robert Lee (Helena)
McFerrin, Robert (Marianna)
Price, Florence B. Smith (Little Rock)
Sanders, Farrell (Little Rock)
Sykes, Roosevelt (Elmar)
Tharpe, Rosetta Nubin (Cotton Plant)
Warfield, William Caesar (West Helena)
Whitman, Essie Barbara (Osceola)
Witherspoon, James (Gurdon)
Wyatt, Kelley E. (Fort Smith)

CALIFORNIA
Ayers, Roy (Los Angeles)
Berry, Charles Edward (San Jose)
Bryant, Joyce (San Francisco)
Crouch, Andrae (Los Angeles)
Dolphy, Eric Allan (Los Angeles)
Duke, George (San Rafael)
Gordon, Dexter Keith (Los Angeles)
Hamilton, Foreststorn (Los Angeles)
Hawes, Hampton (Los Angeles)
Hawkins, Edwin (Oakland)
Hutcherson, Robert (Los Angeles)
Hyers, Anna Madah (Sacramento)
Hyers, Emma Louise (Sacramento)
James, Etta (Los Angeles)
Lewis, Henry Jay (Los Angeles)
Mathis, Johnny (San Francisco)
Simmons, Calvin (San Francisco)
Spencer, Kenneth (Los Angeles)

COLORADO
Lucas, Marie (Denver)
Withers, Mazie Muller (Denver)

CONNECTICUT
Lawson, Warner (Hartford)
Luca Family, The
Silver, Horace Ward M. T. (Norwalk)
Weston, Horace (Derby)

DISTRICT OF COLUMBIA
Balthrop, Carmen Arlene (Washington)
Batson, Flora (Washington)
Cook, Will Marion (Washington)
Dabney, Ford (Washington)
Douglass, Joseph Henry (Washington)
Ellington, Edward Kennedy (Washington)
Ellington, Mercer (Washington)
Evanti, Lillian (Washington)
Fleet, James (Washington)
Gaye, Marvin (Washington)
Hardwick, Otto (Washington)
Jamieson, Samuel (Washington)
Jones, Pearl Williams (Washington)
Layton, Jr., John Turner (Washington)
Lee, Sylvia Olden (Washington)
Lewis, J. Henry (Washington)
McGinty, Doris Evans (Washington)
Mills, Florence (Washington)
Moore, Dorothy Rudd (Washington)
Razaf, Andy (Washington)

Tilghman, Amelia L. (Washington?)
Walker, Frances (Washington)
Walker, George T. (Washington)
White, Andrew Nathaniel (Washington)

FLORIDA
Adderley, Julian Edwin (Tampa)
Adderley, Nathaniel (Tampa)
Blake, "Blind Arthur" (Jacksonville?)
Boyer, Horace C. (Winter Park)
Brown, Lawrence (Jackonsville)
Chappelle, Patrick (Jacksonville)
Daniels, William (Jacksonville)
De Bose, Tourgee (Gainesville)
Edwards, Susie (Pensacola)
Floyd, Samuel (Tallahasee)
Fountain, III, Primous (St. Petersburg)
Goines, Leonard (Jacksonville)
Johnson, James Weldon (Jacksonville)
Johnson, John Rosamond
Knight, Marie (Sanford)
Maultsby, Portia Katrenia (Orlando)
Moorehead, Consuela Lee (Tallahassee)
Navarro, Theodore (Key West)
Norman, Fred (Leesburg)
Pierce, Wilhelmina G. (Marianna)
Shepp, Archie Vernon (Ft. Lauderdale)
Vereen, Benjamin A. (Miami)
Williams, Marion (Miami)

GEORGIA
Bethune, Thomas Green W. (Columbus)
Boatwright, McHenry (Tennille)
Brown, Anita Patti (?)
Brown, James (Augusta)
Brown, John Harold (Shellman)
Brown, Marion (Atlanta)
Charles, Ray (Albany)
Clark, Edgar Rogie (Atlanta)
Clark, James (Burke County)
Cole, Robert Allen (Athens)
Conter, John (DeKalb)
Cox, Ida (Toccoa)
Dobbs, Mattiwilda (Atlanta)
Dorsey, Thomas Andrew (Villa Rica)
Douglass, Fannie Howard (Atlanta)
Edwards, Jody
Fuller, Jesse (Jonesboro)
Greene, John (Columbus)
Hall, Frederick D. (Atlanta)
Hayes, Roland (Curryville)
Hegamin, Lucille Nelson (Macon)
Henderson, Fletcher H. (Cuthbert)
Henderson, Horace (Cuthbert)
Heywood, Edward (Atlanta)
Higginbotham, Jack (Social Circle)
Hillery, Mable (La Grange)
Johnson, Francis Hall (Athens)
Kennedy, Matthew W. (Americus)
King, Juanita (Macon)
Knight, Gladys M. (Atlanta)
Logan, Wendell (Thomson)
Love, Josephine H. (Atlanta)
Martin, Sallie (Pittfield)
McLin, Lena Johnson (Atlanta)
Noble, Jordan
Norman, Jessye (Augusta)
Pace, Harry (Covington)
Penniman, Richard (Macon)
Rainey, Gertrude P. (Columbus)
Redding, Otis (Dawson)
Sirone (Atlanta)
Smith, Cladys (Pembroke)
Swanson, Howard (Atlanta)
Terrell, Saunders (Greensboro)
Turpin, Thomas Million (Savannah)
Watts, Nellie (Atlanta)
Whittaker, Hudson (Smithville)
Williams, Joe (Cordele)
Williams, Mary Lou (Atlanta)
Woodward, Sidney (Stockbridge)
Wyatt, Lucius (Waycross)

IDAHO
Plato Broadley, Desseria (Genesee)

ILLINOIS
Abrams, Richard Louis (Chicago)
Ammons, Albert (Chicago)
Ammons, Eugene (Chicago)
Atkins, Marjorie R. (Chicago)
Baker, La Vern (Chicago)
Banks, Billy (Alton)
Barrett Campbell, Delois (Chicago)
Bohee, George (Chicago)
Bohee, James Douglass (Chicago)
Bonds, Margaret (Chicago)
Braxton, Anthony (Chicago)
Brooks, Tilford (East St. Louis)
Brown, Oscar, Jr. (Chicago)
Cleveland, James (Chicago)
Cooke, Sam (Chicago)
Cooper, Jerome (Chicago)
D'Albert, Marcus (Chicago?)
Davis, Miles Dewey, Jr. (Alton)
Davis, Richard (Chicago)
Donegan, Dorothy (Chicago)
Dulf, George (Springfield)
Dunham, Katherine (Glen Ellyn)
Favors, Malachi (Chicago)
Ferrell, Harrison Hubert (Chicago)
Gaston, Oland (Chicago)
Grant, Micki (Chicago)
Griffin, John Arnold (Chicago)
Hackney, William (Chicago?)
Hancock, Herbert Jeffrey (Chicago)
Harris, Margaret R. (Chicago)
Hathaway, Donny (Chicago)
Haynes, Eugene (East St. Louis)
Hite, Les (Dequoin)
Howard, Darnell (Chicago)
Jackson, Gertrude Smith (Chicago)
Jenkins, Leroy (Chicago)
Johnson, J. C. (Chicago)
Johnson, Lew (Chicago?)
Jones, Harold (Chicago)
Jones, Jonathan (Chicago)
Jones, Quincy Delight (Chicago)
Jordan, Clifford Laconia (Chicago)
Kemp, Emmerlyne J. (Chicago)
King, Betty (Chicago)
LeMon, Lillian Morris (Chicago)
Lewis, John Aaron (La Grange)
Lewis, Meade (Chicago)
Lewis, Ramsey Emanuel (Chicago)
Lincoln, Abbey (Chicago)
Madison, Earl (Chicago)
Matthews, Artie (Minonk)
Mayfield, Curtis (Chicago)
Meadows, Eddie Spencer (La Grange)
Mitchell, Roscoe (Chicago)
Nance, Willis (Chicago)
Peyton, Dave (Chicago?)
Pierson, Edward (Chicago)
Rawls, Louis Allen (Chicago)
Robinson, Florence (Carbondale)
Sears, Albert Omega (Macomb)
Short, Robert Waltrip (Danville)
Smith, Warren I. (Chicago)
Taylor, Tom Theodore (Cairo)
Van Peebles, Melvin (South Chicago)
Walton, Ortiz (Chicago)
Weir, Felix Fowler (Chicago)
Williams, J. Mayo (Monmouth)
Woodard, Nelmatilda R. (Alton)
Yancey, Estelle (Chicago)
Yancey, James Edward (Chicago)

INDIANA
Baker, David N. (Indianapolis)
Brown, Tom (Indianapolis)
Catlett, Sidney (Evansville)
Coston Maloney, Jean (Indianapolis)
De Paris, Sidney (Crawfordsville)
De Paris, Wilbur (Crawfordsville)
Graham Dubois, Shirley (Indianapolis)
Harreld, Kemper (Muncie)
Harrison, Hazel (La Porte)
Hubbard, Frederick D. (Indianapolis)
Jackson Five, The (Gary)
Johnson, James Louis (Indianapolis)
McClain, Billy (Indianapolis)
Montgomery, Charles (Indianapolis)
Montgomery, John Leslie (Indianapolis)
Montgomery, William Howard (Indianapolis)
Polin, Roscoe (Bridgeport)

Ridley, Laurence Howard (Indianapolis)
Shirley, George Irving (Indianapolis)
Simond, Ike (Mount Vernon)
Sissle, Noble (Indianapolis)
White, Donald Edward (Richmond)
Whitney, Salem Tutt (Logansport)

IOWA
Estes, Simon Lamont (Centerville)
Farmer, Arthur (Council Bluffs)
Motts, Robert (Washington)

KANSAS
Clayton, Wilbur (Parsons)
Cooper, Maurice (Kansas City)
Foster, William (Kansas City)
Gerren, Nicholas (Kansas City)
Henry, Lew W. (Leavenworth)
Holt, Nora (Kansas City)
Jessye, Eva (Coffeyville)
Lowery, Perry G. (Reece)
McDaniel, Hattie (Wichita)
Parks, Gordon A. (Fort Scott)
Smith, Nathaniel Clark (Ft. Leavenworth)
Stone, Jesse (Atchison)
Walker, George (Lawrence)
Whitman, Alberta (Pratt)
Whitman, Alice (Lawrence ?)
Whitman, Mable (Lawrence)

KENTUCKY
Barbour, J. Berni (Danville)
Bibbs, Leon (Louisville)
Brown, Thelma Wade (Ashland)
Brown, William Wells (Lexington)
Childers, Lulu (Dryridge)
Cooke, Charles L. (Louisville)
Deppe, Lois (Horse Cave)
Dorsey, William H. (Louisville)
Duncan, Robert Todd (Danville)
Furman, James B. (Louisville)
Griffin Sisters, The (Louisville)
Hampton, Lionel (Louisville)
Hart, Henry (Frankfort)
Henderson, Rosa Deschamps (Henderson)
Hogan, Ernest (Bowling Green)
Humes, Helen (Louisville)
Jones, Robert Elliott (Louisville)
Kirk, Andrew Dewey (Newport)
Lawson, Raymond Augustus (Shelbyville)
Marable, Fate (Paducah)
McCann, Leslie Coleman (Lexington)
McIntosh, Tom (Lexington)
McKinney, William (Cynthia)
Merrifield, Norman L. (Louisville)
Mundy, James Ahlyn (Maysville)
Perry, Julia (Lexington)
Rhea, La Julia (Louisville)
Rhodes, Todd Washington (Hopkinsville)
Smith, Henderson (Frankfort)
Sublett, John William (Louisville)
Taylor, Marshall (Lexington)
Washington, Ford Lee (Louisville)
Williams, Stanley (Danville)
Wilson, Edith (Louisville)

LOUISIANA
Allen, Henry James (Algiers)
Armstrong, Daniel Louis (New Orleans)
Baquet, George F. (New Orleans)
Barbarin, Paul (New Orleans)
Bares, Basile (New Orleans)
Barker, Daniel (New Orleans)
Barrett, Emma (New Orleans)
Bechet, Sidney (New Orleans)
Bigard, Leon A. (New Orleans)
Boatner, Edward H. (New Orleans)
Bolden, Charles (New Orleans)
Braud, Wellman (St. James Parish)
Bryant, William Steven (New Orleans)
Byrd, Henry Roeland (Bogalusa)
Celestin, Oscar (Napoleonville)
Cornmeali, Signor (New Orleans?)
Dede, Edmund (New Orleans)
Delisle, Louis Nelson (New Orleans)
Desdunes, Dan (New Orleans)
Desdunes, Rudolphe Lucien (New Orleans)
Dickerson, Roger Donald (New Orleans)
Dodds, Johnny (New Orleans)
Dodds, Warren (New Orleans)
Domino, Antoine (New Orleans)
Douglas, Minnie (Algiers)
Dudley, Sherman H. (Janesville)
Dutrey, Honore (New Orleans)
Foster, George Murphy (McCall)
Griffin, Bessie (New Orleans)
Guy, George (Lettsworth)
Hall, Edmond (New Orleans)
Handy Miller, D. Antoinette (New Orleans)
Hill, John Leubrie (New Orleans)
Hopkins, Linda (New Orleans)
Jackson, Anthony (New Orleans)
Jackson, Charlie (New Orleans)
Jackson, Mahalia (New Orleans)
Jacobs, Marion Walter (Marksville)
Jacquet, Jean Baptiste (Broussard)
Johnson, Alonzo (New Orleans)
Johnson, William Geary (New Orleans)
Johnson, William Manuel (New Orleans)
Jones, Richard Myknee (New Orleans)
Keppard, Freddie (New Orleans)
Ladnier, Thomas (Mandeville)
Lambert Family, The (New Orleans)
Ledbetter, Huddie (Mooringsport)
Lewis, George Francis (New Orleans)
Lutcher, Nellie (Lake Charles)
McCarty, Victor Eugene (New Orleans)
Montgomery, Eurreal (Kentwood)
Morgan, Albert (New Orleans)
Morton, Ferdinand (New Orleans)
Newman, Joseph Dwight (New Orleans)
Newson, Roosevelt (Rayville)
Nicholas, Albert (New Orleans)
Nickerson, Camille Lucie (New Orleans)
Nickerson, William Joseph (New Orleans)
Noone, Jimmie (New Orleans)
Oliver, Joseph (Abend)
Ory, Edward (La Place)
Perryman, Rufus (Monroe)
Picou, Alphonse F. (New Orleans)
Pierce, Joseph De La Croix (New Orleans)
Piron, Armand J. (New Orleans)
Poindexter, Norwood (New Orleans)
Porter, Olivia Shipp (New Orleans)
René, Leon T. (Covington)
René, Otis J. (New Orleans)
Rosemond, Andrew Fletcher (New Orleans)
Scott, Arthur (New Orleans)
Simeon, Omer Victor (New Orleans)
Singleton, Arthur James (Bunkie)
Snaer, Samuel (New Orleans)
Southall, Geneva Handy (New Orleans)
St. Cyr, John Alexander (New Orleans)
Tio, Lorenzo, Jr. (New Orleans)
Verrett, Shirley (New Orleans)
Williams, Clarence (Plaquemin Delta)
Williams, Robert Pete (Zachary)
Williams, Spencer (New Orleans)

MARYLAND
Anderson, Edward Gilbert (Still Pond)
Bartz, Gary Lee (Baltimore)
Blake, James Hubert (Baltimore)
Brown, Anne Wiggins (Baltimore)
Calloway, Blanche (Baltimore)
Davis, Clifton (Baltimore)
Fax, Mark (Baltimore)
Gibbs, Lloyd (Baltimore)
Hicks, Charles (Baltimore)
Holiday, Billie (Baltimore)
Jackson, Lawrence (Baltimore)
Kerr, Thomas (Baltimore)
Kirby, John (Baltimore)
Long, Avon (Baltimore)

McNeil, Claudia Mae (Baltimore)
Milburn, Richard
Murray, Robert (Baltimore)
Muse, Clarence (Baltimore)
Smith, Amanda (Long Green)
Snowden, Elmer Chester (Baltimore)
Tindley, Charles Albert (Berlin)
Turner, Joe (Baltimore)
Tyler, Veronica (Baltimore)
Webb, William (Baltimore)
Wilson, W. Llewellyn (Baltimore)

MASSACHUSETTS
Benson, Nero (Framingham ?)
Braithwaite, James Roland (Boston)
Byard, John A. (Worcester)
Carney, Harry Howell (Boston)
Clough, Estelle Pickney (Worcester)
Crossman, Simeon (Taunton?)
Dixon, William Robert (Nantucket)
Edet, Edna Smith (Boston)
Haynes, Roy Owens (Boston)
Higginbotham, Irene (Worcester)
Hodges, John Cornelius (Cambridge)
Hodges, M. Hamilton (Boston)
Hunt, Darrold Victor (New Bedford)
Jolly, Jabez (Barnstable)
Lew, Barzilai (Groton)
Lew, William Edward (Dracut)
Lewis, Elma Ina (Boston)
Lewis, Frederick Elliot (Boston)
McIntyre, Kenneth Arthur (Boston)
Middleton, George
Rahn, Muriel (Boston)
Ridley, Florida Ruffin (Boston)
Ruffin, George L. (Boston)
Sawyer, Jacob (Boston)
Stitt, Edward (Boston)
Summer, Donna (Boston)
Tiffany, Cyrus (Taunton)
Tinsley, Pedro T. (Boston)
Vaughn, James A. (Boston)
Washington, Rachel (Boston)
White, Frederick Perry (Boston?)
Williams, Henry F. (Boston)

MICHIGAN
Ashby, Dorothy Jeanne (Detroit)
Burrell, Kenneth Earl (Detroit)
Byrd, Donaldson T. (Detroit)
Carter, Betty (Flint)
Carter, Ronald Levin (Ferndale)
Coltrane, Alice McLeod (Detroit)
Dozier, Lamont (Detroit)
Flanagan, Tommy Lee (Detroit)
Frazier, James (Detroit)
Gillam, Harry (Detroit)
Gordy, Berry, Jr. (Detroit)
Harris, Barry (Detroit)
Holland, Edward (Detroit)
Holland, Brian (Detroit)
Jackson, Milton (Detroit)
Jeffries, Herb (Detroit)
Jones, Elvin Ray (Pontiac)
Jones, Thaddeus Joseph (Pontiac)
LaBrew, Arthur Randolph (Detroit)
McIntosh, Hattie (Detroit)
Oliver, Melvin James (Battle Creek)
Patterson, Willis Charles (Ann Arbor)
Reese, Della (Detroit)
Ross, Diana (Detroit)
Talbert, Florence Cole (Detroit)
Tapley, Daisy (Big Rapids)
Thompson, Eli (Detroit)
Watkins, Julius Burton (Detroit)
Wonder, Stevie (Saginaw)
Wright, Josephine (Detroit)

MINNESOTA
Southern, Eileen Jackson (Minneapolis)

MISSISSIPPI
Boyd, Edward Riley (Stovall)
Broonzy, William Lee C. (Scott)
Brown, William Albert (Jackson)
Burnett, Chester Arthur (West Point)
Butler, Jerry (Sunflower)
Campbell, Lucie (Duck Hill)
Cannon, Gus (Red Banks)
Chatmon, Armenter (Bolton)
Chatmon, Sam (Bolton)
Cotton, James (Tunica)
Crudup, Arthur (Forest)
Dawkins, James (Tchula)
Dixon, Willie James (Vicksburg)
Edwards, David (Shaw)
Fischer, William S. (Shelby)
Frye, Theodore (Fayette)
Gatlin, F. Nathaniel (Summit)
Greenfield, Elizabeth Taylor (Natchez)
Hinton, Milton J. (Vicksburg)
Holmes, Robert (Greenville)
Hooker, John Lee (Clarksdale)
House, Eddie James (Lyon)
Hurt, John (Teoc, Carroll County)
James, Nehemiah (Bentonia)
Johnson, Robert (Hazlehurst)
Johnson, Tommy (Terry)
Jones, Henry (Vicksburg)
King, Albert (Indianola)
King, Riley B. (Itta Bena)
Lewis, Walter (Greenwood)
Luandrew, Albert (Vance)
Lyles, Aubrey (Jackson)
McDaniel, Ellas (Magnolia)
Miller, Willie "Rice" (Glendora)
Morganfield, McKinley (Rolling Fork)
Parker, Herman (Clarksdale)
Patton, Charley (Edwards)
Price, Leontyne (Laurel)
Pride, Charley (Sledge)
Reed, Mathis James (Dunleith)
Rogers, James (Ruleville)
Rush, Otis (Philadelphia)
Selika, Marie (Natchez)
Sellers, John B. (Clarksdale)
Smith, Albert (Bolivar County)
Smith, Leo (Leland)
Smith, Willie Mae Ford (Rolling Fork)
Spann, Otis (Jackson)
Stackhouse, Houston (Wesson)
Still, William Grant (Woodville)
Taylor, Theodore R. (Natchez)
Trotter, James Monroe (Grand Gulf)
Turner, Ike (Clarksdale)
Vinson (or Vincent), Walter Jacob (Bolton)
White, Booker T. Washington (Houston)
Wilkins, Joe Willie (Davenport)
Williams, Joe (Crawford)
Wilson, Gerald Stanley (Shelby)
Young, Lester (Woodville)

MISSOURI
Baker, Josephine (St. Louis)
Billups, Kenneth B. (St. Louis)
Boone, John William (Miami)
Buckner, Milton (St. Louis)
Bumbry, Grace Ann (St. Louis)
Butcher, Vada Easter (St. Louis)
Chauvin, Louis (St. Louis)
Creath, Charles (Ironton)
Davis, William Strethen (Glasgow)
Dyett, Walter Henri (St. Joseph)
Hancock, Eugene Wilson (St. Louis)
Harris, Carl Gordon (Fayette)
Harvey, Georgette (St. Louis)
Hawkins, Coleman (St. Joseph)
Hayden, Scott (Sedalia)
Hughes, Langston (Joplin)
Johnson, Pete (Kansas City)
Lee, George Ewing (Kansas City)
Lee, Julia (Boonesville)
Lee, Pauline James (Louisiana)
Lester, Julius B. (St. Louis)
Liston, Melba Doretta (Kansas City)
Lunceford, James Melvin (Fulton)
Marshall, Arthur (Saline County)
Middleton, Velma (St. Louis)
Mitchell, William (Kansas City)
Morrison, George (Fayette)
Moten, Bennie (Kansas City)
Nelson, Oliver Edward (St. Louis)
Page, Walter Sylvester (Gallatin)
Parker, Charles C. (Kansas City)
Patterson, Sam (St. Louis)

Postlewaite, Joseph William (St. Louis)
Price, Jesse (Kansas City)
Scott, James Sylvester (Neosho)
Sedric, Eugene Hall (St. Louis)
Smith, Richard Joseph (Kansas City)
Smyles, Harry (Kansas City)
South, Eddie (Louisiana)
Sweatman, Wilbur C. (Brunswick)
Taylor, Eva (St. Louis)
Terry, Clark (St. Louis)
Thompson, Charles Hubbard (St. Louis)
Thompson, Dekoven (St. Louis)
Turner, Joseph Vernon (Kansas City)
Walton, Lester Aglar (St. Louis)
Weathers, Felicia (St. Louis)
Webster, Benjamin Francis (Kansas City)
Wilkins, Ernest Brooks (St. Louis)
Wilson, Olly Woodrow (St. Louis)
Wright, Preston T. (Mexico)

MONTANA
Gordon, Taylor (White Sulphur Springs)

NEBRASKA
Harris, Wynonie (Omaha)

NEW HAMPSHIRE
Brown Mitchell, Nellie (Dover)
Fisk, Cato (Epson)
Hagan, Helen Eugenia (Portsmouth)
Pindell, Annie Pauline (Exeter)

NEW JERSEY
Baraka, Imamu Amiri (Newark)
Basie, William (Red Bank)
Bostic, Joe William (Mt. Holly)
Cole, William Randolph (East Orange)
Craig, Walter F. (Princeton)
Davison Watkins, Harriette (Newark)
De Paur, Leonard (Summit)
Gonzales, Babs (Newark)
Greer, William A. (Long Branch)
Hall, Juanita (Keyport)
Huff, Leon (Camden)
Johnson, James Price (New Brunswick)
King, Wallace (Newark)
Layton, Sr., John Turner (Freeport)
O'Fake, Peter (Newark)
Roberts, Howard (Burlington)
Robeson, Paul (Princeton)
Russell, Sylvester (Orange)
Shorter, Wayne (Newark)
Thomas, C. Edward (Vineland)
Tucker, Robert Nathaniel (Morristown)
Van Buren, Catherine (Morristown)
Vaughan, Sarah Lou (Newark)
Warwick, Dionne (East Orange)

NEW YORK
Addison, Adele (New York)
Aldridge, Ira Frederick (New York)
Allen, Sanford (New York)
Alsdorf, Dubois B. (Newberg)
Arle-Tilz, Coretti (New York?)
Arroyo, Martina (New York)
Belafonte, Harold George (New York)
Bland, James (Flushing)
Bonnemere, Edward (New York)
Booth, Alan (New York)
Brady, William (New York?)
Burgie, Irving Louis (New York)
Calloway, Cabell (Rochester)
Capers, Valerie (New York)
Carroll, Diahann (New York)
Carter, Bennett Lester (New York)
Charlton, Melville (New York)
Collymore, Winston (New York)
Cumbo, Marion (New York)
Cunningham, Arthur (Nyack)
Daniel, Billie Lynn (New York)
Davis, Eddie (New York)
Davis, Ellabelle (New Rochelle)
Davis, Sammy, Jr. (New York)
Davy, Gloria (New York)
Dixon, Dean (New York)
Dixon, Lucille (New York)
Douglass, John Thomas (New York?)
Dowdy, Helen (New York)
Drew, Kenneth Sidney (New York)
Eaton, Roy (New York)
Freeman, Bergert C. (Auburn)
Gillam, Joseph (Geneva)
Grist, Reri (New York)
Hailstork, Adolphus (Albany)
Hall, Adelaide (New York)
Havens, Richard Pierce (New York)
Horne, Lena (New York)
Jackson, William (New York?)
Jones, Elayne (New York)
Jones, Irving (New York)
Kersands, William (New York)
Lane, William Henry (New York?)
Lemonier, Tom (New York)
Lymon, Frankie (New York)
McLean, John Lenwood (New York)
McRae, Carmen (New York)
Mando, Alfred F. (Troy)
Martin, David Irwin (New York)
Martin, Eugene Mars (New York)
Martin, Gertrude (New York)
Matthews, Edward (Ossining)
Matthews, Inez (Ossining)
Mitchell, Abbie (New York)
Moore, Melba (New York)
Morton, Henry Sterling (New York)
Nanton, Joseph (New York)
Northup, Solomon (Minerva, Essex County)
Owens, James Robert (New York)
Payne, Cecil McKenzie (New York)
Perkinson, Coleridge Taylor (New York)
Peters, Brock (New York)
Peterson, Elwood (New York)
Plet, A. (New York)
Powell, Earl (New York)
Ray Russell, Carline (New York)
Roach, Maxwell (New York)
Rollins, Theodore Walter (New York)
Sampson, Edgar Melvin (New York)
Schuyler, Philippa Duke (New York)
Shavers, Charles James (New York)
Simpson, Valerie (New York)
Smith, Muriel (New York)
Smith, William Henry J. (Goshen)
Taj Mahal (New York)
Taylor, Cecil Percival (New York)
Thompson, Arthur (New York)
Uggams, Leslie (New York)
Utterback, Clinton
Waller, Thomas Wright (New York)
Washington, Grover (Buffalo)
Weston, Randolph (New York)
White, Christopher (New York)
Wood, Obediah (New York)

NORTH CAROLINA
Brice, Carol (Sedalia)
Brymn, James Timothy (Kinston)
Caesar, Shirley (Durham)
Coltrane, John William (Hamlet)
Cotten, Elizabeth (Chapel Hill)
Dawson, Mary Cardwell (Meridian)
De Wolfe Sisters, The (Charlotte)
Flack, Roberta (Black Mountain)
Fuller, "Blind Boy" (Wadesboro)
Hakim, Talib Rasul (Asheville)
Harris, Hilda (Warrenton)
Heath, Percy (Wilmington)
Jarboro, Caterina (Wilmington)
Johns, Altona Trent (Asheville)
Lovell, John (Asheville)
Mabley, Jackie (Brevard)
McAdoo, Orpheus Myron (Greensboro)
McCoy, Seth (Sanford)
McPhatter, Clyde Lensey (Durham)
Martin, David I. (Asheville)
Monk, Thelonious S. (Rocky Mount)
Roach, Hildred (Charlotte)
Settle, Glenn (Reidsville)
Simone, Nina (Tryon)

Simpson, Eugene Thamon (North Wilkesboro)
Smith, Raymond Lowden (Salisbury)
Spellman, A. B. (Elizabeth City)
Taylor, William (Greenville)

OHIO
Abdul-Rahim, Raoul (Cleveland)
Adams, Armenta (Cleveland)
Adams, Elwyn Albert (Cleveland)
Allen, Betty Lou (Campbell)
Anderson, Walter Franklin (Zanesville)
Atkins, Russell (Cleveland)
Ayler, Albert (Cleveland)
Ayler, Donald (Cleveland)
Bradshaw, Myron (Youngstown)
Bushell, Garvin Payne (Springfield)
Carlisle, Una Mae (Xenia)
Cole, Frances Elaine (Cleveland)
Collins, Cleota (Cleveland)
Cowell, Stanley (Toledo)
Dameron, Tadley Ewing (Cleveland)
Dandridge, Dorothy (Cleveland)
Davis, Gussie (Dayton)
Dickenson, Victor (Xenia)
Dunbar, Paul Laurence (Dayton)
Edison, Harry (Columbus)
Finney, Theodore (Columbus)
Fletcher, Tom (Portsmouth)
Foster, Frank B. (Cincinnati)
Freeman, Harry Lawrence (Cleveland)
Gossette, Walter (Steubenville)
Guy, Harry (Zanesville)
Hendricks, John Carl (Newark)
Hinderas, Natalie (Oberlin)
Isley Brothers, The (Cincinnati)
Jones, Clarence (Wilmington)
Jones, Louia Vaughn (Cleveland)
Jordan, Joe (Cincinnati)
Kirk, Rahsaan Roland (Columbus)
Lucas, Sam (Washington)
McAfee, Charles (Cleveland)
Mills Brothers, The (Piqua)
Moore, Carman Leroy (Lorain)
Moore, Kermit (Akron)
Mundy, James (Cincinnati)
Nolan, Robert L. (Cleveland)
Reed, Addison W. (Steubenville)
Russell, George Allan (Cincinnati)
Scott, Cecil Xavier (Springfield)
Shipp, Jesse A. (Cincinnati)
Smith, Hale (Cleveland)
Smith, Hezekiah Leroy G. (Portsmouth)
Smith, Joe (Ripley)
Smith, Mamie (Cincinnati)
Strayhorn, William (Dayton)
Tatum, Arthur (Toledo)
Tibbs, Roy Wilford (Hamilton)
Tyler, Jesse Gerald (Oberlin)
Walker Turner, Rachel (Cleveland ?)
Williams, Henry (Cleveland)
Wilson, Nancy (Chillicothe)
Womack, Robert Dwayne (Cleveland)

OKLAHOMA
Bostic, Earl (Tulsa)
Byas, Carlos Wesley (Muskogee)
Cherry, Donald E. (Oklahoma City)
Fulson, Lowell (Tulsa)
Grant, Earl (Idabelle)
Love, Hortense (Muskogee)
McGhee, Howard (Tulsa)
McShann, Jay (Muskogee)
Mitchell, Leona (Enid)
Pettiford, Oscar (Okmulgee)
Pittman, Evelyn La Rue (McAlester)
Price, John E. (Tulsa)
Rivers, Samuel Carthorne (El Reno)
Rushing, James Andrew (Oklahoma City)

OREGON
Allen, William Duncan (Portland)

PENNSYLVANIA
Allen, Peter
Allen, Richard (Philadelphia)
Anderson, Joseph G. (Philadelphia)
Anderson, Marian (Philadelphia)
Anderson, Thomas Jefferson (Coatesville)
Appo, Ann (Philadelphia)
Appo, William (Philadelphia)
Augustus, Edward (Philadelphia)
Barron, Kenneth (Philadelphia)
Barron, William (Philadelphia)
Bell, Thom R. (Philadelphia)
Benson, George (Pittsburgh)
Blakey, Art (Pittsburgh)
Blakey, Arthur (Pittsburgh)
Bowers, Thomas (Philadelphia)
Burleigh, Henry Thacker (Erie)
Burris, Andrew (Philadelphia)
Chambers, Paul Laurence, Jr. (Pittsburgh)
Clarke, Kenneth Spearman (Pittsburgh)
Connor, Aaron J. R. (Philadelphia)
Cooper, William Benjamin (Philadelphia)
Creach, John (Beaver Falls)
Dale, Clamma (Chester)
Davis, Arthur D. (Harrisburg)
De Priest, James Anderson (Philadelphia)
Diton, Carl Rossini (Philadelphia)
Eckstine, William Clarence (Pittsburgh)
Eldridge, David Roy (Pittsburgh)
Evans, Ernest (Philadelphia)
Gamble, Kenneth (Philadelphia)
Garland, Phyllis T. (McKeesport)
Garner, Errol L. (Pittsburgh)
Golson, Benny (Philadelphia)
Gordon, Joseph (Philadelphia)
Hairston, Jester (Homestead)
Hazzard, Isaac (Philadelphia)
Heath, Albert (Philadelphia)
Heath, James Edward (Philadelphia)
Hemmenway, James (Philadelphia)
Hines, Earl Kenneth (Duquesne)
Hobson, Ann (Philadelphia)
Jackson, James Albert (Bellefonte)
Jamal, Ahmad (Pittsburgh)
Jefferson, Edgar (Pittsburgh)
Jones, Joseph Rudolph (Philadelphia)
Jones, Robert C. (Philadelphia)
Julius, John (Pittsburgh?)
Kennedy, Joseph J. (Pittsburgh)
Killebrew, Gwendolyn (Philadelphia)
Labelle, Patti (Philadelphia)
Locke, Alain Leroy (Philadelphia)
Moore, Hamilton A. (Philadelphia)
Pankey, Aubrey (Pittsburgh)
Parker, Louise (Philadelphia)
Paul, Billy (Philadelphia)
Payne (or Paine), Benny (Philadelphia)
Porter, Karl Hampton (Pittsburgh)
Prattis Jennings, Patricia (Pittsburgh)
Roberts, Charles L. (Philadelphia)
Scott, Shirley (Philadelphia)
Seymour, Francis V. (Philadelphia)
Smith, James Oscar (Norristown)
Smith, Richard Donald (Philadelphia)
Staton, Dakota (Pittsburgh)
Stewart, Rex William (Philadelphia)
Sullivan, Maxine (Homestead)
Suthern, Orrin Clayton (Renovo)
Thomas, Alfred Jack (Pittsburgh)
Turrentine, Stanley (Pittsburgh)
Tyner, Alfred McCoy (Philadelphia)
Vordey, Will Henry B. (Philadelphia)
Wall, Jessie or Jesse (Erie)
Ward, Clara (Philadelphia)
Waters, Ethel (Chester)
Wilder, Joseph Benjamin (Colwyn)
Wooding, Samuel David (Philadelphia)

PUERTO RICO
Gutierrez y Espinosa, Felipe (San Juan)
Tizol, Juan (San Juan)

RHODE ISLAND
Brown, Scipio
Jackson, Raymond T. (Providence)
Lucas, Carrie Melvin (Newport)

SOUTH CAROLINA
Allen, Cleveland G. (Greenville)
Anderson, Pink (Laurens)
Anderson, William Alonzo (Greenville)
Ashford, Nickolas (Fairfield)
Bates, Clayton (Fountain Inn)
Benton, Brook (Camden)
Blackwell, Francis Hillman (Syracuse)
Blanton, Carol (St. Helena Island)
Bowman, Elmer (Charleston?)
Brown, Morris (Charleston)
Carey, Thomas Devore (Bennettsville)
Cheeks, Julius (Spartanburg)
Dash, St. Julian B. (Charleston)
Davis, Gary D. (Laurens)
Gillespie, John Birks (Cheraw)
Hill, Bertha (Charleston)
Jenkins, Edmund Thornton (Charleston)
Johnson, William Francis (Charleston)
Kenyatta, Robin (Charleston)
Kitt, Eartha Mae (North)
Lawrence, William (Charleston)
McKinney, Nina Mae (Lancaster)
Mikell, Francis Eugene (Charleston)
Miley, James Wesley (Aiken)
Payne, Daniel Alexander (Charleston)
Prysock, Arthur (Spartanburg)
Smith, Chris (Charleston)
Smith, Clara (Spartanburg)
Smith, William McLeish (Charleston)
White, Joshua Daniel (Greenville)
Winters, Lawrence (Kings Creek)

TENNESSEE
Anderson, T. C. (Memphis?)
Armstrong, Lillian Hardin (Memphis)
Austin, Lovie (Chattanooga)
Bland, Robert Calvin (Rosemark)
Blanton, James (Chattanooga)
Brewster, W. Herbert (Somerville)
Carr, Leroy (Nashville)
Chatman, Peter (Memphis)
Cheatham, Adolphus Anthony (Nashville)
Cook, Jean Lawrence (Athens)
Dunn, John (Memphis)
Edmonds, Shepherd (Memphis)
Estes John (Ripley)
Franklin, Aretha (Memphis)
Franklin, William (Memphis)
Frierson, Andrew (Columbia)
Fuller, Walter (Dyersburg)
Hackley, Emma Azalia (Murfreesboro)
Hayes, Isaac (Covington)
Hayes, Robert (Memphis)
Hunter, Alberta (Memphis)
Jones, Booker T. (Memphis)
Jones, J. Wesley (Nashville)
Jones, James Henry (Memphis)
Jordan, Robert (Chattanooga)
Lateef, Yusef (Chattanooga)
Lewis, Mabel Sanford (Memphis)
Little, Vera (Memphis)
Lofton, Clarence (Kingsport)
McDowell, Frederick (Rossville)
McGhee, Walter (Knoxville)
Meadows, Eddie Spencer (La Grange)
Miller, Flournoy (Nashville)
Nixon, Hammie (Brownsville)
Proctor, Henry Hugh (Clifton)
Rachell, James (Brownsville)
Rogers, Alexander C. (Nashville)
Ryder, Noah (Nashville)
Saunders, Theodore D. (Memphis)
Shade, Will (Memphis)
Shines, John Ned (Frayser)
Shook, Ben (Nashville)
Smith, Bessie (Chattanooga)
Smith, Mabel Louise (Jackson)
Snow, Valaida (Chattanooga)
Tate, Erskine (Memphis)
Taylor, Cora Walton (Memphis)
Turner, Tina (Brownsville)
Warfield, Charles (Guthrie)
Wells, Amos (Memphis)
Wells, William (Centerville)
Whalum, Wendell P. (Memphis)
White, Clarence Cameron (Clarksville)
White, Maurice (Memphis)
Williamson, John Lee (Jackson)
Work, Frederick Jerome (Nashville)
Work, John Wesley II (Nashville)
Work, John Wesley III (Tullahoma)
Work, Julian C. (Nashville)

TEXAS
Bledsoe, Julius (Waco)
Bowman, Euday Louis (Fort Worth)
Browning, Ivan Harold (Brenham)
Christian, Charles (Bonham)
Coleman, Ornette (Fort Worth)
Dent, Jessie Covington (Houston)
Dixon, Jessy (San Antonio)
Dorham, McKinley Howard (Fairfield)
Durham, Eddie (San Marcos)
Fuller, Oscar Anderson (Marshall)
Garcia, William (Dallas)
George, Zelma Watson (Hearne)
Glenn, Evans Tyree (Corsicana)
Handy, John (Dallas)
Hare, Maud Cuney (Galveston)
Harrison, Frank (Austin)
Hopkins, Sam (Centerville)
Hunter, Ivory Joe (Kirbyville)
Jackson, Melvin (Barry)
Jefferson, Lemon (Wortham [Near])
Johnson, Albert (Dallas)
Joplin, Scott (Bowie County)
Killingsworth, John Dekoven (Fort Worth)
King, Freddie (Gilmer)
Laws, Hubert (Houston)
Laws, Ronald (Houston)
Lipscomb, Mance (Brazos County)
Love, James L. (Jefferson)
Moten Barnett, Etta (San Antonio)
Nash, John (Houston)
Ousley, Curtis (Fort Worth)
Page, Oran Thaddeus (Dallas)
Phillips, Esther (Galveston)
Preston, William (Houston)
Price, Samuel Blythe (Honey Grove)
Redman, Walter Dewey (Fort Worth)
Robinson, Faye (Houston)
Smith, Henry (Aldorf)
Spivey, Victoria Regina (Houston)
Standifer, James (Itasca)
Stewart, Sylvester (Dallas)
Stone, Theodore (Gainesville)
Tapscott, Horace (Houston)
Tillis, Frederick C. (Galveston)
Vinson, Eddie (Houston)
Walker, Aaron Thibeaux (Linden)
Wallace, Beulah Thomas (Houston)
White, Barry (Galveston)
Wilson, Theodore (Austin)

VIRGINIA
Anderson, Hallie (Lynchburgh)
Bailey, Evangeline G. (Portsmouth)
Bailey, Pearl (Newport News)
Carter, Dennis Drummond (Accomac County)
Chambers, Joseph (Stoneacre)
Creamer, Henry (Richmond)
Dabney, Wendell Phillips (Richmond)
Delany, Martin Robinson (Charleston)
Dupree, William H. (Petersburg)
Fitzgerald, Ella (Newport News)
Freeman, Paul D. (Richond)
Garner, George Robert
Gilliat, Simeon (Richmond)
Gilpin, Charles Sidney (Richmond)
Hines Matthews, Altonell B. (Norfolk)
Holland, Charles (Norfolk)
Holland, Justin Miner (Norfolk County)
Hopkins, Claude (Alexandria)
Jackson, Clifton Luther (Culpeper)
Jackson, Graham W. (Portsmouth)
Jackson, Isaiah (Richmond)
Jones, M. Sissieretta (Portsmouth)
Loving, Walter (Lovingston)
Mack, Cecil (Norfolk)
Maynor, Dorothy (Norfolk)

Moore, Undine Smith (Jarrat)
Nickens, William (Lancaster County)
Northern, Chauncey (Hampton)
Patterson, Ulysses S. Grant (Franklin County)
Perkins, Nimrod (Accomac County)
Ryder, Georgia Atkins (Newport News)
Scott, Robert (Charlottesville)
Smith, Lonnie Liston (Richmond)
Spiller, Isabelle T. (Abingdon)
Spiller, William Newmeyer (Hampton)
Thompson, Leon Evanette (Richmond)
Tyers, William H. (Richmond)
Tynes, Margaret (Saluda)
Von Charlton, Rudolph Everett (Norfolk)
Walker, Aida Overton (Richmond)
Williams, Camilla (Danville)
Work, John Wesley I

WASHINGTON
Hendrix, James Marshall (Seattle)

WEST VIRGINIA
Berry, Leon (Wheeling)
Dixon, Will (Wheeling)
Kennedy, Anne Gamble (Charleston)
Layne, Maude Wanzer (Charleston)
Lee, Everett (Wheeling)
Pinkard, Maceo (Bluefield)
Redman, Donald Matthew (Piedmont)
Smith, Ada Beatrice (Alderson)
Smith, Harry C. (Clarksburg)
Weatherford, Teddy (Bluefield)

WISCONSIN
McNair, Barbara (Racine)

PLACE OF BIRTH UNKNOWN
Accooe, Willis
Alexander, Brooks
Bracken, James
Brown, George
Clough, Inez
Cooper, Clarence
Dickerson, Carroll
Dranes, Arizona
Drury, Theodore
George, Maude Roberts
Graham, Gladys
Jones, Irving
Jones, Mildred Bryant
Overstreet, Benton
Plato, Desseria
Simpson, Frederick
Wall, Jessie
Whitman, Alice

Appendix 3

MUSICAL OCCUPATIONS

BLUES MUSICIANS AND BOOGIE-WOOGIE PIANISTS

Allison, Luther
Ammons, Albert
Anderson, Pink
Austin, Lovie
Blackwell, Francis (''Scrapper'')
Blake, ''Blind Arthur''
Bland, Robert (''Bobby Blue'')
Boyd, Edward Riley (''Eddie'')
Bracken, James (''Jim'')
Broonzy, William (''Big Bill'')
Burnett, Chester (''Howlin' Wolf'')
Byrd, Henry (''Professor Longhair'')
Cannon, Gus (''Banjo Joe'')
Carr, Leroy
Chatman, Peter (''Memphis Slim'')
Chatmon, Armenter (''Bo'')
Chatmon, Sam
Cotten, Elizabeth (''Libba'')
Cotton, James
Cox, Ida
Crudup, Arthur (''Big Boy'')
Davis, Gary (''Blind Gary'')
Dawkins, James (''Jimmy'')
Dixon, Willie (''Big'')
Domino, Antoine (''Fats'')
Dorsey, Thomas (''Georgia Tom'')
Douglas, Minnie (''Memphis Minnie'')
Edwards, David (''Honeyboy'')
Estes, John (''Sleepy'')
Fuller, ''Blind Boy''
Fuller, Jesse (''The Lone Cat'')
Fulson, Lowell
Guy, George (''Buddy'')
Harris, Wynonie (''Mr. Blues'')
Hill, Bertha (''Chippie'')
Hillery, Mable
Hooker, John Lee
Hopkins, Linda
Hopkins, Sam (''Lightnin'')
House, Eddie (''Son'')
Hunter, Alberta
Hunter, (''Ivory'') Joe
Hurt, John (''Mississippi'')
Jackson, Charlie (''Papa'')
Jackson, Melvin (''Little Son'')
Jacobs, Marion Walter (''Little Walter'')
James, Nehemiah (''Skip'')
Jefferson, Lemon (''Blind Lemon'')
Johnson, Alonzo (''Lonnie'')
Johnson, Pete
Johnson, Robert
Johnson, Tommy
King, Albert
King, Freddie
King, Riley (''B. B. King'')
Ledbetter, Huddie (''Leadbelly'')
Lewis, Meade (''Lux'')
Lewis, Walter (''Furry'')
Lipscomb, Mance
Lockwood, Robert (''Junior'')
Lofton, Clarence (''Cripple'')
Luandrew, Albert (''Sunnyland Slim'')
McCoy, Robert
McDaniel, Ellas (''Bo Diddley'')
McDowell, Frederick (''Mississippi Fred'')
McGhee, Walter (''Brownie'')
Miller, Willie (''Rice, Sonny Boy No. 2'')
Montgomery, Eurreal (''Little Brother'')
Morganfield, McKinley (''Muddy Waters'')
Morton, Ferdinand (''Jelly Roll'')
Nixon, Hammie
Parker, Herman (''Little Junior'')
Patton, Charley
Perryman, Rufus (''Speckled Red'')
Phillips, Esther
Rachell, James (''Yank'')
Rainey, Gertrude (''Ma'')
Rawls, Louis (''Lou'')
Reed, Mathis (''Jimmy'')
Rogers, James (''Jimmy'')
Rush, Otis
Rushing, James (''Jimmy'')
Sellers, John (''Brother John'')
Shade, Will (''Son Brimmer'')
Shines, John (''Johnny Shines'')
Smith, Bessie
Smith, Clara
Smith, Clarence (''Pine Top'')
Smith, Mabel (''Big Maybelle'')
Smith, Mamie
Spann, Otis
Spivey, Victoria (''Queen'')
Stackhouse, Houston
Taylor, Cora Walton (''Koko'')
Taylor, Theodore (''Hound Dog'')
Terrell, Saunders (Sonny Terry)
Thornton, Willie Mae (''Big Mama'')
Turner, Joseph (''Big Joe'')
Vinson, Eddie (''Cleanhead'')
Vinson (or Vincent), Walter
Walker, Aaron (''T-Bone'')
Wallace, Beulah Thomas (''Sippie Wallace'')
Waters, Ethel
Wells, Amos (''Junior'')
White, Booker (''Bukka'')
Whittaker, Hudson (''Tampa Red'')
Wilkins, Joe Willie
Williams, Joe
Williams, Joe (''Big Joe'' or ''Po'Joe'')
Williams, Robert
Williamson, John (''Sonny Boy No. 1'')

Blues Musicians and Boogie-Woogie Pianists, continued

Witherspoon, James ("Jimmy")
Wright, Annie Bell
Yancey, Estelle ("Mama")
Yancey, James ("Jimmy, Papa")

CHORAL CONDUCTORS

Adams, Ishmael
Alexander, Brooks
Billups, Kenneth
Brown, Morris
De Paur, Leonard
Hairston, Jester
Jackson, Gertrude Smith
Jessye, Eva
Johnson, Hall
Jones, J. Wesley
Jones, Robert
Lawson, Warner
Lewis, J. Henry
McAdoo, Orpheus
McLin, Lena Johnson
Mundy, James
Roberts, Howard
Stans, Jacob
Tinsley, Pedro
Tyler, Jesse

COMPOSERS

Akpabot, Samuel
Aldridge, Amanda
Amu, Ephraim
Anderson, T. J.
Appo, William
Atkins, Russell
Baker, David N.
Bankole, Ayo
Bethune, Thomas ("Blind Tom")
Boatner, Edward
Bonds, Margaret
Boone, John ("Blind Boone")
Brady, William
Braxton, Anthony
Brindis de Salas, Claudio
Brindis de Salas, Claudio J. D.
Brown, John Harold
Burleigh, Henry ("Harry")
Burris, Andrew
Capers, Valerie
Chauvin, Louis
Clark, Edgar Rogie
Coleman, Ornette
Coleridge-Taylor, Samuel
Coltrane, John
Cook, Will Marion
Cooper, William
Cordero, Roque
Cunningham, Arthur
Da Costa, Noel
Dafora, Asadata
Dawson, William
Dede, Edmund
Dett, Robert Nathaniel
Dickerson, Roger
Duncan, John
El-Dabh, Halim
Elie, Justin
Ellington, Edward ("Duke")
Euba, Akin
Fax, Mark
Fischer, William
Fleet, James
Fountain, III, Primous
Freeman, Harry Lawrence
Furman, James
Geffrard, Robert
Golson, Benny
Grant, Micki
Gutierrez y Espinosa, Felipe
Hailstork, Adolphus
Hakim, Talib Rasul
Hall, Frederick
Hall, Ian
Hancock, Herbert
Handy, William ("W. C.")
Harris, Margaret
Hathaway, Donny
Hazzard, Isaac
Hemmenway, James
Hill, John Leubrie
Jenkins, Edmund
Jenkins, Leroy
Jessye, Eva
Johnson, Francis ("Frank")
Johnson, Francis Hall
Johnson, J. Rosamond
Jones, Quincy
Joplin, Scott
Jordan, Joe
Kay, Ulysses
Kerr, Thomas
King, Betty
Ladipo, Duro
Lake, Oliver
Lamothe, Ludovic
Lateef, Yusef
Lee, William ("Bill")
Leon, Tania
Logan, Wendell
McCarty, Victor
Margetson, Edward
Marshall, Arthur
Matthews, Artie
Meude-Monpas, The Chevalier. J. J. Ode
Moore, Carman
Moore, Dorothy Rudd
Moore, Undine Smith
Murray, Robert
Nelson, Oliver
Norman, Fred
Nunez Garcia, Jose Mauricio N.
Overstreet, W. Benton
Parks, Gordon
Perkinson, Coleridge
Perry, Julia
Pittman, Evelyn La Rue
Price, Florence B. Smith
Price, John
Redman, Donald ("Don")
Rivers, Clarence
Roldan, Amadeo
Russell, George
Ryder, Noah
Saint-Georges, The Chevalier de
Sancho, Ignatius
Sawyer, Jacob
Scott, James
Smith, Hale
Smith, Leo
Smith, N. Clark
Snaer, Samuel
Sowande, Fela
Still, William
Swanson, Howard
Tillis, Frederick
Van Peebles, Melvin
Vodery, Will
Walker, George Theophilus
White, Clarence Cameron
Williams, Henry F.
Williams, Mary Lou
Wilson, Olly
Work, John Wesley II
Work, John Wesley III

CONCERT ARTISTS AND GROUPS

Abdul-Rahim, Raoul
Adams, Armenta
Adams, Elwyn
Addison, Adele
Aldridge, Irene Luranah
Allen, Betty Lou
Allen, William
Anderson, Marian
Arle-Tilz, Coretti
Axelson, Doris Holland
Batson, Flora

Bebey, Francis
Bethune, Thomas ("Blind Tom")
Blanton, Carol
Bledsoe, Julius
Boatwright, McHenry
Bonds, Margaret
Boone, John ("Blind Boone")
Booth, Alan
Bowers, Sarah Sedgwick
Bowers, Thomas ("The Colored Mario")
Brice, Carol
Bridgetower, George
Brindis de Salas, Claudio
Brindis de Salas, José
Brown, Anita Patti
Brown, Anne Wiggins
Brown, Lawrence
Brown, Thelma Wade
Brown, William
Brown Mitchell, Nellie
Carey, Thomas
Cato, Minto
Clough, Estelle Pickney
Clough, Inez
Cole, Frances Elaine
Collins, Cleota
Cooper, Maurice
Coston Maloney, Jean
Craig, Walter
Cumbo, Marion
D'Albert, Marc[us]
Daniel, Billie Lynn
Davis, Ellabelle
Davison Watkins, Harriette
De Bose, Tourgee
De Wolfe Sisters, The
Dent, Jessie Covington
Diton, Carl
Douglass, John
Douglass, Joseph
Duncan, Robert Todd
Eaton, Roy
Elie, Justin
Emanuel, William
Emidee
Evanti, Lillian
Frierson, Andrew
Garner, George
Gibbs, Lloyd
Gordon, Taylor
Greene, John
Greenfield, Elizabeth Taylor ("The Black Swan")
Griffin Sisters, The
Hackley, Emma Azalia
Hagan, Helen Eugenia
Handy Miller, D. Antoinette
Harris, Hilda
Harrison, Hazel
Hart, Myrtle
Harvey, Georgette
Hayes, Roland
Haynes, Eugene
Hinderas, Natalie
Hines Matthews, Altonell B.
Hyers, Anna Madah
Hyers, Emma Louise
Jackson, Raymond
Jamieson, Samuel
Jarboro, Caterina
Jimenez-Berra, Jose Julio
Jimenez-Berra, Jose Manuel
Johnson, J. Rosamond
Jones, Louia Vaughn
Jones, M. Sissieretta ("Black Patti")
Jordan, Robert
King, Coretta Scott
King, Wallace
Lawrence, William
Lawson, Raymond
Lee, Sylvia Olden
Lewis, Frederick
Lewis, Mabel Sanford
Little, Vera
Love, Hortense
Love, Josephine H.
Lucas, Carrie Melvin
McCoy, Seth
McFerrin, Robert
Madison, Earl
Martin, David
Martin, Eugene
Martin, Gertrude
Martinez, Maria Loretto ("The Black Malibran")
Mathis, Joyce
Matthews, Edward
Matthews, Inez
Maynor, Dorothy
Mims, Grace Lee
Mitchell, Abbie
Mitchell, Leona
Moore, Kermit
Moten Barnett, Etta
Newson, Roosevelt
Norman, Jessye
Pankey, Aubrey
Parker, Louise
Patterson, Willis
Peterson, Elwood
Pierson, Edward
Pindell, Annie Pauline ("The Black Nightingale")
Plato Broadley, Desseria
Rahn, Muriel
Rhea, La Julia
Richardson, William
Roberts, Howard
Robeson, Paul
Robinson, Faye
Rosemond, Andrew
Ruffin, George
Saint-Georges, The Chevalier de
Schuyler, Phillippa Duke
Selika, Marie
Shirley, George
Soubise, Julius
Spearman, Rawn
Spencer, Kenneth
Talbert, Florence Cole
Tapley, Daisy
Taylor, Tom
Thompson, Arthur
Tyler, Veronica
Tynes, Margaret
Van Buren, Catherine
Walker, Frances
Walker Turner, Rachel
Warfield, William
Watts, Andre
Weir, Felix
White, Frederick
White, José
White, Portia
Williams, Henry ("Harry")
Winters, Lawrence
Woodward, Sidney

Amphion Glee Club
Choral Study Club
Descendents of Mike & Phoebe
Fisk Jubilee Singers, The
Hampton Singers, The
McMillen and Sourbeck Jubilee Singers
Umbrian Glee Club, The
Williams Colored Singers
Wings Over Jordan

CONSERVATORY FOUNDERS

Lee, Pauline James
Lewis, Elma Ina
Marshall, Harriet Gibbs
Martin, David

EDUCATORS

Akpabot, Samuel
Amu, Ephraim
Anderson, Walter
Aning, Ben Akosa
Atkins, Carl
Axelsen, Doris Holland

Educators, continued

Baker, David
Bankole, Ayo
Billups, Kenneth
Blanton, Carol
Boyer, Horace
Braithwaite, James Roland
Brooks, Tilford
Brown, J. Harold
Brown, Thelma Wade
Butcher, Vada Easter
Caper, Valerie
Carey, Thomas
Childers, Lulu
Cordero, Roque
Da Costa, Noel
Dawson, William
De Bose, Tourgee
Dent, Jessie Covington
Douglass, Fannie Howard
Duncan, John
Duncan, Robert Todd
Dyett, Walter
Edet, Edna Smith
Ekwueme, Lazarus
Euba, Akin
Europe, Mary
Fax, Mark
Ferrell, Harrison
Floyd, Samuel
Foster, Frank
Foster, William
Fuller, Oscar
Furman, James
Garcia, William
Gaston, Oland
Gatlin, F. Nathaniel
Gerren, Nicholas
Goines, Leonard
Grant, Henry
Hancock, Eugene
Harreld, Kemper
Harris, Carl
Harrison, Frank
Haynes, Eugene
Hines Matthews, Altonell
Jackson, Raymond
James, Willis
Jeanty, Occilius
Johns, Altona Trent
Jones, Mildred Bryant
Jones, Pearl Williams
Kay, Ulysses
Kennedy, Anne Gamble
Kennedy, Joseph ("Joe")
Kennedy, Matthew
Kerr, Thomas
Killingsworth, John
King, Betty
Lawson, Warner
Layne, Maude Wanzer
Layton, Sr., John Turner
LeMon, Lillian Morris
Lew, William
Lewis, Elma Ina
Logan, Wendell
Lovell, John
McGinty, Doris Evans
McIntyre, Kenneth ("Ken")
McLin, Lena Johnson
Mando, Alfred
Marshall, Harriet Gibbs
Martin, David
Maultsby, Portia Katrenia
Meadows, Eddie
Merrifield, Norman
Moorehead, Consuela Lee
Nickerson, Camille Lucie
Nketia, Joseph
Nzewi, Emeka Meki
Patterson, Willis
Pittman, Evelyn La Rue
Pittman, Portia Washington
Polin, Roscoe
Reed, Addison
Roach, Hildred
Robinson, Florence Crim
Ryder, Georgia Atkins
Ryder, Noah
Simpson, Eugene
Smith, Hale
Smith, N. Clark
Smith, Richard
Smith, Warren
Southall, Geneva Handy
Southern, Eileen Jackson
Spearman, Rawn
Spiller, Isabelle T.
Standifer, James
Suthern, Orrin
Tapley, Daizy
Thomas, C. Edward
Tibbs, Roy
Tyler, Jesse
Von Charlton, Rudolph
Walker, Frances
Walker, George
Washington, Rachel
Watts, Nellie
Whalum, Wendell
Whatley, John ("Fess")
Wilson, Clarence
Wilson, Olly
Wilson, W. Llewellyn
Woodard, Nelmatilda R.
Work, Frederick
Work, John Wesley II
Work, John Wesley III
Wright, Josephine
Wyatt, Lucius Reynolds

ENTERTAINERS AND ENTERTAINER GROUPS (including rock, rhythm 'n' blues, and popular-music singers)

Aldridge, Ira Frederick
Ashford & Simpson
Baker, Josephine
Baker, Lavern
Banks, Billy
Barbour, J. Berni
Bassey, Shirley
Bates, Clayton ("Peg Leg")
Benton, Brook
Berry, Charles ("Chuck")
Bohee, George
Brooks, Shelton
Brown, James
Brown, Oscar, Jr.
Brown, Tom
Browning, Ivan
Bryant, Joyce
Bryant, William ("Willie")
Butler, Jerry
Carroll, Diahann
Charles, Ray
Cliff, "Jimmy"
Cole, Robert ("Bob")
Cooke, Sam
Cornmeali, Signor
Creach, John ("Papa")
Dandridge, Dorothy
Daniels, William ("Billy")
Davis, Gussie
Davis, Sammy, Jr.
Dixon, Will
Domino, Antoine ("Fats")
Dorsey, William ("Billy")
Dudley, S. H. ("Hapsy")
Edmonds, Shepherd
Edwards, Jody (Butterbeans")
Edwards, Susie ("Butterbeans & Susie")
Evans, Ernest ("Chubby Checker")
Flack, Roberta
Franklin, Aretha
Gaye, Marvin
Grant, Earl
Green, Al
Hall, Juanita
Hathaway, Donny
Hayes, Isaac
Hegamin, Lucille Nelson
Henderson, Rosa Deschamps

Hendricks, Frederick ("King Houdini")
Hendrix, James ("Jimi")
Henry, Lew
Hewlett, James
Hibbert, Frederick ("Fred" or "Toots")
Horne, Lena
Jackson, Graham
James, Etta
Jefferson, Edgar ("Eddie")
Jeffries, Herb
Johnson, Fred ("Deacon")
Johnson, William ("Billy")
Jones, Irving
Jordan, Louis
Kemp, Emmerlyne J. ("Emme")
Kendricks, Edward ("Eddie")
King, William ("Billy")
Kitt, Eartha Mae
Knight, Gladys M.
Labelle, Patti
Layton, Jr., J. Turner
Long, Avon
Lutcher, Nellie
Lyles, Aubrey
Lymon, Frankie
Mabley, Jackie ("Moms")
McDaniel, Hattie
McIntosh, Hattie
McIntosh, Tom
McKinney, Nina Mae
McNair, Barbara
McNeil, Claudia Mae
McPhatter, Clyde
Marley, Robert Nesta
Mathis, Johnny
Mayfield, Curtis
Mercer, Mabel
Milburn, Richard
Miller, Flournoy ("Honey")
Mills, Florence
Moore, Melba
Muse, Clarence
Nash, John ("Johnny")
Ousley, Curtis ("King Curtis")
Overstreet, W. Benton
Paul, Billy
Penniman, Richard ("Little Richard")
Peters, Brock
Pickett, Wilson
Preston, William
Pride, Charley
Prysock, Arthur
Redding, Otis
Ross, Diana
Shipp, Jesse
Short, Robert ("Bobby")
Smith, Ada Beatrice ("Bricktop")
Spiller, Isabelle T.
Spiller, William
Sublett, John ("Buck & Bubbles")
Summer, Donna
Sweatman, Wilbur
Taj Mahal
Taylor, Eva
Turner, Ike and Tina
Uggams, Leslie
Vereen, Benjamin ("Ben")
Walker, Aida Overton
Walker, George
Warwick, Dionne
Weston, Horace
White, Barry
Whitman, Alberta ("Bert")
Whitman, Alice
Whitman, Essie Barbara
Whitman, Mable
Whitney, Salem
Williams, Egbert ("Bert")
Wilson, Edith
Womack, Robert ("Bobby")
Wonder, Stevie

Booker T. & the MGs
Charioteers, The
Crusaders, The
Deep River Boys, The
Dells, The
Delta Rhythm Boys, The
Earth, Wind, and Fire
Gladys Knight and the Pips
Golden Gate Quartets
Hyers Sisters, The
Impressions, The
Ink Spots, The
Isley Brothers, The
Jackson Five, The
Luca Family, The
Martha & the Vandellas
Mills Brothers, The
Miracles, The
O'Jays, The
Platters, The
Southernaires, The
Spinners, The
Staple Singers, The
Supremes, The
Temptations, The
Turner, Ike and Tina
War

FOLKLORISTS AND FOLKSINGERS

Belafonte, Harold ("Harry")
Bibb, Leon
Dunham, Katherine
Gordon, Odetta
Havens, Richard ("Richie")
James, Willis Laurence
Makeba, Miriam Zenzi
Nickerson, Camille Lucie
Ofori, Agyare T.
Olatunji, Michael
Ridley, Florida Ruffin
White, Joshua ("Josh")
Work, Frederick
Work, John Wesley II

GOSPEL GROUPS

Caravans, The
Clouds of Joy, The Mighty, Mighty
Dixie Hummingbirds, The
Five Blind Boys of Alabama, The
Five Blind Boys of Mississippi, The
Gospel Chimes, The
Gospel Harmonettes, The
Mitchell's Christian Singers
Nightingales, The Sensational
Soul Stirrers, The
Swan Silvertone Singers, The
Ward Singers, The

GOSPEL MUSICIANS

Anderson, T. C. ("Queen C.")
Barrett Campbell, Delois
Boyer, Horace C.
Bradford, Alex
Brewster, W. Herbert
Caesar, Shirley
Campbell, Lucie E.
Cheeks, Julius ("June")
Cleveland, James
Coates, Dorothy Love
Cooke, Sam
Crouch, Andrae
Dixon, Jessy
Dorsey, Thomas Andrew
Dranes, Arizona
Franklin, Aretha
Frye, Theodore
Griffin, Bessie
Hawkins, Edwin
Jackson, Mahalia
Jones, Pearl Williams
Knight, Marie
Martin, Roberta
Martin, Sallie
Preston, William ("Billy")
Rawls, Louis ("Lou")
Reese, Della
Sellers, John ("Brother John")
Smith, Willie Mae Ford

Gospel Musicians, continued

Tharpe, Rosetta Nubin ("Sister")
Tindley, Charles
Utterback, Clinton
Washington, Dinah (neé Ruth Jones)
Ward, Clara
Williams, Marion

HYMNBOOK COMPILERS

Allen, Richard
Layton, Sr., John Turner
Soga, John Henderson
Soga, Tiyo
Taylor, Marshall W.

JAZZ ARRANGERS

Capers, Valerie
Cooke, Charles ("Doc")
Dameron, Tadley ('Tadd")
Golson, Benny
Hathaway, Donny
Henderson, Fletcher
Henderson, Horace
Mundy, James ("Jimmy")
Norman, Fred
Oliver, Melvin ("Sy")
Parrish, Avery
Redman, Donald ("Don")
Sampson, Edgar
Stone, Jesse
Strayhorn, William ("Billy" "Sweetpea")
Vodery, Will

JAZZ GROUPS

Art Ensemble of Chicago, The
Coronets, The
Crusaders, The
Int. Sweethearts of Rhythm
Modern Jazz Quartet
Osibisa
Revolutionary Ensemble, The
Swinging Rays of Rhythm, The

JAZZ KEYBOARDS

Abrams, Richard ("Muhall")
Armstrong, Lillian Hardin ("Lil")
Barrett, Emma ("Sweet Emma")
Barron, Kenneth ("Kenny")
Basie, William ("Count")
Bonnemere, Edward
Brand, Adolph ("Dollar")
Buckner, Milton ("Milt")
Carlisle, Una Mae
Cole, Nat "King"
Coltrane, Alice McLeod
Cowell, Stanley
Davis, William ("Wild Bill")
Donegan, Dorothy
Dorsey, Thomas ("Georgia Tom")
Drew, Kenneth ("Kenny")
Duke, George
Ellington, Edward ("Duke")
Flanagan, Tommy
Hancock, Herbert ("Herbie")
Harris, Barry
Hawes, Hampton
Henderson, Fletcher ("Smack")
Heywood, Edward ("Eddie")
Hill, Andrew
Hines, Earl ("Fatha")
Hopkins, Claude
Jackson, Clifton ("Cliff")
Jamal, Ahmad
Johnson, J. C.
Johnson, James ("James P.")
Jones, James ("Jimmy")
Jones, Richard
Lee, Julia
Lewis, John
Lewis, Ramsey
Marable, Fate
McCann, Leslie ("Les")
McShann, Jay
Montgomery, Charles ("Buddy")
Moten, Bennie
Parrish, Avery
Payne, Benny
Peterson, Oscar
Pierce, Wilhelmina G. ("Billie")
Powell, Earl ("Bud")
Price, Samuel ("Sammy")
Rhodes, Todd
Robert, Charles ("Luckey")
Russell, Luis
Scott, Hazel Dorothy
Scott, Shirley
Shirley, Donald
Smith, James ("Jimmy")
Smith, Lonnie
Smith, William ("Willie-The-Lion")
Stone, Jesse
Sun Ra
Tapscott, Horace
Taylor, Cecil
Taylor, William ("Billy")
Tucker, Robert ("Bobby")
Turner, Joe
Tyner, Alfred
Waller, Thomas ("Fats")
Weston, Randolph ("Randy")
Williams, Mary Lou
Wilson, Theodore ("Teddy")
Wooding, Samuel ("Sam")

JAZZ PERCUSSIONS

Ayers, Roy
Barbarin, Paul
Blakey, Art
Bradshaw, Myron ("Tiny")
Campbell, Ambrose
Catlett, Sidney ("Big Sid")
Chambers, Joseph ("Joe")
Clarke, Kenneth ("Kenny" "Klook")
Cobham, William ("Billy")
Cole, William ("Cozy")
Cooper, Jerome
Dodds, Warren ("Baby")
Greer, William ("Sonny")
Hamilton, Foreststorn ("Chico")
Hampton, Lionel
Haynes, Roy
Heath, Albert ("Tootie")
Hutcherson, Robert ("Bobby")
Jackson, Milton ("Milt")
Johnson, Folorunso ("Ginger")
Jones, Elvin
Jones, Jonathan ("Papa Jo")
Jones, Joseph ("Philly Joe")
McKinney, William ("Bill")
Price, Jesse
Roach, Maxwell ("Max")
Santamaria, Ramon ("Mongo")
Saunders, Theodore ("Red")
Shepherd, Berisford ("Shep")
Singleton, Arthur ("Zutty")
Smith, Warren
Warren, Guy
Webb, William ("Chick")

JAZZ SINGERS

Anikulapo-Kuti, Fela
Bailey, Pearl
Calloway, Blanche
Calloway, Cabell ("Cab")
Carter, Betty
Davy, Gloria
Deppe, Lois
Eckstine, William ("Billy," "Mr. B")
Fitzgerald, Ella
Gonzales, Babs
Hall, Adelaide
Hendricks, John ("Jon")
Hibbler, Albert ("Al")
Holiday, Billie
Humes, Helen
Laine, Cleo
Lincoln, Abbey
Lucien, Jon
McRae, Carmen
Middleton, Velma
Simone, Nina

Staton, Dakota
Sullivan, Maxine
Tabu, Pascal
Vaughan, Sarah Lou ("Sissy")
Wilson, Nancy

JAZZ STRINGS

Ashby, Dorothy Jeanne
Baker, David
Barker, Daniel ("Danny")
Benson, George
Blanton, James ("Jimmy")
Braud, Wellman
Burrell, Kenneth ("Kenny")
Carter, Ronald ("Ron")
Chambers, Paul
Christian, Charles ("Charlie")
Davis, Richard
Dickerson, Carroll
Durham, Eddie
Edet, Edna Smith
Ellington II, Edward
Favors, Malachi
Foster, Frank
Foster, George ("Pops")
Franklin, William
Heath, Percy
Hinton, Milton ("Milt")
Jenkins, Leroy
Johnson, William ("Bill")
Kennedy, Joseph ("Joe")
Kirby, John
Lee, William ("Bill")
Mingus, Charles
Montgomery, John ("Wes")
Montgomery, William ("Monk")
Morgan, Albert ("Al")
Morrison, George
Page, Walter
Pettiford, Oscar
Piron, Armand
Ray Russell, Carline
Ridley, Laurence ("Larry")
Scott, Arthur ("Bud")
Sirone
Smith, Hezekiah ("Stuff")
Snowden, Elmer ("Pops")
South, Eddie
St. Cyr, John ("Johnny")
Tate, Erskine
Walton, Ortiz
White, Christopher ("Chris")

JAZZ WINDS

Acquaye, Saka
Adderley, Julian ("Cannonball")
Adderley, Nathaniel
Allen, Henry ("Red")
Ammons, Eugene ("Jug" "Gene")
Anderson, William ("Cat")
Armstrong, Daniel ("Satchmo")
Ayler, Albert
Ayler, Donald
Baquet, George
Barron, William ("Bill")
Bartz, Gary
Bascomb, Paul
Bascomb, Wilbur ("Dud")
Bechet, Sidney
Berry, Leon ("Chu")
Bigard, Leon ("Barney")
Bolden, Charles ("Buddy")
Bostic, Earl
Braxton, Anthony
Brown, Marion
Bushell, Garvin
Byas, Carlos ("Don")
Byrd, Donaldson ("Donald")
Carney, Harry
Carter, Bennett ("Benny")
Celestin, Oscar ("Papa")
Cheatham, Adolphus ("Doc")
Cherry, Donald ("Don")
Clayton, Wilbur ("Buck")
Coleman, Ornette
Coltrane, John
Creath, Charles ("Charlie")
Dash, St. Julian
Davis, Clifton ("Pike")
Davis, Eddie ("Lockjaw")
Davis, Miles
De Paris, Sidney
De Paris, Wilbur
Delisle, Louis ("Big Eye")
Dibango, Manu ("Dibbs")
Dickenson, Victor ("Vic")
Dixon, William ("Bill")
Dodds, Johnny
Dolphy, Eric
Dorham, McKinley ("Kenny")
Dunn, John ("Johnny")
Dutrey, Honore
Edison, Harry ("Sweets")
Eldridge, David ("Little Jazz")
Ellington, Mercer
Farmer, Arthur ("Art")
Fuller, Walter ("Rosetta")
Gillespie, John ("Dizzy")
Glenn, Evans
Gordon, Dexter
Griffin, John
Hall, Edmond
Handy, John
Hardwick, Otto ("Toby")
Hawkins, Coleman ("Bean" or "Hawk")
Hawkins, Erskine
Heath, James ("Jimmy")
Higginbotham, Jack ("Jay C.")
Hill, Theodore ("Teddy")
Hite, Les
Hodges, John ("Johnny" or "Rabbit")
Howard, Darnell
Hubbard, Frederick D. ("Freddie")
Jacquet, Jean
Jarman, Joseph
Johnson, Albert ("Budd")
Johnson, James ("J. J.")
Johnson, William ("Bunk")
Jones, Quincy
Jones, Robert
Jones, Thaddeus ("Thad")
Jordan, Clifford
Kenyatta, Robin
Keppard, Freddie
Kirk, Andrew ("Andy")
Kirk, Rahsaan Roland
Ladnier, Thomas ("Tommy")
Lake, Oliver
Laws, Hubert
Laws, Ronald ("Ronnie")
Lee, A. Clifton
Lee, George
Lewis, George
Liston, Melba Doretta
Lunceford, James ("Jimmy")
McGhee, Howard
McIntyre, Kenneth ("Ken")
McLean, John ("Jackie")
Masekela, Hugh
Mensah, Emmanuel
Miley, James ("Bubber")
Mitchell, Roscoe
Mitchell, William ("Billy")
Morton, Henry ("Benny")
Mundy, James ("Jimmy")
Nance, Willis ("Ray")
Nanton, Joseph ("Tricky Sam")
Navarro, Theodore ("Fats")
Newman, Joseph ("Joe")
Nicholas, Albert ("Al")
Noone, Jimmie
Oliver, Joseph ("King")
Ory, Edward ("Kid")
Osei, Teddy
Owens, James ("Jimmy")
Page, Oran ("Hot Lips")
Parker, Charles ("Charlie" "Bird")
Payne, Cecil ("Zodiac")
Picou, Alphonse
Pierce, Joseph ("Dede")
Poindexter, Norwood ("Pony")
Redman, Walter
Rivers, Samuel ("Sam")
Rollins, Theodore ("Sonny")

Jazz Winds, continued

Sanders, Farrell ("Pharoah")
Scott, Cecil
Sears, Albert("Al")
Sedric, Eugene ("Gene Honey Bear")
Shavers, Charles ("Charlie")
Shepp, Archie
Shorter, Wayne
Simeon, Omer
Smith, Cladys ("Jabbo")
Smith, Henry ("Buster")
Smith, Joe
Smith, Leo
Smith, William ("Willie")
Snow, Valaida
Stewart, Rex
Stitt, Edward ("Sonny")
Tchicai, John
Terry, Clark
Thompson, Eli ("Lucky")
Tio, Lorenzo, Jr.
Tizol, Juan
Turrentine, Stanley
Washington, Grover
Webster, Benjamin ("Ben")
Wells, William ("Dickie")
White, Andrew
Wilkins, Ernest ("Ernie")
Williams, Charles ("Cootie")
Williams, Richard
Williams, Stanley ("Fess")
Wilson, Gerald
Young, Lester ("Prez")

JOURNALISTS/CRITICS

Abdul-Rahim, Raoul
Allen, Cleveland G.
Calloway, Earl
Garland, Phyllis T. ("Phyl")
George, Maude Roberts
Graham, Gladys
Hayes, Robert
Holt, Nora
Nolan, Robert ("Dean")
Russell, Sylvester
Stone, Theodore
Walton, Lester

MILITARY MUSICIANS

Adams, Alton Augustus
Allen, Peter
Anderson, Joseph
Augustus, Edward
Bailey, Evangeline
Bazadier, Philip
Benson, Nero
Brown, George
Brown, Scipio
Brymn, James ("Tim")
Carter, Dennis
Clark, James
Conter, John
Cozzens, Richard
Crossman, Simeon
Dulf, George
Europe, James ("Jim")
Fisk, Cato
Gordon, Joseph
Hammond, Wade
Jeanty, Occide ("Fils")
Jolly, Jabez
Lew, Barzilai ("Zelah" or "Zeal")
Looks, Samuel
Loving, Walter
Middleton, George
Mikell, Francis
Moore, Hamilton
Nickens, William
Noble, Jordan ("Matchless Drummer")
Perkins, Nimrod
Rodriguez, Sebastian
Roland, Edward
Seymour, Francis
Simpson, Frederick ("Fred")
Thomas, A. Jack
Thompson, Egbert
Tiffany, Cyrus
Wall, Jessie or Jesse

MINSTRELS

Bland, James
Bohee, James
Bohee, George
Butler, John ("Picayune")
Fletcher, Tom
Georgia Minstrels, The
Gillam, Harry
Handy, William ("W. C.")
Hicks, Charles ("Barney")
Hogan, Ernest
Johnson, Lew
Kersands, William ("Billy")
Lane, William ("Master Juba")
Love, James ("Daddy")
Lucas, Sam
McClain, Billy
Patterson, Ulysses
Scott, Robert ("The Albemarle Minstrel")
Simond, Ike ("Old Slack")
Smith, Henderson
Weston, Bobby
Weston, Horace
Withers, Mazie Muller ("Lady Trombonist")
Wright, P. T.

MUSICOLOGISTS AND ETHNOMUSICOLOGISTS

Akpabot, Samuel
Ballanta-Taylor, Nicholas
Butcher, Vada Easter
Edet, Edna
Ekwueme, Lazarus
Floyd, Samuel
McGinty, Doris Evans
Maultsby, Portia Katrenia
Nketia, Joseph
Nzewi, Meki
Southall, Geneva
Southern, Eileen Jackson
Wright, Josephine

ORGANISTS

Appo, Ann
Braithwaite, James Roland
Charlton, Melville
Cooper, William
Forbes, Kathleen Holland
Gaston, Oland
Gossette, Walter
Hancock, Eugene
Phillips, T. K. E.
Suthern, Orrin

OPERA/CONCERT SINGERS

Addison, Adele
Allen, Betty Lou
Arle-Tilz, Coretti
Arroyo, Martina
Balthrop, Carmen Arlene
Bledsoe, Julius
Boatwright, McHenry
Brice, Carol
Brown, Anne Wiggins
Brown, William Albert
Bryant, Joyce
Bumbry, Grace Ann
Carey, Thomas
Cato, Minto
Clough, Estelle Pickney
Cooper, Maurice
Dale, Clamma
Davy, Gloria
Davis, Ellabella
Dawson, Mary Cardwell

Dobbs, Mattiwilda
Dowdy, Helen
Drury, Theodore
Duncan, Robert Todd
Estes, Simon
Evanti, Lillian
Franklin, William
Frierson, Andrew
George, Zelma Watson
Grist, Reri
Harris, Hilda
Holland, Charles
Jarboro, Caterina
Killebrew, Gwendolyn
King, Juanita
Little, Vera
McCoy, Seth
McFerrin, Robert
Mitchell, Leona
Parker, Louise
Peters, Brock
Peterson, Elwood
Pierson, Edward
Plato Broadley, Desseria
Price, Leontyne
Rhea, La Julia
Robinson, Faye
Shirley, George
Smith, Muriel
Thompson, Arthur
Tyler, Veronica
Tynes, Margaret
Verrett, Shirley
Warfield, William
Weathers, Felicia
White, Willard
Williams, Camilla

PROFESSIONAL ORGANIZATIONS

Afro-American Music Opportunity Association
Association for the Advancement of Creative Musicians
Clef Club, The
National Association of Negro Musicians

PRODUCERS, PROMOTERS, AND PUBLISHERS

Bell, Thom
Bostic, Joe
Bracken, James ("Jim")
Carter, Vivian
Cumbo, Clarissa Burton
Dawson, Mary Cardwell
Drury, Theodore
Dudley, S. H.
Gamble, Kenneth
Gordy, Berry, Jr.
Holland-Dozier-Holland
Hackley, E. Azalia
Hackney, William
Handy, William ("W.C.")
Huff, Leon
Northern, Chauncey
Pace, Harry
Proctor, Henry Hugh
René, Leon T.
René, Otis J.
Smith, Albert
Van Peebles, Melvin
Watts, Nellie
Williams, Clarence
Williams, J. Mayo ("Ink")

RAGTIME MUSICIANS

Blake, James ("Eubie")
Bowman, Euday
Chauvin, Louis
Cook, Jean Lawrence
Hayden, Scott
Jackson, Anthony
Johnson, James P.
Joplin, Scott
Jordan, Joe
Marshall, Arthur
Matthews, Artie
Morton, Ferdinand ("Jelly Roll")
Patterson, Sam
Roberts, Charles ("Lucky")
Scott, James
Smith, William ("Willie-the-Lion")
Thompson, Charles
Turpin, Thomas ("Tom")
Warfield, Charles ("Charlie")

SOCIETY DANCE-BAND LEADERS AND BRASS-BAND LEADERS

Alsdorf, Dubois B.
Anderson, Hallie
Anderson, Joseph
Brymn, James ("Tim")
Connor, Aaron
Craig, Walter
Dabney, Ford
Dennis, A.
Desdunes, Dan
Dupree, William
Europe, James ("Jim")
Finney, Theodore
Freeman, Bergert
Gillam, Joseph
Gilliat, Simeon
Guy, Harry
Hart, Henry
Hazzard, Isaac
Hemmenway, James
Jackson, William
Johnson, Francis ("Frank")
Johnson, John
Julius, John
Lucas, Marie
Mando, Alfred
McAfee, Charles
O'Fake, Peter
Peyton, Dave
Plet, A.
Porter, Oliva Shipp
Shook, Ben
Smith, Harry
Tinsley, Pedro
Thompson, Egbert
Wood, Obediah

SONGWRITERS

Accooe, Willis
Bell, Thom
Blake, J. Hubert ("Eubie")
Bland, James
Bowman, Elmer
Bowman, Euday
Bradford, Perry ("Mule")
Brewster, W. Herbert
Brooks, Shelton
Burgie, Irving ("Lord Burgess")
Cheeks, Julius ("June")
Connor, Aaron
Creamer, Henry
Crouch, Andrae
Davis, Gussie
Dixon, Jessy
Dorsey, Thomas
Edmonds, Shepherd
Gamble, Kenneth
Holland-Dozier-Holland
Higginbotham, Irene
Hill, John ("J. Leubrie")
Huff, Leon
Jones, Clarence
Jones, Irving
Jordan, Joe
Layton, Jr., J. Turner
Lemonier, Tom
Mack, Cecil
McClain, Billy

Songwriters, continued

Pinkard, Maceo
René, Leon T.
René, Otis J.
Rogers, Alexander ("Alex")
Smith, Chris
Stone, Fred
Thompson, Dekoven
Tindley, Charles
Tyers, William ("Bill")
Vaughan, James
White, Barry
Williams, Clarence
Williams, Spencer

SYMPHONY CONDUCTORS AND INSTRUMENTALISTS

Allen, Sanford
Anderson, Edward
Collymore, Winston
Cumbo, Marion
Davis, Arthur
De Priest, James
Dixon, Dean
Dixon, Lucille
Dunbar, Rudolph
Emidee
Ferrell, Harrison
Frazier, James
Freeman, Paul
Hall, Ian
Handy, D. Antoinette
Harris, Margaret
Hobson, Ann
Hunt, Darrold
Jackson, Isaiah
Jones, Elayne
Jones, Harold
Kennedy, Joseph ("Joe")
Lee, Everett
Leon, Tania
Lewis, Henry
Madison, Earl
Moore, Kermit
Nickerson, William
Porter, Karl
Prattis Jennings, Patricia
Simmons, Calvin
Smith, Raymond
Smyles, Harry
Thompson, Leon
Walton, Ortiz
Watkins, Julius
White, Donald
Wilder, Joseph ("Joe")

SYMPHONY ORCHESTRAS

Philadelphia Concert Orchestra
Symphony of the New World

VAUDEVILLE

Accooe, Willis
Barbour, J. Berni
Batson, Flora
Bowman, Elmer
Brooks, Shelton
Brown, Tom
Chappelle, Patrick ("Pat")
Clough, Inez
De Wolfe Sisters, The
Edmonds, Shepherd
Edwards, Jody ("Butterbeans")
Edwards, Susie ("Butterbeans & Susie")
Gibbs, Lloyd
Gilpin, Charles
Griffin Sisters, The
Hyers, Anna Madah
Hyers, Emma Louise
Johnson, J. Rosamond
Johnson, William ("Billy")
Jones, Irving
Jones, M. Sissieretta ("Black Patti")
King, Wallace
Layton, Jr., J. Turner
Lowery, P. G.
Lucas, Carrie Melvin
Lyles, Aubrey
McDaniel, Hattie
McIntosh, Hattie
Memphis Students, The
Miller, Flournoy ("Honey")
Mitchell, Abbie
Overstreet, W. Benton
Plato Broadley, Desseria
Shipp, Jesse A.
Smart Set, The
Spiller, Isabelle T.
Spiller, William
Sublett, John ("Bubbles")
Sweatman, Wilbur
Tapley, Daisy
Walker, George
Walker Turner, Rachel
Whitman, Alberta ("Bert")
Whitman, Alice
Whitman, Essie Barbara
Whitman, Mable
Whitney, Salem Tutt
Williams, Egbert ("Bert")
Woodward, Sidney

WRITERS/LYRICISTS

Abdul-Rahim, Raoul
Atkins, Russell
Baraka, Imamu Amiri
Brown, William
Dabney, Wendell
Delany, Martin
Desdunes, Rudolphe
Dumervé, Constantin
Dunbar, Paul Laurence
Graham Dubois, Shirley
Hare, Maud Cuney
Hughes, Langston
Handy, D. Antoinette
Johnson, James
LaBrew, Arthur
Ladipo, Duro
Layne, Maude W.
Lester, Julius
Lovell, John
Locke, Alain
Lovinggood, Penman
Northup, Solomon
Payne, Daniel
Razaf, Andy
Roach, Hildred
Shipp, Jesse
Sissle, Noble
Southall, Geneva
Southern, Eileen
Spellman, A. B.
Tilghman, Amelia L.
Trotter, James

SELECTED BIBLIOGRAPHY

BOOKS

The titles in the following list represent the books most frequently consulted in the preparation of this dictionary, alphabetized by author or title. When cited in the biographical entries, the books are indicated by abbreviations as given below. The list also includes a few books that I was unable to use because they were published (or came to my attention) after my research was completed but are nevertheless highly recommended on the basis of my examination.

AbdulBCM — Abdul, Raoul. *Blacks in Classical Music*. New York: Dodd, Mead & Co., 1977.

AbdulFBE — ———. *Famous Black Entertainers of Today*. New York: Dodd, Mead & Co., 1974.

WWAfrica — *Africa Year Book & Who's Who, 1977*. London: Africa Journal Limited, 1976.

AlHen — Allen, Walter C. *Hendersonia: The Music of Fletcher Henderson and His Musicians: a Bio-Discography*. Highland Park, N.J.; Walter C. Allen, 1973.

GMEncy — Anderson, Robert and North, Gail. *Gospel Music Encyclopedia*. New York: Sterling Publishing Co., 1979.

ASCAP — *ASCAP Biographical Dictionary of Composers, Authors, and Publishers*. 1966 ed. Comp. and ed. by the Lynn Farnol Group. New York: American Society of Composers, Authors and Publishers, 1966.

BakBCS — Baker, David N.; Belt, Lida M.; Hudson, Herman C. *The Black Composer Speaks*. Metuchen, N.J.: The Scarecrow Press, 1978.

Baker — *Baker's Biographical Dictionary of Musicians*. Revised by Nicolas Slonimsky. 6th edition. New York: Schirmer Books, 1978.

Berendt, Joachim. *The Jazz Book: From New Orleans to Rock and Free Jazz*. 4th rev. ed. 1973. Transl. by Dan Morgenstern and Helmut and Barbara Bredigkeit. New York: Lawrence Hill & Co., 1975.

WWHarlem — Beresford, Sylvester, and Briggs, Trottman, eds. *Who's Who in Harlem*. New York: Magazine and Periodical Printing & Publishing Co., 1949.

BiogNig — *Biographia Nigeriana: A Biographical Dictionary of Eminent Nigerians*. Ed. by S. A. Orimoloye. Boston: G. K. Hall, 1977.

Blesh — Blesh, Rudi, and Janis, Harriet. *They All Played Ragtime*. 1950. 4th ed. New York: Oak Publications, 1971.

Boardman, Gerald. *The American Musical Theatre*. New York: Oxford University Press, 1978.

Bogle, Donald. *Brown Sugar: Eighty Years of America's Black Superstars*. New York: Harmony Books, 1980.

Brawley, Benjamin. *The Negro Genius: A New Appraisal of the Achievement of the American Negro in Literature and the Fine Arts*. 1937. Reprint. New York: Biblo & Tannen, 1966.

Bull — Bull, Storm. *Index to Biographies of Contemporary Composers*. Vol. 2. Metuchen, N.J.: The Scarecrow Press, 1974.

Burton, Jack. *The Blue Book of Broadway Musicals*. 1952. With additions by Larry Freeman. Watkins Glen, N.Y.: Century House, 1969.

———. *The Blue Book of Tin Pan Alley: A Human Interest Anthology of American Popular Music*. 1950. Expanded new ed. 2

vols. Watkins Glen, N.Y.: Century House, 1962.

Carroll, John M., ed. *The Black Military Experience in the American West.* New York: Liveright, 1971.

CharCB Charters, Samuel. *The Country Blues.* New York: Rhinehart & Co., 1959.

———. *The Bluesmen: The Story and the Music of the Men Who Made the Blues.* New York: Oak Publications, 1967.

CharLB ———. *The Legacy of the Blues.* 1975. Reprint. New York: Da Capo Press, 1977.

——— and Kunstadt, Leonard. *Jazz: A History of the New York Scene.* New York: Doubleday & Co., 1962.

Cherry, Gwendolyn; Thomas, Ruby; Willis, Pauline. *Portraits in Color. The Lives of Colorful Negro Women.* New York: Pageant Press, 1962.

ChilWW Chilton, John. *Who's Who of Jazz: Storyville to Swing Street.* 1970. Reprint. Chicago: Time-Life Records Special Edition, 1978.

Dabney, Wendell P. *Cincinnati's Colored Citizens.* 1926. Reprint. New York: Negro Universities Press, 1970.

DanceWCB Dance, Stanley. *The World of Count Basie.* New York: Charles Scribner's Sons, 1980.

DanceWDE ———. *The World of Duke Ellington.* New York: Charles Scribner's Sons, 1970.

DanceWEH ———. *The World of Earl Hines.* New York: Charles Scribner's Sons, 1977.

DanceWS ———. *The World of Swing.* New York: Charles Scribner's Sons, 1974.

Dannett, Sylvia. *Profiles of Negro Womanhood.* Yonkers, N.Y.: Educational Heritage, Inc., 1964.

Davis, Lenwood C. *The Black Woman in American Society: A Selected Annotated Bibliography.* Boston: G.K. Hall, 1975.

Davis, Russell. *Black Americans in Cleveland.* Washington, D.C.: Associated Publishers, Inc., 1972.

Des Desdunes, Rudolphe. *Nos Hommes et Notre Histoire.* 1911. Transl. by Sister Dorothea McCants. *Our People and Our History.* Baton Rouge: Louisiana State University Press, 1973.

DAB *Dictionary of American Biography.* Ed. by Allen Johnson and Dumas Malone. 20 vols. New York. 1928-37. Supplements, 1944-74.

DiGod Dixon, Robert M. W., and Godrich, Jon. *Blues and Gospel Records, 1902-1942.* Rev. ed. London: Storyville Publications, 1969.

Dumervé Dumervé, Constantin. *Histoire de la musique en Haiti.* Port-au-Prince: Imprimerie des Antilles, 1968.

Dunbar, Ernest. *The Black Expatriates.* New York: E.P. Dutton, 1968.

Ebony Success Library, The. 3 vols. Chicago: Johnson Publications, 1973.

EAB *Encyclopedia of American Biography.* Ed. by John A. Garraty and Jerome L. Sternstein. New York: Harper & Row, 1974.

Ewen Ewen, David. *New Encyclopedia of the Opera.* New York: Hill & Wang, Inc., 1971.

FeaJS Feather, Leonard. *The Encyclopedia of Jazz in the Sixties.* New York: Horizon Press, 1966.

FeaEJ ———. *The New Edition of the Encyclopedia of Jazz.* New York: Horizon Press, 1960.

FeaGitJS ——— and Gitler, Ira. *The Encyclopedia of Jazz in the Seventies.* New York: Horizon Press, 1976.

Fetis Fétis, François J. *Biographie universelle des musiciens.* 2nd ed. Paris, 1866-1870.

Flet Fletcher, Tom. *100 Years of the Negro in Show Business.* New York: Burdge & Co., Ltd., 1954.

Garland, Phyl. *The Sound of Soul.* Chicago: Henry Regnery & Co., 1969.

GWW *Ghana's Who's Who, 1972-73.* Ed. by Charles Bartels. Accra, Ghana: Bartels Publishing Co., 1972.

Git Gitler, Ira. *Jazz Masters of the Forties.* 1966. Reprint. New York: Collier Books, 1974.

Giv Given, Dave. *The Dave Given Rock 'n' Roll Stars Handbook.* Smithtown, New York: Exposition Press, 1980.

Green Green, Robert Ewell. *Black Defenders of America, 1775-1973.* Chicago: Johnson Publications, 1974.

	Green, Stanley. *Encyclopedia of the Musical Theatre*. New York: Dodd, Mead & Co., 1976.
Handy	Handy, D. Antoinette. *Black Women and American Bands and Orchestras*. Metuchen, N.J.: Scarecrow Press, 1981.
Hare	Hare, Maude Cuney. *Negro Musicians and Their Music*. Washington, D.C.: Associated Publishers, 1936.
BWW	Harris, Sheldon. *Blues Who's Who: A Biographical Dictionary of Blues Singers*. New Rochelle, N.Y.: Arlington House Publishers, 1979.
ModJ	Harrison, Max, et al. *Modern Jazz: The Essential Records*. A critical selection by Max Harrison, Alun Morgan, Ronald Atkins, Michael James, Jack Cooke. London: Aquarius Books, 1975.
	Hatch, James V., and Abdullah, Omanii. *Black Playwrights, 1823-1977: An Annotated Bibliography of Plays*. New York: R. R. Bowker Co., 1977.
Hayes	Hayes, Cedric, comp. *A Discography of Gospel Records, 1937-1971*. Copenhagen: Karl Emil Knudsen, 1973.
Heil	Heilbut, Tony. *The Gospel Sound: Good News and Bad Times*. New York: Simon & Schuster, 1971.
	Hipsher, Edward. *American Opera and Its Composers*. 1927. Expanded ed. Philadelphia: Theodore Presser, 1934.
	Horn, David. *The Literature of American Music in Books and Folk Music Collections: A Fully Annotated Bibliography*. Metuchen, N.J.: Scarecrow Press, 1977.
Hughes	Hughes, Langston, and Meltzer, Milton. *Black Magic: A Pictorial History of the Negro in American Entertainment*. Englewood Cliffs, N.J.: Prentice-Hall, Inc., 1967.
JaTi	Jasen, David A., and Tichenor, Trebor. *Rags and Ragtime: A Musical History*. New York: The Seabury Press, 1978.
Jac	Jackson, Irene V. *Afro-American Religious Music: A Bibliography and a Catalogue of Gospel Music*. Westport, Conn. Greenwood Press, 1979.
Jep	Jepsen, Grunnet Jorgen. *Jazz Records: A Discography, 1942-1968*. 11 vols. Copenhagen: Karl Emil Knudsen, 1963-70.
JohnBM	Johnson, James Weldon. *Black Manhattan*. New York: Alfred A. Knopf, 1930.
Kink	Kinkle, Roger D. *The Complete Encyclopedia of Popular Music and Jazz, 1900-1950*. 4 vols. New Rochelle, N.Y.: Arlington House, 1974.
CBDict	Kutsch, Karl Josef, and Riemens, Leo. *Concise Biographical Dictionary of Singers*. 1962. Transl., expanded and annotated by Harry Earl Jones. Fresno, Cal.: Chelton Book Co., 1969.
LaBrew	LaBrew, Arthur. *Studies in Nineteenth-Century Afro-American Music*. Detroit: Published by the author, 1976.
Layne	Layne, Maud Wanzer. *The Negro's Contribution to Music*. Philadelphia: Theodore Presser, 1942.
LeSl	Leadbitter, Mike, and Slaven, Neil, eds. *Blues Records, January 1943-December 1966*. New York: Oak Publications, 1969.
	Leadbitter, Mike, ed. *Nothing But the Blues*. London: Hanover Books, Ltd., 1971.
	McCarthy, Albert, et al. *Jazz on Record: A Critical Guide to the First 50 Years, 1917-1967*, by Albert McCarthy, Alun Morgan, Paul Oliver, Max Harrison, with additional contributions by Ronald Atkins et al. London: Hanover Books, 1968.
	MacGregor, Morris J., and Nalty, Bernard, eds. *Blacks in the Armed Forces: Basic Documents*. Wilmington, Del.: Scholarly Resources, 1980.
Maj	Majors, M.A. *Noted Negro Women*. Chicago: Donohue and Henneberry, 1893.
	Mapp, Edward. *Blacks in the Performing Arts*. Metuchen, N.J.: The Scarecrow Press, 1978.
MeeJMov	Meeker, David. *Jazz in the Movies: A Guide to Jazz Musicians, 1917-1977*. New Rochelle, N.Y.: Arlington House, 1977.
	Mossell, Gertrude Bustill. *The Work of the Afro-American Woman*. Philadelphia: George Ferguson & Co., 1884.
NegA	*Negro Almanac, The*. Comp. and ed. by Harry Ploski and Ernest Kaiser. 2nd rev. ed. New York: Bellwether Co., 1971.
NHB	*Negro Hand Book, The*. Ed. by Florence Murray. New York: Wendell Malliet & Co., 1942-49.

NYB — *Negro Year Book*. Ed. by Monroe N. Work. Tuskegee, Ala. Tuskegee Institute, 1912-1951.

Gro — *The New Grove Dictionary of Music and Musicians*. Ed. by Stanley Sadie. 20 vols. London: Macmillan Publishers Limited, 1980.

New York Times Directory of the Theatre, 1920-1970. New York: Arno Press, 1973.

NAW — *Notable American Women, 1607-1950: A Biographical Dictionary*. Ed. by Edward T. James and Janet Wilson James. 3 vols. Cambridge, Mass. The Belknap Press. 1971.

NAWM — *Notable American Women: The Modern Period*. Ed. by Barbara Sicherman and Carol Hurd Green. Cambridge, Mass., The Belknap Press, 1980.

Oliv — Oliver, Paul. *The Story of the Blues*. Philadelphia: Chilton Book Co., 1969.

Oster, Harry. *Living Country Blues*. Detroit: Folklore Associates, 1969.

Page, James A., comp. *Selected Black American Authors*. Boston: G. K. Hall, 1977.

Richardson, Clement. *The National Cyclopedia of the Colored Race*. Montgomery, Ala., National Publishing Co., 1919.

Roach — Roach, Hildred. *Black American Music: Past and Present*. Boston: Crescendo Publishing Co., 1973.

HNB — Robinson, Wilhelmena S. *Historical Negro Biographies*. Washington, D.C.: Publishers Company, Inc., 1967.

Rom — Romeo, Patricia. *Black America, 1968: The Year of Awakening*. Washington, D.C.: Publishers Company, Inc., 1969.

Souch — Rose, Al and Souchon, Edmond. *New Orleans Jazz: A Family Album*. 1967. Rev. ed. Baton Rouge: Louisiana State University Press, 1978.

Russ — Russell, Ross. *Jazz Style in Kansas City and the Southwest*. Berkeley: University of California Press, 1971.

Rust, Brian. *The American Record Label Book*. New Rochelle, N.Y.: Arlington House, 1978.

RustCED — ———. *The Complete Entertainment Discography*. New Rochelle, N.Y. Arlington House, 1973.

RustJR — ———. *Jazz Records, 1897-1942*. 2 vols. 4th rev. and enlarged ed. New Rochelle, N.Y.: Arlington House, 1978.

Sandbert, Larry, and Weissman, Dick. *The Folk Music Sourcebook*. New York: Alfred A. Knopf, 1976.

Schuller, Gunther. *Early Jazz: Its Roots and Musical Development*. New York: Oxford University Press, 1968.

Scobie, Edward. *Black Britannia*. Chicago: Johnson Publications, 1972.

Scruggs, Lawson. *Women of Distinction*. Raleigh, N.C.: Published by the Author, 1893.

Shapiro, Nat, and Hentoff, Nat, eds. *Hear Me Talkin' to Ya*. New York: Rhinehart, 1955.

ShawHS — Shaw, Arnold. *Honkers and Shouters: The Golden Years of Rhythm and Blues*. New York: Macmillan Publishing Co., 1978.

ShawR5 — ———. *The Rockin' '50s. The Decade That Transformed the Pop Music Scene*. New York: Hawthorne Books, Inc., 1974.

ShawWS — ———. *The World of Soul. Black America's Contribution to the Pop Music Scene*. New York: Cowles Book Co., 1970.

Simmons — Simmons, William. *Men of Mark: Eminent, Progressive and Rising*. 1887. Reprint. Chicago: Johnson Publishing Co., 1970.

Simond — Simond, Ike. *Old Slack's Reminiscence and Pocket History of the Colored Profession, from 1865 to 1891*. 1891. Reprint, with preface by Francis Lee Utley and introduction by Robert C. Toll. Bowling Green, Ohio: Bowling Green University Popular Press, 1974.

SouMBA — Southern, Eileen. *The Music of Black Americans*. New York: W. W. Norton, 1971.

SouRBM — ———, ed. *Readings in Black American Music*. New York: W. W. Norton, 1971.

Spradling, Mary M., ed. *In Black and White: Afro-Americans in Print*. 3rd edition. Detroit: Gale Research Company, 1980.

StamPRS — Stambler, Irwin. *Encyclopedia of Pop, Rock and Soul*. New York: St. Martin's Press, 1975.

StamFCW — ———and Landon, Grelum. *Encyclopedia of Folk, Country and Western Music*. New York: St. Martin's Press, 1969.

	Stewart-Baxter, Derrick. *Ma Rainey and the Classic Blues Singers*. London: Studio Vista, 1970.
Trot	Trotter, James M. *Music and Some Highly Musical People*. 1878. Reprint. New York: Johnson Reprint Corporation, 1968.
TudBM	Tudor, Dean and Tudor, Nancy. *Black Music*. Littleton, Colo.: Libraries Unlimited, Inc., 1979.
TudJ	———. *Jazz*. Littleton, Colo.: Libraries Unlimited, Inc., 1979.
Turn	Turner, Patricia. *Afro-American Singers. An Index and Preliminary Discography of Opera, Choral Music and Song*. Minneapolis: Challenge Productions, Inc., 1977.
WWW	*Who Was Who in America*. 6 vols. Chicago: Marquis Who's Who Inc., 1942-76.
WWBA	*Who's Who Among Black Americans*. Edited by William C. Matney. 2nd ed. Northbrook, Ill.: Who's Who Among Black Americans, Inc., Publishing Co., 1977-78.
WWAfrLit	*Who's Who in African Literature*. Tübingen, West Germany: Horst Erdmann Verlag, 1972.
WWA	*Who's Who in America*. 40th ed. Chicago: Marquis Who's Who, Inc., 1978-79.
WWCA	*Who's Who in Colored America*. 1st, 2nd eds., 1927, 1928, ed. by Joseph J. Boris. 3rd-6th eds., 1930-44, ed. by Thomas Yenser. New York: Who's Who in Colored America Corporation, 1927-1944. 7th ed., 1950, ed. by G. James Fleming and Christian E. Burckel. Yonkers-on-Hudson, N.Y.: Christian E. Burckel & Associates, 1950.
IntWWM	*Who's Who in Music, The International*. Ed. by Ernest Kay. 7th ed. Cambridge, England: Melrose Press, 1975.
WWN	*Who's Who in Nigeria*. Lagos, Nigeria: The Nigerian Printing & Publishing Co., Limited, 1956.
WWOpera	*Who's Who in Opera*. Ed. by Maria F. Rich. New York: Arno Press, 1976.
WWE	*Who's Who in the East*. 16th ed. Chicago: Marquis Who's Who, Inc., 1978-1979.
	Who's Who in the Theatre. Ed. by Ian Herbert. 16th ed. Detroit: Gale Research Co., 1977
WWAW	*Who's Who of American Women*. 11th ed. Chicago: Marquis Who's Who, Inc., 1979-1980.
WWCR	*Who's Who of the Colored Race*. Ed. by Frank Lincoln Mather. Chicago: n.p., 1915.
Wilkes	Wilkes, Laura. *Missing Pages in American History*. Washington, D.C.: Published by the author, 1919.
WilABW	Williams, Ora. *American Black Women in the Arts and Social Sciences*. Rev. ed. Metuchen, N.J.: The Scarecrow Press, 1978.

PERIODICALS AND NEWSPAPERS

The following is a highly selective list of titles of periodicals and newspapers I consulted; it does not include press materials made available to me through subscription to the Black Press Clipping Service. Dates are given in those cases where I used complete runs, but it should be observed that issues sometimes were missing, particularly among the microfilm copies of black newspapers.

	ASCAP Today
	Africa Report
	Baltimore Afro-American
BPIM	Black Prespective in Music, The, 1973-
	Boston Guardian
BMI	*BMI: The Many Worlds of Music*
Cadence	*Cadence Magazine*
CDef	*Chicago Defender*, 1909-
CleveG	*Cleveland Gazette*, 1883-1940
	Colored American Magazine, 1900-1908
ContA	*Contemporary Authors*, 1962-
ContK	*Contemporary Keyboard*, 1975-
	Crisis, The
CurBiog	*Current Biography*, 1940-
	Disc & That, 1978-
	Drum
Ebony	*Ebony*, 1941-
Essence	*Essence*
Encore	*Encore Worldwide News and Review*
IndF	*Indianapolis Freeman*, 1886-1924
	Index to Black Newspapers, 1978-
JNH	*Journal of Negro History*, 1916-
LivBl	*Living Blues*, 1970-
	Master Musician, The, 1919-1921
	Music and Artists, 1968-1972 (merged with the *Music Journal* in 1973).
NHB	*Negro History Bulletin*
	Negro Music Journal, 1902-1903
NYAge	*New York Age*, 1887-1960
AmstN	*New York Amsterdam News*
	New York Clipper
	New York Dramatic Mirror
NYFreeman	*New York Freeman*, 1884-1887
	New York Colored American, 1837-1841
	New York Globe, 1883-1884

NYT *New York Times*
New York Times Biographical Service
Norfolk Journal and Guide
PhilaT *Philadelphia Tribune*, 1912-1919
Record Research
SW *Southern Workman, The*
Sepia *Sepia*, 1953-
Washington, D.C., Bee
West Africa Review

ARCHIVES

The archives listed below undoubtedly have the richest holdings in the nation insofar as Afro-American and African music history are concerned. Moreover, they offer pleasant working conditions in that vertical files and special collections are well indexed. Several of the archives have dictionary catalogues of their holdings in print.

ChiHistSoc Chicago Historical Society, The Claude A. Barnett Collection.

ChiVH Chicago Public Library, Carter G. Woodson Regional Library, Vivian G. Harsh Collection of Afro-American History and Literature.

DetAH Detroit Public Library, E. Azalia Hackley Collection.

Harv Harvard University, Cambridge, Massachusetts, University Library Theatre Collection.

MSCent Howard University, Washington, D. C. Moorland-Spingarn Research Center.

Schom New York Public Library, Schomburg Center for Research in Black Culture.

NYPL New York Public Library, Library and Museum of the Performing Arts at Lincoln Center, Theatre Collection.

PaHistSoc Pennsylvania Historical Society. Leon Gardiner Collection.

INDEX

Boldface numbers refer to major entries.

ABOUT THE AUTHOR

EILEEN SOUTHERN is Professor of Music and of Afro-American Studies at Harvard University in Cambridge, Massachusetts, and editor/co-publisher of *The Black Perspective in Music*. Her earlier books include *The Buxheim Organ Book*, *Anonymous Pieces in the Ms. El Escorial IV.a.24*, *The Music of Black Americans: A History*, and *Readings in Black American Music*.